ISBN 978-1-5281-3497-2
PIBN 10917931

PIEDMONT BAPTIST ASSOCIATION

North Carolina

FORTY-FIRST ANNUAL SESSION

Held With

THE BAPTIST CHURCH

Franklinville, N. C.

October 24-25,

1934

The next session will be held with the Southside Baptist Church, High Point, N. C., Wednesday and Thursday before the fourth Sunday in October, 1935.

Rev. J. S. Hopkins will preach the sermon.

Alternate: Rev. C. N. Royal.

PIEDMONT BAPTIST ASSOCIATION

North Carolina

FORTY-FIRST ANNUAL SESSION

Held With

THE BAPTIST CHURCH

Franklinville, N. C.

October 24-25,

1934

The next session will be held with the Southside Baptist Church, High Point, N. C., Wednesday and Thursday before the fourth Sunday in October, 1935.
Rev. J. S. Hopkins will preach the sermon.
Alternate: Rev. C. N. Royal.

PIEDMONT BAPTIST ASS'N

Associational Directory

OFFICERS

CLARENCE A. SMITH, Moderator..................High Point, N. C.
REV. J. M. HILLIARD, Vice-Moderator...........High Point, N. C.
O. E. LEE, Clerk and Treasurer ....Greensboro, N. C.

EXECUTIVE COMMITTEE

Clarence A. Smith, Chairman......................High Point, N. C.
O. E. Lee, Secretary ....Greensboro, N. C.
Rev. J. M. Hilliard................................High Point, N. C.
Dr. A. B. Conrad...................................High Point, N. C.
M. R. Shields ....High Point, N. C.
Dr. J. Clyde Turner..............................Greensboro, N. C.
Rev. T. L. Sasser................................. Reidsville, N. C.
Williams Cummings ....Reidsville, N. C.

CHURCHES BY DISTRICTS

District 1
High Point, First
Hilliard Memorial
Green Street
North Main
North Park
South Side
West End
Oak Grove
Smith's Grove
Trinity
Cedar Falls
Allen Jay

District 2
Greensboro, First
Asheboro Street
Bessemer
Eller Memorial
Forest Avenue
Florida Street
Latham Park
Magnolia Street
Pomona Mills
Revolution
Lebanon
Summerfield
Stevens Memorial
White Oak
Gibsonville
Tabernacle
Mount Zion
Pleasant Garden
Jessup's Grove
Osborne Chapel
Guilford

District 3
Reidsville, First
Lawsonville Avenue
Calvary
Fairview
Osceola
Ruffin-Stacey
Mount Olive

OFFICERS OF THE PIEDMONT BAPTIST SUNDAY SCHOOL ASSOCIATION

Harry B. Caldwell, Superintendent .... Greensboro, N. C.
E. C. Riggins, Assistant Superintendent .... Greensboro, N. C.
F. F. Blevins, Secretary .... Greensboro, N. C.
W. F. Hearne, Chorister .... Greensboro, N. C.
J. Harvey Mitchell, Supt. Group 1, Dist. 1 .... Franklinville, N. C.
Mrs. T. F. Ashburn, Supt. Group 2, Dist. 1 .... Liberty, N. C.
W. A. Hedrick, Supt. Group 1, Dist. 2 .... High Point, N. C.
M. E. Howell, Supt. Group 2, Dist. 2 .... High Point, N. C.
M. E. Frazier, Supt. Group 1, Dist. 3 .... Greensboro, N. C.
O. Joe Howard, Supt. Group 2, Dist. 3 .... Greensboro, N. C.
Rev. T. L. Sasser, Supt. District 4 .... Reidsville, N. C.
Miss Ruth Scott, Beginners Supt. .... Greensboro, N. C.
Mrs. C. C. Stout, Primary Supt. .... High Point, N. C.
Mrs. J. W. Blexton, Junior Supt. .... Greensboro, N. C.
Mrs. C. A. Lewis, Intermediate Supt. .... High Point, N. C.
Miss Viola Hensley, Young People's Supt. .... High Point, N. C.
E. R. Baldwin, Adult Supt. .... Greensboro, N. C.

OFFICERS OF THE PIEDMONT ASSOCIATION BAPTIST TRAINING UNION

Walter Crissman, President .... High Point, N. C.
Wiley Jones, Vice-President .... Asheboro, N. C.
Miss Thelma Patrick, Secretary-Treasurer .... High Point, N. C.
John Reavis, Vice-President, Dist. 1 .... High Point, N. C.
Talmadge Smith, Vice-President, Dist. 2 .... Greensboro, N. C.
Mrs. C. D. Scoggins, Vice-President, Dist. 3 .... Reidsville, N. C.
George W. Baity, Chorister .... Greensboro, N. C.
Miss Ila Hensley, Pianist .... High Point, N. C.
Miss Mildred Jackson, Junior Leader .... Greensboro, N. C.
J. O. House, Intermediate Leader .... High Point, N. C.

OFFICERS OF THE PIEDMONT ASSOCIATION W. M. U.

Mrs. Nettie Hoge, Superintendent .... Greensboro, N. C.
Mrs. J. D. Schoolfield, Secretary .... Greensboro, N. C.
Mrs. C. E. Siceloff, Treasurer .... High Pont, N. C.
Mrs. R. N. Rumble, Mission Study Lit. Ch'm .... High Point, N. C.
Mrs. W. H. McKeever, Personal Service Chairman .. Greensboro, N. C.
Mrs. Catherine Marley, Stewardship Chairman .... Greensboro, N. C.
Miss Ruth Scott, Young People's Leader .... Greensboro, N. C.
Mrs. A. Lee Gibson, Group Leader Dist. 1 .... High Point, N. C.
Mrs. A. Andrews, Group Leader, Dist. 2 .... Greensboro, N. C.
Mrs. Ellis McCargo, Group Leader, Dist. 3, ... Reidsville, N. C.

Church Directory

ORDAINED MINISTERS (NOT PASTORS)

W. J. Byrum ....Asheboro, N. C.
Dr. C. H. Nash....................................Greensboro, N. C.
J. W. Rose .... Greensboro, N. C.
Dr. W. C. Newton .... China
W. C. Richardson.........................Guilford College, N. C.
C. D. Barton ....Greensboro, N. C.
J. C. DeLancey .... Greensboro, N. C.
W. H. Matherly .... Greensboro, N. C.
L. M. Beaton .... Greensboro, N. C.
S. B. Wilson....................................... High Point, N. C.
Carl Lewis .... High Point, N. C.
D. E. Oates .... High Point, N. C.
J. M. Hilliard .... High Point, N. C.
Thomas Carrick .... High Point, N. C.
R. L. Smith .... High Point, N. C.
T. L. Chamberlin.................................High Point, N. C.
B. T. Gladden..................................... High Point, N. C.
W. F. Arrington .... Liberty, N. C.
J. F. Murray .... Reidsville, N. C.
Paul M. Roberts .... Reidsville, N. C.
B. H. Fairington.. Colfax, N. C.
Clyde James .... Colfax, N. C.
Joe Bullins .... Colfax, N. C.
C. R. Smith..Colfax, N. C.
J. C. Gatewood .... Trinity, N. C.
F. W. Shaw .... Worthville, N. C.

B. Y. P. U. DIRECTORS, PRESIDENTS, AND LEADERS

ASHEBORO—Mrs. M. T. Lambert, B. A. U. President; Roy Williams, Senior President.; Mrs. Halbert Lowe, Intermediate Leader; Miss Daffie Boone, Junior Leader.

BALFOUR—Eugene Moody, Director; Mrs. Richard Kennedy, Senior President; Mrs. E. F. Glass, Intermediate Leader; Mrs. Ernest Moody, Junior Leader.

CENTRAL FALLS—Mrs. S. S. Wallace, B. A. U. President.

FRANKLINVILLE—Margaret Groce, Director; Mrs. Laurie Cox, Senior President; Ester Moon, Intermediate Leader; Lillie Tryden,

Junior Leader.

GIBSONVILLE—Isaiah Dears, Director; Ellen Sears, Senior President.

GLENOLA—Fairy White, Senior President.

GREENSBORO, FIRST—O. E. Lee, Director; Rev. C. D. Barton, Adult President; Elizabeth Campbell, Inez Patterson, Wade Atkins, Senior Presidents; Mrs. Bertha Chapman, Lillian Giles, Mr. and Mrs. August Rouf, Intermediate Leaders; Mildred Jackson, Hallie Sykes, Jane Cates, Junior Leaders.

ASHEBORO STREET—C. W. McLees, Director; M. Nevell Wills, Senior President; J. J. Norwood, Mrs. B. E. Pickard, Madeline Causey, Intermediate Leaders; E. L. Oliver, Emma Mae Cheek, Mesdames O. E. Shields, Sam Welker, John R. Durham, C. W. McLees, Junior Leader.

BESSEMER—Norfleet Dixon, Director; Claude Murray, Adult President; Truman Parks, Senior President; Mary Langley, Intermediate Leader; Mrs. W. H. Holliday, Junior Leader.

ELLER MEMORIAL—J. Carl Bell, Director; C. E. Brady, Adult President; Raymond Kincaid, R. T. Smith, Senior Presidents; Rev. J. S. Hopkins, Nora B. Brady, Mrs. Perry Beall, Intermediate Leaders; Datha Ramsey, Frances Lee, Mesdames J. H. Sharpe, G. O. Basinger, Junior Leaders.

FLORIDA STREET—W. M. Carrell, Director; J. B. Rumley, Adult President; Eulene Collins, Senior President; B. G. Whitley, Intermediate Leader; Mrs. W. M. Carrell, Junior Leader.

FOREST AVENUE—R. L. Bridges, Director; Ethel Osborne, Senior President; Mrs. Draper Leigh, Junior Leader.

MAGNOLIA STREET—Mrs. Jennings Johnson, Director; A. A. Rogers, Adult President; Marshall Durham, Senior President; Mrs. Jennings Johnson, Intermediate Leader; J. M. Johnson, Junior Leader.

REVOLUTION—David Barbour, Senior President.

WHITE OAK—Robert Leonard, Director; Frank Gales, Adult President; L. F. Paris, Intermediate Leader; Opal Ryals, Junior Leader.

GUILFORD—Beulah Martin, Director; Setzer Weston, Senior President.

HIGH POINT, FIRST—Thelma Patrick, Director; Tamsie Knight, Senior President; Addie Lomax, Mrs. H. A. Knight, Intermediate Leaders; Mrs. C. D. Goldsmith, Junior Leader.

GREEN STREET—Woodrow Hill, Director.

HILLIARD MEMORIAL—J. W. Saunders, Intermediate Leader.

NORTH MAIN STREET—J. E. Wade, Director; Mrs. Ethel Fowler, Adult President; Aurilla Kinley, Senior President; Mrs. Selena Parsons, Intermediate Leader; J. B. Shaver, Junior Leader.

NORTH PARK—Paul K. Frye, Director; Mrs. Eva Alson, Senior

President; Floyd Wood, Intermediate Leader; Mrs. O. F. Barnes, Junior Leader.

SOUTH SIDE—G. H. Liner, Director; Mrs. W. T. Shenault, Senior President.

WEST END—J. E. Hedrick, Director; J. E. Hedrick, Intermediate Leader; Vernon Coffey, Junior Leader.

LIBERTY—Miriam Stroud, Senior President; Mrs. J. G. Reitzel, Intermediate Leader; Ann Ridenhour, Junior Leader.

MACEDONIA—F. DeWitt Coble, Senior President.

RAMSEUR—W. H. Leonard, Director; Mrs. Johnny Burgess, Senior President; W. M. Burgess, Intermediate Leader; Mrs. H. M. Stroup, Junior Leader.

RANDLEMAN—Cooper Greter, Senior President.

REIDSVILLE FIRST—J. C. Gillespie, Jr., Director; Margaret Murphy, Senior President; Mrs. T. L. Sasser, Intermediate Leader; Sara Price Kemp, Junior Leader.

TABERNACLE—J. L. Lee, Director; Ruth Davis, Senior President; Mrs. Lenora Waddell, Junior Leader.

WHITE'S MEMORIAL—Jessie Webster, Director; Jessie Webster, Intermediate Leader.

OFFICERS OF W. M. S. AND AUXILIARIES

ASHEBORO—Mrs. H. T. Stevens, W. M. S. P.; Mesdames W. H. Grimes, Maude Allred, Y. W. A. Counselors; Mrs. G. R. Kennedy, G. A. Leader; Mrs. John Morrison, R. A. Leader; Mrs. Arthur Presnell, Sunbeam Leader.

BALFOUR—Mrs. R. C. Caudle, W. M. S. President; Mrs. O. P. Dix, Y. W. A. Counselor; Mrs. George Teague, G. A. Leader; Mrs. J. C. Pearce, Sunbeam Leader.

CALVARY—Mrs. J. E. McCargo, W. M. S. President.

GIBSONVILLE—Mrs. Lela Cable, W. M. S. President.

FRANKLINVILLE—Nettie Moon, W. M. S. President; Mrs. J. H. Mitchell, Y. W. A. Counselor; Rama Liles, G. A. Leader; Mrs. E. S. Thomas, R. A. Leader; Lena Liles, Sunbeam Leader.

CENTRAL FALLS—Mrs. J. A. Cox, W. M. S. President.

GREENSBORO, FIRST—Mrs. Vander Liles, W. M. S. President; Mrs. S. R. Webb, Y. W. A. Counselor; Mrs. J. R. Pegram, Mrs. Joe H. Johnson, G. A. Leaders; W. O. Burnham, R. A. Leader; Mrs. Edwin King, Sunbeam Leader.

ASHEBORO STREET—Mrs. A. Andrews, W. M. S. President; Mesdames J. J. Myer, M. D. Teague, Y. W. A. Counselors; Misses Lily McLees, Margaret Debnam, G. A. Leaders; Mesdames D. F. Stone, D. E. Shelton, W. D. Harrelson, Sunbeam Leaders.

BESSEMER—Mrs. James O. Reynolds, W. M. S. President; Mrs. J. R. Medlin, Y. W. A. Counselor; Juanita Haynes, G. A. Leader; Elizabeth Miller, Sunbeam Leader.

ELLER MEMORIAL—Mrs. G. O. Basinger, W. M. S. President; Mrs. Oakland Morrison, G. A. Leader, Mrs. W. H. Lambert, Sunbeam Leader.

FLORIDA STREET—Mrs. June Johnson, W. M. S. President; Mrs. D. F. Harwell, Y. W. A. Counselor; Mrs. W. W. Spivey, G. A. Leader; W. M. Caswell, R. A. Leader; Miss Emma Hoover, Sunbeam Leader.

FOREST AVENUE—Mrs. B. A. Scott, W. M. S. President; Mrs. Wilson Woodcock, Y. W. A. Counselor; Mrs. Carrol Weaver, G. A. Leader; Carrol Weaver, R. A. Leader; Rebecca Braswell, Sunbeam Leader.

MAGNOLIA STREET—Mrs. L. L. Jarvis, W. M. S. President.

POMONA—Mrs. J. L. Nall, W. M. S. President.

REVOLUTION—Sallie Burgess, W. M. S. President and Y. W. A. Counselor; Nellie Pitchford, G. A. Leader; James Clifton, R. A. Leader; Lora Canter, Sunbeam Leader.

STEVENS MEMORIAL—Mrs. W. A. Gunter, W. M. S. President.

WHITE OAK—Mrs. Morgan Smith, W. M. S. President; Mrs. C. M. Hodges, Y. W. A. Counselor; Mrs. J. E. Garner, G. A. Leader; J. L. Cloey, R. A. Leader; Perla Hayes, Sunbeam Leader.

GUILFORD—Beulah Martin, W. M. S. President and Y. W. A. Counselor.

HIGH POINT, FIRST—Mrs. A. Lee Gibson, W. M. S. President; Mesdames A. M. Richardson, C. E. Siceloof, M. R. Shields, Y. W. A. Counselors; Mesdames L. E. Tinsley, R. M. Hughes, G. A. Leaders; Claude A. Smith, Jr., R. A. Leader; Katie Sue Stanfield, Sunbeam Leader.

GREEN STREET—Mrs. Ila Campbell, W. M. S. President; Mrs. C. C. Stout, Y. W. A. Counselor; Mable Koontz, Mrs. G. M. Koontz, R. A. Leaders.

HILLIARD MEMORIAL—Mrs. J. B. Ellis, W. M. S. President; Mrs. H. O. Miller, Y. W. A. Counselor; Mrs. Mary Conklin, G. A. Leader; Mrs. J. C. Talbert, R. A. Leader; Mrs. C. H. Farmer.

NORTH MAIN STREET—Mrs. K. L. Shipwash, W. M. S. President; Mrs. S. R. Clinard, Y. W. A. Counselor; Mrs. Hal Davis, G. A. Leader.

NORTH PARK—Mrs. O. F. Barnes, W. M. S. President.

SOUTH SIDE—Lillie May Mauldin, W. M. S. President; Daisy Shawe, G. A. Leader; Mrs. R. C. Wade, R. A. Leader; Margaret Oldham, Sunbeam Leader.

WEST END—Mrs. Perlie Presler, W. M. S. President; Carrie Hooper, Y. W. A. Counselor; Mesdames Tom Hedrick, C. W. Harvey, Sunbeam Leaders.

LIBERTY—Mrs. E. C. Williamson, W. M. S. President.

PLEASANT GARDEN—Mrs. Ralph Neely, W. M. S. President.

RAMSEUR—Mrs. C. E. Baldwin, W. M. S. President; Mrs. H. M. Stroupe, Y. W. A. Counselor and R. A. Leader; Mrs. C. E. York, G. A. Leader; Mrs. Madge Caveness, Sunbeam Leader.

RANDLEMAN—Mrs. N. N. Newlin, W. M. S. President.

REIDSVILLE, FIRST—Mrs. M. A. Whitmers, R. T. Burton, Y. W. A. Counselor; Naomi Southard, G. A. Leader; Mrs. Claude Phillips, Sunbeam Leader.

LAWSONVILLE AVENUE—Mrs. M. H. Fitz, W. M. S. President.

SUMMERFIELD—Mrs. W. W. Doggett, W. M. S. President.

LIST OF APPOINTED MESSENGERS

ASHEBORO—

BALFOUR—W. F. Cates, W. I. Jordan, W. N. Green, Mesdames W. A. Underwood, O. P. Dix, D. E. Brown.

CALVARY—J. E. Nance, Lee Duke, Ernest Duke, Irene Duke, Mrs. J. M. Carter.

CARAWAY—C. O. Sawyer, George Ferree, Homer Hammonds.

CEDAR FALLS—

CENTRAL FALLS—

FAIRVIEW—William Cummings, J. P. Mitchell, Wade A. Durham.

FRANKLINVILLE—J. H. Mitchell, J. W. Clark, S. C. Twyden, Carl Brown, J. R. Burrow, Mrs. J. H. Mitchell, M. F. Cheek, C. E. Henson, Miss Nettie Moon.

GIBSONVILLE—E. C. Riggins, W. M. Ferguson.

GLENOLA—Mr. and Mrs. A. M. Smith, Mr. and Mrs. C. R. Stone, W. R. Boyles.

GREENSBORO, FIRST—O. E. Lee, F. D. Whitehead, George Bennett, Mrs. Nettie Hoge, Mrs. J. L. Andoe, Mrs. W. H. McKeever.

ASHEBORO STREET—E. R. Baldwin, C. W. McLees, Mrs. A. Andrews.

BESSEMER—W. P. Haynes, Mesdames J. Frank Layton, J. R. Medlin, L. W. Michael.

ELLER MEMORIAL—Rev. and Mrs. J. S. Hopkins, S. E. May, Geo. W. Baity, Julius Baity.

FLORIDA STREET—C. L. Roberson, Mesdames J. B. Rumley, T. G. Owens.

FOREST AVENUE—

MAGNOLIA STREET—Mr. and Mrs. H. P. Wray, Mr. Bryant, Mesdames J. M. Lashley, E. E. Thompson.

POMONA—Ernest C. Stout, C. G. Coe, Mesdames W. H. Brown, C. C. Patterson.

REVOLUTION—L. Lankford, Mr. and Mrs. Waldo Johnson, Mr. and Mrs. David Barber.

STEVENS MEMORIAL—Mesdames E. E. Welborn, H. H. Sutton, D. M. Brisson.

WHITE OAK—W. A. Straughn, Mrs. Maggie Johnson, Miss Lillian Bush.

GUILFORD—Mr. and Mrs. B. F. Butler, Setzer Weston, Mrs. Cora Martin.

HIGH POINT, FIRST—Dr. and Mrs. A. B. Conrad, G. H. Jones, Mrs. C. E. Siceloff, Miss Thelma Patrick, Clarence A. Smith, M. R. Shields, Mesdames C. D. Goldsmith, A. Lee Gibson.

GREEN STREET—B. G. Leonard, Walter Vrissman, W. E. Meyers, Lee Marshall, Mrs. C. C. Stout.

HILLIARD MEMORIAL—C. J. Hedrick, L. C. Andrews, C. H. Sanders.

NORTH MAIN STREET—S. R. Clinard, E. G. Morris, R. L. Reeves.

NORTH PARK—
SOUTH SIDE—Rev. G. H. Liner, J. R. Ruer, A. M. Garren.
WEST END—Rev. Hoyle Love, C. M. Scott, Z. V. Swain.
JESSUP GROVE—Rev. R. O. Nuckles, Henry Page, C. W. Johnson.
LEBANON—B. G. Yowe, Mrs. J. B. Carter.
LIBERTY—Mr. and Mrs. E. C. Williamson, Mrs. Lydia Peyatte.
MACEDONIA—Rev. W. F. Arrington, B. R. Staley, W. M. Brothers, Mesdames Ray York, Bernice Hill.
MOUNT ZION—Vida Coble, Laura Coble, May Branson.
OAK GROVE—Mr. and Mrs. C. U. Smith, Mr. and Mrs. G. K. Saunders, Mrs. J. R. Bowman.
OSBORNE CHAPEL—Mr. and Mrs. Robert R. Osborne, J. A. Loyal, Will Wall.
OSCEOLA—Floyd Brown, E. R. Brande, L. C. Cole.
PLEASANT GARDEN—Walter J. Smith, Miss Helen Gray, Mesdames J. E. Thompson, Ralph Neely.
RAMSEUR—M. E. Johnson, E. B. Leonard, N. F. Phillips, Mesdames W. M. Burgess, C. E. Baldwin.
RANDLEMAN—Dr. T. L. Helms, A. M. Barker, C. W. Hilliard.
REIDSVILLE, FIRST—Rev. T. L. Sasser, Mesdames R. H. Pleasants, H. L. Morrison, R. T. Burton, C. B. Scoggin.
LAWSONVILLE—Rev. D. W. Overby, T. G. Dixon, G. T. Roberts, A. M. Hatcher.
MOUNT OLIVE—Rev. and Mrs. J. H. Saunders, James Sellars, Miss Hazel Driscoll.
RUFFIN STACEY—M. C. Thomas, Abner Walker, Posey McBryde.
SANDY CREEK—J. M. Williams, Miss Ida Williams.
SMITH GROVE—Drew Smith, Cora Pendry, J. G. Pendry, W. B. Hyatt.
SUMMERFIELD—A. J. Ayers, Mr. and Mrs. Jess Carter.
TABERNACLE—Rev. Grover C. Phillips, W. D. Smithey, H. E. Parker, J. L. Lee, Paton W. Phillips, Miss Edna Phillips, Mesdames Mattie Parker, Lenora Waddell.
TRINITY—Mr. and Mrs. G. G. Clinard, Mesdames E. W. Welborne, J. R. Jordan.
WHITES MEMORIAL—L. J. Davis, E. W. Allred, Miss Jessie Webster.
WORTHVILLE—T. W. Davis, J. L. Wiles, J. W. Jenkins.

MINUTES

of the

FORTY-FIRST ANNUAL SESSION

of the

PIEDMONT BAPTIST ASSOCIATION

Held With

The Baptist Church, Franklinville, N. C.

October 24-25, 1934

1. The Association was opened with a devotional service led by Rev. J. M. Hilliard.

2. Rev. H. M. Stroup, pastor of the Franklinville Baptist Church, gave a hearty welcome to the messengers. The response was given by Rev. J. H. Saunders.

3. A roll of the churches was called and messengers from forty-two churches responded to the roll call. The Association then proceeded to the election of officers for the ensuing year, which resulted as follows: Clarence A. Smith, Moderator; Rev. J. M. Hilliard, Vice-Moderator; O. E. Lee, Clerk and Treasurer.

4. The Moderator appointed the following committee on program: Dr. H. T. Stevens, H. M. Stroup, T. W. Fogleman.

5. The report on Religious Literature was read by J. Ben Eller. On motion to adopt the report, the subject was discussed by N. H. Shepherd, J. M. Hilliard, Dr. A. B. Conrad. The report was adopted.

RELIGIOUS LITERATURE

One of our greatest needs as Baptists is a keener conscience with respect to reading our Baptist papers and magazines. In the social, financial, educational, political and other realms, the literature which treats of the needs and methods in those realms in considered indispensable. Why then should it be necessary to convince Christian people of the value and necessity of constructive Religious Literature?

Religious papers are not an end in themselves. They are a means to an end. They serve our churches, our denominations and our homes. They inspire, inform and indoctrinate. They are unifying and informing forces. They inspire to greater service and greater sacrifice. It is generally true that as the circulation of Baptist papers declines contributions to Missions and Benevolences decline. Is there not a significant connection here?

In our homes religious literature renders a large service. Many influences are at work to undermine and corrupt our homes. Automobiles invite us to spend much time away from them. Moving pictures lure many to gaze upon scenes unfit for youth or age. Daily newspapers full of trash and slush and stores of crime feed the minds of many. Smutty, suggestive, and salacious magazines hold sway with many others. We might well pause and ask what kind of mental diet is being served to our children. A father said, "I have five reasons for taking our Baptist paper." When asked to give them, he pointed to five lovely children. How we do need wholesome, uplifting Christian literature in our homes!

We urgently recommend then that we give a larger place to this kind of reading matter. Of course no book, magazine nor paper can compare with the Bible. This heads the list. Next in order we commend the Biblical Recorder. Founded in 1833 it has rendered a century of conspicuous service. Its greatest opportunity is before it. The Biblical Recorder should be in every Baptist home.

There are other periodicals which we heartily urge our people to read. Home and Foreign Fields, Royal Service, The Window, and World Comrades are all worthy of a much larger circulation. Furthermore, we think, no Baptist Sunday School should be without Charity and Children, and the Kind Word series of our Sunday School Board.

Respectfully submitted,

J. BEN ELLER.

6. The report on Foreign Missions was written by Dr. J. Clyde Turner. In his absence on account of being out of the State, the report was read by the Clerk. Upon motion to adopt the report a Missionary address was delivered by Dr. Charles A. Leonard, missionary to China. The report was adopted.

REPORT ON FOREIGN MISSIONS

For the first time in several years we are able to make a more encouraging report concerning our Foreign Mission work.

Increased Gifts

For the past year the gifts to Foreign Missions by Southern Baptists have been steadily increasing. For the first eight months of this calendar year the receipts of the Foreign Mission Board have been $146,000 more than for the same period last year. Several factors have entered into this increase. Our regular gifts to the Cooperative Program have been larger, the special offering of the women was more, the Hundred Thousand Club has contributed nearly $50,000 and a larger number of churches are undertaking the support of a missionary in addition to their regular gifts. This increase in receipts has enabled the Board to pay more than $100,000 on its indebtedness, thus decreasing the debt to less than a million dollars.

New Missionaries

These increased receipts have made it possible for the Board to send out a number of new missionaries. At the meeting of the Southern Baptist Convention in May, fifteen new missionaries, who had been appointed by the Board, were publicly dedicated to the service. All of them have since gone to their respective fields. At the meeting of the Board last week several more new missionaries were appointed.

Great Opportunities

From the fourteen countries in which Southern Baptists are working there come tidings of growing interest on the part of the people. Multitudes are seeking salvation, and native Christians are assuming a larger share of responsibility in the work. Great revivals with Pentecostal power have swept over northern China, bringing many into the kingdom and leading Christians into a deeper experience of grace. Dr. Maddry, our Secretary, has recently returned from a visit to our European fields, and he brings news of a white harvest. The people are hungry for the gospel. In South America and in Africa multitudes are turning to Christ. The door of opportunity is open to Southern Baptists.

New Books

The Foreign Mission Board is offering three new books on our Foreign Mission work: "WHERE IS HE?" by Mrs. R. K. Redwine, written with special reference to the Christmas Season; "AT THE GATE OF ASIA," by Mrs. J. S. Farmer, the first and only book on our Mission work in Japan; "JAPANESE BOYS AND GIRLS," by Miss Inabelle Coleman, a booklet prepared as a guide for junior teachers. You will notice that all three of these books were written by North Carolinians. In addition to these books there are many splendid tracts which may be had free by writing to the Board for them.

Our Missionaries

We cannot close without saying a word about the self-sacrificing spirit of our missionaries. They have assumed the extra burdens which have been laid upon them without complaint. They have given of their meagre salaries to make up in part for our decreased gifts. When at home on furlough they have given freely of their time and strength in behalf of the cause which is so dear to their hearts. We honor them for their work's sake, and pledge to them our hearty support.

J. CLYDE TURNER.

7. Following the singing of a hymn, Rev. Wilson Woodcock preached the Introductory Sermon. The text was Deut. 8:18, subject, "Establishing the Covenant." The sermon was an inspiration to all.

8. The Moderator appointed the following Committee on Committees: Hoyle Love, Dr. H. T. Stevens, T. W. Fogleman.

Rev. H. M. Stroup made an announcement about plans for the dinner.

The morning session was closed with prayer.

Wednesday Afternoon Session

9. The afternoon session was opened with a devotional service led by Rev. Jennings Johnson.

10. The report on Denominational Program was read by J. L. Coley. Upon motion to adopt the report the discussion of the subject was deferred until after the verbal reports from the churches were made, on account of the speaker being delayed.

11. Interesting verbal reports were made by representatives of the churches. Many interesting facts about the work were presented. The period was in charge of Dr. H. T. Stevens.

12. The report on State Missions was read by J. S. Hopkins. Upon motion to adopt the report the subjects of Denominational Program and State Missions were discussed by M. A. Huggins, Corresponding Secretary of the Baptist State Convention. The reports were adopted.

DENOMINATIONAL PROGRAM

The changing years do not bring any changes in the great program of our Lord. The churches are face to face with the greatest opportunity of all time. The prince of darkness has not slackened his pace a bit. He is rapidly whipping things in shape for the enthronement of the man of sin.

The year 1934 has seen a great pick-up in the economic world, and it ought to witness a forward move on the part of the forces of Christianity. The Baptists of North Corlina and the whole Southland were never better prepared for a united forward move for Christ than now. Think of the training and instruction that we have received. Jesus said, "That servant who knew his Lord's will, and did it not, shall be beaten with many stripes."

The time of the annual every member canvass is close at hand. It is earnestly hoped that each church in the Piedmont Association will put on a thorough canvass this year. Churches that put on a canvass show the best record each year. All funds contributed through the Cooperative Program are divided on a sixty-forty basis. Sixty per cent. is kept in our own state, and forty per cent. is sent for South-wide and world-wide objects.

Respectfully submitted,
J. L. COLEY.

REPORT ON STATE MISSIONS

Within the last twenty-five years the work of State Missions has enlarged so that it now embraces many of the most vital interests of our denominational life. But even today, in most cases, if not all, the aid given each cause is not at all commensurate with the needs. During the years State Missions has majored in helping weak churches and struggling churches, and today Christ's cause is reaping benefits because of those investments. Among the churches aided in the early days we find many of our strongest churches today. A continuous evangelistic program for North Carolina was the aim of our fathers in State Missions, and our rapid growth has been due in a large measure to this aggressive soul-winning effort.

Our present State Mission program includes the following activities: Helping weak churches and struggling churches to maintain pastors, and some churches are being aided with their building programs, supporting the Sunday School and Baptist Training Union departments of our State Convention, aiding one student secretary, Miss Cleo Mitchell, who endeavors to give spiritual guidance to the Baptist students at the State colleges located at Greensboro, Cullowhee and Boone, helping brother W. W. Williams to continue his ministry to sick soldiers at Oteen, and supporting three missionaries to the Indians in North Carolina.

At present we are greatly in need of reinforcing and enlarging the work being done by the State Mission Board in all its endeavors, and there are other needy fields within our State that the Board has thus far been unable to enter. Secretary M. A. Huggins says that at least 200 churches in addition to those being helped are in real need of aid from the State Board to enable them to have the needed pastoral care. And it is impossible to estimate the lasting good that would be accomplished by appropriating a few thousand dollars each year to aid strugling churches with their building programs. Work among our Baptist students is also greatly in need of reinforcements. And work among the Negro churches, which was started a few years ago and was dropped, surely ought to be taken up again. It has often been said that State Missions is the seed corn, and to strengthen State Missions now would, in the future, add inestimable strength to our world-wide mission program.

Respectfully submitted,

J. S. HOPKINS.

13. Report on the Orphanage was read by A. Lincoln Fulk. Upon motion to adopt the report the subject was discussed by R. D. Covington, Treasurer of the Mills Home. The report was adopted.

REPORT ON ORPHANAGE

Baptists of the State have approached in spirit and in deed the true definition of religion as expressed by the apostle James when he said, "Pure religion and undefiled before God and the Father is this, To visit the fatherless and widows in their affliction, and to keep himself unspotted from the world." Under date of January 1, 1934, Baptists of the State were providing care for 491 children at the Thomasville home and 136 at the Kennedy Home. These dependent children are not only being provided with the necessities of life, but are being trained religiously and secularly to the end that they may not only become self-supporting, but that they may make a worthy contribution to society and the Master's Kingdom. Not only are the wholly dependent being "visited" in our support of the Orphanage, but Baptists are "visiting" widows and orphans in the form of Mother's Aid. January 1, 1934, there were 172 children under supervision of this department of orphanage work. It is realized that no orphanage, however efficient, can take the place of a Mother's influence and training; therefore, it is earnestly hoped that more funds may be available for expansion of this phase of our work.

In view of the increased cost of living and the growing number of applications for admission to the orphanage, it is earnestly urged that every Sunday School in this Association set a definite amount to be given to the orphanage each first Sunday and the amount raised without fail. "To keep unspotted from the world," it is further suggested that the pastors of the various churches be as much concerned about this matter as they are about their salaries; that superintendents set apart the first Sunday of each month to make an offering for The Mills Home, and that the membership keep "unspotted" by responding liberally and cheerfully to these appeals.

Respectfully sumbitted,
A LINCOLN FULK.

The Committee on Committees made the following report:

REPORT OF THE COMMITTEE ON COMMITTEES

Committee on Place and Preacher: J. H. Saunders, Jennings Johnson, H. P. Wray.

Committee to Nominate Executive Committee: B. G. Leonard, G. W. Baity, Mrs. A. Andrews.

Committee to Nominate Delegates to State Convention: Jennings Johnson, Mrs. Nettie Hoge, C. S. White.

Committee to Nominate Promotion Committee: Dr. J. T. J. Battle, W. B. Cook, A. Lincoln Fulk.

Auditing Committee: J. H. Hanes, W. J. Jordan, S. R. Clinard.

Program Committee: J. O. Reynolds, Wilson Woodcock, J. S. Hopkins.

Committee on Verbal Reports from Churches: A. N. Hollis, H. O. Miller, J. T. London.

Committee on Resolutions: C. S. White, D. W. Overby, C. M. Oates

HOYLE LOVE
H. T. STEVENS
T. W. FOGLEMAN
Committee.

14. Dr. H. T. Stevens presented a plan for organizing a new Baptist Association. He stated that most of the churches in Randolph County, members of the Piedmont Baptist Association, as well as Baptist Churches, members of other Associations, had expressed a desire to form a new Association. He requested that the Clerk be authorized to grant letters of dismissal to any of the churches in Randolph County desiring to withdraw from

our Association and help form a new Association. A motion was made that the Clerk be so authorized. The subject was discussed by Dr. A. B. Conrad, M. A. Huggins, T. W. Fogleman, W. P. McCarter, J. M. Hilliard, J. Ben Eller, O. E. Lee, Clarence A. Smith. The motion was passed.

Letters of dismissal were requested by Dr. H. T. Stevens for the following churches: Asheboro, N. C., Ramseur, Franklinville, Balfour, Glenola, Carraway, White's Memorial, Central Falls, Liberty, Macedonia, Sandy Creek, Worthville, Randleman.

15. The Committee on Receiving New Churches recommended that the following churches be received: Tabernacle, Osborne Chapel, Pleasant Garden, Allen Jay, and Jessup Grove.

Committee:
J. M. Hilliard,
C. N. Royal,
G. H. Liner.

The report was adopted.

A hearty welcome was given the messengers from the new churches by Dr. A. B. Conrad.

The afternoon session was closed with prayer by C. N. Royal.

Night Session

16. The night session was opened with a devotional service led by W. Wilbur Hutchins.

17. The report on B. Y. P. U. Work was read by Walter E. Crissman. The report was adopted.

The young people from High Point gave a splendid playlet, which closed the night session.

REPORT ON BAPTIST TRAINING UNION

In view of the fact that we now have Adult Unions, that is, the B. A. U. and B. Y. P. U., our leaders of Young People have seen fit to change the name of Baptist Young People's Union to Baptist Training Union, the B. T. U.

General Organizations, 13.

Adult Unions, 6—a gain of two unions.

Senior Unions, 31—a gain of three unions.

Intermediate Unions, 33—a gain of four unions.

Junior Unions, 31—a gain of only one union.

Total number of Unions, 99—a gain of eight unions.

Adult enrollment, 80—a gain of twelve.

Twenty-seven churches were represented at the last B. Y. P. U. Associational Convention which met at Asheboro Street Baptist Church in Greensboro, last April.

Sixty-seven unions held a study course this last year.

Work is being done over the Association now toward organizing unions in other churches and we are looking forward to reporting a Baptist Training Union in each of the 49 churches of our Association by next October.

SECOND DAY

Thursday Morning Session

18. The morning session was opened with a devotional service led by J. O. Reynolds.

19. On account of the pastors and messengers from the churches in Raldolph County having a separate meeting in the afternoon, and because two of the pastors from Randolph County were to read reports during the afternoon, the periods for the discussion of Christian Education and Obituaries were exchanged with the period for the discussion of Home Missions.

20. The report on Woman's Work was read by Mrs. C. E. Siceloff. Upon motion to adopt Mrs. C. L. Steidley delivered an address. The report was adopted.

REPORT ON WOMAN'S WORK

The Lord giveth the word: the women that published the tidings are a great host. Psalm 68:11. Truly the Christian women of our Southland are a great host and our opportunities to publish the tidings are almost unlimited as we meet those in our midst who know not the Lord as Saviour. We rejoice that the women of the Association are a part of this great host and are helping spread the good news to those in the homeland and in the distant lands.

In our theme for the year, "Prayer in the Progress of Christianity," we have been led to see that prayer has played a most important part in every advancement of the kingdom. As we have prayed we have become more and more interested in telling others of His wonderous love and more liberal in giving of our means that others may go to those who have never had the opportunity to hear of our Lord and Master.

Our annual W. M. U. meeting held in April with the Asheboro Street Church was largely attended. Our hearts were stirred as we listened to the reports and future plans for our Associational and State leaders. We were cheered by the good news of many turning to Jesus as our missionaries told of their work in other lands. Surely this was the most spiritual and inspiring meeting in the history of the woman's work.

Years ago our women in the Association, meeting with the men, had only a small part in the work, but as the woman's work grew in interest we found it necessary to have our meeting at another time. For some years the women and the young people have had their meetings together, but last year the program seemed too full for a one-day session, so this year our Young People had their meeting at a separate time and place from the women. In June they had an all-day meeting with the Young People of the First Baptist Church, High Point. The program was entirely in their charge and one felt the earnestness of those taking part on the program. This meeting was well attended, nearly two hundred being present.

We now have 35 W. M. S.'s and 88 Young People's Organizations, a total of 113, with 19 new societies.

While we failey to make our apportionment of $20,197.45, the offering for all objects was $17,429.40. This gift led the State, with the W. M. S. of the First Church, Greensboro, leading the churches with a gift of $7,573.08, with the Young People $8,649.20. The First Church, High Point, supports Miss Alda Grayson in China while the W. M. S. of the First Church, Greensboro, pays most of the salary of Dr. and Mrs. Carey Newton.

Our mission study report was an exceedingly good one, the Association receiving the Mission Study Banner in our Divisional Meeting.

The Personal Service reports showed an increased interest in the welfare of the helpless and needy in our midst.

As we look back over the year's work our hopes are renewed and we press forward in the work of helping spread the good tidings to every land.

MRS. C. E. SICELOFF.

21. The report on Ministerial Relief and Annuity was read by H. M. Stroup. Upon motion to adopt the subject was discussed by Wilson Woodcock and J. M. Hilliard. The report was adopted.

REPORT ON RELIEF AND ANNUITY

"4. The Relief and Annuity Board:

(a) "This Board was organized for the purpose of providing relief (Note the word RELIEF) for retired and aged ministers who have no other means of support. It is aiding about 1,500 each year at present. Often it aids also widows of deceased ministers. The money for this purpose comes from the Co-operative Program and from interest on invested funds.

(b) "It also has an Annuity Plan. This Plan provides that the churches set aside a small amount each year, and that the pastors do likewise. Thus a fund is provided whereby a pastor at age 65 may retire and have an income which will provide at least the minimum necessities of life.

(c) "Recently all the benefits of this Board have been extended to all the Missionaries and already twenty-one have been retired from active service.

(d) "Dr. T. J. Watts, Dallas, Texas, is Secretary of this Board."

—Secretary M. A. Huggins, in "Baptist Work"

Respectfully sumbitted,

H. M. STROUP.

22. The report on the Hospital was read by T. L. Sasser. Upon motion to adopt the subject was discussed by Smith Hagaman and S. F. Morton. The report was adopted.

REPORT ON HOSPITALS

There are two hospitals which share in the gifts of the churches of this Association. One is the Southern Baptist Hospital in New Orleans, La. The report made to the Convention last May shows that 5,981 patients were treated during the year, 634 of whom were given free treatment. The operating cost of this hospital was $26,311.01. All operating expenses were paid, all interest on the bonded debt, and $26,800 was paid on the principal during the year. An addition of $11,674.60 was made to the net worth of the property. The institution is from year to year paying off its debt and is a real missionary asset to Southern Baptists and the Kingdom.

The other hospital is North Carolina Baptist Hospitals, Inc., located in Winston-Salem. During the first half of 1934, 1,472 patients were treated there. Of these 981 were full pay, 355 part pay and 136 free patients. The cost of free service for the year was $14,676.00. Mother's Day Offerings from 1,269 churches provided $13,057.97 toward this expense. The difference of $1,618.03 adds to the liabilities against the income which is not adequate to pay operating expenses of the Hospital and reduce the bonded debt rapidly enough. It must as soon as possible have a larger financial support and this must come from an increased moral support of the churches of the State.

Respectfully sumbitted,

T. L. SASSER.

23. The report on Christian Education was presented by W. Wilbur Hutchins. Upon motion to adopt the report the subject was discussed by W. Wilbur Hutchins. The report was adopted.

CHRISTIAN EDUCATION

Education is one of the most talked of things in America today. Every year thousands of our youth are marshalled upon the campuses of the nation for the first time; and every year thousands of college and university graduates are pouring back into the warp and woof of the fabric of this nation's life. A prominent educator said sometime ago that Christian Education was the hope of the world in many respects. Some of us quite readily agree with him. It ought to be a well accepted fact that Christianity cannot be the religion it claims to be without being vitally interested in the well-rounded education of the youth of the land. That, of course, implies a deeper sense of responsibility for the progress of Christian Education than some of us may have realized before.

The Baptists of North Carolina have made progress in the past years in the realm of Christian Education. There are, at this time, three senior colleges of the Baptist denomination, Wake Forest, Meredith at Raleigh, and Chowan at Murfreesboro. In addition, there are outstanding junior colleges. Mars Hill and Campbell are familiar names to loyal Baptists of the State. They are sending into the class rooms of the senior colleges many outstanding students; and the senior colleges are sending yearly out into the many realms of State and national life men and women who have been touched by the Spirit of Christ.

With these facts in mind, let us resolve that our devotion to the cause of educated Christian youth shall not become as a torch that flickers. State Schools do not attempt to teach religion. Denominaional schools must teach it, and Baptist people must continue to place representatives of the Christ within reach of the youth who attend non-denominational schools.

Today, as never before, we need men and women who have been TRAINED, and trained SPIRITUALLY as well as mentally, physically and socially. Christian Education alone will meet these needs.

Today, the Church is in dire need of a leadership that has been educated in a Christian way. This nation stands in need of more leaders who have not sacrificed righteousness for popularity. Surely the answer to these problems is found in the erection and support, by Christian people, of colleges and universities within whose walls the Spirit of Christ may be found and fostered.

W. WILBUR HUTCHINS.

24. The report on Obituaries was presented by J. C. Edwards. Upon motion to adopt the report remarks were made by J. M. Hilliard. The report was adopted.

REPORT ON OBITUARIES

The Death Messenger has taken from us a great many of our noble brethren and sisters, but we trust they have gone to be with Him whom they loved and served. "I go to prepare a place for you. And if I go and prepare a place for you, I will come again and receive you unto myself, that where I am there ye may be also."

Heaven is a place—a prepared place for a prepared people. There is a time in the history of every person when there comes a change that cannot be averted. That change means parting of the way in which they have been traveling. We trust that when our brethren and sisters came to the parting of the way they could say: "I know whom I have believed, and am persuaded that He is able to keep that which I have committed unto Him against that day."

"And I said unto him, Sir, thou knowest. And he said to me: These are they which came out of great tribulation, and have washed their robes, and made them white in the blood of the Lamb."

Respectfully sumbitted,

J. C. EDWARDS.

25. The Treasurer's report was presented and referred to the Auditing Committee.

TREASURER'S REPORT

To the Piedmont Baptist Association:

I herewith submit my report for the year ending September 30, 1934:

Received from the Churches	$216.78

Disbursements

Greensboro Printing Co., for Programs	$4.75
Balance on Clerk's Remuneration	36.93
To M. A. Huggins, Treasurer, for pledge cards....	19.87

Economy Printing Co., for Minutes	109.19
Postage and Stationery	4.25
Paid on Clerk's Remuneration	41.79
	$216.78
Deficit, Balance due on Clerk's Remuneration	8.21

Respectfully sumbitted,

O. E. LEE, Treasurer.

26. The following new pastors were presented and a hearty welcome given by J. M. Hilliard: C. N. Royal, R. O. Reynolds, and Tom W .Bray.

The following visitors were recognized: N. H. Shepherd, R. E. Heath, and J. C. Kidd.

After announcements the morning session closed with prayer by S. F. Morton.

Afternoon Session

27. The afternoon session was opened with a devotional service led by H. O. Miller.

28. The report on Social Service was presented by C. N. Royal. Upon motion to adopt the report the subject was discussed by C. N .Royal, J. M. Hilliard, H. O. Miller, A. L. Fulk, Dr. A. B. Conrad, Wilson Woodcock. The report was adopted.

SOCIAL SERVICE

Social Service is laboring together with God for the uplift of humanity. In doing this Christians glorify Him. Never in our nation and even in our communities has the challenge sounded more loudly. We rejoice that there has been an improvement in the economic situation but we lament that this is not true of the social and moral realm. Our people have never passed through a greater testing of moral standards and convictions than in the past twelve months.

There is a persistent effort to repeal or weaken all Sunday laws. The proper observance of the Christian Sabbath as a day of rest and worship is fundamental in Christian teaching and life.

The repeal of the Eighteenth Amendment is the greatest backward step in economic sanity and moral welfare legislation ever taken by a great people. While our own State does not by law permit the manufacture and sale of liquor it would be impossible for us to forecast or imagine the evils that will result from the present situation. Drunkenness is everywhere increasing and court dockets are jammed with the ripening fruits of reckless sowing. "You can repeal prohibition but you cannot repeal the nature of alcohol; you cannot repeal its deadening effect upon the brain; its paralyzing power over the nerves. You cannot repeal the beggary and want which always follow in the wake of alcoholic drinks."

There has never been in the history of our nation such an ignoble surrender to an evil group or such a betrayal of the rights of the people as when our lawmakers, both National and State, surrendered to the German brewers and re-established the sale of beer.

At the present time conditions are chaotic but there is already manifest almost everywhere a very strong reaction against the present order. Multitudes of men who joined the parade for repeal are frankly admitting their error and deploring the existing conditions.

Co-incident with increased drinking we meet the serious problem of increased motor car accidents. Licensed alcoholic beverages cannot by any process of reasoning be made to fit into our high-speed motorized civilization.

Other evils are like sores on our social life. Lynching, one of the most barbarous and brutal forms of all lawlessness and crime, has increased in our nation over two hundred per cent. in the past year.

There is an ever increasing ratio of divorces. There must be instilled a deeper realization of the sanctity of marriage and of the home. Our young people must be saved from the far-reaching influence of this evil.

A potent factor in shaping the minds of our youth is the moving picture show. Indecent pictures are a menace to mental and moral life. Christian people must refuse to see or allow their children to see harmful pictures.

From Sunday School, pulpit, and home, Christians must carry on the fight against social evils. We must support for public office men who stand against wrong and who stand for and represent the best Christian and American ideals. "Righteousness exalteth a nation but sin is a reproach to any people."

Respectfully sumbitted,

C. N. ROYAL.

29. The report on Home Missions was presented by Dr. A. B. Conrad. Upon motion to adopt the report the subject was discussed by Dr. A. B. Conrad, H. O. Miller, and Wilson Woodcock.

HOME MISSIONS

The work of the Home Mission Board is one of the most important parts of our denominational work. Its success guarantees the success of all our enterprises in Kingdom building and its failure spells defeat for all that we have undertaken in world-wide evangelization.

In its sphere which includes all our Southern Convention territory, Cuba, Porto Rico and the Panama Canal Zone, it has since its organization in 1845 carried on magnificently and has a glorious record. The Home fires have been kept burning brightly and thus the light has gone round the world.

According to reports sent out from headquarters in Atlanta, it has employed during this period, of itself and in cooperation with State Boards or other organizations, a force sufficient to equal the working of 40,862 missionaries working for one year. They have baptized 785,135 persons, organized 8.570 churches. These 785,135 baptisms are equal to one out of every five of our present total constituency and the 8.570 churches organized are equal to one out of every three of our total number of churches. This is a glorious record, but it by no means represents the greatness of the Board's accomplishment. More than making so great a number of converts and establishing so many churches, it has helped in the development and progress of State organizations, its missionaries on the frontiers have kept pace with the growing population and more than any other agency has made our beloved church the dominant one numerically at least in all this vast territory of our Southern Convention. It has helped to support many thousands of pastors on fields where they could not have stayed without this aid and has given more than a million dollars to help build churches in strategic places.

The glory of its work is revealed in the particular classes to which it has especially ministered and without whose ministry they would have been practically without the gospel. Among foreigners of whom there are more than five million, among the Negroes with more than ten million, among the Indians of whom there are fourteen different tribes, among deaf mutes of whom there are more than forty-five thousand, among Mountain people with more than eight million, and among Seamen, Jews and in rescue missions it has carried on gloriously and trophies of redeemed ones are among all these classes.

During the stressful years of depression through which we have passed and are passing, for we have not yet emerged, the Board has had to carry on in the face of greatly reduced income but it has balanced its budget each year, lived within its income and paid last year $61,346 on its debts and reported more baptisms than in several years.

It has now in the field two hundred and two missionaries and received last year $245,452 for its work. According to the report given at the last session of the Convention in Fort Worth, Texas, the Board was forced to ask its creditors for an adjustment of its debts, which was agreed upon by those creditors, on this basis: a five year extension of the principal was made and it is also allowed to pay on notes at banks and retire bonds at any time without premium. This puts the debts in such shape that they can be handled and at the same time guarantees to the Board an operating budget while paying these debts.

It must be apparent to every Baptist that the work of the Home Mission Board is of most vital importance; if it is not adequately supported, then all our work in Kingdom building must dwindle and will ultimately fail.

The field is large and what has been done, glorious as it is, is only a beginning. Large areas have not been covered in any adequate way. Some sections have not been touched at all. The field is white to the harvest. More workers are needed and all our people ought to awake to a keener sense of responsibility and be aroused to larger giving, more prayer, and the imperative need of more workers, for today, with all these needy, unsaved multitudes, with all the perils of stark materialism, increase in crime, poverty, millions unemployed, strikes, Communism, rampant infidelity and giddy worldliness, the only way out, the only way to peace and order is not by New Deals, N. R. A.'s or any social or political manipulation, but by the gospel of Christ—it alone is the power of God unto personal, social, political, commercial, national and world salvation. And the Home Mission Board is the one agency above all others here in the Homeland, so far as our denomination is responsible, that is organized, equipped and able to cope with all these evil forces and bring in a better order and make Christ King.

, A. B. CONRAD.

30. The report on Sunday Schools was not presented. The subject was discussed by Dr. J. T. J. Battle, O. E. Lee, T. L. Sasser, and Clarence A. Smith.

31. The following reports were made and adopted:

REPORT OF AUDITING COMMITTEE

Your committee has gone over all items and found the statement to be correct.

S. F. MORTON
T. L. SASSER

REPORT OF COMMITTEE TO NOMINATE EXECUTIVE COMMITTEE

Clarence A. Smith
O. E. Lee
Dr. A. B. Conrad
T. L. Sasser
J. M. Hilliard
M. R. Shields
Dr. J. Clyde Turner
William Cummings

B. G. LEONARD
G. W. BAITY
MRS. A. ANDREWS
Committee.

REPORT OF COMMITTEE ON PROGRAM FOR NEXT MEETING

Religious Literature: C. N. Royal
Foreign Missions: J. Ben Eller
Denominational Program: T. L. Sasser
State Missions: Jennings Johnson
Orphanage: B. G. Whitley
Baptist Training Union: Walter Crissman
Woman's Missionary Union: Mrs. B. A. Scott
Ministerial Relief and Annuity: Clyde Glosson
Hospital: Tom W. Bray
Home Missions: Dr. J. Clyde Turner
Social Service: Hoyle Love
Christian Education: A. Lincoln Fulk
Sunday Schools: Dr. A. B. Conrad
Obituaries: W. B. Cook

JAMES O. REYNOLDS
WILSON WOODCOCK
J. S. HOPKINS
Committee

The Committee to nominate delegates to Baptist State Convention reported the names of Wilson Woodcock and Hoyle Love.

Committee on Place and Preacher recommended that the next meeting of the Association be held with the Southside Baptist Church in High Point, and that J. S. Hopkins deliver the Introductory Sermon and that C. N. Royal be the alternate.

The Committee on Resolutions being absent, the Association expressed their thanks and appreciation to the members of the Franklinville Baptist Church and the people of Franklinvlle for their cordial welcome and the splendid way in which the Association was entertained.

Mrs. Morrison, daughter of Rev. F. H. Jones, was recognized.

A motion was made and passed that the Clerk write resolutions of regret to the churches leaving our Association to form the new Association.

RESOLUTIONS SENT TO THE CHURCHES RECEIVING LETTERS OF DISMISSAL

The Piedmont Baptist Association wishes to send the following resolutions to your Church:

First—We regret very much your leaving our Association. Your pastor and members will be greatly missed in our meetings.

Second—We wish to thank you for your cooperation in the great work in which the Association is engaged. Our Association has had a marvelous growth and we appreciate the part that your Church had in the work.

Third—We appreciate the fine Christian fellowship that has existed between the Churches. It has been a joy to all.

Fourth—As your Church unites with other churches in Randolph County in forming a new Baptist Association, it is our hope and wish that the work of our Lord will continue to grow, and that your Church will have a large part in giving the Gospel to the whole world. We want your Church to be assured of our continued interest and prayers.

32. The Committee to Nominate the Promotion Committee made the following report which was adopted:

Clarence A. Smith, Chairman	Mrs. C. E. Siceloff
Harry B. Caldwell	E. R. Baldwin
T. L. Sasser	Dr. J. T. J. Battle
A. L. Fulk	

DR. J. T. J. BATTLE
W. B. COOK
A. LINCOLN FULK

33. After singing "Praise God from Whom All Blessings Flow," the session closed with prayer by Dr. H. T. Stevens.

IN MEMORIAM

ASHEBORO, N. C.:
- Mrs. D. T. Pankey, Deaconess
- Mr. Cuyler P. Green

CALVARY:
- Mr. James P. McCargo
- Mrs. James Roberts

CARAWAY:
- Deacon Benjamin Lanier

GIBSONVILLE:
- Mrs. Lynch
- Mrs. Bradshaw
- Mrs. Eunice Mason
- Mr. C. P. Bradshaw

CENTRAL FALLS:
- Deacon Tom Webster
- Mrs. Walter Ashburn
- Mrs. Jane M. Wallace

GREENSBORO, FIRST:
- Mr. J. L. Harris
- Mr. Claude B. Vestal
- Mr. R. F. Williams
- Mr. C. J. Dillon
- Mr. A. B. Creech
- Mr. Paul G. Welch
- Miss Pearl Gurley
- Mrs. T. L. Chisholm
- Mrs. M. B. Smith
- Mrs. E. T. Scism
- Mrs. Susan Williams
- Mrs. Janie Ridge

ASHEBORO STREET:
- Mr. William Pamplin
- Mrs. A. L. Blalock

BESSEMER:
- Mrs. Mary Teasley

ELLER MEMORIAL:
- Mr. Wiley L. Davis
- Mr. Otis W. Davis
- Mr. Bernard Nuckles
- Mrs. Eliza J. Hall
- Mrs. Eugenia (James) Vaviness
- Mrs. James Jarrell
- Mrs. Carl Ham
- Mrs. Ella (Wesley) Kirkman
- Mrs. Effie J. (J. L.) Beall

FLORIDA STREET:
- Miss Ruth Huffling

FOREST AVENUE:
- Mr. Charles Smith
- Mrs. Elza Westmoreland
- Mr. John Womble

POMONA:
- Mr. T. F. Jenkins
- Mr. James Tugwell
- Mrs. J. B. Tugwell
- Mrs. A. J. Clifton

REVOLUTION:
- Mr. W. M. Leach

GUILFORD:
- Mrs. R. L. Dixon

IN MEMORIAM

WHITE OAK:
- Mr. Henry Manuel
- Mr. Shelly Hart
- Mr. J. M. Stutts
- Mr. W. F. Alberry
- Mr. Henry Hanes
- Mr. W. W. Elkins
- Mr. Frank Talley
- Mr. Paul Taylor
- Mrs. Mary Gaston
- Mrs. B. B. Brafford

HIGH POINT, FIRST:
- Mr. G. A. Ausband
- Mr. J. A. Clinard, Deacon
- Mr. R. L. Loflin
- Mr. L. H. Harwell
- Dr. J. L. Spruill, Deacon
- Mr. W. C. York
- Mrs. W. E. Lloyd
- Mrs. J. Matt Hedgecock
- Mrs. J. N. Rumble
- Mrs. J. W. Quattlebaum
- Miss Kate Phillip

GREEN STREET:
- Mrs. J. R. Shelton
- Miss Katrina Wheelis
- Mrs. W. R. Stacy
- Mrs. H. R. Andrews
- Mrs. A. N. Hill
- Mrs. A. D. Green

HILLIARD MEMORIAL:
- Mr. W. L. Ward

NORTH MAIN:
- Mrs. J. S. Brown

NORTH PARK:
- Mrs. T. M. Wood
- Miss Enola Jackson
- Miss Leola Bean

WEST END:
- Mrs. Dovie Huff

LEBANON:
- Mrs. Margaret Whitley

LIBERTY:
- Mrs. Annie Fowler

MACEDONIA:
- Mrs. Bobbie Jones

MOUNT ZION:
- Miss Lizzie Lineberry

OSCEOLA:
- Mrs. Mary Chrismon

RAMSEUR:
- Mrs. W. O. York
- Mr. W. D. McDaniel
- Mrs. J. M. Whtehead

RANDLEMAN:
- Mrs. A. D. Richardson

REIDSVILLE, FIRST:
- Mr. J. T. Richardson
- Mr. L. B. Barnes

RUFFIN STACEY:
- Mrs. Lula Durham
- Mr. W. M. Frairs

SMITH'S GROVE:
- Mr. J. L. Nuckles, Deacon

SUMMERFIELD:
- Mr. John Smith

WHITE'S MEMORIAL:
- Deacon C. R. Hurley

Constitution

Article 1. The Association shall be called the Piedmont Baptist Association.

Article 2. It shall be composed of the ordained ministers who are members of, and those who may have pastoral charges within the Associational District, and three Delegates from each church in the district aforesaid, and churches having a membership exceeding 300 shall be entitled to one additional delegate for every 200 members or fraction thereof in excess of 300.

Article 3. The said delegates shall, before taking their seats, produce letters from respective churches showing their appointment as delegates.

Article 4. The Associational session shall be held at least once a year.

Article 5. The officers shall be a Moderator, Vice-Moderator, Clerk, and Treasurer. If deemed expedient by the Association the offices of Clerk and Treasurer may be combined.

Article 6. The officers of the Association shall be chosen annually by the Association.

Article 7. Association shall be clothed with authority only to advise the churches touching all things pertaining to their interest but shall in no case presume to direct or control them in reference to their own government or internal policy.

Article 8. A Committee of Arrangements, consisting of three members, shall be appointed on the first day of each session to prepare and report the proceedings and suggest topics proper for the consideration and action of the next Annual Association.

Article 9. Baptist brethren, not members of the Association, who may be present at any session of the body, may, on invitation by the body, take seats and participate in the debates of the Association.

Article 10. The territory embraced in the Association shall be divided into not less than four districts and a committee composed of one pastor and one layman from each district, together with the Moderator, Vice-Moderator, and the Clerk of the Association, shall be appointed at each meeting of the Association, which committee shall compose the Executive Committee of the Association a majority of which shall constitute a quorum. It shall be the duty of the committee to superintend and direct the missionary operations of the Association.

Article 11. All committees shall be appointed by the Moderator unless otherwise ordered by the Association.

Article 12. The Constitution may be altered only at an Annual Session of the Association and by a vote of two-thirds of the whole present.

Article 13. The rules of this body shall follow Mell's Parliamentary Practice.

Article 14. This Association shall cooperate with the Baptist State Convention.

Article 15. The time of the holding of the annual session shall be on Wednesday after the fourth Sunday in October of each year.

Adopted October 17, 1895.
Articles 2, 5, 6, 10, 15 Amended.
Sessions, July 23, 24, 1930.
Article 15 Amended,
Session, July 21, 1932.

W. O. JOHNSON,
A. WAYLAND COOKE,
Committee

MINUTES

of the

PIEDMONT W. M. U.

The W. M. U. of the Piedmont Association met in Annual Session April 26 at the Asheboro Street Baptist Church, Greensboro. Mrs. Nettie Hoge, Supt., presided. "Power" was the theme for the day's program.

Mrs. S. N. White, Reidsville, conducted the devotional. Mrs. J. Lester Lane welcomed the visitors. Mrs. June Johnson responded.

Roll called by Secretary showed 20 churches represented at the opening hour. Group Leader's reports were given. They showed progress in all organizations. Miss Ruth Scott gave Young People's report. She told of plans for an all-day meeting of young people June 28 in High Point. This will be an annual meeting.

The Treasurer, Mrs. C. E. Siceloff, reported $11.12 on hand. Mrs. J. N. Rumble gave report of Mission Study done in the Union.

Mrs. Edna R. Harris took the chair while Mrs. Hoge gave her report. Speaking to her report, Mrs. Hoge appealed to the women to seek the Spirit-filled life.

Mrs. C. R. Leonard of China addressed the morning audence. She told of the great spiritual revival now in progress in China. She stirred the hearts of her hearers as she told of changed lives and homes among all classes of Chinese.

The following committees were appointed by the Superintendent:

Nominating Committee—Mrs. Hoyle Love, Mrs. E. C. Williamson, Mrs. S. N. White, Mrs. Chas. W. Moseley.

Time and Place Committee—Mrs. N. N. Newlin, Mrs. Arthur Presnelll, Mrs. J. N. Armfield.

Afternoon Session

The afternoon session was opened with a devotional led by Mrs. J. S. Moore. Mrs. W. H. McKeever gave report of Personal Service work done.

Mrs. J. M. Whitted, Divisional Superintendent, Durham, addressed the women. Her subject was, "The History and Growth of Divisional Work." Mrs. Edna R. Harris, State Secretary, spoke on "Our State Work" and conducted a questionnaire.

Special days of prayer and the special offerings taken by the W. M. U. during the year were discussed at length by women of the different churches.

A short memorial service was held for those who had died during the year. Mrs. J. T. J. Battle read the names while the audience stood.

The best method of providing lunch for the meeting was discussed. It was moved and carried that each woman bring a box lunch to the next meeting.

The Nominating Committee recommended the following for officers:

Mrs. Nettie Hoge, Superintendent
Mrs. J. D. Schoolfield, Secretary
Mrs. C. E. Siceloff, Treasurer
Mrs. W. H. McKeever, Personal Service Chairman
Mrs. R. N. Rumble, Mission Study
Mrs. Catherine Marley, Stewardship
Miss Ruth Scott, Young People's Leader

Group Leaders:

Mrs. H. T. Stevens, Asheboro Group
Mrs. Ellis McCargo, Reidsville
Mrs. A. Andrews, Greensboro
Mrs. A. Lee Gibson, High Point

The Time and Place Committee reported the next meeting will be held at White Oak Baptist Church, Greensboro.

MRS. J. D. SCHOOLFIELD,
Secretary.

YEAR	WHERE HELD	MODERATOR	[redacted]K	PREACHER	Churches	Baptisms	Church Members	Total Gifts
	[redacted]o	Dr. C. A. Rominger	W. L. Kivett	M. A. [redacted]s	5	....	562	....
1895	Liberty	T. L. Chislom	W. L. Kivett	L. Johnson	12	16		[redacted] 4,695.50
	[redacted]s [redacted]el	R. W. Brooks	W. H. Eller	L. Johnson	14	66	1,194	5,128.94
1897	[redacted]ld	F. H. Jones	W. H. Eller	J. A. [redacted]y	16	73	[redacted]0	7,198.27
1898	Mount Zion	R. W. Brooks	W. H. Eller	L. Johnson	17	67	1[redacted]57	6,883.23
	[redacted]ur	R. W. Brooks	F. P. Tucker	John E. [redacted]ite	19	54	1,570	7,435.43
	[redacted]y Street	R. W. Brooks	W. H. Eller	Thomas Carrick	16	48	1,538	7,970.35
1901	Reidsville	F. H. Jones	W. H. Eller	L. [redacted]n	19	157	1,657	8,282.73
	[redacted]h Steet	F. H. Jones	W. H. Eller	W. C. [redacted]n	19	135	1,774	9,950.97
	[redacted]e	F. H. Jones	W. H. Eller	C. L. [redacted]s	20	185	1,868	12,834.77
	[redacted]y	F. H. Jones	W. H. Eller	H. W. Battle	22	112	1,832	12,807.43
	[redacted]h	F. H. Jones	W. H. Eller	J. M. Hilliard	22	14	2,096	17,674.91
1906	High Point, First	F. H. Jones	W. H. Eller	W. R. Bradshaw	23	201	2,333	29,366.31
1907	[redacted]o Street	F. H. Jones	W. H. Eller	Wm. Hedley	26	372	2,798	29,993.79
1908	Ramseur	F. H. Jones	W. H. Eller	C. E. Maddry	28	[redacted]1	3,086	26,347.57
1909	Greensboro	F. H. Jones	W. H. Eller	Wm. Hedley	30	292	3,429	49,847.28
1910	Mount Zion	F. H. Jones	W. H. Eller	R. G. Hendrick	31	336	3,731	28,531.01
[redacted]1	Asheboro	W. F. Staley	W. H. Eller	W. F. Staley	29	182	3,736	25,887.56
[redacted]2	High Point, Green St	F. P. Hobgood, Jr.	W. H. Eller	J. C. Turner	30	174	3,647	29,697.38
[redacted]3	Liberty	F. P. Hobgood, Jr.	W. H. Eller	R. P. Walker	31	409	3,971	37,700.97
1914	Asheboro [redacted]t	F. P. Hobgood, Jr.	W. H. Eller	A. W. Claxon	31	413	4,202	42,428.44
	[redacted]sville	J. M. Hilliard	W. H. Eller	J. M. Hilliard	42	313	4,491	42,577.68
1916	Forest Avenue	J. M. Hilliard	W. H. Eller	E. N. [redacted]n	36	369	4,854	48,418.92
1917	Green Street	J. [redacted] Hilliard	W. H. Eller	W. R. [redacted]e	39	308	4,760	44,609.05
1918	o[redacted]re's Chapel	I. M. [redacted]	W. H. Eller	J. W. Rose	39	374	5,140	72,538.46
1919	White [redacted]	I. M. Hilliard	W. H. Eller	W. H. [redacted]on	39	339	5,359	76,638.85
1920	Calvary	J. [redacted] Hilliard	W. H. Eller	E. N. Johnson	39	543	5,867	117,682.35
1921	Summerfield	Clarence A. Smith	J. E. Lanier	B. K. [redacted]	39	[redacted]80	6,454	135,561.79
	[redacted]la	[redacted]e A. Smith	J. E. Lanier	Jas. A. [redacted]rk	39	679	7,226	149,955.24
1923	Magnolia Street	Clarence A. Smith	H. O. Miller	E. E. [redacted]e	38	365	7,341	140,553.25
1924	West End	Clarence A. [redacted]h	H. O. Miller	W. E. Goode	40	672	7,489	164,658.19
1925	Fairview	Clarence A. [redacted]h	H. O. Miller	A. T. Howell	41	[redacted]	3,[redacted]56	211,792.21
1926	Ramseur	Clarence A. Smith	S. T. Hensley	L[redacted]d T. Wilson	42	620	9,974	243,500.68
[redacted]	Trinity	Clarence A. Smith	S. T. Hensley	H. T. Stevens	40	6[redacted]	10,223	211,846.40
1928	Bessemer	Clarence A. [redacted]h	O. E. Lee	R. P. Ellington	41	531	10,866	202,002.30
1929	Liberty	Clarence A. Smith	O. E. Lee	C. F. Rogers	44	573	11,496	218,987.61
	[redacted]ro	Clarence A. [redacted]th	O. E. [redacted]e	[redacted] T. Tunstall	44	[redacted]76	12,012	198,077.29
1931	Florida Street	Clarence A. Smith	O. E. Lee	A. B. Conrad	44	827	12,789	178,501.19
	[redacted]e	Clarence A. Smith	O. E. Lee	J. C. [redacted]	46	778	13,485	159,000.60
	[redacted]te Oak	Clarence A. Smith	O. E. Lee	T. L. Sasser	48	1561	15,199	186,041.40
1934	Franklinville	Clarence A. Smith	O. E. Lee	[redacted] [redacted]k	53	757	15,356	172,839.18

TABLE I. CHURCH MEMBERSHIP OF PIEDMONT BAPTIST ASSOCIATION.

CHURCHES	PASTORS AND POST OFFICES	Location	Year constituted	Days of Meeting	Members Last Year	GAINS Baptisms	GAINS Letters	GAINS Statements	GAINS Restorations	LOSSES Letters	LOSSES Deaths	LOSSES Exclusions	LOSSES Erasures	Total Present Membership	Weekly Prayer Meeting Held	Revivals Held	Lord's Supper Observed	Families Taking State Paper
[illegible] Jay	R. L. Smith, [illegible] [illegible], N. C.	O	1934	2 4	...	...	...	...	...	...	...	...	...	32	Yes	...	...	...
[illegible]o, N. C.	Dr. H. T. Stevens, [illegible]o, N. C.	T	1902	Every	391	3	32	1	...	10	2	...	3	412	Yes	...	1	20
Balfour	O. P. Dix [illegible], N. C., Rt. 2	V	[illegible]	Every	57	3	10	3	...	1	...	...	...	72	Yes	1	4	...
Calvary	Jas. C. [illegible]e, [illegible]e, N. C.	O	[illegible]	2 4	189	11	2	...	1	2	2	...	...	199	...	1	2	...
[illegible]y	W. P. [illegible]r, [illegible]-Salem, N. C.	O	1932	1 3	8	...	2	...	...	...	1	...	...	9	Yes	1	...	...
[illegible]r Falls	W. F. Hancock, Bear Creek, N. C.	V	8[illegible]	1 3	31	1	1	...	...	...	...	...	...	32	...	1	...	...
Central Falls	J. A. Cox, Central Falls, N. C.	T	[illegible]93	Every	20	3	14	...	...	3	3	...	...	31	Yes	2	4	...
[illegible]w	J. C. Gillespie, Reidsville, N. C.	O	1904	1 3	132	4	4	...	...	7	...	...	1	132	...	1	2	2
Franklinville	H. M. Stroup, Ramseur, N. C.	T	1877	2 4	239	11	4	...	...	3	...	...	21	220	Yes	1	4	...
Gibsonville	T. W. Fogleman, Greensboro, N. C.	T	1894	......	275	4	...	...	...	...	4	...	...	211	Yes	1	4	1
[illegible]	W. Wilbur H[illegible]s, High Point, N. C.	O	1917	2 4	150	10	1	...	...	6	...	...	...	153	...	1	2	...
[illegible]o, First	Dr. J. Clyde Turner, Greensboro, N. C.	C	1859	Every	1790	76	162	14	...	84	12	9	...	1937	Yes	1	12	...
[illegible]o St.	J. Ben Eller, Greensboro, N. C.	C	8[illegible]	Every	980	26	18	5	...	54	2	...	9	964	Yes	1	4	...
Eller [illegible]orial	J. S. Hopkins, [illegible]o, N. C.	C	1897	Every	863	27	21	4	1	13	9	4	...	890	Yes	1	4	12
Bessemer	J. O. Reynolds, Bessemer Br., G'boro	C	1922	Every	541	31	11	...	...	33	1	...	...	549	Yes	2	12	6
Florida Street	B. G. [illegible]y, [illegible]o, N. C.	C	1916	E[illegible]y	352	27	26	3	...	25	1	...	59	323	Yes	2	4	8
Forest Ave.	[illegible] [illegible]k, [illegible]o, N. C.	C	1906	Every	526	24	30	2	...	26	3	1	...	552	Yes	1	12	30
L[illegible] Park	W. I. J[illegible], Burlington, N. C.	C	1916	Every	29	14	6	...	...	...	...	1	...	52	Yes	1	...	...
Magnolia Street	Jennings [illegible], Greensboro, N. C.	C	1912	Every	398	15	18	...	...	23	...	2	2	400	Yes	2	...	5
Pomona	W. B. [illegible]k, Pomona, N. C.	V	1913	Every	195	5	11	2	7	4	4	1	1	210	Yes	3	2	...

Revolution	A. N. Hollis, Revolution Br., G'boro	C	....	Every	295	2	6	...	2	9	1	...	...	295	Yes	1	1	2
Stevens Memorial	T. W. Fogleman, Greensboro, N. C.	V	1922	Every	155	11	2	...	...	1	...	...	...	167	Yes	1	4	...
White Oak	John L. Coley, Denim Sta., G'boro	C	1907	Every	1138	20	1	...	1	18	8	52	...	1088	Yes	2	10	25
Guilford	Clyde W. Glosson, Greensboro, N. C., R.5	V	1914	Every	64	6	3	1	...	4	1	...	...	77	...	1	2	5
High Point, First	Dr. A. B. Conrad, High Point, N. C.	C	1825	Every	1182	16	34	2	1	31	11	...	28	1165	Yes	1	4	25
Green Street	C. N. Royal, High Point, N. C.	C	1900	Every	1376	56	56	10	...	55	6	...	210	1104	Yes	1	2	4
Hilliard Memorial	Hughey O. Miller, High Point, N. C.	C	1929	Every	257	27	22	...	...	5	1	...	8	280	Yes	1	2	4
North Main Street	A. Lincoln Fulk, High Point, N. C.	C	1908	Every	264	38	6	2	...	20	1	...	55	234	Yes	1	4	6
North Park	O. F. Bass, High Point, N. C.	C	1929	....	142	14	6	1	1	7	3	5	...	149	Yes	2	3	...
South Side	G. H. Liner, High Point, N. C.	C	1916	Every	303	11	6	2	2	3	...	...	...	321	Yes	2	4	2
West End	Hoyle Love, High Point, N. C.	C	1913	Every	344	40	3	...	...	11	1	1	...	374	Yes	1	4	4
Jump Grove	R. O. Nuckels, Rt. 1, Colfax, N. C.		1933	2 4	......	15	...	...	...	...	...	...	...	45	Yes	2	4	...
Lebanon	C. M. Oates, Revolution Br., G'boro	O	1911	Every	107	24	10	2	...	1	1	...	...	141	Yes	2	2	...
Liberty	Wilbur Hutchins, High Point, N. C.	T	1886	1 3	124	...	...	...	...	10	1	...	...	114	...	...	...	5
Macedonia	J. A. Cox, Central Falls, N. C.	O	1880	....	178	9	3	...	...	1	1	...	...	190	...	1	1	...
Mount Zion	W. I. Johnson, Burlington, N. C.	O	....	....	161	...	...	...	...	...	...	...	...	161	...	...	...	2
Oak Grove	J. H. Haynes, Blews Creek, N. C.	O	1916	1 3	51	19	18	...	...	...	...	...	...	88	Yes	1	2	1
Osborne Chapel	Tom W. Bray, Pleasant Garden, N. C.	O	1934	Every	......	7	1	3	...	...	...	...	...	11	Yes	1	...	...
Osceola	D. E. Oates, High Point, N. C.	O	1915	1	42	3	...	1	...	...	1	...	...	45	...	1	...	2
Pleasant Garden	Tom W. Bray, Pleasant Garden, N. C.	V	1933	Every	23	17	13	...	...	...	...	...	...	53	Yes	2	1	14
Ramseur	H. M. Stroupe, Ramseur, N. C.	T	1850	1 3	223	5	...	...	...	3	3	...	5	171	...	1	3	...
Randleman	S. F. Morton, Winston-Salem, N. C.	T	1879	2 4	97	9	5	...	1	8	1	...	...	103	Yes	1	2	5
Reidsville, First	T. L. Sasser, Reidsville, N. C.	C	....	Every	680	7	9	2	...	12	2	...	3	681	Yes	1	4	39
Lawsonville Ave.	D. W. Overby, Reidsville, N. C.	C	1927	Every	87	26	27	...	...	3	...	...	...	140	Yes	1	4	5
Mount Olive	J. H. Saunders, Reidsville, N. C.	C	1929	Every	179	27	20	8	...	6	...	28	...	200	Yes	2	4	4
Ruffin-Stacey	J. T. London, Reidsville, N. C.	O	1931	Every	113	9	...	...	10	3	2	3	...	124	Yes	1	3	3
Sandy Rock	J. C. Edwards, Staley, N. C.	O	1905	2	5	...	...	...	...	...	...	...	...	5	...	1	...	1
Smith Grove	R. O. Nuckels, Colfax, N. C.	O	1921	1 3	100	23	...	...	...	2	1	...	...	124	Yes	3	4	...
Summerfield	E. A. Long, Germantown, N. C.	V	....	2	148	2	2	...	...	...	1	...	...	151	...	1	2	4
Tabernacle	Grover C. Phillips, Altamahaw, N. C.	V	1933	Every	......	2	8	16	...	...	...	...	5	21	Yes	2	...	...
Trinity	B. F. Clark, Thomasville, N. C.	V	1924	1 3	100	6	1	...	...	12	...	...	...	88	Yes	2	1	...
Whites Memorial	J. C. Edwards Staley, N. C.	O	1908	3	40	...	1	...	...	...	1	...	...	40	...	1	...	...
Worthville	S. F. Morton, Winston-Salem, N. C.	V	1891	4	14	5	6	...	1	...	...	...	...	26	Yes	1	1	...
TOTALS					15,135	757	646	154	28	519	92	107	410	15,356	...	66	151	246

39

TABLE II. SUNDAY SCHOOLS OF PIEDMONT BAPTIST ASSOCIATION.

CHURCHES	SUPERINTENDENTS AND POST OFFICES	Beginners 3-5 Years	Primaries 6-8 Years	Juniors 9-12 Years	Intermediates 13-16	Young People 17-24	Adults 25 Years Up	Cradle Roll Under 3	Home Department	Officers and Teachers	Total Enrollment	Average Attendance	Is School Graded?	Teachers Holding Normal Diplomas	Baptisms from School	Have You a Mission Sunday School?	Enrollment of Mission Sunday School	Did You Hold a Daily Vacation Bible Sch?	Enrollment Daily Vacation Bible School	Average Attendance D. V. B. School
Allen Jay	Wade Comby, Trinity, N. C., Rt. 1	8	10	19	17	...	30	...	...	7	91	55	...	...	...	...	...	...	...	...
Asheboro, N. C.	R. S. Allred, Asheboro, N. C.	25	55	52	25	77	114	32	...	19	399	211	Yes	14	3	...	...	...	...	...
Balfour	J. C. Pearce, Randleman, N. C., Rt. 2	15	23	24	17	47	52	10	...	15	188	87	Yes	...	4	...	...	...	...	...
Calvary	C. J. Dilgado, Reidsville, N. C.	31	...	31	21	87	23	...	...	11	193	91	...	1	7	...	...	...	...	...
Caraway	George Ferree, Sophia, N. C., Rt. 1	...	9	...	...	16	20	5	...	4	50	36	...	1	...	...	...	...	...	...
Cedar Falls	...	7	...	15	...	8	12	...	...	8	50	25	...	...	1	...	...	...	...	...
Central Falls	Roy Plummer, Central Falls, N. C.	17	...	...	17	39	33	...	...	6	112	75	...	...	...	...	...	...	...	...
Fairview	A. D. Hopkins, Reidsville, N. C.	...	...	...	...	...	...	...	...	...	70	50	...	...	4	...	...	...	...	...
Franklinville	J. H. Mitchell, Franklinville, N. C.	...	...	...	...	...	...	...	...	22	224	160	Yes	...	11	...	...	...	...	...
Gibsonville	E. C. Riggins, Gibsonville, N. C.	31	45	45	41	46	39	...	...	17	264	153	Yes	17	...	...	...	...	...	...
Glenola	G. H. Tillotson, High Point, N. C.	31	...	32	...	46	61	6	...	11	187	156	...	...	10	...	...	...	...	...
Greensboro, First	O. E. Lee, Greensboro, N. C.	163	146	206	157	184	680	82	199	92	1909	849	Yes	38	57	...	...	1	230	166
Asheboro St.	J. T. True, Greensboro, N. C.	59	133	122	104	76	268	53	36	79	930	467	Yes	...	...	...	...	...	...	...
Eller Memorial	C. E. Brady, Denim Sta., Greensboro	31	76	102	90	125	150	...	...	70	644	370	Yes	30	25	...	...	1	245	167
Bessemer	A. C. Melvin, Bessemer Br., G'boro	30	38	68	117	68	100	18	...	32	471	290	Yes	11	12	...	...	1	244	221
Florida Street	J. L. Roberson, Greensboro, N. C.	38	58	55	53	31	114	...	...	25	374	265	Yes	...	16	...	...	...	...	...
Forest Ave.	Dr. J. T. J. Battle, Greensboro, N. C.	26	58	75	69	134	118	44	45	48	617	360	Yes	40	19	1	72	1	133	85
Latham Park	Ruth Scott, Greensboro, N. C.	...	...	...	...	...	...	...	...	7	105	55	Yes	...	14	...	...	...	...	...
Magnolia Street	H. S. Noah, Glenwood, N. C.	11	39	67	19	63	102	17	...	18	336	223	Yes	...	...	...	...	...	...	...
Pomona	C. C. Patterson, Pomona, N. C.	37	52	70	49	60	63	10	...	13	354	225	Yes	1	...	...	...	...	...	...

Revolution	W. D. Teeter, Revolution Br., G'boro	24	49	63	37	46	81	55	21	26	402	188	Yes	11						
Stevens Memorial	T. E. Hilliard, Greensboro, N. C., Rt. 2	17	38	37	25	23	66	4		20	230	172	Yes							
White Oak	J. B. Brady, Denim Sta., G'sboro, N. C.	37	42	116	66	43	230	26		20	570	357	Yes	4	20					
Guilford	Setzer Weston, Guilford College, N. C.	15	14	12	16	24	13	9	2		115	75	Yes	1	6					
High Point, First	A. E. Tate, High Point, N. C.	77	77	119	116	161	205	30	64	74	923	482	Yes		15			1	133	90
Green Street	B. G. Leonard, High Point, N. C.	96	199	244	168	199	365	53		122	1446	712	Yes	100	28					
Hilliard Memorial		53	19	34	65	48	77	12		24	332	203	Yes	20	22					
North Main Street	Winfred Clinard, High Point, N. C.	23	30	49	36	35	50			20	243	187		6	27					
North Park	Paul K. Frye, High Point, N. C.	36	39	43	35	12	87	16	1	19	288	176	Yes	10						
South Side	B. E. Chandler, Highland Sta., High Pt.	40	46	67	69	48	94	10		15	389	245	Yes							
West End	C. F. Witherspoon, High Point, N. C.	45	32	62	39	38	76	25	30	22	369	224	Yes	3	25					
Jesup Grove	Al Apple, Guilford College, N. C., Rt. 1		15	15	18		17				65	60			2					
Lebanon	B. G. Yow, Denim Sta., Greensboro, N. C.	43	22	26	18	52	71			10	243	140			24					
Liberty	A. E. Dark, Liberty, N. C.	5	15	6	11	30	23	4		10	102	60								
Macedonia		12	12	20	13	28	49	14		12	160	81		1	4					
Mount Zion	George Spoon, Kimesville, N. C.										90									
Oak Grove	L. R. Loflin, Jamestown, N. C.	12	12	15		27	18			9	93	68								
Osborne Chapel	Robert R. Osborne, Greensboro, Rt. 3	4	10	5			6			2	27	20	Yes							
Osceola	Branford Wray, Brown Summit, Rt. 1	12		15	18		14			8	67	46			1					
Pleasant Garden	Walter J. Smith, Pleasant Garden, N. C.	19		19		29	15			5	87	50	Yes		23					
Ramseur	M. E. Johnson, Ramseur, N. C.	17	8	12	19	26	55			18	155	106			5					
Randleman	A. M. Barker, Randleman, N. C.	16	10	23	14	31	46			11	151	110	Yes	5	9					
Reidsville, First	R. I. Burton, Reidsville, N. C.	18	48	77	76	111	109	37		62	538	254	Yes	10	5			1	194	151
Lawsonville Ave.	R. R. Roberts, Reidsville, N. C.	19		14	18	29	30			8	118		Yes	1						
Mount Olive	Elwood Talley, Reidsville, N. C.	31	22	20	18	77	16			10	194	118	Yes			1	45			
Ruffin-Stacey	M. C. Thomas, Reidsville, N. C., Rt. 5										130	80								
Sandy Creek	Miss Ida Williams, Liberty, N. C.		7	5			5			4	21	15								
Smith Grove	Drew Smith, Colfax, N. C.		30		35		35				100	50			6					
Summerfield	A. C. Metz, Germantown, N. C.									11	125	85			1					
Tabernacle	W. D. Smithey, Altamahaw, N. C.	4	10	15	8	10	20			8	67	47			2					
Trinity	J. M. Thomas, High Point, N. C., Rt. 3	5	10	6	16	29	42	11		15	134			6	6					
Whites Memorial	Charlie Walker, Franklinville, N. C.	14		10		20	18			6	68	30								
Worthville																				
TOTALS		1244	1557	2132	1750	2283	3912	583	398	1075	15,610	8644	29	331	414	2	117	6	1179	880

TABLE III. CHURCH PROPERTY OF PIEDMONT BAPTIST ASSOCIATION.

CHURCHES	CHURCH CLERKS AND POST OFFICES	Dos Church own its House of Worship?	When Was it Built?	Materials Used	Persons Seated	Number of Rooms	No. Department Assembly Rooms	No. Separate Class Rooms	Value of Church House and Grounds	Value Mission Chapel	Value of Pastor's Home	Total Value of All Church Property	Indebtedness on All Church Property	Insurance Carried
Allen Jay	Wade Cumby, Trinity, N. C.	No	....	[illegible]d	300	1	...	...	......	......	......	......	....	......
Asheboro, N. C.	Mrs. M. T. Lambert, Asheboro, N. C.	Yes	1934	Brick	700	17	5	17	30,000	......	5,000	40,000	15,000.00	13,000
Balfour	W. F. Cates, Randleman, N. C., Rt. 2	Yes	1933	Brick	250	11	1	9	5,000	......	......	5,000	1,900.00	2,500
Calvary	J. E. McCargo, Reidsville, N. C.	Yes	1898	Wood	375	5	4	4	3,000	......	2,000	5,000	150.00	2,000
Caraway	C. C. Sawyer, Sophia, N. C.	Yes	1889	Wood	150	1	...	...	500	......	......	500	....	......
Cedar Falls	Mrs. J. M. Harmon, Cedar Falls, N. C.	Yes	1844	Wood	200	1	...	...	1,500	......	......	1,500	....	......
Central Falls	Mrs. W. S. Wallace, Central Falls, N. C.	Yes	1893	Wood	500	1	...	...	2,000	......	......	2,000	....	......
Fairview	William Cummings, Reidsville, N. C., R 2	Yes	1907	Wood	300	1	...	...	1,500	......	500	2,000	....	1,400
Franklinville	W. A. Martin, Franklinville, N. C.	Yes	1920	Brick	300	1	1	15	9,000	......	......	9,000	....	2,500
Gibsonville	W. P. Killette, Gibsonville, N. C.	Yes	1894	Wood	350	10	5	8	......	......	......	......	....	2,500
Glenola	Marvin Smith, High Point, N. C., R. 3	Yes	1917	Wood	350	8	...	7	2,500	......	......	2,500	....	1,200
Greensboro, First	A. R. Williams, Greensboro, N. C.	Yes	1906	Brick	1000	48	...	...	130,000	......	15,000	145,000	....	67,000
Asheboro St.	J. B. Wills, Greensboro, N. C.	Yes	1912	Brick	700	32	6	47	30,000	......	6,000	36,000	4,500.25	26,000
Bessemer	W. P. Haynes, Bessemer Br., G'boro	Yes	1922	Wood	400	16	3	16	6,000	......	2,000	8,000	1,500.00	4,500
Eller Memorial	[illegible] W. Baity, Denim Sta., G'boro, N. C.	Yes	1925	Brick	450	48	6	48	41,000	......	......	41,000	....	25,000
Florida Street	Mrs. W. A. Roberts, Glenwood, N. C.	Yes	1930	Brick	450	22	2	12	15,000	......	......	15,000	3,500.00	10,000
Forest Ave.	B. B. Stockard, Greensboro, N. C.	Yes	1906	Brick	275	14	6	14	17,000	100	6,000	41,000	2,500.00	10,500
Latham Park	W. W. [illegible], [illegible], N. C.	Yes	1916	Wood	150	1	...	...	3,000	......	......	3,000	....	......
Magnolia Street	Mrs. G. H. Williamson, Bes. Br., G'boro	Yes	1912	Wood	300	8	...	8	6,000	......	......	6,000	....	4,000
Pomona	C. C. Patterson, Pomona, N. C.	Yes	1913	Wood	350	8	7	7	3,500	......	......	3,500	....	......

Revolution	W. L. Campbell, Greensboro, N. C.	Yes	1907	W[redacted]d	400	5	3	7	10,000	......	5,000	15,000	....	7,500
Stevens [redacted]	J. H. Campbell, [redacted]o, N. C., R. 2	Yes	1922	W[redacted]d	250	11	2	13	10,000	......	......	10,000	....	5,000
White [redacted]	L. F. Paris, Denim Sta., Greensboro	Yes	1907	Brick	500	9	2	9	30,000	......	......	30,000	....	10,000
Guilford	R. F. Bondurant, Guilford College, N. C.	Yes	1914	W[redacted]d	200	1	...	5	3,500	150	......	3,650	....	1,500
High Point, First	C. D. [redacted]h, High Point, N. C.	Yes	1905	Brick	500	16	5	14	98,000	......	10,000	128,000	....	36,000
[redacted]n Street	Clyde Ayers, High Point, N. C.	Yes	1926	Brick	1500	95	6	68	156,000	1,600	5,000	162,600	62,500.00	60,000
Hilliard [redacted]	H. E. Taylor, High Point, N. C.	Yes	1930	Brick	800	22	...	20	20,000	......	......	20,500	650.00	10,000
North Main Street	Mrs. Ethel Clinard, High Point, N. C.	Yes	1924	Brick	350	10	3	10	10,000	......	......	10,400	....	4,000
North Park	D. H. Short, High Point, N. C.	Yes	1929	Wood	300	6	6	6	3,500	......	......	3,500	1,200.00	1 [redacted]0
South Side	J. G. [redacted]s, High Point, N. C.	Yes	1916	W[redacted]d	400	9	...	9	4,500	......	2,500	7,000	2,300.00	......
West End	Z. V. Swain, High Point, N. C.	Yes	1913	W[redacted]d	350	11	...	13	8,500	......	3,500	12,000	....	5,000
J[redacted]p [redacted]e	Jessie Stanley, [redacted] [redacted]ege, N. C.	Yes	1934	W[redacted]d	400	1	...	...	1,050	......	......	1,050	....	......
Lebanon	J. B. [redacted]r, Greensboro, N. C., R. 5	Yes	1911	Wood	250	3	...	...	1,200	......	......	1,400	....	......
Liberty	A. E. Dark Liberty, N. C.	Yes	1911	Brick	300	3	4	4	6,000	......	......	6,000	800.00	4,000
[redacted]ia	Rev. W. F. [redacted]n, Liberty, N. C., R 1	Yes	1930	Wood	600	1	...	...	3,500	......	......	3,500	....	......
[redacted]t Zion	J. C. Lackamy, Liberty, N. C.	Yes	1912	W[redacted]d	500	1	...	...	2,000	......	......	2,000	....	......
Oak Grove	L. R. Loflin, Jamestown, N. C.	Yes	1927	Wood	270	3	2	2	1,500	......	......	1,500	....	......
[redacted]e Chapel	Robt. W. Osborne, Greensboro, N. C., R 3	Yes	....	W[redacted]d	125	1	...	...	150	......	......	150	....	......
[redacted]a	E. R. Brande, Brown Summit, N. C., R 1	Yes	1915	W[redacted]d	300	1	...	4	2,000	......	......	2,000	....	......
Pleasant Garden	Edna Thompson, Pleasant Garden, N. C.	No	....	W[redacted]d	225	1	1	1	800	......	......	800	....	500
Ramseur	D. E. [redacted]d, Ramseur, N. C.	Yes	1894	Brick	400	11	11	11	15,000	......	3,500	18,500	....	9,500
Randleman	A. M. Barker, Randleman, N. C.	Yes	1879	Wood	600	6	5	6	5,000	......	......	5,000	....	1,500
Reidsville, First	T. L. [redacted]r, Reidsville, N. C.	Yes	....	Brick	500	24	5	19	37,000	......	14,000	51,000	....	43,500
Lawsonville Ave.	Mrs. Pearl Boswell, Reidsville, N. C.	Yes	1927	Wood	300	1	...	...	2.000	......	1,600	3,600	900.00	1,500
Mount Olive	Hazel Driscoll, Reidsville, N. C.	...	1929	Wood	275	1	...	5	2,000	......	......	2,000	800.00	1,500
Ruffin-Stacey	R. M. Durham, Reidsville, N. C., R. 5	Yes	1931	W[redacted]d	350	...	...	...	2,000	......	......	2,000	....	......
Sandy Creek	Ida Williams, Liberty, N. C., R. 5	Yes	1905	W[redacted]d	500	1	...	...	700	......	......	700	....	200
Smith Grove	Drew Smith, Colfax, N. C.	Yes	1923	W[redacted]d	......	...	...	...	1,200	......	......	1,500	....	650
Summerfield	M[redacted]s. Myrtle Smith, Summerfield, N. C.	Yes	1904	W[redacted]d	400	1	...	4	6,000	......	......	6,000	....	3,500
Tabernacle	Edna Phillips, Altamahaw, N. C.	Yes	1934	W[redacted]d	400	1	...	...	1,200	......	......	1,200	....	......
Trinity	M[redacted]s. G. G. [redacted]d, Trinity, N. C.	Yes	1925	W[redacted]d	200	7	5	4	2,500	......	......	2,500	....	2,000
Whites Memorial	E. W. [redacted]d, Franklinville, N. C.	Yes	1908	W[redacted]d	400	1	...	...	600	......	......	600	....	......
Worthville	Mrs. J. M. Myrick, Randleman, N. C. R 2	No	....	......	......	...	...	...	......	......	......	......	....	......
TOTALS					20,695	518	106	446	753,900	1,850	81,600	881,650	98,200.25	380,950

TABLE IV. GIFTS FOR [illegible]L CHURCH WORK OF [illegible]ONT BAPTIST ASSOCIATION.

CHURCHES	REGULAR TREASURERS AND POST [illegible]S	Pastor's Salary	Other Salaries	Ministerial Help and Supply	Building and Repairs	Incidentals	Literature for S. S., B.Y.P.U. and W.M.S.	Aid to Local Poor	Association Fund	Other Objects	Given by the W. M. U. Organizations	Given by the Sunday School	Total for Local Purposes by Church and all its organizations
Allen Jay	Hill [illegible]h, High Point, R. 3												
[illegible]o, N. C.	Miss Rilla B. [illegible]n, [illegible]o, N. [illegible]	2,100.00			14,346.30	876.51	248.84	13.00	8.00		421.00		17,592.65
Balfour	W. M. Green, [illegible]o, N. C.	528.26			1,303.69	118.64	53.09			10.00	131.75		2,013.68
Calvary	[illegible]as. F. [illegible]l, Reidsville, N. C.	255.37		41.56	3.95	71.37	23.80		3.00	6.37	24.07	50.80	405.42
[illegible]y	C. O. Sawyer, Sophia, N. C.	70.67					12.80						83.47
[illegible]r Falls	Mrs. J. M. Har[illegible]on, Cedar Falls, N.	147.09		33.76		1.87	10.50	2.00	.75				195.97
Central Falls	W. L. Richardson, Randleman, R 2,	260.00		20.00	320.05								600.05
Fairview	[illegible] T. [illegible]n, Reidsville, N. C., R. [illegible]	158.03		28.00		7.30	40.00		4.00				237.38
Franklinville	J. O. York, Franklinville, N. C.	724.24		51.35	30.35	139.38	135.39		5.00	15.00	390.20		1,100.71
Gibsonville	T. L. Roberson, [illegible]e, N. C.	600.00		57.00	138.00	156.00	151.07	3.00	3.00	15.00			1,123.07
[illegible]a	T. F. Baker, High Point, N. C., R. [illegible]	300.00		70.00	820.00	15.00	60.00		3.00			75.00	1,268.00
[illegible]o, First	Howard Gardner, Greensboro, N. C	4,600.00	4,383.00	[illegible]84	273.44	4,320.36	750.10	528.56	20.00	1,959.59			17,533.99
[illegible]o St.	U. A. [illegible]k, [illegible]o, N. C.	2,625.00	1,027.00	339.75	1,595.99	570.26	537.83	11.69		480.81	6.00		7,188.33
E[illegible]r Memorial	E. G. Parker, Denim [illegible]., [illegible]o	1,300.00		20.32	415.55	211.48	491.26	75.91	4.00			491.26	2,518.52
Bessemer	A. C. Melvin, Bess. Br., [illegible]o	2,350.00		151.11	892.83	1,102.96	364.00	177.42	10.00	115.84			5,164.16
Florida [illegible]t	E. H. Moore, Glenwood, N. C.	1,435.00		92.35	808.99	415.80	141.71	70.47	3.25	226.41	20.70	88.42	3,183.98
Forest Ave.	[illegible] E. Sharp, [illegible]o, N. C.	2,035.16		30.00	401.46	974.57	350.23						3,791.42
Latham Park	[illegible] C. Parish, [illegible]o, N. C.	130.00				25.00	24.00						179.00
Magnolia [illegible]et	Harvey Royal, Greensboro, N. C.	1,560.00		61.50	169.83	80.39	82.96	10.00		106.67		511.35	2,071.35
Pomona	Ernest C. Stout, Pomona, N. C.	1,391.08		84.82	150.00	285.33	79.42		1.25	147.90		287.32	2,139.80

Revolution	Waldo Johnson, Greensboro, N. C.	1,707.50	....	59.59	61.73	223.35	166.50	....	4.00	....	....	153.96	2,822.67
Stevens Memorial	C. B. Brisson, Greensboro, N. C., R.	739.00	....	25.00	5.87	184.56	57.87	....	3.50	7.40	818.57	204.63	1,023.20
White Oak	A. W. Long, Denim Sta., Greensbor	2,353.16	....	76.79	....	1,107.94	216.17	92.40	....	56.74	....	....	3,[illegible]
Guilford	W. L. Hudson, Greensboro, N. C.	234.00	....	18.70	22.10	126.89	42.00	10.00	2.00	20.00	....	....	475.69
High Point, First	Miss Thelma Patrick, High Point, N.	3,300.00	900.00	170.00	6,744.76	1,591.51	[illegible]	113.31	18 00	754.80	....	971.82	14,404.18
Green Street	R. B. Culler, High Point, N. C.	2,103.50	....	175.00	3,950.00	2,600.00	450.00	125.00	5.00	60.00	....	....	9,468.50
Hilliard Memorial	K. F. Moore, High Point, N. C.	1,501.06	....	61.00	2,151.51	225.66	138.11	8.06	3.00	22.00	213.93	187.51	4,150.42
North Main Street	Kester Burrows, High Point, N. C.	960.00	....	60.00	343.07	243.28	146.72	50.57	....	34.19	32.99	329.83	1,837.83
North Park	L. W. Glenn, High Point, N. C.	859.50	....	139.71	731.86	182.62	[illegible]	69.95	4.00	....	....	59.95	2,161.55
South Side	B. E. Chandler, Highland Sta., High P	1,293.17	....	62.00	890.35	156.70	192.00	18.00	....	....	....	....	2,612.22
West End	C. M. Scott, High Point, N. C.	1,357.00	....	45.00	359.18	346.71	129.40	12.28	2.50	130.11	....	259.77	2,382.18
Jesup Grove	Everette Jessup, Guilford College, N.	....	....	....	....	....	....	....	....	....	....	....	....
Lebanon	J. B. Carter, [illegible]sboro, N. C., R. 5	220.90	....	52.25	....	20.00	54.00	....	3.00	132.00	....	....	482.15
Liberty	Miss Clara Stroud, Liberty, N. C.	525.00	....	30.00	12.65	58.71	66.15	....	....	6.35	....	....	698.96
Macedonia	Mrs. Ray York, Liberty, N. C.	142.94	....	....	15.00	....	....	....	....	23.50	....	....	181.44
Mount Zion	Miss [illegible] Branson, Burlington, N.	250.00	....	25.00	37.30	....	16.23	....	5.00	....	....	....	[illegible]
Oak Grove	L. R. Loflin, Jamestown, N. C.	91.42	....	....	126.18	20.99	20.85	....	2.00	....	....	....	261.44
Stone Chapel	....	4.00	....	....	....	....	6.00	....	2.00	7.00	....	....	19.00
Osceola	Mrs. D. A. Green, Brown Summit, R	52.74	....	24.35	173.18	....	25.40	....	2.00	....	....	....	277.67
Pleasant Garden	J. R. Collins, Pleasant Garden, N. C	56.00	....	19.00	51.00	16.00	29.21	16.00	2.00	51.50	....	....	240.71
Ramseur	E. B. Leonard, Ramseur, N. C.	720.00	....	94.88	....	245.12	98.07	....	6.25	....	....	....	1,164.32
Randleman	C. W. Hilliard, Randleman, N. C.	360.00	....	32.00	4.00	102.40	96.20	10.00	4.00	8.00	....	....	616.60
Reidsville, First	K. K. Li[illegible]y, Reidsville, N. C.	2,400.00	82.50	....	3,608.13	736.60	272.52	5.90	10.50	276.76	423.14	887.81	7,392.91
Lawsonville Ave.	R. R. Roberts, Reidsville, N. C.	476.66	....	84.28	....	43.00	25.00	....	1.50	....	....	....	630.44
Mount Olive	James Sellars, Reidsville, N. C.	1,247.33	....	51.00	332.00	196.46	49.70	....	1.50	45.84	....	151.89	1,923.83
Ruffin-Stacey	M. C. Thomas, Reidsville, N. C., R. 5	200.00	....	....	....	10.00	....	....	2.00	....	....	....	212.00
Sandy Creek	Miss Ida Williams, Liberty, N. C.	35.00	....	6.50	....	14.50	5.50	....	.50	.50	....	....	62.50
Smith Grove	Drew Smith, Colfax, N. C.	125.00	....	[illegible]	....	12.00	6.00	11.00	2.00	17.00	....	....	223.00
Summerfield	Mrs. O. E. Shields, Summerfield, N. C	300.00	....	42.61	20.59	65.58	48.00	....	4.00	....	....	....	480.78
Tabernacle	Miss Edna Phillips, Altamahaw, N. C	....	....	....	1,130.10	26.28	4.27	....	2.00	1.50	....	....	1,164.15
Trinity	J. M. Thomas, High Point, N. C., R.	217.23	....	....	....	91.00	89.94	....	2.50	....	....	....	400.67
Whites Memorial	E. W. Allred, Franklinville, N. C.	60.00	....	12.00	....	20.00	15.00	....	....	....	....	....	107.00
Worthville	Mrs. M. J. Myrick, Randleman, N. C.	60.00	....	7.00	....	....	....	....	....	....	....	....	67.00
TOTALS	....	46,512.06	6,452.50	3,201.12	43,040.99	18,040.08	6,949.52	1,474.54	160.00	4,738.78	2,482.35	4,711.32	130,572.59

TABLE V. GIFTS FOR MISSIONS, EDUCATION AND ALL BENEVOLENCES, PIEDMONT BAPTIST ASSOC [illegible]N.

CHURCHES	Total to Co-operative Program	Special to Chowan College	Special to State Missions	Special to Home Missions	Special to Foreign Missions	Special to Christian and Ministerial Education	Special to Orphanage	Special to Hospitals	Special to Old Minister's Relief	Other Special Gifts	Total for Missions, Benevolences, given by the church and all departments	Total by W. M. U.	Given by Sunday School	Grand Total All Gifts for all purposes
Allen Jay	......	......	......	......	......	......	6.35	......	......	......	......	......	6.35	6.35
Asheboro, N. C.	622.65	3.20	18.83	33.84	20.78	12.50	127.11	5.37	......	7.00	303.62	142.20	851.28	18,443.93
Balfour	21.87	......	3.59	......	4.27	......	27.07	5.49	......	......	6.82	36.15	62.29	2,075.97
Calvary	70.77	1.61	9.32	7.66	20.22	2.61	55.14	12.16	4.00	4.90	77.12	43.83	188.39	593.81
Caraway	......	......	......	......	......	......	......	......	......	......	......	......	......	83.47
Cedar Falls	......	......	......	......	......	......	......	......	......	18.34	......	......	18.34	214.31
Central Falls	......	......	......	......	......	......	......	......	......	......	......	......	......	600.05
Fairview	6.40	......	......	......	......	......	......	3.00	......	......	......	3.00	9.40	246.78
Franklinville	303.10	......	......	20.58	......	......	82.71	......	19.90	15.00	235.45	138.19	441.29	1,542.00
Gibsonville	24.00	......	7.45	......	......	......	48.12	15.00	......	......	37.77	......	94.57	1,217.64
Glenola	......	......	30.52	......	......	......	193.12	7.65	......	......	......	93.12	231.29	1,499.29
G'boro, First	2,712.96	......	249.65	351.96	2,106.21	645.22	1,810.30	176.60	......	587.69	9,161.17	2,595.34	18,640.59	36,174.58
Asheboro St.	1,869.78	......	72.43	88.90	147.06	4.55	466.02	40.58	......	74.72	402.26	......	2,764.04	9,952.37
Bessemer	346.70	......	7.40	......	......	......	71.00	12.10	......	......	......	......	437.20	2,955.72
Eller Memorial	855.60	......	14.35	40.35	2074	......	590.67	16.45	......	45.76	19.89	......	1,593.92	6,748.08
Florida Street	263.07	......	7.05	5.60	.60	......	180.42	12.67	......	.98	96.25	104.82	470.39	3,654.37
Forest Ave.	586.61	......	......	......	16.00	......	235.70	59.37	......	......	......	......	897.68	4,689.10
Latham Park	......	......	......	......	......	......	6.00	......	......	......	6.00	......	6.00	185.00
Magnolia Street	53.00	......	10.18	5.00	......	......	84.62	16.26	......	......	8.00	161.06	169.06	2,240.41
Pomona	......	......	......	......	......	......	80.58	16.34	......	......	......	92.32	96.92	2,236.72

Revolution	625.57		29.31	43.74	59.42		186.92	28.53		19.50	570.57	225.71	992.99
Stevens Memorial	.5.33			11.10	42.71		148.23	20.2(		17.00	63.01	176.23	324.57
White Oak	384.69						175.30	30.07			194.69	180.07	590.06
Guilford	50.00		2.50	2.10	11.80		13.91	2.35		8.00	29.90		90.66
High Point, First	3,869.35		70.65	39.37	221.35		1,511.45	370.45		1,833.00	3,858.49	1,714.90	7,935.62
Green Street	953.06						396.41	20.00			234.12		1,369.47
Hilliard Mal	10.50		12.65	2.80	5.00		45.51				18.30	50.61	76.46
Nth Main Street	165.00			8.53	22.03		150.00	18.28		20.65	79.15	55.34	384.49
North Park	43.84		5.00	7.50	7.50		45.00	5.00			5.00	55.00	113.84
South Side	51.96										13.08		51.96
West End	101.90		19.00	1.80			235.35	30.72		25.50	75.05	282.22	414.27
Jesup Grove							10.00						10.00
Lebanon			5.00	5.00			37.04						47.04
Liberty	8.44		1.00	3.50		3.00	42.88	7.56		6.00	21.94	50.44	72.38
Macedonia	17.02									15.35			32.37
Mount Zion							13.43						13.43
Oak Grove	5.00						13.72	2.00				15.72	20.72
Osborne Chapel	2.00												2.00
Osceola	3.00						26.50	2.30					31.80
Pleasant Garden	11.00						17.77				1.00	17.77	28.77
Ramseur	85.00		20.29	12.00	23.33		145.31	41.00		34.50	88.83	187.60	361.43
Randleman		33.12	2.65	13.00	13.00			2.50			47.57	16.70	64.27
Reidsville, First	1,150.00		67.50	41.00	65.04	109.07	290.38	29.23		34.00	943.12	310.11	1,786.22
Lawsonville Ave.			3.00	4.30			9.75						17.05
Mount Olive					48.69		49.07	5.81			9.35	94.31	103.57
Ruffin-Stacey	6.25						7.50	4.25		3.77			21.77
Sandy Creek	5.13		1.00	.60	1.16		2.50	2.37					12.7
Smith Grove							26.00	4.00					30.0
Summerfield	20.00		5.00	11.00		2.00	60.00	13.99		34.93	73.96	72.96	146.9
Tabernacle													
Trinity							95.65	22.40					118.0
Whites Mal			2.00				2.00	4.00					8.0
Worthville			.50	.25	6.00		7.00	2.90	1.00	7.00			24.6
TOTALS	5,390.55	37.93	697.82	761.48	2,862.91	778.95	7,829.51	1,068.95	24.90	2,813.59	16,681.48	6,913.72	42,266.5

TABLE VI. B. Y. P. U.'S. PIEDMONT BAPTIST ASSOCIATION.

CHURCHES	Does Church Have General Organization?	Adult Unions	Senior Unions	Intermediate Unions	Junior Unions	Total Unions	Standard Unions	Adults Enrolled	Seniors Enrolled	Intermediates enrolled	Juniors Enrolled	Total Enrolled	Daily Bible Readers	No. Taking Study Course	Total Systematic Givers in all Unions	Students in College from your church
Allen Jay	...	...	...	...	...	...	...	...	...	...	...	...	...	...	...	...
Asheboro, N. C.	Yes	1	1	1	1	4	1	9	18	19	13	59	24	32	44	4
Balfour	Yes	...	1	1	1	3	...	...	14	20	21	55	37	36	44	...
Calvary	...	...	...	...	...	...	...	...	...	...	...	...	...	...	...	...
Caraway	...	...	...	...	...	...	...	...	...	...	...	...	...	...	...	...
Cedar Falls	...	...	...	...	...	...	...	...	...	...	...	...	...	...	...	...
Central Falls	...	1	...	...	...	1	...	15	...	...	...	15	15	8	7	...
Fairview	...	...	...	...	...	...	...	...	...	...	...	...	...	...	...	...
Franklinville	Yes	...	1	1	1	3	...	...	13	20	16	49	25	34	41	...
Gibsonville	...	...	1	1	1	3	...	...	20	18	15	53	...	...	...	...
Glenola	...	...	1	...	...	1	...	...	16	...	...	16	...	...	...	...
Greensboro, First	Yes	1	3	3	2	9	...	16	47	63	34	160	60	40	104	30
Asheboro St.	Yes	...	1	3	4	8	...	...	13	58	62	133	64	77	79	...
Bessemer	Yes	1	1	1	1	4	...	23	10	20	32	85	22	35	48	5
Eller Memorial	Yes	1	2	4	4	11	...	15	28	35	42	120	62	75	81	3
Florida Street	...	1	1	1	2	5	2	11	15	18	35	79	42	47	44	...
Forest Ave.	Yes	...	4	...	1	5	...	...	81	...	16	97	23	42	46	...
Latham Park	...	...	...	...	...	...	...	...	...	...	...	...	...	...	...	...
Magnolia Street	...	1	1	1	1	4	...	10	22	18	23	73	5	5	38	...
Pomona	...	...	...	...	...	...	...	...	...	...	...	...	...	...	...	...
Revolution	...	...	1	...	...	1	...	...	19	...	...	19	19	14	19	...
Stevens Memorial	...	...	...	...	...	...	...	...	...	...	...	...	...	...	...	...
White Oak	Yes	...	1	1	1	3	...	...	30	30	31	91	28	52	42	1
Guilford	...	...	1	...	...	1	...	...	14	...	...	14	10	11	5	...
High Point, First	Yes	...	1	1	1	3	...	...	27	52	48	127	58	55	68	...
Green Street	...	1	1	2	2	6	...	...	...	...	...	140	96	110	100	2
Hilliard Memorial	...	...	...	1	1	2	...	...	...	19	10	29	9	...	6	2
North Main Street	Yes	1	1	1	2	5	...	21	13	20	23	77	28	37	47	...
North Park	Yes	...	1	1	1	3	...	...	15	18	23	56	35	46	35	...
South Side	...	...	1	1	1	3	...	...	18	16	17	51	...	...	...	...
West End	Yes	...	1	1	1	3	...	...	12	20	18	50	30	29	30	...
Jesup Grove	...	...	...	...	...	...	...	...	...	...	...	...	...	...	...	...
Lebanon	...	...	...	...	...	...	...	...	...	...	...	...	...	...	...	...
Liberty	...	...	1	1	1	3	...	...	13	14	8	35	...	...	...	3
Macedonia	...	1	...	...	1	...	...	...	...	...	...	...	...	...	...	...
Mount Zion	...	...	...	...	...	...	...	...	...	...	...	...	...	...	...	...
Oak Grove	...	...	...	...	...	...	...	...	...	...	...	...	...	...	...	...
Osborne Chapel	...	...	...	...	...	...	...	...	...	...	...	...	...	...	...	...
Osceola	...	...	...	...	...	...	...	...	...	...	...	...	...	...	...	...
Pleasant Garden	...	...	1	...	...	1	...	...	40	...	...	40	...	...	...	...
Ramseur	Yes	...	1	1	1	3	...	...	10	11	8	29	15	19	20	...
Randleman	Yes	...	1	...	1	2	...	...	16	...	16	32	...	10	11	1
Reidsville, First	...	1	1	1	1	4	...	25	20	18	30	93	22	15	33	4
Lawsonville Ave.	...	...	...	...	...	...	...	...	...	...	...	...	...	...	...	...
Mount Olive	...	...	...	1	...	1	...	...	...	15	...	15	...	...	...	...
Ruffin-Stacey	...	...	...	...	...	...	...	...	...	...	...	...	...	...	...	...
Sandy Creek	...	...	...	...	...	...	...	...	...	...	...	...	...	...	...	...
Smith Grove	...	...	...	...	...	...	...	...	...	...	...	...	...	...	...	...
Summerfield	...	...	...	...	...	...	...	...	...	...	...	...	...	...	...	1
Tabernacle	...	...	1	...	1	2	...	...	27	...	30	57	...	...	57	...
Trinity	...	...	1	...	...	1	...	...	...	...	...	...	...	...	...	...
Whites Memorial	...	...	...	1	...	1	...	...	...	25	...	25	...	...	...	...
Worthville	...	...	...	...	...	...	...	...	...	...	...	...	...	...	...	...
TOTALS	15	10	35	31	34	110	3	145	571	547	571	1974	729	829	1049	56

TABLE VII. WOMAN'S WORK. PIEDMONT BAPTIST ASSO.

CHURCHES	Number W. M. S.	Number of Y. W. A.'s	Number of G. A.'s	Number of R. A.'s	Number of Sunbeams	Total W.M.U. Orgs.	W.M.S. Members	Y.W.A.'s Members	G.A.'s Members	R.A.'s Members	Sunbeam Members	Total Member Enrolled	Mission Study Enrollment
Allen Jay	...	...	...	...	...	...	...	...	...	...	...	...	...
Asheboro, N. C.	1	1	1	1	1	5	45	12	14	6	20	97	129
Balfour	1	1	1	...	1	4	12	8	...	...	12	32	...
Calvary	1	...	...	...	...	1	25	...	...	...	...	25	...
Caraway	...	...	...	...	...	...	...	...	...	...	...	...	...
Cedar Falls	...	...	...	...	...	...	...	...	...	...	...	...	...
Central Falls	1	...	...	...	...	1	31	...	...	...	...	31	...
Fairview	...	...	...	...	...	...	...	...	...	...	...	...	...
Franklinville	1	1	1	1	1	5	40	16	15	10	...	81	...
Gibsonville	1	...	...	...	...	1	15	...	...	...	...	15	...
Glenola	...	...	...	...	...	...	...	...	...	...	...	...	...
Greensboro, First	1	1	2	1	1	6	347	43	50	33	46	519	284
Asheboro St.	1	2	2	2	1	8	115	46	41	31	50	283	81
Bessemer	1	1	1	...	1	4	18	18	19	...	16	71	...
Eller Memorial	1	...	1	...	1	3	42	...	37	...	10	89	...
Florida Street	1	1	1	1	1	5	48	10	21	14	10	103	36
Forest Ave.	1	1	1	1	1	5	60	29	10	12	15	126	28
Latham Park	...	...	...	...	...	...	...	...	...	...	...	...	...
Magnolia Street	1	...	...	...	...	1	30	...	...	...	...	30	...
Pomona	1	...	...	...	1	2	15	...	...	...	25	40	...
Revolution	1	1	2	2	1	7	24	15	23	14	40	116	55
Stevens Memorial	1	...	...	...	...	1	27	...	...	...	...	27	...
White Oak	1	1	1	1	1	5	43	17	12	15	25	112	...
Guilford	1	1	...	...	...	2	18	9	...	...	...	27	...
High Point, First	1	1	2	1	1	6	125	80	43	40	50	338	182
Green Street	1	2	1	1	1	6	110	20	50	30	45	255	...
Hilliard Memorial	1	1	1	1	1	5	28	10	25	12	6	81	...
North Main Street	1	1	1	...	...	3	13	9	8	...	...	30	...
North Park	...	...	...	...	...	...	...	...	...	...	...	...	...
South Side	1	...	1	1	1	4	...	...	...	...	...	70	...
West End	1	1	...	...	1	3	25	36	...	...	30	91	7
Jesup Grove	...	...	...	...	...	...	...	...	...	...	...	...	...
Lebanon	...	...	...	...	...	...	...	...	...	...	...	...	...
Liberty	1	...	...	...	1	2	14	...	...	...	...	14	...
Macedonia	...	...	...	...	...	...	...	...	...	...	...	...	...
Mount Zion	...	...	...	...	...	...	...	...	...	...	...	...	...
Oak Grove	...	...	...	...	...	...	...	...	...	...	...	...	...
Osborne Chapel	...	...	...	...	...	...	...	...	...	...	...	...	...
Osceola	...	...	...	...	...	...	...	...	...	...	...	...	...
Pleasant Garden	1	...	...	...	...	1	9	...	...	...	...	9	...
Ramseur	1	1	1	1	1	5	20	10	10	8	35	83	...
Randleman	1	...	...	...	...	1	...	...	...	...	...	...	...
Reidsville, First	1	1	1	...	1	4	150	35	20	...	30	235	...
Lawsonville Ave.	1	...	...	...	...	1	14	...	...	...	...	14	...
Mount Olive	...	...	...	...	...	...	...	...	...	...	...	...	...
Ruffin-Stacey	...	...	...	...	...	...	...	...	...	...	...	...	...
Sandy Creek	...	...	...	...	...	...	...	...	...	...	...	...	...
Smith Grove	...	...	...	...	...	...	...	...	...	...	...	...	...
Summerfield	1	...	...	...	...	1	13	...	...	...	...	13	...
Tabernacle	...	...	...	...	...	...	...	...	...	...	...	...	...
Trinity	...	...	...	...	...	...	...	...	...	...	...	...	...
Whites Memorial	...	...	...	...	...	...	...	...	...	...	...	...	...
Worthville	...	...	...	...	...	...	...	...	...	...	...	...	...
TOTALS	31	20	22	15	20	108	1476	423	398	225	465	3057	802

INDEX

MINUTES

OF THE

PIEDMONT BAPTIST ASSOCIATION

North Carolina

FORTY-SECOND ANNUAL SESSION

Held With The

SOUTH SIDE BAPTIST CHURCH

High Point, N. C.

October 23-24

1935

Next Session will we held with the Calvary Baptist Church, near Reidsville, N. C., Wednesday and Thursday before the fourth Sunday in October, 1936.

Rev. J. Ben Eller will preach the Sermon

Alternate—Rev. Hoyle Love

PIEDMONT BAPTIST ASSOCIATION

North Carolina

FORTY-SECOND ANNUAL SESSION

Held With The

SOUTH SIDE BAPTIST CHURCH

High Point, N. C.

October 23-24

1935

The Next Session will be held with the Calvary Baptist Church near Reidsville, N. C., Wednesday and Thursday before the fourth Sunday in October, 1936.

Rev. J. Ben Eller will preach the Sermon
Alternate—Rev. Hoyle Love

THE 1935 MINUTES ARE A MEMORIAL TO REV. THOMAS CARRICK

Rev. Thomas Carrick was born near High Rock, Davidson, County, April 11, 1850, and died in High Point, N. C., May 22, 1935. He received his education at Abbott's Creek, Wake Forest College, and the Southern Baptist Theological Seminary. In early manhood he was married to Miss Mary Bain, of High Point, N. C. Dr. J. B. Richardson was his intellectual and spiritual father. He prepared him at Abbott's Creek for college and led him into Christian service. In his youth he entered the ministry and for forty-seven years he served Baptist churches in North Carolina. His first pastorates was in Greenville, N. C., where he founded the Memorial Baptist Church. After ten years he accepted the pastorate of the First Baptist Church of Lexington. He founded the Main Street Baptist Church in High Point, also served the Green Street Baptist Church, and Baptist churches at Randleman, Ramseur, Abbott's Creek, and others. He rendered a notable service as a charter member of the Board of Trustees of the Baptist Orphanage and attended forty-eight of its annual sessions.

Dr. W. L. Poteat, his college mate, said of him, "He was a good man, widely useful, sincere, and courageous in maintaining an inflexible standard of the upright life."

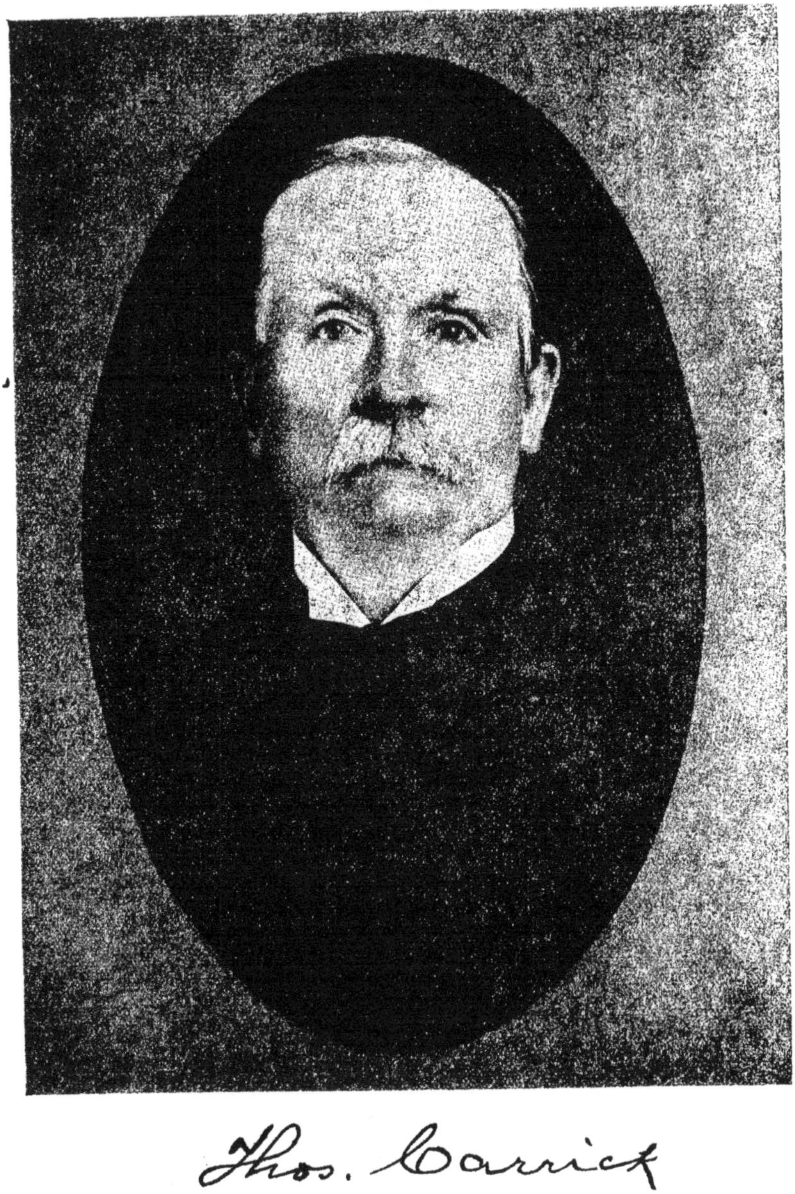

Thos. Carrick

INDEX

MAP
OF THE
PIEDMONT BAPTIST ASSOCIATION

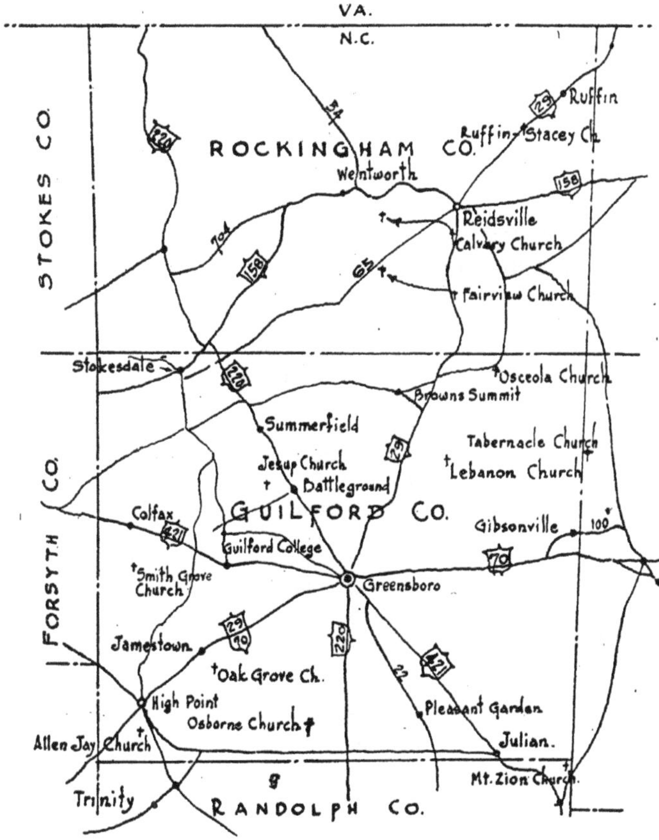

Associational Directory

OFFICERS

Clarence A. Smith, Moderator .... High Point, N. C.
Rev. J. M. Hilliard, Vice-Moderator .... High Point, N. C.
O. E. Lee, Clerk-Treasurer .... Greensboro, N. C.

EXECUTIVE COMMITTEE

Clarence A. Smith, Chairman .... High Point, N. C.
O. E. Lee, Secretary .... Greensboro, N. C.
Rev. J. M. Hilliard .... High Point, N. C.
Rev. C. N. Royal .... High Point, N. C.
C. M. Scott .... High Point, N. C.
Rev. J. C. Gillespie .... Reidsville, N. C.
J. C. Tatum .... Reidsville, N. C.
Rev. J. Ben Eller .... Greensboro, N. C.
Dr. J. T. J. Battle .... Greensboro, N. C.
Mrs. Nettie H. Hoge .... Greensboro, N. C.
F. L. Paschal .... Greensboro, N. C.
Walter Crissman .... High Point, N. C.

CHURCHES BY DISTRICTS

DISTRICT 1:
- High Point, First
- Hilliard Memorial
- Green Street
- North Main
- North Park
- South Side
- West End
- Oak Grove
- Smith Grove
- Trinity
- Allen Jay

DISTRICT 2:
- Greensboro, First
- Asheboro Street
- Bessemer
- Bailey Memorial
- Eller Memorial
- Forest Ave.
- Florida Street
- Latham Park
- Magnolia Street
- Pomona Mills
- Revolution
- Sixteenth Street
- Stevens Memorial
- Gibsonville
- Guilford
- Jessip Grove
- Lebanon
- Mount Zion
- Pleasant Garden
- Osborne Chapel
- Summerfield
- Tabernacle
- Webster Memorial

DISTRICT 3:
- Reidsville, First
- Penn Memorial
- Mount Olive
- Calvary
- Fairview
- Osceola
- Ruffin-Stacey

OFFICERS OF THE PIEDMONT SUNDAY SCHOOL ASSOCIATION

F. L. Paschal, Superintendent .... Greensboro, N. C.
Rev. J. H. Saunders, Assistant Superintendent .... Reidsville, N. C.
W. F. Hearn, Chorister .... Greensboro, N. C.
Mrs. Jewel Williamson, Pianist .... Greensboro, N. C.
Marvin Shields, Supt. Group 1, District 1 .... High Point, N. C.
M. E. Howell, Supt. Group 2, District 1 .... High Point, N. C.
Rev. J .S. Hopkins, Group 1, District 2 .... Greensboro, N. C.
R. E. Hodgin, Group 2, District 2.................. Greensboro, N. C.
William Cummings, Supt. District 3 .... Reidsville, N. C.
Miss Ruth Scott, Supt, Beginners Department ...... Greensboro, N. C.
Mrs. C. C. Stout, Supt. Primary Department ...... High Point, N. C.
Miss Thelma Patrick, Supt. Young People's Dept. .. High Point, N. C.
Mrs. J. S. Moore, Supt. Adult Department .... Greensboro, N. C.

OFFICERS OF THE PIEDMONT ASSOCIATION W. M. U.

Mrs. Nettie Hoge, Superintendent .... Greensboro, N. C.
Mrs. C. R. Harrison, Secretary .... High Point, N. C.
Mrs. C. E. Siceloff, Treasurer .... High Point, N. C.
Miss Ruth Scott, Young People's Leader .... Greensboro, N. C.
Mrs. W. H. McKeever, Personal Service Chairman .. Greensboro, N. C.
Mrs. C. N. Royal, Stewardship Chairman .... High Point, N. C.
Miss Elizabeth Apple, Training School and
Margaret Fund Chairman .... Greensboro, N. C.
Mrs. J. J. Andoe, Mission Study Lit. Chairman ..... Greensboro, N. C.
Mrs. T. C. Robins, Group Leader, District 1 .... High Point, N. C.
Mrs. A. Andrews, Group Leader, District 2 .... Greensboro, N. C.
Mrs. T. L. Sasser, Group Leader, District 3 .... Reidsville, N. C.

PIEDMONT ASSOCIATION B. T. U. OFFICERS

President, Walter Crissman .... High Point, N. C.
Vice-President, Woodrow Hill .... High Point, N. C.
President District No. 1, John Reavis .... High Point, N. C.
President District No. 2, Jimmy Wills .... Greensboro, N. C.
President District No. 3, Mrs. C. B .Scoggins .... Reidsville, N. C.
Secretary and Treasurer, Thelma Patrick .... High Point, N. C.
Junior Leader, Paul Roach .... High Point, N. C.
Intermediate Leader, Miss Estelle Mitchell .... Greensboro, N. C.
Chorister, G. W. Baity .... Greensboro, N. C.
Pianist, Miss Illa Hensley .... High Point, N. C.
For Treasurers .... Table 5

CHURCH DIRECTORY

ORDAINED MINISTERS (NOT PASTORS)

Dr. C. H. Nash .... Greensboro, N. C.
J. W. Rose .... Greensboro, N. C.
C .D. Barton .... Greensboro, N. C.
W. C. Richardson .... Guilford College, N. C.
J. C. DeLancey .... Greensboro, N. C.
Dr. W. C. Newton .... China
Carl E. Gaddy .... Greensboro, N. C.
William H. Matherly .... Greensboro, N. C.
D. L. Temple .... Pomona, N. C.
L. M. Deaton .... Greensboro, N. C.
Clydd Glosson .... Greensboro, N. C.
S. B. Wilson .... High Point, N. C.
Carl Lewis .... High Point, N. C.
D. E. Oates .... High Point, N. C.
J. M. Hilliard .... High Point, N. C.
T. L. Chamberlain .... High Point, N. C
B. T. Gladden .... High Point, N. C.
J. F. Murray .... Reidsville, N. C.
B. H. Fairington .... Colfax, N. C.
C. R. Smith .... Colfax, N. C
Bro. Belle .... Colfax, N. C.
Bro. Cain .... Colfax, N. C.
J. C. Gatewood .... Trinity, N. C.

B. T. U. DIRECTORS, PRESIDENTS AND LEADERS

ALLEN JAY—Arlene Younts, Director; Wade Cumbie, Intermediate Leader; John Younts, Junior Leader .

GIBSONVILLE—Isaiah Seaas, Director; and President Senior Union.
GREENSBORO, FIRST—O. E. Lee, Director; L. R. Smithey, Adult President; Ann Woodward, Senior President; Elizabeth Taylor, Senior President; Mrs. Bertha Chapman, Mrs. J. D. Schoolfield, Loretta Nichols, Jane Cates, Mrs. L. R. Leary, Intermediate Leaders; Lillian Giles, Helen Saleeby, Mildred Jackson, Eva Saleeby,

Junior Leaders; Mary F. Walker, Mabel Fitch, Florence Robinson, Story Hour Leaders.

ASHEBORO STREET—C. W. McLees, Director; Nevelle Wills, Senior President; J. J. Norwood, Madeline Causey, Intermediate Leaders; Emma Mae Cheek, Mrs. Sam Walker, Junior Leaders.

BAILEY MEMORIAL—Robert Mitchell, Director and Senior President.

BESSEMER—Norfleet Dixon, Director; Mary Langley, Senior President; S. R. Butler, Intermediate Leader; Mrs. Gilbert Rumley, Junior Leader.

ELLER MEMORIAL—J .Carl Bell, Director; A. M. Bass, Adult President; Raymond Kincaid, Senior President; Mrs. Perry Beal, Farrell James, Eugene Bates, Intermediate Leaders; Mr. and Mrs. R. Hobbs, Mrs. J. H. Sharp, Junior Leader.

FLORIDA STREET—W. M. Cassell, Director; Mrs. M. W. Spivey, Adult President; Viola Wilson, Senior President; Eulene Collins, Intermediate Leader; Mrs. W. M. Cassell, Junior Leader.

FOREST AVE.—Ethel Osborne, Director.

MAGNOLIA STREET—Mrs. Jennings Johnson, Director; G. D. Oaks, Adult President; Fletcher Sessoms, Senior President; Mrs. Jennings Johnson, Intermediate Leader; Clara Johnson, Junior Leader.

REVOLUTION—Ray Hollis, Senior President.

SIXTEENTH STREET—Franks Gales, Director; L. F. Paris, Adult President; Clarence Hunt, Senior President; Robert Leonard, Intermediate Leader.

STEVENS MEMORIAL—Ethel Brown, Senior President; Mrs. R. A. Newman, Intermediate Leader; Mrs. J. W. Newman, Junior Leader.

GUILFORD—Beulah Martin, Director; Lillie Butler, Senior President.

HIGH POINT, FIRST—Dr. M. L. Slate, Director; Claudd A. Smith, Senior President; Addie Lomax, Mary Vaught, Intermediate Leader; Mrs. C. D. Goldsmith, Junior Leader.

GREEN STREET—John Reavis, Director; A. W. Buck, Adult President; David Shelton, Senior President.

HILLIARD—M. B. Fitzgerald, Director; C. H. Farmer, Adult President; Lloyd Willard, Senior President; C. J. Hedrick, Intermediate Leader; Mrs. H. O. Miller, Junior Leader.

NORTH MAIN—E. R. Highfill, Director; R. L. Reeves, Adult President; Tom Lamar, Senior President; Mrs. Menda McArthur, Intermediate Leader; Myrtle Epps, Junior Leader.

NORTH PARK—L. R. McNeel, Director; J. A. Jones, Adult President;

Floyd Wood, Senior President; Mrs. L. W. Glenn, Intermediate Leader; Mrs. N. F. Britt, Junior Leader.

SOUTH SIDE—Martha Brown, Director; Eva Ward, Senior President; Mrs. C. B. Byrd, Intermediate Leader; Estia Brown, Junior Leader.

WEST END—J. E. Smith, Director; Eugene Gregory, Adult President; J. E. Hedrick, Intermediate Leader; Mrs. J. E. Hedrick, Junior Leader.

OSCEOLA—Robert Flynn, Director; Mrs. D. A. Green, Senior President; Maggie Cole, Junior Leader.

PLEASANT GARDEN—Telza Hamby, Director; Henry Foy, Senior President; Mary Foy, Junior Leader.

REIDSVILLE, FIRST—J. C. Gillespie, Junior Director; Flora Foote, Adult President; W. O. Cantrell, Senior President; Virginia Sluder, Intermediate Leader; Sara Price Kemp, Junior Leader.

MOUNT OLIVE—C. D. Barker, Director.

TABERNACLE—J. Luther Lee, Director; Edna Phillips, Senior President; Mrs. B. C. Hyder, Junior Leader.

OFFICERS OF W. M. S. AND AUXILIARIES

ALLEN JAY—Mrs. R. L. Smith, W. M. S. President.

CALVARY—Mrs. J. E. McCargo, W. M. S. President.

GIBSONVILLE—Lottie White, W. M. S. President.

GREENSBORO, FIRST—Mrs. O. E. Lee, W. M. S. President; Mrs. Stafford Webb, Mrs. T. F. Casey, Y. W. A. Leaders; Mrs. J. R. Pegram, Mrs. I. B. Squier, G. A. Councelors, W. O. Burnham, O. E. Lee, R. A. Councelor; Mrs. August Rouf, Sunbeam Leader.

ASHEBORO STREET—Mrs. A. Andrews, W .M. S. President; Mrs. J. J. Myers, Y. W. A. Councelors; Mrs. M. D. Teague, Margaret Debnam, G. A. Councelors; Virginia Satterfield, Sunbeam Leader; Mrs. D. E. Skelton, R. A. Councelor.

BESSEMER—Mrs. L. M. Gideon, W. M. S. President; Mrs. J. R. Medlin, Y. W. A. Councelor

ELLER MEMORIAL—Mrs. G. O. Basinger, W. M. S. President; Mrs. E. Glen Parker, Y. W. A. Councelor.

FLORIDA STREET—Mrs. J. B Rumley, W M S. President; Mrs. D. D. Harwell, Y. W. A. Councelor; Mrs C. N. Hutchinson, G. A. Councelor; Mrs. C. A. Daniel, R. A. Councelor; Mrs. N. W. Bolejack, Sunbeam Leader.

FOREST AVE.—Mrs. B. A. Scott, W. M. S. President; Mrs. Wilson Woodcock, Y. W. A. Councelor; Ruth Williams, G. A. Councelor; Mrs. J. E. Oliver, R. A. Councelor; Rebecca Braswell, Sunbeam Leader.

MAGNOLIA STREET—Mrs. L. L. Jarvis, W. M. S. President.

POMONA—Mrs. H. L. Nall, W. M. S. President; Mrs. Lelia Way, Sunbeam Leader.

REVOLUTION—Sallie Burgess, W. M. S. President and Y. W. A. Councelor; Nellie Pitchford, G. A. Councelor; Mrs. Audry Clifton, R. A. Councelor; Lora Canter, Sunbeam Leader.

SIXTEENTH STREET—Mrs. C. L. Straughn, W. M. S. President and Y. W. A. Councelor; Helen Straughn, G. A. Councelor; J. L. Coley, R. A .Councelor; Vear Hayes, Sunbeam Leader.

STEVENS MEMORIAL—Mrs. W. A. Gunter, W. M. S. President.

GUILFORD—Beulah Martin, W. M. S. President.

HIGH POINT, FIRST—Mrs. A. Lee Gibson, W. M. S. President; Ila Hensley, Y. W. A. Councelor; Mrs. L. W. Apple, Mrs Fletcher Welch, G. A. Councelors, Claudd A. Smith, Jr., R. A. Councelors; Katie Sue Stanfield, Sunbeam Leader.

GREEN STREET—Mrs. L. F. Robbins, W. M. S. President; Mrs. M. C. Holton, Y. W. A. Councelor; Miss Mabel Kootz, Mrs. J. D. Edmundson, G. A .Councelor; Woodrow Hill, R. A. Leader; Mrs. Carroll, Sunbeam Leader.

HILLIARD MEMORIAL—Mrs. J. B. Ellis, W. M. S. President; Mrs. H. O. Mille, Y. W. A. Councelor; Mrs. W. R. Ward, G. A. Councelor; Mrs. C H Saunders, R. A. Councelor; Mrs. C. H. Foynes, Sunbeam Leader.

NORTH MAIN STREET—Mrs. D. S. King, W. M. S. President; Alice Davis, Y. W. A. Councelor; Mrs. Minda McArthur, Myrtle Epps, G. A. Councelor; Mrs. Hal Davis, R. A. Councelor; Mrs. Wayne McCanless, Sunbeam Leader.

NORTH PARK—Mrs. D. H. Short, W. M. S. President; Mrs. J. A. Jones, G. A .Councelor; Mrs L. R. McNeel, Sunbeam Leader.

SOUTH SIDE—Mrs. Pearl Cameron, W. M. S .President; Mrs. Moad, Y. W. A. Councelor; Daisy Shaw, G. A. Councelor; Mrs. Oldham, Sunbeam Leader.

WEST END—Mrs. Hoyle Love, W. M. S. President; Mrs. W. F. Metcalf G. A. Councelor; Mrs. C. W. Harvey, Sunbeam Leader

OSBORNE CHAPEL—Mrs. Ethel Nelson, W. M. S. President.

PLEASANT GARDEN—Mrs. Ralph Neeley, W. M. S. President.

REIDSVILLE, FIRST—Mrs. R. R. Saunders, W. M. S. President; Mrs. R. H. Pleasants, Y. W. A. Councelor; Mrs. Lane Peters, G. A. Councelor; Mrs. George Schaeffer, R. A. Councelor; Mrs. Claude Phillips, Sunbeam Leader.

MOUNT OLIVE—Mrs. J. H. Saunders, W. M. S. President.

PENN MEMORIAL—Mrs. M. H. Fitz, W. M. S. President and Y. W. A. Councelor.

LIST OF APPOINTED MESSENGERS

ALLEN JAY—John Younts, R. L. Smith, Frank Hunt, Wade Cumbie.

CALVARY—J. F. Carroll, Mesdames Jessie Carter, C. J. Delgado.

FAIRVIEW—Wade Durham, Oscar Powell, William Carter.

GIBSONVILLE—R. K. Craven, Mr. and Mrs. Robert Howard.

GREENSBORO, FIRST—A. A. Chandler, L. R. Smithy, H. B. Caldwell, W. L. Carter, Mr. and Mrs. O. E. Lee, Mesdames Nettie Hoge and Vander Liles.

ASHEBORO STREET—Mrs. J. S. Moore, F. L. Paschal, J. J. Norwood.

BAILEY MEMORIAL—W. J. Mitchell, Mr. and Mrs. Ralph Jackson, Mrs. R. A. Cooke.

BESSEMER—N. P. Haynes, C. L. Casey, W. A. Aydlette.

ELLER MEMORIAL—Mr. and Mrs. Carl Bell, Mesdames J. H. Sharpe, J. B. Bateman, Yancie Francis.

FLORIDA STREET—R. L. Roberson, Mesdames June Johnson and C. N. Hutchinson.

FOREST AVE.—Dr. and Mrs. J. T. J. Battle, Mrs. Geneva Fitzgerald.

MAGNOLIA STREET—Thelma Oaks, Mrs. Jennings Johnson, Mr. and Mrs. H. P. Wray.

POMONA—Rev. and Mrs. W. B. Cooke, Mrs. C. C. Patterson

REVOLUTION—N C. Brown, John Martin, Mesdames Clara Manuel, Jettie Joyce.

SIXTEENTH STREET—J. L. Coley, Vernon Richardson, Mesdames W. A. Straughn, T. W. Michael, C. L. Straughn.

STEVENS MEMORIAL—Mesdames E. E. Welborn, J. B. Brown, J. H. Ham.

WEBSTER MEMORIAL—C. V. Webster, Z. V. Martin, Mrs. W. H. Lucas, Selma Scales.

GUILFORD—Mesdames W. R. Harmon, Butler, Martin.

HIGH POINT, FIRST—A. E. Tate, G. H. Jones, C. E. Goldsmith, Miss Thelma Patrick, W. E. Price, Mesdames W. F. Clayton, C. E. Siceloff, H. A. Knight, Dr. and Mrs. A. B. Conrad.

GREEN STREET—B. T. Leonard, Clyde Ayers, R. B. Culler, Mesdames L. A. Pegg, T. C. Robbins.

HILLIARD MEMORIAL—W. C. Kirkman, W. L. Lewis, P. L. Culp, J. C. Talbert, Mrs. P. L. Culler.

NORTH MAIN—Mesdames Alice Davis, D. S. Ring, Winifred Clinard.

SUMMERFIELD—Mrs. W. W. Doggett, W. M. S. President.

NORTH PARK—J. L. Jones, G. S. Callahan, Floyd Wood.

SOUTH SIDE—G. H. Liner, A. J. Borland, A. M. Gearren.

WEST END—T. L. Chamberland, C. M. Scott, Mrs. Hoyle Love.

OAK GROVE—Mr. and Mrs. C. B. Shackleford, Mr. and Mrs. J. H. Miles, Ellen Hobby, Mrs. Georgia Bowman.

OSBORNE CHAPEL—E. C. White, John May, Mr. and Mrs. Robert R. Osborne, Mrs. Ethel Nelson.

OSCEOLA—A. E. Cook, E. R. Brand and Mrs. D. A. Green.

PLEASANT GARDEN—John Smith, Henry Foy, Mesdames Ralph Neeley, I. F. Anderson, Lillie T. Jordan.

MOUNT OLIVE—Mesdames Odel Delapp, J. H. Saunders, D. P. Drescoll.

PENN MEMORIAL—D. W. Overbey, Thomas Dixon, Mrs. M. H. Fitz, G. S. Hall, J. A. Dunevant.

RUFFIN STACEY—E. B. Poindexter, Mesdames, J. T. Cardwell, J. A. Burton.

SMITH GROVE—Johnny Johnson, Walter Westmoreland, Drew Smith, Roy McCollum, Corah Pender.

SUMMERFIELD__T. D. Carter, Mr. and Mrs. J. C. Doggett.

TABERNACLE—Rev. and Mrs. G. C. Phillips, Jennings L. Phillips, Mesdames Betty Lou Whitt, B. C. Hyder.

TRINITY—J. C. Payne, Mr. Hardle, J. C. Gatewood, Mesdames McDowell, E. W. Welborn.

MINUTES

OF THE

FORTY-SECOND ANNUAL SESSION

OF THE

PIEDMONT BAPTIST ASSOCIATION

HELD WITH

SOUTH SIDE BAPTIST CHURCH
High Point, N. C.

October 23-24, 1935

Wednesday Morning Session

1. The Association was opened with a devotional led by Rev. J. M. Hilliard.

2. Rev. G. H. Liner gave a cordial welcome to the messengers. The response was given by Rev. A. N. Hollis.

3. A roll of the churches was called and the messengers from thirty-three churches responded to the roll call. The Association then proceeded to the election of officers for the ensuing year, which resulted as follows: Clarence A. Smith, Moderator; Rev. J. M. Hilliard, Vice-Moderator; O. E. Lee, Clerk and Treasurer.

4. The Report on Religious Literature was read by C. N. Royal. On motion to adopt the report, the subject was discussed by B. K. Mason. The report was adopted.

RELIGIOUS LITERATURE

The Bible is man's greatest treasure. As we commemorate this year the four hundredth anniversary of the printed English Bible let us seek to give and to lead others to give more earnest attention to the reading and the study of the Holy Scriptures.

By placing our denominational papers in our homes along with the Bible we give Christ first place in our reading. Jesus said to His disciples "Go ye into all the world," "Ye shall be My witnesses," "Lift up your eyes and look on the fields." Why? To see the prevailing conditions and to understand the needs so that they might go about His work intelligently..

For more than a century North Carolina Baptists have had the Biblical Recorder to serve our denomination. This worthy periodical tells us each week of the organized efforts of God's people to bring this world to the feet of Jesus. It records the missionary, educational, and benevolent enterprises of the denomination at home and abroad. It gives the most effective methods for every department of church work. The Home Circle seeks to instill high ideals and to be of real help in the development of Christian character. All of this can be ours for less than four cents a week.

But how are we to go forward with the Lord's work when we have only one out of twelve North Carolina Baptists who has the chance to see the Biblical Recorder? Let us urge more subscribers to our State paper and let us also urge more readers.

There are a number of magazines which are issued by the Baptist Sunday School Board at Nashville, Tennessee: "Home and Foreign Fields," "The Sunday School Builder," "The Young People and Adult's Magazine," and "The Baptist Training Union Magazine."

The Woman's Missionary Union, Auxiliary to the Southern Baptist Convention, at Birmingham, Alabama, publishes "Royal Service," "The Window," and "World Comrades."

We must strive to counteract the flood of evil and worthless literature which is apparently increasing. Our young people are going to read something and I believe God holds us responsible for what we select for them for almost every kind of worldly reading matter is before them on the news stands of today. Do we love our young people enough to place choice Christian literature before them which will not poison their minds but which will instead build character and mold strong minds for the glory of God? Youth never needed the stabilizing, purifying influence of religious literature so much as it does today.

We heartily recommend the Bible and our denominational papers to the homes and hearts of our brethren.

Respectfully submitted,

C. N. ROYAL

5. The following visitors were recognized: Hoyt Blackwell, O. P. Dix, H. M. Stroup, and Miss Alda Grayson.

6. The Report on Foreign Missions was read by J. Ben Eller. On motion to adopt the report the subject was discussed by J. Ben Eller, and Miss Alda Grayson, Missionary in China. The report was adopted.

REPORT ON FOREIGN MISSIONS

On August 4, 1845 our Foreign Mission Board appointed its first missionaries. During the intervening ninety years there have been many encouragements and many discouragements, but the leading of the Holy Spirit has ever been manifest. We come this year with another heartening report.

A word concerning the Lottie Moon offerings of our W. M. U. is timely. These Christmas offerings have seemingly stopped the disastrous retreat of our Foreign Mission work. The objective of offering last year was $150,000.00, but final reports show that it went far beyond the $200,000.00 mark.

Increased income from the Co-Operative Program along with the Lottie Moon offering has enabled the Board to appoint several much needed missionaries. The daily press of recent date carries the announcement of the appointment of thirty. Some of these are replacements; some are returning to former tasks; others are going out for the first time.

The 100,000 club, the sale of mission property, and increased income from our churchces have enabled the Board to largely reduce its indebtedness. The Board at its annual meeting declared a continued policy of economy and debt reduction. At that time it adopted a $659,927.74 budget for the year, including specially supported missionaries.

The leading Mission Study Books for 1935-'36 deal with our work in South America. Four books are heartily commended. They are: "Share with Neighbor America,' "Christ In Silver Lands," "Guitars and Water Jars," and "The Sugar Loaf."

From the region beyond come reports from our 388 missionaries showing a net gain in membership during the year of 21,733 souls. These reports also show that the 204,894 Baptists in these lands gave to the Master's work last year $370,075.66. "The Spirit Of Power" which gives detailed report of our work abroad will be sent free to anyone upon request.

Respectfully submitted,

J. BEN ELLER

7. Following the singing of a hymn and the reading of II. Cor. 8, C. N. Royal led in prayer. Rev. J. S. Hopkins, preached the Introductory Sermon. The text was II. Cor. 8:5, subject "God's Plan for Kingdom Financing." The sermon was deeply spiritual and an inspiration to all.

8. The following committee were appointed:

Program: G. H. Liner, H. O. Miller, A. Lincoln Fulk.

*Committee on Committees*s T. L. Sasser, J. Ben Eller, J. L. Coley.

Committee on New Churches: Dr. J. Clyde Turner, J. M. Hilliard, Wilson Woodcock.

The morning session closed with prayer by J. Ben Eller.

Wednesday Afternoon Session

9. The afternoon session was opened with a devotional service led by Luther Hux.

10. The Report on Denominational Program was read by T. L. Sasser. The Report on State Missions was presented by Jennings Johnson. Upon motion to adopt the subjects were discussed by T. L. Sasser, Jennings Johnson, and B. E. Morris, President of the N. C. Baptist State Mission Board. The report was adopted .

DENOMINATIONAL PROGRAM

The Denominational Program is the co-operative plan of the churches to go into all the world preaching the Gospel to every creature, baptizing and teaching them, in and by the empowering presence of the risen Christ.

There are six definite entities involved in the program: (1) The Holy Spirit; (2) The saved individual; (3) The local church; (4) The district Association; (5) The State Convention; and (6) The Southern Baptist Convention.

The Holy Spirit is the power, the intelligence, the inspiration, and the will to do. The saved individual is the essential person in whom the Holy Spirit abides, leading, empowering, restraining, constraining, inspiring and sending him forth into the harvest. The church is the organism composed of saved persons who walk together in Christian love, helping one another in spiritual life, winning the people of the community to the Lord Jesus, and cooperating with other churches in world-wide missionary work. The fourth entity is the Association of the churches who join hands and local fields, filling in the open places and coming together for fellowship, counsel and inspiration. The State Convention is composed of the messengers of the churches, whose function is to promote missions,

Christian education, and social service. The Southern Baptist Convention is composed also of the messengers from local churches and is designed to carry on home and foreign missions.

Through these organizations redeemed men empowered by the Holy Spirit follow Jesus as he leads in a world-redemption program. For the sake of efficiency and practical effort we divide missions into State, Home and Foreign. To support and complement these we have Christian education, hospitals, ministerial relief and orphanages.

The purpose of this report and the consideration of the point involved is to coordinate and make efficient our organized activities in preaching the Gospel, the power of God unto salvation, to every creature everywhere.

In other years we have followed the God of this world into the bondage of financial debt. We have now, under the leadership of our Lord crossed the Red Sea. The first and immediate item of our denominational program is to gather our people together from our wilderness wanderings and cross the Jordan by paying off all our financial obligations. We will then lengthen the cords and strengthen the stakes for all missions and their supporting causes as we continue to enlist, evangelize, and enlarge.

Respectfully submitted,

T. L. SASSER

STATE MISSION REPORT

Christ taught His disciples that they were to go to the end of the earth carrying the Gospel, but they were to begin at home, and like the leaven work to the ends of the earth. Surely that must mean if we are to do an efficient work in all the world we must make strong the home base of our service. The strength of the Church and its activities at home will largely determine our power and efficiency at the front. As your committee sees it, that, is the specific task of the State Missions.

At present, we are undertaking seven particular tasks in North Caroina, under the head of State Missions. These are as follows:

1. Assisting Missionary Pastors who are carrying the Gospel to the poor. There are 130 churches now being helped. These churches could not have the Gospel preached to them if they were not so helped. Many such churches have developed into self-sustaining useful churches.

2. Churches are assisted in educational centers in order to care for our students who are away from our home church but cannot afford to be away from the preaching of the Gospel.

3. Through State Missions, a Sunday School, and a B. T. U. Department are maintained for the teaching and training of our people.

4. State Missions is, as far as possible, helping poor churches to pay for adequate buildings. Many churches could better serve if they had better plants in which to carry on their work, but are unable to have such plants.

5. For some years the sick veterans at Oteen Government hospital have been ministered to by Rev. Wayne Williams under auspecies of the State Mission Board.

6. The State Mission Board is trying at this time to give the Gospel to the Indians in Robeson and Swain Counties.

7. There was for some time a very limited work done among the negroes, then for a while it was discontinued. Since March of this year we are doing some work with them. At present there is one young negro pastor. He is doing a good work holding conferences with the pastors, and doing what other work he can.

In addition to this, the Board has added this year, one general missionary, M. O. Alexander. He spends his time in holding revivals, attending general meetings, helping churches in forming better fields, etc. There is a real need for three men in the State, one in each division, Eastern, Central and Western.

As a boy, I liked to tie a boat chain to something on land, and then get out and ride the length of the chain in Little Pee Dee River: that was before I could handle a boat. There was one thing I noticed my father was always interested in; that was how solid the object on the land was that the chain was fastened to. If we are to do a lasting work in all the world we must reinforce at home, by teaching studying, and practicing the plan as given in the Bible.

Respectfully submitted,

JENNINGS JOHNSON

11. After announcments by C. N. Royal and G. H. Liner, the Committee on New Churches reported that the Bailey Memorial Baptist Church and the Webster Memorial Baptist Church, of Greensboro had asked to be received into the Association. Motion was passed that the churches be received.

12. The Report on the Orphanage was read by B. G. Whitley. Upon motion to adopt the subject was discussed by B. G. Whitley and J. A. McMillan. The report was adopted.

REPORT ON MILL'S HOME

The Mill's Home has closed its 50th year with 700 children. Of these, 155 are at the Kennedy Home. Through Mother's Aid, 189 were cared for.

The fiftieth annual report of the Home gives very encouraging progress of the various departments of "OUR ORPHANAGE." However, because of the great demand on the Home, we are in need of funds to enlarge our work. We are happy to report that wise efficient and consecrated men and women are at the head of each department.

The report shows the cost per month for each child cared for, to be $19.05. We woud also call your attention to the fact that the counties of Guilford and Rockingham furnish the Home with 59 children. The annual cost for caring for the children from the Piedmont Association is $13,487.40.

The monthly or once a month offering from our Sunday Schools and the Thanksgiving offerings are the only regular support of the Home. Out of nearly 2,500 Sunday schools, less than 1,000 send monthly offerings.

Because of the lack of funds, the Mother's Aid has been unable to carry on this worthy work as desired by the management.

Your committee would offer the following suggestions:

1. That the pastor of each church see that the once a month offering is sent the Home, or get a new Superintendent, or get out himself.

2. That the Treasurer of each church be instructed not to use the money for the Home for paying other bills.

3. That each pastor and Sunday school visit the Home.

4. That we send our prayers to the Lord and send more of our money to the Mills Home.

Respectfully submitted,

B. G. WHITLEY

13. The Treasurers' Report was presented and referred to the Auditing Committee.

TREASURER'S REPORT

To the Piedmont Baptist Association

I herewith submit my report for the year ending September 30, 1935:

Received from the churches		$227.94
Disbursements:		
Greensboro Printing Co.—for Programs	$ 4.00	
Balance due on Clerk's Remuneration	8.21	
To M. A. Huggins, Treasurer, from Ruffin-Stacey Church	6.25	
To M. A. Huggins, Treasurer, from Whites Memorial Church	10.50	
Economy Printing Co.—for Minutes	122.26	
Postage and Stencils	3.01	
Clerk's Remuneration	50.00	
	$204.23	
Balance on Hand	23.71	
		$227.94

Respectfully submitted,

O. E. LEE, Treas.

14. Rev. J. M. Hilliard gave a cordial welcome to the following new pastors: N. F. Britt, C. G. Coe, Grover C. Phillips, M. L. Hux, John U. Garner.

The afternoon session closed with prayer.

Night Session

15. The night session opened with devotional service led by N. F. Britt.

16. The Report on Christian Education was read by A. Lincoln Fulk. Upon motion to adopt the subject was discussed by A. Lincoln Fulk. Dr. A. C. Reid, of Wake Forest College delivered an address on Christian Education. The report was adopted.

CHRISTIAN EDUCATION

Education is our modern shibboleth. More pupils are enrolled and more monies are being expended for the cause of education than ever before in our history. Going to college is no longer regarded as the exception, but as the rule. The question facing modern youth is not, "Should I go to College?" but, "Can I go?"

With over half of our Baptist students now enrolled in State schools, with the religious element largely eliminated from those schools, and with their increased allotment of funds and equipment, the situation facing the denominational schools is grave. J. M. Price, writing in "Home and Foreign Fields" for June, says that there are four tasks awaiting us today. First, that the number of Christian schools should be reduced to the minimum and their efficiency increased to the maximum. Second, that Christian training must be provided for our students enrolled in state schools. Third, that the religious education program of our churches be intensified, and fourth, that as far as possible, Christian teachers be secured in our public schools.

It is earnestly suggested that parents realize that education includes more than mere book-knowledge, and that the Christian school affords the education plus. Our ideas are learned largely from those with whom we associate, and if parents desire their children to be Christian in act and attitude, they must send them where they may be taught from a Christian viewpoint and where they may associate with personalities friendly to and discharged with the Spirit of Christ. If Christ would appear in the educated product, He must be given place in the educational process.

The Christian school must realize that its excuse for being is that it offers the education plus. Its program must include more than the three R's. It is to train the hand to serve, the head to think, and the heart to love. Christian Education must include the three H's. No educational institution can rise higher than the ideals of its faculty and student body. Thus the challenge is two-fold: First, that parents send material out of which character can be formed, and that our schools give back our boys and girls in whom has been instilled the spirit of the Master-Teacher himself.

With the complexity of our modern times, with the increase in invention, and with a greater scientific knowledge than ever before linked with spiritual maladjustments on every hand, the demand for Christian Education is only intensified. Mere education might place in man's hands powerful inventions of science, but Christian Education must direct the proper use of them. Our civilization may end itself by mis-use of powerful instruments unless we bring them under spiritual control. Science invents, Christ directs. Education is a means to an end; Christianity is that end realized. The need for an education that is Christian is great; Christian Education will meet the great need.

Respectfully submitted,

A. LINCOLN FULK

The night session was closed with prayer.

Thursday Morning Session

17. 9:45 A. M. The morning session was opened with a devotional service led by John U. Garner.

18. A visitor, Fred N. Daye, of Winston-Salem, was recognized.

19. The Report on Woman's Work was read by Mrs. Nettie H. Hoge. Upon motion to adopt, the subject was discussed by Mrs. Hoge. The report was adopted.

REPORT OF WOMAN'S WORK

Someone has jokingly said, if you want to publish news, telephone, telegraph and tell a woman. We smile at the joke, but it ceases to be a joke when we remember it was to a woman Jesus first committed the message of His resurrection, and she was to tell the brethren. During the past centuries she has continued by word and deed to proclaim the Gospel in all lands. How much the growth of Christianity owes to the testimony of womanhood is only recorded in the book of rememberance.

To womanhood has been entrusted the mission of ministry beginning in the home and reaching out into all walks of life. Her place of influence and service in the church carries with it unknown possibilities. Part of the Woman's Missionary program is the enlistment into the service of the women and young people, and through prayer, tithing, studying and training, develop the spiritual life of our churches at home and support the mission work in all the fields.

The magnitude of the work accomplished in our South-wide work, of which we are a part can be partially estimated in the combined reports sent to our Southern Baptist Convention. Last year the Woman's Missionary Union reported 93,217 tithers; 31,248 mission study classes; $94,000 for Home Mission Thank Offering; $210,000 Lottie Moon Christmas Offering; with a total of $1,915,882.99 for all gifts to missions and benevolences. $181,423.96 of this was contributed by our North Carolina W. M. U. and $19,602.59 of the State's contribution was made by our Piedmont W. M. U. We are not satisfied with our progress, we do not wish to magnify our own achievements, but our aim is to assist and stimulate the work undertaken by our denomination, and we are dependent upon support and cooperation of our pastors which we most earnestly solicit.

We have 28 W. M. S.; and a large number of Young People's Auxiliaries.

Respectfully submitted,
NETTIE HATCHER HOGE, Supt.

20. A visitor, Mr. Campbell, President of Campbell College was recognized.

21. The Report on Ministerial Relief and Annuity was presented by Wilson Woodcock. Upon motion to adopt, the subject was discussed by Wilson Woodcock. The report was adopted.

REPORT ON RELIEF AND ANNUITY BOARD

To the Piedmont Baptist Association, October 24, 1935

"What will Baptists do about it?" Is the question asked by Secretary, T. J. Watts, of the Relief and Annuity Board.

The Federal Security Bill has been passed and all religious workers have been exempted from its obligations and excluded from its benefits. Since Baptists have been opposed to taxation for the support of ministers while in active service it is consistent to oppose the support of aged or disabled preachers with public money. Thus it is clearly seen that Baptists have a moral responsibility and obilgation to care for the old preachers.

If the Federal Security Bill had included religious institutions each church would have been required by law to pay a percentage of the pastor's salary into the Federal Treasury. Likewise the preacher would have been compelled to pay a percentage of his salary into th Federal Tresury. From this money a pension would have been paid the preacher in proportion to the salary he had been receiving. May we not urge that Baptist Churches, in their freedom to lay aside in the treasury of the Relief and Annuity Board a percentage of the pastor's salary, and that the preacher do likewise? Thus the preacher will be cared for in old age, in proportion to the salaries they have received while in active service.

Full information as to the various plans may be secured from Dr. T. J. Watts, Dallas, Texas.

The money that is contributed through the Co-Operative Program for Ministerial Relief is administered by this Board and amounted to two cents for each Southern Baptist for the entire year of 1934. Only the most destitute ministers have been helped and these have received less than $10.00 per month.

It is said that certain Indian tribes take their old people out in the wilderness and club them to death. We are more civilized. We just starve our old preachers. God forgive us and give us strength to do more for them.

Respectfully submitted,

WILSON WOODCOCK

22. The Report on Hospitals was read by Tom Bray. Upon motion to adopt, the subject was discussed by Smith Hagaman, Superintendent of our North Carolina Baptist Hospital. The report was adopted.

REPORT ON HOSPITALS

Two hospitals in the Southern Baptist Convention are sharing in the gifts of Southern Baptists. One is the Southern Baptist Hospital at New Orleans, La. and the other is our own North Carolina Baptist Hospital Inc, Winston Salem, N. C.

The Southern Baptist Hospital is located at New Orleans and Louis J. Bristow is Superintendent. This Hospital has 198 active beds and during the last year cared for 6,577 patients, giving them 44,218 days of service. Of them, 378 were given free treatment, and 1,811 part free service at a cost to the hospital of $33,684.82. This hospital reported all operating expenses paid. The Hospital is a Christian institution and seeks to magnify Christ.

This Hospital has no regular income with which to help the poor, but is dependent upon voluntary contributions from those who are of a benevolent spirit and who desire to minister to the needy. It has been and is a mighty factor in the Denominational life of New Orleans and all the section in which it is located.

During the year in the Southern Baptist Hospital blind eyes were opened, crippled limbs were made whole, crushed hearts were ministered to.

All of this was done in the Name of Him whose mission was and is Healing Humanity's Hurt." (For the year ending March 31, 1935).

Then we have our own State Hospital which is perhaps nearer our hearts because it is nearer our homes and we are permitted to share in it more vitally.

Since the opening of the Hospital May 28, 1923 to July 15, 1935, 29,000 patients have entered for treatment. In the first half of the year, 1935, 1,760 patients have been treated. At this rate, the Hospital will have 3,520 patients this year, or 31,260 patient days. Of this, 11,882 will be full pay, 9,704 part pay and 9,674 free.

The Hospital has had an average of 86 patients per day for the last six months and is now averaging 300 per month. Almost one-half of patient days are service, or free days.

The Woman's Missionary Union of the State, in addition to their cash contributions, have sent to the Hospital during the first six months of this year 3,635 articles of linen, consisting of sheets, spreads, pillow cases, towels, etc. These are much needed and much appreciated.

Mother's Day (the second Sunday in May) has been designated

by the denomination as "Hospital Day." They are trying to carry on the same program that Jesus gave so much of His life to—relieving suffering humanity. What part have you had in it? What part will you have in it?

Respectfully submitted,
TOM W. BRAY

23. The Committee on Committees made the following report:

PLACE AND PREACHER—J. S. Hopkins, C. N. Royal, J. C. Gillespie.

NOMINATE THE EXECUTIVE COMMITTEE—Mrs. Nettie H. Hoge, G. H. Jones, B. G. Whitley.

NOMINATE DELEGATES TO THE STATE CONVENTION—John U. Garner, Mrs. Alice Davis, Dr. A. B. Conrad.

AUDITING COMMITTEE—Dr. J. T. J. Battle, N. F. Britt, Carl Bell.

PROGRAM COMMITTEE—Dr. J. Clyde Turner, H. O. Miller, A. Lincoln Fulk.

COMMITTEE ON VERBAL REPORTS—Jennings Johnson, T. W. Bray, Mrs. Flora Moore.

COMMITTEE ON RESOLUTIONS—J. M. Hilliard, Hoyle Love, J. Ben Eller.

Respectfully submitted,
J. L. CONLEY
H. O. MILLER
A. LINCOLN FULK

REPORT OF COMMITTEE ON PROGRAM

Religious Literature	J. C. Gillespie
Foreign Missions	T. L. Sasser
Denominational Program	Dr. A. B. Conrad
State Missions	J. Ben Eller
Orphanage	J. H. Saunders
Baptist Training Union	J. W. Robbins
Woman's Missionary Union	Mrs. Lee Gibson
Ministerial Relief and Annuity	C. N. Royal
Hospitals	J. L. Coley
Home Missions	J. S. Hopkins
Social Service	Hughey O. Miller

Christian Education .... J. Clyde Turner
Sunday Schools .... Harry B. Caldwell
Obituaries .... John U. Garner

Respectfully submitted,
DR. J. CLYDE TURNER
H. O. MILLER
A. LINCOLN FULK

REPORT OF COMMITTEE ON VERBAL REPORTS

C. N. Royal to conduct verbal reports.

Respectfully submitted,
JENNINGS JOHNSON
T. W. BRAY
MRS. FLORA MOORE

REPORT OF COMMITTEE ON RESOLUTIONS

Whereas the South Side Baptist Church along with the other Baptist Churches of High Point have made every possible arrangement for our physical and spiritual comfort be it resolved:

1. That we express our thanks and deepest appreciation to this Church and its pastor Brother G. H. Liner for such generous hospitality.

2. That we further thank the other Baptist Churches and their pastors for the assistance rendered in extending such beautiful courtesies.

Respectfully submitted,
HOYLE LOVE
J. BEN ELLER
J. M. HILLIARD

24. The Report on Home Missions was presented by Dr. J. Clyde Turner. Upon motion to adopt, the subject was discussed by Dr. Turner. The report was adopted.

REPORT ON HOME MISSIONS

The Home Mission Board has a large field of service. Its program includes evangelistic and educational work among the foreigners, the Indians, the Negroes, the deaf, and the Jews. It operates a hospital at El Paso, Texas, for tubercular patients. In addition to its work within the bounds of the Southern Baptist Convention, the Board conducts our mission work in Cuba and Panama. The last report of the Board includes the following summary:

"The Board has in all departments and fields of its work more than 200 missionaries. It is maintaining more than 400 mission stations and preaching places; operating in whole or in part five good-will centers, two rescue missions, and a Seamon's Institute; has fifteen schools operated by missionaries in Panama, Cuba and the homeland, and is furnishing the property of eight mountain schools free of charge to local boards of trustees for the operation of schools in the mountains; it is operating the Southern Baptist Sanitarium in El Paso, Texas, which has, since October, 1930, paid its operating expenses, and has a building and loan department with $1,176,000 loaned to churches."

The work of the past year has been marked by many encouraging features. The evangelistic fires have burned brightly, as evidenced by nearly two thousand conversions. The financial receipts have shown a marked increase over the previous year, and a substantial amount has been paid on the debt. The affairs of the Board are being efficiently and economically administered. There are still many difficulties to be faced, and many obstacles to be overcome, but the future of the work of the Board is encouraging.

Respectfully submitted,

J. CLYDE TURNER

After announcements the morning session closed with prayer.

Thursday Afternoon Session

25. 1:30 P. M. The Afternoon session opened with a devotional service led by E. A. Long.

26. The Report on Social Service was read by Hoyle Love. Upon motion to adopt, the subject was discussed by Hoyle Love and J. A. McKoin, Representative of N. C. United Dry Forces. Upon motion the time for discussion was extended ten minutes. Upon motion an offering was taken for the N. C. United Dry Forces which amounted to $14.55. The report was adopted.

REPORT ON SOCIAL SERVICE

Social service cannot take the place of personal evangelism, but aims to correct the evils in the social order and promote conditions favorable to right living.

Its purpose is to cause the mind of Chist to be applied in all human relationships.

In this day standards of morals are very much lowered.

Gambling is on the increase being legalized in several states.

Sunday is being used more and more as a day of sport.

Sunday baseball, golf, moving pictures, riding and beach revelry are becoming more popular.

Sexual laxity and the divorce evils are growing at a rapid rate; and a divorce is almost as easily gotten as a license to get married.

As we face the liquor question we are overwhelmed in shame, men, women, boys and girls are seen in a drunken condition.

As we look in upon the screen we find many pictures presenting the worst forms of vice, fostering disrespect for law, sacredness of the home and tending to destroy virtue. We are told that there are more men under arms now than at the beginning of the World War. Nationalism, fear, suspicion and race hatred urge preparation.

Respectfully submitted,
HOYLE LOVE

27. The Report on Baptist Training Union was presented by Walter Crissman. Upon motion to adopt, the subject was discussed by H. O. Miller. The report was adopted.

REPORT OF BAPTIST TRAINING UNION

It has been very difficult to determine the progress, if any, in the Baptist Training Union of this Association training the past year since the Asheboro district has withdrawn. We have not been able to really get organized and under way during the past year. The President of the B. T. U. of the Association was elected in his absence a year ago last April and again this past April. He has made the best of the situation without being present at the past two Associational meetings of the Baptist Training Union. At the First Baptist Church in High Point this past April, the Associational Convention was attended by three hundred fifty-three young people who registered. Sixteen churches were represented and a very interesting program was rendered, the leading speakers being Rev. Coy Muckle, Miss Winnie Rickett, and Rev. C. N. Royal. No increase in the number of Unions and the enrollment was reported. We feel sure that there was some slight increase in the number of Unions and a more definite check on this is planned for this year.

Respectfully submitted,
WALTER CRISSMAN

28. The Report on Sunday Schools was read by Dr. A. B. Conrad. Upon motion to adopt, the subject was

discussed by Dr. Conrad, F. L. Paschal, and J. Ben Eller. The report was adopted.

SUNDAY SCHOOL REPORT

According to the last annual of our State Convention there are in North Carolina 2,384 Baptist Sunday Schools with a membership of 384,647. These figures show a gain of 39 schools and 4,115 members over the previous year. In the Piedmont Association we have 53 Sunday Schools with an enrollment of 15,404, each church in the Association having a school regularly maintained. During the past year a few schools have been organized. All this is encouraging and shows substantial progress.

The Sunday School is the Churches' chief agency for propagating its work—it is its chief feeder. When we remember that a very large percentage of those who unite with the church on profession of faith come through the Sunday School, and also that a great number of those enrolled in our schools receive no definite religious instruction at home or anywhere outside of the Sunday School, the importance of this part of our work can hardly be over emphasized. All of our churches ought to put a stronger emphasis on and persue with renewed zeal all that relates to our Sunday School work. Many of our strongest and best churches came into being through the organization of a Sunday School. This year several new churches have been admitted into our Association which had their beginning in a Sunday School in some growing or needy section, the work carried on by devoted souls for a time—and then a church.

Three things ought to receive greater attention in our Sunday School work. First, we need a better trained teaching force, and in all our Sunday Schools there ought to be a regularly maintained Teacher Training Class. The teacher, first of all, needs to be taught. Much that goes on in the name of teaching is slipshod and ineffective. Pastors, Superintendents and all officers ought to insist on all who assay to teach that they shall prepare themselves by every possible means for their great and important task.

We need also to get over to all our teachers the need of a deep sense of responsibility. From superintendents and heads of departments comes the lament that the chief problem is to get efficient teachers, who feel their responsibility and are faithful and regular in attendance. For the flimsiest reasons, many leave their classes without teachers, go away on pleasure bent or for some other reason, and soon the class disintergrates and many are lost to the school and the church.

And a third matter of major importance is emphasis on evangelism. The chief object is not to teach simply but to win to Christ. Numbers, organizations, diplomas, awards all fade into insignificance before this. One thing to be guarded against is that in the multiplying of organizations and seeking awards and carrying out convention programs we shall lose sight of and side track from this great objective.

Baptists have a great task. God has given us favor with the masses. We reach more people than any other religious body in North Carolina and we need eyes to see, and wills to do our divinely appointed task. We can do this only as we plan wisely, study diligently, pray fervently, work interestingly, and have a growing sense of the greatness and importance oi our task.

Respectfully submitted
A. B. CONRAD

29. The Report on Obituaries was presented by E. A. Long. The report was adopted. The subject was discussed by A. Lincoln Fulk, and J. M. Hilliard. Motion was passed that the minutes this year be dedicated to the memory of Thomas Carrick.

REPORT ON OBITUARIES

During the past year many of our brethren and sisters in the Lord have passed to their reward. While we miss their presence and their service in the Master's Kingdom we bow humbly and submissively to the Father's will; looking forward with great anticipation to the time when we will all be re-united in that upper and better home, which Christ has gone to prepare for all those who love and serve him.

And while we wait for his coming for us, may we not be slothful in business, but fervent in spirit serving the Lord. Like the five wise virgins who had their lamps trimmed, full of oil, and ready to go at the shout of the coming of the Bridegroom.

Respectfully submitted
E. A. LONG

List of Honored Dead will be found on pages 38 and 39

30. The following reports of committees were made and adopted:

REPORT OF COMMITTEE ON PLACE AND PREACHER

PREACHER—J. Ben Eller
ALTERNATE—Hoyle Love

The place of meeting to be left with the Executive Committee.

REPORT OF COMMITTEE TO NOMINATE EXECUTIVE COMMITTEE

Clarence A. Smith, Chairman; O. E. Lee, Secretary, J. M. Hilliard, C. N. Royal, C. M. Scott, J. C. Gillespie, J. C. Tatum, J. Ben Eller, Dr. J. T. J. Battle.

Respectfully submitted

MRS. NETTIE H. HOGE
G. H. Jones
T. L. SASSER

Motion was passed to changed Article 10 of the Constitution to include the Associational W. M. U. President, Associational Sunday School Superintendent, and the Associational B. T. U. President on the Executive Committee. Motion was passed to include Mrs. Nettie Hoge, F. L. Paschal and Walter Crissman on the Executive Committee. The report was adopted.

REPORT OF COMMITTEES TO NOMINATE DELEGATES TO THE STATE BAPTIST CONVENTION

DELEGATES—T. L. Sasser and G. H. Jones

Respectfully submitted,

JOHN U. GARNER
MRS. ALICE DAVIS
DR. A. B. CONRAD

REPORT OF AUDITING COMMITTEE

Your Auditing Committee finds the Treasurer's report correct.

Respectfully submitted,

DR. J. T. J. BATTLE
N. F. BRITT
J. CARL BELL

The following Committee to Nominate the Promotion Committee was appointed: Wilson Woodcock, T. L. Sasser, Walter Crissman.

REPORT OF COMMITTEE TO NOMINATE PROMOTION COMMITTEE

Clarence A. Smith, Chairman; C. N. Royal, A. L. Fulk, Mrs. C. E. Siceloff, E. R. Baldwin, Dr. J. T. J. Battle, Mrs. R. R. Saunders.

Motion passed to adjourn. The session closed with singing "God Be With You 'Til We Meet Again" and prayer by Brother J. M. Hilliard.

CLARENCE A. SMITH,
Moderator.

O. E. LEE,
Clerk.

CONSTITUTION

Article 1. The Association shall be called the **Piedmont Baptist** Association.

Article 2. It shall be composed of the ordained ministers who are members of, and those who may have pastoral charges within the Associational District, and three Delegates from each church in the district aforesaid, and churches having a membership exceeding 300 shall be entitled to one additional delegate for every 200 members or fraction thereof in excess of 300.

Article 3. The said delegates shall, before taking their seats, produce letters from respective churches showing their appointment as delegates.

Article 4. The Associational session shall be held at least once a year.

Article 5. The officers shall be a Moderator, Vice-Moderator, Clerk, and Treasurer. If deemed expedient by the Association the offices of Clerk and Treasurer may be combined.

Article 6. The officers of the Association shall be chosen annually by the Association.

Article 7. Association shall be clothed with authority only to advise the churches touching all things pertaining to their interest but shall in no case presume to direct or control them in reference to their own government or internal policy.

Article 8. A Committee of Arrangements, consisting of three members, shall be appointed on the first day of each session to prepare and report the pr ceedings and suggest topics proper for the consideration and action of the next Annual Association.

Article 9. Baptist brethren, not members of the Association, who may be present at any session of the b dy, may, on invitation by the body, take seats and participate in the debates of the Association.

Article 10. The territory embraced in the Association shall be divided into not less than four districts and a committee composed of one pastor and one layman from each district, together with the Moderator, Vice-Moderator, Clerk of the Association, Associational W. M. U. Superintendent, Associational Sunday School Superintendent, and Associational B. T. U. President, shall be appointed at meeting of the Association, which committee shall compose the Executive Committee of the Association a majority of which shall constitute a quorum. It shall be the duty of the committee to superintend and direct the missionary operations of the Association.

Article 11. All committees shall be appointed by the Moderator unless otherwise ordered by the Association.

Article 12. The Constitution may be altered only at an Annual Session of the Association and by a vote of two-thirds of the whole present.

Article 13. The rules of this body shall follow Mell's Parlimentary Practice.

Article 14. This Association shall cooperate with the Baptist State Convention.

Article 15. The time of the holding of the annual session shall be on Wednesday after the fourth Sunday in October of each year.

Adopted October 17, 1895.

Articles 2, 5, 6, 10, 15, Amended.

Sessions, July 23, 24, 1930.

Article 15 Amended.

Session, July 21, 1932.

Article 10 Amended.

Session, October 23, 24, 1935.

Committee—W. O. JOHNSON
A. WAYLAND COOKE

W. M. U. ANNUAL SESSION

Morning Session

The W. M. U. of the Piedmont Association met in annual session, April 25, 1935 at Sixteenth Street Baptist Church, Greensboro.

Mrs. Nettie Hoge presided. Theme, "Christian Warfare." Devotional by Mrs. R. R. Saunders, subject "War A Good Warfare," I. Tim. 1:18.

Welcome given by Mrs. W. R. Fuller, response by Mrs. Shipwash.

The roll call was answered by representatives from 17 churches. Group leaders reported new organizations and more zeal in the work.

Mrs. Stevens of the Asheboro Group asked for the release of seven societies to form the Randolph Association, and pleaded for our prayers and continued love as they accept this new challenge.

Report of Young People's Work was given by Miss Scott, who announced an all day Y. P. Meeting at Balfour, June 13th. She laid on our hearts the importance of training our young people.

Mrs. Mosely gave Personal Service report for Mrs. McKeever, to which she spoke, emphasizing the necessity of spiritual living as the beginning of personal service.

The report of Mission Study Work was presented by Mrs. J. J. Andos.

The Superintendent appointed committee on Time, Place, and Resolutions: Mesdames, R. R. Saunders, Jno. E. Walters, Ralph G. Marley. Nominating Committee: Mesdames, A. Lee Gibson, T. L. Sasser, O. E. Lee.

The report of the Superintendent was followed by her message "A Call To Arms" urging all Christians to rekindle revival fires, defend our young people and to fight worldiness in the church.

This was followed by a talk by Clarence A. Smith, he left a question on our hearts, "What Percent of Your Life is Christ's?"

The new leader for young people of the State was presented, Miss Mary Currin. Her address was based on Isa. 13:2, "Lift We His Banner." Some of the imperatives of Jesus were sighted.

The pastors were presented by Dr. J. C. Turner.

Morning sesion closed with prayer by Rev. B. G. Whitley.

Afternoon Session

Devotional by Mrs. C. N. Royal. Minutes of morning session read and approved.

The report of the Treasurer showed a balance of $48.04.

For Stewardship, Mrs. J. J. Meyers presented Margaret Barnes, a prize winner in the declamation contest, who gave her reading, "Filling the Lord's Treasury." Acts 23:5. "Our Special Offering" was the subject of Mrs. Ben Eller, using Micah 4:3. After a song, Rev. C. N. Royal led in prayer for our special offerings.

Business: Apportionment for the 50th. Anniversary.

Address by Mrs. J. B. Hips, Shanghai, China, on Peace. She gave a picture of the life of women of China in the old days, and another of the new problems. She said she was going back to China, leaving us the challenge of world peace.

The Nominating Committee recommended the following who were elected: Mrs. Nettie Hoge, Superintendent; Miss Ruth Scott, Young People's Leader; Mrs. C. R. Harrison, Secretary; Mrs. C. E. Siceloff, Treasurer; Mrs. W. H. McKeever, Personal Service; Mrs. C. N. Royal, Stewardship; Mrs. J. J. Andos, Mission Study, Literature Chairman; Elizabeth Apple, Training School and Margaret Fund. Group Leaders: Mrs. T. C. Robbins, High Point; Mrs. A. Andrews, Greensboro; Mrs. T. L. Sasser, Reidsville.

A touching memorial to Mrs. J. N. Rumble was given by Mrs. A. Lee Gibson. Mrs. Jasper Hutto gave a solo. Names of others who had died during the year were read while the congregation stood.

The Committee on Resolutions, Time and Place, submitted their report. The next meeting will be held with the First Baptist Church in High Point.

The box lunch plan will be used again next year.

The session closed with prayer by Rev. J. L. Coley.

Respectfully submited,
MRS. H. D. MARTIN,
Sec'y. Pro Tem.

OUR HONORED DEAD

CALVARY
- Mr. and Mrs. J. W. Combs

FAIRVIEW
- Mrs. Elizabeth Cummings

GIBSONVILLE
- Mr. Edison Rankin
- Mrs. Mollie Rainey
- Mrs. Orpha Hommer
- Mrs. Fannie Murray
- Miss Jessie Huffines

GREENSBORO FIRST
- Mr. J. M. Durham
- Mr. S. N. Liles
- Miss Audry Heath
- Mrs. Laura Carr
- Mrs. F. A. Paylor
- Miss Beatrice Barton
- Mr. R. F. Burke
- Mr. J. W. Money
- Miss Elvn Gale Fowler
- Mr. A. P. Noell
- Mr. J. B. Peebles
- Miss Mary Whittington
- Mr. W. H. Glamery

ASHEBORO STREET
- Miss Fannie Moorefield
- Mrs. R. E. Satterfield
- Mr. Geo. W. Veron
- Mr. H. M. Howard
- Mr. W. E. Cheek
- Mr. W. H. Matthews

BESSEMER
- Mrs. Benjamin Lowdermilk
- Mr. M. F. Melvin

ELLER MEMORIAL
- Mr. E. O. Nichols
- Mr. E. Lee Hollingsworth
- Mr. Frank A. Clowers
- Mr. Wm. Erwin Goodwin
- Mr. Ernest Smith
- Master Paul Maness
- Mrs. Mary El James
- Mrs. Annie Isley
- Mrs. W. H. Smith
- Mrs. Thomas Pilkenton

FLORIDA STREET
- Mrs. Lucy Johnson
- Mr. W. E. Sewell
- Mr. N. W. Bolejack
- Mr. E. H. Holder
- Mr. E. A. McFarland

FOREST AVE.
- Mr. Ralph Mooney
- Mr. Neil Sigmund
- Miss Bessie Ferguson

MAGNOLIA STREET
- Miss Lucille Jarvis
- Mrs. Lelia Talton
- Mr. Reid Kirkman

POMONA
- Mrs. S. P. Bland

REVOLUTION
- Mr. J. R. Moore

SIXTEENTH STREET
- Mr. W. L. Lineback
- Mrs. W. R. Straughan
- Mr. W. B. Parrish
- Mr. Virgil Carter
- Mr. J. R. Moore

OUR HONORED DEAD

STEVENS MEMORIAL
- Mr. R. A. Vitito
- Mrs. Carrie Pace

GUILFORD
- Deacon J. R. Coggins

HIGH POINT, FIRST
- Deacon T. G. Shelton
- Mrs. J. J. McMurray
- Mrs. Claude A. Smith
- Mrs. T. G. Elliott
- Mr. W. A. Williams
- Mr. G. C. Floyd
- Mr. H. W. Clark
- Mrs. W. S. Phibbs
- Mrs. Nathan Braswell
- Mr. J. Matt Hedgecock
- Mrs. M. H. Russell
- Mr. Jack Holden
- Mrs. Mary I. Tinnin

GREEN STREET
- Deacon A. E. Brimm
- Mr. W. H. Mann
- Mrs. Annie Russell

HILLIARD MEMORIAL
- Mrs. W. L. Ward
- Rev. David L. Miller
- Mrs. Janie Dunning
- Mr. J. H. McKinnon

NORTH MAIN STREET
- Rev. Thomas Carrick
- Mrs. J. B. Shaver
- Mrs. Isadora Vereen

NORTHPARK
- Mrs. Mildred Marley

SOUTH SIDE
- Mr. W. N. Poor

WEST END
- Mr. C. F. Hendrix
- Mrs. Joyce Carmichael

LEBANON
- Mrs. J. W. Saunders
- Mrs. Jessie Waynick

OAK GROVE
- Mrs. C. U. Smith

OSCEOLA
- Mr. R. O. Brande
- Deacon W. H. Brande
- Deacon R. L. Christmon

REIDSVILLE, FIRST
- Mrs. J. W. Jones
- Mrs. Mary Winstead

MOUNT OLIVE
- Mrs. Ollie Cook
- Mrs. J. E. Carter

PENN MEMORIAL
- Mr. W. A. West

RUFFIN STACEY
- Mr. Ray Watlington

SMITH GROVE
- Mrs. Hattie Grey

SUMMERFIELD
- Deacon J. A. Wilson
- Mr. Wm. Parrish

YEAR	WHERE HELD	MODERATOR	CLERK	PREACHER				Total Gifts
1894	Greensboro	Dr. C. A. Rominger	W. L. Kivett	M. A. Adams	5	....	562	....
1895	Liberty	T. L. Chislom	W. L. Kivett	L. Johnson	12	16	112	$ 4,695.50
1896	Moore's Chapel	R. W. Brooks	W. H. Eller	L. Johnson	14	66	1,194	5,128.94
1897	Summerfield	F. H. Jones	W. H. Eller	J. A. Munday	16	73	1,540	7,198.27
	[illegible]nt Zion	R. W. Brooks	W. H. Eller	L. Johnson	17	67	1,557	6,883.23
1899	Ramseur	R. W. Brooks	F. P. Tucker	John E. White	19	54	1,570	7,435.43
1900	Cherry Street	R. W. Brooks	W. H. Eller	Thomas Carrick	16	48	[illegible]538	7,970.35
1901	Reidsville	F. H. Jones	W. H. Eller	L. Johnson	19	157	1,657	8,282.73
1902	Salem Street	F. H. Jones	W. H. Eller	W. C. Newton	19	135	1,774	9,950.97
	[illegible]le	F. H. Jones	W. H. Eller	C. L. [illegible]s	20	[illegible]85	1,868	12,834.77
1904	Calvary	F. H. Jones	W. H. Eller	H. W. Battle	22	112	1,832	12,807.43
1905	Randleman	F. H. Jones	W. H. Eller	J. M. Hilliard	22	114	2,096	17,674.91
1906	High Point, First	F. H. Jones	W. H. Eller	W. R. Bradshaw	23	201	2,333	29,366.31
1907	[illegible]boro Street	F. H. Jones	W. H. Eller	Wm. Hedley	26	372	2,798	29,993.79
1908	Ramseur	F. H. Jones	W. H. Eller	C. E. Maddry	28	311	3,086	26,347.57
1909	Greensboro	F. H. Jones	W. H. Eller	Wm. Hedley	30	292	3,429	49,847.28
1910	Mount Zion	F. H. Jones	W. H. Eller	R. G. Hendrick	31	336	3,731	28,531.01
	[illegible]ro	W. F. Staley	W. H. Eller	W. F. Staley	29	182	3,736	25,887.56
1912	High Point, Green St	F. P. Hobgood, Jr.	W. H. Eller	J. C. Turner	30	174	3,647	29,697.38
1913	Liberty	F. P. Hobgood, Jr.	W. H. Eller	R. P. Walker	31	409	3,971	37,700.97
1914	Asheboro Street	F. P. Hobgood, Jr.	W. H. Eller	A. W. Claxon	31	413	4,202	42,428.44
1915	Reidsville	J. M. Hilliard	W. H. Eller	J. M. Hilliard	42	313	4,491	42,577.68
1916	Forest Avenue	J. M. Hilliard	W. H. Eller	E. N. Johnson	36	369	4,854	48,418.92
	[illegible]en [illegible]eet	J. M. Hilliard	W. H. Eller	W. R. White	39	308	4,760	44,609.05
	[illegible]e's Chapel	J. M. Hilliard	W. H. Eller	J. W. Rose	39	374	5,140	72,538.46
	[illegible]ite Oak	J. M. Hilliard	W. H. Eller	W. H. [illegible]on	39	339	5,359	76,638.85
1920	Calvary	J. M. Hilliard	W. H. Eller	E. N. Johnson	39	543	5,867	117,682.35
1921	Summerfield	Clarence A. Smith	J. E. Lanier	B. K. Mason	39	180	6,454	135,561.79
1922	Glenola	Clarence A. Smith	J. E. Lanier	Jas. A. Clark	39	679	7,226	149,955.24
1923	Magnolia Street	Clarence A. Smith	H. O. Miller	E. E. White	38	365	7,341	140,553.25
1924	West End	Clarence A. Smith	H. O. Miller	W. E. Goode	40	672	7,489	164,658.19
1925	Fairview	Clarence A. [illegible]th	H. O. Miller	A. T. Howell	41	610	8,956	211,792.21
1926	Ramseur	Clarence A. Smith	S. T. Hensley	Lloyd T. Wilson	42	620	9,974	243,500.68
1927	Trinity	Clarence A. Smith	S. T. Hensley	H. T. Stevens	40	656	[illegible]0,[illegible]23	211,846.40
1928	Bessemer	Clarence A. Smith	O. E. Lee	R. P. Ellington	41	531	10,866	202,002.30
1929	Liberty	Clarence A. Smith	O. E. Lee	C. F. Rogers	44	573	11,496	218,987.61
1930	Asheboro	Clarence A. Smith	O. E. Lee	Geo. T. Tunstall	44	676	[illegible]012	198,077.29
1931	Florida Street	Clarence A. Smith	O. E. Lee	A. B. Conrad	44	827	[illegible]	178,501.19
1932	Reidsville	Clarence A. Smith	O. E. Lee	J. C. Turner	46	778	13,485	159,000.60
	[illegible]te Oak	Clarence A. [illegible]th	O. E. Lee	T. L. Sasser	48	1561	15,199	186,041.40
1934	Franklinville	Clarence A. Smith	O. E. Lee	Wilson Woodcock	53	757	15,356	172,839.18
	[illegible]So. Side, [illegible]h Point	Clarence A. Smith	O. E. Lee	J. S. Hopkins	41	623	12,687	164,135.92

CHURCHES	PASTORS	Location *	When Constituted	Days of M	Members Reporte Last Year	Baptisms	Letters	Statements	Restorations	Letters	Exclusions	Erasures	Deaths	Total Membership	Weekly Prayer Meetings	Reviv	Lord's Obser	Families receivin
Allen Jay	R. L. Smith, [illegible] Point, N. C.	V	1934	2 4	32	5	7	...	...	1	...	...	...	43	1	1	12	...
[illegible]y	Jas. C. Gillespie, Reidsville, N. C.	O	[illegible]	2 4	[illegible]99	5	1	...	...	8	...	44	2	151	0	1	2	...
Fairview	Jas. C. Gillespie, Reidsville, N. C.	O	1904	1 3	......	6	...	...	...	...	...	...	1	......	0	1	2	2
Gibsonville	E. A. Long, Germantown, N. C.	T	[illegible]94	2 4	......	4	6	...	...	2	...	1	5	236	0	1	2	...
Greensboro, First	Dr. J. Clydd Turner, [illegible]o, N. C.	C	1859	1 2 3 4	1,927	29	[illegible]00	7	...	87	17	...	13	1,956	1	1	12	...
Asheboro St.	J. Ben Eller, Greensboro, N. C.	C	1899	1 2 3 4	964	47	33	6	...	43	...	5	6	996	1	1	4	...
Bailey Mem.	C. G. [illegible], [illegible]a, N. C.	C	1935	1 2 3 4	......	26	6	4	...	...	...	...	...	51	1	1	4	...
Bessemer	....	V	1922	1 2 3 4	549	11	16	...	...	22	...	1	2	551	1	1	10	9
Eller Mem.	J. S. Hopkins, Denim Br., Greensboro	C	1897	1 2 3 4	890	36	9	7	4	3	...	130	10	803	1	2	4	12
Florida St.	B. G. Whitley, Rt. 5., [illegible]ro, N. C.	C	1916	1 2 3 4	323	26	7	2	2	13	...	...	5	342	1	2	3	5
[illegible]st Av.	Wilson Woodcock, [illegible]o, N. C.	C	1906	1 2 3 4	552	17	18	2	...	45	4	17	3	520	1	1	12	30
Latham Park	W. I. Johnson, Burlington, N. C	C	1916	1 2 3 4	52	5	...	...	...	...	...	...	...	55	...	...	...	...
Magnolia St.	Jennings Johnson, Greensboro, N. C.	C	1912	1 2 3 4	400	18	6	5	...	12	...	...	3	412	1	2	1	5
Pomona	W. B. Cooke, Pomona, N. C.	V	1913	1 2 3 4	210	12	7	10	2	10	...	2	1	228	1	3	3	...
Revolution	A. N. Hollis, Revolution, Greensboro	C	1907	1 2 3 4	2[illegible]	9	2	...	...	6	3	...	1	289	1	2	2	2
Sixteenth St	Jno. L. Coley, Denim Sta., Greensboro	C	[illegible]	1 2 3 4	1,015	37	4	1	7	83	61	...	5	149	1	1	9	10
Stevens Mem.	Jno. U. Garner, Denim Br., Greensboro	V	1922	1 2 3 4	167	11	16	...	...	5	...	52	2	130	1	1	4	...
Webster Mem.	M. L. Hux, Rt. 5, Greensboro, N. C.	O	1935	1 2 3 4	.....	2	34	6	...	...	...	...	...	95	1	...	...	2
[illegible]d	....	V	1914	1 2 3 4	76	5	4	...	...	5	...	...	1	76	0	1	2	5
High Point, 1st.	Dr. A. B. Conrad, High Point, N. C.	C	1825	1 2 3 4	1,168	52	49	3	...	49	...	14	13	1,196	1	1	4	25
Green St.	C. N. Royal, High Point, N. C.	C	1899	1 2 3 4	1,104	54	40	10	...	37	...	...	3	1,168	1	2	4	8
Hilliard Mem.	Hugh Y. O. Miller, High Point, N. C.	C	1929	1 2 3 4	280	22	9	1	2	8	4	...	4	298	1	1	...	3
[illegible]th [illegible]in St.	A. [illegible]n Fulk, High Point, N. C.	C	1908	1 2 3 4	234	18	4	6	...	5	...	25	3	230	1	1	4	6
[illegible]th [illegible]k	N. F. Britt, High Point, N. C.	C	1929	1 2 3 4	194	11	6	4	...	4	...	...	1	165	1	2	2	2
South Side	G. H. Liner, High Point, N. C.	C	1914	1 2 3 4	317	20	10	3	...	1	...	81	1	271	1	2	4	...
West End	Hoyle Love, High Point, N. C.	C	1913	1 2 3 4	374	10	14	...	...	11	3	4	2	340	1	1	4	5
Jessup Grove	....	O	1933	2 4	45	...	...	...	...	...	...	...	...	......	...	...	...	...
[illegible]on	C. M. Oates, Greensboro, N. C.	O	1911	1 2 3 4	141	16	1	...	...	...	...	...	2	155	...	2	2	...
Mount Zion	I. Johnson, Burlington, N. C.	O	....	2 4	......	2	...	...	...	...	...	...	2	......	...	1	1	...
Oak Grove	J. H. Hanes, Belew Creek, N. C.	O	19[illegible]	1 3	88	1	...	...	...	...	...	...	1	88	1	1	2	...
[illegible]e [illegible]pel	Thos. W. Bray, Greensboro, N. C.	O	1934	1 2 3 4	9	2	2	...	...	...	...	...	...	13	1	2	4	...
Osceola	D. E. Oates, Rt. 2, [illegible] Point, N. C.	O	19[illegible]	2 4	46	2	4	...	...	...	...	...	3	49	0	1	2	2
[illegible]nt Garden	Thos. W. Bray, [illegible]o, N. C.	V	1933	1 2 3 4	53	21	6	5	...	...	1	1	...	82	1	1	11	11
[illegible]e, 1st.	T. L. Sasser, Reidsville, N. C.	C	....	1 2 3 4	681	12	16	2	...	15	...	...	2	694	1	...	4	44
Mount Olive	J. H. Saunders, Reidsville, N. C.	C	1929	1 2 3 4	200	32	11	4	...	5	17	6	2	217	1	2	4	4
Penn Mem.	D. W. Oberby, Reidsville, N. C.	C	1927	1 2 3 4	140	1	5	2	...	11	3	14	1	118	1	2	2	6
f [illegible]ey	J. T. [illegible]n, Rt. 5, [illegible]le, N. C.	O	[illegible]31	1 2 3 4	124	6	...	...	1	3	1	...	1	126	1	1	4	4
[illegible]th Grove	R. O. Nuckels, Colfax, N. C.	O	1921	1 3	124	...	...	3	...	15	...	...	1	106	1	2	4	...
Summerfield	E. A. Long, Germantown, N. C.	V	....	1	151	16	...	...	...	...	...	...	2	165	...	1	2	6
[illegible]le	Grover C. Phillips, Altamahaw, N. C.	V	1933	1 2 3 4	21	8	2	9	...	11	...	...	...	29	1	2	2	1
[illegible]ty	B. F. Clark, [illegible]e, N. C.	V	1924	1 3	88	6	2	...	...	2	...	...	...	94	1	1	2	...
TOTALS					13,263	623	457	102	18	522	114	397	104	12,687		52	156	209

(*)—'O', Country; 'V', Village; 'T', [illegible]n; 'C', City.

TABLE II: SUNDAY SCHOOLS OF PIEDMONT BAPTIST ASSOCIATION FOR YEAR ENDING SEPTEMBER, 1935

CHURCHES	SUPERINTENDENTS	SUNDAY SCHOOL ENROLLMENT: Beginners 3-5 Years	Primaries 6-8 Year	Juniors 9-12 Years	Intermediates 13-16 Years	Young People 17-24 Years	Adults 25 Years and Up	Cradle Roll Under 3 Years	Home Department	Officers and Teachers	Total Enrollment Including Officers Teachers & Pupils	SPECIAL INFORMATION: What is your Av'ge. Attendance?	Is the School Graded? *	Is It Standard A-1? *	Teachers Holding Normal Diplomas	Baptisms from School	Have You a Mission Sun. School?	Enrollment of Mission S. S.	Did you Hold a Vacation Bible School	Enrollment of Vacation School	Avr'ge. Attendance Of Vacation School
Allen Jay	Wade Cumbie, Rt. 1, Trinity, N. C.	6	8	12	15	20	37			7	105	70	0		1	5					
Calvary	Chas. F. Delgado, Reidsville, N. C.	20		25	14	80	20			11	170	82	0			5					
Fairview	A. D. Hopkins, Reidsville, N. C.									7	70										
Gibsonville	R. K. Craven, Gibsonville, N. C.	30	44	54	31	36	54	16	20	17	302										
Greensboro, First	O. E. Lee, Greensboro, N. C.	132	132	220	165	279	733	101	208	98	2,068	876	1	0	2	19			1	206	131
Asheboro St.	J. T. True, Greensboro, N. C.	69	109	118	117	67	290	53	25	77	925	450	1	0	25	39					
Bailey Mem.	Jas. T. Smith, Rt. 5, [illegible]o, N. C.									11	135	67	0		2						
Bessemer	Claude L. Murray, Bessemer Br., G'boro.	38	28	35	64	38	98	29		25	355	218	1	0	11	5					
Eller Mem.	C. E. Brady, Denim Br., Greensboro	39	82	87	87	91	127			127	640	324	1		26	22					
Florida St.	J. L. Roberson, Greensboro, N. C.	18	61	73	53	13	85	24		28	355	251	1			18					
Forest Ave.	Dr. J. T. J. Battle, [illegible]o, N. C.	54	40	63	81	108	109	47	25	52	579	360	1		37	17					
Latham Park	Odell Pulley, Greensboro, N. C.										90	55									
[illegible]a St.	H. S. Noah, Glenwood Br., Grensboro	10	28	60	49	60	107	17		20	351	175	1		3	18					
Pomona	C. C. Patterson, Pomona, N. C.	49	56	63	64	93	95	12		13	445	248									
Revolution	N. C. Brown, Greensboro, N. C.	18	51	60	29	44	63	42	21	26	354	193	1		11						
Sixteenth St.	J. V. Brady, Denim Br., Greensboro,	26	29	121	119	52	124	15		22	508	275	1		3	37					
Stevens Mem.	L. A. Mills, Rt. 2., Greensboro, N. C.	11	43	42	27	33	74	4		20	254	195	1			10					
Webster Mem.	R. E. Fitchett, Rt. 5., Greensboro, N. C.	8	8	15	9	15	68	15		11	149	125									
Guilford	W. R. Harmon, Greensboro, N. C.	7	11	14	11	15	26		1	12	97	66			1	5					
High Point, 1st.	A. E. Tate, High Point, N. C.	88	77	118	146	159	217	30	66	72	973	463	1		2	45					
Green St.	B. G. Leonard, Greensboro, N. C.	96	166	231	165	221	377	32		108	1,396	700	1		100	35					
Hilliard Mem.	L. E. Edwards, Sta. A., High Point, N. C.	54	18	56	54	28	74	10		23	317	211	1								
North Main St.	Winfred Clinard, High Point, N. C.	30	36	61	15	53	61			4	260	159	1		6	18					
North Park	Paul K. Fry, High Point, N. C.	29	38	39	36	27	68	15	2	28	282	165	1		10	11					
South Side	W. K. Briggs, High Point, N. C.		98	53	55	53	92			14	365	227	1		5	12					
West End	Eugene Gregory, High Point, N. C.	32	30	54	50	32	74	22	30	22	346	252	1		14	9					
Jessup Grove																					
Lebanon	B. G. Yowe, Denim Sta., Greensboro	24	10	27	12	46	71			10	200	133	1			16					
Mount Zion	Geo. H. Spoon, Kimesville, N. C.		28	23		32	23			7	113	53				2					
Oak Grove	L. R. Loflin, Jamestown, N. C.	10	15	19	31		31			9	115	70									
Osborne Chapel	Robt. R. Osborne, Rt. 3, Greensboro	4	18	25	14	10	35	2		7	115				1	2					
[illegible]la	A. E. Cooke, Gibsonville, N. C.	16		18		20	20			8	82	38				2					
Pleasant [illegible]den	Walter J. Smith, Pleasant Garden	9	18	18	13	12	19	9		9	107	65	1		1	15					
Reidsville, 1st.	R. T. Burton, Reidsville, N. C.	17	46	69	67	106	113	40	112	54	624	260	1			12			1	188	159
Mount Olive	Elwood Talley, Reidsville, N. C.	28	24	22	19	47	30		35	8	213		1								
Penn Mem.	Herbert Ford, Reidsville, N. C.	12		18	12	20	25			8	95	55	1								
Ruffin-Stacey	M. C. Thomas, Rt. 5., Reidsvile, N. C.	27	18	12	9	24	39			9	138	80				3					
Smith Grove	Drew Smith, Colfax, N. C.		50		40		30			5	125	60									
Summerfield	C. V. Furgeson, Summerfield, N. C.									12	125	73									
Tabernacle	J. Frank Hensley, Rt. 1., Elon College	10	10	14	6	9	12	5		8	74	50				8					
Trinity	J. M. Thomas, Rt. 3, High Point, N. C.		9	11	9	22	41	14		14	120				6	6					
TOTALS		1,021	1,439	1,950	1,688	1,965	3,562	554	545	1,023	14,137	7,144			267	396				394	290

Allen Jay	[illegible] [illegible], Rt. 1, Trinity, N. C.	Yes	....	Wood	300	1	...	...	300	......	......	300	....	......
Calvary	J. E. McCargo, Reidsville, N. C.	Yes	1898	Wood	375	5	4	4	3,500	......	2,000	5,[illegible]00	165.00	2,000
Fairview	Wm. Cummings, Rt. 2, Reidsville, N. C.	Yes	1902	Wood	300	5	...	4	2,000	......	1,200	2,[illegible]00	50.00	1,500
Gibsonville	W. P. Killette, Gibsonville, N. C.	Yes	1894	Wood	300	9	9	9	4,000	......	......	4,[illegible]00	....	2,500
[illegible], First	A. R. Williams, [illegible], N. C.	Yes	1906	Brick	1,000	48	8	46	130,000	......	15,000	145,[illegible]00	....	67,000
[illegible] St.	J. B. Wills, Greensboro, N. C.	Yes	1912	Brick	700	32	6	47	30,000	......	6,000	36,000	4,164.23	26,000
Bailey [illegible]	[illegible]s. J. T. Smith, Rt. 3, Gr[illegible], N.C.	Yes	1935	Wood	250	1	...	...	1,500	......	......	1,[illegible]00	537.62	......
Bessemer	W. P. Haynes, Bessemer Br. [illegible]	Yes	1922	Wood	300	16	3	16	6,000	......	2,000	8,[illegible]00	1,375.00	4,000
Eller Mem.	[illegible] W. Baity, Denim Sta., [illegible]	Yes	1925	Brick	450	48	6	48	41,000	......	......	41,000	....	25,000
Florida St.	[illegible] Johnson, Greensboro, N. C.	Yes	1930	Brick	450	22	2	12	15,000	......	......	15,000	2,500.00	10,000
Forest Ave.	B. B. Stockard, Greensboro, N. C.	Yes	1906	Brick	275	14	6	14	17,000	......	8,000	41,000	2,200.00	10,750
Latham Park	W. W. Sutton, Greensboro, N. C.	Yes	1916	Wood	150	1	...	...	3,000	......	......	3,000	....	......
[illegible] St.	[illegible] G. H. Williamson, Greensboro,	Yes	1912	Wood	300	6	1	9	6,000	......	......	6,000	....	4,000
Pomona	C. C. Patterson, Pomona, N. C.	Yes	1913	Wood	350	8	7	7	3,500	......	......	3,500	....	......
Revolution	W. S. Jones, Greensboro, N. C.	Yes	1907	Wood	400	5	3	7	10,000	......	5,000	15,000	....	7,500
Sixteenth St.	Alfred E. Whitt, Denim Sta., Greensboro	Yes	1907	Brick	450	9	2	9	30,000	......	6,000	36,000	....	10,000
Stevens Mem.	J. H. Campbell, Rt. 5, Greensboro, N. C.	Yes	1922	Wood	250	11	2	13	10,000	......	......	10,000	....	5,000
[illegible] Mem.	J. W. Walters, Rt. 5, Greensboro, N. C.	Yes	1935	Wood	240	4	...	4	4,000	......	......	4,000	....	1,800
Guilford	R. F. Bondurant, Rt. 1., Guilford College	Yes	1914	Wood	200	1	...	...	3,500	150	......	3,650	....	1,650
High Point, 1st.	C. D. Goldsmith, High Point, N. C.	Yes	1905	Brick	500	49	6	43	75,000	......	7,000	97,000	33,000.00	36,000
Green St.	Clyde Ayers, High Point, N. C.	Yes	1926	Brick	1,500	95	6	68	156,000	1,600	3,000	160,600	56,300.00	60,000
Hilliard Mem.	J. W. Saunders, High Point, N. C.	Yes	1931	Brick	800	22	...	20	22,500	......	......	22,500	1,260.00	10,000
North Main St.	Mrs. Ethel Clinard, High Point, N. C.	Yes	1924	Brick	350	10	4	10	10,000	......	400	10,400	....	4,000
[illegible]th Park	D. H. Short, High Point, N. C.	Yes	1929	Wood	300	6	...	6	3,[illegible]00	......	......	3,500	1,056.00	1,500
South S[illegible]e	J. G. Williams, High Point, N. C.	Yes	1916	Wood	400	8	...	8	4,500	......	2,500	7,000	....	......
West End	Mrs. C. H. Clodfelter, High Point, N. C.	Yes	1913	Wood	350	11	...	13	8,500	......	3,500	12,000	....	5,000
Jessup Grove	....	Yes	1934	Wood	400	1	...	...	1,050	......	......	1,050	....	......
Lebanon	Pauline Jarvis, Rt. 5, [illegible]	Yes	1911	Wood	250	6	...	5	2,500	......	......	2,500	200.00	......
Mount Zion	J. C. Lackamy, Liberty, N. C.	Yes	1912	Wood	500	1	...	...	2,000	......	......	2,000	....	......
Oak Grove	L. R. Loflin, Jamestown, N. C.	Yes	1927	Wood	270	3	2	2	1,500	......	......	1,500	....	......
[illegible]	Robt. R. Osborne, Rt. 3, Greensboro	Yes	1935	Wood	400	1	...	...	650	......	......	650	125.00	......
[illegible]ola	E. R. Brand, Rt. 1, Brown Summit	Yes	1915	Wood	300	1	...	...	2,[illegible]00	......	......	2,000	....	......
Pleasant Garden	Harvey L. Paschal, Rt. 1, Greensboro	Yes	1918	Wood	220	1	...	...	1,500	......	......	1,500	500.00	500
Reidsville, 1st.	T. L. Gardner, Reidsville, N. C.	Yes	....	Brick	500	24	5	19	37,000	......	14,000	51,000	....	43,500
Mount Olive	Mrs. Patrick DeLapp, Rt. 5, Reidsville	Yes	1929	Wood	275	1	...	4	2,[illegible]00	......	......	2,500	....	2,000
Penn Mem.	Mrs. Pearl Boswell, Reidsville, N. C.	Yes	1935	Brick	300	13	3	10	10,000	......	1,500	11,500	900.00	1,000
Ruffin-Stacey	R. M. Durham, Rt. 5, Reidsville, N. C.	Yes	1931	Wood	350	...	...	...	2,000	......	......	2,000	....	......
Smith Grove	Drew Smith, Colfax, N. C.	Yes	1923	Wood	300	1	...	...	1,000	......	......	1,000	....	600
Summerfield	Mrs. Myrtle Smith, Summerfield, N. C.	Yes	1904	Wood	400	1	...	4	6,000	......	......	6,000	....	3,500
[illegible]lle	Edna Phillips, Alta[illegible]w, N. C.	Yes	1934	Wood	400	1	...	...	1,400	......	......	1,400	....	......
Trinity	Mrs. G. G. Clinard, Trinity, N. C.	Yes	1925	Wood	300	7	5	4	2,500	......	......	2,500	....	2,000
TOTALS					16,405	509	90	465	673,900	1,750	77,100	783,150	104,332.85	348,300

TABLE IV: GIFTS FOR LOCAL CHURCH WORK OF PIEDMONT ASSOCIATION FOR YEAR ENDING SEPTEMBER, 1935

CHURCHES	Pastor's Salary	Other Salaries	Ministerial Help and Supply	Building and Repairs	Church Debt and Interest	Incidentals	Literature for S. S. B.Y.P.U. & W.M.U	Help Given To Local Poor	For Printing the Minutes and Clerk of Association	Other Objects	(Local Work) Given by Church Only	(Local Work) Given by All W. M. U. Organizations	(Local Work) Given by the Sunday School	(Local Work) Total for Local Purposes Given by the Church and All Its Organizations
[illegible]n Jay				30.00	200.00	25.00	40.00				295.00			295.00
Calvary	247.14		26.00	146.50		27.98			3.00	4.89	455.51	17.50	61.49	534.50
Fairview	200.00		50.00								250.00		432.00	682.00
Gibsonville	600.00		20.00			155.43					775.43	13.01	119.35	907.79
[illegible]o, First	4,600.00	4,300.00	[illegible]	[illegible]		3,471.55	1,172.12	740.71	18.00	2,669.61	17,749.97			17,749.97
[illegible]o St.	2,910.30	1,235.00	205.00	[illegible]	1,292.75	516.64	705.18	272.06	12.00	545.35	7,858.52			7,858.52
Bailey [illegible].	50.00		25.00	560.72		13.42				43.51	692.65		58.48	751.13
Bessemer	986.15		94.50	83.77	250.12	165.09	105.42	30.80	5.00	105.75	1,826.60		357.63	2,184.23
Eller [illegible]n.	2,520.00		225.00	369.50		1,072.95	[illegible]	144.50	10.00		4,674.21			4,674.21
Florida St.	1,560.00		134.20	[illegible]	1,275.00	[illegible]	57.45	171.73	5.00	172.19	3,769.06	63.25	103.17	3,935.48
Forest Ave.	2,016.32		35.00	[illegible]	193.43	725.20	307.95			140.48	4,171.68			4,171.68
Latham Park	150.00										150.00			150.00
[illegible]lia St.	1,560.00		110.00	155.00		12.00		5.00	3.00	178.55	2,023.55	25.03	627.65	2,676.23
Pomona	1,234.19		99.92	5.00		57.30		6.15	3.00	2.00	1,407.56	2.00	226.24	1,635.80
Revolution	1,692.50		48.62	[illegible]		310.63	11.50		4.00		2,197.80		255.85	2,453.65
[illegible]th St.	2,372.[illegible]	881.28	50.00						5.00		3,308.28			3,308.28
Stevens [illegible]n.	934.20		85.00	30.10		207.33	14.55		3.00		1,274.18		141.58	1,415.76
[illegible]r Mem.	35.66			1,459.48		49.46			5.00		1,549.60	32.65	192.60	1,774.85
Guilford	234.00		10.00	60.00		[illegible]03	108.00	5.00	2.00	60.00	616.03			616.03
High [illegible]nt, 1st.	3,300.00	1,180.00	260.00	137.49	15,372.07	2,510.04	161.35	45.64	18.00	696.55	23,681.14	195.17	954.26	24,830.57
Green St.	3,120.00		197.00	52.57	5,980.62	1,476.31	560.05	17.00	5.00	666.44	12,074.99			12,074.99
Hilliard [illegible]m.	1,340.26		50.25	1,247.20		153.41		5.00	3.00	35.00	2,834.12	21.75	214.98	3,070.85
North [illegible]in St.	1,196.00			60 00		233.05			9.00		1,498.05	46.00	198.05	1,742.10
North Park	940.00		148.00	296.00	201.50	139.05	149.50	64.00	3.00	4.88	1,945.93			1,945.93
o[illegible]th i[illegible]e	1,153.00		105.11	408.26							1,666.37	47.22		1,713.59
West End	1,300.00		45.00	128.55		240.72		14.81	2.50		1,731.58		263.00	1,994.58
Jessup Grove														
[illegible]n	270.65		47.76		324.47	25.66	46.05		3.00	27.50	745.09			745.09
M[illegible]nt Zion	202.24		36.25	15.48							253.97		28.00	281.97
Oak Grove	105.85			40.00		10.55	27.37		2.55	30.00	216.32			216.32
[illegible]e Chapel	104.00		6.00	150.00			18.00		2.00	10.00	290.00		5.00	295.00
[illegible]a	91.25		23.97				31.70			6.00	152.92			152.92
Pleasant Garden	260.00		26.00	[illegible]	250.00	58.25	50.00	15.00	2.00	50.00	758.25	14.46		772.71
Reidsville, 1st.	2,850.00	416.50		200.85		584.79	74.16	27.00	9.00	249.55	4,411.85	520.53	599.51	5,531.89
Mount Olive	1,473.92		66.65	135.00	863.00	42.50	99.89	5.00	2.00		2,687.96			2,687.96
Penn Mem.	780.00		42.00	2 [illegible]	52.00	33.27		10.00	1.50		3,375.47	65.15	127.18	3,567.80
Ruffin-Stacey	200.00					44.80	41.44		2.00		288.24			288.24
Smith Grove	50.00						6.00		2.00	33.12	91.12			91.12
Summerfield	330.00		[illegible]06			66.19	48.00		4.00	96.73	600.98			600.98
[illegible]e			90.65	237.67		10.21		25.00	1.50	160.00	525.03		26.79	551.82
Trinity	300.00					48.00	49.09				397.09			397.09
TOTALS	43,269.63	8,012.78	2,538.94	10,492.09	26,254.96	12.744.12	4,217.03	[illegible]4.40	150.05	5,988.10	115,272.10	1,063.72	4,992.81	121.328.63

NOTE—Treasurers of Piedmont Association will be found on Page 47

Allen Jay						36.00	6.35			42.35			42.35	337.35
Calvary	55.30	10.67	5.50	25.10	4.00	57.26	[illegible]67		21.05	79.55	70.85	44.15	194.55	729.05
Fairview	19.00			6.50		30.07	7.50			42.57		20.50	63.07	745.07
[illegible]e	47.60									47.60			47.60	955.39
Greensboro, First	12,843.25	306.18	742.81	2,704.93	1,004.25	2,013.43	198.94		780.30	7,851.02	9,730.23	3,012.84	20,594.09	38,344.06
Asheboro St.	1,989.21	53.74	116.41	165.79		407.10	65.69		453.58	2,627.02	624.50		3,251.52	12,110.04
Bailey [illegible]							2.35					2.35	2.35	753.48
Bessemer	201.38					75.75	13.10			239.88	50.35		290.23	2,474.46
Eller Mem.	1,180.25	2.85				[illegible]67	16.54		170.60	1,678.70	148.21		1,826.91	6,501.12
Florida St.	334.95	33.50	14.04	52.04		214.69	22.35		3.50	484.97	59.56	130.54	675.07	4,610.55
Forest Ave.	518.75	61.74	23.00	140.00		205.08	43.71			992,28			992.28	5,163.96
Latham Park														150.00
Magnolia St.	13.00	7.55	4.50	15.00		[illegible]	18.09		31.43		68.23	108.36	176.59	2,852.82
Pomona	4.06		1.85			68.84	18.18		125.35	63.74		154.54	218.28	1,854.08
Revolution	549.82	60.04	32.01	68.99		187.56	37.60		22.03	182.12	512.81	263.12	958.05	3,411.70
Sixteenth St	141.35					36.13				177.48			177.48	3,485.76
Stevens [illegible]			34.40	146.02		[illegible]00	29.20			197.62		137.00	334.62	1,750.38
[illegible]		5.00	10.00		2.50	42.45	11.45		15.00		37.50	48.90	86.40	1,861.25
Guilford	5000	2.05	3.10	10.70		13.15	7.05		29.80	91.00	24.85		115.85	731.88
[illegible]h Point, 1st.	3,646.12	83.32	108.37	1,062.92		1,211.48	124.13		923.22	[illegible].73	599.90	1,867.93	7,159.56	31,990.13
Green St.	564.00					300.00	18.45	137.62		[illegible]20.07			1,020.07	13,095.06
Hilliard [illegible]	15.85	11.55	3.45	6.00		110.41	1.50			2.50	25.85	120.41	148.76	3,219.61
North [illegible]n St.	184.00	5.00	13.00	28.00	5.00	0[illegible]0	30.00			44.00	60.00	211.00	415.00	2,157.10
North Park	11.00	12.00				10.75	5.00			10.75	23.00	5.00	38.75	1,984.68
South Side	38.00					25.00				51.00	12.00		63.00	1,776.59
West End	114.00	54.04	18.32	33.35		270.85	49 01		49.40	69.06	193.20	326.71	588.97	2,583.55
Jessup Grove														
Lebanon				13.20		41.06	9.20			63.46			63.46	808.55
[illegible]t Zion		5.50		3.15		40.48	6.70					55.83	55.83	337.80
Oak Grove		5.00		5.00			2.25		23.32	35.57			35.57	251.89
Osborne [illegible]	15.00					9.00			10.00	34.00			34.00	329.00
Osceola	16.90	.50				25.01	4.07			46.48			46.48	199.40
Pleasant Garden	5.75	5.80				36.55	6.00		42.00	134.55	6.75	5.80	147.10	919.81
[illegible]e, 1st.	1,500.00	38.75	56.50	104.04	191.44	378.42	37.48		78.84	1,699.28	307.80	378.39	2,385.47	7,917.36
[illegible]t Olive			4.40	76.25		83.31	7.11			94.82	76.25		171.07	2,859.03
Penn Mem.		12.11	17.00		2.00	10.25					19.00	22.36	41.36	3,609.16
Ruffin-Stacey	10.00					16.52	3.62			30.14			30.14	318.38
Smith Grove									9.14	9.14			9.14	100.26
Summerfield	69.40	5.00	10.00		1.00	70.00	1200		15.95	49.40	73.95	60.00	183.35	784.33
r[illegible]le						13.31						13.31	13.31	565.13
Trinity			34.80			50.11			24.70	109.61			109.61	506.70
TOTALS	24,188.94	781.89	1,253.46	4,666.98	1,210.19	6,908.71	830.29	137.62	2,829.21	23,093.46	12,924.79	6,989.04	42,807.29	164,135.92

TABLE VI: B. T. U. AND W. M. U. OF PIEDMONT BAPTIST ASSOCIATION

CHURCHES	General B. Y. P. U. Organization?	Adult Unions	Senior Unions	Int. Unions	Junior Unions	Total Unions	Standard Unions	Adults Enrolled	Seniors Enrolled	Intermediates Enrolled	Juniors Enrolled	Total Enrolled	Total No. Daily Bible Readers	No. taking B.Y.P.U. Study Courses	Total Systematic Givers All Unions	Students in college from your church	No. of W's. M. S.	No. Y. W. A's.	No. of G. A's.	No. R. A's.	No. of Sunbeams	Total W. M. U. Organizations	W. M. S. Members	Y. W. A's. Members	G. A's. Members	R. A's. Members	Sunbeam Members	Total Members Enrolled	Total Enrolled in Mission Study
[illegible]h Jay	...	...	...	1	1	2	...	...	...	12	8	20	15	12	15	...	1	...	...	...	...	1	8	...	...	...	...	8	...
Calvary	...	...	...	...	...	...	...	...	...	...	...	...	...	...	...	...	1	...	...	...	...	1	25	...	...	...	...	25	...
[illegible]y	...	...	...	...	...	...	...	...	...	...	...	...	...	...	...	...	...	...	...	...	...	...	...	...	...	...	...	...	...
Gibsonville	...	...	1	1	...	2	...	...	10	18	...	28	...	...	...	...	1	...	...	...	...	1	18	...	...	...	...	18	...
[illegible]o, First	Yes	1	3	3	1	8	...	20	48	40	24	132	43	49	84	...	1	1	2	1	1	6	325	21	39	63	38	486	298
[illegible]o St.	Yes	...	1	2	2	5	...	...	21	53	35	109	42	48	59	1	1	2	2	1	1	7	160	35	35	23	45	298	141
Bailey Mem.	...	...	1	...	...	1	...	...	21	...	...	21	4	...	2	...	...	...	...	...	...	...	...	...	...	...	...	...	...
Bessemer	Yes	...	1	1	1	3	...	...	9	20	25	54	19	37	36	2	...	...	...	...	...	...	...	...	...	...	...	...	...
Eller Mem.	Yes	1	1	3	3	8	...	16	15	41	53	125	56	51	54	2	1	1	...	...	...	2	39	14	...	...	...	53	...
Florida St.	Yes	1	1	2	2	6	1	12	10	25	35	82	50	53	55	...	...	...	...	...	...	...	...	...	...	...	...	...	...
[illegible]st Ave.	Yes	...	2	1	...	3	3	...	66	20	...	86	...	...	...	...	...	...	...	...	...	...	...	...	...	...	...	...	...
[illegible]h Park	...	...	...	...	...	...	...	...	...	...	...	...	...	...	...	...	...	...	...	...	...	...	...	...	...	...	...	...	...
Magnolia St.	Yes	1	1	1	1	4	...	13	22	14	17	66	11	5	24	...	1	...	...	...	...	1	25	...	...	...	...	25	14
Pomona	...	...	...	...	...	...	...	...	...	...	...	...	...	...	...	...	1	...	...	...	1	2	12	...	...	...	28	40	...
[illegible]h	No	...	1	...	...	1	...	...	18	...	...	18	18	16	18	...	1	1	2	1	1	6	25	14	24	14	20	97	45
[illegible]th St.	Yes	1	1	1	2	5	...	17	27	16	42	102	...	68	...	...	1	1	1	1	1	5	45	9	14	18	20	106	26
[illegible]s Mem.	...	...	1	1	1	3	...	...	...	...	...	...	...	...	...	...	1	...	...	...	...	1	34	...	...	...	...	34	...
[illegible]er Mem.	...	...	...	...	...	...	...	...	...	...	...	...	...	...	...	...	1	...	...	...	...	1	37	...	...	...	...	37	...
[illegible]d	...	...	1	...	...	1	...	...	16	...	...	16	8	12	8	1	1	...	...	...	...	1	18	...	...	...	...	18	...
High [illegible]t, 1st.	Yes	...	1	2	1	4	...	...	25	66	20	111	42	...	62	...	1	1	2	1	1	6	173	65	44	15	30	327	186
[illegible]n St.	Yes	1	1	4	4	10	...	...	...	...	...	143	96	110	100	...	1	2	2	1	1	7	75	20	60	30	45	230	...
[illegible]rd Mem.	Yes	1	1	1	1	4	...	15	11	14	17	57	34	19	57	2	1	1	1	1	1	5	24	10	15	10	18	77	8
[illegible]h Main St.	...	1	1	1	2	5	...	16	12	14	15	57	27	29	38	...	1	1	2	1	1	6	10	6	19	12	18	65	...
[illegible]h Park	...	1	1	1	1	4	...	28	11	22	22	83	...	...	...	...	1	...	1	...	1	3	25	...	15	...	24	64	...
South Side	...	1	1	1	1	4	...	20	14	12	16	62	...	...	...	...	1	1	1	...	1	4	25	15	16	...	20	76	...
[illegible]st End	...	1	1	1	1	4	...	10	11	18	16	55	36	51	30	...	1	1	1	...	1	4	20	12	13	...	15	60	50
Jessup Grove	...	...	...	...	...	...	...	...	...	...	...	...	...	...	...	...	...	...	...	...	...	...	...	...	...	...	...	...	...
[illegible]n	...	...	...	...	...	...	...	...	...	...	...	...	...	...	...	...	...	...	...	...	...	...	...	...	...	...	...	...	...
Mount Zion	...	...	...	...	...	...	...	...	...	...	...	...	...	...	...	...	...	...	...	...	...	...	...	...	...	...	...	...	...
Oak Grove	...	...	...	...	...	...	...	...	...	...	...	...	...	...	...	...	...	...	...	...	...	...	...	...	...	...	...	...	...
[illegible]e Chapel	...	...	...	...	...	...	...	...	...	...	...	...	...	...	...	...	1	...	...	...	...	1	5	...	...	...	...	5	...
[illegible]la	...	...	1	...	1	2	...	...	14	...	10	24	4	...	16	...	...	...	...	...	...	...	...	...	...	...	...	...	...
Pleasant Garden	...	...	1	...	1	2	...	...	21	...	17	38	12	20	...	...	1	...	...	...	...	1	15	...	...	...	...	15	5
Reidsville, 1st.	...	1	1	1	1	4	...	20	15	28	35	98	34	23	45	2	1	1	2	2	1	7	150	35	20	15	25	245	37
[illegible]t [illegible]e	...	1	...	1	1	3	...	30	...	15	15	60	...	...	...	...	...	...	...	...	...	...	...	...	...	...	...	...	...
Penn Mem.	...	...	...	...	...	...	...	...	...	...	...	...	...	...	...	1	1	1	...	...	...	2	13	17	...	...	...	30	...
Ruffin-Stacey	...	...	...	...	...	...	...	...	...	...	...	...	...	...	...	...	...	...	...	...	...	...	...	...	...	...	...	...	...
[illegible] Grove	...	...	...	...	...	...	...	...	...	...	...	...	...	...	...	...	...	...	...	...	...	...	...	...	...	...	...	...	...
Summerfield	...	...	...	...	...	...	...	...	...	...	...	...	...	...	...	...	1	...	...	...	...	1	14	...	...	...	...	14	...
Tabernacle	...	...	1	...	1	2	...	...	15	...	20	35	18	...	...	...	...	...	...	...	...	...	...	...	...	...	...	...	...
[illegible]y	...	...	...	...	...	...	...	...	...	...	...	...	...	...	...	...	...	...	...	...	...	...	...	...	...	...	...	...	...
TOTALS		13	27	30	30	100	4	217	432	448	442	1,682	569	603	703		25	15	19	10	13	82	1,320	273	314	200	346	2,453	820

[redacted]	REGULAR TREASURERS
[redacted] [redacted]y	[redacted] White, [redacted]. 3, High [redacted] N. C.
Calvary	J. F. Carroll, Reidsville, N. C.
[redacted]	Guy [redacted] Gordon, Rt. 2, Reidsville, N. C.
[redacted]e	T. L. [redacted]n, [redacted]e, N. C.
[redacted]o, [redacted]st	[redacted]d [redacted]r, [redacted]o, N. C.
[redacted]o St.	U. A. Hedrick, Greensboro, N. C.
Bailey [redacted]n.	R. A. Cooke, Pomona, N. C.
Bessemer	A. C. [redacted]n, Bessemer Br., [redacted]o
Eller [redacted]	E. [redacted]n Parker, Denim Br., [redacted]o
[redacted]a [redacted]	E. H. Moore, Greensboro, N. C.
[redacted]t [redacted]e.	I. E. [redacted], Greensboro, N C.
[redacted]n Park	B. B. Parrish, [redacted]o, N. C.
[redacted]a St.	Harvey [redacted], [redacted]o, N. C.
[redacted]a	Ed. Henry, Pomona, N. C.
Revolution	Waldo [redacted]n, [redacted]o, N. C.
S[redacted]h St.	L. F. [redacted]s, Denim Br., [redacted]
Stevens Mem.	[redacted] C. B. Brisson, [redacted]o, N. C.
[redacted]r [redacted]	I. F. [redacted], Denim Br., [redacted]o
[redacted]d	W. L. [redacted]n, [redacted]o, N. C.
High [redacted]t, 1st.	Thelma Patrick, High Point, N. C.
[redacted]n St.	R. B. Culler, High Point, N. C.
[redacted]d [redacted]n.	K. H. [redacted], [redacted]h Point, N. C.
[redacted]h [redacted]n St.	Kester [redacted]e, High [redacted]t, N. C.
[redacted]h Park	L. W. Glenn, High Point, N. C.
South Side	J. G. Williams, High [redacted]t, N. C.
[redacted]st End	C. M. Scott, High Point, N. C.
[redacted]p [redacted]ve	
[redacted]n	J. B. [redacted]r, [redacted]. 5, [redacted]o, N. C.
[redacted]t Zion	May Branson, Snow Camp, N. C.
[redacted]k [redacted]e	L. R. Loflin, Jamestown, N. C.
[redacted]e Chapel	[redacted]n [redacted], [redacted]. 1, [redacted]o, N. C.
[redacted]a	[redacted] D. A. [redacted], Rt. 1, Brown [redacted]t
[redacted]t [redacted]n	J. E. Thompson, Pleasant [redacted], N. C.
[redacted]e, 1st.	J. F. Smith, [redacted]e, N. C.
[redacted]t Olive	John McCullen, Reidsville, N. C.
[redacted]n Mem.	[redacted]s [redacted], [redacted]e, N. C.
[redacted]y	M. C. [redacted]s, Rt. 5, Reidsville, N. C.
S[redacted]h [redacted]e	Drew [redacted]h, [redacted]x, N. C.
[redacted]ld	[redacted] A. E. [redacted]s, [redacted]eld, N. C.
[redacted]e	Edna Phillips, Altamahaw, N. C.
[redacted]y	[redacted]a [redacted]e [redacted]n, [redacted]y, N. C.

48

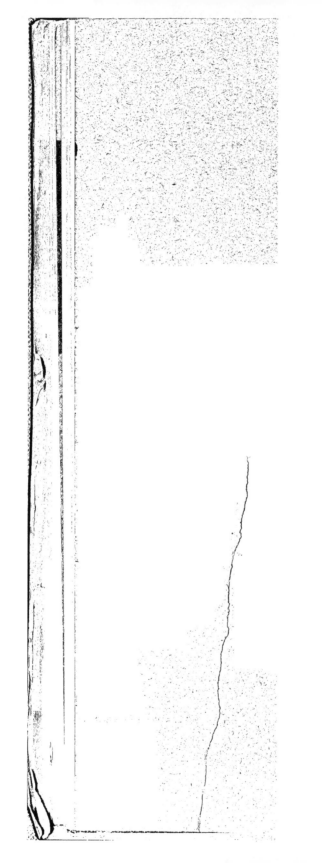

MINUTES

OF THE

PIEDMONT BAPTIST ASSOCIATION

NORTH CAROLINA

FORTY-THIRD ANNUAL SESSION

Held With The

CALVARY BAPTIST CHURCH

Near Reidsville, N. C.

OCTOBER 21-22

1936

The Next Session will be Held with the Eller Memorial Baptist Church, Greensboro, N. C., Wednesday and Thursday before the fourth Sunday in October, 1937.

Rev. C. N. Royal will preach the Sermon
Alternate—Rev. Jones E. Kirk.

MINUTES

OF THE

PIEDMONT BAPTIST ASSOCIATION

NORTH CAROLINA

FORTY-THIRD ANNUAL SESSION

Held With The

CALVARY BAPTIST CHURCH

Near Reidsville, N. C.

OCTOBER 21-22

1936

The Next Session will be Held with the Eller Memorial Baptist Church, Greensboro, N. C., Wednesday and Thursday before the fourth Sunday in October, 1937.

Rev. C. N. Royal will preach the Sermon
Alternate—Rev. Jones E. Kirk.

INDEX

MAP
OF THE
PIEDMONT BAPTIST ASSOCIATION

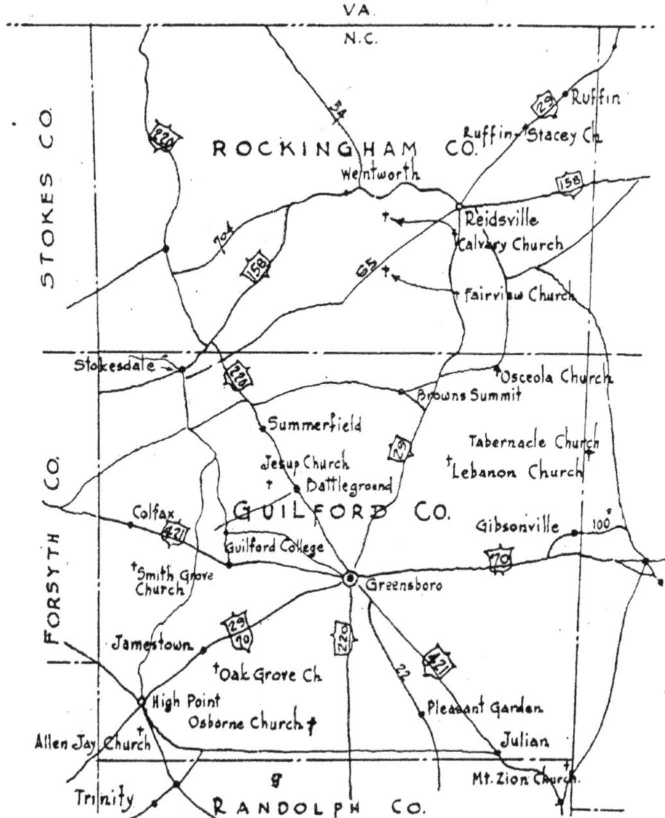

Associational Directory

OFFICERS

Clarence A. Smith, Moderator....................High Point, N. C.
Rev. J. M. Hilliard, Vice-Moderator..............High Point, N. C.
O. E. Lee, Clerk-Treasurer........................Greensboro, N. C.

EXECUTIVE COMMITTEE

Clarence A. Smith, Chairman......................High Point, N. C.
O. E. Lee, Secretary...............................Greensboro, N. C.
Rev. J. M. Hilliard..................................High Point, N. C.
Rev. C. N. Royal.....................................High Point, N. C.
Dr. A. B. Conrad.....................................High Point, N. C.
Rev. J. C. Gillespie...................................Reidsville, N. C.
J. C. Tatum..Reidsville, N. C.
Rev. J. Ben Eller......................................Greensboro, N. C.
Dr. J. T. J. Battle....................................Greensboro, N. C.
Mrs. Nettie H. Hoge,................................Greensboro, N. C.
F. L. Paschal...Greensboro, N. C.
Walter Crissman ....High Point, N. C.

CHURCHES BY DISTRICTS

DISTRICT 1:
- High Point, First
- Hilliard Memorial
- Green Street
- North Main
- North Park
- South Side
- West End
- Oak Grove
- Smith Grove
- Trinity
- Allen Jay

DISTRICT 2:
- Greensboro, First
- Asheboro Street
- Bessemer
- Bailey Memorial
- Eller Memorial
- Forest Ave.
- Florida Street
- Latham Park
- Magnolia Street
- Pomona Mills
- Revolution
- Sixteenth Street
- Stevens Memorial
- Gibsonville
- Guilford
- Jessip Grove
- Lebanon
- Mount Zion
- Pleasant Garden
- Osborne Chapel
- Rocky Knoll
- Summerfield
- Tabernacle
- Webster Memorial

DISTRICT 3:
- Reidsville, First
- Penn Memorial
- Mount Olive
- Calvary
- Fairview
- Osceola
- Ruffin-Stacey

OFFICERS OF THE PIEDMONT BAPTIST SUNDAY SCHOOL ASSOCIATION

F. L. Paschal, Superintendent, ... Greensboro, N. C.
Rev. A. A. Walker, Assistant Superintendent, Secretary
and Treasurer .... Greensboro, N. C.
Genter Shepherd, Chorister .... Greensboro, N. C.
Genter Stephens, Chorister .... Greensboro, N. C.
Rev. A. Lincoln Fulk, Supt., Group 1., District 1——High Point, N. C.
M. E. Howell, Supt. Group 2, District 1 .... Greensboro, N. C.
M. D. Teague, Supt. Group 1, District 2, ... Greensboro, N. C.
Rev. Tom W. Bray, Supt. Group 2, District 2. Pleasant Garden, N. C.
William Cummings, Supt. District 3 .... Reidsville, N. C.
Mrs. T. L. Ogburn, Supt. Cradle Roll Department.. Greensboro, N. C.
Miss Ruth Scott, Supt. Beginners Dept .... Greensboro, N. C.
Mrs. C. C. Stout, Supt., Primary Department ...... High Point, N C.
Mrs. Geo. D. Allred, Supt. Junior Department .... Greensboro, N. C.
Mrs. I. B. Squier, Supt. Intermediate Department.. Greensboro, N. C.
Miss Thelma Patrick, Supt. Young People's Dept. High Point, N. C.
Mrs. J. S. Moore, Supt. Adult Department .... Greensboro, N. C.
Rev. Jones E. Kirk, Supt. Extension Department.. Greensboro, N. C.

OFFICERS OF THE PIEDMONT ASSOCIATION W. M. U.

Mrs. Nettie Hoge, Superintendent .... Greensboro, N. C.
Mrs. C. R. Harrison, Secretary .... High Point, N. C.
Mrs. C. E. Siceloff, Treasurer .... High Point, N. C.
Miss Ruth Scott, Young People's Leader .... Greensboro, N. C.
Mrs. L. M. Gideon, Personal Service Chairman .... Greensboro, N. C.
Mrs. C. N. Royal, Stewardship Chairman .... Hight Point, N. C.
Miss Elizabeth Apple, Training School and
Margaret Fund Chairman .... Greensboro, N. C.
Mrs. J. J. Andoe, Mission Study Lit. Chairman .... Greensboro, N. C.
Mrs. H. A. Knight, Group Leader, District 1 .... High Point, N. C.
Mrs. A. Andrews, Group Leader, District 2 .... Greensboro, N. C.
Mrs. T. L. Sasser, Group Leader, District 3 .... Reidsville, N. C.

BAPTIST TRAINING UNION ASSOCIATIONAL OFFICERS

Walter E. Crissman, President .... High Point, N. C.
Harry Myers, Vice President .... Greensboro, N. C.
Miss Elizabeth Campbell, Secretary-Treasurer ...... Greensboro, N. C.
Miss Mildred Jackson, Junior Leader .... Greensboro, N. C.
Miss Margaret Murphy, Intermediate Leader .... Reidsville, N. C.
C W. Baity, Chorister .... Greensboro, N. C.
Miss Mebane Yarborough, Pianist .... Reidsville, N.C.
John Reavis, District President .... High Point, N. C.
Jimmie Wills, District President .... Greensboro, N. C.
James Gillespie, District No. 3 President .... Reidsville, N. C.

CHURCH DIRECTORIES

ORDAINED MINISTERS (NOT PASTORS)

C. D. Barton, ...Greensboro, Bessemer Br.
Wm. H. Matherly, ...Greensboro
L. M. Deaton...Greensboro
J. M. Hilliard ....High Point
T. L. Chamberlain ....High Point
J. F. Murray ....Reidsville
C. W. Myrick ....Greensboro
C. R. Smith ....Colfax
B. H. Farington ....Colfax
Clyde James ....Colfax
U. C. Bell ....Colfax
O. F. Barnes ....Trinity
B. F. Clark ....Trinity
Dr. C. H. Nash ....Greensboro
Jennings Johnson ....Greensboro
W. C. Richardson ....Greensboro
Dr. W. C. Newton ....China

B. T. U. DIRECTORS, PRESIDENTS AND LEADERS

ALLEN JAY—W. R. Hobson, Director; Glen Smith, S. Pres. Wade Cumbie, I. Leader, Mrs. Frank Rice, J. Leader.

GREENSBORO, First—O. E. Lee, Director, J. G. Oates, A. Pres., Charles Howard, S. Pres., Elizabeth Campbell, S. Pres., Estelle Mitchell, Mrs. L. R. Leary, Mrs. Z. H. Howerton, I. Leaders, Genter Stephens, I. Director, Mildred Jackson, Mrs. P. B. Comer, J. Leaders, Mary F. Walker, S. H.

ASHEBORO STREET—C. W. McLees, Director, Judith Eller, S. Pres., Madeliene Causey, J. J. Norwood, I. Leaders, Louis Oliver, Mrs. John R. Durham, J Leaders, Mrs. J. J. Norwood, S. H.

BESSEMER—Norfleet Dixon, Director, Hulda Dixon, S. Pres., Mrs. W. T. West, J. Leader.

ELLER MEMORIAL—J. Carl Bell, Director, E. G. Parker, A. Pres. Raymond Kincaid, S. Pres. Mrs. J. E. Kirk, Mrs. W. H. Lambert,

I. Leaders, Katherine Short, Mrs. J. H. Sharpe, J. Leaders, Mrs. Wakland Morrison, S. H.

FLORIDA STREET—W. M. Cassell, Director, W. M. Spivey, A. Pres. Lucille Wilson, S. Pres., Eulene Collins, I. Leader, Mrs. W. M. Cassell, J. Leader, Mrs. E. E. Bradley, S. H.

FOREST AVE.—Ethel Osborne, Director, Mary Eliz. Woodcock, S. Pres., E. W. Richardson, I. Leader, Waldo W. Williams, J. Leader.

MAGNOLIA STREET—T. Burchett, Director; A. A. Rogers, A. Pres., Marshall Drushan, S. P., Clara Johnson, I. Leader, Mrs. D. Wrenn, J. Leader, Mrs. Pearl Morris, S. H.

REVOLUTION—Frances Burke, S. Pres.

SIXTEENTH STREET—Harry Moore, Director, Williard Lawson, S. Pres.

STEVENS MEMORIAL—Mrs. R. A. Newman, I. Leader, Ethel Brown, J. Leader.

GUILFORD—Mary Gilbert, J. Leader.

HIGH POINT, FIRST—Claude A. Smith, Jr., Director; Carmala Lewis, S. Pres., Kate Lomax, I. Leader, Mrs. C. D. Goldsmith, J. Leader.

GREEN STREET—John Teavis, Director; V. L. Campbell, A. Pres., Maggie Lee Douglas, S. Pres., Mrs. J. L. Payne, I Leader, J. T Curlee, J. Leader.

HILLIARD MEMORIAL—L. E. Edwards, Director; Mrs. C. J. Hedrick, I. Leader, Mrs. H. O. Miller, J. Leader.

NORTH MAIN—R. L. Reeves, Director, W. L. Woodell, A. Pres., Mrs. Minda McArthur, S. Pres., A. Lincoln Fulk, I. Leader, Mrs. R. L. Reeves, J. Leader, Mrs. Alice Davis, S. H.

NORTH PARK—L. R. McNeil, Director, H. B. Chatham, A. Pres., Mrs. J. H. Axom, Mrs. N. F. Britt, I. Leader, Mrs. L. W. Glenn, J. Leader, Mrs. Paul Frye, S. H.

SOUTHSIDE—Mrs. S. E. Oldham, Director, Daisy Shaw, S. Pres., Martha Brown, I. Leader, Estie Brown, J. Leader.

WEST END—J. E. Smith, Director; Dolan Hedrick, S. Pres., J. E. Hedrick, I. Leader, Mrs. J. E. Hedrick, J. Leader.

PLEASANT GARDEN—Mrs. Vera Riley, J. Leader.

REIDSVILLE, FIRST—Paul Roach, Director; Flora Foote, A. Pres, Jas. C. Gillespie, S. Pres., Helen Small, I. Leader, Sara Kemp Price, J. Leader.

MOUNT OLIVE—Earl Kesley, S. Pres., Sarah De. Leancy, J. Leader

PENN MEMORIAL—Mrs. J. W. Gilly, Director; Thomas Dixon, S.

Pres., Mrs. Nash Wilkins, I. Leader, Mrs. W. H. Ford, J. Leader.

ROCKY KNOLL—R. R. Suddreth, Director; Mrs. Jos. Stamey, J. Leader.

OFFICERS OF W. M. S. AND AUXILIARIES

CALVARY—Mrs. R. H. Terrell, W. M. S. Pres.

GIBSONVILLE—Mrs. O. B. Coble, W. M. S. Pres.

GREENSBORO FIRST—Mrs. O. E. Lee, Pres., Mrs. T. F. Casey, Y. W. A. C., Mrs. R. E. Hodgin, G. A. L., Mrs. August Ruof, G. A. L.. W. O. Burnham, R. A. L., O. E. Lee, R. A. L., Miss Mildred Jackson Sunbeam Band L

ASHEBORO STREET—Mrs. A. Andrews, W. M. S. Pres., Mrs. J. J. Meyers, Y. W. A. C., Mrs. M. D. Teague, G. A. L., Mrs. Leslie Harvey, G. A. L., Mrs. B. L. Pickard, R. A. L., Virginia Satterfield. Sunbeam L.

BESSEMER—Mrs. J. H. Green, W. M. S., Pres., Mrs. J. R. Medlin, Y. W. A. C.

ELLER MEMORIAL—Mrs. G. O. Basinger, W. M. S., Pres., Mrs. E. ,G. Parker, Y. W. A. C.

FLORIDA STREET—Mrs. J. B. Rumbley, W. M. S., Pres., Mrs. D. F. Harwell, Y. W. A. C., Mrs. E. E. Brady, G. A. L., Mrs. J. B. Rumley, R. A. L., Mrs. E. E. Brady, Sunbeam L.

FOREST—Mrs. O. Joe Howard, W. M. S. Pres., Mrs. Wilson Woodcock, Y. W. A. C., Mrs. Ruth Williams, G. A. L., Mrs. J. E. Oliver, R. A. L.

MAGNOLIA STREET—Mrs. L. L. Jarvis, W. M. S. Pres., Mrs. H. S. Noah, W. Y. A. C.

POMONA—Mrs. W. B. Coook, W. M. S. Pres., Mrs. Lelia Waye, Sunbeam L.

REVOLUTION—Sallie Burgess, W. M. S. Pres., Diana Scarlett, G. A. L., Sallie Burgess, R. A. L., Lora Carter, Sunbeam L.

SIXTEENTH—Mrs. C. L. Straughn, W. M. S. Pres.

STEVENS MEMORIAL—Mrs. C. B. Brissom, W. M. S. Pres., Ethel Brown, G. A. L., Mrs. L. M. Deaton, Sunbeam L.

WEBSTER MEMORIAL—Mrs. W. H. Lucas, W. M. S. Pres.

GUILFORD—Bulah Martin, W. M. S. Pres.

HIGH POINT, FIRST—Mrs. W. F. Clayton, W. M. S. Pres., Ila Hensley, Y. W. A. C., Helen Smith, G. A. L., Claude A. Smith, Jr., R. A. L., Katie Sue Stanfield, Sunbeam L.

GREENE STREET—Gladys Ellington, W. M. S. Pres., Mrs. Amos Carroll, Sunbeam L.

HILLIARD MEMORIAL—Mrs. H. O. Miller, W. M. S. Pres., Mrs. Fred Bryant, Y. W. A. C., Mrs. W. R. Ward, G. A. L., Mrs. Cora Hutchens, Sunbeam L.

NORTH MAIN—Mrs. R. L. Reeva, Y. W. A. C., Mrs. Minda McArthur, Myrtle Epps, G. A. Leaders, Mrs. Wayne McCanless, Sunbeam L.

NORTH PARK—Mrs. Paul Frye, W. M. S. Pres.

SOUTH SIDE—Mrs. Pearl Camrey, W. M. S. Pres., Mrs. S. E. Oldham, Sunbeam L.

WEST END&—Mrs. Pearl Preslar, W. M. S. Pres., Mrs. Charlotte Lanier, G. A. L., Mrs. Pled Hughes, Sunbeam L.

PLEASANT GARDEN—Mrs. J. E. Thompson, W. M. S. Pres., and Sunbeam Leader.

REIDSVILLE FIRST—Mrs. R. R. Saunders, W. M. S. Pres., Mrs. R. H. Pleasants, Y. W. A. C., Mrs. Lane Peters, G. A. L., Mrs. Geo. Schaeffer, R. A. L., Mrs. Claude Phillips, Sunbeam L.

MOUNT OLIVE—Mrs. J. H. Saunders, W. M. S. Pres.

PENN MEMORIAL—Mrs. M. H. Fitz, W. M. S. Pres., and Y. W. A. C.

SUMMERFIELD—Mrs. A. C. Lloyd, W. M. S. Pres.

LIST OF MESSENGERS

ALLEN JAY—J. O. Warren, Glenn Smith, Mrs. Henry Burrou.

CALVARY—R. H. Terrell, Alex Setliffe, Mrs. J. E. McCargo.

FAIRVIEW—Wade Durham, Guy T. Gordon, Doughton Hopkins.

GIBSONVILLE—E. A. Long, Melvin Cates, E. C. Riggins.

GREENSBORO FIRST—A A. Chandler, Harry B. Caldwell, J. W. Robbins, Talmage Smith, Genter Stephens, Mr. and Mrs. O. E. Lee, Mesdames W. O. Burnham, Nettie Hoge, Miss Mildred Jackson.

ASHEBORO STREET—J. S. Moore, T. B. Pickard, Mrs. A. Andrews.

BAILEY MEMORIAL—Rev. and Mrs. C, G. Coe, Mr. and Mrs. W. J. Mitchell.

BESSEMER—C. L. Murray, W. P. Haynes, Mesdames J. H. Green, J. F. Layton.

ELLER MEMORIAL—Mr. and Mrs. Carl Bell, Mrs. W. H. Lambert, Miss Kathleen Short.

FLORIDA STREET—J. L. Roberson, Mesdames J. B. Rumbly, W. J. Deal, H. P. Bilyew.

FOREST AVENUE—Rev. Wilson Woodcock, Dr. J. T. J. Battle, S. H. Craver, Mesdames D. W. Leigh, E. W. Richardson.

MAGNOLIA STREET—Mesdames T. H. Williamson, H. P. Wray, Cleo Covington.

POMONA—Rev. and Mrs. W. B. Cook, Mesdames W. G. Teague, W. H. Brown, Mr. C. C. Patterson.

REVOLUTION—John Martin, Malcomn Miller, David Barbour, Elige Lankford.

SIXTEENTH STREET—Mr. and Mrs. W. R. Fuller, Mr. and Mrs. T. W. Michael.

STEVENS MEMORIAL—Mr. and Mrs. S. M. Brissom. L. Y. Straughn, Mesdames J. B. Brown, Chas. Garner.

WEBSTER MEMORIAL—Mesdames J. F. Graves, B. H. Scott, W. H. Lucas, Mr. and Mrs. C. V. Webster.

GUILFORD—Mesdames Hettie Kennedy, Cora Martin, Eugene Hodgin, E. L. Weston.

HIGH POINT FIRST—Dr. and Mrs. A. B. Conrad, G. H. Jones, Miss Thelma Patrick, Mesdames C. D. Goldsmith, W. F. Clayton, C. E. Siceloof.

GREEN STREET—Mr. and Mrs. Walter E. Crissman, Mesdames E. M. Blakley, D. T. Andrews, Mr. J. C. Cross.

HILLIARD MEMORIAL—C. M. Howell, C. J. Hedrick, Mesdames H. O. Miller, C. H. Saunders, J. W. Saunders.

NORTH MAIN STREET—S. R. Clinard, Mesdames Alice Davis, Spencer Epps.

NORTH PARK—H. B. Chatham, L. W. Glenn, Mrs. D. H. Short.

SOUTH SIDE—G. H. Liner, Mesdames E. V. Slack, T. E. Goins, C. R. Rodden, Mrs. Henson.

WEST END—Mr. and Mrs. C. M. Scott, Mrs. J. N. Bowman.

LEBANON—C. M. Oates, B. G. Yow, S. F. Milloway, Mrs. Whitley, Mrs. Carter.

MOUNT ZION—C. V. Branson, Geo. Spoon, Bud Murry, J. C. Lackamy, Jes Foster.

OAK GROVE—Chester Allred, C. B. Shackelford, Walter Shackelford.

OSBORNE CHAPEL—John May, E. C. White, Mrs. Minnie Morgan, Mrs. Ethel May, Mrs. Ben Cheek.

OSCEOLA—E. R. Brande, L. C. Cole, Mrs. D. A. Greene.

PLEASANT GARDEN—Rev. Tom W. Bray, Henry Foy, Harvey L. Paschal, Mesdames I. F. Anderson, Lillian T. Jordan.

REIDSVILLE FIRST—Mr. and Mrs. N. C. Thompson, Mesdames R. H. Pleasants, A. B. Satliffe, R. G. Gladstone, H. L. Morrison, W. H. Bolyn, J. Floyd Moore.

MOUNT OLIVE—Mesdames D. P. Driscoll, A. D. Clifton, Patrick O. DeLapp.

PENN MEMORIAL—Rev. D. W. Overbey, G. S. Hall, R. L. Borland, J. W. Winchester.

ROCKY KNOLL—Rev. L. C. Chandler, Mesdames T. C. Frazier, M. T. Jackson.

RUFFIN STACEY—R. M. Durham, Mesdames Lottie Shrum, J. T. Cardwell.

SMITH GROVE—Drew Smith, Green Pender, Miss Cora Pender.

SUMMERFIELD—Mr. and Mrs. Robert Forbes, Mrs. Stigall.

TABERNACLE—Rev. and Mrs. Grover C. Phillips, Mrs. Annie Sutton, Miss Edna Phillips.

TRINITY—Mesdames J. C. Gatewood, O. F. Barnes, G. G. Clinard.

MINUTES

OF THE

FORTY-THIRD ANNUAL SESSION

OF THE

PIEDMONT BAPTIST ASSOCIATION

HELD WITH

CALVARY BAPTIST CHURCH

NEAR REIDSVILLE, N. C.

OCTOBER 21-22, 1936

Wednesday Morning Session

1. The Association was opened with singing "We are Marching to Zion" led by Genter Stephens. Rev. J. S. Farmer led in prayer.

2. Rev. Jas. C. Gillespie and Rev. D. W. Overbey spoke words of weclome. The response was given by Rev. A. Lincoln Fulk.

3. A roll of the churches was called and messengers from thirty-three churches responded to the roll call. The Association then proceeded to the election of officers for the ensuing year, which resulted as follows: Clarence A. Smith, Moderator; Rev. J. M. Hilliard, Vice Moderator; O. E. Lee, Clerk and Treasurer.

4. The Committee on Program reported that Mr. Harry B. Caldwell, who had written the report on Sunday School work could not be present on Thursday, and that in the absence of Rev. T. L. Sasser, who was absent on account of sickness in his home, that the report on Sunday Schools be considered during thirty minutes of the time assigned to the consideration of Foreign Missions. The report was adopted.

5. The report on Religious Literature was presented by Jas. C. Gillespie. Upon motion to adopt the subject was discussed by Jas. C. Gillespie, J. S. Farmer, J. M. Hilliard. The report was adopted.

REPORT ON RELIGIOUS LITERATURE

In Proverbs 29:18 we have, "Where there is no vision the people perish." Primarily this vision comes from God through the Word. How very important, then, that we should be daily students of God's

Word illuminated by the Holy Spirit! But in a secondary sense vision becomes practical through information. How can people know practically their obligations if they do not know the fields to be occupied and the work to be done on these fields? On the otherhand it is very evident that those who have the true vision in their hearts from God will be ready to do, at least much of what they see to be their duty, when this is practically revealed to them. It generally follows that as the circulation of our Baptist papers declines, contributions to Missions and Benovolences, and also general denominational and Christian work, declines in about like proportions.

Then again as a great factor in the development of Christian character, religious literature renders a large service, among which our own denominational papers stand among the highest.

We urgently recommend a larger place in our homes especially for the Bibical Recorder, Home and Foreign Fields, Royal Service, and Charity and Children.

Respectfully Submitted,
JAS. C. GILLESPIE.

6. The following visitors were recognized: Dr. Walter N. Johnson, A. V. West, Rev. and Mrs. O. P. Dix, Rev. and Mrs. L. R. O'Brian, Mrs. Geo. D. Vick, N. A. Thompson, E. X. Heatherly.

7. The report on Foreign Missions was read by the clerk in the absence of T. L. Sasser. Upon motion to adopt the subject was discussed by Dr. Walter N. Johnson at the request of the Association. The report was adopted.

REPORT ON FOREIGN MISSIONS

The number of baptisms for the last ten years on our foreign fields have been as follows: 1927, 12085; 1928, 12542; 1929, 12264; 1930, 13250; 1931, 14415; 1932, 16568; 1933, 17284; 1934, 15969; 1935, 17794; 1936, 13982. Although there has been a decline in the number of baptisms this year splendid general progress has been made.

Viewed in the large there are four definite and immediate foreign mission needs. 1. To pay off the debt. 2. To adquately support the missionaries we have. 3. To send out additional missionaries. 4. To repair the foreign properties now in a run-down condition.

The hope of reaching these objectives lies in the possibility of increased receipts from the Co-operative Program, the Hundred Thousand Club, The Wade Bryant Plan, The Lottie Moon Christmas Offering, and special gifts. The Lottie Moon offerings went still further beyond anticipations last December than formerly, but the Co-operative Program receipts have declined rather than increased this year over last. This is a cause of serious concern.

The Board is committed to the policy of paying the debt which now stands at $444,000.00 by the end of 1938 at the same time keeping the amount of expenditures safely within the amount of receipts.

A vigorous publicity program is being carried on by the use of denominational periodicals, and the constituency of prospective missionaries and supporters in the churches of the Convention is being enlisted and developed by means of mission study courses. The Foreign Missions Week at Ridgecrest is growing in popularity and spiritual power. Added to the text books used heretofore new ones are being published and studied. Stewardship schools in the churches are beginning to bear fruit to a decidedly noticeable degree.

The cause of foreign missions is still the major interest of informed, consecrated Southern Baptists.

Respectfully Submitted,
T. L. SASSER.

8. The report on Sunday Schools was presented by Harry B. Caldwell. Upon motion to adopt the subject was discussed by Harry B. Caldwell. The report was adopted.

SUNDAY SCHOOL REPORT

The importance of the Sunday School as an agency for Soul winning, Enlistment, Education and Fellowship has steadily grown. Originally the Sunday School was an agency to encourage Bible Study and a majority of the members came from the Church. Today we look upon the Sunday School as an agency for reaching the lost and enlisting members for service. The Sunday School has made steady progress where leaders have recognized the many opportunities for religious services afforded. Success always depends upon consecrated leadership responsive to the Will of God and ready to make any necessary sacrifice in reaching people.

We have made progress during the past year. Many schools have made a net gain in enrollment, fellowship meetings have been held, Souls have been won for Christ and members have been enlisted for service. We now have 41 schools in this Association with approximately 14,000 members enrolled and an average Sunday attendance of about 7,000. According to figures given out by our Sunday School Board, approximately half of the people who reside in the area represented by this Association are not affiliated with any Sunday School. The tragedy of this is that two few of us take this matter seriously. We try to attend Sunday School ourselves and feel little concern for the absence of the other fellow. I would impress you with the fact that Jesus holds us accountable for Souls. When you and I stand before the great Judge glad for our own Salvation and He inquires about those not enlisted in His work, what reply can we make? Have we really done our best? We are His Witnesses, His servants, and if we fail to carry out His program we can expect little reward.

Realizing the responsibility that is ours I wish to make a few suggestions for the consideration of our Sunday Schools and for the Associational Leaders.

1. The Sunday School should do the following things;

(a). Each school should be graded according to the plans outlined by the Sunday School Board in-so-far as it is possible. This classification system creates favorable conditions for effective teaching and the proper spirit of fellowship.

(b). Check rooms and equipment and improve for maximum results. A poorly equipped room hinders the work of the class.

(c). Each member should radiate a friendly spirit. Greet one another with a smile and extend a hearty welcome to all visitors and new members.

(d). Plan suitable outside social activities. This builds class spirit and membership interest.

(e). Make a survey of the community to determine un-enlisted individuals. You will be surprised to find many of your neighbors outside of the work of the church.

(f). See that all unenlisted individuals are invited regularly to attend your services. Don't give up just because the party fails to respond to the first invitation.

(g). Teachers and class officers should always be on time and well prepared to carry out their duties. The success of the school depends upon the whole-hearted co-operation of all.

(h). Lead all members into the work of the Church.

(i). Encourage all members to meet requirements of our Six Point Record System. This will help build a well rounded Christian Life.

(j). Strive to make your school Standard. Do this to improve the effectiveness of your work.

(k). Have business meetings at least quarterly and oftener if possible. Business leaders meet regularly to check their work and plan for the future. It is essential in the work of the Sunday School.

(l). Conduct a training school for teachers and officers. About one-fourth of our teachers have received a Diploma. Teachers are required to prepare for work in our public schools. How much more important that those entrusted with Souls should be properly trained.

(m). Participate in the Associational meetings.

(n). Make your reports to the Association regularly, correctly, promptly and cheerfully.

2. The Associational Leaders should do the following;

(a). Hold quarterly meetings and conduct well planned discussions on current Sunday School problems. A program of work for the entire Association should be planned at the beginning of each year.

(b). District Superintendents and officers should conduct monthly meetings.

(c). The executive committee of the Association, which is the Superintendent of each Department, should meet quarterly and check the entire program.

(d). Training courses should be encouraged and teachers provided.

(e). Every school should be encouraged by visitation and cooperation.

(f). New schools should be established where conditions are favorable. We must reach the lost and enlist Christians for service.

Let us treasure the lessons we have learned from the past, plan wisely for the future and strive to make our work os harmoniously beautiful as are the works of nature's God.

Respectfully Submitted,
HARRY B. CALDWELL.

9. The following new pastors were presented by J. M. Hilliard: J. N. Bowman, Jones E. Kirk, and A. A. Walker. Genter Stephens was recognized.

10. The Moderator appointed the following committee on committees, Dr. A. B. Conrad, Dr. J. Clyde Turner, N. F. Britt.

11. Announcements were made by Jas. C. Gillespie.

12. Following the reading of the scripture, singing a hymn, and prayer by B. G. Whitley, Rev. J. Ben Eller, preached the Introductory Sermon. The text was John 14:16; Acts 1:8, subject "Following the Leading of the Holy Spirit". The sermon was deeply spiritual.

The morning session closed with prayer.

Wednesday Afternoon Session

13. The session was opened with a devotional service led by Genter Stephens and Henry E. Love.

14. The report on Denominational Program was read by Dr. A. B. Conrad, and the report on State Missions was read by J. Ben Eller. Upon motion to adopt, the subjects were discussed by M. A. Huggins. The reports were adopted.

DENOMINATIONAL PROGRAM

The Denominational Program is the plan adopted by Southern Baptists to fulfill Christ's last and great command to evangelize the world.

It relates to all local, adjacent and far removed enterprize. It is the natural fruitage of the best thought, the earnest prayers, and the growing experience of the churches through the years of our history.

It is approved by Associations, State Conventions and the Southern Baptist Convention as the best plan yet devised for the support and furtherance of all the causes embraced in our general work.

Six commendary things may be said about it. First—It is personal. It reaches out and lays urgent hands on every Baptist, calling each one to share in the support of every enterprise which Baptists believe have a place in the great program of Jesus and hence are incumbent on and make imperative demand for support from each disciple.

Second—It is unifying. It crystalizes the many phases of our denominational work into one great cause, and emphasizes the importance of each. In the past some of our causes received emphasis, not too much, but often to the neglect of others that are vitally important and an essential part of the program of Jesus. But in this plan every phase of our work is recognized, receives it's proper hearing and fair share of financial support. It prevents overlapping. We major in missions, city, State, Home, Foreign and rightly so, for to that end was the church conceived in the mind of God. But in this Co-operative Program we recognize and foster as contributing and necessary agencies to the great end of a missioned world. Christian Education, the care of orphans, the ministry of healing and provision and comfort for God's aged and out-worn servants.

As has been well said, it operates on the principle of "Each for all, all for each and all for Christ."

Third—It is Democratic and that is Baptistic. A Baptist church is the purest form of Democracy in the world, and that principle of soul liberty, of spiritual self expression, for which some of our forbears suffered and died, stands out in our Denominational Program. While appeal is made to every member to support the whole program on the ground that Foreign Misions and Christian Education, Home Missions and the care of orphans are so inter-related that they cannot be fairly separated, yet if one becomes obsessed with a hobby for some particular cause, he can give or designate his gifts to that cause in full assurance that all he gives will go to that object.

Fourth—It is Discriminating and wisely so. Some of our causes are larger than others, the expense in carrying them forward is much greater than others so there must be a fair, equitable distribution of all funds among those causes. To this end sixty per cent at the present of the total remains in our State and is divided among these objects.

State Missions 13 percent—Christian Education 42 percent—Baptist Hospital 4 percent—Ministerial Education 1 percent. The Mills Home is not listed. It is not in this Co-operative Program but is well cared for by monthly offerings from Sunday Schools, a Thanksgiving offering, and special gifts from the churches.

The other 40 percent goes to our general Southwide work and is divided as follows—Foreign Missions 20 percent, Home Missions 9.4 percent, Aged Ministers Relief 2.8 percent, Education 6.8 percent, Hospital at New Orleans 1 percent. That seems to be as wise a distribution of all funds as can be arrived at under existing circumstances

Fifth—It is Assuring. That is it gives to every part of our work a sense of security. Leaders in the various organizations know that what ever amount may be raised by the Denomination they will get their fair share. Income does not depend on fervid appeals, nor does the man who is more adept at opening tear ducts on stated occasions get the lion's share as was often the case under the old plan. Bad weather or an announcement that some Superintendent or Secretary was coming to make an appeal for Missions or what not that kept some of the Saints at home with a sudden attack of Morbus Sabbaticus, as an epidemic or some unforseen event does not affect the amount of money received, but steadily under this plan the stream flows—not in the tide it ought, but it flows, and there is in the hearts of those who bear the burden of these various causes a good degree of assurance.

Sixth—It is Spiritual, because it is scriptural. There is nothing haphazard about it. It is done decently and in order. Increasingly our people are coming to realize that they are helping to carry on the program of Christ. They are not giving to a campaign, or an orphanage, or hospital, or Board or a school or what have you, but to Christ and to all the causes that lay hard on His heart—and they are helping to win to His redeeming love and sacrifice the world for which He died.

A. B. CONRAD.

STATE MISSION REPORT 1936

Dr. Livingstone Johnson used to speak of State Missions as "Baptist Seed Corn" and "Denominational Fertilizer." His prophetic insight has proved true. Many of our strong and passionately Missionary Churches of today were aided by our State Mission Board of yesterday.

For one hundred years the objective of State Missions was to win the people of North Carolina to Christ and to the fellowship of our Baptist churches. In more recent years we have been stressing also the training and developing of those coming into our Churches.

At present our State Mission program embraces a number of activities. 160 missionary pastors are receiving assistance while two full-time general missionaries are supported. Efficient Sunday-School and B. T. U. departments are maintained. A timely ministry is still carried on at Oteen. Among the Indians of the State the Board continues a helpful Gospel work while it is now co-operating with our colored brethren in supporting a worker. We are, furthermore, maintaining a limited Student Work among our Young People away from home and the home church in College.

Some few churches are receiving aid in building adequate buildings. The large part of this service is rendered in educational centers where the problem is acute. Our own Association is now sharing this blessing. Forest Avenue is being assisted over a period of four years to the amount of $20,000.00 For this timely and worthy assistance we wish to make grateful acknowledgement..

State Missions has a vital place in our united program. Foreign Missions, Home Missions, and all our benevolent works suffer when State Missions suffers. Let us maintain an aggressive State Mission Program as all other interests are so dependent upon this base of supplies.

Respectfully Submitted,
J. BEN ELLER

15. The report on the Orphanage was read by A. A. Walker. Upon motion to adopt the subject was discussed by A. A. Walker and I. G. Greer. The report was adopted.

ORPHANAGE REPORT

No religion is so kindly disposed to children as Christianity and we rejoice that Jesus said "Whoso receives one such little child in my name receives me." We have therefore actually been a host to the Friend of Children while for the past 51 years we have been welcoming some 4,000 orphans into our arms at Thomasville, for surely it has been done in His name.

Counting the some 140 children on the Mother's Aid, the 135 at the Kennedy Home, and the 455 at Thomasville we have 730 children looking to us to administer the daily bread our heavenly Father has promised them. To provide this bread at Thomasville alone costs us $450 a day or about $22.50 per child per month. For the Associational year ending September 30, 1936, the Piedmont Association has contributed toward this cause the sum of $6,914.39. This is a bare increase over the previous year of $5.68. Our report last year showed that about 16 per cent. of all our convention gifts went to the Orphanage. Our report this year will show a smaller per cent if we have made anything like a substantial increase in our convention gifts. Only two of our churches failed to contribute anything at all for the past twelve months. Of the remaining 39 there are 17 that made a remittance once each month, and 11 others that made regular monthly remittances consecutively for one quarter or more. We have 22 schools taking the Charity and Children, our orphanage paper, for which they have paid the sum of $717.23. No Sunday School should be without this paper.

Let us work and pray that every church in this Association shall make an offering and remit it once each month of the new Associational year; that the orphanage paper be more liberally subscribed to and read; and that the Holy Spirit of God shall continue to guide and bless our orphanage and its administration.

A. A. WALKER.

16. The Committee on Committees made the following report which was adopted:

Place and Preacher—T. L. Sasser, Grover Jones and H. O. Miller.

To Nominate the Executive Committee—J. Ben Eller, Mrs. W. O. Burnham, A. L. Fulk.

To Nominate Delegates to State Convention—J. E. Kirk, B. G. Whitley, W. J. Goldsmith.

Auditing Committee—A. A. Chandler, Walter Mitchell, C. V. Webster.

Program Committee—C. N. Royal, Mrs. O. E. Lee, J. C. Gillespie.

Committee on Verbal Reports—Wilson Woodcock, L. W. Glenn, Mrs. Nettie Hoge.

Committee on Resolutions—A. A. Walker, Mrs. S. N. White, J. N. Bowman.

Committee on New Churches—J. E. Kirk, Jas. C. Gillespie, B. G. Whitley.

Respectfully submitted,
A. B. CONRAD,
J. CLYDE TURNER,
N. F. BRITT.

17. The Verbal Report Period was in charge of C. N. Royal. A large number of churches made verbal reports.

18. Motion was made and adopted that the Financial goals for 1937 be adopted and printed in the minutes.

19. The Treasurer presented his report, which was referred to the Auditing Committee:

TREASURER'S REPORT

I herewith submit my report for the year ending September 30, 1936.

Balance on hand, September 30, 1935		$ 23.71
Received from the churches		166.50
Total		$190.21
DISBURSEMENTS:		
Economy Printing Co., Minutes and Postage to mail and map of Association	$117.35	
Clerks Remuneration	50.00	
Postage and Supplies	2.06	
To M. A. Huggins, Treasurer for Hand Books and Pledge Cards	8.50	
	$177.91	
Balance on Hand Sept. 30, 1936	12.30	
Total		$190.21

Respectfully submitted,
O. E. LEE, Treasurer.

20. A. L. Fulk presents resolutions relative to the ordination of preachers and locating new churches. Upon motion to adopt, the resolutions were discussed by A. L. Fulk and C. N. Royal. The motion to adopt the resolutions was withdrawn and the Moderator stated that they would be referred to the Committee on Resolutions. Motion was then passed that the report on the resolutions be considered at 12:30 on Thursday.

21. Motion was made by J. Ben Eller and passed, that the Moderator confer with the Moderators of the Randolph and Sandy Creek Associations relative to Rev. Shubael Stearns grave at the Sandy, Creek Baptist Church in the Randolph Association.

22. The Moderator appoints the following committee on New Churches: J. E. Kirk, B. G. Whitley and Jas C. Gillespie.

23. Following the singing of a hymn the session closed with prayer by J. M. Hilliard.

Thursday Morning Session

24. 9:45—A devotional service was led by Genter Stephens.

25. Upon motion the report on Home Missions was considered in the place of Hospitals in order to give Mr. Smith Hagaman, Superintendent of the Hospital a larger hearing. The report on Home Missions was presented by Jones E. Kirk. Upon motion the subject was discussed by Jones E. Kirk. The report was adopted.

REPORT ON HOME MISSIONS

The fundamental purpose in missions is the proclamation of the saving grace of our Lord and Saviour Jesus Christ to every creature in all the world. The cause of Missions is the very heart of our denominational program. Our interest in missions is the supreme test of our love and loyalty to Jesus as Saviour and Lord. Our missionary vision and our investments in missions determine our progress as individual christians and as a denomination.

The point of approach to this world-task, for Southern Baptist, is to evangelize the homeland. This is the hope of the world's evangelization. If we fail here missions in far away fields will fail for lack of support. Home Missions are essential to World Missions, Acts 1:8.

Our Home Mission task is greater today than ever. 22 Millions of people in the homeland are waiting for the Word of Life. Our brother in black, 10,000,000 of them, are looking to us for help; 5,000,000 foreigners in our midst are a challenge to our passion for the lost; in Oklahoma and New Mexico 200,000 Indians will never have a chance if we do not send the Gospel to them; the 225,000 Spanish-speaking people in New Mexico will never know about Christ as a personal Saviour unless someone goes to them with the Gospel; 600,000 Mexicans this side the border are crying out for the light; the great Acadian section in French Louisiana with its more than 600,000 souls should know about the Saviour. The opportunities and responsibilities are great.

The Board, during the year, appointed 27 new missionaries, making a total of 283 missionaries working in 894 mission churches and stations. There were over 4,000 conversions and baptisms, 18 new churches were organized and 62 mission stations opened.

In Cuba, the missionaries made 31,855 visits, held 2,802 prayer meetings, and conducted 4,987 preaching services. In the homeland 5,563 individuals were reached by personal evangelism. Of these, 587 were Italians, 1,610 Indians, 1,974 Mexicans, and nearly 1,000 were Negroes. Moreover, 9,326 Bibles and Gospels were distributed.

For lack of space we can but mention the benovolent work being done by the Board such as that of our Sanatorium at El Paso, the orphanage for Mexican children at Bastrop, Texas, the free clinic for poor children in Cuba, and almost innumerable other services, the spiritual ministries back of which Miss Kelly suggests, "Cannot be estimated until the Judgment Day."

In 1936 the Board received from all sources $416,576.85. This was $82,880.82 more than was received in 1934. The budget for 1936 is $150,000.00 for mission work, and $194,896.67 for interest and principal on debts. For over two years the Board has operated within the budget and without borrowing money.

Dr. Lawrence says, "The Home Mission Board was never more conscious of its Stewardship and never more determined to meet that stewardship than it is right now." He believes that the paramount issue before Southern Baptist is whether the homeland is to be made Christian, or is it to become pagan and go the way of all nations that forget God. The Board is set for the saving of the homeland. Shall we fail our Lord in this Glorious task?

Respectfully Submitted, JONES E. KIRK

26. The report on Woman's Work was presented by Mrs. A. Lee Gibson and was discussed by Mrs. C. N. Royal, Dr. A. B. Conrad, J. Ben Eller, and J. M. Hilliard. The report was adopted.

WOMEN'S WORK IN THE PIEDMONT ASSOCIATON

In our missionary endeavors our women of the Piedmont Association work according to the programs adopted by the State and Southern Conventions. The fundamental principles of our order are:

1. Prayer. In our group meetings we learn to pray individually and unitedly. We look at ourselves, and at the fields; and recognize needs. We come together with God's people, in God's name, in the interest of God's Kingdom. So we feel His presence, His love, His attention; and find it easy to approach Him through the prayer channel.

2. Enlistment. Having experienced the joy of togetherness with His believers and with Him, and seeing how we may become "Laborers together with Him," we seek to enlist others, and lead them to know the joy of understanding, of fellowship, of service.

3. Study. We seek to know the missionary message of the Bible. Through our periodicals, State papers, and wonderful study books we see the fields, come to know the workers, their stations, and the various needs and problems.

4. Personal Service. We help actively in Evangelistic work in our churches, and endeavor individually in all personal service activities to win souls to Christ. We manifest Christian fellowship and good will through visits, flowers, letters, lunches, cottage prayer meetings, mission Sunday Schools, and Mission Study classes for remote sections, for the negroes, and for the deaf and blind.

5 Tithes and Offerings. We cannot accept the tithe as the minimum basis of contributing, and encourage special offerings as a means of spiritual growth. To this end we faithfully continue the custom of our Women's Missionary Union through the years of its history, in connection with our three sessions of prayer: the Lottie Moon Christmas Offering for Foreign Missions, the Annie W. Armstrong Offering for Home Missions, and the Special State Mission Offering.

We plan according to our State policy contributions to our co-operative program, the W. M. U. Training School at Louisville, Ky., our Margaret Fund Students, together with expenses of sending delegates to our Junior State meetings. We have a vital part in supporting orphanages, Hospitals, field workers, and mission schools through showers and boxes of supplies.

6. Missionary Education of the Young People. Through Sunbeam Bands, Girls Auxiliaries, Royal Ambassadors, and Young Women's Auxiliaries we give all ages of young people programs and study courses that are informing and challenging. We make possible summer Camp Conferences, State, District, and Association rallies for their inspiration and spiritual growth.

We do all this because, having experienced salvation through grace we have a story to tell to the nations of a Christ who will save to the uttermost all who will call upon Him. This Christ will make new creatures of all who will trust Him. His Gospel will substitute the law of love for the law of hate, and will give to individuals and nations the Golden Rule for a Creed.

MRS. A. LEE GIBSON

27. The report on Hospitals was presented by J. N. Bowman. Upon motion to adopt the subject was discussed by J. N. Bowman and Smith Hagaman. The report was adopted.

REPORT ON HOSPITAL

The North Carolina Baptist Hospital, Inc., located at Winston-Salem, North Carolina, is owned and controlled by the Baptist Denomination and hence, it is state-wide in its service.

Since the Hospital was opened in 1923 a little more than 33,000 patients have entered for treatment. We shall have this year about 4,000 patients; of this number almost one-half will be part-pay and free patients. Hospital had a little more than 14,000 free days last year; this year, as we are now running we shall have a little more than that number. We have at the present rates 19,932 part-pay and free days, or 1,458 free and part-pay patients. This with our present capacity, cannot be increased as we are running as full as possible.

We received from the Duke Endowment last year a little more than $14,000.00. Apart from this, we are dependent upon the Churches and Sunday Schools, through their Mother's Day offerings, for the hospitilization of this vast number of free and part-pay patients.

It cost $3.87 per day to care for patients in the hospital.

The different organizations of our women are rendering an exceedingly valuable service for the Hospital by furnishing linen, such as sheets, pillow cases, tray covers, towels, etc., these are always needed and gratefully received. Hospital will gladly furnish a list, giving the specifications of linens used in the hospital.

We have a fine staff of sixty-six doctors and surgeons; also a school in which nurses are trained with the Christian idea of service. They are trying to carry on the same program that Jesus gave so much of his life to relieving suffering humanity.

But by chance some pastors of certain Churches in the state convention passed by on Mother's day, he saw many suffering in the Hospital but passed by on the other side and his whole church followed him in like manner the Superintendent of the Sunday School and the members, when they saw the sick they passed by on the other side also. But certain pastors with their people journey that way last Mother's Day, stopped and looked upon the sick and the suffering and had compassion on them. These pastors took an offering which the people gladly made and gave it to Smith Hagaman the keeper of the house where the sick people lay and said unto him, take care of them and when we come back next Mother's Day we will repay thee. Jesus ask which of these proved neighborly to them that were sick?—and he said the churches that showed mercy unto them, and Jesus said unto them go and do thou like-wise.

J. N. BOWMAN.

28. The report on Christian Education was presented by Dr. J. Clyde Turner. Upon motion to adopt the subject was discussed by Dr. B. Y. Tyner from Meredith College. The report was adopted.

CHRISTIAN EDUCATION

When the North Carolina Baptist State Convention was organized in 1830, it had a two-fold purpose, Christian Education and Missionary Endeavor. In accord with this purpose Wake Forest Institute, now Wake Forest College, was founded in 1834. For 102 years this institution has trained young men for Christian citizenship and Kingdom work. In the course of the years other institutions have risen to join hands with Wake Forest. In 1846 Chowan College was chartered and has rendered fine service in the education of young women, especially in the eastern part of the state. 1856 Mars Hill opened its doors to both boys and girls. 1887 came Buies' Creek, now Campbell College. In 1899 Meredith College opened for the education of young women. Other schools, such as Wingate College and Boiling Springs, though not a part of our North Carolina system, have rendered fine service. During the past year more than 2500 young men and women were enrolled in these schools. Of that number 163 were studying for the ministry, and many others for definite Christian work.

In addition to these schools located within the state, we have four south-wide institutions for the training of ministers and Christian workers, the Southern Baptist Theological Seminary at Louisville, Ky., the Southwestern Seminary at Fort Worth, Texas, the Baptist Bible Institute at New Orleans, and the Training School for young women at Louisville. During the past year there were more than 1100 students in these institutions.

Never has there been a greater need for Christian Education than now. The work of the Kingdom demands trained men and women as never before. The problems that confront our country call for Christian leadership. Our Christian schools must furnish the greater part of these leaders and workers.

There are two things which we must do concerning our Christian schools. First, we must insist that they be **Christian,** creating a Christian atmosphere, holding up Christian ideals, and doing definite Christian service. There is no place for schools that are only nominally Christian. Second, we must give them better financial support. They cannot continue to exist and serve under present conditions.

J. CLYDE TURNER

29. The Committee to Nominate the Executive Committee made the following report which was adopted.

Members of Executive Committee—Clarance A. Smith, O. E. Lee, J. M. Hilliard, Mrs. Nettie Hoge, F. L. Paschall, Walter Crissman or successors, Dr. A. B. Conrad, C. N. Royal, J. C. Gillespie, J. C. Tatum, J. Ben Eller, Dr. J. T. J. Battle.

The Committee recommends quarterly meetings for the Executive Committee and that the Executive Committee plan for a Simultanous Stewardship Campaign during the year.

J. BEN ELLER,
MRS. W. O. BURNHAM,
A. LINCOLN FULK.

30. The Committee on Resolutions recommended the adoption of the resolution offered on Wednesday by A. Lincoln Fulk relative to the appointment of an Associational Church Advisory Committee, with some change of wording. The subject was discussed by A. L. Fulk and Dr. A. B. Conrad.

The following resolution was adopted:

RESOLUTION

The ordination of new preachers and the organization of new churches is not only of vital importance to the immediate man or church concerned, but reaches out and bears directly upon the work of the Association and conventions.

Therefore, be it resolved:

First, That this association elect annually, seven persons from the association at large to be known as the Associational Church Advisory Committee.

Second, That the duties of this committee shall be as follows:

1. To advise with local churches and groups concerning the formation and location of new churches.
2. To advise with churches in the matter of grouping certain churches into fields that will facilitate the work.
3. To aid and advise with churches in the matter of ordaining men to the ministry.
4. To advise with churches concerning any other work for which the churches might seek counsel.

Third, that it be understood that this committee has no power to force upon any church its advice.

Respectfully submitted,
A. LINCOLN FULK,
A. A. WALKER,
L. N. WHITE,
J. N. BOWMAN,
Committee on Resolutions.

31. Motion was passed that the Moderator appoint the Associational Church Advisory Committee this year.

The morning session closed with prayer by Jones E. Kirk.

Thursday Afternoon

1:30—A devotional service was led by Henry E. Love.

32. The report on Ministerial Relief and Annuity was read by C. N. Royal. Upon motion to adopt the subject was discussed by C. N. Royal. The report was adopted.

REPORT ON MINISTERIAL RELIEF AND ANNUITY

The work of the Relief and Annuity Board of the Southern Baptist Convention located at Dallas, Texas, should find a large place in the thought and concern of every Baptist in the South. They should make it a matter of prayer, of study, and of co-operative effort.

The Board continually faces the great task laid upon it by the the Southern Baptist Convention and by the various States of providing for their ministers who have grown old in the service of Christ, and for the widows ministers who have gone to their Heavenly home.

As to our State, the figures do not tell a pleasant story; for while we have eighteen more on the list of beneficiaries than we had two years ago, this has been made possible by reducing existing allocations so that the average monthly allocations of $6.65 at that time have now fallen to $4.75 for men and a few cents less for women. The figures also tell us that in spite of improved conditions, North Carolina Baptists contributed to the Board last year nearly one fourth less than the year before, and only four-fifths as much as they received from the Board. The amount contributed to this cause by Southern Baptist per capita was less for the year than the price of a two cent stamp. Surely this does not reflect the heart interest of our people. It is not believed that it was intended that the faithful men of God should spend their last days depending upon the mere pittance that is now given them. They gave away every opportunity for earthly gain that we might learn the Story; having learned at their feet let us not forget them. We should not let one of them look to us with pleading eyes and be turned away.

"Let him that it taught in the word communicate unto him that teacheth in all good things." Gal. 6:6.

The Relief and Annuity Board is now asking that a special "Fellowship Offering" be taken by each church at least once a year in conection with the observance of the Lord's Supper.

The Service Annuity is the major plan of the Board for preventing old age dependency. In co-operation with the Foreign Mission Board its benefits have been extended to all missionaries. A similar arrangement has been effected with our orphanages for the relief of their retired workers.

No denominational worker is elegible to enter the Federal Old Age Security Plan. All full-time church or denominational employees are eligible to participate in the Age Security Plan of the Annuity Board. It would seem that our ministers, churches, denominational boards, institutions and agencies whose employees are to a man excluded from participation in the Federal Plan would now be alert to lay hold on a plan through which old age protection can be had by these legions of employees.

Would God that more of our ministers would bring the causes of Ministerial Relief and Annuity squarely and feelingly to the minds and hearts of their church members. We need to create a denominational conscience on this subject.

"Now at this time your abundance may be a supply for their want that their abundance also may be a supply for your want; that there may be equality.' II Cor. 8:14.

C. N. ROYAL.

33. The report on Social Service was presented by Hughey O. Miller. Upon motion to adopt the subject was discussed by Hughey O. Miller. The report was adopted.

SOCIAL SERVICE REPORT

Social service is laboring together with God for the uplift of humanity. It cannot take the place of personal evangelism, but aims to correct the evils in the social order and promote conditions favorable to right living. We rejoice that there has been an improvement in the economic situation, but lament the fact that this is not true of the social and moral realm. There is an alarming disrespect for the Sabbath. Business and pleasure centers stand with outstretched arms to welcome an ungrateful, careless Sabbath day desecrating public. The standards of morals are dropping lower daily. Sexual laxity and the divorce are growing at a desperately rapid rate. It is almost as easy to secure a divorce today as it was to secure marriage license a few years ago. The home life is being broken down until the once boasted American home is in the minority. This machine age presents a perplexing problem. As we think of the liquor question we are overwhelmed, as the liquor forces constantly wrap the chains of bondage about us. The number of excessive drinkers among our men, women, boys and girls is increasing at an alarming rapid rate. There is a growing disrespect for law, sacredness of the home and tending to destroy virtue. There are more men under arms today than at any time in the world. The world is seething with hatred and suspicion.

Respectfully Submitted,
HUGHEY O. MILLER.

34. The report on B. T. U. work prepared by J. W.

Robbins was read by the Clerk. The report of the Associational B. T. U. President, Walter Crissman was read by C. N. Royal. The report was adopted.

REPORT OF BAPTIST TRAINING UNION

The writer, who was appointed to report on the Baptist Training Union of this Association for the past year, regrets very much that he is unable to submit a complete report at this time. Due to the absence of final figures there can be no actual comparison showing the gain or loss in number of unions, in total enrollment, and in other essential points. The writer is informed, however, that there has been a slight decrease in number of Unions and in total enrollment during the past year; but this should not be discouraging at this time, since a number of Unions in various churches were undergoing a reorganization—weeding out the inactive members and consolidating Unions in the separate churches, in order that B. T. U. work might be done among the Young People. We are hoping that during the next year we will be able to see the effects of this re-organization work, to the extent that, at the next Associational meting, a more favorable report may be submitted.

Respectfully Submitted,
J. W. ROBBINS

REPORT OF BAPTIST TRAINING UNION

During the past year, we feel that Baptist Training Union of this Association has made some progress. The number of general organizations has been increased from fourteen to twenty, which is a sure sign that the training union is becoming a real and vital part and necessary department of the churches. The number of Unions in each church has not increased a great deal during the year, but we feel that the quality of training being done is much improved. Study courses have been conducted in practically every church where Baptists Training Unions are in operation.

It is the plan of the Executive Committee of the Piedmont Associational Baptist Training Union to make a special effort during the months of November and December, this year, and January, February and March of next year, to get Baptist Training Unions organized in those churches not now having a Union.

The annual convention of the Associational Baptist Training Union was held last April at the First Baptist Church at Reidsville N. C. We are encouraged with the work and believe that the work will continue to show improvement during the coming year.

Respectfully Submitted,
WALTER E. CRISSMAN.

35. Motion was passed giving F. L. Paschall, Associational Sunday School Superintendent five to ten minutes to make an announcement of plans for the year.

36. The report on Obituaries was presented by John U. Garner. The report was adopted. J. M. Hilliard requests prayer for Mr. Moore. This to be included in the closing prayer.

REPORT ON OBITUARIES

The Death Angel, during the past year, has taken from us many of our brethren and sisters, but we trust they have gone to be with Him whom they loved and served. While we miss their presence and service, we bow submissively to the Father's will, recognizing that His will is always best, always right, and always safe.

We memorialize our dead, those who have given us our ideals and standards of living. The greatest memorial that we can give them is in upholding those standards and ideals. When we fail to uphold them, our memorials are hypocritical.

Let us uphold their standards, let us attain to their ideals; let us memorialize our dead.

Respectfully Submitted,
JOHN U. GARNER

37. The Committee on New Churches recommends that the Rocky Knoll Church be received into the Association. The report was adopted. J. M. Hilliard gives welcome to the representatives of the Rocky Knoll Church.

38. The following reports of Committees were made and adopted.

Committee to Nominate Delegates to State Convention

Delegates J. C. Gillespie and J. M. Hilliard

Respectfully submitted,
J. E. KIRK,
B. G. WHITELY,
W. J. GOLDSMITH.

Report of Auditing Committee

Your Committee finds the Treasurer's report correct.

Respectfully submitted,
A. A. CHANDLER,
WALTER MITCHELL,
C. V. WEBSTER.

REPORT OF COMMITTEE ON PLACE AND PREACHER

Preacher—C. N. Royal.

Alternate—Jones E. Kirk.

The place of meeting to be left with the Executive Committee.

Respectfully submitted,

T. L. SASSER,
GROVER JONES,
H. O. MILLER.

REPORT OF COMMITTEE ON PROGRAM

Religious Literature	D. W. Overby
Foreign Missions	Dr. J. Clyde Turner
Denominational Program	Grover H. Jones
State Missions	N. F. Britt
Orphanage	E. A. Long
Baptist Training Union	W. E. Crissman
Woman's Missionary Union	Mrs. Nettie H. Hoge
Ministerial Relief and Annuity	J. C. Gillespie
Hospitals	A. A. Walker
Home Missions	Wilson Woodcock
Social Service	Dr. A. B. Conrad
Christian Education	T. L. Sasser
Sunday Schools	A. Lincoln Fulk
Obituaries	Tom W. Bray

Committee,

C. N. ROYAL,
MRS. O. E. LEE,
T. C. GILLESPIE.

REPORT OF COMMITTEE ON RESOLUTIONS

The unbounded courtesy and hospitality of the good people of the Calvary Church and community have greatly enhanced the spiritual blessings of this the forty-third annual session of the Piedmont Baptist Association.

Therefore be it resolved:

1. That we express our thanks to these people for the use of their house and church property.

2. That we pay special tribute to the good ladies who prepared and served these tempting, wholesome and bountiful lunches.

3. That we commend our faithful officers for their splendid services and fine spirit with which they have carried on their work,

4. That these resolutions be taken as an expression of our good will, our Christian love, and lasting gratitude to this Church and

community for their kind hospitality and unspared efforts rendered at this meeting.

5. That we express our thanks to the Reidsville, First Church, the Mount Olive, and Penn Memorial Churches for their splendid cooperation with the Calvary Church in helping to entertain the Association.

Respectfully submitted,
A. A. WALKER,
MRS. S. N. WHITE,
J. N. BOWMAN.

Rev. Jas. C. Gillespie, pastor of the Calvary Baptist Church responds with words of appreciation to the report of the Committee on Resolutions.

39. The Moderator appoints the Associational Church Advisory Committee as follows: Dr. J. Clyde Turner, Dr. A. B. Conrad, T. L. Sasser, Mrs. Nettie Hoge, Clarance A. Smith, J. M. Hilliard, O. E. Lee.

Motion passed to adjourn. The session closed with singing "God Be With You 'Til We Meet Again" and prayer by J. M. Hilliard.

CLARENCE A. SMITH,
Moderator.

O. E. LEE,
Clerk

ASSOCIATIONAL AIM FOR 1936-37 CO-OPERATIVE PROGRAM

Allen Jay	$ 20.00	Hilliard Memorial	150.00
Calvary	150.00	North Main Street	350.00
Fairview	50.00	North Park	80.00
Gibsonville	100.00	Southside	150.00
Greensboro, 1st	20,000.00	West End	600.00
Asheboro St.	3,000.00	Jessup Grove	25.00
Bailey Memorial	25.00	Lebanon	75.00
Bessemer	300.00	Mt. Zion	50.00
Eller Memorial	1,800.00	Oak Grove	40.00
Florida St.	700.00	Osborn Chapel	25.00
Forest Ave.	1,200.00	Osceola	40.00
Latham Park	25.00	Pleasant Garden	100.00
Magnolia St.	200.00	Reidsville, First	2,500.00
Pomona	150.00	Mt. Olive	100.00
Revolution	1,200.00	Penn Memorial	50.00
Sixteenth Street	400.00	Ruffin Stacey	50.00
Stevens Memorial	400.00	Smith Grove	50.00
Webster Memorial	100.00	Summerfield	125.00
Guilford	80.00	Tabernacle	10.00
High Point, 1st	8,000.00	Trinity	40.00
Green Street	2,000.00	Total	$40,045.00

OUR HONORED DEAD

GIBSONVILLE
- Mrs. Christine Varner
- Mrs. Eliza Harris
- Mr. B. W. Loy

GREENSBORO, FIRST
- Mrs. Fannie Burton
- Mr. F. F. Blevins
- Mrs. M. R. Williams
- Mrs. Maggie Williams
- Rev. J. C. DeLancey
- Mrs. W. B. Mayes
- Mr. S. L. Strickland
- Mrs. A. B. Walker
- Mrs. C. E. Lanford
- Miss Naomi Case
- Mr. J. T. Morgan
- Mrs. Annie T. Hubbard
- Mrs. R. S. Stephens
- Rev. J. W. Rose
- Mrs. Sabra Getsinger
- Mr. G. B. Phillips
- Mrs. Nora Gathings.

ASHEBORO STREET
- Mrs. C. H. Money
- Mr. A. C. O'Neal, Sr.
- Mrs. Kate Oliver
- Mrs. J. A. Coble
- Miss Sallie Coble

BAILEY MEMORIAL
- Mr. C. H. Hampton

BESSEMER
- Mrs. G. C. Ozment
- Mrs. J. D. Holderfield

ELLER MEMORIAL
- Mr. Jasper J. Richardson
- Mr. Robert Fleming
- Mr. S. E. Mays
- Mrs. Adolphus Boone
- Mrs. Albert C. Chaney
- Mrs. L. W. Hodges
- Miss Alvie Lloyd

FLORIDA STREET
- Mr. J. R. Davis

FOREST AVENUE
- Mrs. J. T. J. Battle
- Mrs. S. A. Harvey
- Mr. Edgar Moore
- Mrs. Ida Reese
- Mrs. Sallie Smith
- Mrs. J. P. Merrell
- Mrs. Mary Spradlin
- Deacon C. S. Harward

MAGNOLIA STREET
- Mrs. James Pergsan
- Mr. R. L. Kirkman
- Mrs. W. R. Warden
- Mr. Marshall Houston

POMONA
- Mrs. Lizzie White
- Mr. E. A. Humphries

OUR HONORED DEAD

REVOLUTION
Mrs. Camilla Mathews
SIXTEENTH STREET
Mrs. Mary Boswell
Mr. Elzie Whitt
Mr. Tonnie Wrenn
Miss Annie Cecil
STEVENS MEMORIAL
Mrs. A. E. Mills.
GUILFORD
Mr. J. N. Peacock
HIGH POINT FIRST
Mrs. C. M. Cox
Mr. M. C. Mason
Mrs. E. C. Smoak
Dr. J. T. Burruss
Mrs. Arthur Wilson
Mrs. Mildred Hendricks
Mr. J. J. Garland.
Miss Bettie Humpries
GREEN STREET
Mrs. A. J. Rutledge
Mrs. Dora Beck
Mrs. G. B. Bridges
NORTH MAIN STREET
Mr. I. S. Hucks
NORTH PARK
N. F. Britt, Jr.

SOUTH SIDE
Mrs. Elbert Culler
Mr. Church
LEBANON
Mr. O. P. Carter
Mr. W. W. Wray
OSBORNE CHAPEL
Deacon J. A. Loyal
Mr. Frank Leonard
REIDSVILLE, FIRST
Miss Doyle Saunders
Mrs. T. R. Whittemore
Mrs. Jennie Hooper
RUFFIN STACEY
Mr. E. E. Robertson
SMITH GROVE
Miss Susie Shields
Mr. Lenn Dillon
Deacon Tom Ballard
SUMMERFIELD
Mrs. Cynthia Lane
Mrs Mernevia Duggins
TABERNACLE
Mr. C. B. Parker
TRINITY
Deacon W. J. Sapp

CONSTITUTION

Article 1. The Association shall be called the Piedmont Baptist Association.

Article 2. It shall be composed of the ordained ministers who are members of, and those who may have pastoral charges within the Associational District, and three Delegates from each church in the district aforesaid, and churches having a membership exceeding 300 shall be entitled to one additional delegate for every 200 members or fraction thereof in excess of 300.

Article 3. The said delegates shall, before taking their seats, produce letters from respective churches showing their appointment as delegates.

Article 4. The Associational session shall be held at least once a year.

Article 5. The officers shall be a Moderator, Vice-Moderator, Clerk, and Treasurer. If deemed expedient by the Association the offices of Clerk and Treasurer may be combined.

Article 7. Association shall be clothed with authority only to advise the churches touching all things pertaining to their interest but shall in no case presume to direct or control them in reference to their own government or internal policy.

Article 8. A Committee of Arrangements, consisting of three members, shall be appointed on the first day of each session to prepare and report the proceedings and suggest topics proper for the consideration and action of the next Annual Association.

Article 9. Baptist brethren, not members of the Association, who may be present at any session of the body, may on invitation by the body, take seats and participate in the debates of the Association.

Article 10 The territory embraced in the Association shall be divided into not less than four districts and a committee composed of one pastor, and one layman from each district, together with the Moderator, Vice-Moderator, Clerk of the Association, Associational W. M. U. Superintendent, Associational Sunday School Superintendent, and Associational B. T. U. President, shall be appointed at meeting of the Association, which committee shall compose the Executive Committee of the Association a majority of which shall constitute a quorum. It shall be the duty of the committee to superintend and direct the missionary operations of the Association.

Article 11. All committees shall be appointed by the Moderator unless otherwise ordered by the Association.

Article 12. The Constitution may be altered only at an Annual Session of the Association and by a vote of two-thirds of the whole present.

Article 13. The rules of this body shall follow Mell's Parlimentary Practice.

Article 14. This Association shall cooperate with the Baptist State Convention.

Article 15. The time of the holding of the annual session shall be on Wednesday after the fourth Sunday in October of each year.

Adopted October 17, 1895.
Articles 2, 5, 6, 10, 15, Amended.
Sessions, July 23, 24, 1930.
Article 15 Amended.
Session, July 21, 1932.
Article 10 Amended.
Session, October 23, 24, 1935.

Committee—W. O. JOHNSON,
A. WAYLAND COOKE.

PIEDMONT ASSOCIATION, W. M. U.

Morning Session

The W. M. U. of the Piedmont Association met in annual session April 30th at the First Baptist Church High Point.

Mrs. Nettie Hoge opened meeting announcing our theme "The King and the Kingdom."

Devotional was conducted by Mrs. L. M. Gideon. "Five Means of Kingdom Coming as Recorded in Luke."

Welcome was given by Mrs. W. L. Clayton. Response by Mrs. C. L. Straughn.

Prayer by Rev. Hopkins.

Roll call was answered by a large delegation from 15 churches.

Excellent reports were then given by the various group leaders.

All Hail the Power, was sung.

Mrs. Turner, our state president made a most interesting talk using as her subject, "Kingdom Work."

Mrs. Miller sang beautifully "The King's Business."

Mrs. Turner introduced Mrs. D. L. Stamps. The theme of her talk being "What God is Doing in China."

Mrs. Hoge ask for a season of prayer, Rev. C. N. Royal opened the prayer, Rev. J. L. Coley closing.

Afternoon Session

Mrs. Ben Eller conducted the devotional. Mrs. Eller led the prayer.

Mrs. Hoge in her message urged that we as citizens of the Kingdom be obedient to the Masters will.

Obituary—Solo—Mrs. W. T. Tice.

Resolutions: *Time and Place by Mrs. S. A. Helms.* Last Thursday in April—First Baptist Church—Greensboro.

Adjournment.

Respectfully submitted,
MRS. C. R. HARRISON, Secretary

42

CHURCHES	Location*	When Constituted	PASTORS	SUNDAY SCHOOL SUPERINTENDENTS
Allen Jay	V	1934	R. L. Smith, High Point, N. C.	Wade Cumbie, Rt. 2., Trinity
Calvary	O	1901	J. C. Gillespie, Rt. 4., Reidsville	C. J. Delgado, Reidsville
Fairview	O	....	J. C. Gillespie, Rt. 4., Reidsville	A. D. Hopkins, Reidsville
Gibsonville	T	1894	E. A. Long, Germantown, N. C.	R. K. Craven, Gibsonville
Greensboro, First	C	1859	Dr. J. Clyde Turner, Greensboro	O. E. Lee, Greensboro
Asheboro Street	C	1899	J. Ben Eller, Greensboro, N. C.	M. D. Teague, Greensboro
Bailey Memorial	C	1935	C. G. Coe, Pomona, N. C.	W. J. Mitchell, Rt. 3., Greensboro
Bessemer	V	1922	A. A. Walker, Bessemer, Greensboro	C. L. Murray, Greensboro
Eller Memorial	C	1897	Jones E. Kirk, Greensboro, N. C.	Raymond Kincaid, Greensboro
Florida Street	C	1916	B. G. Whitley, Rt. 5., Greensboro	J. L. Roberson, Greensboro
Forest Avenue	C	1906	Wilson Woodcock, Greensboro, N. C.	Dr. J. T. J. Battle, Greensboro
Latham Park	..	....	W. I. Johnson, Burlington, N. C.	Odell Pulley, Greensboro
Magnolia Street	C	1912	W. F. Hancock, Greensboro, N. C.	H. S. Noah, Greensboro
Pomona	V	1913		C. C. Patterson, Pomona
Revolution	C	....	T. E. Baber, Greensboro, N. C.	N. C. Brown, Greensboro
Sixteenth Street	C	....	W. B. Cook, Denim Sta. Greensboro	J. V. Brady, Greensboro
Stevens Memorial	V	1922	John U. Garner, Greensboro, N. C.	L. A. Mills, Greensboro, Rt. 2
Webster Memorial	O	1935	M. L. Hux, Rt. 5., Greensboro	R. E. Fitchett, Greensboo, Rt. 5
Guilford	V	1914	Robert Costener, Geensboro	W. R. Harmon, Greensboro
High Point, First	C	1825	Dr. A. B. Conrad, High Point, N. C.	A. E. Tate, High Point
Green Street	C	1899	C. N. Royal, High Point, N.	B. G. Leonard, High Point
Hilliard Memorial	C	1929	Hughey O. Miller, High Point, N. C.	L. E. Edwards, High Point
North Main	C	1908	A. Lincoln Fuik, High Point, N. C.	Winfred Clinard, High Point
North Park	C	1929	N. F. Britt, High Point, N. C.	Paul Frye, High Point
South Side	C	1916	G. H. Liner, High Point, N. C.	W. K. Briggs, High Point
West End	C	1913	J. N. Bowman, High Point, N. C.	Eugene Gregory, High Point
Jessup Grove	O	....	R. O. Nuckels, Rt. 1., Colfax, N. C.	Jasper Highfill, Rt.1, Guilford College
Lebanon	O	1911	C. M. Oates, Greensboro, N. C.	B. G. Yow, Greensboro
Mount Zion	O	....	W. I. Johnson, Burlington, N. C.	George Spoon, Kimesville
Oak Grove	C	1916	J. H. Hanes, Belew Creek, N. C.	L. R. Loflin, Jamestown
Osborne Chapel	O	1934		Robert Osborne, Rt. 3., Greensboro
Osceola	O	....	D. E. Oates, Siler City, N. C.	A. E. Cook, Rt. 1., Gibsonville
Pleasant Garden	V	1933	Tom W. Bray, Pleasant Garden, N. C.	Walter J. Smith, Pleasant Garden
Reidsville, First	C	....	T. L. Sasser, Reidsville, N. C.	R. T. Burton, Reidsville
Mount Olive	C	1929	J. H. Saunders, Reidsville, N. C.	Elwood Talley, Reidsville
Penn Memorial	C	1927	D. W. Overbey, Reidsville, N. C.	Herbert Ford, Reidsville
Rocky Knoll	O	1934	L. C. Chandler, Rt. 1., Greensboro	Ray Chandler, Greensboro Rt. 1
Ruffin Stacey	O	1931	J. T. London, Rt. 5, Reidsville N. C.	R. M. Durham, Reidsville, Rt. 5
Smith Grove	O	1921	R. O. Nuckles Rt. 1, Colfax, N. C.	Drew Smith, Colfax, Rt. 1
Summerfield	V	....	E. A. Long, Germantown, N. C.	C. V. Furgerson, Summerfield
Tabernacle	V	1933	Grove C. Phillips, Altamahaw, N. C.	Paton W. Phillips, Altamahaw
Trinity	V	1924	J. C. Gatewood, Trinity, N. C.	J. M. Thomas, High Point Rt. 3

CHURCH DIRECTORY

CHURCHES	CHURCH TREASURERS	CHURCH CLERKS
Allen Jay	Earl White, High Point, N. C., Rt. 3	Glenn T. Smith, High Point, N. C.
Calvary	J. F. Carroll, Reidsville, N. C.	J. E. McCargo, Reidsville, N. C.
Fairview	Guy T. Gordon, Rt. 2, Reidsville, N. C.	Wm. Cummings, Rt. 2., Reidsville, N. C.
Gibsonville	T. L. Robinson, Gibsonville, N. C.	W. P. Killette, Gibsonville, N. C.
Greensboro, First	Howard Gardner, Greensboro, N. C.	W. O. Burnham, Greensboro, N. C.
Asheboro Street	U. A. Hedrick, Greensboro, N. C.	J. B. Wills, Greensboro, N. C.
Bailey Memorial	W. J. Mitchell, Rt. 3, Greensboro, N. C.	R. A. Mitchell, Rt. 3, Greensboro
Bessemer	A. C. Melvin, Bessemer Br. Greensboro	W. P. Haynes, Bessemer Br. Greensboro
Eller Memorial	E. G. Parker, Denim Sta. Greensboro	Geo. W. Baity, Denim Sta. Greensboro
Florida Street	E. H. Moore, Greensboro, N. C.	J. B. Rumley, Greensboro, N. C.
Forest Avenue	J. E. Sharpe, Greensboro, N. C.	B. B. Stockard, Greensboro N. C.
Latham Park	J. C. Parrish, Geensboro, N. C.	W. W. Sutton, Greensboro
Magnolia Street	Harvey Royals, Greensboro, N. C.	Mrs. Cleo Covington, Greensboro
Pomona	E. E. Henry, Pomona, N. C.	C. [illegible] Patterson, [illegible] N.
Revolution	Waldo Johnson, Revolution, Greensboro	W. L. Jones, Revolution, Greensboro
Sixteenth Street	L. F. Paris, Denim Sta. Greensboro	Alfred E. White, Denim, Greensboro
Stevens Memorial	Mrs. C. B. Brissom, Rt. 2, Greensboro	Mrs. J. B. Brown, Rt. 2., Greensboro
Webster Memorial	J. F. Graves, Denim Br. Greensboro	Miss Selma Scales, Rt 5., Greensboro
Guilford	W. L. Hudson, Guilford, N. C.	R. F. Bondurant, Guilford College, N. C.
High Point, First	Miss Thelma Patrick, High Point	C. D. Goldsmith, High Point, N. C.
Green Street	R. B. Culler, High Point, N. C.	Clyde [illegible]ars, High Point, N. C.
Hilliard Memorial	K. F. Moore, High Point, N. C.	J. W. Saunders, High Point, N. C.
North Main	Kester Burrow, High Point, N. C.	Miss Annie Lawson, High Point, N. C.
North Park	L. W. Glenn, High Point, N. C.	D. H. Short, High Point, N. C.
South Side	J. G. Williams, High Point, N. C.	J. G. Williams, High Point, N. C.
West End	C. M. Scott, High Point, N. C.	Mrs. O. H. Clodfelter High Point
Jessup Grove	Flossie Stanley, Rt. 1., Guilford College	Jess Fuller, Rt. 1. Guilford College
[illegible]	J. B. Carter, Rt. 5, Greensboro, N. C.	Miss Pauline Jarvis, Rt. 5., Grensboro
Mount Zion	Miss May Bronson, Snow Camp, N. C.	J. C. Lackamy, Liberty, N. C.
Oak Grove	L. R. Loflin, Jamestown, N. C.	L. R. Loflin, Jamestown, N. C.
Osborne Chapel	Mrs. Mimie Morgan, Rt. 3, Greensboro	Robert R. Osborne, Rt. 3. Greensboro
Osceola	Mrs. D. A. Greene, Brown Summit, N. C	E. R. Brande, Rt. 1, Brown Summit, N. C.
Pleasant Garden	J. E. Thompson, Pleasant Garden, N. C.	I. F. Anderson, Rt 1, Greensboro, N. C.
Reidsville, First	J. F. Smith, Reidsville, N. C.	T. L. Gardner, Reidsville, N. C.
Mount Olive	Mrs. Lawson Daniel, Reidsville, N. C.	Mrs. Patrick O. De. Lapp, Reidsville,
Penn Memorial	Thomas Dixon, Reidsville, N. C.	Mrs. Pearl Boswell, Reidsville, N. C.
Rocky Knoll	John P. Rieves, Rt. 1, Greensboro, N. C	J. W. Smith, Greensboro, N. C.
Ruffin Stacey	Mrs. Lottie Shrum, Ruffin, N. C.	R. M. Dprham, Rt. 5, Reidsville, N. C.
Smith Grove	Drew Smith, Colfax, N. C., Rt. 1	Drew Smith, Rt. 1., Colfax, N. C.
Summerfield	Mrs. O. E. Shields, Summerfield, N. C.	Mrs. Myrtle Smith Summerfield
Tabernacle	Miss Edna Phillips, Altamahaw, N. C.	Miss Edna Phillips, Altamahaw, N. C.
Trinity	Miss Ora Maie Welbourne, Trinity, N. C.	Mrs. G. G. Clinard, Trinity, N. C.

TABLE I. CHURCH MEMBERSHIP, ETC., PIEDMONT ASSOCIATION YEAR ENDING SEPTEMBER 30, 1936

CHURCHES	Days of Meeting	Church Membership: Members Reported Last Year	Gains: Baptisms	Gains: Letters	Gains: Statements	Gains: Restorations	Losses: Letters	Losses: Exclusions	Losses: Erasures	Losses: Deaths	Total Present Members	Weekly Prayer Meetings	Revival Meetings Held During Year	Observance of Lord's Supper During Year	Families Receiving State Baptist Paper
Allen Jay	2 4	43	7	9	1	...	2	1	...	...	57	1	1	2	3
Calvary	2 4	151	4	...	...	...	2	...	...	...	153	1	1	1	...
Fairview	......	....	3	...	...	...	...	...	...	...	115	0	1	2	2
Gibsonville	2 4	236	6	2	1	...	...	...	1	3	244	0	1	4	...
Greensboro, First	1 2 3 4	1956	56	133	18	...	92	74	...	17	1980	1	1	12	139
Asheboro Street	1 2 3 4	996	48	36	6	...	28	...	7	5	1044	1	1	4	...
Bailey Memorial	1 2 3 4	53	14	12	5	...	26	...	...	1	53	1	2	12	...
Bessemer	1 2 3 4	551	17	18	1	...	34	...	108	2	449	1	1	10	35
Eller Memorial	1 2 3 4	803	18	20	3	...	19	3	...	7	815	1	1	4	20
Florida Street	1 2 3 4	342	10	13	6	1	17	...	4	1	350	1	2	3	6
Forest Avenue	1 2 3 4	520	27	45	5	2	23	...	26	7	543	1	2	12	40
Latham Park	......	55	...	...	...	...	...	...	...	...	45	...	...	...	...
Magnolia Street	1 2 3 4	412	6	1	...	1	43	...	...	4	365	1	1	1	21
Pomona	1 2 3 4	228	6	8	4	3	21	3	92	2	131	1	2	2	...
Revolution	1 2 3 4	287	6	9	...	6	10	1	...	1	292	1	1	1	1
Sixteenth Street	1 2 3 4	915	7	8	...	...	48	34	...	4	844	1	2	7	...
Stevens Memorial	1 2 3 4	130	13	...	3	...	6	...	...	1	139	1	1	4	3
Webster Memorial	1 2 3 4	95	9	18	4	...	...	...	...	...	126	1	1	4	3
Guilford	1 2 3 4	76	...	8	...	4	1	...	...	1	81	0	...	2	5
High Point, First	1 2 3 4	1196	40	56	3	...	60	...	78	8	1149	1	1	4	34
Green Street	1 2 3 4	1168	35	38	10	...	39	...	...	3	1253	1	1	4	10
Hilliard Memorial	1 2 3 4	298	3	5	1	...	6	...	...	...	301	...	...	...	...
North Main	1 2 3 4	230	19	6	3	...	13	...	...	1	242	1	2	4	27
North Park	1 2 3 4	165	15	8	5	...	4	...	...	1	172	1	1	4	15
South Side	1 2 3 4	271	7	10	2	...	5	3	...	2	290	1	2	4	...
West End	1 2 3 4	340	12	12	2	...	9	4	...	...	353	1	1	4	30
Jessup Grove	2 4	....	...	...	...	...	...	...	...	...	45	...	...	...	...
Lebanon	1 2 3 4	155	20	2	...	...	2	...	...	2	173	...	...	...	...
Mount Zion	2 4	150	5	...	...	...	...	...	...	...	155	...	...	...	...
Oak Grove	1 3	88	2	2	...	1	...	...	...	...	93	...	1	1	...
Osborne Chapel	......	11	...	2	...	...	...	...	...	2	12	1	1	2	...
Osceola	2	49	...	...	...	...	...	2	...	...	47	...	1	2	1
Pleasant Garden	1 2 3 4	82	10	...	...	...	1	...	1	...	89	1	1	5	12
Reidsville, First	1 2 3 4	....	14	24	1	...	12	...	...	3	718	1	2	4	49
Mount Olive	1 2 3 4	217	37	6	3	3	6	11	6	...	230	1	3	4	4
Penn Memorial	1 2 3 4	118	12	18	11	...	7	...	...	...	152	1	1	2	3
Rocky Knoll	1 4	....	24	6	2	...	...	...	...	...	90	1	2	2	...
Ruffin Stacey	1 2 3 4	124	19	...	3	...	2	2	...	1	144	1	1	4	...
Smith Grove	1 3	104	24	...	2	...	...	...	...	3	130	...	2	4	...
Summerfield	1	165	5	...	...	...	...	...	...	2	168	...	1	2	6
Tabernacle	1 2 3 4	29	...	...	...	...	...	1	...	1	27	...	...	...	...
Trinity	1 3	....	3	2	...	...	...	...	...	1	99	1	1	2	...
		12809	563	534	105	21	538	139	323	86	13958		46	145	473

Allen Jay	12	15	17	20	24	30	...	...	10	128	70		...	1	7	...	...	...	...	...	....	....	52.70
Calvary	....	10	22	6	69	30	...	...	11	148	66		...	...	4	...	...	...	...	...	45.09	84.61	129.70
Fairview	...	6	10	13	12	12	...	...	7	60	....		...	...	3	...	...	...	...	...	....	16.92	16.92
Gibsonville	24	56	59	30	59	55	...	11	17	311	...		...	...	...	...	...	...	...	...	128.20	....	128.20
Greensboro, First	122	168	214	174	279	806	110	215	102	2190	933	Yes	...	...	42	...	...	1	204	128	847.46	4,075.22	4,922.68
Asheboro Street	60	111	143	126	73	357	50	25	75	1020	491	Yes	...	25	43	...	...	1	235	181	....	....	....
Bailey Memorial	12	....	16	10	35	14	...	...	7	94	72	Yes	...	...	8	...	...	1	9	...	....	....	....
Bessemer	22	38	73	61	35	126	23	...	24	402	218	Yes	...	11	13	...	...	...	...	...	499.60	....	499.60
Eller Memorial	32	97	140	82	104	114	...	...	126	695	311	Yes	...	26	...	...	...	...	...	...	464.80	....	464.80
Florida Street	26	65	78	54	42	92	26	...	30	413	299	Yes	...	...	5	...	...	...	...	...	238.28	136.56	374.84
Forest Avenue	50	50	61	83	117	96	50	30	...	537	355	Yes	...	12	18	...	...	1	129	95	709.80	198.21	908.21
Latham Park	...	...	...	...	...	...	...	...	...	64	45		...	...	...	...	...	...	...	...	....	....	....
Magnolia Street	24	10	23	19	33	75	9	...	16	209	119	Yes	...	...	2	...	...	...	...	...	310.99	13.47	324.46
Pomona	49	30	68	35	71	83	...	...	13	349	201	Yes	...	1	...	...	...	...	...	...	175.54	78.48	254.02
Revolution	20	42	52	35	44	65	53	21	28	360	151	Yes	...	...	...	...	...	...	...	...	201.05	211.35	412.40
Sixteenth Street	32	44	104	50	70	104	15	...	21	440	288		...	...	7	...	...	...	...	...	227.17	120.11	347.28
Stevens Memorial	7	43	43	24	32	80	8	...	19	256	187	Yes	...	1	1	...	...	...	...	...	....	....	....
Webster Memorial	16	15	30	17	15	67	19	...	11	190	128		...	2	...	...	...	...	...	...	199.59	82.08	281.67
Guilford	20	22	15	14	15	30	...	...	11	129	67		...	2	...	...	...	...	...	...	....	....	86.92
High Point, First	49	85	101	163	166	214	43	76	64	961	471	Yes	...	2	32	...	...	...	...	...	1,173.67	1,224.18	2,397.85
Green Street	74	160	273	135	225	371	63	...	101	1402	655	Yes	...	80	25	...	...	1	230	175	....	....	....
Hilliard Memorial	19	45	56	41	20	92	9	...	23	305	...	Yes	...	...	3	...	...	...	...	...	188.08	118.35	306.43
North Main	25	25	35	31	19	88	...	...	15	238	150		...	...	19	...	...	...	...	...	....	....	358.59
North Park	25	54	52	38	30	46	21	6	23	301	177	Yes	...	1	15	...	...	...	...	...	....	....	....
South Side	...	125	61	74	49	91	...	...	14	414	220		...	3	...	...	...	...	...	...	223.19	21.91	245.10
West End	33	36	54	51	37	67	23	30	23	354	180	Yes	...	12	8	...	...	...	...	...	339.78	217.82	557.60
Jessup Grove	...	...	...	...	...	...	...	...	...	64	25		...	...	...	...	...	...	...	...	....	....	....
Lebanon	35	16	20	24	46	70	...	...	10	221	[illegible]		...	...	...	...	...	...	...	...	....	....	....
Mount Zion	35	...	21	...	24	26	...		6	112	55		...	...	4	...	...	...	...	...	....	....	....
Oak Grove	5	7	8	8	...	29	...	...	9	66	48		...	...	...	...	...	...	...	...	10.56	....	31.28
The Chapel	...	...	...	...	...	...	...	...	5	107	40	Yes	...	...	...	...	...	...	...	...	28.34	1.50	29.84
Osceola	23	...	13	12	...	9	...	...	6	63	36		...	1	...	...	...	...	...	...	....	....	39.94
Pleasant Garden	12	16	19	9	16	32	13	...	10	127	60		...	1	5	...	...	...	...	...	....	....	....
Reidsville, First	27	54	97	84	49	275	24	100	57	767	278	Yes	...	4	6	...	...	1	159	124	429.86	347.00	776.86
Mount Olive	20	18	39	32	83	...	...	...	9	201	133	Yes	...	1	...	...	...	...	...	...	....	....	....
Penn Memorial	13	...	13	12	26	51	...	...	...	124	65	Yes	...	...	...	...	...	...	...	...	87.91	2.50	90.41
Rocky Knoll	26	29	20	28	27	60	...	...	...	190	85		...	...	...	...	...	...	...	...	165.84	24.16	190.00
Ruffin Stacey	...	...	...	...	...	...	...	...	...	143	80		...	...	...	...	...	...	...	...	....	....	14.01
Smith Grove	31	25	...	63	...	32	...	...	6	157	80		...	...	...	...	...	...	...	...	10.00	....	10.00
Summerfield	...	...	...	...	...	...	...	...	2	125	75		...	...	...	...	...	...	...	...	48.00	60.00	108.00
Tabernacle	5	5	7	6	9	8	...	...	4	44	24		...	...	...	...	...	...	...	...	7.65	13.20	20.65
Trinity	...	20	8	20	22	41	11	...	13	135	79		...	6	3	...	...	...	...	...	15.00	15.00	75.00
TOTALS	985	1542	2065	1684	1977	3838	570	516	953	14,616	6947		...	192	273	...	...	...	966	703	6,775.45	7,062.63	14,445.96

CHURCHES	Does Your Chu Its House of V	When Wa	Materials Use	Persons Seatec	Numb	Department Rooms	Number Sepa Rooms	Value of Churc and Grounds	Value of Chapel if	Value of Pastor	Total Value Al Property	Indebtedness or Church Propert	Insurance Carr
Allen Jay	Yes	1936	Wood	300	1	...	...	1,200.00			1,200.00	650.00	1,000.00
Calvary	Yes	1898	Wood	375	5	4	4	3,500.00		2,000.00	5,500.00		2,000.00
Fairview	Yes	1902	W[illegible]d	300	5	...	4	2,000.00		1,200.00	2,600.00		1,500.00
Gibsonville	Yes	1894	Wood	300	9	...	9	4[illegible].00			4,[illegible]		2,500.00
Greensboro, First	Yes	1906	Brick	1000	48	...	...	130,000.00		15,000.00	145,[illegible]		67,000.00
Asheboro Street	Yes	1912	Brick	700	32	6	47	30,000.00		6,000.00	36,[illegible]	2,261.63	26,000.00
Bailey Memorial	Yes	1936	Wood	200	1	...	...	1,000.00			1,[illegible]	200.00	750.00
Bessemer	Yes	1922	Wood	350	16	3	16	[illegible].00		2,000.00	8,[illegible]	1,245.00	4,500.00
Eller Memorial	Yes	1925	Brick	450	48	6	16	[illegible].00			41,000.00		25,000.00
Florida Street	Yes	1930	Brick	450	22	2	12	15,000.00			15,000.00	2,000.00	10,000.00
Forest Avenue	Yes	1906	Brick	275	14	6	14	17,000.00		8,000.00	41,000.00	2,000.00	10,750.00
Latham Park	Yes	1912	Wood	150	1	...	...	3,000.00			3,[illegible]		
Magnolia Street	Yes	1912	Wood	300	7	9	16	6,000.00			6,[illegible]		4,000.00
Pomona	Yes	1913	Wood	350	8	6	7	3[illegible].00			3,000.00		
Revolution	Yes	1907	Wood	400	5	3	7	[illegible].00		5,000.00	15,[illegible]		7,500.00
[illegible]h Street	Yes	1907	Brick	400	10	...	9	30,000.00			30,[illegible]		10,000.00
Stevens Memorial	Yes	1922	Wood	250	11	2	13	[illegible].00			10,[illegible]		5,000.00
Webster Memorial	Yes	1935	Wood	240	5	...	4	4,000.00			4,000.00		1,800.00
[illegible]rd	Yes	1914	Wood	200	1	...	...	3,500.00			3,[illegible]		1,650.00
High Point, First	Yes	1905	Brick	500	60	7	40	100,000.00		7,000.00	122,[illegible]	31,350.00	55,000.00
Green Street	Yes	1926	Brick	1500	96	6	68	156,000.00	1,600.00	3,000.00	160,[illegible]	45,550.00	6[illegible]
Hilliard Memorial	Yes	1931	Brick	800	22	...	22	22,500.00			22,500.00	1,000.00	10,000.00
North Main	Yes	1924	Brick	350	10	3	9	10,600.00		400.00	11,000.00		4,000.00
North Park	Yes	1929	Wood	300	7	...	...	3,500.00			3,[illegible]	906.00	1,500.00
South Side	Yes	1916	Wood	400	9	...	8	2,500.00		2,500.00	5,[illegible]	1,721.00	
West End	yes	1913	Wood	350	15	...	13	8,500.00		3,500.00	12,[illegible]		5,000.00
Jessup Grove	Yes	1934	Wood	400	1	...	...	1,050.00			1,050.00		
Lebanon	Yes	1911	Wood	250	6	5	5	2,500.00			3,000.00		
Mount Zion	Yes	1912	Wood	500	1	...	...	2[illegible]0.00			2,[illegible]		
Oak Grove	Yes	1927	Wood	270	3	2	2	1,500.00			1,500.00		
Osborne Chapel	Yes	1935	Wood	400	1	...	...	750.00			750.00		
Osceola	Yes	1912	Wood	300	1	...	...	1,500.00			1,650.00		
Pleasant Garden	Yes	1918	Wood	220	1	...	...	1[illegible]0.00			1,500.00	300.00	1,000.00
Reidsville, First	Yes	....	Brick	550	24	5	19	37,000.00		14,000.00	51,000.00		43,500.00
Mount Olive	Yes	1929	Wood	325	1	...	...	2,000.00			2,000.00		2,000.00
Penn [illegible]al	Yes	1935	Brick	350	13	13	11	10,000.00		1,500.00	11,500.00	1,900.00	3,500.00
Rocky Knoll	Yes	....	Wood	200	1	...	...	1,000.00			1,000.00		500.00
Ruffin Stacey	Yes	1931	[illegible]ood	350	1	...	...	2,000.00			2,000.00		1,500.00
Smith Grove	Yes	1923	Wood	300	1	...	...	1,500.00			1,600.00		650.00
Summerfield	Yes	1904	Wood	400	1	...	4	6,000.00			6,000.00		3,500.00
Tabernacle	Yes	1934	Wood	400	1	...	...	1,500.00			1,500.00	170.32	
Trinity	Yes	1925	Wood	300	2	5	4	2,500.00			2,500.00		2,000.00
				16,705	532	93	409	696,100.00	1,600.00	71,100.00	802,100.00	91,253.95	374,600.00

Churches	FOR SUPPORT OF LOCAL CHURCH WORK										
	Pastor's Salary	Other Salaries	Ministerial Help and Supply	Building and Repairs	Church Debt and Interest	Incidentals	Literature for Sunday School and B. Y. P. U. and W. M. S.	Help Given to Local Poor	For Printin the Minutes and Clerk of Association	Other Objects	(Local Work) Tota for Lo al Purposes Given by the Church and All Its Organizations
Allen Jay	114.69				156.78	20.10	38.50		2.00		332.07
Calvary	260.44		50.35			69.98	24.92		3.00	3.00	411.69
Fairview	125.65		41.00		50.00	6.00			4.00		226.65
Gibsonville	600.00		43.10			183.93	128.20		3.00		958.23
Go., First	4,600.00	4,790.00	260.91	410.57		3,948.30	1,478.18	992.00	18.00	4,027.61	20,525.57
Asheboro Street	3,000.40	740.00	265.00	112.50	1,840.00	1,714.09	802.05	356.68	12.50	93.72	8,936.94
Bailey Memorial	200.00			100.87		16.00	32.72	14.00	2.00		365.59
Bessemer	1,250.00		308.37	334.15	250.12	482.96	223.92	21.50	5.00	72.61	2,948.63
Eller Memorial	2,580.00		286.22	633.45		714.50	348.25	301.04	10.00	197.20	5,070.66
Florida Street	1,560.00		147.88	110.00	656.00	185.64	156.95	57.70		265.24	3,139.41
Forest Avenue	2,104.55		120.00	201.39	1,204.62	547.50	403.08			80.77	4,881.91
Latham Park											
Magnolia Street	1,015.04	55.50		71.68		329.73	71.60	11.00	3.00		1,557.55
Pomona	1,293.85		26.50			213.59	79.52	32.16		39.52	1,685.05
[illegible]	1,655.00		24.60	79.86		253.62	146.04	28.16	4.00	94.04	2,285.32
Sixteenth Street	2,224.24		95.30	462.55		559.38	143.43		5.00		3,4[illegible].90
Stevens Memorial	1,435.00	60.00		273.31		254.34	81.66		3.50		2,1[illegible].81
Webster Memorial	764.32		5.00	97.78	315.19	37.80	86.98	78.67	5.00	109.12	1,499.86
Guilford	234 00			10.00		162.50	132.60	6.00	2.00	40.00	587.10
High Point, First	3,200.00	1,295.00	343.00	61.28	3,352.15	3,512.74	527.44	334.39	18.00	3,305.94	15,949.94
Green Street	3,120,00	624.00	165.00	95.39	10,230.00	1,057.21	485.51	15.00	5.00	24.69	16,221.80
Hilliard Memorial	1,771,94		21.18	448.09	270.00	242.33	131.08		3.00	142.69	3,630.31
North Main	1,300.00		70.60	380.00		357.80	118.87	9.15	3.00	63.90	2,303.32
North Park	1,250.00			66.49	216.00	136.94	232.75	76.20	3.00	44.30	2,025.68
South Side	1,300.00		73.23	12.00	399.91	86.20	275.20	15.00			2,281.54
West End	1,135.00		75.00	34.17		276.15	138.84	7.45	2.50	82.97	1,752.05
Jessup Grove											
Lebanon	286.60		74.12	32.00	200.00		117.55	14.30		1200	736.57
Mount Zion	250.00		50.00			8.00	30.40	2.62	5.00		346.02
Oak Grove	105.31		11.00			10.5[illegible]	18.75		3.00	10.00	158.62
Osborne Chapel					63.64					54.05	117.69
Osceola	79.86		13.65	14.00		6.49	18.85		2.50	18.87	154.19
Pleasant Garden	443.75		13.50		215.00	37.00	48.00		2.00	1.71	760.96
Reidsville, First	3,000.00	2,415.00	434.92	822.06		145.87	406.39	50.00	9.00	1,554.02	8,837.26
Mount Olive	1,692.37		118.50	362.81		86.82	74.51		2.00	125.00	2,[illegible]82.0[illegible]
Penn Memorial	795.00		50.00	817.05	114.00	87.55	47.77	72.00	1.50	24.60	2,009.47
Rocky Knoll	120.00		70.00			90.00	60.00				340.00
Ruffin Stacey	200.00					43.20			2.50		245.70
Smith Grove	51.35		12.00			11.00	10.00	16.04	2.00		102.39
Summerfield	360.00		50.00			76.76	48.00	4.00			58.76
Tabernacle			79.09	107.84		11.17	7.65	20.00			225.75
Trinity	240.00	10.00	26.11	147.00		92.50	36.00	22.00	3.00		576.61
Total	45,718.36	9,989.50	3,425.13	6,298.29	19,533.41	16,366.13	7,212.16	2,557.06	149.00	11,107.57	122,356.61

CHURCHES	Total to Cooperative Pr							Special to Ho	Other Special C	(Missions, Etc. Given for Miss Benevolences b Church and Al	Grand Total fo Purposes—Bot Work and Miss Given by Churc Its Organizatio
Allen Jay			5.00				43.35	4.35		52.70	384.77
Calvary	74.54		14.19	11.54	12.25	10.30	101.16	19.09	40.95	[illegible]	695.71
Fairview	12.45		2.85	3.55	2.00	8.20	5.75			34.80	261.45
Gibsonville	7.00		3.00	2.00			68.50	7.60		88.10	1,046.33
Greensboro, First	14,326.53	212.21	397.48	473.95	2,550.97	792.58	2,335.18	246.21	645.21	21,980.32	42,505.89
Asheboro Street	2,1[illegible]8.84		69.07	97.74	267.45	4.95	459.18	40.14	241.05	3,338.42	12,275.36
Bailey [illegible]rial							34.52		21.09	55.61	421.20
Bessemer	226.09		6.79	18.90	38.85		128.81	20.10		[illegible]54	3,388.17
Eller Memorial	1,267.52			9.00			451.79			1,728.31	6,798.97
Florida Street	308.92		20.70	14.00	53.50		172.06	36.55		605.73	3,745.14
Forest Avenue	595.40		105.73	7.85	157.16		214.60	30.56		1,111.30	5,993.21
Latham Park											
[illegible]olia Street	8.00		2.25	11.22			61.97	33.04		116.48	1,674.03
Pomona	27.61						68.29	10.19	8.00	114.09	1,799.14
Revolution	446.75		37.96	31.36	86.59		162.24	36.15	24.17	825.22	3,110.54
[illegible] Street	304.04		5.00	5.31					120.11	434.46	3,924.36
Stevens Memorial	408.89			17.15	23.06		168.06	70.00	39.05	726.21	2,834.02
Webster Memorial	70.00		8.00	10.00	25.00	10.00	84.59	25.02	6.00	238.61	1,738.47
Guilford	50.00		2.50	4.70	12.70	2.00	5.30	5.80		83.00	670.10
High Point, First	4,220.18		100.06	132.39	266.77	70.00	993.43	84.94	99.00	5,966.77	21,916.71
Green Street	613.90						389.45		2.50	1 [illegible]5 85	17,227.65
Hilliard Memorial	6 [illegible]35		1.55	5.70	6.75		108.03	13.02		141.40	3,171.71
North Main	227.00		22.75	10.00	20.00		150.00	30.00		459.75	2,763.07
North Park	42.00						51.75	15.00		108.75	2,134.43
South Side	21.91				21.00		11.75	2.00		56.66	2,338.20
West End	262.50		51.96	12.00	47.00		249.32	60.92	60.00	743.70	2,495.98
Jessup Grove											
Lebanon			5.00	5.00			74.92			84.92	821.49
Mount Zion	7.00		11.95				[illegible]	3.35		51.58	397.60
Oak [illegible]							20.92	12.00		32.92	191.54
[illegible]he Chapel			4.60				1 [illegible]			6.10	123.79
Osceola	11.95		1.00				13 [illegible]78	5.25		31.98	186.17
Pleasant Garden	39.[illegible]		2.67	12.00			14.00	5.32	3.76	77.15	838.11
Reidsville, First	1,350.00		25.00	105.15	100.00	10.00	347.01	29.36	85.59	2,052.11	10,889.37
Mount Olive					118.00		107.33			225.33	2,857.34
Penn Memorial			2.50		4.00			4.00		10.50	2,019.97
Rocky Knoll							24.16			24.16	364.16
Ruffin Stacey	10.00						20.98	3.00		33.98	279.68
Smith [illegible]e									38.47	38.47	140.86
Summerfield	51.30		5.00	10.00	6.00	1.00	65.00	15.90	9.95	164.15	702.91
Tabernacle							13.20			13.20	238.95
[illegible]		3.00	15.00	22.00			60.00	10.00		110.00	686.61
Total	27,155.77	215.21	929.56	1,032.51	3,819.05	909.03	7,311.16	878.85	14,447.79	43,696.35	166,052.96

'TIST TRAINING UNION & MEN'S BROTHERHOODS—PIEDMONT
IATION FOR THE YEAR ENDING SEPTEMBER 30, 1936

	Baptist Training Unior with Director	THE YOUNG PEOPLE'S WORK																
		Is Baptist Training Union A-1?	3. A. U.'s	Senior B. Y. P. U.'s	Inter. B. Y. P. U.'s	Junior B. Y. P. U.'s	Total B.A.U-B.Y.P.U.	Story Hours	A-1B. Y. P. U.s and B. A. U.'s	Adults Enrolled	Senior's Enrolled	Intermediates Enrolled	Juniors Enrolled	Total Enrolled	Total Number Daily Bible Readers	Number Taking Study Course	Total Systematic Givers in All Unions	Students in College
...	Yes	...	...	1	1	1	3	...	...	...	12	17	15	44	30	30	30	...
...		...	...	...	...	...	...	...	...	...	...	...	...	...	...	...	...	...
...		...	...	...	...	...	...	...	...	...	...	...	...	...	...	...	...	...
...		...	...	...	...	...	...	...	...	...	...	...	...	...	...	...	...	...
...	Yes	...	1	2	3	2	8	1	...	16	42	68	33	159	76	52	118	...
...	Yes	...	...	1	2	2	5	1	...	...	15	50	48	113	39	49	59	5
...		...	...	...	...	...	...	...	...	...	...	...	...	...	...	...	...	...
...	Yes	...	...	1	1	1	3	...	...	...	13	15	35	63	17	18	38	2
...	Yes	...	1	1	2	2	6	1	...	13	20	25	30	88	27	39	68	1
...	Yes	Yes	1	1	2	2	6	1	4	9	10	26	25	70	50	50	39	...
...	Yes	...	...	4	1	1	6	...	...	...	70	18	15	103	...	...	23	1
...		...	...	...	...	...	...	...	...	...	...	...	...	...	...	...	...	...
...		...	1	1	1	1	4	...	...	12	25	20	15	72	...	50	9	...
...		...	...	...	...	...	...	...	...	...	...	...	...	...	...	...	...	...
...		...	...	1	...	...	1	...	...	...	10	...	...	10	...	...	...	...
...	Yes	...	...	1	1	2	4	...	...	...	1	1	2	4	21	24	35	...
...	Yes	...	...	...	...	...	...	...	...	...	...	...	...	31	...	...	...	...
1..		...	...	...	...	...	...	...	...	...	...	...	...	...	...	...	...	...
...		...	...	...	...	1	1	...	...	...	...	...	15	15	5	10	5	...
...	Yes	...	...	1	2	1	4	...	...	...	21	22	19	62	32	36	37	...
...	Yes	...	1	2	2	2	7	...	...	10	35	44	49	138	50	120	101	4
...	Yes	...	1	1	1	1	4	...	...	17	10	18	10	55	32	25	...	...
...	Yes	...	1	1	1	1	4	1	...	10	15	14	12	51	30	31	35	...
...	Yes	...	1	1	1	1	4	1	...	22	17	21	20	80	64	70	80	...
...	Yes	...	...	1	1	1	3	...	...	...	15	14	12	41	24	5	18	...
...	Yes	...	1	1	1	1	4	...	...	16	10	23	22	71	44	61	22	...
..		...	...	...	...	...	...	...	...	...	...	...	...	...	...	...	...	...
...		...	...	...	...	...	...	...	...	...	...	...	...	...	...	...	...	...
		...	...	...	...	...	...	...	...	...	...	...	...	...	...	...	...	...
...		...	...	...	...	...	...	...	...	...	...	...	...	...	...	...	...	...
...		...	...	...	...	...	...	...	...	...	...	...	...	...	...	...	...	...
..		...	...	...	...	...	...	...	...	...	...	...	...	...	...	...	...	...
...	Yes	...	...	...	1	1	2	...	...	...	...	19	10	29	8	7	8	...
...	Yes	...	1	2	1	1	5	...	...	20	33	20	30	103	38	8	47	4
...		...	...	1	...	1	2	...	...	...	20	...	10	30	...	...	...	...
...	Yes	...	...	1	1	1	3	...	...	...	22	22	13	57	16	...	21	1
...	Yes	...	...	...	1	1	2	...	...	...	...	20	10	30	...	...	...	...
...		...	...	...	...	...	...	...	...	...	...	...	...	...	...	...	...	...
...		...	...	...	...	...	...	...	...	...	...	...	...	...	...	...	...	1
...		...	...	...	...	...	...	...	...	...	...	...	...	...	...	...	...	...
...		...	...	...	...	...	...	...	...	...	...	...	...	...	...	...	...	...
...		...	...	...	...	...	...	...	...	...	...	...	...	...	...	...	...	...
....		1	10	26	27	28	93	6	4	145	416	477	450	1519	603	685	793	19

TABLE VII. W. M. U. ORGANIZATIONS AND GIFTS—PIEDMONT BAPTIST ASSOCIATION—YEAR ENDING. SEPT. 30. 1936.

CHURCHES	PRESIDENTS OF W. M. S. AND POST [illegible]	Number of Woman's Missionary Societies	Number of Y. W. A.'s	Number of G. A.'s	Number of R. A.'s	Number of Sunbeams	Total W. M. U. Organizations	W. M. S. Members	Y. W. A.'s Members	G. A.'s Members	R. A.'s Members	Sunbeam Members	Total Members Enrolled	Total Enrolled in Mission Study Courses	Contributions (Local Work) Given by W. M. U.	Contributions (Missions) Given by W. M. U.	Grand Total for All Purposes Given by W. M. U and all its Organizations
Allen Jay																	
Calvary	Mrs. R. H. Terrell, Reidsville	1					1	25					25		23.34	93.25	116.59
Fairview													18				
Gibsonville	Mrs. O. B. Cable, Gibsonville	1					1	18									
Greensboro, First	Mrs. W. H. McKeever, Greensboro	1	1	2	1	1	6	331	40	45	60	70	546	269		11,148.18	11,148.18
Asheboro Street	Mrs. A. Andrews, [illegible]ro	1	2	2	1	1	7	139	52	56	9	35	291	140	190.95	513.56	703.61
Bailey Memorial																	
Bessemer	Mrs. J. H. Green, Bess. Br. Greensboro	1	1				2	30	9				39	10		57.75	57.75
Eller Memorial	Mrs. G. O. Basinger, Denim, Greensboro	1	1				2	32	15				47	15		140.78	140.78
Florida Street	Mrs. J. B. Rumbley, Greensboro	1	1	1	1	1	5	48	14	13	12	6	93	20	30.70	441.28	471.98
Forest Avenue	Mrs. O. Joe Howard, Greensboro	1	1	1	1	1	5	50		12	1		63	25		709.39	709.39
Latham Park																	
Magnolia Street	Mrs. L. L. Jarvis, Greensboro	2	1				3	35	6				41	20			
[illegible]a	Mrs. W. B. Cook, Pomona	1				1	2	14				45	59		3.50	3.30	6.80
Revolution	Miss Sallie Burgess, Greensboro	1	1	2	1	1	6	30	12	20	6	19	87			450.51	450.51
[illegible]h Street	Mrs. C. L. Straughn, Rt. 5, Greensboro	1					1	35					35				
Stevens [illegible]	Mrs. C. B. Brissom, Rt. 2, Greensboro	1		1		1	3	35		15		12	62				
Webster Memorial	Mrs. W. H. [illegible]s, Rt. 5, Greensboro	1					1	39					39		16.90	86.00	102.90
[illegible]	Miss Bulah Martin, [illegible]ord	1					1										
High Point, First	Mrs. W. F. Clayton, High Point	1	1	1	1	1	5	175	56	20	15	25	291	164	2,698.83	3,066.90	5,765.73
Green Street	Miss Gladys Ellington, [illegible]h Point	1	1	1	1	1	5	60	16	36	12	15	139	100		365.00	365.00
Hilliard Memorial	Mrs. H. O. Miller, High Point	1	1	1		1	4	18	12	12		10	48	5	41.00	23.05	64.05
North Main		2	1	2	1	1	7	35	9	19	6	21	90	9	65.00	103.00	168.00
[illegible]th Park	Mrs. Paul Frye, High Point	1				1	2	20				5	25		6.00		6.00
S[illegible]h Side	Mrs. Pearl Camrey, High Point	1				1	2	17				25	42			21.00	21.00
West End	Mrs. Pearl Presler, High Point	1		1		1	3	25		15		17	57	38		221.25	221.25
[illegible] Grove																	
Lebanon																	
Mount Zion																	
Oak Grove																	
Osborne Chapel																	
Osceola																	
Pleasant Garden	Mrs. J. E. Thompson, Pleasant Garden	1				1	2	17				6	23	9	35.00	26.97	61.97
Reidsville, First	Mrs. R. R. Saunders, Reidsville	1	1	2	1	1	6	156	24	14	6	30	230	80	873.00	455.45	1,328.45
Mount [illegible]e	Mrs. J. H. Saunders, Reidsville	1					1										105.00
Penn Memorial	Mrs. M. H. Fitz, Reidsville	1	1				2	13	21				34		7.05	4.00	11.05
Rocky Knoll																	
Ruffin Stacey																	
Smith Grove																	
Summerfield	Mrs. A. C. Lloyd, Summerfield	1					1										
[illegible]e																	
Trinity																	
Total		29	15	17	9	16	87	1397	386	277	127	341	2419	904	3,990.37	17,930.62	22,025.99

YEAR	WHERE HELD	MODERATOR	[redacted]K	PREACHER	Churches	Baptisms	Church Members	Total Gifts
1894	Greensboro	Dr. C. A. Rominger	W. L. Kivett	M. A. Adams	5	....	562	....
	[redacted]y	T. L. [redacted]h	W. L. Kivett	L. [redacted]d	12	16	112	$ 1,695.50
1896	Moore's [redacted]pel	R. W. Brooks	W. H. Eller	L. [redacted]n	14	66	1,194	5,128.94
	[redacted]ld	F. H. Jones	W. H. [redacted]r	J. A. [redacted]ay	16	73	1,540	7,198.27
	[redacted]t Zion	R. W. Brooks	W. H. [redacted]ler	L. [redacted]d	17	67	1,557	6,883.23
1899	Ramseur	R. W. [redacted]ks	F. P. [redacted]	[redacted]h E. [redacted]te	19	54	1,570	7,435.43
	[redacted]y Street	R. W. [redacted]ks	W. H. [redacted]r	[redacted]s Carrick	16	48	1,538	7,970.35
	[redacted]e	F. H. Jones	W. H. Eller	L. [redacted]d	19	157	1,657	8,282.73
	[redacted]m Street	F. H. Jones	W. H. Eller	W. C. [redacted]n	19	135	1,774	9,950.97
	[redacted]le	[redacted] H. Jones	W. H. Eller	C. L. Greaves	20	185	1,868	12,834.77
1904	Calvary	F. H. Jones	W. H. [redacted]r	H. W. Battle	22	112	1,832	12,807.43
19[redacted]	[redacted]h	F. H. Jones	W. H. Eller	J. M. [redacted]	22	114	2,096	17,674.91
	[redacted]h [redacted]ht, First	F. H. Jones	W. H. Eller	W. R. Bradshaw	23	201	2,333	29,366.31
	[redacted]o Street	F. H. Jones	W. H. Eller	Wm. Hedley	26	372	2,798	29,993.79
1908	Ramseur	F. H. Jones	W. H. Eller	C. E. Maddry	28	311	3,086	26,347.57
	[redacted]oro	F. H. Jones	W. H. Eller	Wm. Hedley	30	292	3,429	49,847.28
	[redacted]t Zion	F. H. [redacted]s	W. H. Eller	R. G. [redacted]ck	31	336	3,731	28,531.01
1911	[redacted]	W. F. Staley	W. H. Eller	W. F. Staley	29	182	3,736	25,887.56
1912	H[redacted]h Point, Green St	F. P. Hobgood, Jr.	W. H. Eller	J. C. Turner	30	174	3,647	29,697.38
1[redacted]	Liberty	F. P. Hobgood, Jr.	W. H. Eller	R. P. Walker	31	409	3,971	37,700.97
1914	[redacted] S[redacted]t	F. P. Hobgood, Jr.	W. H. Eller	A. W. Claxon	31	413	4,202	42,428.44
1915	Reidsville	J. M. [redacted]	W. H. [redacted]r	I. M. [redacted]	42	313	4,491	42,577.68
1916	Forest Avenue	J. M. [redacted]	W. H. Eller	E. N. [redacted]on	36	369	4,854	48,418.92
1917	Green S[redacted]t	J. [redacted]	W. H. [redacted]r	W. R. [redacted]te	39	308	4,760	44,609.05
	[redacted]e's Chapel	J. M. [redacted]	W. H. [redacted]r	J. W. [redacted]	39	374	5,140	72,538.46
	[redacted]te O[redacted]	J. M. [redacted]	W. H. [redacted]r	W. H. [redacted]on	39	339	5,359	76,638.85
	[redacted]y	J. M. [redacted]	W. H. Eller	E. N. Johnson	39	543	5,867	117,682.35
	[redacted]ld	[redacted]ce A. Smith	J. E. Lanier	B. K. [redacted]	39	480	6,454	135,561.79
1922	Glenola	Clarence A. Smith	J. E. Lanier	Jas. A. [redacted]k	39	679	7,226	149,955.24
	[redacted]ia Street	[redacted]ce A. [redacted]	H. O. Miller	E. E. [redacted]	38	365	7,341	140,553.25
1924	West End	[redacted]ce A. Smith	H. O. Miller	W. E. Goode	40	672	7,489	164,658.19
	[redacted]ew	Clarence A. Smith	H. O. Miller	A. T. Howell	41	610	8,956	211,792.21
1926	Ramseur	[redacted]e A. Smith	S. F. Hensley	Lloyd T. Wilson	42	620	9,974	243,500.68
1927	Trinity	[redacted]e A. Smith	S. T. [redacted]	H. T. Stevens	40	656	10,223	211,846.40
1928	Bessemer	[redacted]e A. [redacted]	O. E. Lee	R. P. Ellington	41	531	10,866	202,002.30
1[redacted]	Liberty	Clarence A. Smith	O. E. Lee	C. F. Rogers	44	573	11,496	218,987.61
1930	Asheboro	Clarence A. Smith	O. E. Lee	Geo. T. [redacted]stall	44	676	12,012	198,077.29
	[redacted]a Street	[redacted]e A. Smith	O. E. [redacted]e	A. B. [redacted]	44	827	12,789	178,501 19
	[redacted]e	[redacted]e A. Smith	O. E. Lee	J. C. Turner	46	778	13,485	159,000 [redacted]
	[redacted]te [redacted]k	[redacted]e A. Smith	O. E. Lee	T. L. Sasser	48	1561	15,199	186 041.40
	[redacted]le	[redacted]e A. Smith	O. E. Lee	[redacted] [redacted]cock	53	757	15,356	172 839 18
1935	So. S[redacted]e, [redacted]h Point	[redacted]e A. S[redacted]	O. E. Lee	J. S. Hopkins	41	623	12,687	164,135.92
1936	Calvary	Clarence A. Smith	O. E. Lee	J. [redacted] Eller	42	563	13,958	166,052.[redacted]

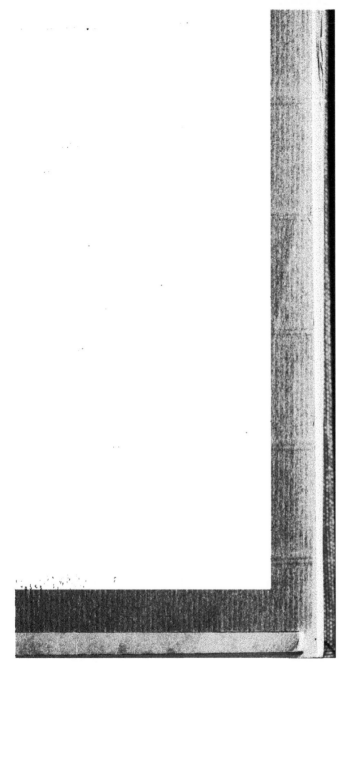

MINUTES

OF THE

Piedmont Baptist Association

NORTH CAROLINA

★ ★ ★

Forty-fourth Annual Session

Held with

ELLER MEMORIAL BAPTIST CHURCH

GREENSBORO, N. C.

October 20, 21

1937

The next session will be held with the Hilliard Memorial Baptist Church, High Point, N. C., Wednesday and Thursday before the fourth Sunday in October, 1938

Dr. A. B. Conrad Will Preach the Sermon

Alternate, Rev. J. C. Gillespie

ECONOMY PRINTING CO. - ROANOKE

MINUTES

OF THE

Piedmont Baptist Association

NORTH CAROLINA

★ ★ ★

Forty-fourth Annual Session

Held with

ELLER MEMORIAL BAPTIST CHURCH

GREENSBORO, N. C.

October 20, 21

1937

The next session will be held with the Hilliard Memorial Baptist Church, High Point, N. C., Wednesday and Thursday before the fourth Sunday in October, 1938

Dr. A. B. Conrad Will Preach the Sermon

Alternate, Rev. J. C. Gillespie

INDEX

The 1937 Minutes Are A Memorial To

CLARENCE A. SMITH

Moderator From 1921 To 1936

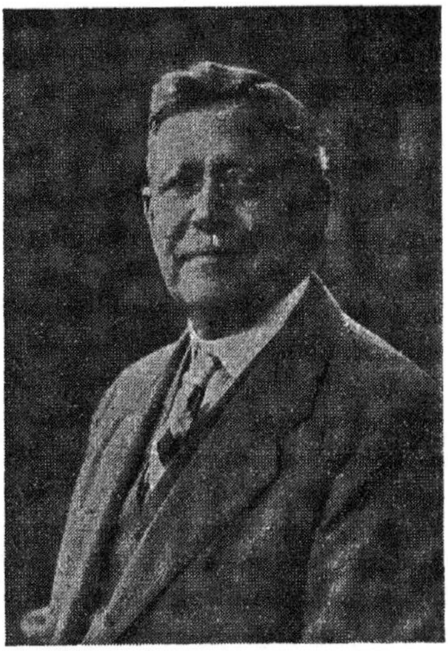

Appreciation

WHEREAS, Brother Clarence A. Smith has served the Piedmont Association for sixteen years as the Moderator but now feels because of the state of his health that it is best for him to relinguish this work,

Therefore, this Association in annual session in the Eller Memorial Baptist Church, Greensboro, desires to make this public record:

First—It expresses to Mr. Smith its admiration of his fine Christian character and social qualities that have endeared him to all as friend and brother.

Second—It voices its appreciation of his excellence as presiding officer and unfailing courtesy in the conduct of all our gatherings.

Third—This body is especially grateful for the earnest zeal, the contribution of much of his time, his frequent visits, for the inspiring advice to the smaller churches, his fatherly help to our young ministers and workers and his unfailing efforts to further every interest that has to do with our common cause.

Fourth—As he retires from this place of leadership, this body assures him of its abiding affection and continued prayers for the full recovery of his health, the full enjoyment of all the rewards that follow faithful service and that all his days may be crowned with happiness and peace.

MAP
OF THE
PIEDMONT BAPTIST ASSOCIATION

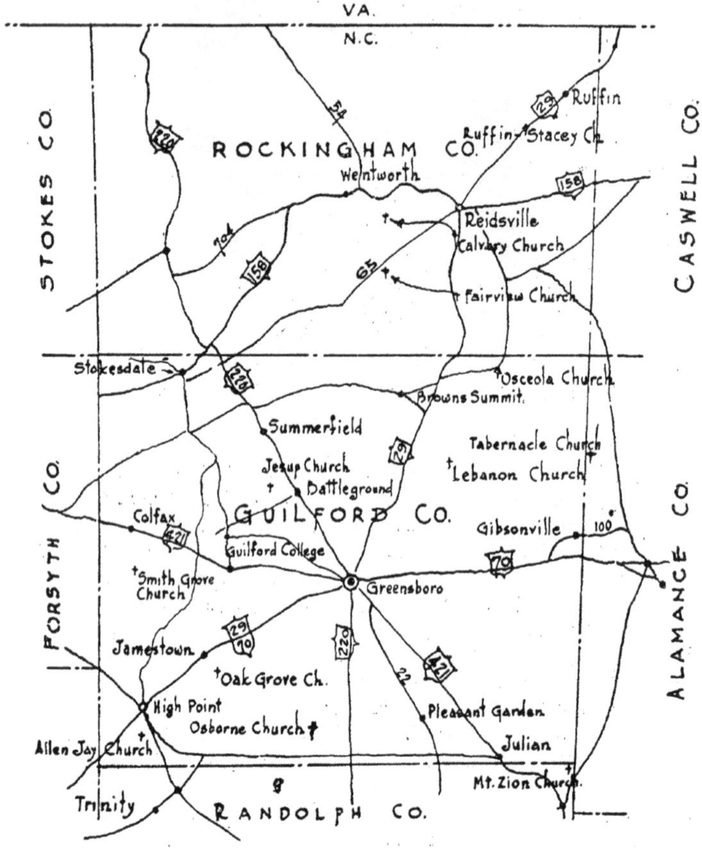

Associational Directory

OFFICERS

Grover H. Jones, Moderator	High Point, N. C.
Dr. J. T. J. Battle, Vice-Moderator	Greensboro, N. C.
O. E. Lee, Clerk-Treasurer	Greensboro, N. C.

EXECUTIVE-PROMOTION COMMITTEE

Grover H. Jones, Chairman	High Point, N. C.
O. E. Lee, Secretary	Greensboro, N. C.
Dr. J. T. J. Battle	Greensboro, N. C.
Rev. C. N. Royal	High Point, N. C.
Dr. A. B. Conrad	High Point, N. C.
Rev. J. C. Gillespie	Reidsville, N. C.
Rev. T. L. Sasser	Reidsville, N. C.
J. C. Tatum	Reidsville, N. C.
Rev. J. Ben Eller	Greensboro, N. C.
Mrs. Nettie Hatcher Hoge	Greensboro, N. C.
F. L. Paschal	Greensboro, N. C.
J. Carl Bell	Greensboro, N. C.

CHURCHES BY DISTRICTS

District 1:

High Point, First
Hilliard Memorial
Green Street
North Main
North Park
South Side
West End
Oak Grove
Smith Grove
Allen Jay

District 2:

Greensboro, First
Asheboro Street
Bessemer
Bailey Memorial
Eller Memorial
Forest Avenue
Florida Street
Latham Park
Magnolia Street
Pomona Mills
Revolution
Sixteenth Street
Stevens Memorial
Gibsonville
Guilford
Jessip Grove
Lebanon
Mount Zion
Pleasant Garden
Osborne Chapel
Rocky Knoll
Summerfield
Tabernacle
Webster Memorial

District 3:

Reidsville, First
Penn Memorial
Mount Olive
Calvary
Fairview
Osceola
Ruffin-Stacey

OFFICERS OF PIEDMONT SUNDAY SCHOOL ASSOCIATION

F. L. Paschal, Superintendent ....Greensboro, N. C.
A. C. Lovelace, Associate Superintendent ....High Point, N. C.
Rev. A. A. Walker, Secretary and Treasurer ......Greensboro, N. C.
Genter Stephens, Chorister ....Greensboro, N. C.
Miss Judith Eller, Pianist ....Greensboro, N. C.
Rev. A. Lincoln Fulk, Supt. Group 1, District 1 ....High Point, N. C.
M. E. Howell, Supt. Group 2, District 1 ....High Point, N. C.
Rev. T. E. Baber, Supt. District 2 ....Greensboro, N. C.
William Cummings, Supt. District 3 ....Reidsville, N. C.
Mrs. T. L. Ogburn, Supt. Cradle Roll Department ..Greensboro, N. C.
Miss Ruth Scott, Beginners Department ....Greensboro, N. C.
Mrs C. C. Stout, Primary Department ....High Point, N. C.
Mrs. Geo. D. Allred, Junior Department ....Greensboro, N. C.
Mrs. I. B. Squier, Supt. Intermediate Department, Greensboro, N. C.
T. L. Ogburn, Supt. Young People's Department ....Greensboro, N. C.
Mrs. J. S. Moore, Supt. Adult Department ....Greensboro, N. C.
Miss Elizabeth Lassiter, Supt. Extension Dept.....Greensboro, N. C.
Rev. C. N. Royal, Supt., Dept. of Evangelism ......High Point, N. C.

OFFICERS OF THE PIEDMONT ASSOCIATION W. M. U.

Mrs. Nettie Hoge, Superintendent ....Greensboro, N. C.
Mrs. C. R. Harrison, Secretary ....High Point, N. C.
Mrs. C. E. Sliceloff, Treasurer ....High Point, N. C.
Miss Ruth Scott, Young People's Leader ....Greensboro, N. C.
Mrs. L. M. Gideon, Personal Service Chairman ....Greensboro, N. C.
Rev. C. N. Royal, Supt. of Evangelism ....High Point, N. C.
Miss Elizabeth Apple, Training School and
Margaret Fund Chairman ....Greensboro, N. C.
Mrs. J. J. Andoe, Mission Study Lit. Chairman....Greensboro, N. C.
Mrs. H. A. Knight, Group Leader, District 1 ....High Point, N. C.
Mrs. A. Andrews, Group Leader, District 2 ....Greensboro, N. C.
Mrs. R. R. Saunders, Group Leader, District 3......Reidsville, N. C.

BAPTIST TRAINING UNION ASSOCIATIONAL OFFICERS

J. Carl Bell, Director ....Rt. 2, Greensboro, N. C.
Miss Thelma Patrick, Associate Director ....High Point, N. C.
Miss Elizabeth Campbell, Secretary-Treasurer....Greensboro, N. C.
Mrs. L. W. Glenn, Junior Leader ....High Point, N. C.
J. J. Norwood, Intermediate Leader ....Greensboro, N. C.
Henry Love, Chorister ....Reidsville, N. C.
Miss Louise Sharpe, Pianist..................Rt. 5, Greensboro, N. C.
Miss Mattie Lee Douglass, Director District 1......High Point, N. C.
Miss Loretta Willis, Director District 2 ....Greensboro, N. C.
Paul Roach, Director District 3 ....Reidsville, N. C.
Rev. C. N. Royal, Pastor Advisor ....High Point, N. C.

Church Directory

ORDAINED MINISTERS NOT PASTORS

W. C. Richardson, Guilford, N. C.
Dr. W. C. Newton, ,
O. F. Barnes, Greensboro, N. C.
B. C. Lamb, Greensboro, N. C.
L. M. Deaton, Greensboro, N. C.
J. M. Hilliard, High Point, N. C.
T. L. Chamberlain, High Point, N. C.
E. W. Netherlain, High Point N. C.
J. F. Murray, Reidsville, N. C.
B. H. Farington, Colfax, N. C.
Rev. Cain, Kernersville, N. C.

B. T. U. DIRECTORS, PRESIDENTS AND LEADERS

ALLEN JAY—Wade Cumbie, Director; Edith Hobson, I. L.; Mrs. Frank Rice, J. L.

GREENSBORO, FIRST—Genter L. Stephens, Director; W. O. Burnham, B. A. U. P; J. R. Sowell, Doris Nowell, H. Kellogg, Sr. P.; Mr. and Mrs. Noel, Mrs. Genter L. Stephens, I. L.: Mildred Jackson, Lorena McManus, J. L.; Helen Saleeby, S. H. L.

ASHEBORO STREET—C. W. McLees, Director; Miss Loetta Willis, Sr. P.; Lorene James, J. J. Norwood, I. L.; Mrs. John Durham, Myrtis Thomas, J. L.; Mrs. J. J. Norwood, S. H. L.

BESSEMER—Norfleet Dixon, Director; C. L. Casey, B.A.U. P.; Louise Sharpe, Sr. P.; Norfleet Dixon, I. L.; Mary Staley, J. L.

ELLER MEMORIAL—Raymond Kincaid, Director; Richard Hobbs, S. P.; Mrs. J. E. Kirk, I. L.; Mrs. G. O. Basinger, J. L.; Mrs. Leonard Bell, S. H. L

FLORIDA STREET—W M. Cassell, Director; J. T. Simmons, B.A.U. P.; W. O. Smith, S. P.; Euline Collins, Lucile Wilson, I. L.; Mrs. W. M. Cassell, Inez Bolejack, J. L.; Mrs. Geo. B. Purcell, S. H. L.

FOREST AVENUE—Mrs. William Fulp, Director; Chas. Talley, S. P.; E. W. Richardson, I. L.; Mr. and Mrs. W. W. William, J. L.

MAGNOLIA STREET—Alma Moore, Jr. L.

POMONA—G. F. Roseberry, Director; Margaret Hudson, S. P.; Mina Lawson, I. L.; Mrs. Velma Lamb, J. L.; Rev. C. M. Oates, S. H. L.

REVOLUTION—J. H. Martin, Sr. P.

SIXTEENTH STREET—Frank Gales, Director; Opal Ryles, S P.; Harry Moore, I. L.; Cathern Caveness, J. L.

STEVENS MEMORIAL—Patsy Harris, Director; Lena Brisson, S. P.; Wm. Brooks, I. L.; Ethel Brown, J. L.; Mrs. B. A. Newman, S. H. L.

HIGH POINT, FIRST—Julia Liles, Director; Ila Hensley, S. P.; Thelma Patrick, I. L.; Rose Goldsmith, J. L.

GREEN STREET—John Reavis, Director; W. R. Denson, B.A.U. P.; Carl Edmonds, S. P.; Mrs. John Reavis, I. L.; J. T. Curlee, J. L.

HILLIARD MEMORIAL—P. E. Grubb, Director; C. H. Farmer, B.A.U. P.; Herbert Miller, S. P.; Mrs. C. H. Saunders, I. L.; Mrs. H. O. Miller, J. L.; Mrs. C. H. Farmer, S. H. L.

NORTH MAIN STREET—R. L. Reeves, Director; Allene Kelly, B.A.U. P.; Mrs. Minda McAruther, S. P.; W. L. Woodell, I. L.; Mrs. W. L. Woodell, J. L.; Mrs. Ed Crisco, S.H.L.

NORTH PARK—L. W. Glenn, Director; H. B. Chatham, B.A.U. P.; Paul Frye, S. P.; Mrs. N. F. Britt, I. L.; Mrs. L. W. Glenn, J. L.

SOUTH SIDE—Huston Williams, Director; W. K. Briggs, S. P.; Martha Brown, I. L.; Estie Brown, J. L.; Mrs. Oldham, S.H.L.

WEST END—J. E. Hedrick, Director; Eugene Gregory, B.A.U. P.; Annie Marie Hedrick, S. P.; Leona Chappell, I. L.; Vernon Coffey, Jr. L.

REIDSVILLE, FIRST—Paul Roach, Director; Mrs. Paul Hubbard, B.-A.U. P.; Mrs. Joe Robinson, S. P.; Mrs. J. Floyd Moore, I. L.; Sarah Price Kemp, J. L.; Mrs. R. W. Justice, S.H.L.

MOUNT OLIVE—C. D. Barker, Director; Odell DeLapp, S. P.; Robt. Allen, I, L.; Earl Kerley, Jr. L.

PENN MEMORIAL—Raymond C. Peters, Director; James Albert Dunevant, S. P.; Mrs. Nash Wilkins, I. L.; Mrs. Herbert Ford, J. L

ROCKY KNOLL—Mrs. T. C. Frazier, Director; Froney Brown, I. L.; Mrs. M. T. Jackson, J. L.

OFFICERS OF W. M. S. AND AUXILIARIES

CALVARY—Mrs. R. H. Terrell, W.M.S. Pres.; Mrs. S. T. McCollum, Y.W.A. Counselor.

GIBSONVILLE—Lelia Coble, W.M.S. Pres.

GREENSBORO, FIRST—Mrs. W. H. McKeever, Pres. W.M.S.; Mrs. T. F. Casey, Y.W.A. Counselor; Mrs. O. E. Lee, Mrs. W. M. Ham, G.A. L.; O. E. Lee, R.A. L.; Miss Mildred Jackson, Sunbeam L.

ASHEBORO STREET—Mrs. A. Andrews, W.M.S. Pres.; Miss Moselle Causey, Mrs. Joe Kirkman, Y.W.A. C.; Mrs. M. D. Teague, Mrs. D. S. Neill, Mrs. U. A. Hedrick, Mrs. A. C. Lowe, G.A. L.; Mrs. B. L. Pickard, R.A. L.; Mrs. Chas. Brown, Sunbeam Leader.

BESSEMER—Mrs. O. F Barnes, W.M.S. Pres.; Mrs. J. R. Medlin, Y.-W.A. C.; Mrs. H C King, G.A. L.; Miss Edna Womack Sunbeam Leader.

ELLER MEMORIAL—Mrs. J. E. Kirk, W.M.S. Pres.; Mrs. E. G. Parker, Y.W.A. C.

FLORIDA STREET—Mrs. C. N. Hutchinson, W.M.S. Pres.; Mrs. W. P. Whitley, Y.W.A. C.; Mrs. E. C. White, G.A. L.; Mrs. W. M. Cassell, R.A. L.; Mrs. N. W. Bolejack, Sunbeam Leader.

FOREST AVENUE—Mrs. J. W. Marsh, W.M.S. Pres.; Mrs. Wilson Woodcock, Y.W.A. C.; Miss Lula Brooks, G.A. L.; Mrs. Geneva Fitzgerald, Sunbeam Leader.

MAGNOLIA STREET—Mrs. L. L. Jarvis, Pres. W.M.S.; Mrs. H. S. Noah, Y. W. A. Counselor.

POMONA—Mrs. W. G. Teague, Pres. W.M.S.; Mrs. Emo Wherry, G.A. Leader.

REVOLUTION—Miss Sallie Burgess, Pres. W.M.S.; Miss Sallie Burgess, Y.W.A. C.; Mrs. Jewel Martin, G.A. L.; Miss Sallie Burgess, R.A. L.; Miss Lora Carter, Sunbeam Leader.

SIXTEENTH STREET—Mrs. T. W. Michael, Pres. W.M.S.

STEVENS MEMORIAL—Mrs. C. B. Brisson, Pres. W.M.S.; Miss Ethel Brown, G.A. L.; Mrs. L. M. Deaton, Sunbeam Leader.

WEBSTER MEMORIAL—Mrs. W. H. Lucas, W.M.S. Pres.; Miss Selma Scales, G.A. L.

GUILFORD—Mrs. E. L. Weston, Pres. W.M.S.

HIGH POINT, FIRST—Mrs. W. F. Clayton, W.M.S. Pres.; Miss Cecile Armentrout, Y.W.A. C.; Miss Helen Smith, G.A. L.; Mr. Claude Smith, Jr., R.A. L.; Miss Katie Sue Stanfield, Sunbeam Leader.

GREEN STREET—Gladys Ellington, Pres. W.M.S.; Mrs. I. W. Daniel, Y.W.A. L.; Esther Harrington, G.A. L.; Nora Haney, R.A. L.; Mrs. Amos Carroll, Sunbeam Leader.

HILLIARD MEMORIAL—Mrs. J. B. Ellis, Pres. W.M.S.; Mrs. Fred Bryant, Y.W.A. C.; Mrs. C. H. Farmer, Sunbeam Leader

NORTH MAIN STREET—Mrs. Alice Davis, Pres. W.M.S.

NORTH PARK—Mrs. Paul Frye, Pres. W.M.S.; Mrs. P. H. Gurley, Sunbeam Leader.

SOUTH SIDE—Mrs. J. S. Cameron, Pres. W.M.S.; Daisy Shawe, G.A. L.; Mrs. W. R. Briggs, Sunbeam Leader.

WEST END—Mrs. T. P. Andrews, Pres. W.M.S.; Mrs. P. A. Snider, Y.W.A. C.; Miss Leona Chappell, G.A. L.; Mrs. Carl Harvey, Sunbeam Leader.

PLEASANT GARDEN—Mrs. J. E. Thompson, Pres. W.M.S.

REIDSVILLE, FIRST—Mrs. T. L. Sasser, Pres. W.M.S.; Mrs. J. M. Gold, Mrs. S. F. Wells, G.A. L.; Henry Love, R.A. L.; Mrs. J. H. Simpson, Sunbeam Leader.

MOUNT OLIVE—Mrs. J. H. Saunders, Pres. W.M.S.

PENN MEMORIAL—Mrs. M. H. Fitz, Pres. W.M.S., and Y.W.A. C.

ROCKY KNOLL—Mrs. L. C. Chandler, Pres W.M.S.

RUFFIN STACEY—Mrs. Lottie Schrum, Pres. W.M.S.

SUMMERFIELD—Mrs. A. C. Lloyd. Pres. W.M.S.

List of Messengers

ALLEN JAY—Rev. C. M. Floyd, Mrs. Henry Burrow, Mary Warren, Mealie Burrow, J. O. Warren.

CALVARY—Womble McCargo, Mrs. J. E. McCargo, Lester Terrell, Mr. and Mrs. J. F. Carroll.

FAIRVIEW—D. E. Trantham, Wade Durham, R. T. Coleman, Mrs. A. D. Hopkins, Miss M. Coleman.

GIBSONVILLE—Mr. and Mrs. W. E. Loy, Will Ferguson, Will Foster, J. R. Edwards, Joe Boggs.

GREENSBORO, FIRST—Mr. and Mrs. O. E. Lee, Genter Stephens, Geo. R. Bennett, Mrs. Nettie Hoge, A. A. Chandler, T. B. Gaskins.

ASHEBORO STREET—F. L. Paschall, J. S. Moore, J. J. Norwood, W. A. Coble, Mesdames M. D. Teague, A. Andrews.

BAILEY MEMORIAL—Mesdames W. D. Stewart, Mabel Kindley and W. J. Mitchell.

BESSEMER—C. L. Casey, C. L. Murray, J. C. Turner, W. P. Haynes, Miss Lila Barton, Mesdames O. F. Barnes, J. F. Layton, W. A. Aydelette, Jr.

ELLER MEMORIAL—Raymond Kincaid, Farrell James, H. M. Angel, John Hobbs, Richard Hobbs, Miss Elizabeth Lassiter, Mesdames G. O. Basinger, W. H. Lambert.

FLORIDA STREET—J. L. Roberson, E. C. White, Jr., Mrs. J. B. Rumbley, P. L. Robinson, Misses Bertha Hall, Inez Bolejack.

FOREST AVENUE—Wilson Woodcock, J. T. J. Battle, Mrs. Geneva Fitzgerald.

LATHAM PARK—Rev. C. D. Barton, Walter Moore, J. C. Parrish.

MAGNOLIA STREET—L. C. Davis, N. J. Jarvis, D. L. Wrenn.

POMONA—Rev. C. M. Oates, Mesdames C. M. Oates, W. H. Brown and H. L. Nall.

REVOLUTION—Rev. T. A. Baber, T. A. Moffett, J. H. Martin, Miss Burgess.

SIXTEENTH STREET—Mesdames Morgan Smith, T. W. Michael, W. R. Fuller, W. B. Cook, Walter Godfrey, Neal Herrin.

STEVENS MEMORIAL—Mesdames J. B. Brown, J. H. Ham, C. A. Self, J. E. Sutton.

WEBSTER MEMORIAL—Mr. and Mrs. C. V. Webster, E. D. Young, Mesdames B. H. Scott, J. F. Graves, W. H. Lucas, G. H. Payne and H. L. Cartledge.

GUILFORD—Rev. Robert Costner, Setzer Weston, Mesdames Hettie Kennedy, B. F. Butler, E. L. Weston, Eugene Hodgin, Miss Mary Gilbert.

HIGH POINT, FIRST—G. H. Jones, A. E. Tate, Miss Thelma Patrick, Mesdames A. B. Conrad, W. F. Clayton, G. L. Asbury, C. E. Siceloff.

GREEN STREET—Carl Edmonds, Clarence Keever, W. E. Myers, Mrs. M. W. Busser.

HILLIARD MEMORIAL—C. M. Howell, H. E. Taylor, J. J. Haywood, Mesdames Margaret E. Hill, H. O. Miller, J. W. Saunders.

NORTH MAIN STREET—R. L. Reeves, Mesdames Alice Davis, Ed Crisco, R. L. Teague, Spencer Epps, S. R. Clinard.

NORTH PARK—L. W. Glenn, Mrs. Paul Frye, Misses Inez Jones, Drucilla Fagg.

SOUTH SIDE—Mr. and Mrs. W. K. Briggs, Mr. and Mrs. G. H. Lines, Mrs. Henson, Miss Daisy Shaw.

WEST END—Mr. and Mrs. C. N. Scott, Mrs. P. A. Snider, W. A. Hedrick, Eugene Gregory, H. W. Smith.

LEBANON—B. G. Yowe, Mrs. J. B. Carter.

MT. ZION—L. L. Spoon, A. C. Lackamy, Wade Durham, C. D. Branson, George Spoon, Roxie Foster, Louis Spoon, Lorena Lackamy.

OAK GROVE—C. W. Smith, Mesdames W. A. Kenan, J. H. Miles.

OSBORNE CHAPEL—Rev. C. W. Myrick, R. R. Osborne, J. C. May, G. S. McCandless.

OSCEOLA—Mr. and Mrs. L. C. Cole, Mr. and Mrs. E. R. Brande.

PLEASANT GARDEN—Mesdames E. L. Rummage, J. E. Thompson, Lillie T. Jordon, Miss Bessie Taylor, Mr. Smith.

REIDSVILLE, FIRST—Henry E. Love, Mesdames M. L. Rice, H. L. Morrison, R. T. Burton, M. A. White, C. H. Pettigrew, R. H. Pleasants, R. L. Hubbard, W. H. Bolyn.

MOUNT OLIVE—Mesdames J. H. Saunders, D. P. Driscoll, Odell Delapp.

PENN MEMORIAL—Rev. Daniel Overbey, James Overbey, Mesdames J. W. Gillie, D. W. Overbey.

ROCKY KNOLL—Rev. L. C. Chandler, Ray Canler, Mesdames R. A. Laughlin, G. L. York, T. C. Frazier, H. A. Morgan, Vera Alred, Pearl Coble.

RUFFIN STACEY—Mr. Pergerson, Earlie Wattlington, W. C. Eavens, Mesdames J. T. Cardwell, Lottie Schrum, Lillie Burton, May E. London, Dora Massey.

SMITH GROVE—Johnny Johnson, Jonah Pitts, R. O. Nuckles, Roy McCollums, C. S. Long, Drew Smith, J. A. Farrington, J. G. Pender.

SUMMERFIELD—Mr. and Mrs. W. E. Strader, Mr. and Mrs. T. F. Tuttle, R. L. Stigall, Mrs. Clyde Robinson.

Proceedings

of the

FORTY-FOURTH ANNUAL SESSION

of the

PIEDMONT BAPTIST ASSOCIATION

Held With The

Eller Memorial Baptist Church

Greensboro, N. C.

October 20, 21, 1937

WEDNESDAY MORNING SESSION

1. The Association was opened with a devotional service led by Rev. J. Ben Eller.

2. The Moderator stated that he would be out of the Association for several months and thought it would be well to appoint a nominating committee to nominate officers for the ensuing year. The following committee was appointed: Wilson Woodcock, T. L. Sasser and J. N. Bowman.

3. H. M. Angel spoke words of welcome. The response was given by Mr. Grover H. Jones, of High Point.

4. A roll of the churches was called and messengers from thirty-eight churches responded to the roll call.

5. The Moderator appoints the following committees:

Committee on Committees—J. Ben Eller and Mrs. Nettie Hoge.

Committee on Program—Hughey O. Miller, D. W. Overbey, and J. H. Saunders.

6. The following visitors were recognized: Tom Bray, E. C. Roach, A. D. Kenette, A. G. Carter, T. H. Biles, T. L. Helms, H. H. Biles, C. W. Hilliard, Mr. Terrell.

7. The Nominating Committee makes the following report:

Moderator—J. Ben Eller.
Vice-Moderator—Dr. J. T. J. Battle
Clerk and Treasurer—O. E. Lee.

Brother Eller stated that he would not have much time to give to the work. After this statement from Brother Eller, Grover H. Jones was nominated. The election resulted as follows: Moderator, Grover H. Jones, Vice-Moderator, Dr. J. T. J. Battle; Clerk and Treasurer O. E. Lee.

8. The report on Religious Literature was presented by D. W. Overbey. Upon motion to adopt the report the subject was discussed by R. F. Terrell, representative of the Biblical Recorder. Brother Terrell stated that he would be glad to have words of appreciation for the services of Brother Clarence A. Smith who had served as Moderator of the Association for the past sixteen years and also words of appreciation for the services of J. M. Hilliard who had served as Vice-Moderator for many years printed in the Biblical Recorder. Motion was passed that the Nominating Committee be asked to prepare words of appreciation for the services of the retiring officers to be sent to the Biblical Recorder.

The report was adopted.

BIBLICAL RECORDER

For a hundred and two years the BIBLICAL RECORDER has sought to serve the Baptists of North Carolina and the world. It seeks in a constructive way to comply with the command of the Master to carry the Gospel to every part of the world. Page five is set aside in almost every issue for this particular work. The sixty-eight Baptists who compose the stockholders in the Biblical Recorder Publishing Company are lending every effort to make The Recorder of interest to our people and to instruct them concerning our Baptist work. For a number of years they received no dividend, but they have received, in later years, six percent on their investment. But for the other interests of the Biblical Recorder Publishing Company, publication of the Biblical Recorder would have been suspended ten years ago; but the income from rent on the building and other sources have been taken to pay the deficit on publishing the paper. The Christian culture of our future Baptist homes depends, in no small degree, upon the contribution the Biblical Recorder makes to that end.

People are largely influenced by what they read. The Biblical Recorder seeks to bring our people weekly a summary of our Baptist news, local and general. It seeks to give a Christian and Baptist interpretation to the events of the day. It seeks to record achievements of our schools, churches, Sunday Schools, B.T.U.'s, W.M.U.'s, and laymen's work. It carries news from our missionaries at home and abroad, and informs the reader of what is being accomplished thru his contributions.

The Home Circle offers help for the development of the spiritual and intellectual needs in every young church member. It seeks to inculcate high ideals in our young people and to be of real help in the development of Christian character. All this means much good for the future generations. Never before was there a time when our boys and girls had greater need for wholesome literature which will instill high ideals, create a desire for pure living, and stimulate them to render unselfish service. The Biblical Recorder seeks to lend aid at this particular point.

The price is $2.00 per year, or a six months' subscription may be taken for $1.00. It is very desirable that the circulation be increased from 13,450 to 25,000 as a minimum. More than three hundred of our churches have the Recorder in the budget, sending the paper to ten per cent, or more, of the church membership.

Respectfully submitted,

D. W. OVERBEY

9. The Committee on Program reported that Dr. J. Clyde Turner could not be present today and that he would make his report on Foreign Missions at 2:25 P. M. tomorrow, and that Wilson Woodcock would make the report on State Missions this morning.

10. The report on Home Missions was presented by Wilson Woodcock. Upon motion to adopt the report the subject was discussed by Wilson Woodcock. The report was adopted.

REPORT ON HOME MISSIONS

The Home Mission Board is lifting up Christ in the homeland among the Indians, the foreigners, the Negroes, the under-privileged in the cities and congested industrial sections, and in Cuba and Panama. In all the departments of work, including the field force, the

Sanatorium, the rescue missions, the goodwill centers, and schools, the Board has 327 missionaries working in 850 mission stations. During the past convention year we have placed in the field 35 missionaries and have opened 36 new mission stations. This enlargement of our work was made possible by the receipts from the Bottoms Trust and unsolicited designations.

The Board has adjusted its budget so as to operate on a cash basis. For the past three and a half years no money has been borrowed for current work.

During the past year $108,313.88 was paid on the principal of the old debt. The Board rejoices that its percentage in the Hundred Thousand Club has been increased. It hopes that added emphasis will be given the Hundred Thousand Club and that a larger amount will be raised each year until all the debts of the agencies of the Southern Baptist Convention have been paid.

Respectfully submitted.
WILSON WOODCOCK

11. After singing a hymn, reading the Scripture, and prayer by Brother J. Ben Eller, Rev. C. N. Royal preached the Introductory Sermon. The text was John 17:18, subject, "The Christian's Mission in the World." The sermon was inspiring and helpful.

12. The following new pastors were presented by J. M. Hilliard: C. W. Myrick, James E. Swinson, and A. C. Lovelace, assistant pastor of the First Church.

13. The Committee on Program reported that the question of the Shubal Stearns Memorial would be the special order at 1:30 P. M.

14. The Committee on Committees reported the following committees:

Committee on New Churches—T. L. Sasser, Dr. A. B. Conrad, and Dr. J. Clyde Turner.

Committee on Resolutions—A. Lincoln Fulk, J. H. Saunders, Mrs. A. Andrews.

15. After announcements were made, the morning session closed with prayer by Brother R. F. Terrell.

AFTERNOON SESSION

16. The question of a memorial at the grave of Shubal Stearns was presented by H. M. Stroup, of the Randolph Baptist Association. The Moderator was instructed last year to confer with the Moderators of the Randolph Baptist Association and the Sandy Creek Association. The following Committee was appointed to cooperate with the other Associations in arranging for the memorial: Grover H. Jones, Dr. J. Clyde Turner, J. Ben Eller.

17. The report on Denominational Program was presented by Grover H. Jones. Upon motion to adopt the report the subject was discussed by Grover H. Jones.

DENOMINATIONAL PROGRAM

The Scriptures make it clear that Jesus came to earth to mediate and interpret God to man and to announce His program to evangelize the world. As evidence of this fact, we have His own words when He said: "As my Father has sent me, even so send I you." "Make disciples of all the nations...baptize...teach, and, lo, I am with you alway, even unto the end of the world." And one who reads the Book of Acts will be convinced that the apostles and early disciples conceived of their task as carrying on the work which Jesus had begun.

Moreover, from a careful reading of the Scriptures, it will be seen that Christ's program included preaching, teaching, healing and ministering to need; that His program was world-wide in scope and that His field of service was humanity.

As Baptists we have adopted what we call our Coöperative Program through which we are undertaking to carry out the fourfold mission of Jesus through State Missions, Home Missions, and Foreign Missions; through Sunday Schools, Christian Colleges and Seminaries; through hospitals; through orphanages and old ministers' relief.

As to content our Cooperative Program is the program of Jesus, begun by Him and committed to us. As to means and methods it is the product of Baptist intelligence. Where two or more individuals, or churches try to work together, a plan of action is necessary. Means and methods must be found; and for this purpose Christian stewards use their God-given intelligence.

It is gratifying to report that the denominational program as a plan by which and through which we must work to the best advantage of all our denominational objects grows in favor. We believe this plan will continue to grow in favor with our people if our Pastors and church leaders take a little more time to explain it definitely to them. May we become more mindful of the fact that we shall have a part in carrying the gospel to the uttermost part of the world in proportion to the measure in which we let our beneficience flow through our Cooperative Program.

Respectfully submitted,
GROVER H. JONES

18. The following committees were appointed by the Committee on Committees:

Committee on Place and Preacher—T. E. Baber, C. M. Scott, D. W. Overbey, Mrs. W. F. Clayton, Walter J. Smith;

Committee on Program—C. N. Royal, F. L. Paschal, J. C. Gillespie, Miss Thelma Patrick, and E. A. Long;

Auditing Committee—A. A. Chandler, J. S. Moore, Miss Ruth Scott;

Committee to Nominate Delegates to the State Convention—J. N. Bowman, Mrs. H. L. Morrison, W. B. Cook;

Committee to Nominate Leader for the Verbal Report Hour—J. U. Garner, C. C. Chandler, Mrs. J. N. Gillie.

19. Rev. James E. Swinson, Pastor of the Trinity Baptist Church, presents a request for a letter from our Association for the Trinity Baptist Church to unite with the Randolph Baptist Association. The letter was granted.

20. The report on State Missions was presented by N. F. Britt. Upon motion to adopt the report, the subject was discussed by M. A. Huggins, General Secretary of the Baptist State Convention. The report is adopted.

STATE MISSIONS

For more than a century the objective of State Missions has been to win the people to Christ and then to the fellowship of our Baptist churches. During more recent years it has sought through establishing Sunday School and B.T.U. Departments to teach and train those who come into the churches for active fellowship and cooperative promotion of Kingdom service.

Many needy and strategic churches have received pastoral and church building assistance which has enabled them to develop strong mission programs and return such investment one hundred fold. Yet, the task is merely begun. A distressing number of worthy pastors must find work to do with their hands in order to support a family of normal Christian size and neglect their visitations while possibly a greater number are well paid for actual service rendered. Yes, we have many weak churches deserving state aid and a few unprepared pastors who need to adapt themselves to cooperative extension and church efficiency.

Rev. and Mrs. M. C. Lunsford, whom our Board has had with our Indians of Robeson County for several years continue to do a great work there.

Our Convention is helping the Negroes pay the salary of Rev. W. C. Somerville, who is achieving notable success with the quarter million North Carolina Negro Baptist. Mr. Clanton has recently been assigned to their Sunday School work.

The increasing number of students in state and denominational institutions demand far more service than our one efficient student secretary, Miss Cleo Mitchell, can hope to render.

For some years our Board has sponsored a splendid work with the sick veterans of Oteen.

We now have two general missionaries to serve the whole state which reveals a self-evident need.

The great Christian general of China has won the admiration of the civilized world with his resistance to Japan's invasion but the unexpected spirit of the people behind the lines has made it possible. We, too, must sustain State Missions if the true spirit of Home and Foreign Missions is to survive.

Respectfully submitted,

N. F. BRITT

21. The report on Social Service was presented by Dr. A. B. Conrad. Upon motion to adopt the report, Dr. Conrad presented Mr. H. L. Koontz, who addressed the Association on the Prohibition Question. Remarks were made by J. M. Hilliard. The report is adopted.

REPORT ON SOCIAL SERVICE

Social service is a part of the program of the church as taught by Christ and enjoined by the writers of the New Testament. It is the gospel at work in human relations.

While the first duty of the church is the winning of men to personal faith in Christ as Savior, yet the Gospel has its social aspects; it is designed to change society as a whole and that by relentless war on every form of evil. It must "render unto Caesar the things that are Caesar's" if it be true to its mission. The church is responsible for conditions that injure and ruin men until it has done its utmost to destroy those conditions, on the level of Christ's teaching and practice there is no middle ground. Men must vote as well as pray. So evil in any form that entrenches itself in domestic, social, commercial or political life is an open challenge to the church to make open and violent attack upon it. The church must save society or lose itself.

Perilous times are upon us. Radical changes have taken place in the various social relations. Society is in a ferment. Sacred and unalienable rights are threatened, holy institutions are imperiled, free government is being undermined and it is not too much to say that liberty as we cherish it is in the balance.

A brief survey will show how true this is. There is a growing disregard for law and the sacredness of human life. Law is openly flouted, the spirit of anarchy stalks abroad. According to government reports our nation has an annual fifteen billion dollar crime bill. There is a death by murder or manslaughter every forty minutes, a larceny every fifty-four minutes, a burglary every two minutes, a car theft every minute and a half, and felonious assault every twelve minutes. The crime wave is apalling. Morals are degenerating; old restraints are thrown off. A subtle philosophy of life termed "self-expression" runs a strong deep current in much of the current literature and is taught in many of our schools. It has gripped the masses. Translated into simple speech it means "live your own life in your own way—do as you please". As a consequence there is alarming increase of vicious habits, sexual laxity, and spread of private disease that can only mean physical deterioration and race suicide in the end.

The foundations of the home are being undermined by many currents of evil, chief among which is the breaking down of parental authority. In multitudes of homes children are a law unto themselves. Hence our courts and prisons are crowded with youths—boys and girls of teen age. Divorce is on the increase, the sanctity of the marriage relation has lost its significance. For trivial reasons men and women break this sacred relation and go their ways and try other experiments. The first institution God set up for man was the home. He bound man and woman by bonds that may be broken for only one cause. A nation can never rise above the home life of its people or long survive the breaking down of its sanctity.

The Christian Sabbath, God's appointment for rest and worship, has largely lost its significance in the life of the world. With multitudes it has gone into discard; it has no significance other than a day for amusements: movies, ball games, golf links, joy rides, travel, feasting, sprees, and general abandon. "All the nations that forget God shall be cast into Hell," the hell of anarchy.

War between capital and labor goes violently on. Strikes, riots, usurpation of property rights, bloodshed are on every side. Events have recently transpired in this conflict that strike at the very foundations of government and all good order in society.

The clamor and tumult and carnage of war are heard and seen round the world—war of aggression inspired by greed for land and lust for gold. Swiftly there is going on reversion to the law of the jungle, of tooth and fang, that might makes right. Thor is in the saddle, booted and spurred for conquest. The spirit of war sweeping like a whirlpool threatens to draw all nations into its vortex. Most of the nations are armed camps and digging in for the day of battle. Most of the statesmen have the jitters dreading what may happen at sunrise.

And the liquor business, what shall be said of that mother of iniquities and prolific breeder of woe, sorrow and despair. The repeal of prohibition was a costly and fearful mistake. Not one of the promises of repeal has been kept. Not one of the prophesies has been fulfilled, but iniquity after iniquity has grown and flourished; the consumption of liquor has greatly increased. Bootlegging is a more flourishing and profitable enterprise than ever before. The saloon is here, only under another name. Women are openly drinking. In one great metropolitan city drunken women increased seventy-five per cent in three months. Inmates of Keely institutes have increased fifty-five per cent. Highways have become shambles and death holds tryst at every crossroads largely because of drunken drivers; automobile accidents pile up. In a neighboring city, $508,260.00 went over the counter of its liquor store in one year; $2,614.00 each day, and doubtless the major portion of that amount was spent by those who could ill afford to use it thus, and sorrowing and suffering, want and woe came to many.

What shall we say more? Surely it is a sad picture and there is a sore need for social service. The church is challenged to face these problems and under God to solve them. No other institution will do it or can do it. The church must awake, gird on its armor, and go forth to battle with these evils. With a new zeal, a holy enthusiasm, a better faith and surer confidence in its great Captain, Christ, it must fight to the death these evils in society that destroy both the souls and bodies of men in hell.

Respectfully submitted,

A. B. CONRAD

22. The report on the Orphanage was presented by E. A. Long. Upon motion to adopt the report the subject was discussed by J. A. McMillan. The report is adopted.

REPORT ON MILLS HOME

On November 11, 1885, the first child was received into our Baptist Orphanage, at Thomasville. Since the beginning, the work has gone steadily forward under the direction of consecrated and wise leadership. And above all, our Heavenly Father has placed His stamp of approval upon the work.

"By adopting and pursuing a wise financial policy the Orphanage has accumulated assets worth more than a million dollars and has rendered aid to more than 4,000 needy children."

The present policy of the Orphanage is that no child be received without careful investigation on the part of the Orphanage. The Orphanage is constantly being confronted with two embarrassments: First, it is impossible to make room for all who apply for admission; and, Second, it is equally impossible for the authorities to investigate all applications as fast as they would like to. For these reasons those making application should be patient with the Orphanage officials.

One of the outstanding problems of the Orphanage is the financial side. Its chief support comes thru once-a-month offerings from the Sunday Schools and the annual Thanksgiving Offering. Therefore we feel that the matter of our once-a-month offering of our Sunday Schools should be kept before our people each month.

In order that our people be better informed as to the work of our Orphanage it would be well for each Sunday School, that has not already done so, to have a goodly supply of "Charity and Children" on hand. This important organ of the Orphanage is full of wholesome reading as well as information about the Home. The circulation of this paper is now 27,870.

We have many things to be thankful for as we sum up the work of the past year, and rejoice that marked progress has been made in the work. May we face the New Year with renewed faith, zeal and courage, "Looking unto Jesus the author and finisher of our faith; who for the joy that was set before him endured the cross despising the shame, and is set down at the right hand of the throne of God."

Respectfully submitted,
E. A. LONG

23. Motion is passed combining the Executive Committee and the Promotion Committee and that the Committee be named the Executive-Promotion Committee.

24. Committee on Committee appoints the Committee to Nominate the Executive-Promotion Committee: Wilson Woodcock, H. O. Miller, Henry Love, A. C. Lovelace, J. E. Kirk.

25. The Treasurer presents his report which was referred to the Auditing Committee.

TREASURER'S REPORT

I herewith submit my report for the year ending September 30, 1937:

Balance on hand September 30, 1936		$ 12.30
Received from the Churches		165.25
		$177.55
DISBURSEMENTS:		
Clerk's Remuneration	$ 50.00	
Economy Printing Company, for Minutes and Postage	120.43	
Postage and Supplies	6.52	
	$176.95	
Balance on hand Sept. 30, 1937	.60	
	$177.55	$177.55

Respectfully submitted,
O. E. LEE

EXAMINED AND FOUND CORRECT
A. A. CHANDLER
J. S. MOORE

26. After announcements, Rev. John D. Newton, a visitor from the Liberty Baptist Association, was recognized.

The afternoon session was closed with prayer by M. A. Huggins.

NIGHT SESSION

27. At 7:15 the devotional service was led by Farrell James.

28. The report on the Baptist Training Union was presented by Miss Elizabeth Campbell. The report is adopted.

REPORT ON BAPTIST TRAINING UNION

During the past year our Baptist Training Union has made considerable progress. There has been two complete new organizations set up of four Unions each, adding about 51 new members. Our B.T.U. Association is next to the highest in seals and diplomas awarded for study courses in this State. We are very proud of the fact that this has been achieved.

There has been much extension work done by different churches which has been appreciated by the smaller churches that have benefitted by this work.

The fellowship enjoyed by the three districts is great. Early last spring a banquet was held at the Masonic Temple, Greensboro, for the Training Union members. There were about 300 present. Then, on August 14, 1937, the unions of this Association enjoyed a watermelon feast at the Battleground Country Park, Greensboro.

The annual Convention of the Associational B.T.U. was held last April at the First Baptist Church, Greensboro, N. C. We had several prominent speakers, one being our own State Secretary, Mr. Nathan C. Brooks.

The quarterly meetings of the Piedmont B.T.U. since that time have been very interesting and beneficial.

Never has there been a greater need for Christian Education than now. The work of our Lord demands trained boys and girls, men and women more than ever before. Our B.T.U.'s must furnish the greater part of the leaders and workers of tomorrow. We beg you pastors to cooperate with the work of the Baptist Training

Union in order that we may make more progress in training young people for tomorrow's leadership. **We are depending on you.**

Respectfully submitted,

ELIZABETH CAMPBELL

29. Vice-Moderator J. M. Hilliard presents Mr. J. Carl Bell, Associational B.T.U. Director, who makes some announcements relative to the Associational work, and then presents Miss Loretta Willis, the Director of the Greensboro District.

The following program is rendered:

The Asheboro Street Baptist Church B.T.U. presents a play, "Aunt Sally Joins the B.T.U."

Rev. A. Lincoln Fulk addresses the Association on "What the Adults Should Mean to the B.T.U."

The night session is closed with prayer by J. U. Garner.

THURSDAY MORNING

30. At 9:45 the devotional service was led by J. U. Garner.

31. The report on Woman' Work was presented by Miss Nettie Hoge. Upon motion to adopt the report the subject is discussed by Mrs. Hoge and J. Ben Eller. The report is adopted.

REPORT ON WOMAN'S WORK

The Woman's Missionary Union, Auxiliary to the Piedmont Association, offers the following report as their contribution in service and money to the year's achievements in Kingdom service.

This report is always made with conflicting emotions—a feeling of gratitude and appreciation for the year's attainments in Kingdom service, mingled with a regret for neglected opportunities and possibilities for greater service. With Paul—"We thank God and take courage", forgetting those things which are behind and reaching forth unto those things which are before, we press toward the mark for the prize for the high calling of God in Christ Jesus.

The calendar year gave to the Union twenty-nine Women's missionary societies and seventy-five auxiliaries. With the addition of six new organizations for the second quarter, it now has one hundred and ten active organizations—the largest number in its history.

This leaves eleven out of the forty churches of our Association without any missionary organizations. These eleven offer a field for enlistment and service to the other twenty-nine—and appeals to their pastors for interest and co-operation in perfecting the organizaion of their women is a work of such great importance.

The gifts of the Piedmont W.M.U. for 1936 amount to $20,537.39. This is $389.00 over the apportionment.

The separate, all-day meeting of the Young People has become an established and an outstanding part of our work.

The organization of a City Y.W.A. in Greensboro is the second organization of its kind in the State.

While the union, as a whole, does excellent work, it is a source of regret that so few attained the Standard of Excellence last year.

The United seasons of prayer, the organized personal service, mission study, enlistment, sacrificial giving and training of the young people are propelling forces in the local churches, which reaches to the uttermost parts of the earth and of which no record can be made or reported.

Respectfully submitted
MRS. NETTIE HATCHER HOGE,
Supt. Piedmont W.M.U.

32. The report on Hospital Work was presented by A. A. Walker. Upon motion to adopt the report the subject was discussed by A. A. Walker, Grover H. Jones and Smith A. Hagaman, Superintendent of the Hospital.

The report was adopted.

THE REPORT ON THE HOSPITAL

For fourteen years the Baptists of this state have assumed the responsibility of ministering to the sick through the medium of a hospital. Not once, when it was possible, have we passed by on the other side closing the doors of our compassion upon the sick. Nearly 40,000 times we have opened the doors of our hospital to the afflicted. In every instance we promised all the help it was humanly possible for us to give, even if it meant our coming this way again to pay an unsettled account. Thousands of these accounts have been paid in full at our own expense while a larger number have been supplemented so that all these patients have been dismissed with unburdened, gratefully free, hearts and the benedictions of our Heavenly Father.

Through the North Carolina Baptist Hospital, Inc., at Winston-Salem, we are reaching hundreds of thousands of people, touching them through the patients they send us, the nurses we train for them, and the donors whose hearts and interests have become a part of their gifts. Our receipts through the Cooperative Program are used to retire the building debt. Charity patients are utterly dependent upon our Mother's Day offerings. Also contributions of towels, sheets, pillow cases, tray covers, etc (according to specifications sent upon request) are a substantial help in this peculiarly Christian endeavor. May we season our gifts with fervent prayers and so cultivate the spirit of the Great Physician that more and more we shall become ministers of mercy to all those who groan under the burden of disease and affliction.

Respectfully submitted
A. A. WALKER

33. The report on Christian Education was presented by T. L. Sasser. Upon motion to adopt the report the subject was discussed by Dr. D. B. Bryan, Grover H. Jones. J. Ben Eller makes motion which is passed, that J. E. Kirk lead in prayer for Dr. R. L. Moore, who is sick. The report is adopted.

REPORT ON CHRISTIAN EDUCATION

The Southern Baptist Convention has two theological seminaries, one Bible institute, and the Woman's Missionary Union, auxiliary to the Convention, has one missionary training school. These are designed and maintained to train leaders for the churches of the Convention and missionaries for the fields at home and abroad. In addition to these four there should be mentioned here the educational institution established and maintained by the Home Mission Board in this country, in Cuba and in Panama, and those by the Foreign Mission Board in foreign lands.

The Southern Baptist Education Commission is the particular agency by which the Convention does its work in the field of what is usually called Christian Education. This Commission studies and interprets the educational activities of the denomination and reports them to the Convention.

The other Baptist schools, colleges and universities not specifically referred to already, which are also of special interest to this

Association, are owned and controlled by the State Convention, district associations, individual Baptists, or groups of individual Baptists. The Commission's 1937 report shows that there are now sixty-five of these institutions training Southern Baptist students.

The 1936 North Carolina Baptist Annual indicates that five of these colleges are under the definite control of the State Convention. They are as follows: Wake Forest, Meredith, Chowan, Mars Hill and Campbell. They have the first and most direct claim upon our financial support, co-operative interest and patronage. The trained leadership and constituency of this Association and its affiliated churches are the products of these North Carolina Baptist, and Southern Baptist, institutions, or similar schools.

We cannot reasonably hope to compete favorably with State schools in financial support and physical equipment, but by great sacrificial giving we must have the best that we can. We can sustain a high standard of scholarship. As touching Christian life and spiritual development we must far excel state schools or we shall nullify the only reason for having strictly denominational or so-called Christian educational institutions. As the churches support our colleges and seminaries, in that degree we shall increase in spiritual power. If we neglect them the churches will all but, if not entirely, perish. A spiritually trained leadership and constituency is imperative. Under the leadership of the Holy Spirit the churches through the proper agencies must train their own.

Respectfully submitted,
T. L. SASSER

33-a The report of the Committee to Nominate the Executive-Promotion Committee is adopted:

REPORT OF COMMITTEE TO NOMINATE MEMBERS OF THE EXECUTIVE-PROMOTIONAL COMMITTEE

Grover H. Jones, Chairman, High Point; O. E. Lee, Secretary, Greensboro; J. T. J. Battle, Greensboro; C. N. Royal, High Point; A. B. Conrad, High Point; J. C. Gillespie, Reidsville; T. L. Sasser, Reidsville; J. C. Tatum, Reidsville; J. Ben Eller, Greensboro; Mrs. Nettie H. Hoge, Greensboro; F. L. Paschal, Greensboro; Carl Bell, Greensboro.

Respectfully submitted,
WILSON WOODCOCK
J. E. KIRK
H. O. MILLER
H. E. LOVE

34. The report on Foreign Missions was presented by Dr. J. Clyde Turner. Upon motion to adopt the report the subject was discussed by Dr. Turner. The report is adopted.

REPORT ON FOREIGN MISSIONS

For ninety-two years Southern Baptists have been engaged in organized Foreign Mission work. It was started in 1845 with the appointment of four missionaries to work in China. Today we have 415 missionaries working in sixteen countries. Our missionaries have followed the example of Jesus in His three-fold ministry of preaching, teaching and healing. On our Foreign Mission fields we have 1715 churches, with a membership of 203,674. More than half of these churches are self-supporting. There are 347 schools and 36 hospitals.

During the past year there have been many evidences of divine favor on the work. The goodly number of 14,882 have been baptized on a profession of faith. For the first time in several years the total receipts of the Foreign Mission Board passed the million dollar mark. The debt, which a few years ago was more than a million dollars, has been reduced to something like $350,000.

In some of the countries the work has been greatly hindered by war and the unfriendly attitude of the governments. For more than a year the work in Spain has been disrupted by civil war. In China, many of our missionaries have been compelled to leave their posts. In Italy and Mexico the hostile attitude of the governments has made mission work difficult. In Roumania, the hand of persecution is being felt. South America is perhaps our most promising mission field today.

The world is still lost. After all the years of Christian history more than half of the people of the world have never heard the name of Jesus. Many of our churches have no part in the world-wide task which our Savior committed to us. During the past year there were more than 6,000 churches within the bounds of the Southern Baptist Convention which made no contribution towards sending the gospel throughout the world. More than 500 of these are in North Carolina, and five or six of them are in this Association. Surely we need to get in earnest about this holy task which the Master has intrusted to us.

Respectfully submitted,
J. CLYDE TURNER

35. Words of appreciation for the long period of faithful service of our retiring Moderator, Brother Clar-

ence A. Smith were presented by Dr. A. B. Conrad and approved. Motion passes that our Minutes this year be dedicated to Brother Smith. Words of appreciation for the long period of service of our Vice-Moderator, Brother J. M. Hilliard, were also spoken.

36. The following reports of committees were made and adopted:

COMMITTEE TO NOMINATE DELEGATES TO STATE CONVENTION

We the Committee recommend as Delegates, Grover H. Jones and Dr. J. T. J. Battle.

Respectfully submitted,
JAMES N. BOWMAN
W. B. COOK

COMMITTEE ON COMMITTEES ON ADVISORY BOARD

Our Committee names the following Committee to Nominate Church Advisory Committee: A. A. Walker, J. C. Gillespie, Mrs. W. H. McKeever.

COMMITTEE ON TIME, PLACE AND PREACHER

Your Committee recommends the following:

TIME—Wednesday and Thursday before the fourth Sunday in October, 1938.

PLACE—Hilliard Memorial Baptist Church, High Point, N. C.

PREACHER—Dr. A. B. Conrad; Alternate, Rev. J. C. Gillespie.

Respectfully submitted,
T. E. BABER
D. W. OVERBEY
C. M. SCOTT
MRS. W. F. CLAYTON
WALTER J. SMITH

The Program Committee announces that Dr. A. B. Conrad will lead the Hour of Prayer and Testimonies at the afternoon session.

The morning session closed with prayer by Brother T. L. Sasser.

THURSDAY AFTERNOON

At 1:30 the devotional service is lead by J. H. Saunders.

37. The report on Sunday Schools is presented by A. Lincoln Fulk. Upon motion to adopt the report the subject is discussed by A. Lincoln Fulk, F. L. Paschal and O. E. Lee. The report is adopted.

SUNDAY SCHOOL REPORT

Teaching, preaching, healing; these three services constituted the main ministry of Jesus. And should one examine the records, he would find Jesus in the role of teacher more than any other. The Gospel must make its appeal to the heart by way of the mind. Thus today our teaching and training programs should stand out in bold relief in the work of the churches. Jesus recognized and we realize that taught people are won people. Nearly all our baptisms for the past year and other years have come through the Sunday School and a great majority of those who join our churches first join our Sunday Schools. But the work of the Sunday School should not stop here. Its task is not only to win souls to Christ but to save lives for Christ. Thus the work of the School is not ended when a person Joins the church. To win to Christ and to build up in Christ are the two main objectives of our Schools. Let us see how we are meeting these two objectives:

The BAPTIST ANNUAL for 1936 shows that we have in the State 2,451 churches with a reported membership of 465,698 members, and that we have 2,437 Sunday Schools with a membership of 391,194. Thus we have more than fourteen churches without Sunday Schools and nearly 75,000 less enrolled in Sunday School than we have members of our churches. Should we make a study of the average attendance in the Schools compared to the enrollment we should find that we are doing little better than 50 per cent in efficiency in attendance.

Therefore, we present a comparative report showing our accomplishments as compared to our responsibilities. According to reports we are just about half-way doing our work as Sunday Schools. Last year our Association reported a membership of 14,616, with an average attendance of 6,947, or much less than half of our enrollment. Subtracting those enrolled in the Home Departments, our average attendance would still be less than half our enrollment. It would seem that our primary problem is not enrollment but enlistment in regular attendance; we do not need to get names to report but pupils to teach. We need to promote regular attendance in our schools.

The report shows that our Association has 13,958 church members with about half that number in Sunday School. How can we hope to reach the outside with a large number of unenlisted church members? Our greatest and most immediate field for Sunday School enlargement lies within the membership of our churches.

There was not a school in the entire Association that was standard last year. Our record system should serve the pupil and our emphasis should be as such. Out of 42 churches, only six held Daily Vacation Bible Schools. Out of 953 teachers and officers, 192 hold study course diplomas.

There were 273 baptisms from the schools last year. If we credit all of these to the efforts of teachers and officers, we shall find that it took nearly four to lead one soul to Christ. Can each teacher and officer do less than lead one soul to Christ in an entire year?

Records of our Association reveal as an average the following astounding summaries:

1. That we have two members enrolled for each regular attendant.

2. That we have one church member unenrolled for each one enrolled.

3. That we have two possibilities for each one enrolled in our schools, or four for each regular attendant.

4. Therefore, we should multiply our present efforts by two.

In the light of the foregoing facts and realizing that a mere insistence on the record systems will not suffice, we feel led to make the following suggestions for our work next year:

1. An enrollment equal to the church membership.
2. An average attendance of 75 per cent of the enrollment.
3. Improved teaching and planned programs that will inspire regular attendance.
4. The enlistment of more church members in the school.
5. At least two study courses annually, one for the teachers and one for officers.
6. That we promote at least 12 D.V.B.S. in our churches.
7. That our schools be definitely evangelistic; that Christ be presented as Lord, Savior, and Keeper in every lesson.
8. That we do not merely "adopt" this report but that we DO something about it.

Respectfully submitted,

A. LINCOLN FULK

38. The report on Minister's Relief and Annuity was presented by J. C. Gillespie. Upon motion to adopt the report the subject is discussed by J. C. Gillespie. The report is adopted.

REPORT ON MINISTERIAL RELIEF AND ANNUITY

The primary interest of the Relief and Annuity Board is in the ministry of the Southern Baptist Convention, and among the services which it seeks to render is that of getting our people to a proper evaluation of this ministry. Ministers are given to help all of us to grow up in Christ. But this service is not limited to ministers alone but is extended to churches as well. The time has come when no church can have the proper respect of the community in which a minister serves, who, when retired, is dependent on the generosity of friends, or public charity. This neccessary provision may be made through the "Age Security Plan" of the Relief and Annuity Board.

And again the service of this Board has been extended to all Boards and institutions within the bounds of the Southern Baptist Convention, for the employees of our Mission Boards, of our Orphanages, of our Hospitals, and of our schools, colleges, and seminaries, all of which are excluded from participation in the government plan. And it will be the part of wisdom for all above mentioned boards, institutions, and agencies of the Convention to utilize the services of the Relief and Annuity Board rather than to apply to commercial companies; because this Board is operated in a purely benevolent way, and performs its services without pecuniary reward. And further, retirement and disability annuities can be obtained through this Board than can be obtained elsewhere for the same amount of money.

We should greatly appreciate the efforts made by the Relief and Annuity Board in their efforts to provide relief for these servants of the Lord, and we recommend that we stand loyally and practically by them in their great work.

Respectfully submitted,

JAS. C. GILLESPIE

39. The following visitors are recognized: V. H. Harrell, N. C. Teague.

40. The hour of Prayer and Testimonies was in charge of Dr. A. B. Conrad, and proved to be most helpful.

41. The report on Obituaries prepared by Tom W.

Bray was read by the Clerk in the absence of Brother Bray. The report was adopted.

REPORT ON OBITUARIES

Jesus said, "Verily verily, I say unto you; except a corn of wheat fall into the ground and die, it abideth alone." Death to the Christian is a call to come home. This call has been answered by many of our beloved brethren and sisters in the Lord since our last Association met a year ago. Many more will pass on to be with Jesus before this body shall meet again. "Therefore, be ye also ready: for in such an hour as ye think not the Son of Man cometh."

Respectfully submitted,
TOM W. BRAY

42. The following reports of committees were made and adopted:

COMMITTEE ON RECEPTION OF NEW CHURCHES

The Committee recommends that the application from the Buchanan Baptist Church be given further consideration by the Committee.

Respectfully submitted,
T. L. SASSER
A. B. CONRAD
J. CLYDE TURNER

COMMITTEE TO NOMINATE CHURCH ADVISORY COMMITTEE

The Committee makes the following recommendation:

Dr. J. Clyde Turner, Dr. A. B. Conrad, T. L. Sasser, Mrs. Nettie Hoge, Grover H. Jones, Dr. J. T. J. Battle, O E. Lee.

The following report was adopted:

REPORT ON PROGRAM FOR 1938

RELIGIOUS LITERATURE—J. H. Saunders.
FOREIGN MISSIONS—J. B. Eller.
INTRODUCTORY SERMON—A. B. Conrad.
DENOMINATIONAL PROGRAM—T. L. Sasser.
STATE MISSIONS—F. L. Paschal.
SOCIAL SERVICE—Wilson Woodcock.
ORPHANAGE—John U. Garner.

WOMAN'S MISSIONARY WORK—Mrs. Nettie H. Hoge.
BAPTIST TRAINING UNION—J. Carl Bell.
HOSPITAL—T. E. Baber.
CHRISTIAN EDUCATON—A. C. Lovelace.
HOME MISSIONS—J. E. Kirk.
SUNDAY SCHOOLS—A. A. Walker.
MINISTERS' RELIEF AND ANNUITY—J. N. Bowman.
OBITUARIES—G. H. Liner.

Respectfully submitted,
C. N. ROYAL
F. L. PASCHAL
J. C. GILLESPIE
MISS THELMA PATRICK
E. A. LONG

COMMITTEE ON VERBAL REPORTS

The Committee recommends Harvey L. Paschal.

Respectfully submitted,
JOHN U. GARNER
MRS. J. W. GILLEY

REPORT OF RESOLUTIONS COMMITTEE

The gracious hospitality and brotherly kindness of the people of Eller Hemorial Church and the sister churches of Greensboro have met every physical and temporal need of this the forty-fourth annual session of the Piedmont Baptist Association,

Therefore, Be it Resolved:

1. That we express to the host church our appreciation for the use of the building and for other gracious kindnesses.

2. That we extend to the other Baptist churches of the city our deep gratitude for their noble assistance in providing bountiful meals,

3. That we pay our special thanks to the women of the host church, and the members of the Y.M.C.A. staff for their untiring efforts to meet our every need.

4. That the officers of the Association be commended for their noble and unselfish services.

Respectfully submitted,
A. LINCOLN FULK
MRS. A. ANDREWS
J. H. SAUNDERS

REPORT OF AUDITING COMMITTEE

The Committee finds the Treasurer's records correct.

Respectfully submitted,
A. A. CHANDLER
J. S. MOORE

Following the singing of "God Be With You" the session closed with prayer by Dr. J. Clyde Turner.

In Memoriam

GIBSONVILLE:

Mrs. Hudgins

GREENSBORO, FIRST:

Mr. James A Barbour
Miss Sallie Brooks
Mrs. C. L. Blanchard
Mrs. A. G. Burgess
Mr. R. A. Clay
Mrs. T. L. Henderson
Mrs. A. T. Morris
Dr. (Rev.) Chas. H. Nash
Mr. S. H. Mitchell
Mr. J. R. Sneed
Mrs. J. E. Seawell
Mrs. J. A. Wright
Mr. A. B. Walker
Mrs. J. S. Wright

ASHEBORO STREET:

Mrs. J. A. Causey
Mr. A. F. Brooks
Mr. H. P. Clarida
Mrs. Wm. Stephenson
Mrs. Lydia Hackney
Mrs. E. C. Moffitt
Mrs. Mary True
Mr. R. D. Samuel
Mrs. Minnie J. Simmons
Mrs. J. J. Meyers
Mr. Ira Scott
Mr. J. W. Mitchell
Mrs. W. H. Matthews

BESSEMER:

Mrs. C. L. Casey

ELLER MEMORIAL:

Mr. Lindo Collins

FLORIDA STREET:

Mrs. Stella Roberst
Mrs. J. L. Inman
Mr. G. H. McMath

FOREST AVENUE:

Mrs. R. C. Prince
Mr. W. L. Andrews
Mr. W. S. Dowd
Mrs. Annie Patterson
Mr. J. E. Brunson

MAGNOLIA STREET:

Mrs. Annie Dabbs
Mrs. George Long
Mr. Al Lanning

REVOLUTION:

Mrs. E. A. Johnson

SIXTEENTH STREET:

Mrs. J. L. Snyder
Mrs. Nettie Jordan
Miss Annie Cecil
Mr. N. C. Smith

STEVENS MEMORIAL:

Mr. A. E. Mills

WEBSTER MEMORIAL:

Miss Mildred Gregory

In Memoriam

HIGH POINT, FIRST:
- Mr. Fletcher Suttenfield
- Mr. J. Knox Wilson
- Deacon C. C. Walker
- Mr. J. W. Wilson
- Mrs. Janie Burch
- Dr. T. Wingate Andrews, Deacon.
- Mrs. T. L. Warford
- Mrs. H. G. Connally
- Mr. W. B. Reese
- Mrs. Bascom Hoskins
- Mrs. A. N. Yowell
- Mr. J. C. Teague
- Deacon A. J. Bolling
- Mr. Andrew Knight
- Miss Alice Palmer
- Mr. E. D. Stephenson
- Mr. W. I. Estes
- Mr. J. P. Rawley
- Deacon W. T. Anderson

WEST END:
- Mr. Walter Bowers
- Mr. J. R. Carter

GREEN STREET:
- Mr. L. C. Stallings
- Mr. P. D. Hutchins
- Mr. Lynn Haney
- Mrs. J. A. Sprinkle

NORTH MAIN:
- Mrs. J. G. Martin
- Mrs. Pearl Kivitte
- Mrs. R. J. Clinard
- Mrs. J. W. Riley
- Mr. M. J. Grissett

OSCEOLA:
- Miss Kate Jones

REIDSVILLE, FIRST:
- Mrs. C. C. Paschall
- Mr. C. C. Paschall
- Mr. T. R. Whittemore

MOUNT OLIVE:
- Mrs. Luke Gilbert
- Mr. Dewey Duggins

PENN MEMORIAL:
- Master George Stroud
- Mrs. F. C. Betts

Constitution

ARTICLE 1. The Association shall be called the Piedmont Baptist Association.

ARTICLE 2. It shall be composed of the ordained ministers who are members of, and those who may have pastoral charges within the Associational District, and three delegates from each church in the district aforesaid, and churches having a membership exceeding 300 shall be entitled to one additional delegate for every 200 members or fraction thereof in excess of 300.

ARTICLE 3. The said delegates shall, before taking their seats, produce letters from respective churches showing their appointment as delegates.

ARTICLE 4. The Associational session shall be held at least once a year.

ARTICLE 5. The officers shall be a Moderator, Vice-Moderator, Clerk, and Treasurer. If deemed expedient by the Association, the offices of Clerk and Treasurer may be combined.

Article 7. Association shall be clothed with authority only to advise the churches touching all things pertaining to their interest but shall in no case presume to direct or control them in reference to their own government or internal policy.

ARTICLE 8. A Committee of Arrangements, consisting of three members, shall be appointed on the first day of each session to prepare and report the proceedings and suggest topics proper for the consideration and action of the next annual Association.

ARTICLE 9. Baptist brethren, not members of the Association, who may be present at any session of the body, may on invitation by the body, take seats and participate in the debates of the Association.

ARTICLE 10. The territory embraced in the Association shall be divided into not less than four districts and a committee composed of one pastor, and one layman from each district, together with the Moderator, Vice-Moderator, Clerk of the Association, Associational W. M. U. Superintendent, Associational Sunday School Superintendent, and Associational B. T. U. President, shall be appointed at meeting of the Association, which committee shall compose the Executive Committee of the Association, a majority of which shall constitute a quorum. It shall be the duty of the committee to superintend and direct the missionary operations of the Association.

ARTICLE 11. All committees shall be appointed by the Moderator unless otherwise ordered by the Association.

ARTICLE 12. The Constitution may be altered only at at an Annual session of the Association and by a vote of two-thirds of the whole present.

ARTICLE 13. The rules of this body shall follow Mell's Parlimentary Practice.

ARTICLE 14. This Association shall cooperate with the Baptist State Convention.

ARTICLE 15. The time of the holding of the annual session shall be on Wednesday after the fourth Sunday in October of each year.

Adopted October 17, 1895.
Articles 2, 5, 6, 10, 15, Amended.
Sessions, July 23, 24, 1930.
Article 15 Amended,
Session, July 21, 1932.
Article 10 Amended,
Session, October 23, 24, 1935.

W. O. JOHNSON
A. WAYLAND COOKE
Committee

Proceedings

of the

WOMAN'S MISSIONARY UNION

of the

PIEDMONT BAPTIST ASSOCIATION

THEME: "THE WAY, THE TRUTH AND THE LIFE

Watchword for year—"*Not by might, nor by power, but by my Spirit, saith the Lord of Host.* Zach. 4:6:

First Baptist Church,
Greensboro, N. C.
April 29, 1937

MORNING SESSION

The W.M.U. of the Piedmont Baptist Association met in annual session April 29th in the First Baptist Church, Greensboro. The session was opened by singing "My Jesus I Love Thee".

Dr. J. Clyde Turner expressed his appreciation of the W.M.U., and spoke a word of welcome. Dr. Turner led the opening prayer.

A most impressive devotional was conducted by Mrs. Jack Medlin, using as the Scripture lesson verses from the 14th chapter of John, basing her talk on "The Way, the Truth, and the Life".

Welcome was extended by Mrs. W. H. McKeever from the hostess church.

Response was made by Mrs. A. C. Lovelance, from High Point.

Roll call by the Secretary was answered by a large group of delegates from twenty-one of the twenty-nine societies.

Splendid reports were given by the officers.

Mrs. J. Clyde Turner led in prayer.

With Mrs. Turner in the chair, Mrs. Hoge reported that there were one hundred and ten active societies in the Association.

Superintendent's Message—Mrs. Hoge based her

talk on the theme, "We Would See Jesus". She stressed the need of a revival of the old time religion. Mrs. Hoge closed her message by reading the words of the song, "Let Others See Jesus in You."

Dr. Turner introduced the visiting pastors.

Mr. Genter Stephens sang beautifully, "I Am Satisfied With Jesus".

Address—Rev. Herman Stevens on the subject, "Behold the Man". Mr. Stevens dismissed the morning session with prayer.

A bountiful lunch was served in the dining room by the ladies of the hostess church.

AFTERNOON SESSION

Devotional—Mrs. Joe Howard gave a most inspiring talk on "The Stewardship of Life".

Minutes read and approved.

Report of Young Peoples' Work by Miss Ruth Scott. She presented Miss Short, who gave a reading, "What Y.W.A. Means to Me".

Mr. Stevens then sang, "Ready".

Mrs. Edna Harris on W.M.U. Methods.

Mrs. Harris explained the Standard of Excellence, also gave us some interesting information on the Hundred Thousand Club, Stewardship and Personal Service.

Business: The Association voted to pay for books to be used in mission study work to be led by Mrs. J. J. Andoe.

Obituary, Mrs. L. L. Jarvis.

Mrs. H. E. Armstrong sang softly, "Those Golden Bells".

Motion to adjourn and Mr. Cook dismissed us with prayer .

Respectfully submitted,
MRS. NETTIE H. HOGE,, Supt.
MRS. C. R. HARRISON, Secretary.

47

CHURCHES	*Location	Constituted	PASTORS	S. S. SUPERINTENDENTS
Allen Jay	V	1934		Wade Cumbie, R. 2, Trinity, N. C.
Calvary	O	1901	J. C. Gillespie, R. 4, Reidsville, N. C.	Chas. J. Delgado, Reidsville
Fairview	O	1904	J. C. Gillespie, R. 4, Reidsville,	A. D. Hopkins, Reidsville
Gibsonville	T	1894	E. M. Long, Germantown	R. K. Craver, Gibsonvile
Greensboro, First	C	1859	Dr. J. Clyde Turner, Greensboro	O. E. Lee, Greensboro
Asheboro Street	C	1899	J. Ben Eller, Reidsville	M. D. Teague, Greensboro
Bailey Memorial	C	1935	C. G. Coe, Pomona	C. C. Stanley, Greensboro
Bessemer	V	192	A. A. Walker, Bessemer, Greensboro	C. L. Casey, R. 2, Greensboro
Eller Memorial	C	1897	Jones E. Kirk, Greensboro	H. E. Whitfield, Greensboro
Florida Street	C	1916	B. G. Whitley, R. 5, Greensboro	J. L. Roberson, Greensboro
Forest Avenue	C	1906	Wilson Woodcock, Greensboro	Dr. J. T. J Battle, Greensboro
Latham Park	C	1914	C. D. Barton, Bessemer, Greensboro	Walter Moore Grensboro
Magnolia Street	C	1912		L. C. Davis, Greensboro
Pomona	V	1906	C. M. Oates, Pomona	C. C. Patterson, Pomona
Revolution	C	....	T. E. Baber, Greensboro	N. C. Brown, Greensboro
Sixteenth Street	C	1907	W. B. Cook, Denim Sta., Greensboro	J. V. Brady, Greensboro
Stevens Memorial	V	1922	John U. Garner, Greensboro	L. A. Mills, R. 2, Greensboro
Webster Memorial	O	1935	M. L. Hux, R. 5, Greensboro	E. D. Young, Greensboro
Guilford	V	1914	Robert Costener, Greensboro	J. Setzer Weston, Guilford
High Point, First	C	1825	Dr. A. B. Conrad, High Point	A. E. Tate, High Point
Green Street	C	1899	C. N. Royal, High Point	B. G. Leonard, High Point
Hilliard Memorial	C	1929	Hughey O. Miller, High Point	L. E. Edwards, High Point
North Main	C	1908	A. Lincoln Fulk, High Point	Winfred Clinard, High Point
North Park	C	1929	N. F. Britt, High Point	L. R. McNeil, High Point
South Side	C	....	G. H. Liner, High Point	W. K. Briggs, High Point
West End	C	1913	J. N. Bowman, High Point	W. A. Hedrick, High Point
Jessup Grove	.	....		
Lebanon	O	1911	S. G. Snider, R. 5, Greensboro	Diamond Davis, Brown Summit
Mount Zion	O	....	W. I. Johnson, Burlington	George Spoon, Kimesville
Oak Grove	O	1916	R. L. Smith, High Point	L. R. Loflin, Jamestown
Osborne Chapel	O	1934	C. W. Myrick, R. 1, Greensboro	R. R. Osborn, R. 3, Greensboro
Osceola	O	....	J. F. Sellars, Charles Stores, Winstoi	A. E. Cook, RFD, Gibsonville
Pleasant Garden	V	1933	L. C. Chandler, R. 1, Greensboro	W. J. Smith, R. 4, Greensboro
Reidsville, First	C	....	T. L. Sasser, Reidsville	R. T. Burton, Reidsville
Mount Olive	C	1929	J. H. Saunders, Reidsville	Elwood Talley, Reidsville
Penn Memorial	C	1927	D. W. Overbey, Reidsville	Herbert Ford, Reidsville
Rocky Knoll	O	1934	L. Chandler, R. 1, Greensboro	R. R. Suddreth, R. 1, Greensboro
Ruffin Stacey	O	1931	J. T. London, R. 5, Reidsville	H. J. Reed, R. 5, Reidsville
Smith Grove	O	1921	R. O. Nuckles R. 1, Colfax	Drew Smith, R. 1, Colfax
Summerfield	V	....	E. A. Long, Germantown	C. V. Ferguson, Summerfield
Tabernacle	.	....	G. C. Phillips, Altamahaw	

*C—City; V—Village; T—Town; O—Country

CHURCH OFFICERS

CHURCHES	CLERKS	TREASURERS
Allen Jay	..rlene Younts	W. R. Hobson, High Point, R 1, Box 239
Calvary	J. E. McCargo	J. F. Carroll, Reidsville
Fairview	William Cummings	G. T. Gordon, Reidsville, R. 2
Gibsonville	W. P. Gillette	T. L. Roberson, Gibsonville
Greensboro, First	W. O. Burnham	Howard Gardener, Greensboro
Asheboro Street	J. D. Mls	U. A. Hedrick, Greensboro
Bailey Memorial	W. J. Mitchell, Sr.	W. J. Mitchell, Greensboro, R. 3
Bessemer	C. L. Murray	C. L. Murrey, Greensboro
Eller Memorial	Carl Ham	Richard Hobbs, Greensboro
Florida Street	J. B. Rumbley, Sr.	E. H. Moore, Greensboro
Forest ue	C. O. Wer	T. E. Sharp, Greensboro
Latham Park	Walter Sutton	J. C. Parrish, Greensboro
Magnolia Street	Mrs. G. L. Williamson	H. S. Noah, o
Pomona	C. C. Patterson	E. E. Henry, Pomona
Revolution	W. L. Jones	Waldo Johnson, Greensboro
Sixteenth Street	Alfred C. Whitt	L. F. Paris, Greensboro
Stevens Memorial	Mrs. J. B. Brown	Ms. C. B. Brisson, Greensboro, R. 2
Webster Memorial	Miss Selma Scales	J. F. Graves, Greensboro, Denim Station
Guilford	F. F. Bondurant	W. L. Hudson, Guilford, Box 52
High Point, First	C. D. Goldsmith	Miss Thelma Patrick, High Point
Green Street	Clyde Ayers	R. B. r, High Point
Hilliard Memorial	J. W. Saunders	K. F. Moore, High Point, R. 4
North Main	Miss Annie Lawson	Kester Burrow, High Point
North Park	Paul Frye	L. W. Glenn, High Point
South Side	J. G. Williams	J. G. Williams, High Point
West End	Mrs. O. H. Clodfelter	C. N. Scott, High Point
Jessup Grove		
Lebanon	Mrs. Pauline Jarvis	J. B. Garner, Greensboro, R. 5
Mount Zion	J. C. Lackamy	Mae Branson, Snow Camp
Oak Grove	L. R. Loflin	L. R. Loflin, Jamestown
Osborne Chapel	R. R. Osborne	Mrs. M. n, R. 3, Greensboro
ela	E. R. Brande	Mrs. D. A. Greene, Brown Summit
Pleasant Garden	I. F. Anderson	J. E. Thompson, Pleasant Garden
Reidsville, First	T. L. Gardner	J. F. Smith, Reidsville
Mount Olive	Mrs. ll Delapp	Mrs. A. D. n, Reidsville
Penn al	Mrs. Pearl Boswell	Thomas Dixon, Reidsville
Rocky Knoll	J. W. Smith	John P. Rieves, Greensboro, R. 1
Ruffin Stacey	Mrs. Lottie Schrum	Mrs. Lottie Schrum, Ruffin
Smith Grove	Drew Smith	Drew Smith, Colfax, R. 1
Summerfield	Mrs. Myrtle Smith	Mrs. Hettie Shields, Summerfield
Tabernacle		Miss Edna Phillips, Altamahaw

CHURCHES		M La	Baptisms	Letters	Statements	Restorations	Letters	Exclusions	Erasures	Deaths		W	I		State Paper
Allen Jay	2 4	57	1	5	...	...	10	...	...	...	53	Yes	2	2	...
Calvary	2 4	153	7	...	...	...	...	...	...	...	160	Yes	1	1	2
Fairview	1 3	115	4	...	...	...	1	...	1	...	117		1	2	2
Gibsonville	2 4	238	...	...	...	...	1	...	2	1	234	Yes	1	4	1
Greensboro, First	1 2 3 4	1980	50	136	16	...	93	15	...	14	2060	Yes	1	12	128
Asheboro Street	1 2 3 4	1044	75	28	8	1	22	...	10	13	1111	Yes	1	4	60
Bailey Memorial	1 2 3 4	56	27	8	2	...	1	...	...	...	92	Yes	2	12	...
Bessemer	1 2 3 4	449	8	7	1	1	10	...	...	1	455	Yes	2	4	37
Eller Memorial	1 2 3 4	815	5	4	...	7	11	...	...	1	819	Yes	2	4	41
Florida Street	1 2 3 4	350	26	15	5	...	23	...	3	3	367	Yes	3	1	2
Forest Avenue	1 2 3 4	543	12	25	...	...	16	2	48	5	509	Yes	1	12	30
Latham Park	1 2 3 4	40	...	3	...	...	9	...	...	...	34		...	...	...
Magnolia Street	1 2 3 4	365	6	9	1	1	6	...	...	3	367	Yes	2	1	10
Pomona	1 2 3 4	132	30	9	3	4	11	...	...	...	167	Yes	2	2	...
Revolution	1 2 3 4	292	19	7	...	3	4	4	...	1	312	Yes	2	1	2
Sixteenth Street	1 2 3 4	844	16	10	3	2	27	361	...	4	452	Yes	2	10	...
Stevens Memorial	1 2 3 4	139	24	8	4	...	...	5	26	1	143	Yes	1	4	3
Webster Memorial	1 2 3 4	126	16	4	3	...	4	...	...	1	144	Yes	1	...	3
Guilford	1 2 3 4	81	...	4	...	...	9	...	...	...	72		...	2	4
High Point, First	1 2 3 4	1149	17	34	2	...	39	...	9	19	1135	Yes	1	4	110
Green Street	1 2 3 4	1253	37	62	5	...	35	...	...	4	1318	Yes	1	4	75
Hillard Memorial	1 2 3 4	301	4	7	...	...	17	3	...	2	290	Yes	1	1	20
North Main	1 2 3 4	242	6	5	2	...	17	...	1	5	232	Yes	2	3	2
North Park	1 2 3 4	172	5	5	1	...	2	1	...	...	180	Yes	...	3	15
South Side	1 2 3 4	290	9	5	6	...	16	...	...	...	304	Yes	2	4	...
West End	1 2 3 4	353	20	26	5	1	8	...	...	2	393	Yes	2	4	...
Jessup Grove	......	45	...	...	...	...	...	...	...	...	45		...	...	...
Lebanon	1 2 3 4	173	33	6	...	...	6	...	...	...	206	Yes	2	1	...
Mount Zion	2 4	155	5	...	...	...	...	...	...	...	166		...	...	...
Oak Grove	1 3	93	...	9	...	...	...	...	...	...	102	Yes	1	1	...
Osborne Chapel	1 2 3 4	12	13	4	4	...	...	...	...	...	29	Yes	1	1	...
Osceola	1 3	47	...	...	...	...	2	...	...	1	44		...	...	1
Pleasant Garden	2 4	89	6	3	...	...	2	...	...	...	96	Yes	1	4	13
Reidsville, First	1 2 3 4	718	73	25	6	...	14	...	1	3	804	Yes	2	4	40
Mount Olive	1 2 3 4	231	7	6	4	1	2	11	2	2	237	Yes	1	4	5
Penn Memorial	1 2 3 4	152	16	1	4	...	9	...	...	2	162	Yes	2	3	3
Rocky Knoll	1 3	90	38	10	3	...	3	...	...	...	144	Yes	1	4	...
Ruffin Stacey	1 2 3 4	144	17	...	2	...	6	...	1	...	154	Yes	2	4	3
Smith Grove	1 3	130	17	...	21	...	2	...	1	2	163	Yes	2	3	...
Summerfield	1	168	8	7	2	...	...	...	...	...	187		1	3	4
Tabernacle		27	...	...	...	...	...	...	...	...	27		1	3	4
Totals		13853	657	497	110	21	438	402	105	90	14086		...	...	...

Allen Jay	8	15	18	21	20	40	6		8	136	77		1	1				500.00	36.00	536.00
Calvary	6	8	15	8	77	20			9	143	63			6				65.92	59.03	124.95
Fairview										92	43			4				30.21	19.00	49.21
Gibsonville	19	20	43	32	35	79	20		17	265								112.32	57.32	170.24
Greensboro, First	84	169	214	182	236	884	186	204	111	2270	936	Yes	2	59	Yes	164	114	907.53	4,474.41	5,381.94
Asheboro Street	62	144	151	144	78	366	49	50	72	1116	474	Yes	1		Yes	260	160	114.99	69.50	184.49
Bailey Memorial	27	17	20	56	35				8	163	60			8						
Bessemer	8	27	50	60	30	117	20		23	335	177	Yes	1	7	Yes	65	53	407.80	228.13	635.93
Eller Memorial	35	78	98	80	94	104	110		71	673	256	Yes		5	Yes			422.70	464.87	887.57
Florida Street	18	46	68	52	43	75	14		34	350	220			23	Yes			303.40	152.56	455.96
Forest Avenue	48	48	60	80	101	124	45	24	5	535	341	Yes	12		Yes	114	87	379.97	261.82	641.79
Latham Park	9		16	11		10			6	52									52.28	52.28
Magnolia Street	13	11	17	12	26	46	9		13	147	110									
Pomona	35	32	63	62	64	61			13	330	205	Yes						221.43	149.64	371.07
Revolution	35	59	70	41	39	69	45	22	27	407	201	Yes						28.90	61.67	90.57
Sixteenth Street	24	59	75	51	64	160	15		23	171	350			12				219.74	131.59	351.33
Stevens Memorial	7	30	30	30	25	80	8		18	228	186	Yes						228.77	200.40	429.17
Webster Memorial	12	24	35	13	18	140	16		12	270	137							215.88	66.55	282.43
Guilford	16		12	7	15				11	61	68									
High Point, First	64	109	127	125	170	307	34	70	60	1066	526	Yes	4	15				2,117.86	1,346.35	3,464.21
Green Street	64	160	264	175	232	359	40		110	1404	644	Yes		20						
Hilliard Memorial	30	40	48	42	22	100	15		23	320		Yes		3				217.90	114.83	332.73
North Main	17	42	44	31	53	27			35	249	148	Yes		4				246.01	208.00	454.01
North Park	18	42	38	26	29	52	19	4	29	257	163			5						
South Side	26	59	56	43	35	76			15	310	214	Yes							103.24	103.24
West End	32	59	69	69	64	104	24	23	23	467	237	Yes		7						
Jessup Grove										64										
Lebanon	20	19	28	33	40	70	21		10	241	118								57.95	57.95
Mount Zion	18	14	25		30	24			6	117	65			5				19.50	36.58	56.08
Oak Grove	13	14	20		22	31			10	110	79							9.60	35.50	45.10
Osborne Chapel	12		9		6	14			6	120	40	Yes						15.00	23.00	38.00
Osceola	8	11	16	12	15	10			10	82	53	Yes						33.20	7.36	40.56
Pleasant Garden	17	14	16	10	28	29	5		11	130	63									
Reidsville, First	27	54	97	84	60	275	24	100	57	778	282	Yes		73	Yes	182	128	532.99	396.27	929.26
Mount Olive	11	15	51	24	47	38			17	203	150	Yes	1	3						
Penn Memorial	12	16	15	12	9	90			10	164	85	Yes						60.57		60.57
Rocky Knoll	27	20	17	33	30	60	14		9	210				20				200.00	60.00	260.00
Ruffin Stacey	24	25	10	16	25	25			10	135	85								26.26	26.26
Smith Grove		30			40	32			6	108	75			17						
Summerfield									12	125								52.00	71.67	123.67
Tabernacle										44										
Total	906	1530	2005	1677	1957	4098	739	497	953	14748	6931	Yes	22	297		785	542	7,664.19	8,972.38	16,636.57

CHURCHES

	Do O[illegible]		Materials Used	Persons Seated	N	D R	N C J			Value of Past Home.	Total Value Al[illegible] Church Proper		Insurance Carr[illegible]
Allen Jay	Yes	1936	Wood	300	1	...	...	1,200	...	....	1,200	255.52	100
Calvary	Yes	1898	Wood	375	5	...	4	3,500	...	2,000	5,500	....	2,000
Fairview	Yes	1902	Wood	300	5	...	4	2,000	...	....	2,000	....	1,500
Gibsonville	Yes	1894	Wood	300	9	2	9	3,500	...	....	3,500	....	2,500
Greensboro, First	Yes	1906	Brick	1000	48	...	48	130,000	...	15,000	145,000	....	67,000
Asheboro Street	Yes	1912	Brick	700	32	6	47	30,000	...	6,000	36,000	....	26,000
Bailey Memorial	Yes	1935	Wood	250	1	...	...	1,000	...	....	1,000	....	750
Bessemer	Yes	1922	Wood	350	16	2	16	6,000	...	2,500	8,500	....	4,000
Eller Memorial	Yes	1925	Brick	450	48	7	32	41,000	...	....	41,000	....	25,000
Florida Street	Yes	1930	Brick	450	22	2	14	15,000	...	....	15,000	1,500.00	10,000
Forest Avenue	Yes	1906	Brick	275	14	6	14	17,000	...	8,000	41,000	1,812.50	10,750
Latham Park	Yes	1914	Wood	150	1	...	...	1,000	...	....	1,000	856.00	....
Magnolia Street	Yes	1912	Wood	300	7	9	9	6,000	...	3,000	9,000	2,520.00	4 000
Pomona	Yes	1906	Wood	350	8	7	7	3,000	...	....	3,000	....	....
Revolution	Yes	1907	Wood	400	5	3	7	10,000	...	5,000	15,000	....	7,500
Sixteenth Street	Yes	1907	Brick	500	23	2	16	39,000	...	....	39,000	....	15,000
Stevens Memorial	Yes	1922	Wood	250	11	2	13	10,000	...	....	10,000	....	6,000
Webster Memorial	Yes	1935	Wood	.....	5	...	4	4,000	...	....	4,000	....	800
Guilford		1914	Wood	200	1	1	1	3,500	...	....	3,500	....	1,500
High Point, First	Yes	1905	Brick	500	46	7	39	100,000	...	7,000	122,000	28,050.00	55,000
Green Street	Yes	1926	Brick	1500	96	6	68	156,000	1,600	3,000	160,600	3,900.00	60,000
Hilliard Memorial	Yes	1931	Brick	800	23	...	23	25,000	...	....	25,000	800.00	5,000
North Main		1924	Brick	350	23	6	17	17,000	...	....	17,400	3,000.00	8,000
North Park	Yes	1929	Wood	300	8	1	16	3,500	...	....	3,500	732.00	500
South Side	Yes	1916	Wood	350	9	...	8	5,000	...	3,000	8,000	2,030.76	1,800
West End	Yes	1913	Wood	350	15	...	13	8,500	...	3,500	12,000	....	5,000
Jessup Grove	Yes	1934	Wood	400	1	...	...	1,050	...	....	1,050	....	....
Lebanon	Yes	1911	Wood	250	7	...	6	3,000	...	....	3,000	....	2,000
Mount Zion	Yes	1912	Wood	500	1	...	...	2,000	...	....	2,000	....	....
Oak Grove	Yes	1927	Wood	270	3	2	2	[illegible]	...	....	1,500	....	1,400
Osborne Chapel	Yes	1934	Wood	200	...	...	...	[illegible]	...	....	1,000	....	....
Osceola	Yes	1915	Wood	300	1	...	10	1,500	...	....	1,650	....	....
Pleasant Garden	Yes	1918	Wood	220	1	...	3	800	...	....	1,800	180.00	1,000
Reidsville, First	Yes	....	Brick	550	24	5	20	37,000	...	14,000	51,000	....	43,500
Mount Olive		1929	Wood	300	15	2	13	500	...	....	5,000	1,350.00	4,000
Penn Memorial		1935	Brick	350	13	13	11	10,000	...	1,500	11,500	2,200.00	4,500
Rocky Knoll	Yes	1934	Wood	250	4	4	4	2, [illegible]00	...	....	2,000	....	1,500
Ruffin Stacey		1931	Wood	[illegible]	1	...	...	2,000	...	....	2,300	....	1,500
[illegible]th Grove	Yes	1923	Wood	300	1	...	...	1,200	...	....	1,500	....	650
Summerfield	Yes	....	Wood	400	1	...	4	6,000	...	....	6,000	....	3,500
Tabernacle		1934	Wood	400	1	...	...	1,500	...	....	1,500	....	....
Totals				16090	556	95	502	7[illegible]3,250	1,600	73,500	825,500	49,186.78	386 650

Allen [illegible]y	127.40		25.00	400.00	191.64	15.00	48.00		2.00	75.96	[illegible]5.00
Calvary	294.78		10.00	9.75		42.13	25.84		3.00	65.29	450.79
Fairview	183.65		10.00	[illegible]		12.21	18.00		3.00		441.86
Gibsonville	626.75		5.00			161.77	112.32		3.00	54.51	963.35
Greensboro, First	4,600.00	6,313.14	170.76	5,321.08		4,285.12	1,654.08	979.79	18.00	1,882.75	25.224.72
[illegible]boro Street	3,000.40	795.00	280.00	1,073.97	2,320.00	1,492.80	803.78	303.86	12.50	165.10	10,247.41
Bailey Memorial	410.00		70.00		[illegible]	62.60		25.30	2.00		699.90
Bessemer	1,535.00		113.86	631.10	457.05	377.97	228.71	105.28	5.00	177.07	3,631.04
Eller Memorial	2,580.00		206.65	622.77		539.97	294.86	166.39	10.00	254.67	4,675.31
Florida Street	1,567.50		267.80	202.20	620.00	85.41	191.26	62.04	5.00	415.78	3,616.99
[illegible] Avenue	2,390.00		96.06	3,131.93	534.86	1,075.81	265.00			65.44	7,559.10
Latham Park	108.00										108.00
Magnolia Street	1,560.00		117.00	82.65	480.00	146.47	55.23	25.36	3.00	68.18	2,537.89
[illegible]a	1,292.57		63.74	94.09		176.00	93.35	3.00	3.00	292.58	2,018.33
[illegible]on	1,780.54		83.44	65.22		266.37	153.62	25.00	4.00	167.48	2,545.67
[illegible]th Street	2,001.37			8,772.74		577.96	227.89	26.00	5.00		11,610.96
Stevens [illegible]al	1,450.00		70.21			39.59	104.43	31.00	4.00	43.00	2,[illegible]
Webster [illegible]al	1,040.00		43.75	3.00		152.32	134.35	114.94	5.00	61.48	1,554.84
Guilford	385.00			10.00		185.50	162.50	8.00	2.00	60.00	813.00
High Point, First	[illegible]00	2,193.33	130.00	982.80	5,166.25	2,329.62	791.69	48.87	18.00	2,453.52	17,514.08
Green [illegible] Street	3,120.00		185.00	85.76	9 [illegible]	1,477.00	440.00	66.06	5.00		14,928.82
Hilliard Memorial	1,692.65		47.77	609.85	270.00	414.64	122.54	6.12	3.00	34.80	3,201.37
North [illegible]	1,560.00		59.88	1,327.26		210.62	97.55	8.55	3.00	55.11	3,321.97
North Park	1,315.00		30.20	550.60	156.50	[illegible]	152.25	32.55	3.00	171.01	2,554.21
South Side	1,300.00		60.00		[illegible]	240.65	75.00	50.00	2.00		1,830.65
[illegible] End	1,560.00		34.70	176.86		260.63	223.47	9.75	2.50	52.90	2,320.81
Jessup Grove											
Lebanon	458.14		59.00	182.44		143.32	61.18	44.35	3.00	1.40	952.83
Mount Zion	204.40		32.60	18.00					5.00		260.00
Oak Grove	124.61			45.00		16.60	22.97		2.00		211.18
Osborne [illegible]el	125.00			86.00	46.00		15.00		1.00		273.00
Osceola	15.85						9.79	19.68		13.52	58.84
Pleasant Garden	427.00		22.50	180.00	300.00				2.00	100.00	1,031.50
Reidsville, First	3,000.00	2,027.50	35.00	[illegible]		761.56	421.80	381.64	9.00	1,257.87	8,316.68
[illegible] Olive	1,358.33		100.00		1,850.00	75.00	85.60		2.00		3,470.93
Penn Memorial	1,083.00		50.00	5.79	872.65	314.03	74.00	14.60	1.50		2,415.57
Rocky Knoll	240.00		43.00	1,000.00		64.00	95.00	30.00	1.50		1,473.50
[illegible]	258.00		37.00			34.34	36.66		2.00	15.00	[illegible]
Smith Grove	37.00	24.93				10.00					71.93
Summerfield	360.00		75.00	141.00		75.47	48.00		4.00		[illegible]3.47
[illegible]ls	[illegible]	11,353.90	2,634.92	26,449.17	23,047.95	16755.58	7345.72	2,588.13	159.00	8,004.42	146,910.73

CHURCHES	Total to Co-operative Pr	Special to Asso tional Missions	Special to Stat Missions	Special to Hom Missions	Special to Fore Missions	Special to Chris Ministerial Edu	Special to Orph	Special to Hosp	Special to Old Ministers' Relie	Other Spe	Total Give sions and ences	Grand Total fo Purposes—Both Work and Miss
Allen Jay	10.00	....	....	....	....	....	36.00	5.00	....	....	51.00	936.00
Calvary	67.31	....	24.07	13.58	87.38	5.00	63.02	28.65	....	17.00	306.01	756.80
Fairview	28.68	....	....	....	35.07	....	30.40	10.00	....	....	104.15	546.01
Gibsonville	51.70	6.30	....	5.00	1.60	....	57.92	6.00	....	....	128.52	1,091.87
Greensboro, First	15,720.08	....	320.49	391.75	3,093.85	72.32	2,439.64	295.84	....	1,744.50	24,078.47	49,303.19
Asheboro Street	2,250.34	....	75.97	121.93	371.09	....	535.66	59.49	....	388.19	3,802.67	14,050.08
Bailey Memorial	29.17	....	....	....	....	....	69.50	1.95	....	46.98	150.60	[illegible]
Bessemer	334.38	....	14.30	....	12.15	....	196.83	17.00	....	....	574.66	4,205.70
Eller Memorial	1,080.43	....	14.76	....	36.08	107.00	564.00	51.69	....	35.00	[illegible]	6,564.27
Florida Street	453 73	....	76.92	3.23	6.00	....	214.00	39.40	....	....	793.28	4,410.27
Forest Avenu	705.01	....	58.16	10.00	101.24	13.53	243.07	39.04	....	109.52	1,279.57	8,838.67
L... m... P...	.....	....	....	....	....	....	....	....	....	....	....	108.00
Ma... o...	0	....	6.50	13.93	14.78	....	22.28	10.58	....	17.24	90.34	2,628.23
[illegible]	3.53	....	....	....	....	....	116.63	11.01	....	27.60	218.77	2,237.10
Re... ut... n	568 24	....	28.73	23.00	....	....	195.19	28.00	....	53.00	[illegible]	3,441.83
S... St...	226.87	....	8.35	3.30	11.40	....	131.59	13.80	....	....	395.31	12,006.27
St...ens M...	579 71	....	12.80	17.80	38.29	....	194.60	30.15	....	60.75	914.10	2,946.33
We...	100.60	....	11.50	10.50	24.00	11.00	76.50	17.45	....	9.00	[illegible]	1,815.39
...uilford	50.00	....	....	....	....	....	10.00	12.00	....	....	72.00	885.00
Hi... ...on F	3,098.75	....	137.63	102.75	1,151.43	60.00	1,033.65	200.00	....	166.19	5,950.40	23,464.48
Green Street	940 00	....	....	....	....	....	360.00	57.90	....	84.86	1,442.76	16,371.58
Hilliard Memorial	9 05	....	15.94	2.00	4.00	....	108.65	6.18	....	....	145.82	3,347.19
North Main	2 0 0	....	31.00	5.00	5.00	....	150.00	23.00	....	1.00	[illegible]	3,776.97
North Park	16.33	....	....	....	....	....	59.25	5.50	10.00	6.15	[illegible]	2,651.44
South Side	61.48	....	....	....	....	....	73.61	....	....	31.60	166.69	1,997.34
West End	347.14	24.00	45.92	21.25	35.00	10.94	246.84	27.14	....	2.35	[illegible]	3,081.39
Jessup Grove	....	....	....	....	....	....	....	....	....	....	....	....
Lebanon	....	....	....	....	....	....	57.95	10.00	....	38.35	106.30	1,059.13
Mt Zion	....	....	....	....	....	....	27.45	....	....	19.28	46.73	306.73
Oak Grove	....	....	....	....	....	....	35.50	4.02	....	....	39.52	250.70
Osborne Chapel	....	....	12.00	....	....	....	11.00	....	....	....	23.00	296.00
Osceola	....	....	....	....	....	....	11.06	....	....	....	11.06	69.90
Pleasant Garden	9 00	....	....	....	....	....	17.74	....	....	30.11	56.85	1,088.35
Reidsville, First	1,750 00	....	42.34	67.60	20.00	25.00	391.93	38.83	....	291.84	2,627.54	10,944.22
Mount Olive	....	....	....	....	240.00	....	109.29	6.20	....	....	355.49	3,826.42
Penn Memorial	....	....	3.00	....	....	....	....	5.00	....	....	8.00	2,423.57
Rocky Knoll	....	....	....	....	....	....	60.00	....	....	....	60.00	1,533.50
Ruffin Stacey	12.00	....	2.00	....	....	....	20.00	3.00	....	6.26	43.26	426.26
Smith Grove	....	....	....	....	....	....	....	14.30	....	....	14.30	86.23
Summerfield	67.70	....	5.00	....	15.50	1.00	80.00	22.67	....	22.25	214.12	917.59
Tabernacle	....	....	....	....	....	....	....	....	....	....	....	....
Totals	28,856.23	30.30	947.38	812.65	5,303.86	305.79	8,050.75	1,103.79	10.00	3,209.02	48,629.77	195,540.50

Allen Jay	Yes				1	1	2					14	11	25	15	20	25	
Calvary																		
Fairview																		
Gibsonville																		
Greensboro, First	Yes		1	3	2	2	9	13		12	45	34	35	139	58	80	118	8
Asheboro Street	Yes			1	2	2	6	18			22	45	41	126	36	38	56	7
Bailey Memorial																		
Bessemer	Yes		1	1	1	1	4			10	12	10	18	50	16	14	26	
Eller Memorial	Yes		1	1	2	1	5			12	17	29	17	75	23	45	29	
Florida Street	Yes		1	1	2	2	7	11	3	11	36	32	20	110	47	58	52	
Forest Avenue	Yes			1	1	1	3				10	19	15	44	14	9	14	8
Latham Park																		
Magnolia Street						1	1						12	12				
Pomona	Yes			1	1	1	4	10			16	21	29	76	22	32	36	1
Revolution				1			1				13			13	11	10	12	
Sixteenth Street				1	1	1	3				15	14	16	45				
Stévens Memorial	Yes			1	1	1	4	8			12	9	14	43	18	26	8	1
Webster Memorial																		
Guilford																		
High Point, First	Yes			1	1	1	3				30	24	24	78	27	36	47	10
Green Street	Yes		1	3	2	2	8			25	48	42	40	155	80	110	140	3
Hilliard Memorial	Yes		1	1	1	1	4			12	14	13	9	48	34	37	37	3
North Main	Yes		1	1	1	3	7	8	2	10	10	9	17	54	32	37	35	
North Park	Yes		1	1	1	1	4			17	16	15	23	71	57	66	62	
South Side	Yes			1	1	1	4	30			10	16	20	76	34	5	60	
West End			1	1	1	1	4			14	13	10	29	66	32	48	47	
Jessup Grove																		
Lebanon																		
Mount Zion																		
Oak Grove																		
Osborne Chapel																		
Osceola																		
Pleasant Garden				1		1	2				10		10	20				
Reidsville, First	Yes		1	2	1	1	6	16		15	49	35	28	143	28	59	50	1
Mt Olive	Yes		1	1	1	1	4			10	12	12	4	38				
Penn Memorial	Yes			1	1	1	3				17	11	17	45	18	9	24	
Rocky Knoll	Yes				1	1	2					24	16	40				
Ruffin Stacey																		
Smith Grove																		
Summerfield																		
Tabernacle																		
Totals			11	26	26	29	100	114	5	148	427	438	465	1592	602	739	878	42

CHURCHES	PRESIDENTS OF W. M. S.	Number of W Missionary S				Number of	Total W. M Organizatio	W. M. S. M	Y. W. A.'s	G. A.'s M			T		Co Gi	C si	Grand Total Purposes Given M.U. and its zations.
Allen Jay																	
Calvary	Mrs. R. H. Terrell	1	1				2	20	24				44			74.75	74.75
Fairview																	
Gibsonville	[illegible] Cable	1					1	18					18			16.20	16.20
[illegible]o, First	Mrs. W. H. McKeever	1	2	2	2	1	8	368	69	88	56	73	654	271		12,362.78	12,362.78
Asheboro [illegible]	Mrs. A. Andrews	1	2	2	1	1	7	160	38	65	20	32	315	194	256.94	583.99	840.93
Bailey Memorial																	
Bessemer	Mrs. O. F. Barnes	1	1	1		1	4	51	10	12		37	110			162.18	162.18
[illegible] Memorial	Mrs. J. E. Kirk	1	1				2	37	15				52	20	443.63	336.24	779.87
Florida Street	Mrs. C. N. Hutchinson	1	1	1	1	1	5	40	10	17	22	15	104	14	50.00	378.92	428.92
Forest [illegible]	Mrs. J. W. Marsh	1	1	1		1	4	50	28	12		20	110	40		926.32	926.32
Latham Park																	
Magnolia Street	Mrs. L. L. Jarvis	1	1				2	20	8				28			48.74	48.74
Pomona	Mrs. W. G. Teague	1		1			2	22		20			42			25.00	25.00
Revolution	Miss Sallie Burgess	1	1	1	1	1	5	30	12	15	7	17	81			478.37	478.37
Sixteenth Street	Mrs. T. W. Michael	1	1	1	1	1	5	38	12	13	13	10	86				
Stevens [illegible]	Mrs. C. B. Brisson	1		1		1	3	35		15		12	62			135.57	135.57
Webster Memorial	Mrs. W. H. Lucas	1		1		1	3	30		9		8	47	31		137.09	137.09
Guilford	Mrs. E. L. Weston	1					1	14					14			44.99	44.99
High Point, First	Mrs. W. F. Clayton	1	1	1	1	1	5	175	43	10	15	35	278	141	1,935.45	3,152.07	5,087.52
Green Street	Gladys Ellington	1	1	2	1	1	6	75	20	18	20	23	156	81	881.37	598.63	1,480.00
Hilliard [illegible]	Mrs. J. B. Ellis	1	1			1	3	9	15			10	34	9	10.00	18.75	28.75
North Main	Mrs. Allice Davis	1					1	12					12		81.90	80.00	161.90
North Park	Mrs. Paul Frye	1				1	2	20				25	45	15		10.33	10.33
South Side	Mrs. J. S. Cameron	1					1	24					24			63.45	63.45
West End	[illegible]s. T. P. Andrews	2	1	1		1	5	33	10				43			218.00	218. 0
Jessup Grove																	
Lebanon																	
Mount Zion																	
Oak Grove																	
[illegible] [illegible]el																	
Osceola																	
Pleasant [illegible]	Mrs. J. E. Thompson	1					1	15					15		30.11		30.11
Reidsville, First	Mrs. T. L. Sasser	1	1	2	2	1	7	154	20	20	15	18	227	40	591.69	1,190.68	1,782.37
[illegible] Olive	[illegible]s. J. H. Saunders	1					1	75					75			263.50	263.50
Penn Memorial	Mrs. M. H. Fitz	1	1				2	20	21				41		9.00	6.00	15. 0
Rocky Knoll	Mrs. L. C. C [illegible]	1					1	12					12		40.00		40.00
Ruffin Stacey	Mrs. Lottie Schrum	1					1	17					17				
Smith Grove																104.50	104.50
Summerfield	Mrs. A. C. Lloyd	1					1	15					15				
Tabernacle																	
Totals		30	18	18	10	15	91	989	355	314	168	335	2761	856	4,330.09	21,417.05	25 747.14

YEAR	WHERE HELD	MODERATOR	CLERK	PREACHER	Churches	Baptisms	Church Members	Total Gifts
1894	Greensboro	Dr. C. A. Rominger	W. L. Kivett	M. A. Adams	5	....	562	....
1895	Liberty	T. L. Chislom	W. L. Kivett	L. Johnson	12	16	112	$ 4,695.50
1896	Moore's Chapel	R. W. Brooks	W. H. Eller	L. Johnson	14	66	1,194	5,128.94
1897	Summerfield	F. H. Jones	W. H. Eller	J. A. Munday	16	73	1,540	7,198.27
1898	Mount Zion	R. W. Brooks	W. H. Eller	L. Johnson	17	67	1,557	6,883.23
1899	Ramseur	R. W. Brooks	F. P. Tucker	John E. White	19	54	1,570	7,435.43
1900	Cherry Street	R. W. Brooks	W. H. Eller	Thomas Carrick	16	48	1,538	7,970.35
1901	Reidsville	F. H. Jones	W. H. Eller	L. Johnson	19	157	1,657	8,282.73
1902	Salem Street	F. H. Jones	W. H. Eller	W. C. Newton	19	135	1,774	9,950.97
1903	Gibsonville	F. H. Jones	W. H. Eller	C. L. Greaves	20	185	1,868	12,834.77
1904	Calvary	F. H. Jones	W. H. Eller	H. W. Battle	22	112	1,832	12,807.43
1905	Randleman	F. H. Jones	W. H. Eller	J. M. Hilliard	22	114	2,096	17,674.91
1906	High Point, First	F. H. Jones	W. H. Eller	W. R. Bradshaw	23	201	2,333	29,366.31
1907	Asheboro Street	F. H. Jones	W. H. Eller	Wm. Hedley	26	372	2,798	29,993.79
1908	Ramseur	F. H. Jones	W. H. Eller	C. E. Maddry	28	311	3,086	26,347.57
1909	Greensboro	F. H. Jones	W. H. Eller	Wm. Hedley	30	292	3,429	49,847.28
1910	Mount Zion	F. H. Jones	W. H. Eller	R. G. Hendrick	31	336	3,731	28,531.01
1911	Asheboro	W. F. Staley	W. H. Eller	W. F. Staley	29	182	3,736	25,887.56
1912	High Point, Green St	F. P. Hobgood, Jr.	W. H. Eller	J. C. Turner	30	174	3,647	29,697.38
1913	Liberty	F. P. Hobgood, Jr.	W. H. Eller	R. P. Walker	31	409	3,971	37,700.97
1914	Asheboro Street	F. P. Hobgood, Jr.	W. H. Eller	A. W. Claxon	31	413	4,202	42,428.44
1915	Reidsville	J. M. Hilliard	W. H. Eller	J. M. Hilliard	42	313	4,491	42,577.68
1916	Forest Avenue	J. M. Hilliard	W. H. Eller	E. N. Johnson	36	369	4,854	48,418.92
1917	Green Street	J. M. Hilliard	W. H. Eller	W. R. White	39	308	4,760	44,609.05
1918	Moore's Chapel	J. M. Hilliard	W. H. Eller	J. W. Rose	39	374	5,140	72,538.46
1919	White Oak	J. M. Hilliard	W. H. Eller	W. H. Wilson	39	339	5,359	76,638.85
1920	Calvary	J. M. Hilliard	W. H. Eller	E. N. Johnson	39	543	5,867	117,682.35
1921	Summerfield	Clarence A. Smith	J. E. Lanier	B. K. Mason	39	480	6,454	135,561.79
1922	Glenola	Clarence A. Smith	J. E. Lanier	Jas. A. Clark	39	679	7,226	149,955.24
1923	Magnolia Street	Clarence A. Smith	H. O. Miller	E. E. White	38	365	7,341	140,553.25
1924	West End	Clarence A. Smith	H. O. Miller	W. E. Goode	40	672	7,489	164,658.19
1925	Fairview	Clarence A. Smith	H. O. Miller	A. T. Howell	41	610	8,956	211,792.21
1926	Ramseur	Clarence A. Smith	S. T. Hensley	Lloyd T. Wilson	42	620	9,974	243,500.68
1927	Trinity	Clarence A. Smith	S. T. Hensley	H. T. Stevens	40	656	10,223	211,846.40
1928	Bessemer	Clarence A. Smith	O. E. Lee	R. P. Ellington	41	531	10,866	202,002.30
1929	Liberty	Clarence A. Smith	O. E. Lee	C. F. Rogers	44	573	11,496	218,987.61
1930	Asheboro	Clarence A. Smith	O. E. Lee	Geo. T. Tunstall	44	676	12,012	198,077.29
1931	Florida Street	Clarence A. Smith	O. E. Lee	A. B. Conrad	44	827	12,789	178,501.19
1932	Reidsville	Clarence A. Smith	O. E. Lee	J. C. Turner	46	778	13,485	159,000.60
1933	White Oak	Clarence A. Smith	O. E. Lee	T. L. Sasser	48	1561	15,199	186,041.40
1934	Franklinville	Clarence A. Smith	O. E. Lee	Wilson Woodcock	53	757	15,356	172,839.18
1935	So. Side, High Point	Clarence A. Smith	O. E. Lee	J. S. Hopkins	41	623	12,687	164,135.92
1936	Calvary	Clarence A. Smith	O. E. Lee	J. Ben Eller	42	563	13,958	166,052.96
1937	Eller Memorial	Grover H. Jones	O. E. Lee	C. N. Royal	41	657	14,086	195,540.50

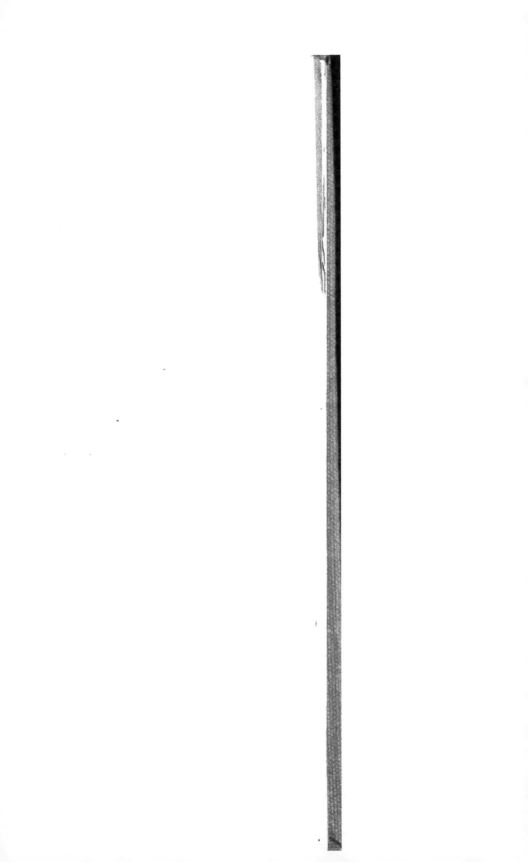

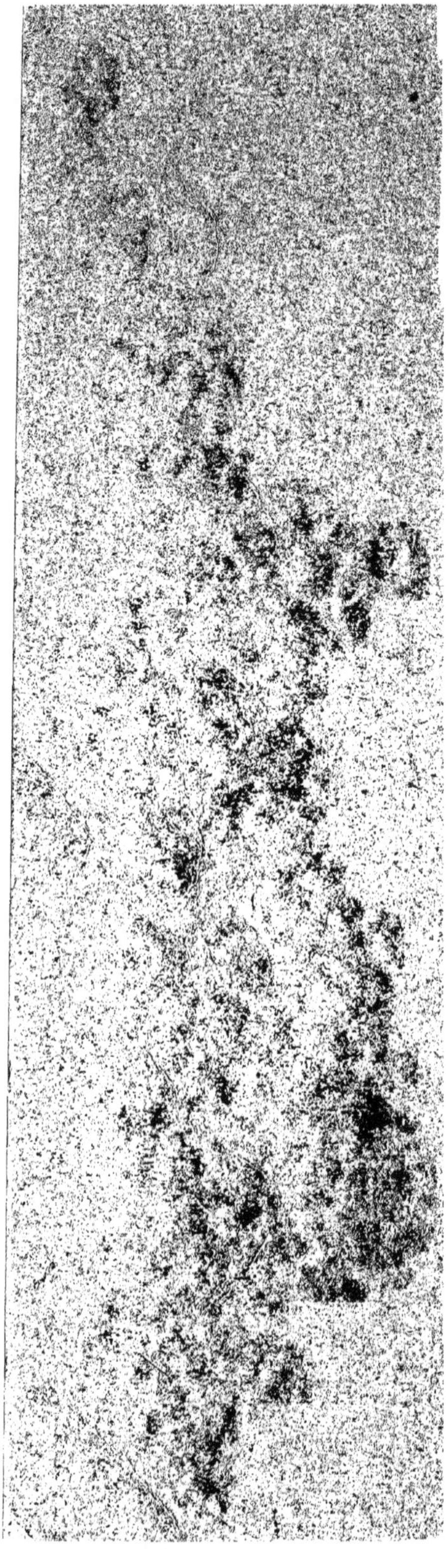

MINUTES
of the

PIEDMONT BAPTIST ASSOCIATION

NORTH CAROLINA

FORTY-FIFTH ANNUAL SESSION

held with

Hilliard Memorial Baptist Church

HIGH POINT, N. C.

OCTOBER 19-20

1938

The next session will be held with the First Baptist Church, Reidsville, N. C.

Wednesday and Thursday before the fourth Sunday in October, 1939

Dr. J. Clyde Turner Will Preach the Sermon

Alternate, Rev. C. E. Parker

MINUTES

of the

PIEDMONT BAPTIST ASSOCIATION

NORTH CAROLINA

FORTY-FIFTH ANNUAL SESSION

held with

Hilliard Memorial Baptist Church

HIGH POINT, N. C.

OCTOBER 19-20

1938

The next session will be held with the First Baptist Church, Reidsville, N. C.

Wednesday and Thursday before the fourth Sunday in October, 1939

Dr. J. Clyde Turner Will Preach the Sermon

Alternate, Rev. C. E. Parker

INDEX

MAP

OF THE

EDMONT BAPTIST ASSOCIATION

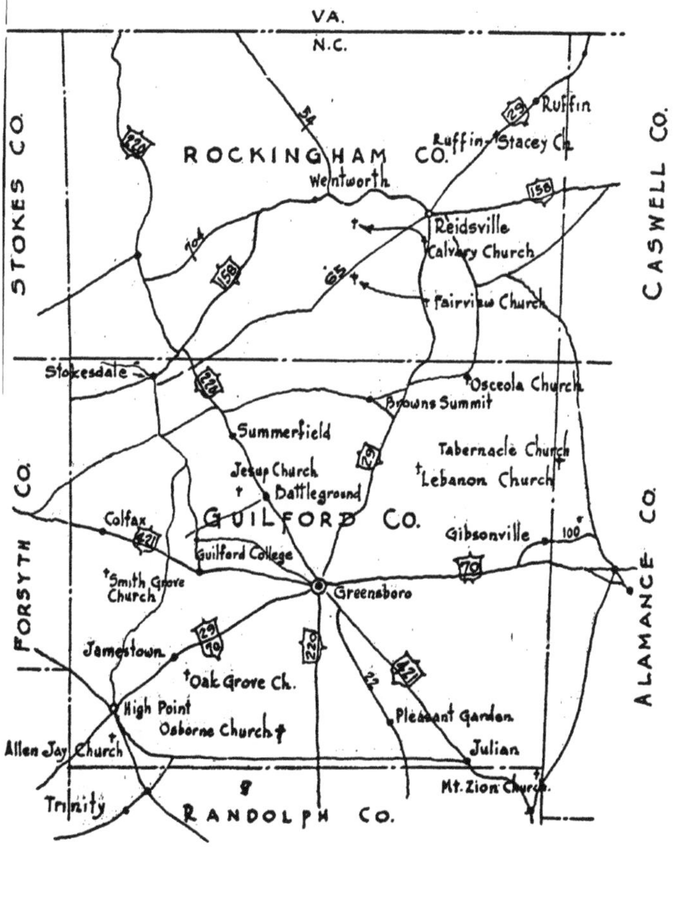

ASSOCIATIONAL DIRECTORY

OFFICERS

Grover H. Jones, Moderator .... High Point
T. L. Sasser, Vice-Moderator .... Greensboro
O. E. Lee, Clerk-Treasurer .... Greensboro

EXECUTIVE- PROMOTION COMMITTEE

Grover H. Jones, Chairman .... High Point
O. E. Lee, Secretary .... Greensboro
Dr. J. T. J. Battle .... Greensboro
Rev. C. N. Royal .... High Point
Dr. A. B. Conrad .... High Point
Rev. J. C. Gillespie .... Reidsville
Rev. T. L. Sasser .... Reidsville
J. C .Tatum .... Reidsville
Rev. J. Ben Eller .... Greensboro
Mrs. Nettie Hatcher Hoge .... Greensboro
F. L. Paschal .... Greensboro
J. Carl Bell .... Greensboro

CHURCH ADVISORY COMMITTEE

Dr. J. Clyde Turner, Chairman .... Greensboro
Dr. A. B. Conrad .... High Point
T. L. Sasser .... Reidsville
Mrs. Nettie H. Hoge .... Greensboro
Grover H. Jones .... High Point
Dr. J. T. J. Battle .... Greensboro
O. E. Lee .... Greensboro

CHURCHES BY DISTRICTS

District 1:
High Point, First
Hilliard Memorial
Green Street
North Main
North Park
South Side
West End
Oak Grove
Smith Grove
Allen Jay

District 2:
Greensboro, First
Asheboro Street
Bessemer
Bailey Memorial
Buchanan
Eller Memorial
Forest Avenue
Florida Street
Latham Park
Magnolia Street
Pomona Mills
Revolution
Sixteenth Street
Stevens Memorial
Gibsonville
Guilford
Jessip Grove
Lebanon
Mount Zion
Pleasant Garden
Osborne Chapel
Rocky Knoll
Summerfield
Tabernacle
Webster Memorial

District 3:
Reidsville, First
Penn Memorial
Mount Olive
Calvary
Fairview
Osceola
Ruffin-Stacey

OFFICERS OF BAPTIST SUNDAY SCHOOL ASSOCIATION

F. L. Paschal, Superintendent	Greensboro
A. C. Lovelace, Associate Superintendent	High Point
Rev. A. A. Walker, Secretary and Treasurer	Greensboro
Miss Judith Eller, Pianist	Greensboro
Rev. A. Lincoln Fulk, Supt. Group 1, District 1	High Point
M. E. Howell, Supt. Group 2, District 1	High Point
William Cummings, Supt. District 3	Reidsville
Mrs. T. L. Ogburn, Supt. Cradle Roll Dept.	Greensboro
Miss Ruth Scott, Supt. Beginners Department	Greensboro
Mrs. C. C. Stout, Supt. Primary Dept.	High Point
Mrs. Geo. D. Allred, Supt. Junior Dept.	Greensboro
Mrs. I. B. Squier, Supt Intermediate Dept.	Greensboro
T. L. Ogburn, Supt. Young People's Dept.	Greensboro
Mrs. J. S. Moore, Supt. Adult Dept.	Greensboro
Henry Love, Supt. Extension Dept.	Reidsville
Rev. C. N. Royal, Supt. of Dept. of Evangelism	High Point

—o—

OFFICERS OF W. M. U. ASSOCIATION

Mrs. Nettie H. Hoge, Superintendent	Greensboro
Mrs. A. Andrews, Secretary	Greensboro
Mrs. Siceloff, Treasurer	High Point
Miss Ruth Scott, Young People's Leader	Greensboro
Mrs. L. M. Gideon, Personal Service Chairman	Greensboro
Mrs. C. N. Royal, Stewardship Chairman	High Point
Mrs. J. J. Andoe, Mission Study Lit. Chairman	Greensboro
Mrs. H. A. Knight, Group Leader, District 1	High Point
Mrs. O. J. Howard, Group Leader, District 2	Greensboro
Mrs. T. L. Sasser, Group Leader, District 3	Reidsville

—o—

OFFICERS OF BAPTIST TRAINING UNION

J. Carl Bell, Director	Greensboro
Miss Thelma Patrick, Associate Director	High Point
Miss Elizabeth Campbell, Secretary-Treasurer	Greensboro
D. W. Overbey, Jr., Pianist	Reidsville
Henry Love, Chorister	Reidsville
Mrs. John Reavis, Junior Leader	High Point
Miss Illa Hensley, Intermediate Leader	High Point
J. E. Hedrick, Director, District 1	High Point
Farrel James, Director, District 2	Greensboro
Paul Roach, Director, District 3	Reidsville
Rev. C. N. Royal, Pastor Advisor	High Point

ORDAINED MINISTERS NOT PASTORS

T. E. Staley	Bessemer Br. Greensboro, N. C.
W. L. Robinson	Gibsonville, N. C.
W. C. Richardson	Guilford, N. C.
Dr. C. W. Newton	Richmond, Va.
O. F. Barnes	Concord, N. C.
W. F. Matherly	Greensboro, N. C.
B. C. Lamb	Mars Hill, N. C.
Rufus Carroll	Greensboro, N. C.
L. M. Deaton	Greensboro, N. C.
Woodrow Hill	High Point, N. C.
J. M. Hilliard	High Point, N. C.
Ben McDowell	High Point, N. C.
T. L. Chamberlain	High Point, N. C.
J. F. Murray	Reidsville, N. C.
T. H. Stamey	Route 1, Greensboro, N. C.
C. R. Smith	Route 3, Kearnersville, N. C.
B. H. Farington	Colfax, N. C.

———oOo———

B. T. U. DIRECTORS, PRESIDENTS AND LEADERS

ALLEN JAY—Wade Cumbie, Director, Mrs. Thomas Gray, S. P.; Edith Hobson, I. L.; Mrs. Avery Perryman, J. L.

GIBSONVILLE—John S. Westmoreland, Sr. P.; Thelma Riggins, I. L.; Theo. Edwards, Jr. L.

GREENSBORO, FIRST—O. E. Lee, Director, Mrs. C. W. Moseley, Miss Netta Liles, Z. H. Howerton, and A. L. Roberson, B. A. U. P.; Misses Sara Kanoy, Elizabeth Taylor, and Vernon Roberts, S. P.; Mr. and Mrs. Edwin Nash, Miss Estelle Mitchell, Mrs. F. A. Hyatt, Mrs. Eula Osborne, and Glenn Toms, I. L.; Misses Mildred Jackson, Eva Saleeby, Mrs. A. P. Lloyd, and Mrs. F. L. Person, J. L.; Mrs. M. E. Wilson, and Mrs. J. R. Simpson, S. H. L.

ASHEBORO STREET—C. W. McLees, Director; W. A. Coble, B. A. U. P.; Alec Cheek, Sr. P.; J. J. Norwood, Lorene James, I. L.; Mrs. Joe Kirkman, Elizabeth Meyers, J. L.; Mrs. J. J. Norwood, S. H. L.

BESSEMER—Norfleet Dixon, Director; W. P. Haynes, A. P.; Horace Johnson, Sr. P.; Lora Cantor, I. L.; Mary Staley, J. L.

ELLER MEMORIAL—Howard May, Director; A. M. Bass, A. P.; Raymond Kincaid, Sr. P.; Mrs. D. L. Redmond, S. H. Mrs. C. E. Parker, I. L.; Mrs. Howard May, J. L.

FLORIDA STREET—W. M. Cassell, Director; Mrs. J. T. Simmonds, A. P.; Lula West, Sr. P.; Mrs. W. W. Williams, Mrs. W. M. Cassell, I. L.; B. H. Mitchell, Mrs. J. B. Rumbley, Jr., J. L.; Mrs. J. H. Saunders, S. H. L.

FOREST AVE.—J. B. Watson, Director; B. B. Stockard, A. P.; Marie Troxler, Sr. P.; E. W. Richardson, I. L.; Mrs. E. W. Richardson, J. L.

LATHAM PARK—Lila Barton, I. L.

MAGNOLIA STREET—Alma Moore, J. L.

POMONA—G. F. Roseberry, Director; J. H. Parrish, Sr. P.; Minor Lawson, I. L.; Mrs. Vela Lamb, J. L.

REVOLUTION—Francis Burke, Sr. P.

SIXTEENTH STREET—Miss Catherine Caviness, Director; Mildred Southern, Sr. P.; Harry Moore, I. L.; R. B. Stacy, Viola Southern, J. L.; Iris Snyder, S. H. L.

STEVENS MEMORIAL—Patsy Harris, Director; Elizabeth Brissen, Sr. P.

HIGH POINT—Julia Liles, Director; Malloye Stanfield, Sr. P.; Leslie Johnson, Moselle Boyles, I. L.; Ora Boyles, J. L.; Mrs. L. A. Dickens, S. H. L.

GREEN STREET—John Reavis, Director; W. E. Crissman, A. P.; Carl Edmundson, Sr. P.; Mrs. John Reavis, I. L.; Lizzie Peeler, J. L.; Mrs. C. C. Stout, S. H. L.

HILLIARD MEMORIAL—P. E. Grubb, Director; Mrs. H. A. Freeman, A. P.; Lloyd Willard, Sr. P.; C. H. Farmer, I. L.; A. H. Dunning, J. L.; Mrs. C. H. Farmer, S. H. L.

NORTH MAIN STREET—Mrs. D. S. Ring, Director; Mr. D. S. Ring, A. P.; Annie Lawson, Sr. P.; J. E. Wade, W. C. Locke, I. L.; Lena McFarland, Lois Kearns, J. L.; Myrtle Mae McCorkle, S. H. L.

NORTH PARK—H. B. Chatham, Director; Coy Elliott, A. P.; Paul K. Frye, Sr. P.; Mrs. Paul K. Frye, I. L.; Mrs. E. M. Smith, Mrs. L. W. Glenn, J. L.

SOUTHSIDE—Daisy Shaw, Sr. P.; J. G. Williams, I. L.; Estie Brown, J. L.

WEST END—J. E. Hedrick, Director; Mrs. J. E. Hedrick, A. P.; Clifford Hedrick, Sr. P.; Vernon Coffey, I. L.; Mrs. Ora Tyler, J. L.

LEBANON—S. L. Carter, A. P.; Frank S. Bettini, Sr. P.; B. G. Yow, J. L.

OSBORNE CHAPEL—Mrs. P. W. Osborne, Director.

REIDSVILLE, FIRST—Paul Roach, Director; Mrs. R. L. Hubbard, A. P.; Mrs. Lane Peters, Lester Wofford, Grey Pettigrew, Sr. P.; Mrs. Hunter Walker, Mrs. Floyd Moore, I. L.; Sarah Kemp, Lucille Windsor, J. L.

MOUNT OLIVE—Mrs. Ruth Jones, Director; Lawson Daniel, Sr. P.; Elwood Talley, I. L.; Mrs. J. H. Saunders, J. L.; Mrs. Elwood Talley, S. H. L.

PENN MEMORIAL—Mrs. Minnie Harrison, Director; James Albert Dunevent, Sr. P.; Mrs. Nash Wilkins, I. L.; Mrs. W. H, Ford, J. L.

ROCKY KNOLL—L. S. Moore, Director; Mrs. L. S. Moore, A. P.; James Stamey, Sr. P.; Ray Chandler, I. L.; Mrs. R. A. Laughlin, S. H. L.

SUMMERFIELD, C. F. Hayes, Sr. P.

———oOo———

OFFICERS OF W. M. S. AND AUXILIARIES

CALVARY—Mrs. Lawrence Setleffe, W. M. S. Pres.; Mrs. J. R. Fulp, Y. W. A. C.

GREENSBORO, FIRST—Mrs. W. H. McKeever, W. M. S. Pres.; Mrs. Mayes Behrman, and Mrs. H. M. Sutherland, Y. W. A. C.; Mesdames Joe Cates, W. M. Ham, O. E. Lee, G. A. L.; Dr. J. C. Turner, O. E. Lee, Sidney Clayton, R. A. L. Miss Mildred Jackson, Sunbeam L.

ASHEBORO STREET—Mrs. J. S. Moore, W. M. S. Pres,; Mrs P. J. Smith, Mrs. Joe Kirkman, Y. W. A. C.; Mrs. M. D. Teague, Mrs. Davis Neal and Mrs. A. W. Edwards, G. A. L. Mrs. J. B. Wills, R. A. L.; Mrs. Chas. T. Brown, Sunbeam L.

BESSEMER—Mrs. J. T. Willett, W. M. S. P. Miss Lora Cantor Y. W. A. C. Mrs. H. C. King, G. A. L., Verla Hayes, Sunbeam L.

ELLER MEMORIAL—Mrs. Lloyd Vonadora, W. M. S. Pres.; Mrs. Glenn Parker, Y. W. A. C., Mrs. D. L. Redmond, Sunbeam L.

FLORIDA STREET—Mrs. C. N. Hutchinson, W. M. S. Pres., Mrs. S. Harcum, Y. W. A. C.; Mrs. E. E. Brady, G. A. L.; Mrs. W. M. Cassell, R. A. L.; Mrs. Edna Thomas, Sunbeam L.

FOREST AVENUE—Mrs. E. W. Richardson, W. M. S. Pres.; Mrs. Wilson Woodcock, Y. W. A. C.; Mrs. Harold Wiles, G. A. L.; Lillian Price, Sunbeam L.

MAGNOLIA STREET—Mrs. L. L. Jarvis, W. M. S. Pres.; Mrs. H. S. Noah, Y. W. A. C.

POMONA—Mrs. W. G. Teague, W. M. S. Pres.; Mrs. Emo Wherry, G. A. L.

REVOLUTION—Sallie Burgess, W. M. S. Pres. and Y. W. A. C.; Mrs. Jewel Martin, G. A. L.; Sallie Burgess, R. A. L.; Mrs. Edna Thornberry, Sunbeam L.

SIXTEENTH STREET—Mrs. W. A. Straughn, W. M. S. Pres.; Mrs. Harry Moore, Y. W. A. C.; Mrs. Rockford Hill, G. A. L.; Mr. Rockford Hill, R. A. L.; Wilma Somers, Sunbeam L.

STEVENS MEMORIAL—Mrs. C. B. Brisson, W. M. S. Pres.; Patsy Harris, G. A. L.; Mrs. L. M. Deaton, Sunbeam L.

WEBSTER MEMORIAL—Mrs. W. H. Lucas, W. M. S. Pres., Selma Scales, G. A. L.; Mrs. Paul Holt, Sunbeam L.

GUILFORD—Mrs. R. B. Ferrell, W. M. S. Pres.

HIGH POINT, FIRST—Mrs. P. Y. Adams, W. M. S. Pres.; Mrs. L. W. Apple, Y. W. A. C.; Mrs. H. D. Sears, G. A. L.; Sue Stanfield; Sunbeam L.

GREEN STREET—Mrs. M. W. Buser, W. M. S. Pres.; Mrs. C. M. Holton, Y. W. A. C.; Mabel Koontz, G. A. L.; Mrs. Nora Haney, R. A. L.; Mrs. Amos Carroll, Sunbeam L.

HILLIARD MEMORIAL—Mrs. J. B. Ellis, W. M. S. Pres.; Mrs. Fred Bryant, Y. W. A. C.; Aldine Edwards, Mrs. Myrtle Willard, G. A. L.; Mrs. C. H. Farmer, Sunbeam L.

NORTH MAIN STREET—Mrs. Alice Davis, W. M. S. Pres.

NORTH PARK—Mrs. J. A. Jones, W. M. S. Pres.; Mrs. E. M. Smith, Y. W. A. C.; Mrs. J. D. Edmonson, G. A. L.; W. H. Brock, R. A. L. Mrs. D H. Short, Mrs. E. E. Hill, Sunbeam L.

SOUTH SIDE—Mrs. Pearl Cameron, W. M. S. Pres.; Daisy Shaw, G. A. L.; Mrs. Caudle, Sunbeam L.

WEST END—Mrs. T. P. Andrews, W. M. S. Pres.; Mrs. J. N. Bowman, Y. W. A. C.; Mrs. P. A Snider, G A. L.; P. A. Snider, Curtis Swain R. A. L.

OSBORNE CHAPEL—Mrs. J. C. May, W. M. S. Pres.

PLEASANT GARDEN—Mrs. J. E. Thompson, W. M. S. Pres.

REIDSVILLE, FIRST—Mrs. T. L. Sasser, W. M. S.; Mrs. G. F. McBrayer, Y. W. A. C.

MOUNT OLIVE—Mrs. J. H. Saunders, W. M. S. Pres.; Mrs. Charlie Griffeth, Sunbeam L.

PENN MEMORIAL—Mrs. Elsie Gailey, W. M. S. Pres.; Doris Lawrence, Y. W. A. C.

ROCKY KNOLL—Mrs. Carl Chandler, W. M. S. Pres.

RUFFIN STACEY—Mrs. Lottie Schum, W. M. S. Pres.

SUMMERFIELD—Mrs. A. C. Lloyd, W. M. S. Pres.

LIST OF MESSENGERS

ALLEN JAY
J. O. Warren
Rev. C. M. Floyd
Mrs. Henry Burrow
Miss Mealie Burrow
Miss Mary Warren

ASHEBORO STREET
J. S. Moore
F. S. Paschall
E. Brightwell
Mrs. J. B. Ellen
L. L. Nash
Mrs. J. S. Moore
Mrs. W. J. Welker

BAILEY MEMORIAL
B. G. Coe
Mrs. Coe
Mrs. E. J. Jarvis
B. J. Mitchell
Mrs. Bessie Foy
Mrs. W. H. Sullivan
Mr. and Mrs. R. Bryant

BESSEMER
C. L. Casey
W. P. Haynes
Mrs. J. T. Willett

BUCHANAN
Mr. Mabe
Mr. Cranc
Mr. Parks

CALVARY
Mrs. George Gum
Mrs. Jesse Carter
Mr. and Mrs. J. E. McCargo
Mrs. C. J. Delgardo

ELLER MEMORIAL
Mrs. H. O. Basinger
Mrs. W. H. Lambert
Mrs. J. H. Sharp
Mrs. Walter Overman
Mrs. H. P. Carson
Mrs. C. E. Brady
Raymond Kincaid
H. E. Whitfield

FAIRVIEW
Ralph Dowell
D. E. Trantham
Wade Durham

FLORIDA STREET
P. L. Roberson
Mrs. C. N. Hutchinson
Mrs. J. B. Rumbley

FOREST AVENUE
J. E. Oliver
Mrs. Oliver
Mrs. E. W. Richardson

GIBSONVILLE
W. M. Fergerson
C. C. Harmon
Mrs. Harmon

GREENSBORO FIRST
O. E. Lee
Mrs. Nettie Hoge
J. Carl Bell
Mrs. W. H. McKeever
A. A. Chandler
Mrs. J. Clyde Turner
V. C. Bradley
Miss Jane Cates
J. D. Wilkins, Jr.
Mrs. R. A. Cates
Hampton Howerton

GUILFORD
Mrs. B. F. Butler
Mrs. W. L. Hudson
W. E. Kirkman
Setzer Weston
Mrs. Ora Weston
Miss Mary Gilbert

GREEN STREET
Mr. J. O. House
Mrs. T. C. Robbins
Mrs. E. M. Blakley
M. E. Howell
Mrs. C. M. Crissman
Haywood Haward

HILLIARD MEMORIAL
J. W. Sarndren
J. N. Slay
C. H. Maynes
Mrs. D. Cachean

HIGH POINT FIRST
A. E. Tate
Mrs. W. F. Clayton
Mrs. R. W. Seward
Fred Whitescaver
E. A. Lockwood
W. E. Price
C. D. Goldsmith

LATHAM PARK
C. D. Barton
Mrs. J. E. Parmar
J. C. Parish
W. W. Sutton

LEBANON
B. G. Yowe
Mrs. D. E. Lashley
Mrs. Larkin Cole
Mrs. F. S. Bettini

MAGNOLIA STREET
Mrs. L. L. Jarvis
Mrs. Author Lewis
H. P. Wray
L. L. Jarvis
Mrs. Wray
Mrs. G. H. Williamson

MOUNT OLIVE
Mrs. Ray Gentry
Mrs. D. P. Driscall
Mrs. A. D. Clifton

MT. ZION
Mr. and Mrs. J. C. Lackarry
L. L. Spoon
John Soats

NORTH MAIN STREET
S. R. Clinard
Mrs. Ed Crisco
Mrs. Alice Davis

NORTH PARK
H. B. Chatham
Mrs. J. D. Edmonson
Mrs. L. W. Glenn

OAK GROVE
John Dennis
Mrs. C. S. Weaver
Mrs. J. H. Blackwill
Mrs. W. A. Curman

OSBORN CHAPEL
Mrs. F. Osborne
Rev. C. W. Myrick
Mrs. M. Morgan
Mrs. Lillian McCandliss

OSCEOLA
Mrs. L. C. Cole
Mr. and Mrs. W. B. Key
Rev. G. F. Sellars
L. C. Cole
Mrs. P. D. McKinney
Mrs. D. A. Greene
Miss Clara Key

PLEASANT GARDEN
Miss Jennie Burton
Mrs. J. B. Gardner
Mrs. W. W. McGee

PENN MEMORIAL
James Overbey
R. L. Borland
Miss Mary Jane Hooper

POMONA
Mrs. R. W. Cox
Mrs. Vela Lamb
Mrs. J. H. Wall
Mrs. C. M. Oates

REIDSVILLE FIRST
T. L. Sasser
Henry Love
Mrs. C. H. Saunders

REVOLUTION
David Barbour
A. C. Hilliard
T. J. Ross
Mrs. Wade Johnson
Alton Riddle
W. L. Parrott

ROCKY KNOLL
Mrs. T. C. Frazier
Mrs. G. L. York
Mrs. R. A. Laughlin

RUFFIN STACY
Mr. and Mrs. E. B. Poindexter
Mrs. J. T. Cardwell

SIXTEENTH STREET
Mrs. W. R. Fully
Mrs. C. C. Hunt
Mrs. W. B. Cook
Mrs. C. L. Straughn
Mrs. T. W. Micheal

SMITH GROVE
George Farington
Johny Johnson
Ray Clark
Drew Smith
Mrs. B. H. Farington
Mrs. Walter Westmorely
Ed Tilly

STEVENS MEMORIAL
C. M. Webster
Mrs. Webster
Mrs. J. H. Ham

SUMMERFIELD
Dr. and Mrs. C. H. Fryar
Mrs. Ida Fryar

TABERNACLE
Miss Mamie Roach
Miss Lillie Bailiff
Mrs. Jean Whitworth
Mrs. Ruth Curl
Mrs. Pauline Rule
Mrs. Diamond

WEBSTER MEMORIAL
Mr. and Mrs. C. V. Webster
Mrs. J. F. Graves
Mrs. W. H. Lucas
Miss Selma Scales
Mr. W. N. Kivet
Mr. E. D. Young
Mrs. G. H. Payne

WEST END
Mr. and Mrs. C. M. Scott
H. W. Smith

CONSTITUTION

—oOo—

ARTICLE 1. The Association shall be called the Piedmont Baptist Association.

ARTICLE 2. It shall be composed of the ordained ministers who are members of, and those who may have pastoral charges within the Associational District, and three delegates from each church in the district aforesaid, and churches having a membership exceeding 300 shall be entitled to one additional delegate for every 200 members or fraction thereof in excess of 300.

ARTICLE 3. The said delegates shall, before taking their seats, produce letters from respective churches showing their appointment as delegates.

ARTICLE 4. The Associational session shall be held at least once a year.

ARTICLE 5. The officers shall be a Moderator, Vice-Moderator, Clerk, and Treasurer. If deemed expedient by the Association, the offices of Clerk and Treasurer may be combined.

ARTICLE 6. The officers of the Association shall be chosen annually by the Association.

ARTICLE 7. Association shall be clothed with authority only to advise the churches touching all things pertaining to their interest but shall in no case presume to direct or control them in reference to their own government or internal policy.

ARTICLE 8. A Committee of Arrangements, consisting of three members, shall be appointed on the first day of each session to prepare and report the proceedings and suggest topics proper for the consideration and action of the next annual Association.

ARTICLE 9. Baptist brethren, not members of the Association, who may be present at any session of the body, may on invitation by the body, take seats and participate in the debates of the Association.

ARTICLE 10. The territory embraced in the Association shall be divided into not less than four districts and a committee composed of one pastor, and one layman from each district, together with the Moderator, Vice-Moderator, Clerk of the Association; Associational W. M. U. Superintendent, Associational Sunday School Superintendent, and Associational B. T. U. President, shall be appointed at meeting of the Association, which committee shall compose the Executive Committee of the Association, a majority of which shall constitute a quorum. It shall be the duty of the committee to superintend and direct the missionary operations of the Association.

ARTICLE 11. All committees shall be appointed by the Moderator unless otherwise ordered by the Association.

ARTICLE 12. The Constitution may be altered only at an Annual session of the Association and by a vote of two-thirds of the whole present.

ARTICLE 13. The rules of this body shall follow Mell's Parlimentary Practice.

ARTICLE 14. This Association shall cooperate with the Baptist State Convention.

ARTICLE 15. The time of the holding of the annual session shall be on Wednesday before the fourth Sunday in October of each year.

Adopted October 17, 1895.
Articles 2, 5, 6, 10, 15, Amended.
Sessions, July 23, 24, 1930.
Article 15 Amended,
Session, July 21, 1932.
Article 10 Amended,
Session, October 23, 24, 1935.

W. O. JOHNSON
A. WAYLAND COOKE
Committee

PROCEEDINGS

of the

FORTY-FIFTH ANNUAL SESSION

of the

PIEDMONT BAPTIST ASSOCIATION

Held With the

HILLIARD MEMORIAL BAPTIST CHURCH

High Point, N. C.

October 19, 20, 1938

———o———

WEDNESDAY MORNING SESSION

1. The Association was opened with a devotional service led by Rev. J. H. Saunders.

2. Rev. Hughey O. Miller spoke words of welcome. Rev. A. Lincoln Fulk responded with words of appreciation for the hearty welcome given.

3. A roll of the churches was called and messengers from 37 churches responded to the roll call.

4. The Moderator appoints the following committees:

Committee on present program: F. L. Paschal, C. N. Royal, J. C. Gillespie.

Committee on Committees: T. L. Sasser, C. E. Parker, A. Lincoln Fulk.

Nominating Committee: Wilson Woodcock, J. Ben Eller, J. N. Bowman.

5. The Report on Religious Literature was presented by J. H. Saunders. Upon motion to adopt the report the subject was discussed by R. F. Terrell, representative of the Biblical Recorder, Dr. J. C. Turner, and J. M. Hilliard. Bro. Terrell requested that a committee be appointed to report the meeting to the Recorder, and to represent the Recorder during the session. Also that a representative be appointed to represent the Record-

er during the year. The following were appointed on the committee: A. Lincoln Fulk, O. E. Lee, and J. H. Saunders. The report was adopted.

Religious Literature

In Hosea 4:6 we read "My people are destroyed because of the lack of knowledge." This does not mean that they need knowledge about life in general, but knowledge about God. This could not have been more true then, than it is now. Our generation is probably educated as well as any people have ever been, on things in general. But our ignorance concerning the Bible and the christian faith is appalling. Where ever we are succeeding in getting the truth on the minds of the people there is an immediate turning to God on the part of many. If we succeed in having the great Southwide revival now being advocated by our denominational leaders, the reading of God's word and other Christian literature is going to play a great part in bringing it about.

We recognize that it is largely the minister's responsibility to lead the people into this reading. Therefore, we recommend more expository preaching, and a constant and varied appeal to our people to read God's word. Those who read the Bible will naturally read some Christian literature. The Biblical Recorder and Charity and Children can hardly be excelled in this field. Therefore, we heartily recommend them to our people. We urge a continued effort to put the Recorder in the homes which can afford it and a liberal distribution of Charity and Children by our Sunday Schools to those unable to pay for a paper.

Respectfully submitted.
J. H. Saunders

RECOMMENDATION:—That the Piedmont Association approve the club plan of subscribing to the Biblical Recorder and that the moderator appoint an association representative to contact pastors, S. S. superintendents and W. M. S. presidents for making effective this plan in the churches of our association.

———o———

6. The nominating committee makes the following report:
Moderator—Grover H. Jones
Vice-Moderator—T. L. Sasser
Clerk and Treasurer—O. E. Lee.

The report was approved and the officers elected.

7. The report on Foreign Missions was presented by J. Ben Eller. Upon motion to adopt the report the subject was discussed by Rev. Henry C. K. Djang from China who is doing post-

graduate work at the University of North Carolina. This was a splendid spiritual message. The report was adopted.

Report On Foreign Missions

In ninety three years of service our Foreign Mission Board has not faced more uncertain times. Wars and rumors of war are the order of the day. Nations are in commotion. We know not what a day will bring forth. But in our fear we turn to our Lord who still guides in the affairs of men and nations.

Some of our mission fields are facing trying ordeals. In Spain and China the work is greatly hindered by war. In Central, Interior, and North China Missions most of our property is in the hands of Japanese military authorities. Many of our missionaries have had miraculous escapes but the Lord has enabled them to render great service to a suffering people. When the war is over the problem of building and repairing will be acute.

However, we have much to encourage us. Our Foreign Mission Board has 422 missionaries working in sixteen nations. We have in these fields 1,802 churches and 2,798 out-stations. Our church membership on Foreign fields is 208,794. Last year 14,027 baptisms were reported. Furthermore, we now have 26,799 students enrolled in our schools and seminaries, while during the past year our hospitals treated 88,599 patients.

The loyalty of our women is cause for special gratitude. The goal of the Lottie Moon offering for the past year was $190,000.00. The goal was surpassed by $100,000.00. This generous and unselfish gift has been a great blessing in a time of great need.

The Board would call attention to the annual Foreign Mission Conference held in August at Ridgecrest. This Conference is growing in power and far reaching influence and we urge our people to attend it where it is possible.

A mission magazine, "The Commission", is now being published by our Foreign Mission Board. After Jan. 1, 1939, it will be issued monthly. We commend "The Commission" and also our mission study books to our churches.

Respectfully submitted,
J. Ben Eller.

8. After prayer by J. S. Hopkins, the Introductory sermon is preached by Dr. A. B. Conrad. The text was Rev. 19:10. Subject: "The Testimony of Jesus is the Spirit of Prophecy." The sermon was a great spiritual message, inspiring and helpful.

After singing "There Is A Fountain Filled With Blood," the session was closed with prayer by H. M. Stroup.

AFTERNOON SESSION

1:30. The devotional service was led by H. R. Starling.

9. The visitors from the Liberty and Sandy Creek Associations were recognized.

Henry Love made announcement about the evening session.

10. The report on the Denominational Program was presented by T. L. Sasser. The report on State Missions was presented by Frank L. Paschal. Upon motion to adopt the reports the subjects were discussed by Rev. Arthur Gillespie, Missionary to China, and W. Perry Crouch, Secretary of Christian Education for the State Mission Board. The reports were adopted.

Denominational Program

The program of Jesus is our denominational program. It is the program of a New Testament Church whose members "engage to promote its prosperity and spirituality, to sustain its worship, ordinances, discipline and doctrines, to contribute cheerfully and regularly to the support of the ministry, the expense of the church, the relief of the poor and the spread of the gospel through all nations".

Section One of the Constitution of the Baptist State Convention of North Carolina states: "The object of the Convention shall be to promote Missions, Education, Social Service, the distribution and study of the Bible and sound religious literature; and to co-operate with the Southern Baptist Convention in its work." The State Convention was organized in Greenville, North Carolina in 1830.

"The messengers from missionary societies, churches and other religious bodies of the Baptist denomination in various parts of the United States, met in Augusta, Georgia, May 8, 1845, for the purpose of carrying into effect the benevolent intention of our constituents by organizing a plan for eliciting, combining, and directing the energies of the denomination for the propagation of the gospel."

These three quotations set out our denominational program. The annual report on this program is confined to the particular activities of the churches, conventions and their agencies that are in immediate process and early contemplation.

We are constantly engaged in sustaining and expanding the work of the churches at home and abroad, endeavoring to preach the gospel to all people everywhere. To support and to make effective this primary enterprise we have auxiliary institutions. They are schools, colleges, seminaries, hospitals and orphanages. These institutions give expressive demonstration of our spiritual life.

Immediately following the world war twenty years ago we made concerted effort to buy up a large opportunity. We are yet paying large sums on the obligations inevitably incurred in that advance step. The money has been coming, and must still come, from the treasuries of the churches and from individual givers. For these twenty years we have been working under what we now call the Co-operative Program. In it we seek to "elicit, combine, and direct the energies of the denomination for the propagation of the gospel."

Designated gifts by individuals to denominational objects are used as the giver directs. Designated gifts by churches are used as the church directs. Undesignated gifts are used according to the schedule fixed and published from year to year by the General Board of the State Convention. The Convention instructs the Board to make equitable division of receipts with the Southern Baptist Convention with an equal division as the ideal. As to the division of that part which is retained for State Convention objects the Board is instructed to safe-guard the debts of the Convention, reducing them all possible and at the same time keep the work of Convention institutions advancing as rapidly as reasonably possible.

As to the division of that part which the Southern Baptist Convention receives it is divided according to a schedule fixed by the Executive Committee and approved by the Convention. Next year Southern Baptist Undesignated Funds are to be used as follows:

Foreign Mission Board	50%
Home Mission Board	23 1-3
Relief and Annuity Board	7
Education Board	3 1-3
Southern Baptist Theological Seminary	4 1-5
Southwestern Baptist Theological Seminary	4 1-5
Baptist Bible Institute	4 1-5
W. M. U. Training School	0 8-15
American Baptist Theological Seminary	1
New Orleans Baptist Hospital	2 1-5
	100%

Five years ago it had become very apparent that the funds of the Co-operative Program would not retire Southern Baptist Debts unless the funds were very materially augmented. The Hundred Thousand Club was therefore turned to as an expedient to reduce the principal of the debts. The overhead expenses of the Club are born by the Sunday School Board and the whole dollar goes to reduce the debt proper, the interest on the debts must still come from the Co-operative Program funds. However, interest as well as principal is being materially reduced. In 1933 Southern Baptist Convention debts were $5,880,351,63. May 1, 1938 they had been reduced to $3,465, 274.06.

By mutual agreement of our State Convention and the Southern Baptist Convention the funds given by North Carolina Baptists to the Hundred Thousand Club are divided equally between the two conventions so that our State debts might also be reduced by this method.

Both the Co-operative Program and the Hundred Thousand Club must have our very vigorous support to reduce our debts and expand our work.

The Southern Baptist Convention this year instituted a southwide evangelistic work for the year 1939. It is earnestly expected that a mighty impetus will be given to soul-winning preaching throughout the land, that all the churches will give emphasis to this objective, throwing ourselves into work and prayer with such spiritual zeal as we have never done before. Plans are in the making to reach remote places as well as strategic centers. Southern Baptists, North Carolina Baptists, Piedmont Baptists are called to the high privileges of soul winning. This is the primary meaning of "eliciting, combining and directing the energies of the denomination for the propagation of the gospel". It is the principal item of the denominational program.

Respectfully submitted,
T. L. Sasser.

Report On State Missions.

For more than one hundred years it has been the objective of the Baptists of North Carolina through State Missions to win the people of our great State to Christ, and in the more recent years we have sought to provide proper facilities for the training and development of those who have been won. We now realize that it is possible for people to gain membership in our churches without ever having been converted—that is genuinely, and we consider this a very serious problem, but we are convinced that it is just as serious to take in genuinely converted new members, and give them no training or responsibilities except that which, by chance may happen to fall to their lot.

To properly administer teaching and training so essential in the State Mission Program, we depend particularly upon our Sunday Schools and Baptist Training Unions, both of which do so much to keep alive the scared fires and the spirit of evangelism, missions, and training, without which our work would soon become stale and lacking in the desirable results necessary for the growth of Chris's Kingdom here. It is equally true that "Woe be unto us" if we fail to continue our militant program of winning the lost to Christ, or fail to train and use them after they have been won.

Our State Mission Board, under the stellar leadership of M. A. Huggins, is doing a great work, and richly deserves the cooperation of every Baptist in North Carolina.

Briefly stated, the work done by the Board in the State is as follows:

(a) Pastoral assistance to Churches which are unable to properly support their pastors, which in many cases is helping many local units to get on their feet, and thereafter go forward and build up their home base and help others to build up in strength where no further financial assistance is required.

(b) The splendid assistance given to the Sunday Schools and Baptist Training Unions.

(c) Aid in building Churches in strategic centers.

(d) Carrying the gospel to the Indians in Robeson County under the leadership of Rev. and Mrs. M. C. Lunsford.

(e) Cooperation with and encouragement to our Negro brethren.

(f) Work among the students in the colleges of our State is a very essential part of the program. Miss Cleo Mitchell is doing work of this type here in Greensboro at the Womans College which is of incalculable value.

(g) We are also ministering to those sick in body and mind, and soul at Oteen Hospital, North Carolina Sanitorium at Black Mountain; our State Sanitorium in Moore County, and in our Hospital in Winston-Salem.

(h) We are also happy that we have the services of M. O. Alexander and J. C. Pipes who are doing notable missionary work in building up our denomination by holding revivals, attending general meetings, formation of fields, and performing other miscellaneous tasks.

Furthermore, we present the following resolution, and urge its adoption:

Whereas, a major emphasis of the Southern Baptist Convention and of our State Mission Program during 1939 is to be on evangelism,

BE IT RESOLVED

First:—That a committee on evangelism be instructed to make a survey of the evangelistic needs of this associational area, and inaugurate a well defined program of evangelism.

Second:—That more prayer and effort be made for winning the lost; that at least one evangelistic meeting be urged for every church; that evangelistic preaching be promoted over radio, in school buildings, tents, harbors, and in every advantageous way in unchurched communities; that emphasis be placed on development of personal soul-winners; that stress be given to establishing family altars; and that there be an adequate program of conservation of the results of evangelism through enlistment, training, indoctrination, and stewardship.

Third:—That this committee plan an associational rally during 1939, for prayer, preaching, and promotion of the objectives mentioned above.

Respectfully submitted,
Frank L. Paschal

11. The report on Home Missions prepared by J. E. Kirk was read by the clerk in the absence of Brother Kirk. Upon motion to adopt the report the subject of Evangelism and the Southwide Revival for 1939 was discussed by Dr. J. Clyde Turner. The report was adopted.

Report On Home Missions

"And I, if I be lifted up from the earth, will draw all men unto me," (John 12:32).

The primary purpose of missions is to lift Christ up and to proclaim His saving grace to every creature in all the world. Missions is the very heart of the gospel, and of our denominational program. The supreme test of our love and loyalty to Jesus is our missionary interest and our investment in world-wide missions. This determines our spiritual progress as an individual and as a denomination.

The approach to this world-task is through our efforts to evangelize the homeland. This is our surest hope of the world's evangelization. (Acts 1:8). The Home Mission Board, which has functioned so effectively at this task for 93 years, deserves a conspicuous place in the thoughts, the prayers, and the support of every loyal Baptist in our association.

Very few people understand the magnitude and the importance of our Home mission work. It may be realized somewhat by a consideration of the vast number of people in our midst who are unevangelized. They are divided as follows: Native of native white parentage 30,000,000. Foreign and alien people, aggregating approximately 6,100,000, divided as follows: 5,000,000 foreign-born, 600,000 French-speaking Americans, 500,000 Spanish-speaking Americans, 200,000 American Indians, and 11,000,000 Negroes. In Cuba 2,500,000 and in the Canal Zone 50,000.

During 1937 the Board employed 23 new missionaries, built 22 mission chapels and pastor's homes, over 100 new mission stations opened, and more than 5,000 professed faith in Christ. The Board has 332 missionaries working in 886 mission stations. Also, it revived the department of Evangelism with Dr. Rowland Q. Leavell as superintendent.

Continued progress, both in increased receipts and payment on the debt, is shown in the Board's financial report as follows: "Received from all sources $508,454.67, an increase of $64,999.40, and paid $145,560.37 on principal of the debt. This was the largest amount paid in any year since 1929.

This is the fifth year the Board has operated without borrowing for current work, staying within its budget. The Board's fixed policy is that no new missionaries are appointed until the money for salaries is in hand or in sight.

Respectfully submitted,
Jones E. Kirk.

12. The report on the Orphanage written by John U. Garner was read by the clerk in the absence of Brother Garner. The report was adopted.

Report On Orphanage

No denominational institution in North Carolina has had such wonderful growth as our Baptist Orphanage. From "Facts About the Baptist Orphanage of North Carolina" we quote;

"The purpose of the Baptist Orphanage of North Carolina as provided in the charter, section four, is to prepare poor and promising orphans for the duties and responsibilities of life. The orphanage therefore, is not an institution for the feeble minded neither is it a reformatory. In functions in the field where it can be of the greatest service."

Therefore every Baptist in North Carolina must admit that our Orphanage is an institution that is performing a work that is both basic and fundamental. Through our Orphanage we are giving boys and girls who have been robbed of their birthright a chance in life.

There were 688 children cared for last year by our Orphanage, Mills and Kennedy Home. "The expense bill averages $452.14 per day". The annual cost per child is about $300.00. This is the amount of financial interest per child that about 500,000 Baptist in North Carolina demonstrate for our orphanage children each year.

The annual Report for the 1937 term gives names of 43 from Guilford county in our orphanage. We have more than any county in North Carolina. The minutes of our association for 1937 show we gave $8,050.75, by this we lacked some over $5,000 taking care of the children from Guilford county alone last year.

"To North Carolina Baptists the Thanksgiving season and orphan child are inseparable. The orphanage is a channel through which men and women who want to do something in the name of Jesus may enrich their spiritual lives. What shall the harvest be? You have the answer."

Since November 11, 1885 when the first child was received, God has stamped His approval upon the work. Out of the large family in the two homes only one child has died in over six years. God is in this work, are you? If so let us place greater emphasis upon the monthly offerings in our Churches. Let us make preparation now for a larger Thanksgiving offering.

Let us give these our orphan children a chance, for "we are laborers together with God."

Respectfully submitted,
John U. Garner

13. Upon motion Dr. M. A. Adams was given ten minutes to speak on the subject of Social Service. An offering was taken for the work.

14. Rev. J. A. Neilson, pastor of the Orphanage Church, presented the work of the Orphanage.

15. The Treasurer's report was presented and referred to the Auditing Committee.

Treasurer's Report

I herewith submit my report for the year ending September 30, 1938.

Balance on hand September 30, 1937		$ .60
Received from the Churches		166.60
		$167.20
DISBURSEMENTS:		
Clerk's Remuneration	$ 50.00	
Paid Economy Printing Co. on account	117.20	
	$167.20	$167.20
BALANCE DUE:		
Economy Printing Co.	$13.69	
Due Clerk for Postage and supplies	4.15	
	$17.84	

Respectfully submitted,
O. E. Lee, Treasurer.

16. The Committee on Committees reported as follows:

Committee on New Churches—J. Ben Eller, J. C. Gillespie, Dr. A. B. Conrad.

Committee on Resolutions—A. A. Walker, D. W. Overbey, Mrs. Nettie H. Hoge.

Committee on Place and Preacher—Wilson Woodcock, J. N. Bowman, E. A. Long.

Committee on Program for Next Year—O. E. Lee, H. R. Starling, Hughey O. Miller.

Committee to Nominate Delegates to State Convention—C. N. Royal, G. H. Liner, Miss Thelma Patrick.

Committee to Nominate Leader for Verbal Report Hour—J. H .Saunders, W. B. Cook.

Committee to Nominate the Executive-Promotion Committee—Dr. J. Clyde Turner, C. E. Parker, A. L. Fulk.

Committee to Nominate Church Advisory Committee—T. L. Sasser, A. E. Tate, A. A. Chandler.

Auditing Committee—W. M. Cummings, F. L. Paschal, H. M. Angel.

Committee to Nominate Committee on Evangelism—Grover H. Jones, A. A. Walker, Mrs. W. H. McKeever.

17. The Association gave a rising vote of appreciation to the Moderator and Clerk for the faithful service rendered.

The afternoon session closed with prayer by A. A. Walker.

oOo

WEDNESDAY NIGHT

B. T. U. ASSOCIATIONAL NIGHT

7:15. Everybody sing!

Devotional period led by J. E. Hedrick.

B. T. U. Report of Secretary to Association.

Report Of B. T. U.

The main object this year of the Piedmont B. T. U. was study courses to be held in each District. This having been accomplished, we, as B. T. U. members, feel as if we have really made a step forward in promoting the work of training young and old. There have been more study courses given in our Piedmont Association B. T. U. than any in the state for the 1937-1938 church year.

Our annual conference was held in the Green St. Baptist Church, High Point, April 23 and 24, 1938. At that time we heard from such splendid speakers as Rev. Wilbur Hutchins, of Durham, Rev. J. A. Neilson of Mills Home and Dr. J. Clyde Turner, Pastor, First Baptist Church, Greensboro.

In June at our Associational meeting we had as our speaker Rev. Gillespie, missionary to China, and in September at our second quarterly meeting we enjoyed a debate on the subject "Resolved that the

B. T. U. should receive as much emphasis in the local church as the Sunday School."

We would like to report at this time six new adult unions in our Association. Our adult work is being stressed greatly throughout the three districts. I believe if we get the adults in B. T. U. we will have the Juniors, Intermediates, and Seniors. We have one entire new organization, that of Latham Park. Some splendid work is being done in that church as well as some others I might mention.

We, as B. T. U. members, pledge ourselves to better service in the coming year and need the prayers of each member of the Piedmont Baptist Association.

Respectfully submitted,
Elizabeth Campbell, Secretary

Play, "The Prodigal Comes Home"—Mary Moncure Parker (Asheboro Street B. T. U.)

Special music rendered by quartettes from Green Street and First Church, Reidsville, and Asheboro Street B. T. U. Orchestra.

Benediction.

———oOo———

THURSDAY MORNING

19. 9:45—The devotional service was led by A. A. Walker.

20. The report on Woman's Work was presented by Mrs. Nettie H. Hoge. Upon motion to adopt the report the subject is discussed by Mrs. J. Clyde Turner, State W. M. U. President. The report was adopted.

Report Of Woman's Work

"Behold how great a matter a little fire kindleth."

Fifty years ago in the basement of a Methodist Church in Richmond, a small band of women (30 in all) in fear and timidity and with little encouragement from the men, organized the woman's Missionary Union, Auxiliary to the Southern Baptist Convention. With the courage of their faith they were to "expect great things from God and attempt great things for God." The watchword chosen was "Let us consider one another to provoke unto love and good works". Their motto "Go Forward" was their marching orders. Miss Annie Armstrong read a paper—"The Special Obligation of Women to Spread the Gospel." As we review this Jubilee Year, the fruits of these fifty years, we marvel at the assumed responsibility of this obligation and the high standards maintained, as the Union has gone forward in every field of service.

Its work of ministry, enlistment and training the young has been a benediction to the home, churches and its influence has gone out to the uttermost parts of the earth. Schools and hospitals have been built and equipped and maintained; missionaries sent out and salaries paid thousands of members from the Training School, Missionary Unions organized in Foreign lands and thousands have been brought to saving knowledge of Christ.

As a mighty river gathers force as it flows toward the sea, so the Missionary Union during the passing years has accumulated an ever widening field in Kingdom service and is now a mighty force in the church of Christ.

It numbers 34,594 societies and its gifts through these fifty years amounts to $53,232,555.00. The total gifts for 1937 alone was $2,357,000.00.

The W. M. U. of North Carolina has ever made a noble contribution in unexcelled leadership and gifts. The beloved Miss Fannie Heck, not only led the women of North Carolina, but served three terms as President of the Southern Woman's Missionary Union. Mrs. Wesley Jones, Mrs. Clyde Turner and others have been foremost in leadership.

The Piedmont W. M. U. has long led the State in gifts. Last year $24,116.85 was contributed by the 105 societies of the Association. Eleven out of the forty-one churches in the Association have no organizations.

The trumpet was chosen as the symbol of the Jubilee. Its high notes have ever called the people to action. Its Jubilee call continues "Go forward to meet the special obligation of women to spread the Gospel" and "Expect great things from God and attempt great things for God."

Respectfully submitted,
Mrs. Nettie Hoge, Supt.

21. The report on Hospitals was presented by C. E. Parker. Upon motion to adopt the report the subject was discussed by Smith Hagaman, Superintendent of the Baptist Hospital. The report was adopted

Report On Baptist Hospital

It seems almost superfluous to read a report on the Baptist Hospital in Piedmont North Carolina where so much of its effective work is being done, but for the benefit of those who have not seen much of the Hospital's results, we wish to record a few startling facts about its ministry.

In fifteen years, forty-odd thousand patients have received treatment at the Hospital. An average of fifteen hundred annually of these have been part or no-pay patients. The annual estimate cost of the charity patients for hospitalization, medical and free surgical treatment, is a hundred and ninety thousand dollars. This charity work is provided for by North Carolina Baptists through our Mother's Day offerings. There is a dollar a day provided by the Duke Foundation Fund, but this is only about one-fourth of the cost of a charity patient.

Due to the service that our Hospital has rendered to North Carolina, the applications for treatment are far greater than its capacity. There is constantly a group of patients waiting for entrance into the Hospital, many of them seriously ill. The Hospital Staff seeks to accommodate every patient who comes and if possible turns away none, but the scarcity of space almost demands that some be turned away.

The challenge to North Carolina Baptists is to rise up in response through a program to double the capacity of our Hospital in order that everyone who comes might find a bed waiting.

Therefore, this committee wishes to recommend to this Association that it go on record as pledging its whole-hearted support to this great cause.

Respectfully submitted,
Charles E. Parker.

22. The report of the Committee on New Churches was presented and adopted as follows:

Report of Committee On Reception of Churches

Application for membership in our association has come from two churches, Antioch and Pisgah. Neither church submitted to your committee the Church Covenant and Articles of Faith adopted, nor reported any offering to any couse of our denominational program during the past associational year.

Therefore, your committee would first assure these churches of our earnest desire to see them fully cooperate with all our work. We would commend their zeal for the Lord and their desire to be a member of our association.

Your committee would recommend, first, that the matter of receiving these churches be held in abeyance for the present; and second, that the Church Advisory Committee of this association be requested to investigate the Church Covenants and Articles of Faith adopted by these Churches and their attitude toward orderly worship and our denominational program; and third, that this committee be given authority to act for the Association.

Fraternally submitted,
J. Ben Eller,
A. B. Conrad,
J. C. Gillespie.

23. The report on Christian Education was presented by A. C. Lovelace. Upon motion to adopt the report the subject was discussed by A. C. Lovelace and J. M. Hayes. The report was adopted.

Christian Education

In the minutes of this association for the year 1936, Dr. J. Clyde Turner gave a brief history of our Christian colleges and other institutions. I wish you would read that report again in order that it may serve as a foundation for the present report.

May we now look back of these institutions to another phase of Christian Education. I refer to the influence of the home and the church. Most students will become Christians before they enter college. All should be won to Christ before the college age. This is a responsibility and obligation of the home and the church. Then Christian Education should and will start long before students enter college. This training should be such that these students will be able to stand firm in the faith during college days.

It is my sincere belief that the home and the church, in a large measure, have failed in Christian Education. Our church leaders are largely responsible for this deplorable condition. To remedy this situation, we need more dependable fathers and mothers; we need preachers who will stand for the right rather than cater to certain so-called influential members. We need teachers who will not only teach the truth but who will practice the same every day.

The standard back home will have to be raised higher before we may expect our colleges to do their best. The late Dr. W. L. Poteat, some years ago, told the following story:

A certain young man from our own state came to Wake Forest College. He registered as a ministerial student. He spent his four years and graduated in due form. On his way home he stole a horse and ran away from the state. Dr. Poteat said the boy was not a minister when he came to college and he was not one when he went away, for, said he: "We do not make preachers at Wake Forest; we help those who are already preachers." The same might be said about Christian Education. Let us raise the standard in our local communities and churches and then we may rightly expect a higher standard in our colleges. For our leaders, O Lord, give us both MORE MEN and MORE MAN!

A. C. Lovelace.

24. Following the singing of "Trust and Obey" the report on Social Service was presented by Wilson Woodcock. Upon motion to adopt the report the subject was discussed by Wilson Woodcock. The report was adopted.

Social Service

The basis of all Social Service as it is interpreted by the Social Service Commission of the Southern Baptist Convention may be found in Romans 14:17, "For the kingdom of God is not meat and drink; but righteousness, and peace, and joy in the Holy Ghost." This and many other teachings of God's Word present the fundamental principles by which we seek to understand and purify all social relations.

Dr. E. Y. Mullins says "The teachings of the Gospel of Christ deal directly or indirectly with all the social institutions of men."

The divorce evil is distinctly anti-Christian since Christ recognized only one ground for divorce. (Matt. 5:32.)

While modern economic problems were not discussed in their technical aspects by any of the writers of the New Testament it is evident that all forms of social wrong and injustice are opposed to the ends of the Gospel and the kingdom of God. The spirit of brotherhood, in which every right enjoyed entails a corresponding obligation, is the central truth in God's teaching concerning human relationships.

Class consciousness as indicated by the terms, labor and capital is unchristian. When all men, whether they be employers or employees, are brothers in Christ, and walk together in righteousness then, and only then will labor troubles cease.

Race consciousness, or persecutions because of race, will find no commendation from our Lord Jesus Christ. Our particular racial problem concerns the Negroes. Eight of them were lynched last year. White landlords charge them exorbitant rent for disease breeding hovels. Wages paid them are so low as to be a contributing factor to disease and crime. And these spectres are no respecters of racial or community lines.

Nationalism, or any narrow form of patriotism, violates the principles of Christian brotherhood. There are four powerful nations of the world which are openly preaching this anti-Christian doctrine. Other nations are practicing the doctrine without so openly declaring it. Hence there are wars and rumors of wars. All nations live in fear of invasion by an enemy. Nations impoverish themselves in buying war material and maintaining armies and navies. And they that live by the sword shall die by the sword.

As never before, religious liberty as guaranteed by our national constitution is threatened. "The National Advisory Committee on Education has just recently recommended that large federal appropriations be made to education, with specific provisions that a good portion of the funds may be used for sectarian institutions." This is a quotation from the report of the Social Service Commission to the Southern Baptist Convention in May, 1938. This opens the way for governmental control of sectarian institutions of all kinds. The government at present exercises such control in the resettlement projects.

When the government controls religious institutions, then the religious body which has the most votes will govern all other religious bodies. Therefore, let us keep religion free in the United States, by keeping the Church and the State separate.

Our most immediate social problem is that dealing with the liquor traffic, with its attendant evils, vice and gambling.

We recommend: That total abstinence be taught from our pulpits, and in all church organizations,

That we do not support any candidate for office who favors the legal sale of any alcoholic beverages.

That our churches be urged to give more liberal support to the prohibition agencies in our state and nation.

Respectfully submitted,
Wilson Woodcock.

25. Motion was passed that the Church Advisory Committee serve as the Committee on the Reception of New Churches.

26. Upon motion the report of the Committee considering the reception of the Buchanan Baptist Church was approved and the Church received into the Association.

The morning session was closed with prayer.

———oOo———

THURSDAY AFTERNOON

27. 1:30—The devotional service was led by Rev. E. F. Mumford.

28. The report on Sunday Schools was presented by A. A. Walker. Upon motion to adopt the report the subject was discussed by A. A. Walker and Frank L. Paschal. The report was adopted.

Sunday School Report

In this association the work of the Sunday School as well as that of the Woman's Missionary Union and the Training Union has assumed such proportions as to necessitate a separate associational organization. For some time the Sunday School Association has been meeting on Fifth Sunday afternoons with a rather poor attendance. The last meeting was held on the Friday evening before Fifth Sunday and with such signal success that it was voted to hold all regular meetings on the Friday evening before each Fifth Sunday. To our regret we are not reaching the goals of a Standard Sunday School Association. This is due in part to the fact that we have not even one Standard Sunday School in the Association, and also to the possibility that we have not yet become associationally minded enough to make the sacrifices necessary to reach an associational standard.

The statistical table will show our enrollment, average attendance, Vacation Bible schools, baptisms, and other such achievements. In this report we would emphasize two urgent needs and one golden opportunity. First, we need to make the local school a truly Bible teaching agency. This necessitates a well prepared lesson on the part of both the teacher and the pupil, with an enthusiasm that exceeds that of the week-day school. Second, we need each school cooperating with every other school in making possible an ideal, healthy, happy and zealous Sunday School Association. This will require attendance from each school, complete reports, and an effort born of zeal, prayer and vision. Third, surely every church will use the opportunity her school offers in the great cause of evangelism. Here at hand is a faculty of talent, influence and consecration. Let each teacher be a soul winner. Let every Christian work through the Sunday School organization. When we come to teach the Word as Philip taught it to the Eunuch some one will say "see, here is water; what doth hinder me to be baptized?"

Respectfully submitted,
A. A. Walker.

29. The report on Minister's Relief and Annuity was presented by A. Lincoln Fulk. Upon motion to adopt the report the subject was discussed by Walter Crissman and J. M. Hilliard. The report is adopted.

Report on Ministerial Relief and Annuity

One of the most appealing and most neglected phases of our organized work is that of relief for old and disabled ministers of the Cross of Christ. Because we do not wish to forget these needy Soldiers of the Cross and have them become objects of charity, the Relief and Annuity Board was organized in 1918. The aim of this Board has been to be able to give security to our worthy veterans of the Gospel; this has been realized in part in direct relief and in annuities.

The work of the Board, therefore, is two fold. First, to give direct relief to ministers and their widows as the funds will permit, and, secondly, to furnish the annuity plan for churches and ministers who are willing to cooperate to assure the minister an income at retirement age. However, only eighteen churches in the state have enlisted with their pastors under this plan. In most cases the salaries of the pastors have been too low to permit them to enter such plan; therefore, Secretary Huggins is working on a plan whereby the Mission Board will become one of the contracting parties to the plan and thus lessen the cost to both pastor and church.

Irregardless of the plan adopted, Southern Baptists need to become conscious of their responsibility to aged ministers. As a class, ministers are not rich, but receive salaries too small to permit adequate provision for old age or loss of health; it is not suggested that these brethren be made rich, but that they be released from anxiety concerning their support in old age.

This is a time when the nation is pension-conscious. But let us keep in mind that the minister is not included in any of the legislative plans now before congress. He is still the responsibility of those to whom he has given his years of service. Shall the government, corporations, and business concerns in general be more conscious of their responsibility to those who give years of service than are the churches themselves? Should the minister continue to feel that the business world offers more old-age security than does the church? Should the government have to step in and take care of neglected preachers who have been forsaken by those to whom they have given their lives? Let each church in the Association either increase its gifts to Ministerial Relief or cooperate in the annuity plan whereby the security of the old servant of God may be assured. The minister is worthy of his hire and of his keep.

Respectfully submitted,
A. Lincoln Fulk.

30. The following recommendation presented by J. Ben Eller was approved:

"I move that the Piedmont Baptist Association commend to our General Board and to our North Carolina Baptist State Convention a favorable consideration of some plan of cooperation with our Ministers' Relief and Annuity Board similar to that now followed in South Carolina; and that our Clerk be requested to send a copy of this motion to Brother M. A. Huggins.

31. The Verbal Report Hour was in charge of Harvey L. Paschal. Representatives from eighteen Churches reported.

32. The report on Obituaries was presented by C. D. Barton. The report was adopted.

Report on Obituaries

Jesus left to His Bride, the Church the ordinance of the Lord's Supper lest She forget Him and His death and His suffering, and His coming again. So it is fitting that we should not forget those who have toiled and sacrificed and suffered that the cause of Christ should thus far be advanced. May we take up the torch of faith flung to us by their failing hands, and bear it high in loving memory of their devotion to Him who shall come again to receive His Bride.

May He find us watching, for in such an hour as we think not He cometh.

Respectfully submitted,
C. D. Barton.

33. The following reports of committees were presented and adopted:

The Committee to Nominate the Promotion-Executive Committee. The committee nominates the present committee: J. C. Turner, C. E. Parker, A. L. Fulk.

The Committee on Place and Preacher. We recommend as Preacher, Dr. J. Clyde Turner; Alternate, C. E. Parker. That the place of meeting be referred to the Executive Committee.

Committee—Wilson Woodcock, J. N. Bowman.

Committee to Nominate Church Advisory Committee—We recommend the election of the present committee.

Committee—T. L. Sasser, A. E. Tate, A. A. Chandler.

Auditing Committee—The committee finds the Treasurer's records correct.

Committee—F. L. Paschal.

The Committee on Resolutions—

Report of Resolutions Committee

Whereas the Piedmont Association meeting with the Hilliard Memorial church, October 19, 20, 1938, has experienced one of the finest sessions in its history, be it therefore resolved:

First, that we express our appreciations to the hostess church and her pastor, H. O. Miller ,and all the Baptist churches in High Point that assisted her, for every effort on their part to entertain the association in the gracious way they have.

Second, that we acknowledge the charitable, untiring and wise efforts of our Moderator, Grover H. Jones, who has personally visited the majority of the churches in our association during the past year and made possible in many other ways the success of this meeting; and to our Clerk, O. E. Lee, qualified with an experience and concern peculiar to no other, who so gladly has made himself available to every demand that has arisen throughout the year.

Third, that we heartily commend the work of the Woman's Missionary Union, the Sunday School, and especially that of the Young People as demonstrated in the Wednesday evening program of this meeting. We urge all our young people to lay their various talents upon the altar of service.

Fourth, that we acknowledge our debt of gratitude to God for all the spiritual contributions made in this meeting through every person taking part on the program.

Respectfully submitted,
A. A. Walker, Chm.
Mrs. Nettie Hatcher Hoge,
D. W. Overby.

Committee on Program for Next Session

Religious Literature	John U. Garner
Foreign Missions	Dr. A. B. Conrad
Denominational Program	C. E. Parker
State Missions	Wilson Woodcock
Social Service	C. N. Royal
Orphanage	H. R. Starling
B. T. U.	J. Carl Bell
Woman's Missionary Work	Mrs. Nettie H. Hoge
Hospital	D. W. Overbey
Christian Education	Hughey O. Miller
Home Missions	A. L. Fulk
Sunday Schools	F. L. Paschal
Ministers' Relief and Annuity	J. H. Saunders
Obituaries	J. N. Bowman

Respectfully submitted,
O. E. Lee, H. R. Starling, H. O. Miller.

A. Lincoln Fulk was elected to represent the Biblical Recorder in the Association.

Committee to Nominate Delegates to the State Convention—We nominate the following: Grover H. Jones and T. L. Sasser.
Committee: C. N. Royal, G. H. Liner, Miss Thelma Patrick.

The matter of the Leader of the Verbal Report Hour was referred to the Executive Committee.

The Committee to Nominate Members of the Committee on Evangelism—We recommend the following: Mrs. Nettie H. Hoge, C. N. Royal, D. W. Overbey.

Respectfully submitted,
Committee: Grover H. Jones, A. A. Walker, Mrs. W. H. McKeever.

After singing "God Be With You Till We Meet Again" the session closed with prayer by Brother J. M. Hilliard.

IN MEMORIAM

CALVARY:
Mr. C. J. Delgardo, Deacon
Mr. J. L. Hudson
FAIRVIEW:
Mr. C. H. Pearson, Deacon
Mrs. Cassie M. Griffin
GREENSBORO, FIRST:
Mr. Riley Ely
Mr. A. F. Heath
Mr. R. G. Hill
Mr. W. E. Grovenor
Mr. W. H. Foster
Mrs. L. C. Shaw
Mrs. I. W. White
Mrs. G. F. Blackmon
Mrs. Ida Rieves
Mrs. J. L. Spencer
Mrs. Henry Hunter
Mrs. W. M. King
Mrs. John Williams
Mrs. Ella Carr Liles
Mrs. Wm. Rightsell
ASHEBORO STREET:
Mr. Charles Snead
Mr. Charles T. Brown
Mrs. G. W. Vernon
Mrs. H. T. Rider
Mrs. H. M. Howard
Mrs. Julia Fogleman
BESSEMER:
Mrs. C. T. West
FOREST AVENUE:
Mr. W. R. Byrd
Mr. W. W. Williams
Mrs. Nettie Fay
LATHAM PARK:
Mr. M. L. Shirrell, Deacon
MAGNOLIA STREET:
Mrs. Emma Durham
Mrs. Holyfield
POMONA:
Mrs. Emma Bradley
REVOLUTION:
Miss Marion Caddell
Mr. N. A. Murray
SIXTEENTH STREET:
Mr. J. E. Hayes
Mrs. J. R. Watkins
Mrs. J. C. Wright
Miss Thelma Micheal
STEVENS MEMORIAL:
Mr. John Ledbetter
Mrs. Bessie Bivins
WEBSTER MEMORIAL:
Mrs. W. F. Ball
Mr. E. J. Stenson
Mr. Jim Snyder

IN MEMORIAM

HIGH POINT, FIRST:
- Mr. J. L. Chernault
- Mr. R. T. Chappell, Deacon
- Mr. G. W. Clark
- Mrs. J. W. Wilson
- Mrs. R. L. Loflin
- Mr. Herbert Wilson
- Mrs. Dora Fruitt

GREEN STREET:
- Mrs. Chas. Farrington
- Miss Louise Huffham
- Mr. J. D. Smith, Jr.
- Mrs. J. D. Priest
- Mr. J. B. Bridges, Deacon
- Mr. E. A. Yates
- Mr. D. A. Fowler

HILLIARD MEMORIAL:
- Mr. H. E. Taylor, Deacon

NORTH MAIN STREET:
- Mrs. W. R. Hargrove
- Mrs. Effie Smith

SOUTH SIDE:
- Mrs. Lela Cates
- Mrs. J. I. Campbell
- Mrs. M. H. Dorsett
- Mrs. M .O. Huntsinger
- Mrs. Essie Stone

WEST END:
- Mrs. Nora Cecil
- Mrs. Anna Cecil

LEBANON:
- Mr. S. F. Miloway, Deacon

OAK GROVE:
- Mr. L. H. Jackson
- Mr. L. F. Patton

OSBORNE CHAPEL:
- Mr. Robert McCandless

PLEASANT GARDEN:
- Mrs. Worsham
- Mrs. Lillie Taylor Jordan

REIDSVILLE, FIRST:
- Mr. George E. Barber
- Mrs. S. N. White
- Mrs. Lucy Sluder
- Mr. R. W. Justice
- Mr. T .I. Duke

ROCKY KNOLL:
- Mrs. J. M. Kellam

RUFFIN STACEY:
- Mrs. Effie Baker

SUMMERFIELD:
- Mr. Thomas Moore

TABERNACLE:
- Mr. Broadus Roach

W. M. U. ANNUAL REPORT

Theme: Entrusted Tasks—John 14:15

The Woman's Missionary Union of the Piedmont Baptist Association held its regular annual session with the Reidsville church April 28, 1938, the Supt. Mrs. Nettie H. Hoge, presiding.

After the devotional period order of business was taken up. The minutes of last meeting were omitted. Leaders of the three districts brought reports showing much interest and activity, Miss Ruth Scott brought a report from the young people's work, Mrs. J. J. Andoe spoke on Mission Study, and Mrs. C. N. Royal, Stewardship Chairman, gave her report.

Two committees were appointed by the chair and asked to report at the afternoon session. Nominating Committee—Mrs. J. S. Moore, Mrs. Morrison, Mrs. H. M. Fitts, Mrs. H. L. Koontz. Committee on Time and Place and Resolutions—Mrs. O. J. Howard, Mrs. F. L. Conrad, Mrs. J. H. Saunders.

After the singing of hymn "To The Work," Mrs. J. Clyde Turner was asked to take the chair while the Supt. made her report and gave her message. Mrs. Hoge's theme was "Our Entrusted Task." She expressed gratitude to God for blessings on the year's work; paid tribute to the Pioneers and spoke of larger plans for the new year. Enlistment and development of those enlisted were stressed, and the value of having goals for each organization in the churches was emphasized. Mrs. Hoge stated her belief that the most vital task before the church today is the homeland. Preserving our entrusted heritage and propagation of our Christian ideals and principles. She spoke of the evil forces at work in our country to tear down what we have wrought and urged that the situation not be accepted passively, but that Christ's followers be alert to the dangers on every hand.

Dr. J. Clyde Turner was next presented and brought a message on "Soul Winning." The importance of winning people to Christ, the cry of a lost world and the command of Christ were the three points stressed. "I think we are making a failure if we fail in this supreme task of winning souls to Christ," was Dr. Turner's concluding thought.

The meeting then adjourned and the ladies of the hostess church graciously served lunch to the assembly.

The meeting was called to order at 1:45 for the afternoon session. Devotional period was led by Miss Thelma Patrick, who stressed individual responsibility in winning souls to Christ.

Mrs. L. M. Gideon, Chairman of Personal Service, was called on for her report. She emphasized work among the Jews and Negroes, and gave her report in the form of a reading entitled "The Heavenly Guest."

Reports of committees was next asked for, and Mrs. J. S. Moore, Chairman of the Nominating Committee offered the following names for election: Supt., Mrs. Nettie H. Hoge; Leaders of Districts: Reidsville, Mrs. T. L. Sasser; High Point, Mrs. H. A. Knight; Greensboro, Mrs. O. J. Howard; secretary, Mrs. A. Andrews; treasurer, Mrs. C. E. Siceloff; Leader of Young People, Miss Ruth Scott; Stewardship Chairman, Mrs. C. N. Royal; Personal Service Chairman, Mrs. L. M. Gideon; Mission Study, Mrs. J. J. Andoe.

Mrs. O. J. Howard, Chairman on Resolutions and Time and Place, submitted resolutions and reported time for next meeting last Thursday in April, 1939.

Mrs. J. Clyde Turner presided over a memorial service, the Union standing for a brief time in memory of those who had died since last meeting. Mrs. Turner read a beautiful tribute to Mrs. N. R. White, a beloved member of the Reidsville church, who had served long and faithfully. Mrs. H. E. Armstrong sang "Those Golden Bells." After the singing of hymn "How Firm A Foundation" a Golden Jubilee Pageant was given under the direction of Miss Netta Liles, assisted by members of the First Church, Greensboro.

The meeting then adjourned.

MRS. CHAS. A. TUCKER, Secretary Pro-tem.

HISTORICAL TABLE — PIEDMONT BAPTIST ASSOCIATION

YEAR	WHERE HELD	MODERATOR	CLERK	PREACHER	Churches	Baptisms	Church Members	Total Gifts
1894	Greensboro	Dr. C. A. Rominger	W. L. Kivett	M. A. [illegible]	5	....	562	....
1895	Liberty	T. L. Chislom	W. L. Kivett	L. [illegible]	12	16	112	$ 4695.50
1896	Moore's [illegible]apel	R. W. Brooks	W. H. Eller	L. Johnson	14	66	1194	5128.94
1897	Summerfield	F. H. Jones	W. H. Eller	J. A. [illegible]	16	73	1540	7198.27
1898	Mount Zion	R. W. Brooks	W. H. Eller	L. Johnson	17	67	1557	6883.23
1899	Ramseur	R. W. Brooks	F. P. Tucker	John E. [illegible]ite	19	54	1570	7435.43
1900	Cherry Street	R. W. Brooks	W. H. Eller	[illegible] Carrick	16	48	1538	7970.35
1901	Reidsville	F. H. Jones	W. H. Eller	L. Johnson	19	157	1657	8282.73
1902	Salem [illegible]	F. H. Jones	W. H. Eller	W. C. [illegible]	19	135	1774	9950.97
1903	[illegible]	F. H. Jones	W. H. Eller	C. L. [illegible]	20	185	1868	12834.77
1904	[illegible]	F. H. Jones	W. H. Eller	H. W. Battle	22	112	1832	12807.43
1905	Randleman	F. H. Jones	W. H. Eller	J. M. Hilliard	22	114	2096	17674.91
1906	High Point, First	F. H. Jones	W. H. Eller	W. R. Bradshaw	23	201	2333	29366.31
1907	Asheboro Street	F. H. Jones	W. H. Eller	Wm. [illegible]	26	372	2798	29993.79
1908	Ramseur	F. H. Jones	W. H. Eller	C. E. Maddry	28	311	3086	26347.57
1909	Greensboro	F. H. Jones	W. H. Eller	Wm. Hedley	30	292	3429	49847.28
1910	[illegible] Zion	F. H. Jones	W. H. Eller	R. G. Hendrick	31	336	3731	28531.01
1911	[illegible]	W. F. Staley	W. H. Eller	W. F. Staley	29	182	3736	25887.56
1912	High Point, Green St.	F. P. Hobgood Jr.	W. H. Eller	J. C. Turner	30	174	3647	29697.38
1913	Liberty	F. P. Hobgood, Jr.	W. H. Eller	R. P. [illegible]	31	409	3971	37700.97
1914	Asheboro Street	F. P. Hobgood, Jr.	W. H. Eller	A. W. Claxon	31	413	4202	42428.44
1915	Reidsville	J. M. Hilliard	W. H. Eller	J. M. Hilliard	42	313	4491	42577.68
1916	Forest Avenue	J. M. Hilliard	W. H. Eller	E. N. Johnson	36	369	4854	48418.92
1917	Green Street	J. M. Hilliard	W. H. Eller	W. R. White	39	308	4760	44609.05
1918	Moore's Chapel	J. M. Hilliard	W. H. Eller	J. W. Rose	39	374	5140	72538.46
1919	White Oak	J. M. Hilliard	W. H. Eller	W. H. Wilson	39	339	5359	76638.85
1920	Calvary	J. M. Hilliard	W. H. Eller	E. N. Johnson	39	543	5867	117682.35
1921	Summerfield	Clarence A. Smith	J. E. Lanier	B. K. [illegible]	39	480	6454	135561.79
1922	[illegible]	Clarence A. Smith	J. E. Lanier	Jas. A. Clark	39	679	7226	149955.24
1923	Magnolia Street	Clarence A. [illegible]	H. O. Miller	E. E. [illegible]	38	365	7341	140553.25
1924	West End	Clarence A. Smith	H. O. [illegible]	W. E. [illegible]	40	672	7489	164658.19
1925	Fairview	[illegible] A. Smith	H. O. Miller	A. T. Howell	41	610	8956	211792.21
1926	Ramseur	Clarence A. Smith	S. T. Hensley	Lloyd T. Wilson	42	620	9974	243500.68
1927	Trinity	Clarence A. Smith	S. T. Hensley	H. T. [illegible]	40	656	10223	211846.40
1928	Bessemer	Clarence A. Smith	O. E. Lee	R. P. Ellington	41	531	10866	202002.30
1929	Liberty	Clarence A. Smith	O. E. Lee	C. F. Rogers	44	573	11496	218987.61
1930	Asheboro	Clarence A. Smith	O. E. Lee	Geo. T. [illegible]	44	676	12012	198077.29
1931	Florida Street	Clarence A. Smith	O. E. Lee	A. B. Conrad	44	827	12789	178501.19
1932	Reidsville	Clarence A. Smith	O. E. Lee	J. C. [illegible]	46	778	13485	159000.60
1933	White Oak	Clarence A. Smith	O. E. Lee	T. L. Sasser	48	1561	15199	186041.40
1934	Franklinville	Clarence A. Smith	O. E. Lee	Wilson Woodcock	53	757	15356	172839.18
1935	[illegible], High Point	Clarence A. Smith	O. E. Lee	J. S. Hopkins	41	623	12687	164135.92
1936	Calvary	Clarence A. Smith	O. E. Lee	J. Ben Eller	42	563	13958	166052.96
1937	Eller [illegible]	Grover H. Jones	O. E. Lee	C. N. Royal	41	657	14086	195540.50
1938	Hilliard Memorial	Grover H. Jones	O. E. Lee	A. B. Conrad	42	814	14793	200246.20

CHURCHES	Village, Town, City or Country?	When Constituted	PASTORS AND POST OFFICES	Days of Meeting	Members Reported Last Year	CHURCH MEMBERSHIP Gains: Baptisms	Gains: Letters	Gains: Statements	Gains: Restorations	Losses: Letters	Losses: Exclusions	Losses: Erasures	Losses: Deaths	Total Present Members	Weekly Prayer Meet'gs	Revivals Held	Obs. Lord's Supper	Rec. State Bap. Paper
1. Allen Jay	V	1934	C. M. Floyd, R. 2, [illegible]	2 4	53	33	22	...	...	4	...	1	...	103	*	2	3	5
2. Buchanan	O	......	J. B. Clifton, [illegible]	All	32	10	23	1	...	...	...	...	...	66	*	2	1	...
3. [illegible]	O	1901	J. C. [illegible], R. 4, Reidsville	2 4	160	2	1	...	...	...	...	...	2	161	...	1	2	21
4. Fairview	O	1904	J. C. [illegible], R. 4, Reidsville	1 3	117	3	3	...	...	...	...	2	2	119	...	1	2	8
5. [illegible]	T	1894	E. A. Long, Germanton	2 4	238	8	5	...	...	3	...	...	...	248	*	1	4	...
6. [illegible]boro, First	C	1859	Dr. J. [illegible] Turner, [illegible]	All	2060	83	133	5	1	83	12	...	15	2172	*	1	12	124
7. [illegible] Street	C	1899	J. Ben Eller, Greensboro	All	1111	18	39	4	...	37	...	7	6	1122	*	1	4	63
8. Bailey [illegible]	C	1935	C. G. Coe, Pomona	All	92	10	8	3	...	15	1	...	...	97	*	2	12	...
9. Bessemer	V	1923	A. A. Walker, Bessemer, [illegible]boro	All	455	...	12	3	...	21	...	...	1	448	*	1	4	1
10. Eller [illegible]	C	1897	C. E. Parker, [illegible]	All	815	22	9	4	...	20	...	2	3	825	*	1	4	40
11. Florida [illegible]	C	1916	J. H. Saunders, [illegible]	All	367	7	34	3	...	36	1	3	...	371	*	1	4	...
12. Forest Avenue	C	1906	[illegible]	All	509	34	19	1	...	26	...	...	3	534	*	1	12	25
13. [illegible] Park	C	1914	C. D. Barton, Bessemer Br., Gr'nsboro	All	34	23	8	3	...	7	...	...	1	60	*	1	1	...
14. [illegible] Street	C	1912	W. F. Hancock, [illegible]	All	367	12	5	6	1	13	...	1	2	380	*	2	...	2
15. Pomona	V	1906	C. M. [illegible], Pomona	All	167	20	6	7	...	1	...	...	1	198	*	2	2	...
16. Revolution	C	......	H. R. Starling, Greensboro	All	312	8	5	...	...	11	...	...	2	312	*	1	1	...
17. [illegible] Street	C	1907	W. B. [illegible], Denim Sta., [illegible]boro	All	452	40	17	8	7	2	...	...	4	518	*	2	11	...
18. Stevens Memorial	V	1922	John U. Garner, [illegible]	All	143	4	8	2	...	3	3	...	2	149	*	1	4	15
19. [illegible]	O	1935	M. L. Hux, R. 5, Greensboro	All	144	10	1	2	...	6	1	2	3	145	...	...	4	11
20. Guilford	V	1914	Robt. [illegible], [illegible]	2 4	72	...	1	...	...	2	...	...	2	70	...	...	2	2
21. High Point, First	C	1825	Dr. A. B. Conrad, High Point	All	1135	51	49	5	...	46	...	35	7	1152	*	1	4	57
22. [illegible]	C	1899	C. N. Royal, High Point	All	1318	76	38	7	...	59	...	3	6	1272	*	2	4	65
23. Hilliard Memorial	C	1929	Hughey O. Miller, High Point	All	290	22	...	1	...	1	3	...	1	302	*	1	1	13
24. North [illegible]	C	1908	A. [illegible] Fulk, High [illegible]	All	232	12	23	1	...	6	...	5	2	255	*	1	3	2
25. North Park	C	1929	E. M. Smith, High Point	Al	180	46	7	...	...	3	...	5	...	225	*	2	3	12
26. South Side	C	......	G. H. Liner, High Point	All	304	30	10	3	1	11	...	...	5	332	*	1	4	...
27. West End	C	1913	J. N. Bowman, High Point	All	393	23	7	5	2	7	...	4	2	417	*	2	4	5
28. Jessup Grove	O	......	Estel Cain, Kernersville	All	45	...	...	...	...	...	...	...	...	35	...	...	...	...
29. Lebanon	O	1911	S. G. Snyder, [illegible]	All	206	30	8	...	...	2	...	...	1	242	*	2	...	...
30. [illegible] Zion	O	......	L. H. Nall, Burlington	......	166	6	...	...	...	...	...	...	...	166	...	...	...	...
31. Oak Grove	O	1916	R. L. [illegible], High [illegible]	All	102	40	5	2	1	6	...	1	2	141	*	2	4	...
32. [illegible]	O	1934	C. W. [illegible], R. 1, [illegible]	All	29	3	6	1	...	6	...	...	1	35	*	1	1	...
33. [illegible]	O	......	J. F. Sellars, Mt. Airy	1 3	40	12	1	2	...	1	...	7	...	47	...	2	4	1
34. [illegible] Garden	V	1933	L. C. [illegible], R. 1, [illegible]	All	92	8	2	2	...	1	...	...	2	101	*	1	4	12
35. Reidsville, First	C	......	T. L. Sasser, Reidsville	All	804	17	20	...	...	15	...	...	5	821	*	1	4	40
36. [illegible] Olive	C	1929	......	All	237	11	1	4	...	1	7	...	...	245	*	1	4	5
37. Penn [illegible]	C	1927	D. W. Overbey, Reidsville	All	162	14	1	4	...	4	...	2	...	175	*	2	4	...
38. Rocky Knoll	O	1934	L. C. Chandler, R. 1, [illegible]	All	144	8	7	2	...	4	...	1	1	155	*	1	4	15
39. Ruffin [illegible]	O	1931	J. T. London, R. 5, Reidsville	All	154	27	1	1	1	...	...	...	1	183	*	2	4	3
40. Smith Grove	O	1921	R. O. [illegible], R. 1, [illegible]	1 3	163	2	...	...	...	...	...	...	...	163	*	2	4	...
41. [illegible]	V	......	E. A. Long, Germantown	1	187	21	3	...	...	...	1	...	1	210	...	1	2	2
42. [illegible]	V	1933	L. D. [illegible], R. 1, Graham	All	27	8	11	9	...	7	5	...	1	21	...	2	0	...
TOTALS	...	......	......	......	14110	814	559	101	14	470	34	81	87	14793	...	54	151	549

TABLE TWO — SUNDAY SCHOOLS

CHURCHES	SUPERINTENDENTS AND POST OFFICES	Cradle Roll Under 3	Beginners 3-5 Years	Primaries 6-8 Years	Juniors 9-12 Years	Intermediates 13-16	Young People 17-24	Adults 25 and Up	Extension Department	Total Enrollment	Average Attendance	Baptisms from S. S.	Is School Graded?	Teachers Holding Diplomas	Enrollment V. B. S	Average Attendance
1. Allen Jay	Wade Cumbie, R. 1, Trinity	10	15	20	35	38	24	92	...	234	133	28	*	...	...	...
2. Buchanan	Harry L. Mabe, Bessemer Br., G'boro.	...	26	....	40	....	41	58	...	165	105	...	...	...	...	...
3. Calvary	George Gunn, Reidsville	...	....	10	15	16	50	49	...	140	75	2	...	...	...	...
4. Fairview	A. D. Hopkins, Reidsville	...	....	....	....	....	....	....	...	92	....	...	...	...	...	...
5. Gibsonville	C. C. Hammer, Gibsonville	...	19	28	48	42	42	76	16	271	150	8	...	10	...	...
6. Greensboro, First	O. E. Lee, Greensboro	160	92	175	266	208	237	1015	206	2359	995	70	*	3	202	141
7. Asheboro Street	M. D. Teague, Greensboro	31	62	106	144	151	93	372	50	1009	484	...	*	7	...	...
8. Bailey Memorial	C. C. Stanley, Greensboro	...	....	17	22	16	58	35	...	148	....	...	...	...	...	...
9. Bessemer	C. L. Casey, Bessemer Br., Greensboro	20	21	33	69	61	52	121	...	377	188	...	...	1	92	64
10. Eller Memorial	A. M. Bass, Greensboro	25	34	90	108	77	107	129	...	570	326	...	*	...	...	...
11. Florida Street	J. B. Rumbley, Greensboro	12	22	48	56	49	22	69	...	278	....	...	...	...	...	...
12. Forest Avenue	Dr. J. T. J. Battle, Greensboro	46	18	57	55	62	163	118	...	519	308	...	*	15	122	88
13. Latham Park	A. C. Melvin, Bessemer Br., Greensboro	...	....	....	....	....	....	....	...	113	70	23	...	...	...	...
14. Magnolia Street	D. L. Wrenn, Greensboro	14	19	25	26	11	50	83	...	228	130	...	...	...	...	...
15. Pomona	C. C. Patterson, Pomona	...	36	33	72	54	64	78	...	337	218	15	*	...	...	...
16. Revolution	Grady Phillips, Greensboro	45	37	39	46	53	36	62	22	340	175	...	...	...	...	...
17. Sixteenth Street	Fred Hester, Greensboro	15	37	55	89	64	82	238	...	580	398	...	...	...	221	132
18. Stevens Memorial	L. A. Mills, Greensboro	4	8	36	27	19	33	92	...	219	180	...	*	...	...	...
19. Webster Memorial	E. D. Young, Greensboro	16	16	19	22	39	32	77	...	221	134	2	*	...	65	50
20. Guilford	J. Setzer Weston, Guilford College	...	15	....	12	....	15	73	...	115	....	...	...	...	...	...
21. High Point, First	A. E. Tate, High Point	42	72	131	152	139	97	435	66	1134	565	45	*	3	...	...
22. Green Street	Walter Crissman, High Point	57	74	120	254	161	179	477	...	1322	....	...	...	...	...	...
23. Hilliard Memorial	L. E. Edwards, High Point	...	47	25	45	100	24	124	...	365	204	19	*	...	83	...
24. North Main	Winfred Clinard, High Point	...	27	43	55	45	59	41	...	270	196	11	*	...	...	...
25. North Park	L. R. McNeill, High Point	20	20	31	51	20	52	53	7	254	168	46	...	...	...	...
26. South Side	D. A. Howard, High Point	...	11	38	57	49	38	66	...	259	182	...	*	...	...	...
27. West End	W. A. Hedrick, High Point	45	28	60	76	56	96	115	25	501	....	...	*	...	...	...
28. Jessup Grove	Charley Johnson, Guilford College	...	....	....	....	....	....	....	...	63	25	...	...	...	...	...
29. Lebanon	Diamond Davis, R. 2, Brown Summit	32	18	....	19	9	38	68	...	184	152	...	...	...	...	...
30. Mount Zion	C. D. Branson, Snow Camp	...	27	....	17	....	39	22	...	105	....	...	...	...	...	...
31. Oak Grove	L. R. Loflin, Jamestown	...	24	24	25	....	23	74	...	170	120	...	...	...	...	...
32. Osborne Chapel	R. R. Osborne, R. 3, Greensboro	...	31	....	13	....	31	33	...	108	70	...	*	...	...	...
33. Osceola	P. D. McKinney, R. 1, Gibsonville	...	11	11	19	13	10	13	...	77	47	...	...	...	...	...
34. Pleasant Garden	H. L. Paschal, R. 1, Greensboro	9	13	18	10	6	20	23	...	99	54	8	...	...	...	...
35. Reidsville, First	R. T. Burton, Reidsville	52	34	66	103	75	66	282	50	728	308	15	*	...	177	143
36. Mount Olive	Odell Delapp, Reidsville	8	20	14	52	34	61	45	...	234	164	...	*	1	35	25
37. Penn Memorial	Herbert Ford, Reidsville	...	14	20	14	11	11	64	...	134	75	5	...	...	...	...
38. Rocky Knoll	G. L. York, Greensboro	28	26	....	25	32	47	71	...	229	164	...	...	...	...	...
39. Ruffin Stacey	Dewey London, R. 5, Reidsville	...	....	....	....	....	....	....	...	258	112	...	...	...	...	...
40. Smith Grove	Dovie Clark, Colfax	...	30	32	25	....	35	25	...	147	70	2	...	...	...	...
41. Summerfield	C. V. Furgerson, Summerfield	...	....	....	....	....	....	....	...	124	....	...	...	...	...	...
42. Tabernacle	E. W. Hunt, Elon College	...	....	20	21	....	16	22	...	79	....	...	...	...	...	...
TOTALS		691	1004	1444	2185	1710	2143	4890	442	15159	6745	299	...	40	997	643

TABLE THREE — BAPTIST TRAINING UNION

CHURCHES	B.T.U. With Director	B. A. U.'s	Sr. B. Y. P. U.'s	Intermediate Unions	Junior Unions	Total Unions	Adults Enrolled	Seniors Enrolled	Intermediates Enrolled	Juniors Enrolled	Total Enrolled	Story Hours	T't'l Daily Bible R'd'rs	Study Course	Total Systematic Givers All Unions	No. A-1 for 1 Quarter	Students in College	Brotherhoods	Enrollment of Brotherhoods
1. Allen Jay	Yes	...	1	1	1	3	...	18	20	12	50	...	13	12	34	...	...	...	...
2. [redacted]e		...	1	1	1	3	...	...	...	...	61	...	...	...	...	...	...	...	...
3. [redacted]o, First	Yes	4	4	3	4	15	54	61	64	49	244	16	97	51	161	...	4	1	46
4. [redacted]o Street	Yes	1	1	2	2	6	30	28	49	34	161	20	47	55	90	...	3	...	...
5. Bessemer	Yes	1	1	1	1	4	14	10	21	15	63	3	21	20	48	...	1	...	...
6. Eller Memorial	Yes	1	1	1	2	5	25	16	19	24	94	10	29	...	39	...	...	...	...
7. Florida Street	Yes	1	1	2	2	6	16	8	26	25	85	10	46	46	49	...	1	...	...
8. Forest Avenue	Yes	1	8	1	1	11	17	133	13	20	183	...	15	33	38	...	...	...	...
9. Latham Park	...	...	...	1	...	1	...	...	20	...	20	...	...	6	...	...	...	...	...
10. Magnolia Street	...	...	...	...	1	1	...	...	...	12	12	...	...	...	...	...	...	...	...
11. Pomona	Yes	...	1	1	1	3	...	12	16	35	63	...	...	...	...	...	...	...	...
12. Revolution	...	...	...	1	...	1	...	12	...	...	12	...	10	10	12	...	...	...	...
13. Sixteenth Street	Yes	...	1	1	2	4	...	16	14	35	80	15	...	...	...	...	...	...	...
14. [redacted]s [redacted]rial	Yes	...	1	...	1	2	...	8	...	14	22	...	9	12	7	...	5	...	...
15. [redacted]l [redacted]d	...	...	...	...	...	...	...	...	...	...	...	...	...	...	...	...	1	...	...
16. High Point, First	Yes	...	1	2	1	4	...	25	33	26	102	18	35	41	57	...	6	...	...
17. [redacted]n Street	Yes	1	3	4	2	10	12	51	58	28	157	8	71	75	93	1	2	...	...
18. Hilliard [redacted]orial	...	1	1	1	1	4	14	15	18	19	78	12	28	53	45	...	1	...	...
19. [redacted]th Main	[redacted]s	1	1	2	2	6	9	15	25	18	82	15	25	29	36	...	...	...	...
20. North Park	Yes	1	1	1	2	5	22	25	22	33	102	...	46	86	68	...	4	...	...
21. South [redacted]le	Yes	...	1	1	1	3	...	10	25	20	55	...	13	18	21	...	...	...	...
22. [redacted]t End	[redacted]s	1	1	2	2	6	13	24	22	32	91	...	39	74	60	...	...	...	...
23. Lebanon	...	1	1	1	1	4	16	20	10	10	56	...	...	...	...	...	...	...	...
24. Osborne [redacted]pel	Yes	...	1	...	...	1	...	12	...	...	12	...	...	25	...	...	...	...	...
25. Pleasant Garden	...	...	1	...	1	2	...	15	...	5	20	...	...	12	...	...	...	...	...
[redacted]e, First	Yes	1	3	2	2	8	15	50	44	42	151	...	46	53	70	...	...	...	...
27. Mount l[redacted]e	Yes	...	1	1	1	3	...	24	17	12	73	20	...	...	...	...	...	...	...
28. Penn [redacted]rial	...	...	1	1	1	3	...	15	21	17	53	...	24	6	24	...	...	...	...
29. [redacted]k Knoll	Yes	1	1	1	...	3	25	28	28	...	101	20	...	...	...	...	...	...	...
30. [redacted]ld	...	...	1	...	1	2	...	29	...	12	41	...	8	7	...	...	...	...	...
TOTALS	...	7	140	35	37	129	282	680	585	549	2324	213	622	724	952	1	28	1	46

TABLE FOUR — WOMAN'S MISSIONARY UNION

CHURCHES	PRESIDENTS OF W. M. S. AND POST OFFICES	No. W's. M. Societies	No. of Y. W. A's.	No. of G. A's.	No. of R. A's.	No. of Sunbeams	Total W. M. U. Org's.	W. M. S. Members	Y. W. A's. Members	G. A's. Members	R. A's. Members	Sunbeam Members	Total Members Enr'led	Total Enr'led M. S. C.	Contributions to Local Work by W. M. U.	Contributions to Missions by W. M. U.	Grand Total Given by W. M. U.
1. Calvary	Mrs. [illegible]ce [illegible]e, Reidsville	1	1	...	...	...	2	20	15	...	...	...	35	...	5.16	165.14	170.30
2. [illegible]e	...	1	...	...	...	...	1	30	...	...	...	...	30	...	....	17.80	17.80
3. [illegible]o, First	Mrs. W. M. McKeever, [illegible]	1	2	2	3	1	9	413	36	81	44	65	[illegible]	311	407.33	13015.78	13423.11
4. [illegible]o Street	Mrs. J. S. Moore, [illegible]o	1	2	3	1	1	8	162	43	65	18	27	[illegible]	103	163.60	1735.56	1899.16
5. Bessemer	Mrs. J. T. Willett, Bess. Br., G'boro	1	1	1	...	1	4	26	22	14	...	20	82	6	....	181.77	181.77
6. [illegible]r [illegible]ial	Mrs. Lloyd Vonadore, [illegible]o	1	1	...	...	1	3	38	18	...	...	16	72	16	10.00	199.00	2[illegible]9.00
7. Florida [illegible]et	Mrs. C. N. Hutchinson, [illegible]o	[illegible]	1	1	1	1	5	41	9	10	15	22	97	30	....	109.76	109.76
8. [illegible]t A[illegible]e	Mrs. E. W. Richardson, [illegible]o	1	1	1	...	1	4	50	35	11	...	8	104	...	....	793.62	793.62
9. Magnolia Street	[illegible]s. L. L. Jarvis, [illegible]o	1	1	...	...	...	2	25	10	...	...	...	35	...	24.73	41.67	66.40
10. Pomona	Mrs. W. G. [illegible]e, Pomona	1	...	1	...	...	2	28	...	22	...	...	50	...	4.70	52.09	56.79
11. Revolution	[illegible]s Salie Burgess, [illegible]o	1	1	1	1	1	5	22	9	21	6	25	83	...	....	465.54	465.54
12. [illegible]h Street	[illegible] W. A. Straughn, [illegible]	1	1	1	1	1	5	38	20	15	14	10	97	...	.. -	....	....
13. Stevens [illegible]orial	Mrs. C. B. Brisson, R. 2, [illegible]o	1	...	1	...	1	3	30	...	14	...	12	56	...	.. -	150.18	150.18
14. [illegible]r Me[illegible]il	Mrs. V. H. Lucas, R. 5, [illegible]o	1	...	1	...	1	3	48	...	14	...	10	72	33	....	152.70	152.70
15. [illegible]d	[illegible] R. B. Ferrell, Guilford	1	...	...	...	...	1	14	...	...	...	...	14	...	....	....	....
16. High Point, First	Mrs. P. Y. Adams, High Point	1	1	1	...	1	4	189	20	14	...	34	[illegible]	23	701.37	3381.17	4082.54
17. Green Street	[illegible] M. W. Buser, High Point	7	2	2	1	1	13	86	31	25	12	8	[illegible]	86	527.00	....	527.00
18. [illegible]d Memorial	Mrs. J. B. [illegible]s, High P[illegible]t	1	1	2	...	1	5	15	10	26	...	12	63	9	....	46.68	46.68
19. North Main	Mrs. [illegible]e Davis, R. 1, High Point	1	...	...	...	...	1	15	...	...	...	...	15	12	43.00	70.00	113.00
20. North Park	Mrs. J. A. Jones, High Point	1	1	1	1	2	6	16	17	14	7	25	79	...	.. -	9.00	9.00
21. South Side	[illegible]s. Pearl [illegible]h, High Point	1	...	1	...	1	3	25	...	22	...	23	70	...	24.10	8.60	32.70
22. [illegible]st End	[illegible] T. P. [illegible]s, High Point	2	1	2	1	1	7	29	12	16	10	15	82	29	18.61	194.95	213.56
23. [illegible]e [illegible]hapel	[illegible] J. C. [illegible]y, R. 3 [illegible]o	1	...	...	...	...	1	...	...	...	...	...	...	...	....	....	....
24. Pleasant [illegible]h	Mrs. J. E. Thompson, Pleasant Garden	1	...	...	...	...	1	15	...	...	...	15	...	...	....	....	....
25. [illegible]e, First	Mrs. T. L. Sasser, Reidsville	1	1	...	...	...	2	150	16	...	...	...	[illegible]	66	4360.95	1221.55	5582.50
26. Mount Olive	[illegible] J. H. Saunders, Reidsville	5	...	...	...	1	6	95	...	...	...	20	15	...	....	....	....
27. [illegible]h [illegible]ial	[illegible]s. [illegible]e [illegible]y, Reidsville	3	1	...	...	...	4	37	9	...	...	...	46	...	734.25	17.40	751.65
28. Rocky Knoll	Mrs. Carl [illegible]r, R. 1, Greensboro	1	...	...	...	...	1	17	...	...	...	...	[illegible]	...	16.95	5.00	21.95
29. Ruffin Stacey	Mrs. [illegible]e Schum, Ruffine	1	...	...	...	...	1	22	...	...	...	...	22	...	....	....	....
30. [illegible]d	Mrs. A. C. Lloyd, Summerfield	1	...	...	...	...	1	18	...	...	...	...	18	...	....	....	99.65
[illegible]S	...	43	20	22	10	18	113	1714	332	384	126	352	2908	724	7041.75	22034.96	29176.36

CHURCHES	CHURCH CLERKS AND POST OFFICES	Own House Worship?	When Was it Built?	Materials Used	Persons Seated	Number of Rooms	Dept. Assembly Rooms	No. Sep. Class Rooms	Value Church House and Grounds	Value Mission Chapel	Value Pastor's Home	Total Value All Church Property	Indebtedness on All Church Property	Insurance Carried
1. Allen Jay	[illegible] Younts, [illegible]	Yes	[illegible]	[illegible]	300	8	8	7	2000	....	.....	2000	200.00	1500
2. [illegible]	E. C [illegible], R. 2 [illegible]	Yes	1886	[illegible]	150	5	4	4	3000	....	.....	3250	....	.....
3. Calvary	J. E. McCargo, [illegible]	Yes	1898	[illegible]	275	5	4	4	5000	....	1000	6000	....	2000
4. Fairview	[illegible] Cummings, R. 2, [illegible]sville	Yes	1901	[illegible]	300	5	...	4	2000	....	1000	3000	....	1500
5 [illegible]	W. P. Killette, [illegible]	Yes	1894	[illegible]	300	9	9	9	3000	....	.....	3000	....	2500
6 [illegible], First	[illegible] R. Bennette, [illegible]	Yes	[illegible]	Brick	1000	48	9	48	145000	....	15000	160000	....	70000
[illegible] Street	J. B. Wills, Greensboro	Yes	1912	Brick	700	32	6	47	30000	....	6000	36000	....	26000
8. Bailey [illegible]	W. J. [illegible], [illegible]	Yes	[illegible]35	[illegible]	250	1	...	...	1000	....	.....	1000	....	700
9. Bessemer	C. L. Murray, Box 688, [illegible]	Yes	1923	[illegible]	350	16	2	16	5500	....	2000	7500	1000.00	4500
10. Eller [illegible]	Carl Ham, Greensboro	Yes	1925	Brick	700	48	7	48	41000	....	9000	50000	....	25000
[illegible] Street	J. B. [illegible], Sr., [illegible]	Yes	1930	Brick	450	22	2	21	15000	....	.....	15000	1000.00	10000
12. Forest [illegible]	Carroll O. [illegible], [illegible]	Yes	1906	Brick	275	14	6	14	17000	....	8000	41000	2800.00	10750
[illegible] Park	W. W. Sutton [illegible]	Yes	[illegible]	[illegible]	150	1	...	...	1000	....	.....	.....	....	..
14. Magnolia Street	[illegible] G. [illegible], Greensboro	Yes	1912	[illegible]	300	10	10	10	6000	....	4500	10500	2385.81	[illegible]
15. Pomona	C. C. Patterson, [illegible]	Yes	1906	[illegible]	350	8	...	7	3000	....	.....	3000	....	.....
[illegible]. Revolution	W. L. Jones, [illegible]	Yes	1907	[illegible]	400	5	3	7	10000	....	5000	15000	....	7500
[illegible]	Alfred E. [illegible], Greensboro	Yes	1907	Brick	500	23	2	16	39000	....	.....	39000	....	15000
18. Stevens [illegible]	Mrs. J. B. Brown, [illegible]	Yes	1922	Wood	250	11	2	13	10000	....	.....	10000	....	6000
[illegible]	Selma Scales, R. 5, [illegible]	Yes	1935	[illegible]	300	10	2	8	5500	....	.....	5500	....	2500
20. Guilford	[illegible] College	Yes	1914	WandB	200	1	1	1	3195	300	.....	4500	....	1500
21. High Point, First	C. D. [illegible], High [illegible]	Yes	'05 '35	Brick	500	46	7	42	110000	....	7000	132000	25273.13	55000
22. Green Street	Clyde Ayers, [illegible]	Yes	[illegible]26	Brick	1500	96	6	68	156000	1500	2500	160000	....	60000
23. Hilliard Memorial	J. W. Saunders, [illegible]	Yes	[illegible]31	Brick	800	22	...	22	25000	....	.....	25000	35.00	5000
24. North [illegible]	[illegible] Lawson, High [illegible]	Yes	1924	Brick	350	23	6	17	17000	....	.....	17000	3000.00	8000
25. North Park	[illegible] B. [illegible], High [illegible]	Yes	[illegible]29	[illegible]	300	19	1	18	3500	....	.....	3500	525.00	1500
26. South Side	I. G. [illegible], [illegible] Point	Yes	[illegible]	[illegible]	450	10	10	10	3500	....	.....	3500	136.00	..
27. West End	O. H. [illegible], High [illegible]	Yes	[illegible]	Wood	350	20	...	18	9500	....	2500	12000	....	[illegible]
28. Jessup Grove	Bertha [illegible], [illegible] 1, [illegible] College	Yes	1934	[illegible]	250	1	...	...	1050	....	.....	1050	....	.....
29. Lebanon	Mrs. Pauline Jarvis, R. 5, [illegible]boro	Yes	[illegible]	[illegible]	200	6	...	5	3000	....	.....	3500	....	2000
[illegible] Zion	J. C. Lackamy, Liberty	Yes	1912	....	500	...	...	1	2000	....	.....	2000	....	.....
31. Oak Grove	L. R. Loflin, Jamestown	Yes	[illegible]27	Wood	270	3	2	2	2000	....	.....	2000	....	1400
32. Osborne [illegible]	R. R. Osborne, R. 3, [illegible]	Yes	1934	[illegible]	250	1	...	...	1500	....	.....	1500	78.00	.....
33. Osceola	E. R. Brande, R. 1, Brown [illegible]	Yes	1915	[illegible]	300	1	...	...	2000	....	.....	2150	....	.....
34. Pleasant [illegible]	[illegible], R. 1, [illegible]	Yes	[illegible]	[illegible]	220	1	...	...	1800	....	.....	1800	125.00	1000
35. Reidsville, First	T. L. Gardner, Reidsville	Yes	1871	Brick	550	24	5	20	37000	....	14000	51000	....	43500
36 [illegible] Olive	W. C. [illegible], Reidsville	Yes	1929	[illegible]	300	13	2	13	5000	....	.....	5000	450.00	4000
[illegible]	Sam [illegible], Reidsville	Yes	1935	Brick	350	13	13	11	10000	....	1500	11500	2200.00	4500
[illegible]	[illegible] Rieves, R. 1, [illegible]	Yes	[illegible]	[illegible]	250	5	4	4	2000	....	.....	2500	....	1500
[illegible] Stacey	[illegible]	Yes	[illegible]	[illegible]	350	1	...	...	2000	....	.....	2300	....	1500
40. Smith Grove	Dovie Clark, Colfax	Yes	1923	[illegible]	300	1	...	...	1500	....	.....	1500	....	600
[illegible]	Mrs. Myrtle Smith [illegible]	Yes	.....	[illegible]	400	1	...	...	7500	....	.....	7500	....	3500
42. [illegible]	[illegible] Roach, [illegible] College	Yes	1933	[illegible]	350	1	...	...	1500	....	.....	1500	119.00	..
TOTALS	....	.....	......	....	16590	590	133	535	751445	1800	79000	849750	40026.94	39[illegible]

CHURCHES	REGULAR [illegible]S AND POST OFFICES	Pastor's Salary	Other Salaries	Ministerial Help and Supply	Building and Repairs	Church Debt and Interest	Incidentals	Literature for Sunda[y] School and B.Y.P.U and W.M.S	Help Given to Local Poor	For Printing the Minutes and Clerk of Association	Other Objects	
1. Allen Jay	W. R. [illegible]s[illegible]h, [illegible]h [illegible]t, [illegible] 1	407.21		70.12	577.54	243.56	74.00	78.94	25.13	2.00		
2. Buchanan	E. C. West, R. 2 Greensboro	263.87		9.00	210.95		163.32	37.54	20.00			
3. Calvary	J. F. Carroll, Reidsville	281.10		45.00	428.59		59.85	29.31	10.00	3.00	70.87	
4. Fairview	D. E. Trantham, R. 2, Reidsville	200.00		35.00			38.61		13.65	3.00	68.05	
5. Gibsonville	T. L. Robertson, Gibsonville	600.00		50.00			194.34	144.43		3.00		
6. Greensboro, First	Howard [illegible]r, [illegible]o	4600.00	6325.00	139.03	1272.20	13384.38	4407.79	1755.41	908.46	18.00	1397.05	3
7. Asheboro Street	[illegible] H[illegible]k, [illegible]o	3219.16	1310.00	290.00	320.49		736.03	877.50	682.19	12.50	1521.97	
8. Bailey Memorial	[illegible] H. [illegible]S[illegible], R. 3, Greensboro	812.86				219.40	14.13	53.07	25.15	2.00	105.66	
9. Bessemer	A. C. [illegible]h, Bessemer Br., G'boro	1560.00	120.00	71.50	270.78	207.58	106.60	166.83	38.61	5.00	709.58	
10. Eller Memorial	[illegible]t Burgess, Greensboro	2580.00	460.00	403.80	274.44		660.83	350.25	199.71	10.00		
1[1]. Florida Street	D. M. [illegible]r, [illegible]o	1894.57		87.08	625.88	590.00	348.35	211.93	99.01	5.00	179.44	
12. Forest Avenue	J. E. Sharp, [illegible]	2155.00		84.95	4098.70	453.25	1134.82	333.87			20.00	
13. Latham Park	W. W. Sutton, Greensboro	195.54		45.00	4.80	105.00	7.66				106.82	
14. Magnolia Street	H. S. Noah, Greensboro	1560.00		72.70	1787.05	1180.50	230.31	35.09	20.85	3.00	122.81	
15. Pomona	E. E. Henry, Pomona	1433.50		77.81	126.00		110.18	114.21	42.60	3.00	111.78	
16. Revolution	Waldo Johnson, Greensboro	1445.50		98.30	67.86		287.33	151.63	48.46	4.00	228.73	
17. Sixteenth Street	L. F. Paris, Greensboro	2060.00		78.90			622.61	152.69		5.00		
18. Stevens Memorial	Mrs. C. B. Brisson, R. 2, Greensboro	1560.00		60.00			206.60	83.91		4.00	42.45	
19. Webster Memorial	J. F. Graves, Denim Sta., Greensboro	1040.00			963.70		163.39	263.39	20.00	5.00	40.00	
20. Guilford	W. L. Hudson, Guilford	385.00			21.00	21.00	185.50	170.00	8.00	2.00	50.00	
21. High Point, First	Miss Thelma Patrick, High Point	3025.00	2218.40	25.00	934.17	4305.23	3016.24	707.92	144.12	18.00	833.67	1
22. Green Street	R. B. Culler, High Point	3120.00	1140.00	29.00	607.26	4345.00	1787.29	506.26	76.23	5.00		1
23. Hilliard Memorial	F. W. Metcalf, High Point	1344.23		29.91	239.23	270.00	115.50	71.10	113.80	3.00	31.80	
24. North Main	W. C. Ward, High Point	1612.00		35.00		1672.32	510.36	156.84	56.87	3.00	357.35	
25. North Park	L. W. Glenn, High Point	945.00		18.50	237.58	258.00	125.23	227.18	12.21	3.00	76.39	
26. South Side	J. G. Williams, High Point	1300.00		30.00	508.00	372.00	172.00	79.33	25.00	1.50		
27. West End	C. M. Scott, High Point	1560.00		85.81	1288.89	13.50	317.77	240.45	11.27	3.00	95.05	
28 [illegible]p Grove	Miss Bertha [illegible]p, [illegible]d											
29. Lebanon	J. B. Carter, [illegible] [illegible]o	707.95		92.54	116.49		73.53	141.15		3.00		
30. M[illegible]t Zion	Mae Branson, Snow [illegible]	198.75		40.00	96.00					5.00		
31. Oak Grove	L. [illegible] [illegible]h, [illegible]n	287.37		19.23			24.48	38.71	8.00	2.00	28.75	
32 [illegible]e [illegible]l	Mrs. Renzie [illegible]h, R. 3, Greensboro	47.00		14.50	72.95		18.00	19.03				
33 [illegible]a	Mrs. Irvin Powell, Brown Summit	213.13		86.03	.95		22.85	32.43	9.85		34.36	
34 [illegible]t [illegible]h	J. E. [illegible]h, Pleasant [illegible]n	110.00				100.00	30.00	52.00		2.00		
35. Reidsville, First	J. F. Smith, Reidsville	3000.00	2120.00	45.00	567.20		1027.65	324.30	251.22	9.00	1237.28	
36. Mount Olive	Mrs. [illegible] t[illegible]h, Reidsville	1800.00		17.00		954.00	182.01	79.96		2.00	246.99	
[3]7. Penn Memorial	[illegible]s G. [illegible]n, [illegible]e	1300.00			931.80	291.18	215.62	77.55	18.82	2.00		
38. Rocky Knoll	Johnny Rieves, R. 1, Greensboro	400.00		25.00			80.99	110.90	15.00	1.50		
39. Ruffin Stacey	Mrs. Lottie Schrum, Ruffin	350.00		85.28			56.00	49.54		2.00	157.90	
40. Smith Grove	Drew Smith, Colfax	83.27		48.72			12.40	10.00	5.00	2.00		
[4]1. Summerfield	Mrs. Hettie Shields, Summerfield	360.00		51.56	15.00		76.52	43.43		4.00	3.09	
42. Tabernacle		150.27		42.00	16.00		15.00	23.54		1.00	29.00	

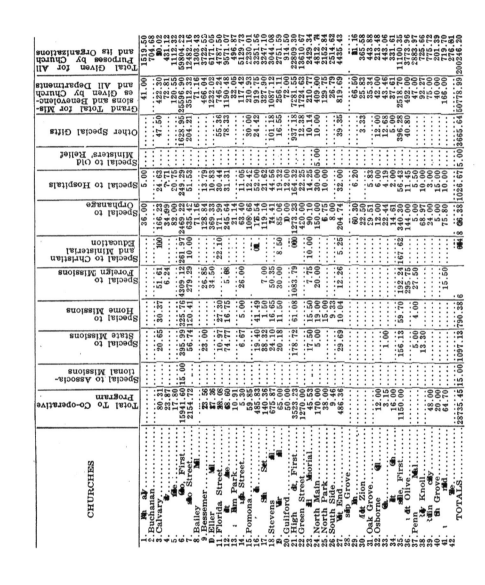

CHURCHES	Total To Co-operative Program	Special to Associational Missions	Special to State Missions	Special to Home Missions	Special to Foreign Missions	Special to Christian and Ministerial Education	Special to Orphanage	Special to Hospitals	Special to Old Ministers' Relief	Other Special Gifts	Grand Total for Missions and Benevolences Given by Church and All Departments	Total Given for All Purposes by Church and its Organizations
1. [illegible]							36.00	5.00			41.00	1519.50
2. Buchanan												704.68
3. Calvary	80.31		20.65	30.37	51.61	[illegible]	166.23	24.63		47.50	422.30	[illegible]0.02
4. [illegible]	23.87				6.24		34.99	7.71			72.81	431.12
5. [illegible]	17.80						82.00	20.75			120.55	1112.32
6. [illegible]o, First	15941.60	15.00	395.99	325.76	4309.12	261.97	2469.22	249.29		1628.95	25596.90	59804.22
7. [illegible]o Street	2154.72		56.74	120.41	279.29	10.00	635.42	51.53		204.21	3512.32	12482.16
8. Bailey [illegible]							71.16				71.16	1303.43
9. Bessemer	[illegible]3.56		23.00		26.85		128.84	13.79			466.04	3722.52
10. Eller [illegible]	[illegible]7.36				34.50		369.33	10.83			1232.02	6171.05
11. Florida Street	[illegible].08		10.97	27.30		22.10	171.99	30.44		55.36	746.24	4787.50
12. [illegible]	[illegible]8.60		74.77	16.75	5.08		245.64	31.31		78.33	1190.48	9571.07
13. [illegible] Park	10.91						21.14				32.05	496.87
14. [illegible] Street	5.30		6.67	5.00	26.00		63.40	11.05			117.42	5129.73
15. Pomona	59.85						108.66	12.42		30.00	210.93	2230.01
16. [illegible]	485.83		19.40	41.49		[illegible]	1[illegible].54	52.00		24.42	919.75	3251.56
17. [illegible]	140.36		38.32	1.50	7.00		119.10	21.62			327.90	3247.10
18. Stevens [illegible]	675.87		24.10	16.65	50.35		[illegible].41	44.56		101.18	1087.12	3044.08
19. [illegible]	65.00		20.18	11.50	30.00	8.50	85.06	19.32		16.55	256.11	2751.59
20. Guilford	50.00						[illegible].00	12.00			72.00	914.50
21. High [illegible]t, First	3523.23		178.72	61.08	1083.79	[illegible]	1273.23	164.32		937.18	7281.55	22809.30
22. Green Street	1270.00						420.00	22.25		12.38	1724.63	13610.67
23. [illegible] [illegible]orial	45.53		17.50	15.50	7.75	10.00	90.10	14.25		10.14	210.77	2429.34
24. North Main	170.00		5.00	19.00	20.00		150.00	30.00	5.00	10.00	409.00	4812.[illegible]
25. North Park	38.00			15.00			[illegible].75	10.00			129.75	2152.84
26. South Side	9.46			9.33			8.00				26.79	2514.62
27. [illegible]t End	486.36		29.69	10.04	12.26	5.25	204.74	32.00		39.35	819.69	4435.43
28. [illegible]p Grove												
29. [illegible]							60.30	6.20			66.50	[illegible]1.16
30. [illegible]t Zion							22.50			3.33	25.83	365.58
31. Oak Grove							29.51	5.83			35.34	443.88
32. Osborne [illegible]	12.00						12.00	6.00		12.00	42.00	213.48
33. [illegible]	3.15		1.00				22.44	4.19		12.68	43.46	443.06
34. [illegible]	16.00						14.61	2.00		5.00	37.61	331.61
35. [illegible]le, First	1150.00		156.13	59.70	192.24	167.62	340.30	56.43		396.28	2518.70	11100.35
36. [illegible]t Olive					295.75		144.00	11.45		40.80	492.00	3773.96
37. Penn [illegible]			5.00	4.00	27.50		5.00	5.50			47.00	2883.97
38. [illegible] Knoll			13.30				68.97	10.00			92.27	725.66
39. [illegible]	48.00						24.00	3.00			75.00	775.72
40. [illegible] Grove	20.00						5.00	15.00			40.00	201.39
41. [illegible]	64.70				15.50		75.80	10.00			166.00	719.70
42. [illegible]												276.81
TOTALS	28735.45	15.00	1097.13	790.38	6[illegible]	[illegible]	8[illegible]6.38	1026.67	5.00	3665.64	50778.99	200246.20

THE RECORD PUBLISHING CO.,
ZEBULON, N. C.

MINUTES

PIEDMONT BAPTIST ASSOCIATION

NORTH CAROLINA

FORTY-SIXTH ANNUAL SESSION

FIRST BAPTIST CHURCH

Reidsville, N. C.

OCTOBER 18-19,

1939

The next session will be held with the Florida Street Baptist Church, Greensboro, N. C., Wednesday and Thursday before the fourth Sunday in October, 1940.

Rev. Chas. E. Parker will preach the sermon.
Alternate, Rev. A. Lincoln Fulk.

MINUTES

of the

PIEDMONT BAPTIST ASSOCIATION

NORTH CAROLINA

FORTY-SIXTH ANNUAL SESSION

Held With The

FIRST BAPTIST CHURCH
Reidsville, N. C.

OCTOBER 18-19,

1939

The next session will be held with the Florida Street Baptist Church, Greensboro, N. C., Wednesday and Thursday before the fourth Sunday in October, 1940.

Rev. Chas. E. Parker will preach the sermon.
Alternate, Rev. A. Lincoln Fulk.

CONTENTS

J. M. HILLIARD

To whom this Volume of the Minutes is Dedicated by order of the Association.

Reverend Joseph Marcellus Hilliard, born in Wake County near Raleigh, March 17, 1850. His parents were James Wilford and Harriet Broadwell Hilliard. He grew up in the Green Level neighborhood in the western part of Wake County. Baptized into the fellowship of Mount Pisgah Baptist Church by Rev. Patrick W. Doud, September, 1865.

Mr. Hilliard was educated at Yates Academy and Wake Forest College. He entered the ministry November 10, 1871. During his ministerial life he served as pastor 18 village, town and city churches.

Among these town and city churches are: West Raleigh, Raleigh; Cherry Street, Greensboro; and in High Point, Green Street, Southside, Mechanicsville, Hilliard Memorial. Other town churches include Thomasville, Ramseur, Summerville, Franklin, Swannanoa, Morrisville, and many other small village churches. Among the country churches in Wake County, he was pastor of Green Level, Mt. Moriah, Wakefield, Leesville, Forestville, Cross Roads and Bethany. In Davidson County the historic old Abbott's Creek Church, Liberty, and Reed's Cross Roads. In Durham County, Red Mountain, and Berry's Grove. In Buncombe County, Berea, Cave Creek, Beaver Dam, North Fork, and Mt. Carmel. In Macon County, Cowee and Mt. Hope. He also served other small Baptist Churches too numerous to mention.

Mr. Hilliard was married three times. He first married Mary Colon Hinton, October 24, 1879. To this union were born two daughters and two sons. The daughters who are now living in High Point are Mrs. C. E. Siceloff and Mrs. Bascom Hoskins. The sons, Jim and Eugene, died several years ago. The second marriage was to Tranquilla Johnson, September 25, 1900. The third marriage was to Mrs. Elizabeth R. Knight, December, 1906. To this union was born one daughter, Ruth Hilliard.

He baptized more than a thousand in the above churches, and built more than ten houses of worship.

He was Moderator of the Piedmont Association for seven or eight years, worked with the State Mission Board for about 50 years, and was once Vice-President of this board. He was elected Secretary and Treasurer of the Mills Home, Thomasville, North Carolina, in 1891. He was also, while working with the late lamented J. H. Mills, pastor of the Orphanage Church.

Although eighty-nine years of age he was interested and active in the Lord's work until he passed to his Heavenly Home, April 1, 1939. Two weeks before his death he preached at the Green Street Baptist Church, and the Sunday before his home going he attended Sunday School and Worship Service at the First Baptist Church in High Point. His daughter said of him — "He was far too feeble to get out, but his greatest joy was preaching God's Word and going to His house."

MAP
OF THE
PIEDMONT BAPTIST ASSOCIATION

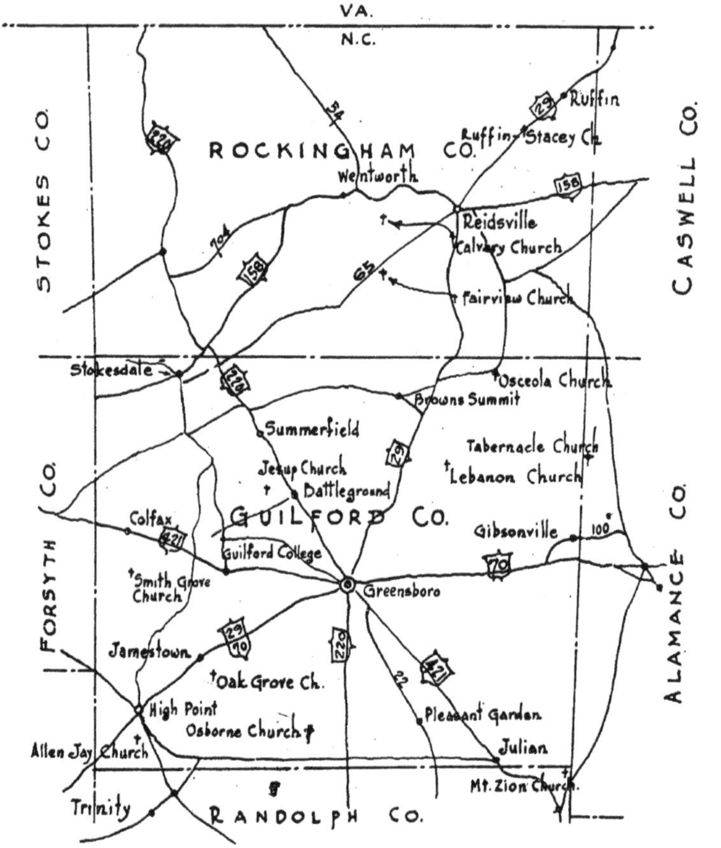

ASSOCIATIONAL DIRECTORY

OFFICERS

Grover H. Jones, Moderator	High Point
T. L. Sasser, Vice Moderator	Reidsville
O. E. Lee, Clerk-Treasurer	Greensboro

EXECUTIVE PROMOTION COMMITTEE

Grover H. Jones, Chairman	High Point
O. E. Lee, Secretary	Greensboro
Rev. T. L. Sasser	Reidsville
Rev. D. W. Overbey	Reidsville
R. R. Saunders	Reidsville
Rev. C. N. Royal	High Point
S. R. Clinard	High Point
J. Ben. Eller	Greensboro
Dr. J. T. J. Battle	Greensboro
Mrs. Nettie Hatcher Hoge	Greensboro
F. L. Paschal	Greensboro
J. Carl Bell	Greensboro

By Committee
J. B. Eller
Clenton Oats
A. A. Walker

CHURCH ADVISORY COMMITTEE

Dr. J. Clyde Turner, Chairman	Greensboro
Dr. A. B. Conrad	High Point
Rev. J. Ben Eller	Greensboro
Rev. Wilson Woodcock	Greensboro
Mrs. Nettie Hatcher Hoge	Greensboro
Grover H. Jones	High Point
O. E. Lee	Greensboro

LIST OF COMMITTEES

COMMITTEES SERVING DURING THE ASSOCIATIONAL YEAR

Executive-Promotion Committee
Church Advisory Committee
Committee to Revise the Constitution
Committee on Evangelism

COMMITTEES SERVING DURING THE ANNUAL MEETING OF THE ASSOCIATION

Committee on Committees
Committee on Arrangements
Committee on Place and Preacher
Auditing Committee
Committee on Resolutions
Program Committee for This Year and Next Year
Committee to Nominate Officers
Committee to Nominate Executive-Promotion Committee
Committee to Nominate Church Advisory Committee
Committee to Nominate Delegates to the Baptist State Convention
Committee to Nominate Leader for the Verbal Report Hour
Committee to Nominate Committee on Evangelism

COMMITTEE TO REPORT AT NEXT ANNUAL MEETING

Committee to Revise the Constitution

CHURCHES BY DISTRICTS

District 1:

High Point, First
Hilliard Memorial
Green Street
North Main
North Park
South Side
West End
Oak Grove
Pisgah
Smith Grove
Allen Jay

District 2:

Greensboro, First
Asheboro Street
Bessemer
Bailey Memorial
Buchanan
Eller Memorial
Forest Avenue
Florida Street
Latham Park
Magnolia Street
Pomona Mills
Revolution
Sixteenth Street
Stevens Memorial
Tabernacle
Gibsonville
Guilford
Jessup Grove
Lebanon
Pleasant Grove
Mount Zion
Pleasant Garden
Osborne Chapel
Rocky Knoll
Summerfield
Tabernacle
Webster Memorial

District 3:

Reidsville, First
Penn Memorial
Mount Olive
Calvary
Fairview
Osceola
Ruffin-Stacey
Antioch

NAMES AND ADDRESSES PIEDMONT BAPTIST SUNDAY SCHOOL ASSOCIATIONAL OFFICERS FOR 1940

Superintendent	F. L. Paschal, Banner Bldg.,	Greensboro
Associate Supt.	A. A. Walker, Bessemer Branch,	Greensboro
Supt. of Evangelism	Mrs. Nettie Hoge, 1406 W. Market,	Greensboro
Secretary	Mrs. Joe A. Kirkman, Asheboro,	Greensboro
Pianist	Miss Louise Sharpe, 2320 E. Market,	G'boro
Group Supt.	Rev. A. L. Fulk, 1407 Welborn,	High Point
	Rev. Ferrell F. James, 47 Walnut St. Proximity,	Greensboro
	Rev. W. I. Johnson	Reidsville

Department Leaders

Cradle Roll .... **Mrs. T. L. Ogburn, 412 Northridge, G'boro**
Beginners .... Miss Ruth Scott, 1503 Spring Garden, G'boro
Primary .... **Miss Stella Lea, 414 Guilford, Greensboro**
Juniors .... **Mrs. George F. Allred, 1216 Randolph, G'boro**
Intermediate .... Miss Leah Andrews, Greensboro
Young People .... **Mr. T. L. Ogburn, 412 Northridge, G'boro**
Adult .... **Rev. L. C. Burgiss, 103 E. Wendover, G'boro**
Extension .... **Mrs. J. B. Eller, 409 Asheboro, Greensboro**
Vacation Bible School Mrs. Charles E. Parker, 1307 Summit, G'boro

OFFICERS OF W. M. U.

Mrs. Nettie Hatcher Hoge, Superintendent .... Greensboro
Mrs. A. Andrews, Secretary .... Greensboro
Mrs. C .E. Siceloff, Treasurer .... High Point
Miss Ruth Scott, Young People's Leader .... Greensboro
Mrs. L. M. Gideon, Personal Service Chairman .... Greensboro
Mrs. C. N. Royal, Stewardship Chairman .... High Point
Mrs. J. J. Andoe, Mission Study-Lit. Chairman .... Greensboro
Mrs. H. A. Knight, Group Leader, District 1 .... High Point
Mrs. O. Joe Howard, Group Leader, District No. 2 .... Greensboro
Mrs. R. R. Saunders, Group Leader, District No. 3 .... Reidsville

OFFICERS BAPTIST TRAINING UNION ASSOCIATION

J. Carl Bell, Director .... Greensboro
Miss Thelma Patrick, Associate Director .... High Point
Miss Elizabeth Campbell, Secretary-Treasurer .... Greensboro
Miss Louise Sharpe, Pianist .... Greensboro
G. R. Ford, Chorister .... Reidsville
Miss Mildred Jackson, Junior Leader .... Greensboro
Rev. L. Grady Burgiss, B. A. U. Leader .... Greensboro
Burgess Leonard, Director, District 1 .... High Point
Rev. Ferrell James, Director, District No. 2 .... Greensboro
Mrs. — — Moore, Director, District No. 3 .... Reidsville

ORDAINED MINISTERS NOT PASTORS

W. L. Robinson .... Gibsonville
L. M. Hamilton .... Gibsonville
W. C. Richardson .... Guilford
Dr. W. C. Newton .... Richmond, Va.
C. D. Barton .... Greensboro
W. F. Matherly .... Greensboro
B. C. Lamb .... Mars Hill
O. F. Barnes .... Greensboro
Alton Riddle .... Greensboro
Rufus Carroll .... Greensboro

T. L. Chamberlain	High Point
R. J. Davis	High Point
Leo. Hudson	Belews Creek
J. F. Murray	Reidsville
J. C. Gillespie	Reidsville
Dr. A. S. Gillespie	Reidsville
T. A. Stamey	Greensboro
B. H. Fairrington	Jamestown
Joe Ballins	Winston Salem

MINISTERS ORDAINED DURING THE YEAR

James C. Varner	Gibsonville
Alton Riddle	Greensboro
Ferrell James	Greensboro
Leo Hudson	Belews Creek
Melvin Faulkner	Reidsville

BAPTIST TRAINING UNION DIRECTORS

ALLEN JAY, Mrs. W. W. Page	Rt. 3 High Point
GIBSONVILLE, W. E. Apple	Gibsonville
GREENSBORO, First, O. E. Lee	Greensboro
ASHEBORO STREET, C. W. McLees	Greensboro
BAILEY MEMORIAL, Roland Mitchell	Greensboro
BESSEMER, Miss Norfleet Dixon	Greensboro
ELLER MEMORIAL, Farrell James	Greensboro
FLORIDA STREET, W. M. Cassell	Greensboro
FOREST AVE., J. B. Watson	Greensboro
MAGNOLIA STREET, Mrs. R. L. Yow	Greensboro
REVOLUTION, David Barbour	Greensboro
SIXTEENTH STREET, Harry Moore	Greensboro
STEVENS MEMORIAL, Blanche Campbell	Greensboro
TABERNACLE (Greensboro), Euline Collins	Greensboro
GUILFORD, Rev. Farrell James	Greensboro
HIGH POINT, FIRST, W. O. Burnham	High Point
GREEN STREET, Burgiss Leonard	High Point
HILLIARD MEMORIAL, P. E. Grubb	High Point
NORTH MAIN, Mrs. D. S. Ring	High Point
NORTH PARK, H. B. Chatham	High Point
SOUTH SIDE, Houston Williams	High Point
WEST END, Mrs. Ora Tyler	High Point
OSBORNE CHAPEL, Hubert Bennett	Rt. 1 Greensboro
REIDSVILLE, FIRST, W. O. Kelley	Reidsville
MOUNT OLIVE, B. J. Harvey	Reidsville
PENN MEMORIAL, James Overbey	Reidsville
ROCKY KNOLL, L. J. Moore	Rt. 1 Greensboro
SUMMERFIELD, C. T. Adams	Summerfield

LIST OF MESSENGERS

ALLEN JAY—
Mr. and Mrs. J. O. Warren
Mary Warren
Mealie Burrow
Mrs. Henry Burrow

ANTIOCH—
Mrs. Ray Vanter
Mrs. Hobart Carter
Ray Moore

BUCHANAN—
R. M. Crane
C. C. Parks
Mrs. Rhew

CALVARY—
J. F. Carroll
Alex Delancy
J. E. McCargo

FAIRVIEW—
D. E. Trantham
Wm. Dorris Sharon
Mrs. Florence DeLapp

GIBSONVILLE—
J. M. Edwards
Ruby Wooderd
W. L. Robertson

GREENSBORO, FIRST—
O. E. Lee
James Wilkins
J. Carl Bell
Edwin Nash
A. A. Chandler
Mrs. Nettie Hoge
Mrs. Stafford R. Webb
Mrs. Chas. A. Tucker
Mrs. J. H. Shuford

ASHEBORO STREET—
J. S. Moore
Mrs. E. R. Baldwin
Mrs. A. Andrews
Miss Lorene James
Mrs. B. S. Cheek

BAILEY MEMORIAL—
Mr. C. C. Stanley
Mrs. C. C. Stanley
Mrs. E. J. Jarvis
Mrs. A. G. Coe

BESSEMER—
Mr. E. E. Banner
Mr. Huber Dixon
Mrs. J. R. Medlin
Miss Norfleet Dixon

ELLER MEMORIAL—
Otis Bowden
Fred Newman
Wiley Patterson
Mrs. G. O. Basinger

FLORIDA STREET—
Mrs. L. H. Holton
Mrs. A. W. Watson
Mr. J. H. Watson

FOREST AVE.—
Mrs. E. W. Richardson
Mrs. J. W. Marsh
Mrs. J. B. Watson
L. E. Ogburn

MAGNOLIA STREET—
Mrs. L. Grady Burgiss
Mrs. T. J. Kelley
Mrs. R. A. Smith
N. J. Jarvis

POMONA—
Rev. C. M. Oates
J. H. Parrish
Mrs. Hattie McDaniel
Mrs. Ila Thornlow

REVOLUTION—
Mrs. David Barbour
W. E. Moore
A. A. Rogus
Mrs. Elijah Lankford

SIXTEENTH STREET—
Mrs. W. M. Smith
Mrs. W. A. Straughn
Mrs. Webster Owens
Mrs. T. W. Michel
Mrs. W. L. Lineback
Mrs. Harry Moore
Mrs. W. B. Cook

STEVENS MEMORIAL—
Mrs. W. P. Brown
Mrs. Ruby Campbell
Rev. John U. Garner

TABERNACLE—
E. H. Moore
J. E. Wiggs
Mrs. J .L. Shouse
B. R. Ward, Sr.
WEBSTER MEMORIAL—
Mr. C. B. Webster
Mrs. C. B. Webster
Mrs. W. H. Lucas
Miss Selma Scales
GUILFORD—
Rev. Ferrell James
Mrs. Hettie Kennedy
Mrs. B. F. Buller
Mrs. E. L. Weston
HIGH POINT, FIRST—
Dr. A. B. Conrad
Virginia Clinard
Mrs. A. B. Clinard
Mrs. A. B. Conrad
A. E. Tate
G. H. Jones
Mrs. J. D. Biggs
HIGH POINT, GREEN ST.—
Mr. and Mrs. A. N. Smith
Mrs. M. W. Buser
Mrs. L. A. Pegg
Mrs. C. E. Crismon
Miss Ollie Rimmer
HILLIARD MEMORIAL—
Mrs. L. L. Grout
C. H. Maynor
J. W. Saunders
NORTH MAIN—
Mrs. Ed Criscoe
Mrs. Alice Davis
Mrs. F. S. Wall
Mrs. S. R. Clinard
NORTH PARK—
L. W. Glenn
Mrs. J. D. Edmondson
Mrs. J. L. Jones
SOUTH SIDE—
Rev. G. H. Liner
Mrs. F. E. Caudle
Mr. J. G. Williams.
WEST END—
Mr. C. M. Stott
Vernon Coffey
T. L. Chamberlain
LEBANON—
Mrs. J. L. Coble
Mrs. Ethel Clutz
B. G. Yow
MT. ZION—
Jessie Foster
L. L. Spoon
Mrs. L. L. Spoon
Mrs. Cora Coble
C. D. Branson
OAK GROVE—
Mrs. L. H. Jackson
Mrs. L. R. Loflin
John Dennis
Mrs. Wayne Auman
OSBORNE CHAPEL—
R. S. Law
Hubert Bennett
Mrs. J. C. May
Mrs. R. R. Osborne
OSCEOLA—
Mr. and Mrs. L. C. Cole
Mrs. D. A. Green
PISGAH—
W. L. Smith
F. P. Vaughn
Z. V. Lanier
L. C. Madden
PLEASANT GARDEN—
Mrs. Anderson
Mrs. Burton
Miss Pauline Barber
Miss J. E. Thompson
PLEASANT GROVE—
Mrs. J. M. Allred
F. M. Atkins
J. H. Collins
D. R. Robertson
REIDSVILLE, FIRST—
T. L. Garner
W. O. Kelley
H. L. Morrison

N. C. Thompson
Mrs. C. A. Penn
Mrs. R. T. Burton

MT. OLIVE—
Mrs. Roy Gentry
Mrs. C. A. Griffith
Mrs. A. D. Clifton
Mrs. Odell Delapp

PENN MEMORIAL—
D. W. Overbey
James Overbey
Mrs. D. W. Overbey
Mrs. M. H. Fitz

ROCKY KNOLL—
R. R. Sudderth
Mrs. R. A. Laughlin
Mrs. Grady Walker
Mrs. Carl Chandler

RUFFIN-STACEY—
Mrs. Lillie Burton
Mrs. Nannie Lovelace
Mrs. J. T. Cardwell
Mrs. Lottie Scrum

SMITH GROVE—
Mr. Ed Alley
Mr. Jonah Pitts
Mr. Clifton Atkinson
Mr. Drew Smith

SUMMERFIELD—
Mrs. Myrtle Smith
Mr. and Mrs. Marvin Truitt

TABERNACLE—
Rev. H. P. Gauldin
Miss Mamie Roach
Mrs. W. H. Fetts
Mr. and Mrs. R. C. Fetts

———o———

CONSTITUTION

———o———

ARTICLE 1. The Association shall be called the Piedmont Baptist Association.

ARTICLE 2. It shall be composed of the ordained ministers who are members of, and those who may have pastoral charges within the Associational District, and three delegates from each church in the district aforesaid. and churches having a membership exceeding 300 shall be entitled to one additional delegate for every 200 members or fraction thereof in excess of 300.

ARTICLE 3. The said delegates shall, before taking their seats, produce letters from respective churches showing their appointment as delegates.

ARTICLE 4. The Associational session shall be held at least once a year.

ARTICLE 5. The officers shall be a Moderator, Vice-Moderator, Clerk. and Treasurer. If deemed expedient by the Association, the offices of Clerk and Treasurer may be combined.

ARTICLE 6. The officers of the Association shall be chosen annually by the Association.

ARTICLE 7. Association shall be clothed with authority only to advise the churches touching all things pertaining to their interest but shall in no case presume to direct or control them in reference to their own government or internal policy.

ARTICLE 8. A Committee of Arrangements, consisting of three members, shall be appointed on the first day of each session to prepare and report the proceedings and suggest topics proper for the consideration and action of the next annual Association.

ARTICLE 9. Baptist brethren, not members of the Association, who may be present at any session of the body, may on invitation by the body, take seats and participate in the debates of the Association.

ARTICLE 10. The territory embraced in the Association shall be divided into not less than four districts and a committee composed of one pastor, and one layman from each district, together with the Moderator, Vice-Moderator, Clerk of the Association, Associational W. M. U. Superintendent, Associational Sunday School Superintendent, and Associational B. T. U. President, shall be appointed at meeting of the Association, which committee shall compose the Executive Committee of the Association, a majority of which shall constitute a quorum. It shall be the duty of the committee to superintend and direct the missionary operations of the Association.

ARTICLE 11. All committees shall be appointed by the Moderator unless otherwise ordered by the Association.

ARTICLE 12. The Constitution may be altered only at an Annual session of the Association and by a vote of two-thirds of the whole present.

ARTICLE 13. The rules of this body shall follow Mell's Parliamentary Practice.

ARTICLE 14. This Association shall cooperate with the Baptist State Convention.

ARTICLE 15. The time of the holding of the annual session shall be on Wednesday before the fourth Sunday in October of each year.

Adopted October 17, 1895.

Articles 2, 5, 6, 10, 15, Amended.
Sessions, July 23, 24, 1930.

Article 15 Amended,
Session, July 21, 1932.

Article 10 Amended,
Session, October 23, 24, 1935.

W. O. Johnson
A. Wayland Cooke
Committee

PROCEEDINGS

of the

FORTY-SIXTH ANNUAL SESSION

of the

PIEDMONT BAPTIST ASSOCIATION

Held with the

FIRST BAPTIST CHURCH

Reidsville, N. C.

October 18-19, 1939

Theme: "Magnifying Christ and His Church"

WEDNESDAY MORNING SESSION 10:00 A. M.

"Magnifying Christ As Savior And Lord"

1. The Association was opened with a song service led by G. R. Ford, and a devotional service led by Rev. Chas. E. Parker.

2. A roll of the churches was called and messengers from 37 churches responded to the roll call.

3. The following committees were appointed by the Moderator:

Committee on Arrangements—O. E. Lee, C. N. Royal.

Committee on Committees—Wilson Woodcock, D. W. Overbey, Dr. A. B. Conrad.

4. Message of Moderator

MESSAGE OF MODERATOR

Moderator Grover H. Jones delivered a brief message to the Association. His message, in part, is as follows:

"The supreme business of God in this age is the gathering of the church. Christ positively identifies Himself with the church. Indeed, He gave up His life that He might found the church. The Apostle Paul sacrificed himself in his endeavors to build up the church. He was willing to do anything, dare anything, endure anything if only he might honor and magnify Christ by establishing churches to embody the teaching, philosophy, Spirit and mission of Jesus.

"America was founded upon New Testament principles, and our civilization in America is held together by principles, by convictions and conceptions of duty regarding the family, the state and nation. As Baptists we believe that there can be no true stability, no permanence in civilization apart from Christianity; that without God a nation is without the one force that insured integrity in office holders, law observance by the people and adequate standards and objectives for a great national life.

"We are living in a great age, a marvelous day. Today is a summing up of all the centuries. It is a storehouse into which the ages have poured their treasures. Into this day are packed all the success, all the achievement, and all the progress of the past. Surely Baptists have the opportunity of aspiring to a grander destiny than has opened before any other denomination."

In concluding his message the Moderator suggested that the following should characterize the members of our churches during this associational year:

1. A deeper, richer experience in our prayer life.
2. A more earnest and a more constant study of the Bible.
3. A more devoted loyalty to the church.
4. A more faithful stewardship.
5. A more earnest effort to make our churches more influential and effective in the communities in which they are located.
6. A more cooperative Spirit among the churches of our association.

5. The report on Religious Literature was presented by John U. Garner.

Upon motion to adopt the report the subject was discussed by Dr. John C. Slemp, and G. H. Jones.

The report was adopted.

REPORT ON RELIGIOUS LITERATURE

There is no book in all the world that can take the place of the Bible, God's Holy word. We would urge our Baptist people to spend much time in the reading of this great Book. It is here we find a solution to all our problems. Surely every Christian should read a part of God's word every day.

We could not confine our reading to the Bible alone but all of our Baptist periodicals. "Commission," "Home Missions," "Royal Service," "Charity and Children" and last but not least "Biblical Recorder."

The Biblical Recorder is our paper, owned now by North Carolina Baptists. It would be a new day in North Carolina if we could get every Baptist family taking and reading the Biblical Recorder.

Our Baptist people will do when they know what to do. They will gladly support our work when they understand our work. I am convinced that the best source of information we have in North Carolina is our own Baptist Paper.

We would urge that all Baptists who are not already reading our Baptist Papers, subscribe for them to-day, and especially the Biblical Recorder, our own denominational paper, and the bureau of information for our State.

Respectfully submitted,

John U. Garner

—o—

6. The report on Social Service was presented by C. N. Royal. Upon motion to adopt the report the subject was discussed by State Senator L. A. Martin of Lexington, Dr. M. A. Adams, and A. L. Fulk.

The report was adopted.

SOCIAL SERVICE

A great deal is said in the Bible about one's relation to another. It is also revealed in the Scriptures that no man liveth unto himself and no man dieth unto himself. We are taught by the greatest of all teachers that our neighbor is the person who needs help, whoever or wherever that person may be found.

True religion has to do with our relationship to God and man. Our relationship to God is not right until it is right toward mankind. So social service is of vital concern to our churches and to our Association. Our part as a group of united churches is to encourage and support all that is good with our influence, our money and our prayers. At the same time, we are to put up a solid front against all that is bad. There is much that is evil in the world today. If a person is inclined to be a pessimist and look on the dark side there is enough to encourage him in his belief. In fact, it would be hard for him to overstate his case.

As earnest Christians our Baptist people are interested in everything that affects human life and freedom and the on-going of the Kingdom of Christ. If we look into the internal affairs and relations, at the present time the picture is not at all bright or encouraging. We can only hope and pray, and this we must earnestly do, that behind the dim unknown God does, indeed, stand within the shadows keeping watch above his own, and out of this war and international confusion a gracious God may somehow bring peace and order, that the Gospel of Christ may have free course and may run and be glorified.

The liquor situation in North Carolina is the most confusing and difficult situation with which the people have ever been called upon to deal. In yesterday's Charlotte Observer we observed this heading" "Liquor sales in North Carolina higher for September." The State ABC Board reported today that liquor stores in 27 counties sold $610,629.55 worth of intoxicants during September, a gain of $6,451.15 over September, 1938. Sales for the first quarter of the fiscal year were $1,742,845.44. Durham County led in September sales with $88,755.55, and Wake was next, with $86,941.95. You can see that drinking in North Carolina is on the increase. We are to carry forward in a ceaseless and persistent manner the work of informing and educating all of our people, old and young, concerning the evil and havoc of intoxicating liquors, and that we do not support any candidate for office who favors the legal sale of any alcoholic beverages.

It is impossible to include all the vices that are affecting the public morals of this day in one brief report. There is an ever increasing ratio of divorce. It is easier to get a divorce now than it is to get license to get married. There must be instilled a deeper realization of the sanctity of marriage and of the home. Moral standards are lowered today. Gambling is on the increase. The Lord's Day is being used more and more as a day of sport. Sunday baseball, golf, moving pictures, and other forms of Sabbath desecration are becoming more popular.

We must do all within our power to raise the moral and Spiritual life of our day and generation. Righteousness exalteth a nation but sin is a reproach to any people.

Respectfully submitted,

C. N. Royal

7. After singing "Love Divine" Chas. E. Parker led in prayer.

The Introductory sermon was preached by Dr. J. Clyde Turner..

The Scripture was Phil. 2:5-11; subject "Magnifying Jesus As Savior and Lord." The sermon was deeply spiritual and an inspiration to all.

8. The following visitors were recognized: J. S. Hopkins, L. A. Nall, C. E. Baker, Wilbur Hutchins, R. H. Weaver, S. T. Morris, Dr. J. C. Slemp.

9. Rev. T. L. Sasser speaks words of welcome. The response is made by Rev. A. A. Walker.

The session is adjourned with prayer by J. S. Hopkins.

AFTERNOON SESSION

Theme—The Church and Its World Program

1:30 The devotional service is led by E. M. Smith.

10. The Committee on Committees makes the following report:

COMMITTEE ON PROGRAM FOR THIS YEAR AND NEXT YEAR—O. E. Lee, Dr. A. B. Conrad, D. W. Overbey.

COMMITTEE TO NOMINATE OFFICERS—C. N. Royal, H. R. Starling, J. H. Saunders.

COMMITTEE ON RESOLUTIONS—H. O. Miller, W. B. Cooke, John U. Garner.

COMMITTEE ON PLACE AND PREACHER—Dr. J. Clyde Turner, E. M. Smith, L. C. Chandler.

COMMITTEE TO NOMINATE MESSENGERS TO THE STATE CONVENTION—Mrs. Nettie Hoge, L. E. Ogburn, J. C. Gillespie.

COMMITTEE TO NOMINATE LEADER FOR VERBAL REPORT HOUR—Grady Burgiss, G. H. Liner, Ferrell James.

COMMITTEE TO NOMINATE EXECUTIVE PROMOTION COMMITTEE—J. Ben Eller, A. A. Walker, C. M. Oates.

COMMITTEE TO NOMINATE CHURCH ADVISORY COMMITTEE—Chas. E. Parker, G. H. Jones, O. E. Lee.

AUDITING COMMITTEE—F. L. Paschal, L. E. Ogburn.

COMMITTEE TO NOMINATE COMMITTEE ON EVANGELISM—A. A. Walker, W. I. Johnson.

COMMITTEE TO REVISE CONSTITUTION—F. L. Paschal, J. H. Saunders, C. V. Webster.

Wilson Woodcock
A. B. Conrad
D. W. Overbey

11. Announcement is made by S. T. Morris relative to radio temperance programs to be given over a net-work including Charlotte, Salisbury, Winston-Salem and Raleigh.

12. Motion is passed asking the Church Advisory Committee to act as the Committee on New Churches this year and next year.

13. The following reports were presented and upon motion to adopt the reports the subjects were discussed by Rev. W. Perry Crouch, Secretary of Christian Education for the Baptist State Convention, and Rev. A. R. Gallimore, Missionary to China.

The reports were adopted.

STATE MISSIONS

1. We are aiding about 160 churches in helping to pay a part of the pastor's salary. So far as we can see, if this aid should be withdrawn, many if not all, of these churches would hardly be able to continue their work.

2. As rapidly as we can we are aiding churches here and there in small amounts to enable them to provide better buildings and a little Sunday School equipment. But we have on hand applications for some $40,000 from needy and strategic places that we cannot meet at all for lack of funds.

3. We are carrying on the Sunday School, B. T. U. and B. S. U. departments of our work; and you know these agencies are trying to lead in the teaching and training of our people in the churches and provide a normal religious life for the Baptist students while they are away from home.

4. We are providing for missionaries, on part time basis, whose business it is to visit the sick in the state tuberculosis sanitoriums and in the school for wayward girls near Aberdeen.

5. We are providing also, through Mr. and Mrs. Lunsford, a ministry to the Indians in Robeson County.

6. We are providing for a Pastor's School at Meredith and at Mars Hill; and these we know are providing a great blessing to the pastors who attend.

7. We are aiding the Negroes in North Carolina, and the progress they have made since we undertook this work some years ago is wellnigh marvelous.

8. State Missions make it possible for the Board to keep Mr. Alexander and Mr. Pipes on the field as general missionaries, who all during the year seek to aid the pastors in vitalizing the churches.

9. We mention also the task of ministering to the prisoners, not because we have done anything about it but because for three years we have wanted to and could not because of lack of funds. Here, in our opinion, is a golden opportunity which we are neglecting. A great offering for State Missions would help us to undertake this task next year.

10. We recommend that each church plan for an annual special offering to State Missions over and above the percentage from the unified budget or the amount subscribed at the beginning of the year.

And that this special offering be fostered by the Sunday School, the B. T. U. and in the regular church services as well as in the W. M. S.

Respectfully submitted,
Wilson Woodcock

———o———

REPORT ON HOME MISSIONS

"Beginning at Jerusalem."

Jesus taught that religion begins at home and so does our missionary task. Only for convenience and identification do we divide our mission work and label it as city, state, home, and foreign. In the sight of God there is in reality no such division, for a soul out of Christ is lost whether it be next door or on the remotest isle of the sea, and all souls are equally precious in the sight of God. Thus our missionary task begins wherever there is one lost soul. Therefore, we do not to leave the homeland to find a great field of human need. Millions here in the homeland are without Christ and thousands have never even heard the Gospel. These are cut off by social, economic, racial, and language barriers from the services of our churches. We have a great and inviting challenge for missionary service to the five million foreign born, six hundred thousand French-speaking Americans, one half million Spanish-speaking Americans, two hundred thousand Indians, eleven million negroes, and the mountain peoples in our midst; and the two and one half million Cubans and fifty thousand residents of the Canal Zone. These are crying "come over next door and help us."

For ninety-four years the Home Mission Board has been carrying the light of the Gospel to many of these millions of our neighbors. This Board has experienced the joy of seeing thousands find the Christ, and in its program of evangelism under the leadership of Dr. Roland Q. Leavell has not only seen many new converts in Christ but has also been instrumental in reclaiming and reenlisting many of the wandering Christians within our own southern churches. While we usually think of the Home Mission task as restricted to this continent, it is, in reality, state, national, and foreign in its reaches. In reaching the foreigner in our midst, Home Missions has very often sent back to their native lands Christians to do a work that no other missionary could do.

The Cooperative Program is the chief source of financial support for the Home Mission task. Dr. J. E. Dillard says, "Without Home Missions the Cooperative Program would fall to pieces. If you should cut out Home Missions from the Program it would bleed to death." Home Missions is necessary to the success of Foreign Missions. If we do not win the homeland, we cannot win foreign lands. Thus our mission program is inseparably linked with our whole mission task. Home Missions is the center from which all our missionary activity radiates. Christ commands each one of us to be a missionary, and we can do so by beginning at our very doors. "The light that shines fartherest, shines brightest at home."

Respectfully submitted,

A. Lincoln Fulk

REPORT ON FOREIGN MISSIONS

Ninety-four years ago the Foreign Mission Board of the Southern Baptist Convention was organized. The achievements of these years have been glorious and their story reads like a romance. The present world situation, with many lands rent and torn by the ravages of war, and civilization itself threatened by the terrible conditions that prevail, give a gloomy outlook. These are perilous times and no one can tell what a day may bring forth. So our Foreign Mission Board is facing one of the most, if not the most, distressing period of its history.

But in such a dark hour there are many things to encourage and give hope and cause rejoicing.

The last report of the Board reveals these interesting facts. There are 437 missionaries in active service, or fifteen more than last year. There are also 64 on pension, several of whom are still on the fields and helping to carry on the work.

There are 1794 churches, 1,053 of these are self supporting, there are also 3,046 out-stations,—on the various fields, there are 959 ordained natives and 1990 unordained natives who are actively engaged in the work.

During the year there have been 16,207 Baptisms and the churches have a total membership of 214,975—with 1,497 houses of worship, 2,457 Sunday Schools with 107,005 scholars enrolled—there are 1,397 womens societies with a membership of 31,373 members. There are also 1,473 Young Peoples societies—with 34,733 members who are being trained for service. The total native contributions for the year amount to $394,439.—When we think of all this and the terrible conditions under which much of this work has been carried on we have great reason to thank God and take courage.

In China, Japan, Spain and the nations of Europe the work is greatly hindered by war and the hostile attitude of the governments. Our missionaries are facing great perils—much of our missionary property has been destroyed or is in the hands of the enemies of Christianity, but the sacrifices the missionaries and native workers and members of the churches are making, their steadfast devotion and loyalty make one of the most glorious pages in our missionary history.

The most distressing feature of the whole situation is the attitude of multitudes of our American Christians and very many of our churches. They seemingly have no concern for a lost world and feel no responsibility as to that last word of Jesus, "Go ye into all the world and preach the Gospel to every creature." If our home churches would become alert and enlisted and give themselves to prayer and provide the means—which is their God given duty and responsibility—then in spite of wars and hostile governments, and all the base forms of heathenism there would be glorious victories and the lands now in the darkness and shadow of death would arise and shine in the radiant light of a serving gospel. Christianity is the only hope—It is Christ in every land or chaos in all the world.

The W. M. U. is carrying on a persistent work of study and training and generous giving. In most of our churches and more than any other organization they are "keeping the home fires burning."

We would command a wider distribution of missionary literature and urge that "The Commission" our fine Foreign Missionary Magazine be put as far as possible in the homes of all our people. At such a time as this our people need the information it carries month by month—information begets interest and interest stirs to action.

The cause of Foreign Missions is the greatest obligation of Southern Baptists.

Respectfully submitted,

A. B. Conrad

THE CHALLENGE OF OUR CO-OPERATIVE PROGRAM

Born in the heart of God, cooperation in service has continued down through the Ages and will continue because of its Divine origin. In this Divine Cooperation we see God the Father, God the Son, and God the Holy Spirit. God the Father—Law, God the Son—Love, God the Holy Spirit—Comforter. Each of these Divine Attributes has his own Dispensation but works together to one end—the salvation of man.

Man being created in the image of God caught something of his Spirit and therefore has worked together consciously or unconsciously throughout the centuries carrying on the progress of this world. A part of the cooperation of man has been to build communities, towns, cities, states, nations and empires together. Men have suffered, sacrificed and died together for worthy causes. And one might go on pointing out concrete examples of this cooperation without end, but neither time or space will permit.

At different periods in history Christianity has shown its strength and made its greatest strides through cooperation. Perhaps our own Denomination made its most forward step in the work of Luther Rice in the early part of the Nineteenth Century. At that time, our State Conventions, General Associations, and local Associations were organized. Our Baptist Colleges, Denominational Papers, Bibles and pamphlet societies were brought into existence. In addition to this, a great missionary consciousness stirred the whole world and in particular the South-land.

Catching up the loose threads from there, our Denomination has gone forward in a great Denominational Program. The missionary Spirit that was born then grew in momentum until we built our Foreign Mission Board in Richmond, and hundreds of missionaries are preaching the Gospel of the Lord Jesus Christ in all parts of the world. We have added to that, our Seminaries where men and women are trained for the purpose of preaching the Gospel at both home and abroad. We are likewise sending missionaries to the Jews, Italians, Chinese and Japanese, Indians, and Negroes here in our Homeland. Here within our own State, we are sending missionaries to some of the remote sections where preaching could not be heard otherwise. We have a great system of Christian education in the Sunday School, Training Union and Educational Department of our State Convention.

The effort is being put forth to preach the Gospel to the Indians within our own borders, to help with the Negro work and to do part-time work at the State prisons and Tubercular Sanitariums. Then, in our own State and throughout the entire Southern Baptist Convention, the Gospel of caring for orphan children and ministering to the sick is being effectively done.

I am sure we have mentioned only in part the work of our Denominational Program, very likely leaving out one of our most active services. However, there must be a word said about how all of this is done. When we give a dollar to benevolent causes, our State keeps sixty per cent of that for work done in our own Convention. The other forty per cent is sent directly to the Executive Committee of the Southern Baptist Convention where it is apportioned out to the various causes.

There is a deep and abiding conviction among all of us that the division of this dollar should be fifty-fifty and we pray for the day when it shall be divided that way. But at present, there are pressing needs at home and we must take care of the home base in defense of the battle line.

Would you say the ministries enumerated in this report are worthy to challenge us? If this program is not a challenge, then spiritually our consciences are void and without feeling.

Respectfully submitted,

Charles E. Parker

———o———

REPORT ON MINISTERIAL RELIEF AND ANNUITY

After a number of years in which some efforts have been made to awaken a conscience and concern on the subject of worthy ministerial relief and annuities for our Southern Baptist ministry, we have at last made a real beginning.

A plan is now operating in many states including our own which is meeting with the approval of most of our churches and ministers. This is a group plan and therefore makes a strong appeal to our benevolent nature. It not only provides adequate provisions for our old age and for any total disability which might come to us, but also makes possible more funds for the help of our old preachers who have finished their work and are now on someone's charity.

This plan is flexible enough for us to pay from two to four per cent of our salary with our church or churches paying the same proportion and the convention paying twenty-five per cent of the amount the pastor pays.

This contract will then pay us twenty-five per cent of our salary if we become totally disabled anytime after eighteen months of participation. And fifty per cent of our previous salary any time we retire after reaching the age of sixty-five, if this is after 1953 and a smaller proportion if before.

Now that the Federal government has put into effect a similar plan in which all public employees are forced to participate, it should be easy for our churches to appreciate this plan and enter heartily into it.

In the past year our Annuity board has paid out in relief to ministers and their widows more than ninety thousand dollars. In Annuity benefits $233,748. It now stands ready to serve all of our ministers and churches.

Let us urge every church in the Piedmont association with her pastor to enter the plan before the end of this month in order that they may enjoy the full benefits of the plan. Because each pastor who enters after the first of November will have his benefits reduced in proportion to the time he delays.

Respectfully submitted,
J.H.Saunders

---o---

14. The following recommendation was made and adopted.

Whereas we have no part-time nor full-time paid associational missionary, and whereas associational missionary work is being effectively done by the associational Training Union and associational Sunday School organization, and whereas there is no fund available from which necessary expenses may be obtained,

Be it resolved that the Moderator or Clerk of the Association be instructed to request the churches to provide an associational missions fund of $150.00 for the ensuing associational year to be used for necessary expenses of the Training Union and Sunday School Associations or Moderator of the Association at the discretion of the Executive Committee.

T. L. Sasser
O. E. Lee
J. Carl Bell,
Committee appointed by the Ex. Committee

---o---

15. The following resolution was presented by A. Lincoln Fulk and adopted.

RESOLUTION

Whereas, Rev. J. M. Hilliard has given six years as moderator and many other years as Vice-Moderator;

Whereas. He has given many years of unselfish service to the churches in and near this Association;

Whereas, He has built and helped to build over forty houses of worship, giving much of his own money to this work;

Whereas, God in His Wisdom and Providence has transplanted this soldier of the cross from his earthly labors to the Land of Service Eternal;

Therefore, Be it Resolved:

1. That this Association in annual session the year 1939 bow in submission to God's Will.

2. That the minutes of this associational year be dedicated to his memory and a suitable picture of our deceased brother be included in said minutes.

Respectfully submitted,
A. Lincoln Fulk

---o---

16. The Treasurer's report was presented and referred to the Auditing Committee.

TREASURER'S REPORT

I herewith submit my report for the year ending September 30, 1939.

Received from the Churches		$173.25
DISBURSEMENTS		
Economy Printing Co.	$13.69	
Postage and supplies for 1937-1938	4.15	
The Record Publishing Co.	95.33	
Clerk's Remuneration	50.00	
Postage and Supplies	2.29	
	$165.46	
Balance on hand	7.79	
	$173.25	$173.25

Respectfully submitted,
O. E. Lee, Treasurer

---o---

17. The Moderator extends the hand of fellowship to representatives of the Pisgah and Antioch Baptist Churches. These Churches were received into the Association by the Church Advisory Committee of the Association. The Committee having been given authority to act, by the Association at the last Annual Meeting.

18. Brother A. E. Tate presents questions relative to the Ministers Retirement Plan and the subject is given further consideration.

19. The Committee to revise the Constitution reported and the report is held in abeyance for further consideration.

The afternoon session is adjourned. Rev. J. Ben Eller leads in prayer.

WEDNESDAY NIGHT

"The Church In Its Ministry Of Training"

7:30 The session is opened with a devotional service led by W. I. Johnson.

The report on Training Union work is read by Miss Elizabeth Campbell, Secretary of the Training Union of the Association.

The report is adopted.

ANNUAL

B. T. U. SECRETARY'S REPORT TO:

PIEDMONT ASSOCIATION

For the year October 1938 to October 1939 we have had four quarterly meetings as required with one special meeting at Hilliard Memorial Baptist Church High Point. This meeting was "B. T. U. Night" with a playlet given by the Asheboro St. Bapt. Church. Greensboro. This church furnished music by their B. T. U. orchestra.

Our Annual Convention was held in the first Baptist Church, Reidsville, with a week-end session.

The Piedmont Associational B. T. U. is still on top in study courses given in the State. Our State is second in the South in study courses.

We have 30 general organizations, 23 Adult unions, 37 Senior Unions, 36 Intermediate Unions, 40 Junior Unions and 12 Story Hour groups. A total of 148 unions, making a total membership of 2400.

Respectfully submitted,
Elizabeth Campbell Sec.- Treas.

———o———

20. A play "Alice Through The Envelope" was presented by the young people of the First Baptist Church, Reidsville.

Special music is rendered by a quartet.

Special prayer is made by Grady Burgiss for Brother Nathan C. Brooks who has been very sick for sometime.

The night session is closed with prayer by N. F. Britt.

MORNING SESSION THURSDAY, OCTOBER 19, 1939

Theme: "The Church In Its Ministry To Human Need"

9:45 The session opened with singing "Help Somebody To-day" and "I Must Tell Jesus" after which C. N. Royal leads in prayer remembering the ladies hurt in the automobile accident yesterday.

The Moderator brings words of greetings from Clarence A. Smith, the former Moderator.

21. By special arrangements the report on Sunday Schools is presented at this time by F. L. Paschal. Upon motion to adopt the report the subject is discussed by L. L. Morgan, S. S. Secretary for the North Carolina Baptist State Convention.

The report is adopted.

REPORT ON SUNDAY SCHOOLS

Time marches on and our Sunday Schools are still growing and making the advancement of Christ's Kingdom on earth by teaching as the real objective of the work.

In our churches special efforts were made in Evangelistic work for 1939. We find that they have been very successful according to information furnished us, and our Sunday School leaders, teachers and officers have co-operated by making special efforts to bring the unsaved to know Jesus as Saviour and Lord. and to quicken the consciences of the rank and file, to exercise their faith and love by bringing the millions of starving, helpless, unsaved peoples to the Saviour.

Still we have just begun to find ourselves in this service. The success of the special program of Evangelism should encourage those who have met with success, to try to attain to greater heights, and to those of us who have not plunged ourselves into the work unreservedly to be aroused and inspired by the achievements of others and put ourselves wholly into the leading of His Spirit for service to win the lost to Him who gave his Life that all might have the Abundant Life.

In our Sunday School Associational work for this year, we have had quarterly meetings which have been well attended by those churches participating and we feel that a great deal of lasting good has been accomplished. Good programs have been rendered and we are grateful for the loyalty of so many who have contributed to the success of these meetings and for the good accomplished by work in the individual Sunday Schools. Our hope is that we can have more to attend these helpful meetings.

For the ensuing year we make the following recommendations:

1. That we continue with fervor and enthusiasm our program of Evangelism. An enlargement program including census taking, visitation day and special Evangelistic efforts in the classes are effective methods in accomplishing results.

2. That we continue to have Vacation Bible Schools, if possible, in every church of the Association.

3. That we have as our aim and objective at least one training course taught in every Sunday School.

4. The organization of new Sunday Schools in unchurched communities and assistance to our recently organized Sunday Schools.

5. That in all things we depend on Christ's leadership and magnify His Name for all victories won.

Respectfully submitted,

Frank L. Paschal

---o---

22. The report on Hospitals is made by D. W. Overbey. Upon motion to adopt the report the Hospital work is discussed by Smith Hagaman, Superintendent of our Baptist Hospital.

The report is adopted.

BAPTIST HOSPITAL REPORT

The Baptist Denomination owns and operates 20 hospitals in 14 Southern States. These have a total bed capacity of 3,000. About 100,000 patients were treated in this last year.

Our own Baptist Hospital, located in Winston-Salem, received its first patients May 28, 1923. Since that date 44,635 patients have been treated (July 14, 1939). A little more than 4,000 were treated last year. This number will not be increased this year as we have gone the limit. A little more than one-third of these were service patients, that is, they paid little or nothing.

About 90 per cent of these came from outside Winston-Salem.

It is always interesting to note the large number of mothers who have families of children at home. More than 1,000 of these were this year blessed to return to their more than 3,000 children.

The hospital treated last year about 100 preachers, missionaries and ministerial students. Almost all of these were free service.

The hospital with its fine staff of 72 doctors and four internes rendered during last year $196,177.00 of free service. We have 42 specialists on our free service staff.

The hospital has a staff of 82 nurses—51 are students in training. The Nurses Training School can accept only 16 in its September Class. They have already been selected from a little more than 500 applicants.

It is interesting to note that these patients come from almost every county in the state. A fair idea can be obtained any day by a check up of any of the large wards. A few days ago it was demonstrated that the seven patients in a ward were an average of 102 miles from home.

It is little less than a tragedy that during the past year the hospital has been compelled to turn away more than 2,000 patients for lack of room. During the year, it is estimated that 1,000 patients in Winston-Salem, who could pay their bills, were turned away in order that the hospital might take those who could not pay a hospital bill.

Plans are going forward to immediately add 100 more bed space to the hospital, giving the hospital a bed capacity of 212. This will enable the hospital to treat 8,000 patients each year. This ought not to be a difficult task for a denomination comprising a membership of almost a half million—One half the entire membership of all denominations of our state. For the expense of caring for these multitudes of sick who cannot pay, we must look largely to the Mother's Day offering and free donations of the hospital linen by the W. M. U. and other organizations.

Respectfully submitted,

D. W. Overbey

———o———

23. The report of the Orphanage is presented by H. R. Starling.

Upon motion to adopt the report the subject is discussed by J. A. McMillan.

The report is adopted.

REPORT ON MILLS HOME

The Baptist Orphanage at Thomasville, N. C., was founded in 1885. The following men have served as Superintendent of the Mills Home: J. H. Mills, 1885-1889; J. B. Boone, 1895-1905; M. L. Kesler, 1905-1932; I. G. Greer, 1932—began his service and is faithfully doing his best to serve in the greatest possible way.

The first child was received for care in the home on November 11, 1885. Mills Home had a small beginning compared with the home today. For at the present there come to the home about one hundred applications each month from worthy children who so badly need Mills Home care. However our Orphanage is not able to take in but a small part of these applicants because there is no room for so many children there.

The purpose of our Orphanage is to prepare orphan boys and girls for the duties and responsibilities of life in a world of opportunity. As a result every possible effort is put forth to provide the best conditions for these boys and girls to prepare physically, mentally and spiritually for places of noble service to humanity.

It is the duty of North Carolina Baptists to make possible for our Orphan children a condition in which they may prepare for leadership tomorrow. At the present the conditions are not what they ought to be if we are able to meet the needs of the advancing demands. The public demands more of her leaders today than was demanded twenty years ago. Therefore if we fail to make more provisions whereby the increasing demands may be met, then we are consenting for our children to take some secondary place in life.

Perhaps the greatest way that we can help in our Orphan work is to increase the monthly offering taken for the Orphanage in our Sunday Schools. For it is upon these offerings and the Thanksgiving offering that the greater part of the work depends.

Let me commend to you the "Charity and Children as possibly the best means through which you may learn each week the work that is going on in our Orphanage System. Have this paper come to your Sunday School each week, for it will help you and through it you will help the Orphanage.

"Do unto others as you would have them do to you" is still a golden rule to live by.

Respectfully submitted,

H. R. Starling

———o———

24. The Verbal Report Hour is in charge of J. Ben Eller. Following the reports Dr. J. Clyde Turner leads in prayer. Rev. R. E. Adams and Rev. J. M. Hayes are recognized.

25. The committee on Resolutions reports as follows. The report is adopted.

REPORT OF COMMITTEE ON RESOLUTIONS

Whereas the Piedmont Baptist Association meeting with the First Baptist Church Reidsville, October 18-19, 1939, has engaged in one of its finest sessions, be resolved:

First· that we express our gratitude to this church and her

Pastor, Rev. T. L. Sasser, and all the Baptist Churches in the Reidsville group for their cooperation in every effort to entertain the Association in this gracious way.

Second, that we express our appreciation of the untiring and wise efforts of our most efficient moderator—Grover H. Jones, who has shown a deep interest in all our churches, and to our clerk, O. E. Lee, qualified with both experience and concern.

Third, that we commend the work of the W. M. U., the Sunday Schools, and the young people's work, calling special attention to the fine program given by our Training Union under the direction of J. Carl Bell last evening. Surely it calls out the best there is in our young people. We urge all our young people to use their talents for the Master.

Fourth, that we acknowledge our debt of gratitude to God for all the information and inspiration brought to us in these meetings.

Respectfully submitted,
H. O. Miller
W. B. Cook
John U. Garner

—————o—————

26. The report of the Church Advisory Committee is presented and adopted.

Two new churches have made application for admission into the association, the Tabernacle Church, Greensboro, N. C., and the Pleasant Grove six miles south of Greensboro.

Representatives of these churches appeared before your committee and gave satisfactory evidence that the churches were duly organized and functioning as Baptist churches. Your committee recommends that they be received into the association. However, we make two suggestions to the Tabernacle Church. First, that they give earnest and prayerful consideration to the selection of a site further removed from Florida Street Church. Second, that they select another name for the church since there is already one church in the association bearing the name Tabernacle.

Respectfully submitted,
A. B. Conrad
T. L. Sasser
Mrs. Nettie Hoge
J. Clyde Turner
Members of Advisory Committee present at meeting.

—————o—————

27. The report of the Committee to Nominate the Church Advisory Committee was presented and adopted.

REPORT OF COMMITTEE TO NOMINATE CHURCH ADVISORY COMMITTEE

Dr. J. Clyde Turner, Dr. A. B. Conrad, J. Ben Eller, Mrs. Nettie Hoge, Grover H. Jones, Wilson Woodcock, O. E. Lee.

Respectfully submitted

Chas. E. Parker
O. E. Lee
Grover H. Jones

28. An address on "The Challenge of the Cooperative Program Accepted" was made by Col. F. P. Hobgood.

The morning session was closed with prayer by Dr. A. B. Conrad.

THURSDAY AFTERNOON

"The Church In Its Ministry Of Teaching"

1:30 The session was opened by singing "Amazing Grace" and "Come, Thou Fount."

29. The report of the Committee on Place and Preacher was made and adopted.

Your COMMITTEE ON PLACE AND PREACHER makes the following report:

Place—Florida Street Baptist Church, Greensboro
Preacher—Charles E. Parker
Alternate—A. Lincoln Fulk

E. M. Smith
L. C. Chandler
J. Clyde Turner
Committee

30. Following prayer by J. C. Gillespie the report on W. M. U. Work was presented by Mrs. Nettie Hoge. Upon motion to adopt the report, the subject was discussed by Mrs. Hoge.

The report was adopted.

REPORT ON WOMAN'S WORK PIEDMONT W. M. U.

The greatest commendation that could be bestowed was given to Mary by Christ. Constrained by her love for Christ, she poured her greatest treasure upon his head and feet. In answer to her critics, Christ said, "She hath done what she could."

The Woman's Missionary Union in its fifty years of loving service has not attained all it desired, nor probably all that was expected of it, possibilities unattained, yet with its marvelous growth, surely Christ says, "Well done good and faithful servant." —"She hath done what she could."

Steadfastly, persistently has the Union followed its first Motto, "Go Forward" in magnifying Christ through enlistment and service at home, and in all the world, until it has grown in numbers and objectives and has become a part of the Church as a praying, educating, studying and giving force in Kingdom work.

Its great strength is in its Union—united in purpose, methods. plans and interest that are carried out co-operatively in churches, associations, states and southwide work.

Never has its first purpose been changed, that of being an "Auxiliary to the Southern Baptist Convention, in stimulating the Missionary Spirit and grace of giving among women and children of the churches and aiding in collecting funds for Missionary purposes to be disbursed by the Boards of the Southern Baptist Convention."—In this has the Union magnified Christ and grown in the knowledge of the world's needs, and made great contributions to meet these needs through service, money, time and talent.

In the Piedmont Association the W. M. U. has become an inseparable part of its work. There are 112 organizations, 81 of which are for the Young People. An offering of $24,790.11 was made last year to the cooperative program, $3,513.39 of this amount was given by the Young People.

The far reaching influence, through service for good cannot be reported in figures. A working force in the churches, Laborers together with God, around the world through prayer, gifts and service is the task of the Woman's Missionary Union in Magnifying Christ.

Respectfully submitted,
(Mrs.) Nettie Hatcher Hoge

—o—

31. The report on Christian Education was made by Hughey O. Miller, and upon motion to adopt the report J. M. Hayes, Representative of Meredith College was presented and discussed the subject.

The report was adopted.

REPORT ON CHRISTIAN SCHOOLS

It is heartening to know that the enrollment in our Christian Schools is increasing year by year throughout the south land. The report of the Education Commission to the Southern Baptist Convention last May show an enrollment in our schools and Seminaries of 33,795, a gain of 7,422 in the last four years.

Many of our schools are placing greater emphasis upon religious training and its correlation with liberal and practical application, than in many years. This emphasis is rightly placed for today, perhaps as never before, we need men and women trained, and trained Spiritually as well as mentally and socially. Christian Education of the right sort will meet this need.

The work of the Kingdom demands trained men and women. The problems that confront our country call for Christian leadership Our Christian Schools must furnish the greater part of these leaders and workers.

There is no place for schools that are only nominally Christian. If we hope to make Democracy safe for the world, we must develop a citizenry who will not sacrifice righteousness for popularity, but will rise up in defense of the principles of Jesus Christ. Surely our hope in attaining these ideals is within our schools and Seminaries under the direction of God fearing, Spirit filled servants of the King of Kings and Lord of Lords.

Respectfully submitted,

Hughey O. Miller

—————o—————

32. The clerk gave a general report of the work done by the churches during the associational year showing that there had been gains made in about every department of the work.

33. The report on Obituaries presented by A. A. Walker was adopted..

OBITUARY

It is appointed unto men once to die, and only once, if they are the redeemed of the Lord. Blessed are the dead who die in the Lord. We yield most high praise and hearty thanks to our heavenly Father for the wonderful grace and virtue declared in all His saints who this year have gone on before us, who have been the chosen vessels of His grace, who have been examples of steadfastness in faith and of obedience to His holy commands. Like a refreshing shadow in the heat of the day, we pause in the memory of these deceased to, lift our eyes to a far country from whose bourn a Traveler shall return when we shall enter with them into the joys of our Lord.

Respectfully submitted,

A. A. Walker

34. The following reports of committees were made and adopted:

COMMITTEE ON PROGRAM FOR NEXT YEAR

Religious Literature	A. Lincoln Fulk
Foreign Missions	Dr. J. Clyde Turner
Denominational Program	T. L. Sasser
State Missions	C. N. Royal
Social Service	Wilson Woodcock
Orphanage	J. Ben Eller
Hospital	A. A. Walker
Training Union	J. Carl Bell
Woman's Missionary Union	Mrs. Nettie Hoge
Christian Education	W. I. Johnson
Home Missions	Dr. A. B. Conrad
Sunday Schools	F. L. Paschal
Ministers' Relief and Retirement Plan	Hughey O. Miller
Obituaries	L. C. Chandler

Respectfully submitted,
O. E. Lee
Dr. A. B. Conrad
D. W. Overbey

REPORT OF COMMITTEE TO AMEND CONSTITUTION

A committee composed of Frank L. Paschal; J. H. Saunders, and C. V. Webster having been appointed to consider the matter of amending the Constitution of the Piedmont Baptist Association, and the committee having met and carefully considered the matter respectfully reports: That notwithstanding the fact that the only committee actually named in the constitution is the committee on arrangements we believe that article (11) eleven sufficiently authorizes the moderator to appoint any and all other committees which may be necessary, and we commend the method now used by the committee on committees, and we therefore offer no resolution for the amendment of our constitution, believing its present provisions are adequate.

Respectfully submitted,
Frank L.Paschal.Chairman

Motion was passed to continue the committee and have the committee bring recommendations at the next annual meeting.

Motion was passed instructing the clerk to have a list of the committees printed in the front of the minutes.

REPORT OF COMMITTEE TO NOMINATE EXECUTIVE PROMOTION COMMITTEE

Members ex-offocio: Grover H. Jones, O. E. Lee, T. L. Sasser; Mrs. N. H. Hoge or successor, F. L. Paschal or successor, J. Carl Bell or successor; S. R. Clinard, C. N. Royal, J. T. J. Battle, J. Ben Eller, R. E. Saunders, D. W. Overbey.

—o—

REPORT OF AUDITING COMMITTEE

The committee consisting of Frank L. Paschal and L. E. Ogburn having been duly appointed to examine and audit the financial report of O. E. Lee, Clerk-Treasurer of the Piedmont Baptist Association for the current year ending with the convening of this association respectfully submits the following report:

We have examined the receipts and vouchers and the books kept by O. E. Lee and we find the same to be neatly and correctly kept and in proper order in every respect, and we therefore recommend the acceptance and adoption of this report.

Respectfully submitted,
Frank L. Paschal
For the Committee

—o—

COMMITTEE TO NOMINATE COMMITTEE ON EVANGELISM

Mrs. Nettie H. Hoge, Chairman; D. W. Overbey, C. N. Royal.

Respectfully submitted,
Committee A. A. Walker
W. I. Johnson

—o—

COMMITTEE TO NOMINATE LEADER FOR VERBAL REPORT HOUR

The committee recommends C. N .Royal.

Committee L. Grady Burgiss
Grover H. Jones
Farrell James

The Committee to nominate officers for next year nominates the following:

Moderator Grover H. Jones, Vice Moderator T. L. Sasser, Clerk and Treasurer O. E. Lee.

Respectfully submitted,
Committee C. N. Royal
H. R. Starling
J. H. Saunders

Motion was passed giving the Committee to Nominate

the Delegates to the Baptist State Convention authority to advise the clerk of the nominations.

The nominations were as follows: Grover H. Jones, and T. L. Sasser.

Committee: Mrs. Nettie H. Hoge
L. E. Ogburn
J. C. Gillespie

The following new Pastors were introduced and welcomed into the fellowship of the Association by Dr. J. Clyde Turner: J. C. Shore, L. Grady Burgiss, and W. I. Johnson.

The session closed with singing "God Be With You" and prayer by Rev. J. Ben Eller.

---o---

MINUTES OF THE W. M. U. PIEDMONT ASSOCIATION

The Piedmont W. M. U. met with 1st. Baptist church High Point, April 27, 1939 with the Superintendent, Mrs. Nettie Hatcher Hoge presiding.

The devotional was led by Mrs. O. E. Lee.

The theme for the day was a "Spiritual Revival." All the addresses and reports of the Group Leaders and Associational Chairmen were made under two divisions of the theme. The morning theme "A Spiritual Revival in the Church," and the afternoon theme "A Spiritual Revival in the Home."

The two guest speakers were Dr. Ralph Herring, who spoke on the Holy Spirit and Miss Wilma Bucy, who presented the work of the Home Mission Board.

Mrs. T. C. Robbins led the devotional for the afternoon session. The Young People's Work was presented by Miss Ruth Scott. Mrs. M. L. Morris conducted the Obituary. Mrs. Stafford Webb discussed the needs of the Hospital, Orphanage and the Fannie Heck Offering.

Mrs. J. H. Saunders expressed the appreciation of the Union for the hospitality of the hostess church, the presence of the guest speakers and faithful services of the officers of the Union.

Nominating Committee reported the following officers:

Superintendent -------------- Mrs. Nettie Hatcher Hoge
Secretary ------------------------------- Mrs. A. Andrews
Treasurer ------------------------------ Mrs. C. E. Siceloff
Young People's Leader -------------------- Miss Ruth Scott
Group Leaders:
High Point -------------------- Mrs. H. A. Knight
Greensboro ---------------------- Mrs. Joe Howard
Reidsville --------------------- Mrs. R. R. Saunders
Mission Study Chairman ----------------- Mrs. J. J. Andoe
Stewardship Chairman -------------------- Mrs. C. N. Royal
Personal Service Chairman -------------- Mrs. L. M. Gideon

The Union reported 112 Organizations and the gift of $24,790.11 for 1938.

Time and place for next meeting, last Thursday in April 1940 with North Main Church, High Point.

An inspiring service of prayer and praise was followed by a pageant written by Miss Netta Liles and presented by the W. M. S. of First Baptist Church of Greensboro. The attendance was large and the meeting inspiring.

Respectfully submitted,
Mrs. A. Andrews, Sec.

BUCHANAN—
Deacon James C. West
Miss Mary Ellen Donnell
CALVARY—
Mr. Layton Ford
GIBSONVILLE—
Mrs. Robert Montgomery
GREENSBORO, FIRST—
Mrs. S. B. Adams
Mr. Allen Adams
Mr. T. M. Boone
Mr. J. M. Church
Mr. J. W. Daniel
Mrs. G. E. Deffenbaugh
Mr. C. M. Edwards
Mr. W. B. Isham
Mrs. Hattie Jackson
Dr. W. J. Meadows
Mrs. C. W. Myers
Mr. C. A. McMillan
Miss Mary Prather
Mr. William Rightsell
Mrs. J. B. Raybon
Mrs. W. F. Sides
Mrs. E. E. Thompson
Mrs. Howard Thompson
Mrs. Hannah J. Utt
ASHEBORO STREET—
Mr. J. T. Lane
Miss Lois Wolfe
Mrs. C. B. Hall
Mr. Thomas Williams
Mr. W. H. Apple
Mr. A. A. Coble
Mr. Austin Pamplin
BESSEMER—
Mr. R. T. Register
ELLER MEMORIAL—
Mr. Eugene Bates
Mrs. Sherman Alberty
Mr. J. B. Bateman
FLORIDA STREET—
Mr. J. S. Wallace
Mrs. E. C. Causey
FOREST AVE—
Mrs. J. W. Bloxton
Mr. J. W. Bloxton
Mrs. W. R. Byrd
Mr. John E. Sharp
Mrs. Fannie Fryer
Mrs. Alice Cooper
MAGNOLIA STREET—
Mrs Mollie Apple
POMONA—
Mrs. J. C. Combs
Mrs. Mollie Flinton
Mr. A. G. Henley
REVOLUTION—
Miss Ruby Phillips
Mr. W. O. Murray
SIXTEENTH STREET—
Mrs. N. W. Whittington
Mrs. T. F. Talley
Mrs. C. C. Roberts
Mr. G. L. Guffey
Mr. W. M. Nickerson
Mrs. Evelyn Lewey Nance
STEVENS MEMORIAL—
Mr. R. A. Newman
TABERNACLE (Greensboro)—
Mrs. Freddie Pridgen
WEBSTER MEMORIAL—
Mr. Z. V. Martin
GUILFORD—
Mrs. N. A. Jones
Mr. Charlie Browden
Mrs. — — Taylor
Miss Mozelle Harris
HIGH POINT FIRST—
Mr. Westcott Roberson
Mr. Earl Jones
Mr. J. M. Simmerson
Mrs. J. D. Hedgecock
Mrs. Lola Moon
Mrs. T. C. Barker
Mr. James Culler
Mrs. Ella Dennis
Mrs. Ella Stewart

IN MEMORIAM

GREEN STREET—
- Mrs. D. T. Andrews, Dea'ness
- Mr. W. A. Howell
- Mr. D. A. Fowler
- Mr. Martin Andrews
- Mr. Frank Ivey
- Mr. J. R. Shelton, Deacon
- Mrs. Jesse Stacy
- Mr. T. S. Clayton
- Mr. W. L. Teague

HILLIARD MEMORIAL—
- Mrs. Mary Bowling

NORTH MAIN STREET—
- Rev. J. M. Hilliard
- Mrs. Katherine Brooks

NORTH PARK—
- Deacon Ed. J. Welch

SOUTH SIDE—
- Mrs. Lee Cranford
- Mr. M. H. Dorsett
- Mrs. M. O. Huntsinger

WEST END—
- Mrs. L. G. Campbell
- Mrs. Nora Norman
- Mrs. Matilda Johnson
- Mrs. Eva Mae Stevenson

MOUNT ZION—
- Mrs. Emily G. Wiatt

OSBORNE CHAPEL—
- Mrs. Rebecca Lenard

OSCEOLA—
- Mr. Harmon Cook

REIDSVILLE, FIRST—
- Mrs. J. R. Webster
- Mrs. N. C. Thompson
- Mrs. J. C. Gillespie
- Mrs. Loyd Manly

MOUNT OLIVE—
- Miss Geraldine Crites

BENN MEMORIAL—
- Mrs. C. V. Watkins

ROCKY KNOLL—
- Mrs. Pearl Coble

SMITH'S GROVE—
- Mr. Albert Farrington

SUMMERFIELD—
- Mr. Ernest Proctor
- Garrett Parrish
- Mr. W. D. Lane
- Miss Martha Baker
- Miss Sarah Highfill

CHURCHES	Is It Village, Town, City or Country?	When Constituted	PASTORS AND POST OFFICES	Days of Meeting	Members Reported Last Year	Gains: Baptisms	Gains: Letters	Gains: Statements	Gains: Restorations	Losses: Letters	Losses: Exclusions	Losses: Erasures	Losses: Deaths	Total Present Members	Weekly Prayer Me[eting]	Revivals Held	Obs. Lord's Supper	Rec. State Bap. Pa[per]
1. Allen Jay	V	1934	C. M. [illegible]d, R2, Thom'ville	2 4	103	16	13	4	...	2	...	...	...	134	*	2	4	2
2. Antioch	O	1934	E. T. Bailey, [illegible]n	1 3	58	7	1	1	...	1	...	...	...	66	*	2	1	...
3. [illegible]	O	1886	J. B. Clifton, Greensboro	All	66	13	6	1	...	3	...	...	2	81	*	2	1	...
4. Calvary	O	1901	J. C. Shore, R4, Reidsville	2 4	161	...	...	...	...	2	...	...	1	158	...	1	2	9
5. Fairview	O	1904	J. C. Shore, Reidsville R4	1 3	119	1	4	...	...	4	...	3	...	117	...	1	1	7
6. [illegible]le	T	1894	E. A. Long, [illegible]n	2 4	243	7	2	...	...	...	2	...	1	249	*	1	4	2
7. [illegible]o, [illegible]st	C	1859	Dr. J. Clyde [illegible], G'boro	All	2172	111	132	13	...	116	13	86	19	2194	*	1	12	122
8. [illegible]o Street	C	1899	J. Ben Eller, Greensboro	All	1122	58	35	2	...	49	...	14	7	1147	*	1	4	60
9. Bailey Memorial	C	1935	C. G. [illegible]e, [illegible]na	All	97	7	...	...	...	1	...	...	...	103	*	2	12	...
10. Bessemer	V	1923	A. A. [illegible]r, [illegible]o	All	448	36	20	2	1	27	...	4	1	477	*	1	4	22
11. [illegible]ler [illegible]al	C	1897	Chas. E. Parker, [illegible]oro	All	825	57	16	4	1	23	...	4	3	873	*	1	4	48
12. Florida Street	C	1916	J. H. Saunders, [illegible]ro.	All	367	51	67	6	5	119	...	91	2	284	*	2	4	27
13. [illegible]t Avenue	C	1906	Wilson W. [illegible]k, G'boro	All	534	21	41	1	1	21	...	3	5	569	*	1	12	33
14. [illegible]n Park	C	1914	R. O. [illegible]s, [illegible], Jamest'n	All	60	...	...	...	...	...	...	...	...	64	*	1	1	...
15. Magnolia Street	C	1909	L. Grady Burgiss, G'boro	All	380	24	18	5	...	18	...	201	1	207	*	2	2	13
16. Pomona	V	1906	C. M. [illegible], [illegible]	All	198	26	7	3	6	5	1	...	3	231	*	2	2	...
17. Revolution	C	1907	H. R. Starling, [illegible]ro.	All	312	25	5	3	5	4	...	2	2	342	*	2	2	18
18. Sixteenth S[illegible]et	C	1907	W. B. [illegible]k, [illegible]	All	518	19	8	10	9	11	24	77	6	446	*	2	12	...
19. Stevens [illegible]	V	1922	John U. Garner, [illegible]oro	All	149	7	4	...	...	9	...	...	1	150	*	1	4	15
20. Tabernacle	C	1938	B. G. [illegible]y, R5, G'boro	All	...	37	133	13	...	...	...	...	1	182	*	1	1	8
21. Webster [illegible]orial	V	1935	M. L. Hux, [illegible]	All	145	12	3	1	...	11	...	3	1	146	*	2	1	7
22. [illegible]d	V	1914	Ferrell James, [illegible]o	All	70	3	4	3	...	4	...	...	4	72	...	...	2	3
23. High Point, First	C	1825	Dr. A. B. Conrad, High Pt.	All	1152	68	103	5	2	41	...	2	9	1278	*	1	4	90
24. [illegible]n Street	C	1900	C. N. [illegible]l, High Point	All	1372	50	24	3	...	54	...	5	9	1381	*	2	4	58
25. Hilliard Memorial	C	1929	Hughey O. Miller, High Pt.	All	301	5	13	1	...	12	...	6	1	301	*	1	1	30
26. [illegible]h [illegible]in	C	1908	A. Lin oln Fulk, R1, H. Pt.	All	255	32	9	3	...	6	...	1	2	290	*	2	4	15
27. [illegible]h Park	C	1929	E. M. Smith, High Point	All	225	10	9	1	...	9	...	3	1	232	*	1	4	17
28. South Side	C	1916	G. H. Liner, [illegible]h Point	All	332	10	7	1	...	6	...	...	3	341	*	3	4	7
29. [illegible]st End	C	1913	T. H. Biles, High Point	All	417	9	1	...	...	45	...	1	4	377	*	...	...	...
30. [illegible]p [illegible]ve	C	1933	E. B. Cain, Kernersville	All	29	6	5	...	1	...	...	...	...	41	*	2	2	...
31. [illegible]n	O	1911	Melvin Faulkner, [illegible]ille	All	242	2	2	1	...	24	...	69	1	120	*	1	4	...
32. M. Zion	O	1824	...	2 4	166	1	...	...	...	2	...	...	1	164	...	1	...	...
33. Oak Grove	O	1916	R. L. Smith, High [illegible]t	All	141	22	5	4	...	10	...	...	...	162	*	2	4	...
34. Osborne Chapel	O	1934	C. W. Myrick, R1, G'boro	All	35	14	11	1	...	...	...	...	1	60	*	2	1	...
35. [illegible]la	O	1915	J. F. Sellars, [illegible]nt Airy	1 3	47	24	4	4	...	...	...	...	1	78	...	2	2	1
36. Pisgah	O	1938	W. L. Smith, High Point	All	42	25	20	4	...	...	...	...	...	91	*	1	3	...
37. [illegible]t Garden	V	1933	L. C. [illegible]r, [illegible], G'boro.	All	101	7	3	1	...	1	...	...	...	111	*	1	4	10
38. Pleasant Grove		...	...	All	30	39	16	1	...	...	...	...	...	86	*	2	1	...
39. [illegible]le, [illegible]st	C	184?	T. L. Sasser, Reidsville	All	821	14	24	3	...	11	...	...	4	847	*	...	4	51
40. [illegible]t Olive	C	1929	W. I. [illegible]n, Reidsville	All	245	28	14	4	2	4	1	66	1	221	*	2	4	2
41. Penn [illegible]l	C	1927	D. W. Overbey, Reidsville	All	175	11	2	6	...	2	...	...	1	191	*	2	4	...
42. Rocky Knoll	O	1934	L. C. [illegible]r, [illegible], G'boro.	All	155	19	13	4	...	5	...	1	1	184	*	2	4	8
43. Ruffin Stacey	O	1888	J. T. London, R5, Reidsville	All	186	6	1	...	1	4	1	1	...	188	*	2	4	3
44. Smith [illegible]e	O	1921	R. O. Nuckles, R1, Jamest'n	2 4	163	3	3	...	...	7	...	...	1	161	*	2	4	...
45. Summerfield	V	...	E. A. Long, [illegible]	1	210	8	...	1	...	...	...	...	5	214	...	1	...	2
46. Tabernacle	V	1933	H. P. Ga ldin, [illegible]haw.	All	21	24	15	10	...	...	2	...	...	68	*	2	...	...
TOTALS		...	...	...	14910	975	823	130	34	673	44	643	106	15479	...	68	158	690

43

1. Allen Jay	Wade Cumbie, R1, High Point	6	15	20	50	55	45	99		12			302	188	15	*		
2. Antioch	Roy Moore, R2, Reidsville		15			20		40					75	50	2			
3. Buchanan	....		39		21	26	48	51					185	105				
4. Calvary	Geo. Gunn, Rt., Reidsville			9	6	7	46	60					128	74				
5. Fairview	A. D. Hopkins, Reidsville												80	66	1			
6. Gibsonville	C. C. Hanner, Gibsonville		18	19	49	39	40	82		17			264	160	7		10	
7. Greensboro, First	O. E. Lee, Greensboro	168	88	156	242	208	187	959	190	48			2246	979	94	*	4	
8. Asheboro Street	M. D. Teague, Greensboro	35	56	79	134	156	143	409	60	5			1077	527		*	6	
9. Bailey Memorial	E. J. Jarvis, Greensboro		28		37		43	23					131	76	6			
10. Bessemer	E. E. Hanner, Greensboro	25	26	53	53	65	65	133		6			426	213	33	*	1	
11. Eller Memorial	G. O. Basinger, Greensboro	170	26	115	128	125	171	162	11	13			921	419	50	*	3	2
12. Florida Street	J. B. Rumbley, Greensboro	103	15	50	53	62	34	162		12			491	259	41	*		1
13. Forest Avenue	B. B. Stockard, Greensboro	45	23	49	57	64	147	145		5			535	293		*	15	1
14. Latham Park	R. A. Anderson, Greensboro												57	47	1			
15. Magnolia Street	D. L. Wrenn, Greensboro	20	14	41	45	29	53	101		4			304	152	26			
16. Pomona	C. C. Patterson, Pomona		35	36	70	60	70	84		13			368	233				
17. Revolution	Grady Phillips, Greensboro	45	20	48	44	51	47	97	18	6			376	234	14	*	3	1
18. Sixteenth Street	Fred Hester, Greensboro	15	37	55	75	59	67	205		8			521	390				1
19. Stevens Memorial	L. A. Mills, Greensboro	3	10	22	32	23	29	80		1			200	145		*		
20. Tabernacle	W. O. Smith, Greensboro	15	17	25	29	21	14	45	15	5			186	119	17	*	5	
21. Webster Memorial	L. P. Pearman, Greensboro	9	16	17	32	28	30	61		4			197	142				
22. Guilford	Setzer Weston, Guilford College		18	10	5	27	15	25		9			109	70	4	*		
23. High Point, First	A. E. Tate, High Point	24	39	120	180	142	155	478	75	4			1217	609	61	*		
24. Green Street	W. E. Crissman, High Point	27	73	126	241	135	160	440		15			1217	620	20	*		
25. Hilliard Memorial	L. E. Edwards, High Point		25	40	34	50	25	86		5	*	40	325	187	4	*		
26. North Main	Winfred Clinard, High Point	13	28	51	66	42	67	72					339	220	30	*		
27. North Park	L. R. McNeill, High Point	23	21	33	58	22	36	52	4	6			255	180	10			
28. South Side	Houston Williams, High Point		14	15	47	28	52	51		6			213	175		*		
29. West End	Vernon Coffey, High Point	44	35	36	64	29	67	84	30	19			408	234		*		
30. Jessup Grove	Charlie Johnson, R1, Guilford College		15		14		12	21		4			66					
31. Lebanon	Jim McDaniels, R5, Greensboro	10	15	12	35	18	30	25					145	150				
32. Mt. Zion	C. D. Branson, Snow Camp		25		20	43	18			6			112	50	1			
33. Oak Grove	L. R. Loflin, Jamestown		12	16	26		30	43		2			129	103				
34. Osborne Chapel	Hubert Bennett, R1, Greensboro		30		23		46	31		12			142	70		*		
35. Osceola	D. A. Greene, R1, Brown Summit		12	15	17	19	16	23		2			94	50				
36. Pisgah	F. P. Vaughn, High Point		30		61		32	64					187	125				
37. Pleasant Garden	W. J. Smith, Pleasant Garden	16	12	6	12	8	12	19	7	12			104		7			
38. Pleasant Grove	F. M. Atkins, R3, Greensboro	8	11	9	15	14	32	36		2			127	68	35	*		
39. Reidsville, First	R. T. Burton, Reidsville	49	38	66	103	76	82	308	50				772	327	14	*		1
40. Mount Olive	Odell Delapp, Reidsville	9	25	28	42	40	24	75		11			254	168		*		
41. Penn Memorial	W. Herbert Ford, Reidsville		11	11	16	16	13	67		2			136	80	6			
42. Rocky Knoll	R. R. Sudderth, R2, Greensboro	26	31		16	38	44	52	36	10			253	175				
43. Ruffin Stacey	Dewey London, R5, Reidsville		24	34	45	26	45	67		15			256	150		*		
44. Smith Grove	Walter Westmoreland, R1, High Point		25		27		42	30					124	55	2			
45. Summerfield	Marion Ayers, Summerfield												144	81	8			

1. Allen Jay	Yes			1	1	2			25	18	43		18	9	26			
2. Antioch																		
3. Buchanan																		
4. Calvary																		
5. Fairview																		
6. Gibsonville	Yes		1	1	1	3		15	15	20	50							
7. Greensboro, First	Yes	3	3	4	4	14	44	48	76	63	231	16	87	49	166			5
8. Asheboro Street	Yes	1	2	2	2	7	16	50	40	43	149	23	85	81	149			6
9. Bailey Memorial	Yes		1	1	1	3		10	12	9	31		19	16	21			
10. Bessemer	Yes	1	1	1	1	4	10	15	27	2[illegible]	75	8	6	2	42			
11. Eller Memorial	Yes	1	1	2	3	7	15	14	32	42	103	9	40	40	54			
12. Florida Street	Yes	2	1	2	2	7	28	12	29	22	91	10	48	58	67		1	1
13. Forest Avenue	Yes		2	1	1	4		112	10	12	134	4	25	27	55			2
14. Latham Park																		
15. Magnolia Street	Yes	1	1	1		3	23	13	17		53	23	10	3	25			
16. Pomona																		
17. Revolution	Yes	1	1	1		3	10	12	18		40	17	19	23				
18. Sixteenth Street			1	1	1	3		12	15	28	55	12	24	21				
19. Stevens Memorial	Yes		1	1		2		12	6		18		6	5	5			
20. Tabernacle	Yes	1	2	1	1	5	11	12	11	18	52	8	32	31	39			1
21. Webster Memorial																		
22. Guilford			1			1		12			12							
23. High Point, First	Yes		1	2	3	6		33	72	76	181	29	62	54	89			3
24. Green Street	Yes		2	1	1	4		22	28	22	72	20	30	33	41			6
25. Hilliard Memorial	Yes	1	1	1	1	4	16	14	9	16	55	8	41	45	37			
26. North Main	Yes	1		1	1	3	15		10	14	39	14						
27. North Park	Yes	1	1	2	2	6	20	20	38	30	108	15	49	82	73			
28. South Side	Yes		1	1	1	3		10	29	25	55	15	2		2			
29. West End	Yes	1	1	1	2	5	12	11	16	28	67		30	39	36			
30. Jessup Grove																		
31. Lebanon																		
32. Mt. Zion																		
33. Oak Grove																		
34. Osborne Chapel	Yes			1		1			12		12							
35. Osceola																		
36. Pisgah																		
37. Pleasant Garden			1		1	2												
38. Pleasant Grove																		
39. Reidsville, First	Yes	1	2	2	2	7	15	36	43	45	139		42	52	66			
40. Mount Olive	Yes	1	1	2	2	6	15	11	25	24	75	10	19		28			
41. Penn Memorial	Yes		1	1	1	3		12	11	8	31		20	10	16			
42. Rocky Knoll	Yes	1	1	1	1	4	20	19	14	19	72			19				
43. Ruffin Stacey																		
44. Smith Grove																		
45. Summerfield	Yes		1	1	1	3		21	12	12	45		23	21				
46. Tabernacle																		
TOTALS		18	33	37	37	125	270	558	643	617	2088	211	737	720	1037		1	24

	POST OFFICES							W. M. S	Y. W. A	G. A.'s							Total Cont by W. M.
1. Allen [illegible]hy																	
2. [illegible]h																	
3. Buchanan																	
4. [illegible]	Mrs. J. E. McCargo, Reidsville, R2	1	1				2	20	23				43		10.00	174.64	184.6
5. [illegible]																	
6. [illegible]e	Mrs. [illegible] [illegible]mmer, Gibsonville	1					1	31					31			19.21	19.2
7. [illegible]o, First	Mrs. Stafford R. Webb, [illegible]nsboro	1	2	2	2	1	8	38	52	80	63	70	648	304		13211.64	13211.6
8. [illegible]o Street	Mrs. E. R. Baldwin, [illegible]oro, R1	1	2	2	1	1	7	171	42	68	9	30	320	162	497.85	2257.65	2755.5
9. [illegible]y Memorial	Mrs. W. J. Mitchell, [illegible]o	1					1									26.97	26.9
10. Bessemer	Mrs. J. R. [illegible]n, [illegible]o	1	1	1		1	4	42	8	18		25	93	33		211.19	211.1
11. Eller [illegible]	Mrs. Ethel [illegible]n, Greensboro	1	1	1	1	1	5	40	15	18	16	15	104	79	359.05	125.37	484.4
12. Florida Street	Mrs. J. H. Saunders, [illegible]oro	1	1	2	1	1	6	69	9	39	15	35	167	50		348.93	348.9
13. Forest [illegible]e	Mrs. J. W. [illegible]n, [illegible]o	1	1	1		1	4	48	47	12		18	125	44		697.40	697.4
14. [illegible]n Park																	
15. [illegible]a Street	Mrs. L. L. [illegible]s, [illegible]o	1	1	1		1	4	25	12	12		10	59		1.00	28.62	29.6
16. Pomona	Mrs. W. G. [illegible]e, [illegible]a	1		1		1	3	33		23		25	81			85.95	85.9
17. Revolution	Mrs. H. R. Starling, [illegible]oro	1	1	1	1	1	5	25	13	24	9	20	91	12		471.19	471.1
18. Sixteenth Street	Mrs. W. A. Straughn, [illegible]boro	1	1	1	1	1	5	47	20	12		12	91	53	15.38	210.13	225.5
19. Stevens Memorial	Mrs. C. B. Brisson, [illegible]ro	1				1	2	35				10	45	15		102.60	102.6
20. Tabernacle	Mrs. E. C. [illegible]e, [illegible]o	1	1	1		1	4	16	9	9		11	45	20		6.50	6.5
21. [illegible]r [illegible]orial	Selma Scales, Rt. 5, [illegible]oro	1	1	2		1	5	35	9	20		12	76	30		275.31	275.3
22. Guilford	Mrs. R. B. Ferrall, Guilford	1		1		1	3	10		14		10	34				40.0
23. High Point, First	Mrs. G. H. [illegible]s, High Point	1				1	2	225				39	264	90	657.71	3071.17	3728.8
24. [illegible]n Street	Mrs. T. C. Robbins, High Point	1	2	2	1	1	7	85	27	25	10	23	170	45	1015.16	399.53	2853.8
25. Hilliard Memorial	Mrs. J. B. Ellis, High Point	1	1	1	1	1	5	18	12	13	8	13	64	14	9.00	52.27	61.2
26. [illegible]h [illegible]	Mrs. H. S. Smith, High [illegible]t	1					1								100.87	127.00	227.8
27. [illegible]h Park	Mrs. J. A. [illegible]s, High Point	1	1	1	1	1	5	20	18	17	12	16	89	42	11.32	36.56	47.8
28. South Side	Mrs. J. G. Williams, High Point	2		1			3	19		12			31	15		15.00	15.0
29. West [illegible]																	
30. [illegible] Grove																	
31. [illegible]n																	
32. M. Zion																	
33. Oak Grove																	
34. [illegible]e Ch[illegible]l																	
35. [illegible]a																	
36. Pisgah																	
37. [illegible]t [illegible]	Mrs. I. F. Anderson, Greensboro Rt.1	1					1	20					20		18.45	16.10	34.3
38. [illegible]nt Grove																	
39. Reidsville, [illegible]	Mrs. T. R. Burton, Reidsville	1	1			1	3	175	20			17	212	67	4578.95	1574.20	6153.1
40. [illegible]	Mrs. A. C. Griffith, Reidsville																
41. [illegible]	Mrs. Elsie Gailey, Reidsville	3	1				4	38	12				50			38.23	38.2
42. Rocky Knoll	Mrs. R. A. [illegible]n, [illegible]oro, Rt1																
43. [illegible]	Mrs. Nannie [illegible]e, Reidsville, R5																
44. Smith Grove																	
45. Summerfield	Mrs. A. C. [illegible], [illegible]ld																
46. Tabernacle																	
TOTALS		29	20	22	10	19	100	1636	245	416	149	411	2953	1081	7274.74	23583.36	32237.9

CHURCHES	CHURCH CLERKS AND POST OFFICES	Own House Worship?	When Was It Built?	Materials Used	Persons Seated	Number of Rooms	Dept. Assembly Rooms	No. Sep. Class Rooms	Value Church House and Grounds		Value Pastor's Home	Total Value All Church Property	Indebtedness	Insurance Carried
1. Allen [illegible]	[illegible] [illegible]s, [illegible]ty	Yes	1936	Wd	300	8	8	7	3000.00			3000.00	332.28	2000.00
2. [illegible]h	[illegible] [illegible]t [illegible]r, Reidsville, [illegible]	Yes	1934	Wd	300	1			900.00			900.00		800.00
3. [illegible]n	E. C. [illegible]t, Rt. 2, [illegible]o	Yes	1886	Wd	150	5		4	3000.00			3000.00		1500.00
4. [illegible]y	I. E. [illegible]o, [illegible]e, R2	Yes	1898	Wd	275	5	4	4	5000.00		2000.00	7000.00		2000.00
5. [illegible]	[illegible] [illegible]s, [illegible]e 2	Yes	[illegible]1	Wd	300	5		4	2000.00			2000.00		1000.00
6. [illegible]e	W. O. [illegible]le, [illegible]e	Yes	1894	Wd	300	9	9	9	2500.00			2500.00		2000.00
7. [illegible]o, First	[illegible]o. R. Bennette, [illegible]o	Yes	[illegible]6	Brk	1000	48			[illegible]		15000.00	160000.00		70000.00
8. [illegible]o S[illegible]t	I. B. [illegible]s, [illegible]o	Yes	1912	Brk	700	61	10	69	51000.00		6000.00	57000.00	15000.00	43000.00
9. Bailey Memorial	W. J. Mitchell, [illegible]o	Yes	1935	Wd	250	1			1000.00			1000.00		700.00
10. Bessemer	[illegible] Leroy Casey, [illegible]o	Yes	1923	Wd	350	16	2	16	5500.00		[illegible]00.00	7500.00	750.00	4500.00
11. Eller Memorial	W. L. Thornburg, [illegible]o	Yes	1925	Brk	750	50	7	48	42000.00		9000.00	51000.00		25000.00
12. [illegible]a Street	[illegible]r [illegible], [illegible]o	Yes	1930	Brk	450	23	2	22	15000.00		4500.00	19500.00	4000.00	12700.00
13. [illegible]t Avenue	[illegible] O. [illegible]r, [illegible]o	Yes	[illegible]6	Brk	275	14	6	14	17000.00		8000.00	25000.00	2461.87	10750.00
14. [illegible]	[illegible] W. [illegible]n, [illegible]o	Yes	1916	Wd	150	1			2500.00			2500.00	714.00	
15. [illegible]a S[illegible]t	[illegible] G. H. [illegible]n, [illegible]sb'ro	Yes	1912	Wd	300	10		9	7500.00		3000.00	10500.00	2837.57	6000.00
16. P[illegible]a	C. C. [illegible]n, [illegible]a	Yes	[illegible]6	Wd	350	8		8	3000.00			3000.00		
17. Revolution	N. C. [illegible]n, [illegible]o	Yes	[illegible]7	Wd	400	5	3	7	10000.00		5000.00	15000.00		7500.00
18. [illegible]h [illegible]t	Alfred E. [illegible]t, [illegible]o	Yes	1907	Brk	500	23	2	16	39000.00			39000.00		15000.00
19. Stevens [illegible]	[illegible] J. B. [illegible]n, [illegible]o	Yes	1922	Wood	250	11	2	13	10000.00		2500.00	12500.00	560.00	7500.00
20. Tabernacle	Mrs. E. C. [illegible]e, Jr., [illegible]boro	Yes	1938	Wd	200	3		2	3000.00			3000.00	1501.25	2000.00
21. [illegible] Memorial	[illegible]s [illegible]a Scales, [illegible]o, 5	Yes	1935	Wd	300	10	2	8	5500.00			5500.00		2500.00
22. Guilford	R. F. [illegible]t, [illegible]d College	Yes	[illegible]4	Brick	200	1	3	4	3500.00	300.00		3800.00		1500.00
23. High [illegible]t, First	C. D. [illegible]h, [illegible]h [illegible]t	Yes	[illegible]5	Brick	500	49	7	46	110000.00		[illegible]00.00	132000.00	23988.51	55000.00
24. [illegible]n Street	[illegible]e [illegible]s, [illegible]h Point	Yes	1926	Brick	1500	96	6	68	5[illegible]00.00	1500.00	[illegible]00.00	160000.00		60000.00
25. [illegible]d Memorial	I. W. [illegible]s, [illegible]h [illegible]t	Yes	[illegible]1	Brk	800	22		20	25000.00			27000.00	1500.00	5000.00
26. North Main	[illegible]e [illegible]n, [illegible]h [illegible]t	Yes	1924	Brick	350	23	6	17	17000.00			17000.00	2375.75	8000.00
27. N[illegible]h [illegible]k	H. B. [illegible]n, High [illegible]nt	Yes	[illegible]9	[illegible]	300	17	1	16	3500.00			3500.00		1500.00
28. [illegible]h Side	I. G. Williams, High Point	Yes	[illegible]6	Wd	350	11		10	3500.00			3500.00		
29. [illegible]t End	[illegible] O. H. [illegible]r, High Point	Yes	1913	Wd	350	20			9500.00		2500.00	12000.00	200.00	[illegible]0.00
30. Jessup Grove	[illegible]s. [illegible]a [illegible]p, R1, [illegible]l. Col.	Yes	1933	Wd	250	1			1050.00			1050.00		
31. Lebanon	Maggie [illegible]n, [illegible]e, 1	Yes	[illegible]1	[illegible]	350	7	1	7	3500.00			3500.00		[illegible]0.00
32. [illegible] Zion	[illegible]o. [illegible] Spoon, Rt. 3, [illegible]	Yes	[illegible]1	Wd	500	1			2000.00			2000.00		
33. [illegible]k Grove	L. R. Loflin, [illegible]n	Yes	1927	Wd	270	2		2	2000.00			2000.00		1400.00
34. [illegible]e Chapel	R. [illegible] [illegible], [illegible]o, R3	Yes	1934	Wd	250	1			1600.00			1600.00	27.00	
35. [illegible]a	E. R. [illegible]e, [illegible]n [illegible]it, R1	Yes	[illegible]5	Wd	300	1			2000.00			2150.00		
36. [illegible]h	T. W. [illegible], High [illegible]t	Yes	1937	[illegible]d		1			1500.00			1500.00		
37. [illegible]t [illegible]h	I. [illegible] [illegible], [illegible]o R1	Yes	[illegible]7	Wd	220	1	4	4	1800.00			1800.00	75.00	[illegible]0.00
38. [illegible]t Grove	[illegible] A. M. Heilig, [illegible]n, Rt.	Yes	1920	Wd	350				1800.00			1800.00	792.15	[illegible]0.00
39. [illegible]lle, First	T. L. [illegible]r, [illegible]e	Yes	1871	Brick	550	24	5	20	37000.00		1[illegible]00.00	51000.00		[illegible]0.00
40. [illegible]t [illegible]e	[illegible] [illegible]a Baker, [illegible]e	Yes	1929	Wd	300	13	2	13	5000.00			5000.00		[illegible]0.00
41. [illegible]	[illegible]s Overbey, [illegible]	Yes	1935	Brick	300	13		10	10000.00		[illegible]00.00	11500.00	2200.00	[illegible]0.00
42. [illegible]	R. O. [illegible]d, [illegible]o, R1.	Yes	1934	Wd	250	5	4	4	2000.00			2500.00		[illegible]0.00
43. [illegible]n [illegible]y	Mrs. [illegible]e Schrum, [illegible]n	Yes	1931	Wd	300	1			2500.00			2500.00		[illegible]0.00
44. Smith Grove	[illegible] Dovie [illegible]k, [illegible]n, R1	Yes	1923	Wood	300	1			1500.00			1700.00		[illegible]0.00
45. Summerfield	[illegible] Myrtle Smith, [illegible]field.	Yes		Wd	400	1			8388.69			8388.69		[illegible]0.00
46. [illegible]e	[illegible]e [illegible]h, Elon College	Yes	1933	[illegible]d	350	1			1500.00			1500.00	119.00	
TOTALS					17440	631	96	[illegible]1	[illegible]8 69	1800.00	34500.00	890688.69	59434.38	417450.00

TABLE [illegible]R — WOMAN'S MISSION [illegible]Y [illegible]N

CHURCHES	PRESIDENTS OF W. M. S. AND POST OFFICES	Number of W. M. S.	Number of Y. W. A.'s	Number of G. A.'s	Number of R. A.'s	Number of Sunbeams	Total W. M. U. Org's.	W. M. S. Members	Y. W. A.'s Members	G. A.'s Members	R. A.'s Members	Sunbeam Members	Total Members Enrolled	Total Enrolled M. S. C.	Contributions to Local Work by W. M. U.	Contributions to Missions by W. M. U.	Total Contributions by W. M. U.
1. Allen [illegible]y																	
2. [illegible]h																	
3. [illegible]h																	
4. [illegible]y	Mrs. J. E. McCargo, Reidsville, R2	1	1				2	20	23				43		10.00	174.64	[illegible]4.64
5. [illegible]v																	
6. [illegible]e	[illegible]s. Lottie [illegible]r, Gibsonville	1					1	31					31			19.21	19.21
7. [illegible]o, First	Mrs. [illegible] R. [illegible]b, [illegible]oro	1	2	2	2	1	8	38[illegible]	52	80	63	70	[illegible]8	304		13211.64	13 [illegible]1.64
8. [illegible]o Street	[illegible]s. E. R. Baldwin, [illegible]o, R1	1	2	2	1	1	7	171	42	68	9	30	[illegible]0	162	497.85	2257.65	2 [illegible]5.50
9. [illegible]y [illegible]n	[illegible]s. W. I. [illegible]l, [illegible]o	1					1									26.97	26.97
10. Bessemer	[illegible]s. J. [illegible] [illegible]n, [illegible]o	1	1	1		1	4	42	8	18		25	93	33		211.19	211.19
11. Eller [illegible]l	[illegible]s. [illegible]l [illegible]n, [illegible]oro	1	1	1	1	1	5	40	15	18	16	15	[illegible]4	79	359.05	125.37	[illegible]4.42
12. [illegible]a Street	[illegible]s. J. [illegible] Saunders, [illegible]oro	1	1	2	1	1	6	69	9	39	15	35	[illegible]7	50		348.93	348.93
13. [illegible]t [illegible]e	[illegible]s. J. W. [illegible]h, [illegible]o	1	1	1		1	4	48	47	12		18	[illegible]5	44		697.40	[illegible]7.40
14. [illegible]m [illegible]																	
15. [illegible]a Street	[illegible]s. L. L. [illegible]s, [illegible]o	1	1	1		1	4	25	12	12		10	59		1.00	28.62	29.62
16. [illegible]a	[illegible]s. W. G. [illegible], [illegible]a	1		1		1	3	33		23		25	81			85.95	85.95
17. [illegible]n	[illegible]s. H. R. Starling, [illegible]oro	1	1	1	1	1	5	25	13	24	9	20	91	12		471.19	[illegible]1.19
18. [illegible]h Street	[illegible]s. W. A. [illegible]n, [illegible]boro	1	1	1	1	1	5	47	20	12		12	91	53	15.38	210.13	225.51
19. Stevens [illegible]l	[illegible] C. B. Brisson, [illegible]ro	1				1	2	35				10	45	15		102.60	102.60
20. [illegible]e	[illegible]s. E. C. [illegible]e, [illegible]o	1	1	1		1	4	16	9	9		11	45	20		6.50	6.50
21. [illegible]r [illegible]l	Selma Scales, [illegible]t. 5, [illegible]oro	1	1	2		1	5	35	9	20		12	76	30		275.31	275.31
22. Guilford	[illegible]s. R. B. [illegible]l, [illegible]l	1		1		1	3	10		14		10	34				40.00
23. High Point, First	Mrs. G. H. [illegible]s, [illegible]h [illegible]nt	1				1	2	225				39	[illegible]4	90	657.71	3071.17	3 [illegible]8.88
24. [illegible]n [illegible]	Mrs. T. C. [illegible]s, [illegible]h [illegible]int	1	2	2	1	1	7	85	27	25	10	23	[illegible]0	45	1015.16	399.53	2 [illegible]3.80
25. [illegible]l [illegible]orial	Mrs. J. B. Ellis, High Point	1	1	1	1	1	5	18	12	13	8	13	64	14	9.00	52.27	61.27
26. [illegible]h [illegible]h	Mrs. [illegible] S. [illegible]h, [illegible]h [illegible]t	1					1								100.87	127.00	227.87
27. [illegible]h [illegible]k	[illegible]s. I. A. [illegible], [illegible]h Point	1	1	1	1	1	5	26	18	17	12	16	89	42	11.32	36.56	47.88
28. South Side	[illegible]s. I. G. [illegible]s, [illegible]h Point	2		1			3	19		12			31	15		15.00	15.00
29. [illegible]t [illegible]																	
30. [illegible]p Grove																	
31. [illegible]n																	
32. [illegible]t. [illegible]h																	
33. [illegible]k Grove																	
34. [illegible]e C [illegible]l																	
35. [illegible]a																	
36. [illegible]h																	
37. [illegible]t [illegible]n	Mrs. I. F. Anderson, Greensboro Rt.1	1					1	20					20		18.45	16.10	34.35
38. [illegible]t [illegible]e																	
39. [illegible]e, First	Mrs. T. R. Burton, [illegible]lle	1	1			1	3	173	20			17	[illegible]2	67	4578.95	1574.20	6153.15
40. [illegible]t Olive	Mrs. A. C. Griffith, Reidsville																
41. [illegible]n [illegible]l	Mrs. [illegible]e [illegible]y, [illegible]e	3	1				4	38	12				50			38.23	38.23
42. [illegible]y [illegible]	Mrs. R. A. [illegible]n, [illegible]oro, Rt1																
43. Ruffin Stacey	[illegible]s. [illegible]e [illegible]e, [illegible]lle, R5																
44. [illegible]h [illegible]e																	
45. Summerfield	Mrs. A. C. Lloyd, Summerfield																
46. Tabernacle																	

	CHURCHES	CHURCH CLERKS AND POST OFFICES	Own House Worship?	When Was It Built?	Materials Used	Persons Seated	Number of Rooms	Dept. Assembly Room	No. Sep. Class Rooms	Value Church House and Grounds		Value Pastor's Home	Total Value All Church Property	Indebtedness	Insurance Carried
1.	Allen Jay	[illegible]e Younts, Trinity	Yes	1936	Wood	300	8	8	7	3000.00			3000.00	332.28	2000.00
2.	Antioch	Mrs. [illegible]t [illegible], [illegible]e, 2	Yes	1934	Wood	300	1			900.00			900.00		800.00
3.	[illegible]n	E. C. [illegible]t, Rt. 2, [illegible]o	Yes	1886	W[illegible]d	150	5		4	3000.00			3000.00		1500.00
4.	[illegible]	I. E. [illegible]o, [illegible]e, R2	Yes	1898	W[illegible]d	275	5	4	4	5000.00		2000.00	7000.00		2000.00
5.	[illegible]	[illegible]n [illegible]s, [illegible]e 2.	Yes	1901	W[illegible]d	300	5		4	2000.00			2000.00		1000.00
6.	[illegible]e	W. O. [illegible]e, [illegible]e	Yes	1894	W[illegible]d	300	9	9	9	2500.00			2500.00		2000.00
7.	[illegible]o, First	[illegible] R. [illegible]e, [illegible]o	Yes	1906	Brick	1000	48			145000.00		15000.00	160000.00		70000.00
8.	[illegible]o Street	I. B. Wills, [illegible]o	Yes	1912	Brick	700	61	10	69	51000.00		6000.00	57000.00	15000.00	43000.00
9.	Bailey [illegible]l	W. J. Mitchell, [illegible]o	Yes	1935	W[illegible]d	250	1			1000.00			1000.00		700.00
10.	[illegible]r	W. [illegible]y Casey, [illegible]o	Yes	1923	W[illegible]d	350	16	2	16	5500.00		2000.00	7500.00	750.00	4500.00
11.	[illegible]r [illegible]l	W. L. [illegible]g, [illegible]o	Yes	1925	[illegible]k	750	50	7	48	42000.00		9000.00	51000.00		25000.00
12.	[illegible]a Street	[illegible]r [illegible]n, [illegible]o	Yes	1930	Brick	450	23	2	22	15000.00		4500.00	19500.00	4000.00	12700.00
13.	[illegible]t Avenue	[illegible]l O. [illegible], [illegible]o	Yes	1906	Brick	275	14	6	14	17000.00		8000.00	25000.00	2461.87	10750.00
14.	[illegible]n Park	W. W. [illegible]n, [illegible]o	Yes	1916	W[illegible]d	150	1			2500.00			2500.00	714.00	
15.	[illegible]a S[illegible]t	Mrs. G. H. [illegible]n, [illegible]sb'ro	Yes	1912	W[illegible]d	300	10		9	7500.00		3000.00	10500.00	2837.57	6000.00
16.	Pomona	C. C. [illegible], [illegible]a	Yes	1906	W[illegible]d	350	8		8	3000.00			3000.00		
17.	Revolution	N. C. [illegible]n, [illegible]o	Yes	1907	W[illegible]d	400	5	3	7	10000.00		5000.00	15000.00		7500.00
18.	[illegible]h S[illegible]t	[illegible]d E. [illegible]t, [illegible]o	Yes	1907	Brick	500	23	2	16	39000.00			39000.00		15000.00
19.	Stevens [illegible]l	Mrs. J. B. Brown, [illegible]o	Yes	1922	Wood	250	11	2	13	10000.00		2500.00	12500.00	560.00	7500.00
20.	Tabernacle	Mrs. E. C. [illegible]e, Jr., [illegible]boro	Yes	1938	W[illegible]d	200	3		2	3000.00			3000.00	1501.25	2000.00
21.	[illegible]r [illegible]l	[illegible]s [illegible]a Scales, [illegible]o, 5	Yes	1935	W[illegible]d	300	10	2	8	5500.00			5500.00		2500.00
22.	Guilford	R. F. Bondurant, Guilford College	Yes	[illegible]4	Brick	200	1	3	4	3500.00	300.00		3800.00		1500.00
23.	[illegible]h Point, [illegible]st	C. D. [illegible]h, [illegible]h Point	Yes	1905	Brick	500	49	7	46	110000.00		7000.00	132000.00	23988.51	55000.00
24.	[illegible]n Street	[illegible]e [illegible]s, High Point	Yes	1926	Brick	1500	96	6	68	156000.00	1500.00	2500.00	160000.00		60000.00
25.	Hilliard Memorial	I. W. [illegible]s, [illegible]h [illegible]	Yes	1931	Brick	800	22		20	25000.00			27000.00	1500.00	5000.00
26.	North Main	[illegible]e [illegible]n, High Point	Yes	1924	Brick	350	23	6	17	17000.00			17000.00	2375.75	8000.00
27.	[illegible]th Park	H. B. [illegible]n, [illegible]gh [illegible]t	Yes	1929	W[illegible]d	300	17	1	16	3500.00			3500.00		1500.00
28.	[illegible]h [illegible]e	I. G. [illegible]s, [illegible]h [illegible]t	Yes	[illegible]6	W[illegible]d	350	11		10	3500.00			3500.00		
29.	West [illegible]	Mrs. O. H. [illegible]r, [illegible]h Point	Yes	1913	W[illegible]d	350	20			9500.00		2500.00	12000.00	200.00	5000.00
30.	Jessup Grove	[illegible]s. [illegible]a J[illegible]p, R1, Guil. Col.	Yes	1933	W[illegible]d	250	1			1050.00			1050.00		
31.	Lebanon	[illegible]e [illegible]n, [illegible]lle, 1	Yes	1911	W[illegible]d	350	7	1	7	3500.00			3500.00		1800.00
32.	Mt. Zion	[illegible]o. H. [illegible]n, Rt. 3, [illegible]y	Yes	1911	W[illegible]d	500	1			2000.00			2000.00		
33.	[illegible]k [illegible]	L. R. Loflin, [illegible]n	Yes	1927	W[illegible]d	270	2		2	2000.00			2000.00		1400.00
34.	[illegible]e [illegible]l	R. R. [illegible]e, [illegible]o, R3	Yes	1934	W[illegible]d	250	1			1600.00			1600.00	27.00	
35.	[illegible]a	E. R. [illegible]e, [illegible]n [illegible]t, R1	Yes	1915	W[illegible]d	300	1			2000.00			2150.00		
36.	Pisgah	T. W. [illegible], [illegible]h [illegible]t	Yes	1937	W[illegible]d		1			1500.00			1500.00		
37.	[illegible]t [illegible]en	I. F. [illegible]n, [illegible]o R1	Yes	1917	W[illegible]d	220	1	4	4	1800.00			1800.00	75.00	1000.00
38.	[illegible]t [illegible]ve	Mrs. A. M. [illegible]g, [illegible]n, Rt.	Yes	1920	W[illegible]d	350				1800.00			1800.00	792.15	1400.00
39.	[illegible]e, [illegible]st	T. L. [illegible]r, [illegible]e	Yes	1871	Brick	550	24	5	20	37000.00		14000.00	51000.00		43500.00
40.	Mount Olive	Mrs. [illegible]a [illegible]r, [illegible]e	Yes	1929	Wood	300	13	2	13	5000.00			5000.00		4000.00
41.	Penn [illegible]l	[illegible]s [illegible]y, [illegible]e	Yes	1935	Brick	300	13		10	10000.00		1500.00	11500.00	2200.00	4500.00
42.	Rocky Knoll	R. O. [illegible], [illegible], R1.	Yes	1934	W[illegible]d	250	5	4	4	2000.00			2500.00		1500.00
43.	Ruffin Stacey	Mrs. [illegible]e [illegible]n, [illegible]n	Yes	1931	W[illegible]d	300	1			2500.00			2500.00		1800.00
44.	Smith Grove	Mrs. Dovie [illegible]k, Jamestown, R1	Yes	1923	Wood	300	1			1500.00			1700.00		600.00
45.	[illegible]d	Mrs. [illegible]e r [illegible]h, [illegible]ield.	Yes		W[illegible]d	400	1			8388.69			8388.69		3500.00
46.	[illegible]e	[illegible]e [illegible]h, Elon College	Yes	1933	W[illegible]d	350	1			1500.00			1500.00	119.00	
	TOTALS					17440	631	96	501	786538.69	1800.00	84500.00	890688.69	59434.38	417450.00

Church	Pastor	Pastor's S		V	Building	Church D Interest	Incidental	L	H		
1. Allen Jay	W. R. Hobson, High Point, R1	719.00		82.10	547.37	96.78	393.01	114.27	100.00	2.00	53.06
2. [illegible]		150.00		25.00			15.00		8.00		
3. [illegible]	E. C. West, [illegible], R2	422.39		31.43	86.83		45.82	47.08	4.00	3.00	13.48
4. [illegible]	J. F. Carroll, [illegible]	4299		50.00	70.50		53.30	32.60		3.00	88.13
5. Fairview	D. E. [illegible]anthram, [illegible]dsville, R2	92.49		46.38	17.87		43.81	19.35		3.00	4.00
6. Gibsonville	T. L. Robertson, [illegible]ille	600.00		53.00	39.84		87.89	114.05		3.00	86.66
7. [illegible], First	Howard [illegible], [illegible]	4600.00	5523.00	752.41	15622.05		3840.48	1656.19	817.33	18.00	3374.25
8. Asheboro Street	U. A. Hedrick, [illegible]	3300.44	1525.00	310.00	5163.88	33.33	513.63	641.36	187.50	12.50	1078.19
9. Bailey [illegible]	W. H. [illegible], [illegible]	[illegible]		56.12	144.05		34.39	35.00	6.00	4.00	
10. Bessemer	C. L. Murray, [illegible]	1560.00		94.32	796.84	250.12	397.35	251.13	45.00	5.00	226.07
11. Eller Memorial	Mrs. Robt. Burgess, [illegible]nsboro	2580.00	502.35	127.00	776.42		537.18	717.91	110.77	10.00	440.28
12. Florida Street	D. M. Frazier, [illegible]	1997.00		113.88	1480.98	1114.81	511.92	283.35	4.12	5.00	498.51
13. [illegible]est Avenue	L. E. Ogburn, [illegible]	2060.00	100.00	50.00	16.21	338.13	1487.98	274.14	17.08	10.00	105.61
14. Latham Park	W. W. Sutton, [illegible]boro	260.00		11.00		50.00	13.00				15.00
15. Magnolia Street	H. S. [illegible]h, Greensboro	1197.00		114.41	382.30	653.50	210.94	106.95	5.00	3.00	139.99
16. Pomona	E. E. [illegible]y, Pomona	1489.66		117.74	32.27		159.50	100.37	60.00	3.00	143.61
17. Revolution	[illegible] [illegible]n, [illegible]boro	1630.00		67.98	51.41		301.67	193.53	125.79	4.00	209.77
18. Sixteenth Street	L. F. Paris, [illegible]	2060.00		137.50	26.76		687.54	150.66		5.00	58.50
19. Stevens Memorial	Mrs. C. B. [illegible]n, [illegible]nsboro, R2	1560.00		5.00	64.43	754.00	200.22	105.49		4.05	139.61
20. Tabernacle	E. H. [illegible]e, [illegible]	1395.00		124.42	1849.60	514.68	395.13	219.45	35.00		35.68
21. [illegible]er [illegible]orial	R. H. King, [illegible]	1040.00		65.00		276.00	267.88	115.24	300.00	5.00	
22. Guilford	W. L. Hudson, Guilford	227.00			210.00		201.00	35.60	10.00	1.00	70.00
23. H[illegible]h [illegible]t, First	M. [illegible]a Patrick, High Point	3575.00	1720.00	326.12	362.71	4180.48	3644.91	1149.72	431.11	18.00	1623.89
24. Green Street	R. B. [illegible], [illegible]h Point	2810.00	1140.00	343.00	777.92	4123.00	1120.34	511.01	239.00		15.00
25. Hilliard [illegible]morial	J. W. [illegible]alf, High Point	1516.20		60.11	1123.94	270.00	125.42	88.48	48.00	3.25	113.25
26. North [illegible]	W. C. Ward, High Point, R1	1820.00		150.00	38.53	774.81	510.43	236.49	7.80	3.00	26.37
27. North Park	L. W. Glenn, High Point	1300.00		0.50	110.20	596.16	246.55	124.98	24.95	3.00	294.19
28. South [illegible]e	J. G. [illegible]s, High Point	1052.18		155.71			412.36	82.19	30.00	1.50	65.00
29. West End	C. M. Scott, [illegible]h Point	1283.00		101.92	43.14	300.00	308.34	191.42		4.00	28.00
30. Jessup Grove	Mrs. [illegible]d Jessup, Guil. Col., R1				12.88	5.00	16.91				
31. Lebanon	L. R. Chilton, Brown Summit, R2	684.00			190.00		103.70	15.72	40.00		
32. Mt. Zion	Mae Branson, S[illegible]ow [illegible]p	350.00	12.50	40.00	199.30		12.00	23.50		5.00	
33. Oak [illegible]e	L. R. Loflin, [illegible]	456.07		14.00	5.00		33.07	36.85	12.00	2.00	
34. [illegible]ne Chapel	Mrs. Mima [illegible]n, Rt. 3, [illegible]nsbo.	[illegible]		34.99	100.00	51.00	32.81	43.66		2.00	
35. [illegible]a	Mrs. A. D. [illegible], Brown Summit, 1	[illegible]		[illegible]	11.20		19.56	35.20	15.00	1.85	25.40
36. Pisgah	Z. V. Lanier, High Point	240.77			641.30		20.49	40.16	14.00	2.00	
37. [illegible]	A. T. Tilley, [illegible], R1	240.00		10.91		11.00	20.00	49.39		2.00	34.77
38. Pleasant Grove	Mrs. A. M. Heilig, Jamestown, R1			103.30	208.56	178.20	41.07	32.54			
39. [illegible]e, First	J. P. Kemp, Reidsville	3000.00	1200.00	13.30	373.56		1461.29	489.02	209.95	10.00	1249.58
40. Mount [illegible]	Mrs. A. D. Clifton, Reidsville	1020.00		[illegible]	19.05	450.00	329.07	124.04	9.55	2.00	
41. Penn [illegible]	W. [illegible]t Ford, Reidsville	1300.00		120.00	720.68	1093.16	381.02	91.92	49.89	2.00	12.88
42. Rocky Knoll	A. L. Price, [illegible]	520.00		80.00	243.93		[illegible]	152.04	32.25	1.50	170.47
43. Ruffin Stacey	Mrs. [illegible]e Schrum, Ruffin	350.00		56.77	250.00		48.00	200.00		2.00	
44. Smith Grove	Drew Smith, Jamestown, R1	76.00		25.00	15.00		12.00	12.28	12.78	2.00	
45. Summerfield	Mrs. Hettie Shields, [illegible]field	360.00		50.00	888.69			34.79		4.00	45.58
46. Tabernacle	Mrs. W. H. Fitts, Elon College	344.60		47.31	75.00		76.90	33.81		1.00	19.15

CHURCHES	Total to Co-operat Program	Special, to Associational Missi	Special to State Missions	Special to Home Missions	Special to Foreign Missions	Special to Schools and Colleges	Special to Theologi Seminaries	Special to Orphana	Special to Hospitals	Special to Old Ministers' Relief	Other Special Gifts	Total Given Missio and Benevolences	Grand Total for Al Purposes Given By Church
1. Allen Jay	20.00							48.00	11.00			79.00	2186.59
2. Antioch					12.00			15.00				27.00	225.00
3. Buchanan	52.00							26.00	11.67			89.67	743.70
4. Calvary	40.72		4.15	10.82	53.00	3.30		137.80	22.80	7.36	69.20	349.15	881.67
5. Fairview			12.45					35.05	7.71			55.21	282.11
6. [illegible]e	6.00	10.63	6.00		13.35			52.73	13.58			102.29	1086.73
7. Greensboro, First	15961.56		460.84	502.63	3514.90	436.61		2449.73	248.51		1290.10	24864.88	61068.59
8. Asheboro Street	2179.57							536.91	55.39		127.00	2898.87	15664.70
9. Bailey Memorial				11.51	15.40			16.66				43.57	1239.95
10. Bessemer	315.67		11.00		9.60			55.51	8.87			400.65	4026.48
11. Eller Memorial	1199.21		60.00					358.05	150.00			1767.26	7569.17
12. Florida Street	301.78		18.29	10.55	181.88			168.35	10.45	27.20	146.33	864.83	6874.40
13. Forest [illegible]e	523.43		65.74	29.50	87.87	9.29		264.88	33.01		96.04	1109.76	5588.91
14. Latham Park								17.00				17.00	366.00
15. Magnolia Street	17.00			5.00	18.00			109.88	16.80			166.68	2979.77
16. Pomona	38.91				11.48			112.49	16.57		38.74	218.19	2324.34
17. Revolution	533.93		15.85	24.80	112.13			186.16	60.15		35.25	968.27	3552.42
18. Sixteenth Street	3[illegible]6.95		22.45	4.49	16.50			97.93	16.80			525.12	3651.08
19. Stevens Memorial	569.49		12.18	26.99	59.12	20.00		162.60	15.20		13.60	879.18	3881.93
20. Tabernacle	128.20		6.50					87.09	21.50			243.29	4812.25
21. Webster Memorial	145.64		27.57	29.05	42.31	11.50		100.50	20.75		26.69	404.01	2473.13
22. Guilford	50.00											50.00	804.60
23. High Point, First	3858.47	26.09	187.52	60.13	1043.54		50.00	1631.34	180.26		565.71	7603.06	24635.00
24. Green Street	988.59		128.14					440.00	26.00		23.46	1606.19	12685.46
25. Hilliard Memorial	64.30		6.50	20.76	16.09			80.03	13.78			201.46	3550.11
26. North Main	265.00				17.40			184.30	25.00		206.11	697.81	4265.24
27. North Park	95.50			18.14	11.10			65.00	26.55			216.29	2956.82
28. South Side			16.64									16.64	1815.58
29. West End	317.43		25.00	11.40	18.50			285.81	16.55		74.57	749.26	3009.08
30. Jessup Grove									3.24			3.24	38.03
31. Lebanon								42.57				42.57	1075.99
32. Mt. Zion								19.52	3.11			34.63	676.93
33. Oak Grove	10.00		2.00					41.98	5.60			47.58	606.57
34 [illegible]e Chapel				5.00				5.00	2.30	9.60	6.18	28.08	407.84
35. Osceola								37.23	3.90		1.25	42.38	398.75
36. Pisgah								34.90				34.90	993.62
37. Pleasant Garden	10.00		6.91					14.00	4.00			34.91	402.98
38. Pleasant Grove					9.18			37.87				47.05	610.72
39. Reidsville, First	1827.45		30.00	65.00	143.50	100.00		409.79			671.00	3246.74	11253.44
40. Mount Olive	120.00		23.00	15.00	60.50			144.00	17.75	6.00	135.00	521.25	2645.71
41. Penn [illegible]al			12.60	9.87	10.00				12.85	13.00	2.42	60.74	3834.29
[illegible]ky Knoll			6.25	7.20	10.00			67.65	24.15		19.45	134.70	1442.70
43. Ruffin Stacey	48.00				5.00			24.00	5.00			82.00	988.77
44. Smith Grove									4.00			4.00	159.06
45. Summerfield	73.94		12.10	7.00	17.05	1.00		80.00	17.89		30.30	239.28	1687.96
46. Tabernacle											2.40	2.40	600.17
TOTALS	30128.74	36.72	1179.68	874.84	5509.40	581.70	50.00	8683.31	1132.69	63.16	3580.80	51821.04	213024.34

HISTORICAL TABLE — PIEDMONT BAPTIS T ASSOCIATION

YEAR	WHERE HELD	MODERATOR	CLERK	PREACHER	Churches	Baptisms	Church Members	Total Gifts
1894	Greensboro	Dr. C. A. Rominger	W. L. Kivett	M. A. Adams	5	....	562	....
1895	Liberty	T. L. Chislom	W. L. [illegible]	L. Johnson	12	16	112	$ 4695.50
1896	Moore's Chapel	R. W. Brooks	W. H. Eller	L. Johnson	14	66	1194	5128.94
1897	[illegible]ld	F. H. Jones	W. H. Eller	J. A. Munday	16	73	1540	7198.27
1898	Mount Zion	R. W. Brooks	W. H. Eller	L. Johnson	17	67	1557	6883.23
1899	Ramseur	R. W. Brooks	F. P. [illegible]ker	John E. White	19	54	1570	7435.43
1900	Cherry Street	R. W. Brooks	W. H. Eller	Thomas Carrick	16	48	1538	7970.35
1901	Reidsville	F. H. Jones	W. H. Eller	L. Johnson	19	157	1657	8282.73
1902	Salem [illegible]eet	F. H. Jones	W. H. Eller	W. C. [illegible]on	19	135	1774	9950.97
1903	Gibsonville	F. H. Jones	W. H. Eller	C. L. Greaves	20	185	1868	12834.77
1904	Calvary	F. H. Jones	W. H. Eller	H. W. Battle	22	112	1832	12807.43
1905	Randleman	F. H. Jones	W. H. Eller	J. M. Hilliard	22	114	2096	17674.91
1906	High Point, First	F. H. Jones	W. H. Eller	W. R. Bradshaw	23	201	2333	29366.31
1907	[illegible] Street	F. H. Jones	W. H. Eller	Wm. Hedley	26	372	2798	29993.79
1908	Ramseur	F. H. Jones	W. H. Eller	C. E. Maddry	28	311	3086	26347.57
1909	[illegible]	F. H. Jones	W. H. Eller	Wm. Hedley	30	292	3429	49847.28
1910	[illegible] Zion	F. H. Jones	W. H. Eller	R. G. Hendrick	31	336	3731	28531.01
1911	[illegible]	W. F. Staley	W. H. Eller	W. F. [illegible]ley	29	182	3736	25887.56
1912	High Point, Green St.	F. P. Hobgood Jr.	W. H. Eller	J. C. Turner	30	174	3647	29697.38
1913	Liberty	F. P. Hobgood, Jr.	W. H. Eller	R. P. [illegible]er	31	409	3971	37700.97
1914	[illegible] Street	F. P. Hobgood, Jr.	W. H. Eller	A. W. [illegible]	31	413	4202	42428.44
1915	Reidsville	J. M. Hilliard	W. H. Eller	J. M. Hilliard	42	313	4491	42577.68
1916	Forest Avenue	J. M. Hilliard	W. H. Eller	E. N. Johnson	36	369	4854	48418.92
1917	Green Street	J. M. Hilliard	W. H. Eller	W. R. White	39	308	4760	44609.05
1918	Moore's [illegible]el	J. M. Hilliard	W. H. Eller	J. W. Rose	39	374	5140	72538.46
1919	[illegible]te Oak	J. M. Hilliard	W. H. Eller	W. H. Wilson	39	339	5359	76638.85
1920	Calvary	J. M. Hilliard	W. H. Eller	E. N. Johnson	39	543	5867	117682.35
1921	Summerfield	Clarence A. Smith	J. E. Lanier	B. K. Mason	39	480	6454	135561.79
1922	Glenola	Clarence A. Smith	J. E. Lanier	Jas. A. [illegible]k	39	679	7226	149955.24
1923	Magnolia Street	[illegible]ce A. [illegible]h	H. O. Miller	E. E. White	38	365	7341	140553.25
1924	West End	Clarence A. Smith	H. O. Miller	W. E. [illegible]e	40	672	7489	164658.19
1925	Fairview	Clarence A. Smith	H. O. Miller	A. T. Howell	41	610	8956	211792.21
1926	Ramseur	Clarence A. Smith	S. T. Hensley	Lloyd T. Wilson	42	620	9974	243500.68
1927	Trinity	[illegible]ce A. [illegible]h	S. T. Hensley	H. T. Stevens	40	656	10223	211846.40
1928	Bessemer	Clarence A. Smith	O. E. Lee	R. P. Ellington	41	531	10866	202002.30
1929	Liberty	Clarence A. [illegible]	O. E. Lee	C. F. Rogers	44	573	[illegible]	218987.61
1930	[illegible]o	Clarence A. Smith	O. E. Lee	[illegible] T. [illegible]all	44	676	12012	198077.29
1931	Florida [illegible]eet	Clarence A. [illegible]h	O. E. Lee	A. B. Conrad	44	827	12789	178501.19
1932	Reidsville	Clarence A. [illegible]h	O. E. Lee	J. C. Turner	46	778	13485	159000.60
1933	White Oak	[illegible]ce A. Smith	O. E. Lee	T. L. Sasser	48	1561	15199	186041.40
1934	Franklinville	[illegible]ce A. [illegible]h	O. E. Lee	Wilson [illegible]k	53	757	15356	172839.18
1935	[illegible], High Point	[illegible]ce A. Smith	O. E. Lee	J. S. Hopkins	41	623	12687	164135.92
1936	Calvary	Clarence A. [illegible]th	O. E. Lee	J. Ben Eller	42	563	13958	166052.96
1937	Eller Memorial	Grover H. Jones	O. E. Lee	C. N. Royal	41	657	14086	195540.50
1938	Hilliard Memorial	Grover H. Jones	O. E. Lee	A. B. Conrad	42	814	14793	200246.20
1939	Reidsville, First	Grover H. Jones	O. E. Lee	J. C. Turner	46			213024.34

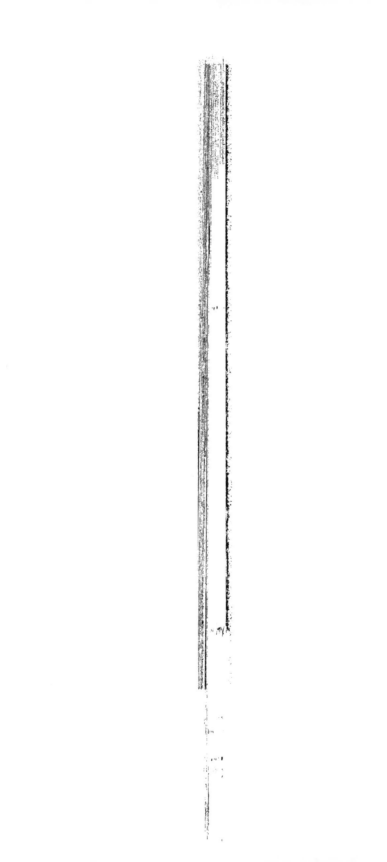

From O. E. Lee Greensboro N. C.

MINUTES

FORTY-SEVENTH ANNUAL SESSION

PIEDMONT BAPTIST ASSOCIATION

NORTH CAROLINA

FLORIDA STREET BAPTIST CHURCH

Greensboro, N. C.

OCTOBER 23-24

1940

The next session will be held with the Green Street Baptist Church, High Point, N. C., Wednesday and Thursday before the fourth Sunday in October, 1941.
Rev. A. Lincoln Fulk will preach the sermon.
Alternate, Rev. A. A. Walker.

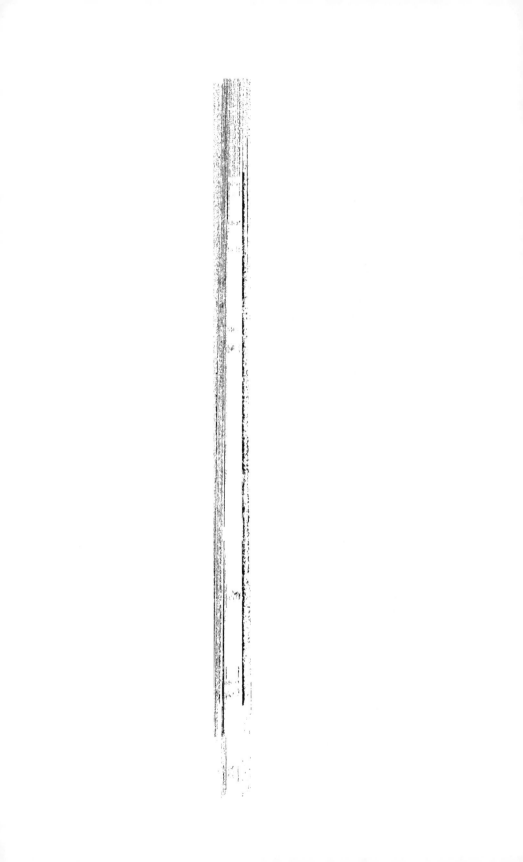

MINUTES

of the

FORTY-SEVENTH ANNUAL SESSION

of the

PIEDMONT BAPTIST ASSOCIATION

NORTH CAROLINA

Held With the

FLORIDA STREET BAPTIST CHURCH

October 23-24

1940

The next session will be held with the Green Street Baptist Church, High Point, N. C., Wednesday and Thursday before the fourth Sunday in October, 1941
Rev. A. Lincoln Fulk will preach the sermon.
Alternate, Rev. A. A. Walker

INDEX

DR. J. T. J. BATTLE

To Whom This Volume of the Minutes is Dedicated by Order of the Association

Doctor John Thomas Johnson Battle, born in Wake Forest, N. C., April 14, 1859, died in Greensboro, N. C., September 29, 1940. He was the son of John Applewhite and Anne Capell Battle. He received his M. A. from Wake Forest College and his M. D. from the College of Physicians and Surgeons in Baltimore, Maryland.

In 1896 he married Miss Dora L. Burns of Wadesboro, N. C., who died February 14, 1936. They had no children.

He moved to Greensboro, N. C., in 1898 to practice medicine and in 1901 was made Medical Director of the Security Life and Annuity Co., a forerunner of the Jefferson Standard Life Insurance Co. of which he was medical director at the time of his death.

He united with the First Baptist Church on coming to Greensboro and moved to Forest Avenue Baptist Church in 1907 soon after that church was organized.

He was regular attendant of all the services of the church, giving at least one-fifth of his income to the Kingdom work, and holding some office in the church at all times. He was particularly interested in young people. There are more than forty young people of record whom he sent through college either by direct gift or by loans. How many more no one knows.

Through his gifts of time, energy, money and thought to church, community and school he lives on in the lives he influenced.

ASSOCIATIONAL DIRECTORY

—o—

OFFICERS

Grover H. Jones, Moderator .... High Point
T. L. Sasser, Vice-Moderator .... Reidsville
O. E. Lee, Clerk-Treasurer .... Greensboro

EXECUTIVE PROMOTION COMMITTEE

Grover H. Jones, Chairman .... High Point
O. E. Lee, Secretary .... Greensboro
Rev. T. L. Sasser .... Reidsville
Rev. D. W. Overby .... Reidsville
R. R. Saunders .... Reidsville
Rev. J. S. Hopkins .... High Point
S. R. Clinard .... High Point
Dr. J. Clyde Turner .... Greensboro
O. Joe Howard .... Greensboro
Mrs. Nettie Hatcher Hoge .... Greensboro
Rev. A. A. Walker .... Greensboro
J. Carl Bell .... Greensboro

CHURCH ADVISORY COMMITTEE

Grover H. Jones, Chairman .... High Point
J. H. Hopkins .... High Point
Rev. J. Ben Eller .... Greensboro
Rev. Wilson Woodcock .... Greensboro
Mrs. Nettie Hatcher Hoge .... Greensboro
T. L. Sasser .... Reidsville
O. E. Lee .... Greensboro

LIST OF COMMITTEES

COMMITTEES SERVING DURING THE ASSOCIATIONAL YEAR

Executive-Promotion Committee
Church Advisory Committee
Committee on Evangelism

COMMITTEES SERVING DURING THE ANNUAL MEETING OF THE ASSOCIATION

Committee on Committees
Committee on Arrangements
Committee on Place and Preacher

Auditing Committee
Committee on Resolutions
Program Committee for This Year and Next Year
Committee to Nominate Officers
Committee to Nominate Executive-Promotion Committee
Committee to Nominate Church Advisory Committee
Committee to Nominate Delegates to the Baptist State Convention
Committee to Nominate Committee on Evangelism

CHURCHES BY DISTRICTS

District 1

High Point, First
Fairmont Park
Hilliard Memorial
Green Street
North Main
North Park
South Side
West End
Oak Grove
Pine Grove
Pisgah
Smith Grove
Temple
Allen Jay

District 2

Fair Grove
Greensboro, First
Asheboro Street
Bessemer
Bailey Memorial
Buchanan
Eller Memorial
College Park
Florida Street
Latham Park
Magnolia Street
Pomona Mills
Revolution
Sixteenth Street
Stevens Memorial
Tabernacle
Gibsonville
Guilford
Jessup Grove
Lebanon
Pleasant Grove
Mount Zion
Pleasant Garden
Osborne Chapel
Rocky Knoll
Summerfield
Tabernacle
Webster Memorial

District 3

Reidsville, First
Penn Memorial
Mount Olive
Calvary
Fairview
Osceola
Reedy Fork
Ruffin-Stacey
Antioch

PIEDMONT BAPTIST SUNDAY SCHOOL ASSOCIATION OFFICERS

Rev. A. A. Walker, Superintendent .... Greensboro
F. L. Paschal, Associate Superintendent .... Greensboro
Rev. L. Grady Burgiss, Secretary-Treasurer .... Greensboro
Miss Louise Sharpe, Pianist .... Greensboro
Rev. H. R. Starling, Chorister .... Greensboro
Rev. J. S. Hopkins, Superintendent of Evangelism ...... High Point
Rev. E. M. Smith, Superintendent Group 1 .... High Point
Joe J. Norwood, Superintendent Group 2 .... Greensboro
Rev. J. C. Shore, Superintendent Group 3 .... Reidsville, Rt. 4

Department Leaders

Mrs. T. L. Osborne, Cradle Roll .... Greensboro
Miss Ruth Scott, Beginners .... Greensboro
Mrs. I. F. Anderson, Primary .... Pleasant Garden
Mrs. J. H. Saunders, Juniors .... Greensboro
Mrs. R. B. Terry, Intermediate .... High Point
Walter E. Crissman, Young People .... High Point
H. A. Helms, Adults .... Greensboro
Mrs. Walter J. Welker, Extension Department .... Greensboro
O. E. Lee, Vacation Bible School .... Greensboro

OFFICERS WOMAN'S MISSIONARY UNION

Mrs. Nettie Hatcher Hoge, Superintendent .... Greensboro
Mrs. A. Andrews, Secretary .... Greensboro
Mrs. C. E. Siceloff, Treasurer .... High Point
Miss Ruth Scott, Young People's Leader .... Greensboro
Mrs. L. M. Gideon, Personal Service Chairman .... Greensboro
Mrs. Grover H. Jones, Stewardship Chairman .... High Point
Mrs. J. J. Andoe, Mission Study-Lit. Chairman .... Greensboro
Mrs. H. A. Knight, Group Leader, District 1 .... High Point
Mrs. O. Joe Howard, Group Leader, District 2 .... Greensboro
Mrs. H. L. Morrison, Group Leader, District 3 .... Reidsville

OFFICERS BAPTIST TRAINING UNION

J. Carl Bell, Director .... Greensboro
Miss Thelma Patrick, Associate Director .... High Point
Miss Julia Liles, Secretary-Treasurer .... High Point
Miss Louise Sharpe, Pianist .... Greensboro
Miss Helen Saleeby, Story Hour Leader .... Greensboro
Mrs. Grady Burgiss, Junior Leader .... Greensboro
Mrs. Chas. E. Parker, Intermediate Leader .... Greensboro
J. E. Hedrick, Young People's Leader .... High Point
Rev. Grady Burgiss, Adult Leader .... Greensboro
Dolan Hedrick, Director District 1 .... High Point
Mrs. Joe Kirkman, Director District 2 .... Greensboro
Paul Roach, Director District 3 .... Reidsville
Rev. J. H. Saunders, Pastor Advisor .... Greensboro

ORDAINED MINISTERS NOT PASTORS

T. S. Raban ...... Thomasville
J. C. Varner ...... Gibsonville
W. L. Robinson .... Gibsonville
Dr. W. C. Newton Richmond, Va.
C. D. Barton ...... Greensboro
T. L. Chamberlain .. High Point
H. P. Billings ..... Jamestown
J. F. Murray .... Reidsville
Dr. A. S. Gillespie ..... China
J. C. Gillespie ..... Reidsville

W. F. Matherly ....Greensboro
Rufus Carroll ......Greensboro
O. P. Dix ....High Point
B. H. Farrington ...Jamestown
C. R. Smith ......Kernersville

MINISTERS ORDAINED DURING THE YEAR

W. T. Smith ....Reidsville
J. Huber Dixon ...Greensboro
Worth Grant ....Greenville, S. C.

LIST OF MESSENGERS

ASHEBORO STREET—
- Mrs. A. C. Lowe
- M. D. Teague
- Mrs. J. B. Mims
- F. L. Paschal
- J. S. Moore
- Mrs. John Carter

BAILEY MEMORIAL—
- Mrs. W. J. Mitchell
- Rev. C. G. Coe
- Mrs. E. J. Jarvis
- George Dorset

BESSEMER—
- W. P. Haynes
- H. M. Lloyd
- Mrs. J. R. Medlin
- Miss Norfleet Dixon

COLLEGE PARK—
- Laura Bateman
- Mrs. O. Joe Howard
- L. E. Agburn
- C. O. Weaver

ELLER MEMORIAL—
- Otis Bowden
- Wiley Patterson
- Archie Maness
- Mrs. Eli Craven
- Mrs. C. E. Brady

FLORIDA STREET —
- J. B. Rumley, Jr.
- C. H. Dodd
- D. M. Frazier

LATHAM PARK—
- Rev. J. Huber Dixon

MAGNOLIA STREET—
- Mrs. G. H. Williamson
- Mrs. L. L. Jarvis
- Mrs. H. S. Nash
- Mrs H. P. Wray

POMONA—
- Mrs. F. C. Moorhead
- Miss Frances Melvin
- D. V. Wilhoit
- Mrs. C. M. Oates
- James Albert

ALLEN JAY—
- J. O. Warren
- Mrs. J. O. Warren
- Mary Warren
- Elsie Burrow

ANTIOCH—
- Mrs. Ray Vanter
- Mrs. Hobart Carter
- Ray Moore

BUCHANAN—
- R. M. Crane
- R. P. Johnson
- Mrs. R. P. Johnson

CALVARY—
- F. A. Delancey
- Mrs. Cora A. Vance
- Mrs. Geo. Gunn
- Mrs. C. J. Delgardo
- J. C. Shore

FAIR GROVE—
- A. R. Riddle
- S. G. Alvis
- W. D. Fields

FAIRMONT PARK—
- Mr. & Mrs. J. E. Copple
- Rev. & Mrs. J. E. Swinson
- W. F. Thomas

GIBSONVILLE—
Morton Edwards
Ellen Edwards
Willie Foster
GREENSBORO, FIRST—
M. E. Frazier
A. A. Chandler
J. Carl Bell
Howard M. Sutherland
Mrs. Nettie H. Hoge
Mrs. Stafford R. Webb
Mr. & Mrs. O. E. Lee
REVOLUTION—
Waldo Johnson
Colon Hinson
Miss Lucille Newton
SIXTEENTH STREET—
Mrs W. L. Linebock
Mrs. W. M. Smith
Mrs. W. R. Fuller
Mrs. Harry Moore
Mrs. C F. Vestal
Mrs. Webster Owens
STEVENS MEMORIAL—
W. S. Burns
Mrs. J. H. Ham
Mrs. W P. Brown
Sadie Garner
TABERNACLE—
W. O. Smith
Mrs. E. H. Moore
Mrs. E. C White, Sr.
WEBSTER MEMORIAL—
Mrs. W. H. Lucas
Mrs. Paul Schaarachmitt
Mrs. T. S. McCadams
Mrs. C. L. Straughan
GUILFORD—
Mrs. Alic Ferrell
Mrs. Ora Weston
Mrs. B. F. Beeler
Mrs. Emma Coggins
HIGH POINT, FIRST—
Mrs. H. A. Knight
Mrs. W. O. Burnham
Thelma Patrick
Mrs. A. M. Terry
Mrs. S. H. Jones
Mrs. C. E. Siceloff
Dr. and Mrs. A. B. Conrad
GREEN STREET—
B. G. Leonard
R. B. Culler
Mr. and Mrs. Marvin Howell
Ollie Rimmer
W. E. Crissman
Mrs. T. L. Payne
Mrs. T. C. Robbins
Mrs. Raymond Campbell
HILLIARD MEMORIAL—
P. E. Grubb
J. J. Haywood
Mrs. J. W. Saunder
Mrs. C. H. Farmer
NORTH MAIN STREET—
Mrs. D. S. Ring
Mrs. Alice Davis
Mrs. Ed Crisco
NORTH PARK—
Mrs. J. D. Edmonson
Mrs. J. L. Jones
Mrs. R. A. Davis
SOUTH SIDE—
Mrs C. A. Conn
Mrs. Saltz
Mr. and Mrs. F. E. Caudle
Mrs. Auman
WEST END—
Mr. and Mrs. C. M. Scott
Mrs. P. A. Snider
LEBANON—
Maggie Kirkman
Mrs. S. R. Coleman
Mrs. J. L. Cole
Mrs. J. L. Goodwin
Mrs. L. R. Chilton
Mrs. Cleo Whitley

MOUNT ZION—
J. C. Lockamy
C. D. Branson
Mrs. C. M. Johnson

OAK GROVE—
G. K. Saunders
W. L. Shackelford
Mrs. D. H. Gruff

OSBORNE CHAPEL—
Mr. and Mrs. Hubert Bennett
Mr. and Mrs. R. R. Osborne
Mr. and Mrs. Law

OSCEOLA—
Mr. and Mrs. L. C. Cole
Mrs. D. A. Greene

PINE GROVE—
Mr. and Mrs. E. H. Eller
Rev. T. H. Myers
Mrs. Loflin
J. E. Leonard

PISGAH—
Richard Church
L. J. Mabe
Mrs. John Cox
Mrs. Manners

PLEASANT GARDEN—
Mrs. Edgar Burton
Cecil Burton
Mrs. I. F. Anderson
Henry Foy

PLEASANT GROVE—
Mr. and Mrs. J. H. Collins
Rev. H. J. Billings
Mrs. W. A. Kenon

REEDY FORK—
Rev. L. J. Hight
Alvin L. Bullard
Mrs. W. T. Smith
Mrs. Lester Carter
Mrs. E. E. Purvis

REIDSVILLE, FIRST—
Mrs. C. H. Saunders
Mrs. H. L. Morrison
Mrs. R. G. Gladstone
Rev. J. F. Murray
W. H. Wilkerson

MOUNT OLIVE—
Mrs. Odell Deloff
Mrs. D. C. Driscoll
Elmo Meadow
Mrs. Lucille Driscoll
Rev. W. D. Johnson
B. J. Harvey

PENN MEMORIAL—
Rev. D. W. Overbey
Mrs. W. H. Ford
Magdolene Gosney
Mrs. M. H. Fitz

ROCKY KNOLL—
W. H. Bullock
Mrs. F. B. Mooney
Mrs. G. L. York

RUFFIN STACEY—
Mrs. Lottie Schrum
Mrs. J. T. Cardwell
Mrs. A. S. London
Mrs. J. A. Burton

SMITH GROVE—
J. C. Pitts
Drew Smith
Rev. R. O. Nuckles

SUMMERFIELD—
Mrs. Myrtle Smith
Mrs. Clyde Robinson
T. D. Carter

TABERNACLE—
Mr. and Mrs. W. E. Collins
Mrs. Jennie Steele
Mamie Roach

CONSTITUTION

ARTICLE 1. The Association shall be called the Piedmont Baptist Association.

ARTICLE 2. It shall be composed of the ordained ministers who are members of, and those who may have pastoral charges within the Associational District, and three delegates from each church in the district aforesaid, and churches having a membership exceeding 300 shall be entitled to one additional delegate for every 200 members or fraction thereof in excess of 300.

ARTICLE 3. The said delegates shall, before taking their seats, produce letters from respective churches showing their appointment as delegates.

ARTICLE 4. The Associational session shall be held at least once a year.

ARTICLE 5. The officers shall be a Moderator, Vice-Moderator, Clerk, and Treasurer. If deemed expedient by the Association, the offices of Clerk and Treasurer may be combined.

ARTICLE 6. The officers of the Association shall be chosen annually by the Association.

ARTICLE 7. Association shall be clothed with authority only to advise the churches touching all things pertaining to their interest but shall in no case presume to direct or control them in reference to their own government or internal policy.

ARTICLE 8. A Committe of arrangements, consisting of three members, shall be appointed on the first day of each session to prepare and report the proceedings and suggest topics proper for the consideration and action of the next annual Association. It shall be the duty of this committee to outline and publish a program for the next annual associational meeting or for any special or called meeting of the association.

ARTICLE 9. Baptist brethren, not members of the Association, who may be present at any session of the body, may on invitation by the body, take seats and participate in the debates of the Association.

ARTICLE 10. The territory embraced in the Association shall be divided into not less than three districts and a committee composed of one pastor, and one layman from each district, together with the Moderator, Vice-Moderator, Clerk of the Association, Associational W. M. U. Superintendent, Associational Sunday School Superintendent, and Associational B. T. U. President, shall be appointed at meeting of the Association, which committee shall compose the Executive Committee of the Association, a majority of which shall constitute a quorum. It shall be the duty of the committee to superintend and direct the missionary operations of the Association.

ARTICLE 11. All committees shall be appointed by the Moderator either directly or indirectly with the approval of the association, unless otherwise authorized by the association from time to time.

ARTICLE 12. The Constitution may be altered only at an Annual session of the Association and by a vote of two-thirds of the whole present.

ARTICLE 13. The rules of this body shall follow Mell's Parliamentary Practice.

ARTICLE 14. This Association shall cooperate with the Baptist State Convention.

ARTICLE 15. The time of the holding of the annual session shall begin on Wednesday before the fourth Sunday in October of each year.

Adopted October 17, 1895.
Articles 2, 5, 6, 10, 15 Amended Sessions, July 23, 24, 1930.
Article 15 Amended Session July 21, 1932.
Article 10 Amended, Session October 23, 24, 1935.
Articles 8, 10, 11 Amended Sessions October 23, 24, 1940.

FRANK L. PASCHAL
C. V. WEBSTER
J. H. SAUNDERS

Committee.

Proceedings

of the

FORTY-SEVENTH ANNUAL SESSION

of the

Piedmont Baptist Associaton

Held With the

FLORIDA STREET BAPTIST CHURCH

Greensboro, N. C.

OCTOBER 23-24, 1940

WEDNESDAY MORNING SESSION — 10:00 A. M.

1. The Association opened with a song service led by Rev. J. C. Shore, and a devotional service led by Rev. Wilson W. Woodcock. Rev. J. H. Saunders speaks words of welcome.

2. A roll of the churches was called and messengers from forty-two churches responded to the roll call.

3. The report of the Moderator was made as follows:

REPORT OF MODERATOR

In my report to the last association, I suggested a few things that I though should characterize us during the associational year which has just come to a close. The things suggested were:

1. A deeper, richer experience in our prayer life.
2. A more earnest and a more constant study of the Bible.
3. A more devoted loyalty to the church.
4. A more faithful stewardship.
5. A more earnest effort to make our churches more influential and effective in the communities in which they are located.
6. A more cooperative spirit among the churches of our association.

It has been a joy to me to work with our churches the past year. I think there is a finer spirit of cooperation among the churches of our association now than at any time since I have been serving as Moderator. The churches of the association have been exceedingly kind to me.

In the brief time allotted to me I desire to report the following:

1. During the associational year just closed, I visited and spoke in twenty-seven of the churches in the association. All of these visits have been made at the invitation of the pastors of the churches visited. I am glad to report that I have been able to visit every church to which I have been invited during the year. In addition to visiting twenty-seven of our churches that are members of the association, I also visited the Fairmont Baptist Church, just west of High Point, Temple Baptist Church, about a mile and a half east of High Point and Pine Grove Baptist Church, about 4 or 5 miles east of High Point. I understand that at least two of these churches will make application at this session for membership in the association.

2. As I have visited the churches, I have emphasized the need for closer cooperation among the churches of the association, of the state and Southland. You will listen, I am sure, to the report of the clerk at 3:15 this afternoon when he brings his report furnishing us figures that we may compare what we have done during the year just closed with the previous year with respect to practically all phases of our work.

3. Shall we not set as a goal for this year:

(a) A more devoted loyalty to our association, our state convention, southern convention and to Christ.

(b) Every church in the association contributing to our denominational program.

(c) Every church duly represented at the next association.

Respectfully submitted,

G. H. JONES, Moderator.

The Moderator stated that Mr. Clarence A. Smith, the former Moderator of the Association, was in the hospital at Sumter, S. C. At the request of the Moderator Dr. J. Clyde Turner led in prayer remembering Brother Smith in his illness. Motion was passed that a telegram of greetings be sent to Brother Smith.

Telegram

Clarence A. Smith, Patient DAY LETTER
c/o Hospital
Sumter, S. C.

The Piedmont Association in session sends greetings and sympathy. May you soon be restored to your usual health. May our Heavenly Father watch over and care for your during your illness. Philippians four nineteen.

O. E. LEE, Clerk.

4. The Moderator appoints the Committee on Committees as follows: Dr. J. Clyde Turner, H. O. Miller, and J. Ben Eller.

5. The report on Hospitals was presented by A. A. Walker. Upon motion to adopt the report the subject was discussed by Chas. E. Parker, Hospital Pastor. The report was adopted.

REPORT ON BAPTIST HOSPITAL

The program of Jesus includes caring for the sick. The Baptists of North Carolina provide for this part of the Master's Program in the hospital at Winston-Salem. It was instituted in 1923. The present capacity, with 108 beds, is entirely inadequate to the ever growing demands made upon it. New buildings are now in the process of construction which when completed will comfortably house 300 beds and provide place for consultation, examination, operations, etc., as needed. This, we are told, will increase the overhead expense some fifteen percent, as against approximately a two-hundred per cent increase in beds. This means that we can care for about 10,000 patients annually, where in the past we have been able to care for little more than 4,000, at a reduced expense per patient per day. The Bowman Gray School of Medicine of Wake Forest College is also in construction on these grounds and in conjunction with the hospital buildings. Together these buildings will present an elaborate display of architectural beauty and be a veritable haven of relief to the physically distressed. Beginning the first of October, Rev. C. E. Parker, retiring pastor of the Eller Memorial Church of this association became pastor of our hospital. He will be director of religious activities for the medical school, will visit the patients, will instruct both nurses and medical students in Bible study—in short he will have spiritual oversight of these two institutions. He also will serve the hospital and denomination in general where this institution is concerned. Let it be remembered that what we do to aid those unable to pay is provided by our Mother's Day offerings. What we give through the Co-operative Program is applied to the liquidation of bonds and cannot be used for operating expenses. Let us make worthy and very liberal Mother's Day offerings.

Respectfully submitted,
A. A. WALKER.

Mr. C. M. Scott, member of the West End Church, High Point, was given special recognition by the messengers standing, for having made it possible for the Baptist Hospital in Winston-Salem to have a pastor.

6. The report on Religious literature was prepared by A. Lincoln Fulk. In his absence the report was read by J. S. Hopkins. Upon motion to adopt the report the subject was discussed by J. Ben Eller, Wilson W. Woodcock, C. E. Parker, David Morgan, representative of the Biblical Recorder, T. L. Sasser and Dr. J. Clyde Turner. The report was adopted.

REPORT ON RELIGIOUS LITERATURE

If Tennyson is right when he makes Ulysses to say, "I am a part of all that I have met," then all literature is of spiritual significance. Whether it be called "religious" or "secular" that reading done by man will have its inevitable spiritual results. For this reason then we ought to give heed to Paul's advice to young Timothy "to give attention to reading." Since our people cannot, and should not, read everything that is printed, then intelligent choices should be encouraged.

It goes without saying that the peer of all literature is the Bible. Widespread ignorance of God's Word and its teachings should cause every lover of the Bible grave concern. Recent surveys conducted in various schools reveal that many of our high school pupils do not even know the names of many prominent Bible characters and therefore have not experienced the great moral teachings to be deducted from their lives. Let us encourage the reading of the Bible in the home, the church, and the schools and insist on making it the center of all our reading habits.

With an unread Bible it is easy to understand why our people, by and large, are not reading religious magazines and periodicals. The fact that the people do not have a taste or a desire for religious reading should give Christian workers grave concern. This lack of taste indicates two possibilities: First, that our people may not be Christian enough to have an abiding interest in the Christian press; and, Second, that the Christian press is not meeting the literary and spiritual needs of modern Christians. However, when Christians manifest a deeper interest in public affairs as related to the teachings and spirit of Christ and manifest such interest by giving a greater support to Christian periodicals, there will be a corresponding increase in the influence and value of those periodicals to the individual Christian. Constant effort is being made to increase the value of our religious papers to our Baptist constituency and that value is increased largely in proportion to the increased circulation of our papers.

It is suggested, therefore, that we redouble our efforts to increase the circulation of our religious periodicals in general, and our state paper in particular, and that we encourage our people constantly to read good literature; and that we call our people back to a daily and systematic reading of the Bible. It is further suggested that we re-assert our unwavering conviction and belief in the freedom of the press with the consequent right of expression, under the rules of clean journalism, for each individual Baptist; and that we give our mental, moral, and financial support to the newest of our institutions, THE BIBLICAL RECORDER. Also THE COMMISSION and HOME MISSIONS.

Respectfully submitted,
A. LINCOLN FULK.

---

7. Following the announcements Dr. John W. Lowe, Missionary to China, brought a message on Foreign Missions and especially of his work in China.

8. Following the singing of a hymn the Introductory Sermon is delivered by Rev. Chas. E. Parker. The Scripture reading is John 4:31-36. The text is John 4:35; the subject, "Lift Up Your Eyes and Look." The sermon was an inspiration to all.

9. The report of the Committee on Committees was presented and adopted as follows:

REPORT OF COMMITTEE ON COMMITTEES

COMMITTEE ON PLACE AND PREACHER—J. S. Hopkins, W. I. Johnson, M. E. Frazier.

AUDITING COMMITTEE—J. S. Moore, A. A. Chandler, J. J. Hagwood.

COMMITTEE ON RESOLUTIONS—T. L. Sasser, L. G. Burgiss, C. M. Scott.

COMMITTEE ON PROGRAM FOR NEXT YEAR—A. A. Walker, D. W. Overby, T. H. Biles.

COMMITTEE TO NOMINATE OFFICERS—H. R. Starling, J. C. Shore, Mrs. Ed Criscoe.

COMMITTEE TO NOMINATE EXECUTIVE PROMOTION COMMITTEE—Wilson Woodcock, A. B. Conrad, Mrs. C. H. Saunders.

COMMITTE TO NOMINATE CHURCH ADVISORY COMMITTEE-F. L. Paschel, L. C. Chandler, H. O. Miller.

COMMITTEE TO NOMINATE DELEGATES TO BAPTIST STATE CONVENTION—L. C. Madden, Mrs. O. E. Lee.

COMMITTEE TO NOMINATE LEADER FOR THE VERBAL REPORT HOUR—Referred to Committee on Program.

COMMITTEE TO NOMINATE COMMITTEE ON EVANGELISM—J. H. Saunders, W. L. Smith.

J. Clyde Turner
H. O. Miller
J. Ben Eller

The morning session was closed with prayer by J. C. Gillespie.

AFTERNOON SESSION — 1:30 O'CLOCK

10. The devotional period was in charge of J. C. Gillespie.

11. The report on State Missions was presented by T. H. Biles. Upon motion to adopt the report the subject was discussed by M. A. Huggins, Secretary representing the Baptist State Mission Board. The report was adopted.

STATE MISSION REPORT

Let us look at our State Mission task. There are 2,532 Baptist Churches in North Carolina with 506,370 members. This numbers nearly half the people who are members of any religious organization in the state. Of these members about one-fourth attend worship regularly. Nearly one-half never attend any service of the church to which they belong. One-fourth of the members bear all the burden of the leadership and of financing the Kingdom. It takes twenty-three of us to win one soul to Christ each year including all the efforts of the preachers. Enlistment of the members is one of the great tasks of the churches ond of State Missions.

Let us see again the communities needing Baptist Churches. We at once think of eastern North Carolina. These needs are kept constantly before us. But here in Piedmont North Carolina and even in the western part of the state are whole industrial communities numbering hundreds and thousands of souls without the privilege of a Baptist church in the midst. In some communities where there are hundreds of Baptist students in college there is no Baptist Church near enough to the college for the studentsto walk to worship. There are also rural communities where the people have to go to other denominations if they attend church at all. There are yet hundreds of needy places in North Carolina.

We have been told recently that North Carolina leads all the states in the union in homicides. In other crimes it ranks well up towards the top. Crime is on the increase. Lawlessness flourishes if not to say it is popular. Worldliness and sensuality is on the upgrade. These conditions open to every church and every Christian a wide field of missionary endeavor.

The State Mission Board is now attempting to do some missionary endeavor in the places here mentioned:

Taking care of headquarters in Raleigh.

Paying part of the salaries of pastors in many needy places where the churches themselves could not adequately support a pastor.

Sending two general missionaries up and down the state.

Making it possible for a Negro preacher to help the underprivileged Negro preachers and churches to do better work.

Providing spiritual ministration thru a pastor to those in institutions at Samarcand, State Sanatoriums, and Oteen.

Supervising Sunday School Work, the Training Union, and the Student Union.

Teaching and leading the Indians in their churches.

Building or helping to build churches in strategic places.

Under the leadership of the Holy Spirit we Baptists should rise to the occasion and minister in an adequate and worthy manner to the needs of the Kingdom of Christ within the bounds of our noble State. Under His banner we move on.

Respectfully submitted,

T. H. Biles

---

12. The verbal Report Hour was in charge of J. H. Saunders. A large number of representatives made reports.

13. The following new pastors were given special recognition: Melvin Faulkner, B. C. Lamb, and J. S. Hopkins.

14. The clerk gave a general report of the work done by the churches during the associational year. The report was encouraging, especially the financial part. The number received for baptism was less and special attention was called to this part of the report. The report was adopted.

15. The report of the Committee on Evangelism was presented by Mrs. Nettie H. Hoge. The report included the resolutions sent by Dr. Roland Q. Leavell. Motion was made that the resolutions be adopted. The motion was discussed by Mrs. Hoge and Hughey O. Miller. The motion was passed.

RESOLUTION ON EVANGELISM FOR AN ASSOCIATION

(Suggested by Roland Q. Leavell, Supt. of Evangelism, Home Mission Board, 315 Red Rock Bldg., Atlanta, Ga.)

WHEREAS:

The experience of Southern Baptists has been that the associations which have planned and promoted perennial programs of evangelism have shown the greatest advance in soul-winning, and
WHEREAS:

Our association needs an aggressive, comprehensive, intensive and extensive program of evangelism during the coming year,
BE IT RESOLVED:

FIRST, that our evangelistic committee organize as follows:
(1) One member shall act as leader or chairman,
(2) The second member shall promote publicity in the county papers and in the churches,
(3) The third person shall promote the organization of an "Andrew Club" of personal soul-winners under the leadership of the pastor in every church,
(4) The fourth member shall promote having a study course in personal soul-winning in every church and
(5) The fifth member shall promote "highways and hedges" evangelism in out-of-the-church efforts, such as shop preaching, street meetings, radio revivals, brush arbor and schoolhouse meetings, mission Sunday schools, deputation work for testimony and soul-winning, and so forth, and

SECOND, That our evangelistic program shall include
(1) At least one revival meeting in every church,
(2) An evangelistic effort in every unchurched community,
(3) "Highways and hedges" evangelism,
(4) A census or survey in every church community,
(5) The organization of an "ANDREW CLUB" or some other soul-winning group in every church,
(6) A study course in soul-winning in every church,
(7) An associational evangelistic rally and

THIRD, That we seek to present the Gospel to every person within our associational territory, and endeavor to win the largest possible number of souls to Christ, - at least one for each ten members in every church.

16. The Moderator calls special attention to the night session.

17. The report of the Committee to Nominate the Church Advisory Committee was made and adopted. (See page 5.)

18. The report on Home Missions, prepared by Dr. A. B. Conrad, was read by Grady Burgiss in the absence of Dr. Conrad, who was sick and could not attend. Upon motion to adopt the report the subject was discussed by Grady Burgiss and M. A. Huggins. The report was adopted.

REPORT ON HOME MISSIONS

Home Missions is the very center of all our Missionary enterprise. For convenience we divide the great task of world evangelization into city, state, home and Foreign Missions- but all Missions are one, but it is true that the strategic point of approach to the great world task is the homeland, we must Christianize America or the forces of unrighteousness at home and abroad will heathenize us. The religion of Jesus must be triumphant at home before it can win any great victories abroad.

The great task of our Home Mission Board is to make America Christian. It is therefore preaching the Gospel among the Negroes, Indians, Foreigners- and in the congested areas and centers of our land and in Cuba and Panama.

The past year has been one of the best in the ninety-five years of the society's history. Our missionaries have been richly blessed on every field. There are 411 of them working in 863 Mission stations. During the past year 40 workers have been added to our Mission force. 93 new Mission stations have been opened and 14 pieces of property strategically located for our work have been acquired.

During the year our Missionaries have distributed 40,362 Bibles, testaments and portions of Scripture and 660,847 tracts. They have preached 34,008 sermons and led over 9000 to make profession of faith in Christ, and received into fellowship with the Church 4,672 persons.

The year has also been one of the best financially for many years for the Home Mission Board. The receipts were larger than the year before and marked progress has been in the payment of the debt. The Board received from all sources in 1939, $544,289.04 and the treasurer's report shows that $159,585.15 was paid on the principal of the debt, and a debt payment program has been mapped out which will liquidate all the debts of the Home Mission Board by 1945. provided the receipts per annum do not fall below that of the past year.

The various departments of the work of the Board are organized as follows:

Dr. J. W. Beagle is field secretary in the department of Missions in the homeland, and under him we have 269 Missionaries which is 17 more than last year.

In Cuba Dr. M. N. McCall is superintendent. New fields have been entered and many conversions reported and conditions generally are favorable for great advance.

Dr. Roland Q. Leavell, Supt. of Evangelism, has devoted much time to the organization and promotion of city-wide simultaneous evangelistic meetings and promoting such campaigns in Assciational areas. In many sections splendid results have followed these efforts.

There are more unsaved souls in the Southland today than there were when the Home Mission Board was organized in 1845. Our cities, many of them have large foreign population- our smaller churches with infrequent services are losing out, and with the increasing number and zeal of unscriptural sects, it is of the first importance that the spirit of evangelism must recapture the hearts of our people and the work of our Home Mission Society be carried on in urban and rural sections with utmost vigor.

During the past year a wonderful work has been going on among the Jews. The greatest ingathering of them that the society has ever witnessed. Rev. Jacob Gartenhouse, field secretary, reports great numbers of them turning to Christ.

The Board's cooperative work with Negroes, headed by Dr. Noble Y. Beall, has been outstanding. Several thousand were enrolled in all types of classes on and off the campuses in the work of 21 teacher Missionaries, and one of the chief accomplishments of these men has been in directing the student activities of more than 9000 students in the schools where they teach.

Attention should be called to the Home Mission Magazine. It should be in every Baptist home. All our people should know the facts as they are in our Southland, and there is no better medium for the dissemination of these facts than in this magazine of which 431,600 copies were circulated during the year. All our people should read this splendid magazine which is only 25c a year.

The task is great, and it issues a mighty challenge to the faith and loyalty of our people— in the Southland there are five million foreign born, 600 thousand French speaking Americans, 500 thousand Spanish speaking Americans, 200 thousand Indians, eleven million Negroes, and a great number of mountain people unevangelized, all these with the millions in Cuba and Panama and the Canal Zone issue a tremendous call. The Baptists are responsible for them and in all our churches special stress should be laid on the cooperative program which is the chief source of financial support, that the work and workers may be largely increased.

The field is white to the harvest and the need and call is for reapers.

---

19. Rev. Vickery Anderson of the Randolph Association was recognized.

20. After singing a hymn the afternoon session was closed with prayer by H. R. Starling.

NIGHT SESSION — 7:30 O'CLOCK

(The Night Session was held with the College Park Baptist Church)

21. The devotional service was in charge of Mrs. Joe Kirkman.

22. The Training Union report was presented by Mrs. J. Carl Bell. The report was adopted.

REPORT OF BAPTIST TRAINING UNION

During the year ending in September, 1940, the work of the Baptist Training Union in the Association has gone forward under the direction of J. Carl Bell. In accordance with the action taken by the Training Union, the quarterly meetings in 1940 have been held on Friday evenings instead of Sunday afternoons and meetings were held on January 12th, June 7th, and September 6th.

The Annual Associational Banquet was held on March 15th in Greensboro. At this time the associational elimination in the Training Union contests was held. These winners were representatives in the Regional contests, where they won first places throughout and went on to Ridgecrest to compete in the State contests. Two Juniors were winners in the State Memory Work Drill.

The Twentieth Annual Session of the Training Union was held at the First Baptist Church in Greensboro on April 21st and 22nd. Included in the goals presented at the Saturday evening session were these:

That a spirit of revival be prayed for throughout our churches.

That our God might call at least one ideal preacher out of the Association within the year.

An increased attendance in the Training Union this year of 25 percent, and number of Unions of 20 percent,

500 registered delegates present at the 1941 Associational Convention of the Training Union.

A new plan of meeting for the 1941 Convention was adopted. This plan is that the annual benquet and associational convention be combined, having an afternoon meeting for conferences, contests, etc., and climaxing the meeting with the banquet in the evening with an outstanding speaker. This action was taken due to the increased number of meetings throughout the Church program.

A plan was also adopted to award banners in efficiency and attendance at each quarterly meeting and a committee was appointed to secure the necessary banners.

Some progress has already been made toward increased attendance in the Training Union and the number of Unions as some extension work has already been done and new Unions organized.

The amount of $50.00 appropriated by the Piedmont Association for the Training work during this past year has been a great help in the furtherance of this cause. Training Course books have been purchased for the Director to use in conducting Training Courses in the smaller churches and new banners purchased for the purpose of stimulating interest in the quarterly meetings.

The cooperation in its work of each Church of the Piedmont Association is earnestly requested and will be sincerely appreciated by the Training Union.

Respectfully submitted,
Julia M. Liles, Secretary.

---

23. The Moderator presents Mr. Carl Bell, the Associational B. T. U. Director, who has charge of the program.

24. Two selections were rendered by the orchestra from the Asheboro Street Baptist Church.

25. After singing "Stepping In the Light" by the audience, a group of students from the Woman's College of the University of North Carolina presented a playlet "Two Masters". The playlet was given under the direction of Miss Laura Bateman, Secretary of the Baptist Student Work. The playlet presented a splendid Missionary message.

26. Rev. J. S. Hopkins delivered a splendid message on the subject "Loyalty to the Church".

The night session was closed with prayer.

THURSDAY MORNING SESSION — 9:45

27. The song and praise service was in charge of J. S. Hopkins.

28. The report of the Ministers' Relief and Retirement Plan was read by Hughey O. Miller. Upon motion to adopt the report the subject was discussed by Hughey O. Miller, Wilson W. Woodcock, J. Ben Eller, T. L. Sasser and Mr. --- --- Copple. The report was adopted.

MINISTERS' RELIEF AND RETIREMENT PLAN

For a number of years a strong effort has been made to awaken a deep concern for the relief of worthy faithful ministers. The progress has been slow, but has gained momentum with each succeeding year.

The Annuity Board fosters eleven different plans, but it appears that the Ministers' and Workers' Retirement Plan, which has been in force for a year is being received by pastors and churches very graciously.

We have now about 350 members representing approximately 650 churches. Instead of 25 per cent, at least half of our churches ought to be enlisted before the close of another year.

It is a fact deserving special emphasis that although nearly four million dollars have been paid out to beneficiaries since 1918 the reserves are now nearly five million dollars, which indicates a steady growth.

There are nearly four thousand members in the Retirement Plan in the Southern Baptist Convention. The total paid out from the several plans of the Annuity during 1939 to beneficiaries amounted to $253,794.94.

Under the Retirement Plan the pastor and church may pay cooperatively 2 3-4 per cent of salary, to which the State Mission Board adds $18 annually. For those reaching the age of retirement in 1941, operation on a 4-4 basis as of January 1, 1940, would be entitled to 25 per cent of salary, with $600.00 maximum. Those reaching retirement age later will be entitled to an additional 1 per cent per year up until 1961, at which time the beneficiary will be entitled to 50 per cent, provided, however, that he served in churches affiliated with the Southern Baptist Convention for thirty-three and a third years, with a maximum of $2000.00.

The task before us is to enlist all the churches and pastors in this worthy program, to the end that the dread of inevitable old age and infirmity may be lessened, and the churches appreciate more fully the inestimable value of these saints of God.

HUGHEY O. MILLER.

---o---

29. The report on Sunday Schools was presented by F. L. Paschal. Upon motion to adopt the report the subject was discussed by A. A. Walker, O. E. Lee, F. L. Paschal, and Grady Burgiss. The report was adopted.

REPORT ON SUNDAY SCHOOLS

"I was glad when they said unto me, "Let us go into the House of the Lord'." This kind of spirit should possess us about the wonderful possibilities which we have in the teaching part of the Kingdom work.

It is amazing to observe the illiteracy of so many of our church members today in reference to the teachings of the Holy Bible. Many of them know nothing about whether Paul's letter to the Ephesians is in the Old or New Testament. Many could not name the four Gospels, nor could they call by name more than two of the twelve disciples. So few of our leaders know enough about the scripture to be able to discuss them intelligently or as well as they could the events discussed in the newspapers of today. The reason for this plight is that we do not have more than approximately 75 per cent of our members actively enrolled in Sunday Schools. In most instances, less than one-half of those who go attend regularly and only a few of those who attend regularly prepare their lessons. In most of our schools, only a half hour is actually used for class discussion.

Then what is the solution of our problem of Religious Education? Certainly we should not say that we might as well stop, for although we admit that we are not doing well enough, to stop trying would be failure within itself. We should strive to make progress as we have done for many years past, and because our progress is slow it should not dampen our ardor and enthusiasm, rather it should constitute a challenge to the best that is within us.

Our study of the need for better religious training and education in our Sunday Schools causes us to make these general, practical suggestions and urge that our churches make a determined effort to carry them out.

(1) Select consistent Christian teachers and officers and always operate our schools under church control.

(2) Organize new classes and thereby provide opportunities for greater student participation in the classes.

(3) Have regular training classes and officers' and teachers' clinics.

(4) Make room for expansion.

(5) Keep departments well organized and cooperating with each other.

(6) Attend associational meetings which provide fellowship, new ideas and inspiration.

(7) Enlist the unenlisted and have a constant program for the enrollment of new members.

(8) Win the unsaved and always serve those who may have physical or spiritual needs.

Respectfully submitted,

FRANK L. PASCHAL.

———o———

30. After singing a hymn the following visitors were rec-

ognized: R. E. Adams, J. A. McMillan and A. A. Lockee.

31. The report on W. M. U. Work was presented by Mrs. Nettie H. Hoge. Upon motion to adopt the report the work was discussed by Mrs. H. A. Knight. The report was adopted.

REPORT OF WOMAN'S WORK

The organized Woman's Work in our denomination needs no recommendation other than its past achievements. "Her own works praise her in the gates."

It covers all fields of Kingdom service. In enlistment it includes all ages from Sunbeams to old age, and has grown in numbers of organizations to 39,720.

The objectives of these organizations are Mission Study, Personal Service, Prayer and Stewardship.

To realize the strength in unity, there was reported last year 46.465 classes for the study of the Gospel need of the world and how to meet this need; 67,000 days and seasons of prayer for the spread of the gospel at home and abroad; 20,011 societies engaged in organized personal service in "going about doing good," visiting the sick and distressed, and ministering and providing for the needy. Stewardship reports 141,129 tithers.

Besides literature to meet various needs, Royal Service, the W. M. U. magazine with its programs and information has reached the enormous circulation of 99,000.

The gifts of the South wide Union last year amounted to over one million. The Christmas offering alone was over $330,000, $100,000 of which paid the salary of 125 Foreign Missionaries.

In our Association we have 122 of these organizations, 33 of our churches co-operating in all W. M. U. programs. Pleasant Grove, Lebanon and Fairview have recently been added. Thirteen churches have no organizations. The offering last year was $24,218.79. There are 10,740 churches with no organizations in our Southern Baptist Convention.

The past achievements are but the foundation for the future.

Respectfully submitted,

MRS. NETTIE HATCHER HOGE,

Supt. W. M. U., Piedmont, Ass'n

---

32. The report of the Committee to Nominate the Executive-Promotion Committee was made as follows. The report was adopted. (See Report in Associational Directory.)

33. The Church Advisory Committee reports as follows:

The Church Advisory Committee recommends that the following new churches be received into this Association: Pine Grove Baptist Church, organized November 20, 1938; Temple Baptist Church, Reedy Fork Baptist Church, Fairmont Park Baptist Church and Fair Grove Baptist Church.

Grover H. Jones, J. Ben Eller, Wilson W. Woodcock, Mrs. Nettie H. Hoge, O. E. Lee, J. S. Hopkins, T. L. Sasser, Committee.

The report was adopted and the hand of fellowship was extended by the Moderator to the representatives from the churches.

34. The Treasurer's report was presented and referred to the Auditing Committee.

REPORT OF AUDITING COMMITTEE

We, the undersigned committee appointed to audit the books of Brother O. E. Lee, treasurer, are glad to report we found same correct and very neatly kept, and recommend his report be accepted with thanks for his accuracy, and work of love.

Respectfully submitted,

J. C. MOORE
A. A. CHANDLER
J. J. HAWOOD

Committee.

Oct. 24, 1940.

———o———

REPORT OF TREASURER—EXPENSE FUND

I herewith submit my report for the year ending September 30, 1940.

Balance on hand September 30, 1939	$ 7.79
Received from the churches	177.31
Total	$185.10

DISBURSEMENTS

Postage and Supplies	$ 6.88
Record Pub. Co. for Minutes	100.00
Clerk's Remuneration	50.00
Total	$156.88
Balance on Hand	28.22

Grand Total	$185.10	$185.10

Respectfully submitted,
O. E. LEE, Treasurer.

REPORT OF TREASURER—MISSION FUND

I herewith submit my report for the year ending September 30, 1940.

Received from the churches $107.30

DISBURSEMENTS

The Piedmont Baptist Association Training Union, Treasurer	$ 50.00	
The Piedmont Baptist Sunday School Association, Treasurer	10.00	
Total	$ 60.00	
Balance on Hand	47.30	
Grand Total	$107.30	$107.30

Respectfully submitted,
O. E. LEE, Treasurer.

———o———

35. The report of the Committee on the Constitution was made by F. L. Paschal and adopted.

REPORT OF COMMITTEE ON REVISION OF CONSTITUTION

We, the undersigned committee to revise the constitution of the PIEDMONT BAPTIST ASSOCIATION, do hereby respectfully submit the following as amendments to the Constitution:

FIRST: We recommend that Article 8 be amended by adding at the end of said Article 8, after the word "Association," the following: "It shall be the duty of this committee to outline and publish a program for the next annual associational meeting or for any special or called meeting of the association."

SECOND: That the word "four" in line 2 of Article 10 be stricken out and that the word "Three" be substituted in lieu thereof.

THIRD: That Article 11 be amended as follows: By adding after the word "Moderator" in line 2 the following: "either directly or indirectly with the approval of the association" and by striking out the word "ordered" in line 2 thereof and substituting in lieu thereof the word "authorized" and by striking out the period in line 2 after the word "association" and by adding the following words: "from time to time" so that said Article 11 shall, when amended, read as follows: Article 11. "All committees shall be appointed by the Moderator either directly or indirectly with the approval of the association, unless otherwise authorized by the association from time to time."

FOURTH: That Article 15 be amended by striking out the word "be" in line 2 and substituting in lieu thereof the word "begin."

Respectfully submitted,
FRANK L. PASCHAL
C. V. WEBSTER
J. H. SAUNDERS

---o---

36. The report on Forelgn Missions was presented by Dr. J. Clyde Turner. Upon motion to adopt the report a splendid message was delivered by Dr. Turner. The report was adopted.

REPORT ON FOREIGN MISSIONS

At the meeting of the Southern Baptist Convention last June the Foreign Mission Board completed ninety-five years of service. It began its work with four missionaries; it now has more than 450 on the field. It started its work in one country, China; it now has missionaries in sixteen countries. The receipts of the Board the first year were $11,689.05; last year the receipts amounted to $1,149,-251.87. This is more than the Board received during the first thirty-five years of its work. In the beginning there were no churches on the foreign fields; now there are 1,803 churches, with a total membership of 236,265. Last year 18,606 were received on a profession of faith. Thirty years ago all the churches on the foreign fields did not have that many members.

At the present time the work of our Board is facing many difficulties and obstacles. The wars that are in progress have greatly retarded the work in China, Japan, and the European countries, and give promise of even greater hindrances. Much of our mission property has been destroyed and the members of the churches have been scattered. There is still a debt of more than $200,000 resting on the Board. Interest in the work has lagged on the part of some in the homeland.

But there are many encouraging features. The people in the war-torn countries, especially China, are turning to the Lord in large numbers. Never has the gospel been so enthusiastically received as it is now. The debt is being gradually reduced, and plans are on foot to wipe it out entirely within the next few years. The annual receipts of the Board are increasing year by year. Last year the Board received $268,678.16 more than it received seven years ago.

The Board publishes a monthly missionary magazine, The Commission, which brings missionary news from all over the world. There are now 16,131 paid-up subscribers to this publication. The price is fifty cents a year.

The Board now has a graded series of mission study books covering the fields in which Southern Baptists are at work. These books not only provide splendid mission study courses for all ages, but will give to the church a good foreign mission library.

Respectfully submitted,
J. CLYDE TURNER.

The morning session closed with prayer by Wilson W. Woodcock.

THURSDAY AFTERNOON SESSION—1:30 O'CLOCK

37. The devotional service was conducted by D. W. Overby.

38. The report on Social Service was presented by Wilson W. Woodcock. Upon motion to adopt the report the subject was discussed by Dr. O. T. Binkley of Wake Forest College. The report was adopted.

REPORT ON SOCIAL SERVICE

Report to the Piedmont Association meeting in Greensboro, N. C., with the Florida Street Church, October 23, 1940. "But wilt thou know, O vain man, that faith without works is dead?" James 2:20.

Southern Baptists have been saying for generations: "Yes, we know that." And they have been appointing commissions to study the best methods of combating drunkenness and gambling and vice, which lead to poverty and destruction.

Their pastors have been taught in the seminaries that the moral ideal has two aspects. The ethical ideal which has to do with the acceptance of Christ as Saviour and Lord, and the growth in grace which should follow.

The social ideal which leads Dr. E. Y. Mullins to write: "There can be no question that Christianity contemplates the purification of all social relations."

We have fought and are continuing to fight for the abolition of the liquor traffic. We are giving increasing attention to race relations. Lynching of Negroes has almost disappeared from the Southland.

There are many other social relationships which demand the

attention of Baptists. Shall we follow the leadership of those who do not know Christ? Or shall we study such questions in the light of God's word and under the guidance of the Holy Spirit? Can the Gospel of Christ be spread through the world by war? If Christ were in the world today in His human body would He defend His gospel by force of arms?

The monastic system arose when men thought it was necessary to turn a deaf ear to the social problems of the world. They separated themselves from the world that they might live holy lives.

In this world of tragedy we are tempted today to shut ourselves away from the facts and dwell in sweet contemplation of the love of God and our own security.

Let us awake out of sleep and seek the New Testament answer to the ills of the world.

Respectfully submitted,
WILSON WOODCOCK.

---

39. The report on Christian Education was presented by W. I. Johnson. Upon motion to adopt the report the subject was discussed by Dr. O. T. Binkley, F. L. Paschal, J. Ben Eller.

The congregation stood with bowed heads for a brief period in memory of Dr. J. T. J. Battle, who passed on to the Heavenly Home a few weeks ago, and who, in his will, left a large sum of money to Wake Forest College and Meredith College. The Baptist Orphanage of N. C. was also remembered in the will. The report was adopted.

REPORT ON CHRISTIAN EDUCATION

Christian education has its origin in Christ and its beginning in the home. Many homes fail to realize these facts and thus neglect the greatest opportunity offered to establish the fundamentals of true Christian education. More Christian homes are needed and more thought should be given to the basic principals that are firmly established in the early years of each life.

Our Baptist schools have rendered an unestimable service in training and guidance of youth for every walk of life. Their service and influence speak out through the lives of their illustrious sons and daughters. These institutions should have our continual support and patronage, not only by our organizations but by every Baptist in North Carolina.

Often our Baptist schools have done for our boys and girls what our homes and churches have failed to do, but may we look back of these to another phase of Christian education that is more important. I refer to the church. The church has a greater responsibility and obligation than the higher institutions of learning. The church touches more lives than any other organization in the world. It should grasp every opportunity to win and to train these people Most of our churches have organizations and programs to train its people, but I am conscious of the fact that we are not making the most of the opportunity. A little here and a little there in our programs and we say the task is done. We need to realize that Christian education is a continual process from birth to death of each life. It is THE basic principal, THE controlling factor, and THE only channel through which Christ and Christianity will ever reach all the world. Without Christ there is no life and without life there is no channel for Christ to be manifested and glorified. The word educate comes from two Latin words: e, which means out, and ducere, which means lead. Thus we have the true meaning of the word, which is: "lead out." Christian education means Christ let out through the channels of one's life. Thus we have the whole Baptist program as a result of Christian education. I commend unto you a greater program in our churches and a loyal support for the maintenance of all its institutions.

Respectfully submitted,
W. I. JOHNSON.

---o---

40. Motion was passed that our Associational Minutes this year be dedicated in honor of Dr. J. T. J. Battle.

41. The report on the Orphanage was presented by J. Ben Eller. Upon motion to adopt the report the subject was discussed by J. Ben Eller and J. A. McMillan, Editor of Charity and Children. The report was adopted.

REPORT OF BAPTIST ORPHANAGE

James defined "Pure religion and undefiled" as this: "To visit the fatherless and the widows in their affliction and keep himself unspotted from the world." Jesus associated Himself with the unfortunate ones of this world. As we minister to them, He said we minister to Him. Hear His word: "I was an hungered and ye gave me meat; I was thirsty and ye gave me drink; I was a stranger and ye took me in; naked and ye clothed me; I was sick and ye visited me."

Last year North Carolina Baptists fed, clothed, and furnished educational and religious opportunities for 648 children. That was "pure and undefiled religion." That was ministering unto Jesus.

The annual report of our Baptist Orphanage is very encouraging. Health conditions for the year have been good. Schools have done splendid work and have been well attended. Spiritual conditions have been excellent. That is attested by the fact that every member of the graduating class was a Christian. Worthy gifts and bequests continue to come to the institution.

Three things we would urge upon our churches. First, be sure that you send a worthy offering to the orphanage at least once a month. Second, plan for a great love offering for Thanksgiving. And, Third, secure a large number of subscriptions for Charity and Children.

Respectfully submitted,
J. BEN ELLER.

———o———

42. The report on Obituaries was presented by L. C. Chandler. The messengers stood and Wilson W. Woodcock led in prayer.

REPORT ON OBITUARIES

Again we bow ourselves before the unerring will of God, who has called home from our fellowship a number of His redeemed whose names will appear in the minutes. Some of these were church officers and leaders and each of them rendered a distinct service in his own God-endowed manner. Precious memories and a sense of great loss overflood our hearts in this moment in which we now pause to pay tribute to our honored dead. Surely the influence of the faithful servants of God hovers over us as a benediction to urge us on to greater heights of achievement in the cause of Christ.

Respectfully submitted,
L. C. CHANDLER.

---

43. The following reports of Committees were presented and adopted.

Report of Committee on Place and Preacher

We recommend that the Association meet next year with the Green Street Baptist Church, and that A. Lincoln Fulk preach the sermon, with A. A. Walker serving as alternate.

JULIAN S. HOPKINS
M. E. FRAZIER
W. I. JOHNSON

Report of Committee to Nominate Delegates to Baptist State Convention

The committee recommends the following: Grover H. Jones and A. A. Walker.

L. C. MADDEN
MRS. O. E. LEE
Committee.

Report of Committee to Nominate Officers

The Committee on the Nomination of Officers for Next Year makes the following report: Grover H. Jones, Moderator; T. L. Sasser, Vice-Moderator; O. E. Lee, Clerk-Treasurer.

H. R. STARLING
MRS. ED. CRISCO
J. C. SHORE
Committee.

Report of Committee to Nominate Committee on Evangelism

The committee recommends the following: J. S. Hopkins, Chairman; Mrs. Nettie Hoge, Study Chairman; Grady Burgiss, Publicity; Howard Sutherland, Andrew Club; Walter E. Crisman, Highway and Hedges Evangelism.

T. L .SASSER
J. H. SAUNDERS
Committee.

REPORT OF COMMITTEE ON PROGRAM FOR NEXT YEAR

Religious Literature .... J. Clyde Turner
Foreign Missions .... J. Ben Eller
Denominational Program .... J. S. Hopkins
State Missions .... E. M. Smith
Social Service .... J. H. Saunders
Orphanage .... J. C. Shore
Hospital .... W. T. Johnson

Training Union ....J. Carl Bell
Woman's Missionary Union ....Mrs. Nettie Hoge
Christian Education ....Wilson Woodcock
Home Missions ....A. B. Conrad
Sunday Schools ....A. A. Walker
Ministers' Relief and Retirement Plan ....A. L. Fulk
Obituaries ....Huber Dixon
Verbal Report Leader ....T. L. Sasser

Respectfully submitted,

A. A. WALKER
D. W. OVERBEY
T. H. BILES
Committee

---o---

The following telegram from Clarence A. Smith, former Moderator of the Association, was read: Sumter, S. C. "Greetings from you greatly appreciated, God Answering His Sustaining Grace is Abundant."—Clarence A. Smith.

REPORT OF COMMITTEE ON RESOLUTIONS

WHEREAS, The Piedmont Baptist Association, meeting with the Florida Street Baptist Church, Greensboro, October 23-24, 1940, has engaged in a splendid session, be it resolved:

First, that we express our gratitude to this church and its pastor, Rev. J. H. Saunders, and all the Baptist churches of the Greensboro group for their co-operation in entertaining the association in a gracious way.

Second, That we express our appreciation of the zealous and wise efforts of our able and very active moderator, Grover H. Jones, who has been instrumental in bringing about so many fine things in our association, and to our efficient and untiring clerk, O. E. Lee

Third, That we commend the work of the W. M. U., the Sunday schools, and the young people's work, and urge that these phases of our work be further emphasized and strengthened.

Fourth, That we acknowledge our debt of gratitude to God for the many spiritual feasts brought to us in these meetings.

Respectfully submitted,

T. L. SASSER, Chairman
L. G. BURGISS
T. C. SCOTT

44. A special offering was taken for the work of the United Dry Forces of North Carolina. The offering amounted

to $9.56.

45. Following the singing of "I Love to Tell the Story" the report on the Denominational Program was presented by T. L. Sasser. Upon motion to adopt the report the subject was discussed by T. L. Sasser. The report was adopted.

REPORT ON DENOMINATIONAL PROGRAM

Our denominational program has its foundation in the New Testament. The members of our churches "engage to promote the prosperity and spirituality" of the body, "to sustain its worship, ordinances, discipline, and doctrine, and to spread the gospel through all nations."

The object of the North Carolina Baptist State Convention is to "promote Missions, Education, Social Service, the distribution and study of the Bible and sound religious literature, and to co-operate with the Southern Baptist Convention in its work of 'eliciting, combining, and directing the energies of the denomination for the propagating of the Gospel.' " These conventions give expression to our corporate spiritual life.

We are constantly engaged in sustaining and expanding the work of the churches at home and abroad, endeavoring to preach the gospel to all people everywhere. To support and make effective this primary enterprise we have auxiliary institutions. They are schools, colleges, seminaries, hospitals, and orphanages.

Twenty years ago we made concerted effort to buy up a large opportunity. We greatly expanded our program. We are yet paying large sums on the obligations incurred in the advance steps we made then. The one source of our income is still the self-sacrificing giving on the part of the people "of like precious faith." For these twenty years the plan of finance which we call the co-operative program has afforded the churches and individuals the opportunity and the facilities to give systematically and proportionately to the whole work of Southern Baptists as well as to the conventions of their respective States. Convention boards and committees expend the funds as designated by the givers. Undesignated funds are used according to schedules worked out, adopted and published by the conventions through their authorized agencies. The current division of undesignated offerings through the Co-operative Program is 60 per cent to the work of the State Convention and 40 per cent to the work of the Southern Baptist Convention. The money used for State Convention work is divided as follows:

State Missions	.23 1/3
Education—Debt Service	.65
Hospital	.06 2/3

Ministerial Education	.01 2/3
Retirement Fund	.03 1/3
	1.00

The money used for Southern Baptist Convention work is divided as follows:

Foreign Missions	.50
Home Missions	.23 1/3
Relief and Annuity	.10 1/3
Southern Baptist Seminary	.04 1/5
Southwestern Baptist Seminary	.04 1/5
Baptist Bible Institute	.04 1/5
W. M. U. Training School	.00 8/15
American Baptist Seminary	.01
New Orleans Baptist Hospital	.02 1/5
	1.00

Seven years ago it had become very apparent that the gifts to the co-operative program would not retire Southern Baptist Convention debts unless the funds were materially increased. The Hundred Thousand Club was organized to help pay off the principal, which was $5,880,351.63 in 1933. The club members have given to May 1, 1940, a total of $1,157,295.72. The co-operative program proper has continued to pay and reduce the interest on the debt as well as materially reduce the principal and it is hoped that the Southern Baptist Convention will be debt-free in 1945.

By mutual agreement of our State Convention and the Southern Baptist Convention the funds given by North Carolina Baptists to the Hundred Thousand Club are divided equally between the two conventions so that our State debts are also reduced by this method.

Both the Co-operative Program and the Hundred Thousand Club must have our very vigorous support to reduce our debts and expand our work.

Respectfully submitted,
T. L. SASSER.

46. After singing "Take My Life and Let It Be" the session was closed by Dr. O. T. Binkley.

W. M. U. PROCEEDINGS — PIEDMONT ASSOCIATION

The Piedmont W. M. U. held its annual meeting April 25, 1940, with North Main Church, High Point, with around 250 members attending.

Mrs. J. I. Phillips had the morning devotional and Mrs. S. H. Smith welcomed the Union.

All reports and addresses centered around the theme for the day, "Christ's Concern, Our Concern."

The presence of ten pastors was appreciated.

The Memorial service was conducted by Mrs. J. Ben Eller.

Mr. I. G. Greer brought the morning message.

The afternoon devotional was led by Mrs. Chas. E. Parker.

The Treasurer's report by Mrs. C. E. Siceloff showed a balance of $84.76.

Mrs. W. D. Briggs conducted a Workers' Council.

Mrs. Frank Woodward, Missionary to China, made an appeal for China.

Mrs. J. Clyde Turner presented special objects—Annie Armstrong, Lottie Moon and Fannie Heck offerings, and the $100,000 Club.

On motion of Mrs. H. A. Knight the Union voted to give, in honor of Mrs. Hoge, $150 to furnish a room in the new hospital.

The following officers were elected:

Superintendent	Mrs. Nettie Hoge
Secretary	Mrs. A. Andrews
Treasurer	Mrs. C. E. Siceloff
Personal Service Chairman	Mrs. L. M. Gideon
Mission Study Chairman	Mrs. J. J. Andoe
Stewardship Chairman	Mrs. Grover Jones
Young People's Leader	Miss Ruth Scott

Group Leaders:

Mrs. H. A. Knight	High Point
Mrs. O. J. Howard	Greensboro
Mrs. H. L. Morrison	Reidsville

The next meeting to be held in the Eller Memorial Church, the last Friday in April, 1941.

The meeting closed with an inspirational praise and prayer service.

MRS. A. ANDREWS, Secretary.

IN MEMORIAM

ASHEBORO STREET—
Mrs. J. E. Robbins
Deacon J. N. Cheek
Mrs. R. M. Spoon
Mr. R. M. Spoon
Mr. J. E. Vowell
Mrs. Josie Andrews

BESSEMER—
Mrs. O. S. Purcell
Mrs. J. T. Willett

CALVARY—
Mr. Willie Lee Cole
Mrs. James A. Carter

COLLEGE PARK—
Mr. S. F. Johnson
Rev. J. E. Greene
Deacon Dr. J. T. J. Battle
Miss Donnis Miller
Mr. L. Winfrey

ELLER MEMORIAL—
Mrs. Lazz Caviness
Mrs. Eli Smith
Mr. W. C. Hill
Mr. Dan Beaker
Mrs. Marshall Anderson

FLORIDA STREET—
Mrs. D. F. Harwell

GIBSONVILLE—
Mrs. Jennie Morene

GREENSBORO FIRST—
Mrs. E. Meyers
Mrs. Vincent Bargamin
Mrs. J. H. Combs
Mr. Wade Atkins
Mrs. Lena Coble
Mrs. H. S. Martin
Mr. Geo. F. Daly
Mrs. E. A. Johnson
Mrs. Maude Reitzel
Mrs. Adda Joplin
Mrs. Evelyn Butler
Mr. O. B. Scism
Rev. W. C. Richardson
Mr. R. L. Mitchell
Mrs. Emma H. Gurley
Mr. R. E. Weaver
Mrs. Geo. B. McPherson
Mr. Chas. Grogan
Mr. J. A. Pendergrass
Mr. John Thomas, Deacon
Mrs. H. W. Dettmering
Mrs. B. R. Long
Mr. A. W. Cooke, Deacon

GREEN STREET—
Mr. C. L. Cecil
Mr. D. H. Combs
Mr. T. P. Cates

GUILFORD—
Pastor T. H. Stamey
Deacon J. A. Case

HIGH POINT, FIRST—
Mr. T. P. Hardie
Mrs. F. J. Spearman
Deacon A. E. Tate
Mr. T. F. Wrenn
Mr. J. E. Whichard
Mrs. A. P. Cliatt
Mrs. J. D. Cheves, Jr.

HILLIARD MEMORIAL—
Mr. P. L. Culler, Deacon
Mr. T. L. Morton, Deacon
Mrs. K. F. Moore
Mrs. D. E. Vaughn

LATHAM PARK—
Mr. J. W. Austin

MAGNOLIA STREET—
Deacon H. P. Wray
Mr. A. E. Cain

MOUNT OLIVE —
Mrs. Frank Cantrell
Mrs. R. H. Warf
MOUNT ZION—
Mrs. Fannie Allred
Mrs. Sarah Foster
NORTH MAIN STREET—
Mrs. Martha Boggs
Miss Inez Davis
NORTH PARK—
Miss Beatrice Broadway
Mr. Charlie Elliott
Mrs. Louisa Panther
Mrs. Fannie Wilson
PLEASANT GARDEN—
Mrs. Cora Swain
Mrs. Laura Lenons
POMONA—
Miss May Demmitte
Mr. C. Self
REIDSVILLE, FIRST—
Mrs. W. J. Cardwell
Mrs. H. E. Link
Mrs. J. W. Pillow
Miss Nettie Stephens
Mrs. Mary Terry
Mr. John P. Bennett
Mr. James Robinson, Jr.
Mr. R. B. Gladstone
Mr. Alvin Cook
REVOLUTION—
Mr. Larkin Dixon
Mrs. Amanda Jones
RUFFIN STACEY—
Mr. C. T. Lovelace, Deacon
SIXTEENTH STREET—
Mrs. Mary Carroll
Mrs. Sarah Owens
Mr. N. W. Whittington
Mrs. M. S. Hayden
Mr. Buck Walters
Mrs. Mamie Brown
Mrs. Sallie Southern
SOUTH SIDE—
Mrs. Frye
STEVENS MEMORIAL—
Mrs. Fannie Seymore
SUMMERFIELD—
Mr. Walter Rice
Mrs. Della Ellington
TABERNACLE—
Mrs. W. B. Dixon
Mr. A. A. Hanner
TABERNACLE—
Mr. Frank Hensley
WEST END—
Mrs. Ollie Groce
Mr. B. W. Jenkins, Sr.

TABLE ONE — [redacted]RCH [redacted]HIP

CHURCHES	City Vill., Town, Country	When Constituted	PASTORS AND POST OFFICES	Days of Meeting	CHURCH MEMBERSHIP: Members Reported Last Year	Gains: Baptisms	Gains: Letters	Gains: Statements	Gains: Restorations	Losses: Letters	Losses: Exclusions	Losses: Erasures	Losses: Deaths	Total: Total Present Members	Weekly Prayer Meet's	Revivals Held	Obs. Lord's Supper	Rec. State Bap. Paper
1. Allen Jay	V	1934	C. M. Floyd, Thomasville, R.1	2 4	13[redacted]	22	17	4	...	1	...	..	..	176	*	2	4	6
2. [redacted]h	O	1934	[redacted]in Faull [redacted]r, Reidsville	2 4	66	1	...	1	...	2	...	...	..	66	*	2	2	...
3. Buchanan	O	1886	J. B. Clifton, G'boro, Bessemer, Br.	All	81	11	13	...	...	10	...	2	...	93	*	1	1	...
4. Calvary	O	1901	J. C. Shore, Reidsville, R.4	2 4	158	7	3	...	...	2	...	...	2	164	...	1	...	9
5. Fair Grove	O	1940	A. R. Riddle, [redacted]	All	.....	27	29	5	...	1	...	...	...	60	*	1	1	...
6. Fairview	O	1904	J. C. Shore, Reidsville, R.4	1 3	117	7	2	...	...	1	...	...	...	125	...	...	2	8
7. Fairmont Park	V	1940	J. E. Swinson, Hanes	2 4	52	14	...	15	...	...	...	...	1	80	*	2	...	4
8. Gibsonville	T	1884	E. A. Long, [redacted]n	2 4	249	...	5	...	...	7	...	8	...	239	*	1	4	1
9. Greensboro, First	C	1859	Dr. J. Clyde Turner, Greensboro	All	2172	37	114	5	2	91	12	...	23	2204	*	...	12	124
10. Asheboro Street	C	1899	J. [redacted]n Eller, Greensboro	All	1147	45	30	5	...	37	...	9	6	1175	*	1	4	65
11. Bailey Memorial	C	1935	C. G. [redacted]e, [redacted]	All	103	3	1	...	...	...	...	2	1	104	*	2	10	...
12. Bessemer	V	1923	A. A. Walker, [redacted]o	All	477	15	21	...	1	29	...	3	2	480	*	2	4	4
13. College Park	C	1906	[redacted]n W. Woodcock, [redacted]boro	All	569	6	26	3	1	16	...	6	5	578	*	...	...	35
14. Eller Memorial	C	....	Chas. E. [redacted]r, Greensboro	All	873	21	7	1	...	16	...	1	5	882	*	1	4	64
15. Florida Street	C	1916	J. H. Saunders, Greensboro	All	284	39	30	4	...	7	...	27	1	322	*	1	4	35
16. Latham Park	C	1916	J. [redacted]her Dixon, [redacted]	All	64	...	...	...	...	3	...	...	1	60	...	1	2	...
17. Magnolia Street	C	1912	Grady Burgiss, Greensboro	All	207	3	3	...	...	19	...	4	2	182	*	2	2	11
18. Pomona	V	1906	C. M. Oates, Pomona	All	231	11	6	3	...	8	...	...	2	241	*	2	2	...
19. Revolution	C	1907	H. R. Starling, Greensboro	All	349	22	3	1	1	16	4	24	2	328	*	2	2	3
20. Sixteenth Street	C	1907	W. B. Cook, Greensboro	All	446	18	7	3	5	6	3	...	7	463	*	2	12	...
21. Stevens Memorial	V	1922	B. C. Lamb, Greensboro	All	150	8	1	...	...	15	...	5	1	138	*	1	4	12
22. Tabernacle	C	1938	B. G. [redacted]y, Greensboro	All	182	17	25	15	...	3	...	3	2	231	*	2	3	2
23. [redacted]er [redacted]orial	V	1935	M. L. Hux, Greensboro	All	146	9	2	...	...	3	...	7	...	147	*	...	2	...
24. Guilford	V	1914	O. F. Barnes, Greensboro	1 2 3	72	2	5	1	...	6	...	...	2	72	...	1	1	3
25. High Point, First	C	1825	Dr. A. B. Conrad, High Point	All	1278	54	78	5	...	53	...	...	7	1355	*	1	4	77

26. Green Street	C	1900	J. S. Hopkins, High Point	All	1381	17	10	...	...	61	...	...	3	1344	*	...	4	58
27. Hilliard Memorial	C	1929	Hughey O. Miller, High Point	All	301	40	14	...	...	16	...	4	4	331	*	2	2	18
28. North Main Street	C	1908	A. Lincoln Fulk, High Point	All	290	29	16	1	...	2	...	...	2	332	*	1	3	18
29. North Park	C	1929	E. M. Smith, High Point	All	232	9	3	...	2	4	...	48	4	190	*	2	4	15
30. South Side	C	1916	G. H. Liner, High Point	All	332	3	3	1	...	19	...	1	1	318	*	2	4	...
31. West End	C	1913	T. H. Biles, High Point	All	377	27	18	1	...	10	...	6	2	405	*	1	4	3
32. Jessup Grove	O	1933	...	...	...	...	...	...	...	...	...	...	...	...	...	...	...	...
33. Lebanon	O	1911	Melvin Faulkner, Reidsville	All	120	28	18	7	8	1	...	...	...	190	*	2	4	...
34. Mount Zion	O	1826	J. T. Swinson, High Point, R.3	2 4	164	5	...	...	...	1	...	...	2	166	...	1	1	10
35. Oak Grove	O	1916	R. L. Smith, High Point	All	162	21	2	3	...	30	9	2	...	147	*	2	4	...
36. Osborne Chapel	O	1934	C. W. Myrick, [illegible]o, R.1	1	54	...	1	...	...	2	...	...	...	53	*	2	2	...
37. Osceola	O	....	J. F. Sellars, White Plains	1 3	78	3	...	...	...	...	...	...	...	81	*	2	2	1
38. Pine Grove	O	1938	T. H. Myers, High Point, R.3	All	32	34	15	...	...	6	...	...	...	75	...	...	...	...
39. Pisgah	C	1937	W. L. Smith, High Point	All	91	82	38	15	...	...	...	1	...	225	*	2	4	...
40. Pleasant Garden	V	1933	J. [illegible]er Dixon, Greensboro	All	111	8	3	1	...	7	...	...	2	117	*	1	3	...
41. Pleasant Grove	O	1938	J. M. Allred, Pomona	All	86	4	...	2	...	2	...	...	...	90	*	2	10	...
42. Reedy Fork	O	1940	L. J. Hight, [illegible]o	All	.....	...	14	2	...	...	...	...	...	16	...	...	...	...
43. Reidsville, First	C	1844	T. L. Sasser, Reidsville	All	847	24	23	5	...	20	...	...	9	870	*	1	4	54
44. Mount Olive	C	1929	W. I. [illegible]son, Reidsville	All	221	23	3	5	...	3	...	34	2	214	*	2	2	14
45. Penn Memorial	C	1927	D. W. Overby, Reidsville	All	191	3	2	21	...	3	...	...	...	214	*	1	4	...
46. Rocky Knoll	C	1934	L. C. Chandler, [illegible]o, R.1	All	184	16	14	2	...	4	...	...	...	212	*	2	...	4
47. Ruffin Stacey	C	1931	J. T. [illegible], Reidsville, R.5	All	186	...	...	...	...	6	1	1	1	159	*	2	4	3
48. Smith Grove	C	1921	R. O. Nuckles, [illegible]n, R.1	1 3	161	11	4	...	...	1	...	...	1	170	*	2	4	...
49. Summerfield	V	....	E. A. Long, Germanton	1	214	3	...	...	...	13	...	1	2	201	...	1	3	10
50. Tabernacle	V	1933	H. P. Gauldin, Altamahaw	All	68	5	6	3	...	...	...	...	1	81	*	2	...	...
51. Temple	O	1939	Ben S. McDowell, High Point	.....	.....	...	...	...	...	...	...	...	...	40	...	...	...	...
TOTALS	..	....	....	.....	15490	804	635	140	...	563	29	199	108	16206	...	...	...	671

43

TABLE TWO — SUNDAY SCHOOLS

CHURCHES	SUPERINTENDENTS AND POST OFFICES	Cradle Roll Under 3	Beginners 3-5 Years	Primaries 6-8 Years	Juniors 9-12 Years	Intermediates 13-16	Young People 17-24	Adults 25 and Up	Extension Dept.	Departmen al Officers	Total Enrollment	Average Attendance	Baptisms from S. S.	Is School Graded?	Teachers Hold'g. Dip.	Enrollment V. S.	Av. Attendance V. S.
1. [illegible]n Jay	Wade H. [illegible]e, High Point, R.1	7	20	30	51	40	42	127	...	12	329	212	22	*	...	....	....
2. Antioch	Ray Moore, Reidsville, R.2	...	....	11	....	....	35	30	...	...	76	35	...	...	...	....	....
3. Buchanan	R. M. [illegible]e, Greensboro, R.5	...	46	....	23	21	34	52	...	...	176	90	...	...	...	....	....
4. Calvary	[illegible]o. Gunn, Reidsville, R.4	...	12	19	20	21	48	84	...	...	204	95	6	...	...	....	....
5. Fair Grove	S. G. Alvis, Greensboro, R.2	...	....	....	....	....	....	....	...	...	....	....	...	...	...	....	....
6. Fairview	A. D. Hopkins, Reidsville, R.1	...	10	17	27	26	25	19	...	...	124	64	6	...	...	....	....
7. Fairmont Park	O. E. Snow, Thomasville, R.1	16	15	15	30	8	8	48	...	8	148	72	30	...	...	92	73
8. Gibsonville	C. C. Hammer, Gibsonville	...	14	18	34	35	43	65	16	...	225	150	...	...	9	....	....
9. Greensboro, First	O. E. Lee, Greensboro	184	93	136	236	225	255	1037	222	47	2435	929	30	*	4	139	100
10. Asheboro Street	M. D. Teague, Greensboro	50	54	118	161	153	135	407	60	4	1142	513	...	*	10	110	80
11. Bailey Memorial	E. J. Jarvis, Greensboro	...	21	....	15	19	59	21	...	...	135	....	3	...	...	....	....
12. Bessemer	H. M. Lloyd, Greensboro, R.5	63	28	45	60	56	33	124	...	10	419	213	15	*	...	....	..
13. College Park	B. B. Stockard, Greensboro	30	24	36	56	77	109	166	...	5	503	278	...	*	...	80	51
14. Eller [illegible]rial	G. O. Barringer, Greensboro	19	46	105	129	101	78	274	17	13	782	380	...	*	...	317	301
15. Florida Street	J. B. Rumby, Sr., [illegible]o	21	48	61	70	77	58	151	...	12	498	282	29	*	5	144	110
16. Latham Park	R. A. Anderson, Greensboro	...	....	....	....	....	....	....	...	...	....	....	...	...	...	....	....
17. Magnolia Street	H. S. Noah, [illegible]	15	12	36	22	29	27	86	...	3	230	133	...	*	2	56	40
18. Pomona	C. C. Patterson, Pomona	...	35	38	47	46	79	64	...	13	322	219	...	*	...	45	43
19. Revolution	Grady Phillips, Greensboro	40	19	39	49	56	48	97	15	5	368	200	...	*	3	107	74
20. Sixteenth Street	Fred Hester, Greensboro	15	37	65	83	65	71	186	...	8	530	338	...	...	2	205	155
21. Stevens [illegible]al	L. A. Mills, Greensboro	3	8	15	25	32	25	52	...	13	173	135	...	*	...	....	....
22. Tabernacle	W. O. Smith	36	25	25	31	34	27	50	20	5	253	124	8	*	...	108	80
23. Webster Memorial	T. P. Pearman, Greensboro	10	15	9	24	20	25	48	...	3	154	115	...	*	...	35	25
24. Guilford	Setzer Weston, Greensboro	...	6	4	4	12	15	20	...	8	69	61	2	...	...	....	....
25. High Point, First	Dr. W. F. Clayton, High Point	64	53	110	193	143	157	459	50	4	1233	650	51	*	12	....	....

26. Green Street	W. E. Crissman, High Point	30	50	108	180	175	161	436	...	3	1143	537	...	*	...	329	290
27. Hilliard Memorial	L. E. Edwards, High Point	19	25	17	48	40	30	65	...	6	250	....	38	*	...	65	63
28. North Main Street	Tom Lamar, High Point	9	25	36	59	25	108	64	...	4	330	243	29	*	...	....	....
29. North Park	L. R. McNeill, High Point	23	14	26	56	31	27	73	3	4	257	169	9	*	...	....	....
30. South Side	Huston Williams, High Point	...	15	19	41	20	67	55	...	6	223	138	...	*	...	....	....
31. West End	Vernon Coffey, High Point	42	27	30	68	35	59	81	30	22	394	198	21	*	5	....	....
32. Jessup Grove	....	...	....	....	....	....	....	....	...	...	....	....	...	...	...	....	....
33. Lebanon	Jim McDaniels, Greensboro, R.5	9	20	17	23	25	42	71	...	...	207	142	...	*	...	....	....
34. Mount Zion	Geo. H. Spoon, Liberty, R.3	...	30	....	17	....	29	25	...	6	107	47	5	...	...	....	....
35. Oak Grove	A. L. Saunders, High Point, R.4	...	9	18	21	....	35	32	...	...	115	72	21	...	...	....	....
36. Osborne Chapel	Mr. Law, Greensboro, R.1	...	....	29	12	....	34	28	12	...	115	61	...	*	...	....	....
37. Osceola	D. A. Greene, Brown Summit, R.1	...	7	7	11	22	16	22	...	11	96	54	...	*	...	....	....
38. Pine Grove	Johnnie Bryan, High Point, R.3	...	23	20	16	40	34	65	...	9	207	150	20	*	...	....	....
39. Pisgah	F. P. Vaughn, High Point	...	10	47	27	86	70	134	...	...	374	180	...	...	...	....	....
40. Pleasant Garden	Walter J. Smith, Greensboro	7	17	12	16	10	27	30	...	11	130	62	8	*	...	....	....
41. Pleasant Grove	F. M. Atkins, Greensboro, R.3	20	....	14	21	25	32	33	...	...	145	85	...	*	...	....	....
42. Reedy Fork	Alvin L. Bullard, Greensboro	...	....	....	....	....	....	....	...	...	....	....	...	...	...	....	....
43. Reidsville, First	R. T. Burton, Reidsville	46	36	51	84	89	96	380	50	46	878	328	23	*	...	130	87
44. Mount Olive	Odell Delapp, Reidsville	7	27	12	43	33	9	54	..	7	192	120	15	*	...	....	....
45. Penn Memorial	W. Herbert Ford, Reidsville	...	22	15	17	11	50	55	...	2	172	125	...	...	...	....	....
46. Rocky Knoll	R. R. Sudderth, Greensboro, R.2	40	16	14	17	60	17	108	...	12	284	180	...	...	...	....	....
47. Ruffin Stacey	....	...	10	15	30	20	30	40	..	14	159	91	...	*	...	....	....
48. Smith Grove	Walter Westmoreland, High Point	...	....	....	....	....	....	....	..	...	....	....	...	...	...	....	....
49. Summerfield	Marian Ayers, Summerfield	...	9	18	20	33	29	45	..	...	154	72	3	...	...	....	....
50. Tabernaele	W. F. Collins, Burlington, R.4	...	24	....	17	....	32	33	...	...	106	65	...	...	...	....	....
51. Temple		...	....	....	....	....	....	....	...	...	59	....	...	...	...	....	....
TOTALS	....	825	1057	1477	2234	2076	2470	5596	495	336	16625	8407	394	...	52	1962	1572

TABLE THREE — BAPTIST TRAINING UNION

CHURCHES	DIRECTORS AND POST OFFICES	Adult Unions	Young People's Unions	Intermediate Unions	Junior Unions	Story Hours	Total Unions, St. Hrs.	Adults Enrolled	Young People Enrolled	Intermediates Enr'l'd.	Juniors Enrolled	Story Hours Enrolled	Total Enrolled Unions	No. Daily Bible R'd'rs.	No. Taking St. C'rse.	Tot. Systematic Givers		Students in College
1. Allen Jay	Thomas Knight, High Point	1	1	1	1	1	5	19	9	20	25	6	79	52	53	73	...	...
2. Gibsonville		...	1	1	1	...	3	...	21	10	19	...	50	16	20	27	...	1
3. Greensboro, First	O. E. Lee, Gboro	2	3	4	3	1	13	38	75	80	68	21	282	75	33	162	...	6
4. Asheboro Street	C. W. McLees, Greensboro	...	2	2	2	1	7	...	55	64	48	12	179	35	42	57	...	4
5. Bailey Memorial	Roland Mitchell, [illegible]	...	1	1	1	...	3	...	12	9	14	...	35	16	20	31	...	...
6. Bessemer	Miss Norfleet Dixon, Gboro	1	1	1	1	1	5	10	14	30	18	6	78	15	32	....	...	...
7. College Park	J. W. Watson, E. W. Richardson	1	2	1	1	...	5	12	53	14	11	...	90	21	48	66	...	...
8. Eller Memorial	Howard May, Greensboro	1	1	1	2	1	6	26	15	15	39	22	117	19	29	48	...	1
9. Florida Street	H. M. Cassell, Gboro	2	1	2	2	1	8	29	18	22	24	15	108	59	56	74	2	...
10. Magnolia Street	Mrs. G. H. Williamson, Gboro	1	1	1	...	1	4	22	10	19	...	15	66	10	12	22	...	...
11. Pomona	Mrs. Lois Rierson, Pomona	...	1	...	...	...	1	...	11	...	...	...	11	...	6	....	...	...
12. Revolution	A. A. Rogers, Greensboro	1	1	1	...	1	4	12	12	29	...	12	65	18	20	25	...	...
13. Sixteenth Street	Harry Moore, Greensboro	...	1	1	1	1	4	...	16	27	17	8	68	22	43	31	...	...
14. Tabernacle	Mrs. Howard Phillips, Greensboro	1	1	1	1	1	5	16	6	12	18	...	47	28	25	31	...	...
15. High Point, First	W. O. Burnham, High Point	...	1	2	3	1	7	5	18	69	107	20	219	70	73	70	...	4
16. Green Street	Burgess Leonard, High Point	...	2	1	2	1	6	...	36	14	35	12	97	30	60	40	...	3
17. Hilliard Memorial	Hubert Williard, High Point	1	1	1	1	1	5	18	10	18	19	10	75	35	...	34	...	3
18. North Main	W. L. Woodell, High Point, R.2	1	1	1	1	1	5	11	10	10	18	5	54	24	21	42	...	...
19. North Park	W. H. Brock, High Point	1	1	2	2	2	8	23	16	35	19	15	108	49	62	72	...	...
20. West End	R. G. Barlowe, High Point	1	1	1	2	1	6	17	16	14	47	6	100	19	32	34	...	...
21. Pleasant Garden	....	...	1	...	1	...	2	...	14	...	12	...	26	6	13	11	...	...
22. Reidsville, First	W. O. Kelley, Reidsville	1	2	2	2	...	7	19	43	40	40	...	142	36	39	54	...	2
23. Mount Olive	B. J. Harvey, Reidsville	1	1	1	1	1	5	12	7	11	15	4	49	12	21	39	...	...
24. Penn Memorial	C. D. Barker, Jr., Reidsville	1	1	1	1	...	4	15	10	6	15	...	46	25	28	17	...	...
25. Rocky Knoll	Ray Chandler, Greensboro	1	1	1	1	1	5	16	14	19	17	16	82	24	...	35	...	...
26. Summerfield	....	...	1	1	1	...	3	...	12	14	12	...	38	22	...	12	...	...
TOTALS	....	19	32	32	34	19	136	315	533	601	657	205	2311	738	788	1107	2	25

TABLE FOUR [illegible]MAN'S MISSIONARY UNION

CHURCHES	PRESIDENTS OF W. M. S. AND POST OFFICES	No. W. M. Societies	No. of Y. W. A.'s	Number of G. A.'s	Number of R. A.'s	Number of Sunbeams	Total W. M. U. Org's.	W. M. S. Members	Y. W. A.'s Members	G. A.'s Members	R. A.'s Members	Sunbeam Members.	Tot. Members Enr'led	Total Enr'led M. S. C.	Contributions (Local Work) by W. M. U.	Contributions (Missions) by W. M. U	Total Given by W. M. U. and its Orgs.
1. Calvary	[illegible] J. E. McCargo, Reidsville, R.4	1	1	...	...	...	2	31	23	...	...	...	54	....	33.01	102.27	135,28
2. Fair ([illegible]	Mrs. Ella Harris, Greensboro	1	...	...	...	...	1	28	...	...	...	...	28	....	....	....	....
3. Fairview	Mrs. Frances Colman, Reidsville, R.2	1	...	...	...	...	1	11	...	...	...	...	11	....	....	....	....
4. Gibsonville	Mrs. E. C. Riggins, Gibsonville	1	...	...	...	...	1	25	...	...	...	...	25	....	....	30.00	30.00
5. Greensboro, First	Mrs. S. R. Webb, Greensboro	1	2	2	2	1	8	417	51	77	93	92	730	151	....	13513.07	13513.07
6. [illegible] Street	Mrs. E. R. Baldwin, Greensboro, R.2	1	2	2	1	1	7	172	45	35	10	10	272	129	....	1854.34	1854.34
9. Bailey Memorial	Mrs. E. R. Mitchell, [illegible]	1	...	...	...	...	1	12	...	...	...	...	12	....	12.00	4.50	16.50
8. Bessemer	Mrs. J. R. Medlin, [illegible]	1	...	1	...	1	3	41	...	18	...	40	99	11	18.21	214.24	232.45
9. College Park	Mrs. J. W. Marsh, Greensboro	1	2	...	...	1	4	47	58	...	...	16	121	79	....	251.25	251.25
10. Eller Memorial	Mrs. Ethel Morrison, [illegible]boro	1	1	1	1	1	5	36	22	16	12	12	98	110	317.37	151.60	468.97
11. Florida Street	Mrs. J. T. Watts, Greensboro	1	...	2	1	1	5	83	...	35	13	30	161	45	....	2 4970	249.70
12. Magnolia Street	Mrs. Grady Burgess, Greensboro	2	1	1	...	1	5	24	9	11	...	35	79	....	....	132.90	132.90
13. Pomona	Mrs. W. H. Brown, Pomona	1	...	1	...	1	3	42	...	21	...	45	108	....	....	65.00	65.00
14. Revolution	Mrs. H. R. Starling, Greensboro	1	1	1	1	1	5	43	8	20	5	23	99	19	....	229.82	229.82
15. Sixteenth Street	Mrs. W. A. Straughn, Greensboro	1	1	1	1	1	5	34	20	18	...	25	97	27	....	252.44	252.44
16. [illegible]ns Memorial	Mrs. J. H. Ham, Greensboro, R.2	1	...	...	...	...	1	30	...	...	...	...	30	....	....	109.65	109.65
17. Tabernacle	Mrs. E. C. White, Sr., Greensboro	1	1	1	...	1	4	22	10	8	...	15	55	24	1223.02	39.45	1262.47
18. Webster Memorial	Miss Selma Scales, Greensboro, R.5	1	1	2	...	1	5	41	11	21	...	15	88	....	....	311.34	311.34
19. Guilford	Mrs. Alice Farrell, Guilford	1	...	...	...	1	2	14	...	...	...	12	26	....	1.97	27.15	29.12
20. High Point, First	Mrs. G. H. Jones, High Point	1	1	2	2	1	7	240	18	49	39	54	400	251	700.00	3541.42	4241.42
21. [illegible]en Street	Mrs. T. C. Robbins, High Point	1	2	2	1	1	7	95	35	40	10	12	192	120	3302.42	511.49	3813.91
22. Hilliard Memorial	Mrs. J. B. Ellis, High Point	1	1	1	1	1	5	19	13	8	5	20	65	23	19.66	53.96	73.62
23. North Main	Mrs. H. S. Smith, High Point	1	...	1	...	...	2	15	...	23	...	...	38	....	30.02	105.00	135.02
24. North Park	Mrs. J. A. Jones, High Point	1	1	2	1	1	6	17	14	23	12	7	73	91	960.64	173.34	1133.98
25. S[illegible]th Side	Mrs. F. E. Caudle, High Point	1	...	1	...	...	2	20	...	30	...	...	50	17	54.48	7.21	61.69
26. West End	Mrs. R. T. Presslar, High Point	2	...	2	1	1	6	25	...	25	...	20	70	50	....	137.40	137.40
27. Lebanon	Mrs. S. R. Colman, Greensboro, R.5	1	...	...	...	...	1	10	...	...	...	...	10	....	....	15.00	15.00
28. Pleasant Garden	Mrs. Ira Anderson, Greensboro, R.1	1	...	...	...	...	1	20	...	...	...	...	20	....	7.50	5.36	12.86
29. Pleasant Grove	Mrs. W. A. Kenan, [illegible]boro, R.3	1	...	...	...	...	1	14	...	...	...	...	14	....	....	4.00	4.00
30. Reidsville, First	Mrs. R. T. Burton, Reidsville	1	1	...	...	1	3	163	24	...	...	43	230	84	3203.92	1196.91	4400.83
31. Mount Olive	Mrs. D. P. Driscold, Reidsville	6	...	...	...	...	6	78	...	...	...	...	78	25	....	314.95	314.95
32. Penn [illegible]rial	Mrs. Elsie Gailey, Reidsville	1	1	...	...	...	2	42	12	...	...	...	54	15	44.25	33.35	77.60
33. Rocky Knoll	Mrs. E. F. Wrenn, Greensboro, R.1	2	1	...	...	...	3	20	7	...	...	...	27	....	41.42	23.60	65.02
34. Summerfield	Mrs. Myrtle Smith, Summerfield	1	...	...	...	...	1	17	...	...	...	...	17	....	....	125.19	125.19
TOTALS	....	42	21	26	13	19	121	1948	380	478	199	526	3531	1271	9969.89	23786.90	33756.79

TABLE FIVE — [illegible]

CHURCHES	CHURCH CLERKS AND POST OFFICES	Own House Worship?	When Was It Built?	Materials Used	Persons Seated	Number of Rooms	Dept. Assembly Rooms	No. Sep. Class Rooms	Value Church House and Grounds	Value Mission Chapel If Any	Value Pastor's Home	Total Value of All Church Property	Indebtedness on All Church Property	Insurance Carried
1. Allen Jay	Miss [illegible] Younts, Trinity, Rt. 3	*	1936	Wood	300	10	9	9	3000	....	.....	3000	....	2000
2. [illegible]	[illegible] Hobert Carter, Reidsville	*	1935	Wood	300	1	...	...	1200	....	.....	1200	....	800
3. Buchanan	R. P. Johnson, Greensboro, Rt. 6	*	1886	Wood	150	5	...	4	3000	....	.....	3250	225.00	1500
4. [illegible]	J. E. [illegible], Reidsville, Rt. 2	*	1898	Wood	275	5	4	...	5000	....	2000	7000	....	2000
5. Fair [illegible]	[illegible] A. L. [illegible], Greensboro, Rt. 2	*	1940	Brick	250	1	...	...	3000	....	.....	3000	500.00	1500
6. Fairview	William Cummings, Reidsville, Rt. 2	*	1901	Wood	300	5	...	4	2250	....	.....	2250	....	1500
7. Fairmont Park	J. S. [illegible], High Point	*	1940	Wood	260	1	...	...	1200	....	.....	1350	....	.....
8. Gibsonville	W. P. Killette, Gibsonville	*	1884	Wood	300	9	9	9	2500	....	.....	2500	....	2000
9. [illegible], First	George Bennett, [illegible]	*	1906	Brick	1000	48	...	...	145000	....	15000	160000	....	70000
10. Asheboro Street	J. B. Wills, Greensboro	*	1912	Brick	700	61	10	69	51000	....	6000	57000	14000.00	43000
11. Bailey Memorial	E. J. Jarvis, Greensboro	*	1935	Wood	250	1	1	6	1300	....	.....	1300	....	700
12. Bessemer	[illegible]	*	1923	Wood	350	16	2	16	5500	....	2000	7500	500.24	4500
13. College Park	Carroll O. Weaver, [illegible]	*	1940	Brick	300	57	8	42	55000	....	8000	63500	15000.00	48500
14. Eller Memorial	[illegible] L. Thornburg, [illegible]	*	1925	Brick	750	53	7	51	43000	....	9000	52000	....	30000
15. Florida Street	Miss Eleanor [illegible], [illegible]	*	1930	Brick	350	23	2	22	15000	....	4500	19500	2500.00	13000
16. Latham Park	W. W. Sutton, Greensboro	..	....	.....	....	..	..	..	.....	....	.....	.....	....	.....
17. [illegible] Street	[illegible] G. H. Williamson, Greensboro	*	1912	Wood	300	9	12	8	6000	....	4000	10000	2346.72	6000
18. Pomona	C. C. Patterson, Pomona	*	1906	Wood	350	8	...	8	3000	....	.....	3000	....	.....
19. Revolution	N. C. Brown, [illegible]	*	1907	Wood	400	5	3	7	10000	....	5000	15000	....	7500
20. [illegible] Street	[illegible] E. Whitt, Greensboro	*	1907	Brick	500	23	2	16	39000	....	.....	39000	....	18000
21. Stevens Memorial	Mrs. J. B. Brown, [illegible], Rt. 2	*	1922	Wood	250	11	2	13	10000	....	2500	12500	180.00	7500
22. [illegible]	Mrs. E. C. White, Jr., [illegible]	*	1938	Wood	200	3	...	2	3000	....	.....	3000	958.76	2000
23. Webster Memorial	Albert West, [illegible], Rt. 5	*	1936	Wood	300	10	2	8	5500	....	.....	5500	....	2500
24. Guilford	R. F. Bondurant, Guilford College	*	1914	Br.-V.	200	1	4	...	3500	300	.....	3900	....	1500
25. High Point, First	C. D. [illegible], High Point	*	1905	Brick	880	49	7	46	110000	....	8000	128000	21703.83	55000

26. Green Street	Clyde Ayers, High Point	*	1926	Brick	1500	96	6	68	156000	1500	2500	160000	31000.00	60000
27. Hilliard Memorial	J. W. Saunders, High Point	*	1931	Brick	800	...	...	22	25000	400	.....	29000	1330.00	5000
28. North Main Street	Annie Lawson, High Point	*	1924	Brick	350	23	6	17	17000	....	.....	17000	1650.00	8000
29. North Park	H. B. Chatham, High Point	*	1929	Wood	300	17	1	16	3500	....	.....	3500	....	1500
30. South Side	J. G. Williams, High Point	*	1916	Wood	350	11	...	10	3500	....	.....	3500	....	.....
31. [illegible]st End	Mrs. O. H. Clodfelter, High Point	*	1913	Wood	350	24	2	20	9500	....	2500	12000	....	5000
32. Jessup Grove	....	..	....	.....	....	...	...	...	.....	....	.....	.....	....	.....
33. Lebanon	Maggie Kirkman, McLeansville, Rt. 1	*	1911	Wood	350	7	1	7	3500	....	.....	3500	....	1800
34. Mount Zion	George H. Spoon, Liberty, Rt. 3	*	1911	Wood	500	1	...	...	2000	....	.....	2000	....	.....
35. Oak Grove	G. K. [illegible]rs, High Point	*	1927	Wood	270	7	...	6	2500	....	.....	2500	271.71	1400
36. Osborne Chapel	R. R. Osborne, Greensboro, Rt. 3	*	1934	Wood	250	1	...	...	1600	....	.....	1600	27.00	.....
37. Osceola	T. J. Brooks, Brown Summit	*	1915	Wood	300	1	...	...	1500	....	.....	1650	....	.....
38. Pine Grove	E. H. Eller, High Point, Rt. 4	*	1938	Wood	300	5	...	5	2000	....	.....	2000	185.06	1000
39. Pisgah	Clyde Lawing, High Point	*	1939	Wood	400	4	...	4	0007	....	.....	7000	....	3000
40. Pleasant Garden	Ira F. [illegible]n, Greensboro	*	1917	Wood	220	1	...	...	1800	....	.....	1800	....	1000
41. Pleasant Grove	D. R. Robertson, Greensboro, Rt. 3	*	1920	Wood	350	...	...	...	1800	....	.....	1800	720.00	1400
42. Reedy Fork	Alvin L. Bullard, Greensboro	..	....	.....	....	...	...	...	250	....	.....	514	....	.....
43. Reidsville, First	T. L. [illegible]r, Reidsville	*	1871	Brick	550	24	5	20	37000	....	14000	51000	....	43500
44. Mount Olive	Mrs. [illegible]a Baker, Reidsville	*	1929	Wood	300	13	2	13	5000	....	.....	5000	....	4000
45. Penn Memorial	James Overby, Reidsville	*	1935	Brick	300	13	...	11	10000	....	1500	11500	2200.00	6000
46. Rocky Knoll	R. O. Creede, Greensboro, Rt. 1	*	1934	Wood	250	9	8	8	2800	....	.....	3000	....	2500
47. Ruffin Stacey	R. M. Durham, Reidsville	..	....	.....	....	...	...	...	1800	....	.....	1800	....	1800
48. Smith Grove	Dovie Clark, Jamestown, Rt. 1	*	1923	.....	300	1	...	...	2000	....	500	2500	....	600
49. Summerfield	Mrs. Myrtle Smith, Summerfield	*	....	Wood	400	...	...	7	8388	....	.....	8388	....	3500
50. Tabernacle	[illegible]ie Roach, Elon College	*	1933	Wood	350	1	...	...	1500	....	.....	1500	119.00	.....
51. Temple	Mrs. R. L. Rodden	..	....	.....	....	...	...	...	1225	....	.....	1225	153.50	.....
TOTALS	....	..	....	.....	....	...	...	...	835113	2200	87000	939527	95570.82	471500

TABLE SIX GIFTS FOR LOCAL CHURCH WORK

CHURCHES	REGULAR TREASURERS AND POST OFFICES	Pastor's Salary	Other Salaries	Ministerial Help and Supply	Building and Repairs	Debt and Interest	Incidentals	Literature for Sunday School and B. Y. P. U. and W. M. S.	Help Given to Local Poor	For Printing the Minutes and Clerk of Association	Other Objects	Total for Local Purposes Given by the Church and its Orgs.	Pledged to Association
1. Allen Jay	W. R. Hobson, High Point, Rt. 1	746.00	....	154.50	....	332.28	354.27	172.83	217.02	....	263.62	2240.52	50.00
2. Antioch	Roy Vanter, Reidsville, Rt. 2	179.70	....		....	....	13.75	25.50	20.00	....	....	238.95	....
3. Buchanan	R. P. Johnson, Greensboro, Rt. 6	390.00	....	35.00	468.20	343.20	55.10	56.70	4.00	3.00	20.41	1375.61	26.00
4. Calvary	J. F. Carroll, Reidsville, Rt. 4	300.00	....	54.80	....	....	45.24	40.84	3.00	....	57.57	501.45	....
5. Fair Grove	W. L. Lee, [illegible]ro, Rt. 2	50.00	....	41.00	....	1050.56	15.00	16.77	3.50	....	....	1176.83	....
6. Fairview	D. E. Trantham, Reidsville, Rt. 2	200.00	....	55.28	64.32	....	30.[illegible]	24.85	5.00	3.00	24.50	407.35	....
7. Fairmont Park	H. J. Willard, Thomasville, Rt. 1	380.00	....	19.56	....	....	59.77	43.40	75.00	....	....	577.73	....
8. Gibsonville	T. L. Roberson, Gibsonville	600.00	....	49.00	4.00	....	176.83	111.43	3.00	....	23.00	967.26	....
9. Greensboro, First	Howard [illegible]er, Greensboro	4600.00	5786.25	120.00	18704.44	....	4546.39	1847.97	1017.22	30.00	3136.54	39788.81	....
10. [illegible]o Street	R. R. Todd, Greensboro	3363.91	1030.00	270.00	242.33	2575.27	1244.82	671.85	152.77	12.50	819.15	10382.60	....
11. Bailey Memorial	Bill Stevens, Greensboro	1055.02	....	74.96	....	172.68	52.80	65.00	12.00	4.00	46.71	1483.17	70.00
12. Bessemer	C. L. Murray, Greensboro	1560.00	....	161.00	1255.46	363.69	250.36	261.84	43.44	5.00	53.21	3954.00	....
13. College Park	L. E. Ogburn, Greensboro	2204.66	220.00	....	5290.41	....	1821.67	297.05	....	12.50	....	9846.29	1200.00
14. Eller Memorial	Mrs. Robert Burgess	2690.00	483.15	175.00	1292.19	....	733.15	698.59	122.19	10.00	430.28	6634.55	....
15. Florida Street	Mrs. D. M. Frazier, Greensboro	2120.00	30.00	70.00	1356.34	1004.05	702.58	472.15	12.00	5.00	482.98	6255.10	....
16. Latham Park	W. W. Sutton, Greensboro	....	....	....	....	....	....	....	....	....	....	387.00	....
17. Magnolia Street	H. S. Noah, Greensboro	1300.00	....	89.61	197.98	675.81	467.49	102.80	70.58	3.00	262.48	3169.75	....
18. Pomona	E. E. Henry, Pomona	1549.50	....	130.00	227.94	....	160.50	99.93	147.66	3.00	77.57	2396.10	....
19. Revolution	Waldo Johnson	1725.00	....	137.44	11.73	....	311.16	175.36	52.92	5.26	251.55	2670.42	....
20. Sixteenth Street	L. F. Paris, Greensboro	2090.00	....	90.00	....	....	663.82	150.15	18.04	5.00	61.00	3078.01	....
21. Stevens Memorial	Mrs. C. B. Brisson, Greensboro, Rt. 2	1530.00	40.00	96.01	49.32	406.00	310.95	82.22	....	4.00	22.66	2541.16	....
22. Tabernacle	E. H. Moore, Greensboro	1820.00	....	163.20	....	819.42	488.78	206.98	147.29	5.00	141.74	3792.41	....
23. Webster Memorial	R. H. King, Greensboro	978.50	....	....	5.65	....	182.29	99.03	350.00	5.00	18.10	1638.57	300.00
24. Guilford	W. L. Hudson, Guilford	314.50	....	10.00	....	....	62.00	40.85	....	2.00	41.00	470.35	50.00
25. High Point, First	Miss Thelma Patrick, High Point	3525.00	1770.00	305.00	140.31	8015.95	3676.62	936.26	252.25	33.00	538.48	19192.87	....

26. Green Street	R. R. Holder, High Point	2367.90	511.20	43.70		4184.08	1224.18	484.38	210.00			
27. Hilliard Memorial	J. W. Metcalf, High Point	1656.10		97.45	87.67	547.79	405.65	226.25	30.50	3.00	65.71	
28. North Main Street	W. C. Ward, High Point, Rt. 1	1820.00		109.58	167.00	888.86	508.74	299.99	40.00	3.00	338.40	
29. North Park	L. W. Glenn, High Point	1504.00		101.32	122.69		176.41	178.33	12.25	4.50	847.15	
30. South Side	J. G. Williams, High Point	1521.64		101.90	125.90		191.58	79.02	25.00	3.00	32.00	
31. West End	C. M. Scott, High Point	1477.90		81.54	51.42	200.00	356.74	183.13	26.11	4.00	238.04	
32. Jessup Grove												
33. Lebanon	L. R. Chilton, Brown Summit, Rt. 2	1185.00		53.77			193.94	59.74	45.00			
34. Mount Zion	Mrs. C. M. Johnson, Burlington, Rt. 4	350.00		40.00	63.00			21.13		6.00		
35. Oak Grove	W. L. Shackelford, High Point, Rt. 3	401.00		11.25	329.29	212.61	35.00	40.00	40.00	2.00		
36. Osborne Chapel	Mr. Whitaker, Greensboro, Rt. 1	120.00					8.85	22.42	3.62	2.00		
37. Osceola	Mrs. D. A. Greene, Brown Sum't, Rt. 1	323.90		128.84	.50		19.30	42.11	1.00		28.92	
38. Pine Grove	L. R. Tuttle, High Point, Rt. 3	180.00				371.78	60.00	60.00	25.00		25.00	
39. Pisgah	L. C. Madden, High Point	960.08		87.31	3200.00		68.50	80.00	100.00	2.00		
40. Pleasant Garden	Cecil Burton, Pleasant Garden	205.00	7.00	21.81	15.00	79.56	46.56	79.75		1.00	52.81	
41. Pleasant Grove	D. R. Robertson, Greensboro, Rt. 3	169.27		39.39	145.82	165.00	122.53	32.07				
42. Reedy Fork	Mrs. W. T. Smith, Brown Sum't, Rt. 2											
43. Reidsville, First	J. P. Kemp, Reidsville	3000.00	1525.00	298.78	306.50		1243.44	449.21	765.74	10.00	495.78	
44. Mount Olive	Mrs. Odell Delapp, Reidsville	1639.50		220.00	1249.24		335.91	162.13	10.00	2.00	41.69	
45. Penn Memorial	Thos. G. Dixon, Reidsville	1300.00		61.70	1871.98	152.00	153.66	123.79	28.15	2.00	193.16	
46. Rocky Knoll	Mrs. R. A. Laughlin, Greensboro, Rt. 1	600.00		62.00	532.69		144.73	161.29	34.00		61.29	
47. Ruffin Stacey	Mrs. Lottie Schrum, Ruffin	350.00			450.00		68.50	65.00		2.00	150.00	
48. Smith Grove	Drew Smith, Jamestown, Rt. 1	84.46		60.85	4.00		12.83	8.61	32.95	2.00	53.35	
49. Summerfield	Mrs. Hettie Shields, Summerfield	360.00		40.00	3.00		129.11	67.67		5.00		
50. Tabernacle	W. E. Collons, Burlington, Rt. 4	452.60		82.32			108.45					
51. Temple												
TOTALS		57300.14	11402.60	4044.87	38036.32	22560.59	22040.35	9626.37	4158.20	203.76	9395.85	17

TABLE SEVEN — MISSIONS, EDUCATION, AND ALL BENEVOLENCES

CHURCHES	Total to Cooperative Program	Special to Associational Missions	Special to State Missions	Special to Home Missions	Special to Foreign Missions	Special to Schools and Colleges	Special to Theological Seminaries	Special to Orphanage	Special to Hospitals	Special to Old Ministers' Relief	Other Objects	Total Given Missions and Benevolences	Grand Total for All Purposes Given By Church
1. Allen Jay	25.00	......	......	......	......	......	......	67.73	19.00	......	......	111.73	2352.25
2. Antioch	......	......	......	12.63	......	......	......	5.48	7.15	......	......	25.26	264.21
3. Buchanan	26.00	......	......	......	......	......	......	26.00	6.45	......	......	58.45	1434.06
4. Calvary	72.15	......	24.00	32.50	56.05	18.55	......	152.25	28.20	5.00	47.39	436.09	937.54
5. Fair Grove	......	......	......	......	......	......	......	......	......	......	......	......	1176.83
6. Fairview	4.42	......	4.75	5.00	10.00	......	......	51.28	10.00	......	5.50	90.95	498.30
7. Fairmont Park	......	......	......	......	......	......	......	......	6.06	......	37.00	43.00	620.73
8. Gibsonville	6.00	30.00	10.00	10.00	......	......	......	55.39	9.08	......	......	120.47	1087.73
9. Greensboro, First	16536.24	......	419.23	468.18	4277.36	334.72	35.00	2678.09	1264.22	......	1347.94	27360.98	67149.79
10. Asheboro Street	2143.58	11.00	57.0	120.33	332.88	16.50	......	578.65	50.42	99.00	101.50	3510.86	13893.46
11. Bailey Memorial	24.50	......	......	10.00	38.00	......	......	78.33	1.51	......	......	152.34	1635.51
12. Bessemer	331.45	4.00	11.55	......	......	......	......	100.00	......	......	......	447.00	4401.00
13. College Park	531.16	......	47.31	38.39	111.28	......	......	333.42	41.79	......	48.00	1151.35	10997.64
14. Eller Memorial	1812.22	......	......	......	......	......	......	390.00	189.00	......	70.80	46 202	9096.57
15. Florida Street	......	9.00	......	......	519.54	......	......	282.29	......	52.40	40.39	903.62	7158.72
16. Latham Park	......	......	......	......	......	......	......	......	......	......	......	......	387.00
17. Magnolia Street	56.00	37.00	7.20	31.45	40.25	......	......	133.63	17.35	......	......	322.88	3492.63
18. Pomona	......	......	......	13.46	50.23	......	......	121.34	22.51	......	......	207.54	2603.64
19. Revolution	443.97	......	15.62	22.72	138.98	12.36	......	178.95	71.76	......	3.00	887.36	3557.78
20. Sixteenth Street	360.00	......	53.0	9.00	16.50	......	......	113.17	83.92	......	......	635.59	3713.60
21. Stevens [illegible]ial	490.00	3.00	31.50	24.90	50.60	......	......	179.14	23.51	......	19.15	821.80	3362.96
22. Tabernacle	150.00	......	.50	4.86	10.34	......	......	123.15	16.40	......	......	305.25	4097.66
23. Webster Memorial	211.05	......	22.60	24.10	68.39	5.00	......	82.72	17.35	......	34.00	465.21	2103.78
24. Guilford	10.00	......	......	......	......	......	......	......	5.94	......	......	15.94	486.29
25. High Point, First	4196.61	......	216.61	164.58	1194.02	230.75	51.00	1801.24	241.57	......	664.32	8760.70	27953.57

26. Green Street	865.34							473.64	32.18		7.00	1378.16	10403.60
27. Hilliard Memorial	78.60	.95	12.55	7.60	10.45			84.16	10.00			204.31	3324.43
28. North Main Street	320.00	2.00	40.25	5.00	20.00			173.26	30.15	54.60	49.18	694.44	4870.01
29. North Park	116.62	1.50	25.41	13.29	16.10			74.50	37.50			284.92	3231.57
30. South Side			19.00	15.15	15.15			21.0	30.12		15.88	116.30	2196.34
31. West End	303.30	2.00	18.77	27.52	32.87			226.57	225.15	48.00	48.00	932.18	3551.06
32. Jessup Grove													
33. Lebanon	3.00		2.00	51.55				48.52				105.07	1642.52
34. Mount Zion								28.01	3.09			31.10	511.23
35. Oak Grove								25.0				25.0	1096.15
36. Osborne Chapel				8.00					27.59			35.59	192.48
37. Osceola			5.60		8.40			37.32	16.79			68.11	612.68
38. Pine Grove								7.15	5.20			12.35	734.13
39. Pisgah			10.00		10.00			12.0	14.65			46.65	4544.54
40. Pleasant Garden			2.00					28.0				30.0	538.49
41. Pleasant Grove	24.00							43.94				67.94	742.02
42. Reedy Fork													
43. Reidsville, First	1535.45	10.00	76.00	81.50	442.90	136.10		353.98	62.64		91.00	2789.57	10884.02
44. Mount Olive	225.00		15.80	13.13	21.19			144.0		31.75	12.50	463.37	4123.84
45. Penn Memorial	14.00		13.89	11.87				20.00	20.50			80.26	3966.70
46. Rocky Knoll			9.28	3.50	30.00			84.87	22.37		41.42	191.44	1787.44
47. Ruffin Stacey	48.00							24.00	5.00			77.0	1162.50
48. Smith Grove								19.75	27.00		5.60	52.35	311.40
49. Summerfield	71.49		27.67		20.00	1.00		80.00	15.59		71.15	286.90	891.68
50. Tabernacle													643.37
51. Temple													
TOTALS	31035.15	110.45	1199.09	1230.21	7541.48	754.98	86.00	9541.92	2718.65	290.75	2760.62	57269.40	236425.45

HISTORICAL TABLE — PIEDMONT BAPTIST ASSOCIATION

YEAR	WHERE HELD	MODERATOR	CLERK	PREACHER	Churches	Baptisms	Church Members	Total Gifts
1894	Greensboro	Dr. C. A. Rominger	W. L. Kivett	M. A. [illegible]s	5	....	562	....
1895	Liberty	T. L. Chislom	W. L. Kivett	L. Johnson	12	16	112	$ 4695.50
1896	Moore's Chapel	R. W. Brooks	W. H. Eller	L. Johnson	14	66	1194	5128.94
1897	Summerfield	F. H. Jones	W. H. Eller	J. A. Munday	16	73	1540	7198.27
1898	Mount Zion	R. W. Brooks	W. H. Eller	L. Johnson	17	67	1557	6883.23
1899	Ramseur	R. W. Brooks	F. P. Tucker	John E. White	19	54	1570	7435.43
1900	Cherry Street	R. W. Brooks	W. H. Eller	Thomas Carrick	16	48	1538	7970.35
1901	Reidsville	F. H. Jones	W. H. Eller	L. Johnson	19	157	1657	8282.73
1902	Salem Street	F. H. Jones	W. H. Eller	W. C. Newton	19	135	1774	9950.97
1903	Gibsonville	F. H. Jones	W. H. Eller	C. L. [illegible]es	20	185	1868	12834.77
1904	Calvary	F. H. Jones	W. H. Eller	H. W. Battle	22	112	1832	12807.43
1905	Randleman	F. H. Jones	W. H. Eller	J. M. Hilliard	22	114	2096	17674.91
1906	High Point, First	F. H. Jones	W. H. Eller	W. R. Bradshaw	23	201	2333	29366.31
1907	Asheboro Street	F. H. Jones	W. H. Eller	Wm. Hedley	26	372	2798	29993.79
1908	Ramseur	F. H. Jones	W. H. Eller	C. E. [illegible]y	28	311	3086	26347.57
1909	Greensboro	F. H. Jones	W. H. Eller	Wm. Hedley	30	292	3429	49847.28
1910	Mount Zion	F. H. Jones	W. H. Eller	R. G. Hendrick	31	336	3731	28531.01
1911	Asheboro	W. F. Staley	W. H. Eller	W. F. Staley	29	182	3736	25887.56
1912	High Point, Green St.	F. P. Hobgood, Jr.	W. H. Eller	J. C. [illegible]	30	174	3647	29697.38
1913	Liberty	F. P. Hobgood, Jr.	W. H. Eller	R. P. [illegible]r	31	409	3971	37700.97
1914	Asheboro Street	F. P. Hobgood, Jr.	W. H. Eller	A. W. Claxon	31	413	4202	42428.44
1915	Reidsville	J. M. Hilliard	W. H. Eller	J. M. Hilliard	42	313	4491	42577.68
1916	Forest Avenue	J. M. Hilliard	W. H. Eller	E. N. Johnson	36	369	4854	48418.92
1917	Green Street	J. M. Hilliard	W. H. Eller	W. R. White	39	308	4760	44609.05
1918	Moore's Chapel	J. M. Hilliard	W. H. Eller	J. W. Rose	39	374	5140	72538.46
1919	White Oak	J. M. Hilliard	W. H. Eller	W. H. Wilson	39	339	5359	76638.85
1920	Calvary	J. M. Hilliard	W. H. Eller	E. N. Johnson	39	543	5867	117682.35
1921	[illegible]ld	Clarence A. Smith	J. E. Lanier	B. K. Mason	39	480	6454	135561.79
1922	Glenola	Clarence A. Smith	J. E. Lanier	Jas. A. [illegible]k	39	679	7226	149955.24
1923	[illegible] Street	Clarence A. Smith	H. O. Miller	E. E. [illegible]	38	365	7341	140553.25
1924	West End	Clarence A. Smith	H. O. Miller	W. E. [illegible]e	40	672	7489	164658.19
1925	Fairview	Clarence A. Smith	H. O. Miller	A. T. Howell	41	610	8956	211792.21
1926	Ramseur	Clarence A. Smith	S. T. Hensley	Lloyd T. Wilson	42	620	9974	243500.68
1927	Trinity	Clarence A. Smith	S. T. Hensley	H. T. Stevens	40	656	10223	211846.40
1928	Bessemer	Clarence A. Smith	O. E. Lee	R. P. Ellington	41	531	10866	202002.30
1929	[illegible]y	Clarence A. Smith	O. E. Lee	C. F. Rogers	44	573	11496	218987.61
1930	Asheboro	Clarence A. Smith	O. E. Lee	Geo. T. [illegible]hall	44	676	12012	198077.29
1931	[illegible]da Street	Clarence A. Smith	O. E. Lee	A. B. Conrad	44	827	12789	178501.19
1932	Reidsville	Clarence A. Smith	O. E. Lee	J. C. [illegible]r	46	778	13485	159000.60
1933	White Oak	Clarence A. Smith	O. E. Lee	T. L. Sasser	48	1561	15199	186041.40
1934	[illegible]lle	Clarence A. Smith	O. E. Lee	Wilson Woodcock	53	757	15356	172839.18
1935	So. Side, High Point	Clarence A. Smith	O. E. Lee	J. S. Hopkins	41	623	12687	164135.92
1936	Calvary	Clarence A. Smith	O. E. Lee	J. Ben Eller	42	563	13958	166052.96
1937	Eller Memorial	Grover H. Jones	O. E. Lee	C. N. Royal	41	657	14086	195540.50
1938	Hilliard Memorial	Grover H. Jones	O. E. Lee	A. B. [illegible]d	42	814	14793	200246.20
1939	Reidsville, First	Grover H. Jones	O. E. Lee	J. C. Turner	46	975	15479	213024.34

MAP
OF THE
PIEDMONT BAPTIST ASSOCIATION

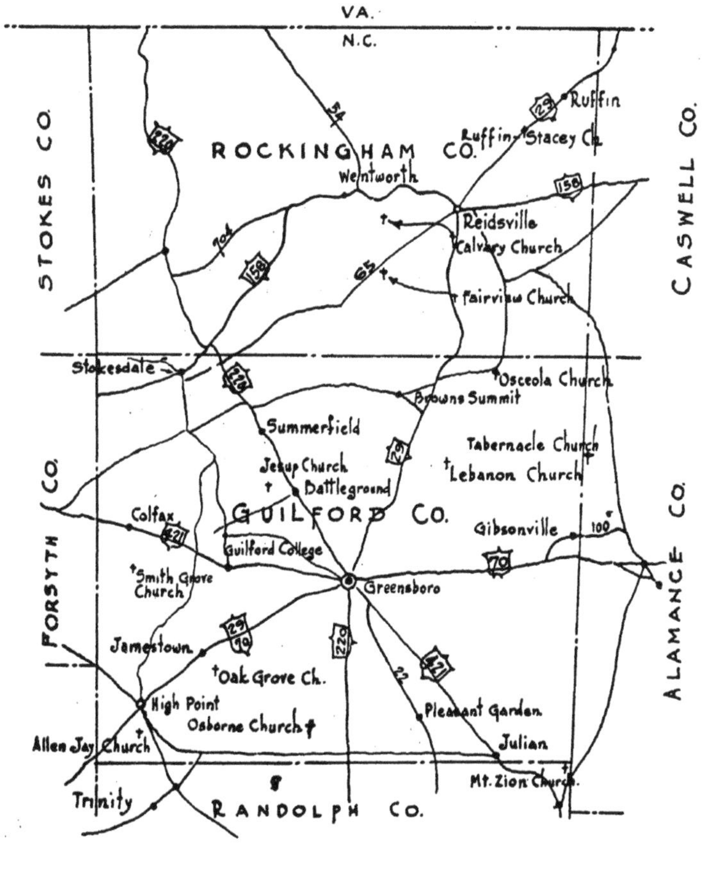

NORTH CAROLINA

Forty-Eighth Annual Session

Green Street Baptist Church

October 22-23, 1941

The next session will be held with the Mount Zion Baptist Church near Liberty Wednesday and Thursday before the fourth Sunday in October, 1942

REV. A. A. WALKER *will preach the sermon*
Alternate, REV. HUGHEY O. MILLER

MINUTES

Piedmont Baptist Association

NORTH CAROLINA

Forty-Eighth Annual Session

Green Street Baptist Church

October 22-23, 1941

The next session will be held with the Mount Zion Baptist Church near Liberty Wednesday and Thursday before the fourth Sunday in October, 1942

REV. A. A. WALKER *will preach the sermon*
Alternate, REV. HUGHEY O. MILLER

MAP

OF THE

PIEDMONT BAPTIST ASSOCIATION

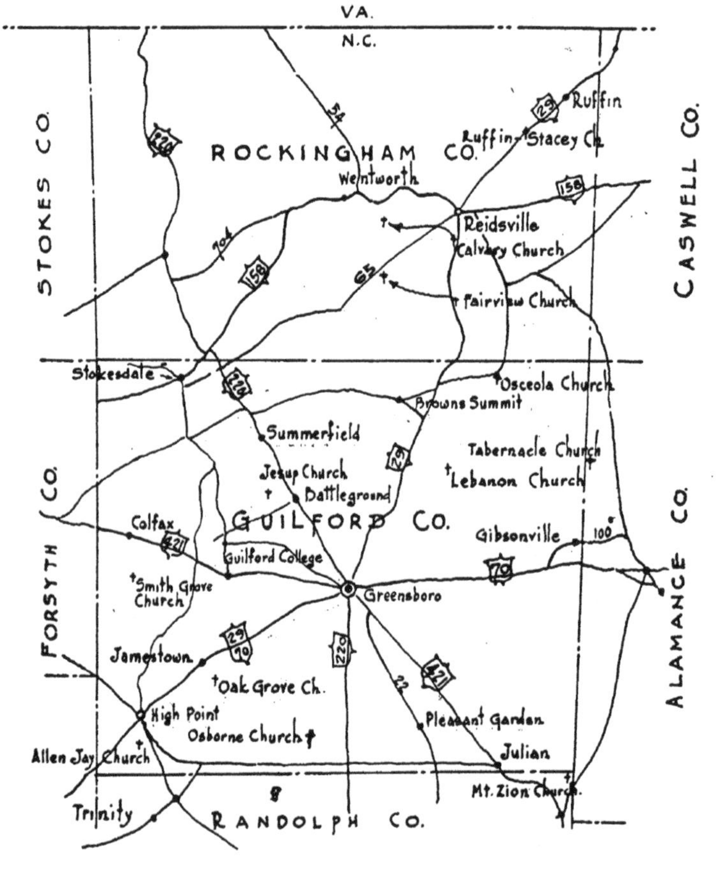

INDEX

ASSOCIATIONAL DIRECTORY

OFFICERS

Grover H. Jones, Moderator ____________________ High Point
Rev. T. L. Sasser, Vice-Moderator ______________ Reidsville
O. E. Lee, Clerk-Treasurer

EXECUTIVE PROMOTION COMMITTEE

Grover H. Jones, Chairman ____________________ High Point
O. E. Lee, Secretary __________________________ Greensboro
Rev. T. L. Sasser _____________________________ Reidsville
Rev. J. Earl Bryant ___________________________ Reidsville
R. R. Saunders ________________________________ Reidsville
Rev. E. M. Smith ______________________________ High Point
Marvin Howell _________________________________ High Point
Dr. J. Clyde Turner ___________________________ Greensboro
F. L. Paschal _________________________________ Greensboro
Mrs. Nettie Hatcher Hoge ______________________ Greensboro
Rev. A. A. Walker _____________________________ Greensboro
J. Carl Bell __________________________________ Greensboro

CHURCH ADVISORY COMMITTEE

Dr. J. Clyde Turner, Chairman _________________ Greensboro
Dr. A. B. Conrad ______________________________ High Point
Rev. J. S. Hopkins ____________________________ High Point
Rev. J. Ben Eller ______________________________ Greensboro
Rev. Wilson Woodcock __________________________ Greensboro
Mrs. Nettie Hatcher Hoge ______________________ Greensboro
Rev. T. L. Sasser _____________________________ Reidsville
O. E. Lee _____________________________________ Greensboro

COMMITTEE ON EVANGELISM

Rev. J. H. Saunders, Chairman _________________ Greensboro
Mrs. Nettie Hatcher Hoge, Study Chairman ______ Greensboro
Rev. A. Lincoln Fulk, Publicity _______________ High Point
Rev. Grady Burgiss, Andrew Club _______________ Greensboro
Walter Crissman, Highway and Hedges Evangelism, High Point

PROGRAM COMMITTEE

Rev. T. L. Sasser, Chairman ---------------------- Reidsville
Rev. L. Grady Burgiss ------------------------ Greensboro
Rev. A. C. Lovelace -------------------------- High Point

LIST OF COMMITTEES SERVING DURING THE ASSOCIATIONAL YEAR

Executive—Promotion Committee
Church Advisory Committee
Committee on Evangelism
Program Committee
Committees Serving During the Annual Meeting of the Association
Committee on Committees
Committee on Time, Place and Preacher
Auditing Committee
Committee on Resolutions
Program Committee for This Year and Next Year
Committee To Nominate Officers
Committee To Nominate Executive-Promotion Committee
Committee To Nominate Church Advisory Committee
Committee To Nominate Delegates to the Baptist State Convention
Committee To Nominate Committee on Evangelism

CHURCHES BY DISTRICTS

District 1

Allen Jay
Fairmont Park
Green Street
High Point, First
Hilliard Memorial
Jewell
North Main
North Park
Oak Grove
Pine Grove
Pisgah
Smith Grove
South Side
Temple
West End

District 2

Asheboro Street
Bailey Memorial
Bessemer
Greensboro, First
Guilford
Jessup Grove
Reedy Fork
Revolution
Rocky Knoll

Brightwood
Buchanan
College Park
Eller Memorial
Fair Grove
Florida Street
Gibsonville
Latham Park
Lebanon
Magnolia Street
Mount Zion
Osborne Chapel
Pleasant Garden
Pleasant Grove
Pomona Mills
Sixteenth Street
Stevens Memorial
Summerfield
Tabernacle (Greensboro)
Tabernacle (Ossipee)
Webster Memorial

District 3

Antioch
Calvary
Fairview
Mount Olive
Osceola
Penn Memorial
Reidsville, First
Ruffin Stacey

OFFICERS OF PIEDMONT BAPTIST ASSOCIATION W.M.U.

Mrs. Nettie Hatcher Hoge, Superintendent ------ Greensboro
Mrs. A. Andrews, Secretary -------------------- Greensboro
Mrs. C. E. Siceloff, Treasurer -------------------- High Point
Mrs. J. C. Shore, Personal Service Chairman ----- Greensboro
Mrs. J. J. Andoe, Mission Study Chairman -------- Greensboro
Mrs. J. M. Cates, Stewardship Chairman ---------- Greensboro
Miss Ruth Scott, Young People's Leader ---------- Greensboro
Mrs. H. A. Knight, Group Leader -------------- High Point
Mrs. O. Joe. Howard, Group Leader ------------ Greensboro
Mrs. H. L. Morrison -------------------------- Reidsville

OFFICERS BAPTIST TRAINING UNION

J. Carl Bell, Director ------------------------ Greensboro
Miss Thelma Patrick, Associate Director -------- High Point
Miss Julia Liles, Secretary-Treasurer ------------ High Point
Miss Jewel Hyatt, Pianist ---------------------- Greensboro
Miss Florence Sneed, Chorister ----------------- Greensboro
Mrs. J. J. Norwood, Story Hour Leader -------- Greensboro
Mrs. J. E. Bryant, Junior Leader ----------------- Reidsville
Mrs. J. F. Moore, Intermediate Leader ------------ Reidsville
Dolan Hedrick, Young People's Leader ---------- High Point
Raymond Kincaid, Adult Leader ---------------- Greensboro
Everett Grubb, Director District No. 1 ---------- High Point

Mrs. Joe Kirkman, Director District No. 2 ------ Greensboro
C. H. Saunders, Director District No. 3 ---------- Reidsville
Rev. J. S. Hopkins, Pastor Advisor ------------ High Point

ORDAINED MINISTERS NOT PASTORS

Taft Raban ---------- Thomasville
J. C. Varner ---------- Gibsonville
C. D. Barton ---------- Greensboro
Ernest Matherley ---------- Greensboro
Dr. W. C. Newton ---------- Richmond, Va.
W. B. Cook ---------- Pomona
Rufus Carroll ---------- Greensboro
O. P. Dix ---------- High Point
Woodrow Hill ---------- High Point
Worth Grant ---------- Louisville, Ky.
Herbert Miller ---------- Sunberry
H. P. Billings ---------- Jamestown
T. H. Myers ---------- High Point
J. F. Murray ---------- Reidsville
J. C. Gillespie ---------- Reidsville
C. R. Smith ---------- Kernersville
B. H. Fairrington ---------- Colfax
B. S. McDowell ---------- High Point
John Burger ---------- Burlington
Estal Cane ---------- Kernersville
Joe Bullins ---------- Winston-Salem

MINISTERS ORDAINED DURING THE YEAR

C. O. Talley, Jr. ---------- Greensboro
J. E. Wiggs ---------- Greensboro
David Shelton ---------- High Point
Herbert Miller ---------- Sunberry
Hubert Bennett ---------- Greensboro
W. L. Owens ---------- High Point

STUDENTS FOR THE MINISTRY

Austin Lovin ---------- Louisville, Ky.
Carl Compton ---------- Wake Forest

John Sykes ---------- Louisville, Ky.
Harold McManus ---------- Louisville, Ky.
Billy Hatton ---------- Mars Hill
John U. Garner ---------- Louisville, Ky.
Roland Swink ---------- High Point
Worth Grant ---------- Louisville, Ky.
J. C. Newsome ---------- Reidsville
J. H. Boles ---------- Greensboro

List of Messengers

ALLEN JAY—Mr. and Mrs. Jim Warren, Mealie Burrow, Mary Warren, Mrs. C. R. Mickey

ANTIOCH—Hattie Roberts, Lee Lewis, Ray Moose

BRIGHTWOOD—H. L. Pruitt, B. G. Yowe, J. W. Holder, Jesse Alberty

BUCHANAN—Mrs. L. W. Michael, Mrs. J. B. Chilton, Mrs. Charles Albright, Mrs. R. L. Mays

CALVARY—Mrs. C. J. Delgado, Mrs. J. F. Carroll, George Gunn

FAIRVIEW—Mrs. H. P. Griffin, George Booker, William Cummings

FAIRMONT PARK—Mr. and Mrs. J. E. Copple, Mr. and Mrs. W. F. Thomas

Greensboro

ASHEBORO STREET—J. S. Moore, J. L. Fox, Mrs. Lettie Jordan, Mrs. H. S. Sherwood, F. L. Paschal, Mrs. A. C. Lowe, Mrs. D. F. Stone, Mrs. J. S. Moore, J. B. Wills

BAILEY MEMORIAL—C. C. Stanley, Mrs. C. C. Stanley, Mrs. E. J. Jarvis, W. H. Sullivan

BESSEMER—A. C. Melvin, Mrs. J. R. Medlin, Miss Norfleet Dixon, Maurice Bunting

COLLEGE PARK—Mrs. J. B. Watson, Miss Willa Marks, B. B. Stockard, L. E. Ogburn, Mrs. Norman Moury

ELLER MEMORIAL—Raymond Kincaid, Leah Andrews, Loretta Phillips, Marie Sykes

GREENSBORO FIRST—Mrs. F. A. Hyatt, James M. Cates, Jr., Mrs. B. L. Spencer, Mrs. W. M. Ham, Mrs. Nettie Hoge,

Geo. R. Bennette, A. A. Chandler, Carl Bell, S. A. Helms, O. E. Lee

FLORIDA STREET—T. H. Truelove, Mrs. J. B. Rumble, Sr., Mrs. A. W. Watson

MAGNOLIA STREET—Mrs. V. U. Blevins, Mrs. Cleo Covington, Mrs. H. P. Wray

POMONA—Miss Frances Melvin, Mrs. F. C. Morehead, Mrs. C. M. Oates, W. B. Roberson

REVOLUTION—Mrs. Ida Strickland, Junius Teeler, Lee Newton, Mrs. Lee Newton

SIXTEENTH STREET—Fred Hester, Mrs. Fred Hester, Harry Moore, Mrs. Harry Moore

STEVENS MEMORIAL—Mrs. C. A. Self, Mrs. J. H. Ham, Mrs. W. P. Brown, W. S. Burns

TABERNACLE—Mrs. J. L. House, Mrs. W. J. Deal, Mrs. N. W. Bolejack

WEBSTER MEMORIAL—Mrs. Norman Straughn, R. Cole Lee, Mrs. W. H. Lucas, C. V. Webster

GUILFORD—C. R. Pierce, Mrs. Ora Weston, Mrs. B. F. Butler, Mrs. Hettie Kennedy

High Point

HIGH POINT FIRST—Mrs. W. F. Clayton, Miss Thelma Patrick, Mrs. A. B. Conrad, Mrs. Fred Flager, Mrs. Grover H. Jones, Mrs. C. D. Goldsmith, Mrs. W. O. Burnham, Mrs. Herman Robinson, Mrs. C. E. Sicesloff

GREEN STREET—J. C. Cross, R. B. Busser, R. B. Culler, W. E. Crissman, Mrs. C. M. Crissman, Mrs. Laura Smith, Miss Lizzie Peeler

HILLIARD MEMORIAL—H. B. Chatham, Mrs. L. L. Grant, Mrs. C. J. Hedrick

NORTH MAIN—Mrs. D. S. Ring, Mrs. L. R. Allen, S. B. Clinard

NORTH PARK—Mrs. P. K. Frye, Mrs. J. L. Jones, Mrs. Davis

SOUTH SIDE—A. J. Borland, Mr. and Mrs. F. E. Caudle, Mrs. Saltz, Mrs. George Tate

WEST END—C. M. Scott, Mrs. Pearl Presler, Mrs. Agnes Carmichael

JESSUP GROVE—James Wiggs, Mrs. James Wiggs, Miss Dora Mason, Mrs. Henry Bryson, Mrs. Frances Jessup

JEWELL—Miss Esther Brown, Hubert Willard, S. P. Stultph

LEBANON—Mrs. Y .H. Carter, Mrs. A. O. Stewart, Mrs. Cleo Whitley, Miss Maggie Kirkman

MT. ZION—J. C. Loakamy, J. T. Swinson, L. L. Spoon

OAK GROVE—G. K. Saunders, W. L. Shackleford, D. H. Grubb, Mrs. L. G. Smith, Mrs. Harry Roberson

OSBORNE CHAPEL—Miss Julia Yowe, Miss Ethel May, R. R. Osborne

OSCEOLA—O. A. Green, Mrs. O. A. Green, L. C. Cole, Mrs. Ruth Huffines

PINE GROVE—R. L. Loflin, Mrs. R. L. Loflin, E. H. Eller, Mrs. E. H. Eller

PISGAH—D. O. Goude, Mrs. W. L. Smith, Mrs. L. C. Madden, Vance Lanier

PLEASANT GARDEN—Mrs. C. T. Burton, Mrs. J. E. Thompson, Henry Foy

PLEASANT GROVE—D. R. Robertson, Mrs. D. R. Robertson, F. M. Atkins, J. H. Collins

REEDY FORK—Mrs. Emily E. Purvis, Mrs. R. P. Everage, Miss Lois Canter, A. L. Bullard

REIDSVILLE FIRST—Mrs. R. L. Hubbard, R. R. Saunders, C. H. Saunders, Mrs. W. H. Bolyn

MOUNT OLIVE—Mrs. Jessie Carter, Mrs. Odell Delapp, Mrs. Lucy Walker

PENN MEMORIAL—Howard Barham, Mrs. Herbert Ford

ROCKY KNOLL—Mrs. Carl Chandler, Mrs. E. F. Wrenn, Mrs. R. A. Laughen, Mrs. Arthur Tilley

RUFFIN STACY—Mrs. Pergason, Mrs. Golden, Mrs. Motley, Mrs. Mary London

SMITH GROVE—Jonah Pitts, Reed Hyatt, Frances Holt, Dona Clark

SUMMERFIELD—Mrs. C. H. Fryar, Mrs. Marvin Truitt, W. W. Doggett

TABERNACLE—R. C. Fitts, Mamie Roach, Mrs. R. C. Fitts, W. C. Collins

TEMPLE—Mr. and Mrs. M. G. Powell, Mr. and Mrs. R. L. Radden, Mr. and Mrs. Watson Wagoner, Rev. and Mrs. J. T. Swinson

Constitution

ARTICLE 1.—The Association shall be called the Piedmont Baptist Association.

ARTICLE 2.—It shall be composed of the ordained ministers who are members of, and those who may have pastoral charges within the Associational District, and three delegates from each Church in the district aforesaid, and Churches having a membership exceeding 300 shall be entitled to one additional delegate for every 200 members or fraction thereof in excess of 300.

ARTICLE 3.—The said delegates shall, before taking their seats, produce letters from respective Churches showing their appointment as delegates.

ARTICLE 4.—The Associational session shall be held at least once a year.

ARTICLE 5.—The officers shall be a Moderator, Vice-Moderator, Clerk and Treasurer. If deemed expedient by the Association, the offices of Clerk and Treasurer may be combined.

ARTICLE 6.—The officers of the Association shall be chosen annually by the Association.

ARTICLE 7.—Association shall be clothed with authority only to advise the Churches touching all things pertaining to their interest but shall in no case presume to direct or control them in reference to their own government or internal policy.

ARTICLE 8.—A Committee of arrangements, consisting of three members, shall be appointed on the first day of each session to prepare and report the proceedings and suggest topics proper for the consideration and action of the next annual Association. It shall be the duty of this committee to outline and publish a program for the next annual associational meeting or for any special or called meeting of the Association.

ARTICLE 9.—Baptist brethren, not members of the Association, who may be present at any session of the body, may on invitation by the body, take seats and participate in the debates of the Association.

ARTICLE 10.—The territory embraced in the Association shall be divided into not less than three districts and a committee composed of one pastor, and one layman from each district, together with the Moderator, Vice,Moderator, Clerk of the Association, Associational W. M. U. Superintendent, Associational Sunday School Superintendent, and Associational B. T. U. President, shall be appointed at meeting of the Association, which committee shall compose the Executive Committee of the Association, a majority of which shall constitute a quorum. It shall be the duty of the committee to superintend and direct the missionary operations of the Association.

ARTICLE 11.—All committees shall be appointed by the Moderator, either directly or indirectly with the approval of the Association, unless otherwise authorized by the Association from time to time.

ARTICLE 12.—The Constitution may be altered only at an Annual session of the Association and by a vote of two-thirds of the whole present.

ARTICLE 13.—The rules of this body shall follow Mell's Parliamentary Practice..

ARTICLE 14.—This Association shall cooperate with the Baptist State Convention.

ARTICLE 15.—The time of the holding of the annual session shall begin on Wednesday before the fourth Sunday in October of each year.

Adopted October 17, 1895.

Articles 2, 5, 6, 10, 15 Amended Sessions, July 23, 24, 1930.

Article 15 Amended Session July 21, 1932.

Article 10 Amended Sessions October 23, 24, 1935.

Articles 8, 10, 11 Amended sessions October 23, 24, 1940.

FRANK L. PASCHAL
C. V. WEBSTER
J. H. SAUNDERS
Committee.

PROCEEDINGS

of the

FORTY-EIGHTH ANNUAL SESSION

of the

Piedmont Baptist Association

Held With the

GREEN STREET BAPTIST CHURCH

High Point, N. C.

October 22-23, 1941

WEDNESDAY MORNING SESSION—10:00 A. M.

1. The Association opened with singing "He Leadeth Me," led by A. A. Walker. The Devotional service was in charge of E. M. Smith. Rev. J. S. Hopkins, pastor of the Green Street Baptist Church, speaks words of welcome.

2. A roll of the churches was called and messengers from forty-four churches responded to the roll call.

3. Mr. Archibald M. McMillan of the Foreign Mission Board was recognized and presented the work of the "Commission," and received subscriptions for the magazine.

4. The Moderator appoints the following members on the Committee on Committees: J. B. Eller, J. S. Hopkins and D. W. Overbey.

5. Rev. T. L. Sasser, vice-moderator, presides as the moderator delivers his annual message.

MODERATOR'S REPORT

The last day of September brought to a close another year in our Association.

At the outset I desire to express my appreciation for the fine spirit of cooperation among the Churches of our Association. From the Churches and organizations in the Churches I received numerous invitations and I am glad to report that I was able to accept all of these invitations, with the exception of one.

A few days ago I received a letter from the Department of Evangelism of the Southern Baptist Convention urging me to emphasize at this session of the Association the importance of the most spiritual, far-reaching and Christ-centered crusade in soul-winning for the next associational year. I have acceded to this request and shall spend the time allotted to me on this program in discussing the matter of evangelism.

World affairs today illustrate the perpetual battle between mankind's spiritual interest and selfish advantage. This present war is an acute expression of the eternal strife between the higher and the lower natures of men. All life is a continuous struggle between good and evil, light and darkness, the higher and the lower.

The salvation of souls, the advancement of the Kingdom; and the life of our Baptist denomination depends on sane, scriptural, spiritual soul-searching evangelism.

Dr. Roland Q. Leavell, superintendent of the Department of Evangelism of our Southern Convention points out that in 1940 we let the war, the draft, the defense program and the election crowd out the most important thing and that Southern Baptists fell back in soul-winning in the year 1940. In this connection Dr. Leavell suggested the following:

1.—Adopt a resolution which plans a program that will cover fifty-two weeks.

2.—Plan to reach unchurched areas, new communities, underprivileged areas, camps, prisons, etc.

3.—Promote Andrew Soul-Winning Clubs in each Church.

4.—Plan an evangelistic rally or preacher's school of evangelism during the winter or spring months.

5.—Aid and encourage pastorless Churches, weak Churches and any Churches that have not been baptizing any new converts.

As you know we have in our Association a Committee on Evangelism and during the sessions of the Association that Committee will submit its recommendations with respect to ways and means for making effective soul-winning in the Association.

Respectfully submitted,
G. H. JONES, Moderator.

6. The report on the work of the Woman's Missionary Union was presented by Mrs. Nettie H. Hoge. Upon motion to adopt the report the work was discussed by Mrs. Hoge. The report was adopted.

REPORT OF WOMAN'S MISSIONARY UNION

The Psalmist prayed with an unselfish purpose, "God be merciful unto us and bless us, and cause His face to shine upon us—

that thy way may be known upon the earth and thy salvation among all nations".

This has been chosen as the watch word of the Woman's Missionary Union for 1941, and expresses the incentive for this splendid organization which has grown in numbers, gifts and influence during the past 53 years, until it has become the greatest enlistment force for missions in our denomination. It's enlistment includes women and young people of all ages.

It's influence has gone out into all the world.

It's gifts have built and equipped schools, hospitals and Churches, kept missionaries on the field, both home and abroad; trained workers in its training school and developed members in the local Churches.

The Union is an auxiliary to all South-wide objects, with it's missionary literature, mission study classes, seasons of prayer, gifts and training the young people in carrying out the great commission.

It numbers around one million members and, it's gifts are counted in the millions.

The Union has never made a debt, but has been a generous contributor to the debts of the denomination.

In response to the slogan adopted at the Baltimore Convention "A Debtless Denomination by 1945", the Union, in it's annual session adopted the following motion.

"That in view of the proposed effort of the Southern Baptist Convention for a debtless denomination by 1945, which necessitates the raising of approximately three million dollars, Woman's Missionary Union, auxiliary to the Southern Baptist Convention, undertake, as it's objective toward the clearance of all debts on southwide causes by 1945, the sum of one million dollars."

Plans have been formed for enlisting, through the One Hundred Thousand Club, the Baptist women of the South in this undertaking.

In the 51 Churches of the Piedmont Association, 14 have no missionary organization. Many of these are small country Churches, with a scattered membership and few leaders.

These have recent organizations: Fairgrove, Buchanan, Bailey Memorial, Reedy Fork and Jessup Grove.

$25,180.53 was last year's gift from Piedmont W. M. U.

Respectfully submitted,
NETTIE H. HOGE,
Superintendent.

7. The report on Home Missions was made by Dr. A. B. Conrad. Upon motion to adopt the report the subject was discussed by Dr. Conrad. The Report was adopted.

REPORT ON HOME MISSIONS

The past year has been one of the most notable in the history of our Home Mission Society, in all departments the work has been signally blessed.

Home Missions have a pecular relation to all forms of missions, city, state and foreign, and there is no place in all the world where there is greater need for evangelization than here in the homeland.

It has been well said that "as goes America so goes the world." If Christianty fails of conquest here and this land goes pagan, and there is a terrible drift in that direction, then there is little hope for the world.

Emerson said "Our whole history seems like the last effort of Divine Providence on behalf of the human race" and, if this nation loses its moral and spiritual integrity and is swallowed up in materialism then it is doomed. So making this land Christian is the great task of the Home Mission Society.

More than fifty per cent of the population of our convention territory has no affiliation with the Church, that majority must be won to Christ or there will be moral and spiritual collapse, that is inevitable;a nation cannot exist for long half Christian and half pagan.

So to the end of saving America the Home Mission Society sets itself. Statistics do not and cannot tell all that has been accomplished, they cannot reveal the moral and spiritual forces unloosed—the hearts touched and lives changed. But this summary is illuminating as to the greatness of the work done. There have been during the year 391 Missionaries, 915 mission stations, 71 new stations opened, 31,403 sermons preached, 5,375 professions of faith, 77,440 souls dealt with in personal work, 4,443 Bibles and 724,505 tracts distributed and $560,168.00 raised from all sources. Heaven alone can reveal the results of all this. It is a matter of rejoicing that during the year $181,130.00 have been paid on the debt that has been such a burden and hindrance to the work, and a debt paying program projected which it is believed will liquidate the whole debt by 1945. The whole debt has been refinanced during the year at a lower rate of interest, which will mean a saving of about $9,000 a year.

This brief report does not admit of any any special mention of our work in Cuba or among the foreign speaking people within our borders, or among the Negroes, Mexicans, Indians, Jews, deaf and in the Rescue Missions and Good Will Centers—but in all fields blessed results have been achieved.

In the Department of Evangelism, under the direction of Dr. Roland Leavell there have been glorious victories in soul winning, full reports of the number saved are not available but a vast number have been won to Christ and doubtless the Southern Baptist Convention has gone over the mark of five million members.

The world situation and impending wars has made national defense imperative, multitudes of young men are being enlisted and trained, so it has come to pass that our Army, Navy, Marine and CCC camps are among our greatest mission fields, and at a meeting of the Administrative Committee of the Southern Baptist Convention held in Nashville, Tenn., in April last, this all important work was assigned to the Home Mission Society.

The Church is challenged today as never before. The calls from every side are great. It is Christ or chaos now, Christianity or back to paganism and in the great fight for all the precious rights and interests that are ours—and for the overthrow of evil and the establishment of righteousness and justice in all the world. The Home Mission Society is doing its full part and is one of the chief agencies.

Respectfully submitted,
A. B. CONRAD.

8. The following visitors were recognized: Rev. Wilbur Hutchins, Rev. E. C. Roach, L. A. Hall and S. G. Snyder.

9. The report of the Committee on Committees was presented and adopted.

REPORT OF COMMITTEE ON COMMITTEE

Committee on Place and Preacher: A. Lincoln Fulk, chairman; R. R. Saunders, Mrs. Nettie Hoge.

Auding Committee: R. B. Culler, J. S. Moore, Wm. Cummings.

Committee on Resolutions: A. A. Walker, Miss Thelma Patrick, J. E. Bryant.

Committee on Program for Next Year: T. L. Sasser, A. C. Lovelace, Grady Burgiss.

Committee to Nominate Officers: Wilson Woodcock, E. M. Smith, Mrs. R. P. Everage.

Committee to Nominate Executive-Promotion Committee: J. C. Gillespie, Mrs. A. C. Lowe, H. O. Miller.

Committee to Nominate Delegates to Baptist State Convention: B. S. Whitley, Mrs. T. C. Robbins, Mrs. E. J. Jarvis.

Committee to Nominate Committee on Evangelism: A. B. Conrad, Mrs. O. E. Lee, Huber Dixon.

Committee on Committeess J. Ben Eller, J. S. Hopkins, D. W. Overby.

10. The Treasurer's report was made and referred to the Auditing Committee.

REPORT OF TREASURER—EXPENSE FUND

I herewith submit my report for the year ending September 30, 1941.

Balance on hand September 30, 1940		$ 28.22
Received from the Churches		194.90
Total		$213.12
Disbursements		
United Dry Forces of N. C.	$ 9.56	
The Record Publishing Co. [Printing]	117.55	
Clerk's Remuneration	50.00	
Postage and Supplies	3.68	
Total	$180.79	
Balance on hand	42.33	
	$223.12	$223.12

Respectfully submitted,
O. E. LEE, Treasurer.

Report of Treasurer—Mission Fund

I herewith submit my report for the year ending September 30, 1941.

Balance on hand September 30, 1940		$47.30
Received from the Churches		8.26
		$55.56
Disbursements		
Piedmont Baptist Training Union Treasurer	$20.00	
Piedmont Baptist Sunday School Treasurer	20.03	
Total	$40.03	
Balance on hand	15.53	

Respectfully submitted,
O. E. LEE, Treasurer.

11. The following new pastors in the Association were recognized and given words of welcome by the moderator: Z. W. Rotan, C. R. Pierce, J. Earl Bryant, James E. Wiggs.

12. Following the singing of a hymn and the announcement about the lunch by J. S. Hopkins, a motion was passed instructing the clerk to write a letter to Brother Clarence A. Smith, the former moderator who is now in Melbourne, Fla.

13. Rev. A. A. Walker reads the scripture and leads

in prayer. Rev. A. Lincoln Fulk delivers a most helpful sermon on the subject, "Our Supreme Problems." The text is James 1: 22: "Be ye doers of the Word and not hearers only."

WEDNESDAY AFTERNOON SESSION—1:30 P. M.

14. The devotional service is led by J. H. Saunders.

15. The report on Foreign Missions is presented by J. Ben Eller. Upon motion to adopt the report the subject is discussed by Brother Eller. The report is adopted.

REPORT ON FOREIGN MISSIONS

The assurance of Jesus: "Lo I am with you always, even unto the end of the world" is being verified in these days of world upheaval. Despite war, faminine, and earthquake our Foreign Mission Board has had one of the best years of its long history.

Through 457 missionaries and 3,000 native workers the Board has been teaching, preaching and healing. During the year 18,542 people were baptised, 35,291 students were taught, and 136,-994 patients received treatment.

The financial reports are encouraging. Members of our Foreign Mission Churches gave during the year $379,896.00. The indebtedness of the Board is now $205,000.00, having been reduced $40,000.00 during the year. Our women have had a vital part in making this possible. Their Lottie Moon offering this last year amounted to $363,743.30 enabling the Board to meet many emergency calls.

In Europe and the Near East a state of uncertainty exists. War, earthquake, and famine have taken an awful toll. Our missionaries have stayed with their work on these fields as long as possible but in most places they have been removed or withdrawn for the present.

In Africa unprecedented opportunities are knocking at our doors. The work in Nigeria, for instance, has expanded to such an extent that it has overflowed into neighboring colonies. From the "outside" areas there come insistent calls for help and leadership.

It is generally conceded that there are no more fruitful fields anywhere than in South America. The Lord is greatly blessing our work there. Recently Dr. S. L. Watson wrote: "As a field of missionary opportunity Brazil is unsurpassed. Even the much talked of nationalism is no hindrance as compared with the unlimited, outstretched rich harvest fields." Then he added: "The workers are committed heart and soul to the mammoth task of national evangelization."

The Orient presents a picture of mixed colors. There is much to sadden and discourage; there is much to gladden and encourage. In Japan the doors seem to be closing. Of all our missionaries only Dr. Maxfield Garrott remains. We must wait for light and leading there. China has suffered much from war, desolation and famine. In recent months the Board has been compelled to remove many missionaries, but the ones that remain are being greatly blessed by the Lord. Never have their services been more appreciated, more fruitful. Dr. M. T. Rankin writes: "If I could tell all that I have seen I question whether my report would be believed. I have never had more opportunities for preaching the gospel of Christ, and I have never spoken to larger groups of people who have heard the word so eagerly".

We would urge our people to take a greater interest in Foreign Missions. Let us give more, let us pray more. Mission Schools and and Mission Classes should be conducted in all our Churches, while our Mission journal, *The Commission*, should be in every home.

Respectfully submitted,

J. BEN ELLER.

16. The clerk presented a digest of the forty-nine church letters received showing that the membership in the churches and the organizations about the same as last year. The Training Unions made some gains in membership. There was a decrease of about eighty in the number of baptisms during the year. There was a gain of about $41,000.00 in contributions to local work and a gain of about $5,700.00 in contributions to benevolences. Thirty-four churches had an increase in their contributions to Benevolences. There was a gain of about $300.00 in the contributions to the Orphanage.

17. The report of the Auditing Committee was presented and adopted as follows:

REPORT OF AUDITING COMMITTEE

We the undersigned committee appointed to audit the books of Brother O. E. Lee, treasurer, are glad to report we found same correct and very neatly kept, and recommend his report be accepted with thanks for his accuracy, and work of love.

Respectfully submitted,

R. B. CULLER,

J. S. MOORE,

WILLIAM CUMMINGS.

18. The report on Denominational Program was presented

by J. S. Hopkins. Upon motion to adopt the report the subject was discussed by J. S. Hopkins:

REPORT ON DENOMINATIONAL PROGRAM

Our denominational program is what we are doing to carry out the great commission in all the work of all our Churches at home and "unto the uttermost parts of the earth". But this report, I take it, is to set forth our efforts in Kingdom finance which program we call the "Co-operative Program".

The Co-operative Program is simply a systematic plan of work developed by Southern Baptists in recent years for promoting and supporting in a more effective way all the causes fostered by them. This program continues to grow in favor with our people, and should have the hearty support of all our Churches because:

1.—It is scriptural. It's aim is to carry out the Great Commission, and this is done on a voluntary co-operative basis.

2.—This program is concrete. All the causes in it are concrete, and they consist of the work our Lord has assigned to us. We do not give to the program but through it to the causes of Christ.

3.—The program is equitable. The funds are distributed to the causes according to their relative needs—all are benefitted alike or all suffer in the same proportion. The state conventions determine the ratio of division between state and southwide causes. The states determine the percentage of distribution to state causes; and the Southern Baptist Convention determines the distribution to southwide causes. In our state at present sixty percent of each dollar is used for state causes and forty percent for southwide causes.

Our state's distributable dollar is divided as follows: State Missions, 23 1-3 percent; education and debt service, 65 percent; hospital, 6 2-3 per cent; ministerial education, 1 2-3 percent; retirement fund, 3 1-3 percent; total, 100 percent.

The distributable southwide dollar is divided thus: Foreign Missions, 50 percent; Home Missions, 23 1-3 percent; Relief and Annuity Board, 10 1-3 percent; Southern Seminary 4 1-5 percent; Southwestern Seminary, 4 1-5 percent; Baptist Bible Institute, 4 1-5 percent; New Orleans Hospital, 2 1-5 percent; Woman's Missionary Union, 8-15 percent; American Seminary, 1 percent; total, 100 percent.

4.—The Co-operative Program is Baptistic. It recognizes the right and independence of every Church and person. No coercion is suggested or implied. It presents a fair, scriptural plan of voluntary co-operation in carrying out the command of our Lord. It enables every Church, large or small, every person rich or poor to have a part in all the co-operative work of his denomination in all the world.

5.—This program is economical and business-like. Instead

of promoting each cause separately and by direct appeal to Churches and individuals, it seeks to promote all together and proportionally. The pastor is expected to represent and present all the causes. This does away with extra appeals, employees, and expense, and does not interfere with the regular work and program of the Church as this is in itself a most vital part of the whole Church program.

In order to keep faith with the commands of our Lord and to promote His work through the Co-operative Program the following recommendations are made:

1.—That the fires of evangelism be kept burning brightly all the year.

2.—That we stress continuously Christian stewardship with the tithe as the minimum standard of Christian giving.

3.—That the Every Member Canvass be put on in every Church during November and December unless for special reason some other period seems better.

4.—That each Church help in the realization of "a debtless denomination by 1945" either by providing for it in the budget or by a special effort in January and February.

5.—That all denominational funds be remitted promptly and properly marked each month to the state secretary-treasurer.

Respectfully submitted,
JULIAN S. HOPKINS.

19. The report on State Missions was made by E. M. Smith. Upon motion to adopt the report the subject was discussed by Dr. Louis Gaines, President of the Baptist State Mission Board, and Pastor of the First Baptist Church, Lexington, N. C. Following the discussion of State Missions, Dr. Gaines presented Dr. Theo. F. Adams, Pastor of the First Baptist Church, Richmond, Va., and member of the Foreign Mission Board, who was assisting Dr. Gaines in evangelistic services. Dr. Adams discussed our foreign mission work. The report was adopted.

STATE MISSION REPORT

The Baptist State Convention has always been interested in helping the Churches to provide a ministry to the lost people in North Carolina. This ministry has been greatly effective. The task, however is far from complete. There are perhaps a million people in North Carolina who do not recognize Christ at all. In keeping with this great need State Missions has reached out her hands.

At present the salaries of about 160 pastors are paid in part from our State Mission fund. These pastors serve in strategic places where they preach the gospel to the poor.

Recently the Board has adopted the policy of buying, or helping to buy, choice lots in growing sections where Churches may be properly located.

We are promoting the Sunday School, B. T. U. and B. S. U. departments of our work. These agencies are undertaking to teach and train the people in our Churches and colleges.

For several years Mr. M. O. Alexander and Mr. J. C. Pipes have been giving the major portion of their time to the development of all the Churches they can reach through the teaching of stewardship and through emphasis on missions.

We are also providing through Mr. and Mrs. Lunsford a ministry to the Indians in Robeson County. Indirectly we are giving aid to our Negro brethren in the state.

Schools are being provided for the pastors, one at Meredith College and the other at Mars Hill. This endeavor has proved a distinct blessing not only to the pastors but to the Churches.

We are providing a ministry to the sick, the veterans' hospital at Oteen and Western North Carolina Sanatorium at Black Mountain. At present Rev. and Mrs. E. M. Harris provide a ministry for the sick at the State Sanatorium near Aberdeen. It might be stated also that Mr. and Mrs. Harris are doing a great work among the wayward girls at Samarcand.

At this time the Board is faced with a two-fold problem that has been brought about as a result of the times in which we live. There are now about 100,000 men in camp in North Carolina. They must receive spiritual aid from the Baptists of the state. Also in these areas there has been a great increase in population. Church buildings and pastors are needed for these areas. State Missions is facing thse problems now. Today, the men of Macedonia are standing and saying, "Come over into Macedonia and help us". And Macedonia is not as far away as it was when Paul heard the cry. Jesus said, "Lift up your eyes and look on the fields; for they are white already unto harvest."

Respectfully submitted,
ERNEST M. SMITH.

20. The Committee to nominate officers made the following report which was adopted.

REPORT OF COMMITTEE TO NOMINATE OFFICERS

Grover H. Jones, Moderator
Rev. T. L. Sasser, Vice-Moderator
O. E. Lee, Clerk-Treasurer
Rev. A. A. Walker, Sunday School Superintendent

J. Carl Bell, Training Union Director
Wilson Woodcock, Mrs. R. P. Everage, E. M. Smith,
Committee

21. Mr. Grover H. Jones, Chairman of the Church Advisory Committee, brings the recommendation of the committee, recommending that the Brightwood Baptist Church, located on the Reidsville Road about three miles from Greensboro, be received into the Association. The recommendation is adopted. The moderator gives the right hand of fellowship to the messengers of the church.

22. The afternoon session is closed with prayer.

WEDNESDAY NIGHT SESSION—7:30 O'CLOCK

23. A service of songs was directed by the Orchestra from the Asheboro Street Baptist Church.

The devotional service was in charge of Raymond Kincaid.

24. The Training Union report and the report of the Training Union Treasurer were presented by Miss Julia Liles, Secretary-Treasurer. The reports are adopted.

REPORT OF BAPTIST TRAINING UNION

Under the direction of Mr. J. Carl Bell, the Training Union work of the Association has been carried on in a commendable manner.

Quarterly meetings were held on January 17, March 15, June 6 and September 12. The programs of these meetings were made up of devotionals, special music, inspirational addresses and conferences with the exception of the March meeting.

The meeting on March 15 was the highlight of the year. The annual Associational Training Union Convention was held in the afternoon at the First Baptist Church, Greensboro, and was followed by a banquet at the Masonic Temple in Greensboro. During the afternoon session the nominating committee brought a recommendation that the present officers be re-elected to serve until the annual Associational Convention in October of the present year, and that new officers be elected during the Training Union session of the Convention in order that terms of future officers might run from October to October in line with other Associational officers and most Church officers. This recommendation was accepted. The Associational elimination of the annual Training Union contests was held during the afternoon. The three entrants in the Junior Memory

Work Drill won out and went on to win state honors. The Intermediate who won in the Piedmont Association also went on to win out in the state, and the Better Speakers Contest also competed in the state finals. The creditable showing which all entrants in the contests made was very gratifying. The attendance at the banquet session was three hundred which was the largest yet attending one of these meetings. Both fellowship and inspiration were in evidence throughout the evening.

A great deal of work has been done by the director, with many others assisting him, to conduct and promote Training Union Study Courses in the Churches of the Association.

Training Unions have been organized in eight Churches during the year, but twenty Churches in the Association are still without a Training Union. This fact should be a challenge to a greater work during the coming year.

Respectfully submitted,
JULIA M. LILES,
Secretary.

Report of the Treasurer of the Associational Training Union

Balance on hand, October 1, 1940		$20.39
Received from the Piedmont Association		20.00
Disbursements:		
Banners [Adult, Senior, Intermediate, Junior]	$ 7.63	
Expenses for March Training Convention and Banquet	12.65	
Program for meeting June 6	2.50	
Stamps, stencils for letters to Churches	3.56	
Note book	.35	
		$26.69
Balance on hand 9-30-41		$13.70

Respectfully submitted,
JULIA M. LILES,
Treasurer.

25. Special music is rendered by the Orchestra from the Asheboro Street Baptist Church.

The Association expresses appreciation of the Orchestra music by standing.

26. The following report of the nominating committee was adopted.

J. Carl Bell, Director
Miss Thelma Patrick, Associate Director
Miss Julia Liles, Secretary and Treasurer
Miss Jewel Hyatt, Pianist
Mrs. J. J. Norwood, Story Hour Leader
Mrs. J. E. Bryant, Junior Leader
Mrs. J. F. Moore, Intermediate Leader
Dolen Hedrick, Young People's Leader
Raymond Kincaid, Adult Leader
Everett Grubb, Director District Number 1
Mrs. Joe Kirkman, Director District Number 2
C. H. Saunders, Director District Number 3
Rev. J. S. Hopkins, Pastor Advisor
Miss Florence Sneed, Chorister

T. L. Sasser, Grady Burgiss, J. E. Hedrick,
Committee

27. The quartet from the Green Street Baptist Church rendered special music.

28. A playlet—"This Night Shall End"—was given by the Training Union Department of the Green Street Baptist Church.

29. Following singing "Our Best" a splendid address on the subject, "Conquering Covetousness," was given by Rev. Grady Burgiss.

The session was closed with prayer by Rev. T. L. Sasser.

THURSDAY, OCTOBER 23, 1941

MORNING SESSION—9:45 O'CLOCK

30. The devotional service was led by C. R. Pearce.

31. The report on Social Service was presented by J. H. Saunders. Upon motion to adopt the report the subject was discussed by J. H. Saunders, V. H. Harrell, Field Representative of the United Dry Forces of N. C.; A. L. Fulk, Dr. A. B. Conrad, James E. Wiggs, Wilson Woodcock, J. Ben Eller. The report was adopted.

REPORT ON SOCIAL SERVICE

It is obvious that the time has come for the Church to do one of two things, with regards to our ideals and standards. We should either retreat to some new position where we wish to wrestle for a while or enter a counter offensive and seek to regain the place of influence and power the Church once possessed.

I understand the assigned subject of Social Service to refer to the Church's responsibility to society. Therefore, we can only mention a few of the things which are covered by this subject.

Our first responsibility is to set a standard of living which will be an encouragement to righteous living and a rebuke to all unrighteousness. Our next obligation is to firmly condemn all forms of sin so as to create a consciousness on the part of the world concerning its character. We are further to use our influence to abolish all forms of commercialized evil.

We have been so lax concerning these things and so afraid of offending, that the world has lost respect for our wishes. An example of this was seen in Greensboro recently when ninety per cent of the ministers came out publicly against Sunday movies and the next day the city authorities met and opened the city to Sunday movies.

The moving picture industry has spent much money and effort to destroy our Sunday laws. The bulk of her pictures have glorified crime and lust. The result of her work is being seen in the increase of crime and immorality in our nation. Our Churches do not have soul winners among those of her members who practice attending this institution.

Gambling is becoming a fad with the American people and needs to be singled out for more attention. Bank night at the movies together with the lotteries operated in most pool rooms are helping to popularize this evil. A Gallup poll report on gambling given in the Greensboro Daily News Oct. 4, 1941, reveals that 54% of the adults in our country gambled in the last year. The most startling part of the report was that 24% of these gambled on Church raffles.

Divorces continue to wreck one out of each five or six homes in our country. So far the only Church to firmly oppose this evil and check its progress among its constituency is the Catholic Church. This should be a rebuke and a stimulus to us.

This is an hour when every sermon should have a word in it about racial hatred. All the news agencies of our time are spreading the propaganda which calls for a fear and hatred of the German people.

We never had a greater opportunity to help men physically than today. Millions are facing starvation in Europe and the Orient. Our missionaries are in a position to distribute all the food and medicine we make available. Therefore, we should curtail unnecessary expenditures and give more than ever to feed starving men, women, and children.

I recommend that we take a new stand against all forms of

sin. A concerted effort on the part of all of our Churches will make a worthy impression on the cities and counties in which we live and enable us to enter the position of power and influence which we should hold.

Society is listening for an authoritative voice. Let the Church speak.

Respectfully submitted,
J. HARVEY SAUNDERS.

32. Upon the recommendation of the Church Advisory Committee the Association voted to receive the Jewel Baptist Church, which is located near High Point, into the Association. The Moderator gives the hand of fellowshp to the messengers of the church.

33. The report on Religious Literature prepared by Dr. J. Clyde Turner was read by the clerk. Dr. Turner was unable to attend. Upon motion to adopt the report the subject was discussed by R. H. Satterfield, Circulation Manager for the Biblical Recorder. The report was adopted.

RELIGIOUS LITERATURE

We are living in a day when literature is abundant. Never in the history of the world have there been so many books, magazines and papers published as there are today. Some of them are good, some are indifferent, some are bad.

We speak of religious literature in contrast with secular literature. Religious literature is literature which is inspired by religion, and has a religious appeal. But not all religious literature is good, because not all religions are good. There are as many kinds of religious literature as there are religions. Some of the most deadly poisons of the mind and soul are to be found in some of the so-called religious literature. We, of course, are interested in Christian literature, literature that has the Christian appeal. Every home ought to have that kind of literature.

In this report, we are especially concerned about the literature which our denomination is producing. Apart from the many books and tracts which are being published, we have literature representing every phase of our denominational work. From the Sunday School Board there comes the literature which we use in the Sunday School and Training Union. The Foreign Mission Board publishes *The Commission,* a monthly magazine which carries information and inspiration concerning our foreign mission work. The price is only fifty cents a year. The Home Mission Board issues a monthly publication called *Southern Baptist Home Missions,* which tells of the work being done by the Home Mission Board. The subscription price of this magazine is only twenty-five cents. The Woman's Missionary Union publishes monthly magazines for the various missionary organizations.

In North Carolina, we have two publications—*Charity and Children* and *The Biblical Recorder*. *Charity and Children* is published by Mills Home, and has a field of its own. *The Biblical Recorder,* owned and controlled by the Baptist State Convention, is the one organ of North Carolina Baptists. *The Recorder* has had a long and honorable history. Its publication was begun in 1833, three years after the State Convention was organized. In the 108 years of its history, it has had only twelve editors. It was owned and published by private interests until three years ago, when it was purchased by the convention. Dr. John C. Slemp, who has been editor and business manager for the past two years, has offered his resignation to become effective November 15.

As the organ of the Convention, the *Biblical Recorder* has wielded a wide influence. It has been the medium through which information concerning the work of the Kingdom has gone out to the people. It has been a leading factor in helping to mold the policies of the convention and promote its interests. It comes weekly with its message of information and inspiration for all the family. The price in single subscriptions is $2.00 per year. In clubs of at least five per cent of the Church membership the price is only $1.50 per year. Churches in increasing numbers are putting *The Recorder* in the Church budget and sending it to every family in the Church.

Respectfully submitted,
J. CLYDE TURNER.

34. The report on Sunday Schools was made by A. A. Walker. Upon motion to adopt the report the subject was discussed by A. A. Walker and J. S. Hopkins. The report was adopted.

SUNDAY SCHOOL REPORT

The statistical tables carry a report both full and concise on all the main phases of our church work and deserve more attention than they usually get. Figures fail to report some things, however. Bible teaching can not be measured in figures and so it is that the best report on Sunday School work can not be reported either verbally or in figures.

We do well, perhaps, to observe some of our weak points for the purpose of correction. There is a vast throng that the Sunday School is not reaching and perhaps some fifty per cent of those reached are barely touched. The opportunity to really study the Bible is lightly regarded by many and wholly neglected by more.

There is the distressing tendency to substitute Sunday School for worship. These and many other defects and temptations give us reason to be ever on our guard. We rejoice, however, that there is a growing interest in the work of Sunday School. For a long time this Association has had a school for every church in her membership. This is indicative of the value we attach to this praiseworthy work. Each of these schools seem to be particularly concerned about increased enrollment and attendance. The place of teacher training is more generally recognized. The departments of Cradle Roll, Extension, and Vacation Bible School are gaining more recognition and reaching more people. It is very significant that nearly all our conversions are Sunday School pupils.

For some time we have had a Sunday School Associational organization which has functioned reasonably well. Two meetings are scheduled each quarter for each of the three districts of the association with one general meeting quarterly. Under the leadership of Associate Superintendent Rev. Mr. J. S. Hopkins, assisted by the district Associational committee on evangelism, one of these quarterly meetings was turned into an Evangelistic Rally held in the Greensboro First church. By many this was regarded the best attended and most promising service ever held in the association. This organization has not been able to do its best work in many instances because of insufficient information and the lack of sustained attendance upon its regular meetings. It is to be hoped that each school will adopt and use faithfully the six-point-record-system, or a system its equal, and that monthly reports be made as requested according to these records. The program committee using these records as indices can provide programs that will more nearly meet the most pressing needs before us. Then it is to be hoped that each school will enthusiastically attend these programs, sharing, studying, and praying together until there shall arise in our midst a Sunday School consciousness that will make us all measure up to the standard God has set for us to reach.

Respectfully submitted,
A. A. WALKER.

35. The report on the Ministers Relief and Retirement Plan was presented by A. L. Fulk. The report was adopted.

REPORT ON MINISTERS' RELIEF AND RETIREMENT PLAN

The Relief and Annuity Board, now in its twenty-fourth year, is an agency responsible for investing funds for the care of retired ministers, their wives, missionaries, and other servants of the denomination. During the year of 1941 this board will disburse benefits of over a half million dollars. There has been a steady increase in the membership of the several plans under which the Board operates. The last reports show a total membership of 6,680. However, this is but a small percentage of the pastors in the Southern Convention who some day will become disabled and who will have to look to others for security in old age. The Board operates under twelve different plans which are designed to meet the needs of any and all our Christian workers.

The major plan now being administered is known as the Convention Ministers Retirement Plan. It is a state unit plan adopted by all the states in the Southern Convention. In this state the plan operates as follows: The Church contributes 4% and the minister 4% of his monthly salary to, which the State Mission Board adds $18.00 annually. The benefits of this operation are to be 50% of the average salary received by the minister during the last 25 years of service if such plan has been in operation for as much as 12 years. $2,000 per annum is the maximum benefit available regardless of salary. The plan also carries a disability benefit providing a maximum of $500 per annum according to the salary received.

Every pastor and Church should at once begin to cooperate with this plan. Delay means decreased benefits. While the Churches who pay larger salaries have been among the first to enter the plan, it is to be regretted that many of the Churches who pay their ministers a small salary seemingly have not been interested. The lower the salary given the minister, the more incumbent it is for that Church to help provide for his security in old age. If the Churches who have been the recipients of their labors do not provide for their ministers, who else will do it?

Respectfully submitted,
A. LINCOLN FULK.

36. The report of the Committee to Nominate the Committee on Evangelism was made and adopted as follows: J. H. Saunders, Chairman; Mrs. Nettie Hoge, Study Chairman; A. Lincoln Fulk, Publicity; Grady Burgiss, Andrew Club; and Walter Crissman, Highway and Hedges Evangelism.

37. The report on Christian Education was made by Wilson Woodcock. Upon motion to adopt the report the subject was discussed, after singing "Draw Me Nearer," by Dr. Carlyle Campbell, President of Meredith College. The report was adopted.

REPORT ON CHRISTIAN EDUCATION

"Baptists have now in the South five types of schools: Theological seminaries, three in number, for the education of the Christian ministry; one training school for women who are being educated for definite Christian service in the homeland and, for the foreign fields; 26 colleges and universities; 24 junior colleges; and 11 academies, making a total of 65 schools." This factual statement is from the report of the Education Commission of the Southern Baptist Convention, May 1941.

It is reported that indebtedness has been decreased and endowments have been increased. New buildings have been erected and new departmnts have been inaugurated. The beginnings of Christian Education among Baptist was to train preachers. Now it is more inclusive. Our colleges have instituted pre-medical, predental and pre-engineering courses, and entire medical courses are offered by some of our Baptist schools.

Our North Carolina Baptist colleges are: Wake Forest, Meredith, Chowan, Mars Hill, Campbell, Wingate and Boiling Springs. The observation of an annual Christian Education Day is suggested when the pastor will preach upon the subject, or that a suitable program be presented.

In each Church the high school seniors should be informed concerning the advantages of our Baptist schools.

Endowments, the erection of new buildings and the remodelling of old buildings call for our utmost financial support.

Our Baptist leadership comes from Baptist schools or from state schools under the influence of the local Churches and the organized Baptist student work. Therefore let us give our influence and our money to the ample support of these agencies.

Respectfully submitted,
WILSON WOODCOCK.

38. Announcement about the lunch was made by the host Pastor, J. S. Hopkins.

The morning session was closed with prayer by Brother A. A. Walker.

THURSDAY AFTERNOON SESSION—1:30 O'CLOCK

39. The devotional service was led by C. M. Floyd.

40. The committee to Nominate the Executive Promotion Committee made the following report which was adopted:

See report in Associational Directory.

41. The report on the Orphanage was presented by J. S. Shore. Upon motion to adopt the report the work of the Orphanage was discussed by R. D. Covington. A large group of children from the Orphanage gave a program under the direction of Mr. and Mrs. W. B. Lord. The report was adopted.

REPORT ON N. C. BAPTIST ORPHANAGE

Surely one of the institutions closest to the hearts of the people of this Association, is the North Carolina Baptist Orphanage. For the past fifty-six years it has stood rendering for us the good service which we so desire to see accomplished and yet are unable to render for ourselves. During those years our Orphanage has given aid to nearly five thousand children. It has not only provided these unfortunate children a place to rest their weary heads, but has done a commendable job in preparing them for the duties and responsibilities of life. This is verified best by the fact that so many of the boys and girls dismissed from the Orphanage have become leaders of the communities in which they took up their abode, whether at home or abroad. Who can tell what would have been the fate of these five thousand lives and souls, without the sheltering influence of this Christian institution?

Since the Orphanage is almost entirely dependent upon the Churches and Sunday School for its support, we appeal to the delegates gathered here to see to it that their people are given the opportunity to share the blessing of this good work through the following channels:

1.—Let the Sunday School offering once a month be sent to the Orphanage.

2.—Collect a truck load of fruits, farm products and canned goods occasionally and send it to the children.

3.—Prove your gratitude to God by sending a real Thanksgiving offering in November.

4.—Be sure a club of the *Charity and Children* comes to your Church every Sunday and appoint someone to be responsible for its distribution. Reports show that the 1-3 of our people who read the *Charity and Children* give 2-3 of the total contributions to the Orphanage.

The eyes of both the officials and the children are looking to us in faith and confidence. Let us match their trust with gifts worthy of our Master's name.

Respectfully submitted,
J. C. SHORE.

42. The report on Obituaries was made by Huber Dixon. The congregation stands as Brother Dixon leads in prayer. The report was adopted.

It is with profound reverence that we pause to pay our respects to those, who, though they have departed, still live in the hearts and lives of many. No eulogy of human origin is adequate to express our gratitude and respect for their influence which is still existent in the work of this Association. As always, we must go to God's Word to find expression to the deepest thoughts and emotions of our hearts. We see John yonder on the Isle of Patmos, surrounded by the heavenly glory, receiving a divine message. Let the heavenly messenger bespeak the profound thoughts and feelings of our hearts. "Blessed are the dead which die in the Lord from henceforth: Yea, saith the Spirit, that they may rest from their labors; and their works do follow them."

Respectfully submitted,
J. HUBER DIXON.

43. The report on the Hospital was presented by B. C. Lambe. Upon motion to adopt the report the work of the Hospital was discussed by Mr. Smith Hagaman, Superintendent of the Hospital. The report was adopted.

REPORT ON BAPTIST HOSPITAL

The Baptist Hospital is just now completing additions to its plant that increase its bed capacity from 108 to 300. This will enable the hospital to treat 10,000 patients each year. Of this number, we may expect 3.300 of them to be service patients; that is, not able to pay a hospital bill. 3,300 will be mothers who have waiting for their return home 10,000 children. If the present rate is maintained, 200 will be preachers for whom no charge has been made for the last two years or more.

The hospital has a staff of 100 doctors: these are all specialists in the many fields of medicine and surgery.

The hospital runs a well-equipped standard Training School for Nurses. These are taken from as nearly every section of the state as possible. A class of about 50 will be taken each year, making a school of 150.

The Medical Building of the Bowman Gray School of Wake Forest College is now completed and the school opened the first of September of this year. While the Medical School and th Hospital will be closely related and mutually helpful in every department, they will remain separate institutions, controlled by separate Boards of Directors and supported from different sources.

Everything contributed to the hospital goes to the support of the hospital exclusively. The Mother's Day Offering by the churches is used entirely for the service of patients not financially able to pay for treatment.

The spiritual side of the hospital's service is stressed always. The Hospital has a fulltime pastor supplied by the generous donation of Mr. C. M. Scott of High Point. This pastor, Rev. Charles E. Parker, in addition to his many activities with the patients and their families and friends, teaches a course in Bible in the Nurses Training School.

The various organizations of our women and young people

are rendering a vast service to the hospital in supplying linens of all kinds—such as sheets, pillow cases, towels, washcloths, etc.

Our vastly enlarged program, of course, will require increased support.

Respectfully submitted,
B. C. LAMB.

44. The report of the Committee on Evangelism was made by J. S. Hopkins. Upon motion to adopt the report the subject was discussed by J. S. Hopkins. The report was adopted.

REPORT ON EVANGELISM

Early last spring your committee set out to encourage all the Churches of the Association in evangelism and soul-winning. Several hundred letters were mailed to pastors, Sunday School superintendents, Training Union directors, and W. M. S. presidents. An evangelistic rally was held in each of the districts of the Association. The first with North Main Street Church in High Point, the second with Magnolia Street Church in Greensboro, and the third with Penn Memorial Church in Reidsville. Following these an associational-wide rally was held in Greensboro. Large crowds attended all of these rallies and great interest in evangelism was manifested in each of the meetings. We are sure that these meetings were worthwhile and helpful, and we feel that a greater Associational program of evangelism should be undertaken in 1942. With this in mind we submit the following resolution:

WHEREAS: The salvation of souls, the advancement of the Kingdom, and the life of our Baptist denomination depends on sane, scriptural, spiritual, soul-searching evangelism, and

WHEREAS: Southern Baptists baptized only 245,500 in 1940, falling below the 269,155 of 1939, thus decreasing 8% in one year, and

WHERAS: Our own state, North Carolina, baptized 21,893 in 1940, a loss of 3,674 as compared with 1939 and a ratio of only one baptism for every 24 members, thus showing a 14% decrease in one year, and a 6% greater loss than that shown by all Southern Baptists in the same period ,and

WHEREAS: Our own Association baptized 804 in 1940, a loss of 171 as compared with 1939, and 714 in 1940, a loss of 90 as compared with 1940, thus showing a decrease of 27% in a period of two years,

BE IT RESOLVED:

FIRST: That we follow Dr. Roland Q. Leavell's suggestion in electing an evangelistic committee, as of last year, composed of a chairman, a publicity man, a survey or census man, one to promote soul winning study courses and Andrew soul-winning clubs, and one to promote out-of-the-church evangelism such as missions, radio, school house or arbor meetings, street preaching, working in camps, and the like, and,

SECOND: That we endeavor to win and baptize a minimum of one for every ten members, and,

THIRD: That our evangelistic program include the following for every Church:

(1) A revival meeting
(2) Report baptisms
(3) A census or survey
(4) One or more Andrew Soul-winning Clubs
(5) A soul-winning study course
(6) Evangelistic efforts through the S. S., B. T. U., W. M. U., and Brotherhood, and,

FOURTH: That our Association hold an evangelistic rally early next spring, the program for such meetings or meetings to be set up by the evangelistic committee.

Respectfully submitted,
JULIAN S. HOPKINS.

45. The following reports were made and adopted:

REPORT OF COMMITTEE ON TIME, PLACE AND PREACHER

Time—Wednesday and Thursday, October 23-24, 1942.

Place to be decided by the Executive-Promotion Committee.

Preacher—Rev. A. A. Walker, Alternate Rev. Hughey O. Miller.

Respectfully submitted,
A. LINCOLN FULK,
MRS. NETTIE HOGE,
R. R. SAUNDERS, Committee

REPORT OF COMMITTEE TO NOMINATE MESSENGERS TO THE BAPTIST STATE CONVENTION

Your committee on nomination of messengers to the Baptist State Convention, do place in nomination the following brethren: Z. W. Rotan and J. C. Shore.

B. G. WHITLEY,
MRS. E. J. JARVIS,
MRS. T. C. ROBBINS, Committee

REPORT OF COMMITTEE ON PROGRAM

Religious Literature	J. Ben Eller
Foreign Missions	J. S. Hopkins
Denominational Program	Wilson Woodcock
State Missions	J. C. Shore
Home Missions	J. E. Bryant
Social Service	Dr. J. C. Turner
Orphanage	E. M. Smith
Hospitals	H. R. Starling
Training Union	J. Carl Bell
W. M. U.	Mrs. Nettie Hoge
Christian Education	H. O. Miller
Sunday Schools	Grady Burgiss
Ministerial Relief and Retirement	D. W. Overby
Obituaries	Melvin Faulkner

Respectfully submitted,
T. L. SASSER,
A. C. LOVELACE,
L. G. BURGISS.

REPORT OF RESOLUTION COMMITTEE

WHEREAS, we, the Piedmont Baptist Association, have held our forty-eighth annual session with the Green Street Church of High Point, October 22-23, 1941, and

WHEREAS, we are mindful that many agencies, personalities, and love labors have entered into the success of this session under the leadership of the Holy Spirit, be it resolved:

First, that we acknowledge our indebtedness to the Green Street Church and her pastor, Rev. J. S. Hopkins, for all the comforts, conveniences, and hospitality so graciously afforded us.

Second, that we express our hearty approval of the work of the Committee on Evangelism and urge its continued and intensified activity.

Third, that we commend all who have contributed to the success of the program this year, especially the work of our most efficient and faithful servants, our Moderator and our Clerk.

Fourth, that we urge upon our church leaders to give emphasis to more prayer and meditation in all departments of our Church work to the end that there be a deepening of our spiritual life.

Respectfully submitted,
A. A. WALKER,
THELMA PATRICK,
EARL BRYANT.

46. Following singing "Bless Be the Tie That Binds," the session closed with prayer by Brother T. L. Sasser.

IN MEMORIAM

Asheboro Street—
Mrs. A. L. Sparrow
Miss Elois Smith
Mr. D. L. Smith
Mrs. J. M. Peace

Bailey Memorial
Mrs. Bessie Loy

Bessemer—
Mrs. Emily Hartness
Mrs. J. M. Sharpe
Mr. J. N. Stout

Calvary—
Mr. Glen Hancock

College Park—
Mr. Charlie Andrews
Mr. J. G. Osborne
Miss Virginia Shepherd

Fairview—
Mrs. Belle Whitted

Florida Street—
Mr. J. W. Allred, Sr.
Miss Betty Holton
Mrs. V. M. Kirkman
Mr. Eddie Sewell
Mrs. J. S. Wallace
G. G. Watts

Greensboro, First
Mr. J. W. Trimble
Mr. R. L. Patterson
Mr. A. W. Robinson
Mr. J. O. Applewhite
Mr. J. B. Wright, Jr.
Miss Nannie Kivett
Mr. J. R. Webb
Mrs. A. A. Johnson
Mr. Frances Hancock
Mr. H. W. Dettmering
Dr. B. R. Long

Green Street—
Mr. F. B. Culler
Mr. J. C. McCreary
Mr. Walter Suckler
Mr. J. C. Young
Mrs. H. J. Ward
Mr. J. R. Rickart

High Point, First—
Mr. M. S. Barbee
Mrs. E. R. Gary
Mr. J. Wesley Smith
Mrs. Harriett Gurley
Mrs. F. M. Pickett
Mr. E. C. Plummer

Lebanon—
Mr. Jessie Mitchell
Mr. B. C. Goodwin

Magnolia Street—
Mrs. James Overbey

Mount Zion—
Mr. S. M. Martin
Miss Mattie Foster

North Main—
Mrs. R. S. Welborn

North Park—
Mr. Joe Smith

Osborne Chapel—
Mr. J. R. McCandless

Osceola—
Mrs. Annie Brande

Penn Memorial—
Mr. Bud Bailey

Pomona—
Mrs. Fannie Bradley
Mrs Alice Ward

Pleasant Garden—
Mrs. H. A. Eddy
Jennie Swaim

Reidsville, First—
Mrs. J. F. Murray
Mr. Henry Southard
Mr. George W. Martin

Sixteenth Street
Mr. E. L. Dixon
Mr. John H. Garner

Smith Grove—
Mr. Robert Westmoreland

Stevens Memorial—
Mrs. R. A. Vetito

South Side—
Mr. Lewis King
Mrs. Eulis Meredith
Mrs. A. M. Garren

Summerfield—
Mrs. Lela Rice
Mr. J. T. Ellis

Tabernacle [Ossipee]—
Mr. C. E. Diamond

Tabernacle [Greensboro]—
Mrs. Mittie Whitfield
Mrs. J. S. Moore
Mr. J. C. Curran
Mr. J. R. Ward

Temple—
F. M. Jarvis
Mr. Forest Hankins

MINUTES OF THE PIEDMONT ASSOCIATION W. M. U.

Annual Meeting April 25, 1941

The W. M. U. of the Piedmont Association met with the Eller Memorial Baptist Church in Greensboro, Friday, April 25, 1941. The theme for the meeting was "The Great Commission."

The morning session opened at 10:00 with Mrs. Hoge, Superintendent, presiding. The devotional was in charge of Mrs. Grady Burgess. Words of welcome were spoken by Mrs. Ethel Morrison. The response was made by Mrs. J. S. Hopkins.

The work of Stewardship and the Hundred Thousand Club was presented by Mrs. Grover H. Jones.

Mrs. J. J. Andoe made an announcement about the book display. After singing "Jesus Saves" Mrs. B. K. Mason spoke on "Telling the Story." This was followed by a solo by Mrs. J. Q. Seawell.

The Superintendent gives her annual report. There are now 37 active societies. The report included a discussion of the Program of Jesus.

The appointment of committees was made by Mrs. Hoge. The meeting was adjourned for dinner.

The afternoon session was called to order by the Superintendent. Mr. Rutledge of Charlotte sang "Satisfied with Jesus." Mrs. B. K. Mason leads in prayer. The devotional service was led by Mrs. Jack Medlin.

Rev. Wilbur Hutchins of Winston-Salem brought an inspirational message on the subject "The Task of Evangelizing the World."

The Treasurer's report is presented by Mrs. C. E. Siceloff.

In the absence of Mrs. J. S. Farmer, Mrs. J. Clyde Turner, President of the North Carolina W. M. U., presented the work of Mission Study and Personal Service."

The work of the Orphanage, Hospital, and Fannie Heck Memorial was presented by Mrs. O. E. Lee. Rev. C. E. Parker, Pastor of the Hospital, discussed the work of the Hospital and the need for a larger Mother's Day offering.

Mrs. Dearing Stone conducted the Memorial.

The report on Young People's report was made by Miss Ruth Scott. A Playlet was given by a group from the College Park Baptist Church. Miss Mary Currin, State Young People's Leader, discusses the young people's work.

The report of the Nominating Committee is presented and the officers elected as follows:

REPORT OF NOMINATING COMMITTEE

Superintendent	Mrs. Nettie Hoge
Secretary	Mrs. A. Andrews
Treasurer	Mrs. C. E. Siceloff
Personal Service Chairman	Mrs. J. C. Shore
Mission Study Chairmen	Mrs. J. J. Andoe
Stewardship Chairman	Mrs. J. M. Cates, First Greensboro
Young People's Leader	Miss Ruby Scott

Group Leaders

Mrs. H. A. Knight	High Point
Mrs. O. J. Howard	Greensboro
Mrs. H. L. Morrison	Reidsville

Respectfully submitted,
MRS. BEN SPENCER,
MRS. T. C. ROBBINS,
MRS. T. L. SASSER,
Committee.

The meeting was closed with a consecration service.

MRS. A. ANDREWS, Secretary.

Churches	*Regular Treasurers and Post Offices*
Allen Jay	W. R. Hobson, Rt. 1, High Point
Antioch	Ray Vauter, Reidsville
Brightwood	J. M. Crabtree, Rt. 5, Box 323, Greensboro
Buchanan	R. P. Johnson, Rt. 6, Box 272, Greensboro
Calvary	J. I. Carroll, Rt. 4, Reidsville
Fair Grove	W. L. Lee, Rt. 2, Greensboro
Fairview	D. E. Trantham, Rt. 2, Reidsville
Fairmont Park	R. A. Teague, High Point
Gibsonville	T. L. Robinson, Gibsonville
GREENSBORO	
Asheboro Street	R. R. Todd, 2608 Springwood Drive
Bailey Memorial	W. H. Stevenson, 2405 High Point Rd.
Bessemer	C. L. Murray, Box 688, Greensboro
College Park	L. E. Ogburn, Greensboro
Eller Memorial	Mrs. Robert Burgess, 1214 Walnut St.
First	Howard Gardner, 405 Sunset Drive
Florida Street	D. M. Frazier, 1319 Florida St.
Lathan Park	R. A. Anderson, 1312 Wendover Ave.
Magnolia Street	H. S. Noah, Greensboro
Pomona	E. E. Henry, Pomona
Revolution	Waldo Johnson, 2211 Shober St.
Sixteenth Street	L. F. Paris, 1608 15th St.
Stevens Memorial	Mrs. C. B. Brisson, Rt. 2
Tabernacle	E. H. Moore, 1704 Grove St.
Webster Memorial	R. H. King, 1505 14th St.
Guilford	W. L. Hudson, Guilford
HIGH POINT	
First	Miss Thelma Patrick, 309½ Church St.
Green Street	R. R. Holder, High Point
Hilliard Memorial	J. W. Metcalf, High Point
North Main Street	W. C. Ward, High Point, Rt. 1
North Park	L. W. Glenn, 805 Dayton St.
South Side	F. E. Caudle, 403 Coltrane St.
West End	C. M. Scott, 1009 Ferndale Drive
Jessup Grove	Dan H. Jessup, Guilford College
Jewel	Mrs. L. Weatherman, High Point, Rt. 2
Lebanon	L. R. Chilton, Brown Summit, Rt. 2
Mount Zion	Mrs. C. M. Johnson, High Point, Rt. 3
Oak Grove	W. L. Shakleford, High Point, Rt. 3
Osborne Chapel	Roy Whitaker, Greensboro, Rt. 1
Osceola	Mrs. D. A. Green, Brown Summit, Rt. 1
Pine Grove	R. F. Handy, High Point, Rt. 3
Pisgah	L. C. Madden, 414 Winslow St., High Point
Pleasant Garden	Cecil T. Burton, Pleasant Garden

Pleasant Grove .... D. R. Robertson, Box 175, Greensboro, Rt. 3
Reedy Fork .... Lee Elder, Brown Summit, Rt. 2
REIDSVILLE
First .... J. P. Kemp, Reidsville
Mount Olive .... Mrs. Odell Delapp, Box 283, Reidsville
Penn Memorial .... Thomas G. Dixon, Reidsville
Rocky Knoll .... Mrs. R. A. Laughlin, Greensboro, Rt. 1
Ruffin Stacy ....
Smith Grove .... Drew Smith, Colfax, Rt. 1
Summerfield .... Mrs. Hattie Shields, Summerfield
Tabernacle .... W. E. Collins, Burlington, Rt. 4
Temple .... M. A. Tysinger, High Point, Rt. 4

OFFICERS OF THE PIEDMONT BAPTIST SUNDAY SCHOOL ASSOCIATION

Superintendent—A. A. Walker, 507 Delancy Street, Greensboro
Associate Supt. in Charge of Evangelism—J. S. Hopkins, 324 Woodrow Avenue, High Point
Associate Supt. in Charge of Training—F. L. Paschal, 2420 Camden Road, Greensboro
Sec.-Treas.—L. G. Burgiss, 103 E. Wendover Ave., Greensboro
Choirster—H. R. Starling, 2218 Shober St., Greensboro
Department Superintendents:
Junior—Ralph Slate, 817 Rotary Drive, High Point
Intermediate—Mrs. Norman B. Moury, 2809 Sherwood St., Greensboro
Young People—T. L. Ogburn, Asheboro St. Ex., Greensboro
Adult—M. D. Teague, 608 Scott Avenue, Greensboro
Extension—Mrs. D. S. Ring, 909 Granby St., High Point
Vacation B. S.—O. E. Lee, c-o First Church, Greensboro
Group Superintendents:
Reidsville—J. C. Shore, R. F. D. 4, Reidsville
High Point—E. M. Smith, 520 Bridges St., High Point
Greensboro—J. J. Norwood, 1600 Asheboro St., Greensboro

Cradle Roll—Mrs. J. W. Preston, 1534 McCormick St., Greensboro
Beginner—Miss Ruth Scott, 1503 Spring Garden St., Greensboro
Primary—Miss Lila Barton, 619 Waugh St., Greensboro

TABLE ONE—CHURCH MEMBERSHIP

CHURCHES	Village, Town, or Country	When Constituted	PASTORS AND POST OFFICES	Days of Meeting	CHURCH MEMBERSHIP GAINS: Members Rep't'd. Last Year	Baptisms	Letters	Statements	Restorations	LOSSES: Letters	Exclusions	Erasures	Deaths	Total Present Members	Weekly Prayer Meets	Revivals Held, Year	Obs. Lord's Supper	Fam. Rec. Bap. Paper
Allen Jay	V	1934	E. M. Floyd, Thomasville, R. 2	All	176	26	16	...	1	...	...	...	...	219	*	2	4	...
Antioch	O	1934	Melvin Faulkner, Reidsville	1 3	64	...	2	...	...	...	...	...	...	66	*	2	...	...
Brightwood		....	H. P. Gauldin, Greensboro, R. 5	All	.....	7	25	2	...	2	...	...	...	34	*	2	...	...
Buchanan	O	1936	J. B. Clifton, Greensboro		93	29	9	8	...	...	5	...	...	134	*	1	2	...
Calvary	O	1901	J. C. Shore, Reidsville, R. 4	2 4	164	3	...	1	...	...	...	...	1	162	...	1	2	9
Fair Grove	O	1940	A. R Riddle, Greensboro, R. 2	All	69	4	1	...	...	12	...	...	...	62	*	2	1	...
Fairview	O	1904	J. C. Shore, Reidsville, R. 4	1 3	125	7	5	...	...	2	...	30	1	104	...	1	2	8
Fairmont Park	V	1940	James E. Swinson, Hanes	All	80	9	22	4	...	...	...	...	...	115	*	3	3	14
Gibsonville	T	1884	E. A. Long, Germantown	2 4	249	6	3	1	...	5	...	1	...	253	*	...	4	3
GREENSBORO		....			.....	...	...	...	...	...	...	...	...	.....	...	...	...	...
Asheboro Street	C	1899	J. Ben Eller, 709 [illegible]o St.	All	1175	35	32	6	...	41	...	7	4	1196	*	2	4	65
Bailey Memorial	C	1937	G. C. Coe, Pomona	All	104	5	1	...	...	...	...	...	1	109	*	2	12	...
Bessemer	V	1923	A. A. Walker, Greensboro	All	480	29	12	4	...	10	...	5	3	507	*	1	4	3
College Park	C	1906	Wilson W. Woodcock, Greensboro	All	578	28	36	...	...	22	...	18	3	599	*	1	12	35
Eller Memorial	C	1897	B. K. Mason	All	837	20	17	...	...	7	...	7	...	860	*	2	4	...
First	C	1859	Dr. J. [illegible]le Turner, Greensboro	All	2204	53	124	2	...	111	20	...	12	2240	*	1	12	88
Florida Street	C	1916	J. H. Saunders, 1110 Glenwood Ave.	All	322	58	44	4	1	6	...	...	6	417	*	2	4	20
Latham Park	C	1916	Hubert Dixon, Pleasant Garden	All	60	1	...	...	...	1	...	...	...	60	*	1	...	...
Magnolia Street	C	1912	Grady Burgess, Greensboro	All	182	20	7	...	...	15	...	1	1	208	*	2	2	8
Pomona	V	1906	C. M. Oates, Pomona	All	241	3	11	...	...	14	...	2	2	239	*	3	2	...
Revolution	C	1907	H. R. Starling, 2218 Shober St.	All	328	14	6	...	...	4	...	1	...	343	*	2	2	...
Sixteenth Street	C	1907	Z. W. Rotan, 0[illegible]-16th St.	All	463	...	9	2	1	40	3	...	2	430	*	2	8	1
Stevens Memorial	V	1922	B. C. Lambe, Greensboro, R. 2	All	138	7	8	...	...	8	...	...	1	144	*	2	4	...
Tabernacle	C	1938	B. G. [illegible]y, 1200 Elwell Ave.	All	231	7	15	7	...	17	...	1	4	238	*	3	4	...
Webster Memorial	C	1935	R. Cole Lee, Greensboro, R. 5	All	147	4	14	1	3	2	...	...	...	169	*	1	3	...
Guilford	V	1914	C. R. Pierce, 336½ S. Elm St.	All	81	8	6	...	...	6	...	...	...	87	...	...	1	3
HIGH POINT		....			.....	...	...	...	...	...	...	...	...	.....	...	...	...	...
First	C	1825	Dr. A. B. Conrad, 225 Lindsay St.	All	1355	16	37	...	...	49	...	6	6	1347	*	...	2	55
Green Street	C	1900	J. S. Hopkins, High Point	All	1344	52	38	2	...	33	...	...	7	1396	*	1	4	50
Hilliard Memorial	C	1929	Hughey O. Miller, 2233 Edgewood	All	331	..	6	3	...	22	...	2	...	306	*	1	2	...

North Main Street	C	1908	A. John [illegible]k, Oak View Rd.	All	332	1	9	...	...	3	...	...	1	338	*	...	3	22
North Park	C	1929	E. M. Smith, 520 Bridge St.	All	184	3	...	1	...	7	...	...	1	180	*	2	4	12
South Side	C	1916	G. [illegible] Liner, 407 Highland	All	318	9	2	...	1	12	...	...	3	315	*	2	4	1
West End	C	1913	A. C. Lovelace, Montlieu Ave.	All	405	20	12	...	...	5	...	3	...	429	*	2	4	...
Jessup Grove	O	1933	James E. Wiggs, 1515 Grove St.	All	48	45	13	8	2	2	...	...	...	113	*	3	1	2
Jewell	O	1941	...	All	...	...	17	1	...	...	...	...	...	18	*	2	...	...
Lebanon	O	1911	Melvin G. Faulkner, Redisville	All	190	13	5	3	1	18	...	...	2	192	*	2	4	...
Mount Zion	O	1826	J. T. Swinson, High Point, R. 3	2 4	166	3	1	...	...	...	...	...	2	168	...	1	1	...
Oak Grove	O	1916	R. L. Smith, 613 [illegible] High Pt.	All	147	11	6	5	...	1	...	...	...	165	*	2	4	...
Osborne Chapel	O	1934	Hubert Bennett, Greensboro	1	54	...	1	...	...	4	...	...	1	50	*	2	2	...
Osceola	O	....	R. L. Kizer, 810 N. Mebane, Burlington	1 3	81	8	6	1	...	3	2	...	1	90	*	1	2	1
Pine Grove	O	1938	W L Campbell, 2211 Maple, Greensboro	All	75	4	3	3	...	8	...	1	...	76	*	2	4	...
Pisgah	C	1939	W. L. Smith, Box 1772, High Point	All	225	52	10	2	...	3	...	1	...	285	*	1	4	...
Pleasant Garden	V	1933	J. Huber Dixon, Pleasant Garden	All	117	2	5	...	...	2	...	...	1	75	*	1	3	...
Pleasant Grove	O	1938	I. M. [illegible]d, Pomona, Box 119	All	90	6	10	1	...	1	...	...	...	106	*	2	11	...
Reedy Fork	O	1940	Elige Lankford, Greensboro	All	16	3	13	...	...	6	...	...	...	26	*	1	...	...
REIDSVILLE																		
First	C	1844	F. L. Sasser, Reidsville	All	870	19	11	...	...	10	...	...	3	887	*	1	4	49
Mount Zion	C	1929	J. Earl Bryant, Box 224, Reidsville	All	214	7	23	1	...	16	...	20	...	209	*	1	2	14
Penn Memorial	C	1929	D. W. Overby, Reidsville	All	204	19	6	3	...	4	...	3	1	224	*	1	4	...
Rocky Knoll	O	1934	L. C. Chandler, Greensboro, R. 1	All	212	19	6	...	...	4	...	...	1	237	*	1	4	...
Ruffin Stacey	O	1931	I. T. London, Reidsville, R. 5	All	186	3	1	1	...	1	...	...	...	190	*	2	4	3
Smith Grove	O	1921	R. O. Nuckles, Colfax, R. 1	All	178	...	...	...	...	1	...	...	1	176	...	2	1	...
Summerfield	V	....	E. A. Long, Germantown	1	202	4	1	1	...	6	...	...	2	200	...	1	3	7
Tabernacle	V	1933	Eugene Hancock, Graham	All	81	11	2	...	...	8	...	4	1	81	*	2	...	...
Temple	O	1939	J. T. Swinson, High Point, R. 3	All	40	11	7	7	...	10	...	...	2	55	*	2	3	...
			Total		16256	724	676	85	10	564	30	113	77	16929	...	82	...	473

TABLE TWO—SUNDAY SCHOOLS

CHURCHES	SUPERINTENDENTS AND POST OFFICES	Cradle Roll, Under 3	Beginners, 3-5 Years	Primaries, 6-8 Years	Juniors, 9-12 Years	Intermediates, 13-16	Young People, 17-24	Adults, 25 and Up	Extension Dept.	Gen., Dep'tal. Officers	Total Enrollment Incl. Of'cers. T'chers.	What is Average Att.?	Baptisms from S. S.	Is School Graded?	Teachers Holding Dip.	Enrollment Vac. Sch.	Av. Att. Vac. Sch.	S. S. Teachers and Officers
[illegible]n Jay	Wade H. [illegible]e, High Point	13	20	25	52	40	35	150	...	12	347	236	...	*	...	...	...	...
Antioch	Lee Lewis, Reidsville	...	...	15	...	24	...	30	...	...	69	...	...	...	...	...	...	...
Brightwood	B. G. Yowe, Greensboro, Rt. 5	...	13	24	...	23	31	35	...	3	129	71	...	...	...	...	...	...
Buchanan	R. M. [illegible]e, [illegible]o	13	33	...	30	29	46	60	...	...	211	113	7	...	...	...	...	...
Calvary	J. W. McCargo, Reidsville, Route 2	...	19	14	14	13	48	85	...	10	203	102	3	...	...	...	...	...
Fair [illegible]e	G. W. Johnson, Greensboro, Route 2	4	23	...	12	...	30	20	...	6	95	50	...	...	...	...	...	...
Fairview	A. D. Hopkins, Reidsville, Route 1	...	18	25	19	35	20	24	...	...	141	95	7	...	...	...	...	...
Fairmont Park	W. R. Moose, High Point, Route 2	30	...	30	...	34	40	60	...	3	197	119	...	...	...	58	47	8
Gibsonville	E. C. Riggins, Gibsonville	...	19	19	38	32	47	65	16	...	236	140	4	*	...	...	...	...
GREENSBORO																		
Asheboro Street	M. D. Teague, Greensboro	40	45	117	156	150	166	389	60	5	1128	462	...	...	6	...	...	...
Bailey Memorial	E. J. Jarvis, Greensboro	9	26	...	...	35	47	20	...	1	138	75	5	...	...	...	...	...
Bessemer	A. C. [illegible]n, Greensboro	3[illegible]	23	38	45	68	38	116	...	6	366	208	27	*	...	65	45	...
College Park	B. B. Stockard, [illegible]oro	57	27	39	47	47	127	145	...	4	493	284	...	*	...	...	...	...
Eller Memorial	C. E. Brady, Greensboro	15	54	91	143	101	95	208	5	32	744	368	...	*	3	166	139	28
First	O. E. [illegible]e, Greensboro	164	83	130	214	205	209	925	225	43	2198	889	44	*	4	127	94	...
Florida Street	J. B. Rumby, Sr., Greensboro	32	35	73	71	66	43	182	10	12	524	300	33	*	...	162	125	16
Latham Park	R. A. Anderson, [illegible]oro	...	10	...	...	19	...	17	...	...	46	35	...	...	...	...	...	4
Magnolia Street	D. L. Wrenn, Greensboro	6	13	21	21	16	27	54	...	3	161	115	14	...	...	...	...	15
Pomona	C. C. Patterson, Pomona	...	35	32	71	55	68	86	...	3	350	194	...	*	...	91	76	13
Revolution	Grady Phillips, [illegible]boro	22	25	39	56	42	26	43	15	6	274	183	14	*	...	109	65	...
Sixteenth Street	Fred Hester, [illegible]boro	15	37	43	80	65	46	139	...	8	433	232	...	...	2	131	96	24
Stevens Memorial	L. A. [illegible]s, Greensboro	8	10	15	40	18	16	55	...	...	162	135	...	*	...	44	34	17
Tabernacle	W. O. [illegible], Greensboro	35	28	21	30	30	36	41	26	5	252	125	5	*	...	78	58	10
Webster Memorial	[illegible]m Pearman, [illegible]boro	10	10	18	20	12	34	58	...	14	176	102	3	...	4	...	...	...
Guilford	[illegible]es Case, Greensboro, Route 3	...	6	6	6	20	12	36	...	8	94	60	8	*	...	...	...	8
HIGH POINT																		
First	Dr. W. F. Clayton, High Point	55	60	107	176	156	160	506	75	4	1299	661	13	*	15	...	...	88
Green Street	W. E. Crissman High Point	38	70	88	171	185	192	459	...	41	1244	582	40	*	...	412	290	35
Hilliard Memorial	L. E. Edwards, High Point	...	24	11	45	37	24	76	6	...	223	168	...	*	...	...	...	27

North Main Street	S. R. Clinard, High Point, Route 1	10	21	48	68	51	73	76	...	4	351	...	...	...	...	...	...	...
North Park	L. R. McNeill, High Point	16	16	21	32	52	16	59	3	3	218	150	3	*	...	...	...	...
South Side	W. R. Bray, High Point	...	17	15	39	30	67	50	...	8	226	148	...	*	...	...	...	...
West End	V. S. Coffey, High Point	38	29	30	95	48	31	106	25	6	408	222	...	*	3	...	...	...
Jessup Grove	Peel Stanley, Guilford College	...	25	...	35	...	40	68	...	...	168	150	45	*	...	...	...	6
Jewel	S. P. Stutts, Sr., High Point	...	...	...	38	...	...	20	...	...	58	55	5	...	...	...	...	12
Lebanon	Diamond Davis Brown Summit, Rt. 2.	10	11	17	21	19	40	66	...	4	188	127	...	...	...	...	...	12
Mount Zion	George H. Spoon, Liberty, Rt. 3	...	...	20	13	22	32	30	...	7	124	76	3	...	...	...	...	...
Oak Grove	A. L. Saunders, High Point, Rt. 1	...	7	11	20	9	25	32	...	...	104	71	11	...	2	...	...	10
Osborne Chapel	R. S. Law, Greensboro Rt. 1	...	20	...	13	36	...	26	...	...	95	50	...	...	...	106	...	8
Osceola	D. A. Greene, Brown Summit, Rt. 1	...	16	9	15	22	25	21	...	2	110	66	7	*	...	...	...	...
Pine Grove	L. R. Loflin, Jamestown	...	18	...	11	15	17	45	...	8	114	99	...	*	...	...	...	...
Pisgah	F. P. Vaughn, High Point	15	10	54	31	58	54	129	...	1	352	225	...	*	...	...	...	...
Pleasant Garden	W. J. Smith, Pleasant Garden	10	21	8	22	13	29	27	...	2	132	55	2	*	...	...	...	9
Pleasant Grove	F. M. Atkins, Greensboro, Rt. 3	...	15	13	16	31	29	25	22	...	151	92	...	*	...	...	...	11
Reedy Fork	Alvin L. Bullard, Greensboro	10	17	13	22	41	...	26	...	6	135	55	...	...	...	...	...	8
REIDSVILLE	...	...	...	...	...	...	...	...	...	...	...	...	...	...	...	...	...	...
First	R. T. Burton, Reidsville	57	35	50	90	72	106	409	50	12	881	352	19	*	...	142	111	29
Mount Olive	Earl Gammon, Reidsville	...	25	25	44	28	7	47	...	6	182	99	3	*	3	...	...	20
Penn Memorial	W. H. Ford, Reidsville	...	20	28	16	20	17	76	...	4	181	140	10	...	...	...	...	...
Rocky Knoll	R. R. Sudderth, G'boro, Rt. 1	32	25	25	50	40	35	140	...	15	362	207	...	...	...	...	...	...
Ruffin Stacey	...	...	...	...	...	...	...	...	...	...	...	...	...	...	...	...	...	...
Smith Grove	J. A. Farrington, Colfax, Rt. 1	...	25	...	27	...	43	30	...	...	125	64	...	...	...	...	...	...
Summerfield	Marion Ayers, Summerfield	...	9	18	20	23	29	40	...	...	139	85	4	...	...	...	...	13
Tabernacle	W. E. Collins, Burlington	...	20	...	20	...	32	25	...	4	101	75	...	...	...	...	...	...
Temple	Van Wagoner, HighPoint	...	...	15	12	...	18	17	...	3	65	56	...	...	...	...	...	...
	TOTALS	796	1168	1461	2327	2187	2428	5674	538	324	16903	8817	339	...	42	1691	1180	431

TABLE THREE—BAPTIST TRAINING UNION

CHURCHES	DIRECTOR OF TRAINING UNION	Adult Unions	Yng. People's Unions	Intermediate Unions	Junior Unions	Story Hours	Total Unions, St. Hrs.	Adults Enrolled	Yng. People Enrolled	Int. Enrolled	Jrs. Enrolled	Story Hours Enrolled	Total Enrolled Unions and Story Hours	Daily Bible Readers	Taking Study Course	Systematic Givers	Students in College
Allen Jay	Thomas Knight, Thomasville	1	1	1	1	1	5	30	10	15	25	8	88	21	...	88	...
Fairmont Park	R. A. Teague, High Point	1	1	...	1	1	4	13	24	...	16	13	66	...	50	...	...
GREENSBORO	...	...	...	...	...	...	...	...	...	...	...	...	...	...	...	...	...
Asheboro Street	J. J. Norwood, Greensboro	...	2	2	2	1	7	...	49	67	37	9	162	5	64	48	11
Bailey Memorial	Royland Mitchell, Greensboro	...	1	1	1	...	3	...	11	8	9	...	28	23	27	28	...
Bessemer	Miss Nórfleet Dixon, Greensboro	...	1	2	1	...	4	...	9	26	12	...	47	11	17	30	...
College Park	Miss [illegible]la Marks, Greensboro	1	2	1	1	...	5	6	44	6	10	...	66	7	6	8	5
Eller Memorial	Miss Leah Andrews	1	1	1	2	1	6	18	18	18	30	8	92	31	30	37	2
First	O. E. Lee, Greensboro	3	3	4	3	1	14	47	70	65	53	27	262	73	52	143	50
Florida Street	J. W. Bolejack, Greensboro	2	1	2	4	2	11	36	14	21	30	20	121	61	58	78	2
Magnolia Street	Mrs. G. H. Williamson, Greensboro	1	1	1	...	1	4	12	8	15	...	15	50	10	13	40	...
Pomona	J. A. Culberson, Pomona	1	...	...	...	...	1	12	...	...	...	...	12	...	...	...	...
Revolution	Mrs. Lois Rieson, Greensboro	1	1	1	...	1	4	9	14	14	...	20	57	3	11	26	...
Sixteenth Street	Harry Moore, Greensboro	...	1	1	1	...	3	...	17	9	10	...	36	19	15	27	...
Tabernacle	Mrs. Howard Phillips, Greensboro	1	1	1	1	1	5	10	10	14	12	...	46	29	26	32	2
Webster Memorial	R. B. Stacey, Greensboro	1	1	...	1	1	4	14	14	...	10	8	46	11	17	12	1
HIGH POINT	...	...	...	...	...	...	...	...	...	...	...	...	...	...	...	...	...
First	W. O. Burnham, High Point	...	1	2	4	1	8	6	22	71	119	30	248	51	67	87	25
Green Street	Burgess Leonard, High Point	2	2	1	2	1	8	42	44	13	38	11	148	38	99	66	...
Hilliard Memorial	Everett Grubb, High Point	1	1	1	1	1	5	18	9	16	12	8	63	17	29	49	...
North Main Street	Lucien Williams, High Point	1	1	2	2	1	7	12	14	16	14	10	66	...	...	...	1
North Park	W. H. Brock, High Point	1	1	2	2	1	7	10	16	33	32	5	96	52	44	59	...
West End	R. G. Barlowe, High Point	1	1	1	1	1	5	11	9	14	13	5	52	23	38	24	1
Jessup Grove	Paul C. Ward, Guilford College	1	1	...	1	...	3	10	30	...	36	...	76	41	31	55	...
Lebanon	Harry Gregory	...	1	...	...	...	1	...	20	...	...	...	20	...	...	...	...
Pisgah	L. J. Mabe, High Point	1	1	1	1	1	5	25	18	20	15	9	87	37	25	...	...
Pleasant Garden	Mrs. M. E. Johnson, Pleasant Garden	...	1	...	...	...	1	...	49	...	...	...	49	...	...	...	...
Reedy Fork	Lewis [illegible]r, Brown Summit, Rt. 2	...	1	1	...	...	2	...	21	16	...	...	37	...	27	...	...
REIDSVILLE	...	...	...	...	...	...	...	...	...	...	...	...	...	...	...	...	...
First	W. O. Kelley, Reidsville	1	3	2	1	...	7	15	51	41	17	...	124	64	55	104	6
Mount Olive	B. J. Harvey, Reidsville	1	...	1	1	1	4	17	...	10	23	12	62	19	8	43	...
Penn Memorial	Edgar Bray, Reidsville	1	1	1	1	1	5	17	7	9	12	4	49	20	37	31	...
Rocky Knoll	L. S. Moore, Greensboro, Rt. 1	1	1	1	1	1	5	15	20	18	18	12	83	30	31	29	...
Summerfield	Ivan Angel, Summerfield	1	...	1	1	...	3	18	...	22	20	...	60	...	32	38	1
Temple	Mrs. R. L. Radden, High Point	1	1	1	1	1	5	25	12	12	8	6	63	42	...	...	...
	TOTALS	28	36	36	39	22	161	448	654	589	631	240	2562	738	909	1182	107

TABLE FOUR—WOM

CHURCHES	PRESIDENTS OF W. M. S. AND POST OFFICES	Number W. M. S.	Number Y. W. A.'s	Number G. A.'s	Number R. A.'s	Number Sunbeams	Total W. M. U. Orgs.	W. M. S. Members	Y. W. A.'s Members	G. A.'s Members	R. A.'s Members	Sunbeam Members	Tot. Members Enr'l'd	Tot. Enr'l'd. M. S. C.	Contributions (Local Work) Given by W. M. U.	Contributions (Missions) by W. M. U.	Grand Total All Purposes by W. M. U. and All Its Orgs.
Buchanan	Mrs. J. B. Clifton, Bessemer	1	1	...	...	...	2	14	15	...	...	...	29	...	$........	$ 13.10	$ 13.10
Calvary	Mrs. J. E. McCargo, Reidsville	1	1	1	...	...	3	29	25	14	...	...	68	...	36.51	128.49	165.00
Fair Grove	Mrs. Ella Harris, Greensboro, Route 2	1	...	...	...	...	1	...	...	...	...	...	...	...	...	...	...
Fairview	Mrs. R. [illegible] Coleman, Reidsville	1	...	...	...	...	1	15	...	...	...	...	15	8	35.00	12.04	47.04
Fairmont Park	Mrs. Willus Jones, High Point	1	...	...	...	...	1	30	...	...	...	...	30	...	265.00	27.50	292.50
Gibsonville	Mrs. E. C. Riggins, Gibsonville	1	...	...	...	...	1	...	...	...	...	...	...	...	...	17.00	17.00
GREENSBORO																	
[illegible] Street	Mrs. D. F. Stone, Greensboro	1	2	2	1	1	7	180	44	39	19	17	299	118	268.99	2735.35	3004.34
Bailey Memorial	Mrs. W. J. Mitchell, [illegible]	1	...	...	...	...	1	16	...	...	...	...	16	...	15.90	35.40	51.30
Bessemer	Mrs. J. R. Medlin, [illegible]	3	...	2	...	1	6	45	...	21	...	40	106	18	...	259.27	259.27
College Park	Mrs. J. B. Watson, Greensboro	1	2	...	...	1	4	40	60	...	...	8	108	35	172.55	197.37	369.92
Eller Memorial	Mrs. [illegible] Thornburg, [illegible]	1	1	1	1	1	5	39	15	12	10	27	103	12	964.84	52.15	1016.99
First	Mrs. Ben L. Spencer, [illegible]	1	2	2	2	1	8	390	122	74	22	81	689	150	...	14141.08	14141.08
Forida Street	Mrs. J. T. [illegible], Greensboro	1	...	2	1	1	5	87	...	25	9	12	133	40	...	232.41	232.41
Magnolia Street	[illegible] Burgiss, [illegible]	1	1	1	...	1	4	26	8	14	..	25	73	27	19.65	72.35	92.00
Pomona	Mrs. W. H. Brown, Pomona	1	...	1	...	1	3	42	...	20	...	16	78	...	...	...	...
Revolution	Miss Sallie Burgess, [illegible]	1	1	1	1	1	5	34	7	7	6	20	74	...	431.97	249.21	681.18
Sixteenth Street	Mrs. W. M. Smith, Greensboro	1	1	1	...	1	4	30	14	21	...	12	77	35	...	...	340.73
Stevens Memorial	Mrs. S. M. Brissen, Greensboro	1	...	...	...	...	1	35	...	...	...	...	35	...	...	126.25	126.25
Tabernacle	Mrs. L. W. Driver, [illegible]	1	1	1	...	1	4	22	9	17	...	16	64	12	...	34.50	34.50
[illegible] Memorial	Mrs. C. L. Straughn, [illegible]	1	1	1	1	1	5	43	10	8	6	15	82	...	...	95.03	195.35
Guilford	Mrs. Alice Ferrell, [illegible] College	1	...	1	...	1	3	12	...	8	...	10	30	...	...	37.36	37.36
HIGH POINT																	
First	Mrs. Fred G. Flagler, High Point	1	1	2	2	1	7	148	20	52	48	28	296	84	1920.27	3750.89	5671.16
Green Street	Mrs. L. A. [illegible], High Point	1	2	1	1	1	6	100	28	12	9	14	163	91	4419.75	804.52	5224.27
Hilliard Memorial	Mrs. J. B. Ellis, High Point	1	1	1	1	1	5	14	9	13	10	20	66	12	...	114.68	114.68
North Main Street	Mrs. S. R. [illegible], High Point	1	...	...	...	...	1	18	...	...	...	...	18	...	8.25	141.00	149.25
North Park	Mrs. L. W. Glenn, High Point	1	1	2	1	1	6	16	12	30	10	15	83	...	1073.04	187.38	1260.42
South Side	Mrs. F. E. Caudle, High Point	1	...	...	...	...	1	24	...	...	...	...	24	13	84.31	17.96	102.27
West End	Mrs. Pearl Presslar, High Point	1	...	2	...	1	4	35	...	25	...	20	80	...	151.00	99.90	250.90
Jessup Grove	Mrs. James E. Wiggs, [illegible]	1	...	...	...	...	1	10	...	...	...	...	10	...	...	...	...
[illegible]	Mrs. A. P. Jarvis, [illegible]	1	...	...	...	...	1	30	...	...	...	...	30	...	...	50.00	50.00
Pleasant Garden	Mrs. Ida [illegible], Pleasant Garden	1	...	...	...	...	1	21	...	...	...	...	21	...	41.55	3.00	44.55
Pleasant Grove	Mrs. W. H. Kenan, Greensboro	1	...	...	...	...	1	14	...	...	...	...	14	...	...	47.05	47.05
Reedy Fork	Mrs. Romie Everage, Brown Summit	1	...	...	...	...	1	10	...	...	...	...	10	...	...	2.00	2.00
REIDSVILLE																	
First	Mrs. J. C. [illegible], Sr., Reidsville	1	1	1	...	1	4	145	17	15	...	24	201	...	4541.98	1686.80	6228.78
Mount Olive	Mrs. Numa Baker, Reidsville	1	...	...	...	...	1	75	...	...	...	...	75	15	19.99	250.63	270.62
Penn Memorial	Mrs. W. H. Ford, Reidsville	1	1	...	...	...	2	52	7	...	...	...	59	12	...	125.58	125.58
Rocky Knoll	Mrs. R. A. Laughlin, [illegible]	1	...	...	...	...	1	25	...	...	...	...	25	...	8.96	105.20	114.16
Summerfield	Mrs. Myrtle Smith, Summerfield	1	...	...	...	...	1	20	...	...	...	...	20	...	...	158.61	158.61
	TOTALS	40	21	28	12	19	120	1947	422	427	149	420	3243	682	$14479.51	$26011.06	$40931.62

TABLE FIVE—CHURCH PROPERTY

CHURCHES	CHURCH CLERKS AND POST OFFICES	Does Church Own House of Worship?	When Was It Built?	Materials Used	Persons Seated	Number of Rooms	Dept. Assembly Rms.	No. Sep. Class Rooms	Value Church House and Grounds	Value of Mission Chapel if Any	Value Pastor's Home	Total Value of All Church Property	Indebtedness on All Church Property	Insurance Carried
Allen Jay	[illegible] R. Yountz, [illegible], Rt. 2	Yes	1936	Wood	300	10	10	9	3000.00			3000.00		2000.00
[illegible]	Mrs. T. H. [illegible]	Yes	1935	Wood	300	1			1200.00					800.00
Brightwood	G. M. Hicks, [illegible]	Yes	1941	Wood	300	1			2500.00			3000.00	309.00	500.00
Buchanan	R. P. [illegible], [illegible]	Yes	1886	Wood	150	5		4	3000.00			3250.00		1500.00
[illegible]	J. E. McCargo, Reidsville, Rt. 2	Yes	1898	Wood	275	9	3	8	5000.00		2000.00	7000.00		3000.00
Fair [illegible]	Mrs. W. L. Lee, Rt. 2, [illegible]ro	Ycs	1939	Brick	250	1			5000.00			5000.00	400.00	1500.00
Fairview	[illegible] Cummings, Reidsville	Yes	1901	Wood	300	11		10	3000.00			3000.00	360.00	2000.00
Fairmont Park	Mrs. Earl A. Yates, High Point, Rt. 2	Yes	1940	Wood	260	1			1200.00			1350.00		1000.00
[illegible]	W. P. Kill [illegible], [illegible]	Yes	1884	Wood	300	9	9	9	2500.00			2500.00		2000.00
GREENSBORO														
[illegible] Street	J. B. Wills, Greensboro	Yes	1912	B[illegible]ck	700	61	10	69	51000.00		6000.00	57000.00	12900.00	43000.00
[illegible]	E. J. Jarvis, Greensboro	Yes		Wood	300	1		6	2300.00					750.00
Bessemer	Maur[illegible] Bunting, Greensboro	Yes	1923	Wood	350	16	2	16	10000.00		2000.00	12000.00	6107.00	4500.00
[illegible] Park	Carroll O. Weaver, Greensboro	Yes	1940	Brick	300	57	8	42	55000.00		8600.00	63600.00	9925.89	50000.00
Eller [illegible]	[illegible] L. Thornburg, [illegible]ro	Yes	1925	Brick	750	50	7	48	42000.00		9000.00	51000.00		30000.00
First	[illegible] Liles, [illegible]	Yes	1906	Brick	1000	48			145000.00		15000.00	160000.00		70000.00
Florida Street	Eleanor Watson, [illegible]	Yes	1930	Brick	350	23	2	22	16500.00		4500.00	21000.00	2350.00	14000.00
[illegible] Park	W. W. [illegible], [illegible]	Yes	1916	[illegible]	150	1			2500.00			2500.00	750.00	
Magnolia Street	Mrs. G. H. [illegible], Greensboro	Yes	1912	Wood	300	6	7	13	6000.00		4000.00	10000.00	1213.02	6000.00
Pomona	C. C. Patterson, Pomona	Yes	1906	Wood	370	8		8	3000.00			3000.00		
[illegible]	N. C. Brown, [illegible]	Yes	1907	Wood	400	5	3	7	10000.00	5000.00		15000.00		7500.00
Sixteenth Street	[illegible] E. Whitt, [illegible]	Yes	1907	[illegible]ck	500	23	2	16	39000.00			39000.00		18000.00
[illegible]	Mrs. J. B. Brown, [illegible]	Yes	1922	Wood	250	11	2	13	10000.00		2500.00	12500.00		7500.00
[illegible]	Mrs. E. C. White, Jr., [illegible]ro	Yes	1938	Wood	200	3		2	3000.00			3000.00		2000.00
[illegible] Memorial	[illegible]rt West, [illegible], Rt. 5	Yes	1935	Wood	300	10	2	8	4000.00		4000.00	8000.00	3100.00	5400.00
Guilford	W. L. Hudson, Guilford College	Yes	1914	Brick	200	1		4	3500.00	300.00		3900.00		1500.00
HIGH POINT														
First	C. D. [illegible], High Point	Yes	1941	Brick	900	70	7	54	150000.00		8000.00	168000.00	81500.00	100000.00
[illegible] Street	Clyde Ayers, High Point	Yes	1926	B[illegible]ck	1500	96	6	68	156000.00		2500.00	160000.00	29460.00	60000.00
Hilliard Memorial	J. W. Saunders, High Point	Yes	1931	Brick	800	24		22	25000.00			25000.00	1060.00	5000.00

North Main Street	Amie L. [illegible]t, High [illegible]t, Rt. 1	Yes	1924	Brick	350	23	6	17	17000.00	....	....	17000.00	1050.00	8000.00
North Park	Miss Drusilla Fagge, High Point	Yes	1929	Wood	300	...	1	17	3500.00	....	....	3500.00	....	1500.00
South Side	F. E. [illegible]e, High Point	Yes	1916	Wood	350	10	...	9	3500.00	....	....	3500.00	30.59	2000.00
West End	Mrs. A. H. [illegible]er, High Point	Yes	1913	Wood	350	24	2	20	10000.00	....	2500.00	12500.00	....	5000.00
Jessup Grove	Mrs. Frances Jessup, [illegible]d College	Yes	1933	Brick	280	1	...	...	2000.00	....	....	2000.00	192.00	1500.00
Jewell	Hubert [illegible], High Point, Rt. 2	Yes	....	Wood	150	...	...	...	500.00	....	....	500.00	....	....
Lebanon	Maggie Kirkman	Yes	1911	Wood	350	7	1	7	3500.00	....	....	3500.00	....	1800.00
Mount Zion	George H. Spoon, Liberty, Rt. 3	Yes	1911	[illegible]	500	1		...	2000.00	....	....	2000.00	....	....
Oak [illegible]ove	G. K. Saunders, High Point, Rt. 4	Yes	1927	Wood	270	7	...	6	2500.00	....	....	2500.00	....	1500.00
O[illegible] Chapel	R. R. Osborne, [illegible]o Rt. 3	Yes	1934	[illegible]	250	1	...	...	1600.00	....	....	1600.00	....	....
Osceola	T. J. Brooks, Brown Summit, Rt. 1	Yes	1915	Wood	300	1	...	9	1650.00	....	....	1650.00	....	1000.00
Pine Grove	[illegible] A. Pickard, [illegible] [illegible]t, Rt. 3	Yes	1938	[illegible]	400	5	...	4	3000.00	....	....	3000.00	169.80	1000.00
Pisgah	[illegible]e Lawing High Point	Yes	1939	Wood	400	...	...	8	8500.00	....	....	8500.00	....	5000.00
Pleasant Garden	J. [illegible] Foy, Pleasant [illegible]	Yes	1917	Wood	220	1	...	...	1800.00	....	....	1800.00	....	1000.00
Pleasant Grove	D. R. Robertson, [illegible]o, Rt. 3	Yes	1920	Wood	350	...	...	..	1800.00	....	....	1800.00	610.00	1400.00
Reedy Fork	[illegible]is [illegible], Brown [illegible]t, Rt. 2	Yes	1941	Brick	275	1	...	...	2544.78	....	....	2544.78	878.29	2000.00
REIDSVILLE	....		....		....	...	...	...	....	....	....	....	....	....
First	T. L. Gardner, Reidsville	Yes	1871	Brick	550	24	5	20	37000.00	....	14000.00	51000.00	....	43500.00
Mount Olive	Mrs. Numa Baker, Reidsville	Yes	1929	[illegible]	300	13	2	13	5000.00	....	4500.00	9500.00	1960.10	6750.00
[illegible] [illegible]rial	James Overbey, Reidsville	Yes	1935	[illegible]	300	13	...	12	10000.00	....	1500.00	11500.00	400.00	....
Rocky Knoll	R. O. [illegible]e, [illegible]o, Rt. 1	Yes	1934	[illegible]	300	11	...	11	3000.00	....	....	3000.00	....	2500.00
Ruffin Stacey	[illegible]s. Esther Schrum, Ruffin	Yes	1931	[illegible]	350	1	...	...	2250.00	....	....	....	....	2250.00
Smith Grove	Dona [illegible], [illegible]x, Rt. 1	Yes	1923	Wood	300	3	...	2	2000.00	....	....	2500.00	....	600.00
Summerfield	[illegible] Myrtle S[illegible]h, [illegible]d	Yes	....	Brick	400	8	...	7	9800.00	....	....	9800.00	800.00	3500.00
Tabernacle	[illegible] Roach, [illegible]n College	Yes	1933	[illegible]	350	5	4	4	2000.00	....	....	2000.00	....	1000.00
Temple	Mrs. R. L. Radden	Yes	1939	[illegible]	400	1	...	...	2000.00	....	....	2000.00	....	1500.00
	TOTALS		....		20280	723	101	624	$898644.78	$5300.00	$90600.00	1001794.78	$155525.69	$533750.00

TABLE SIX—GIFTS FOR LOCAL CHURCH WORK

CHURCHES	Pastor's Salary	Other Salaries	Ministerial Help and Supply	Building and Repairs	Church Debt and Interest	Incidentals	Literature for S. S. and B. Y. P. U. and W. M. S.	Help Given to Local Poor	For Printing the Minutes and Clerk of Association	Other Objects	Total for Local Purposes Given by Church and All Orgs.	Pledged to Cooperative Program
Allen Jay	1424.85	....	110.00	80.92	....	126.40	175.00	200.00	4.00	800.00	2930.17	50.00
A[illegible]h	270.00	....	70.00	45.00	....	15.00	....	....	1.30	....	401.30	....
Brightwood	420.00	....	25.00	1000.00	....	20.05	16.09	....	....	....	1481.14	....
Buchanan	912.00	....	45.29	....	225.00	73.91	63.74	28.00	3.00	82.78	1433.72	....
Calvary	310.00	....	50.00	929.07	....	50.77	49.87	....	3.00	199.27	1591.98	....
F[illegible]r Grove	....	....	....	....	....	....	....	....	....	....	....	....
Fairview	256.22	....	42.00	530.00	....	60.90	47.65	....	3.00	....	939.77	75.00
Fairmont Park	780.00	....	100.00	....	....	36.34	90.00	80.00	3.00	65.00	1154.34	....
[illegible]e	600.00	....	80.00	....	....	210.18	108.40	....	3.00	275.40	1276.98	....
GREENSBORO	....	....	....	....	....	....	....			....	....	....
Asheboro Street	3300.44	1710.00	290.48	500.99	1940.00	723.98	757.79	268.27	12.50	732.51	10236.96	....
Bailey M[illegible]ial	1095.89	....	52.76	1322.11	....	69.14	70.00	47.50	4.00	38.17	2699.57	100.00
Bessemer	1560.00	....	85.00	1328.20	504.96	282.62	348.34	25.00	5.00	308.81	4537.93	....
College Park	2080.00	100.00	100.00	....	31[illegible]2.71	1824.81	434.27	21.28	12.50	211.18	7916.75	1200.00
Eller M[illegible]ial	2250.00	....	838.59	725.65	....	955.05	561.52	51.03	10.00	469.14	5860.98	1500.00
First	4600.00	6495.50	220.63	25057.25	....	4973.11	1181.93	870.89	18.00	1020.27	44437.58	....
[illegible]a Street	2190.00	891.50	393.24	2276.33	....	706.28	469.73	80.76	5.00	235.04	7247.88	....
Latham Park	240.00	....	....	24.96	35.00	45.00	23.50	....		....	368.46	....
Magnolia Street	1560.00	....	102.55	74.19	836.00	336.35	96.93	77.07	3.00	264.08	3340.17	....
Pomona	1609.18	....	201.58	46.42	....	171.10	171.86	52.86	3.00	67.65	2323.65	....
Revolution	1727.25	....	165.08	9.86	....	265.28	203.03	72.00	5.26	301.30	2749.06	....
[illegible]h Street	2187.98	....	86.00	53.56	....	357.06	157.12	17.76	5.00	104.00	2968.48	....
Stevens M[illegible]l	1235.00	....	74.22	244.07	521.41	436.29	91.76	18.85	3.00	60.33	2684.93	....
Tabernacle	1865.00	....	148.00	....	950.62	888.11	214.85	125.46	5.00	....	4197.04	....
[illegible]er Memorial	1105.00	....	32.53	422.80	422.80	204.00	51.00	15.00	5.00	905.02	3163.15	....
[illegible]d	274.00	....	....	....	....	61.30	35.23	....	2.00	8.68	381.21	....
HIGH POINT	....	....	....	....	....	....	....	....	....	....	....	....
First	3600.00	1800.00	81.85	1465.22	23825.92	3841.41	1129.96	159.65	18.00	2465.03	38387.04	....
[illegible]n Street	3120.00	1497.00	25.00	466.99	5490.00	812.01	699.35	140.66	10.00	1059.45	13320.46	....
Hilliard Memorial	1845.99	....	58.67	421.31	270.00	247.49	157.91	47.17	3.00	64.50	3116.04	....

North Main Street	1855.00	185.50	9.00	305.34	688.99	551.27	276.95	26.25	3.00	422.32	4323.62	
North Park	1664.00		77.67	38.05		129.70	296.64	87.81	4.50	257.32	2555.99	
South Side	1869.19		207.57	388.58		190.40	85.21	28.60		8.14	2777.69	
West End	1309.53	144.14		486.09		410.19	187.45		4.00	76.30	2617.70	
Jessup Grove	1040.00		227.58	715.00	223.00	50.00	61.79		2.00	110.08	2429.45	
Jewell			76.00	25.00		25.00	28.62	12.00			166.62	
Lebanon	1300.00		67.43	24.46		88.21	58.15	33.93	4.00		1576.18	
Mt Zion	375.00		40.00	310.00		12.69	45.40				783.09	
Oak Grove	566.13		23.15	21.00	349.41	38.45	41.03	40.00			1079.17	
Osborne [illegible]	101.00	198.00		3.00	27.00	10.34	31.15		2.00		372.49	15.00
Osceola	459.13		33.23	138.01		68.86	45.74	10.00	2.05	46.22	803.24	
Pine Grove	240.00		86.98		125.50	25.56	51.34			24.63	554.01	
Pisgah	1465.75		62.50	1106.81		148.00	100.21	98.00			2981.27	
Pleasant [illegible]	416.00		35.00	10.76		66.17	52.76	15.00	2.00	154.23	751.92	
Pleasant Grove	250.00		40.08	275.00	160.00	53.49	47.27			73.77	899.61	
Reedy Fork	47.54		33.36	650.78	165.00	106.46	44.06		1.00		1048.20	25.00
REIDSVILLE												
First	3000.00	768.00	15.00	2078.95		1572.71	527.70	238.51	10.00	620.04	8830.91	
Mount Olive	1679.00		307.28	721.49	39.90	645.98	118.71	9.52	2.00	44.94	3568.82	275.00
Penn [illegible]	1380.00		312.32	246.51	1442.00	524.20	151.15	34.05			4090.23	
Rocky Knoll	1061.65		50.00	707.02		272.40	162.77	116.15	3.00		2372.99	
Ruffin Stacey	350.00			150.00		68.50	65.00		2.00	150.00	785.50	
[illegible]	122.18		163.50	373.47		27.23	12. 0		2.00		700.38	
Summerfield	360.00		57.00	1114.00	24.00		65.82		5.00	26.95	1652.77	200.00
Tabernacle	467.44		141.09	379.60		28.37	31.46				1047.96	10.00
Temple	290.00		44.72	48.00	152.60	39.16	32.59				607.07	25.00
	$64372.34	$13789.64	$5623.93	$47350.82	$41766.82	$22964.10	$10035.51	$3149.03	198.11	$11752.55	$221002.85	$3475.00

TABLE [illegible]EN—MISSIONS, EDUCATION, ALL BENEVOLENCES

CHURCHES	Total to Cooperative Program	Special to Associational Missions	Special to State Missions	Special to Home Missions	Special to Foreign Missions	Special to Schools and Colleges	Special to Theological Seminaries	Special to Orphanage	Special to Hospitals	Special to Old Ministers' Relief	Hundred Thousand Club	Other Special Gifts	Total Given for Missions, Benevolences by Church and All Departments	Total All Purposes, Local Work and Missions, Given by the Church and All Orgs.
[illegible]en Jay	$ 50.00	$	$	$ 3.00	$	$	$	$ 95.01	$ 186.00	$	$	$	$ 334.01	$ 3264.18
Antioch				5.90				6.64	9.10				21.64	422.94
Brightwood								25.91					25.91	1507.05
Buchanan	52.00							26.00	16.52				94.52	1528.24
Calvary	81.00		19.50	26.85	41.00	10.50		165.92	35.76	5.00	62.00	2.90	450.43	2042.41
Fair Grove									7.18				7.18	486.41
Fairview	82.00				10.00			60.00	17.61		12.00		181.61	1121.38
Fairmont Park								33 00	9.00				42.00	1196.34
Gibsonville	67.00				17.00			69.16	12.00				165.16	1442.14
GREENSBORO														
[illegible]o Street	2368.12		226.83	160.29	366.85	19.15		662.50	86.46	32.00	186.95	1.00	4110.15	14347.11
Bailey Memorial	34.86		10.00	10.00	36.00			151.49	10.45	1.00	6.00	4.00	263.80	2963.37
Bessemer	301.90		5.50		35.33		12.43	108.43	27.00				490.59	5028.52
College Park	520.00		72.47	105.27	150.67	26.15	41.25	288.16	49.05		73.50		1326.52	9243.27
Eller Memorial	1524.76							450.00	252.00			278.85	2505.61	8366.59
First	16289.51		591.07	1342.19	4265.78	246.17	69.95	2533.67	327.14		1799.03	160.20	27624.71	72062.29
Florida Street				47.64	882.28			300.00	100.00	113.15			1443.07	8690.95
Latham Park														368.46
Magnolia Street	64.00	42.60	2.25	10.00				120.00	25.00			42.90	306.75	3646.92
Pomona				17.34	65.99			177.20	51.25			100.95	412.73	2736.38
Revolution	807.29		21.56	31.32	158.57	30.95		148.74	74.25		27.72	10.00	1310.40	4059.46
Sixteenth Street	738.80		51.61	50.00	50.00			160.40	30.00		15.00		1095.81	4064.29
Stevens Memorial	400.00		8.00	24.00	66.85			185.30	23.80		7.40		715.35	3400.28
Tabernacle	150.00		16.19	10.98	25.63			120.00	55.50			10.00	388.30	4585.34
Webster Memorial	112.20		67.43	67.43	67.43	5.00		100.32	10.00		24.00	100.00	553.81	3716.96
[illegible]	10.00	2.00	1.00	5.46	10.00	2.00		5.00	6.26			2.50	44.22	425.43
HIGH POINT														
First	2159.54		730.88	1006.77	1783.66	249.06	50.00	1791.32	294.11		316.48	43.43	8425.25	46812.29
Green Street	1423.78		60.00	35.00	106.00	57.00		428.07	336.40		127.08		2573.33	15893.79
Hilliard Memorial	110.02	.85	12.77	9.10	9.22			122.68	30.93		25.50		321.07	3437.11

North Main Street	296.00			15.00	29.00		5.00	170.00	62.50	72.80	72.00	76.00	798.30	5121.92
North Park	224.00		17.57		10.28		31.55	70.50	30.00		48.00		431.90	2987.89
South Side			15.00	3.95	35.02			26.00	25.50		6.00		11.47	2889.16
West End	404.06	4.00	53.78		23.54	69.25	44.75	249.98	44.00	18.00	72.50	7.25	991.11	3608.81
Jessup Grove			11.39					46.00	16.11				73.50	2502.95
Jewell								5.95				4.61	10.56	177.18
Lebanon				164.25	75.50			38.69					278.44	1854.62
ount Zion			9.05	53.93				20.62	6.03				89.63	872.72
k Grove	15.00							35.47	8.41				58.88	1138.05
borne Chapel								12.97	5.11				18.08	390.57
ceola		8.35		28.50				41.05	8.65			24.00	110.55	913.79
ne Grove				2.06				21.00	5.78				28.84	582.85
sgah			10.00	8.43				26.36	10.00				54.79	3036.06
easant Garden	30.00		3.90					24.00	2.00				59.90	811.82
easant Grove	29.00							54.11	5.70			47.05	135.86	1035.47
edy Fork		1.00	1.00			3.00			7.53				12.53	1060.73
IDSVILLE														
First	1810.71		57.00	105.00	219.75	34.00		395.35	169.20		164.00	152.00	3107.01	11937.92
Mount Olive	213.95		15.43	7.50	8.59			144.00	2.10	24.00		34.50	450.07	4018.89
Penn Memorial	55.40		42.50	5.00	47.18			25.10	25.00		6.00		206.18	4296.41
cky Knoll			99.75	101.65	19.50			100.00	100.00				420.90	2793.89
ffin Stacey	24.00							24.00	5.00				53.00	838.50
ith Grove					1.00			17.50	7.81				26.31	726.69
mmerfield			43.22	10.00		1.00		94.00	19.25			63.03	230.50	1883.27
bernacle														1047.96
mple			4.00					4.34	5.00				13.34	620.41
	$30448.90	$58.80	$2280.65	$3473.81	$8617.62	$ 753.23	$ 254.93	$9981|91	$2653.45	$ 265.95	$3051.16	$1165.17	$63005.58	$284008.43

HISTORICAL TABLE — PIEDMONT BAPTIST ASSOCIATION

YEAR	WHERE HELD	MODERATOR	CLERK	PREACHER	Churches	Baptisms	Church Members	Total Gifts
1894	Greensboro	Dr. C. A. Rominger	W. L. Kivett	M. A. [illegible]	5	....	562	....
1895	Liberty	T. L. Chislom	W. L. [illegible]	L. Johnson	12	16	1[illegible]	$ 4695.50
1896	Moore's Chapel	R. W. Brooks	W. H. Eller	L. Johnson	14	66	1[illegible]4	5128.94
1897	Summerfield	F. H. [illegible]	W. H. Eller	J. A. [illegible]	16	73	1540	7198.27
1898	[illegible]Mt Zion	R. W. Brooks	W. H. Eller	L. [illegible]	17	67	1557	6883.23
1899	Ramseur	R. W. [illegible]	F. P. Tucker	John E. White	19	54	1570	7435.43
1900	Cherry Street	R. W. Brooks	W. H. Eller	Thomas Carrick	16	48	1538	7970.35
1901	Reidsville	F. H. [illegible]	W. H. Eller	L. Johnson	19	157	[illegible]	8282.73
1902	Salem Street	F. H. Jones	W. H. Eller	W. C. Newton	19	135	1774	9950.97
1903	[illegible]	F. H. Jones	W. H. Eller	C. L. Greaves	20	185	1868	[illegible]4.77
1904	Calvary	F. H. Jones	W. H. Eller	H. W. Battle	22	112	1832	1[illegible]07.43
1905	Randleman	F. H. Jones	W. H. Eller	J. M. Hilliard	22	114	2096	[illegible]74.91
1906	High Point, First	F. H. [illegible]	W. H. Eller	W. R. Bradshaw	23	201	2333	29366.31
1907	Asheboro Street	F. H. Jones	W. H. Eller	Wm. Hedley	26	372	2798	[illegible]93.79
1908	Ramseur	F. H. Jones	W. H. Eller	C. E. Maddry	28	311	3086	6[illegible]47.57
1909	Greensboro	F. H. Jones	W. H. Eller	Wm. Hedley	30	292	3429	4[illegible]47.28
1910	[illegible]t Zion	F. H. Jones	W. H. Eller	R. G. [illegible]	31	336	3731	[illegible]1.01
1911	Asheboro	W. F. [illegible]	W. H. Eller	W. F. Staley	29	182	3[illegible]	2[illegible]87.56
1912	High [illegible], Green St.	F. P. Hobgood, Jr.	W. H. Eller	J. C. Turner	30	174	[illegible]	2[illegible]97.38
1913	Liberty	F. P. Hobgood, Jr.	W. H. Eller	R. P. Walker	31	409	3971	37700.97
1914	Asheboro Street	F. P. Hobgood, Jr.	W. H. Eller	A. W. Claxon	31	413	4202	4[illegible]28.44
1915	Reidsville	J. M. Hilliard	W. H. Eller	J. M. Hilliard	42	13[illegible]	4[illegible]1	42577.68
1916	Forest Avenue	J. M. Hilliard	W. H. [illegible]	E. N. Johnson	36	369	8[illegible]4	4[illegible]18.92
1917	Green Street	J. M. Hilliard	W. H. Eller	W. R. White	39	308	4760	4[illegible]09.05
1918	Moore's [illegible]	J. M. Hilliard	W. H. Eller	J. W. Rose	39	374	5140	2[illegible]38.46
1919	White Oak	J. M. [illegible]	W. H. Eller	W. H. Wilson	39	339	5[illegible]	7638.[illegible]5
1920	Calvary	J. M. Hilliard	W. H. Eller	E. N. [illegible]	39	543	5867	117682.35
1921	Summerfield	Clarence A. Smith	J. E. Lanier	B. K. Mason	39	480	6454	[illegible]61.79
1922	[illegible]	Clarence A. Smith	J. E. Lanier	Jas. A. Clark	39	679	7226	[illegible]55.24
1923	Magnolia S[illegible]	Clarence A. Smith	H. O. Miller	E. E. White	38	365	7341	[illegible]53.25
1924	[illegible]est End	Clarence A. Smith	H. O. Miller	W. E. Goode	40	672	7489	[illegible]658.19
1925	Fairview	Clarence A. Smith	H. O. Miller	A. T. Howell	41	610	8956	[illegible]92.21
1926	Ramseur	Clarence A. Smith	S. T. Hensley	[illegible] T. Wilson	42	620	9974	[illegible]00.68
1927	Trinity	Clarence A. Smith	S. T. Hensley	H. T. Stevens	40		[illegible]3	[illegible]46.40
1928	Bessemer	Clarence A. Smith	O. E. Lee	R. P. Ellington	41		[illegible]6	2002.30
1929	[illegible]	Clarence A. Smith	O. E. Lee	C. F. Rogers	44		[illegible]6	[illegible]87.61
1930	Asheboro	Clarence A. Smith	O. E. Lee	Geo. T. [illegible]	44			[illegible]77.29
1931	Florida Street	Clarence A. Smith	O. E. Lee	A. B. Conrad	44		[illegible]89	178501.19
1932	Reidsville	Clarence A. Smith	O. E. Lee	J. C. Turner	46		[illegible]85	[illegible]00.60
1933	White Oak	[illegible] A. Smith	O. E. Lee	T. L. Sasser	48	1561		[illegible]41.40
1934	Franklinville	Clarence A. Smith	O. E. Lee	Wilson Woodcock	53	757		[illegible]39.18
1935	So. Side, High Point	[illegible] A. Smith	O. E. Lee	J. S. Hopkins	41		[illegible]7	[illegible]35.92
1936	Calvary	Clarence A. Smith	O. E. Lee	J. Ben Eller	42	563	13958	[illegible]52.96
1937	Eller Memorial	Grover H. Jones	O. E. Lee	C. N. Royal	41	657		[illegible]40.50
1938	Hilliard Memorial	Grover H. Jones	O. E. Lee	A. B. [illegible]	42	814	4[illegible]93	[illegible]46.20
1939	Reidsville, First	Grover H. [illegible]	O. E. Lee	J. C. Turner	46	975	1[illegible]79	[illegible]4.[illegible]4
1940	Florida Street	Grover H. Jones	O. E. Lee	Chas. E. Parker	51	804		[illegible]5.45
1941	Green Street	Grover H. Jones	O. E. Lee	A. Lincoln Fulk	53			[illegible]08.43

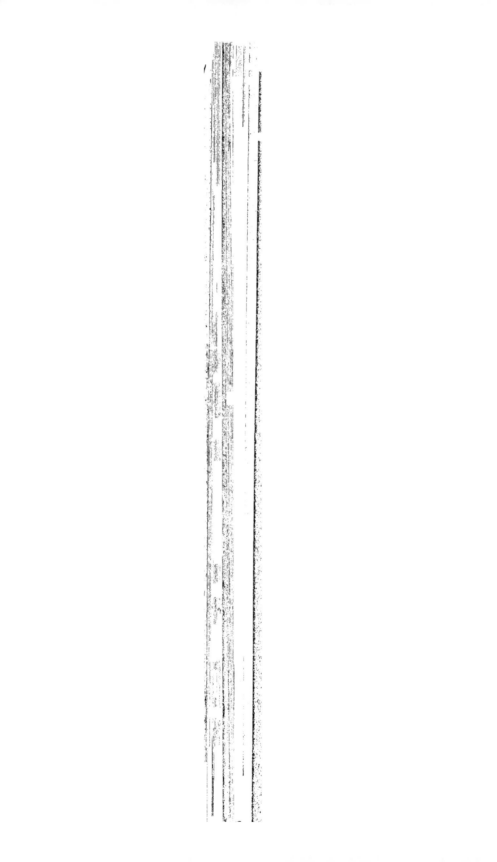

★ ★ ★ ★ ★

MINUTES

Piedmont Baptist Association

NORTH CAROLINA

★ ★ ★

FORTY-NINTH ANNUAL SESSION

FIRST BAPTIST CHURCH

GREENSBORO

OCTOBER 21, 1942

★ ★ ★

TIME AND PLACE OF NEXT MEETING TO BE DETERMINED BY THE EXECUTIVE COMMITTEE

Rev. Irby B. Jackson, High Point, will preach the sermon.
Rev. James H. Smith, Greensboro, Alternate

★ ★ ★ ★ ★

★ ★ ★ ★

Index

★ ★ ★ ★

MR. ORA E. LEE

to Whom This Volume of the Minutes is Dedicated by Order of the Association

Mr. Ora E. Lee was born at Alexandria, Indiana, April 12th, 1886. In his early manhood, he moved to Charleston, West Virginia, where he held a position with a manufacturing firm. When the United States entered the World War, in 1917, Mr. Lee went to San Antonio, Texas, to serve in the army Y. M. C. A. At the close of the war, he entered the Southwestern Seminary at Fort Worth, Texas, to take a course in Religious Education.

Immediately after his graduation at the Seminary Mr. Lee was

married to Miss Ethel Sowell, who had also been a student in the institution, and came with his bride to Greensboro, North Carolina, to accept the position of Educational Director in the First Baptist Church. For twenty years he served in this capacity giving himself to his work with a holy enthusiasm. Under his wise and consecrated leadership, the Sunday School grew from a rather small group to the largest in the city, and one of the largest in the state.

In 1928 Mr. Lee was elected Clerk and Treasurer of the Piedmont Association, a position he held until his death, December 31st, 1941. He also served for several years as Superintendent of the Piedmont Baptist Sunday School Association, and took an active part in the work of the Training Union.

Mr. Lee was a man of highest ideals and unblemished character. His one passion was to serve his divine Master. Up to the very day of his death, he gave himself without reservation to the work that was dear to his heart. He is survived by his wife, who is now Church Hostess of the First Baptist Church, and four children—Earl David, Jennie Rebecca, Page, and Johnnie.

ASSOCIATIONAL DIRECTORY

OFFICERS

Grover H. Jones, Moderator ---------------------- High Point
Rev. T. L. Sasser, Vice-Moderator ---------------- Reidsville
Rev. L. Grady Burgiss, Clerk -------------------- Greensboro

EXECUTIVE PROMOTION COMMITTEE

Grover H. Jones, Chairman ----------------------- High Point
Rev. L. Grady Burgiss, Secretary ---------------- Greensboro
Mrs. Nettie Hoge -------------------------------- Greensboro
Rev. A. A. Walker ------------------------------- Greensboro
J. Carl Bell ------------------------------------ Greensboro
Rev. H. O. Miller ------------------------------- High Point
R. B. Culler ------------------------------------ High Point
Rev. J. H. Smith -------------------------------- Greensboro
R. R. Saunders ---------------------------------- Reidsville
F. L. Paschal ----------------------------------- Greensboro
Rev. T. L. Sasser ------------------------------- Reidsville

CHURCH ADVISORY COMMITTEE

Dr. J. Clyde Turner ----------------------------- Greensboro
Dr. A. B. Conrad -------------------------------- High Point
Rev. J. S. Hopkins ------------------------------ High Point
Rev. J. Ben Eller ------------------------------- Greensboro
Rev. Wilson Woodcock ---------------------------- Greensboro
Mrs. Nettie H. Hoge ----------------------------- Greensboro
Rev. T. L. Sasser ------------------------------- Reidsville
Rev. L. Grady Burgiss --------------------------- Greensboro

COMMITTEE ON EVANGELISM

Rev. H. R. Starling, Chairman ------------------- Greensboro
Rev. Irby Jackson, Study Chairman --------------- High Point
Rev. J. C. Shore, Publicity ---------------------- Reidsville
Rev. J. S. Hopkins, Andrew Club ----------------- High Point
Rev. J. Earl Bryant, Highway and Hedges Evan. ---- Reidsville

OFFICERS OF PIEDMONT W. M. U.

Mrs. Nettie Hatcher Hoge, Superintendent -------- Greensboro
Mrs. J. H. Smith, Secretary ---------------------- Greensboro
Mrs. W. O. Burnham, Treasurer ------------------- High Point
Mrs. Draper Leigh, Personal Service -------------- Greensboro
Mrs. J. J. Andoe, Mission Study ----------------- Greensboro
Mrs. W. H. Wright, Stewardship ------------ Guilford College
Miss Ruth Scott, Young People ------------------ Greensboro
Mrs. H. A. Knight, Group Leader ---------------- High Point
Mrs. Grady Burgiss, Group Leader -------------- Greensboro
Mrs. H. L. Morrison, Group Leader --------------- Reidsville

PROGRAM COMMITTEE

Rev. J. H. Saunders, Chairman ------------------ Greensboro
Clyde Ayers ------------------------------------ High Point
Rev. L. Grady Burgiss -------------------------- Greensboro

LIST OF COMMITTEES SERVING DURING THE ASSOCIATIONAL YEAR

Executive—Promotion Committee
Church Advisory Committee
Program Committee

COMMITTEES SERVING DURING THE ANNUAL MEETING OF THE ASSOCIATION

Committee on Committees
Committee on Time, Place and Preacher
Auditing Committee
Committee on Resolutions
Program Committee for This Year and Next Year
Committee to Nominate Officers
Committee to Nominate Executive-Promotion Committee
Committee to Nominate Church Advisory Committee
Committee to Nominate Delegates to the Baptist State Convention
Committee to Nominate Committee on Evangelism

CHURCHES BY DISTRICTS

District 1

Allen Jay	North Main Street	Smith Grove
Fairmont Park	North Park	South Side
Green Street	Oak Grove	Temple
High Point, First	Pine Grove	West End
Hilliard Memorial	Pilot View	
Jewell	Pisgah	

District 2

Asheboro Street	Gibsonville	Pleasant Grove
Bailey Memorial	Greensboro, First	Pomona Mills
Bessemer	Guilford	Sixteenth Street
Brightwood	Jessup Grove	Stevens Memorial
Buchanan	Latham Park	Summerfield
College Park	Lebanon	Tabernacle
Edgeville	Magnolia Street	Ossippee
Eller Memorial	Mount Zion	Webster Memorial
Fair Grove	Osborne Chapel	
Florida Street	Pleasant Garden	

District 3

Antioch	Baptist Temple	Reidsville, First
Calvary	Osceola	Ruffin Stacey
Fairview	Penn Memorial	

OFFICERS BAPTIST TRAINING UNION

J. Carl Bell, Director ---------------------------- Greensboro
Miss Thelma Patrick, Associate Director ---------- High Point
Miss Julia Lyles, Secretary-Treasurer ------------ High Point
E. C. White, Jr., Pianist ------------------------- Greensboro
C. S. Hodge, Chorister -------------------------- Greensboro
------------------, Story Hour Leader --------------------
Miss Sadie Garner, Junior Leader --------------- Greensboro
Wakeland Morrison, Intermediate Leader -------- Greensboro
Mrs. Joe Kirkman, Young People's Leader -------- Greensboro
W. O. Kelly, Adult Leader ------------------------ Reidsville
J. E. Hedrick, Director District No. 1 ------------ High Point
J. J. Norwood, Director District No. 2 ----------- Greensboro

C. H. Saunders, Director District No. 3 .... Reidsville
Rev. E. M. Smith, Pastor Adviser .... High Point

ORDAINED MINISTERS NOT PASTORS

John Burger .... Thomasville
Ben S. McDowell .... High Point
C. R. Smith .... Kernersville
Estell Cane .... Kernersville
J. F. Murray .... Reidsville
Dr. A. S. Gillespie .... Shanghai, China
H. P. Billings .... Jamestown
R. J. Davis .... High Point
Hubert Bennett .... Route 1, Greensboro
T. H. Biles .... Chaplain in Army
O. P. Dix .... Rt. 3, High Point
W. F. Matherly .... 1207 Walnut St., Greensboro
C. D. Barton .... Greensboro
Rufus Carroll .... Greensboro
D. E. Oates .... Greensboro
George Dorsett .... Greensboro
V. D. Peedon .... Greensboro
Clinton Baker .... Asheboro

MINISTERS ORDAINED DURING THE YEAR

Joe Bullins .... Winston-Salem
C. R. Pierce .... Rt. 1, Greensboro
A. H. Dunning .... High Point
W. H. Barker .... Rt. 3, Box 362, High Point
David Shelton .... Louisville, Ky.
A. R. Snipes .... Rt. 2, Elon College
John Sykes .... Roanoke, Va.
George Dorsett .... Greensboro
V. D. Peedon .... Greensboro
Clinton Baker .... Asheboro

STUDENTS FOR THE MINISTRY

B. H. Farrington .... Rt. 1, Colfax
J. H. Boles .... Rt. 3, Greensboro
Daniel Lowe .... Rt. 5, Greensboro

Felton Carter ---------------------------- Rt. 1, McLeansville
Charlie W. Johnson ---------------------- Rt. 1, Summerfield
Maurice Courtner ------------------------ High Point College
Charles Coffey -------------------------- High Point College
Billy Holton --------------------------------- Louisville, Ky.
Austin Lovin ------------------- 910 Douglas St., Greensboro
Carl Compton ---------------------------------- Greensboro

LIST OF MESSENGERS

ALLEN JAY—Rev. C. M. Floyd, Jim Warren, Luther George, Claude Mickey, Miss Mealy Burrow, Miss Mary Warren

ANTIOCH—Mrs. Joe Carter, Mrs. Minnie Hudson, Mrs. Curtis Lalimore

BRIGHTWOOD—J. W. Holder, G. B. Cocklereese, Mrs. H. P. Gauldin, Miss Mabel Gauldin

BUCHANAN—Mrs. L. W. Michael, Mrs. J. B. Clifton, Mrs. R. P. Johnson, Mrs. W. P. Haynes, Mrs. Clyde Albright, Mrs. J. T. Ellis

CALVARY—Alex Setliff, Mrs. George Gunn, Rev. J. C. Shore, Mrs. J. C. Shore

FAIR GROVE—

FAIRVIEW—Mrs. Thelma Griffin, D. E. Trantham, William Cummings, Mrs. S. D. Whitlow.

FAIRMONT PARK—Mr. and Mrs. J. E. Copple, Ray Moose, Mr. and Mrs. Floyd Thomas, Mrs. A. L. McGee.

GIBSONVILLE—R. L. Seaford, Mrs. Lois Ferguson, E. C. Riggins

Greensboro

ASHEBORO STREET—F. L. Paschal, O. B. Teague, Mrs. A. C. Lowe, L. C. Satterfield, J. B. Mims, Mrs. J. L. Wray, Mrs. T. C. Crutchfield, Mrs. R. P. Royall.

BAILEY MEMORIAL—Mrs. E. J. Jarvis, Miss Jessie Stanley, Mrs. W. C. Heilig, Mrs. J. D. Payne, C. C. Stanley, Miss Ruby Payne.

BESSEMER—A. C. Melvin, Maurice Bunting, Miss Norfleet Dixon, Mrs. J. R. Medlin, Mrs. C. L. Murray, Mrs. J. F. Layton, Sr.

COLLEGE PARK—Mrs. B. A. Scott, Mrs. D. W. Leigh, Mrs. Roy Scott, Mrs. S. S. Johnson, Mrs. J. W. Marsh, Mrs. B. B. Stockard, Mrs. L. E. Ogburn, Mrs. J. B. Watson.

EDGEVILLE—H. E. Whitfield, J. M. Page, Mrs. J. M. Page, O. J. Giddins.

ELLER MEMORIAL—Mrs. C. E. Brady, Mrs. W. H. Oakes, Miss Leah Andrews, Wiley Patterson, Mrs. Russell Noah, David Oakes, Mrs. Nettie Caviness, Mrs. Sarah Overman.

FIRST CHURCH—Mrs. O. E. Lee, Mrs. J. H. Shuford, Mrs.

Stafford Webb, George Bennet, A. A. Chandler and C. S. Hodge.

FLORIDA STREET—Mrs. J. I. Phillips, Mrs. Mary Allred, J. L. Robertson, Mrs. C. N. Hutchinson, Mrs. E. R. Fruitt, Mrs. H. B. Allen.

LATHAM PARK—Mrs. Andrews, Mrs. Sutton, Mrs. Bratley, Mrs. Nelson, Mrs. Broome, Mrs. Trip.

MAGNOLIA STREET—Mrs. H. P. Wray, J. E. Poore, Mrs. John Fountain, Mrs. H. E. Lovings, Mrs. G. H. Williamson, Mrs. H. R. Grogan, Mrs. V. Y. Blevins.

POMONA—Mrs. Vela Godwin, C. M. Oates, Mrs. Ada Folds, Mrs. W. H. Brown, Mrs. C. M. Oates, Mrs. W. G. Teague.

REVOLUTION—G. L. Watkins, Wilbur Parrot, David Barbour, Miss Sallie Burgess, Mrs. Ida Strickland.

SIXTEENTH STREET—Mrs. Webster Owens, Mrs. Fred Hester, Fred Hester.

STEVENS MEMORIAL—

TABERNACLE—W. O. Smith, Ves Craig, E. C. White, A. D. Peacock, Mrs. N. W. Bolejack, Mrs. E. H. Moore.

WEBSTER MEMORIAL—Mrs. A. Andrews, Mrs. C. L. Straughan, Mrs. W. B. Burke.

GUILFORD—Mrs. Alice Ferrell, Mrs. B. F. Butler, Mrs. Hettie Kennedy.

High Point

FIRST—Mrs. A. B. Conrad, Miss Thelma Patrick, Mrs. W. O. Burnham, Mrs. C. R. Harrison, Mrs. W. F. Clayton, Mrs. A. J. Bolling, Mrs. F. J. Flagler, Mrs. C. D. Goldsmith, Mrs. Herman Robinson, Mrs. W. O. Burnham, J. E. Hedrick, Mrs. W. F. Hester.

GREEN STREET—Mrs. I. W. Daniels, Mrs. J. C. Saunders, B. G. Leonard, Mrs. J. L. Kivette, Mrs. C. E. Crissman, Mrs. Laura Smith, Clyde Ayers.

HILLIARD MEMORIAL—

NORTH MAIN STREET—Mrs. Alice Davis, Mrs. Ed Criscoe, Mrs. W. L. Woodell.

NORTH PARK—Mrs. J. L. Jones, Mrs. R. A. Davis, D. H. Short, Mrs. J. D. Edmondson, Mrs. Paul K. Frye, Mrs. D. H. Short.

SOUTH SIDE—Mrs. Saltz, Mrs. Caudle, Mrs. Tate, Mrs. Cameron, Rev. and Mrs. Barker, Mrs. Teague, Mrs. Sykes, Mrs. R. L. Everheart.

WEST END—Mrs. C. M. Scott, C. M. Scott, Mrs. Pearl Preslar, Mrs. P. A. Snider, Mrs. A. C. Lovelace, Mrs. Tom Hedrick.

JESSUP GROVE—Mrs. Ruth Lewis, Mrs. Henry Bryson, Mrs. James E. Wiggs, Peel Stanley, C. W. Johnson, Mrs. V. W. Marshall, Mrs. Johnnie Marshall, Mrs. Bertha Jessup, Mrs. Lucy Price, Mrs. C. W. Johnson.

JESSUP GROVE—T. H. Willard, Mrs. T. H. Willard, Lela Weatherman.

LEBANON—L. R. Chilton, Mrs. Y. H. Carter, Mrs. Willie Craig, Mrs. Jim McDaniels.

MOUNT ZION—Edgar Smith, George Spoon, C. D. Branson.

OAK GROVE—W. L. Shackleford, Mrs. A. L. Saunders, Mrs. Harry Robertson.

OSCEOLA—Mr. and Mrs. D. A. Greene, Rev. and Mrs. R. L. Kizer, L. C. Cole, Mrs. T. J. Brooks, Mrs. William Brooks.

PINE GROVE—Mr. and Mrs. Campbell, Mr. and Mrs. Hubert Bennet, Mr. and Mrs. R. A. Pickard.

PILOT VIEW—

PISGAH—Mrs. John Cox, Mrs. Sam Williamson, Mrs. Sim McNabor, J. O. Spears, Miss Ruby Mae Cooley, Ray Piner, Mrs. Maggie Harris, Miss Lucile Davis.

PLEASANT GARDEN—Mrs. C. P. Burton, Mrs. J. E. Thompson, Mrs. Ira Anderson, Mrs. Tinsley, Miss Bessie Taylor, Mrs. Doris Lambe.

PLEASANT GROVE—Rev. H. P. Billings, F. M. Atkins, Rev. J. H. Boles, Mrs. J. D. Shackleford, Mrs. F. M. Atkins, J. D. Shackleford, Miss Dorothy Preston, Miss Fay Shackleford.

REEDY FORK—Mrs. W. T. Smith, Mrs. E. E. Purvis, Mrs. Lester Canter, Elijah Lankford, Donnie Smith, Jane Bullard, A. L. Bullard.

Reidsville

BAPTIST TEMPLE—Rev. and Mrs. J. C. Gillespie, Mrs. Jesse Carter, Mrs. J. Earl Bryant, Mrs. D. P. Driscoll.

FIRST—R. R. Saunders, Mrs. R. L. Hubbard, Mrs. W. J. Pettigrew, Mrs. J. W. Gilley, Mrs. C. H. Saunders, Mrs. C. B.

Scoggin, Mrs. H. L. Morrison, Rev. J. F. Murray, Mrs. R. R. Saunders, T. L. Sasser, J. C. Tatum, Mrs. J. C. Tatum.

PENN MEMORIAL—

ROCKY KNOLL—Mrs. Charlie Cooper, Mrs. R. A. Laughlin, Mrs. F. B. Mooney, Mrs. W. T. Apple.

RUFFIN STACEY—Mrs. J. T. Cardwell, Mrs. Mam London, Mrs. Lillie Burton, Mrs. Poindexter, Mrs. Helen Schrumm.

SMITH GROVE—Charlie V. Smith, Reid Hiatt, Fairmae Pitts, Daisy Robertson, Linabell Westmoreland, Dora Clark, Frances Holt, Wilma Farrington.

SUMMERFIELD—Mr. and Mrs. T. D. Carter, Mrs. J. A. Wilson, Mrs. Guy Ayers, Mrs. Howard Pope, Mrs. Hettie Shields.

OSSIPEE—A. E. Lewis, Mrs. A. E. Lewis, Mrs. Walter Brown, Mrs. R. C. Fitts, R. C. Fitts, Mrs. A. R. Snipes, Mrs. E. W. Hunt, Mrs. Wayne Fitts.

TEMPLE—Mr. and Mrs. M. T. Powell, M. A. Tysinger, Rev. and Mrs. J. T. Swinson, Mrs. R. L. Radden.

CONSTITUTION

ARTICLE 1.—The Association shall be called the Piedmont Baptist Association.

ARTICLE 2.—It shall be composed of the ordained ministers who are members of, and those who may have pastoral charges within the Associational District, and three delegates from each Church in the district aforesaid, and Churches having a membership exceeding 300 shall be entitled to one additional delegate for every 200 members or fraction thereof in excess of 300.

ARTICLE 3.—The said delegates shall, before taking their seats, produce letters from respective Churches showing their appointment as delegates.

ARTICLE 4.—The Associational session shall be held at least once a year.

ARTICLE 5.—The officers shall be a Moderator, Vice-Moderator, Clerk and Treasurer. If deemed expedient by the Association, the officers of Clerk and Treasurer may be combined.

ARTICLE 6.—The officers of the Association shall be chosen annually by the Association.

ARTICLE 7.—Association shall be clothed with authority only to advise the Churches touching all things pertaining to their interest but shall in no case presume to direct or control them in reference to their own government or internal policy.

ARTICLE 8.—A Committee of arrangements, consisting of three members, shall be appointed on the first day of each session to prepare and report the proceedings and suggest topics proper for the consideration and action of the next annual Association. It shall be the duty of this committee to outline and publish a program for the next annual associational meeting or for any special or called meeting of the Association.

ARTICLE 9.—Baptist brethren, not members of the Association, who may be present at any session of the body, may on invitation by the body, take seats and participate in the debates of the Association.

ARTICLE 10.—The territory embraced in the Association shall be divided into not less than three districts and a committee composed of one pastor, and one layman from each district, together with the Moderator, Vice-Moderator, Clerk of the Association, Associational W. M. U. Superintendent, Associational Sunday School Superintendent, and Associational B. T. U. President, shall be appointed at meeting of the Association, which committee shall compose the Executive Committee of the Association, a majority of which shall constitute a quorum. It shall be the duty of the committee to superintend and direct the missionary operations of the Association.

ARTICLE 11.—All committees shall be appointed by the Moderator, either directly or indirectly with the approval of the Association, unless otherwise authorized by the Association from time to time.

ARTICLE 12.—The Constitution may be altered only at an Annual session of the Association and by a vote of two-thirds of the whole present.

ARTICLE 13.—The rules of this body shall follow Mell's Parliamentary Practice.

ARTICLE 14.—This Association shall cooperate with the Baptist State Convention.

ARTICLE 15.—The time of the holding of the annual session shall begin on Wednesday before the fourth Sunday in October of each year, except where prevailing conditions make it advisable to change this date, in which event the executive Committee shall be empowered to determine the date of meeting.
Adopted October 17, 1895.

Articles 2, 5, 6, 10, 15 Amended Session, July 23, 24, 1930.

Article 15 Amended Session July 21, 1932.

Article 10 Amended Sessions October 23, 24, 1935.

Articles 8, 10, 11 Amended Sessions October 23, 24, 1940.

FRANK L. PASCHAL

C. V. WEBSTER

J. H. SAUNDERS

Committee.

PROCEEDINGS

of the

FORTY-NINTH ANNUAL SESSION

of the

PIEDMONT BAPTIST ASSOCIATION

Held With the

FIRST BAPTIST CHURCH

Greensboro, N. C.

October 21, 1942

WEDNESDAY MORNING SESSION—9:30 A. M.

1. The Association opened with singing "Standing On The Promises of God" and "Draw Me Nearer," led by C. S. Hodge. The devotional period was in charge of Rev. J. T. Swinson, pastor of the Mount Zion Baptist Church. Words of welcome were spoken by Dr. J. Clyde Turner, pastor of the host church.

2. In the absence of Grover H. Jones, the Moderator, who was in Washington, D. C., the sessions were presided over by Rev. T. L. Sasser, vice-Moderator.

3. A roll of the churches was called and messengers from 43 churches responded to the call.

4. A motion was made and carried that those present constitute the body of the Association.

5. The vice-Moderator appoints the following members on the Commttee on Committees: J. S. Hopkins, R. R. Saunders, and H. R. Starling.

6. The Program was presented and adopted.

7. The report on State Missions was presented by Rev. J. C. Shore, of Reidsville. Upon motion to adopt the report the work was discussed by Rev. M. O. Alexander. The report was adopted.

State Missions

By State Missions we mean the program of work carried on under the supervision of our State Mission Secretary, for the purpose of winning to Christ and enlisting in Christian Service the people within our State. Last year there was made available for this program from the Co-operative Program, Regular Designations, interest from Invested Funds, Baptist Book Store, Sunday School Board, and other sources a total of $99,255.03. These funds were expended in carrying on the following phases of the work:

1. General Missionaries $5,667.

The three Missionaries are Rev. M. O. Alexander, Rev. J. C. Pipes, and Rev. Douglas M. Branch. Their activities consist of preaching, teaching, and promoting all phases of Baptist work in as many churches and associations as is possible.

2. Associational Missionaries $2,000.

In co-operation with four associations, the State Mission Board is helping to supply the following associational missionaries: Miss Ruth Keller in the Caldwell, Miss Ellen Daniel in the Surry, Miss Madge Daniel in the Haywood, and Rev. Tom S. Lawrence in the Pilot Mountain.

3. Missionary Pastors $24,583.

Through State Missions our Convention gives aid to churches in needy and strategic locations, making it possible for pastors to live and labor on many fields which would otherwise be neglected. One hundred sixty pastors are now receiving part of their salary from these funds. The average assistance given is about twenty-five dollars per month.

4. Aid on Lots and Buildings $15,543.

In years past the State Mission Board has done much to encourage and support the construction of houses of worship through the state. Some of these are at Chapel Hill, Boone, Cullowhee, Greensboro, Raleigh, Murfreesboro and Wingate, and were designed to provide a place of worship for students of educational institutions. Recently the Board has been buying, or helping to buy, choice lots in growing sections. Such purchases have been made in Durham, High Point and Kannapolis. This is proving to be a very valuable policy.

5. Christian Education in the Churches $34,234.

This item consists of the Sunday School, Training Union, and B. S. U. work.

6. Ministry to Other Races $3,324.

To encourage the work of the Negro Baptists the Board pays part of the salary of their Convention Secretary and the Secretary of Sunday School and B. T. U. Work. Help is also exended to workers among the Indians of Robeson County.

7. Ministering to the Sick $1,065.

Part-time chaplains are provided for veterans at Oteen and the Western North Carolina Sanatorium at Black Mountain, and Rev. and Mrs. E. M. Harris minister to the sick at the Sanatorium at Aberdeen.

8. Pastor Schools and Conferences $1,566.

The vision and outlook of scores of North Carolina pastors has been enlarged by the two Pastor Schools held each year, one at Mars Hill and the other at Meredith.

9. Work Around the Camps $18,000.

The newest and possibly the greatest opportunity facing our State Mission Board is the work in the defense areas of the state. There are perhaps two hundred thousand men in military camps in our state. The areas surrounding these camps have suddenly become filled with civilian population and the families of the army officers. As speedily as is possible lots are being purchased, buildings erected, and pastors provided for these areas.

10. Other State Mision Work $7,624.

This includes the cost of the Southern Baptist Radio Hour, Convention minutes, salaries, materials and postage, insurance and incidentals.

Seeing that the work of State Missions is so vital and the needs so great, let us meet the growing opportunities by increasing our offering to this cause.

J. C. Shore

---

8. The report on Christian Education was presented by Rev. H. O. Miller of High Point. Upon motion to adopt the report it was spoken to by Rev. J. B. Willis, of Hamlet. The report was adopted.

Christian Education

When we think of Christian Education we naturally associate the thought with our denominational Colleges, secondary schools and seminaries, for out of these have come a large percent of leadership in our churches and denominational life. These great institutions have trained and sent out multitudes of the finest Christian men and women to carry on the work of the Kingdom. But back of these great institutions is another phase of Christian Education that plays no small part in paving the way for the achievements of these institutions. I refer to the influence of the home and the church. Most students become Christians before they enter college. All of them should be won to Christ before they are old enough to enter college. This is a responsibility upon the home and the church. With the proper training in the home and in the church, the students will be able to stand firm in the faith during college days.

It is my sincere belief that the home and the church, in a large measure, have failed in Christian Education. To remedy this situation, we need more dependable Christian fathers and mothers. We need a church leadership concerned about high standards of Christian living, rather than a large number on the church roll. We need teachers who will not only teach the truth, but practice the same every day.

The standard set in the home and the church determines, largely, the quality of men and women turned out by our colleges, Seminaries and Training Schools. Let us raise the standard in our local communities and churches and then we may rightly expect a higher standard in our Colleges.

The depletion of our schools, brought about by the terrible conditions thrust upon us shall surely present a crisis in the field of Christian Education. May God give us grace to face it.

We recommend that the Association endorse the action of the Trustees of Wake Forest College in admitting women to the Junior and Senior years of that school.

Respectfully submitted,

Rev. Hughey O. Miller.

---

9. A motion was made by Rev. Wilson Woodcock that the Association approve the reception of girl students at Wake Forest College, and that this be an amendment to the report of Rev. H. O. Miller. The amendment was adopted. The report was adopted.

10. The report on the Hospital was made by Rev. H. R. Starling, of Greensboro. Upon motion to adopt the report it was spoken to by Rev. Chas. E. Parker, of Winston-Salem. The report was adopted.

The Baptist Hospital

The last three years have been eventful in the expansion of the hospital. Three years ago the hospital had a bed capacity of 100 and by overcrowding, we were caring for about 4,000 patients per year.

Today, we have a modernly constructed and equipped hospital with a bed capacity of almost 10,000 patients annually, and now are caring for about 650 patients per month. Owing to a shortage of nurses caused by war conditions, the hospital has been unable to open a few rooms.

We shall have this year not less than 2,500 service or free patients. This will represent, inculding hospital and medical service, about $250,000 in free service for this year.

The hospital has a staff of 26 internes and about 100 doctors practicing in the hospital. In addition, it has the free service of the entire staff of the Medical School whenever desired for consultation and diagnosis. Every department is thoroughly organized to give most efficient service possible.

The equipment, as well as the building, is entirely modern. The hospital recently added $20,000 worth of new instruments to the operating rooms and $44,000 worth of new X-Ray equipment, making an X-Ray department "None better in the South".

The hospital, in conjunction with the Medical School, has a floor-space of four acres and represents a value to the denomination of $2,000,000 with only a very small amount of indebtedness.

The purpose of the hospital shall remain as ever—to give hospital treatment to those who are unable to pay for same, educate nurses with Christian ideals, and at the same ime, maintain a standard of scientific efficiency "second to none in the country". It is the abiding purpose of the management that it shall be definitely a Christian Institution with all that it implies.

This greatly expanded service which is growing more and more into every section of the state, of course, requires an increased support. This, we are glad to report, is growing year by year. In addition to the Mother's Day offering by the churches and Sunday Schools, which has increased in the last few years from $11,500 to about $38,000 this year, the hospital linens contributed by the W. M. U.'s and other church agencies has increased year by year.

H. R. Starling

11. The report on the Orphanage was presented by Rev. E. M. Smith, of High Point. Upon motion to adopt the report it was spoken to by Dr. I. G Greer, of Thomasville, in a marvelous address. The report was adopted.

Orphanage Report

The children who compose the population of the Baptist Orphanage of North Carolina may be classified under three heads: full orphans, half orphans and victims of desertion and wrecked homes. These children are being cared for by three well recognized methods of child caring: Mother's Aid, Boarding Homes and the Orphanage proper.

The demands upon the Orphanage authorities have never been greater. They receive upon an average of 45 applications every month during the year. No matter how urgent the demands, however, the policy of the Orphanage is not to make special appeals. Special appeals for other causes may come and special appeals may go, but this constant stream of human need must go on day after day, and year after year until the purpose of Christ through His church has been fulfilled.

The past year was one of the best in the history of the Orphanage, but imperative needs continue to increase. The care of the orphan child was intrusted to us by Christ Himself. We cannot shun this Christian responsibility and claim to be practicing "pure religion". When appeals are made to the orphanage authorities they have nowhere to go other than individuals, Sunday schools and churches.

We suggest as a goal for the Association for next year: a monthly contribution from each church or Sunday school, gifts of produce in season, a real Thanksgiving offering in November and a club of Charity and Children in each Sunday school.

Respectfully submitted;

Ernest M. Smith.

---

12. The report on Christian Literature was made by Rev. J. Ben Eller, of Greensboro. Upon motion to adopt the report Dr. L. L. Carpenter, the new Editor of the Recorder, was introduced to the Association by Bro. Eller, who then spoke to the report. The report was adopted.

Christian Literature

The books, papers and magazines which we read greatly influence our lives. The forces of unrighteousness have recognized this truth and flooded our nation with unwholesome and hurtful literature. Many of us constantly lament this fact; but we do little about it. Surely we should frankly face the problem by placing the very best reading material in the hands of our people.

Certainly if we are to be intelligent and competent Christians we must read literature that will feed our souls and inform our minds. Our Baptist periodicals and papers are meant to do these things. To read them regularly will save us from much ignorance and strengthen us spiritually. Through them we may keep in touch with our great world-wide Baptist brotherhood. In them we get a glimpse of our workers and their work, and learn the possibilities and needs of our mission fields both at home and abroad. In short as we read them we become a living part of a great religious body striving to do the will of Christ.

We would then urge our people to give a larger place in their home to Christian literature. The Bible of course should come first. But we also commend our Baptist magazines and papers. "Home Missions", "The Commission", "Royal Service" and "Charity and Children" should come to our homes.

At this time, however, special attention should be given to the Biblical Recorder. After a long search Dr. L. L. Carpenter, a North Carolinian by birth and training, has been secured as editor. As pastor, teacher, and writer, he is well prepared for his task. Our leaders know him and trust him. Therefore, we heartily commend him to our Churches. "Forgetting those things which are behind, and reaching forth unto those things which are before" we should gladly rally to the Biblical Recorder in its present great opportunity for service.

Respectfully submitted.

J. Ben Eller.

---

13. Dr. J. Clyde Turner, host pastor, made an announcement about the noon-day meal.

14. The report of the Committee on Committees was presented and adopted.

Report of Committee on Committees

COMMITTEE ON PLACE AND PREACHER: A. A. Walker, Mrs. W. O. Burnham and Z. W. Rotan.

COMMITTEE TO NOMINATE COMMITTEE ON EVANGELISM: Wilson Woodcock, H. O. Miller and D. W. Overbey.

COMMITTEE TO NOMINATE CHURCH ADVISORY COMMITTEE: A. C. Lovelace, J. C. Shore, and A. A. Walker.

COMMITTEE TO NOMINATE EXECUTIVE PROMOTION COMMITTEE: J. B. Eller, E. M. Smith, and J. E. Bryant.

COMMITTEE TO NOMINATE OFFICERS: R. R. Saunders, I. B. Jackson, and J. H. Smith.

COMMITTEE ON RESOLUTIONS: Miss Thelma Patrick, Mrs. Grady Burgiss, and J. C. Gillespie.

AUDITING COMMITTEE: A. A. Chandler, A. L. McGee and J. Huber Dixon.

PROGRAM COMMITTEE: J. H. Saunders, Chm. Clyde Ayers and Grady Burgiss.

COMMITTEE TO NOMINATE DELEGATES TO BAPTIST STATE CONVENTION: B. C. Lamb, W. L. Smith, and Mrs. J. C. Shore.

---

15. Following a 10 minute relaxation period the hymn "Loyalty to Christ" was sung, then a trio from the Bessemer Baptist church sang "Holy Spirit From On High." Rev. H. O. Miller, of High Point, read the scripture, John 6:59-71, and led in prayer. Rev. A. A. Walker then delivered a most inspiring message, the Annual Sermon, from the topic "Loyalty to Christ." The closing prayer was led by Rev. J. S. Hopkins.

16. Dr. A. B. Conrad led in returning thanks for the noon meal.

WEDNESDAY AFTERNOON SESSION

17. The session was opened by singing "How Firm A Foundation." The devotional period was led by Rev. I. B. Jackson, the new pastor of North Main St. Church, High Point.

18. The report on Home Missions was presented by Dr. J.

C. Gillespie, of Reidsville. Upon motion to adopt the report, he also spoke to the report. The report was adopted.

Report on Home Missions

If there was ever a period in the world history when we needed light—spiritual light—it is today. The world is in spiritual darkness, It seems to be moving backward toward the tyranny and oppression and slavery and paganism of the past ages.

Our task as a denomination in America is to prepare our Home-and spiritually to meet its obligations to the world with the gospel of Christ when peace may have been declared and order in the world established. Whatever else we do, the evangelization of our land and its mobilization for the world's evangelization must not be sidetracked. This is the task to which the Board has set itself and for this task it is girding its strength.

There are signs of progress. During the past year we have added 31 missionaries to our force, opened 64 mission stations, constituted 13 new churches; our missionaries have distributed 17,250 Bibles, Testaments and portions of Scripture; have given out more than 785,000 tracts; have preached approximately 35,000 sermons; have led more than 7,000 people to accept Christ and received into the fellowship of the churches 2,863 members.

We are today preaching the gospel to Indians, Mexicans, Spanish, Jews, Italian, French, Cubans,, Chinese, the underprivileged in the crowded industrial sections, in the slums of cities, in the neglected mountain areas, to the millions of negroes in the homeland and are carrying Christ to the camps in our service to and with the chaplains. We have begun a City Mission Department which we will enlarge, when our debts are paid, and have begun a work in the vitalization of the country church and are now working out a program which will, if carried into effect, re-establish the country church as a potent factor in our denominational life.

In addition to the enlarging of our mission work we are paying our debts. Last year the Board paid $355,000.00 on the principal of its debt, and at the present rate of debt payments and on the basis of receipts for the past year the Board expects to fully pay the balance of $495,000.00 due before the end of the calendar year of 1943.

CLASSIFICATION OF WORKERS: The ninety-seventh annual report of the Board, made to the annual meeting of the Southern Baptist Convention last spring, shows a total of 424 workers classified as to fields as follows: Spanish speaking, 127; French, 27; Italian, 11; Chinese, 7; Negro, 19; Indian, 74; Cuban, 95; Canal Zone, 6; Office and Field, 21; Miscellaneous, 37.

MAGAZINES AND BOOKS WIDELY USED. The Board's monthly magazine, "Southern Baptist Home Missions", had an average circulation during last year of 53,673, an average increase per month over the previous year of 1050. Income from magazine subscriptions and advertising and book sales netted a small profit to the Board above cost of publication of the magazine and some 60,000 mission study books. This profit was $1,085.40.

AN IMPERATIVE TASK. No country can be better than its citizens, and if Christianity is to become effective in changing national life, then it must root itself in the lives of the citizens who compose the nation. To embody these principles in law is not enough, for the law may not be obeyed. It is not legal, but moral rights that must be established. The main trouble now with the world is sin and selfishness rooted in individuals. These must be supplanted by love and kindness. Christ must become regnant in the life of the people.

When Christ reigns in the life of the people then will He rule in the social, economic, political and moral life of the world. Nothing else will save the world. It is Christ or chaos. We must Christianize the world or else the social order of the world will rot us in our own wickedness. As Christians we believe that the solution for the world's hurt is Christian religion.

Respectfully submitted,

J. C. Gillespie

---

19. The following visitors were recognized: Rev. A. R. Gallimore, Rev. L. A Nall, Rev. Mr. Beene.

20. The report on Foreign Missions was presented by Rev. J. S. Hopkins, of High Point. Upon motion to adopt the report it was spoken to by Rev. A. R. Gallimore, who had just returned from occupied China. The report was adopted.

Report on Foreign Missions

Our Foreign Mission Board, through its 464 missionaries and its thousands of native workers, has been engaged in a program of education, evangelism, and healing in Africa, Asia, Europe, South

America, and the Hawaiian Islands. During the current year mission work has been inaugurated in two fields, namely, Columbia and the Hawaiian Islands.

In 1933 the Board had an indebtedness of $1,110,000.00. The debt now stands at $90,000.00. That means that $115,000.00 has been given during the current year to debt reduction. It looks as if this burden of indebtedness will have been rolled away by the middle of 1943. The response to appeals arising out of the present emergence is most encouraging. Already more than $390,000.00 has been received. The Lottie Moon Christmas offering this year reached the unprecedented sum of $449,162.48.

THE COMMISSION has enjoyed phenomenal growth during the past year. Last year a circulation of 23,190 was reported while this year we can count a circulation of 39,313. Pastors and other religious leaders would confer a great benefit upon themselves and their people if they would make an effort to get this publication into every home. The price is only $ .50 per year.

AFRICA: Southern Baptists have the largest number of missionaries under appointment they have ever had in Africa—a total of sixty. From this field come glowing reports that both pagan and Mohammedans are finding and following the conquering Christ in this land of desperate darkness, and that the progress of our work has been impeded in no way by world conditions.

*EUROPE AND NEAR EAST*s Since total war enveloped Europe and threatened to lay waste the Near East, it has been necessary for all our American missionaries to withdraw from these areas. Our lone missionary remaining in Europe is Mrs. N. J. Bengtson of Barcelona.

THE ORIENT: Present world conditions have restricted our work in many parts of the Orient but Free China still opens to us one of the great opportunities of all time for mission work. Our mission secretary says that after the war there will be waiting for us in the Orient such an opportunity for preaching the gospel as Baptists have not known since Pentecost.

LATIN AMERICA: Every door swings wide for the entrance of the gospel in Latin America. Here our challenge is great to implement our "good neighbor policy" with the spiritual reality and the saving grace of the gospel of Christ.

Respectfully submitted,

Julian S. Hopkins

21. The report on Relief and Annuity was made by Rev. D. W. Overby, of Reidsville. Upon motion to adopt the report it was spoken to by Rev. M. O. Alexander, our General Missionary to Eastern N. C. The report was adopted.

Report on Relief and Annuity Board

The Relief and Annuity Board has entered upon the twenty-fifth year of its work. During the twenty-four years, which ended at the meeting of the Southern Baptist Convention last spring, the Board has made a great record of service and growth. Its assets grew from a little over $100,000 at the end of the first year's operation to approximately $5,500,000 by the close of 1941.

The Board is serving through its Relief Department and its several Annuity Plans more than 10,000 ministers, missionaries, denominational workers, and widows of ministers. Two thousand five hundred of these are already receiving benefits and 7,500 others are due to receive benefits in the years ahead.

A host of Southern Baptist pastors, with their churches, are participating in the Ministers' Retirement Plan. The number of preachers is rapidly approaching 6,000 and the number of churches approaching approximately 8,000.

Through other Annuity Plans of the Board, such as the (old) Annuity Fund, the Foreign Mission Board Pension Plan, the plan for Home Mission Board and the State Boards, together with the plans of the various agencies and Institutions of the Southern Baptist Convention, the employees are being protected against the vicissitudes of old age and permanent illness.

There are still scores and even hundreds of pastors in the Southern Baptist Convention, and in every state, who have not been awakened to their privileges and duty in connection with the Ministerial Relief Plan through which plan they have been urged to make provision for their old age or disability.

Young pastors should enroll promptly and he with the church or churches he serves should pay their dues regularly each month.

The unenlisted may receive full information as to enlistment by writing to

Secretary M. A. Huggins
Recorder Building
Raleigh, N. C.

Respectfully submitted,

D. W. Overbey

22. The report of the Committee to Nominate the Committee on Evangelism was made and adopted as follows: H. R. Starling, Chairman; Irby Jackson, Study Chairman; J. C. Shore, Publicity; J. S. Hopkins, Andrew Club; and J. E. Bryant, Highway and Hedges Evangelism.

23. The Committee to Nominate Officers made the following report which was adopted:

Grover H. Jones, Moderator

Rev. T. L. Sasser, Vice-Moderator

Rev. L. Grady Burgiss, Clerk-Treasurer

Rev. A. A. Walker, Sunday School Superintendent

J. Carl Bell, Training Union Director

RICHARD R. SAUNDERS, Sr., Chmn.,

JAMES H. SMITH and

IRBY B. JACKSON, Committee.

Report of Committee on Time, Place and Preacher

First—for preacher, Rev. Irby B. Jackson; alternate, Rev. James H. Smith.

Second—that the matter of a place be left in the hands of the Executive Committee.

Third—that the Association now in session amend the Article No. 15 of the Constitution so as to make it read as follows:

ARTICLE 15.—The time of the holding of the annual session shall begin on Wednesday before the fourth Sunday in October of each year, except where prevailing conditions make it advisable to change this date, in which event the Executive Committee shall be empowered to determine the date of meeting.

The report was adopted.

---

24. The Committee to Nominate the Church Advisory Committee made its report as follows: Dr. J. Clyde Turner, Chairman, Dr. A. B. Conrad, Rev. J. S. Hopkins, Rev. J. Ben Eller, Rev. Wilson Woodcock, Mrs. Nettie H. Hoge, Rev. T. L. Sasser and Rev. L. Grady Burgiss.

A. C. LOVELACE, Chmn.

A. A. WALKER

J. C. SHORE

25. A motion was made and carried that the Minutes of the Association of 1942 be dedicated to Mr. O. E. Lee, who for 16 years served efficiently and faithfully as Clerk of the Association.

26. A motion was made and carried that a letter of greeting and sympathy be sent to Mr. J. S. Moore, of Greensboro, who had attended the Association for 40 years, but was unable to attend this year.

27. Rev. Wilson Woodcock spoke for the Baptist Bible Institute of New Orleans.

28. Dr. J. Clyde Turner, who had just returned from the Seminary at Louisville, spoke briefly on the work there. He said that more than 500 male students are now enrolled there, and that the ladies of the Training School are taking part of their classes on the campus of the Seminary.

29. The report on the Co-operative Program was presented by Rev. Wilson Woodcock. Upon motion to adopt the report it was spoken to by him. The report was adopted.

Report on Co-operative Program

During 1941 the gifts by Southern Baptists to the Co-operative Program were $1,318,572.77, which is an increase of $183,530.36 over the gifts of 1940. The total, including $672,106.21 designations and $261,143.63 for the Hundred Thousand Club was $2,251,822.61, or an increase over the total of 1940 of $265,105.34.

Fair dealing is one of the principles on which the Co-operative Program is based. The needs and possibilities of each agency of our Convention is carefully weighed and allotment made accordingly. This prevents the agency with the best field representative securing more funds in proportion to its needs than another agency without such effecive promotional activity.

Faithful giving is the success of the program. Week by week giving is more satisfactory and produces more funds than spasmodic offerings made under high pressure.

Steadfastness in giving is the Scriptural method. Therefore those who follow this method because of their conviction that it is God's will are the joyous givers. As a rule they are the effective members of the churches.

Fundamental principles underlie the Program. The unity of missions is kept in the forefront. There is one command to go into all the world. The divergence in emphasis arises simply from the fact of geography. We learn the importance of the whole mission program by becoming familiar with the needs of the various mission fields, State, Home and Foreign.

Therefore the special days for special offerings have their place in the Program and they should be supported.

Hnery Ward Beecher said "A church debt is the devil's salary." And Paul said "Owe no man anything, but to love one another." (Rom. 13:8) In 1933 Southern Baptists began to do something about the six million dollar debt. The various agencies began to set aside a percentage of their receipts from the Co-operative Program for debt retirement. In May of that year the Southern Baptist Convention inaugurated the Baptist Hundred Thousand Club. Since then the debt has been reduced to less than one and three quarter million dollars. For the entire time since 1933 North Carolina stands seventh in the list according to the amount of the gifts. But for the first four months of this year our state is third, only Georgia and Texas exceed us.

In the first eight months of this year, that is, from January 1, to September 1, the receipts for the Hundred Thousand Club were $259,914.86, which is $95,274.73 more than the same period last year. A new slogan is suggested, viz. "Debt-free in 1943—count on me."

Respectfully submitted,

Wilson Woodcock.

---

30. The report on Social Service was presented by Dr. J. Clyde Turner. Upon motion to adopt the report it was spoken to by him. The report was adopted.

REPORT ON SOCIAL SERVICE

In times of war, the enemies of righteousness become stronger and more threatening. The baser passions are unleashed, and greed, and hate and prejudice take control; profanity, and prostitution, and drunkenness abound; holy things are desecrated. In the many social evils that confront us, we can mention only a few.

Desecration of the Lord's Day

The Lord's Day has been captured by the spirit of secularism and worldliness. Under the plea of war emergency, it has been turned into a day of revelry. Many professing Christians have been caught in the tide and swept from their moral moorings. If the present tendency is not checked, it will not be long until Sunday will be little different from the other days of the week. Let that day be stript of its sacred character, and Christianity will be wounded in its very heart.

Economic Evils

The business and industrial life of the nations is permeated with the spirit of greed and covetousness. Class is arraigned against class in an economic warfare that grows more threatening with each passing year. Competition instead of cooperation marks the spirit of the times. Extreme wealth and extreme poverty dwell side by side. Never will these evils be corrected until men come to realize that "none of us liveth to himself," but everyone has a social responsibility.

Racial Prejudice

In a time when all the people of our country should stand together, there are those who fan the fires of racial prejudice, and seek to stir up racial misunderstanding. The word of God declares that "There can be neither Jew nor Greek, there can be neither bond nor free, there can be no male and female; for ye are all one in Christ Jesus." The proper relation between the races can exist only when injustices are removed and the spirit of love prevails. Just when the people of the south were rejoicing in the fact that lynchings had almost ceased within our borders, three Negroes, two of them fourteen-year old boys, were lynched by angry mobs in one of our southern states. Crime can never be blotted out by the commission of other crimes. Right relations between races can never be established by prejudice and injustice.

The Liquor Traffic

The legalized liquor traffic continues to hold a favored place in our land. The beer barons and liquor dealers are using the conditions accompanying war to enlarge their patronage and increase their sales. Drunken drivers are menacing the highways in ever-increasing numbers. Social gatherings are characterized by drunken revelry. Areas around army camps are still flooded with liquor and vice in spite of the repeated protests of the forces of righteousness. Now that the young men from eighteen to twenty years of age are to be called to the army, it is all the more necessary that such conditions should be corrected.

The Christian church cannot escape its responsibility. It must hold high the standard of righteousness in a time of moral decay. It must seek to abolish the social evils that threaten our country, and create conditions in which life can be lived at its fullest.

J. Clyde Turner

---

31. A motion was made that telegrams be sent from the Association to our Congressmen, Rep. Carl T. Durham, Senator Josiah W. Bailey and Senator Robert R. Reynolds, urging them to support the bill now before congress to eliminate the sale of beer, wine and liquor from the army camps and their environs.

32. The Committee to Nominate the Executive Committee made its report as follows: Grover H. Jones, Chairman, T. L. Sasser, L. Grady Burgiss, Mrs. Nettie H. Hoge, A. A. Walker, J. Carl Bell, H. O. Miller, R. B. Culler, J. Earl Bryant, R. R. Saunders, J. H. Smith and F. L. Paschal. The report was adopted.

J. BEN ELLER, Chairman

E. M. SMITH

J. E. BRYANT.

33. The Committee to Nominate Delegates to the Baptist State Convention reported as follows: J. E. Bryant, Reidsville; W. H. Barker, High Point; and J. H. Saunders, Greensboro. The report was adopted.

B. C. LAMB

MRS. J. C. SHORE

W. L. SMITH.

34. The Treasurer's report was made and referred to the Auditing Committee.

Report of Treasurer

EXPENSE FUND

I herewith submit my report for the year ending September 30, 1942.

Balance on hand, Sept. 30, 1941		$ 42.33
Received from the Churches		180.97
Total		$223.30

Disbursements

Nov., 1941, Clerk's Remuneration	$ 50.00	
Feb. 11, 1942, Printing Minutes	132.28	
Sept. 21, 1942, Printing Programs	5.50	
Postage and Supplies	3.00	
Total	$190.78	
Balance on hand	32.52	
	$223.30	$223.30

MISSION FUND

I herewith submit my report for the year ending September 30, 1942.

Balance on hand Sept. 30, 1941		$15.53
Received from the Churches		37.20
Total		$52.73

Disbursements

Piedmont Baptist Training Union Treasurer	$20.00	
Piedmont Baptist Sunday School Treasurer	10.00	
Total	$30.00	
Balance on hand Sept. 30, 1942	22.73	
	$52.73	$52.73

Respectfully submitted,

L. Grady Burgiss, Treasurer

35. The report of the Committee on Resolutions was presented and adopted.

Report of Committee on Resolutions

Whereas, the Piedmont Baptist Association, meeting with the First Baptist Church, Greensboro, October 21, 1941, has engaged in a splendid session, be it

RESOLVED:

First, that we express our gratitude to this church and its pastor, Dr. J. Clyde Turner, and all the Baptist churches of the Greensboro group for their co-operation in entertaining the Association in a gracious way.

Second, that we express our appreciation to Mr. G. H. Jones, our very efficient Moderator, for his untiring efforts in serving the Association throughout the year. And to our vice-Moderator, Rev. T. L. Sasser, for his excellent service rendered as Moderator of this present session in the absence of Mr. Jones. Also to Rev. L. Grady Burgiss, for the plendid manner in which he has carried out the duties of clerk, completing the unexpired term of the former clerk.

Third, that we commend the work of the various organizations of the churches of the Association and urge that we give serious consideration to the appeal of Dr. Greer relative to the training of our young people for future service.

Fourth, that we express our sincere thanks to the Program Committee for the splendid program furnished us. And be it resolved that we as followers of Christ accept the opportunities and responsibilities that challenge us in these uncertain times.

Respectfully submitted,

Miss Thelma Patrick, Chm.

Mrs. L. Grady Burgiss

Mr. J. C. Gillespie

35-A. The report of the Auditing Committee was presented.

Report of the Auditing Committee

We the undersigned Committee appointed to audit the books of Brother L. Grady Burgiss, Treasurer, are grad to report that we found the same correct and very neatly kept, and recommend that his report be accepted with thanks for his accuracy and work of love.

Respectfully submitted,

A. A. Chandler

A. L. McGee

J. Huber Dixon

36. The report of the Church Advisory Committee was read and adopted.

Report of Church Advisory Committee

On January 19, 1942, the Advisory Committee met for the purpose of considering the advisability of Brother C. R. Pierce, of the Rocky Knoll church being a candidate for the ministry. Bro. Pierce was approved.

On June 18, 1942, at 3:00 p.m., the Advisory Committee met for the purpose of hearing the request of Allie R. Snipes, of the First Baptist Church, High Point, that he be ordained to the ministry, he having been called as pastor of the Ossipee Baptist Church. Motion was made by Mrs. Nettie H. Hoge, and seconded by Rev. J. S. Hopkins, that he be approved. Motion carried.

On Sept. 15, the Advisory Committee met at the First Baptist Church at 3:20 p.m. for the purpose of considering the establishment of a new church on Battle Ground Road near the junction of the old Hillsdale Road. A motion made by J. Ben Eller was carried that Dr. J. Clyde Turner and Grady Burgiss be a committee to represent the Advisory Committee to the group already carrying on work in that locality, and hear their requests and work with them in fostering the work.

The Church Advisory Committee in session today has heard the requests of the Edgeville and Pilot View Baptist Churches, has approved their requests and recommended their reception into the Piedmont Baptist Association.

Respectfully submitted,

L. Grady Burgiss, Sect. of Com.

37. The Edgeville and Pilot View Baptist Churches were welcomed into the fellowship of the Piedmont Baptist Association as Rev. T. L. Sasser, Vice-Moderator, extended the right hand of fellowship to the representatives from those churches.

38. The following new pastors were welcomed into the Association: Rev. A. L. McGee, Rev. I. B. Jackson, Rev. A. J. Swinson, Rev. W. H. Barker, and Rev. James H. Smith.

39. The session was closed with prayer.

WEDNESDAY EVENING SESSION

40. The session opened by singing "At the Cross," "Glory to His Name," and "When I survey the Wondrous Cross." The worship period was led by Rev. C. R. Pierce, pastor of Guilford Baptist Church. He read John 20:21, and led in prayer.

41. The report on Sunday Schools was presented by L. Grady Burgiss. Upon motion to adopt the report it was spoken to by Rev. L. L. Morgan. The report was adopted.

Report of Sunday Schools of Piedmont Baptist Association

A survey of records of our Sunday school work in this Association will reveal some facts that should give us some occasion for serious reflection and vigorous planning for the future.

Our records show that 46 Sunday schools in the year 1939 reported 16,270 pupils enrolled, with a total average attendance of 8894, while the records for this year of 1942 show 53 Sunday schools reporting an enrollment of 16,320, or a gain of only 50 pupils in four years. The enrollment for the years of 1940 and 1941 shows 16,625 and 16,903 respectively. The average attendance for those years was 8,407 and 8,817, both of which are below the 1939 average of 8,894. The total average attendance for 1942 is not yet computed, but the indications are that the figures will fall below those of the other years mentioned above.

All of this means that in spite of the fact that new Sunday schools and churches are coming into being at the rate of two r three a year our total enrollment and our average attendance do not increase materially.

Two questions immediately arise: 1, Are these new churches and Sunday schools made up and carried on by people who have withdrawn from other churches? 2, Is this an indication that if new churches and Sunday schools had not been established in these four years we would have suffered a definite decline in our Sunday school work?

Perhaps more than we realize it, the condition of the Sunday school is an index to the condition of the church. To what extent this is true we cannot say accurately. But there is enough relatior ship between them to cause us to pause and ponder when there is an indication that our Sunday school work may be slipping.

Let us each investigate conditions in our own church and

Sunday school, as well as in the community in which we serve, and see what can be done to enlarge our work all we can by employing the most vigorous efforts, and relying upon the help of the Lord.

Respectfully submitted,

L. Grady Burgiss.

42. The report on W. M. U. work was presented by Mrs. J. Ben Eller, in the absence of Mrs. Nettie H. Hoge. Upon motion to adopt the report it was spoken to by Mrs. Eller. The report was adopted.

Report of W. M. U. of Piedmont Association

At no time in the history of our denomination, probably in the history of the world, has there been so great a call for cooperation in all Christian work.

The watchword of the Woman's Missionary Union, "Laborers together with God," suggests the supreme task of not cooperating with each other but with God in his plan for the salvation of the human race.

Statistics of dollars and numbers are evidences of growth and activity, yet are soon forgotten. The Woman's Missionary Union of the Southern Baptist Convention is cooperating in all material things, but the abiding work of this organization, so blessed by God, is its imperishable influence at home and abroad through its emphasis on the importance of prayer, the enlistment and training of the women and young people in active service, the study of the world's need for gospel, stewardship of self and substance, ministering to the suffering and destitute and the systematic training of the young people in the missionary work.

A church whose women and young people are so organized will be a spiritual missionary church.

In these days of distress and confusion, the church may well say with the apostles when Christ asked them, "Will ye also go away?" and they replied, "Lord to whom shall we go? Thou hast the words of eternal life." To *whom* and to *what* must the world in its distress turn today?

The Woman's Missionary Union is as a beacon or sentinel through prayer and service pointing to Christ, the world's greatest need.

In the Piedmont Association there are thirty-eight churches with missionary organizations, some fully organized with all the auxiliaries. They report for the year through the cooperative program, gifts amounting to $130,106.20.

Respectfully submitted,

(Mrs.) Nettie Hatcher Hoge

43. The report on the Baptist Training Union was presented by Mrs. J. Carl Bell. Upon motion to adopt the report it was spoken to by Rev. J. S. Hopkins in a stirring address. The report was adopted.

Report of the Baptist Training Union to the Piedmont Baptist Association—Year Ending Sept. 30, 1942

A survey of the work of the Training Union of the Piedmont Association for the year ending September 30, 1942, shows that some progress has been made and some honors won. The efforts of the Director, Mr. J. Carl Bell, have been praiseworthy and untiring.

During the year the Director has conducted or assisted in twelve study courses and promoted the organization of two new Baptist Training Unions. Other work has also been done along this line by other leaders in the Association.

In spite of the transportation situation, quarterly meetings have been held as usual. At one of these meetings Mrs. Charles Leonard brought the inspirational message and at another Miss Ola Lee brought a stirring message.

Again an outstanding event of the year was the meeting at the First Baptist Church, Greensboro, on the afternoon of March 14th, which was climaxed by a banquet in the Masonic Temple. During the afternoon session, the associational eliminations of the various contests of the Training Union were held. At the banquet session, 366 persons were present for a record attendance. Group singing and skits were enjoyed during the meal and the evening was brought to a close with an inspiring address by Mrs. John Lane.

The Piedmont Associational Training Union is very proud of the fact that the winners of the contests held in Greensboro went on to win out in the Region and were winners of all the state contests held at Ridgecrest. The Better Speakers Contest was won by the representative of the First Baptist Church, Greensboro. The Intermediate Sword Drill by Asheboro Street Church, Greensboro, and the Adult Readers, the Junior Memory Work Drill, and the Music

Contests by the First Baptist Church, High Point. The entire Association should be proud of these winners.

As a new year stretches ahead, plans are being made that the work of the Training Union of the Association be carried on in the best way possible, in spite of existing conditions, that Christians may be trained for service.

Respectfully submitted,

Julia M. Liles, Secretary

Treasurer's Report of the Baptist Training Union of the Piedmont Association—Year Ending Sept. 30, 1942

October 1, 1941, Balance on hand		$13.70
RECEIPTS		
Piedmont Association		20.00
Total		$33.70
DISBURSEMENTS		
Flowers	$ 5.15	
Stamps, etc. for notices	2.26	
Banquet expense	18.41	
		25.82
Balance on hand September 30, 1942		$ 7.88

Respectfullly submitted,

Julia M. Liles, Treasurer.

Obituaries

During the past year sixty-one members of the churches in our Association departed this life. One of our most beloved ministers in the Southern Baptist Convention fittingly said while conducting the funeral of a man who had been devoted to his home, Christ and the church: "The best day any of us will see in this world is the day we leave it, provided we are Christians. In every sense it is triumph for the Christian. One is absent from the body in order to be present with the Lord."

We know not what a day may bring forth, and certainly we cannot tell which of us may go or who will be listed with the departed a year from now. But we do know that Jesus is the Resurrection and the life, that to live is Christ and to die is gain. Our God and Father is the God and Father of the living. Whether we live or whether we die we are His in Christ Jesus, the Alpha and the Omega.

Respectfully submitted,

J. H. Smith.

Report of Committee on Program

Religious Literature	J. Earl Bryant
Foreign Missions	Dr. J. Clyde Turner
Denominational Program	T. L. Sasser
State Missions	J. H. Smith
Home Missions	Z. W. Rotan
Social Service	B. C. Lamb
Orphanage	J. S. Hopkins
Baptist Hospital	I. B. Jackson
Baptist Training Union	C. S. Hodge
W. M. U.	Mrs. Nettie Hoge
Christian Education	Wilson Woodcock
Sunday Schools	J. Ben Eller
Ministerial Relief and Annuity	D. W. Overbey
Obituaries	J. B. Clifton

Respectfully submitted,

J. H. Saunders, Chairman

Clyde Ayers

Grady Burgiss

In Memoriam

ALLEN JAY—Mr. Walter Hawks.

CALVARY—J. E. Nance, Deacon.

FAIR GROVE—Mr. Clifton Doss.

GIBSONVILLE—Mr. W. T. Goodman.

ASHEBORO STREET—Mr. A. L. Self, Mrs. Geo. W. Causey, Mrs. W. E. Brightwell, Mrs. A. C. Burgess, Mr. Bill Hopkins, Mr. P. M. Sharpe, Mr. J. A. Nave, Mrs. W. H. Goodwin.

BESSEMER—Clarence Harris.

COLLEGE PARK—Miss Margaret Hollifield.

ELLER MEMORIAL—Mr. C. N. Shaw, Mrs. Myrtle Overly, Mr. J. H. Sharpe.

GREENSBORO, FIRST—Luther W. Herbin, Mrs. A. R. Williams, Mrs. J. B. Johnstun, Annie Seymour Edwards, Mrs. Virginia Sneed, J. G. Russell, O. E. Lee, Mrs. Vander Liles, Mrs. T. M. Boone, J. H. Riley, Dr. W. C. Moseley, Miss Betty Harrison, G. M. Kirkman, and Henry M. Durham.

FLORIDA STREET—Mrs. J. W. Austin.

LATHAM PARK—Mr. J. E. Broome, Deacon.

MAGNOLIA STREET—Mr. W. D. Neal, Deacon.

REVOLUTION—Mrs. Mary Parrot.

SIXTEENTH STREET—Mr. John Gaster.

STEVENS MEMORIAL—Mrs. J. W. Newman, Mr. W. A. Gunter.

TABERNACLE—Mr. J. C. Parrish.

WEBSTER MEMORIAL—Mr. S. T. Bryson.

HIGH POINT, FIRST—Mrs. C. A. Barbee, Mr. O. W. Forrest, Mrs. R. B. White, Mr. T. G. Elliot, Mr. D. L. Hayes, Mrs. Carl Edmonds, Mr. W. C. Kirkman.

GREEN STREET—Mr. E. D. Turner, Mrs. Laura Smith, Mrs. Mack Smith.

NORTH MAIN ST.—Mrs. Joseph Teague.

NORTH PARK—Miss Mary Blizzard.

SOUTH SIDE—Mr. Shaw.

WEST END—Mr. J. M. Glover, Mr. J. C. Swaim, Mrs. W. G. Slack, Mrs. J. W. Kivett.

LEBANON—Mr. S. R. Coleman.

REEDY FORK—Mrs. G. A. Canter.

BAPTIST TEMPLE—Mrs. Ernest Vaughn.

REIDSVILLE, FIRST—Miss Ella Johnson, Mr. H. L. Morrison, Mr. R. J. Fargis, Mr. E. M. Jones, Mr. O. A. Smith.

PENN MEMORIAL—Mrs. Lonnie Lemmons, Mr. Benton Holmes.

SMITH GROVE—Mrs. Louise Nuckles, Mr. Walter McCormick, Mr. Larken Frazier.

SUMMERFIELD—Mrs. Candis Groce.

OSSIPEE—Mr. E. W. Hunt.

Officers of the Piedmont Baptist Sunday School Association

SUPERINTENDENT—A. A. Walker, 507 Delancy St., Greensboro.

ASSOCIATE SUPT. in charge of Evangelism—J. S. Hopkins, 324 Woodrow St., High Point.

ASSOCIATE SUPT. in charge of Training—F. L. Paschal, 2420 Camden Rd., Greensboro.

SEC.-TREAS.—L. G. Burgiss, 103 E. Wendover Ave., Greensboro.

CHORISTER—H. R. Starling, 2218 Shober St., Greensboro.

DEPARTMENT SUPERINTENDENTS:

Junior—Ralph Slate, 817 Rotary Drive, High Point.

Intermediate—Mrs. Norman B. Moury, 2809 Sherwood St., Greensboro.

Young People—T. L. Ogburn, Asheboro St. Ext., Greensboro.

Adult—M. D. Teague, 608 Scott Ave., Greensboro.

Extension—Mrs. D. S. Ring, 909 Granby St., High Point.

Vacation B. S.—C. S. Hodge, First Church, Greensboro.

GROUP SUPERINTENDENTS:

Reidsville—J. C. Shore, Rt. 4, Reidsville.

High Point—E. M. Smith, 520 Bridges St., High Point.

Greensboro—U. A. Hedrick, Greensboro.

Cradle Roll—Mrs. J. W. Preston, 1534 McCormick St., Greensboro.

Beginner—Miss Ruth Scott, 1503 Spring Garden St., Greensboro.

Primary—Miss Lila Barton, 619 Waugh St., Greensboro.

MINUTES OF THE PIEDMONT ASSOCIATION W. M. U.

Annual Meeting April 24, 1942

The Piedmont Association of the Woman's Missionary Union met Friday, April 24, 1942, at the First Baptist Church, High Point, N. C.

Mrs. Nettie Hatcher Hoge, Superintendent, called the meeting to order, emphasizing the theme of the year, "When Christ Reigns—Peace."

Hymn, "We Praise Thee, O God."

Mrs. Paul Wrenn led the devotional.

Mrs. F. J. Flagler gave the welcome and Miss Judith Eller responded.

The roll call of the churches of the Association was taken with 105 present.

Mr. Grover Jones, Moderator of the Piedmont Association, made a talk on "Cooperation."

The $100,000 Club was discussed by Mrs. Edgar Howell.

Mrs. J. H. Smith brought us a delightful message in song, "Jesus, Savior, Pilot Me."

A season of prayer was held beseeching Christ's presence and guidance, followed by singing of Hymn, "All Hail the Power of Jesus' Name."

Mrs. Nettie H. Hoge, Superintendent, gave her report of the Association, which was approved.

Mrs. Hoge then brought us a most stirring message, using as her theme "The Kingdom of God." She emphasized that the Kingdom is written in our hearts and she glorified "Christ, the Wonderful."

Visitors were recognized.

Mrs. Hoge appointed the following committees:

Nominating Committee: Mrs. Ben Eller, Mrs. Paul Wrenn, Mrs. T. L. Sasser.

Resolution, Time and Place: Mrs. J. B. Clifton, Mrs. J. B. Ellis, Mrs. L. G. Burgiss.

Mrs. Chas. Leonard brought us a most inspiring message on "Peace." She challenged us to "Cast all our cares on Him daily," who can only bring the Christian Peace.

After a prayer by Mrs. Hoge, the meeting was adjourned for lunch until 2:30 P. M.

Respectfully submitted,

MRS. NETTIE HATCHER HOGE, Supt.

MRS. W. H. WRIGHT, Acting Secretary.

The afternoon session of the Piedmont Association of the Woman's Missionary Union was called to order by Mrs. Nettie Hatcher Hoge, Superintendent, with the singing of the hymn "The Light of the World."

Mr. Grady Burgiss gave the devotional.

The minutes of the morning session were read.

Reports were made as follows:

Mission Study—Mrs. J. J. Andoe

Personal Service—Mrs. Gover Jones

W. M. U.—Mrs. Ben Spencer

Stewardship and $100,000 Club—Mrs. H. A. Knight.

Mrs. W. D. Briggs outlined W. M. U. Methods and Specials for the ensuing year. She urged each W. M. U. to try a little harder this year to come up with our Standard of Excellence.

Mrs. C. E. Siceloff made her Treasurer's report, showing a balance on hand to date of $50.86.

Hymn, "All Hail the Pow'r of Jesus' Name."

Miss Ruth Scott gave the report of the Young People's Work, with Mrs. C. B. Brasinger representing the Sunbeams; Mrs. W. M. Ham, G. A.; Rev. E. M. Smith, R. A.; and Mrs. J. B. Ellis, Y. W. A.

Mrs. B. B. Stockard offered Resolution in memory of our deceased. Mrs. Marvin L. Slate sang, "When I Come to the End of the Road."

The Nominating Committee presented the following names of officers for the coming year:

Mrs. Nettie Hatcher Hoge	Superintendent
Mrs. J. H. Smith	Secretary
Mrs. W. O. Burnham	Treasurer
Mrs. Draper Leigh	Personal Service
Mrs. J. J. Andoe	Mission Study
Mrs. W. H. Wright	Stewardship
Miss Ruth Scott	Young People
Group Leaders	Mrs. H. A. Knight, Mrs. Grady Burgiss, Mrs. H. L. Morrison

Resolution report was read by Mrs. Burgiss.

The Committee on Time and Place recommended that the next annual meeting of our Associational Woman's Missionary Union be held the last Friday in April, which was voted on at a previous meeting, and that we accept with pleasure the invitation of the Asheboro Street Baptist Church of Greensboro to meet with them.

The meeting was then adjourned.

Respectfully submitted,

MRS. NETTIE HATCHER HOGE, Supt.

MRS. W. H. WRIGHT, Acting Secretary.

TABLE ONE—CHURCH MEMBERSHIP

CHURCHES	Village, Town, City or Country	When Constituted	PASTORS AND POST OFFICES	Days of Meeting	CHURCH MEMBERSHIP GAINS: Mem. Last Year	Baptisms	Letters	Statements	Restorations	LOSSES: Letters	Exclusions	Erasures	Deaths	Tot. Pres. Mem.	Weekly Prayer Meets.	Revivals Held, Year	Obs. Lord's Supper	Fam. Rec. Bap. Paper
Allen Jay	V	1934	C. M. Floyd, R.2, Thomasville	All	219	17	6	1	...	...	...	...	1	241	*	2	4	...
Antioch	O	1935	Melvin Faulkner, Guilford College	1 3	66	...	...	1	...	1	...	1	...	65	...	1	...	...
Brightwood	V	1940	H. P. Gauldin, R.5, Greensboro	All	34	11	31	8	...	7	...	1	...	76	*	2	1	...
Buchanan	O	1936	J. B. Clifton, Bessemer Branch, G'boro	All	134	1	4	1	...	1	1	...	...	138	*	1	2	1
Calvary	O	1901	J. C. Shore, R.4, Reidsville	2 4	162	17	5	2	...	...	...	...	1	185	...	1	2	9
Fair Grove	V	1940	A. R. Riddle, 2202 Spruce St., G'boro	All	60	2	5	...	...	10	6	...	1	50	*	2	2	...
Fairview	O	1904	J. C. Shore, R.4, Reidsville	1 3	102	19	1	1	...	3	...	...	...	120	...	1	2	1
Fairmont Park	V	1939	A. L. McGee, R.2, High Point	All	115	15	6	7	...	22	...	...	...	121	*	2	4	...
Gibsonville	T	1884	E. A. Long, Germanton	2 4	253	4	7	...	...	1	...	4	1	258	*	1	1	3
GREENSBORO—																		
Ashebore St.	C	1899	J. Ben Eller, 709 Asheboro St., G'boro.	All	1196	53	25	...	...	51	...	13	8	1202	*	2	4	...
Bailey Memorial	C	1937	Marion Beene, (Temporary)	All	109	1	...	...	...	12	...	2	...	96	*	...	6	...
Bessemer	C	1923	A. A. Walker, 507 Delancy St., G'boro	All	507	21	27	3	...	24	...	3	1	540	*	1	4	2
College Park	C	1906	Winson Woodcock, 508 Forest Ave, G'b	All	599	25	38	...	...	32	...	2	1	627	*	1	12	25
Edgeville	C	1942	L. J. Hight, 1406 Tucker, Greensboro.	All	.....	15	3	5	...	1	...	...	...	22	*	2	...	1
Eller Memorial	C	1897	J. H. Smith, 1307 Summit, Greensboro.	All	860	16	11	1	...	23	...	2	3	860	*	2	8	1
First	C	1859	J. Clyde Turner, 2601 W. Market, G'bor	All	2240	57	135	3	2	94	10	...	14	2319	*	1	12	97
Florida Street	C	1916	J. H. Saunders, 1110 Glenwood Ave.	All	417	34	47	3	3	12	...	...	1	491	*	2	4	...
Latham Park	C	1916	Lester D. Curl, Burlington	**All	60	2	8	...	...	1	...	...	1	68	...	1	...	...
Magnolia Street	C	1912	Grady, Burgiss, 103 E. Wendover, G'b.	All	208	5	4	1	...	7	...	3	1	207	*	2	3	11
Pomona	V	1906	C. M. Oates, Pomona	All	239	8	6	3	...	15	...	1	...	240	*	1	2	...
Revolution	C	1907	H. R. Starling, 2218 Shober St., G'boro	All	343	30	2	...	2	21	...	1	1	354	*	2	4	21
Sixteenth Street	C	1907	Wade H. James, 1504 16th St., Gr'boro	All	430	3	...	...	3	20	...	241	1	174	*	1	3	9
Stevens Memorial	V	1922	B. C. Lambe, R.2, Greensboro	All	144	13	7	...	...	1	...	...	2	161	*	2	4	5
Tabernacle	C	[illegible]	[illegible]	[illegible]	[illegible]	[illegible]	[illegible]	[illegible]	[illegible]	[illegible]	[illegible]	[illegible]	[illegible]	[illegible]	[illegible]	[illegible]	[illegible]	[illegible]

First			A. B. Conrad, 225 Lindsey, High Point	All	1347	52	47	2	...	48	...	4	8	1388	*	1	4	55
Greene Street			J. S. Hopkins, High Point	All	1396	44	42	1	...	20	...	...	3	1460	*	1	4	50
Hilliard Memorial			H. O. Miller, High Point	All	306	25	18	1	...	22	...	2	...	326	*	2	2	2
North Main Street	C	1908	I. B. Jackson, 200 Parkway, High Pt.	All	338	12	9	...	...	16	...	3	1	349	*	2	3	24
North Park	C	1929	E. M. Smith, 520 Bridges St., High Pt.	All	180	17	3	...	2	...	...	...	1	201	*	2	4	10
South Side	C	1916	W. H. Barker, R.3, Box 362, High Pt.	All	318	3	7	...	1	14	...	...	1	314	*	2	1	1
West End	C	1913	A. C. Lovlace, Mont Lieu Ave., High P.	All	414	9	2	1	...	4	...	4	4	414	*	2	4	...
Jessup Grove	O	1940	James E. Wiggs, 1515 Grove St., G'boro	All	113	12	...	...	...	...	...	2	...	123	*	3	2	1
Jewell	O	1941	A. H. Dunning, 811 Tryon St., High Pt.	All	18	8	3	1	...	...	...	...	...	30	*	1	1	...
Lebanon	O	1911	Melvin Faulkner, 55 Wentworth, R'ville	All	192	7	...	...	...	18	...	7	1	173	*	2	3	...
Mount Zion	O	....	J. T. Swinson, 613 Woodberry Av. H. P	2 4	174	6	...	...	...	...	...	...	2	178	...	1	1	...
Oak Grove	O	1916	R. L. Smith, High Point	All	165	17	2	...	1	2	4	53	...	106	*	2	4	2
Osborne Chapel	..	....	.....	.....	.....	...	...	...	...	...	...	...	...	.....	...	...	...	...
Osceola	O	....	R. L. Kizer, 810 N. Mebane St., Bur'ton	1 3	90	3	...	1	...	4	...	...	...	90	*	2	2	1
Pine Grove	O	1938	W. L. Campbell, R.3, High Point	All	76	8	7	1	...	1	...	1	1	90	*	2	1	...
Pilot View	V	1941	A J. Swinson, Box 402, High Point	All	29	11	12	6	...	...	...	...	...	58	*	2	...	5
Pisgah	C	1939	W. L. Smith, Box 1772, High Point	All	285	31	19	1	...	4	4	4	...	324	*	2	4	...
Pleasant Garden	V	1933	J. Huber Dixon, Pleasant Garden	All	75	10	2	...	...	2	...	...	...	85	*	1	4	...
Pleasant Grove	O	1937	J. M. Allred, Box 119, Pomona	All	106	3	...	1	...	...	...	...	...	93	*	2	11	...
Reedy Fork	O	1940	Elijah Lankford, Denim Sta., G'boro.	All	26	13	16	5	...	...	...	...	1	59	*	2	1	...
REIDSVILLE—																		
First	C	1844	T. L. Sasser, Reidsville	All	887	45	19	12	...	30	...	...	5	927	*	1	4	54
Baptist Temple	C	1929	.....	All	209	21	8	...	3	1	...	4	1	235	*	1	1	...
Penn Memorial	C	1929	D. W. Overby, 83 Lawsonville, Av., R'v	All	224	5	2	1	...	2	...	3	2	225	*	2	4	...
Rocky Knoll	V	1934	Geo. Tucker, R.1, Greensboro	All	238	8	10	1	...	11	...	...	...	246	*	2	2	4
Ruffin Stacey	O	1931	J. T. London, R.5, Reidsville	2 4	186	2	1	...	...	6	...	...	...	183	*	2	4	...
Smith Grove	O	1921	R. O. Nuckles, R.1, Colfax	1 3	176	5	1	...	...	...	...	...	3	179	*	2	1	...
Summerfield	O	....	E. A. Long, Germanton	1	200	6	2	1	...	...	...	...	1	208	...	1	3	...
Ossippee	V	1933	A. R. Snipe, R.2, Elon College	All	81	9	9	5	...	11	...	...	1	92	*	1	1	...
Temple	O	1939	J. T. Swinson, R.3, High Point	All	55	7	10	3	...	...	...	...	...	77	*	2	1	4
TOTALS	..	....	.....	.....	16888	794	646	87	17	588	25	361	76	17307	...	85	168	396

**Every P M.

TABLE TWO—SUNDAY SCHOOLS

ASSOCIATIONAL SUPT.
Rev. A. A. Walker
507 Delancey St.
Greensboro, N. C.

CHURCHES	SUPERINTENDENTS AND POST OFFICES	Cradle Roll, Under 3	Beginners, 3-5 Years	Primaries, 6-8 Years	Juniors, 9-12 Years	Intermediates, 13-16	Young People, 17-24	Adults, 25 Years Up	Extension Dept.	Gen., Dept. Officers	Tot. Enrollment, Officers, Teachers, Pup.	What is Av. Attend.?	Baptisms from SS	Is School Graded?	Teachers Holding Dip.	Enrollment Vac. Sch.	Av. Att. Vac. School
Allen Jay	Wade Cumbie, R.1, Box 239, High Pt.	19	17	26	44	57	37	108	...	12	320	218	...	*	...	....	....
Antioch	Roy Moore, Reidsville	...	....	....	....	....	....	....	...	8	.....	45	...	...	...	....	....
Brightwood	C. M. McGhee, R.5, Greensboro	...	14	21	....	53	31	37	...	3	159	80	...	...	...	....	....
Buchanan	L. E. Bush	18	28	....	17	30	44	50	...	....	187	115	...	...	...	....	....
Calvary	J. W. McCargo, R.2, Reidsville	...	20	19	16	25	55	93	...	11	239	103	14	...	...	....	....
Fair Grove	G. W. Johnson, R.2, Greensboro	8	11	....	4	10	....	16	...	9	52	50	2	...	...	....	....
Fairview	A. D. Hopkins, Reidsville	...	15	25	20	33	25	24	...	....	142	106	15	...	...	....	....
Fairmont Park	Ray Moore, R.2, High Point	16	46	....	34	....	38	84	...	3	221	130	15	...	...	....	....
Gibsonville	E. C. Riggins, Gibsonville	...	20	19	38	32	47	65	16	14	237	130	1	...	...	....	....
GREENSBORO—																	
Ashebore St.	M. D. Teague, 608 Scott Ave., G'boro.	38	51	89	148	152	148	378	55	70	1059	423	...	*	10	124	91
Bailey Memorial	E. J. Jarvis, 2018 Asheboro St., G'boro	10	14	....	15	16	30	16	...	7	107	72	1	...	...	....	....
Bessemer	A. C. Melvin, 3817 E. Market St., G'bor.	47	30	54	35	56	32	118	...	40	387	246	21	*	...	109	87
College Park	B. B. Stockard, Greensboro	29	40	34	55	69	98	134	18	61	498	299	25	*	19	79	60
Edgeville	H. E. Whitfield, 1234 Elmer, Gr'boro.	...	....	22	21	25	....	21	...	7	92	50	...	...	...	....	....
Eller Memorial	C. E. Brady, 1217 Homeland Ave., G'b.	16	33	89	130	110	80	195	8	56	681	290	...	*	...	230	177
First	C. S. Hodge, First Bapt. Ch., Gr'boro.	183	82	137	218	211	188	902	221	160	2146	893	45	*	...	185	154
Florida Street	H. A. Schuman, 1414 Ella St., G'bor.	33	35	60	78	74	35	177	...	32	524	335	22	*	...	198	137
Latham Park	....	...	14	....	....	19	....	21	...	5	50	35	2	...	...	....	....
Magnolia Street	J. E. Loving, 1419 Fairview St., G'boro	3	9	15	14	16	17	37	...	13	114	111	4	*	...	....	....
Pomona	C. C. Patterson, Pomona	...	34	38	73	46	73	65	...	13	342	209	...	*	...	....	....
Revolution	Grady Phillips, Greensboro	22	38	53	68	43	23	35	18	....	306	176	24	...	3	147	128
Sixteenth Street	Fred Hester, 1204 17th St., Greensboro	5	14	50	63	37	24	54	...	45	247	177	2	*	3	155	112
Stevens Memorial	L. A. Mills, R.2, Greensboro	15	10	15	20	15	25	90	...	17	190	135	...	*	...	....	....
Tabernacle	W. O. Smith, 1542 Lovett St., Gr'boro.	32	11	19	27	23	17	37	25	17	196	98	8	*	...	43	39
Webster Memorial	Tom Pearman, Denim Sta., Greensboro	10	12	23	26	14	31	14	...	....	180	94	...	...	1	....	....

Greene Street	W. E. Crissman, High Point	40	81	84	198	181	164	486	...	110	1240	588	34	*	...	343	231
Hilliard Memorial	T. E. Edwards, 1004 Stanton, High Pt.	...	34	15	56	31	17	85	...	25	244	170	25	*	...	...	...
North Main Street	S. R. Clinard, R.1, High Point	...	30	62	54	57	81	63	6	18	371	226	12	*	...	...	...
North Park	L. R. McNeil, 915 Forrest Ave., Hi. Pt.	11	22	23	35	48	19	45	7	28	214	150	...	*	6	...	...
South Side	Arthur Bean, 501 Highland, High Point	4	17	25	36	24	62	57	...	20	233	135	...	*	...	...	...
West End	Vernon Coffey, Barker St., High Point	28	28	42	60	40	52	81	...	6	337	187	...	*	...	...	...
Jessup Grove	Peel Stanley, R.1, Guilford College	...	27	...	30	...	40	56	...	6	159	128	12	...	...	...	...
Jewell	S. P. Stutts, Sr., R.2, High Point	...	...	25	...	20	...	15	...	20	60	48	8	...	...	...	...
Lebanon	Diamond Davis, R.2, Brown Summit	9	6	9	11	14	30	51	...	13	130	98	...	...	...	...	...
Mount Zion	George Spoon, Kinsville	...	...	12	12	30	30	30	...	8	117	74	6	*	...	...	...
Oak Grove	A. L. Saunders, R.3, Box 78, Archdale	...	15	12	15	8	31	41	...	10	122	84	...	...	...	...	...
Osborne Chapel	......	...	...	...	...	...	...	...	...	...	...	...	...	...	...	...	...
Osceola	D. A. Greene, R.1, B rwn Summit	...	7	12	10	18	28	20	...	2	97	60	2	*	...	...	...
Pine Grove	R. L. Loflin, Jamestown	...	28	...	18	19	12	26	...	8	105	63	...	*	...	...	...
Pilot View	H. L. Hill, R.2, High Point	...	18	...	28	...	26	18	...	7	90	70	...	...	...	20	18
Pisgah	J. J. Lowe, R.4, Box 284, High Point	5	8	20	43	56	64	134	...	28	330	230	...	*	...	...	...
Pleasant Garden	W. J. Smith, 1011 Caldwell St., G'boro	9	15	11	13	32	29	29	...	...	138	60	6	*	...	...	...
Pleasant Grove	F. M. Atkins, R.3, Greensboro	8	10	19	24	22	23	30	...	21	136	78	...	*	...	...	...
Reedy Fork	Worth Smith, R.2, Greensboro	13	21	13	17	39	...	29	...	10	133	88	...	...	...	...	...
REIDSVILLE—																	
First	R. T. Burton, Reidsville	79	33	40	88	83	78	326	75	46	814	317	45	*	...	113	92
Baptist Temple	Earl Gammon, Reidsville	12	18	29	39	34	17	68	...	6	223	110	15	*	...	...	...
Penn Memorial	W. Herbert Ford, Box 988, Reidsville	...	14	15	20	22	15	65	...	14	155	103	7	*	...	...	...
Rocky Knoll	F. B. Mooney, R.1, Greensboro	23	22	20	39	41	25	83	...	14	256	195	...	...	...	...	...
Ruffin Stacey	C. L. Schrumm, Ruffin	...	15	18	12	18	25	40	...	11	132	50	...	*	...	...	...
Smith Grove	J. A. Farrington, R.1, Colfax	...	38	...	22	...	62	50	...	6	172	62	5	...	...	...	...
Summerfield	Marion Ayers, S mmerfield	...	25	14	12	16	26	30	...	...	123	106	...	...	...	...	...
Ossippee	R. C. Fitts, R.2, Elon College	...	25	...	17	...	30	15	...	6	93	75	...	...	...	...	...
Temple	Miss Callie Cook, R.3, High Point	...	15	8	16	...	23	29	...	14	94	60	...	...	...	...	...
TOTALS	......	815	1241	1426	2270	2184	2283	5273	524	1160	16325	8947	429	...	67	1746	1326

TABLE THREE—BAPTIST TRAINING UNION

CHURCHES	Director of Training Union J. Carl Bell, Greensboro / DIRECTOR OF TRAINING UNION	Adult Unions	Yng. People's Unions	Intermediate Unions	Junior Unions	Story Hours	Tot. Unions, Sto. Hrs.	Adults Enrolled	Young People Enrol'd.	Intermediates Enrol'd	Juniors Enrolled	Story Hours Enrolled	Tot. Enrolled, Unions and Story Hours	Daily Bible Readers	No. Taking St. Course	Tot. Systematic Givers	Students in College	No. Gen. Dept. O'cers.
Allen Jay	Early White, Rt. 4, High Point	1	...	1	1	...	3	19	...	20	19	...	58	35	34	49	...	4
Calvary	Harry Conner, Rt. 2, Reidsville	...	1	1	...	1	3	...	...	...	...	...	...	...	...	...	1	...
Fairmont Park	R. A. Teague, Rt. 2, High Point	1	1	...	1	1	4	17	21	...	17	21	76	...	...	...	...	...
GREENSBORO—																		
Asheboro St.	J. J. Norwood, 1318 Oak, Greensboro	...	1	2	2	1	6	...	25	62	25	5	117	33	39	117	14	6
Bailey Mem.	Roland Mitchell, Rt. 7, Greensboro	...	1	...	1	...	...	...	15	...	8	...	23	19	17	23	...	1
Bessemer	Miss Norfleet Dixon, Greensboro	1	1	1	1	1	5	6	9	19	15	9	58	18	28	36	1	3
College Park	C. C. Gamble, Greensboro	...	...	...	...	...	...	...	...	...	...	...	...	...	...	...	...	...
Eller Memorial	Raymond Kincaid, 1214 F'rview, G'boro	1	1	1	2	1	6	16	16	12	24	8	76	53	48	52	1	6
First	C. S. Hodge, Greensboro	2	4	4	2	1	13	41	90	74	36	28	269	51	70	160	20	...
Florida Street	C. H. Walker, 1009 Haywood, G'boro	2	1	1	4	3	11	27	19	12	36	24	118	49	56	72	1	7
Magnolia Street	J. E. Poore, 203 E. Wendover, G'boro	1	1	1	...	1	4	8	9	10	...	6	33	18	...	26	...	3
Pomona	Mrs. W. H. Brown, Pomona	1	...	...	...	...	1	14	...	...	...	...	14	14	5	10	...	...
Revolution	Mrs. Lois Reirson, Greensboro	1	1	1	...	1	4	11	10	7	...	...	28	13	13	16	...	5
Sixteenth Street	Willard Lawson, Rt. 5, G'boro	2	1	1	1	1	6	19	7	12	10	11	59	29	33	59	...	6
Stevens Memorial	Miss Ethel Brisson, Rt. 2, Greensboro	...	...	...	...	...	...	...	...	...	...	...	...	...	...	...	4	...
Tabernacle	Miss Lucile [illegible]n, 1408 Fla. St. G'boro	1	...	1	1	...	3	8	...	20	9	...	37	21	25	28	...	9
Webster Memorial	Mrs. R. Cole Lee, Rt. 2, Bx. 116, G'boro	1	1	1	1	1	5	14	9	20	12	7	62	30	19	37	...	3
HIGH POINT—																		
First	W. O. Burnham, 309 [illegible]ch, H. Point	...	2	3	4	1	10	...	22	72	67	17	183	48	63	83	25	5
Greene Street	Clarence Keever, High Point	2	2	3	2	1	10	36	33	43	26	9	147	57	99	126	6	13
Hilliard Memorial	H. B. Chatham, 2108 English, High Pt.	2	1	1	1	1	6	25	8	20	15	11	79	25	...	37	...	3
North Main Street	Lucian Williams, 205 Lex. Ave., H. Pt.	1	1	1	2	1	6	20	9	12	20	15	76	23	28	32	...	22
North Park	Mrs. J. A. Jones, High Point	1	1	2	1	1	6	20	15	20	19	8	82	39	53	58	...	...
South Side	Miss Daisy Shaw, Highland Sta., H. Pt.	1	1	...	1	...	3	29	9	...	7	...	45	8	...	12	...	3
West End	R. G. Barlow, Barker, St., High Point	2	2	1	1	1	7	20	17	20	18	15	90	28	47	50	...	...
Jessup Grove	James Albert, 907 Englewood St. G'boro	2	...	...	1	1	4	34	...	...	14	3	51	22	12	48	...	6
Jewell	Mrs. T. H. Willard, Rt. 2, High Point	...	...	...	...	...	...	...	...	...	...	...	30	7	10	...	...	[illegible]

REIDSVILLE—																		
Baptist Temple	Mrs. Leonard Gammon, Reidsville	1	...	1	1	1	4	...	...	...	...	...	88	8	9	49	...	13
First	W. O. Kelley, Reidsville	1	3	2	1	...	7	16	54	46	30	...	146	59	54	90	8	8
Penn Memorial	Mrs. Nash Wilkins, Reidsville	1	1	1	1	1	5	11	7	11	8	3	40	18	21	19	...	...
Rocky Knoll	Sam Carrick, Rt. 1, Greensboro	1	1	1	1	1	5	15	11	14	10	11	61	...	...	27	1	...
Summerfield	Ivan Angel, Summerfield	1	...	1	1	...	3	13	...	12	11	...	36	15	35	22	2	...
TOTALS		36	32	35	36	24	157	452	535	583	481	221	2395	771	826	1424	84	158

TABLE FOUR—WOMAN'S MISSIONARY UNION

CHURCHES	PRESIDENTS OF W. M. S. AND POST OFFICES	Number W. M. S.	Number Y. W. A.'s	Number G. A.'s	Number R. A.'s	Number Sunbeams	Total W. M. S. Orgs.	W. M. S. Members	Y. W. A.'s Members	G. A.'s Members	R. A.'s Members	Sunbeam Members	Tot. Members Enrol'd	Tot. Enr. Mis. St. Cse.	Contributions (Local Work) By W. M. U.	Contributions (Missions) By W. M. U.
Brightwood	Mrs. Frank Bettini, Rt. 1, B[illegible]n S[illegible]mit	1	...	...	...	...	...	9	...	...	...	...	9	...	6.00	....
Buchanan	Mrs. J. B. Clifton, Bessemer Branch, Greensboro	1	1	...	...	1	3	16	14	...	...	22	52	21	....	93.16
Calvary	Mrs. J. E. McCargo, Rt. 2, Reidsville	1	1	1	...	...	3	28	22	19	...	...	69	...	37.60	180.10
Fairview	Mrs. R. E. DeLapp, Rt. 2, Reidsville	1	...	...	...	...	...	...	...	...	...	...	16	15	9.27	26.35
Fairmont Park	Mrs. Willus Jones, Rt 1, Thomasville	1	...	...	...	...	...	...	...	...	...	...	42	...	438.00	50.00
Gibsonville	Mrs. Westmoreland, Gibsonville	1	...	...	...	...	...	...	...	...	...	...	26	...	63.50	85.42
GREENSBORO—																
Asheboro Street	Mrs. D. F. Stone, No. 3 Scott Apt., Greensboro	1	2	2	1	1	7	166	45	41	20	22	294	132	....	1759.78
Bailey Memorial	Mrs. W. J. Mitchell, Rt 7, Greensboro	1	...	...	...	...	1	...	...	...	...	...	15	...	35.60	34.00
Bessemer	Mrs. J. R. Melvin, 200 Sykes, [illegible]o	2	...	2	...	1	5	45	...	23	...	10	78	14	72.52	380.07
College Park	Mrs. W. J. Marsh, Greensboro	1	1	1	...	1	4	40	10	50	...	8	108	35	....	....
Eller Memorial	Mrs. W. L. Thornburg, 1600 Fairview, G'boro	1	1	...	1	...	3	50	17	...	17	...	84	26	....	877.06
First	Mrs. Ben Spencer, 751 Chestnut St., Greensboro	1	3	3	2	1	10	394	66	52	61	69	642	271	6209.20	12088.95
Florida Street	Mrs. [illegible] Allred, 1510 Elwood, Greensboro	1	1	1	1	1	5	74	25	15	10	10	134	15	....	273.88
Magnolia Street	Mrs. R. A. Smith, 916 Cherry, Greensboro	1	1	1	...	1	4	20	7	12	...	30	69	15	6.80	86.94
Pomona	Mrs. F. C. Morehead, Pomona	1	...	1	...	1	3	25	...	22	...	30	77	...	....	50.15
Revolution	Miss Sallie Burgiss, [illegible]o	1	1	1	1	1	5	30	6	15	5	21	56	22	....	1011.97
Sixteenth Street	Mrs. W. A. Straughan, [illegible]h St., Greensboro	1	1	2	1	1	6	33	8	20	12	12	95	47	....	1610.69
Stevens Memorial	Mrs. R. A. [illegible]n, Denim Station, Greensboro	1	...	...	...	...	1	25	...	...	...	...	25	12	....	....
Tabernacle	Mrs. T. W. Driver, 1604 Grove St., Greensboro	1	1	1	...	1	4	16	9	8	...	12	45	11	1675.79	232.00
Webster Memorial	Mrs. C. L. Straughan, Rt. 5, Greensboro	1	1	1	1	1	5	48	8	9	8	15	88	...	151.30	378.74
Guilford	Mrs Alice Ferrel, Guilford	1	...	...	...	1	2	14	...	...	...	12	26	...	....	58.05
HIGH POINT—																
First	Mrs. F. J. Flagler, 321 Montlieu Ave., High Point	1	1	2	2	1	7	148	21	50	31	14	264	...	766.74	4186.18
[illegible]e S[illegible]eet	Mrs. L. A. Pegg, 500 Chandler, High Point	1	2	2	1	1	7	120	32	22	6	10	244	65	5695.00	1488.03
Hilliard Memorial	Mrs. C. J. Hedrick, Rt. 2, High Point	1	1	1	1	1	5	15	12	8	13	15	63	22	9.64	115.43
North Main Street	Mrs. G. L. Thompson, High Point	2	...	1	...	...	3	32	...	9	...	...	41	12	....	193.38
North Park	Mrs. L. W. Glenn, Bx. 702, High Point	1	1	1	1	1	5	15	10	10	8	6	49	...	1411.06	278.54

TABLE FIVE — CHURCH PROPERTY

CHURCHES	CHURCH CLERKS AND POST OFFICES	Own House Worship?	When Was It Built?	Materials Used	Persons Seated	Number of Rooms	Dept. Assem. Rooms	No. Sep. Class Rooms	Value Church House and Grounds	Value Mission Chapel, if Any	Value Pastor's Home	Total Value All Church Property	Indebtedness on All Church Property	Insurance Carried
Allen Jay	Hoy Yarborough, Rt. 3, Bx. 152, H. Pt.	*	1936	wood	300	10		9	4000.00			4000.00		2000.00
Antioch	Mrs. T. H. Carter, Rt. 2, Reidsville	*	1935	wood	300	4		3	1500.00			1500.00		
Brightwood	G. M. Hicks, 1503-18th St., G'boro	*	1941	wood	300	8		6	5000.00			5000.00	15.00	2000.00
Buchanan	E. C. West	*	1886	wood	150	5	1	4	3000.00			3250.00		1500.00
Calvary	J. E. McCargo, Rt. 2, Raidsville	*	1898	wood	275	9	1	8	5000.00		2000.00	7000.00		3000.00
Fair Grove	Mrs. W. L. Lee, Rt. 2, Greensboro	*	1940	brick	225	1	1	6	6000.00			6500.00		1500.00
Fairview	William Cummings, Rt. 2, Reidsville	*	1901	wood	300	11		10	3000.00			3000.00		2000.00
Fairmont Park	Mrs. I. A. [illegible], Rt. 1, Thomasville	*	1942	wood	540	7		5	6000.00			7025.00	860.00	2000.00
Gibsonville	C. M. Seaford, Gibsonville	*	1884	wood	300	9	9	9	2500.00			2500.00		2000.00
GREENSBORO—														
Ashebore St.	J. B. Wills, 1026 Pearson, G'boro	*	1912	brick	700	61	10	69	51000.00		6000.00	57000.00	11500.00	43000.00
Bailey Memorial	E. J. Jarvis, 2018 Asheboro, G'boro	*	1935	wood	300		1	6	2300.00			2300.00	35.00	750.00
Bessemer	Maurice Bunting, 3705 Cam'r'n Av. G'b'o	*	1923	w-b	350	25	5	20	10000.00		2000.00	12000.00	2688.74	12500.00
College Park	Carrol O. [illegible], Greensboro	*	1940	brick	300	57	8	42	52000.00	200.00	8000.00	63600.00	8000.00	50000.00
Edgeville	Mrs. J. M. Page, 1326 [illegible], G'boro	*	1942	wood	200	1			1500.00			1600.00		
Eller Memorial	W. L. Thornburg, 1600 Fairview, G'boro	*	1925	brick	800	50	7	48	42000.00		9000.00	51000.00		30000.00
First	Vander Liles, Greensboro	*	1906	brick	1000	43		48	100000.00		15000.00	115000.00		70000.00
Florida Street	Eleanor [illegible], 1514 Elwood, G'boro	*	1930	brick	350	23	2	22	17000.00		4500.00	21500.00		14000.00
Latham Park	W. W. Sutton, Greensboro	*	1916	wood	150	1			2500.00			2500.00	750.00	
Magnolia Street	Mrs. G. H. Williamson, 3700 Oak Grove	*	1912	wood	300	11	1	11	6000.00	1000.00	4000.00	11000.00		6500.00
Pomona	C. C. Patterson, Bx. 102, Pomona	*	1906	wood	350	8		8	3000.00			3000.00		
Revolution	N. C. Brown, 1902 Poplar St., G'boro	*	1907	wood	400	5	3	8	10000.00	5000.00		15000.00		7500.00
Sixteenth Street	J. Vaughn Brady, 2408 Spruce St.	*	1907	brick	400	5	4	17	39000.00			39000.00		18000.00
Stevens Memorial	Mrs. J. B. Brown, Rt. 2, [illegible]boro	*	1922	wood	250	11	2	13	10000.00		2500.00	12500.00		750.00
Tabernacle	Mrs. E. C. White, Jr., 1006 Hertford St.	*	1938	wood	200	3		2	5000.00			5000.00	100.00	2000.00
Webster Memorial	Albert West, Rt. 5, Bx. 204, G'boro	[illegible]	[illegible]	[illegible]	[illegible]	[illegible]	[illegible]	[illegible]	[illegible]	[illegible]	[illegible]	[illegible]	[illegible]	[illegible]

yes

TABLE SIX — GIFTS FOR LOCAL CHURCH WORK

CHURCHES	REGULAR TREASURERS AND POST OFFICES	Pastor's Salary	Other Salaries	Ministerial Help and Supply	Building and Repairs	Church Debt and Interest	Incidentals	Literature for S. S., B. Y. P. U., W. M. S.	Help Given to Local Poor	For Printing Minutes and Clerk of Assn.	Other Objects	Total for Local Purposes Given By Church and Its Orgs.	Number of Tithers
Allen Jay	W. R. Hobson, R.1, Box 239, High Pt.	2279.50	....	135.00	777.56	....	142.88	170.90	232.35	5.00	664.60	4407.79	40
Antioch	Mrs. Hobart Carter, Reidsville	195.00	....	115.00	175.00	....	9.00	20.00	....	1.30	....	514.00	...
Brightwood	J. M. Crabtree, R.5, Box 232, G'boro	1385.00	....	185.83	479.90	....	63.00	....	45.00	......	....	2158.73	...
Buchanan	E. C. West, Greensboro	1300.00	....	40.00	109.67	....	71.69	65.91	....	3.00	230.49	1820.76	14
Calvary	J. F. Carroll, R.3, Reidsville	360.00	....	80.00	894.87	....	91.90	89.53	....	4.00	103.82	1614.22	...
Fair Grove	W. L. Lee, R.2, Greensboro	150.00	....	60.00	350.00	268.04	25.68	16.00	5.00	......	....	875.72	...
Fairview	D. E. Trantham, R.2, Reidsville	302.00	....	100.00	....	360.00	63.55	85.48	....	3.00	5.50	919.53	...
Fairmont Park	R. A. Teague, R.2, High Point	660.00	....	102.75	3734.26	....	131.53	82.50	50.00	5.00	142.00	4908.04	16
Gibsonville	T. L. Robinson, Gibsonville	600.00	....	69.02	6.50	....	240.37	100.00	....	3.00	....	1018.89	3
GREENSBORO—													
Ashebore St.	Earl L. Johnson, 2012 Asheboro, G'boro	3300.44	1792.50	538.30	533.01	2174.00	514.19	922.46	753.36	12.50	1305.67	11846.53	...
Bailey Memorial	Simon W. Bryant, R.3, Box 444, G'boro	820.00	....	68.42	530.86	178.95	158.29	71.47	12.50	4.00	109.41	1953.90	30
Bessemer	C. L. Murray, Box 688, Greensboro	1690.00	....	125.00	1365.88	4556.00	385.35	244.65	221.20	10.00	....	8201.06	...
College Park	L. E. Ogburn, Greensboro	2400.00	340.00	446.89	1229.42	2940.48	1837.85	434.29	6.89	12.50	421.56	10069.88	100
Edgeville	H. E. Whitfield, 1234 Elmer St.	....	....	81.60	1298.06	....	4.00	31.07	....	1.00	....	1415.73	...
Eller Memorial	Mrs. Robert Burgess, 1214 Walnut, G'b	2100.00	470.00	380.00	655.27	....	1897.13	409.14	44.50	10.00	422.20	6388.24	...
First	Howard Gardner, 405 Sunset Drive, G'b	4600.00	6595.59	128.87	736.72	23864.47	4605.93	1245.13	959.59	......	4436.57	47172.87	...
Florida Street	D. M. Frazier, 1319 Florida St.	2385.00	1092.00	270.43	1479.31	2257.31	808.47	634.00	5.00	......	3798.56	12730.08	...
Latham Park	R. A. Anderson, Greensboro	328.06	....	....	....	26.86	46.95	32.26	....	......	....	434.13	...
Magnolia Street	H. S. Noah, 1700 Grove, Greensboro	1560.00	....	107.00	457.36	1486.92	389.77	96.57	39.98	3.00	326.46	4467.06	41
Pomona	E. E. Henry, Pomona	1652.00	....	85.84	316.63	....	175.50	155.38	56.48	3.00	43.24	2488.07	...
Revolution	Waldo Johnson, 2241 Shober St., G'boro	2060.00	....	110.44	252.36	....	255.20	244.34	53.00	5.20	432.03	3412.57	...
Sixteenth Street	L. F. Paris, 1608 15th St., Greensboro	2135.00	....	....	445.14	....	707.42	194.99	41.13	9.00	310.00	3842.68	50
Stevens Memorial	Mrs. C. B. Brisson, R.2, Greensboro	1560.00	....	96.44	491.19	....	278.54	128.97	11.51	4.00	97.52	2668.17	...
Tabernacle	[illegible]	[illegible]	[illegible]	[illegible]	[illegible]	[illegible]	[illegible]	[illegible]	[illegible]	[illegible]	[illegible]	[illegible]	[illegible]

TABLE SEVEN—MISSIONS, EDUCATION, ALL BENEVOLENCES

CHURCHES	Total to Cooperative Program	Special to Associational Missions	Special to State Missions	Special to Home Missions	Special to Foreign Missions	Special to Schools and Colleges	Special to Theological Seminaries	Special to Orphanage	Special to Hospitals	Special to Old Ministers' Relief	Hundred Thousand Club	Other Objects	Total Given for Missions and Benevolences by Church and All Depts.	Grand Total, All Purposes, Given By the Church and All Orgs.
Allen Jay	50.00			90.00				96.06	30.00				266.06	4673.85
Antioch								10.00	15.00				25.00	539.00
Brightwood	10.00							24.00						2158.73
Buchanan	111.01							26.00	19.10		8.00	14.01	178.12	1998.88
Calvary	70.00	1.00	28.65	26.50	55.60	11.00		200.12	37.15	5.00	68.25	3.00	506.27	2121.09
Fair Grove									7.00					
Fairview	98.00							54.25	15.94		9.00		177.19	1096.72
Fairmont Park				40.30	5.00			30.00	15.00				90.30	4998.34
Gibsonville	50.00							30.67	17.00				97.67	1116.56
GREENSBORO—														
Ashebore St.	2464.35	.40	120.33	102.06	276.20		7.00	799.58	148.10	132.00	232.93	284.16	4567.11	16413.54
Bailey Memorial	82.55		10.00		17.00			199.63	8.75	1.00	12.00		330.93	2284.83
Bessemer	360.00		10.50	14.35	15.00	8.00	5.00	100.00	43.65		14.00		570.50	8771.56
College Park	600.00		138.24	32.32	433.83	111.68		355.40	43.57		134.40	17.94	1867.38	11937.26
Edgeville														
Eller Memorial	1713.95							450.00	131.76		306.05	95.45	2697.21	9085.45
First	17520.74	342.51	814.03	556.72	5692.99	238.00	77.48	2855.10	504.80		2268.37	181.82	31052.56	78225.43
Florida Street				38.35	1189.13			300.00	52.48	139.00		222.91	1941.87	14671.95
Latham Park									5.00			17.91	22.91	457.04
Magnolia Street	147.46	42.20			25.00			110.00	35.00		22.50	41.60	423.76	4890.82
Pomona			45.30	53.11	77.93			436.16	38.00		12.00	182.16	871.66	3359.73
Revolution	1172.04	17.47	57.45	32.25	215.35			191.59	119.65		143.44	233.94	2183.18	5595.75
Sixteenth Street	2149.93		127.50	50.00		17.50		312.85	33.21		163.50	127.85	2982.34	6825.02
Stevens Memorial	600.00		10.00	44.00	91.00	28.35		197.66	38.30		15.65	70.52	1095.48	3763.65

Greene Street	2021.30	......	133.21	......	......	60.50	......	521.15	[illegible]	[illegible]	[illegible]	[illegible]	[illegible]	[illegible]
Hilliard Memorial	129.43	.75	6.50	12.50	10 75	......	......	150.17	24.40	......	46.62	......	381.12	4486.77
North Main Street	400.00	......	70.60	......	11.50	......	......	160.00	60.77	......	42.00	203.02	947.89	5484.02
North Park	315.00	......	70.55	......	36.20	......	......	97.00	31.00	......	58.25	166.00	772.50	4792.29
South Side	......	......	16.71	14.00	......	......	......	......	......	......	36.10	......	81.81	2674.68
West End	291.07	5.00	37.32	28.80	179.50	......	2.25	302.07	55.00	......	81.00	90.13	1072.14	3719.06
Jessup Grove	16.11	......	......	......	......	......	......	84.00	12.11	......	......	800.00	912.22	3035.54
Jewell	25.00	......	......	......	......	......	......	8.50	5.01	......	......	......	38.51	419.80
Lebanon	......	......	......	63.93	74.30	......	......	62.78	10.00	......	......	......	211.01	2158.51
Mount Zion	......	......	......	161.05	......	......	......	21.25	4.05	......	......	......	186.35	783.45
Oak Grove	18.00	......	......	......	......	......	......	57.00	10.00	......	......	......	85.00	1504.50
Osborne Chapel	......	......	......	......	......	......	......	......	......	......	......	......	......	......
Osceola	......	......	13.50	4.30	8.65	......	......	76.56	12.61	......	......	12.86	128.48	676.24
Pine Grove	......	......	10.81	7.50	7.71	......	......	11.47	6.51	......	......	......	44.00	736.71
Pilot View	......	......	......	......	......	......	......	14.44	14.00	......	......	......	28.44	744.54
Pisgah	25.00	......	10.00	......	......	......	......	25.00	25.00	......	......	......	85.00	4372.13
Pleasant Garden	24.00	......	......	......	10.00	......	......	24.00	......	......	......	......	58.00	1364.00
Pleasant Grove	39.65	......	......	......	......	......	......	50.00	6.05	......	......	48.92	144.62	1687.47
Reedy Fork	64.90	......	7.00	......	7.65	4.45	......	12.00	19.00	......	......	7.90	122.90	1934.28
REIDSVILLE—														
Baptist Temple	294.53	......	35.31	27.96	33.72	......	......	144.00	......	2.00	9.00	393.86	940.38	5887.59
First	1818.99	......	57.00	95.00	189.00	52.50	......	427.17	85.86	......	326.00	341.96	3393.48	13141.92
Penn Memorial	55.76	......	91.83	36.00	43.46	......	......	53.00	35.00	......	12.00	......	327.05	3762.63
Rocky Knoll	......	......	57.11	138.73	40.00	......	......	150.00	75.00	......	......	......	460.84	2731.40
Ruffin Stacey	......	......	......	......	......	......	......	24.00	5.00	......	......	......	29.00	1006.40
Smith Grove	......	......	10.70	1.10	2.24	......	......	14.00	14.94	......	......	......	42.98	601.99
Summerfield	86.93	......	25.16	25.00	45.63	1.00	......	95.00	10.00	......	24.00	......	312.72	1841.38
Ossippee	......	......	......	......	......	......	......	......	......	......	......	......	928.79	928.79
Temple	60.94	......	6.04	......	......	......	......	24.50	13.00	......	......	......	104.48	1414.84
TOTALS	38115.44	419.33	2336.34	2064.26	10241.90	581.78	141.73	11232.11	2300.73	663.84	5221.25	......	79224.70	324184.15

Minutes Of The

Piedmont Baptist Association

North Carolina

Fiftieth Annual Session

Held With The

First Baptist Church

Greensboro, N. C.

Thursday, October 21st

1943

Next Meeting Will Be Held With The First Baptist Church, Greensboro, Thursday, October 19, 1944.

Rev. J. H. Smith, Greensboro............Preacher

Rev. G. G. Lanter, Reidsville............Alternate

—Index Will Be Found On Last Page—

Associational Directory

Grover H. Jones, Moderator ---------------- High Point

Rev. J. Ben Eller, Vice Moderator ------------- Greensboro

Rev. L. Grady Burgiss, Clerk ----------------- Greensboro

EXECUTIVE PROMOTION COMMITTEE

Grover H. Jones, Chm. ---------------------- High Point

Rev. L. Grady Burgiss, Clerk ---------------- Greensboro

Mrs. J. Ben Eller ----------------------------- Greensboro

J. Carl Bell ---------------------------------- Greensboro

C. S. Hodge ---------------------------------- Greensboro

Rev. J. Ben Eller ----------------------------- Greensboro

Harry B. Caldwell ----------------------------- Greensboro

R. B. Culler ---------------------------------- High Point

Rev. H. O. Miller ----------------------------- High Point

R. R. Saunders ------------------------------- Reidsville

T. L. Gardner -------------------------------- Reidsville

Rev. J. H. Smith ------------------------------ Greensboro

Rev. E. A. Long ------------------------------ Germanton

Rev. R. R. Jackson ---------------------------- High Point

CHURCH ADVISORY AND MISSIONS COMMITTEE

Dr. J. Clyde Turner, Chm. ------------------- Greensboro

Rev. L. Grady Burgiss, Clerk ---------------- Greensboro

Grover H. Jones ------------------------------ High Point

Mrs. J. Ben Eller ----------------------------- Greensboro

Mrs. R. R. Saunders ---------------------------- Reidsville

Rev. J. S. Hopkins ---------------------------- High Point

Rev. J. C. Shore ---------------------------- Reidsville

OFFICERS OF PIEDMONT W. M. U.

Mrs. J. Ben Eller, Superintendent, 709 Asheboro St., Greensboro.

Mrs. Nettie Hatcher Hoge, Superintendent Emeritus, 1406 West Market St. Greensboro.

Mrs. W. F. Clayton, Associate Superintendent, 223 Lindsay St., High Point.

Mrs. T. C. Robbins, Young Peoples Leader, 321 Louise St. High Point.

Mrs. J. H. Smith, Secretary, 1307 Summit Ave., Greensboro.

Mrs. W. O. Burnham, Treasurer, 309 Shurch St., High Point.

Mrs. J. J. Andoe, Mission Study, 923 North Eugene St., Greensboro.

Mrs. Draper Leigh, Community Missions, 1511 Spring Garden, Greensboro.

Mrs. W. H. Wright ,Stewardship, Guilford College.

Mrs. R. R. Saunders, Margaret Fund and Training School, 401 Main St. Reidsville.

Mrs. H. A. Knight, Group Leader, 1100 North Main St. High Point.

Mrs. Grady Burgiss, Group Leader, 103 East Wendover Ave., Greensboro.

LIST OF COMMITTEES SERVING DURING THE ASSOCIATIONAL YEAR

Executive—Promotion Committee

Church Advisory and Missions Committee

Program Committee

COMMITTEES SERVING DURING THE ANNUAL MEETINGS OF THE ASSOCIATION

Committee on Committees

Committee on Time, Place, and Preacher

Auditing Committee

Committee on Resolutions

Program Committee for this year and next year

Committee to Nominate Officers

Committee to Nominate Executive—Promotion Committee

Committee to Nominate Church Advisory and Missions Committee

Committee to Nominate Delegates to the Baptist State Convention

CHURCHES BY DISTRICTS

District 1

Allen Jay; Fairmont Park, Greene Street, High Point, First; Hilliard Memorial, Jewell, North Main Street, North Park, Oak Grove, Pine Grove, Pilot View, Pisgah, Smith Grove, South Side, Temple, West End.

District 2

Asheboro Street, Bailey Memorial, Bessemer, Brightwood, Buchanan, College Park, Edgeville, Eller Memorial, Fair Grove Florida Street, Gibsonville, Greensboro, First; Guilford, Jessup

Grove, Latham Park, Lebanon, Magnolia Street, Mount Zion, Osborne Chapel, Pleasant Garden, Pleasant Grove, Pomona Mills, Sixteenth Street, Stevens Memorial, Summerfield, Tabernacle, Ossippee, Webster Memorial.

District 3

Antioch, Calvary, Fairview, Baptist Temple, Osceola, Penn Memorial, Reidsville, First; Ruffin Stacey.

OFFICERS OF BAPTIST TRAINING UNION

J. Carl Bell, Director	Greensboro
Miss Thelma Patrick, Asso. Director	High Point
Miss Julia Lyles, Sect. Treas.	High Point
E. C. White, Jr., Pianist	Greensboro
C. S. Hodge, Chorister	Greensboro
Mrs. Crutchfield, Story Hour Leader	Greensboro
Miss Martha Jane Mitchell, Jr. Leader	Greensboro
Miss Myrtis Thomas, Int. Leader	Greensboro
Miss Mable Starnes, Young Peoples Leader	Greensboro
C. S. Hodge, Adult Leader	Greensboro
J. E. Hedrick, Director Dist. No. 1	High Point
J. J. Norwood, Director District No. 2	Greensboro
Mrs. Marvin Jones, Director Dist. No. 3	Reidsville
Rev. T. L. Sasser, Pastor Advisor	Greensboro

PROGRAM COMMITTEE

C. S. Hodge, Chairman	Greensboro
Rev. L. Grady Burgiss	Greensboro
Miss Mabel Starnes	Greensboro

ORDAINED MINISTERS NOT PASTORS

Ben S. McDowell	High Point
Guy Funderburke, Chaplain	Washington, D. C.
Gilmer, Proctor, Chaplain	Fort Benning, Ga.
Clinton R. Baker,	Asheboro
V. D. Peedon	Greensboro
Geo. F. Dorsett	Greensboro
C. D. Barton	Greensboro
A. A. Walker, Chaplain, Hensley Fld.	Dallas, Tex.
Dr. C. A. Leonard, Missionary	China
W. F. Matherly	Greensboro
C. C. Cross, Student	Louisville, Ky.
T. L. Sasser, City Miss. Supt. 611-5th Ave.,	Greensboro
D. E. Oates,	Fargis St., Greensboro
John U. Garner, Chaplain	U. S. Army
O. P. Dix,	High Point
Charles Coffey,	High Point
T. H. Biles, Chaplain	U. S. Army
E. L. Hutchins	115 E. Bragg, Greensboro
A. E. Lewis,	Rt. 2, Elon College
Hubert Bennet,	Rt. 1, Greensboro
H. P. Billings	Jamestown
J. F. Murray	Reidsville
A. S. Gillespie, Missionary	Stovall
C. R. Smith	Kernersville
B. H. Farrington,	Colfax

MINISTERS ORDAINED DURING THE YEAR

Rev Irl E. Kerley -------------- 1704 Florida St., Greensboro

Rev. Charles C. Cross, (Bapt. Seminary)---- Louisville, Ky.

Rex. Tem Bryant ------------------------------ Reidsville

Rev. Fred Koerber ---------- 1512 Glenwood Ave. Greensboro

Rev. Odell Pulley ------------------------- Hampton, Va.

NEW PASTORS WELCOMED TO ASSOCIATION

Ray W. Harrington ------------------------------ Bessemer

Irl E. Kerley ------------------------------------ Guilford

R. R. Jackson ---------------------------------- West End

Fred Koerber ----------------------- Tabernacle, (Assist.)

G. G. Lanter ---------------------------- Baptist Temple

John Gamble ------------------------------- Gibsonville

J. C. Gillespie ------------------------------------ Antioch

G. A. Tucker ------------------------------- Rocky Knoll

L. J. Tribble ------------------------------------ Ossipee

Geo. H. Wallace ------------------------------- Allen Jay

J. D. Fuller ---------------------------------- Community

Dewey Armstrong ---------------------------- North Park

Howard L. Weeks ------------------------ Reidsville, First

W. C. Bearden ------------------------------ Bailey Mem.

Wade H. James ----------------------------- Sixteenth St.

STUDENTS FOR THE MINISTRY

Austin Lovin ------------ Sou. Bapt. Seminary, Louisville, Ky.

Carl Compton ---------- Sou. Bapt. Seminary, Louisville, Ky.

Billy Holton ---------------------------------- Greensboro

Charles Coffey --------------- High Point Col. High Point

Felten Carter -------------------------------- McLeansville

J. H. Boles ---------------------------- Rt. 3, High Point

LIST OF MESSENGERS

ALLEN JAY—Rev. Geo. H. Wallace, Jim Warren, Miss Mary Warren, Miss Mealie Burrow, Mrs. Claude Mickey, Mrs. Thomas Gray, Thomas Gray, Mrs. Hoy Yarborough.

ANTIOCh—Mrs. Joe Carter, Mrs. T. H. Carter, Raymond Lovelace

BRIGHTWOOD—H. G. Coleman, Mrs. G. B. Cocklereese, J. W. Holder, Mrs. H. P. Gauldin, B. G. Yow

BUCHANAN—Mrs. R. P. Johnson, Mrs. J. T. Ellis, Mrs. J. B. Clifton

CALVARY—J. C. Shore, Mrs. J. C. Shore, Mrs. J. E. McCargo, Mrs. Charles Lynn, Eugene Hancock, Mrs. J. R. Fulp.

COMMUNITY—Mr. and Mrs. Robert Osborne, Mr. and Mrs. John May

FAIRVIEW — Mrs. H. P. Griffin, D. E. Trantham, William Cummings, Mrs. D. E. Trantham, Mrs. William Cummings.

FAIRMONT PARK—Mr. and Mrs. J. E. Copple, Mr. and Mrs. A. S. McGee, O. E. Snow, W. F. Thomas.

GIBSONVILLE—E. C. Riggins, Mrs. Willie Summers, Miss Thelma Riggins, Mrs. Thompson, Mrs. C. C. Hancock, R. L. Seaford

GREENSBORO:

ASHEBORO St.—Rev. J. Ben Eller, Mrs. E. R. Baldwin, Mrs. J. S. Moore, Miss Mable Starnes, Mrs. A. C. Lowe, Mrs. W. S. Sherwood, Mrs. Clayton Sneed, Mrs. Lettie Jordan, Frank Paschal, J. J. Norwood, V. E. Jones, Joe Fox, Page Mann, L. C. Satterfield

BAILEY MEM.—Mrs. E. J. Jarvis, Mrs. C. C. Stanley, C. C. Stanley, Miss Ruby Payne, Mrs. W. C. Heilig

BESSEMER—C. L. Murray, Mrs. C. E. Brady, Mrs. W. A. Aydelette, Mrs. R. F. Pace, Mrs. J. F. Layton, Mrs. Ray W. Harrington, R. F. Pace

COLLEGE PARK—E. N. Sharpe, C. O. Weaver, L. E. Ogburn, P. R. Venable, Mrs. B. A. Scott.

EDGEVILLE—J. H. Lineberry, Webster Mahaffey, Mrs. W. Lineberry, Mrs. D. B. Eaton

ELLER MEM.—Wyley Patterson, Mrs. Lloyd Varnadore, Mrs. Russell Noah, Miss Leah Andrews, Albert Duggins, Mrs. James Overman, Mrs. Helen Shepherd, Mrs. T. M. Obrien

FIRST—

FIRST—Dr. and Mrs. J. Clyde Turner, Mrs. B. L. Spencer, Mrs. E. T. Howell, Mrs. S. R. Webb, Mrs. O. E. Lee, J. D. Wilkins, C. S. Hodge, George Bennet, T. B. Gaskins, and Ronald Reid.

FLORIDA ST.—Mrs. C. L. Robertson, Mrs. W. L. Jones, Mrs. H. L. Holton, Mrs. John Turner, Mrs. J. I. Phillips, Mrs. A. W. Watson

LATHAM PARK—Mrs. Anderson, Mrs. Leslie D. Curl, Mrs. Permar, Mrs. Bradley

MAGNOLIA STREET—Mrs. R. G. Henry, Mrs. L. L. Jarvis, Mrs. H. S. Noah, Geo. Apple, Mrs. J. A. Lewis

POMONA—Mrs. R. M. Causby, Mrs. Hattie McDaniels, Mrs. E. E. Henry, Mrs. C. M. Oates, L. E. Parschal, Rev. C. M. Oates

REVOLUTION—Mrs. H. R. Starling, Mrs. Waldo Johnson, Mrs. L. G. Mannuel, W. L. Parrot, N. C. Brown

SIXTEENTH ST.—J. V. Brady, Mrs. Harry Moore, Willard Lawson, L. F. Parris, Harry Moore

STEVENS MEM.—Mrs. J. H. Ham, Mrs. H. E. Whitfield, H. E. Whitfield, Mrs. W. P. Brown, Mrs. A. C. Hilliard, Mrs. B. C. Lambe

TABERNACLE—J. T. Berry, A. B. Green, E. C. White, Jr., Mrs. J. L. Shouse, Mrs. Ella King, Mrs J. T. Berry

WEBSTER MEM.—Mrs. A. Andrews, Mrs. W. H. Lucas; R. L. Bell

GUILFORD—Mrs. I. E. Kerley, Mrs. B. F. Butter, Mrs. Hettie Kennedy

HIGH POINT:

FIRST—Mrs. W. F. Clayton, Mrs. A. B. Conrad, Mrs. C. E. Siceloff, Miss Thelma Patrick, Mrs. W. O. Burnham, Mrs. H. A. Knight, J. E. Hedrick, Mrs. A. J. Bolling, Mrs. M. L. Slate

QUEEN ST.—W. E. Crissman, B. G. Leonard, Clyde Ayers, Mrs. J. C. Saunders, Miss Gladys Ridgill, A. M. Smith, Mrs. T. C. Robbins, B. E. Mixon, W. S. Lewis ,Mrs. Robert Winfrey

HILLIARD MEM.—C. H. Maynor, C. R. Manis, Mrs Ralph Elkins, Mrs. Carl Barnes, H. B. Chatham, Miss Ruth Sledge, Mrs. C. H. Jasmer, Mrs. H. O. Miller, Mrs. Gertrude Garver, Mrs. J. J. Haywood

NORTH MAIN ST.—Mrs. E. H. Parker, Mrs. Ed Crisco, Mrs. Homer A. Seachrest, Mrs. R. D. Langston, Mrs. Alice Davis, Mrs. Irby Jackson

NORTH PARK—Mrs. A. Davis, D. H. Short, Mrs. D. H. Short, Mrs. C. J. Elliot, Mrs. P. K. Frye, Mrs. J. L. Jones

SOUTHSIDE—Mrs. C. R. Saltz, Mrs. Geo. Tate, Mrs. Will Hinson, Miss Daisy Shaw

WEST END—C. M. Scott, Mrs. R. R. Jackson, Mrs. T. D. Hedrick, Mrs. C. M. Scott, Talmadge Smith, Mrs Talmadge Smith

JESSUP GROVE—Mrs. Ruth Lewis, Mrs. James E. Wiggs, Rev. James E. Wiggs, Mrs. D. H. Bryson, Mrs. V. W. Marshall, Mrs. Johnny Marshall, Clarence Marshall, Miss Dora Mason

JEWELL—E. L. Rhyne, S. P. Stutts, Marvin Stutts, Mrs. E. L. Rhyne, Mrs. S. P. Stutts, Estie Brown

LEBANON—Mrs. J. L. Cole, Mrs. M. G. Faulkner, Mrs. J. McDaniel, Mrs. J. P. Lindsay, Mrs. S. R. Coleman, Miss Maggie Kirkman, Miss Margie Carter

MOUNT ZION—Rev. J. T. Swinson, Edgar Smith

OAK GROVE—C. S. Weaver, Mrs. Harry Robertson, W. L. Shackleford, H. T. Holder, Mrs. A. L. Saunders, Mrs. H. T. Holder, Mrs. D. H. Grubb, Mrs. C. S. Weaver

OSCEOLA—Mr. and Mrs. E. R. Brande, Mrs. Ora Whicker, Elmer Haynes

OSSIPEE—Huston Steele, R. C. Fitts, R. E. Barker, H. D. Smith, Mrs. R. C. Fitts, Miss Maude Barker

PILOT VIEW—Rev. and Mrs. A. J. Swinson, Mr. and Mrs. H. L. Hill, Mrs. J. A. Hussy, Miss Roxie Thomas, Charlie Parker, Marion Leviner, Mrs. David Cannon

PINE GROVE—Mr. and Mrs. O. A. Peryman, Mrs. W. L. Camppell, Mrs. L. R. Loflin, Mrs. R. A. Packard

PISGAH—Winifred Powers, L. C. Adden, Mrs. L. C. Madden, Mrs. C. R. Byrd, Mrs. Z. V. Lanier, W. A. Moore, Ray Riner, Mrs. T. W. Moore

PLEASANT GROVE—D. R. Robertson, Mrs. D. R. Robertson, J. H. Foy, Clarence Yow, Mrs. J. E. Thomason, Walter J. Smith

PLEASANT GROVE—D. R. Robertson, Mrs. D. R. Robertson, J. D. Shackleford, Mrs. W. H. Smith, J. H. Boles, Mrs. John Nunn, F. M. Atkins, Mrs. F. M. Atkins

REEDY FORK—G. A. Canter, Mrs. O. H. Pressnell, Mrs. E. A. Snyder, Mrs. L. G. Greer, Rev. Elijah Lankford

REIDSVILLE:

BAPTIST TEMPLE—Mrs. Odell Dellap, Mrs. J. C. Gillespie, Mrs. Jesse Strader, Milton Warf, Wilson Hudson, Mrs. Wilson Hudson

FIRST—Mrs. R. H. Pleasants, Mrs. T. L. Gardner, Mr. and Mrs. R. R. Saunders, Mrs. C. H. Saunders, Mrs. C. B. Scoggin, and Mrs. J. C. Tatum.

PENN MEMORIAL—D. W. Overbey

ROCKY KNOLL—Mrs. F. B. Mooney, E. L. Maness, A. L. Price, Mrs. G. A. Tucker, Mrs. E. P. DeLong, Vernon Williams, W. T. Apple, Mrs. R. A. Laughlin

RUFFIN STACEY—Mrs. J. T. Cardwell, Mrs. John Burton, Mrs. Dewey London, Mrs. John Childress, Robert Baker, Mrs. John Childress

SMITH GROVE—Dora Clark, Pearl Rayle, Wilma Farrington, Jonah Pitts, Walter Westmoreland, Willy Midkiff, Daisy Robertson, Hettie Westmoreland

SUMMERFIELD—Mr. and Mrs. Marvin Truitt, Mrs. Mrytle Smith, Mrs. Monroe Winfree, Mrs. J. A. Wilson, Mrs. Suda Doggett

TEMPLE—Rev. and Mrs. J. Tommy Swinson, Miss Callie Cook, Roy Yarborough, Mrs. R. L. Rodden

Constitution

ARTICLE 1.—The Association shall be called the Piedmont Baptist Association.

ARTICLE 2.—It shall be composed of the ordained ministers who are members of, and those who may have pastoral charges within the Associational District, and three delegates from each Church in the district aforesaid, and Churches having a membership exceeding 300 shall be entitled to one additional delegate for every 200 members or fraction thereof in excess of 300.

ARTICLE 3.—The said delegates shall, before taking their seats, produce letters from respective Churches showing their appointment as delegates.

ARTICLE 4.—The Associational session shall be held at least once a year.

ARTICLE 5.—The officers shall be a Moderator, Vice-Moderator, Clerk and Treasurer. If deemed expedient by the Association, the offices of Clerk and Treasurer may be combined.

ARTICLE 6.—The officers of the Association shall be chosen annually by the Association.

ARTICLE 7.—Association shall be clothed with authority only to advise the Churches touching all things pertaining to their interest but shall in no case presume to direct or control them in reference to their own government or internal policy.

ARTICLE 8.—A Committee of arrangements, consisting of three members, shall be appointed on the first day of each session to prepare and report the proceedings and suggest topics proper for the consideration and action of the next annual Association. It shall be the duty of this committee to outline and publish a program for the next annual associational meeting or for any special or called meeting of the Association.

ARTICLE 9.—Baptist brethren, not members of the Association, who may be present at any session of the body, may on invitation by the body, take seats and participate in the debates of the Association.

ARTICLE 10.—The territory embraced in the Association shall be divided into not less than three districts and a committee composed of one pastor, and one layman from each district, together with the Moderator, Vice-Moderator, Clerk of the Association, Associational W. M. U. Superintendent, Associational Sunday School Superintendent, and Associational B. T. U. President, shall be appointed at meeting of the Association, which committee shall compose the Executive Committee of the Association, a majority of which shall constitute a quorum. It shall be the duty of the committee to superintend and direct the missionary operations of the Association.

ARTICLE 11.—All committees shall be appointed by the Moderator, either directly or indirectly with the approval of the Association, unless otherwise authorized by the Association from time to time.

ARTICLE 12.—The Constitution may be altered only at an Annual session of the Association and by a vote of two-thirds of the whole present.

ARTICLE 13.—The rules of this body shall follow Mell's Parliamentary Practice.

ARTICLE 14.—This Association shall cooperate with the Baptist State Convention.

ARTICLE 15.—The time of the holding of the annual session shall begin on Wednesday before the fourth Sunday in October of each year, except where prevailing conditions make it advisable to change this date, in which event the executive Committee shall be empowered to determine the date of meeting.

Adopted October 17, 1895.

Articles 2, 5, 6, 10, 15 Amended Session, July 23, 24, 1930.

Article 15 Amended Session July 21, 1932.

Article 10 Amended Sessions October 23, 34, 1935.

Articles 8, 10, 11 Amended Sessions October 23, 24, 1940.

FRANK L. PASCHAL

C. V. WEBSTER

J. H. SAUNDERS

Committee

Proceedings

of the

FIFTIETH ANNUAL SESSION

of the

PIEDMONT BAPTIST ASSOCIATION

Held With The

FIRST BAPTIST CHURCH

Greensboro, N. C.

October 21, 1943

THURSDAY MORNING SESSION—9:30 A. M.

1. The Association opened with singing "All Hail the Power of Jesus Name," led by C. S. Hodge, Educational director of the host church. Rev. J. Huber Dixon, pastor of Pleasant Garden Church, then read Psalms 22, 23 and 24 as a devotional, and led the body in prayer.

2. The sessions were presided over by the Moderator, Grover H. Jones, assisted at times by the Vice-Moderator, Rev. T. L. Sasser.

3. Words of welcome were spoken by Dr. J. Clyde Turner, pastor of the host church.

4. The printed program was presented for the sessions and adopted.

5. Rev. T. L. Sasser, Vice-Moderator, was then called to

the chair while Grover H. Jones, the Moderator, made his report. The report was adopted.

MODERATOR'S REPORT

Today we pause to consider some of the accomplishments of the last year's work in our association, in our state, in the south and on our mission fields and to gather information and inspiration that shall gird us for the tasks that are upon us. From the churches in this association and organizations in the churches, I have received numerous invitations during the past year. With few exceptions, I have been able to accept these invitations. Due to war conditions, it has been harder to contact the churches during the past year than at any time since I have been your moderator.

A fine spirit of cooperation prevails among the churches in our association and with the associational mission program under the leadership of Rev. T. L. Sasser, this year should prove to be the greatest year in the history of our association. During this session you will be advised fully concerning the program for associational missions.

I received a report from Brother L. L. Carpenter, Editor and Business Manager of the Biblical Recorder, relative to the Recorder. There are some encouraging facts set forth in this report. It is stated, "The circulation of the paper since August 1942 has increased rapidly. The present circulation is 18,591 which means a net gain since August 1942 of more than 7,000.

The Biblical Recorder is a good, wholesome and attractive weekly paper and gives much information concerning the work of Baptists in North Carolina and throughout the south. It is an organ of our Baptist State Convention and ought to be in every North Carolina Baptist home. One of the great needs for our people is that they be informed, trained and enlisted in the whole program of the church and of the Kingdom of God. The Biblical Recorder can be of immense value in this respect.

Never before in the history of the world have christian men and women been challenged as they are now challenged by national and world conditions. I fear that many professed christians have commonly thought of Christ's teachings as lovely, idealistic and beautiful to hold; that we have discussed His doctrine as though we could merely accept it or not as we pleased and have segregated it into a special realm called religious as though it were an ideal dream of the world as it ought to be. This attitude has sprung from our failure to realize the alternatives that confront us; that there are other doctrines in the field that will dominate the world if His does not. With new consecration, new zeal and new courage, may we more fully devote ourselves to Christ and His cause.

Respectfully submitted,
G. H. Jones, Moderator.

6. The Moderator appointed the following as members of the Committee on Committees; Rev. H. O. Miller, Chm. Rev. J. H. Smith and Rev. J. C. Shore.

7. The report on State Missions was made by Rev. J. H. Smith, of Greensboro. Upon motion to adopt the report, the discussion of it was postponed until the report on the Cooperative Program, which followed immediately. The report was adopted.

REPORT ON STATE MISSIONS, OCTOBER 21, 1943
PIEDMONT BAPTIST ASSOCIATION

Baptist people in North Carolina have a tremendous responsibility and a glorious opportunity in regard to a million lost souls in this state. In our "Judea" about one out of every two belonging to a church belongs to a Baptist church. More than 500,000 (432,-823) are enrolled in our 2,634 churches of 72 associations. If each member would accept the privilege of being a personal witness as commanded in Acts 1:8 how many days would be required to reach this million who are condemned and abiding under the wrath of God? The answer is, only one day, if each one could see two persons. But you say that 90 percent of these church members never seriously attempt to win another to Christ. How about the more than 2,000 Sunday School superintendents and the 2,107 ordained minisers in our state convention, then? If our ordained ministers could see an average of two a day, it would require about 238 days (less than a year) to reach the million. I seriously wonder how many of these who are lost-lost-lost have been approached by a minister, deacon, Sunday School superintendent, teacher or some member of a Baptist church. How much longer shall we hear them saying: "Why do you wait, dear brother; why do you tarry so long? Your Saviour has bidden you tell us of One who can save us from wrong. There is danger and death in delay."

Under the Lordship of Jesus who came to seek and save the lost, may we heartily and enthusiastically cooperate with our beloved state secretary, M. A. Huggins, in his great vision for our state to be Christian. Our three general missionaries, the 73 pastors in mission churches, associational missionaries, missionaries in our camp areas and every servant of the state convention ought to be remembered in our daily prayers. Our witnessing to the unsaved, our spiritual guidance in the life of each believer and our ministry to the sick are as essential in "ALL Judea" as the sun is to the earth. If one in our territory should be lost may it not be necessary for Him to say, "His blood will I require at your hand!"

Fort Bragg, the largest Army Post in America and largest Artillery Post in the world, and these other camps in our midst must not be neglected in this dark and crucial hour. More soldiers are being trained in this state than in any other state in the union. The men and women stationed at these strategic points need additional funds to carry out their heavenly visions. Surely we are going back to our churches and lead our people Sunday in a worthy offering for STATE Missions! With reference to special offerings for state missions and a budget for the coming year, I recommend that each pastor and each Sunday school superintendent study carefully and use the table on page 80 of the 1942 *North Carolina Baptist Annual.* (The same table is found on page 75 in *Kingdom Building in North Carolina* by M. A. Huggins.) According to the table the vision of our servants who are trying to lead us in a worthy program for Jesus, our Saviour and Lord, calls for at least $147,900.00 more than we are giving them now. We should be obedient to their vision! May our glorious privilege to witness in every area and to every person in this fair state and the spirit of the Christ in us lead us in exclaiming, "Take my life and let it be consecrated, Lord, to Thee. Here is my silver and gold, too. Use me and what I have to help make North Carolina a Christian state.

Respectfully submitted,

J. H. Smith

8. The report on the Co-operative Program and the 100 Thousand Club was made by Rev. Wade H. James, of Greensboro. Upon motion to adopt the report it was spoken to by Rev. E. L. Spivey, our new General Missionary for Central N. C. The report was adopted.

REPORT ON THE COOPERATIVE PROGRAM

The Cooperative Program is the tried, true, and increasingly successful plan of Southern Baptist for enlisting all our people in the support of all our work.

The Purpose of the Program

1. To include all denominational work in one comprehensive plan.

2. To enlist all our people in the intelligent, cheerful, systematic, and adequate support of this plan.

3. To distribute the funds to the several causes in proportion to their relative importance and needs as determined by the denomination itself.

How it Works

1. The individual member contributes through his church for both the local expenses of his church and the causes included in the Cooperative Program.

2. The church treasurer sends the co-operative funds to the state secretary-treasurer.

3. The state secretary-treasurer retains a portion to care for the expenses of his office and divides the balance into two parts: State and Southwide according to the percentages agreed upon (50-50 is considered ideal though some states do not observe this ratio now, and some states take out for certain preferred items before dividing the funds).

4. The state secretary-treasurer distributes the state portion to the state causes and sends the Southwide portion to the Executive Committee of the Southern Baptist Convention, Nashville Tennessee.

5. The Executive Committee of the Southern Baptist Convention distributes the Southwide funds to the agencies of the Southern Baptist Convention according to the instructions of the Convention. Nothing is taken out for the expense of the Executive Committee, these are born by the Sunday School Board .

How the Funds Are Divided

The state Convention determines how the state funds are divided. In our state it is as follows: Southwide objects 40 percent; Ministerial Aid 1 percent; Convention Debt for Educational Institutions 23 percent; Current Support for Colleges 14 percent; State Missions 15 percent; Hospital 5 percent; Ministers' Retirement Fund 2 percent.

The Southern Baptist Convention determines how the Southwide distributable dollar is divided. In 1944 it will be as follows: Foreign Mission Board, 50 percent; Home Mission Board, 23 1-3 percent; Relief and Annuity Board, 10 1-3 percent; Southern Baptist Theological Seminary, 4 1-5 percent; Southwestern Baptist Theological Seminary, 4 1-5 percent; Baptist Bible Institute, 4 1-5 percent; W. M. U. Training School, 8-15 percent; American Baptist Theological Seminary, 1.5 percent; New Orleans Baptist Hospital, 1.7 percent. Total 100 percent.

Conditions of Successs Our people must be informed about the Program; what it is; how it came about, how it works, what causes are included, etc. A consistent effort must be made to enlist all the people in its systematic support while also caring for the local expenses of their church. An all-year-round effort must be made to keep the people informed, to cultivate the spiritual life and indoctrinate them in the principles of our faith, including the glorious doctrine of Christian Stewardship.

The stressing time through which we are passing and the unprecedented opportunities and imperative needs of a post-war world demand that an all-out effort be made to enlist all our people in a larger support of all our work.

REPORT ON HUNDRED THOUSAND CLUB

The old Southwide debt of $6,500,000 is now (Oct. 1) only $235,000.00.

On March 12 our Foreign Mission Board got out of debt for the first time in forty years. On May 12 our Home Mission Board paid the last dollar of its $2,500,000 debt. On August 14 our Southern Baptist Hospital for the first time in its history was debt free. (While paying its debt it has also given $694,427.92 in free service and added $700,000 to its capitol improvements). On August 24 our Baptist Bible Institute paid out and is now free for the first time since it started. Our Southwestern Seminary is also now free of debt.

We now have only two other debt obligations to meet by December 31 in order to reach our goal. The Southern Seminary owes $25,000 the total of which will be paid November 1, which will leave only one more debt of $210,000.

This happy situation has been brought about by the exercise of rigid economy, by the sale of property, by some special gifts, and by the receipts of the Hundred Thousand Club every cent of which is applied upon the principal of the debts of the denomination.

We hope to be entirely free of debt by the end of the year. We, therefore, most earnestly urge:

1. That all members of the Hundred Thousand Club stay in and keep up their payments until the last dollar is paid.

2. That effort be made in all our churches and all our organizations to increase the number of members in the Hundred Thousand Club.

3. That wherever possible special offerings be taken urging our people to contribute at least one dollar a piece so as to be Club members at least one month and to have some part in ridding our denomination of its back-breaking debt.

4. That all money for Southwide debts be sent by the church treasurers to the state secretaries before December 15 to as to pay on the debt before Dec. 31.

Let us work and pray and pay that we may be entirely *DEBT-FREE IN '43—COUNT ON ME.*

The income through the Hundred Thousand Club this year in North Carolina will run close to $100,000 provided we do not fall off during the remainder of the year. Of this amount we keep one half in the state for debts of our own Convention and the other half goes to Southwide debts. Just give us one more year and North Carolina will be out of debt PROVIDED—and mark this well— the gifts to the Cooperative Program continue to rise and the people do not drop their Hundred Thousand Club Memberships. Let us not get the idea that it is not needed now that the Southwide debt is almost paid. We urge the people wherever possible to continue their memberships in the Hundred Thousand Club for one more year, and, the Lord willing, we shall not have to do this another year.

Respectfully submitted,

Wade H. James

9. The report on Christian Education was made by Rev. W. W. Woodcock, of Greensboro. Upon motion to adopt the report it was spoken to by Dr. M. H. Kendall, Head of Bible Department, of Mars Hill College. The report was adopted.

REPORT ON CHRISTIAN EDUCATION,

The report of the Education Commission of the Southern Baptist Convention for 1943 gives the number of Baptist Academies as nine with an enrollment of 2,126. Twenty-two Junior colleges are being maintained with 6,001 students. There are 26 Senior Colleges with an enrollment of 18,509 which is a decrease of 14 percent. The call to arms has been answered by our students from all colleges. The number of students listed above does not include the large number of service personnel being trained in many of our collges. It is gratifying to report that when the enrollment of regular students for the year is supplemented by the enrollment of the various units now in our Baptist colleges the total exceeds that of any other year in all our Baptist educational history. The opportunity that our colleges have in influencing the men and women in these units for Christian ideals and practices is unprecedented.

The enrollment in our three seminaries compares favorably with last year, the decrease in attendance being less than that of the Junior and Senior colleges.

The Baptist Student Union is bringing the Christian message to many other campuses. By its spread to South America and the Orient this part of our work has become International and the Foreign Mission Board has designated Dr. and Mrs. Edgar Hallock as student workers in Brazil.

It is recommended that our pastors and churches support the general program of Christian education and the particular projects inaugurated by the State and the Southern Baptist Convention.

Respectfully submitted,

Wilson Woodcock

10. The report on the Baptist Hospital was made by Rev. R. R. Jackson, of High Point. Upon motion to adopt the report it was spoken to by Dr. Smith Hagaman, of the Hospital. Dr. Hagaman stated in his address that our Baptist Hospital is now equal in rating to any other hospital in the entire south. The report was adopted.

THE BAPTIST HOSPITAL

The Baptist Hospital has completed a full year with its enlarged facilities. Instead of caring for 4,000 patients as formerly.

We have had 12,000 the past year—1942. It is again becoming increasingly difficult to provide for the growing numbers of sick who come for treatment—**an average of 33 each day.**

Of these 12,000 patients who were treated last year 4,000 were service patients; that is, were unable to pay a hospital bill. These are the sick for whom our Mother's Day Offering is made. It is also interesting to note that 4,000 of this 12,000 patients were mothers who had, here and there in our state, 12,000 children waiting anxiously for their return. We had also about 175 ministers, returned missionaries, ministerial students and children from our orphanage for whom no charge was made.

The Hospital Training School for Nurses has 116 students in training, 51 staff and graduate nurses, with an **addition of 22** nurses and Red Cross Aids, making a nursing staff of 189.

It is one of the functions of the Baptist Hospital to educate as many nurses as possible with the Christian ideal of service. These are always selected so as to represent as nearly as possible every section of our state.

Although quite a number of our medical staff are constantly going into the service of our country, we still have a staff of about 75 doctors, almost all of whom are specialists in several fields of medicine and surgery.

These two institutions—Hospital and Medical School—represent a money value to the denomination of $2,000,000.

It is with a just pride, we trust, that the American Medical Association has given the Baptist Hospital the highest rating of any hospital in the entire south, save one.

The hospital desires to express to the members of this association their appreciation for the best Mother's Day offering ever, and also to the W. M. U.'s and other church agencies this same appreciation for their generous contributions of hospital linen.

The hospital was built and has operated for these 20 years with one great fundamental purpose: that it shall be an institution through which the half million Baptists of our state may render a definite Christian Service to sick and suffering humanity who could not, in most instances, have hospital treatment otherwise. It is the purpose of the denomination and the management that it shall forever remain true to this one purpose in addition to its wide service.

Respectfully submitted,
R. R. Jackson.

11. The report on the Orphanage was made by Rev. J. S. Hopkins, of High Point. Upon motion to adopt the report it was spoken to by Dr. W. C. Reid, new Superintendent of the Kennedy Home, at Kinston. The report was adopted.

ORPHANAGE REPORT

Article 1 of the constitution says: "This institution shall be known as the Baptist Orphanage of North Carolina, Incorporated, formerly known as Thomasville Baptist Orphanage and later known as the Mills Home, according to its amended charter, and shall have for its object the support and caring for and training of dependent children of the white race."

There are two officials of the Orphanage, a general superintendent and a treasurer. Mr. I. G. Greer is the general superintendent and Mr. R. D. Covington is treasurer. Their offices are in Thomasville.

The Orphanage maintains two homes, the Mills Home in Thomasville and the Kennedy Home near Kinston. These are not two orphanages but are the homes of the North Carolina Baptist Orphanage. Each of these homes has a superintendent but neither has a separate treasurer, for the Orphanage treasurer handles all the finances of both homes. Miss Sarah E. Elmore is superintendent of the Mills Home and Rev. W. C. Reed is superintendent of the Kennedy Home. The Social Service Department, Miss Hattie Edwards, director, receives all applications for the entrance of children into the Orphanage and after investigation makes recommendation to the general superintendent, who makes the final decision. He says whether the child is to be accepted and if so into which home. If it seems best, he places the child in a boarding home or establishes a mothers' aid home.

The Orphanage cared for, during 1942, 687 in the two homes, 35 in the boarding homes, and 74 in their own homes. During the year more children were placed than ever before.

Attendance in school reached almost 99 percent, due to the general good health of the children and the almost total absence of contagious diseases.

A graded Sunday School, B. T. U., and W. M. U., both at Mills Home and Kennedy Home helps to round out the lives of the boys and girls.

General superintendent Greer says: "The greatest asset of this Orphanage are the many friends who love it. That mighty Thanksgiving offering whose echoes are still sweetly ringing in our hearts was the most heartening and uplifting thing in a financial way that has ever come to our Orphanage life. The continuation of the monthly offerings from the Sunday school climaxed by another Thanksgiving offering as good or better than the one last year will make it possible for us to meet the demands being placed upon us in these strenuous times."

Respectfully submitted,

Julian S. Hopkins

12. A roll of the churches was called and messengers from 52 churches responded to the call, with a total of 283 messengers reporting.

13. A hymn, "When I Survey the Wondrous Cross," was then sung.

14. The report of the Committee on Committees was presented and adopted.

REPORT OF COMMITTEE ON COMMITTEES

COMMITTEE ON PLACE AND PREACHER: J. H. Saunders, Mrs. J. E. McCagro, C. E. Snow.

COMMITTEE ON RESOLUTIONS: W. H. James, G. G. Lanter, Mrs. J. S. Hopkins.

AUDITING COMMITTEE: R. R. Jackson, J. H. Dixon, and R. R. Saunders.

PROGRAM COMMITTEE: C. S. Hodge, L. Grady Burgess, and Miss Mabel Starnes.

COMMITTEE TO NOMINATE OFFICERS: A. L. McGee, D. W. Overly, and Mrs. Nettie Hoge.

COMMITTEE TO NOMINATE EXECUTIVE PROMOTION COMMITTEE: W. W. Woodcock, and William Cummings.

COMMITTEE TO NOMINATE DELEGATES TO BAPTIST STATE CONVENTION: C. H. Maynor, Mrs. Leah Andrews, and Mrs. J. C. Shore.

CITY AND ASSOCIATIONAL COMMITTEE: Dr. A. B. Conrad, Mrs. J. B. Eller and J. H. Smith.

Respectfully submitted,

H. O. Miller
J. H. Smith
J. C. Shore

15. Reports of the Executive and Promotion Committee, and of the City and Associational Missions Committee were made by the Clerk. A motion to adopt the reports was carried, after a motion to postpone action on the matter until later was lost.

REPORT OF EXECUTIVE COMMITTEE

I Jan. 1, 1943, The Executive Committee met at 19:00 a. m. at First Baptist Church, Greensboro.

1. A motion, by F. L. Paschal, seconded by A. A. Walker, was passed to approve the applications of College Park church for $600.00, and the Pleasant Garden Church for $300.00 to supplement the pastors' salary to the State Missions Board.

2. A motion, by F. L. Paschal, seconded by A. A. Walker, was passed that the churches be asked for one half a cent per member for the Missions Fund.

3. A motion was passed that the next Annual Session of the Association be held with the First Baptist Church of Greensboro, for one day, Thursday, Oct. 21.

A motion to adjourn was entertained.

Grover H. Jones, Mod.

L. G. Burgiss, Clerk

II May 17, 1943, The Executive Committee of the Association met at 9:30 a. m. at the First Baptist Church, Greensboro.

1. A motion was made to recommend to the pastors and churches of the Association that the necessary Committee and

official organization be set up to direct the work of an Associational Supt. of Missions, and to assume any incidental expense that may occur in the performance of the duties of such a Supt. of Missions.

2. A motion to adjourn was entertained.

Grover H. Jones, Mod.

L. Grady Burgiss, Clerk

III May 31, 1943, The Executive Committee of the Piedmont Baptist Association met at 11:00 a. m. at the First Baptist Church, Greensboro, with the following members present;

—Grover H. Jones, Mod., L. Grady Burgiss, Clerk, F. L. Paschal, J. H. Smith, T. L. Sasser, R. R. Saunders, H. O. Miller, Mrs. J. Ben Eller, and C. S. Hodge, for Carl Bell.

1. A motion was passed to hold Annual Session for one day, Oct. 21, Thursday, with First Baptist Church, Greensboro.

2. A motion was passed to elect the following as members of the Temporary City and Associational Missions Committee; —Dr. J. Clyde Turner, J. S. Hopkins, T. L. Sasser, J. C. Shore, L. G. Burgiss, Mrs. J. Ben Eller Mrs. R. R. Saunders, Mrs. W. F. Clayton and J. Carl Bell.

3. A motion to adjourn was entertained.

Grover H. Jones, Mod.
L. Grady Burgiss, Clerk.

IV. Friday, Oct. 15, 1943, the Executive Committee of the Association met at 3:00 p, m, at First Baptist Church, Greensboro.

1. On motion the Committee adopted the following recommendations to the Annual Meeting of the Association:—

1. That a permanent City and Associational Missions Committee consisting of at least seven members be set up.

2. That one General Fund be set up for all Associational Expenses.

3. That the Associational Fund for the coming year be set at $1,050.00, $300.00 of which to be applied toward supplementing the travel expenses of the Supt. of City and Associational Missions, and that the fund be apportioned to the churches of the Association.

4. The Committee further recommends that each church of the Association put a definite amount in its annual budget for the General Fund of the Association .

2. A motion to adjourn was entertained.

Grover H. Jones, Mod.
L. Grady Burgiss, Clerk

REPORT OF CITY AND ASSOCIATIONAL MISSIONS COMMITTEE

I. Monday, June 7, 1943, The City and Associational Missions Committee appointed by the Executive Committee met at the First Baptist Church of Greensboro, at 3:00 p. m.

Members present were Dr. J. Clyde Turner, Chm., L. Grady Burgiss, Sect., J. S. Hopkins, T. L. Sasser, J. C. Shore, J. Carl Bell, Mrs. J. Ben Eller and Mrs. R. R. Saunders; absent was Mrs. W. F. Clayton.

Dr. J. Clyde Turner was elected Chm., L. G. Burgiss, Sect. The secretary read a letter from Grover H. Jones naming T. L. Sasser as a prospect for Superintendent of Missions. The name of J. Ben Eller was also mentioned.

A special committee of J. C. Shore, J. S. Hopkins and J. Carl Bell was elected to survey the field for available material and report back to the whole Committee.

A motion to adjourn was entertained.

J. C. Turner, Chm.
L. G. Burgiss, Sect.

11 Monday, June 14, The City and Associational Missions Committee met at 4:45 p. m. at First Baptist Church, Greens-

boro. Members present were, Dr. J. Clyde Turner, Chm. L. G. Burgiss, Sect., J. S. Hopkins J. C. Shore, Mrs. J. Ben Eeller and Mrs. R. R. Saunders.

On motion Rev. T. L. Sasser was recommended to the Home Mission Board as Supt. of City and Associational Missions.

A motion was adjourn was entertained.

J. C. Turner, Chm.
L. G. Burgiss, Sect.

III Tuesday, Sept. 21, 1943, The City and Associational Missions Committee met at 3:00 p. m. at First Baptist church, Greensboro, with the following members present;—Dr. J. Clyde Turner, Chm. L. Grady Burgiss, Sect., J. S. Hopkins, J. C. Shore, Mrs. J. Ben Eller, Mrs. R. R. Saunders and T. L. Sasser..

Rev. J. S. Hopkins made a report on the Home Missions Conference at Ridgecrest.

The Committee adopted the following recommendations to the Executive Committee of the Association:

1. That the Temporary City and Associational Missions Committee has employed through the sponsorship of the Home Missions Board Rev. T. L. Sasser as Superintendent of City and Associational Missions of the Piedmont Association, and recommends that the Association set up the work in the Association and appoint a permanent City and Associational Missions Committee consisting of at least five members.

2. The Committee recommends that one fund be set up for all Associational Expenses.

3. The Committee Recommends that the Associational Fund for the coming year be set at $1,050.00, $300.00 of which to be applied toward supplementing the travel expenses of the Supt. of City and Associational Missions, and that the fund be apportioned to the churches of the Association.

4. The Committee further recommends that the churches put a definite amount in the annual budget of each for the General Fund of the Association.

REPORT OF CHURCH ADVISORY COMMITTEE

I Sunday, Jan. 31, 1943, A group of ministers and two members of the Church Advisory Committee of the Association met at 3:00 p. m. at Guilford Battle Ground to assist in the organization of a Baptist, later called the Battle Ground Road Baptist Church. Members of the Committee were Dr. J. Clyde Turner, Chm., and L. Grady Burgiss, Clerk. Other ministers were Revs. B. C. Lambe, J. B. Clifton, L. J. Hight, Wade H. James, J. Huber Dixon, and C. M. Oates.

II. August 2, 1943, The Church Advisory Committee of the Association met at 11:00 a. m. at First Baptist Church, Greensboro, with the following members present, Dr. J. Clyde Turner, Chm. L. Grady Burgiss, Clerk, W. W. Woodcock and Mrs. Nettie Hoge.

1. A motion was passed that Irl E. Kerley, of the Florida St. Baptist Church, be recommended as a candidate for the ministry.

2. A motion was passed that Charles C. Cross, pastor of the Spring Garden St. Friends Church, be recommended as a candidate for the Baptist Ministry.

3. A motion to adjourn was entertained.

Dr. J. Clyde Turner, Chmn.
L. Grady Burgiss, Clerk.

---

16. Beginning at 12:20 the Annual Sermon was delivered. Rev. J. H. Smith, Alternate, read the Scripture, Acts 20: 17-38, and led in prayer. The Sermon, " The Value of the Church" was then delivered by Rev. I. B. Jackson, pastor of North Main St. Church of High Point.

17. Rev. D. W. Overby, of Reidsville, led the closing prayer, as the body adjourned for lunch.

THURSDAY AFTERNOON SESSION

18. The session was opened by singing "Draw Me Nearer," led by Rev. J. C. Shore, of Reidsville.

19. Announcements were made and several Committees were called to meet.

20. The devotional period was led by Rev. William C. Bearden, the new pastor of Bailey Memorial Church. He also led in prayer.

21. The report on Foreign Missions was presented by Dr. J. Clyde Turner. Upon motion to adopt the report it was spoken to by Dr. E. C. Routh, of the Foreign Mission Board. The report was adopted.

REPORT ON FOREIGN MISSIONS

In the last chapter of his First Letter to the Corinthian church Paul gave two reasons for remaining at Ephesus for a while longer:— "For a great and effectual door is opened unto me, and there are many adversaries." It was the challenge of a great opportunity, and the challenge of many difficulties. This is the two-fold challenge which the Foreign Mission Board faces.

In spite of the difficulties, the past year has been one of real achievements. The last dollar of the indebtedness which has burdened the Board for many years has been paid. The financial receipts for the past year reached the high mark of $2,117,672.26, an increase of $689,032.57 over the preceding year. During the past year the Board received nearly $500,000 for World Emergency Relief. This money has been spent in bringing relief to the people in many lands, but especially in stricken China. The call has gone forth for another $500,000 for use in the immediate future, and we are sure the churches will make a liberal response to that call.

Since the organization of the Foreign Board 98 years ago, over 1200 missionaries have been appointed. We now have more than 460 active missionaries, and 80 retired, or emeritus missionaries. On account of conditions in the war zones, many of our missionaries have been called home. Forty were repatriated from China last year, and thirty-eight are now on their way home. A few are still interned in war areas. A faithful group still carries on the work in Free China, and a flourishing mission has been developed in the Hiwaiian Islands. In the mission fields outside of the war zones the work goes on in a satisfactory manner, though every land is feeling the effects of the war.

Five years ago the Board started a new publication—THE COMMISSION, a monthly missionary magazine. From the beginning it has been a publication of unusual merit, and its subscription list has grown to more than 50,000. Dr. E. C .Ruth, forfer Editor of THE BAPTIST MESSENGER of Oklahoma, has recently been elected Editor of THE COMMISSION. Under his direction the publication is already showing marks of improvement. We expect the subscription list to pass 100,000 within the next few months.

The Board has a splendid Book Department under the direction of Miss Nan Weeks. Graded study books have been prepared and others are in the making.

No one knows what the years just ahead will bring, or how the work of our Foreign Mission Board may be affected. The years following the war will be years of great missionary opportunity, as well as years of great difficulties. It looks as if God may use the mailed fist of war to open doors that have been closed to the gospel. The Board is making preparation to enter into those doors as soon as they are open, and to rebuild the work destroyed by war. This will call for large sums of money and a greatly increased missionary force. We call on our people for their prayers and wholehearted support.

Respectfully submitted,

J. Clyde Turner

22. The report on Relief and Annuity was made by Rev. D. W. Overbey. Upon motion to adopt the report it was spoken to by Rev. Wilson Woodcock. The report was adopted.

REPORT ON RELIEF AND ANNUITY BOARD

At the annual meeting of the Relief and Annuity Board in Dallas last March the Board observed its twenty-fifth anniversary. An eighty-page pamphlet prepared by the executive secretary, Dr. T. J. Watts, revealed at every turn striking evidences of Divine Favor. Note the following:

FINANCIAL GROWTH

The total assets of the Board at the end of March, 1943, stood at $6,166,766.37. In addition to this figure five and one half million more have been paid out through the years in relief and annuity benefits. Thus for every one dollar assets at the close of the first year's work, the Board has paid out in benefits fifty dollars and has in assets today $58.17.

In 1942 income was well beyond $1,383,000, while the relief and annuity benefits paid totaled $629,000. More than 1,200 aged preachers and preachers' widows received relief grants totaling $115,000. The progress of the past few years has been phenominal.

MINISTERS' RETIREMENT PLAN

More than ten thousand ministers, missionaries, denominational workers, and ministers' widows are participating in one or more of the Board's plans, while over twenty-six hundred of these are now receiving benefits from the Board and all of the others are due to receive benefits in the years that lie ahead. The Relief and Annuity Board has already become and is destined to become increasingly a strong stabilizing force in the life of our denomination. It offers a stability of economic security to every denominational worker and employee throughout the Southern Baptist Convention, asking only the cooperation of all that it may render the largest possible service.

Already more than ten thousand churches are participating and more than seven thousand preachers hold certificates of membership. The percentage of pastors enlisted in North Carolina April 30, 1943, is .49. While reports show the enthusiastic reception of the Ministers' Retirement Plan by our preachers, at the same time they show much enlistment work yet to be done. In every district association the goal should be, "Every Baptist church cooperating—and every Baptist Pastor a member."

There are still in the Southern Baptist Convention, and in every state thereof, scores and even hundreds of pastors who do not yet realize their privilege and duty in connection with the Ministers' Retirement Plan, through which plan they have been urged to aid in making provision for their old age or disability.

Some noble pastors may have hesitated lest they be understood to be making an attempt to secure something equivalent to an increase in salary. But there need not be any hesitancy here. The fact is the churches do not contribute anything that goes to the credit of any particular pastor, but into the State Reserve Fund, out of which the members of the Plan receive a part of their benefits when they retire because of old age after 65 or because of disability before 65. Many pastors will pass on without having retired in either of these ways and in such cases the money paid in by them will be returned to their widows or their families or to their estates with interest thereon. Hence any pastor can present this matter to his church and ask his people to cooperate in it for the sake of the entire ministry participating in the Plan, and so without a semblance of selfishness.

A WORD TO THE YOUNG PASTOR

The Young Pastor should remember that he will grow old if he lives long enough, and ministers who do not make provisions for old age usually suffer want. Hence the Young Pastor who is not in the Plan should enroll promptly, pay his dues with promptness along with the church or churches he serves, and then at the age of 65 or thereafter or earlier in case of total permanent disability, his provision, along with the others participating in the Plan, *will be a worthy one.*

Respectfully submitted,
D. W. Overby

23. Rev. W. W. Woodcock made some remarks in regard to the Baptist Bible Institute.

24. A hymn, "Revive Us Again" was sung, being led by Rev. J. C.Shore.

25. The report on Social Service was read by Rev. L. J. Hight, having been prepared by Rev. B. C. Lambe. Upon motion to adopt the report Rev. T. L. Sasser, the vice-Moderator took the chair, and the report was spoken to by Grover H. Jones. The report was adopted.

REPORT ON SOCIAL SERVICE

Any program for the promotion of social service must be related to the serious conditions now prevailing in the world. Mankind is in the midst of a dark and dangerous period. Enemies from without and from within would break down and destroy the Church and all she has been able to accomplish through the years. We are near the zero hour ,and may the people of God arouse themselves to a reassertion of their faith in God and a rededication to His program.

There is a great deal said in the Bible about our relation one to another, showing us that no man liveth to himself and no man dieth to himself. We can not live apart from others if we would, and in a large measure we are our brother's keeper.

True religion has to do with our relationship to God and man, and that relationship is not as it should be so long as we fail in our responsibilities to either. Therefore, social service is of vital concern to us, our churches and our Association. As associated churches, we are to promote that which is good and support the program of Christ with our influence, money and prayers. At the same time, we are to stand against evil in all of its deadly forms, even when it is not popular to do so. There is much that is evil in the world today. In fact it would be hard for one to overstate the real conditions that exist here in our own land. Of the many social evils that confront us we can state only a few.

In our humble opinion, desecration of the Sabbath has become a real menace. It is no longer the exception but the accepted rule. The Lord's Day has become merely another day. There remains very little of the sanctity by which God intended it to be characterized. Even Christians are guilty of using it as time to be devoted to their own pleasure and recreation rather than to the service and worship of God. The war effort has been used as a reason for this secularism to a large extent. We are in great need of a call to the correct observance of God's Day. If it loses its meaning and sacred character, Christianity will have suffered an irreparable loss.

Divorce is ever increasing numbers continue to be the arch enemy of the home. One out of every four or five marriages will eventually be terminated in the divorce court. Should not some part of our ministry be devoted to the building and maintaining of substantial Christian homes? There must be some way in which the churches can help with this great problem.

The use of alcoholic beverages still remains a problem. The production of these has been curtailed in some measure by the war, but this nefarious business usually is given precedence over other business enterprise by the authorities. Other monarchs may have to bow, but King Alcohol reigns on unmolested. Let us rise up against him in a mighty effort to destroy this great and deadly monster. There is only one safe position for us to take in dealing with alcohol and its use as a beverage. And that is war to the death.

In a report on social service it would be impossible for us to ignore the alarming situation among our youth. The latest reports from the Federal Bureau of Investigation tell us that juvenile delinquency is increasing by leaps and bounds.

Arrest of young girls on moral charges in 1942 almost doubled those of the year before, and recent reports show an increase of 78 per cent over last year. This should be cause for deep concern on the part of Christians everywhere. There are many causes for such a condition, and we are wondering if a want of real religious training in the home has not been responsible in many cases. On our youth rests the future of all our institutions, and we must do something to aid them in getting their bearings and becoming useful members of society. We urge that our Baptist people be given to prayer for guidance and wisdom in ministering to our boys and girls from pulpit and classroom that we may lead them in paths of righteousness.

Let the standard be raised by all Christians for we are in the midst of a moral let-down, and the Christian church must face her responsibility.

Respectfully submitted,

B. C. Lamb

26. The report on the W. M. U. was presented by Mrs. Nettie Hatcher Hoge, who also made some remarks on it. Upon motion to adopt the report it was spoken to by Mrs. J. Ben Eller. The report was adopted.

REPORT ON WOMAN'S WORK

Woman's place in evangelism was approved by Christ and began when Christ and the twelve disciples went forth preaching, and "showing glad tidings of the Kingdom of God" and certain women ministered unto him of their substance.

The service of ministry in the home and in the church is the given task of womanhood, and throughout the centuries the history of the church has recorded her faithful ministering spirit in the promotion of the Kingdom of God. This gift of ministry through the years has developed and materialized into the organization of women in all denominations and today is the most out-standing promoter of all missionary and benevolent causes.

In our Baptist denomination we have the Woman's M. U. which only aspires to be an auxiliary to the program of the church as a whole.

It has but one purpose and that is to stimulate a missionary spirit by enlisting women and young people in the all important ministry of private and united prayer, the necessity of studying the world's needs and God's call for stewardship of self and substance. These aims are inclusive of so much good and so far reaching in their influence that no local church can afford to ignore nor neglect having the women and young people organized into service societies. In the state of North Carolina we have 1,346

Woman's Missionary Societies, 2,729 Young People's organizations leaving 1,067 churches with no organizations.

In the Piedmont Association according to the Associational minutes, there are 55 churches with 48 reporting Woman's Societies with 91 auxiliaries.

It has long been the desire to have a society in every church and the goal appears near with only 7 more churches to organize.

The W. M. U. watchword "Laborers together with God" is an invitation to all women every where to enlist in this missions movement.

Respectfully submitted,

Mrs. Nettie Hatcher Hoge

27. The report on Obituaries was made by Rev. Geo. A. Tucker, who also made some remarks on the report.

OBITUARIES

During the past year, eighty of our association members, three deacons, and four of our soldiers departed this life, and joined hands on the other shore, our loss is their eternal gain. As Job said, "Man that is born of woman is of few days and full of trouble. Job: 14:1.

We know not what another association year will bring to pass. Under these trying days—if we are listed in with God's family it is all well, "Whereby are given unto us exceeding great and precious promises," that by these ye might be partakers of the divine nature.

Respectfully submitted,

G. A. Tucker

28. The report of the Auditing Committee was presented by Rev. R. R. Jackson. The report was adopted.

REPORT OF AUDITING COMMITTEE

Your auditing committee has examined the treasurer's books and found them to be correctly balanced.

R. R. Jackson,
Chairman for the Committee.

29. The report of the Resolutions Committee was presented by Rev. J. Melvin Faulkner. The report was adopted.

REPORT OF THE COMMITTEE ON RESOLUTIONS

PIEDMONT BAPTIST ASSOCIATION, 10-21-'43

Whereas, the Piedmont Baptist Association, meeting with the First Baptist Church of Greensboro, has engaged in a splendid session;

Be it Resolved:

First, that we express our gratitude to this church and its pastor, Dr. J. Clyde Turner, for the privilege of meeting here.

Second, That we express our appreciation to Mr. Grover H. Jones, our very efficient moderator, for his untiring efforts, in serving the Association throughout this year, also to Rev. L. Grady Burgiss for the splendid manner in which he has carried out the duties of clerk.

Third: That we commend the various organizations of the churches of the Association for their splendid support of the Baptist program.

Fourth: That we express our sincere thanks to the program committee for the wonderful program,

And be it resolved that we as followers of Christ give ourselves unreservedly to the cause of Christ in these uncertain times.

Respectfully submitted,

Melvin Faulkner, *Chmn.*
Mrs. J. S. Hopkins
G. G. Lanter

30. The Committee to Nominate Officers made the following report, which was adopted:

Grover H. Jones, Moderator
Rev. J. Ben Eller, Vice-Moderator
Rev. L. Grady Burgiss, Clerk-Treasurer
C. S. Hodge, Sunday School Superintendent
J. Carl Bell, Training Uuion Director.

Respectfully submitted

Rev. A. S. McGee
Rev. W. D. Overbey
Mrs. Nettie Hoge

31. The report of the Committee to Nominate Delegates to the Baptist State Convention was presented as follows:

Rev. A. H. Dunning, High Point
Rev. D. W. Overbery, Reidsville
Rev. L. Grady Burgiss, Greensboro

Respectfully submitted,

C. H. Maynor
Mrs. J. C. Shore
Miss Leah Andrews

32. The report of the Committee on Time, Place and Preacher was read by the Clerk, as follows:

PREACHER, Rev. J. H. Smith, Greensboro

ALTERNATE, Rev. G. G. Lanter, Reidsville

PLACE, First Baptist Church, Greensboro

TIME, Thursday October 19, 1944

Rev. J. H. Saunders
O. E. Snow
Mrs. J. E. McCargo

The report was adopted.

33. A motion was passed that a letter be sent to Clarence A. Smith, a former moderator.

34. A number of new pastors were recognized.

35. The closing prayer was led by Dr. J. Clyde Turner.

Adjourned until Evening Session.

THURSDAY EVENING SESSION

36. The session opened by singing "Higher Ground." The devotional was led by Rev. J. C. Shore, of Reidsville, who read some verses from Luke 24. The prayer was led by Rev. H. O. Miller, of High Point.

37. The report on the Sunday Schools was presented by Rev. J. Ben Eller. Upon motion to adopt the report it was spoken to by Rev. J. H. Smith. The report was adopted.

REPORT ON SUNDAY SCHOOLS

It is difficult to place a proper estimate upon the work of a Sunday School in the life of a Church. As a disseminator of Bible knowledge, as an evangelistic agency, and as an interpreter of a Church to the unchurched it has no equal among our Church organizations. Multitudes get their impressions of the Church and whatever scripture knowledge they have from the Sunday School. Many of our Church members belong to this group. Such an organization, then, should not be neglected.

The task of keeping our Sunday Schools properly graded and functioning calls for eternal vigilance. Like other organizations they will not run themselves. Our associational reports for 1942 show that 27 of our Sunday Schools are not graded, while only 67 teachers were reported as holders of Sunday School diplomas. The average attendance of our Sunday School enrollment was only a little over 55%.

During the year before us let us fully cooperate with our associational leaders in a program of training. With the courses now offered by our Sunday School Board there is no excuse for uninformed and inefficient Sunday School workers. We should see to it that every Church has a season—or seasons—of Sunday School training.

We should also utilize our Sunday Schools to the fullest as soul-saving agencies. No other organization in our Church set up has an equal opportunity for this essential work. Here are found the unsaved; here, too, are the workers. Of the 794 baptisms reported last year in our Association 429 came from the Sunday Schools.

May we, then, address ourselves with renewed energy during the coming months to the great opportunities which the Sunday School presents and at the close of the associational year may we be able to say "Under God it was the best year of all."

Respectfully submitted,
J. Ben Eller

38. The B. T. U. report was presented by Miss Julia Liles. The report was adopted.

REPORT OF THE BAPTIST TRAINING UNION OF THE PIEDMONT BAPTIST ASSOCIATION

For the year Ending September 30, 1943.

The Baptist Training Union of the Piedmont Baptist Association in closing its year's work can report some accomplishments during the year.

Outstanding is the fact that a complete organization of the Training Union was instituted at Pleasant Grove Church by Mr. J. Carl Bell, Associational Director, and one at Pilot View Church by Mr. J. E. Hedrick, President of the High Point District of the Association. Other churches have been aided in the teaching of study courses by various Training Union leaders during the year. The enrollment of the Training Union has increased approximately 200.

Quarterly meetings have been held, though transportation facilities cut down the attendance of those coming from a distance. The work of Mr. J. J. Norwood with the Greensboro District and Mr. J. E. Hedrick with the High Point District has been most noteworthy.

At the twenty-third annual session of the Piedmont Associational Training Union in Greensboro on March 13, 1943, there was a record attendance. The theme of the meeting was: "Living Faith in a World at War." The afternoon meeting was held at the First Baptist Church, and the banquet at the Masonic Temple close by. Reservations for the banquet numbered 405. As usual the afternoon session was taken up with conferences, business, and contests. Following the banquet the group heard Mr. Nathan C. Brooks, Jr., then State Training Union Director.

This report would not be complete without an expression of gratitude to Mr. J. Carl Bell, Associational Director, for his untiring efforts and continued splendid work.

Respectfully submitted,
Julia M. Liles, *Secretary.*

TREASURER'S REPORT OF THE BAPTIST TRAINING UNION
OF THE PIEDMONT BAPTIST ASSOCIATION
For the year ending September 30, 1943

October 1, 1942—Balance on hand		$ 7.88
RECEIPTS		
Piedmont Association—3-13-43	$20.00	
Greensboro District—toward cost of banquet	6.68	
		26.68
Total		$34.56
DISBURSEMENTS		
For banquet 3-13-43		$22.13
Balance on hand September 30, 1943		$12.43

Respectfully submitted,
Julia M. Liles, *Treasurer.*

39. J. E. Hedrick presented the report of the Committee

to nominate B. T. U. Officers of the Association. The report was adopted.

40. Miss Mable Starnes then spoke from the topic, "Thy Will Be Done in Our Training Union.

41. The report on Home Missions was presented by Rev. T. L. Sasser, our new City and Associational Missionary. Upon motion to adopt the report it was spoken to by Dr. S. F. Dowis, of the Home Mission Board, Atlanta.

REPORT ON HOME AND ASSOCIATIONAL MISSIONS

Home Missions is the corporate term of expression by Southern Baptists as to the base of world-wide Christian conquest. We must project and sustain an ever expanding foreign mission movement. The commission to preach the gospel to all the nations is emphasized by revealing events of every passing year. Strengthening the stakes is complementary to lengthening the cords and is of increasing importance. Every year demands new emphasis on Home Missions.

The Home Mission Board of the Southern Baptist Convention steadily grows in spiritual power. New missionaries are added to the large number of faithful workers and new support comes from the increased financial gifts of the churches.

The last annual report, May, 1943, of the Board to the convention covers forty-three pages of the minutes in compact statement. The work is wide-spread and far-reaching. It shows 435 full-time missionaries working among our native peoples and among the many thousands of foreign people who live here and in Cuba and Panama. The work includes teaching, preaching, healing, helping the underprivileged and rescuing the fallen.

While this mission work has continued expanding the heavy burden of debt on the Board has in recent years been diminishing. May 12, 1943, marks the end of an epoch in Home Mission Board history. The last of the long-standing debt was paid in full and the cause of home missions was liberated to expand into the large and waiting fields of the South.

This annual report to the Piedmont Association is this year combined with a report on associational missions because the Home Mission Board has entered the Association by a new approach and support. Upon the proffer of the Board to the Association this year to enter this field the Executive Committee of the Association appointed a missions committee to nominate a missionary and with him promote the work.

The writer of this report was elected to this new position and began his work as such in the Association August first. He is supported by the Board in cooperation with the Association and gives his full time to work strictly missionary in character. Activities to date have been toward acquainting the churches and prospective workers in the mission projects with the proposed purpose and plans. The objective is to make effective Jesus' commissions to us, "For the perfecting of the saints, for the work of the ministry, for th edifying of the body of Christ; Till we all come in the unity of the faith, and of the knowledge of the Son of God, unto a perfect man, unto the measure of the stature of the fullness of Christ."

Respectfully submitted,
T. L. Sasser.

---

43. The Clerk-Treasurer presented his annual report.

REPORT OF TREASURER

EXPENSE FUND

I herewith submit my report for the year ending September 30, 1943.

Balance on hand, Sept. 30, 1942		$ 32.52
Received from the Churches		251.34
Total		$283.86
Disbursements		
Nov. 5, Clerk's Remuneration	$ 50.00	
Jan. 25, 1943, Printing Minutes	150.25	
Sept. 1, 1943, Printing Programs	5.75	
Postage and Supplies	10.99	
Total	$216.99	
Balance on hand	66.87	
	$283.86	$283.86

MISSIONS FUND

I herewith submit my report for the year ending Sept. 30, 1943.

Balance on hand Sept. 30, 1942		$22.73
Received from the Churches		52.35
Total		$75.08
Disbursements		
Piedmont B. T. U. Treasurer	$20.00	

Piedmont Baptist S. S. Treasurer	5.20	
Total	$25.20	
Balance on hand Sept. 30, 1943	49.88	
	$75.08	$75.08

Respectfully submitted,
L. Grady Burgiss, *Treasurer.*

44. The Committee on Committees made a report on nominations for the City Missions & Church Advisory Committee, and the Executive Promotion Committee. These Committees are listed in the Associational Directory on preceding pages.

45. Some remarks made by Rev. J. S. Hopkins as to the purpose and functions of the Church Advisory Committee. Rev. J. Ben Eller made further remarks on the subject.

46. Grover H. Jones, the Moderator, called attention to the printed Digest of Church Letters.

47. The session was closed by singing "God Be With You."

48. The closing prayer was led by Rev. J. Ben Eller.

Minutes of the Piedmont W. M. U.

The annual session of Piedmont W. M. U. was presided over by Mrs. Nettie Hatcher Hoge on April 30, 1943 at Asheboro St. Baptist Church, Greensboro, N. C.

The program theme was "For Such An Hour as This." Guest speakers were Mrs. Chas. A. Leonard, past missionary to China and, now, of Hawaii; Rev. J. H. Smith, pastor of Eller Memorial; and Mrs. J. S. Farmer, State President. The afternoon meeting was in the hands of the various chairmen and officers.

At this meeting Mrs. Hoge completed her sixteenth year if faithful, loyal service as superintendent. When she asked to be relieved she was made Superintendent Emeritus. Also, Miss Ruth Scott, rounded out ten years of devoted service as Young Peoples Leader. Both were honored at a tea on June 10 and were presented gifts of love and appreciation by the association.

During the summer quarter, Mr. David Byrd, Field Worker for Royal Ambassadors was heard in many churches. His presence was very beneficial and inspiring, especially, to those boys who came in touch with him personally.

Rev. Edwin Perry was a welcome guest speaker in many churches for State Missions.

In spite of hindrance and shortages, our W. M. U. program is receiving earnest emphasis.

"Where there is **no vision** the people perish;" but, if all pastors, leaders, chairmen, and members will cooperate fully and loyally, an enlarged vision of Christ's Kingdom will spread among us.

Respectfully submitted,

Mrs. J. Ben Eller, Supt.

In Memoriam

CALVARY—
Mr. R. M. Boaz
Mr. F. A. Delancy
Mrs. Mattie Cantrell
COMMUNITY—
Mrs. Ava Myers
FAIRMONT PARK—
Mr. Vance Lee Shaw
GIBSONVILLE—
Mr. Joe Christman
ASHEBORO ST.—
Mr. W. H. Pamplin
Mr. D. M. Sullivan, Deacon
Mr. Sam Collins
Mrs. R. H. Davis
Mr. C. B. Lewis, Jr., Soldier
Mrs. W. B. Lane
Mrs. O. N. Walton
BAILEY MEM.—
Mr. Charles Mitchell
BESSEMER—
Mrs. Albert Gossett
COLLEGE PARK—
Mrs. Ethel Kiser
Mr. Charlie Johnson
Mrs. J. C. Mabry
Mr. J. M. Wright
Mrs. C. L. Young
ELLER MEM.—
Mrs. A. J. Stanley
Mr. Russell Arthur
Mr. Floyd Bain
Mr. J. T. Ratliffe
Mr. D. L. Redmond
GREENSBORO FIRST—
Mrs. W. H. Foushee
Mrs. A. N. Gardner
Mr. Howard Gardner
Mr. Jos. W. King
Mrs. J. B. Johnston
Judge S. B. Adams
Mr. J. B. Parker, Soldier
Mr. Thos. W. Minor
Mrs. O. W. Monroe
Miss Lillie Matthews
Mr. John Faw, Soldier
Mrs. J. Yates Parker
Miss Rebecca Gold
Dr. H. T. Aydelette
Mrs. F. O. Mangum
Mrs. J. B. Wright
FLORIDA ST.—
Mrs. John Mooney
MAGNOLIA ST.—
Miss Ida Lee Long
Mr. G. D. Oakes, Deacon
Mrs. N. J. Jarvis
POMONA—
Miss Viola Hudson
REVOLUTION—
Mrs. S. A. Roberts
SIXTEENTH ST.—
Mrs. H. B. Haynes
Mr. A. F. Stewart
Mr. A. G. Jones
TABERNACLE—
Mrs. Henry Pike
Mrs. H. J. Bland
Mrs. J. R. Pike
WEBSTER MEM.—
Mrs. Roxie Bishop
HIGH POINT FIRST—
Mrs. A. T. Moffitt
Mrs. W. L. Seigler
Mrs. J. E. Squires
Mrs. E. H. Parker
Mrs. Mabel Brown
Mrs. J. M. Gordon
Mr. Jack Hunter Gibson
Mr. E. P. Jacobs
Mrs. Clay Clinard
Mr. J. T. Dickens
Mrs. William J. Bryant
Mrs. N. C. Cranford
Mr. W. G. Bridges

In Memoriam

GREENE ST.—
Mrs. F. A. Comer
Mrs. Clyde Spry
HILLIARD MEM.—
Mr. A. E. Whidden
NORTH MAIN ST.—
Mrs. Rena Watts
Mr. C. E. Alverson
SOUTHSIDE—
Mrs. N. O. Brown
Mrs. Church
Mr. M. A. Swaim
WEST END—
Mrs. Minnie Davis
LEBANON—
Mrs. J. S. Brown
Mrs. McDaniels
OAK GROVE—
Mr. C. M. Lance
PINE GROVE—
Mr. John Leonard, Deacon
PISGAH—
Mrs. F. P. Vaughn
REIDSVILLE FIRST—
Mrs. W. T. Pickerell
Mrs. R. H. Satterfield
Mr. James Lee Cobb
Mr. J. B. Pipkin
PENN MEM.—
Mrs. G. W. Denny
SUMMERFIELD—
Mrs. Sallie Carter
Mr. William Duggins
Mrs. Annie Winfree

TABLE ONE — CHURCH MEMBERSHIP

CHURCHES	City, Town, Country?	When Constituted	PASTORS AND POST OFFICES	Days of Meeting	[illegible]H MEMBERSHIP										Weekly Prayer Meets	Revivals Held, Year	Obs. Lords Supper	Fam. Rec. Bap. Paper	Enr. Min. Ret. Fund
						[illegible]NS				LOSSES									
					Mem. Last Year	Baptisms	Letters	Statements	Restorations	Letters	Exclusions	Erasures	Deaths	Tot. Pres. Mem.					
Allen Jay	V	1934	Geo. H. Wallace, R.3, High Point	All	241	29	17	...	...	10	...	2	...	275	*	2	3	...	......
[illegible]	O	1935	J. C. Gillespie, Reidsville	2 4	66	21	...	1	...	2	...	...	...	84	...	1	1	...	......
Brightwood	V	1940	H. P. Gauldin, R.5, Greensboro	All	77	...	...	...	...	...	...	...	...	126	*	2	1	1	......
Buchanan	O	1936	J. B. Clifton, R.6, Box 334-B, Gr'boro.	All	138	2	9	...	...	3	5	...	...	141	...	1	2	9	62.40
Calvary	O	1901	J. C. Shore, R.4, Reidsville	2 4	185	...	2	...	...	1	...	...	3	183	...	1	2	13	......
[illegible]ty	O	....	John D. Fuller, 1812 Fr'm'n M. Rd, Gbo	All	50	5	9	1	3	2	1	...	...	65	...	1	1	1	......
Fair [illegible]	V	1940	......	......	......	...	...	...	...	...	...	...	...	.....	...	...	...	...	......
Fairview	O	1904	[illegible], R.4, Reidsville	1 3	120	21	2	...	...	...	...	...	...	143	...	1	2	16	......
Fairmont Park	V	1939	A. L. [illegible], R.2, High Point	All	121	32	32	10	...	3	...	...	1	191	*	2	4	7	40.80
Gibsonville	T	1884	John S. Gamble, Raleigh	All	258	8	10	...	...	2	...	...	1	273	*	1	2	6	......
GREENSBORO—																			
[illegible] St.	C	1899	J. Ben [illegible], 709 Asheboro St., G'boro.	All	1202	30	44	3	...	49	...	10	7	1212	*	2	4	...	141.00
—Bailey [illegible]orial	C	1937	W. C. Bearden, 2809 H. Pt. Rd., G'boro	All	96	2	4	2	...	...	...	4	1	99	*	3	4	...	......
—Bessemer	C	1923	Ray W. Harrington, 509 Del. St., G'bor	All	507	15	13	2	...	17	...	...	1	519	*	2	3	3	......
—College Park	C	1906	W. W. Woodcock, 508 For'st St., G'boro	All	627	19	34	...	...	18	...	1	5	656	*	1	12	30	......
—Edgeville	C	1942	L. J. Hight, 1406 Tucker St., G'boro	All	22	7	9	...	...	9	...	10	...	19	*	2	...	...	......
—Eller Memorial	C	1897	J. H. Smith, 1307 Summit Ave., G'boro	All	860	9	10	1	1	17	...	4	5	855	*	...	12	25	124.80
—First	C	1859	J. Clyde [illegible], [illegible]	All	2319	[illegible]	14	5	...	112	10	...	16	2343	*	2	12	160	198.11
—Florida St.	C	1916	J. H. Saunders, 1110 Glenw'd Av., Gbor	All	491	24	22	3	...	23	...	3	1	515	*	2	4	...	149.09
—Latham Park	C	1916	[illegible] D. [illegible], R.5, Greensboro	All	66	...	5	...	...	...	...	...	...	71	*	2	4	1	......
—Magnolia St.	C	1912	L. Grady Burgiss, 103 E. [illegible], Gb	All	207	7	6	...	...	3	...	25	3	188	*	3	4	9	56.78
—Pomona	V	1906	C. M. Oates, Pomona	All	240	4	6	1	...	6	...	1	1	243	*	2	2	...	......
—Revolution	C	1907	S. L. Riddle, 2218 Shobe St.	All	355	2	2	2	...	5	...	...	1	355	*	2	4	21	......
—Sixteenth St.	C	1907	[illegible] H. James 1504 16th St., G'boro.	All	174	32	8	...	30	5	...	...	3	236	*	2	4	5	......
—Stevens Mem.	V	1922	P. M. Hutchinson, Rt. 5	All	161	9	4	1	...	2	...	...	...	173	*	2	4	7	......
—Tabernacle	C	1938	B. G. Whitley, 1200 Elwell Ave., G'boro	All	243	9	12	...	...	13	...	...	3	248	*	2	4	...	......
—Webster Mem.	V	1935	......	All	190	...	...	...	...	4	1	51	1	133	...	1	4	...	......
Guilford	V	1914	I. E. Kerley, 1704 Florida Av., G'boro	All	84	...	4	...	...	3	...	...	..	85	*	1	1	5	......
HIGH POINT—																			
—First	C	1825	A. B. Conrad, 225 Lindsay, St. High Pt.	All	1388	70	72	3	...	60	...	1	13	1459	*	1	4	72	520.40

TABLE TWO — SUNDAY SCHOOLS

[illegible]L SUPT.
C. S. Hodge, First Church, Greensboro

[illegible]ES	SUPERINTENDENTS AND POST OFFICES	Cradle Roll, Under 3	Beginners, 3-5 Years	Primaries, 6-8 Years	Juniors, 9-12 Years	Intermediates, 13-16	Young People, 17-24	Adults, 25 and Up	Extension Dept.	Gen., Dept. Officers	Total Enr'm't, Of'cers, Teachers, Pupils	What Is Av. Attend.?	Baptisms from S. S.	Is the School Graded?	Is It Standard A-1?	Teachers Holding Dip.	Enr'ment Vac. School	Av. Att. Vac. School
Allen Jay	Wade [illegible]e, Rt. 1, High Point	17	20	29	58	56	21	129	...	12	330	210	...	...	...	...	...	...
Antioch	Roy [illegible]re, Rt. 2, Reidsville	5	10	...	...	12	...	20	...	7	173	38	21	...	...	...	60	...
Brightwood	C. M. McGehee, Rt. 5, Greensboro	12	...	25	16	15	35	51	3	10	157	130	...	...	...	...	...	...
Buchanan	J. C. Small, R.6, Greensboro	16	23	...	25	...	51	41	...	21	158	97	...	...	...	...	...	...
Calvary	Harry Conner, R.2, Reidsville	...	12	14	19	24	55	90	...	12	217	90	...	...	...	...	...	...
Community	Ralph Jackson, 1812 F'm'n Mill Rd., Gb	...	13	...	12	...	13	25	...	9	63	45	...	...	...	...	...	...
Fair Grove	...	...	...	...	...	...	...	...	...	...	...	...	...	...	...	...	...	...
Fairview	A. D. Hopkins, Reidsville	...	22	15	18	33	18	20	...	21	126	85	17	...	...	...	...	...
Fairmont Park	W. R. Moose, R.2, High Point	12	22	34	30	21	31	89	...	3	242	141	18	...	...	...	78	53
Gibsonville	Willie Summers, Gibsonville	...	20	26	40	13	34	62	...	13	199	108	8	...	...	...	...	...
GREENSBORO—																		
[illegible]ro St.	Frank Paschal, 2420 Camden Rd., Gbo.	42	38	85	163	153	96	339	55	93	977	406	25	*	...	15	159	120
—Bailey [illegible]morial	W. H. Stevenson, 2405 Hi. Pt. Rd., Gb.	7	...	16	...	32	27	19	...	11	103	68	2	...	...	...	...	...
—Bessemer	D. M. Johnson, 3604 E. Bes. Av., G'boro	32	29	58	48	62	27	105	...	18	379	201	...	*	...	6	...	...
—College Park	B. B. Stockard, [illegible]ro	93	24	35	57	71	63	112	102	59	557	212	18	*	*	21	62	49
—Edgeville	J. H. Lineberry, 1508 Ball St., G'boro	...	...	12	10	15	...	12	...	5	49	40	...	...	...	...	...	...
—Eller Memorial	Raymond Kincaid, 1213 Fv. St., G'boro	80	35	80	125	98	47	164	25	72	676	237	6	*	...	...	198	155
—First	C. [illegible]e, Greensboro	171	70	125	193	212	145	815	220	31	1982	795	...	*	...	12	202	170
—Florida St.	H. A. Schuman, 1414 Florida St., G'bor.	27	40	50	61	54	20	145	40	31	445	296	15	*	...	...	137	105
—Latham Park	Roy Andrews, R.2, Greensboro	...	8	...	14	5	18	19	...	7	71	43	...	...	...	...	...	...
—Magnolia St.	J. E. Lovings, Bessemer Br., Gr'boro	3	22	21	26	19	18	64	...	16	175	93	7	...	...	1	46	33
—Pomona	C. C. Patterson, Pomona	...	34	26	78	35	40	86	...	13	312	159	...	*	...	...	...	...
—Revolution	Grady Phillips, 209 [illegible]in St., G'boro	32	27	57	82	41	25	69	18	18	354	166	2	...	...	3	...	...
—Sixteenth St.	Fred Hester, 1204 17th St., Greensboro	12	10	36	69	32	16	68	...	35	249	117	30	*	...	2	125	75
—Stevens Mem.	L. A. Mills, R.2, [illegible]o	15	8	10	20	20	12	70	...	17	172	126	...	...	...	...	...	...
—Tabernacle	W. O. Smith, 1542 Lovett St., Gr'boro	48	16	14	23	15	12	41	30	28	204	87	3	*	...	...	44	42
—Webster Mem.	Tom Pearman, 2404 [illegible]ple St., G'boro	10	11	20	22	10	28	76	...	14	177	98	...	...	...	1	...	...
Guilford	Clyde Harvey, Guilford	22	12	...	15	8	10	20	...	7	87	45	...	...	...	...	...	...
HIGH POINT—																		
—First	Dr. W. F. Clayton, 223 Lindsay St., HP	61	65	97	122	174	123	484	71	3	1200	580	62	*	...	15	...	...

—Greene St.	W. E. Crissman, High Point	36	76	86	227	149	127	457	...	18	1176	549	95	*	*	...	502	227
—Hilliard M.	C. R. Morris, High Point, R.1	...	26	7	34	35	20	70	...	24	200	148	5	...	...	...	...	...
—North Main St.	S. R. Clinard, R.1, High Point	...	26	57	85	47	25	115	6	34	377	205	21	*	...	...	125	90
—North Park	L. R. McNeil, High Point	5	21	22	33	27	19	43	4	...	182	123	...	*	...	...	...	...
—South Side	Arthur Bean, Highland Ave., High Pt.	7	12	17	47	17	56	61	...	15	223	172	2	*	...	...	...	...
—West End	R. G. Barlowe, Barker St., High Point	16	25	17	45	33	40	65	17	6	264	186	...	*	...	...	...	...
J[illegible]p Grove	E. L. Hutchins, 115 E. Bragg St., G'bor	...	30	...	25	30	16	50	...	12	163	124	26	*	...	...	...	...
Jewell	S. P. Stutts, Sr., R.2, High Point	...	22	...	14	42	...	20	...	15	98	53	7	*	...	...	...	...
Lebanon	Diamond Davis, R.2, Brown Summit	8	10	15	9	14	25	47	...	13	128	66	...	...	...	...	...	...
Mount Zion	Winfred Shaffner, R.2, Snow Camp	...	15	...	15	20	43	42	...	17	152	95	9	...	...	...	...	...
Oak Grove	Mrs. A. L. Saunders, Bx. 928, High Pt.	...	12	7	19	10	15	35	...	10	98	72	...	...	...	...	...	...
Osceola	D. A. Greene, R.1, Brown Summit	...	11	11	13	21	33	22	...	11	113	61	8	*	...	...	...	...
Ossipee	Huston Steele, R.2, Elon College	...	12	...	15	...	17	14	...	6	64	45	...	...	...	...	...	...
Pine Grove	L. R. Loflin, Jamestown	...	21	9	26	16	20	22	...	8	114	67	...	...	...	...	...	...
Pilot View	H. L. Hill, R.2, High Point	...	16	...	30	...	20	16	...	8	82	68	...	...	...	...	...	...
Pisgah	C. R. Byrd, 415 Tate St., High Point	...	...	...	...	...	...	...	...	23	196	140	...	...	...	...	...	...
Pleasant Garden	Walter J. Smith, R.4, Greensboro	13	25	16	24	30	22	35	...	12	159	69	1	...	...	...	...	...
Pleasant Grove	F. M. Akins, R.2, Box 201, Greensboro	10	10	10	18	21	17	22	...	20	108	61	14	*	...	...	...	...
Reedy Fork	Worth Smith, R.2, Greensboro	9	22	11	25	25	17	26	...	10	145	92	...	...	...	...	...	...
REIDSVILLE—																		
—Baptist [illegible]e	Milton Warf, Wentworth St., R'dsville	17	20	26	36	30	18	60	...	10	217	100	16	*	...	...	...	...
—First	R. T. Burton, Reidsville	87	30	38	93	79	63	293	75	46	770	297	11	*	...	...	123	98
—Penn Memorial	W. H. Ford, Reidsville	...	13	11	19	22	32	37	...	4	138	95	...	...	...	...	...	...
Rocky Knoll	C. G. May, R.1, [illegible]o	14	40	22	35	18	26	108	...	3	266	165	...	...	...	...	...	...
Ruffin S[illegible]y	C. L. Schrumm, Ruffin	10	8	15	12	18	12	25	...	10	98	54	...	*	...	...	...	...
Smith Grove	J. A. Farrington, Colfax	...	39	...	25	...	46	42	...	6	152	65	...	...	...	...	...	...
Summerfield	Marion Ayers, Summerfield	25	12	16	10	23	33	...	...	...	119	90	...	...	...	...	...	...
[illegible]e	R. C. Clodfelter, R.4, High Point	14	...	10	16	19	14	19	...	15	92	62	...	...	...	...	...	...
TOTALS		988	1145	1308	2296	1976	3642	4981	666	942	15728	8037	449	...	...	76	1721	1217

TABLE 3—BAPTIST TRAINING UNION

[redacted]L DIRECTOR

J. Carl Bell, Concord Ave., [redacted]o

Church	TRAINING UNION DIRECTORS AND POST OFFICES	Adult Unions	Young Peop. Unions	Intermediate Unions	Junior Unions	Story Hours	Tot. Unions, St. Hrs.	Adults Enrolled	Young Peop. Enrolled	Intermediates Enroll'd	Juniors Enrolled	Story Hours Enrolled	Tot. En., Un., St. Hrs.	Daily Bible Readers	No. Tak. Study Course	Tot. Systematic Givers	No. Unions A-1 1 Qr.	No. Gen., Dept. Of'cers
Allen Jay	P. E. White, R.4, High Point	1	...	1	2	...	4	13	...	15	40	...	68	34	...	68	...	4
Fairmont Park	R. A. Teague, R.2, High Point	1	1	...	1	1	4	32	18	...	15	15	84	...	...	...	...	6
GREENSBORO—																		
—College Park	J. B. Watson, 2416 Walker Ave., G'boro	...	1	1	...	...	2	...	45	24	...	...	69	27	11	67	...	10
—Asheboro St.	J. J. Norwood, 3118 Oak St., Gr'nsboro	...	2	2	2	1	7	...	37	60	52	10	168	20	60	40	...	18
—Bailey [redacted]	C. C. Stanley, Box 741, [redacted]	...	1	1	...	...	2	...	12	10	...	...	22	20	13	22	...	4
—Bessemer	J. W. [redacted], 122 W. Sycamore, G'bo	1	1	2	1	1	6	18	10	17	6	11	61	8	6	25	...	3
—Eller Mem.	Mrs. Russell Noah, 1208 Park [redacted], [redacted]o	1	1	1	2	1	6	11	9	16	29	5	70	19	25	28	...	7
—First	C. S. Hodge, 1st [redacted], [redacted]	3	4	4	2	1	14	65	64	60	35	15	239	74	67	189	...	12
—Florida St.	C. H. [redacted], 1009 Haywood St., [redacted]	1	1	2	3	3	10	14	15	15	28	20	92	32	38	46	...	3
—Magnolia St.	J. E. Poore, 203 E. Wen'ver Ave., [redacted]	1	1	1	1	1	5	8	8	8	10	9	43	11	11	24	...	6
—Pomona	J. A. Culberson, Pomona	1	...	...	...	...	1	10	...	...	...	...	10	10	10	10	1	...
—Sixteenth St.	Williard Lawson, R.2, Box 113, G'boro	1	1	1	1	1	5	14	7	17	17	10	65	39	35	55	1	6
—Tabernacle	Miss Lucile [redacted], 1408 Fla. St., G'bo.	1	...	1	1	...	3	11	...	17	9	...	37	18	20	23	...	5
HIGH POINT—																		
—First	W. O. Burnham, 309 Ch. St., High Pt.	...	1	3	3	1	8	...	23	77	67	25	198	...	...	...	...	6
—Greene St.	T. C. Robbins, High Point	3	2	3	4	1	13	67	26	65	56	25	243	57	71	97	...	12
—Hilliard Mem.	H. B. Chatham, 2108 English St., H. Pt.	1	1	1	1	1	5	15	4	18	18	5	60	29	33	55	...	3
—N. Main St.	Lucien Williams, 205 W. Lex'ton, H.P.	1	1	1	2	1	6	12	12	18	29	15	86	18	26	32	...	4
—North Park	W. H. Brock, High Point	1	1	1	1	1	5	12	7	11	15	10	55	19	24	28	...	3
—South Side	Miss Daisy Shaw, Highland St., H. Pt.	1	...	1	1	1	4	9	...	19	9	12	49	12	23	23	...	5
—West End	Miss Marjorie Macy, Barker St., H. Pt.	1	...	1	1	1	4	14	...	13	15	14	56	17	...	30	...	1
Jessup Grove	James S. Albert, 907 Eng'w'd Av., [redacted]	1	...	2	1	1	5	11	...	31	24	7	73	37	66	73	...	8
Jewell	Miss Estie Brown, High Point	...	...	...	...	...	1	...	...	...	...	...	58	...	...	...	...	...
Lebanon	J. L. Goodwin, R.5, Greensboro	...	1	...	...	...	1	...	15	...	...	...	...	...	...	...	...	3
Pilot View	David [redacted], R.2, High Point	1	1	...	1	...	3	15	20	...	15	...	50	20	...	15	...	...
Pisgah	W. O. Howard, 2217 E. Greene St., HP	1	1	1	1	1	5	...	...	...	...	...	63	17	...	25	...	12
Pleasant Garden	Miss Ora Scott, Pleasant Garden	1	1	1	1	...	4	...	...	...	...	...	...	...	...	...	...	...
Pleasant Grove	F. M. [redacted], R.3, Greensboro	1	...	1	1	...	3	12	...	17	14	...	43	21	20	...	...	6

Reedy Fork........	Parks Gregory, 1514 Upland Dr., G'bo	1	...	1	...	1	3	18	...	18	...	23	59	6	...	41	...	3
REIDSVILLE—																		
—Baptist Temple...	Mrs. Leonard Ganmon, W'w'th St., Rv.	1	1	1	1	1	5	21	9	11	24	19	84	9	18	28	...	3
—First............	Paul Roach, Reidsville................	1	1	2	1	1	6	20	34	40	28	15	137	57	59	83	...	9
—Penn Mem........	Mrs. Nash Wilkins, Reidsville.........	...	1	1	1	...	3	...	10	12	6	...	28	8	18	9	...	5
Rocky Knoll.......	W. T. Apple, R.1, Greensboro..........	1	1	...	1	1	4	15	17	...	21	21	74	17	25	39	...	2
Summerfield........	Ivan Angle, Summerfield..............	1	...	1	1	...	3	8	...	22	18	...	48	...	...	...	...	...
TOTALS........	....	31	27	38	39	23	154	445	402	631	604	286	2492	656	679	1175	2	159

TABLE FOUR — W. M. U. ORGANIZATIONS AND GIFTS

CHURCHES	PRESIDENTS OF W. M. S. AND POST OFFICES	Number of W. M. S.	Number of Y. W. A.'s	Number of G. A.'s	Number of R. A.'s	Number of Sunbeams	Total W. M. U. Orgs.	W. M. S. Members	Y. W. A.'s Members	G. A.'s Members	R. A.'s Members	Sunbeam Members	Total Mem. Enrolled	Tot. En. Miss. St. Crse	Contributions (Local Work) by W. M. U.	Contributions (Missions) by W. M. U.
Buchanan	Mrs. J. B. Clifton, Bessemer Br., G'bor	1	1	...	1	...	4	13	10	...	8	20	51	10	....	139.66
[illegible]	Mrs. J. E. [illegible]o, Rt., Reidsville	1	1	1	...	...	3	25	15	...	...	...	40	...	9.99	136.25
Fairview	Mrs. A. D. [illegible]s, R.1, Reidsville	1	...	...	...	...	1	18	...	...	...	...	18	18	1.22	35.25
Fairmont Park	Mrs. Joe Edwards, R.2, High Point	1	...	...	...	...	...	35	...	...	...	...	35	...	263.70	....
Gibsonville	Mrs. John [illegible]d, Gibsonville.	1	...	...	...	...	1	28	...	...	...	...	28	...	652.25	77.87
GREENSBORO—																
—[illegible]o St.	Mrs. E. R. Baldwin, Rand'n Rd., G'bor	1	1	2	2	1	7	132	14	42	36	25	239	126	4697.88	2107.17
—Bailey M[illegible]n	Mrs. W. H. Stevenson, 2405 HP Rd., Gb	1	...	...	...	...	1	15	...	...	...	...	15	...	9.83	20.30
—Bessemer	Mrs. J. R. [illegible]n, 200 [illegible]s Av., G'bor	1	...	1	...	1	3	30	...	14	...	43	87	...	1741.90	459.66
—Eller M[illegible]	Mrs. Ethel Morrison, [illegible]o	1	...	...	...	...	1	2	35	...	...	10	45	18	....	1021.73
—First	Mrs. E. T. Howell, 210 N. Men'hall, [illegible]	1	3	3	2	1	10	400	41	44	44	37	566	237	5748.82	10249.24
—Florida St.	Mrs. D. S. [illegible]y, 1104 Fla. St., Gr'boro	1	1	1	1	1	5	61	18	21	6	...	106	25	16.04	333.04
—[illegible]a St.	Mrs. L. G. Burgiss, 103 E. W'over Av.	1	1	1	...	1	4	16	6	10	...	30	62	12	49.50	61.80
—Pomona	Mrs. W. H. Brown, Pomona	1	...	...	...	1	2	30	...	...	...	15	45	...	....	150.87
—Revolution	Miss Sallie Burgess, [illegible]e St., Rev., G	1	1	1	1	1	5	25	6	10	3	10	54	...	706.47	522.60
—Sixteenth St.	Mrs. Harry [illegible], 1508 17th, Gr'boro	1	1	1	1	1	5	35	12	30	9	14	100	32	....	1199.98
—Stevens M[illegible]	Mrs. Jack Caudle, R.2, [illegible]	1	...	...	...	...	1	25	...	...	...	...	25	...	....	180.67
—Tabernacle	Mrs. T. W. Driver, 1604 Grove, Gr'boro	1	1	...	...	1	3	16	10	...	...	19	43	...	....	46.00
—Webster M[illegible]	Mrs. A. [illegible]s, R.5, [illegible]o	1	1	1	2	1	6	46	10	10	12	13	91	19	174.10	701.90
Guilford	Mrs. [illegible]e Kennedy, R.7, [illegible]o	1	...	...	...	1	2	16	...	...	...	12	28	...	....	58.00
HIGH POINT—																
—First	Mrs. W. F. Clayton, 223 Lind'y St., HP	1	1	2	2	1	7	225	17	24	25	...	292	102	500.00	4785.85
—[illegible]e St.	Mrs. C. C. Stout, High Point	1	1	2	1	1	6	120	20	22	25	10	197	103	3702.71	1322.62
—Hilliard M[illegible]	Mrs. Joe Tolbert, Joshua St., High Pt.	1	1	1	1	1	5	12	7	7	...	22	48	...	570.79	102.94
—N. M[illegible]in St.	Mrs. G. L. Thompson, R.1, Guilf. Col.	2	...	1	1	...	4	24	...	10	10	...	44	...	....	182.10
—North Park	....	1	1	1	1	1	5	12	10	13	8	6	49	...	607.36	40.48
—S[illegible]i[illegible]e	Mrs. J. S. [illegible], 307 [illegible], High P.	1	...	...	...	...	1	26	...	...	...	...	26	15	6.50	101.34
—West End	Mrs. T. P. [illegible]s, [illegible]ps St., H. Pt.	1	...	2	...	...	3	20	...	16	...	...	36	...	133.20	136.60
Jessup Grove	Mrs. James E. Wiggs, 1515 [illegible]. St., [illegible]	1	...	...	...	...	1	12	...	...	...	...	12	...	20.00	....
Jewell	....	...	...	...	1	...	1	20	...	...	...	...	20	...	....	....

TABLE VI.—CHURCH PROPERTY

CHURCHES	CHURCH CLERKS AND POST OFFICES	Own House Worship?	When Was It Built?	What Materials Used?	How Many Seated?	Number of Rooms	Dept. Assembly Rms.	No. Sep. Class Rooms	Value Church House and Grounds	Value Mission Chapel If Any	Value Pastor's Home	Total Value All Church Property	Indebtedness on All Church Property	Amount of Insurance Carried
Allen Jay	Hoy Yarborough, R.3, Box 152, Hi. Pt.	Yes	1936	Wood	300	10	...	9	4000	.....	.....	4000	....	3000
Antioch	Mrs. T. M. [illegible], R.2, Reidsville	Yes	1935	Wood	300	4	...	3	1500	.....	.....	1500	101.00	......
[illegible]	H. G. [illegible], R.2, Brown Summit	Yes	1941	Wood	300	8	...	6	6000	.....	1800	7800	206.00	508
Buchanan	R. F. [illegible], R.6, [illegible]	Yes	1877	Wood	200	5	1	4	3500	.....	.....	3500	....	1500
[illegible]	J. E. [illegible], R.2, Reidsville	Yes	1898	Wood	275	9	1	8	5000	.....	2000	7000	....	3000
Community	Mrs. Nina Morgan, R.3, Greensboro	Yes	1943	Cind.	350	1	...	...	2500	.....	.....	2500	1250.00	2500
Fair Grove	......	....	.....	.....	.....	...	...	...	.....	.....	.....	.....	....	......
Fairview	William [illegible], R.2, Reidsville	Yes	1901	Wood	300	11	...	10	3000	.....	.....	3000	....	2000
Fairmont Park	Joe Edwards, R.5, High Point	Yes	1942	Wood	540	11	...	9	8500	.....	.....	9525	....	5000
Gibsonville	C. W. Seaford, Gibsonville	Yes	1884	Wood	300	9	9	9	5000	.....	.....	5000	....	3500
GREENSBORO—														
—[illegible] St.	L. C. [illegible]sterfield, 214 E Lee St., G'boro	Yes	1912	Brick	700	61	10	69	51000	.....	6000	57000	6000.00	43000
—Bailey Memorial	W. C. Heilig, 2018 Asheboro St., G'boro	Yes	1935	Wood	250	...	1	6	2500	.....	.....	2500	....	750
—Bessemer	R. F. [illegible]e, 607 Sykes, Greensboro	Yes	1923	Wood	350	25	5	20	13400	.....	2000	15600	....	12500
—College Park	Carroll C. Weaver, [illegible]	Yes	1940	Brick	300	57	8	42	55000	600	8000	63600	5236.00	50000
—Edgeville	Mrs. [illegible] Hight, 1406 [illegible] St., G'bor	Yes	1943	Wood	200	1	...	...	2500	.....	.....	2500	....	2000
—Eller Memorial	Eli Craven, 1510 [illegible] Dr., Gr'boro	Yes	1925	Brick	800	50	7	48	42000	.....	9000	51000	....	30000
—First	Vander Liles, Greensboro	Yes	1906	Brick	1000	48	...	48	130000	.....	.....	130000	....	70000
—Florida St.	[illegible], 1514 Elwood Av., Gbo	Yes	1930	Brick	350	23	2	22	17000	1700	6000	23000	....	24000
—[illegible]	W. W. Sutton, [illegible]	Yes	1916	Wood	250	1	...	...	2500	.....	.....	2500	686.19	......
—Magnolia St.	[illegible], 1121 [illegible] St., Gb.	Yes	1912	Wood	300	6	1	11	6000	1000	4000	11000	....	6500
—Pomona	C. C. Patterson, Pomona, Box 102	Yes	1906	Wood	350	8	...	8	3000	.....	.....	3000	....	......
—Revolution	N. C. Brown, 1902 Poplar St., Gr'boro	Yes	1907	Wood	400	5	3	9	10000	5000	.....	15000	....	7500
—Sixteenth St.	J. V. Brady, 2408 Spruce St., Gr'boro.	Yes	1907	Brick	500	5	4	16	39000	.....	.....	39000	....	18000
—Stevens Mem.	Mrs. J. B. Brown, R.2, Greensboro	Yes	1922	Wood	250	11	2	13	10000	.....	2500	12500	....	7500
—Tabernacle	Mrs. E. C. White, Jr., 1003 Hert. St., G.	Yes	1938	Wood	200	3	...	2	5000	.....	.....	5000	....	......
—Webster Mem.	Albert S. West, R.5, Greensboro	Yes	1935	Wood	200	10	1		4000	.....	4000	8000	2000.00	5500
Guilford	Mrs. Dora Farrar, Guilford College	Yes	1914	Brick	200	1	4		3500	300	.....	3800	....	3000
HIGH POINT—														
[illegible]	C. D. Goldsmith, 113 Briggs Ave. H.-Pt.	Yes												

TABLE SEVEN — GIFTS FOR LOCAL CHURCH WORK

CHURCHES	REGULAR TREASURERS AND POST OFFICES	Pastor's Salary Paid This Year	Other Salaries	Ministerial Help and Supply	Building and Repairs Spent This Year	Church Debt and Interest	Incidentals	Literature for Church Use, S. S., etc.	Help Given to Local Poor	For Printing Minutes and Clerk of Assn.	Other Objects	Total, Local Purposes, Given by Church and All Its Organizations	Number of Tithers
Allen Jay	W. R. Hobson, R.3, High Point	2302.67	....	292.00	....	....	637.68	196.68	313.86	5.00	2000.00	5747.89	60
Antioch	Mrs. Hobart Carter, R.2, Reidsville	207.64	....	40.00	200.00	101.00	9.00	....	12.00	1.50	....	570.74	....
Brightwood	J. M. Crabtree, R.5, Greensboro	1790.50	....	185.60	800.00	509.85	256.57	52.84	28.00	2.00	....	3625.46	....
Buchanan	R. F. Carter, R.6, Greensboro	1560.00	....	50.00	....	....	107.93	73.00	....	3.00	272.43	2128.76	....
Calvary	J. F. Carroll, R.3, Reidsville	495.00	....	81.00	63.75	....	142.72	72.77	1.30	4.00	111.12	971.39	....
Community	Miss Julia Yow, R.1, Greensboro	243.80	....	46.62	....	....	44.05	26.21	52.89	1.50	....	415.47	....
Fair Grove	....	....	....	....	....	....	....	....	....	....	....	....	....
Fairview	D. E. Trantham, R.2, Reidsville	450.00	....	75.00	12.09	....	69.12	52.73	....	3.00	15.88	677.82	....
Fairmont Park	R. A. Teague, R.2, High Point	1555.00	....	68.00	2080.30	....	317.11	123.92	50.00	5.00	129.00	4369.13	20
Gibsonville	T. S. Robinson, Gibsonville	1275.00	....	240.98	1000.00	....	211.14	83.46	21.50	3.00	70.23	2905.31	3
GREENSBORO—													
—Asheboro St.	Earl Johnson, 2012 Asheboro St., G'bor	3525.08	1770.28	370.16	257.30	6169.00	1727.74	861.10	150.80	12.50	2469.77	17454.79	19
—Bailey Memorial	Roland Mitchell, R.7, Greensboro	1080.00	....	358.29	202.63	53.00	160.78	99.36	40.00	4.00	249.75	2247.81	....
—Bessemer	Claude L. Murray, 406 DeLan. St., G'b	1860.00	....	492.30	841.43	2688.74	861.54	299.95	....	10.00	1200.00	8253.96	....
—College Park	L. E. Ogburn, Greensboro	2400.00	105.00	....	....	3140.79	2851.43	643.47	105.60	12.50	....	9258.79	100
—Edgeville	J. H. Lineberry, 1508 Ball, Greensboro	260.48	....	4.00	301.60	....	67.76	22.86	....	1.00	....	657.70	5
—Eller Memorial	Mrs. Robert Burgess, 1214 Walnut, G'b	3125.00	1510.70	35.00	1437.32	....	1196.85	411.33	147.64	10.00	210.36	8204.00	61
—First	Mrs. R. W. Morton, 4005 Peterson, G'b	4903.67	7138.23	565.00	836.96	22472.93	4688.73	1930.99	1218.89	....	5211.03	49164.54	....
—Florida St.	D. M. Frazier, 1319 Fla. St., Gr'boro	2585.00	798.00	406.63	894.65	....	565.75	493.57	21.50	10.00	6459.10	12383.29	....
—Latham Park	R. A. Anderson, Greensboro	520.00	....	54.83	228.18	203.35	43.94	39.64	43.80	2.00	....	1135.74	....
—Magnolia St.	H. S. Noah, 1700 Grove, Greensboro	1840.00	....	227.00	19.75	2509.86	436.47	151.68	79.89	3.00	358.60	5683.03	46
—Pomona	E. E. Henry, Pomona	1768.00	....	170.38	66.06	....	170.39	154.10	36.25	3.00	48.70	2416.88	....
—Revolution	Waldo Johnson, 2211 Shober St., G'bor	2290.00	....	264.95	32.24	....	307.44	223.31	40.00	5.20	603.68	3766.82	....
—Sixteenth St.	L. F. Paris, 1608 15th St., Greensboro.	2340.00	225.00	....	283.45	....	1326.52	424.07	102.50	9.00	265.00	4975.54	50
—Stevens Mem.	Mrs. C. B. Brisson, R.2, Goldsboro	1820.00	....	184.86	25.43	....	324.32	150.41	....	4.00	55.78	2564.80	....
—Tabernacle	E. H. Moore, 1704 Grove, Greensboro	2105.00	720.00	367.54	364.14	103.00	395.86	212.69	146.76	5.00	411.11	4831.10	....
—Webster Mem.	R. H. King, 1505 14th St., Greensboro.	1100.00	....	154.00	434.00	1375.45	157.14	89.88	134.25	5.00	548.97	3997.69	....
Guilford	Mrs. Dora Farrar, Guilford College	260.00	....	125.00	....	....	79.67	32.98	....	2.00	....	499.65	2
HIGH POINT—													
—First	Thelma Patrick, High Point	3600.00	2901.00	670.35	767.[illegible]	[illegible]	5312.22	1302.45	279.18	25.00	2142.82	35874.69	150

—Greene St.	R. R. Holder, High Point	3380.00	906.00	1191.78	333.49	20642.22	2261.34	780.58	135.28	10. 0	....	29775.45	150
—Hilliard Mem.	J. W. Metcalf, R.2, High Point	1820.00	....	54.00	....	1446.73	393.41	202.07	29.53	3.00	156.27	5154.01	..
—North Main St.	J. E. Brawley, 1619 N. Main, High Pt.	2340. 0	499.65	96.00	2201.62	573.68	404.02	291.78	14.71	3.00	135.00	6559.46	30
—North Park	L. W. Glenn, Box 702, High Point	770.00	....	590.00	....	....	416.92	204.05	15.00	5.00	511.32	2512.29	25
—South Side	F. E. Caudle, 1403 King, High Point	1580. 0	....	185.51	216.93	....	181.79	126.58	135.92	7.08	369.85	2803.66	50
—West End	C. M. Scott, 1009 Ferndale Dr., High P.	1340.00	....	69.31	92.22	1652.41	469.67	228.47	....	4.00	341.91	4249.99	...
Jessup Grove	Ruth Lewis, Rt. 1, Summerfield	1541.77	....	245.41	20.15	....	275.03	102.46	....	2.00	2793.18	4980.00	30
J well	Mrs. Lela Weatherman, R.2, High Pt.	243.76	....	63.52	46.25	....	79.86	102.56	20.25	2.80	....	559.00	5
Lebanon	L. R. Chilton, R.2, Brown Summit	1560.00	....	214.30	50.13	....	149.97	55.85	29.20	4.00	....	2063.45	20
Mount Zion	Eugenia Lockamy, R.2, Liberty	639.19	....	124.70	241.49	....	34.28	41.50	10.50	5.00	1.39	1098.05	...
Oak Grove	W. L. Shackleford, R.3, High Point	1375.94	....	213.57	69.96	....	196.42	45.21	....	......	86.39	1987.49	9
Osceola	Mrs. D. A. Greene, R.1, Brown Summit	385.04	....	268. 0	310.44	....	80.52	60.10	....	3.00	159.23	1266.33	...
Ossipee	Rev. W. E. Lewis, Elon College	1055.00	....	156.00	....	128.00	40.00	35. 0	....	1.00	....	1415.00	6
Pine Grove	E. H. Eller, R.2, Trinity	520. 0	....	93.37	26.21	....	119.22	31.96	53.93	2.50	42.08	889.27	8
Pilot View	Mrs. H. L. Hill, R.2, High Point	1300. 0	....	108.74	....	....	66.43	68.22	17.00	......	45.00	1605.39	15
Pisgah	L. C. [illegible], 414 Winslow St., H. Pt.	1805.00	....	240.50	390.21	....	215.10	124.00	93.85	3.00	36.24	2907.90	36
Pleasant Garden	C. L. Yow, Pleasant Garden	858. 0	120.00	50.00	....	198.00	52.00	85.00	30.00	2.00	10.00	1405.00	12
Pleasant Grove	Virgil Ward, R.3, Greensboro	461.00	....	74.61	615.00	249.55	272.38	58.04	....	......	....	1730.58	20
Reedy Fork	Miss Lora Canter, R.2, Brown Summit	816.00	....	46.00	288.82	765.55	122.40	123.19	6.75	3.00	7.12	2178.83	14
REIDSVILLE—													
—Baptist Temple	Mrs. Dell [illegible], Box 283, [illegible]ville	2422.00	....	786.34	1007.40	1347.05	468.82	251.75	5.14	7.50	587.87	6883.87	30
—First	J. P. Kemp, Reidsville	3000. 0	653.50	105.00	2897.90	....	2007.30	707.68	260.00	10. 0	3045.00	12806.38	25
—Penn Memorial	T. G. Dixon, Reidsville	180 0. 0	....	260.00	2670.29	....	449.32	122.02	231.17	5.00	....	5610.60	...
Rocky Knoll	Mrs. R. A. Laughlin, R.1, [illegible]boro.	1500. 0	162.05	92.05	1575.88	250.00	225.43	242.26	375.66	3.00	397.02	4823.35	30
Ruffin Stacey	Dewey London, R.5, Reidsville	390. 0	....	116.00	305.00	....	111.85	40. 0	....	3.00	30. 0	995.85	14
Smith Grove	Drew Smith, R.1, Colfax	240.34	....	69.56	186.50	....	44. 0	12.21	....	......	20.30	572.91	4
Summerfield	Mrs. T. D. Carter, Summerfield	520.00	....	58.58	136.71	17.54	144.67	84.05	....	5.00	87.47	1054.02	...
Temple	Roy Yarborough, R.4, High Point	1130.75	....	495.19	591.39	....	100. 0	49.08	103.00	2.00	5.71	2477.12	20
TOTALS		82050.63	17509.41	11587.53	25422.67	84681.63	31852.12	12591.52	4593.50	238.08	31701.68	305681.71	1069

TABLE EIGHT — GIFTS FOR MISS IONS, EDUCATION AND ALL BENEVOLENCES

CHURCHES	Total to Cooperative Program	Special to Associational Missions	Special to State Missions	Special to Home Missions	Special to Foreign Missions	Special to Schools and Colleges	Special to Theological Seminaries.	Special to Orphanage	Special to Hospitals	Special to Old Ministers' Relief	Hundred Thousand Club	Red Cross and Foreign Relief	Other Objects	Total Given for Missions and Benevolences by Church and all Departments	Grand Total, All Purposes, Given by the Church and All Orgs.
Allen Jay	75.00		9.25	51.00	100.00			100.52	50.00					385.77	6133.66
Antioch								5.75		5.09				10.84	581.58
Brightwood	10.00							123.09	31.60					1.69	3790.15
Buchanan	104.00							65.66	50.00				62.70	282.36	2411.12
Calvary	100.00		32.00	22.00	113.00	9.50		193.05	66.55	5.00	81.50		82.80	705.40	1676.79
Community								11.00	11.13					22.13	437.60
Fair Grove															
Fairview	169.00		10.00	8.75	14.50			96.88	22.00		12.00			333.13	1010.95
Fairmont Park	25.00		89.41					45.50	25.00					184.91	4554.04
Gibsonville	50.00							114.75	10.00					174.75	3080.06
GREENSBORO—															
—Asheboro St.	2971.82	6.50	185.26	95.87	467.97	288.31		793.18	159.92		292.02		170.80	5431.65	22886.44
—Bailey Memorial	73.00		20.00	89.65	10.00			182.78			7.0			392.43	2640.24
—Bessemer	378.00		12.00	148.46	18.35	25.00		100.00	25.00		45.13		35.25	787.19	9041.15
—College Park	791.69		286.08	75.86	171.50			374.67	68.55		278.08		450.05	2496.49	11755.28
—Edgeville	91.10							26.67	27.04					144.81	802.50
—Eller Memorial	1645.45				290.78	110.00		450.00	68.16		381.85		30.00	2976.24	11180.24
—First	18260.91		891.25	1556.22	7231.81	565.15	50.00	3412.84	676.49		2361.71		1098.48	36104.86	85269.40
—Florida St.	1398.98							300.00					59.00	1757.98	14141.27
tham Park	25.00				12.00				16.00					53.00	1188.74
—Magnolia St.	114.00		25.00	25.00	39.80			152.50	35.00		17.00		10.0	418.30	6101.33
—Pomona	159.49		284.72	30.00				567.14	108.00		12.00		279.53	1432.88	3849.76
—Revolution	1297.83		83.03	24.95	312.86	75.00		239.85	194.36		184.16		192.05	2604.09	6370.91
—Sixteenth St.	2388.67		108.65	63.27	15.90	100.00		344.76	44.78	50.00	205.41		102.42	3423.86	8399.40
—Stevens Mem.	700.00		15.65		206.55			258.16	75.64		100.00		49.57	1405.67	3970.37
—Tabernacle	200.00	1.25	43.23	10.35	57.51			147.05	45.85				46.0	551.24	5382.34
—Webster Mem.	560.87		2.37	43.03	56.10	10.00		159.72	5.00		157.14		12.00	1031.16	5028.85
Guilford	26.45		4.00		2.00			15.00	24.40					71.85	571.50
HIGH POINT—															
—First	5034.34	13.40	358.21	263.43	1684.53	510.00		1729.99	413.22		554.43		178.17	10739.72	46614.41

—Greene St.	2650.00			73.98	163.90	300.00		530.65	45.80		317.62			4081.95	33857.40
—Hilliard Mem.	118.98	1.00	5.95	5.00	12.85			175.99	30.48		46.30		14.30	410.90	5564.91
—North Main St.	528.00		137.42		2.00			172.10	83.70	91.60	33.20	220.00		1268.02	7827.48
—North Park	325.75		30.05	12.75	14.15			106. 0	35.00		40.75		20.00	584.45	3096.75
—South Side			10.11	15.00	15.00			20.70	30.15		45.00		5.75	141.71	2945.37
—West End	501.71		208.35	37.39	50.85		125.00	350.52	62.00		123.00		2.00	1460.82	5710.81
Jessup Grove			16.43	66.20				126.00	20.00				51.01	279.64	4259.64
Jewell								52.45	8.42				25.15	86.02	645.02
Lebanon				146.00		60.00		65.86	25.00					296.86	2360.31
Mount Zion			12.46	43. 0	5.00			50.92						111.38	1109.43
Oak Grove	21.00							63.88	16.50					101.38	2088.87
Osceola			18.36	5.27	10.80	6.13	21.82	102.10	23.25			16.59		204.32	1470.65
Ossipee	10.00													10.00	1425.00
Pine Grove			19.30	5.11				10.59	17.00				56.50	108.50	996.77
Pilot View			52.81					100.51	20.37					173.69	1779.08
Pisgah	50.00		25.00					40.00	22.00					137.00	3044.90
Pleasant Garden	24.00			4.00				24.00			5.00			57.00	1562.00
Pleasant Grove	36.00							84.84					74.77	195.61	1926.19
Reedy Fork	98.77		16.84	6.19	40.18			26.00	65.06				26.72	279.76	2458.59
REIDSVILLE—															
—Baptist Temple	272.00		40.00	28.33	58.21			144. 0	36.60		24.00		14.61	617.95	7501.82
—First	2470.89	20.00	202.00	117.85	408.95	519.00		531.03	191.39		558.70		380.00	5399.81	18206.19
—Penn Memorial	79.50		24.96	11.00	16.50	6.00		28.00	25.00		12.00		60.00	262.96	5873.56
Rocky Knoll			225.47	107.51	25.00			75. 0	127.50				22.75	583.55	5406.90
Ruffin Stacey						24.00		24. 0	11.00					59.00	1054.85
Smith Grove			4.83	11.83	1.83			34.87	22.37					75.73	648.64
Summerfield	100.92		11.50	25. 0	255.00			92.31	35.16		39.00		52.05	611.94	1665.96
Temple	100.00	9.00		78.25				6.00	11.50					204.75	2681.87
TOTALS	44038.32	51.15	3547.20	3307.50	11849.38	2608.09	196.82	13058.83	3218.94	151.69	5934.01	236.59	3564.43	91091.27	396139.14

HISTORICAL TABLE — PIEDMONT BAPTIST ASSOCIATION

Year	Where Held	Moderator	Clerk	Preacher	Churches	Baptisms	Members	Gifts
1894	Greensboro	Dr. C. A. Rominger	W. L. Kivett	M. A. Adams	5	....	562	....
1895	Liberty	T. L. Chislom	W. L. Kivett	L. Johnson	12	16	1112	4695.50
1896	Moore's Chapel	R. W. Brooks	W. H. Eller	L. Johnson	14	66	1194	5128.94
1897	Summerfield	F. H. Jones	W. H. Eller	J. A. Munday	16	73	1540	7198.27
1898	Mount Zion	R. W. Brooks	W. H. Eller	L. Johnson	17	67	1557	6883.23
1899	Ramseur	R. W. Brooks	F. P. Tucker	John E. White	19	54	1570	7435.43
1900	Cherry Street	R. W. Brooks	W. H. Eller	Thomas Carrick	16	48	1538	7970.35
1901	Reidsville	F. H. Jones	W. H. Eller	L. Johnson	19	157	1657	8282.73
1902	Salem Street	F. H. Jones	W. H. Eller	W. C. Newton	19	135	1774	9950.97
1903	Gibsonville	F. H. Jones	W. H. Eller	C. L. Greaves	20	185	1868	12834.77
1904	Calvary	F. H. Jones	W. H. Eller	H. W. Battle	22	112	1832	12807.43
1905	Randleman	F. H. Jones	W. H. Eller	J. M. Hilliard	22	114	2096	17674.91
1906	High Point First	F. H. Jones	W. H. Eller	W. R. Bradshaw	23	201	2333	29366.31
1907	Asheboro Street	F. H. Jones	W. H. Eller	Wm. Hedley	26	372	2798	39993.79
1908	Ramseur	F. H. Jones	W. H. Eller	C. E. Maddry	28	311	3086	26347.57
1909	Greensboro	F. H. Jones	W. H. Eller	Wm. Hedley	30	292	3429	49847.28
1910	Mount Zion	F. H. Jones	W. H. Eller	R. G. Hendrick	31	336	3731	28531.01
1911	Asheboro	W. F. Staley	W. H. Eller	W. F. Staley	29	182	3736	25887.56
1912	Hi Point, Green St.	F. P. Hobgood, Jr.	W. H. Eller	J. C. Turner	30	174	3647	29697.38
1913	Liberty	F. P. Hobgood, Jr.	W. H. Eller	R. P. Walker	31	409	3971	37700.97
1914	Asheboro Street	F. P. Hobgood, Jr.	W. H. Eller	A. W. Claxon	31	413	4202	42428.44
1915	Reidsville	J. M. Hilliard	W. H. Eller	J. M. Hilliard	42	313	4491	42577.68
1916	Forest Avenue	J. M. Hilliard	W. H. Eller	E. N. Johnson	36	369	4854	48418.92
1917	Green Street	J. M. Hilliard	W. H. Eller	W. R. White	39	308	4760	44609.05
1918	Moore's Chapel	J. M. Hilliard	W. H. Eller	J. W. Rose	39	374	5140	72538.46
1919	White Oak	J. M. Hilliard	W. H. Eller	W. H. Wilson	39	339	5359	76638.85
1920	Calvary	J. M. Hilliard	W. H. Eller	E. N. Johnson	39	543	5967	117682.35
1921	Summerfield	Clarence A. Smith	J. E. Lanier	B. K. Mason	39	480	6454	135561.79
1922	Glenola	Clarence A. Smith	J. E. Lanier	Jas. A. Clark	39	679	7226	149955.24
1923	Magnolia St.	Clarence A. Smith	H. O. Miller	E. E. White	38	365	7341	140553.25
1924	West End	Clarence A. Smith	H. O. Miller	W. E. Goode	40	672	7489	164658.19
1925	Fairview	Clarence A. Smith	H. O. Miller	A. T. Howell	41	610	8956	211792.21
1926	Ramseur	Clarence A. Smith	S. T. Hensley	Lloyd T. Wilson	42	620	9974	243500.68
1927	Trinity	Clarence A. Smith	S. T. Hensley	H. T. Stevens	40	656	10223	211846.40
1928	Bessemer	Clarence A. Smith	O. E. Lee	R. P. Ellington	41	531	10866	202002.30

1941	Green Street........	Grover H. Jones......	O. E. Lee.............	A. Lincoln Fulk.......	53	724	16929	284008.43
1942	Greensboro, First..	Grover H. Jones......	L. Grady Burgiss.....	A. A. Walker..........	55	794	16922	324184.15
1943	Greensboro, First..	Grover H. Jones......	L. Grady Burgiss......	I. B. Jackson..........	55	772	17268	396139.14

—INDEX—

Minutes Of The

Piedmont Baptist Association

North Carolina

Fifty-First Annual Session

held with the

First Baptist Church

Greensboro, N. C.

Thursday, October 19

1944

Next Meeting Will Be Held With The First Baptist Church, Greensboro, Thursday, October 25, 1945

Dr. John W. McGennis, Reidsville ---------------- Preacher
Ray W. Harrington, Greensboro --------------- Alternate

Minutes Of The

Piedmont Baptist Association

North Carolina

Fifty-First Annual Session

held with the

First Baptist Church

Greensboro, N. C.

Thursday, October 19

1944

Next Meeting Will Be Held With The First Baptist Church,
Greensboro, Thursday, October 25, 1945

Dr. John W. McGennis, Reidsville ---------------- Preacher
Ray W. Harrington, Greensboro ---------------- Alternate

Index

ASSOCIATIONAL DIRECTORY

Grover H. Jones, Moderator ------------------ High Point
J. Ben Eller, Vice Moderator ------------------ Greensboro
Ray W. Harrington, Clerk ---------------------- Greensboro

EXECUTIVE PROMOTION COMMITTEE

Grover H. Jones, Chmn. ------------------------- High Point
J. Ben Eller ------------------------------------ Greensboro
Mrs. J. Ben Eller ------------------------------ Greensboro
C. S. Hodge ------------------------------------ Greensboro
Carl Bell --------------------------------------- Greensboro
Ray W. Harrington ----------------------------- Greensboro
Harry B. Caldwell ----------------------------- Greensboro
Wilbur W. Hutchins ---------------------------- High Point
H. O. Miller ------------------------------------ High Point
D. W. Overby ----------------------------------- Reidsville
T. L. Gardner ---------------------------------- Reidsville
E. A. Long -------------------------------------- Germantown
R. R. Jackson ---------------------------------- High Point
Dr. J. Clyde Turner ---------------------------- Greensboro
C. W. Scott ------------------------------------- High Point
Dr. John McGinnis ----------------------------- Reidsville
Mrs. C. W. Moseley ---------------------------- Greensboro
J. C. Shore ------------------------------------- Reidsville

CHURCH ADVISORY AND MISSIONS COMMITTEE

Dr. J. Clyde Turner, Chm. ---------------------- Greensboro
Grover H. Jones -------------------------------- High Point
Mrs. C. W. Moseley ---------------------------- Greensboro
T. L. Gardner ---------------------------------- Greensboro
J. C. Shore ------------------------------------- Reidsville
J. S. Hopkins ---------------------------------- High Point
Wilbur W. Hutchins ---------------------------- High Point
Ray W. Harrington ----------------------------- Greensboro

OFFICERS OF PIEDMONT W. M. U.

Mrs. J. Eller, Supt. ——————— 709 Asheboro St. Greensboro
Mrs. Nettie Hoge, Supt. Emeritus 1406 W. Mkt. St. Greensboro
Mrs. T. L. Sasser, Asso. Supt. ------------------ Greensboro
Mrs. T. L. Sasser, Acting Sec. ---------------- Greensboro
Mrs. W. O. Burnham, Treasurer -------------- High Point
Mrs. T. C. Robins, Y. P. L. ------ 321 Louise St. High Point
Mrs. H. A. Knight, Mission Study, ------------ High Point
Mrs. W. H. Wright, Stewardship ---------- Guilford College
Mrs. C. W. Moseley, Community Missions ------ Greensboro
Mrs. R. P. Royal, Literature ------------------ Greensboro
Mrs. R. R. Saunders, Training School and Margaret Fund
Reidsville
Rev. Ray W. Harrington, R. A. Counselor of Asso. Greensboro

COMMITTEES SERVING DURING THE ASSOCIATIONAL YEAR

Executive—Promotion Committee
Church Advisory and Missions Committee
Program Committee

COMMITTEES SERVING DURING THE ANNUAL MEETINGS OF THE ASSOCIATION

Committee on Committees
Committee on Committees
Committee on Time, Place, and Preacher
Auditing Committee
Committee on Resolutions
Program Committee for this year and next year
Committee to Nominate Officers
Committee to Nominate Executive—Promotion Committee
Committee to Nominate Church Advisory and Missions Committee
Committee to Nominate Delegates to the Baptist State Convention

CHURCHES BY DISTRICTS

District 1

Allen Jay; Fairmont Park, Greene Street, High Point First; Hilliard Memorial Jewell, North Main Street, North Park, Oak Grove, Pine Grove, Pilot View, Pisgah, Smith Grove, South Side, Temple, West End.

District 2

Asheboro Street, Bailey Memorial, Bessemer, Brightwood, Buchanan, College Park, Edgeville, Eller Memorial, Fair Grove, Florida Street, Gibsonville, Greensboro, First; Guilford, Jessup Grove, Latham Park, Lebanon, Magnolia Street, McLeansville, Mount Zion, Osborne Chapel, Pleasant Garden, Pleasant Grove, Pomona Mills, Sixteenth Street, Stevens Memorial, Summerfield, Tabernacle, Ossippee, Webster Memorial.

District 3

Antioch, Calvary, Fairview, Baptist Temple, Osceola, Penn Memorial, Reidsville, First; Ruffin Stacey.

OFFICERS OF BAPTIST TRAINING UNION

J. Carl Bell, Director	Greensboro
Miss Thelma Patrick, Asso. Director	High Point
Miss Julia Lyles, Sec. Treas.	High Point
E. C. White, Jr., Pianist	Greensboro
Harry Wester, Chorister	High Point
Mrs. C. W. Crutchfield, Story Hour Leader	Greensboro
Miss Eva Saleeby, Jr., Leader	Greensboro
Miss Myrtis Thomas, Int. Leader	Greensboro
Miss Mabel Starnes, Young People's Leader	Greensboro
C. S. Hodge, Adult Leader	Greensboro
J. E. Hedrick, Director Dist. No. 1	High Point
J. J. Norwood, Director Dist. No. 2	Greensboro
Mrs. Arnett Gourley, Director Dist. No. 3	Reidsville
Rev. T. L. Sasser, Pastor Advisor	Greensboro

PROGRAM COMMITTEE

J. Ben Eller, Chairman	Greensboro

L. Grady Burgiss	Greensboro
Harry O. Wester	Greensboro

ORDAINED MINISTERS NOT PASTORS

Barnes, O. F.	Greensboro
Barton, C. D.	Greensboro
Bennett, Hubert	Greensboro
Biles, T. H., Chaplain	U. S. Army
Billings, H. P.	Jamestown
Blanchard, Henry N., Chaplain	Greensboro
Boles, J. H.	Greensboro
Bray, Sgt. Thomas E.	Fort Bragg
Coe, C. G.	Pamona
Diggs, Capt. Harold C., Chaplain	U. S. Army
Dix, O. P.	High Point
Farrington, D. H.	Colfax
Funderburk, 1st. Lt. Guy B., Chaplain	U. S. Army
Garner, John U., Chaplain	U. S. Army
Gatewood, J. C.	Greensboro
Gillespie, Cr. A. S.	Wake Forest
Gillespie, J. C.	Reidsville
Havner, Dr. Vance	Greensboro
Hight, L. J.	Greensboro
Hutchins, Leo.	
Leonard, Dr. C. A., (Missionary)	Honolulu
Lewis, A. E.	Elon College
Matherly, W. T.	Greensboro
McDowell, Ben S.	High Point
Montgomery, Floyd, Chaplain	U. S. Army
Murray, J. F.	Reidsville
Oates, D. E.	Greensboro
Peedon, V. D.	Greensboro
Plybon, C. T.	Greensboro
Proctor, Mag. Gilmer, Jr., Chaplain	U. S. Army
Smith, J. H., Chaplain	U. S. Army
Smith, C. R.	Kernersville
Talley, Lt. (jg) C. O., Jr., Chaplain	U. S. Navy

MINISTERS ORDAINED DURING THE YEAR

Williamson, George E., (Bapt. Seminary) Seminary Hill, Texas

NEW PASTORS WELCOMED TO ASSOCIATION

Armstrong, Neil .... Steven's Memorial, Greensboro
Clemmons, D. M. .... Baptist Temple
Hutchins, Wilbur .... First, High Point
Hutchinson, Philip .... Webster Memorial, Greensboro
McGinnis, John M. .... First, Reidsville
Rainey, L. J. .... North Main St., High Point
Riddle, S. L. .... Revolution, Greensboro
Roberts, C. C. .... Pilot View, High Point
Stokes, H. M. .... Temple Baptist, High Point
Thompson, J. R. .... Florida Street, Greensboro

STUDENTS FOR THE MINISTRY

Carter, Felton .... P. B. T. S.
Coffee, Charles, (Bapt. Seminary .... Louisville, Ky.
Compton, Carl, (Bapt. Seminary) .... Louisville, Ky.
Dunevent, J. A. .... Reidsville
Hanner, Richard .... Bob Jones College
Harrison, James .... U. S. Navy
Holton, Billy Steed .... Guilford College
Lovin, Austin, (Bapt. Seminary) .... Louisville, Ky.
Ozement, Robert .... Greensboro
Pike, Wentworth .... Bob Jones College
Taylor, Robert .... High Point

Messengers

ALLEN JAY—T. Bennison, Robah Corder, P. E. White.
ANTIOCH—Roy Moore, Mrs. Roy Moore, Audrey Lovings.
BRIGHTWOOD—Mrs. C. M. McGehee, Mrs. G. B. Cocklereece, Mrs. Carl Ham, A. C. Maness.
CALVARY—Mrs. Bob Cole, Mrs. George Gunn, Mrs. J. E. McCargo.
COMMUNITY— Lester Landreth, T. M. Marsh, Mrs. Morgan, Mrs. Mamie Dodson.
FAIRMONT PARK—W. F. Thomas, O. E. Suan, W. R. Moose, T. E. Copple, Mrs. T. E. Copple, M. B. Fitzgerald, Mrs. A. L. McGee.
FAIRVIEW—Bernard B. Pearson, Mrs. R. E. DeLapp, Frances Sharon.
GIBSONVILLE—Thelma Riggins, E. C. Riggins, R. K. Craven.
GREENSBORO:
ASHEBORO STREET—F. L. Paschal, Mrs. A. C. Lowe, O. B. Teague, Mrs. Goodwin, Mrs. J. Ben Eller, Mrs. J. J. Norwood.
BAILEY MEMORIAL—C. C. Stanley, Mrs. C. C. Stanley, Mrs. E. J. Jarvis, Mrs. Bryant, Mrs. Roland Mitchell.
BESSEMER—W. P. Haynes, Mrs. R. F. Pace, C. L. Murray, Mrs. J. Frank Layton, Mrs. Ray W. Harrington.
COLLEGE PARK—Joe Howard, C. O. Weaver, P. R. Venabee, Laura Durant, B. B. Steward.
EDGEVILLE—Webster Mahaffey, R. L. Purett, Mrs. W. H. Lineberry, Ruth Greason, Mrs. D. B. Eaton.
ELLER MEMORIAL—Mrs. Melvin Caveness, Mrs. L. V. Matthews, Mrs. H. M. Angel, Wylie Patterson, Mrs. D. C. Morgan.
FIRST BAPTIST—C. S. Hodge, Mrs. E. T. Howell, Mrs. Nettie Hoge, Wilson Mitchell, Mrs. O. E. Lee.
FLORIDA STREET — C. H. Dodd, T. E. Trelove, Mrs. J. N. Reele.
LATHAM PARK—Mrs. C. J. Trull, Mrs. Charlie Bradley, Mrs.

Elizabeth Nelson, Mrs. Leslie Curl, Mrs. Hugh Lovings.

MAGNOLIA STREET—L. Grady Burgiss, T. L. Sasser, J. E. Poore, J. A. Lewis, Mrs. J. W. Fountain, Mrs. Odell Scott.

PAMONA—Mary Melvin, Mrs. Ada Folds, Mrs. W. G. Teague, Mrs. E. E. Henry, Vela Godwin.

REVOLUTION—Waldo Johnson, W. L. Parrolle, Grady Phillips, Mrs. Campbell Smith.

SIXTEENTH STREET—Willie Straughn, Fred Hester, Carrie Crutchfield, Mrs. W. M. Smith.

STEVENS MEMORIAL—H. E. Whitfield, Neil J. Armstrong, Mrs. H. E. Whitfield.

ABERNACLE—Mrs. J. L. Shonse, Mrs. E. C. Howard.

WEBSTER MEMORIAL—Mrs. A. Andrews, Paul Schaarschmidt, Phillip Hutchinson, Mrs. Paul Schaarschmidt.

GUILFORD — T. E. Kerley, Mrs. Hettie Kennerly, Mrs. B. F. Butler, Mrs. Setzer Weston.

HIGH POINT:

FIRST—W. W. Hutchins, Mrs. W. W. Hutchins, Thelma Patrich, Mrs. G. L. Asbury, Mrs. W. F. Clayton.

GREEN STREET—Mrs. J. S. Hopkins, Walter E. Crisman, P. P. Hartsell, A. M. Smith, Mrs. Walter Whaley, Mrs. J. L. Payne, Mrs. J. C. Saunders, Mrs. R. J. Winfrey, Mrs. R. L. Smith, Mrs. R. B. Culler.

HILLIARD MEMORIAL — Mrs. C. H. Hedrick, Mrs. J. B. Ellis, Mrs. O. E. Hampton, H. B. Chatman, Mrs. G. W. Underwood.

NORTH MAIN STREET—Mrs. Alice Davis, Mrs. Ed Crisco, Mrs. Bessie Teague, Mrs. J. W. Ledwell, Mrs. S. J. O'Neal.

NORTH PARK—Mrs. D. H. Short, Mrs. R. A. Davis, Mrs. J. L. Jones.

SOUTHSIDE — Mrs. J. S. Cameron, Mrs. George Tate, Mrs. C. R. Salty.

WEST END—Mrs. T. D. Hedrick, Mrs. R. R. Jackson, Mr. C. M. Scott.

JESSUP GROVE—Rev. and Mrs. James E. Wiggs, Mrs. D. H. Bryson, Miss Dora Mason, Eugene Mason, Mrs. Ruth Lewis.

JEWELL—Marvin Strutts, Lloyd Gurley, Walter Trotter.

LEBANON—Mrs. Cleo Whitley, Mrs. S. R. Coleman, Miss

Marylin Taylor, Mrs. Nellie Talley, Miss Maggie Kirkman.

OAK GROVE—W. L. Shackleford, Mrs. Henry Holder, A. L. Saunders, Mrs. A. L. Saunders, Mrs. J. E. Rodgers.

OSCEOLA—Mr. and Mrs. Frank Huffines, Mrs. O. O. Whicker, D. A. Greene, T. J. Brooks.

OSSIPEE—H. D. Smith, Mrs. Jennie Steele, A. E. Lewis.

PILOT VIEW—Mrs. V. E. Webb, Mrs. Ruby Waggoner, Mrs. Fletcher.

PINE GROVE—R. L. Tuttle, Mrs. R. L. Tuttle, Mrs. R. A. Pickard, Mrs. L. R. Loflin, Mrs. E. H. Eller.

PISGAH—Mrs. Ray Liner, Mrs. Charlie Weaver, Mrs. D. H. Grubb, Mr. Bill Moore, Mrs. L. C. Madden.

PLEASANT GARDEN—Mrs. Dixon, Mrs. G. T. Burton, Mrs Thompson.

PLEASANT GROVE—F. M. Atkins, Mrs. W. H. Smith, Mrs F. M. Atkins, Mrs. D. V. Ward, Mrs. D. R. Robertson.

REEDY FORK—Mrs. Ernest Kivett, Mrs. Lester Canter, Mrs. Ella Harris, Elijah Lankford.

REIDSVILLE:

BAPTIST TEMPLE—Mr. Bert Elliot, Mrs. Bert Elliot, Mrs. Jesse Carter, Mrs. Pink King.

FIRST—Mrs. R. H. Pleasants, Mrs. J. C. Tatem, Mrs. Houston Saunders.

PENN MEMORIAL—D. W. Overby, Mrs. W. B. Gosney, Mrs. George Pennington.

ROCKY KNOLL—Mrs. C. F. Cooper, Mrs. G. A. Tucker, Mr. and Mrs. Laughlin, Mrs. Joe Spoon.

RUFFIN STACY—C. L. Schrum, Dewey London, John Childers, J. T. London.

SMITH GROVE—J. C. Pitts, Walter Westmoreland, Mrs. Wilma Fairrington, Mrs. Virginia Westmoreland, Mrs. Dora Clark.

SUMMERFIELD—Mr. and Mrs. A. J. Ayers, Mr. Robert Forbes.

TEMPLE—H. M. Stokes, Mrs. R. L. Rodden, Mrs. Wagner, Mr. Yarborough, Mrs. Hanes.

Constitution

ARTICLE 1.—The Association shall be called the Piedmont Baptist Association.

ARTICLE 2.—It shall be composed of the ordained ministers who are members of, and those who may have pastoral charges within the Associational District, and three delegates from each Church in the district aforesaid, and Churches having a membership exceeding 300 shall be entitled to one additional delegate for every 200 members or fraction thereof in excess of 300.

ARTICLE 3.—The said delegates shall, before taking their seats, produce letters from respective Churches showing their appointment as delegates.

ARTICLE 4.—The Associational session shall be held at least once a year.

ARTICLE 5.—The officers shall be a Moderator, Vice-Moderator, Clerk and Treasurer. If deemed expedient by the Association, the offices of Clerk and Treasurer may be combined.

ARTICLE 6.—The officers of the Association shall be chosen annually by the Association.

ARTICLE 7.—Association shall be clothed with authority only to advise the Churches touching all things pertaining to their interest but shall in no case presume to direct or control them in reference to their own government or internal policy

ARTICLE 8.—A Committee of arrangements, consisting of three members shall be appointed on the first day of each session to prepare and report the proceedings and suggest topics proper for the consideration and action of the next annual Association. It shall be the duty of this committee to outline and publish a program for the next annual Associational meeting or for any special or called meeting of the Association.

ARTICLE 9.—Baptist brethren, not members of the Association, who may be present at any session of the body, may on invitation by the the body, take seats and participate in the debates of the Association.

ARTICLE 10.—

Section 1. The territory of the Association shall be divided into not less than three districts.

Section 2. A committeee composed of the Moderator, the Vice-moderator, the Clerk of the Association, the Associational W M. U. Superintendent, the Associational Sunday School Superintendent, the Associational B. T. U. Director, and twelve other members of churches in the Association, giving fair representation to the three districts, shall constitute the Executive Committee of the Association. This committee at its first meeting shall decide the number required for a quorum.

Section 3. Seven of the members of the Executive Committee shall be named by the Association as members of the Church Advisory and Missions Committee.

Section 4 The duties of the Executive Committee are to act for the Association between the annual sessions of the Association. The Church Advisory and Missions Committee is charged with the task of seeking the cooperation of churches in the ordination of ministers, the location and organization of new churches, and the management of the Associational Mission Program in our Association.

ARTICLE 11.—All committees shall be appointed by the Moderator, either directly or indirectly with the approval of the Association, unless otherwise authorized by the Association from time to time.

ARTICLE 12.—The Constitution may be altered only at an Annual session of the Association and by a vote of two-thirds of the whole present.

ARTICLE 13.—The rules of this body shall follow Mell's Parliamentary Practice.

ARTICLE 14.—This Association shall cooperate with the Baptist State Convention.

ARTICLE 15.—The time of the holding of the annual session shall begin on Wednesday before the fourth Sunday in October of each year, except where prevailing conditions make it advisable to change this date, in which event the Executive Committee shall be empowered to determine the date of meeting.

Adopted October 17, 1895.

Article 2, 5, 6, 10, 15 Amended Session, July 23, 24, 1930.

Article 15 Amended Session July 21, 1932.

Article 10 Amended Sessions October 23, 24, 1935.

Articles 8, 10, 11 Amended Sessions October 23, 24, 1940

Article 10 Amended Session October 19, 1944.

———o———

Proceedings

of the

FIFTY-FIRST ANNUAL SESSION

of the

PIEDMONT BAPTIST ASSOCIATION

Held With he

FIRST BAPTIST CHURCH

Greensboro, N. C.

October 19, 1944.

THURSDAY MORNING SESSION—9:30 A. M.

1. The Association was called to order at 9:30 a. m. by Moderator Grover H. Jones and Joined in singing "Our Best" and "Stand Up For Jesus," led by Harry O. Wester, High Point; C. S. Hodge, Greensboro, accompanist. After reading the second chapter of Jeremiah, Rev. James R. Thompson, Florida Street Baptist Church, led the invocation.

2. Moderator Jones recognized Dr. J. Clyde Turner, pastor of the host church, who welcomed the Association.

3. The moderator appointed the following:

Committee on Committees: W. W. Woodcock, chm., D. W. Overby, and J. S. Hopkins.

4. The Committee reported, and the printed program was adopted.

5. Vice Moderator J. Ben Eller presiding—the moderator reporting using the Church Letter Digest, and report was adopted.

6. The Sunday School report given by C. S. Hodge, and adopted. The report was spoken to by C. S. Hodge.

SUNDAY SCHOOL REPORT

One year ago you elected me as Associational Sunday School Superintendent. Soon after the first of the year the new organization was set up after a lapse of two years and Quarterly meetings have been held, more than 40 Sunday Schools being represented at the Spring meeting.

The reports of the Sunday Schools this year show that 52 Schools have an enrollment of 14,654, as compared with last year when 55 Schools reported an enrollment of 15,728. The average attendance this year has been 7,335, about 50 per cent of the enrollment and just the average over the South. When we consider the thousands from our Schools in armed services, these figures compare rather favorably.

Some indication of the work of the Sunday School may be gathered from the report of baptisms from the Schools, which was about 500 this year. Another indication of work is the record of Study Course Awards According to the record in the office in Raleigh, 14 churches held study classes last year with 348 awards. First Church High Point led in number of awards with 102.

As far as we can learn, 20 Vacation Bible Schools were held, as compared with 12 last year. There were 2,248 enrolled, an average of 113.

The year 1945 promises to be one of the greatest in Baptist history. The goal of "a million souls for Christ" places added responsibility on the Sunday School, from which fully 80 per cent of the baptisms come. If the goal is to be reached in our Association, our Sunday Schools must win and baptize next year about 2,500 instead of about 500 reported this year. This stupendous task calls for the combined efforts and prayers of us all.

Respectfully submitted,
C. S Hodge, Asso. Supt.

7. The Baptist Training Union report read by Miss Thelma Patrick, and the report was adopted. Miss Mabel Starnes spoke to the report.

Dr. John McGinnis read nominations for the B. T. U. Associational officers for the year, and they were elected.

REPORT ON BAPTIST TRAINING UNION

The close of the Associational year found the Training Union of the Piedmont Association an A-1 organization.

Regular quarterly meetings were held with programs planned

by the Executive Committee headed by Mr. J. Carl Bell, Director. Five new training unions have been organized.

Since November 1, 1943 study courses have been conducted in 28 churches A total of 996 awards have been issued to those completing these studies.

The twenty-fourth annual session of the Training Union was held in Greensboro on April 1, 1944. At this session 490 were in attendance at the banquet. This was the largest attendance on record. In an address following the banquet Dr. A. S. Gillespie, recently returned from China, held the group spellbound. At the conclusion a great host of the young people signified their desire to live a life of service for Christ.

The Association stood well in the Annual Training Union contests Miss Madeline Phillips of Asheboro Street Church, Greensboro, won first place in the Southside Better Speakers' Tournament. Miss Wilma Jones of the same church was winner of the State Intermediate Sword Drill. Miss Doris Craven and Mr. Robert Prince of First Church, High Point, were winners in the State Junior Memory Work Drill.

At the various Training Union weeks at Ridgecrest during the summer, there were more than 200 from this Association in attendance.

While the year just past has seen some accomplishments in the Training Union work of the Association, it is the desire of this organization that the year ahead may show worthwhile advancement in the service of the Master.

Respectfully submitted,
Julia M. Liles, Secretary

---

8. The Committee on Committees reported, making a motion to amend article No. 10 of the Baptist Piedmont Associational Constitution, and report was adopted.

9. The W. M. U. report read by Mrs. J. Ben Eller. Mrs. Nettie H. Hoge spoke to the report. Report adopted.

W. M. U. REPORT

The Piedmont Association is composed of the churches of Guilford and Rockingham counties and is considered one of the largest and best Associations in the State. The W. M. U. has a full quota of efficient and loyal officers. These meet in a quarterly session to pray and plan for progress and in cooperation with other like organizations over the state and southland.

The W. M U. follows the calendar year of four quarters. In

1943 Piedmont W. M. U. lacked only 2 points in its effort to attain the A-1 Standard of Excellence.

In January, we observed W. M. U. Leadership Day at Asheboro Street Church, Greensboro. Conferences on each phase of W. M. U. work were held and each society was presented with a Standard of Excellence Chart to stimulate better and more careful work. The Chairmen were introduced to the delegation. They became people instead of names. As a result, all year reports have been coming in on time and with increases along every line.

On April 20, the Annual Meeting was held at College Park Church, Greensboro. Only 23 churches sent delegates with the small attendance 115. Miss Olive Lawton, China, and Miss Kathryn Abee, Raleigh, were our guest missionary and official representative. The program was unique and planned to inform and inspire

In July, Piedmont W. M. U. sent two delegates to the Interracial Institute held at Shaw University and, also, paid the expense of sending two negro women from Greensboro. The meeting was adjudged to be of very high inspiration and a worthy "Good Neighbor Project."

In August, at Ridgecrest, delegates from Business Womens' Circles over the southland came together for a great Conference. Your superintendent and two young ladies from Greensboro attended. These came back from their mountain-top experience to the valley of service and organized the first B. W. C. Federation in the state on September 28. Their purpose is to encourage many other business women to use their talents to help promote Christ's Kingdom on Earth through the channels of W. M. U.

The Biblical Recorder prints the quarterly reports on gifts and intelligent members check their societies and compare results for themselves. The past four quarters, all gifts totaled $34747.22.

Mission Study among the societies has been given a recent boost by the simultaneous schools of missions promoted by Missionary T. L Sasser.

Stewardship awaits our most earnest efforts and unfailing support in October and November when each society should have a church Stewardship Night with young and old alike having part.

Community Missions is gaining ground in the thinking and plannings of our women. The final end of our services is to win someone to Christ. If every woman will win one other to Christ the Centennial Crusade for souls will soon become a reality. There is much work yet to be done by W. M. U. in our honored Association. Some 15 or 16 churches without active, promptly-reporting, missionary societies, offer every pastor and every loyal missionary-hearted woman a challenge in service to Christ. Only 8 of the 55 churches in Piedmont have full graded unions. Many churches have too few junior organizations, and many needlessly let these organizations languish and die.

There are 39 active W. M. S. and 56 junior organizations at present. Our three A-1 societies for 1943 were High Point First Church W. M. S.; High Point Green Street Church Y. W. A and G. A. These waiting to see how many more will make the grade in '44.

Women, we are "Laborers together with God." "That the generations to come might know." Let us pledge ourselves to a more constant and more faithful endeavor to live up to our high calling in Christ Jesus

Respectfully submitted,
Mrs. J. Ben Eller, Asso. Supt.

———o———

10. The report of Committee on Committees presented and adopted.

REPORT OF COMMITTEE ON COMMITTEES

COMMITTEE ON PLACE AND PREACHER: Wade H. James, R. R. Saunders, T. C. Robbins

COMMITTEE ON RESOLUTIONS: J. Huber Dixon, C M. Floyd, D. M. Clemmons

AUDITING COMMITTEE: C. M. Scott, J. C. Shore, Miss Mabel Starnes.

PROGRAM COMMITTEE: J. Ben Eller, L. Grady Burgiss, Harry O Wester.

COMMITTEE TO NOMINATE OFFICERS: J. Clyde Turner, B. G. Leonard, J. C. Gillespie.

COMMITTEE TO NOMINATE EXECUTIVE COMMITTEE AND CHURCH ADVISORY COMMITTEE: R. R. Jackson, Ray W. Harrington, Raymond Kincaid.

COMMITTEE TO NOMINATE MESSENGERS TO THE BAPTIST STATE CONVENTION: Wilbur W Hutchins, A. L. McGee, T. B. Clifton.

Respectfully submitted,
Wilson Woodcock, Chairman
J. S. Hopkins
D. W. Overby

11. The clerk called the roll of churches. 53 of the 55 churches were represented. 318 messengers were recognized.

12. The report of obituaries by I. E. Kerley was adopted.

The Association stood one minute in silent prayer in memory of the deceased.

OBITUARIES

In the churches of the Piedmont Association ninety-nine members departed this life during the past year. These included one pastor, one deacon and ten service men. These ninety and nine left the fields we trust, to live in the fold with the Great Shepherd of the sheep, to abide in the house of the Lord forever.

We can say with Paul that they, benig absent from the body, are present with the Lord. It is better for them to depart, if their trust be in Christ Jesus.

Too, the living shall not precede them in glory, for "the dead in Christ shall rise first, then we which are alive and remain shall be caught up into the clouds to meet the Lord in the air; and so shall we ever be with the Lord." (I Thessalonians 4:16-17).

Respectfully submitted,
I. E. Kerley

13. Visitors were recognized.

14. Rev. T. L. Sasser introduced all pastors of the Association including the new-comers.

15. Two churches, McLeansville, and Friendly with representatives seeking admission into the Association.

16. While standing, the Association sang, "On Jordan's Stormy Banks."

17. The Associational Missions reported by T. L. Sasser, who spoke to his report. The report was adopted.

REPORT ON ASSOCIATIONAL MISSIONS

The churches of Piedmont Baptist Association are located in the area taking in Guilford and about half of Rockingham counties. Forty-seven of the fifty-five churches are in Guilford and eight are in Rockingham. Available dependable figures from federal, connty and city governments, and the church statistics of all local denominations yield the following:

In Guilford and half of Rockingham counties 186,719 (Federal census 1940)

Church Members in this area (counting all denominations and all races) 78,419 (42 per cent of population)

Non-Members of Church (including people who, if they are members anywhere, have not become members here) 108,300 (58 percent of population)

Members of local Baptist Churches 17,610 (22 per cent of all church members in this area)

Members of Other denominations 60,809 (78 per cent of all church members in this area)

Baptist Prospects 23,826 (22 per cent of 108,300)

Add to the Baptist prospects the unknown number who have no church preference and all others who should hear the Gospel of salvation and we have a reasonable estimate of the field of Piedmont Associational missions.

Looking at the number of church members only one marvels at the great achievement of winning and enlisting so large number. It is beyond the limits of our imagination to picture what conditions might have prevailed had there been no evangelistic fervor, no efforts, and no churches in this territory.

But there is much yet to be possessed. A study of the latest surveys reveals many hundreds of Baptists living near, or in reach of, the churches whose memberships have been left at their former places of residence. Many of them were doubtless active and useful members of their churches until they moved from their church communities. To re-enlist them is a big task and an important one.

Despite the fact that we have fifty-five churches there are still thousands of people of Baptist persuasion, inclination and preference who are unattached to any church or Sunday School. It follows that we are not as efficient as we should be or we do not have enough churches or mission stations to reach and hold the people. The solution is to strengthen what we have and establish others also. The number of laborers for the harvest must be multiplied. This is the objective and the task of Associational missions.

A summary of a year's work by the Associational missionary toward this objective follows:

Days spent on the field 342. On other fields 23.

Miles traveled 10,685

Visits to communities 295

Communities surveyed 22

Conferences on work 516

Committee meetings attended 48.

New church organization assisted in 1

Number pieces literature distributed 1500

Circular letters prepared and sent out 1790

Visits to churches 191
Letters to individuals 177
Subscriptions secured for Southern Baptist Home Missions 173
Classes taught 48
Sermons and addresses 219

Simultaneous schools of missions were held in thirty-nine churches of the Association the week of September 17-22. Nineteen foreign and nine home missionaries and two army chaplains delivered 234 addresses in the churches during the week. The number enrolled in the mission study classes in addition to the Sunday congregations who heard the missionaries was 1723.

RECOMMENDATION:—It is hereby recommended that each church of the Association have an authorized missions committee to work with the general missions committee of the Association.

Respectfully submitted,
T. L. Sasser

---

18. Southern Baptist Centennial report made by T. L. Sasser and adopted.

REPORT ON THE SOUTHERN BAPTIST CENTENNIAL

For several years Southern Baptists have been considering plans for a worthy observance in 1945 of their hundred years of history. In the 1944 Convention the messengers were made seriously aware of the imperative necessity of a new emphasis on evangelism. Plans were made to endeavor prayerfully and devotedly to win 1,000,000 souls to Christ in the year 1945. The centennial meeting of the Convention May 8-13 will be keyed to this objective. Our Association's co-operative part in the centennial is to support whole-heartedly the whole work of the Southern Baptist Convention which will include renewed efforts in evangelism.

The Home Mission Board was instructed by the Convention to promote the movement to win a million souls. The Board has asked and secured Dr. M. E. Dodd's leadership in this big task. The various Southern, State, and Associational boards and committees will carry forward the plans. The vital leadership and personnel to do the work are of course in the local churches. To the churches the denominational agencies are suggesting a calendar of activities for the year as follows:

Sunday, December 31, 1944. A day of contrition, confession and consecration in all the churches and services.

January, 1945. Week of Prayer in all churches for all. Month of Bible study with a view to soul-winning.

February. Planning and organization month. Evangelistic meetings in colleges. Evangelistic conferences.

March-April. City and Association-wide evangelistic crusades. Enlistment of unaffiliated Baptist members. Evangelistic conferences.

May-June. Evangelistic meetings in the churches. Promote evangelism through Sunday School and Training Union, W. M. U. and Vacation Bible School organizations.

July-August-September. Rural church meetings. Extension meetings to evangelize outlying districts.

October-November. Gleanings months. Reaching places not yet evangelized. Supplemental meetings in churches and institutions.

December. Enlistment month for all members, new and old, for the completion of the task and to prepare for the following year.

Literature carrying suggestions in detail is being prepared and will be available shortly. The general denominational committee earnestly requests the prayers of the churches for divine guidance and power, and for the scriptural co-operation in reaching the objective.

It is hereby recommended that this Association approve the general plan and affirm our purpose to co-operate in the movement by doing our full part in organizing for, and setting forward, this evangelistic work in 1945.

Respectfully submitted,
T. L. Sasser

19. Wilbur W. Hutchins brought words of greeting from Clarence A. Smith, and Dr. A. B. Conrad.

The Clerk L. Grady Burgiss, was instructed to reciprocate messages of greeting to them.

20. T. L. Sasser was commended by the Association for the fine work in the promotion of the Associational School of Missions.

21. The hymn, "Draw Me Nearer" was sung.

22. After Scripture reading, Luke 23: 33-53, and prayer led by Wade H. James, Greensboro, the Associational sermon was preached by the appointee, George H. Wallace, High Point. Theme: "The Place Called Calvary."

23. The closing prayer was led by Charles E. Parker, Bap-

tist Hospital, Winston-Salem.

AdJourned until afternoon Session.

THURSDAY AFTERNOON SESSION

24. The Association assembled at two o'clock, vice moderator, J. Ben Eller in the chair. "All Hail the Power of Jesus Name" was included in the song service conducted by C. S. Hodge, and Mrs. O. E. Lee, accompanist. D. M. Clemmons conducted the devotional, reading Luke 12:13-20, and leading the Association in prayer.

25. The following report on Christian Literature was made by L. J. Rainey, High Point, and adopted. Dr. L. L. Carpenter spoke to the report.

THE REPORT ON DENOMINATIONAL LITERATURE

"As a man thinketh in his heart, so is he." What one reads has a great deal to do with what one thinks; and what one thinks has much to do with what one is or *does*. Since this is true, our churches should not fail to encourage their members to read good Christian literature, and especially Baptist Christian literature.

We place first on the list of Baptist Christian literature the Bible, and especially the New Testament, our Baptist creed. Every individual should have his own Bible and he ought to read it prayerfully every day. He should seek the aid of the Holy Spirit to help him understand it and to live it.

Next on the list should be the Biblical Recorder. It is our State Baptist paper. It is a splendid Christian publication, and should be read by every Baptist. It should be in every home among their members. The rate is $1.20 per year per home. Other churches are offering it to their members on the Club Plan for $1.50 per year. A great many churches have done nothing to assist their people in getting this Christian paper. We recommend more reading of the Biblical Recorder by our people.

We are proud of our Baptist orphanage, but the majority of our churches do not give it the proper financial support that they should. "Charity and Children," the weekly publication of our orphanage, by informing our people, will cause them to become more interested in the Mills Home and the Kennedy Home, and all the work of our Baptist orphanage. We recommend a club of "Charity and Children" in every Sunday School.

We commend to the churches and to our people the use of the following Baptist literature:

1. The Sunday School and B. T. U. literature and many books published by our Sunday School board.

2. The mission magazines published by the W. M. U.

3. The "Home Missions" published by the Home Mission Board.

4. and, "The Commission" published by the Foreign Mission Board.

With this abundance of good material, our people need not lack for information and inspiration of good Christian literature. In fact, the church should see to it that no one perishes for lack of Christian knowledge.

Respectfully submitted.
L. J. Rainey

26. The following report on Christian Education was mdae bv Miss Maxine Garner, and adopted. Mrs. R. Bruce Wilkins, Durham, spoke to the report.

REPORT ON CHRISTIAN EDUCATION

According to the latest State Convention report, Christian Education work in the churches and in the colleges has not been critically crippled by the war. In both divisions there have been, of course, changes in personnel. Every officer in the Sunday School, Training Union, and student work labors in the terrible knowledge that those who will make tomorrow's world are themselves being made by the world we are giving them today.

Seventy-one Associations had the benefit of a Sunday School leadership conference last year. More than five hundred Vacation Bible Schools were held. Seven hundred schools were planned for the present year. Indiations at the beginning of the year were that ten thousand persons will receive Sunday School training awards in 1944. Work is going forward to increase Sunday School attendance throughout the state even in this year of war.

Ten regional conventions are reported by the Training Union division. Southwide Training Union leaders participated in two training meetings in the state last year. Plans for the current year include an emphasis on spiritual growth to promote a consciousness of world brotherhood.

Baptist student work in the colleges of the state grows apace under the guidance of R. T. Howerton, Jr. Piedmont Baptists will be interested in the coming of Miss Laura Durant as student secretary to the Woman's College of the University of North Carolina. Miss Durant, a native af Alabama, comes from Atlanta, Georgia, to succeed Mrs. Laura Bateman Lawrence, now on the staff of

First Church, Raleigh. Miss Cleo Mitchell who is well remembered for her work at Woman's College and was more recently connected with Meredith College is now Mrs. R. H. Edwin Espy of 31 Washington Square West, New York City. The student department in general assists the churches and the colleges in developing leadership and commitment among young Baptists in the state.

Each of these departments merit the most lavish support that we can provide. It is recommended that each pastor urge his people to strengthen these forces for good in our midst.

Respectfully submitted,
Maxine Garner

27. The following report on State Missions, and the Co-operative Program was made by J. S. Hopkins, High Point, and adopted. The report was spoken to by M. A. Huggins.

REPORT ON STATE MISSIONS AND THE COOPERATIVE PROGRAM

Surely every informed Baptist in North Carolina rejoices over the splendid progress our Convention has made in the field of State Missions in recent years. Limited space forbids any attempt in this report to review this progress in detail. In view of this fact, only a comprehensive statement as to State Mission activities is given which includes the following: (1) General Missionaries, (2) Associational Missionaries, (3) Aid to Missionary Pastors, (4) Aid on Buildings and in the Purchase of Lots, (5) Teaching and Training as carried on by the Sunday School, Training Union and Student Union Divisions, (6) Ministry to Other Races, the Negro and the Indian, (7) Ministry to the Sick in State Institutions, (8) Promotion of Schools and Conferences for Pastors, (9) Promotion of Work in and around Military Camps, (10) Support of Allied Church League, (11) General Mission Work not included in the above.

As to the Co-operative Program, it is growing in favor with our people all the time. The increase in gifts this year is about 20 per cent over last year, and will exceed last year's total perhaps $100,000 by the end of the calendar year. Hundreds of churches are accepting increased goals for 1945. Our goal for the State is one million dollars. The goal for our Association is $104,625. This is certainly within our reach with all our churches whole-heartedly cooperating.

The Southern Baptist Convention will celebrate the one hundredth anniversary of its organization May 1945. A great program is being prepared, and a Centennial Crusade is being launched seeking to complete, celebrate, climax, and crown the century for Christ.

In promotion of this great crusade all our people are urged to give full-length cooperation. All the causes, state and southwide, are included; the distribution of funds will be according to the Cooperative Program percentages. The southwide all inclusive Centennial goal is ten million dollars which is approximately double the receipts of last year. The states will suggest corresponding goals for state causes and institutions.

To help realize those high and holy objectives we call upon all churches and people:

1. To magnify the Cooperative Program for the financial support of all our work.

2. To make the Centennial Crusade with all of its objectives, state, southwide, and world-wide a matter of constant prayer and effort.

3. To observe the special days and seasons as listed in the Calendar of Denominational Activities.

4. To put on the Every Member Canvass prayerfully, patiently, and persistently seeking to enlist all our people in the larger support of all our work.

5. To stress Christian stewardship and to enroll as tithers all who will contribute at least one-tenth of their net income to the Lord's work.

6. To take the great Centennial Thank offering on April 15 or nearest convenient Sunday for the causes included in the Cooperative Program to help in the strengthening and enlarging of our work and for worthily CROWNING A CENTURY FOR CHRIST.

Respectfully submitted,
Julian S. Hopkins

28. The report on the Baptist Hospital was read by Dr. J. Clyde Turner in the absence of Mrs. Turner, and adopted. The report was spoken to by Charles E. Parker.

THE BAPTIST HOSPITAL

The Baptist Hospital in Winston-Salem was established to meet a very definite need in the ministry of Baptists to the people of North Carolina. Its aim has ever been to furnish a Christian ministry to those who are sick in body, and especially to those who are unable to meet the expenses of such sickness. This ministry has been greatly blessed. The hospital has been enlarged, and yet, with increased facilities, it is always overcrowded and has a waiting list.

When Wake Forest Medical School was moved to Winston-Salem, it became closely associated with the hospital, and, with its staff of highly trained specialists it has increased the ministry of the hospital. Dr. Lynch, in his report, says: "We now have an institution that is equipped, and provides the medical talent to care for practically any illness that may be encountered. We are happy to report the addition to the staff during the year of a brain surgeon."

The hospital is now fully approved by the American College of Surgeons and has the approval of the American Medical Association for the training of internes and advanced courses along many lines.

In June, 1943, Mr. Ray E. Brown was elected administrator, thus relieving Mr. Hagaman from routine duties that he might be able to contact the Baptist constituency in the interest of the hospital.

In [illegible] more than ten thousand patients were treated. Of this number more than three thousand were service patients. It was largely to meet the need of this group that the hospital was founded, and it is still this group which appeals most keenly to the Baptist people. For the care of this group our Mother's Day offering is used. This year the goal for the offering was $150,000. Of this amount, $75,000 was designated for use of service patients, while all over this amount was to be applied to the debt on the hospital. The offering exceeded $90,000, including linens from various organizations. This is our largest offering for this work and is evidence of the appreciation of the work of the hospital.

There are 119 nurses enrolled. Or this number, 101 are "cadet nurses," that is, they receive certain expenses for their training from the government in consideration of their needed service in the present emergency. At present the home for the nurses is being enlarged.

Many are the expressions of appreciation and approval that have come from patients treated in the hospital. These have come, not only from Baptists, but from those of other denominations. We rejoice in this ministry, in the high standards our hospital has attained, and in its enlarged service. We covet for it even greater usefulness. To this end we urge your continued support and your constant prayers that it may be kept true to the purpose that brought it into being.

Respectfully submitted,
Mrs. J .Clyde Turner

---

29. The following report on the Orphanage was presented by Frank Paschal, and adopted. R. D. Covington, Treasurer of the Home, spoke to the report.

REPORT ON ORPHANAGE

The heart of every loyal Baptist in North Carolina swells with pride whenever the splendid record of the Baptist Orphanage of North Carolina is reviewed.

The Orphanage maintains two homes, The Mills Home in Thomasville, and The Kennedy Home near Kinston. These are not two Orphanages, but are the two homes of the Baptist Orphanage. Each of these two homes has a Superintendent, but neither has a separate treasurer, for the Orphanage treasurer handles all of the finances of both homes. Our beloved Dr. I. G. Greer is General Superintendent of the Orphanage and Mr. R. D. Covington is the efficient treasurer, and their offices are in Thomasville located on the Mills Home grounds.

The Orphanage cares for a large number of children in the two homes, several in boarding homes and in their own homes. A large number of the boys and girls are now in military service of the United States and some are giving a good account of themselves at the front, giving their last full measure of devotion and loyalty to the land and country which they love.

Many of the Sunday Schools in our Baptist Churches in North Carolina have one Sunday per month as Orphanage day and the offerings for that day are remitted direct to the Orphanage Treasurer in Thomasville. Practically all of the Churches have the special Thanksgiving offering to be applied exclusively for the Orphanage which is highly commended, and is a practice which should be followed universally by all of our Churches. Many Churches have placed the Orphanage on a percentage basis in their budget from which a remittance is made at the end of each calendar month which is also a systematic and proportionate method of making regular contributions to the Orphanage, and this practice is to be highly commended and is probably a better method than having the once a month collection.

We are exceedingly fortunate in having as executives and leaders in charge of these Homes, men and women who are not only well trained, but who are outstanding Christians. They are carrying on the work in such a splendid manner in caring for our fine boys and girls. They provide not only good training and religious instruction, but they also provide from the farms of the institution themselves and from the different farming sections of North Carolina, the best of selected foods. Splendid medical care and attention is given to every boy and girl, and the health record of the children is excellent. Charity and Children published once a week at Thomasville brings us the news of their activities

This situation challenges us, therefore, to give of our very best to this great cause, and we should make a special effort for the ensuing year to have every Baptist Church in North Carolina give regular and systematic support. In so doing, we will be carrying out the sublime words of Jesus, when he said: "Suffer little children to come unto me and forbid them not, for of such is the Kingdom."

Respectfully submitted,

Frank L. Paschal

30. The following report on Social Service was presented by Walter Crissman. Mr. Crissman spoke to his report. L. A. Martin, Lexington, also spoke to the report. A motion to amend this report to approve, and favor the program of the Allied Church Movement of this state was adopted.

REPORT ON SOCIAL SERVICE

The first two sentences of last year's report still apply. They are as follows: "Any program for the promotion of Social Service must be related to the serious condition now prevailing in the world. Mankind is in the midst of a dark and dangerous period."

What should worry and concern us is that there seems to be no Social Service program among our Churches. Therefore, this is not a report, for I can find nothing worthy of a report.

Yes, desecration of the Sabbath, divorce, broken homes, evils of alcohol, parent and juvenile delinquency, immorality among girls and married women are all still with us, and present more serious problems now than they did a year ago. Is the fact that these problems have multiplied during the past year an indictment of the Church? What has the Church done about any of them? What is the Church doing today?

Our Churches have ministered unto only the very rare cases that have been brought to them. We have programs all right, perhaps too many, but we have no program which enables us to familiarize ourselves with the conditions in the homes, iin the communities where our Churches are supposed to render service.

Less than fifty percent of the ministers or pastors make any attempt to solve these social problems in the manner taught by precept and example by the lowly Nazarene. The other fifty percent do not have enough help in the Churches they serve to put on the needed programs. Pastor clinics or schools are needed, not to teach preachers how to preach, but to point out to them how the Master met the social problems of His day, and how those same simple methods are practical and powerful today.

Too many of us, preachers and laymen alike, have come to the view: "Here is the Church, the Preacher and the messages, come and get it. It is here for you." Christ "went about doing good." He went about in the neighborhood. He walked from house to house in the community, and from community to community. He saw how they lived. He learned their individual problems and He learned their family problems. He, therefore, knew how to approach and solve the problems. He took the Gospel to them.

The time has come for local Church Missionaries—Christlike visitors—if you please. The leaders of our Sunday School Board have been preaching visitation for a number of years. Some pastors have not considered this Sunday School program for the Church at all. Some Pastors and laymen have considered this program for the Sunday School but not practical for the Church. There may be a Church here and there that has caught the vision. Many of our larger Churches need a staff of missionaries, men and women who give their full time to visiting in the communities which should be ministered unto by the particular Church. Pastors need to give more heed to a systematic method of visitation. In our cieies and in our larger Churches there is so much danger of people being overlooked. I lay particular stress upon this visitation, because I think that the day has come when the peoples' faith in the Church must be restored and I know of no way to restore that faith other than to help with the social problems, and we'll not help with these problems unless we know about them.

People do not report their social and domestic problems. They are inclined to keep these problems smothered up and to themselves. Few have been close enough to the Pastor or to any persons of our Churches to confide in them. Local Church Missionaries.

or visitors, will get closer to these people and come in contact with the various problems. These Missionaries, if the right kind, will also encourage deacons and the ladies of the Missionary Union to do more visiting, to become more acquainted with the people in the various communities. This will restore faith in the Church and this will justify that faith in the Church. And there must be more God-called local Church missionaries if our Churches establish a social service program in keeping with Christ's plan. Pleas must be made among our membership for Christians to answer God's call to full time local Church missionary service. The whole life must be laid upon the altar in this field just as much as preaching.

Just having Sunday School, Worship Services, Training Union, Missionary Union and many meetings will not minister to the needs of our communities. Christ met needs, furnished the solution to problems of those around Him. A real Social Service Program by our Churches will in no manner conflict with the Welfare Department of our Counties. It is entirely a different problem. Many of those who need assistance of one nature or another most seriously, never go to the Welfare Agencies, and never will. They will never tell their troubles or admit the presence of problems, except to someone whom they recognize as having a heartful of love and the spirit of Christ within.

Yes, the problems are with us. We say we know it, but I doubt if we really do. We could point out many of the cases which have come to light in our experiences, but we do little about these isolated cases. Our program must generate and develop a genuine interest. It is such a program for which I plead. The lightening has been striking in various places ever since we can remember, but none of us take it very seriously, untli it strikes our home. I think it is time for our Churches to launch a definite Social Service Program, and I hope it will be done during this Associational year, so that a real report can bemade one year from now.

Respectfully submitted,
Walter E. Crissman

———o———

AMENDMENT TO SOCIAL SERVICE REPORT

Resolved that the Piedmont Baptist Association endorse the Allied Church League against alcohol, and recommend the organization of county units of this organization in Guilford and Rockingham counties.

31. RECOMMENDATION:

The Executive Committee recommended that the Clerk-treasurer be paid $100.00 annually including the Associational year 1943-44.

32. The following report of the Committee on Resolutions was adopted.

REPORT OF THE COMMITTEE ON RESOLUTIONS

Whereas, the Piedmont Baptist Association, meeting with the First Baptist Church of Greensboro, has engaged in a splendid session;

Be it Resolved:

First, that we express our gratitude to this church and its pastor, Dr. J. Clyde Turner, for the privilege of meeting here.

Second, that we express our appreciation to Mr. Grover H. Jones, our very efficient moderator, for his untiring efforts, in serving the Association throughout this year, also to Rev. L. Grady Burgiss for the splendid manner in which he has carried out the duties of clerk.

Third: That we commend the various organizations of the churches of the Association for their splendid support of the Baptist program.

Fourth: That we express our sincere thanks to the program committee for the wonderful program.

And be it resolved that we as followers of Christ give ourselves unreservedly to the cause of Christ in these uncertain times.

Respectfully submitted,
C. M. Floyd
D. M. Clemmons

---

33. The following report of the committee on time, place and preacher, was made and adopted.

REPORT OF COMMITTEE ON PLACE AND PREACHER

Place—To be left in the hands of the Executive Committee.
Preacher—Dr. John W. McGennis
Alternate—Rev. Ray W. Harrington

34. The committee to nominate officers of the Association submitted the following report, which was adopted.

Moderator ---------------------------------- Grover S. Jones
Vice Moderator ------------------------------ J. Ben Eller
Clerk-Treasurer ----------------------- Ray W. Harrington
Supt. of Asso. S. S. work ---------------------- C. S. Hodge

Dr. of Asso. Training Union ------------------- J. Carl Bell

J. C. Gillespie
B. G. Leonard
J. Clyde Turner

Committee

35. The following report of the church Advisory Committee was adopted.

The Advisory Committee of the Association recommends that the application of the McLeansville Baptist Church for admission into the Association be approved, and that action on application of the Friendly Church be deferred for one year.

36. The following reports—the Executive and Missions Committees—were made and adopted.

REPORT ON THE EXECUTIVE COMMITTEE

Dec. 31. 1943

1. Approved an appropriation of $360.00 from the State Board to Pleasant Garden Church, for pastoral help.

2. Approved an appropriation of $600.00 to College Park Church from the State Board.

3. Approved a motion to set up a fund of $25.00 for Clerk help.

Sept. 8, 1944.

1. Motion passed that a request for eight cents per member be continued to the churches for the General Fund.

REPORT OF MISSIONS COMMITTEE

Nov. 1, 1943

1. Motion that General Fund be apportioned to the churches on the basis of 8c member.

Nov. 27, 1943

1. Motion that Bro. Geo. Williamson be recommended to a presbytery for examination for the ministry.

2. Motion that the Committee approve the organization of a church at McLeansville.

3. Motion that supplement of $25.00 per month be paid to Rev. T. L. Sasser beginning as of Oct. 1, 1943.

Feb. 4, 1944

Feb. 4, 1944

1. Motion that Committee approve an appropriation of $200.00 to McLeansville Church for purchase of lot.

2. Motion that T. L. Sasser be paid $50.00 for Convention Expense.

Aug. 7, 1944

1. Motion that Committee recommend to Eller Mem. Church that Bro. Bill Kincaid be licensed as a minister of Gospel.

2. Motion that Committee recommends to Florida St. Church that Bro. Billy Holton be ordained to the ministry upon condition that he be called as pastor of a church, or that he enter the seminary.

Sept. 28, 1944

1. In view of the increased work placed upon the Clerk, a motion was passed recommending that the Asso. pay him an additional $50.00 for the Associational year of 1943-44.

37. The Clerk-Treasurer presented his annual report which was adopted.

REPORT OF TREASURER

I herewith submit my report for the period of time between Oct. 1, 1943 and 10:00 p. m. Oct. 18, 1944, which is as follows:

Balance on Hand Oct. 1,1943		$116.75
RECEIVED FROM THE CHURCHES:		
For Minutes and Clerk 1943	$261.56	
For General Fund, (Supplement)	973.84	
For School of Missions	893.62	
For General Fund (Since Sept. 18, 1944)	434.14	
	$2,563.16	
GROSS FUNDS		$2,679.91
PAID OUT:		
Supplement to T. L. Sasser, (13 months)	$325.00	
Remuneration of Clerk, Nov. 10, 1943	50.00	
Incidentals	82.79	
Clerk Help	11.10	
Printing Programs	5.00	
Printing of Minutes	168.20	
B. T. U. Work	25.00	
Convention Expense for T. L. Sasser	50.00	
Expense of School of Missions	966.59	
Total	$1,683.68	
BALANCE ON HAND 10:00 p. m. Oct. 18, 1944		$996.23
CONDITION OF FUNDS:		
In Bank	$990.96	
Check	12.50	

Currency	2.00
Change	1.31
Total	$1,006.77

A surplus of $10.54 exists, perhaps due to an unfound error.

Respectfully submitted,

L. Grady Burgiss, Treas.

38. Report of the Committee on Messengers to the State Baptist Convention was made and adopted.

MESSENGERS

H. O. Miller	High Point
W. W. Woodcock	Greensboro
D. M. Clements	Reidsville

Respectfully submitted,

W. Wilbur Hutchins
A. L. McGee
J. B. Clifton

39. The following report of the Auditing Committee was made and adopted.

REPORT OF AUDITING COMMITTEE

The Auditing Committee has examined the treasurer's books and found them to be as represented in his report.

Respectfully submitted,

J. C. Shore, Chm.
C. M. Scott
Miss Mabel Starnes

40. Dr. J. Clyde Turner led the closing prayer. The Association adJourned until the evening session.

THURSDAY—EVENING SESSION

41. The Association assembled at seven-thirty o'clock, Moderator Jones in the chair. "I Need Thee Every Hour" was led by C. S. Hodge, and the choir followed with "When I Survey the Wondrous Cross," and Dr. John McGinnis conducted the devotional reading Psalm 46 and leading in prayer.

42. The following report on Relief and Annuity was presented by H. O. Miller, and adopted.

REPORT ON MINISTERIAL RELIEF AND ANNUITY

We, your committee, beg to submit the following report on the work of the Relief and Annuity Board. The growth of this Board has been steady since it was founded in 1918. Its ministry of protection against old age and infirmity is offered to all those gainfully employed in our complex denominational life. Pastors, Missionaries, employees of state and southwide Boards, Orphanages, Hospitals, also faculties and staffs of Seminaries, and colleges are included in this protection.

During 1943 the Board collected $1,087,395.26, Benefits, Relief and Annuity during 1944 will aggregate $824,556.00. The total assets of the Board December 1943 was $6,771,184.31 June 1944 the assets were over $7,000,000.

The Board earned 4.22 per cent on its total investments for the year 1943. Its mortgage loans are amply protected by property value. It is confronted with the problem of low interest, but the finance committee is dilligently seeking to make the funds produce as much as possible, consistent with the safety of principal. The Board is actively supporting the war effort by purchasing U. S. Government Bonds. It now has $1,200,000 invested in these bonds.

The increased cotributions from the churches through the cooperative program during 1943 made it possible to give two extra checks to every one on the beneficiary roll, and no application for aid, properly attested, was denied. Receipts in this department went beyond $168,000, which was $48,000 more than the previous year. In addition to the above, the sum of $30,000 was added to the special relief fund, in anticipation of lean years in the post-war period. Twelve hundred aged workers, many of them with no other source of income, look to Southern Baptists and to the Relief fund of our Board.

Concerning the Ministers' Retirement Plan, Secretary Huggins reports this fund in good condition, there being 70 new applications between January and June of this year, bringing the total to 524 at that time. We are confident the number is much larger at this time. Most of these who are coming into the plan now are among the younger men, which adds strength to the plan. He further reports that the benefits paid on annuities, age, disability and widows, are far below the estimates made by the actuary. It is safe to say that during the last twelve months the interest on our invested funds, paid in by the churches, ministers, and the convention, has been sufficient to meet fully 50 per cent of all the benefits. This may not be true another year, as a number of the older men, who have been receiving larger salaries, will retire. At any rate we can see that this department is in excellent condition.

During the past year there were fifteen receiving Age annuity, four disability and five widows, receiving a total of $8,350.08. This was not a large sum, but it was a great comfort and help to the participants. We urge every pastor and church who have not done so to get into this worthy program as early as possible.

Respectfully submitted,
Hughey O. Miller

42. The following report on Southern Baptist Institutions was made by Ray W. Harrington and adopted.

SOUTHERN BAPTIST INSTITUTIONS

Like the experience of Israel is the situation of Southern Baptist theological education today. The training of religious workers had developed to the point that the school of the prophets had outgrown its bounds: "And the sons of the prophets said unto Elisha, Behold now, the place where we dwell with thee is too straight for us. Let us go, we pray thee, unto Jordon, and take thence every man a beam, and let us make us a place there, where we may dwell. And he answered, Go ye." (II Kings 6:1-2.) In ancient days, the prophets "Go ye' 'was all that was needed to provide commodious accommodations for the increasing enrollment, but today the hands of all three of our theological seminaries are tied until Southern Baptists, with one united voice, speak the words which will open the doors of expanding usefulness.

BAPTIST BIBLE INSTITUTE

There are 219 enrolled in the Baptist Bible Institute in the opening of the 1944-45 session, and scores of students have been turned away, because there is no room in either dormitories or apartment buildings. That means that many of our young men and women must go on unprepared.

The Executive Committee of the Southern Baptist Convention has approved a campaign for $200.00 to build a new men's dormitory and a new library building for the Baptist Bible Institute. Already $40,000 has been secured. The buildings now used by the Institute were abandoned by Sophie Newcomb College twenty-six years ago. Money for replacement must be secured now, or an emergency will occur to embarrass all Southern Baptists.

This session of the Baptist Bible Institute finds a new arrangement of courses. The degrees offered: in the Seminary Department, Bachelor of Divinity, Master of Theology, Doctor of Theology, in the Christian Training Department, Bachelor of Religious Education, and Master of Religious Education. A wider variety of elective courses has been introduced.

Professor W. Plunkett Martin succeeds Professor E. O. Sellers, retired, as head of the Music Department. Miss Charlotte Reed has been added to music faculty. Dr. Frank P. Lide ,professor in Baptist Seminary in China is teaching on a temporary arrangement.

Southern Louisiana is being captured from the Catholic Church, and turned to Christ by the preaching and teaching of the students.

SOUTHERN BAPTIST SEMINARY

Today the Southern Baptist Seminary is the biggest strictly Theological Seminary among evangelical Christians anywhere upon the earth. This seminary has enrolled for the session 1944-45, 603 men. In addition to these men, the 125 girls in the Training School, the 20 students of the Music School, and about 225 wives of young preachers are studying in the classrooms of the Seminary.

People generally think that the Southern Baptist Seminary with its lovely campus and comparatively new buildings is in need of nothing. The fact is, it is in need of practically everything. It has only four major classrooms with a student body of approximately 900. There are only twelve faculty members to carry the excessively heavy load of teaching. One-third of the Seminary family can get into the room the Seminary is now using for its chapel services and other assemblies. At least a hundred and twenty-five married students are unable to find living quaretrs on the campus. The dining room and the kitchen are altogether inadequate to meet the needs of this enlarged student body. The lobby in the Library should be doubled in size to provide adequate room for the students.

To sum up, the Seminary needs at least one million dollars for capital improvements and it needs to increase its present endowment of $1,750,000 to $5,000,000 in order that it may be assured of a steady, dependable annual income sufficient to maintain the faculty that is sorely needed.

From the Southern Seminary have gone about 8,500 trained men to carry the gospel to the ends of the earth.

SOUTHWESTERN BAPTIST THEOLOGICAL SEMINARY

For the first semester of the current session Southwestern Seminary has enrolled 758, far beyond any previous record for the first semester. The enrollment for the summer school and the first semester of this session, without duplications, totals 979.

The needs of Southwestern: a library, costing approximately $200,000.00, including building and equipment. A health building designed to help the students build sound bodies for sound minds. A modernized kitchen with up-to-date equipment. A fund provided for the upkeep of the campus, an increased endowment, a necessity for growth and service. The endowment to date is $1,436,296.84 which is far too small. It should be $4,000,000.00.

A movement is under way to erect an Administration-Library building calling it The George W. Truett Memorial.

SOUTHERN BAPTIST HOSPITAL

During the year 1943 the Southern Baptist Hospital admitted 19,920 patients and gave them 134,791 days of service. Nine hundred and fifty-one persons were given 15,166 days of free service, at a cost to the Hospital of $90,996.84. There were 2,426 births, and 4,417 emergency room cases which were not hospitalized. A class of 46 nurses was graduated. The capital debt of $149,000.00 was paid, and $50,000 of United States certificates of indebtedness were purchased The year was closed with all operating expenses paid, and cash balance in the bank

The hospital has given service to 35 Foreign Missionaries, and 14 Home Missionaries.

Miss Bonnie Jean Ray is hospital missionary. The students have the Young Woman's Auxiliary, Student Union, Sunday School class, and worship services are conducted in the chapel every morning.

According to figures published in the Journal of the American Medical Association for March 25th, Southern Baptist Hospital in New Orleans in 1943 admitted a larger number of patients than were admitted to any other non-government-owned hospital in the territory of the Southern Baptist Convention: and only one church-owned hospital in the United States admitted a larger number—Methodist at Indianapolis, Indiana. The hospital was fourth in number of patients admitted.

Respectfully submitted,
Ray W. Harrington

44. The following report on Home Missions was presented by A. L. McGee, and adopted.

REPORT ON HOME MISSIONS

The Home Mission Board now has 514 missionaries working in 1050 churches and mission stations in every state in the territory of the Southern Baptist Convention and in Cuba and Central America. In 1943 these missionaries preached 36,000 sermons, led more than 122,000 to make a profession of faith in Christ and received 8,200 members into the fellowship of Baptist Churches. Seventy-four missionaries have been added since January 1, 1943.

We rejoice that the debt which so burdened the Board for many years has been paid and the fredeom from debt has made possible an enlarged missionary program. The receipts of the Board in 1943 were $992,708.76 which is more than $225,000 in excess of the 1942 offerings. The Annie Armstrong Offering amounted to $290,111.82.

Missionaries of the Board are working among the Spanish, Indians, French, Italians, Negroes, Jews, Deaf, Chinese, Japanese, Mountain peoples and underprivileged groups. Workers are supported in mission churches. Good-will centers, kindergartens, rescue homes, preachers institutes, and in house to house evangelism. More than 125 missionaries are serving in Cuba and Central America. The Board has cooperated with the government by certifying 1139 Southern Baptist preachers for the chaplaincy.

The Home Mission Board is now cooperating with the respective state mission boards in the selection and support of workers for the City Mission Program and the Country Church Program. Work is now being done in thirty-one cities and rural workers are serving in this cooperative effort in six states.

Never have the Baptists of the Southland been so challenged by the task to be accomplished and by the opportunities for missionary service. The world now looks to America for Christian leadership. Southern Baptists have a peculiar responsibility in furnishing such leadership. The progress of the Kingdom throughout the world can be helped or hindered by the response of Southern Baptists. The Home Mission Board is challenged to help establish and maintain a strong spiritual front at home from which the Gospel may be effectively sent to the ends of the world.

Think of the evangelistic opportunities in the Southland! Of a population of 45,000,000, about 20,000,000 have come to the years of accountability without a profession of faith in Christ. There are 11,000,000 Negroes, 5,000,000 foreigners, nearly 1,000,000 Jews and 250,000 Indians in the territory of the Convention. The harvest truly is great — the time for reaping is at hand.

To meet this challenge, the year of 1945, which is the Centennial year of the Southern Baptist Convention, has been designated as a time for a special Southwide evangelistic campaign. Other southwide Boards and Agencies are joining the Home Mission Board to make this an all-out soul winning effort. Dr. M. E. Dodd, pastor of the First Baptist Church of Shreveport, has been chosen to lead in this great crusade for souls. Every Association will be asked to cooperate. Pastors and laymen alike are asked to consecrate themselves and dedicate their talents and resources to this great soul winning effort.

The Home Mission Board desires to thank Southern Baptists for their fine spirit of cooperation and their increased support and to ask that they continue to pray for the workers of this Board and especially for the special evangelistic effort that is being planned for our Centennial year.

Respectfully submitted,
A. L. McGee

---

45. The following report on Foreign Missions was presented by Mrs. R. R. Saunders, and adopted.

FOREIGN MISSION REPORT

"As the day of victory draws nearer in this tragic war, Southern Baptists face the greatest missionary needs in their history. We shall be called upon to minister to millions around the world who will be hungry for physical food and for spiritual food. Southern Baptists should have an understanding of the times to know that they ought to do in such a day of opportunity." So reads the yearly report of the Foreign Mission Board as of May 1st. 1944.

The war does not lesson but rather enlarges our missionary obligations. If we are far sighted enough to capitalize on these obligations and opportunities we may rest assured that our rewards will be in the same proportion as our efforts. We have come a long way since the first American foreign Missionary Society was formed back in 1812. Since then the battle for Christ on the far flung mission fields of the world has been not unlike the battle for freedom in the present conflict of war. We who are so far away and not realizing what hazardous undertakings confront them cannot appreciate or fairly estimate the progress we are making—the same conditions hold true in our missionary work.

Since 1937 Southern Baptists have given $1,340,820.14 for relief purposes around the world. Since Jan .1st 1943 one-half million dollars has been spent for this purpose, of which $100,000 was spent in Europe and $100,000 in China.

I might add that in 1943 the board paid up its indebtedness in full, which at one time exceeded $1,600,000 and a year later had accumulated a reserve of approximately $1,000,000. Every dollar of this, however, will be required to rebuild our missionary work in Europe and the Orient. Besides the task of rehabilitation, we are confronted with the heavy costs of getting missionaries to and from mission fields and to care for the increased expenses due to inflation.

The income for the current work of the Board for 1943 was $1,530,318.48. The total Lottie Moon offering for 1943 amounted to $761,269.79.

Southern Baptists have mission work in seventeen countries: China, Japan, Africa, Brazil, Argentina, Chile, Uruguay, Colombia, Mexico, Hungary, Italy, Rumania, Spain, Yugoslavia, Palestine, Syria, Hawaii, with plans to enter Paraguay when the way is open.

Southern Baptists have nearly 1000 chaplains in the army, a great many have signified their desire to return to those stricken fronts after the war as missionaries.

The COMMISSION has increased its circulation from 45,000 to 60,000 and many churches are placing it in their budget with other Sunday School and Missionary Literature.

May we at home arouse ourselves, our churches, and our denomination to the great opportunity that awaits us—stir our hearts and souls to the needs and demands of a stricken world. "When you have done it unto the least of these my brethren ,you have done it unto me."

Respectfully submitted,
Mrs. R. R. Saunders

46. The clerk read the following telegram from John Lowe.

Please urge Association receive generous offering to help send the Commission to 600 Chaplains. Request churches to take offerings for World Relief immediately.

Affectionately,
John Lowe

47. The report of the Committee to Nominate the Executive, Church Advisory, and Mission Committees was made and adopted. See page 2, 3.

48. Special music was rendered by the quartet of the host church.

49. Dr. A. S. Gillespie, returned missionary to China, brought the closing message. Theme: "World Missions."Scripture, Acts 1:8 was read in Chinese. Dr. Gillespie sang choruses in Chinese.

50. Dr. J. Clyde Turner led the closing prayer.

51. The Association adjourned from its 1943-44 Session.

IN MEMORIAM

ANTIOCH—
Mrs. Annie Crawford
BUCHANON—
Mr. John Evans
CALVARY—
Miss Laura Cantrell
Mrs. D. M. Moore
Mr. David Nance
GIBSONVILLE—
Mrs. Annie Robertson
Miss Mary Boone
Mr. John Pitts
Mrs. S. V. May
Mrs. Lessie Thomas
ASHEBORO STREET—
Mrs. C. S. White
Mr. John Dewey Wold
William C. Cagle,
Soldier killed in action
David Lee Smith, Jr.,
Soldier killed in action
BESSEMER—
Lt. John D. Chandler, Marine
COLLEGE PARK—
Mrs. C. T. Carter
Mrs. J. C. Hebron
Mrs. Grace Jenkins
Mr. R. C. Prince
Miss Enna Weaver
Mrs. J. M. Wright
ELLER MEMORIAL—
Mrs. J. C. Phillips
Mrs. Russ ll Kemp
Mr Zollie Nichols
Mrs. Charlie Jones
GREENSBORO FIRST—
Mrs. Ellen M. Sutton
Miss Mary E. Blair
Harold Dean Howell
C. W. Green
Mrs. Araminta Bush
Mrs. J. A. Hopper
Mrs. Bertie Temple
J. E. Yarboro
Grover C. Griffin
Mrs. Chas. H. Nash
Tom Sasser
N. C. Covington
Mrs W. A. Schrock, Jr.
F. A. Burroughs
A. S. Cate
Stafford W. Webb
Mrs. Tom L. Henderson
Mrs. F. P. Solomon
D. Frank Stone
Henry H. Blanchard, Jr.
Mrs. C. E. Glass
FLORIDA STREET—
Mrs. W. R. Gill
Sgt. Thomas Daniels, Soldier
LATHAM PARK—
Mr. John Broome
Mrs. Lula East
MAGNOLIA STREET—
Mr. N. J. Jarvis, Deacon
POMONA—
Mr. Eddie Batton
Mr. George Dean
Mr. Sidney Humphrey
Mrs. Martha Booker
REVOLUTION—
Sister Judia Ferguson
W. F. Johnson
SIXTEENTH STREET—
Mrs. R. T. Southern
Mr. J. R. Watkins
Mr. Cletus White
killed in action
STEVENS MEMORIAL—
Mr. S. M. Brisson
TABERNACLE—
Rev. B. G. Whitley, Pastor
Mrs. Maggie Brooks
Mr. W. M. Stevenson
WEBSTER MEMORIAL—
R. H. King
S. T. Bryson
HIGH POINT FIRST—
Mrs. Bertha Lawdermilk
Mrs. Levi Ring
Mr. C. C. Muse
Pvt. Robert Lebman
Mr. C. O. Wiley
Mrs. J. B. Lyda
Mr. Jack Squives
Mr. L. C. Lomax
T-S Willia, Shelton
Lt. A. D. Brockett, Jr.
Pvt. James W. Potts
Mr. H. A. Petty
Mrs. J. H. Petty
GREEN STREET—
Miss Ruth Stallings
Mr. F. P. Conrad
Albert Primm, Jr.
Mrs. M. T. Ellis
W. M. Turner
HILLIARD MEMORIAL—
Mr. Gilbert Young
NORTHT MAIN STREET—
Mrs. W. T. Metters
WEST END—
Mr. J. T. Chaney
Mr W. C. Robertson
JESSUP GROVE—
Mrs. Roby Greene
LEBANON—
Pvt. John Frank Clemmons
Mrs. Hattie Davis
OSCEOLA—
Mrs. Connie Hall
PILOT VIEW—
Pvt. James C. Hussey
PISGAH—
Hollis Presswood
PLEASANT GARDEN—
Mrs. B. F. Spry
Mrs. B. F. Foy
REIDSVILLE FIRST—
Mr. N. C. Thompson
Mr. J. C. Allison
Mrs. Fred Degrotte
Mrs. R. G. Gladstone
Mrs. C. W. Swann
Grey Pettigrew
Haywood Southard
PENN MEMORIAL—
Mr. W. B. Gosney
Mrs. Herbert Ford
Mr. H. A. Busick
Mr. E. R. Parrish
ROCKY KNOLL—
Mrs. Ethel Allen
RUFFIN STACY—
Mr. W. C. Evans
SMITH GROVE—
Mrs. H. A. Frazier
SUMMERFIELD—
Mrs. Jennie Case

Statistical Tables Begin

TABLE ONE — CHURCH MEMBERSHIP

CHURCHES	Town, Vill., Country?	When Constituted	PASTORS AND POST OFFICES	Days of Meeting	Memb. Last Year	CHURCH MEMBERSHIP GAINS: Baptisms	GAINS: Letters	GAINS: Statements	GAINS: Restorations	LOSSES: Letters	LOSSES: Exclusions	LOSSES: Erasures	LOSSES: Deaths	Non-Res. Memb.	Tot. Present Members	Weekly Prayer M't'gs.	Revivals Held, Year	Obs. Lords Supper, Yr.	Fam. Rec Bapt. Paper	Enrld. Min. Ret. Fund
Allen Jay	O	1934	Geo. H. Wallace, R.3, High Point	All	275	11	31	6	...	2	...	...	...	35	321	*	2	4	...	...
Antioch	O	1935	J. C. Gillespie, Reidsville	2 4	83	1	2	...	...	...	...	2	1	...	83	*	1	1	9	...
Brightwood	V	1940	H. P. Gauldin, R.5, Greensboro	All	126	21	19	4	...	2	...	...	...	...	168	*	4	1	...	...
Buchanan	C	....	J. B. Clifton, R.6, B 334-B, Greensboro	All	138	3	2	...	...	3	4	...	1	...	132	...	2	4	...	*
Calvary	O	1901	J. C. Shore, R.4, Reidsville	2 4	183	2	...	...	...	...	...	...	3	...	182	...	1	2	17	...
Community	O	1934	John D. Fuller, R.1, [illegible]o	All	63	25	4	4	...	1	...	...	...	1	94	...	1	4	1	...
Fair Grove	C	....	...	...	...	...	...	...	...	...	...	...								
Fairmont Park	V	1940	A. L. McGee, P.O.B. 1081, High Point	All	91	16	5	2	11	...	...	...	...	...	225	*	1	4	22	*
Fairview	O	1904	J. C. Shore, R.4, Reidsville	1 3	139	...	...	...	...	1	...	1	...	15	137	...	...	2	15	...
Gibsonville	V	1884	John S. Gamble, Gibsonville	All	273	...	...	1	...	7	...	...	5	...	262	*	1	1	...	...
GREENSBORO—																				
Asheboro St.	C	1899	J. Ben Eller, 709 Asheboro St., Gr'boro	All	121	51	27	3	...	42	...	8	4	116	1239	*	1	4	41	*
Bailey Mem.	C	1935	A. C. Lawson, [illegible]o	All	98	...	2	3	...	4	...	...	...	...	99	*	1	3	...	...
Bessemer	C	1922	Ray W. Harrington, 507 Delancey St.	All	519	16	24	2	...	26	...	2	1	...	550	*	2	2	4	...
College Park	C	1906	W. W. Woodcock, 508 For'st St., G'boro	All	628	12	30	4	...	33	3	...	6	32	636	*	1	12	38	...
Edgeville	C	1942	A. R. Riddle, 2202 Spruce St., [illegible]	All	19	2	6	4	...	2	...	...	...	8	29	*	2	2	...	...
Eller Mem.	C	1897	Von King, Greensboro	All	855	15	3	...	...	23	...	...	3	...	847	*	2	11	12	...
First	C	1859	J. Clyde [illegible]r, Greensboro	All	2343	52	96	10	...	101	...	13	21	...	2366	*	1	12	884	*
Florida St.	C	1916	Leslie D. [illegible], R.4, Greensboro	All	513	28	20	4	...	20	...	2	2	...	541	*	2	4	100	*
Latham Park	C	1916	James R. Thompson, 1110 Glenwood	All	71	8	2	1	...	1	...	...	2	...	79	...	2	2	1	...
Magnolia St.	C	1909	L. Grady Burgess, 102 E. Wendover Av	All	188	8	5	1	...	5	...	2	1	...	194	*	2	4	40	*
Pomona	C	1906	C. M. Oates, Pomona	All	243	5	3	2	1	3	...	1	4	116	246	*	2	2	...	...
Revolution	C	1907	S. L. Riddle, 2218 Shober St., Gr'boro	All	355	8	8	4	...	6	...	2	2	...	365	*	2	4	...	*
Sixteenth St.	C	1907	Wade H. James, 1504 16th St., G'boro	All	236	23	9	4	8	11	1	1	3	...	264	*	1	4	1	...
Stevens Mem.	V	1922	[illegible]il J. Armstrong, R.2, Greensboro	All	173	13	4	...	...	5	4	...	1	...	180	*	2	1	12	...
Tabernacle	C	1938	Fred Koerber, Greensboro	All	249	7	13	3	...	4	...	1	3	55	264	*	3	4	...	*
Webster Mem.	V	1935	Philip Hutchinson, Greensboro	All	133	7	8	...	...	5	1	29	2	...	111	*	2	4	2	...
Guilford	V	1914	T. E. Kerley, 1704 Florida Ave., Gr'boro	All	72	1	...	...	...	6	...	...	...	...	57	*	...	1	6	...
HIGH POINT—																				
First	C	1825	W. Wilbur Hutchins, 225 Lindsay St.	All	1459	25	66	...	1	44	...	10	13	359	1484	*	...	4	90	*

Green St.	C	....	Julian S. Hopkins, High Point	All	1460	70	52	9	52	38	...	22	5	202	1170	*	1	4	70	154.27
Hilliard Mem.	C	....	Hughey O. Miller, High Point	All	326	21	10	1	...	8	...	1	1	....	355	...	2	3	....	71.80
N. Main St.	C	....	L. J. Rainey, 111 Hillcrest Dr., H. Pt.	All	349	4	15	...	...	18	...	4	1	....	377	*	1	3	25	76.00
North Park	C	1929	Dewey Armstrong, High Point	All	129	10	10	...	...	4	...	1	...	....	207	*	2	4	10	......
Southside	C	1916	W. H. Barker, R.3, High Point	All	334	23	10	...	...	4	...	1	...	....	147	*	2	4	7	......
West End	C	1913	R. R. Jackson, 918 Ridding St., H. Pt.	All	414	7	4	3	2	26	...	2	...	....	428	*	1	4	8	*
Jessup Grove	O	1933	James E. Wiggs, 1515 Grove St., G'boro	All	149	14	4	2	...	...	...	...	1	....	169	*	1	2	7	......
Jewell	O	1947	A. H. Dunning, High Point	All	36	2	4	1	...	2	...	...	...	....	41	*	2	1	....	......
Lebanon	O	1911	M. G. Faulkner, 55 Wentworth, R'ville	All	178	5	3	3	...	8	...	2	2	48	177	...	1	2	28	......
Mount Zion	O	....	J. T. Swinson, R.1, Burlington	All	191	29	21	3	...	...	...	...	...	....	231	*	2	1	20	......
McLeansville	O	....	J. B. Clifton, R.6, B. 334-B, Gr'boro	All	.....	8	10	1	...	...	...	...	...	....	19	*	2	1	....	......
Oak Grove	O	1916	R. L. [illegible], 613 Woodbury Ave., H. Pt.	All	110	8	...	2	...	9	...	...	...	....	111	*	2	4	1	......
Osceola	O	1915	Paul M. Roberts, R.4, Reidsville	1 3	84	...	...	...	...	4	...	...	1	....	79	...	...	2	1	......
Ossippee	V	1933	E. J. Tribble, R.1, Burlington	All	46	...	...	2	...	1	...	12	...	....	35	*	2	2	1	*
Pine Grove	O	1938	W. L. Campbell, Pilot Mountain	2 4	95	2	1	...	...	3	...	...	...	....	95	...	2	1	....	......
Pilot View	O	....	J. C. [illegible], 309 Polk St., Thom'ville	All	58	8	...	...	...	2	...	27	1	....	54	*	3	4	5	......
Pisgah	C	1938	J. M. [illegible], 1104 [illegible]ro St., H. Pt.	All	128	...	...	...	...	...	...	...	1	....	127	*	2	4	10	......
Pleasant Garden	V	....	J. Juber Dixon, Pleasant Garden	[illegible]	85	9	8	...	...	2	...	...	1	....	114	*	1	4	1	......
Pleasant Grove	O	1938	J. M. Allred, Pomona	All	103	10	1	3	...	1	...	1	...	5	112	*	2	10	....	......
[illegible] Fork	O	....	Elijah Lankford, R.2, B[illegible]n S[illegible]it.	All	59	11	8	...	2	1	...	...	...	....	104	*	2	1	....	......
REIDSVILLE—																				
Baptist Temple	C	1929	D. M. Clemmons, Reidsville	All	255	8	7	...	1	3	...	1	...	....	267	*	2	1	12	......
First	C	....	Dr. John McGinnis, 220 Piedmont St.	All	927	7	14	1	...	7	...	...	7	....	941	*	...	4	....	214.00
Penn Mem.	C	1926	D. W. Overby, Reidsville	All	212	3	1	...	1	5	...	...	4	13	208	*	1	4	6	*
Rocky Knoll	C	1934	G. A. [illegible]r, R.1, Greensboro	All	249	12	4	...	...	13	...	...	2	....	250	*	2	2	1	......
Ruffin Stacey	O	1931	J. T. London, R.5, Reidsville	2 4	186	5	1	...	...	...	...	...	...	....	192	...	...	...	....	......
Smith Grove	O	1921	R. O. Nuckles, Colfax	1 3	176	7	...	...	1	...	...	...	1	....	184	*	2	2	....	......
Summerfield	V	....	E. A. Long, Germantown	2 4	203	2	2	...	...	...	...	...	...	....	205	...	1	3	6	......
Temple	V	1939	H. M. [illegible]s, 112 Marshall St., W-Sal.	All	107	4	...	1	...	8	...	...	...	35	104	*	3	3	....	......
TOTALS	..	....		.....	[illegible]	640	579	94	80	524	13	148	108	1040	17958	...	85	183	1514	......

TABLE TWO — SUNDAY SCHOOLS

ASSOCIATI[illegible] SUPT.
C. S. Hodge, First [illegible], Greensboro

CHUHCHES	SUPERINTENDENTS AND POST OFFICES	Cradle Roll, Under 3	Beginners, 3-5 Years	Primaries, 6-8 Years	Juniors, 9-12 Years	Intermediates, 13-16	Young People, 17-24	Adults, 25 Yrs. and Up	Extension Dept.	Gen., Dep'tal Officers	Total Enrollment, Officers, Teachers, Pupils	What Is Av Attend.?	Baptisms from S. S.	Is the School Graded?	Is It Standard A-1?	Teachers Holding Dip.	Enrollment Vac School	Av. Attend. Vac. Sch.
[illegible] Jay	[illegible], R.1, Box 239, H. Point	7	13	17	53	47	20	143	...	2	302	213	11	...	...	...	...	...
[illegible]	...	...	...	...	...	...	...	...	...	...	53	35	...	...	...	...	...	...
Brightwood	C. M. McGehee, [illegible], Greensboro	...	12	22	...	33	48	57	...	3	175	140	...	...	...	...	...	...
[illegible]	R. M. Crane, R.5, Greensboro	12	23	...	23	...	45	47	...	18	150	99	...	...	...	...	...	...
Calvary	Harry Conner, R.2, [illegible]	...	10	14	16	20	21	130	...	...	211	88	...	...	...	...	...	...
[illegible]	Ralph Jackson, Greensboro	...	...	35	24	35	...	47	...	...	141	80	18	...	...	...	...	...
Fair [illegible]	...	...	...	...	...	...	...	...	...	...	...	...	...	...	...	...	...	...
Fairmont Park	W. R. Moose, R.5, B. 391, High Point	12	19	35	25	27	22	73	...	3	216	135	10	...	...	...	...	...
Fairview	A. D. Hopkins, R 2, Reidsville	...	12	18	21	30	25	25	...	...	131	89	...	...	...	...	...	...
Gibsonville	C. C. Hammer, Gibsonville, N. C.	...	20	21	10	15	52	57	...	...	175	100	...	...	...	...	...	...
GREENSBORO—																		
[illegible]ro St.	F. L. Paschal, 2420 Camden [illegible], G'bor.	42	52	68	132	147	96	328	55	6	926	391	39	*	...	15	210	152
Bailey Mem.	W. H. Stevenson, 2405 H. P. [illegible], G'bor	...	...	21	...	35	36	22	...	4	118	68	...	...	...	...	...	...
Bessemer	Walter Jackson, 3802 Oak Gr. St., G'bo.	14	26	55	52	59	39	84	...	5	334	185	5	*	...	...	155	97
College Park	B. B. Stockard, Greensboro	84	24	45	50	74	68	110	134	4	593	204	11	*	*	24	70	50
Edgeville	H. M. Barber, 1512 Ball St., [illegible]	...	...	16	10	10	...	14	...	...	50	45	...	...	...	...	...	...
Eler Mem.	[illegible] Kincaid, 1103 [illegible] Ave.	5	24	69	78	69	41	40	11	20	356	178	11	*	...	...	178	138
First	C. S. Hodge, Greensboro	121	80	125	176	220	131	804	180	33	1870	[illegible]	47	*	...	12	204	161
Florida St.	F. E. [illegible], 1412 Florida St., G'boro.	20	20	43	56	35	13	182	101	6	476	275	3	...	...	...	100	75
Latham Park	...	...	3	6	12	8	29	27	...	10	85	47	8	...	...	...	...	...
Magnolia St.	J. E. Lovings, Greensboro	1	32	14	20	18	13	38	...	4	136	86	8	...	...	...	46	35
Pomona	C. C. Patterson, Pomona	...	...	30	30	27	30	86	...	13	236	37	...	...	...	...	...	...
[illegible]	[illegible] Phillips, 209 Newlyn St., [illegible]	18	24	43	65	20	17	73	18	...	278	132	...	...	...	...	91	83
Sixteenth St.	J. U. Brady, 2408 Spruce St., Gr'boro.	12	13	49	84	43	16	74	...	4	305	163	23	*	...	2	191	150
[illegible] Mem.	Jack Caudle, Greensboro	15	10	19	33	28	34	65	...	13	217	[illegible]	...	...	...	...	95	65
Tabernacle	W. O. [illegible]	43	30	18	28	16	25	45	20	5	210	90	4	...	...	...	42	36
Webster [illegible]	Thomas Pearman, 2404 Maple St., G'bo	4	8	15	21	10	15	44	...	14	131	92	...	...	...	4	63	55
Guilford	Clyde Harvey, Guilford	18	12	...	12	...	12	20	...	...	84	40	...	...	...	...	...	...
HIGH POINT—																		
First	Dr. W. F. Clayton, 223 [illegible] St., HP	71	63	93	120	177	130	516	65	3	1238	546	22	*	...	22	189	160

Green St.	W. E. Crissman, High Point	31	75	99	184	162	199	475	...	5	1150	543	44	*	...	...	206	152
Hilliard Mem.	H. B. t[illegible]m, High Point	...	21	8	29	20	39	71	25	7	220	111	19	*	...	1	57	46
N. Main St.	W. C. Edwards, 204 W. Lelington Ave.	...	28	48	68	50	29	109	...	12	344	151	4	*	...	...	...	...
North Park	J. B. Hugg, High Point	5	17	20	43	27	32	53	3	4	204	122	...	...	...	...	...	...
Southside	A. L. Bean, 501 Highland Ave., Hi. Pt.	8	12	23	53	32	66	70	...	6	270	160	...	...	...	...	...	...
West End	R. G. Barlowe, 522 Barker St., Hi. Pt.	15	18	35	37	43	52	66	20	6	286	154	7	...	...	4	91	71
Jessup Grove	Oscar Lewis, R.1, Summerfield	...	25	...	35	...	30	45	...	3	138	99	14	...	...	...	...	...
Jewell	S. P. Stutts, Sr., R.2, High Point	...	...	...	44	30	24	31	...	...	129	45	2	...	...	...	...	...
Lebanon	Diamond Davis, R.2, Brown Summit	18	12	15	9	28	31	60	...	2	175	85	3	...	...	...	...	...
Mount Zion	N. H. Blackburn, McLeansville	...	12	...	18	...	20	22	...	2	74	...	...	...	...	...	...	...
McLeansville	Winfred Shoffner, R.2, Snow Camp	...	...	...	...	...	...	...	...	...	...	89	29	...	...	...	...	...
Oak [illegible]e	A. L. Saunders, 928, High Point	...	15	7	20	13	14	38	...	...	107	80	...	...	...	...	...	...
Osceola	D. A. Green, Brown Summit	...	11	13	13	21	19	22	...	2	101	49	...	...	...	...	...	...
Ossippee	Walter Brown, R.2, Elon College	...	8	...	12	...	14	8	...	6	48	35	...	...	...	...	...	...
Pine Grove	R. L. Loflin, Jamestown	...	13	12	16	...	11	32	...	2	86	56	...	...	...	...	...	...
Pilot View	U. E. [illegible]bb, R.2, High Point	...	12	...	25	...	21	20	...	3	81	45	4	...	...	...	...	...
Pi.gah	Z. V. Lanier, 2213 E. Greene St., H. Pt.	...	19	16	35	37	30	75	38	2	252	125	...	...	...	...	...	...
Pleasant Garden	......	10	24	20	29	23	24	35	...	5	170	60	9	*	...	...	25	23
Pleasant [illegible]e	F. M. Atkins, R.3, B. 145, Greensboro.	10	10	13	13	22	22	35	...	...	125	65	10	...	...	...	38	35
Reedy Fork	Worth Smith, R.2, Greensboro	14	12	12	20	12	23	35	...	...	128	89	...	...	...	...	138	89
REIDSVILLE—																		
Baptist Temple	Milton Warf, Wentworth St., R'ds'ville	27	24	38	35	48	19	77	...	4	272	94	4	...	...	...	...	...
First	S. F. Wells, 233 Lindsay St., Reidsville	30	32	53	61	58	78	233	...	7	565	225	6	*	...	...	136	127
Penn Mem.	E. L. Jones, Reidsville	...	10	9	20	24	9	51	...	3	126	57	3	...	...	...	...	...
Rocky Knoll	R. A. Chandler, R.1, Greensboro	20	36	18	25	18	20	115	...	3	255	150	...	...	...	...	62	55
Ruffin Stacey	C. L. Schrum, Ruffin	10	8	15	12	18	12	25	...	...	98	41	...	...	...	...	...	...
Smith Grove	J. A. Fairrington, R.1, Colfax	...	20	...	17	...	48	50	...	...	135	62	7	...	...	...	...	...
Summerfield	Marion Ayers, Summerfield	...	...	...	...	...	...	...	...	...	124	60	2	...	...	...	...	...
Temple	Willie Wilson, R.4, High Point	...	17	12	17	...	11	32	...	2	91	60	...	...	...	...	...	...
TOTALS	......	697	991	1377	2041	1889	1795	5036	670	256	14951	7446	387	...	...	84	2387	1855

TABLE THREE — BAPTIST TRAINING UNION

ASSOCIATIONAL DIRECTOR

J. Carl Bell, Greensboro

CHURCHES	TRAINING UNION DIRECTORS AND POST OFFICES	Adult Union	Young People's Unions	Intermediate Unions	Junior Unions	Story Hours	Tot Unions, Story Hrs.	Adults Enrolled	Young People Enrolled	Intermediates Enrolled	Juniors Enrolled	Story Hours Enrolled	Tot. Enr., Un. St. Hrs.	No. Daily Bible Read's	No. taking Study C'rse	Tot. Systematic Givers	A-1 for One Quarter?	Students in College	No. Gen., Dept. Of'c'rs
Buchanon	Mrs. R. P. Johnson, R.6, Greensboro	...	...	...	...	...	...	...	...	...	...	...	33	7	7	33	...	...	...
Calvary	Mrs. Joe Roberts, R.2, Reidsville	1	...	...	...	...	1	24	...	...	...	...	24	...	...	...	...	...	...
Fairmont Park	J. R. Edwards, R.5, Box 414, High Pt.	1	1	1	1	1	5	29	9	14	20	22	94	...	...	...	...	...	7
GREENSBORO—																			
Aboro St.	Jim R. Durham, 309 Burtner St., G'b.	1	1	2	2	1	7	18	23	44	43	30	165	22	48	46	...	6	7
Bailey Memorial	C. C. Stanley, Box 741, Greensboro	...	1	1	1	...	3	...	12	13	6	...	31	17	23	31	...	3	1
Bessemer	J. W. Morrison, 122 W. Sycamore, G'b.	1	1	1	1	1	5	14	13	13	17	4	61	13	23	38	...	1	6
College Park	Mrs. G. W. Williams, Greensboro	...	2	1	...	...	3	...	21	5	...	...	26	3	7	...	...	23	7
Eller Memorial	Raymond Kincaid, 1103 Summit Ave.	1	1	1	1	1	5	11	6	10	17	4	48	18	23	26	...	...	6
First	C. S. Hodge, Greensboro	3	3	4	2	1	13	68	60	63	36	12	239	74	94	185	...	18	15
Florida Street	W. F. Murchison, 1318 Oak St., G'boro	1	1	1	2	3	8	20	11	12	17	15	75	42	32	55	*	1	...
Magnolia Street	J. E. Poore, 203 E. Wendover Ave., G'b	1	1	1	1	...	4	12	10	8	9	...	39	13	26	33	...	...	12
Pomona	J. A. Culberson, Pomona	...	...	...	1	...	1	...	...	...	15	...	15	12	10	15	...	...	5
Revolution	Doris Johnson, 2211 Shober St., Gr'boro	...	1	...	...	1	2	...	46	...	...	...	...	11	18	18	...	...	12
Sixteenth St.	Betty Paris, 1508 15th St., Greensboro.	1	...	1	1	1	4	11	...	18	7	10	56	33	31	44	...	2	7
Stevens Memorial	Carolyn Pickard, Greensboro	...	1	...	...	...	1	...	14	...	...	...	14	...	...	...	...	3	...
Tabernacle	Lucille Wilson, Greensboro	1	1	1	1	...	4	13	9	8	9	...	39	19	16	24	...	1	1
Webster Memoria	Mrs. C. L. Straughn, Greensboro, R.5.	1	...	1	1	1	4	35	...	...	...	...	35	3	...	14	...	...	16
HIGH POINT—																			
First	W. O. Burnham, 309 Church St., Hi. Pt.	...	1	3	2	1	7	5	39	92	73	34	243	...	95	...	...	...	...
Green St.	T. C. Robbins, High Point	3	1	2	4	1	11	57	14	51	68	24	214	65	91	121	...	3	20
Hilliard Memoria	C. H. Farmer, R.5, High Point	1	1	1	1	1	5	12	10	12	10	3	47	16	39	47	...	...	3
North Main St.	Vivian Blackwell, 1416 Welbom St., HP	1	...	1	1	1	4	...	...	...	...	...	35	25	...	30	...	2	11
North Park	C. J. Elliott, High Point	1	1	1	1	1	5	15	10	8	11	16	60	14	20	22	...	...	2
Southside	Daisy Shaw, 398 Walker St., High Pt.	1	...	...	1	...	2	10	...	...	15	...	25	15	11	15	...	...	1
West End	...	1	...	1	1	1	4	11	...	9	11	9	40	16	20	31	...	...	...
Jessup Grove	Rev. J. S. Albert, 907 Englewood, G'bor	1	2	...	1	1	5	12	23	...	19	6	60	22	20	23	...	...	6
Jewell	Marvin Stutts, R.2, High Point	1	...	1	1	...	3	25	...	15	17	...	57	...	...	...	...	...	...
Pisgah	W. O. Powers, 2217 E. Green St., Hi. P.	2	1	1	1	1	6	43	16	14	12	7	92	38	53	17	...	...	...
Pleasant Garden	Gertrude Tow, R.1, Greensboro	1	1	1	1	1	5	2	5	4	5	12	28	10	13	12	...	...	9

Pleasant Grove....	F. M. Atkins, R.3, Box 145, Greensboro	1	...	1	1	...	3	9	...	13	[illegible]	...	31	20	20	21	...	...	8
Reedy Fork........	Parks Gregory, 1514 Upand Drive, G'bo	1	...	1	1	1	4	17	...	14	14	12	57	...	...	....	...	...	6
REIDSVILLE—																			
Baptist Temple..	Odell Dellap, Reidsville....	2	1	1	1	1	6	21	8	16	14	12	71	14	16	42	...	...	8
First............	R. T. Gillespie, 118 Lindsay St., R'ville	1	1	1	1	1	5	8	23	24	32	10	97	36	30	97	...	8	9
Penn Memorial..	Mrs. Nash Wilkins, Reidsville.........	1	...	1	1	...	3	4	...	4	5	...	13	9	13	12	...	1	6
Rocky Knoll.......	G. E. Faucette	1	1	1	1	1	5	10	6	10	15	3	54	16	20	30	...	...	6
Summerfield.......	Howard Pope, Summerfield	1	...	1	1	...	3	...	...	...	...	...	36	9	20	....	...	...	...
TOTALS.....	....	34	26	35	37	24	156	516	388	494	536	255	2254	612	839	1082	...	72	197

TABLE FOUR — W. M. U. ORGANIZATIONS AND GIFTS

CHURCHES	PRESIDENTS OF W. M. S. AND POST OFFICES	Number W. M. S.	Number of Y. W. A.'s	Number of G. A.'s	Number of R. A.'s	Number of Sunbeams	Total W. M. U. Orgs.	W. M. S. Members	Y. W. A.'s Members	G. A.'s Members	R. A.'s Members	Sunbeam Members	Tot. Members Enr'l'd.	Tot. Enr. Mis. St. C'se.	Contributions (Local Work) by W. M. U.	Contributions (Missions) by W. M. U.
[redacted]h	Mrs. J. C. Gillespie, Reidsville	1	...	...	...	...	1	...	...	...	...	...	...	...	13.35	6.00
Buchanan	Mrs. J. B. Clifton, R.6, Greensboro	1	1	...	...	...	2	16	12	...	...	...	28	27	...	137.05
Calvary	Mrs. J. E. McCargo, R.2, Reidsville	1	1	...	...	...	2	21	18	...	...	...	39	...	47.00	144.25
Fairmont Park	Mrs. T. R. ([redacted]s, R.5, High Point	1	1	...	...	...	2	20	15	...	...	...	35	23	50.00	79.00
Fairview	Mrs. A. D. Hopkins, R.1, Reidsville	1	...	...	...	...	1	20	...	...	...	...	20	14	7.50	82.45
Gibsonville	Mrs. W. C. White, Gibsonville	1	...	...	...	...	1	23	...	...	...	...	23	...	415.50	53.77
GREENSBORO—																
Asheboro St.	Mrs. A. C. [redacted]e, 1500 Randolph Ave.	1	2	2	2	1	8	134	16	41	21	43	255	234	5388.61	2278.49
Bailey Mem.	Mrs. C. C. [redacted]y, Box 741, Gr'boro	1	...	...	...	...	1	15	...	...	...	...	15	9	...	20.65
Bessemer	Mrs. J. R. Medlin, 200 Sykes [redacted]e., G'bo	2	1	...	...	1	4	42	15	...	...	55	112	60	43.82	587.27
College Park	Mrs. B. A. Scott, 1318 Spring Gard, G'b	1	1	...	...	1	3	71	15	...	...	10	96	40	3151.48	1102.99
Eller Memorial	Mrs. Eli [redacted]n, 1510 [redacted]d Dr., G'bo	1	...	1	...	1	3	28	...	11	...	20	57	34	...	923.40
First	Mrs. E. T. Howell, [redacted]o	1	3	4	4	1	13	368	36	44	59	38	545	225	7291.00	12704.92
Florida St.	Mrs. Mary Allred, 1510 Elwood Ave.	1	1	2	...	1	5	56	12	30	...	...	98	50	2063.92	439.28
Latham Park	Jane Wilkie, R.2, Box 24A, Gr'boro	1	...	...	...	...	1	17	...	...	...	...	17	...	...	20.00
Magnolia St.	Mrs. L. L. Jarvis, 2401 Lawndale Dr.	1	1	1	...	1	4	18	8	13	...	25	64	21	...	140.00
Pomona	Mrs. E. E. Henry, Pomona	1	...	...	...	1	2	30	...	...	...	12	42	...	...	58.35
Revolution	Miss Sallie Burgess, 2103 Maple St., G'b	1	...	1	...	1	3	22	...	12	...	...	34	12	...	1244.62
Sixteenth St.	Mrs. Harry L. [redacted]e, 1508 17th St., G'b	1	1	1	1	1	5	33	9	12	13	10	77	104	1619.64	1176.69
Stevens Mem.	Mrs. [redacted]k [redacted]e, R.2, [redacted]	1	1	...	...	...	2	15	12	...	...	...	27	...	...	117.94
Tabernacle	Mrs. W. J. Deal, 1410 Berwick St., G'b	1	1	1	...	1	4	21	14	13	...	13	61	...	...	83.25
[redacted]er [redacted]morial	Mrs. A. Andrews, R.5, [redacted]o	1	1	1	1	1	6	30	8	8	10	5	61	...	75.00	319.19
Guilford	Mrs. Hettie Kennedy, Guilford	1	...	...	...	...	1	2	16	...	...	...	12	28	...	...
HIGH POINT—																
First	Mrs. W. F. [redacted]n, 223 Lindsay St.,	1	1	2	1	1	6	228	13	27	10	...	278	315	...	5934.53
Green St.	[redacted] C. C. Stout, High Point	1	2	2	2	2	9	116	19	35	23	12	205	227	4152.90	2454.80
Hilliard Mem.	Mrs. J. B. Ellis, High Point	1	1	1	1	1	5	19	9	7	10	15	60	24	451.13	131.13
[redacted]th Main St.	Mrs. G. L. Thompson, 1306 Oak Ave.	1	...	...	1	...	2	15	...	...	10	...	25	15	15.59	222.50
North Park	Mrs. D. H. Short, High Point	1	1	1	...	1	4	17	12	16	...	25	70	29	655.50	57.84
Southside	Mrs. J. S. Cameron, 307 [redacted]er St., H.P.	2	...	...	...	...	2	26	...	...	...	...	26	26	...	209.32

West End	Mrs. F. M. Houser, W. [illegible]n St., H.P.	1	...	2	...	1	4	17	...	19	...	18	54	13	22.00	155.90
Jewell	......	...	...	...	1	...	1	...	...	...	15	...	15	15	....	....
Lebanon	Mrs. N. G. Carter, R.5, Greensboro	1	...	...	...	...	1	...	...	...	...	...	...	9	....	22.55
Mt. Zion	......	1	...	...	...	...	1	20	...	...	...	...	20	...	....	33.91
Ossipee	Mrs. A. E. Lewis, R.1, Elon College	1	...	...	...	...	1	12	...	...	...	...	12	...	....	43.01
Pisgah	Mrs. C. F. Beachamp, 1305 Thissell, HP	1	...	...	...	...	1	8	...	...	...	...	8	10	....	....
Pleasant Garden	M[illegible]. J. E. [illegible]h, Pleasant Garden	1	...	...	...	...	1	12	...	...	...	...	12	8	50.00	50.00
Pleasant Grove	Mrs. W. A. Kenan, R.3, [illegible]o	1	...	1	...	...	2	13	...	12	...	...	25	...	16.00	10.23
Reedy Fork	Mrs. Ella Harris, R.2, Greensboro	1	...	...	...	...	1	7	...	...	...	...	7	...	1293.35	236.85
REIDSVILLE—																
Baptist Temple	Mrs. Nuna Baker, Oak St., Reidsville.	1	...	3	...	1	5	100	...	35	...	15	150	66	119.63	312.35
First	Mrs. J. C. Tatem, Reidsville	1	1	1	...	1	4	200	22	8	...	32	262	56	442.95	641.50
Penn Mem.	M[illegible]s. Gilmer Dalton, Box 414, R'dsville	1	...	...	...	...	1	35	...	...	...	...	35	18	271.50	219.15
Rocky Knoll	Mrs. W. T. [illegible]e, R.1, Greensboro	2	1	1	...	...	4	25	15	8	...	...	48	...	6.00	112.00
Summerfield	Mrs. Clyde Robinson, Summerfield	1	...	...	...	...	1	18	...	...	...	...	18	...	219.70	225.70
Temple	Mrs. Gagner, High Point	1	...	...	...	...	1	9	...	...	...	...	9	...	12.00	30.00
TOTALS	......	45	23	27	14	20	130	1899	296	351	171	348	3057	1712	27895.07	32822.83

TABLE SIX — CHURCH PROPERTY

CHURCHES	CHURCH CLERKS AND POST OFFICES	Does your Church Own House of Worship?	When Was It Built?	What Materials Were Used?	No. Persons Seated	Number of Rooms	Dept. Assembly Rooms	No. Sep. Class Rooms	Value Church House and Grounds	Value Mission Chapel If Any	Value Pastor's Home	Total Value All Church Property	Indebtedness on All Church Property	Amount of Insurance Carried
Allen Jay	Hoy Yarborough, R.4, B. 589, High Pt.	Yes	1936	Wood	300	10	13	9	4500	....	4500	9000	....	6000
Antioch	......	Yes	1935	Wood	300	4	...	3	1500	....	......	1500	....	......
Brightwood	Roy Beal, Greensboro	Yes	1940	Wood	300	7	7	7	8000	....	2500	10500	....	......
Buchanan	R. F. Carter, R.6, Greensboro	Yes	....	Wood	150	4	1	4	3000	....	......	3000	....	1500
Calvary	J. E. McCargo, R.2, Reidsville	Yes	1898	Wood	275	9	...	8	5000	....	2000	7000	....	3000
Community	T. M. Marsh, Randleman	Yes	1913	C. Bl.	350	1	...	...	4500	....	......	4500	698.66	2500
Fair Grove	......	...	....	......	......	...	...	...	......	....	......	......	....	......
Fairmont Park	J. R. Edwards, R.5, B. 414, High Point	Yes	1942	Wood	510	11	...	9	9000	....	......	10025	....	10000
Fairview	Williams Cummings, R.2, Reidsville	Yes	1901	Wood	300	11	...	10	3000	....	......	3000	....	2000
Gibsonville	C. W. Seaford, Gibsonville	Yes	1884	Wood	300	9	9	9	4500	....	......	4500	....	3500
GREENSBORO—														
Asheboro St.	R. Paul Greason, 1200 Bellevue, G'boro	Yes	1912	Brick	700	61	10	69	51000	....	6000	57000	....	43000
Bailey Mem.	Walter Heilig, R.6, B. 334-A, Gr'boro	Yes	1935	Wood	250	7	...	6	2500	....	......	2500	....	750
Bessemer	R. F. Pace, 607 Sykes, Greensboro	Yes	1923	Wood	350	25	5	20	16000	....	3000	19000	....	19500
College Park	P. R. Venable, Greensboro	Yes	1940	Brick	400	57	8	42	55000	....	8000	63000	....	50000
Edgeville	Ruth Greason, 1508 Ball St., Gr'boro	Yes	1942	Wood	175	1	...	...	2000	....	......	2300	....	2000
Eller Mem.	E. P. Hinson, 1203 Homeland Ave., G'b	Yes	1925	Brick	800	50	7	48	42000	....	9000	51000	....	30000
First	Vander Liles, Greensboro	Yes	1906	Brick	1000	48	...	48	130000	....	......	130000	....	70000
Florida St.	Eleanor Watson, 1404 Lexington Ave.	Yes	1930	Brick	350	23	2	22	22000	....	4500	24500	....	26000
Latham Park	Mary L. Anderson, 1048 Battle Gr. Av.	Yes	1916	Wood	240	1	...	...	3000	....	......	3000	400.00	3000
Magnolia St.	Thelma Covington, 1121 Magnolia St.	Yes	1912	Wood	250	7	...	11	6000	1000	4000	11000	....	6500
Pomona	C. C. Patterson, Pomona	Yes	1906	Wood	350	8	...	8	3000	....	......	3000	....	......
Revolution	N. C. Brown, 1902 Poplar St., Gr'boro.	Yes	1907	Wood	400	5	3	9	10000	....	5000	15000	....	7500
Sixteenth St.	Harry L. Moore, 1508 17th St., Gr'boro	Yes	1907	Brick	500	5	5	16	39000	....	......	39000	....	18000
Stevens Mem.	Mrs. J. B. Brown, Greensboro	Yes	1922	Wood	250	11	...	13	10000	....	2500	12500	....	7500
Tabernacle	Mrs. E. C. White, Jr., Greensboro	Yes	1938	Wood	200	3	...	2	5000	....	3500	8500	2923.25	8500
Webster Mem.	Albert S. West, R.5, B. 294, Greensboro	Yes	1935	Wood	200	10	9	9	4000	....	4000	8000	....	5500
Guilford	Mrs. Dora Farrar, Guilford College	Yes	1914	Brick	200	7	4	4	3500	300	......	3800	....	3000
HIGH POINT—														
First	C. D. Goldsmith, 113 Briggs Ave., H. P.	Yes	'35-'41	Brick	900	70	7	54	150000	....	7000	161720	42000.00	100000

Green St.	Clyde Ayers, High Point	Yes	1926	Brick	1500	106	7	80	164500	1500		166000		60000
Hilliard Mem.	J. W. Saunders, High Point	Yes	1931	Brick	600	24		22	30000			30000		5000
N. Main St.	Mrs. Homer Sechrest, R.1, High Point	Yes	1924	Brick	350	26	6	20	19500		7000	26500	4000.00	16500
North Park	D. H. Short, High Point	Yes	1929	Wood	300			17	4900		3500	8400	2800.00	4250
Southside	Mrs. D. A. Parlier, 205 W. Springdole	Yes	1916	Wood	250	10		9	3500			3500		2000
West End	Mrs. Maud Harrison, 507 Amos St., HP	Yes	1913	Wood	350	24	3	20	10000		2500	12500		5000
Jessup Grove	Mrs. D. H. Bryson, R.5, Greensboro	Yes	1933	Brick	280	1			3000			4000		3000
Jewell	W. E. Kirkman, R.2, High Point	Yes	1941	Wood	100	4	4	4	1000			1000		
Lebanon	Miss Maggie Kirkman, McLeansville	Yes	1911	Wood	350	7	1	7	3500			3500		1800
McLeansville	C. H. Blackburn, McLeansville	No												
Mount Zion	Norman Linens, R.4, Snow Camp	Yes	1817	Wood	500	1	6	6	2000			2000		2000
Oak Grove	Mrs. Harry Robertson, B. 1622, H. Pt.	Yes	1927	Wood	270	8		7	3000			3000		2400
Osceola	T. J. Brooks, Brown Summit	Yes	1915	Wood	300	1		9	2000			2000		2000
Ossippee	H. D. Smith, Elon College	Yes	1933	Wood	350	5		4	2000			2400		1000
Pine Grove	R. H. Pickard, R.3, High Point	Yes	1938	Wood	400	5	5	5	3000			3000		2500
Pilot View	J. E. Rollins, R.2, High Point	Yes	1941	Wood	200	1	4	4	1800			1800		1200
Pisgah	M. J. Bowen, 1902 Franklin St., H. Pt.	Yes	1939	Wood	340	9	9	9	8000		3000	11000	850.00	8000
Pleasant Garden	J. Henry Foy, Pleasant Garden	Yes	1900	Wood	220	7		6	3500			3500	700.00	2000
Pleasant Grove	Vergil Ward, R.3, B. 2860, Greensboro	Yes	1920	Wood	350	8	1	7	4000			4000		3000
Reedy Fork	A. L. Bullard, Greensboro	Yes	1940	Brick	350	1	1		5000		3125	8125	1300.00	6000
REIDSVILLE—														
Baptist Temple	Mrs. Jessie Strader, 55 Wentworth St.	Yes	1929	Brick	300	16	2	16	5500		4500	10000		6750
First	T. L. Gardner, Reidsville	Yes	1871	Brick	550	24	5	24	36000		13300	49300		43500
Penn Mem.	Ruth Gosney, Reidsville	Yes	1934	Brick	300	15	1	11	10000		3000	13000		8500
Rocky Knoll	F. B. Mooney, R.1, Greensboro	Yes	1934	Wood	300	11	11	11	3000		2500	5500	282.96	4000
Ruffin Stacey	Mrs. Lottie Schrumm, Ruffin	Yes	1931	Wood	300	1	8		3000			3000		3000
Smith Grove	Dona Clark, R.1, Box 240, Colfax	Yes	1923	Wood	300	4		3	2000			2500		2000
Summerfield	Mrs. Myrtle Smith, Summerfield	Yes		Brick	400	7		6	9800			9800		3500
Temple	Mrs. R. L. Dodden, Box 1545, H. Point	Yes	1940	Wood	300	5		4	2500			2500		2000
TOTALS					20440	796	164	751	943000	2800	107925	59670	55954.87	630150

TABLE SEVEN — GIFTS FOR LOCAL CHURCH WORK

CHURCHES	Pastor's Salary Paid This Year	Other Salaries	Ministerial Help and Supply	Building and Repairs Spent This Year	Church Debt and Interest	Incidentals	Literature for Church Use, Sun. School, Etc.	Help Given to Local Poor	For Printing Minutes and Clerk of Assn.	Other Objects	Total for Local Purposes given by Church and All Organizations	Pledged to Co-operative Program	Pledged to Associational Missions	Number of Tithers	Mem. Sub. to Ch Bud.	Ev.-Mem. Can. B'get?	Value Food and Clothing Given Orphanage	Ch. Enr. in Min. Ret.?
[illegible]n Jay	2600.00	....	[illegible]00	3825.00	....	583.02	255.78	500.74	11.42	1082.00	9152.96	....	......	75	....	...	......	...
Antioch	335.00	....	110.00	....	....	43.25	48.00	....	6.64	....	542.89	50.00	......	....	....	...	......	...
Brightwood	2600.00	....	702.24	863.64	897.37	247.06	127.17	32.00	6.00	....	5469.48	....	......	30	....	...	199.79	...
Buchanan	1900.00	....	176.98	414.18	....	115.80	66.76	....	11.28	....	2685.00	365.00	......	....	....	...	......	*
Calvary	590.00	....	80.00	121.05	....	94.81	74.97	37.30	......	134.36	1132.49	....	......	....	....	...	......	...
[illegible]ty	578.47	....	65.12	....	561.34	49.95	47.66	31.44	7.60	990.56	2332.14	....	......	....	....	...	......	...
Fair Grove	....	....	....	....	....	....	....	....	......	....	....	....	......	....	....	...	......	...
Fairmont Park	1850.00	....	187.15	1125.56	....	601.29	343.18	....	5.00	923.00	5035.18	250.00	......	31	....	...	......	*
Fairview	450.00	....	....	....	....	66.68	71.19	....	......	....	587.87	....	......	....	....	...	......	...
[illegible]e	1500.00	....	258.35	668.61	....	263.39	106.87	70.00	19.24	202.68	3089.14	75.00	......	....	....	...	......	...
GREENSBORO—																		
Asheboro St.	3599.96	3937.20	482.00	1272.58	6247.62	1033.05	1560.73	184.00	15.00	3101.98	21434.21	3407.68	100.00	54	645	...	......	*
Bailey Mem.	1680.00	....	306.00	277.18	....	379.00	81.68	70.00	4.00	244.29	3042.65	150.00	......	....	....	...	......	...
Bessemer	2400.00	315.00	100.00	565.02	....	1089.20	332.16	43.82	10.00	2000.00	6855.21	480.00	40.00	....	....	...	......	*
[illegible]e Park	2400.00	250.00	210.00	417.98	5304.38	2491.57	416.90	....	12.50	....	11503.33	1200.00	40.00	100	260	...	......	...
Edgeville	523.09	....	126.29	145.08	....	39.30	24.27	....	2.00	....	860.03	....	......	5	....	...	......	...
Eller Mem.	3000.00	1742.00	310.00	324.00	....	1093.01	341.30	237.01	10.00	413.87	7471.29	....	......	40	....	...	......	*
First	5300.00	9495.00	320.66	470.29	27705.06	5013.35	2413.71	1335.50	25.00	5233.34	57311.91	....	......	....	....	...	......	*
Florida St.	2300.00	....	456.53	1725.20	....	1906.56	693.20	25.06	40.00	5365.96	12512.45	....	......	100	....	...	......	*
Latham Park	630.00	....	121.94	109.50	317.68	129.03	35.65	7.00	......	....	1350.80	....	......	4	....	...	......	...
Magnolia St.	2047.50	....	143.00	2283.68	....	592.20	117.86	52.25	4.00	103.37	5343.86	150.00	15.00	45	120	...	179.50	*
Pomona	1713.00	....	112.65	30.72	....	175.18	171.74	60.41	19.44	80.27	2363.41	....	......	19	....	...	......	...
Revolution	1937.50	....	72.00	425.77	....	283.89	222.12	35.00	5.20	319.33	3300.81	....	......	....	....	...	......	...
Sixteenth St.	2600.00	....	130.00	2938.50	....	1357.72	230.45	82.99	10.00	189.50	7539.24	....	......	50	....	...	......	...
Stevens Mem.	975.00	322.50	322.06	1008.00	....	425.20	122.90	....	4.00	234.37	3414.83	800.00	249.38	35	110	*	......	...
Tabernacle	2275.00	1670.50	837.88	6.93	485.91	1450.91	242.34	52.11	......	244.84	7273.42	300.00	21.12	....	....	...	......	...
Webster [illegible]	1530.00	25.00	178.05	300.00	3325.15	421.21	152.52	75.00	33.88	55.00	6095.81	350.00	8.88	16	65	*	......	...
[illegible] f[illegible]d	520.00	32.00	....	....	....	64.44	32.90	....	5.36	2.00	655.60	....	......	....	....	...	......	...
HIGH POINT—																		
First	3766.65	3300.00	....	1877.16	22086.66	6591.41	1569.55	61.00	116.72	5691.33	45060.48	....	......	150	....	...	......	3

Green St.	3575.00	3553.00	37.05	4181.69	7331.09	3034.81	961.40	22.23	10.00		22756.27	25 pct.	100.00	200	900	*	
Hilliard Mem.	2030.00		191.00	43.09	2049.00	498.86	176.75	41.20	15.00	131.76	5215.66			19			
N. Main St.	2600.00		36.95	404.55	1075.00	959.57	233.37	63.50	8.00		4380.94	1000.00	28.00				
North Park	2275.00		227.59	891.87		276.50	297.50	25.00	5.00	251.77	4160.62		11.00				
Southside	2260.00		481.34	55.50	1000.00	435.00	170.00	239.78	10.00		4651.12			20			30.
West End	2196.44		143.00	83.07		811.38	234.27	38.05	5.00	133.59	3644.80						
Jessup Grove	1694.00		271.14	33.44		234.53	95.00	36.50	2.00	830.00	3196.61	25.00	16.00			*	
Jewell	266.79		77.80	665.85		77.48	68.83		3.28		1160.03			10			
Lebanon	1560.00		204.00			53.00	55.13		4.00	41.35	1917.48			30			
McLeansville	115.80		135.86			25.00	35.00	6.53			318.19	52.00					
Mount Zion	2031.16		119.92			118.97	59.77	50.00	5.00		2384.82						
Oak Grove	1813.96		340.29			262.14	44.76			32.25	2496.40	18.00		12		1	
Osceola	612.00		256.08	1.15		77.59	62.50	22.50		11.84	1073.66						
Ossippee	720.00		50.00			55.00	19.50		2.80		847.50						
Pine Grove	520.00		53.42			68.29	38.55		2.50	69.00	751.76						
Pilot View	1470.00		115.66			97.68	60.00	15.00			1758.34			5			100
Pisgah	2340.00		245.00	984.15	1760.40	512.61	128.67	188.15	9.90	270.74	6440.12	75.00		36		*	
Pleasant Garden	1040.00		25.00	240.00	-198.00	200.00	125.00		7.00	50.00	1865.00			12			
Pleasant Grove	1300.00		151.96	436.00	175.00	80.00	74.63		9.20	143.26	2370.05	60.00		12			
Reedy Fork	1130.00		112.03	3125.00	1825.00	211.29	109.32		8.32	133.03	3528.99	104.00		26			
REIDSVILLE—																	
Baptist Temple	2645.00		531.69	1183.55		934.82	497.58		27.40	422.34	6242.38						
First	3437.50	609.90	233.15	1407.11		1690.92	820.73		10.00	112.12	8321.43						
Penn Mem.	1820.00		245.89	3069.11		560.88	120.27	229.72	5.00	809.05	6895.92					*	
Rocky Knoll	1950.00		194.82	310.96	575.00	379.42	260.00	367.82	5.00	213.72	4256.74						
Ruffin Stacey	575.00					122.53			4.00		851.58			6			
Smith Grove	466.00		287.31	15.00		49.75	20.00		3.00	32.00	873.56			7			
Summerfield	625.00		127.30	72.05		239.76	92.64		16.00	26.32	1049.07						
Temple	935.00		380.81	54.72	303.79	311.76	96.84	50.00	2.00		2134.61	150.00	25.00	7			75
TOTALS	100604.82	25252.19	11379.96	38523.70	82273.45	36739.07	14743.56	4388.55	566.68	30359.19	336628.00	8961.68	654.38	1156	2100	...	584

TABLE EIGHT — GIFTS FOR MISSIONS, EDUCATION AND ALL BENEVOLENCES

CHURCHES	REGULAR TREASURERS AND POST OFFICES	Total to Co-operative Program	Special to Association-al Missions	Special to State Missions	Special to Home Missions	Special to Foreign Missions	Special to Schools and Colleges	Special to Theological Seminaries	Special to Orphanage	Special to Hospitals	Special to Ministers' Retirement Fund	Red Cross and Foreign Relief
Allen Jay	W. R. Hobson, R.1, B. 239, High Point	376.20	36.26	40.00	....	726.00	....	....	126.00	100.00	....	....
Antioch	Mrs. T. H. Carter, Reidsville	....	....	7.00	12.75	9.00	....	....	21.63	17.34	....	....
Brightwood	W. L. Johnson, R.2, Brown Summit	....	....	....	1040.00	....	51.00	....	199.79	16.76	....	6.00
Buchanan	R. F. Carter, R.6, [illegible]boro	156.00	....	50.00	....	....	....	....	52.00	36.89	76.00	....
Calvary	J. F. Carroll, R.3, Reidsville	300.00	29.50	14.50	8.00	22.00	43.50	....	227.36	77.25	....	106.60
Community	Mrs. John P. Fuller, R.1, [illegible]nsboro	....	....	....	....	....	....	....	26.50	50.51	....	....
Fairmont Park	R. A. Teague, R.5, B. 400, High Point	....	11.00	....	....	....	....	....	100.00	75.00	28.00	....
Fairview	D. E. Tranthan, R.2, Reidsville	177.42	32.00	12.57	35.50	35.55	20.00	....	142.52	39.75	....	36.00
Gibsonville	T. L. Robertson, Gibsonville	75.00	....	....	....	....	....	....	199.74	13.53	....	31.93
GREENSBORO—												
Asheboro St.	Earl L. Johnson, 2012 Asheboro St., G'b	3307.68	75.27	163.81	166.78	205.95	107.49	....	807.49	172.48	144.00	315.26
Bailey Mem.	Roland Mitchell, R.7, Greensboro	66.00	....	52.00	....	15.00	....	....	238.77	18.42	....	....
Bessemer	C. L. Murray, 3909 E. Bessemer, G'boro	480.00	....	....	229.27	300.00	....	....	100.00	126.50	....	34.50
College Park	Joe Howard, Guilford College	819.04	40.00	125.80	83.76	297.73	254.72	11.00	509.78	143.05	....	351.48
Edgeville	Ruth Greason, 1508 Ball St., Gr'boro	37.24	....	....	....	....	....	....	42.68	20.02	....	....
Eller Mem.	Mrs. Robert Burgess, 512 E. Bess., G'b.	1720.33	89.00	37.11	....	....	....	....	631.50	62.80	....	179.63
First	C. A. McKeel, Greensboro	19911.75	130.00	697.24	967.45	5066.31	890.91	3235.35	4017.83	552.26	1620.39	585.01
Florida St.	D. M. Frazier, 1319 Florida St., G'boro	....	50.00	....	....	900.00	....	100.00	300.00	80.00	95.37	129.33
Latham Park	R. A. [illegible]n, [illegible]boro	35.00	5.56	19.00	....	....	....	....	....	30.00	....	....
Magnolia St.	H. S. Noah, 1700 Grove St., Greensboro	138.00	12.00	13.10	15.73	25.00	25.00	....	179.50	[illegible]	81.87	39.00
Pomona	E. E. Henry, Pomona	132.29	....	36.00	66.67	66.68	....	....	651.33	[illegible]	....	....
Revolution	Waldo Johnson, 2211 Sheber, Gr'boro	1180.64	....	27.24	36.35	419.46	....	....	230.12	188.13	84.00	58.00
Sixteenth St.	L. F. Paris, 1608 15th, Greensboro	2555.14	57.46	19.95	27.39	41.45	....	....	346.01	100.00	....	....
Stevens Mem.	Mrs. C. B. Brisson, Greensboro	700.00	25.00	18.70	13.40	74.34	....	....	257.51	57.83	....	....
Tabernacle	E. H. Moore, Greensboro	240.00	19.84	27.38	7.58	16.10	....	....	196.92	29.60	13.00	....
[illegible]r Mem.	B. H. Scott, R.5, Greensboro	459.71	....	....	....	....	....	....	169.08	10.00	....	....
Guilford	....	48.75	....	1.00	17.00	3.00	....	....	25.00	30.00	....	....
HIGH POINT—												
First	Thelma Patrich, 309 1-2 Ch. St., Hi. Pt.	6064.25	50.00	346.62	410.07	1859.50	....	....	1922.26	382.55	422.84	527.88
Green St.	R. R. Holder, High Point	5513.80	100.00	17.20	213.75	283.87	600.00	....	679.00	45.80	154.27	....

Hilliard Mem.	G. W. Underwood, High Point	139.59	15.00	18.60	42.95	14.75			133.93	30.00	71.80		10.15	475.77	5691.43
N. Main St.	I. E. Brawley, 1916 N. Main St., Hi. Pt.	700.00	30.80	81.24	32.13	142.00	52.00	52.00	215.96	142.78	76.00	82.00	47.00	1653.41	6034.35
North Park	L. W. Glenn, High Point	314.00		30.00		17.78			106.00	6.00			26.00	499.78	4660.41
Southside	W. R. Grant, 901 Granda St., High Pt.	32.90		33.75	16.00	16.55			30.00	35.25				164.45	5024.89
West End	C. M. Scott, 1009 Ferndale Dr., Hi. Pt.	470.52	33.60	162.45	76.00	76.00		125.00	396.37	13.85	41.60		159.11	1678.50	5501.20
Jessup Grove	Mrs. Ruth Lewis, Summerfield		16.00	102.65					124.28	21.34			2106.33	2370.60	5567.21
Jewell	Lela Weatherman, High Point								96.00	15.28				111.28	1271.31
Lebanon	Mrs. O. L. Hanes, R.5, Greensboro		10.00	6.00	13.00	72.81	96.00		79.00	28.05		35.00		339.86	2257.34
Mount Zion	Eugenia Lockamy, R.2, Liberty	442.73			266.88	115.85			101.32	7.54		45.00		979.32	2384.82
Oak Grove	W. L. Shackleford, R.1, Greensboro	18.00							78.30	10.00				106.30	2602.70
Osceola	Mrs. D. A. Green, Brown Summit		21.94	11.26		8.34			92.24	17.64		33.75	49.26	234.43	1308.09
Ossippee	H. D. Smith, R.1, Elon College	6.33								8.00	30.00			44.33	891.83
Pine Grove	E. H. Eller, R.2, Trinity			10.11					29.84	15.39				55.34	807.10
Pilot View	Mrs. Ruby Waggoner, R.2, High Point			11.25	16.00				100.00	21.00				148.25	1906.59
Pisgah	L. C. Madden, 414 Winslow St., Hi. Pt.	50.00	67.67	25.00					125.30	61.80				329.77	6769.89
Pleasant Garden	Geo. Denny, R. 1, Greensboro	57.00		12.00		30.00				10.00			5.00	114.00	1979.00
Pleasant Grove		61.85							125.03	10.00			26.23	223.11	2593.16
Reedy Fork	Parks Gregory, 1514 Upland Dr., G'bor.	125.00	7.20	12.45	10.50	33.15			63.16	87.11		15.00		353.57	3882.56
REIDSVILLE—															
Baptist Temple	Mrs. Odell Dellap, B. 283, Reidsville	547.57	8.50	47.60	45.66	52.00			177.70	19.00		33.00		931.03	7173.41
First	James P. Kemp, Reidsville	2326.43	130.50	99.50	104.00	425.00			529.69	130.29	214.00	26.00	294.50	4279.91	12601.34
Penn Mem.	G. V. Dalton, Box 414, Reidsville	184.15		26.05	41.38				25.96	50.00	72.80	90.00	495.10	985.44	7845.36
Rocky Knoll	Mrs. R. A. Laughlin, R.1, Greensboro			101.00	265.04	25.00			100.00	127.70				618.74	4875.48
Ruffin Stacey	Dewey London, R.5, Reidsville								24.00	11.00				35.00	886.58
Smith Grove	Drew Smith, R.1, Colfax			2.64	11.88	6.12			65.00	39.00			16.00	140.64	1014.20
Summerfield	Mrs. T. D. Carter, Summerfield	117.35		20.13		200.00			61.68	21.95		5.43	225.70	696.80	1755.87
Temple	Roy Yarborough, R.4, High Point	18.50			25.00	30.00			20.00	18.00				110.00	2245.61
TOTALS		50106.26	1104.10	2539.90	4317.87	11632.34	2143.62	3523.35	15211.08	3730.34	3226.85	2765.80	8114.11	108021.48	446131.10

HISTORICAL TABLE — PIEDMONT BAPTIST ASSOCIATION

Year	Where Held	Moderator	Clerk	Preacher	Churches	Baptisms	Members	Gifts
1894	Greensboro	Dr. C. A. Rominger	W. L. Kivett	M. A. Adams	5	....	562	....
1895	Liberty	T. L. Chislom	W. L. Kivett	L. Johnson	12	16	1112	4695.50
1896	Moore's Chapel	R. W. Brooks	W. H. Eller	L. Johnson	14	66	1194	5128.94
1897	Summerfield	F. H. Jones	W. H. Eller	J. A. Munday	16	73	1540	7198.27
1898	Mount Zion	R. W. Brooks	W. H. Eller	L. Johnson	17	67	1557	6883.23
1899	Ramseur	R. W. Brooks	F. P. Tucker	John E. White	19	54	1570	7435.43
1900	Cherry Street	R. W. Brooks	W. H. Eller	Thomas Carrick	16	48	1538	7970.35
1901	Reidsville	F. H. Jones	W. H. Eller	L. Johnson	19	157	1657	8282.73
1902	Salem Street	F. H. Jones	W. H. Eller	W. C. Newton	19	135	1774	9950.97
1903	Gibsonville	F. H. Jones	W. H. Eller	C. L. Greaves	20	185	1868	12834.77
1904	Calvary	F. H. Jones	W. H. Eller	H. W. Battle	22	112	1832	12807.43
1905	Randleman	F. H. Jones	W. H. Eller	J. M. Hilliard	22	114	2096	17674.91
1906	High Point First	F. H. Jones	W. H. Eller	W. R. Bradshaw	23	201	2333	29366.31
1907	[illegible] Street	F. H. Jones	W. H. Eller	Wm. Hedley	26	372	2798	39993.79
1908	Ramseur	F. H. Jones	W. H. Eller	C. E. Maddry	28	311	3086	26347.57
1909	Greensboro	F. H. Jones	W. H. Eller	Wm. Hedley	30	292	3429	49847.28
1910	Mount Zion	F. H. Jones	W. H. Eller	R. G. Hendrick	31	336	3731	28531.01
1911	Asheboro	W. F. Staley	W. H. Eller	W. F. Staley	29	182	3736	25887.56
1912	Hi Point, Green St.	F. P. Hobgood, Jr.	W. H. Eller	J. C. Turner	30	174	3647	29697.38
1913	Liberty	F. P. Hobgood, Jr.	W. H. Eller	R. P. Walker	31	409	3971	37700.97
1914	[illegible] Street	F. P. Hobgood, Jr.	W. H. Eller	A. W. Claxon	31	413	4202	42428.44
1915	Reidsville	J. M. Hilliard	W. H. Eller	J. M. Hilliard	42	313	4491	42577.68
1916	Forest Avenue	J. M. Hilliard	W. H. Eller	E. N. Johnson	36	363	4854	48418.92
1917	Green Street	J. M. Hilliard	W. H. Eller	W. R. White	39	308	4760	44609.05
1918	Moore's Chapel	J. M. Hilliard	W. H. Eller	J. W. Rose	39	374	5140	72538.46
1919	White Oak	J. M. Hilliard	W. H. Eller	W. H. Wilson	39	339	5359	76638.85
1920	Calvary	J. M. Hilliard	W. H. Eller	E. N. Johnson	39	543	5967	117682.35
1921	Summerfield	Clarence A. Smith	J. E. Lanier	B. K. Mason	39	480	6454	135561.79
1922	Glenola	Clarence A. Smith	J. E. Lanier	Jas. A. Clark	39	679	7226	149955.24
1923	Magnolia St.	Clarence A. Smith	H. O. Miller	E. E. White	38	365	7341	140553.25
1924	West End	Clarence A. Smith	H. O. Miller	W. E. [illegible]	40	672	7489	164658.19
1925	Fairview	Clarence A. Smith	H. O. Miller	A. T. Howell	41	610	8956	211792.21
1926	Ramseur	Clarence A. Smith	S. T. Hensley	Lloyd T. Wilson	42	620	9974	243500.68
1927	**Trinity**	Clarence A. Smith	S. T. Hensley	H. T. Stevens	40	656	10223	211846.40
1928	**Bessemer**	Clarence A. Smith	O. E. Lee	R. P. Ellington	41	531	10866	202002.39

1929	Liberty	Clarence A. Smith	O. E. Lee	C. F. Rogers	44	573	11496	218987.61
1930	Asheboro	Clarence A. Smith	O. E. Lee	Geo. T. [illegible]all	44	676	12012	198077.29
1931	Florida St.	Clarence A. Smith	O. E. Lee	A. B. Conrad	44	827	12789	178501.19
1932	Reidsville	Clarence A. Smith	O. E. Lee	J. C. Turner	46	778	13485	159000.60
1933	White Oak	Clarence A. Smith	O. E. Lee	T. L. Sasser	48	1561	15199	186041.40
1934	Franklinville	Clarence A. Smith	O. E. Lee	[illegible]n Woodcock	53	757	15366	172839.18
1935	So. Side, Hi. Point	Clarence A. Smith	O. E. Lee	J. S. Hopkins	41	623	12687	164135.92
1936	Calvary	Clarence A. Smith	O. E. Lee	J. Ben Eller	42	563	13958	166052.96
1937	Eller [illegible]orial	Grover H. Jones	O. E. Lee	C. N. Royal	41	657	14086	195540.50
1938	Hilliard Memorial	Grover H. Jones	O. E. Lee	A. B. Conrad	42	814	14793	200246.20
1939	Reidsville	Grover H. Jones	O. E. Lee	J. C. Turner	46	975	15479	213024.34
1940	Florida St.	Grover H. Jones	O. E. Lee	Chas. E. Parker	51	804	16206	236425.45
1941	Green Street	Grover H. Jones	O. E. Lee	A. [illegible]ln Fulk	53	724	16929	284008.43
1942	Greensboro, First	Grover H. Jones	L. Grady Burgiss	A. A. Walker	55	794	16922	324184.15
1943	Greensboro, First	Grover H. Jones	L. Grady Burgiss	I. B. Jackson	55	772	17268	396139.14
1944	Greensboro, First	Grover H. [illegible]	Ray W. Harrington	G. H. Wallace	56	640	17958	446131.10

MINUTES

of the

Piedmont Baptist Association

North Carolina

Fifty-Second Annual Session

held with the

FIRST BAPTIST CHURCH

Greensboro, N. C.

Thursday, October 25

1945

Next meeting to be in High Point October 23 and 24, 1946, as follows: 1. Green Street first day; 2. Hilliard Memorial, second day; 3. North Main Street evening session.

Wilbur W. Hutchins .... Preacher
James R. Thompson .... Alternate

Edited for the

Piedmont Baptist Association

by

Ray W. Harrington

INDEX

ASSOCIATIONAL DIRECTORY

Grover H. Jones, Moderator .... High Point
Dr. John W. McGinnis, Vice-Moderator .... Reidsville
Ray W. Harrington, Clerk .... Greensboro

EXECUTIVE PROMOTION COMMITTEE

Grover H. Jones, Chairman .... High Point
Dr. John W. McGinnis .... Reidsville
Mrs. J. Ben Eller .... Greensboro
C. S. Hodge .... Greensboro
Carl Bell .... Greensboro
Ray W. Harrington .... Greensboro
Wilson Woodcock .... Greensboro
Wilbur W. Hutchins .... High Point
H. O. Miller .... High Point
D. W. Overby .... Reidsville
T. L. Gardner .... Reidsville
E. A. Long .... Germantown
J. S. Hopkins .... High Point
Dr. J. Clyde Turner .... Greensboro
C. W. Scott .... High Point
C. S. Norwood .... Greensboro
Mrs. C. W. Moseley .... Greensboro
D. M. Clemmons .... Reidsville

CHURCH ADVISORY AND MISSIONS COMMITTEE

Dr. J. Clyde Turner, Chairman .... Greensboro
Grover H. Jones .... High Point
Mrs. C. W. Moseley .... Greensboro
T. L. Gardner .... Greensboro
D. M. Clemmons .... Reidsville
J. S. Hopkins .... High Point
Wilbur W. Hutchins .... High Point
Ray W. Harrington .... Greensboro

OFFICERS OF PIEDMONT W. M. U.

Mrs. J. Ben Eller, Supt. .... 709 Asheboro St., Greensboro
Mrs. Nettie Hoge, Supt. Emeritus
1406 W. Market St., Greensboro
Mrs. T. L. Sasser, Asso. Supt. .... Reidsville
Mrs. J. N. Turner, Sec. .... 2403 Walker Ave., Greensboro
Mrs. W. O. Burnham, Treas. .. 309 Church St., High Point
Mrs. Jas. R. Thompson, Y. P. L.
1110 Glenwood Ave., Greensboro

Chairmen

Mrs. H. A. Knight, Mission Study
1100 N. Main St., High Point
Mrs. W. H. Wright, Stewardship .... Guilford College
Mrs. C. W. Moseley, Community Missions
438 S. Mendenhall St., Greensboro
Mrs O. J. Howard, Literature .... Guilford College
Mrs. R. R. Saunders, Training School and Margaret Fund
Main St., Reidsville

Group Leaders

Mrs. J. Grady Colson, Greensboro City .. Guilford College
Mrs. T. L. Sasser, Greensboro Outside .... Reidsville
Mrs. J. C. Gillespie, Reidsville . 319 Lindsey St., Reidsville
Mrs. Julian S. Hopkins, High Point
324 Woodrow Ave., High Point

Nominating Committee for Year

Mrs. A. C. Lowe, Chm. .. 1500 Randolph Ave., Greensboro
Mrs. W. O. Burnham .... 309 Church St., High Point
Mrs. John McGinnis .... Piedmont St., Reidsville

COMMITTEES SERVING DURING THE ASSOCIATIONAL YEAR

Executive—Promotion Committee
Church Advisory and Missions Committee
Program Committee

COMMITTEES SERVING DURING THE ANNUAL MEETING OF THE ASSOCIATION

Committee on Committees
Committee on Time, Place, and Preacher
Auditing Committee
Committee on Resolutions
Program Committee for this year and next year
Committee to Nominate Officers
Committee to Nominate Executive — Promotion Committee
Committee to Nominate Church Advisory and Missions Committee
Committee to Nominate Delegates to the Baptist State Convention

---

CHURCHES BY DISTRICTS

District 1

Allen Jay; Fairmont Park, Green Street, High Point First, Hilliard Memorial, Jewell, North Main Street, North Park, Oak Grove, Pine Grove, Pilot View, Pisgah, Smith Grove, Southside, Temple, West End.

District 2

Asheboro Street, Bailey Memorial, Bessemer, Brightwood, Buchanan, College Park, Edgeville, Eller Memorial, Florida Street, Gibsonville, Greensboro First, Guilford, Jessup Grove, Latham Park, Lebanon, Magnolia Street, McConnell Road, McLeansville, Mount Zion, Osborne Chapel, Pleasant Garden, Pleasant Grove, Pomona, Sixteenth Street, Stevens Memorial, Summerfield, Tabernacle, Ossipee, Webster Memorial.

District 3

Antioch, Calvary, Fairview, Baptist Temple, Oceola Penn Memorial, Reidsville First, Ruffin Stacey.

OFFICERS OF BAPTIST TRAINING UNION

J. Carl Bell, Director .... Greensboro
Miss Thelma Patrick, Asso. Director .... High Point
Miss Julia Lyles, Secretary-Treasurer .... High Point
E. C. White, Jr., Pianist .... Greensboro
J. W. Morrison, Chorister .... Greensboro
Miss Pearl Womack, Story Hour Leader ...... Greensboro
Miss Eva Saleeby, Junior Leader .... Greensboro
Mrs. W. A. Aydelette, Intermediate Leader ... Greensboro
Miss Mabel Starnes, Young People's Leader .. Greensboro
C. S. Hodge, Adult Leader .... Greensboro
C. V. Coffey, Director District No. 1 .... Reidsville
J. J. Norwood, Director District No. 2 .... Greensboro
Mrs. Arnett Gourley, Director District No. 3 ... Reidsville
Mrs. Marvin Jones, Asso. Director District No. 3, Reidsville
Rev. T. L. Sasser, Pastor Advisor .... Reidsville

PROGRAM COMMITTEE

Rev. W. W. Woodcock, Chairman .... Greensboro
Mrs. John McGinnis .... Reidsville
Rev. Wilbur Hutchins .... High Point
Ellis McCargo .... Reidsville

ORDAINED MINISTERS NOT PASTORS

Barton, C. D. .... Greensboro
Biles, T. H., Chaplain .... U. S. Army
Billings, H. P., Evangelist .... Jamestown
Blanchard, Henry N., Chaplain .... Greensboro
Bowles, J. H., Evangelist .... Greensboro
Bray, T. E. .... Reidsville
Coe, C. G. .... Pomona
Diggs, Harold C., Chaplain .... U. S. Army
Dix, O. P. .... High Point
Farrington, B. H., Evangelist .... Reidsville
Funderburk, Guy B., Chaplain .... U. S. Army
Garner, John U., Chaplain .... U. S. Army

Grant, Wirth, Chaplain .... U. S. Army
Gatewood, J. C. .... Greensboro
Hartsell, P. P. .... High Point
Havner, Vance, Evangelist .... Greensboro
Hight, L. J. .... Greensboro
Hutchins, Edgar .... Greensboro
Lewis, A. E. .... Snow Camp
Matherly, W. F. .... Greensboro
McDowell, Ben S. .... High Point
Montgomery, Floyd, Chaplain .... U. S. Army
Murray, J. F. .... Reidsville
Oates, D. E. .... Greensboro
Peedon, D. E. .... Greensboro
Plybon, C. T. .... Greensboro
Sasser, T. L., Associational Missionary .... Reidsville
Talley, Charles, Jr., Chaplain .... U. S. Navy
Truelove, T. A. .... Greensboro

MINISTERS ORDAINED DURING THE YEAR

Dunevant, J. A. .... Reidsville
Fore, Bennie .... Draper
Lowe, Donnie .... Greensboro
Moffitt, F. E. .... Greensboro
Snow, O. E. .... Winston-Salem
Taylor, Robert L. .... High Point

NEW PASTORS WELCOMED TO ASSOCIATION

Adams, W. T., Magnolia Street .... Greensboro
Atkinson, W. C., Sixteenth Street .... Greensboro
Gupton, B. L., Webster Memorial .... Greensboro
Guth, W. C., West End .... High Point
Scalf, J. H., Fairmont Park .... High Point
Turner, W. D., Calvary .... Reidsville

STUDENTS FOR THE MINISTRY

Boyan, Clarence	**Wake Forest**
Carter, Felton	**Guilford**
Cassell, Paul	**High Point**
Fleet, James B., Jr.	**Wake Forest**
Hancock, Lewis	**Gardner Webb**
Hanner, Richard	**Bob Jones**
Harrison, Jimmie	**In Navy**
Holten, William Steed	Southern **Seminary**
Kincaid, Bill	Wake Forest
Love, Austin	Southern **Seminary**
Mason, James E.	**Moody**
McRae, Maurice	**Bob Jones**
Miller, H. P.	**Wake Forest**
Pike, Wentworth	**Bob Jones**
Williamson, Geo. E.	Southwestern **Seminary**

MESSENGERS

ALLEN JAY—T. Bennison, Jim Warren, L. J. Summey.
ANTIOCH—L. L. Lewis, John Carter, Virginia Carter.
BRIGHTWOOD—Mrs. Carl Ham, A. C. Maness, J. W. Holder, Mrs. Gilmer Cocklereece.
BUCHANON—Mrs. R. P. Johnson, Mrs. Arthur West, Mrs. J. B. Clifton.
CALVARY—Rev. W. D. Turner, Mrs. W. D. Turner, Alex Setliffe, Eugene Hancock, Mrs. Chas. Delgardo.
COMMUNITY—Mr. and Mrs. G. B. Dodson, Z. S. McCanless, Paul Ashborn.
FAIRMONT PARK—Mr. and Mrs. J. E. Copple, Mr. and Mrs. L. G. Campbell, Mrs. John H. Scalf.
FAIRVIEW—D. E. Trantham, Mrs. H. O. Griffin, Dorothy Handy.
GIBSONVILLE—R. K. Cravin, Edd Riggins, Mrs. John Westmoreland.
GREENSBORO:
ASHEBORO STREET—F. L. Paschal, J. J. Norwood, Mabel Starnes, Mrs. C. T. Brown, Mrs. W. A. Aydelette, Jr., Mrs. S. B. Stapleton.
BESSEMER—Mrs. G. H. Williamson, Mrs. C. E. Brady, Mrs. R. F. Pace, Mrs. J. F. Layton, Mrs. E. C. Coble.
COLLEGE PARK—G. W. Williams, C. O. Weaver, E. W. Sharpe, O. J. Howard, P. R. Venable.
EDGEVILLE—Ruth Greeson, G. W. Mahaffy, Marie Lineberry.
ELLER MEMORIAL—Mrs. Eli Craven, Mrs. Melvin Caviness, Mrs. Wiley Patterson, Mrs. R. Von King, Miss Leah Andrews.
FIRST—C. S. Hodge, A. A. Chandler, Howard Sutherland, T. B. Gaskins, F. L. Miles, Mrs. B. L. Spencer.
FLORIDA STREET—Mrs. J. P. Pugh, Mrs. J. N. Reele, Mrs. T. A. Truelove, Mrs. R. W. Spivey, Mrs. E. G. Adams, J. H. Kennedy.
MAGNOLIA STREET—Rev. W. T. Adams, Mrs. W. T. Adams, Mrs. V. Y. Blevins, Mrs. H. S. Noah, Mrs. J. A. Lewis.

POMONA—Rev. C. M. Oates, Mrs. E. E. Henry, Mrs. Vela Godwin, Mrs. W. H. Brown, Mrs. H. L. Nall.

REVOLUTION—N. C. Brown, Waldo Johnson, Hermon Johnson, Clara Mannuel.

SIXTEENTH STREET—Mrs. Webster Owens, Mrs. John Starling, Mrs. Harry Moore, Mrs. Winfield Lowe, Fred Hester, W. G. Somers.

STEVENS MEMORIAL—Rev. Neil Armstrong, H. E. Whitfield, Mrs. J. H. Ham, Mrs. A. C. Hilliard.

TABERNACLE—Mrs. J. L. Shouse, Mrs. Fred Koerber.

WEBSTER MEMORIAL—Mrs. A. Andrews, Mrs. B. H. Scott, Mrs. C. S. Straughan.

GUILFORD—B. F. Butler, Mae Jones, Ora Weston, Mrs. C. E. Gough, Mrs. Clellie Glass.

HIGH POINT:

FIRST—Rev. W. W. Hutchins, Thelma Patrick, Mrs. C. E. Siceloff, Mrs. C. D. Goldsmith, Mrs. W. W. Morton, Mrs. J. M. Lancaster, J. M. Lancaster, Mrs. W. F. Ellis, H. R. Williamson, Mrs. W. F. Clayton, Mrs. G. L. Asbury, Mrs. P. D. Haynes.

GREEN STREET—B. G. Leonard, J. L. Causby, Mrs. J. C. Saunders, P. P. Hartsell, Arthur Whaley.

HILLIARD MEMORIAL—A. L. Slate, Myrtle Williard, P. E. Grubb, Mrs. J. B. Ellis.

NORTH MAIN—Mrs. S. J. Oneal, Alice Davis, R. L. Reeves, Minda McArthur, Ethel Fowler.

NORTH PARK—Mrs. L. W. Glenn, Myrtle Jones, D. H. Short.

SOUTHSIDE—Mrs. G. Tate, Mrs. W. M. Sexton, Daisy Shaw, Mrs. T. Gains.

WEST END—C. M. Scott, W. A. Hedrick, Pearl Preslar, F. A. Moser.

JESSUP GROVE—Mrs. V. W. Manhall, Mrs. W. E. Brightwell, Mrs. D. H. Bryan.

JEWELL—S. P. Stutts, Bessie Hill, Lela Weatherman.

LEBANON—Mrs. Cole, Ruth Carter, Emmalee Goodwin, Felton Carter, Rev. C. C. Cross.

MT. ZION—Chester Branson, Rev. J. T. Swinson.

McCONNELL ROAD—W. H. Bullock, Mrs. J. T. Ellis, Jr.

McLEANSVILLE—S. B. Murphy, Mrs. Beatrice Howard, E. U. Snow, J. W. King, Mrs. W. R. Fuller.

OAK GROVE—A. L. Saunders, Mrs. Mary Barbee, Miss Marion Boleman, W. L. Shackelford, Mrs. John Haynes.

OSCEOLA—L. C. Cole, Frank Huffines, D. A. Greene.

OSSIPEE—T. J. Tribble, Mrs. Gennie Steele, Mrs. Alene Gerringer, H. D. Smith.

PINE GROVE—Larston Tuttle, Mrs. Georgie Tuttle, Mrs. Bertha Pickard, Mrs. Francis Leonard, Willie Leonard.

PILOT VIEW—Arnold Ward, Mrs. Arnold Ward, Mrs. H. S. Fletcher, Mrs. D. F. Kestler, Mr. and Mrs. J. H. Miles.

PISGAH—L. C. Madden, Mrs. D. H. Grubb, Mrs. Lena Maness, Mrs. U. H. Morris, Mrs. Charlie Weaver.

PLEASANT GARDEN—George Denny, Mrs. J. C. Thompson, Mrs. Burton.

PLEASANT GROVE—F. M. Atkins, Mrs. F. M. Atkins, J. H. Boles, Mrs. W. H. Smith, Mrs. Clyde Burce.

REEDY FORK—Lee A. Beach, Mrs. Lee A. Beach, Mrs. Lee Elder, Mrs. Canter, Mrs. A. L. Bullard.

REIDSVILLE:

BAPTIST TEMPLE—George Elliott, Gordon Roberts, Miss Janie Mangum, Mrs. Jesse Strader, Rev. and Mrs. D. M. Clemmons.

FIRST—Not listed.

PENN MEMORIAL—Mrs. W. B. Gosney, Mrs. W. H. Ford, Mrs. Geo. Pennington.

ROCKY KNOLL—Mrs. Cooper, Mrs. R. A. Laughlin, Mrs. R. O. Creede, Mrs. G. A. Tucker, Mrs. F. B. Mooney.

RUFFIN STACY—B. R. Massey, Rev. J. T. London, Lillie Burton.

SMITH GROVE—Mrs. Ray Clark, Pvt. Cleo Holt, J. C. Pitts, Mrs. Tom Holt, Johnny Johnson.

SUMMERFIELD—Mr. and Mrs. T. D. Carter, H. J. Wilson.

TEMPLE—Rev. John Burger, Mrs. John Burger, Robert Taylor, Mrs. Watson Wagner, Mrs. R. L. Radden.

CONSTITUTION

ARTICLE 1.—The Association shall be called the Piedmont Baptist Association.

ARTICLE 2.—It shall be composed of the ordained ministers who are members of, and those who may have pastoral charges within the Associational District, and three delegates from each Church in the district aforesaid, and Churches having a membership exceeding 300 shall be entitled to one additional delegate for every 200 members or fraction thereof in excess of 300.

ARTICLE 3.—The said delegates shall, before taking their seats, produce letters from respective Churches showing their appointment as delegates.

ARTICLE 4.—The Associational session shall be held at least once a year.

ARTICLE 5.—The officers shall be be a Moderator, Vice-Moderator, Clerk and Treasurer. If deemed expedient by the Association, the offices of Clerk and Treasurer may be combined.

ARTICLE 6.—The officers of the Association shall be chosen annually by the Association.

ARTICLE 7.—Association shall be clothed with authority only to advise the Churches touching all things pertaining to their interest but shall in no case presume to direct or control them in reference to their own government or internal policy.

ARTICLE 8.—A Committee of arrangements, consisting of three members shall be appointed on the first day of each session to prepare and report the proceedings and suggest topics proper for the consideration and action of the next annual Association. It shall be the duty of this committee to outline and publish a program for the next annual Associational meeting or for any special or called meeting of the Association.

ARTICLE 9.—Baptist brethren, not members of the Association, who may be present at any session of the body, may on invitation by the body, take seats and participate in the debates of the Association.

ARTICLE 10.—

Section 1. The territory of the Association shall be divided into not less than three districts.

Section 2. A committee composed of the Moderator, the Vice-moderator, the Clerk of the Association, the Associational W. M. U. Superintendent, the Associational Sunday School Superintendent, the Associational B. T. U. Director, and twelve other members of churches in the Association, giving fair representation to the three districts, shall constitute the Executive Committee of the Association. This committee at its first meeting shall decide the number required for a quorum.

Section 3. Seven of the members of the Executive Committee shall be named by the Association as members of the Church Advisory and Missions Committee.

Section 4. The duties of the Executive Committee are to act for the Association between the annual sessions of the Association. The Church Advisory and Missions Committee is charged with the task of seeking the cooperation of churches in the ordination of ministers, the location and organization of new churches, and the management of the Associational Mission Program in our Association.

ARTICLE 11. — All committees shall be appointed by the Moderator, either directly or indirectly with the approval of the Association, unless otherwise authorized by the Association from time to time.

ARTICLE 12.—The Constitution may be altered only at an Annual session of the Association and by a vote of two-thirds of the whole present.

ARTICLE 13.—The rules of this body shall follow Mell's Parliamentary Practice.

ARTICLE 14.—This Association shall cooperate with the Baptist State Convention.

ARTICLE 15.—The time of the holding of the annual session shall begin on Wednesday before the fourth Sunday in October of each year, except where prevailing conditions make it advisable to change this date, in which event the Executive Committee shall be empowered to determine the date of meeting.

Adopted October 17, 1895

Articles 2, 5, 6, 10, 15 Amended Session, July 23, 24, 1930.

Article 15 Amended Session, July 21, 1932.

Article 10 Amended Sessions, October 23, 24, 1935.

Articles 8, 10, 11 Amended Sessions, October 23, 24, 1940.

Article 10 Amended Session, October 19, 1944.

PROCEEDINGS

of the

FIFTY-SECOND ANNUAL SESSION

of the

PIEDMONT BAPTIST ASSOCIATION

Held With the

FIRST BAPTIST CHURCH

Greensboro, N. C.

October 25, 1945

THURSDAY MORNING SESSION—9:30 A. M.

1. The Association was called to order at 9:30 A. M. by the Moderator, Grover H. Jones, and joined in singing, "All Hail the Power," led by C. S. Hodge, accompanied by Mrs. O. E. Lee. After reading Matthew 7:15-29, Rev. J. B. Clifton, Buchanon Baptist Church, led the invocation.

2. The Program Committee reported, and the printed program was accepted.

3. While the Vice-Moderator, J. Ben Eller, was presiding the Moderator presented his report using the Church Letter Digest.

4. The Moderator appointed the following Committee on Committees: C. S. Hodge, Chairman; Dr. John W. McGinnis, and Wilbur W. Hutchins.

5. The Report on Denominational Literature was prepared by Miss Mabel Starnes, read by Ray W. Harrington, spoken to by Dr. J. Clyde Turner, and the report was accepted.

REPORT ON DENOMINATIONAL LITERATURE

Literature is a tremendous force whether it be good or bad. It is one of the most potent factors in modern life. It is so available to everybody. It is so attractively presented. The minds of the people are exposed daily. What they read will largely make them or ruin them.

Great issues are before us. Gigantic problems confront us. A vast deluge of literature dealing with these is released daily. All kinds of points of view are being exploited. Good ideas, crazy ideas, and dangerous ideas are being presented. Many minds are being poisoned while others are being confused.

We, as Baptists need a real crusade in the dissemination of good literature. Herein lies our great opportunity as a Baptist people. We must teach people to read and to know, or we will perish. By getting into our homes our denominational papers and periodicals and establishing in our churches good libraries we will guide our people in the reading of good books and Christian literature. We have then the opportunity of turning our membership away from the vile and vicious habit of reading material that will harm and destroy. What do people read? I stopped in front of one of our news stands and glanced through the magazine section. This is what our people are reading, murder, intrigue, sex, filth, depravity. One is almost persuaded that the entire thought-life and heart-life of the American people is immoral to the extreme.

A few years ago one of our scholarly men made an extensive study of all the best sellers of recent years and here is what he wrote as his conclusion: "I have never found one single best seller of any recent year, the name of Diety referred to except in blasphemy and profanity. There is no exception to this. Why the modern books that I have read in late years make me blush for shame and weep in sorrow." Says Dr. Criswell of the First Baptist Church, Dallas. "The filth that they call literature. You would think that the nicest thing in life is the cesspool, and the garbage heap and the incinerator! Who could blind himself to the evil and dirt and insinuation that characterizes modern intelligent life."

Too long has the church overlooked our responsibility in this field. Too long have Christian leaders failed to provide for the need of Christian literature in our homes and in our churches. And, too long have we left unguarded the ports where so many evil influences enter.

Baptists are creating a wealth of good literature in books, state papers and in magazines, periodicals and tracts of our Sunday School Board. We should expose our people of all ages to the best in Christian literature. We should urge them from the pulpit, the class room, and through personal contact to subscribe to and to read faithfully our denominational papers and magazines.

I would go further in this report and urge the churches of Piedmont Association to build adequate church libraries.

A good church library of carefully selected books will inspire the readers with high ideals, that will open new fields of thought and activities. It will help the young people to discover themselves, and will challenge them to their best. Wonderful things are books. They are the only opportunity and the only means of educating the great rank and file of our people. We have built our great colleges, seminaries and universities for the education of our preachers and leaders among our laity. But not all our people are able to attend our universities and colleges; we must bring the universities to them. One of the great definitions of a university is this: "A university is a collection of books." Maybe not as effective, but the same great opportunity that our schools have in Wake Forest, Meredith, Mars Hill, and the rest, to educate our students, we have in our libraries to educate our people, if we will take advantage of it. After all, the wisdom of the ages is not found in any man's head, it is found in the books that have been left behind.

We therefore commend to the churches that we use widely in all our church programs in every organization our Baptist Literature published by our Sunday School Board; that we encourage the circulation of all W. M. U. publications and of the current mission periodicals namely, "Home Missions" and "The Commission," that we endeavor to have many more clubs for "Charity and Children," our weekly Orphanage paper; and we urge every family in our church membership to subscribe to our State Baptist paper, the "Biblical Recorder."

Second, we commend to each church the importance of having a good church library, urging that each church give its best effort to the promotion of building an adequate church library that will meet the needs of its young people and its leaders in very phase of the church work.

Respectfully submitted,

Mabel Starnes.

---

6. The Christian Education report was presented by Rev. J. R. Thompson, spoken to by Dr. J. A. Easily, Wake Forest College, and the report was accepted.

CHRISTIAN EDUCATION

Christian Colleges do their best work when they minister to students sent to them from the background of Christian homes and the active church. Our schools fare badly when the misguided boys and girls of weak churches and failing homes are sent to them with the hope that a miracle will be worked. Our finest young people ought to be pointed to our Baptist schools.

Christian education, in broad application, includes the teaching fostered in Christian homes, both in deed and in word. No substitute can be found to match the effectiveness of parental Bible instruction in the home. Every effort to magnify the home and make it more Christian deserves our attention. Also the whole church program, but more especially the Sunday School, the Training Union and the mission organizations have to do with Christian education as Christ's teachings and our Baptist program through these agencies reach the masses of people—both Christian and non-Christian. When teachers engage in study courses and when program planning meetings are held primarily we are aiming at Christian education. How well we are educating our Baptist people in the Scriptures and in support of a program worthy of Christ each may judge as he asks how well his home church is doing the job.

Christian education has new mediums of expression in religious broadcasts and visual aids, such as sound films and film strips.

For trained leadership for our churches and our homes we look to our Christian colleges. North Carolina has Wake Forest, Meredith, Mars Hill, Wingate, Campbell, and Gardner-Webb last school year enrolling for all sessions 3,400 students. Of these students 15 were ministerial students and 152 student volunteers. Enrollment this year is record-breaking, nearly every school reporting capacity enrollment with many students turned away. Mars Hill with 748 enrolled of which 36 are ministerial students reports about 275 turned away. Wake Forest had 761 enrolled last year. The interest in spiritual things is manifested by a voluntarily attended evening vesper service at the church recently when 150 were present. Meredith has 586 young women enrolled this year. Her $565,000 expansion program is progressing, our Association having pledged in this project. Meredith has supplied 23 Foreign missionaries, one State W. M. U. President, six of the seven Executive Secretaries of the State and many pastors' wives and splendid teachers and home builders. Last year Campbell College enrolled 333 students, and Wingate 120. Newest among our colleges is Gardner-Webb, with 143 students, and launching a building program of 13 new buildings. Teaching in these colleges are 257 faculty members, God called men and women, proven by their standing by their tasks when war jobs with big salaries were alluring.

Your seminaries, three for white and one for colored, and our W. M. U. Training School offer advanced education for ministers, missionaries, and educational workers. South Western Seminary with record enrollment had student pastors serving 446 churches. This year 58 North Carolina students are enrolled there. Southern Seminary turned away 40 married students this year because there was no place for them to live, yet they report 550 men enrolled. Two North Carolina men this year completed 25 years service on the faculty there. They are Dr. Hersey Davis, and Dr. Gaines S. Dobbins.

B. B. I. has 276 enrolled, 119 from North Carolina. Her correspondence department continues to expand.

Every one of these colleges and seminaries have enlargment programs in view. All are building. All need our help. B. B. I. asks $200,000 for new men's dormitory, Southern Seminary Alumni have $170,000 on the new $250,000 proposed chapel. The crowding of our seminaries has raised the question of the advisability of establishing another one. Ridgecrest has been mentioned as the place.

In our public schools and colleges we work in keeping with our principles of separation of church and state. In local schools Christian teachers are sought. In our colleges the B. S. U. is linking the student with the church. B. S. U. work is beginning to show results. This year 22 of the 38 new missionaries appointed in April came from our State or other than Baptist colleges. The B. S. U. which reaches Baptist students or state campuses for Christ explains the 22 who came to service as foreign missionaries from other than Baptist schools.

Submitted by,

James R. Thompson.

---

7. N. C. Baptist Hospital report was presented by T. Bennison, Dr. C. C. Carpenter, Dean of Wake Forest Medical School, spoke to the report, and the report was accepted.

THE BAPTIST HOSPITAL

The North Carolina Baptist Hospital located at Winston-Salem received its first patient May 28, 1923. At that time it was a 100-bed institution. Today it has 247 beds and 55 bassinets.

The fundamental purpose of our hospital has been to render a medical service to those who were not able to pay for it.

It has demonstrated over and over again its adherence to this purpose by admitting patients from all sections of the State regardless of their financial status.

When the four year medical school of Wake Forest College was moved to the hospital campus the service of the hospital was enhanced many fold.

Our hospital now carries out the two-fold purpose of teaching and healing.

At the present time 150 of our finest girls are in training for a real service to their fellowman—that of nursing.

While they learn the techniques of nursing they are further grounded in the principles of Christ.

Out of 8,000 patients admitted last year fully 4,000 paid no doctor's fee and only a small portion of their hospital expense. Out of the 4,000 only 1,000 paid anything on their expenses.

In addition to the free service mentioned above 20,000 persons were given free diagnostic examinations.

The cost to the hospital of free services rendered during 1944 was $198,648.92.

All Baptists should know that our hospital at Winston-Salem is among the top ranking hospitals of our nation today.

While the hospital has developed physically the emphasis on the spiritual atmosphere has kept pace with the physical. The religious program is under the direction of a full-time chaplain and student secretary. This service is made possible by the generosity of Mr. C. M. Scott of High Point, N. C. The chaplain is able, through the nature of his contacts, to lead many patients to conversion and others to rededication.

North Carolina Baptists have developed in their hospital one of the greatest medical centers in our country, and at the same time one of the strongest influences for the cause of Christ that exists in any land. Its huge opportunities for serving as an agency of mercy, as a means of teaching, and as a means of spreading the influence of Christ are a challenge to the generous heart of our great denomination that its program will not be restricted for lack of finances. All of its activities are operated on the highest of standards, and hence it requires a tremendous budget. It is self-supporting with the exception of its charity work, and it is for this merciful side of its program that North Carolina Baptists this year are giving over $100,000 through the Mother's Day program.

Respectfully sumbitted,

Tennor Bennison.

---

8. The following report was presented by Rev. E. A. Long, and spoken to by Paul Lovengood. The report was accepted.

ORPHANAGE REPORT

The memorable year of 1945 has almost come to its close. This year has witnessed the end of one of the most horrible, the most devastating, the most destructive, and most costly wars in all the annals of history.

But God, whose wisdom is faultless, whose love is perfect, whose power is supreme and whose resources are inexhaustible, still sits upon his throne in the heavens, keeping watch over his little ones and supplying their every need.

One of the most impressive scenes in the life of our Lord, was when he took the little ones up into his arms and blessed them and said, "Suffer the little children to come unto me, and forbid them not: for of such is the kingdom of God."

In no phase of our denominational work is the guiding hand

of God more clearly seen and his stamp of approval upon the work, than in the work of the orphanage.

The past year has been a good year for the orphanage, in spite of the war. No serious illness; no epidemic of contagious diseases have disturbed the peace or interfered with the work in any way.

Wars have always been tragic to homes and to childhood. During the past two years many children have been born in this country who have never seen, and who never will see their fathers. Others, through dissipation and neglect have shirked their responsibility as parents and left helpless children dependent on Christian citizens. Shall we be faithful to these children?

During the past year, in spite of the increased cost of living, we cared for approximately 700 children in the Mills Home and Kennedy Home, through Mother's Aid and in Boarding homes. In addition to this, orphanage representatives rendered splendid service to more than 300 children, by helping families work out their domestic problems, thus preventing the necessity of having to take these children into the institution.

It cost $675.00 a day to care for the large family now in the orphanage. This large sum cannot be met by a few but by the united efforts of the Baptists of North Carolina, through the once a month offering, and the Thanksgiving offering, it can very easily be done. We cannot build orphanages large enough to care for all needy children. But we can help the situation by laying greater emphasis upon the importance of building better and stronger Christian homes.

May we all give ourselves more fully and completely to the task of building more Christ-like homes. Wrecked homes are the greatest tragedies of the present generation.

Respectfully submitted,

E. A. Long.

9. The Committee on Committees presented the following report which was accepted.

REPORT OF THE COMMITTEE TO NOMINATE COMMITTEES

COMMITTEE ON TIME, PLACE AND PREACHER:
Rev. Lawyer Rainey, Chairman
F. L. Paschal
Rev. S. L. Riddle.

AUDITING COMMITTEE:
Miss Thelma Patrick, Chairman
T. Bennison
Rev. D. M. Clemmons.

COMMITTEE ON RESOLUTIONS:
Rev. E. A. Long, Chairman
Rev. C. M. Floyd
Mrs. J. C. Tatum.

PROGRAM COMMITTEE:
Rev. W. W. Woodcock, Chairman
Mrs. John McGinnis
Rev. Wilbur Hutchins
Ellis McCargo.

NOMINATING COMMITTEE:
Rev. J. Ben Eller, Chairman
Mrs. R. T. Burton
Rev. Huey Miller.

COMMITTEE TO NOMINATE EXECUTIVE-PROMOTION COMMITTEE:
Rev. J. S. Hopkins, Chairman
T. L. Gardner
Rev. J. B. Clifton.

COMMITTEE TO NOMINATE CHURCH ADVISORY AND MISSIONS COMMITTEE:
Rev. J. R. Thompson, Chairman
Mrs. Stafford Webb
Rev. Elijah Lankford.

COMMITTEE TO NOMINATE DELEGATES TO THE BAPTIST STATE CONVENTION:
Rev. R. Von King, Chairman
Mrs. James R. Thompson
Rev. George Wallace.

Respectfully submitted,

C. S. Hodge, Chairman
W. W. Hutchins
John W. McGinnis.

10. The report on Social Service was presented by Rev. W. W. Woodcock, and Woodcock spoke to his report. The report was accepted.

SOCIAL SERVICE

Looking back over the Social Service reports presented to this Association during the past eighteen years we find the following problems stressed with considerable hopelessness: Liquor, divorce, labor and management, war, the radio, moving pictures, lynching, gambling, nationalism, race prejudice, the machine age, automobiles and good roads. Rather than waste the brief time allotted to this subject by repeating the lurid descriptions of these which have so ably been given in the former reports let us consider the remedies they demand.

The first remedy suggested in the former reports is evangelism. But the New Testament adds something to the task of getting people to accept Christ as Saviour. In I Corinthians 3:1-3, Paul is talking to babes in Christ, real born again people, people who have been evangelized. But he tells them in effect they have not the moral nor intellectual teeth to chew the strong meat of the Gospel. Their relations with other people are incorrect. There are divisions and strife among them, so even though they are babes in Christ the carnal nature is still in power.

In Hebrews 5:12-14, the writer is stern with the born again people who ought to be teachers but they are dwelling in the glow of their first acquaintance with Christ and have not gone forward to the full Gospel. He says, "But strong meat belongeth to those that are of full age, even those who by reason of use have their senses exercised to discern both good and evil."

Our Lord Jesus Christ was very definite about this when he gave the great commission to the churches and individuals who have been born again saying, Go . . . make disciples . . . baptize . . . and teach. Evangelism must be followed by education if the full Gospel is to be presented.

Family life, divorce, drunkeness, juvenile delinquency, and such immoral conduct are all related. In this church beginning Sunday afternoon will be held a Family Life Institute. Our churches should appoint representative members to attend and report back to the churches their impressions. The Baptist Sunday School Board sends out a program called Christian Home Week which should be observed in all the churches. The Home Mission Board publishes a tract called Home Fellowship Hour which is valuable. Allied Youth and the Allied Church League are fighting liquor and furnish inspiration and information in this area. Pre-marital clinics should be held in the churches to acquaint young people with the psychological, physical and moral privileges and obligations of family life. Let us grow some moral and intellectual teeth with which to chew the strong meat of the Gospel.

War, nationalism, race prejudice, economic greed, labor and management are causes of strife and suffering in relations outside the family. In spite of the fact that President Truman, General Marshall and others have advised us to continue compulsory military training and to continue to build war machines, it remains a fact that the peace of the world will be established only on terms laid down by the full Gospel. General MacArthur, speaking at the signing of the Japanese surrender, said of the peace, "If it is not of the Spirit it will not save the flesh." The day after the first Atomic Bomb was dropped on Japan a Professor of Chemistry said to a teacher of religion, "Now it is up to you fellows." The world is looking to the Christian Church to make peace, peace between nations peace between races, and peace between economic groups. Therefore we should grow some strong intellectual teeth to chew the strong meat of the Gospel. Jesus said, "Blessed are the peacemakers, for they shall be called the children of God." It is not making peace to repeat condemnations and criticisms of other races, nations or economic groups without knowing whether they are justified. It is making peace when we seek to understand other people and seek to convince them of our desire to do them good. Therefore our churches should conduct or support classes and conferences regarding race relations, international relations, and the differences between management and labor, with eyes open seeking the truth.

Baptists are primarily interested in individuals. We believe that the individual may approach God on his own behalf, and that he is responsible to God for his conduct. Baptists also believe that the Christian will grow in grace and the knowledge of God as he puts the Gospel into his relations with other people. Baptists believe that Christ may be revealed to the world through the words and works of individual Christians in their political activities, their daily labor and their home life. Therefore it seems self evident that individual Christians have a responsibility to God to pass beyond the sincere milk of the word to the strong meat of the Gospel and learn to apply it to every human relationship.

Wilson Woodcock.

---

11. State Missions and Cooperative Program was presented by Rev. W. Wilbur Hutchins, and spoken to by Rev. Earl Bradley. The report was accepted.

STATE MISSIONS AND THE COOPERATIVE PROGRAMME

The purpose of State Missions is to provide a program of activities in which each of the churches can share to the end that Christ may become regnant in North Carolina in all areas of life. In order to do this many activities, briefly stated, are listed in this report.

Aid is provided for part payment of the salaries of missionary pastors in needy and strategic places. During the year ending September of 1944, the latest figures we have available, we had sixty-five pastors who were being thus aided. They were serving 121 churches, had preached about 6,000 sermons, made around 22,000 visits, and reported 902 baptisms. Apart from the amount which these 121 churches paid on pastors' salaries and church buildings, namely $135,760, they gave to Convention causes $34,292. Incidentally, during the past calendar year, that is, 1944, we paid a little over $29,000 in salaries to these pastors.

The State Mission program provides for three general missionaries who work with the General Secretary in promoting all the projects of the mission program. They are J. C. Pipes, E. L. Spivey, and Earle L. Bradley.

With reference to the matter of church building let it be said that the Convention does not have money to help in church buildings, except in unusual situations. It does seek, however, to buy lots in growing sections of our cities and in the rural sections where a new church is being established, or an old church is desirous of moving its location in order to be near a good highway. The fund for this is admittedly inadequate. We could use to very good advantage $100,000 each year in stimulating churches to erect better buildings and better educational facilities.

In the matter of racial relationships we are attempting the practical approach of promoting work among the Indians in Robeson County, and are joining with the Negro Baptists of the State in a limited support of their work; helping them to provide for a General Secretary, and a Sunday School and Training Union Secretary.

A visitation program for the sick in the Veteran's Hospital at Oteen, and in the sanatoriums at Aberdeen and Black Mountain, is also provided. The ministry to the girls at Samarcand is carried on through the ministry of Mr. E. M. Harris. The return to the hospitals of our State of more wounded veterans of this recent war should not find Baptists negligent of their Christian responsibilities in this work of remembrance and mercy.

The Convention, through State Missions, also cooperates with many of the Associations in providing for Associational missionaries. Usually the Convention provides about $750.00 a year toward the salary and expenses, and the Association provides the rest. There are about twenty of these Associational missionaries now employed—but there ought to be about fifty.

Our State Convention also cooperates with the Home Mission Board of the Southern Convention in the work of City Missions. We now have four such centers in North Carolina: Raleigh, Greensboro, Durham, and Charlotte.

The State Mission program also seeks to work with the churches in developing a more effective approach to the opportunities for Christian Education in the local churches, which includes the work of the Sunday School, the Training Union, and the Student Union Divisions.

Of particular interest is a new and enlarged work which has been undertaken during the past summer. About one hundred of our finest young people from our colleges have been working in many of the churches and Associations during the summer. It would be difficult to overestimate the value of the work that these well trained young people have been doing in some of the churches.

Other important items which also have the financial support of our State Mission work are the work of the Allied Church League, Pastors' Schools and Conferences, and the North Carolina Radio Hour. It is perhaps true that Baptists are, at the present time, giving the bulk of support for the work of the Allied Church League, which is attempting to defeat the liquor traffic in North Carolina, and to educate the citizenship of the State to the evils of intemperance. But the amount spent by the Convention for this is pitifully small when it is remembered that not long ago Judge E. Yates Webb was authority for the statement that, last year, North Carolina people spent 20 million dollars for their churches, twenty-six million dollars for their educational system, and sixty-six millions of dollars for alcoholic beverages.

For all the activities referred to above, the State Mission account was provided, during the year 1944 with 11% of the Undesignated Cooperative Program funds, plus the special designations for State Missions. The total amount received from these two sources was $182,862.22. We believe the amount this year, 1945, will be more than $200,000. The W. M. U. has set their goal for the offerings during the month of September, just past, at $30,000.

Let it be remembered that we are still in the midst of our Centennial Crusade for Christ, perhaps one of the most comprehensive spiritual efforts ever undertaken by Baptists. The moral and spiritual results of this undertaking cannot be measured statistically, but some of the financial reports can be, and they are encouraging. Total receipts for 1944 were $76,599,420—an increase of $13,532,336 over 1943; mission receipts were $17,303,519, an increase of $3,847,-879, or 28.6% over 1943. Our per capita mission gift in 1944 was $3.05, in 1933 it was only 93 cents. Receipts the first half of 1945 were approximately 30% larger than for the corresponding period in 1944. This is good, but it ought to be better and it can be. The reports just quoted are, of course, for the churches of the Southern

Baptist Convention as a whole. What about our record at home in North Carolina?

The Undesignated Cooperative Program so far this year is about 30% above the same period last year. Our total gifts, counting both designated and un-designated are up about 15%. We think the un-designated Cooperative Program funds this year will go around a million dollars. Our goal for the year 1946 is $1,250,000 for the Un-designated Cooperative Program, which means a step-up of about 25%. Based on last year's goal for the Piedmont Association, I would suggest then, that our goal be approximately $130,000, since last year's figure was $104,000. We must remind ourselves that, within the last year, or thereabouts, we have had three heavy special offerings—the Wake Forest Chapel, the Hundred Thousand Club, and the Centennial Thank Offering. In 1946 not any of this is expected to be promoted, and this means that the people ought to be encouraged to give more to the Un-designated Cooperative Program, therefore helping to reach the goal of $1,250,000. I am informed by Mr. Huggins, our State Secretary, that more and more, we are hoping to get away from the need of these special offerings, and concentrate on the Cooperative Program as the financial method of raising our funds. If the churches, in making their budgets for this next year, will attempt to increase their gifts by 25%, our financial goals for the Coöperative Program can be reached easily.

Two simple recommendations seem appropriate as a part of this report: (1) Since the Cooperative Program seems to be the most effective instrument we have for supporting the current work of our denomination, State and Southwide, we concentrate upon its use as the most effective and fruitful means of financial support for our Christian opportunities; (2) Since Stewardship lies at the basis of Christian character, and is needed to undergird all the causes of our churches and denomination, we recommend that larger and larger emphasis be laid upon Christian stewardship, and that each church, whenever possible, set aside special periods of time for emphasis upon the total stewardship of life, including its material aspects.

Respectfully submitted,

W. Wilbur Hutchins.

---

12. The hymn, "Onward Christian Soldiers," was sung, led by C. S. Hodge.

13. After reading John 2:23-25; 3:1-12, the Associational sermon was preached by the appointee—Dr. John W. McGinnis, Reidsville. The subject: "The New Birth."

14. Dr. A. B. Conrad, High Point, led the closing prayer.

Adjourned until the afternoon.

THURSDAY AFTERNOON—2:00 P. M.

15. The afternoon session opened with the hymn, "When I Survey the Wondrous Cross," led by C. S. Hodge. After Rev. A. H. Dunning read Matthew 13:45-46, he led the invocation.

16. The Committee on delegates to the State Convention reported. The report was accepted as follows:

Rev. W. Wilbur Hutchins
Dr. John W. McGinnis
Ray W. Harrington

17. The Committee on Time, Place and Preacher reported, and the report was accepted.

Time: October 23 and 24, 1945.
Place: High Point.

1. Green Street, first day.
2. Hilliard Memorial, second day.
3. North Main Street, evening session.

Preacher .... Rev. Wilbur W. Hutchins
Alternate .... Rev. James R. Thompson

18. The report of the Committee to Nominate Officers of the Association presented, and accepted:

Moderator .... Grover H. Jones
Vice-Moderator .... John W. McGinnis
Clerk-Treasurer .... Ray W. Harrington
Superintendent of Associational Sunday School, C. S. Hodge
Director of Associational B. T. U. .... J. Carl Bell

---

19. Annuity Board and Retirement Plan report presented by Rev. J. S. Hopkins. The report was accepted, and Rev. Hopkins also spoke to his report.

ANNUITY BOARD AND RETIREMENT PLAN

The Relief and Annuity Board of the Southern Baptist Convention was organized in 1918. In those days few ministers were able to save anything from their meager incomes. Relief work for the aged and disabled preachers was not organized on a convention wide scale, and the disabled brother received sympathy but little financial aid. Old age frequently meant retirement from labor and retirement with insecurity, worry, suffering, and want.

Today the Board is extending aid to more than twelve hundred aged preachers and widows.

The income of the Board in 1944 was $2,136,867.98, three times the income of the year 1939. The total assets, almost $8,000,000.00 at the close of the year, are now well beyond that figure.

During 1944 the relief and annuity benefits paid were $774,142.99, or far more than twice as much as in 1939.

In the Ministers Retirement Plan there were, at the close of 1944, 7,970 active members, while in all plans 10,836 active members. There were 11,480 cooperating churches, boards and institutions

In the North Carolina Ministers Retirement Plan we had 552 active members March 8, 1945, and 696 cooperating churches. This represent a gain of 99 members and 50 churches over the preceding year.

Every salaried employee in our entire denominational working force is eligible for membership in the Retirement Plan.

Any Baptist pastor can become a member of the Ministers Retirement Plan by paying 2, 3 or 4 per cent of his salary to the Board provided the church he is serving pay a like amount. The benefits to be derived will be proportionate to the amount paid. Our State Convention pays $18.00 per year for every active member.

Any pastor paying four per cent over a period of twenty years or more will be eligible to retire at 65 years of age and draw approximately half of his computed salary for the rest of his life. The plan also provides benefits for the pastor's widow and children in case of his death.

We would recommend and urge that all churches and pastors in our Association cooperate, if possible, with our denomination in this forward movement by becoming active members of the Ministers Retirement Plan.

Respectfully submitted,
Julian S. Hopkins.

---

20. The Home Missions report was presented by D. M. Clemmons, who also spoke to the report. The report was accepted.

HOME MISSION REPORT

Every resource we have in people and money, every institution and every church should be mobilized for and dedicated to the God-given task of preaching Jesus Christ and Him crucified to a lost and dying world. The strategic point of approach to this task is our Homeland. Christ must conquer in the Homeland if we expect to win victories for Him in the lands beyond the seas. Let us make the religion of Jesus Christ triumphant at home if we hope to make it triumphant abroad. We must make our own land a demonstration station, revealing what the Gospel can do for a nation which accepts it. When we show that the Gospel of Jesus Christ is solving our problems in the modern world, we shall then make the work of our missionaries vastly easier.

Let us notice the fields of labor on which our Home Mission forces are working. The missionaries of the Home Mission Board are preaching the Gospel to the Indians, the Mexicans, the Spanish-Americans, the Jews, the Italians, the French, the Cubans, the Chinese, the Russians, the under-privileged in our own crowded industrial sections and the slums of our cities, the people in the neglected mountain areas, the boys in military service, and the Negroes. We also have work in Panama and Central America, and among the Japanese in the South.

The last report of the Home Mission Board shows that there are now 489 missionaries working in 1,037 mission stations. Last year 49 missionaries were added to the forces. During the year our missionaries distributed over 60,000 Bibles, Testaments and portions of the Scripture. They gave out more than 925,000 tracts; they preached over 36,000 sermons; they led more than 12,000 people to make a profession of faith in Christ and received into the fellowship of the churches 8,200 members.

The debt, which has hampered the Board for the past fifteen years, has been paid. Relieved of this burden, the Board is now ready and is making plans to enlarge its work in all of the fields.

Let us thank the Lord for Mrs. Ida M. Bottoms and for what she has done in the work of Home Missions. She established a trust for maintaining the Home Mission work in a most difficult period in our work. Out of her generosity, she put into the treasury of the Home Mission Board, an average of $40,000 per year for the last twelve years. The income from this trust goes for work among the foreigns and aliens in the South and in Cuba. Out of this income chapels are built and missionaries are employed. In addition to the work done, this generous soul has inspired enthusiasm in many to do more for the Lord and His cause. We thank the Lord for her.

Right now we ought to thank our missionary-minded women for the noble part they play in this work. Not only do they stand by the work and pay, but they pray for its success. The Woman's Missionary Union has rendered signal service in the field of Home Missions.

The work of Home Missions is very re-assuring at this time. The star of Bethlehem shall not go down now. Nations may grow corrupt and fall to pieces, but others strong in righteousness will arise to take their place. Freedom may be painfully wounded in her temples, but her banner, torn but flying, will at last stream triumphantly over the grave of tyranny. The black night of barbarous ignorance may endanger the world, but our Eternal God will cause the day to dawn when every demon of greeed and need shall have been exercised, when love shall have universal sway and Christ shall be crowned King of Kings and Lord of Lords. Our God is marching on to victory; let us follow in His train.

Respectfully submitted,

D. M. Clemmons.

---

21. The Foreign Missions report was presented by Rev. R. Von King, and spoken to by Rev. Bon Olive. The report was accepted.

FOREIGN MISSION REPORT

To declare war means we are at war but does not mean the war is won. To declare peace means that a state of war has ceased to exist but does not mean that peace is won. By declaration the war is over, but in effect it will not be over for many years. We should strive as earnestly to estabilsh the principles of peace by the world-wide preaching of the Gospel as we have to win our great military victory. In the war's backwash, we face the alternative of becoming victors or victims. We face a world where multiplied millions are hungry for bread and in greater need for the Bread of Life. Old fields are re-opening and many new fields challenge us with wide-open doors.

China awaits with expectancy our return with a more adequate force of laborers, where, we quote, "Children drop by the roadside in China and die of starvation because there is not enough rice to mix with the mud they eat." Children in India wait at our mission stations to see if one more handout of wheat or bowl or soup may come. Japan, Europe, Africa, Latin America, Asia, and many of the Islands are ready harvest fields for the message of the living Christ.

Southern Baptists have now approximately 540 active missionaries under appointment, one to every 10,000 Baptists in our membership. We average about fifty cents per capita for foreign missions annually. With so few laborers and such meager giving we cannot hope to meet present world missionary needs which we face as Southern Baptists. We need at once 300 new missionaries, to say nothing of replacements. Hundreds more might easily be absorbed in needy fields in the near future. Down through the years comes God's call, fresh to the youth of our day, "Whom shall I send, and who will go for us?"

Mr. E. P. Buxton, Treasurer, reports that our income for the year 1944, exclusive of relief funds, amounts to $2,747,207, of which $950,000 came through the Lottie Moon Christmas offering.

Our present financial need is fourfold: (1) a current budget of approximately $2,500,000, (2) funds for replacing destroyed mission property and equipment not less than $2,000,000, (3) an emergency fund of not less than $2,000,000 to be used only under circumstances which will compel us to borrow money from banks if we do not have such a fund, (4) we must have money to finance the growth and development of the Baptist groups which we have helped to found in 19 countries abroad and for enlargement of such program, estimated at $3,000,000. Such a four-fold program is indeed a challenge, but still does not come up to that of which we are worthy and able to do. Funds are also needed to continue our relief work, for which $323,315.47 was received in 1944.

The Commission, E. C. Routh, Editor-in-Chief, and Miss Marjorie Moore, Managing Editor, has had a net increase of fifty per cent in circulation during the past two years. It is urgent and wise that more of our churches include The Commission in our regular list of church literature and send it into the homes of our people on the Church budget plan. Informed and inspired Baptists are Missionary Baptists.

Respectfully submitted,

R. Von King.

---

22. The report of the Auditing Committee.

The Auditing Committee has examined the Treasurer's books and found them to be as represented in his report.

Miss Thema Patrick, Chairman
W. C. Adkinson
D. M. Clemmons.

23. The Church, Mission, and Advisory Committee recommended that the McConnell Road Zion Baptist Church be accepted into the Association, and the committee urged that the word Zion be dropped from the name because the name as it stands is too long. The recommendation was accepted.

24. The Executive Promotion Committee presented their report which was accepted (see index).

25. The Committee on Resolutions presented their report which was accepted.

RESOLUTIONS

Whereas, the Piedmont Baptist Association, meeting with the First Baptist Church of Greensboro, has engaged in a splendid session;

Be it Resolved:

First, that we express our gratitude to this church and its pastor, Dr. J. Clyde Turner, for the privilege of meeting here.

Second, that we express our appreciation to Mr. Grover H. Jones, our very efficient moderator, for his untiring efforts, in serving the Association throughout this year, also to Ray W. Harrington for the splendid manner in which he has carried out the duties of clerk.

Third, that we commend the various organizations of the Churches of the Association for their splendid support of the Baptist Program.

Fourth, that we express our sincere thanks to the program committee for the wonderful program.

And be it resolved that we as followers of Christ give ourselves unreservedly to the cause of Christ in these uncertain times.

Respectfully submitted,

C. M. Floyd
E. A. Long
Mrs. J. C. Tatem.

---

26. Rev. T. L. Sasser presented the new ministers (see index).

27. The Clerk-Treasurer presented his report, which was accepted.

THE FINANCIAL REPORT

Received from Grady L. Burgiss

In Bank	$ 988.02	
Cash	8.99	
Check	10.00	
Total	$1007.01	$1007.01

Received from Churches

For General Fund	$ 558.59	
For McLeansville Chairs	791.52	
Total	$1350.11	$1350.11
Grand Total		$2357.12

LESS EXPENSES

Supplement to T. L. Sasser	$ 275.00	
Rev. L. Grady Burgiss (Clerk Compensation)	100.00	
Compensation of Clerk	100.00	
Dr. Ralph Herring (Expenses)	15.00	
Printing of Minutes	202.50	
Clerk Help	11.00	
Printing Programs	6.50	
Incidentals	182.61	
Mcleansville Chairs	775.25	
Bank Charges	.70	
Total	$1668.56	$1668.56
		$ 688.56

Balance in treasury to date $688.56.

Respectfully submitted,

Ray W. Harrington.

28. While standing C. S. Hodge led the messengers in the hymn, "Send the Light."

29. Address—Baptist Centennial Crusade—by Dr. J. Clyde Turner.

Chaplain Clay Landis, U. S. Army, led the closing prayer.

Adjourned until the evening session.

EVENING SESSION

30. The Association assembled at seven-fifteen o'clock with the singing of the hymn, "I Am Thine O, Lord," led by C. S. Hodge—Carry Davis, accompanist. After reading John 14:1-15, and the singing of one verse of, "Blest Be the Tie," Rev. A. H. Dunning led the invocation.

31. The following report presented by C. S. Hodge was accepted. Paul Crandall, Winston-Salem, spoke to the report.

SUNDAY SCHOOL REPORT

One of our great Baptist laymen has said that two major factors accounted for Southern Baptist progress—continued teaching of the fundamental beliefs of the New Testament and improved methods to meet the needs of the changing times in which we live. If this be true, our Sunday Schools hold the key to even greater successes in our denomination.

Another has said that, "When the world is at its worst, the church must be at its best." Surely, no other age ever called for better Bible teaching. Never was there a time when our efforts ought to be re-doubled in enlisting the unenlisted.

During the year we have held three Associational meetings, a Better-Teaching Clinic and Little Ridgecrest. Added to that 17 churches have held study courses with 325 awards.- First Church High Point again leads with 103 awards.

In the 53 churches reporting there was a Sunday School enrollment of 15,411 as compared with 14,399 last year—an increase of 1012. The average attendance was 8051 compared with 7303 last year—an increase of 748. There were 574 baptisms reported from 32 Schools, an increase of 187 over last year.

Vacation Bible Schools were reported in 27 churches, compared with 21 last year. The enrollment was 3051 and average attendance 2393 as compared with 2387 enrolled last year and 1855 attending.

Only one Sunday School, College Park, reached the Standard this year.

It would seem that these figures, every one of which is an increase over last year, would call for gratitude to God for His blessings and for renewed consecration on our part to the all-important task of winning the lost to Christ through the teaching of God's Word in our Sunday Schools.

Respectfully submitted,

C. S. Hodge, Association Supt.

---

32. The following report was prepared by Julia M. Liles, and presented by J. J. Norwood. The report was accepted. Rev. J. S. Hopkins spoke to the report.

THE BAPTIST TRAINING UNION

The work of the Training Union of the Piedmont Association has been under the direction of Mr. J. Carl Bell again this year. Due largely to his untiring efforts the Associational Training Union has met the Standard of Excellence and has continued to be an A-1 organization throughout the year. A recent report of the Southern Baptist Convention showed only one other Association in North Carolina to be A-1.

The three districts, Reidsville, Greensboro, and High Point, have been working under the leadership of the District Directors. Study Courses have been held in the various churches, with the officers and leaders of the Association lending help wherever possible. Mr. Bell, with some of his co-workers, has organized four new Training Unions.

Quarterly meetings have been held, as well as the Twenty-fifth Annual Spring Session on March 10th. During the afternoon period of this session at the First Baptist Church, Greensboro, the different Associational contests of the Training Union were held. The winners, however, were not able to participate in any further eliminations as all Regional and Ridgecrest meetings were cancelled upon the request of the Office of Defense Transportation. The banquet of the Twenty-fifth Session was held in the Masonic Temple and 532 were in attendance which was the largest attendance ever. Rev. W. Wilbur Hutchins who had been former State Training Union Director and who had recently come into the Association as Pastor of the First Church, High Point, brought the inspirational message.

Due to the fact that there were no meetings at Ridgecrest some churches of the Association tried to promote "Ridgecrest at Home" during the summer. Greensboro had a city-wide meeting and one was also held by the First Church, High Point. Each of these was pronounced a success and some feeling has been expressed that something of the kind might be continued in the future, even after Ridgecrest, itself, is available.

With the returning of many veterans to the communities of the Association, a great challenge is presented to each of us. Each of them should be or become a member of a Christian Church and it is the task of the Training Union to enlist and train those affiliated with the Baptist churches.

Respectfully submitted,

Julia M. Liles, Secretary.

---

33. The W. M. S. report was presented by Mrs. J. Ben Eller, and Mrs. Stafford Webb spoke to the report. The report was accepted.

W. M. U. REPORT

In the book of reports issued by the State Executive Committee at the opening of the year of 1945, we read figures which give the comparative strength of the sixty-eight Associations in North Carolina. Consider these figures:

Number of Churches	56
Number of Societies	126
Number of Members	2713
Number of Young People and Women	4100
Number of New Societies	13
Number of Societies Doing Community Missions	71
Number of Mission Study Classes	195
Number of Tithers	717

In striving for high grade of service we made ten points of twelve on the Standard of Excellence.

At Leadership Conferences in January W. M. U. accepted and entered heartily into southwide plans for "Consecrating the Centennial to Christ."

Piedmont officers continue to meet quarterly and press toward the goals for the Centennial Celebration in beautiful harmony. While the usual 5% increase in gifts allows the society to mark the standard, the higher goal of 20% increase is hoped for in this great year, We are reasonably sure to reach our financial goal.

We aim for twenty new societies. If the churches will feel the proper interest in their young people and commission godly leaders to train them in the needed organizations we shall also reach this aim.

About 550 new members should be enlisted and enrolled in our missionary organizations and, at least, 150 tithers should be won along with a great number of souls won to Christ.

After all of this has been done, there will still be plenty room for improvement in every phase of W. M. U. work.

Our outstanding project in Community Missions was the employment of a Negro Field Worker from the Religious Department of Shaw University. She spent two weeks in High Point and Reidsville with four weeks in Greensboro aiding the Negro churches in Vacation Bible Schools and church visitations.

Miss Mary Christian, Southwide Field Worker was our guest speaker for the Annual Meeting in April at Florida Street Church.

The Business Woman's Federation of Greensboro was organized September 28, 1944, and has properly functioned for one year. It is the aim of this organization to bring a greater missionary zeal and high inspiration to those women who are denied the privilege of the monthly W. M. U. meeting.

Piedmont W. M. U. most urgently needs a revival of consuming passion for winning, enlisting and training the great army of lost and churchless souls in our midst. Let us all address ourselves afresh to this challenging task and truly "consecrate the Centennial year of Baptist Missions to Christ."

Mrs. J. Ben Eller, Superintendent.

---

34. The Obituary report by D. W. Overby, read by Rev. J. M. Allred, was accepted. The Association stood in memory of the deceased, and Dr. J. Clyde Turner led the prayer.

OBITUARIES

Since our last Association 121 of our members have passed to their Heavenly home. And it is with profound reverence that we pause to pay our respects to them; for while they have departed from us they still live in our hearts and lives. We shall greatly miss them, but our loss is their eternal gain and we humbly bow to the will of our Heavenly Father.

We greatly rejoice in the great truth expressed by John the Revelator relative to the redeemed, which is as follows: "Blessed are the dead which die in the Lord henceforth: yea saith the Spirit, that they rest from their labors; and their works do follow them."

Respectfully submitted,

D. W. Overby.

35. The hymn, "My Faith Looks Up to Thee," was sung.

36. A motion was made, carried, that Fairgrove Baptist Church be dropped from the Association.

37. The following report, presented by Rev. T. L. Sasser was accepted. Rev. Sasser also spoke to his report.

ASSOCIATIONAL MISSIONS

The logical unit of corporate missionary activity is the District Association. A church being a body of baptized believers bound together by the strong tie of Christian fellowship can by the power of the Holy Spirit evangelize its local community. Each church is an authoritative source of missionary endeavor. A church can send missionaries to other communities or places like the church at Antioch sent Barnabas and Paul. The establishing of churches by the missionaries makes the association of the churches immediately vital to the orderly and efficient propagation of the Gospel of Christ.

If one local church could send out and supervise all the missions it would not be a New Testament church but a hierarchy of evil type, of which the world has had sufficient example to convince.

A New Testament church looks beyond the borders of its community. In the very looking it must unite with other scriptural churches in associational missions. Hence associational missions becomes the first and the fundamental unit of corporate missionary activity. This concept is scriptural, historic, and by no means new. It antedates missionary societies, church conventions and mission boards but does not preclude them. It underlies and produces them.

Late decades, if not generations, have tended to lessen rather than increase the emphasis on associational missions, leaving the practical performance of the work to State and Southwide agencies. Not in competition against, but in cooperation with these agencies, we should promote missions in the associational territory with increased zeal and spiritual power. This is scriptural and logical. There are signs of a renewal of emphasis. Many associations are employing associational missionaries and promoting association-wide missionary movements. They are kindling anew the fires of evangelism that the light and heat of these fires might be seen and felt to the ends of the earth.

The work in our Association is progressing steadily, if not rapidly. In the three cities of the Piedmont and in rural places the churches are sending out their workers. Missions are being established and functioning with renewed power.

I herewith offer a summary of my personal activities from October

1, 1944 to September 30, 1945 toward the objective indicated in the above paragraphs:

Days on field, 307.
Days on other fields, 49.
Miles traveled, 13,708.
Visits to communities, 200.
Communities surveyed, 29.
Personal conferences on work, 566.
Committee meetings attended, 110.
Associational committee meetings attended, 20.
Pieces literature distributed, 1650.
Circular letters sent out, 4200.
Visits to churches, 133.
Letters to individuals, 216.
Subscriptions to Southern Baptist Home Missions, 175.
Classes taught, 74.
Sermons and addresses, 177.
Revival meetings conducted, 3.
Associational schools of missions (other associations), 3.
Sunday School enlargement campaigns (other associations), 2.
Miscellaneous services, 85.
Visits and services in mission stations, 20.

I wish to express my thanks to all for the unfailing kindness to me throughout the Association.

Respectfully submitted,

T. L. Sasser.

---

38. C. H. Hodge led the closing hymn, "Blest Be the Tie."

39. Mrs. Nettie Hoge led the closing prayer.

40. The Association adjourned from its 1944-45 session.

IN MEMORIAM

ALLEN JAY
2nd Lt. John T. Smith, Jr.
BRIGHTWOOD
Mr. J. M. Crabtree
CALVARY
Mrs. Jones Gunn
Mrs. Virginia Stiers
COMMUNITY
Rev. J. P. Fuller, Pastor
Rev. T. C. Hodgin
Mr. Thomas Garner Marsh
Hope McCandless
GIBSONVILLE
Rev. J. C. Varner
H. L. Webster
W. D. Hammer
ASHEBORO STREET
Mrs. G. W. Hill
Mrs. T. T. Winstead
James Kent Williams, killed in action
Mrs. J. W. Shaw
Mrs. J. S. Moore
Mr. M. C. Oliver
Mr. Chas. F. Scott
Mrs. Harmon Sullivan
Mrs. David Phoenix
Mrs. E. W. Mitchell
BESSEMER
Tech. Sgt. Clay L. Young, killed in action
Miss Dorothy Pitts
Mr. J. F. Brown
COLLEGE PARK
Mr. H. N. Hill
Mr. John H. Buckner
Mr. A. C. Hudson
Mr. T. W. Joines
ELLER MEMORIAL
Mr. J. T. Gregory, Jr.
Mr. Vance Seawell
Mr. R. C. Stutts
Mr. A. C. Chaney
Mrs. Charlie Danford
Mr. A. R. West
GREENSBORO FIRST
Mr. A. P. Ruth
Mrs. A. Cheek
Dr. W. L. McManus
Mrs. Bettie Ballard
Mrs. Eliza Siler
Mr. E. J. Brown
Mr. I. W. White
Mr. Harold Smothers
Mr. H. M. Sykes
Mr. Richard Stone, Jr.
Mr. J. T. True, Deacon
Mrs. R. A. Cates
FLORIDA STREET
Mr. Charles Edmondson
Mrs. Troy Heath
MAGNOLIA STREET
Mr. Wright Barton
Mr. J. H. Lashley
POMONA
Mr. Wm. E. Stanley, Jr.
Mrs. Ida Rich
Mrs. Mollie Watkins
REVOLUTION
Harold Jones
Junior Hillilard
Mrs. N. B. Manley
SIXTEENTH STRTET
Mrs. Eddie Southern
Mrs. Mary D. Wray
Mrs. Collie Walters
Mrs. Pearl Coe
Mr. W. R. Straughn
TABERNACLE
Mrs. J. W. Lackey
Mrs. Edna Thornlow
Mrs. Daisy Lockamy
GUILFORD
Mrs. Grace Lomax
Mrs. Jane Setser
FIRST HIGH POINT
Mr. T. C. Barker
Clayton Holt, ACMM
Mrs. Arthur Ellison
Miss Lillian W. Thrift
Sgt. Clyde Griffith
Miss Hilda Sink
Mrs. Wilma Prevo
Mr. J. Earle Gibson
Mrs. C. C. Hooks
Mrs. R. T. Chappell
S/Sgt. Banks Hamilton
Mr. W. B. Goldsmith, Deacon
Mrs. J. D. Lewis
Ens. Charles Coleman
GREEN STREET
Mrs. Clyde Spry
Johnnie Pendry
Mrs. Laura I. Smith
Harold Seckler
J. M. Smith
Mrs. F. M. Hall
Mrs. Fannie Alice Duggins
Mrs. J. J. Johnson
Jack D. Stout
W. I. Dickens
NORTH MAIN STREET
Private John Mobley
H. E. Sloan
WEST END
Mr. E. L. Chambulin
Mr. Robert Cox
LEBANON
Mrs. B. C. Goodwin
Mr. Earl Reaves
Mrs. Mary E. Stewart
MT. ZION
Mrs. J. T. Swinson (Pastor's Wife)
Mr. J. C. Lockamy, Deacon
Mr. Eddie H. Bunton
Mr. William Soots
OAK GROVE
Mrs. J. H. Hicks
Mrs. James Hubbard
PISGAH
Mrs. C. L. Hunsucker
Mr. W. T. Harrel
PLEASANT GROVE
Mrs. A. M. Heilig
Mr. F. J. Brown
REEDY FORK
Mr. S. J. Fulk
Mrs. Alison Tripp
BAPTIST TEMPLE
Mrs. Ernest Gammon
M. B. J. Harvey
REIDSVILLE FIRST
Mrs. Chares Stanfield
Mr. Paul White
Mr. Haywood Southard
Mrs. Mahola Durham
Henry Arthur, Jr.
SMITH GROVE
Mrs. Jean McCollum
Mr. Clyde Canada
Rev. C. R. Smith
SUMMERFIELD
Mrs. Ida Fryar
Mr. Floyd Stigall
Mr. Robert Parrish

STATISTICAL TABLES

TABLE ONE—CHURCH MEMBERSHIP

CHURCHES	Town, Vill., Country?	When Constituted	PASTORS AND POST OFFICES	Days of Meeting	[redacted]EH GAINS Total Members Reported Last Year	Baptisms	Letters	Statements	Restorations	H[redacted]P LOSSES Letters	Exclusions	Erasures	Deaths	TOTAL Members (Including Non-Resident)	Non-Resident Members	Weekly Prayer M'tings	Revival Meetings During Year	Observances of Lord's Supper During Year	Families Receiving State Baptist Paper	Does Church Have Musical Director?	Does Church Have Library?
Allen Jay	O	1934	[redacted]. H. Wallace, Rt. 3, High Point	All	321	28	9	3	...	4	...	...	1	361	40	52	3	4	....	*	†
[redacted]h	O	1935	J. C. Gillespie, Reidsville	2, 4	62	4	...	...	...	...	...	21	...	66	12	....	2	1	7	†	†
Brightwood	V	1[redacted]0	H. P. [redacted]in, Rt. 5, Greensboro	All	168	21	11	19	2	9	3	13	1	217	....	52	4	3	1	*	†
Buchanon	O	1936	J. B. Clifton, 619 Waugh St., Greensboro	All	137	3	5	1	...	4	3	...	...	139	....	52	2	4	....	*	†
Calvary	O	1901	W. D. Turner, Rt. 4, Reidsville	All	182	5	6	2	...	4	...	...	2	189	....	3	1	1	17	†	*
Community	O	1934	R. O. [redacted]s, Colfax	2, 4	95	...	...	...	...	...	...	...	4	92	....	50	1	....	3	*	†
Fairmont Park	V	1[redacted]0	John H. Scalf, Rt. 5, Box 391, High Point	All	225	10	7	10	...	11	...	...	...	241	12	52	1	2	21	†	†
Fairview	O	1904	No Pastor	1, 3	137	12	3	2	...	2	...	...	...	152	17	....	1	2	18	†	†
Gibsonville	T	1884	John L. Gamble, Gibsonville	All	262	25	12	...	...	7	...	...	3	290	54	52	2	4	....	*	*
1 3[redacted]—																					
[redacted]o Street	C	1899	J. Ben Eller, 709 [redacted]ro St., [redacted]ro	All	1239	45	56	2	...	37	...	11	10	1284	120	52	1	4	62	*	*
Bailey [redacted]ial	C	1935	A. C. [redacted]n, 1016 S. [redacted]k St., G'boro	All	99	...	5	1	...	7	...	...	...	98	....	52	1	2	....	....	....
Bessemer	C	1922	Ray W. Harrington, 507 Delancey, G'boro	All	550	24	17	...	...	12	...	3	2	555	....	52	2	4	4	*	*
[redacted]e [redacted]rk	C	1906	[redacted]on Woodcock, [redacted]08 [redacted]st St., G'boro	All	636	19	18	5	...	25	...	8	4	637	52	52	2	12	24	*	*
Edgeville	C	1942	A. R. [redacted]e, 2202 Spruce St., G'boro	All	29	...	1	4	...	...	...	...	...	39	....	52	3	1	....	†	†
Eller [redacted]orial	C	1897	R. [redacted]n King, 1307 Summit Ave., G'boro	All	847	45	7	1	1	13	...	6	6	876	....	52	....	....	....	....	*
First	C	1859	J. [redacted]e Turner, [redacted]o	All	2366	72	110	10	...	94	...	14	12	2438	....	52	....	12	219	*	*
Florida Street	C	1906	J. R. Thompson, 1110 [redacted]d, G'boro	All	541	56	34	2	...	20	...	...	2	611	34	52	2	4	167	*	*
Latham a[redacted]k	C	1916	....	...	...	...	...	...	...	...	...	...	...	...	...	....	....	....	....	....	....
Magnolia Street	C	1912	W. T. [redacted]s, 103 [redacted]r Ave., G'boro	All	194	15	1	1	...	11	...	...	2	198	....	52	1	3	30	*	*
Pomona	C	1906	C. M. [redacted]s, Pomona	All	246	2	5	...	...	5	...	1	3	244	112	52	2	2	....	†	†
Revolution	C	1907	S. L. Ri[redacted]dle, 2218 Shober, [redacted]o	All	365	17	3	2	1	4	...	2	3	379	....	48	2	4	....	*	*
Sixteenth St.	C	1907	W. C. [redacted]n, 504 16th St., [redacted]	All	264	34	8	6	11	12	...	...	5	306	....	52	2	4	2	†	†
Stevens M[redacted]ial	V	1922	[redacted]il J. [redacted]g, Greensboro	All	180	19	8	...	...	4	1	...	...	202	....	52	2	4	12	*	*
Tabernacle	C	1938	Fred W. Koerber, 100 Marion, [redacted]o	All	264	16	6	...	...	23	...	...	3	260	75	52	3	4	....	†	†
Webster Memorial	V	1935	B. L. Gupton, Rt. 5 Greensboro	All	111	2	...	...	...	1	...	...	...	112	....	52	3	4	3	*	†
[redacted]rd	O	1914	F. E. Kerley, 1704 [redacted]a Ave., G'boro	All	57	16	7	...	...	...	...	...	2	89	....	52	2	2	6	....	*

[illegible]H POINT—																					
First	C	1825	W. Wilbur Hutchins, High Point	All	1484	53	61	2	...	50	...	...	14	1536	347	52	1	4	96	*	*
[illegible]en Street	C	1900	J. S. [illegible]s, Box 1584, High Point	All	1600	119	49	13	...	48	...	13	10	70	201	52	2	4	93	*	*
Hilliard [illegible].	C	1929	H. O. [illegible], 2333 Edgewood Ave., H. P.	All	355	8	11	...	...	19	3	46	...	306	....	52	2	2	14	....	*
North Main	C	1908	L. J. Rainey, 111 [illegible]st [illegible], H. P.	All	377	10	9	...	...	5	...	...	...	289	17	52	1	4	25	....	†
[illegible]h [illegible]k	C	1929	J. W. Loy, Rt. 3, Salisbury	All	207	4	5	...	...	12	...	...	...	204	....	52	1	3	10	*	*
Southside	C	1916	W. H. Barker, 415 [illegible]th St., High Point	All	334	11	6	...	1	4	...	...	...	347	....	52	3	4	10	*	†
West End	C	1913	W. C. Guth, 918 Redding St., High Point	All	411	18	6	...	...	8	...	3	2	422	....	52	2	4	8	*	*
Jessup Grove	O	1933	James E. Wiggs, 1515 Grove St., G'boro	All	172	9	1	...	...	...	...	...	...	182	2	52	1	2	10	†	*
Jewel	O	1937	A. H. Dunning, High Point	All	41	7	10	...	...	3	...	...	...	55	....	52	3	1	....	†	†
Lebanon	O	1911	C. C. Cross, Rt. 5, [illegible]o	All	177	9	5	2	...	4	...	...	2	181	....	†	1	2	13	*	†
Mt. Zion	O	1826	J. T. Swinson, Rt. 1, Burlington	All	131	10	6	1	...	...	...	...	...	233	....	52	....	....	....	*	†
McConnell Road	O	1945	J. F. [illegible]s, Jr., 101 Dockery St., G'boro	All	.....	3	7	...	1	2	...	...	4	233	....	52	2	1	11	*	†
[illegible]e	V	1[illegible]4	J. B. Clifton, 619 Waugh St., [illegible]o	All	19	8	...	...	...	...	...	...	...	27	....	52	1	1	....	....	....
Oak Grove	O	1916	R. L. Smith, 613 [illegible]y Ave., H. P.	All	111	8	2	...	1	...	...	2	2	118	....	52	2	4	....	....	....
Osceola	O	1915	[illegible]l M. [illegible]s, Rt. 4, Reidsville	½	79	2	...	...	...	3	...	...	...	80	....	....	....	....	....	....	†
Ossipee	V	1933	[illegible]r [illegible], Rt., Elon [illegible]e	All	35	...	2	...	...	5	...	...	...	42	8	52	2	4	1	*	†
Pine Grove	O	1938	No Pastor	2, 4	95	...	...	...	...	5	...	1	...	87	....	52	2	1	....	....	....
Pilot View	V	1941	C. C. Roberts, 309 Polk, Thomasville	All	54	3	14	1	3	2	...	...	...	75	....	52	1	1	7	*	†
Pisgah	C	1938	C. M. Floyd, 508 [illegible]r St., High Point	All	127	18	6	2	...	1	...	1	4	155	....	52	4	4	10	*	†
Pleasant Garden	V	1933	No Pastor	All	114	7	6	...	...	6	...	...	...	90	6	52	1	4	....	*	*
Pleasant Grove	O	1938	J. M. Allred, Box 119, Pomona	All	115	5	8	1	...	2	...	2	2	123	....	52	2	8	....	*	†
[illegible]y [illegible]k	O	1940	Elijah Lankford, Rt. 2, [illegible]n [illegible]t	All	104	33	3	...	...	3	...	...	2	135	....	3	2	2	....	*	†
REIDSVILLE—																					
Baptist [illegible]e	C	1929	D. M. Clemmons, Reidsville	All	267	14	1	...	1	5	...	2	2	274	....	52	1	3	12	†	*
First	C	1844	John McGinnis Reidsville	All	941	21	16	1	...	9	...	...	6	965	....	52	2	4	....	....	....
[illegible]n [illegible]l	C	1926	D. W. Overby, [illegible]dsville	All	208	6	5	...	...	5	...	...	1	220	12	52	2	12	6	†	*
[illegible]ky [illegible]ll	O	1934	G. A. Tucker, Rt. 1, Greensboro	All	250	25	12	1	...	6	...	...	...	264	....	52	2	2	....	*	†
Ruffin Stacey	O	1931	J. T. London, Rt. 5, Reidsville	All	192	7	1	...	...	...	...	...	...	200	....	52	1	4	3	†	†
Smith Grove	O	1921	R. O. Nuckles, Rt. 1, Colfax	1, 3	184	5	...	1	...	1	...	2	3	184	....	52	2	3	....	†	†
Summerfield	V	....	E. A. Long, Germantown	1, 3	205	3	...	...	...	...	...	1	3	204	....	....	....	....	....	....	....
[illegible]e	V	1939	John Burger, Rt. 4, High Point	All	104	5	...	...	...	22	...	...	...	85	....	2	3	2	....	†	*
TOTALS		....			18070	921	591	96	20	539	10	152	122	18988	1121	2446	94	176	925	....	....

* Yes. † No.

TABLE TWO—SUNDAY SCHOOLS

[illegible]	ASSOCIATIONAL SUPT. C. S. Hodge, Greensboro, N. C. SUPERINTENDENTS [illegible]	Cradle Roll 3 Years and Under	Beginners 3-5 Years	Primaries 6-8 Years	Juniors 9-12 Years	Intermediates 13-16 Years	Young People 17-24 Years	Adults 25 Years and Up	Extension Department	General and Department Officers	Have You a Mission Sunday School?	Enrollment of Mission Sunday School	Total Enrollment—Mission, Officers Teachers and Pupils	What Is Your Average Attendance?	Baptisms from Sunday School	Is the School Graded?	Is it Standard A-1?	Teachers Holding Diplomas (New Series)	Enrollment of Vacation School	Average Attendance of Vacation School
Allen Jay	Wade Cumbie, R. 1, [illegible]	8	17	16	55	53	19	155	....	5	....	....	327	245	....	*	†	....	....	....
[illegible]	L. L. Lewis, Rt. 4, Reidsville	7	....	8	10	9	8	24	....	3	....	....	66	45	4	†	†	....	....	....
[illegible]	C. M. [illegible], Rt. 5, [illegible]	18	....	....	22	44	47	50	....	3	....	....	184	136	....	†	†	....	....	....
[illegible]	[illegible] Lloyd, Rt. 6, [illegible]	12	23	....	29	6	55	47	....	....	....	....	172	96	....	†	†	....	....	....
Calvary	[illegible], Rt. 2, [illegible]	....	12	23	20	26	21	130	....	....	....	....	232	109	5	†	†	....	....	....
[illegible]ty	Charlie Landreth, Rt. 2, Randleman	....	....	30	20	....	25	53	....	....	....	....	128	72	....	†	....	....	....	....
[illegible]t Park	R. E. Biles, 2[illegible]7 Tipton St., [illegible]h Point	8	16	28	34	23	11	65	....	4	....	....	189	139	8	†	†	....	40	40
Fairview	H. D. [illegible]s, [illegible]	....	20	15	10	50	40	30	....	....	....	....	165	112	9	†	†	....	....	....
[illegible]e	W. J. Blythe, Whitsett, N. C.	....	18	25	40	10	45	60	....	....	....	....	202	124	25	†	†		65	60
GREENSBORO—																				
[illegible]	L. F. Paschal, 420 Camben Rd., G'boro	67	51	71	40	118	130	367	150	5	....	....	1099	370	....	*	†	....	195	159
Bailey [illegible]	L. S. Stanley, Greensboro	....	....	....	....	....	....	....	....	....	....	....	....	....	....	....	....	....	....	....
[illegible]mer	C. [illegible], [illegible]1 Willard St., Greensboro	19	29	44	63	37	54	105	....	7	....	....	351	193	9	*	†	7	15	150
[illegible]e Park	E. W. Sharpe, 306 Isabelle St., G'boro	63	24	45	50	73	21	107	125	4	....	....	512	225	13	*	*	....	65	48
Edgeville	W. L. Lee, Rt. 2, Box 83, Greensboro	....	....	20	12	....	20	15	....	....	....	....	67	45	....	*	†	....	....	....
Eller [illegible]	[illegible], 1103 [illegible]t Ave., G.	10	20	86	[illegible]	87	35	125	12	20	....	....	495	211	35	*	†	....	194	151
[illegible]st	C. S. [illegible]e, [illegible]	210	87	140	186	195	126	801	160	....	....	....	1905	834	62	*	†	12	220	175
[illegible]a [illegible]	V. A. Wilson, 1013 [illegible]k St., G'boro	23	34	49	44	37	22	210	112	7	....	....	458	282	37	*	†	2	154	125
Latham Park	....	....	....	....	....	....	....	....	....	....										
[illegible]a Street	J. [illegible], [illegible]r Br., Greensboro	3	14	12	20	20	15	39	....	3	....	....	126	85	13	*	†	....	39	36
[illegible]a	C. C. [illegible], Box 102, [illegible]	....	20	40	22	35	32	86	....	13	....	....	235	138	....	*	†	....	50	47
[illegible]on	[illegible] Phillips, 209 Newlyn St., G'boro	23	21	31	62	23	44	75	16	....	....	....	295	164	17	†	†	3	91	83
S[illegible] St.	I. V. Brady, 4[illegible]8 Spruce St., G'boro	9	12	47	85	45	23	71	....	22	....	....	298	166	31	*	†	4	158	124
Stevens M[illegible]	S. G. Alvis, Greensboro	12	10	23	23	20	31	70	....	5	....	....	194	125	17	†	†	....	127	83
[illegible]cle	[illegible] Holden, 1004 [illegible]k St., [illegible]	63	33	32	31	15	23	48	45	5	....	....	290	108	6	*	†	....	56	47
W[illegible]r Memorial	[illegible] P. [illegible], 2404 Maple St., [illegible]	7	7	18	21	10	15	45	....	15	....	....	133	106	2	*	†	4	45	39
Guilford	Setzer W[illegible], 635 S. Cedar St., G'boro	12	15	8	8	....	15	50	....	....	....	....	108	52	....	....	....	....	....	....

HIGH POINT—																				
First	W. F. [illegible]on, 223 Lindsay St., Hi. Pt.	95	68	86	117	172	139	525	72	3	....	....	1277	627	48	*	†	32	221	174
[illegible]n S[illegible]t	W. E. [illegible]n, 827 Lexington Ave., H. P.	45	88	129	185	190	158	542	....	5	....	....	1342	640	109	*	†	....	282	198
Hilliard [illegible]	A. L. S[illegible]e, Rt. 5, High Point	4	4	16	32	26	30	67	30	....	....	....	215	132	8	*	†	....	64	....
[illegible]rth Main	W. C. Edwards, 202 W. Lex. Ave., H. P.	10	19	43	82	45	47	116	7	21	....	....	366	67	8	*	†	2	102	92
North Park	I. B. Huff, High Point	9	12	34	15	11	27	49	....	4	....	....	161	112	4	*	†	....	....	....
Southside	D. A. Howard, Rt. 2, H[illegible]h Point	....	10	25	49	25	60	72	....	6	....	....	247	180	....	*	†	....	....	....
West End	R. G. r[illegible]w, Barker St., H[illegible]h [illegible]t	21	27	21	40	30	17	87	20	26	....	....	289	153	16	*	†	4	....	....
J[illegible]p [illegible]e	[illegible]ul Duggins, Freeman Mill Rd., [illegible]oro.	....	31	....	15	....	53	54	....	3	....	....	157	104	9	†	†	....	....	....
Jewel	S. P. Stutts, Rt. 5, High Point	....	....	40	....	....	32	20	....	....	....	....	92	67	7	*	†	....	62	54
Lebanon	Diamond Davis, Rt. 2, [illegible]n Summit	28	7	11	16	16	26	49	....	4	....	....	157	82	9	†	†	....	....	....
M. Zion	Winfred [illegible]r, Rt. 2, Snow Camp	....	18	....	25	25	30	30	....	2	....	....	130	69	8	*	†	....	....	....
[illegible]ll Road	W. H. Bullock, Rt. 6, Greensboro	....	11	....	8	....	9	5	....	....	....	....	33	21	....	†	†	....	....	....
McLeansville	S. B. Murphy, McLeansville	....	22	....	10	....	15	13	....	....	....	....	60	41	8	†	†	....	....	....
Oak Grove	A. L. [illegible]s, Box 928, H[illegible]h Point	....	15	....	13	14	12	30	....	....	....	....	84	6	....	*	†	....	....	....
[illegible]a	E. J. Brown, Rt. 1, Brown Summit	....	7	5	13	12	16	22	....	2	....	....	77	41	....	*	†	....	....	....
Ossipee	R. H. [illegible]h, Box 686, High [illegible]t	....	9	....	14	11	6	13	....	2	....	....	44	18	....	†	†	....	....	....
Pine Grove	J. W. Breedlove, Jamestown	....	12	9	....	8	7	21	....	2	....	....	59	36	....	*	†	....	....	....
Pilot [illegible]w	V. E. [illegible]b, Rt. 2, H[illegible]h Point	....	26	....	26	17	24	32	....	....	....	....	125	70	3	†	†	....	....	....
Pisgah	R. C. h[illegible]h, Box 686, High Point	13	15	18	35	40	32	60	....	....	*	20	233	131	....	†	†	1	90	65
Pleasant Garden	[illegible]il Burton, Pleasant Garden	7	10	7	22	16	9	28	....	....	....	....	99	50	7	†	†	....	40	35
Pleasant [illegible]e	F. M. Atkins, Greensboro	13	12	11	13	21	13	45	....	....	....	....	128	68	5	*	†	....	40	37
Reedy Fork	L. A. 3[illegible]h, Rt. 2, Box 114, Greensboro	19	15	21	29	11	25	52	....	....	....	....	172	99	....	†	†	....	....	....
REIDSVILLE—																				
Baptist [illegible]e	Milton Warf, 212 [illegible]h, Reidsville	13	18	19	47	35	15	67	18	15	....	....	247	116	13	*	†	....	100	80
First	S. F. Wells, [illegible]e	35	40	55	60	60	100	250	....	3	*	25	625	254	15	*	†	....	170	125
Penn Memorial	E. L. Jones, Reidsville	....	10	10	24	13	19	54	....	3	....	....	133	88	6	†	†	....	....	....
Rocky Knoll	E. H. Peele, Troy St., Reidsville	24	27	25	30	22	15	92	....	4	....	....	242	149	....	†	†	....	100	75
Ruffin Stacey	Edmond Poindexter, Ruffin	....	8	10	18	12	25	48	....	4	....	....	123	....	....	*	†	....	123	70
Smith Grove	Homer [illegible]l, Guilford [illegible]e	....	20	....	17	....	48	50	....	2	....	....	137	62	5	†	†	....	....	....
Summerfield	Marion Ayers, Summerfield	....	21	18	27	9	20	44	....	17	....	....	139	80	....	†	†	....	....	....
Temple	R. L. Taylor, Rt. 4, High Point	3	10	16	7	....	17	27	....	....	....	....	90	72	....	†	†	....	45	32
TOTALS		893	1075	1410	2096	1777	1903	5392	767	247	....	45	15514	7977	581	....	....	71	3113	2374

* Yes. † No.

[illegible]E [illegible]OUR—W. M. U. I[illegible]ATIONS AND GIFTS

CHURCHES	PRESIDENTS OF W. M. S. AND POST OFFICES	Number of Woman's Missionary Societies	Number of Y.W.A.'s	Number of G.A.'s	Number of R.A.'s	Number of Sunbeams	Total W. M U. Organizations	W. M. S. Members	Y. W. A.'s Members	G. A.'s Members	R. A.'s Members	Sunbeam Members	Total Members Enrolled	Total Enrolled in Mission Study Courses	Contributions (Local Work) Given by W. M. U.	Contributions (Missions) Given by W. M. U.
Allen Jay																
[illegible]ch		1		1		1	3	6		9		11	26	12	34.60	33.08
[illegible]																
Buchanon	Mrs. J. B. Clifton, 619 Waugh, G'boro	1	1	1	1	1	5	17	14	12	4	15	62	41		[illegible]
Calvary		1	1				2	27	12				39		29.62	9.[illegible]2
[illegible]ty																
Fairmont Park		1	1				2	16	10				26		25.00	302.41
[illegible]w	Mrs. C. S. Booker, Rt. 2, Reidsville	1					1	22					22	13		61.26
[illegible]e	Mrs. W. C. White, [illegible]ville	2					2	23					23	15	355.85	247.98
[illegible]—																
[illegible]o Street	Mrs. A. C. Lowe, 1500 Randolph, G'boro	1	1	2	1	1	6	173	17	50	20	66	326	253	6029.58	2851.85
Bailey Memorial																
Bessemer	Mrs. J. R. Medlin, 200 Sykes Ave., G'boro	1	1	1		1	4	51	15	18		40	124		44.23	296.35
[illegible]e Park		1	1			1	3	71	11			12	94	20	3260.60	1139.18
Edgeville																
Eller [illegible]al	Mrs. Eli[illegible], 1510 Upland Dr., G'boro	1	1			1	3	30	14			20	64	25		883.46
First	Mrs. E. T. Howell, Gr[illegible]boro	1	2	5	5	1	14	388	30	59	61	49	587	340	7493.56	11840.93
Florida S[illegible]t	Mrs. C. D. Foster, 1510 McCormick, Gr.	1	1	2	1	1	5	103	12	35	10	12	172	80		387.57
[illegible]a S[illegible]t		1	1	1		1	4	25		12		15	52	24	1050.00	189.66
Pomona		1				1	2	30				20	50			141.64
[illegible]n	Mrs. Waldo Johnson, 2211 [illegible]r, G'boro	1		1		1	3	25		15		10	50			1220.41
S[illegible]h St.	Mrs. Harry L. [illegible]e, Greensboro	1	1	1	1	1	5	32	12	18	13	10	85	64	1882.54	9[illegible]75
Stevens M[illegible]ial		1	1				2	12	10				22			[illegible]85
[illegible]cle	Mrs. W. J. [illegible]l, 1403 Bersick, [illegible]o	1	1	1		1	4	21	12	12		20	65		6812.96	1000.93
[illegible]r Memorial	Mrs. A. An[illegible]s, Rt. 5, Greensboro	1	1		1		3	37	12	8			57	26	34.24	166.19
[illegible]d	Mrs. C. E. Gough, Guilford	1				1	2	18				11	29			53.00

HIGH POINT—																
First	M[illegible] W. F. Ellis, Jr., W. Lex., H. P.	1	1	2	1	1	6	207	25	40	15	30	317	520	430.21	6043.08
[illegible]n Street	M[illegible] Grover S[illegible]y, 905 Thissell, H. P.	1	3	2	2	1	10	144	19	35	23	20	241	227	6361.32	3985.64
Hillia[illegible]m.	M[illegible]s. J. B. Ellis, 1006 Stanton St., H. P.	1	1	1	1	1	5	15	14	9	12	9	59	23	968.05	123.91
N[illegible]h M[illegible]n	M[illegible] L. J. [illegible]ey, 111 Hillcrest, H. P.	1	....	....	....	....	....	24	....	....	....	....	24	12	673.10	6[illegible]25
N[illegible]h Park	....	1	....	2	1	1	5	17	....	....	9	29	55	34	469.88	287.17
Southside	M[illegible] J. S. [illegible]on, 307 [illegible], H. P.	2	....	....	....	....	....	26	....	....	....	....	26	26	....	8[illegible]23
W[illegible]t End	M[illegible] F. M. Houser, W. Green St., H. P.	1	....	2	1	1	5	15	....	17	7	18	57	27	112.73	171.83
Jessup Grove	....	....	....	....	....	....	....	....	....	....	....	....	....	....	....	....
Jewel	M[illegible] H. L. Hill, Rt. 2, High Point	1	....	....	....	....	1	18	....	....	....	....	18	....	10.00	8.77
Lebanon	....	....	....	....	....	....	....	....	....	....	....	....	....	....	....	....
M[illegible] Zion	Mrs. J. C. Lockamy	1	....	....	....	....	1	15	....	....	....	....	15	....	15.45	45.00
McConnell Road	....	....	....	....	....	....	....	....	....	....	....	....	....	....	....	-
[illegible]le	....	....	....	....	....	....	....	....	....	....	....	....	....	....	....	....
Oak Grove	....	....	....	....	....	....	....	....	....	....	....	....	....	....	....	....
[illegible]a	....	....	....	....	....	....	....	....	....	....	....	....	....	....	....	....
Ossipee	Mrs. Marie Tysinger, Rt. 2, Elon Col.	1	....	....	....	....	1	9	....	....	....	....	9	....	....	....
P[illegible]ie Grove	....	....	....	....	....	....	....	....	....	....	....	....	....	....	....	....
P[illegible]t [illegible]ew	M[illegible] C. C. R[illegible]s, [illegible]masville	1	....	....	....	....	1	16	....	....	....	....	16	....	35.00	34.00
P[illegible]h	M[illegible] C. F. Beachamp, 1305 [illegible]sel, H. P.	1	....	....	....	....	1	14	....	....	....	....	14	8	25.00	30.68
B[illegible]t [illegible]n	M[illegible] J. E. [illegible]pson, Pl[illegible]nt Garden	1	....	....	....	....	1	9	....	....	....	....	9	8	36.00	33.18
P[illegible]t Grove	M[illegible] Clyde Burris, Rt. 3, [illegible]sboro	1	....	1	....	....	2	8	....	8	....	....	16	....	....	17.75
[illegible]y [illegible]k	M[illegible] Ella [illegible]s, Rt. 2, G[illegible]o	1	....	....	....	....	1	12	....	....	....	....	12	7	1019.74	174.00
REIDSVILLE—																
[illegible]t Temple	[illegible]s. Numa [illegible]r, 16 Oak St., Reidsville	1	....	3	....	1	5	74	....	38	....	33	145	68	104.36	349.00
First	Mrs. J. C. [illegible], Reidsville	1	1	2	....	1	5	150	17	15	....	20	202	50	133.10	2645.43
Penn [illegible]l	[illegible]s. G. V. Dalton, Reidsville	1	....	....	....	....	1	22	....	....	....	....	22	16	....	162.57
Rocky Knoll	M[illegible] W. T. Apple, Rt. 1, Greensboro	1	1	1	....	....	3	20	....	....	....	....	20	....	57[illegible]44	57.65
[illegible]n Stacey	....	....	....	....	....	....	....	....	....	....	....	....	....	....	....	....
S[illegible]h Grove	....	....	....	....	....	....	....	....	....	....	....	....	....	....	....	....
Summerfield	M[illegible] Clyde Robinson, Summerfield	1	....	....	....	1	2	17	....	....	....	19	36	....	....	280.75
[illegible]le	M[illegible] R. L. [illegible]n, P. O. Box [illegible]5, H. P.	1	....	1	1	1	4	7	....	11	9	15	42	....	3.25	36.50
TOTALS	....	43	22	34	16	23	135	1966	256	421	183	504	3330	1939	37507.41	37493.04

TABLE SIX—CHURCH PROPERTY

CHURCHES	CHURCH CLERKS AND POST OFFICES	Does Church Own House of Worship	When Was It Built?	What Materials Were Used?	How Many Persons Can Be Seated?	Number of Rooms	Department Assembly Rooms	Number Separate Class Rooms	Value of Church House & Grounds	Value of Mission Chapel if Any	Value of Pastor's Home	Total Value All Church Property	Indebtedness on All Church Property	Amount of Insurance Carried
Allen Jay	Hoy Yarborough, Rt. 4, Box 589, H. P.	*	1934	Wood	300	10	2	15	5000		5000	1 0 0	0	6000
[illegible]ch	Mrs. T. H. Carter, Rt. 2, Reidsville	*	1935	Wood	300	3	3	3	2089			2089		
Brightwood	Mrs. Dewey Fuller, 1501 18th St., G'boro	*	1940	Wood	300	7	7	7	10000		3500	13500		4500
Buchanon	R. F. Carter, Rt. 6, Greensboro	*	....	Wood	200	5	1	5	3000			3000		1500
Calvary	J. E. [illegible]o, Rt. 2, Reidsville	*	1898	Wood	275	9		8	5000		2000	7000		3000
[illegible]ty	Luther McCanless, Rt. 3, Greensboro	*	1943	C. Blk	350	1			4750			4750		2500
Fairmont Park	Ray Moose, Rt. 5, Box 391, High Point	*	1942	Wood	540	11		12	15260			15260		10000
Fairview		*	1901	Wood	300	11		10	3000			3000		2000
Gibsonville		*	1894	Wood	300	9		9	5000			5000		
GREENSBORO—														
Asheboro Street	R. Paul [illegible], 1200 [illegible] St., [illegible]ro	*	1912	Brick	700	61	10	69	51000		6000	57000		43000
Bailey Memorial	Mrs. W. C. Heilig, 1630 Rainbow Dr., G.	*	1935	Wood	250	6		6	2500			2500		750
Bessemer	R. F. Pace, 607 Sykes Ave., Greensboro	*	1923	Wood	350	25	5	20	20000		3000	23000		19500
College Park	P. R. [illegible]le, 1720 W. Lee St., G'boro	*	1940	Brick	400	57	8	42	55000		8000	63000		50000
Edgeville	Marie [illegible]y, 1508 Ball St., [illegible]ro	*	1942	Wood	200	1	1	4	2000			2750		2000
Eller Memorial	E. P. Hinson, 1203 Homeland Ave., G'boro	*	1925	Brick	800	50		48	42000		9000	51000		30000
First	Vander Liles, Greensboro	*	1906	Brick	1000	48		48	130000			130000		70000
Florida Street	Miss Eleanor Watson, 1404 Lexington, G.	*	1930	Brick	350	24	2	24	27000		6000	35000		26000
Latham Park														
Magnolia Street	[illegible]ry Scott, 1110 [illegible]t St., [illegible]ro	*	1912	Wood	250	7		11	6000	1000	4000	11000		[illegible]
Pomona	C. C. Patterson, Box 102, Pomona	*	1906	Wood	350	8		8	3000			3000		
Revolution	N. C. Brown, 1902 Poplar St., Greensboro	*	1907	Wood	400	5	3	9	10000		5000	15000		7500
Sixteenth St.	Harry L. Moore, 1508 17th St., G'boro	*	1907	Brick	500	5		16	39000			39000		18000
Stevens Memorial	Mrs. J. B. Brown, Rt. 2, Greensboro	*	1922	Wood	250	11	2	13	10000			10000		6000
Tabernacle	Lucille [illegible]n, 1408 Florida St., '[illegible]o	*	1938	Wood	200	3		2	5000		3500	8500	2294	8500
[illegible]ter Memorial	Mrs. Kermit Payne, Box 145 Den. Sta.,	*	1935	Wood	200	10	2	9	4000		5500	9500		3000
Guilford	Mrs. Dora Farrar, Guilford College	*	1914	Brick	200	1		4	3500	300		3800		3000

HIGH POINT—														
First	Mrs. W. [illegible] [illegible]ns, 310 [illegible] [illegible], H. P.	*	1935	Brick	900	70	7	54	150000	5000	7000	162000	17000	100000
[illegible] Street	Clyde [illegible]s, High Point	*	1926	[illegible]k	1500	106	7	80	171000	1500	......	172000	......	65000
Hilliard Mem.	[illegible]e Saunders, 345 Wrenn St., H. P.	*	1931	Brick	800	22	.....	.....	35000	.....	.....	35000	.....	5000
[illegible]	Dallas S. [illegible] [illegible]y St., H. P.	*	1924	Brick	350	26	6	20	19500	.....	7000	26500	3100	16500
North Park	[illegible] K. Frye, High [illegible]nt	*	1929	Wood	300	.....	.....	17	4900	.....	.....	4900	.....	1500
[illegible]side	Mrs. D. A. [illegible]r, 205 W. Sp'dale, H. P.	*	[illegible]6	Wood	300	10	.....	10	3500	.....	.....	3500	.....	2000
West [illegible]	H. A. Hedrick, 406 Rotary Dr., H. P.	*	1913	Wood	350	24	3	20	10000	.....	2500	12500	.....	5000
[illegible]	Mrs. D. H. Bryan, Rt. 5, [illegible]o	*	1935	Brick	280	1	.....	.....	5000	.....	.....	5000	.....	3000
[illegible]	Mrs. H. L. [illegible]ll, High [illegible]t	*	...	Wood	25	4	4	3	2000	.....	.....	2000	.....	1500
[illegible]	....	*	[illegible]	Wood	250	8	5	5	3500	.....	.....	4000	.....	1800
Mt. Zion	Norman [illegible]ns, Rt. 2 Snow [illegible]	*	[illegible]	Wood	500	1	.....	.....	2500	.....	3000	5500	.....	2000
[illegible]ll Road	I. T. [illegible]s, Jr., 101 [illegible]y St., G'boro	*	....	C. Blk	250	1	.....	.....	3000	.....	.....	3800	.....	..
[illegible]e	N. H. [illegible]ah, [illegible]o	*	1945	Brick	200	1	.....	.....	6000	.....	.....	7000	1800	.....
Oak Grove	[illegible]ch Boleman, P. O. Box 1622, H. P.	*	1927	Wood	270	8	.....	7	3500	.....	.....	3500	.....	2400
[illegible]	T. I. Brooks, Rt. 1, Brown [illegible]nt	*	1915	Wood	300	1	.....	9	2000	.....	.....	2000	.....	2000
Ossipee	H. D. Smith, Rt. 1, Elon College	*	1933	Wood	350	5	5	4	2500	.....	.....	2900	.....	[illegible]
[illegible]le Grove	R. A. [illegible]d, High Point	*	1938	Wood	400	5	4	5	2500	.....	.....	2500	.....	2500
[illegible]	I. [illegible] [illegible]ngs, Rt. 2, High [illegible]t	*	1941	Wood	200	1	1	1	1800	.....	.....	1800	300	1200
Pisgah	M. J. [illegible]h, 1902 Franklin St., H. P.	*	1939	Wood	340	9	.....	9	8000	.....	3500	11500	.....	11500
[illegible]t Garden	J. H. Foy, Pleasant Garden	*	1900	Wood	220	6	7	7	3500	.....	.....	3500	500	2000
Pleasant Grove	Mr. [illegible] Ward, [illegible] 3, [illegible]o	*	1920	Wood	350	8	1	7	4000	.....	.....	4000	.....	3000
Reedy Fork	A. L. Bullard, [illegible] St., [illegible]o	*	1940	Brick	350	1	.....	1	6000	.....	4265	10265	.....	6000
REIDSVILLE—														
Baptist Temple	Mrs. [illegible]e Strader, 55 [illegible], [illegible]	*	1929	W&B	300	18	2	18	6000	.....	4500	10500	.....	[illegible]750
First	E. S. Powell, Reidsville	*	...	Brick	500	26	3	.....	75000	.....	15000	90000	.....	[illegible]5150
[illegible]h Memorial	Mrs. L. C. Gailey, [illegible]	*	[illegible]4	Brick	300	15	1	11	11000	.....	3000	14000	.....	1 [illegible]00
[illegible]	F. B. [illegible]y, Rt. 1, [illegible]o	*	1934	Wood	300	11	11	11	3000	.....	2500	5500	.....	4000
[illegible]h Stacey	Mrs. Ernest Lee, Ruffin	*	1935	Wood	300	1	8	8	3000	.....	.....	3000	.....	3000
Smith Grove	Mrs. Ray Clark, Rt. 1, Colfax	*	1923	Wood	300	4	.....	3	2000	.....	.....	2500	.....	20[illegible]0
[illegible]eld	[illegible]e Smith, Summerfield	*	...	Brick	400	.....	7	7	9800	.....	.....	9800	.....	3500
Temple	Mrs. R. L. Rodden, P. O. Box 1545, H. P.	*	[illegible]9	Wood	300	5	.....	5	3500	.....	.....	3500	.....	2500
TOTALS				....	20850	786	128	723	26099	7800	112764	71113	24994	655050

* Yes. † No.

TABLE SEVEN—GIFTS FOR LOCAL CHURCH WORK

CHURCHES	Pastor's Salary Paid this Year	Other Salaries	Ministerial Help and Supply	Building and Repairs Spent This Year	Church Debt and Interest	Incidentals	Literature for Church Use, Sunday School, Etc.	Help Given to Local Poor	For Printing the Minutes and Clerk of Association	Building Reserve Fund	Other Objects	(Local Work) Total for Local Purposes Given by the Church to Organizations	Pledged to Cooperative Program	Pledged to Associational Missions	Number of Tithers	Members Subscribed to Church Budget	Every-Member Canvass for Annual Budget	Value of Food and Clothing Given To Orphanage	Church Enrolled in Ministers Retirement?
Allen Jay	2915.00		593.55	801.16		481.86	342.72	261.42		17843.28	61.00	11018.71			100				
[illegible]ch	300.00		138.00	257.60		9.60	27.57	8.00	4.32		34.47	575.56	50.00		6				
Brightwood	2600.00		653.31	1885.92	2000.00	535.50	84.19	235.15	6.00	65.00	346.28	8403.35			30		*		
[illegible]	2080.00		149.24	94.75		157.05	69.35	353.83	10.96	1715.70		4630.88	365.00						
[illegible]	378.00		214.00	116.93		115.06	104.75	99.40	3.00		110.67	1141.81							
[illegible]ty	942.00		113.58	243.0	443.76	21.00	47.92	17.36				1585.52			10				
[illegible]t Park	1760.00		619.87	4035.25		366.72	247.61		18.50		2149.85	9197.80							
Fairview	363.75		100.00			74.04	29.72		9.00	589.23	17.74	594.25							
[illegible]le	1800.00	[illegible]	292.48	49.95	400.00	422.58	137.17	256.00	21.92	5905.55		9445.65							
GREENSBORO—																			
Asheboro Street	3804.52	4384.69	524.00	997.78		680.31	1020.28	860.32		5601.79	3728.15	21601.84		100.00	57	706		108.00	*
Bailey Memorial	1520.00		155.56	5.69		242.12	94.88		8.00		178.59	2204.84							
[illegible]er	2400.00	720.00	120.00	135.48		1434.39	323.24	100.23	10.00	3553.00	154.91	8951.25	480.00			250			*
College Park	2753.76	150.00	385.49	706.66		2934.96	311.81	285.25	12.50	4486.85	601.71	12628.94	2800.00	40.00	100	218	*		*
Edgeville	420.00	122.00	112.00	388.89		25.44	23.12		2.00		60.00	1153.45			12				
Eller [illegible]	2100.00	2023.30	530.00	406.59		1190.38	374.40	222.42	10.00	789.80	1222.07	8877.96	2000.00	55.00	75				*
First	5400.00	10460.00	220.84	2114.23	33140.71	5277.60	3138.94	1487.09			5468.74	67112.01							
Florida Street	3180.00	306.40	393.08	941.96		1318.49	649.71	112.76		5220.00	429.57	12551.97	2800.00	60.00	100	300			*
Latham Park																			
Magnolia Street	1920.00		292.50	149.28		969.59	104.51	206.80	4.00	203.75		3850.43	150.00	15.00	45				*
Pomona	2182.50		210.00	83.15		201.10	124.46	18.74	19.68		373.86	3213.49							
Revolution	2355.00		352.00	132.72		368.88	218.40	156.61	31.70	9436.23	530.31	13581.85							
Sixteenth Street	2549.00		200.00	196.00		1179.11	349.75	154.56	21.72	3662.87	100.00	8372.44	2100.00	100.00	50				
[illegible]s [illegible]	2120.00	75.00	198.59	223.14		345.65	261.58	48.30	4.00		151.70	3407.96	800.00						
Tabernacle	2340.00	1040.00	1001.52	147.33	860.93	659.10	267.66	202.81		148.47	145.14	6812.96	300.00						
Webster Memorial	1982.36	68.22	141.00	21.50		431.81	125.76	34.24		722.00	76.00	3602.89	400.00		16	65	*		
Guilford	710.00		116.34	367.75		129.79	54.75		5.36		13.30	1397.29			10				

HIGH POINT—																			
First	4124.98	3926.90	409.27	1649.05	26922.61	6872.26	1184.00	292.60	118.72	1591.68	3664.81	50756.88			150	843	*		*
Green Street	3835.00	3323.70	2832.95	6954.03		3301.18	1288.67	166.63	120.00	9034.34	4665.63	35630.13		120.00	220		*		*
Hilliard Mem.	[illegible]		157.00	605.40		770.40	239.34	100.00	12.00		534.99	4499.15							
[illegible]h [illegible]n	2650.00		123.00	112.00	2808.02	878.57	337.43	106.35	8.00	49.51		7072.88							
[illegible]h Park	1350.00		660.00	112.82	375.00	346.68	202.92	26.06	[illegible]	6744.77	293.82	8628.07							
Southside	2260.00	17.00	[illegible]	142.48	500.00	486.55	134.57	[illegible]	5.00	3000.00	101.20	7633.28	100.00		30			120.00	
West End	2204.55		159.50	532.22		[illegible]	453.76		32.96		590.48	4539.91			16				*
[illegible]p Grove	1979.00	45.00	330.14	13.73		220.42	137.19	15.00	6.00	612.01	2667.77	4025.86	35.00	16.00	30	110	*	10.00	
Jewel	793.56	92.00	158.85		624.71	188.46	163.09	43.14	[illegible]	174.17	49.48	2300.46			15				
[illegible]an	1960.00	160.00	85.00			114.75	58.20			1090.89	295.78	2573.73			13				
Mt. Zion	2600.00		145.13	162.00		159.18	78.50	73.62	[illegible]	840.00		4043.43	[illegible]						
[illegible]l Road				1000.00								1000.00			2	10			
McLeansville	232.00		55.00		1485.18	104.55	32.74		2.50		125.60	2038.07							
[illegible]k Grove	2153.72		[illegible]			178.34	43.86				31.32	2527.59	18.00		12				
Osceola						35.08						35.08							
[illegible]ee	[illegible]		[illegible]			65.39	18.61		2.00			[illegible]			5				*
Pine Grove	110.00		66.85	7.20		98.16	33.97			44.15		360.33							
Pilot [illegible]w	950.00	20.00	52.00	1296.00		98.46	38.76	7.10	1.46	420.00	[illegible]	3112.37			11				
Pisgah	2852.00		[illegible]	70.09	3247.75	476.83	179.31	432.04	10.00	168.25		7911.27	75.00		36			120.85	
Pleasant Garden	700.00		65.00	[illegible]	[illegible]	200.00	[illegible]	[illegible]			50.00	2016.70	104.00		15				
Pleasant Grove	1500.00		114.28	116.35		161.27	88.73		10.00	208.96	126.00	2325.59	72.00	10.00					
Reedy Fork	[illegible]		100.00	1139.91	1356.44	181.26	110.14		3.00		63.44	5054.19	104.00		23				
REIDSVILLE—																			
Baptist Temple	2965.00			303.95		789.70	270.16		21.36	1961.74	1946.81	[illegible]							
First	3600.00	1296.72	300.00	487.99		1850.32	589.31	34.00	10.00	9976.25	429.24	18573.83							
Penn Memorial	1820.00		256.85	84.03		518.89	104.97	236.55			2000.76	5022.05					*		*
Rocky Knoll	1995.00		230.00	207.43	447.46	354.96	315.73	769.43	5.00	525.00	309.95	5159.96							
Ruffin Stacey	900.00					150.00	[illegible]		4.00			1184.00			8				
Smith Grove	786.00		339.70	144.00		51.50	12.00		3.00		456.88	1793.08							
Summerfield	770.50		147.50			155.85	130.04		16.00			1220.19							
[illegible]le	1225.00		500.00	212.00		154.26	66.73	60.00				2218.00			10		*		
TOTALS	101136.90	35788.93	16598.65	30440.64	74810.57	39003.84	14339.12	6838.83	617.66	96394.24	34583.61	428297.23	[illegible]			[illegible]03		358.85	

* Yes. † [illegible].

TABLE EIGHT—GIFTS FOR MISSIONS, EDUCATION AND ALL BENEVOLENCES

CHURCHES	REGULAR TREASURERS AND POST OFFICES	Total to Co-operative Program	Special to Associational Missions	Special to State Missions	Special to Home Missions	Special to Foreign Missions	Special to Schools and Colleges	Special to Theological Seminaries	Special to Orphanage	Special to Hospitals	Special to Ministers' Retirement Fund	Red Cross and Foreign Relief	Other Objects	Total Given for Missions and Benevolences by Church and All Its Departments	Grand Total, All Purposes, Given by the Church and Its Orgs.
Allen Jay	W. R. [illegible]n, Rt. 1, High Point	600.00	28.88	28.50			98.50		160 00	[illegible]	18.00		239.00	1282.88	12298.59
[illegible]h	Mrs. T. H. Carter, Reidsville			14.75	4.00	7.00			71.00	37.00			34.47	163.17	738.73
Brightwood	Carl Ham, 1216 Fairview St., Greensboro				1040.00		[illegible]		211.82	20.00		8.00		1370.82	9774.17
Buchanon	R. F. Carter, Rt. 6, Greensboro	365.00							52.00	[illegible]	83.20			543.38	5174.26
Calvary	J. F. Carroll, Rt. 3, Reidsville	294.00	11.56	21.12	15.00	55.10	10.00		204 80	68.75		183.70	27.00	891.03	2032.84
[illegible]ty	Julia [illegible], Rt. 1, [illegible]								[illegible]	60.00				120.00	1705.52
Fairmont Park	R. A. Teague, Box 400, High Point			100.00	100.00	100.00			216 50	100.00	74.00			690.50	9888.30
Fairview	T. E. Trantham, Reidsville	245.86		43.76	41.00	60.00	20.00		75 35	41 87		27.00		554.84	1149.09
[illegible]e	T. L. Robertson, Gibsonville	[illegible]							227.40	44.82		31.15	279.00	657.17	4197.27
GREENSBORO—															
Asheboro Street	Mrs. A. C. Lowe, 1500 Randolph Ave., Gr.	1542.79	102.02	179.75	195.00	900.00	239.29	153.01	1138.56	[illegible]	144.00		50.10	7795.57	[illegible]
Bailey [illegible]	[illegible] [illegible], Rt. 7, Box 78, [illegible]			30.00	60.00	41.61			207.82	28.31			47.63	370.37	2575.21
Bessemer	[illegible] L. Murray, P. O. Box 688, G'boro	480.00		35.75	15.00	35.80			100.00	135.00		191.49	5.00	998.04	9949.29
College Park	O. J. Howard, Greensboro	719.12	40.00	150.11	1 [illegible]	[illegible]	100.20	18.31	467.30	108.58	38.65	68.00	45.00	2965.46	15594.42
Edgeville			36.00												1189.45
Eller [illegible]	Mrs. R. R. Burgess, 512 E. Bessemer, Gr.	1962.11	55.00	34.90		63.85	113.00		523.50	279.26		224.59	41.00	3297.21	12175.17
First	C. A. [illegible], [illegible]	26164.37	150.00	1059.96	2053.32	6876.25	906 75	1 145.01	4582.79	743.49		1808.38	1 175.43	46965.75	114077.76
Florida Street	D. M. [illegible]r, 1319 Florida St., G'boro			23.05	387.57	1676.00	225.00		[illegible]	75.15	135.20		1305.93	4352.90	16904.87
Latham Park															
Magnolia Street		150.00	15.00	50.00	75.00	150.00	25.00		150.00	50.00	83.16			748.16	4598.50
Pomona	E. E. Henry, Pomona	391.39		38.00	38.62	38.62			817.00	150.00			33.00	1468.00	4681.50
Revolution	[illegible] Johnson, [illegible]	2260.03		11.97	19.65	242.90			230.67	188.96		29.51	181.13	3164.82	1[illegible]45.67
Sixteenth Street	L. F. Paris, 1507 15th St., Greensboro	2435.55		10.20	13.46	20.80	25.00		362.89	100.00		12.65	12.00	2992.55	1[illegible]65.02
Stevens Memorial		800.00		18.50	23.06	[illegible]	4.10	15.00	235.00	38.41			63.02	1270.94	4678.90
Tabernacle	E. H. Moore, 1704 Grove St., Greensboro	300.00	41.12	25.59	[illegible]	22.85			268.23	43.70			288.69	1000.93	7813.89
[illegible]er Memorial	B. H. Scott, [illegible]	400.00		10.00	20.00	65.00			223.00	37.50		20.00	41.19	816.69	4419.58
Guilford		82.35		4.00	4.00	20.00			33.42	42.50			7.00	193.27	[illegible]

HIGH POINT—															
First		7031.08	50.00	357.20	226.75	1879.26	534.84		2012.53	547.98	301.78		484.42	13425.84	64182.72
Green Street	R. [illegible] Holder, High Point	7200.00	120.00	28.21		1391.23	300.00		1200.00	268.53		70.18		10578.15	46208.28
[illegible]	C. H. Farmer, High Point	217.68	13.00	22.17	22.00	15.85	3.00		229.50	50.27	93.00	3.70	2.00	671.17	5170.32
North Main	I. E. [illegible]	940.63	50.00	[illegible]	60.00	109.98			262.84	100.00	104.00		4.50	1658.95	8731.83
North Park		443.25		29.30	13.90	20.50			194.08	50.00		8.00	16.56	775.59	9403.66
Southside	W. R. Grant, High Point	[illegible]		35.00	25.00	20.63			120.00	26.61				275.13	7908.41
West End		833.17		121.19	144.79		154.23		439.42	1614.71	38.00			3295.51	8119.98
Jessup Grove	Ruth [illegible], Summerfield	35.00	16.00	151.25	92.06				[illegible]	[illegible]			1930.48	2432.80	6458.56
Jewel		40.00							52.44	35.18			10.00	137.62	2438.00
[illegible]				62.78	49.29	99.27			128.08	38.40				773.82	2961.64
Mt. Zion	[illegible], Rt. 1, [illegible]	50.00	5.00	[illegible]	35.00	545.00			[illegible]	7.55				741.59	4785.02
[illegible] Road	J. T. Ellis, Jr., [illegible]														1000.00
McLeansville		39.00							19.50	19.50				78.00	2116.07
Oak Grove	W. L. [illegible], High Point	18.00							73.80	16.00				107.80	2635.39
[illegible]	D. A. Greene, Brown Summit			8.35	2.40	6.75	1362		[illegible]	10.00			13.00	121.04	156.12
Ossipee	H. D. Smith, Elon College			6.54						4.25	30.00			40.79	907.12
Pine Grove	Larston [illegible], High Point								30.63	5.88				36.51	396.84
Pilot View	Mrs. I. E. [illegible], [illegible] Point	69.12							67.20	35.77				172.09	3284.46
Pisgah	L. C. Madden, High [illegible]	85.20		[illegible]		33.00			[illegible]	40.00		49.39	22.28	363.37	8274.64
[illegible] Garden		44.05		26.95	25.00	25.00			83.86	26.00			25.00	286.86	2303.56
Pleasant Grove	Virgil Ward, [illegible]	60.00			17.75				140.00	10.00				227.75	2553.34
Reedy Fork	Parks Gregory, [illegible]	106.00	8.32	13.25	23.90	15.90	18.50		[illegible]	107.50		12.00		383.37	5437.56
REIDSVILLE—															
Baptist [illegible]	Mrs. Odell DeLapp, Reidsville	[illegible]	23.75	[illegible]	44.70	47.75			177.70	[illegible]	105.16	9.00	248.79	1417.18	9705.90
First	J. P. Kemp, Reidsville	3291.16		152.50	304.03	570.00	130.00		[illegible]	132.72	140.00			5573.28	24147.11
Penn Memorial	G. V. Dalton, Reidsville	[illegible]			14.00				60.00	[illegible]	72.80	60.00	311.00	641.49	5663.54
Rocky Knoll				147.00	117.60	48.40	6.65		150.00	125.00				594.65	5754.61
Ruffin Stacey	Lillie Burton, Reidsville								36.00	10.00				46.00	1230.00
Smith Grove	Drew Smith, Colfax			15.00	[illegible]	5.00			90.00	[illegible]				175.00	1968.08
[illegible]	Mrs. T. B. Carter, Summerfield	110.00		[illegible]	35.50	300.00			142.30	25.20		69.80	32.50	[illegible]	1977.80
Temple					25.00	45.00				12.00				107.00	2325.00
TOTALS		63710.67	764.65	3190.54	5568.17	16616.48	3018.68	1631.33	18167.58	6183.69	1460.95	2886.54	6976.12	129842.82	544603.36

HI[redacted]RICAL TABLE—PIEDM[redacted] [redacted] ASSOCIATION

[redacted]	Where Held	Mode[redacted]	Clerk	[redacted]	Churches	Baptisms	Members	Gifts
[redacted]	[redacted]	Dr. C. A. [redacted]	W. L. [redacted]	M. A. [redacted]	5	....	562	....
1895	Liberty	T. L. Chislom	W. L. [redacted]	L. [redacted]	12	16	1112	4695.50
1896	Moore's Chapel	R. W. Brooks	W. H. Eller	L. Johnson	14	66	1194	5128.94
1897	Summerfield	F. H. [redacted]	W. H. Eller	J. A. [redacted]	16	73	1540	7198.27
[redacted]	[redacted] Zion	R. W. Brooks	W. H. Eller	L. [redacted]	17	67	1557	6883.23
1899	[redacted]	R. W. Brooks	F. P. Tucker	John E. [redacted]	19	54	1670	7435.43
[redacted]	[redacted] Street	R. W. Brooks	W. H. Eller	[redacted]	16	48	1538	7970.35
1901	[redacted]	F. H. Jones	W. H. Eller	L. [redacted]	19	157	1657	8282.73
1902	Salem [redacted]	F. H. [redacted]	W. H. Eller	W. [redacted]	19	135	1774	9950.97
[redacted]	Gibsonville	F. H. Jones	W. H. Eller	C. L. Greaves	20	185	1868	12834.77
[redacted]	Calvary	F. H. [redacted]	W. H. Eller	H. W. [redacted]	22	112	1832	12807.43
1905	[redacted]	F. H. Jones	W. H. Eller	J. M. Hilliard	22	114	2096	17674.91
[redacted]	[redacted] First	F. H. [redacted]	W. H. Eller	W. R. Bradshaw	23	201	2333	29366.31
1907	[redacted]	F. H. [redacted]	W. H. Eller	[redacted] Hedley	26	372	2798	39993.79
1908	Ramseur	F. H. Jones	W. H. Eller	C. E. [redacted]	28	311	3086	26347.57
[redacted]	Greensboro	F. H. Jones	W. H. Eller	Wm. Hedley	30	292	3429	49847.28
[redacted]	[redacted] Zion	F. H [redacted]	W. H. Eller	R. G. Hendrick	31	336	3731	28531.01
[redacted]	[redacted]	W. F. Staley	W. H. Eller	W. F. Staley	29	182	3736	15887.56
1912	High Point, Green St.	F. P. [redacted], Jr.	W. H. Eller	J. C. Turner	30	174	3647	29697.38
[redacted]	[redacted]	F. P. [redacted]	W. H. Eller	R. P. Walker	31	409	3971	37700.97
[redacted]	[redacted]	F. P. [redacted]	W. H. Eller	A. W. [redacted]	31	413	4202	42428.44
1915	Reidsville	J. M. [redacted]	W. H. Eller	J. M. Hilliard	42	313	4491	42577.68
[redacted]	[redacted] Avenue	J. M. [redacted]	W. H. Eller	E. N. [redacted]	36	369	4854	48418.92
[redacted]	[redacted]	J. M. Hilliard	W. H. Eller	W. R. White	39	308	4760	44609.05
1918	[redacted]'s Chapel	J. M. Hilliard	W. H. Eller	J. W. [redacted]	39	374	5140	72538.46
[redacted]	[redacted] Oak	J. M. [redacted]	W. H. Eller	W. H. Wilson	39	339	5359	76638.85
[redacted]	[redacted]	J. M. Hilliard	W. H. Eller	E. N. [redacted]	39	543	5967	117682.35
[redacted]	[redacted]field	[redacted] A. Smith	J. E. Lanier	B. K. Mason	39	480	6454	135561.79
[redacted]	[redacted]	[redacted] A. Smith	J. E. Lanier	Jas. A. [redacted]	39	679	7226	149955.24
1923	[redacted] St.	[redacted] A. [redacted]	H. O. Miller	E. E. White	38	365	7341	140553.25
[redacted]	West End	[redacted] A. [redacted]	H. O. Miller	W. E. [redacted]	40	672	7489	164658.19
1925	[redacted]	[redacted] A. Smith	H. O. Miller	A. [redacted] Howell	41	610	8956	211792.21
[redacted]	Ramseur	[redacted] A. [redacted]	S. [redacted]	[redacted]	42	620	9974	243500.68
1927	[redacted]	[redacted] A. Smith	S. T. [redacted]	H. T. Stevens	40	656	10223	211846.40
1928	Bessemer	[redacted] A. [redacted]	O. E. [redacted]	R. P. Ellington	41	531	10866	202002.30

1929	Liberty	[illegible]ce A. [illegible]th	O. E. Lee	C. F. Rogers	44	573	11496	218987.61
1930	Asheboro	[illegible]ce A. [illegible]th	O. E. Lee	[illegible]G. T. Tunstall	44	676	12012	198077.29
1931	Florida St.	[illegible]ce A. [illegible]th	O. E. Lee	A. B. Conrad	44	827	12789	178501.19
1932	Reidsville	[illegible]ce A. Smith	O. E. Lee	J. C. Turner	46	778	13485	159000.60
1933	W[illegible]te Oak	[illegible]ce A. Smith	O. E. Lee	T. L. Sasser	48	1561	15199	186041.40
1934	Franklinville	[illegible]ce A. Smith	O. E. Lee	Wilson [illegible]	53	757	15365	172839.18
1935	So. Side, Hi. Point	Clarence A. Smith	O. E. Lee	J. S. Hopkins	41	623	12687	164135.92
1936	Calvary	[illegible]ce A. [illegible]th	O. E. Lee	J. Ben Eller	42	563	13958	166052.96
1937	Eller [illegible]	Grover H. Jones	O. E. Lee	C. N. Royal	41	657	14086	195540.50
1938	Hilliard Memorial	Grover H. Jones	O. E. Lee	A. B. Conrad	42	814	[illegible]	200246.20
1939	Reidsville	Grover H. Jones	O. E. Lee	J. C. Turner	46	975	15479	213024.34
1940	Florida Street	Grover H. J[illegible]es	O. E. Lee	Chas. E. [illegible]	51	804	16206	236425.45
1941	Green [illegible]	Grover H. Jones	O. E. Lee	A. L[illegible]n Fulk	53	724	16929	284008.43
1942	Greensboro, First	Grover H. Jones	L. Grady Burgiss	A. A. Walker	55	794	16922	324184.15
1943	Greensboro, First	Grover H. Jones	L. Grady Burgiss	I. B. Jackson	55	772	17268	396139.14
1944	[illegible]o, First	Grover H. Jones	Ray W. Harrington	G. H. Wallace	56	640	17958	[illegible]1.10
1945	[illegible]o, First	Grover H. Jones	Ray W. Harrington	John McGinnis	56	921	18988	544603.36

MINUTES

of the

Piedmont Baptist Association
North Carolina

FIFTY-THIRD ANNUAL SESSION

held with the

Green Street, North Main, Hilliard
Memorial Baptist Churches

High Point, N. C.

October 23-24

1946

★

Next meeting to be at Mt. Zion Baptist Church, October 22-23, 1947

R. Von King .... Preacher
D. M. Clemmons .... Alternate

MINUTES

of the

Piedmont Baptist Association

North Carolina

FIFTY-THIRD ANNUAL SESSION

held with the

Green Street, North Main, Hilliard
Memorial Baptist Churches

High Point, N. C.

October 23-24

1946

★

Next meeting to be at Mt. Zion Baptist Church, October 22-23, 1947

R. Von King .... Preacher
D. M. Clemmons .... Alternate

Edited for the

Piedmont Baptist Association

by

Ray W. Harrington

INDEX

ASSOCIATIONAL DIRECTORY

Grover H. Jones, Moderator .... High Point
Dr. John W. McGinnis, Vice-Moderator .... Reidsville
Ray W. Harrington, Clerk .... Greensboro

EXECUTIVE PROMOTION COMMITTEE

Grover H. Jones, Chairman .... High Point
Dr. John W. McGinnis .... Reidsville
Mrs. E. T. Howell .... Greensboro
R. Von King .... Greensboro
Carl Bell .... Greensboro
Ray W. Harrington .... Greensboro
Wilson Woodcock .... Greensboro
Wilbur W. Hutchins .... High Point
H. O. Miller .... High Point
W. S. Holton .... Reidsville
T. L. Gardner .... Reidsville
Mrs. C. H. Fryar .... Summerfield
J. S. Hopkins .... High Point
Dr. J. Clyde Turner .... Greensboro
C. M. Scott .... High Point
J. J. Norwood .... Greensboro
Mrs. C. W. Moseley .... Greensboro
D. M. Clemmons .... Reidsville

CHURCH ADVISORY AND MISSIONS COMMITTEE

Dr. J. Clyde Turner, Chairman .... Greensboro
Grover H. Jones .... High Point
Mrs. C. W. Moseley .... Greensboro
T. L. Gardner .... Reidsville
D. M. Clemmons .... Reidsville
J. S. Hopkins .... High Point
W. W. Hutchins .... High Point
Ray W. Harrington .... Greensboro
Mrs. Edgar T. Howell .... Greensboro

COMMITTEES SERVING DURING THE ASSOCIATIONAL YEAR

Executive Promotion Committee
Church Advisory and Missions Committee
Program Committee
Committee on Committees
Committee on Time, Place, and Preacher
Auditing Committee
Committee on Resolutions
Program Committee for this year and next year
Committee to Nominate Officers
Committee to Nominate Executive Promotion Committee
Committee to Nominate Church Advisory and Missions Committee
Committee to Nominate Delegates to the Baptist State Convention

---

CHURCHES BY DISTRICTS

District 1

Allen Jay, Conrad Memorial, Fairmont Park, Green Street, High Point First, Hilliard Memorial, Jewell, North Main Street, North Park, Oak Grove, Pine Grove, Pilot View, Pisgah, Smith Grove, Southside, Temple, West End, Woodlawn.

District 2

Asheboro Street, Bessemer, Brightwood, Buchanan, College Park, Edgeville, Eller Memorial, Florida Street, Gibsonville, Greensboro First, Guilford, Immanuel, Jessup Grove, Latham Park, Lebanon, Magnolia Street, McConnell Road, McLeansville, Mount Zion, Pleasant Garden, Pleasant Grove, Pomona, Rankin, Sixteenth Street, Stevens Memorial, South Elm, Summerfield, Ossipee, Webster Memorial, Woodard Memorial.

District 3

Antioch, Calvary, Fairview, Baptist Temple, Oceola, Penn Memorial, Reidsville First, Ruffin-Stacey.

OFFICERS OF BAPTIST TRAINING UNION

J. Carl Bell, Director .... Greensboro
Miss Thelma Patrick, Asso. Director .... High Point
Miss Julia Lyles, Secretary-Treasurer .... High Point
E. C. White, Jr., Pianist .... Greensboro
J. W. Morrison, Chorister .... Greensboro
Miss Pearl Womack, Story Hour Leader .... Greensboro
Mrs. W. C. Adkinson, Junior Leader .... Greensboro
Mrs. W. A. Aydelette, Intermediate Leader .... Greensboro
J. E. Hedrick, Young People's Leader .... High Point
Miss Katherine Roddick, Adult Leader .... Reidsville
C. V. Coffey, Director District No. 1 .... Reidsville
J. J. Norwood, Director District No. 2 .... Greensboro
Mrs. Marvin Jones, Director District No. 3 ...... Reidsville
Rev. T. L. Sasser, Pastor Advisor .... Reidsville

PROGRAM COMMITTEE

J. S. Hopkins, Chairman .... High Point
James R. Thompson .... Greensboro
D. M. Clemmons .... Reidsville
Miss Thelma Patrick .... High Point

OFFICERS OF PIEDMONT W. M. U.

Mrs. Edgar T. Howell .... Superintendent
1250 Westover Terrace, Greensboro

Mrs. Nettie Hoge .... Superintendent Emeritus
1406 W. Warket St., Greensboro

Mrs. J. C. Gulispie .... Associate Superintendent.
Reidsville

Mrs. W. C. Adkinson .... Secretary
1504 16th St., Greensboro

Mrs. W. O. Burnham .... Treasurer
32 Irvin St., Reidsville

Mrs. Jas. R. Thompson .... Y. P. L.
1110 Glenwood Ave., Greensboro

Chairmen

Mrs. H. A. Knight .... Mission Study
1100 N. Main St., High Point

Mrs. W. H. Wright .... Stewardship
Guilford College

Mrs. C. W. Moseley .... Community Missions
438 S. Mendenhall St., Greensboro

Mrs. O. J. Howard .... Literature
Guilford College

Mrs. Grover Jones .... Training School and Margaret Fund
635 W. Lexington Ave., High Point

Rev. James B. Clifton .... R. A. Counselor
619 Waugh St., Greensboro

Group Leaders

Mrs. B. A. Teague .... 204 Waverly Way, Greensboro
Mrs. J. N. Turner .... 705 Northridge, Greensboro
Mrs. C. C. Stout .... 900 6th St., High Point
Mrs. J. E. Kirk .... Route 2, Reidsville
Mrs J. C. Gulespie .... 319 Lindsay St., Reidsville

Nominating Committee for Year

Mrs. T. L. Sasser, Chairman .... Reidsville
Mrs. H. D. Martin ...... 216 S. Mendenhall St., Greensboro
Mrs. W. F. Ellis, Jr., ... Lexington Ave. Ext., High Point

ORDAINED MINISTERS NOT PASTORS

Barton, C. D., Retired	Greensboro
Blanchard, Chaplain Henry N., Retired	Greensboro
Billings, H. P.	Jamestown
Boles, J. H.	Greensboro
Coe, C. C.	Greensboro
Cook, W. B.	Greensboro
Davis, F. E.	Greensboro
Dix, O. P.	High Point
Farrington, B. H., Evangelist	Colfax
Fort, B. B.	Summerfield
Gatewood, J. C. R.	Greensboro
Hartsell, P. P.	High Point
Havner, Vance, Evangelist	Greensboro
Hight, W. J., Retired	Greensboro
Leonard, Dr. C. A., Missionary	Hawaii
Lowe, Danny	Greensboro
Matherly, W. F.	Greensboro
Montgomery, Floyd, Evangelist	Greensboro
McDowell, B. S.	High Point
McGee, John S.	Missionary to Nigera
Oates, C. M.	Greensboro
Overbey, D. W., Retired	Reidsville
Penguson, Luther	Reidsville
Plybon, C. T., Retired	Greensboro
Sasser, T. L., Associational Missionary	Reidsville
White, Claude, Chaplain	Greensboro

MINISTERS ORDAINED DURING THE YEAR

J. T. Ellis	Greensboro
N. H. Blackburn	Greensboro
Bill Kincaid	Thomasville
J. M. Teeter	Wake Forest
A. B. Ashill	High Point

STUDENTS FOR THE MINISTRY

John H. Lineberry	Moody Bible Institute
James B. Fleet, Jr.	Wake Forest
Henry Ratledge	Moody
Connie Salios	Bob Jones
Richard Hanner	Bob Jones
Charles Clifton Belch	Prairie Bible Institute
Paul Cassell	High Point College
Lonnie Shaw	Moody
Avery Tintheaum	Atlanta Bible Institute
James E. Mason	Moody
Felton Carter	Guilford College
Clarence Boyan	High Point College
Troy Robbins	Southern Seminary

MESSENGERS

ALLEN JAY—Mrs. U. L. Mabry, Jim Warren, Claude Mickey, Mary Warren, Joe Bennett.

ANTIOCH—John Carter, Joe Lasley, Roy Moore.

BRIGHTWOOD—Frank Gales, J. W. Holder, Mrs. Carl Ham, Mrs. Raymond Harner, Mrs. Catherine Gardner.

BUCHANON—Mrs. J. B. Clifton, Rev. J. B. Clifton.

CALVARY—Mrs. Jesse Carter, Alex Settiff, J. E. McCargo.

COMMUNITY—Mrs. Ethel May, Lester Landreth, Mamie Dodson, Mrs. Lester Landreth, T. M. Marsh.

CONRAD MEMORIAL—Mrs. Mildred Jester, Mrs. R. F. Mickey, Mrs. J. N. Rodgers, George Richman.

FAIRMONT PARK—No messengers listed.

FAIRVIEW—Mrs. A. D. Hopkins, Mrs. J. V. Moore, D. E. Trantham.

GIBSONVILLE—J. P. Edwards, Theo Edwards, Ann Blythe.

ASHEBORO STREET—M. D. Teague, F. L. Paschal, Mrs. J. Ben Eller, Mrs. A. C. Lowe, Miss Mabel Starnes, B. A. Teague, Mrs. C. E. Lovin, O. B. Teague.

BESSEMER—Mrs. G. H. Williamson, W. P. Haynes, Mrs. Ray W. Harrington, Mrs. C. L. Murray, Mrs. C. E. Brady, Mrs. J. Frank Layton.

COLLEGE PARK—Mrs. B. B. Stockard, Fred L. Bell, Geo. W. Williams, Miss Sarah Moses, Mrs. C. C. Gamble.

EDGEVILLE—No messengers listed.

ELLER MEMORIAL—Mrs. Ira McQueen, Mrs. R. Von King, Mrs. T. R. Noah, Mrs. W. H. Lambert, Miss Leah Andrews, W. P. Malone.

GREENSBORO FIRST—Frank L. Stubbs, Mrs. H. D. Martin, A. A. Chandler, Mrs. E. T. Howell, Carl Bell, F. D. Whitehead, Mrs. Gus Ruof, S. A. Helms, Mrs. J. Clyde Turner, Dr. J. Clyde Turner.

FLORIDA STREET—Mrs. W. M. Spivey, J. B. Rumbley, Sr., Mrs. J. B. Rumbley, Sr., A. B. Coffey, T. A. Trulove.

IMMANUEL—Forrest L. Fraser, Mrs. F. L. Fraser, E. J. Jarvil, Mrs. S. W. Bryant, Mrs. W. J. Mitchell.

LATHAM PARK—No messengers listed.

MAGNOLIA STREET—W. T. Adams, L. L. Jarvis, Mrs. L. L. Jarvis, Mrs. J. A. Lewis, Mrs. H. S. Noah, Mrs. R. L. Yow.

POMONA—C. M. Oates, Mrs. E. E. Henry, Mrs. W. H. Brown, Mrs. C. M. Oates, C. C. Patterson.

REVOLUTION—S. L. Riddle, Mrs. A. L. Stevens, Grady Phillips, Mrs. Waldo Johnson.

SIXTEENTH STREET—W. C. Adkinson, Mrs. W. C. Adkinson, Mrs. Harry Moore, Mrs. John Starling, Fred Hester, Norman Pinkleton.

STEVENS MEMORIAL—H. E. Whitfield, Mrs. H. E. Whitfield, Mrs. N. N. Sutton, Mrs. J. H. Ham, Mrs. R. U. Thornberry.

RANKIN—Mrs. B. H. Scott, Mrs. Banner Bishop, Mrs. A. Andrews.

GUILFORD—McGary, Mrs. McGary, Mrs. G. F. Butler.

HIGH POINT FIRST—W. Wilbur Hutchins, Mrs. W. F. Clayton, Mrs. J. M. Lancaster, Miss Thelma Patrick, Mr. M. R. Shields.

GREEN STREET—B. G. Leonard, A. M. Smith, J. O. House, Walter E. Crissman, Mrs. J. L. Payne.

HILLIARD MEMORIAL—Mrs. O. A. Taylor, Mrs. W. A. Copley, A. L. Slate, Boyce Moore, Mrs. C. H. Farmer.

NORTH MAIN STREET—Neil J. Armstrong, Mrs. Alice Davis, Mrs. Ed. Crisco, R. L. Reeves, Mrs. J. W. Ledwell.

NORTH PARK—H. B. Chatham, D. H. Short, Mrs. L. W. Glenn.

SOUTHSIDE—Mrs. T. E. Gaines, Mrs. C. A. Conn, Mrs. Carl Saltz.

WEST END—C. M. Scott, Vernon Coffey, Mrs. D. R. Harrison, Mrs. Reuben Presslar.

JESSUP GROVE—No messengers listed.

JEWEL—Mrs. Bessie Hill, Chas. Panker, Lila Weatherman.

LEBANON—C. C. Cross, Mrs. A. O. Stuart, Mrs. E. S. Reeves, Mrs. Ezra Lashley, Mrs. Emma Goodwin.

MT. ZION—J. T. Swinson, C. D. Branson, Geo. H. Spoon.

McCONNELL ROAD—W. H. Bullock, Mrs. J. T. Ellis, R. F. Snyder.

McLEANSVILLE—W. R. Fuller, Mrs. W. R. Fuller, Mrs. W. J. Howard, Earl Howard.

OAK GROVE—Mrs. Mary Barbee, Miss Marion Boleman, W. L. Shackelford, Archie Saunders, Mrs. Archie Saunders.

OSCEOLA—Mrs. D. A. Greene, W. S. Young, T. J. Brooks, L. C. Cole, Miss Francis Cole.

OSSIPEE—Luther King, H. D. Smith, R. C. Fitts, Mrs. R. C. Fitts.

PINE GROVE—Robert Taylor, Mrs. Robert Taylor, Mrs. R. A. Richard, Larston Tuttle, Mrs. Larston Tuttle.

PILOT VIEW—Mrs. Joe Edwards, Mrs. U. E. Webb, Mrs. H. S. Fletcher, Mrs. D. G. Kestler, D. F. Kestler.

PISGAH—Mrs. L. C. Madden, Mrs. H. F. Maness, Mrs. D. H. Grubb, Mrs. Charlie Weaver.

PLEASANT GARDEN—No messengers listed.

PLEASANT GROVE—Mrs. W. A. Kinan, F. M. Atkins, Mrs. F. M. Atkins, Mrs. W. H. Smith, Clyde Burris.

REEDY FORK—Mrs. Lee A. Beech, Mrs. O. H. Presnell, Mrs. Lee Elder, Mrs. Lester Canter, Mrs. R. P. Everage.

BAPTIST TEMPLE—D. M. Clemmons, Mrs. D. M. Clemmons, Gordon Roberts, Mrs. M. S. Hayth, Mrs. Jesse King, Mrs. J. P. King.

REIDSVILLE FIRST—No messengers listed.

PENN MEMORIAL—D. W. Overbey, Mrs. C. E. Moricle, Mrs. Maxel Thore.

ROCKY KNOLL—Mrs. G. E. Faucette, G. A. Tucker, Mrs. G. A. Tucker, Mrs. Vera Aldridge.

RUFFIN STACEY—Mrs. A. J. Burton, Mrs. J. T. Cardwell, Mrs. A. S. London, J. T. London.

SMITH GROVE—Mrs. Pearl Rayle, Johnnie Johnson, Fairmae Pitts.

SUMMERFIELD—Dr. C. H. Fryar, W. W. Doggett.

BAPTIST TEMPLE—A. J. Swinson, Watson Wagner, Mrs. Watson Wagner, R. S. Edwards, Mrs. Eva Stevens, R. L. Rodden, Mrs. R. L. Rodden.

WOODWARD MEMORIAL—Mrs. W. R. Smith, Mrs. C. G. Rumley, F. A. O'Briant.

WOODLAWN—No messengers listed.

CONSTITUTION

ARTICLE 1.—The Association shall be called the Piedmont Baptist Association.

ARTICLE 2.—It shall be composed of the ordained ministers who are members of, and those who may have pastoral charges within the Associational District, and three delegates from each Church in the district aforesaid, and Churches having a membership exceeding 300 shall be entitled to one additional delegate for every 200 members or fraction thereof in excess of 300.

ARTICLE 3.—The said delegates shall, before taking their seats, produce letters from respective Church showing their appointment as delegates.

ARTICLE 4.—The Associational session shall be held at least once a year.

ARTICLE 5.—The officers shall be a Moderator, Vice-Moderator, Clerk and Treasurer. If deemed expedient by the Association, the offices of Clerk and Treasurer may be combined.

ARTICLE 6.—The officers of the Association shall be chosen annually by the Association.

ARTICLE 7.—Association shall be clothed with authority only to advise the Churches touching all things pertaining to their interest but shall in no case presume to direct or control them in reference to their own government or internal policy.

ARTICLE 8.—A Committee of arrangements, consisting of three members shall be appointed on the first day of each session to prepare and report the proceedings and suggest topics proper for the consideration and action of the next annual Association. It shall be the duty of this committee to outline and publish a program for the next annual Associational meeting or for any special or called meeting of the Association.

ARTICLE 9.—Baptist brethren, not members of the Association, who may be present at any session of the body, may on invitation by the body, take seats and participate in the debates of the Association.

ARTICLE 10.—

Section 1. The territory of the Association shall be divided into not less than three districts.

Section 2. A committee composed of the Moderator, the Vice-moderator, the Clerk of the Association, the Associational W. M. U. Superintendent, the Associational Sunday School Superintendent, the Associational B. T. U. Director, and twelve other members of churches in the Association, giving fair representation to the three districts, shall constitute the Executive Committee of the Association. This committee at its first meeting shall decide the number required for a quorum.

Section 3. Seven of the members of the Executive Committee shall be named by the Association as members of the Church Advisory and Missions Committee.

Section 4. The duties of the Executive Committee are to act for the Association between the annual sessions of the Association. The Church Advisory and Missions Committee is charged with the task of seeking the cooperation of churches in the ordination of ministers, the location and organization of new churches, and the management of the Associational Mission Program in our Association.

ARTICLE 11.—All Committees shall be appointed by the Moderator, either directly or indirectly with the approval of the Association, unless otherwise authorized by the Association from time to time.

ARTICLE 12.—The Constitution may be altered only at an Annual session of the Association and by a vote of two-thirds of the whole present.

ARTICLE 13.—The rules of this body shall follow Mell's Parliamentary Practice.

ARTICLE 14.—This Association shall cooperate with Baptist State Convention.

ARTICLE 15.—The time of the holding of the annual session shall begin on Wednesday before the fourth Sunday of October of each year, except where prevailing conditions make it advisable to change this date, in which event the Executive Committee shall be empowered to determine the date of meeting.

Adopted October 17, 1895.

Articles 2, 5, 6, 10, 15 Amended Sessions, July 23, 24, 1930.

Article 15 Amended Session, July 21, 1932.

Article 10 Amended Sessions, October 23, 24, 1935.

Articles 8, 10, 11 Amended Sessions, October 23, 24, 1940.

Article 10 Amended Session, October 19, 1944.

PROCEEDINGS

of the

FIFTY-THIRD ANNUAL SESSION

of the

PIEDMONT BAPTIST ASSOCIATION

Held With the

GREEN STREET, HILLIARD MEMORIAL, AND NORTH MAIN STREET BAPTIST CHURCHES

High Point, N. C.

October 23-24, 1946

WEDNESDAY MORNING SESSION—10:00 A. M.

1. The Piedmont Baptist Association was called to order at 10:00 A. M. by the Moderator, Grover H. Jones, and joined in singing, "What a Friend We Have in Jesus," led by S. A. Helms, accompanied by Mrs. J. S. Hopkins. After reading I Ccr. 1:18, Rev. S. L. Riddle, Revolution Baptist Church, let the invocation.

2. Rev. J. S. Hopkins, Green Street Baptist Church, gave the welcome address.

3. The Program Committee reported, and the printed program, with a minor change, was accepted.

4. While the Vice-Moderator, Dr. John W. McGinnis, was presiding the Moderator presented the following report which was accepted.

REPORT OF THE MODERATOR

Again I desire to express my appreciation to the churches of the Association for the many courtesies shown me during the past year. I express also my appreciation for the fine spirit of cooperation that prevails among the churches of the Association. I believe it is safe to say that our churches are working together more as a unit now than perhaps ever before in the history of the Association.

I attribute the spirit of fine cooperation among our churches and the way they are working together largely to the fact that for the past three years we have had the full time services of Brother T. L. Sasser, our Associational Missionary. He has had more time and more opportunities to do effective work along this line than anyone else. We are fortunate to have Brother Sasser to lead in this capacity.

While our Association is comparatively small in territory, in population it is one of the largest in the State.

The work of Brother Sasser has revealed to the churches the fact that there are thousands of people in the Association who have no church affiliation and that this is one of the most fertile fields in the State for mission work.

As a result of the mission work done in the Association during the past three years, I am convinced that our Association should have not only an Associational program, but a budget to carry out that program. With such a program and budget, I am convinced that we will do more even in a financial way, for our local churches and for our denominational program.

I believe that the Church of Christ today has the greatest opportunity, that it has had perhaps in its history. Doors of opportunity are open today to the church to about eighty-five percent of the population of the earth. The big question is whether the conventional church of today will dare to catch and share the spirit and message of Christ to the ends of the earth.

I like to think of each new Associational year as a time of beginning again in our churches. As we think about what we are going to do and where we are going in our work during the new year, it is well that we should review briefly what was accomplished, so far as the figures may show, during the last Associational year.

(Here discussion was made of the digest of church letters for 1946.)

Respectfully submitted,

G. H. Jones, Moderator.

5. Dr. L. L. Carpenter, editor, spoke on the Biblical Recorder.

6. J. E. Miller, field representative of Meredith College, gave an oral report on the College.

7. The following report, presented by T. L. Sasser, Associational Missionary, was accepted. Mr. Sasser spoke to his report.

ASSOCIATIONAL MISSIONS

The local church is the primary corporate unit of scriptural missions. This is true as touching local, associational, state, south-wide, and world-wide missions. Southern Baptists as such have a far broader vision of missions than the Baptists of this nation had in the years of Judson and Rice. The vision of these men and a few others has become the visions of our denomination as a whole.

No local church can neglect its community or the distant mission fields without serious loss all the way round. Neither can the whole obligation be discharged with monetary support alone. We must not only give to missions but we must also do missions. Keeping a balance between giving and doing is difficult but it must be done. The two are complimentary. No part of Acts 1:8 is to be neglected and the whole program is to be emphasized.

There are signs of a growing sense of local missionary obligation in the churches of our Association, but many of our people have not yet lifted up their eyes and looked upon the fields which are already ripe unto harvest. Nor have they themselves entered the fields. It is a joy to observe, however, that some have and the associational field is more and more becoming a force.

Not to mention several new churches that have become affiliated with our Association, in recent years, there are now ten missionary Baptist churches in the general area of the Association that as yet have not entered our Piedmont fellowship. All these churches began as missions. Some of them were promoted by individuals and others of them were sponsored by churches. Some have been organized churches several years and others of them have been organized this year.

As a rule the church-sponsored missions become active missionary churches and identify themselves with the denomination. Some that are promoted by individuals continue as separate church and take no active part in our denominational organizations. It is therefore obvious that the best way to promote missions and to organize new churches is by the sponsorship of the churches.

Newly organized churches call attention to the mission work of the churches in the area of the Association. The people of the territory are responsive and the opportunities are large. There are still 107,000 people in Guilford and half of Rockingham counties who are not church members. Aggressive churches are winning and enlisting some of these but in comparative small numbers. Mission points with capable and qualified leadership are productive of definite spiritual profit to individuals and to the denomination. There are many adversaries to overcome but most other fields have barriers that we of the Piedmont do not have. Our responsibilities are therefore greater.

For many years denominational debts have required a large percentage of our financial offerings and our work. A debtless time has finally come and with it greatly increased offerings through the regular channels. The three bodies, Piedmont Association, The State Convention, and the Southern Baptist Convention, through which our local churches co-operate must have the full support of the churches. But I am taking occasion here to mention particularly the Association whose financial and missionary program for its local work should be greatly strengthened.

The expense account of the Association should be expanded into a budget. In all the church sponsored mission projects in recent years it has been necessary to solicit personal gifts from the givers in the churches. The work can not be done without financial sponsorship and it should be on a corporate basis.

Through the generous over and above gifts of several individuals a tent was purchased this year to be used in places where no buildings are available. Fine meetings were held under it in Greensboro, Pleasant Garden and in High Point. We shall need new seats and other equipment for it next summer.

Vacation Bible Schools have proven to be fine mission projects and it is expected that we shall have a larger number next year than heretofore. The Home Mission Board has been furnisching student missionaries to aid in this work during ten weeks of summer. It is necessary to supplement the financial aid the Board has been giving and it is hoped that the churches will provide funds to enlarge this profitable enterprise.

I herewith offer a summary of my personal activities from October 1, 1945 to September 30, 1946.

Days on field	282
Days on other fields (For State and Home Boards)	59
Miles travelled on this and other fields	16,175
Individual conferences	471
Group conferences	105
Committee meetings	39
Associational meetings	2
Pastors conferences	19
State meetings	4
South-wide meetings	2
Census directed	3

Fields surveyed	6
Visits to churches	116
Visits to mission stations	27
Visits to homes	165
Visits to hospitals	33
Funerals conducted or assisted in	13
Assisted in church organizations	3
Miscellaneous services spoken in	60
Assisted in schools of missions (other fields)	2
Revival meetings conducted or assisted in	1
Tracts and circular letters sent out	2250
Sermons preached	92
Addresses delivered	51
Prayer meetings conducted	8
Classes taught	16
Professions of faith	6
Number personally baptized	1

I wish to thank all for their unfailing kindness to me throughout the Association.

Respectfully submitted,

T. L. Sasser.

---

8. The following report, presented by Dr. John W. McGinnis, chairman of the committee with W. Wilbur Hutchins, and Ray W. Harrington, was accepted.

PIEDMONT BAPTIST ASSOCIATION SUGGESTED ANNUAL EXPENSE AND MISSIONS BUDGET FOR 1947

Recommended by Executive Committee

Associational Missionary's Salary	$2100.00
(To be supplemented by State and Home Mission Boards)	
Associational Missionary's Local Travel and Expense	600.00
Clerk's Compensation	100.00
Associational Minutes	300.00
Office Supplies and Expense	200.00
Tent Fund for Insurance, Equipment and Repairs	300.00
Compensation Student Missionaries for Summer Work	300.00
Associational Pastor's School (A new project)	500.00
Associational Sunday School and Training Union Expense	200.00
Associational Schools of Missions	250.00
Aid Fund for Mission Churches	1000.00
Incidental and Unanticipated Expense Fund	150.00
Total	$6000.00

9. The following report, presented by R. Von King, spoken to by B. E. Morris, West End Baptist Church, Durham, N. C., was accepted.

HOME MISSIONS

The primary task of the Home Mission Board is to evangelize the homeland. We must save America for Christ if we are to fulfill our highest obligations of the gospel to foreigners in foreign lands. To a large degree the Christians of our country must accept the world responsibility implied in the great commission of our Lord. For many reasons we are logically and providentially the nation that now holds the preeminet place of responsibility in a new world order. Let the Baptists of our land assume their part of the responsibility for advancing the Kingdom of God to the ends of the earth as we face says: "The strategic point of approach to this world task is the homeland. Keep the homeland evangelized and mobilized for service and our unparalleled opportunity at home and abroad. Dr. J. B. Lawrence we have the hope and assurance of a world evangelization."

The Home Mission Board has work among Spanish-speaking Americans, Indians, French, Italians, Chinese, and other language groups. The foreigners in our homeland present a foreign mission challenge at home and offer to us an indirect approach to foreign missions abroad. A Chinese responsibility at home today may mean a Chinese missionary to China in the near future if won to Christ. Work is sponsored by the Home Mission Board in 587 churches and missions and needs 327 more. It has 700 missionaries and workers and needs 389 more. We have mission centers, work among the deaf and among Negroes, Cuban missions, and work in Panama, Costa Rica, and the Canal Zone. We need more than two million dollars for mission properties and over a million dollars a year for operation. The Board is now housed in its own building at 161 Spring Street, N. W., Atlanta, Ga.

A brief summary of certain types of Home Mission work is taken from a recently published pamphlet:

"The Department of Jewish Work is helping to plan and work for the salvation of 1,000,000 Jews in the southland.

The Department of Evangelism is cooperating with churches and other denominational agencies in reaching the 20,000,000 unevangelized for Christ.

The Department of Camp Work is cooperating with our Baptist chaplains in ministering to our service men. About 91,750 were won to the Lord by our chaplains in 1945.

The Department of Schools of Missions and the Department of Missionary Education are seeking to give missionary information and stimulate mission interest among our Baptist people throughout the South.

Our Field Workers of the Home Mission Board assist the churches and denominational groups with mission programs and serve in general missionary activities."

The official monthly publication of the Board is "Southern Baptist Home Missions." The subscription rate is twenty-five cents per year to individuals or it can be sent to all families in a church on the budget plan at twenty cents per family. "Trust the Lord and tell the people."

Respectfully submitted,

R. Von King.

---

10. Visitors were recognized by the Moderator.

11. T. L. Sasser presented the Pastors of the Association.

12. The Messengers joined in singing, "All Hail the Power," led by S. A. Helms, accompanied by Mrs. J. S. Hopkins.

13. After James R. Thompson, the Alternate, read Isaiah 53:1-12, Acts 4:12, Matt. 16:21-25, James 1:21-27, Phil. 4:8, he led the invocation; then the Associational sermon was preached by the appointee—W. Wilbur Hutchins, High Point. The subject: "Rebuilding Bridges."

14. Adjournment until the afternoon.

WEDNESDAY AFTERNOON SESSION—2:15 P. M.

15. The afterooon session opened with singing of "Love Divine," led by S. A. Helms and accompanied by Mrs. J. S. Hopkins.

16. J. H. Saunders conducted the devotional service, reading I Cor. 13th Chapter.

17. The following report, presented by W. C. Guth, pastor of West End, was accepted. Rev. Guth spoke to his report.

REPORT ON FOREIGN MISSIONS

In a time when the world is steeped in sin, filled with unrest and chaos, and yearns for the realization of peace, the Foreign Mission Board of the Southern Baptist Convention finds itself surrounded by many challenging problems.

The millions of unfortunate war-stricken people are still crying out for food and shelter, the doors of nations heretofore unopened to the gospel now welcome its message, the fields of established mission work are in need of reinforcements, and the demands for an ever enlarging mission program to meet these current needs, are a few of the problems now confronting the Foreign Mission Board.

Southern Baptists always have been missionary in practice and have striven to meet the demands of foreign mission enterprise. The following cold, contemporaneous and statistical facts substantiate this statement. The receipts for foreign missions in 1945 reached an all-time high figure of $3,592,000. Only two weeks ago we were made to rejoice in learning that the goal of $3,500,000 to be raised by our denomination for relief and rehabilitation for the war-stricken peoples of Europe and Asia had been reached. The Lottie Moon offering last Christmas being $1,200,000, began the gifts to foreign missions in 1946 on a higher level than that of 1945. If the proposed goal for 1946 is achieved, we are informed that the Foreign Mission Board's income for this year, will exceed the high record of 1945 by approximately $1,000,000. In addition to the annual over-all of $3,000,000 during the past year, the Board set aside from current funds approximately $2,700,000 against a total of $7,000,000. This enormous sum is needed in addition to the current annual budget to rehabilitate and enlarge the proposed missionary program.

Southern Baptists must do far more in the future than they have in the past. Dr. M. T. Rankin, Executive Secretary of the Foreign Mission Board states, "In the light of the world's urgent need, the Foreign Mission Board's present program can be seen in its tragic smallness. If the whole world was ever in need of Christ, it is now. If people were ever in need of salvation, it is now. If suffering humanity ever needed the help of five and a half million Southern Baptists, with all their great resources, it is now." While there are retirements and appointments that keep the figure in constant change, there are now a few more than 550 missionaries in active service. This means we have only one missionary for every 10,000 members in our great denomination. In view of the world's need of salvation it is unthinkable that we should send out so few foreign missionaries with the trasforming message of Christ. As soon as sufficient funds make it possible, more appointments will be made by the Board. Our gifts of only an average of seventy cents per person per year to foreign missions, does not suffice in this hour of spiritual crisis.

Therefore, Southern Baptists must pray more fervently, give more liberally, and "go" more willingly if we as a denomination by means of Foreign Missions are to fulfill the task assigned to us by our Lord and Saviour Jesus Christ.

Respectfully submitted,

W. C. Guth.

18. The W. M. U. report, presented by Mrs. Edgar T. Howell was accepted. Mrs. James R. Thompson spoke to the report.

THE W. M. U. REPORT

The following figures were published in the book of reports by the State Executive Committee for the year ending December 31, 1945:

Number of Churches	56
Number of Societies	138
Number of Members	3,013
Number of New Societies	14
Number of Societies doing Community Missions	58
Number of Tithers	1,102

In February the Greensboro Division which includes five Associations met in High Point for a successful missions study and community missions Institute.

The Associational mission study chairman was successful in her efforts to have at least one mission study class in every society during the year.

This year, the Association, as a community missions project, employed three young Negro women who have had religious training at Shaw University to work in High Point, Greensboro, and Reidsville, conducting Vacation Bible Schools and training leaders.

Realizing the value of such work one of the Negro churches in Greensboro has engaged a part time worker.

Early in the year the State Young People's Director suggested to the various Associations that a camp be planned for the Junior R. A's. and Junior G. A's. Realizing the need of supervised recreation for our Junior boys and girls, the Associational Director of young people planned and directed a successful camp with the cooperation of the churches and their leaders. Thus giving these young people both inspiration and recreation. Of the 96 attending, 3 of them accepted Christ as their personal Saviour and 4 others dedicated their lives for Christian service.

Let us pray earnestly that a world revival will begin in our community, our Association as we tell the story of salvation to the lost about us.

Respectfully submitted,

Mrs. Edgar T. Howell, Supt.

19. The State Missions and Co-operative program report, presented by W. C. Adkinson, was accepted. M. A. Huggins spoke to the report.

STATE MISSIONS AND COOPERATIVE PROGRAM

The Aim or Purpose of State Missions is a three-fold one. In the first place, those activities are promoted which develop a Christian State, that is, evangelism and training. In the winning of the lost and the teaching of those who are won, we develop a Christian citizenship. In the second place, an aggressive State Missions program is essential to the growth of the denomination and its morale. In the third place, all missions, State, Home and Foreign, all colleges and school and seminaries, and all benevolent agencies depend upon State Missions as their base of supply. For example, through State Missions, people are won for Christ, churches are established, and membership trained. As the churches grow and their membership becomes informed, they in turn support not State Missions alone, but through the Baptist Program all missions, all Christian Education, and all benevolences.

The scope and task of State Missions has constantly increased with the growth of the denomination. The original task of State Missions was to provide evangelists who created a desire for churches, and as these churches grew, came the desire for new churches and new sites for re-location, aid for pastors, colleges and schools to educate and train preachers as well as other Christian laymen. Then came the development of Sunday Schools, Training Unions, and the Baptist Student Union, hospitals and other benevolent agencies. Also there has been recognized in recent years the need for additional training for ministers already in the service. Hundreds of them have never had the privilege of attending college or seminary. To meet this need, schools for pastors running for a week to six weeks have been inaugurated.

Perhaps the newest addition to the task and scope of State Missions is the development of Visual Education and Radio. Many are just beginning to realize the value of these instruments in an effective and teaching program.

The task of State Missions is not complete while we yet have within the Southern Baptist territory as many as 10,000,000 Baptist possibilities yet unreached, and North Carolina has her share of these.

Now as to our work in more detail: Our State Missions provides for three general missionaries who assist our General Secretary in promoting all missionary projects. They are, J. C. Pipes in Western North Carolina; E. L. Spivey, in Piedmont North Carolina; and Earle L. Bradley in Eastern North Carolina.

There are 66 missionary pastors who serve in needy and strategic places that have their salaries supplemented by the State Mission program during 1945. These 66 pastors served 107 churches which in return gave for all missionary and local projects $147,390.

The church extension service continues to have numerous calls for help on church buildings. During 1945, there were thirty churches helped during the year to the extent of $35,095.54. Much of this was used to purchase lots for new churches, and for re-locations of older churches. A greater sum than this could be used to great advantage in helping the weaker churches to have more adequate equipment.

State Missions helps to carry on an active program among the different racial groups within our state, especially among the Indians and the Negroes. Last year there were more than 300 professions of faith among the Indians with 328 baptized. Part of the salaries of the Negro leaders are paid by our State Missions.

Realizing the importance of Christian Education, and having a person to represent all of our colleges, we now have a full-time director in the person of Mr. Claude F. Gaddy whose time will be given to our Baptist Schools. Last year, we gave $325,000 for our Christian Colleges in North Carolina.

Other benevolent institutions included the Baptist Hospital in Winston-Salem, and the Baptist Orphanage at Thomasville and Kinston, although the Orphanage was not supported by State Missions, we feel our closeness to it as we give liberally for its support. The Relief and Annuity Board shares with the State Mission money.

Other fields of service aided by the State Mission Program are the Rural Church and evangelism work with Rev. J. C. Canipe as director, and Visual Education and Radio with Rev. Fon H. Schofield as its director.

All these along with Christian Education in the churches, with Mr. L. L. Morgan Secretary of the Sunday School and Mr. Harvey Gibson secretary of the Training Union, and the Baptist Student Union in the Colleges are supported by our State Missions Program. Pastors in some of the college towns are aided in their ministry to our boys and girls in the colleges.

The Convention through State Missions and the Home Missions Board, provide a program of City and Associational Missions. Thus they help expand the work of the Gospel and establish and organize new churches.

The Cooperative Program works because of what it is, what it includes, and what it excludes. In 1926 the Cooperative Program was adopted and approved by all the State Conventions and now continues to be the best plan we have in dividing the missionary dollar and make it do the most good in the most places. It assures each agency of the Southern Baptist Convention a proportionate income.

The Cooperative Program includes missions, education, benevolences and it includes all the cooperative work of our denomination.

It is our understanding of a great program Christ gave to his church. It is the safest and the best method yet devised for growth of a well balanced program of service.

It excludes the clamor of one cause to present its needs before the churches to the exclusion of others. It excludes the possibility of a church being lop-sided by being interested only in certain phases of outside Kingdom work. It excludes high pressure offerings, and allows the pastor to present a plan by which one church may share in every missionary project sponsored by the Southern Baptist Convention.

Last year, ending September 30, 1945, our portion of gifts for the Cooperative Program reached $623,991.87. This was a gain of $111,-247.79 over the previous year, and from all reports there will be another gain this year over last year. Much of this gain will be due to the World Relief and Re-habilitation offerings given during the year. Southern Baptists have exceeded their original goal of $3,000,-000 by more than $136,000 to date, even though we in North Carolina have fallen below our goal by $50,000.

By way of recommendation, I would suggest (1) that each individual Christian will pledge to acknowledge the whole stewardship of Christ for your life. (2) That each church continue to concentrate more and more upon the Cooperative Program as we firmly believe that this is the best method yet devised to spend our mission money, and thus with the most opportunities to propagate the Gospel of Christ.

Respectfully submitted,

W. C. Adkinson.

---

20. The Church Advisory and Missions Committee recommended that Conrad Memorial, South Elm, and Woodard Memorial Baptist Churches be accepted into the Association. The recommendation was accepted.

21. The Committee on Committees presented the following report which was accepted.

REPORT OF THE COMMITEES TO NOMINATE COMMITTEES

COMMITTEE ON TIME, PLACE AND PREACHER:
Dr. J. Clyde Turner, Chairman
Floy Cox
R. R. Saunders.

AUDITING COMMITTEE:
T. L. Gardner, Chairman
W. T. Adams
R. L. Reeves

COMMITTEE TO NOMINATE CHURCH ADVISORY AND MISSIONS COMMITTEE:
Dr. John W. McGinnis, Chairman
S. L. Riddle
Dr. Forest Frazer.

COMMITTEE TO NOMINATE DELEGATES TO STATE CONVENTION:
John H. Scalt, Chairman
J. M. Allred
Miss Leah Andrews.

COMMITTEE TO NOMINATE EXECUTIVE PROMOTION COMMITTEE:
B. L. Gupton, Chairman
W. C. Guth
W. W. Woodcock.

NOMINATING COMMITTEE:
J. Ben Eller, Chairman
Mrs. J. R. Thompson
J. B. Clifton.

PROGRAM COMMITTEE:
J. S. Hopkins, Chairman
James R. Thompson
D. M. Clemmons
Miss Thelma Patrick.

COMMITTEE ON RESOLUTIONS:
W. C. Adkinson, Chairman
Miss Mabel Starnes
W. H. Barker.

Respectfully submitted,

R. Von King, Chairman
Neil J. Armstrong
John W. McGinnis.

22. The following report on Obituaries, presented by W. D. Turner, was accepted. The Association stood in memory of the deceased, and Dr. J. Clyde Turner led the prayer.

OBITUARIES

It has pleased God in His wise providence to take out of this world 109 of our members since we last met. It is with profound reverence that we pause to pay our respects to them; for while they have departed from us they still live in our hearts and lives. Let us thank God, that he has not left us comfortless. The question asked by Job of old, "If a man die shall he live again" was answered by the Lord Jesus when He said, "I am the resurrection and the life. He that believeth in me though he were dead, yet shall he live" and "He that liveth and believeth in me shall never die."

May we be reminded that we too are strangers and pilgrims here. "Our citizenship is in heaven from whence also we look for the Saviour, the Lord Jesus Christ, Who shall change our vile body that it may be fashioned like unto his own glorious body whereby he is able to subdue all things unto Himself."

Respectfully submitted,

W. D. Turner.

---

23. D. M. Teague led the closing prayer.

24. Adjourned until the evening session.

24a. The report of the Auditing Committee.

The Auditing Committee has examined the Treasurer's books and found them to be as represented in his report.

T. L. Gardner, Chairman
W. T. Adams
R. L. Reeves.

WEDNESDAY EVENING SESSION—7:30 P. M.

NORTH MAIN STREET BAPTIST CHURCH

25. The Wednesday Evening Session opened with the hymn, "He Leadeth Me, O Blessed thought," led by Floy Cox, accompanied by Doris Heath.

26. After reading the 23rd Psalm, I. E. Kerley, made some remarks, and then led the invocation. Then the hymn, "Sun of My Soul, Thou Saviour Dear," was sung.

27. The Training Union report, by Miss Julia M. Liles, presented by Miss Kathlene Roddick, was accepted.

THE BAPTIST TRAINING UNION

With the close of the fiscal year, September 30, 1946, there were six new Training Unions functioning in the Piedmont Association. While at the writing of this report several churches have not been heard from, annual reports from the churches to the Association indicate that the enrollment of the Training Unions has been increased considerably during the year.

Four mass meetings have been held this past year in addition to the Twenty-sixth Annual Convention which was held in April. The evening session of this Convention was given over to a banquet at which time it was the privilege of the Association to have as guests, Dr. and Mrs. J. E. Lambdin of Nashville, Tenn. Dr. Lambdin is South-wide Director of the Training Union work of our Southern Baptist Convention and was speaker for the occasion. Associational eliminations in the Training Union contests were held during the afternoon session. The winners in these competed later in the Regional and State contests. The Young People's Choir and the two Juniors from First Church, High Point, were winners in the State contests held at Ridgecrest.

During North Carolina week and the three South-wide weeks at Ridgecrest, during the summer, many Training Union members of the various churches of the Association were in attendance.

In March of this year Greensboro District held a City-wide Study Course which was pronounced most successful with a big attendance. The Reidsville District also held a splendid City-wide Study Course in September. The High Point District elected to conduct Study Courses in the individual churches.

Again this year the Training Union of the Piedmont Association has the distinction of being one of the few organizations in the entire South to be A-1, having met the requirements of the Standard of Excellence.

Behind the program of work done in this past year have been the untiring efforts of the Associational Director, Mr. J. Carl Bell. For the new year he asks each church of the Association to adopt this slogan: "EVERY CHURCH ADOPT A CHURCH," and holds up before us these goals for the year 1946-1947:

1. At least 200 in attendance at each Associational Mass meeting.
2. 2,000 Study Course awards.
3. 100 volunteer workers for Study Courses in March, 1947.

May the end of another year find that we have surpassed these goals and that our Training Program has made us more efficent laborers in the work of the Master.

Respectfully submitted,

Julia M. Liles, Secretary.

28. J. Carl Bell directed the group meeting, and the Training Union officers were elected (See index).

29. The chorus, "Into My Heart," and the hymn, " 'Tis So Sweet to Trust in Jesus," were sung.

30. Address—"That We Come Behind On No Gift"—by James R. Thompson, Florida Street Baptist Church.

31. Adjourned until Thursday morning.

THURSDAY MORNING—9:45 A. M.

32. The morning session opened with the hymn, "Take My Life and Let it Be." Rev. W. S. Holton, Penn Memorial, conducted the devotional service.

33. The Biblical Recorder report, presented by S. L. Riddle, Revolution, was accepted. Rev. Riddle spoke to his report.

REPORT ON THE BIBLICAL RECORDER

The report on the Biblical Recorder this year is very encouraging. The circulation of the paper during the past year has shown a good increase. The present circulation is approximately 38,000 which means a net gain for the past twelve months of approximately 5,000. For this increase we are profoundly grateful to God and to the pastors and leaders of North Carolina Baptists who have supported the paper enthusiastically and have done what they could to get it into the homes of the people.

The paper has also shown good progress financially. It is now self-supporting and has been for the last year or two. However, we would not emphasize this matter too much for, after all, the important thing is to get out a good wholesome, true to the Bible, Christ-centered paper and to get it into the homes of our Baptist people, even if at times it might not be financially self-supporting.

The Recorder has three simple subscription plans: $2.00 a year for individual subscription; $1.50 a year in clubs—a minimum of at least 3 subscriptions is required for every church reporting less than 100 members and 5 subscriptions for every church reporting more than 100 members; $1.20 a year for the budget of Every-Family Plan—one subscription for each resident church family is required. We hope that pastors, superintendents, deacons, Training Union, and W. M. U. leaders will do what they can to encourage a good club in every Baptist church; or better still, to persuade the churches to inaugurate the Every-Family Plan. At the present time there are 245 churches which have the Recorder in every resident family. There are 855 churches which have Recorder clubs.

We hope our Baptist people will remember Dr. L. L. Carpenter, Editor and Business Manager along with his co-workers in prayer and offer any material or suggestions for the good of the paper. One of the great needs of our people is that they be informed, trained, and enlisted in the whole program of the church and the Kingdom of God; and we feel that the Biblical Recorder is of immense value in this great cause. We would follow the injunction of Paul and Timothy: "Study to shew thyself approved unto God, a workman that needeth not to be ashamed, rightly dividing the word of truth."

Respectfully submitted,

S. L. Riddle.

---

34. The report on Christian Education, presented by B. L. Gupton, Rankin, was accepted. Sankey L. Blanton, Wake Forest College, spoke to the report. A motion was made to put on a Visual Aid program for the Association, but the motion was lost.

REPORT ON CHRISTIAN EDUCATION

Christian Education is not an acquired virtue but a direct command from our Lord. In Matthew 28:19 and 20 we read, "Go ye therefore and teach all nations, baptizing them in the name of the Father, and of the Son, and of the Holy Ghost: Teaching them to observe all things whatsoever I have commanded you."

Certainly every Baptist is proud of our schools and we should realize the challenge of the present conditions. In our two Senior Colleges and four Junior Colleges we have enrolled more than 4000 students for the present school session, but these colleges were forced to turn away hundreds of other worthy students because of the lack of room and facilities. Someone may say, "This is an abnormal time. The G. I. Bill is responsible for this condition."

True. But we must realize that this very condition is going to enable thousands of prospective fathers and mothers to appreciate the need of higher education, who will in turn wish to send their children to college. Also, in this age of specialized training, when employers demand special trained employees, higher education is a necessity. Therefore, more and more of our young people are going to want to enter college and we must provide for them.

But, let us remember that providing colleges is not all we Baptists should do about Christian Education. The home is the foundation of all Christian Education and unless a boy or girl has instilled in his or her heart a Reverence for God and lofty ideals there is not much the Christian school can do for them, more than any other school. We should do everything to establish family devotions and personal Bible Study in our homes.

Again every church should have a definitely Christian Educational program. Naturally we would expect it to incorporate such things as seeking and training personal workers, finding and developing teachers and leaders, but the writer feels that it should go even further than that, it should reach out into the recreational life of the young people. Such a program will develop such things as honesty and sportsmanship as well as bring into our churches converts and leaders. Under the sponsorship of my Sunday School I organized a baseball team this summer and from that team I have baptized five young men, got one personal worker and one R. A. leader and choir leader.

Lestly, our Association can have, and does have, a big part in the Christian Education program. We appreciate the very fine work being done by our Associational worker, Brother Sasser, also of other persons and organizations. The B. T. U. training course last spring was very successful and we hope they will be repeated, but the writer has a further suggestion to make and attached to this report will be a recommendation to the Association.

In the Army we learned the great value of Visual Education. Our soldiers were not only taught the rudimentary elements of a soldier's work, but it was put on the screen, so that he could see a practical application of what he had learned. As a result of this we were able to put on the field, in a few short months, the best trained men and most efficient army in the history of the world.

If the Association would buy one or two sound projectors and by properly grouping the churches, a training program for each one of our major organizations, Sunday School, B. T. U., and W. M. U., could be put on in every church of the Association during one year.

This would probably cost $1500 to $2000 (using part-time operators), but the returns from such a program would make it one of, if not the best, investment we ever made as a Baptist Association.

Submitted by,

(Rev.) B. L. Gupton.

35. The Hospital report, presented by J. Ben Eller, Asheboro Street, was accepted. W. R. Grigg, Winston-Salem, spoke to the report.

REPORT ON THE NORTH CAROLINA BAPTIST HOSPITAL

Our Baptist Hospital has had another good year. In recent years its facilities to care for the sick have been greatly increased. However, the truth remains that due to lack of space the hospital cannot minister to all who want to come and who need to be admitted.

At present our hospital does far more free service than any other denominational hospital in the South. In fact it stands among the first in this work in America. Last year this service cost $167,000. This was made possible by our Mother's Day offerings and we are delighted that the Baptist Church of this Association had a worthy part in that great service.

We should ever keep in mind the fact that our Baptist Hospital was established, and is maintained, primarily to give hospital service to those unable to pay. North Carolina Baptists have invested large sums of money in this great institution and, under God, we trust they will invest much more. Therefore, we would urge those responsible for directing her policies to be vigilant in keeping her doors open to needy sufferers.

Our hospital now operates one of the best schools of Nursing in the South. It affords a great opportunity for young women to give their lives in the ministry of healing. It invites the very best from our homes and churches to go there for training.

The Department of Religion is also rendering an effective ministry. This includes among other things visits to patients, Bible and religious instruction for students, and helping to create a Christian atmosphere throughout the hospital.

The outstanding need of the hospital is the construction of the proposed South Wing. This would provide 140 new beds and other needed facilities. The cost would be near a million dollars. The advisability of permitting the hospital to construct this building, and thus incur a large debt, will be considered by the Baptist State Convention at Asheville in November. The messengers from our churches should be considering prayerfully the wisdom, or lack of wisdom, of this proposition.

Respectfully submitted,

J. Ben Eller.

36. The report on Social Service, presented by A. B. Conrad, High Point, was accepted. Dr. Conrad spoke to his report.

While Dr. John McGinnis was presiding. Grover H. Jones presented the following resolution which was accepted.

RESOLUTION

Whereas a large group of the citizens of the State of North Carolina have undertaken for the past five sessions of the General Assembly of the State to obtain necessary legislation for a state-wide referendum on the liquor stores of the State, and

Whereas the legislature has declined to pass the necessary legislation to submit this question to the people of the State, and

Whereas it is the feeling of the proponents of such legislation that this is a great moral question upon which all the people of the State should have a right to vote.

NOW, THEREFORE, BE IT RESOLVED BY THE PIEDMONT BAPTIST ASSOCIATION IN MEETING DULY ASSEMBLED ON THIS 24th DAY OF OCTOBER, 1946:

First; That this Association hereby requests the Baptist State Convention of North Carolina in its forth-coming meeting in November, 1946, to adopt a resolution directed to the general assembly of North Carolina memorializing the said General Assembly to enact the necessary legislation to submit the question of liquor stores in North Carolina to a state-wide referendum.

Second; That the Baptist State Convention name a committee of such number as it may determine to present such resolution to the General Assembly.

Third; That three copies of this Resolution be furnished Reverend Casper Warren, President of the Baptist State Convention, for reference by him to such committee of the Convention as he may determine.

REPORT ON SOCIAL SERVICE

The world is in general disorder. There is confusion and tumult in every land.

Former civilizations have risen to great heights, then through the enervating influence of indulgence, corruption, malfeasance, and dishonor have largely destroyed themselves. Such is the story of Babylon, Egypt, Israel, Greece and Rome and the conclusion is inescapable that if America walks in the same path it will reach the same end. God's red light signal warning is set full against us, saying, "All the nations that forget God shall be cast into hell," the hell of anarchy and moral disorder.

Briefly let us consider some of the blights upon our civilization:

The Social Evil. Immorality in all of its forms is gnawing at the vitals of our life and reaching for the heartstrings.

War. The war through which we have just passed, the most terrible in all history, threatened the suicide not only of Europe but of the world. War cheapens human life and lowers the morality of people.

Sabbath Desecration. The great majority of our people hold it is no regard, but God has written the necessity of the Sabbath in the very nature of man. Its sanctity is profaned with baseball, football, golf, questionable movies, feasting, travel and general hilarity.

Juvenile Delinquency. The spirit of the age is self-expression and personal liberty with the result that a large part of youth has thrown off all the bands of moral restraint and plunged into excess and crime. Much of the responsibility must be laid at the doors of the parents of our land.

Bad Literature. Altogether too much of current literature is cheap and degrading in its moral effect upon those who read it.

Growing Disregard for Law. Too many laws are violated openly and wilfully. Our jails are full of offenders of every sort and the crime bill of the nation is staggering.

Corrupt Politics and Venial Politicians. We have at the seat of government a multitude of voices advocating silly panaceas for our national life, seeking class favoritism, multiplying overlapping boards, squandering public funds, and in reality it all amounts to "a babel of confusion and bedlam of stupidities."

Divorce. The home is the very foundation of all well ordered society. Yet we have come to a time when divorce has become a curse not only to the home but to our civilization.

Strikes—both by employee and employer are menacing production, tying up trasportation and producing want and misery as to the needful things of life.

Liquor. The liquor business is a breeder of iniquity, crime, woe, sorrow and despair.

Growing Spirit of Worldliness in the Church. Multitudes in our churches have come down to the level of the world with the result that church has become conventional and has in large measure lost its spirit of militancy in the matter of lifting moral and spiritual standards before the gaze of men.

Respectfully submitted,

Dr. A. B. Conrad.

37. The Orphanage report, presented by G. A. Tucker, was accepted. W. C. Reed, Kinston, spoke to the report.

REPORT ON BAPTIST ORPHANAGE

The Baptist Orphanage of North Carolina opened its doors to the first small member of its vast family on November 11' 1885—nearly 61 years ago. Since that time the Orphanage has, under wise management accumulated assets worth more than a million dollars, and has made life secure and happy for thousands of needy children.

The Convention of 1928 changed the name from THE THOMASVILLE ORPHANAGE to THE HILLS HOME, in honor of its founder John H. Mills. At the Convention in 1934, however the name was changed to THE BAPTIST ORPHANAGE OF NORTH CAROLINA.

The Orphanage operates two homes—The Mills Home at Thomasville, and the Kennedy Home at Kinston. These two with the Mother's Aid Department scattered over the State constitute the system. The Orphanage receives children between the ages of two and twelve. Unlike many other institutions it does not dismiss their children at any given age. Rather, they are allowed to leave only when the Orphanage feels that they are able to face the world on their own.

From practically the founding of the institution, its main support has come from the once a month offering from our Sunday Schools. In more recent years the Thanksgiving offerings have proved helpful means by which the work has been greatly extended.

While we are proud of our Orphanage, and thankful that we are privileged to play a part in its existence, we must stop to realize that there are many worthwhile applicants for worthy consideration. Yet there is no room for them.

No matter how urgent the demands, however, the policy of the Orphanage is not to make special appeals. Special appeals for other causes may come and special appeals may go, but this constant stream of human need must go on day after day, and year after year until the purpose of Christ through His church has been fulfilled.

Growing, healthy children must eat. They need clothing and shelter, physical, educational, and spiritual guidance. This means that we must never cease to give our very best to them. And best means sacrificial giving.

Surely no sight on earth can cause the milk of human kindness to flow more quickly and abundantly, than that of little children in need.

There is no institution in our state today of which the Baptists are more justly proud nor more deeply interested in than our Orphanage.

The care of the orphan child was intrusted to us by Christ

Himself. We cannot shun this Christian responsibility and claim to be practicing "pure religion." When appeals are made to the orphanage authorities they have nowhere to go other than individuals, Sunday Schools and churches.

Respectfully submitted,

G. A. Tucker.

---

38. Perry Morgan was recognized who introduced Robert Guy, manager of Ridgecrest.

39. Report of Committee to nominate officers for the Association presented the following who were accepted.

Grover H. Jones, Moderator
Dr. John McGinnis, Vice-Moderator
Ray W. Harrington, Clerk.

The Associational Sunday School officers left in the hands of the Executive Committee.

Committee
J. Ben Eller
J. B. Clifton
James R. Thompson.

40. The Committee to nominate the Church Advisory and Missions Committee reported (see index). The committee was elected.

John W. McGinnis, Chairman
S. L. Riddle
Forrest Frazier.

41. An Associational Budget of $6,000 was adopted by the Association by adopting 1½% of the total gifts.

John W. McGinnis, Chairman
W. Wilbur Hutchins
Ray W. Harrington.

42. Dr. A. B. Conrad led the closing prayer.

43. Adjourned until the afternoon.

THURSDAY AFTERNOON—2:15 P. M.

44. Dr. John W. McGinnis, presiding. The afternoon session began with the singing of the hymn, "A Charge to Keep," led by James Kirk, accompanied by Mrs. O. E. Lee.

45. James E. Kirk, Reidsville, conducted the devotional service.

46. The Sunday School report, presented by Fred Bell, was accepted. Mr. Bell spoke to his report.

REPORT ON SUNDAY SCHOOLS

Statistics are revealing if they are given careful scrutiny and genuinely studied. A statistical chart of the Sunday Schools is to be found elsewhere in the minutes, and at the individual's leisure ought to be used for serious reflection. For the purpose of this report it will suffice to say that generally the Sunday School attendance is on the increase. The enrollment is up, the average attendance is better, study courses are going strong, many baptisms and new church members have come via the Sunday School, and Vacation Bible Schools have proved to be the best in years.

The figures found in the chart are encouraging, and yet, the full pitcure can never be envisioned without the use of the imagination. Behind the digits, if one has eyes to see, there are children being introduced to Jesus and His way of life; young womanhood is being inspired to live decent lives; young men are being led to dedicate their lives to the Kingdom; the character of men is being transformed and renewed; women are being persuaded to strive for a Christian family and to rear their children in the nurture of the Lord; and all are being led into a saving knowledge of Jesus through the teaching of the Bible.

Statistics can actually block our vision unless with penetrating eyes we can look beyond to see the evils which might have been and yet which have been prevented. Through our Sunday Schools ignorance and Bible illiteracy have been banished; much crime has been prevented; indecency, immorality, and sexual promiscuity have been mitigated; hatreds and prejudices have been squelched; dishonesty, greed, and injustice have been dealt a severe blow; and cynicism has undergone defeat. All this has been accomplished by the simple teaching of the Bible and Jesus and the more complex application of Him to everyday life. With keen eyes those figures become transparent enough so that we may see an enlightened constituency and redeemed attitudes that shall overlook the barriers of race, nation, and class which have kept us enemies for so long.

All of this a Christian with his God-given imagination may see because the Bible, its teachings, its principles, and its spirit is being taught. This is cause for elation. However, let us be fair in analyzing our year's work. Let us be careful that we no not cry "Peace, peace, when there is no peace." Let us not say "a grand Sunday School year" and at the same time close our eyes to our deficiencies. Can we be content with a slight increase in view of the population increase in the United States and in the Piedmont Association Area? Can we be complacent in view of the increased potential brought about by the returned service men? We are happy about our gains and spiritual results, but with renewed consecration let us press forward for a greater year in these critical times.

Respectfully submitted,

Fred L. Bell.

---

47. Grover H. Jones, presiding. The Relief and Annuity Board—Widows Aid Report, presented by W. W. Woodcock, was accepted.

RELIEF AND ANNUITY BOARD

The Relief and Annuity Board was organized and chartered with headquarters at Dallas, Texas, in 1918. Its total assets at the end of the first year were $100,000 contributed by the Sunday School Board of the Southern Baptist Convention and $4,545.42 received from the churches. On December 31, 1945 the assets of the Board reached the total of $9,449,256.09. By making application to the Baptist State Convention of North Carolina any church worker can be assured of a living income after retirement. The church pays four percent of the worker's salary, which payment goes to the permanent endowment of the Relief and Annuity Board. The worker pays four percent of his salary, which is kept to his individual account until such time as he retires, or becomes disabled, when it becomes a part of the capital assets of the Board. By paying one or one and a half percent of his income, the pastor may assure his widow an annuity, if he should die before reaching the retirement age.

The churches have an obligation to see that pastors do not become public charges when they are too old to work. The pastors have an obligation to themselves and their children to provide for themselves, so that they will not be a burden to the state or the community. Every pastor and church worker is urged to take advantage of the retirement plan offered jointly by the Relief and Annuity Board and the Baptist State Convention of North Carolina.

Wilson Woodcock.

48. The Clerk-Treasurer presented the financial report, which was adopted.

THE FINANCIAL REPORT

Balance		$ 688.56
Received from Churches	$1,058.38	
For Tent	550.00	
Total	$1,600.86	$1,600.86
Grand Total		$2,289.42

LESS EXPENSES

Supplement to T. L. Sasser	$ 325.00	
Compensation to Clerk	100.00	
Bank Charge	.15	
Dr. Ralph Herring	20.00	
Dr. Arthur Gellespie	20.00	
Printing Minutes	310.00	
Southern Baptist Convention (Sasser)	72.40	
Relief and Annuity (T. L. Sasser)	18.00	
B. T. U. Associational Work	40.00	
Printing Program	8.00	
For Associational Tent	550.00	
Insurance on Tent	49.65	
Clerk Help	10.00	
Postage, Paper, Etc.	79.85	
Incidentals	11.81	
Total	$1,614.86	$1,614.86
		$ 674.56

Balance in treasury to date $674. 56

Respectfully submitted,

Ray W. Harrington.

---

49. The Committee to nominate delegates to the State Baptist Convention presented the following who were elected.

D. M. Clemmons
Neil Armstrong
J. Ben Eller.

50. The report on time, place, and preacher was accepted.

Time: Wednesday and Thursday following the third Sunday in October, 1947.

Place: Mt. Zion Baptist Church.

Preacher: R. Von King.

J. Clyde Turner, Chairman
R. R. Saunders, Sr.
Floy Cox.

51. The report on Resolutions was accepted.

RESOLUTIONS

Whereas the Piedmont Baptist Association meeting in its fifty-third annual session with the Green Street, The North Main Street, and the Hilliard Memorial Baptist Churches of High Point in a very spiritual and beneficial session,

Be it resolved:

First, that we express our sincere gratitude to these churches and their Pastors for making our visit in High Point one of joy and welocme, and for the meals and other courtesies extended.

Second, That we express our continued appreciation to our very efficient Moderator, Mr. Grover H. Jones, and our very able Clerk, Rev. Ray W. Harrington.

Third, That we express out thanks to the Program Committee for making this Program one of the best.

Be it resolved, that we shall use every effort to promote a better understanding with members of other races, and that we shall use every opportunity to promote better race relations that we may have a better Christian Society.

Be it resolved that we shall continue to support and endorse all agencies of our State and Southern Baptist Convention.

Respectfully submitted,

E. O. Lankford
W. H. Barker
W. C. Adkinson, Chairman.

52. The Messengers joined in singing, "Close to Thee."

53. The Address, "The Call of the Cross," by Dr. J. Clyde Turner.

54. Dr. J. Clyde Turner led the closing prayer.

55. Adjourned from the 1945-1946 session.

IN MEMORIAM

ALLEN JAY
Mrs. Bryant Harrison
BRIGHTWOOD
Mr. Eli Brewer
Mr. Claude C. Hanner
BUCHANON
Mr. R. L. Mays
FAIRVIEW
Mr. Robert Coleman, Deacon
GIBSONVILLE
Mr. R. T. Foster
Mr. Irwin Marton
ASHEBORO
Miss Margaret Harris
Mr. R. L. Kirkman
Mr. Ralph U. Spoon
Mr. C. E. Lovin
Mr. J. A. Coble
BESSEMER
Mr. Joe C. Turner, Deacon
COLLEGE PARK
Mr. R. D. Mayer
Mr. W. B. Sigmond
ELLER MEMORIAL
Mrs. Vera Maness
Mr. W. W. Hobbs
GREENSBORO FIRST
Mrs. E. B. Gresham, Sr.
Mrs. H. R. White
Mr. J. L. M. Smith
Miss Anebel P. Blair
Mrs. N. A. Wilkinson
Mr. C. S. Paris
Mrs. S. W. Blackburn
Mrs. W. S. Rolph
Miss Martha B. Woodroof
Miss Elizabeth Mulford
Mrs. J. D. Suttonfield
Mrs. Nina L. Jones
W. D. Mott
Mr. B. W. Lancaster
Mrs. J. L. Spruill
Mrs. Ida B. Hudson
Mr. R. E. Jordan
Mrs. A. A. Crutchfield
Mrs. M. J. Warren
Mr. W. J. Fulp
Mr. W. B. Webb
FLORIDA STREET
Mr. John L. Roberson, Deacon
Mr. John W. Preston, Deacon
Lawrence Regan
MAGNOLIA STREET
Mr. Alex Frye
Mr. Jack Lashley
SIXTEENTH STREET
Mr. Frank Furlough
Mr. John L. Snider
Mr. J. C. Wright
Mrs. Addie Seagraves
Mrs. Isabelle McDaniel
Mrs. T. A. Cecil
STEVENS MEMORIAL
Mrs. J. P. Scott
Mrs. Ella Alvis
Mr. C. R. Spivey
HIGH POINT FIRST
Lt. Gilbert Clark
Mr. John Raper
Mr. J. Vassie Wilson
Mrs. J. T. Dickens
Mr. R. W. Seward, Deacon
Mr. J. W. Clary
Mr. W. J. Goldsmith, Deacon
Mr. J. W. Quattlebeaum
Mr. Fitshugh Perry
Miss Catherine Smith
Mrs. E. S. Darr
Mr. J. T. Lotts
Mr. Miller Armentrout
Miss Sallie Bolling
GREEN STREET
Mrs. S. H. Hartgrove
Mrs. M. T. Cranford
Mrs. Letha Parton
Miss Daisy Stepp
Mrs. Marie Loving
Mrs. R. L. Winfrey
Alten Phillips
Mrs. Maggie McKinney
J. L. Bobbins
John A. Smith
S. R. Joines
NORTH MAIN STREET
Mrs. C. V. McLendon
Mrs. J. R. Teague
Mr. Carl P. Hines
Mr. Ed. Daniels
SOUTH SIDE
Mr. C. A. Conn
Mr. S. A. Deford
Mr. G. W. Powell
Mr. D. G. Patterson
WEST END
Mr. Solomon S. White
JESSUP GROVE
Mrs. Sarah Marshall
JEWEL
Mr. Robert L. Deaton
LEBANON
Mr. J. L. Brown
MT. ZION
Mr. J. F. Murray
Mr. Cicero Linnens
Miss Rebecca Lineberry
McCONNELL ROAD
Mrs. James A. Heath
OAK GROVE
Mrs. Hoyte Saunders
OSSIPEE
Mrs. C. T. Hopkins
PILOT VIEW
Mr. Odell Fletcher
PISGAH
Mrs. J. W. Hanes
PLEASANT GROVE
Mr. R. J. Eaton
BAPTIST TEMPLE
Mr. H. W. Hudson, Deacon
Robert Talley
REIDSVILLE FIRST
Mr. Les Clymer
Mrs. John A. Kemp
Mrs. Delmar Idol
Mrs. John Grogan
PENN MEMORIAL
Mrs. Elizabeth Rice
RUFFIN-STACEY
Mr. Raymond Simpson
SUMMERFIELD
A. C. Lloyd, Deacon
Mrs. Joy W. Parrish
TEMPLE
Mr. Jessie French

TABLE ONE—CHURCH MEMBERSHIP

CHURCHES	Town, Vill., Country?	Year Organized	PASTORS AND ADDRESSES	GAINS: Dates of Meeting	GAINS: Baptisms	GAINS: By Letter	GAINS: Other Additions	LOSSES: By Letter	LOSSES: By Death	LOSSES: Other Losses	TOTAL: Present Resident Membership	TOTAL: Non-resident Membership	TOTAL: Grand Total Present Membership	SPECIAL INFORMATION: Are Weekly Prayer Meetings Held?	SPECIAL INFORMATION: Number of Revival Meetings Held	SPECIAL INFORMATION: Spent on Building or Remodeling Last Year	SPECIAL INFORMATION: Value of Pastor's Home	SPECIAL INFORMATION: Total Value of All Church Property	SPECIAL INFORMATION: Total Debt on Church Property
Allen Jay	V	1934	V. L. Mabry, Rt. 3, Box 316, H. P.	all	7	7	...	26	1	4	...	...	344	yes	2	...	5000	10000	...
Antioch	C	1935	J. C. Gillespie, Reidsville	½	1	...	...	2	...	...	40	20	60	...	2	...	...	3000	...
[illegible]od	V	1940	H. P. [illegible]n, Rt. 5, [illegible]o	all	14	13	11	10	2	37	209	...	209	yes	4	3700	6500	23500	1603
Buchanon	O	1936	J. B. Clifton, 619 [illegible]h, Greensboro	all	16	1	2	1	1	...	147	...	147	yes	2	2898	...	7000	...
Calvary	O	1901	W. D. Turner, Rt. 4, Reidsville	all	24	8	1	4	...	...	...	...	222	yes	1	328	2000	7000	...
Community	O	1934	R. O. Nuckles, Colfax	2-4-5	1	...	...	...	...	1	...	...	...	no	3	504	...	4750	...
Conrad Memorial	C	1946	George Richman, Rt. 1, High Point	all	2	8	...	...	...	...	...	...	...	yes	1	...	...	7000	...
Fairmont Park	V	1940	John H. Scalf, Rt. 2, High Point	all	9	9	1	20	...	...	225	15	240	yes	2	2675	...	25000	...
Fairview	O	1904	J. E. Kirk, Rt. 2, Reidsville	½	...	3	...	1	1	...	...	...	...	...	...	...	...	...	...
Gibsonville	C	1884	John L. Gamble, Box 85, Raleigh	all	5	1	...	5	2	...	283	...	283	yes	1	...	...	4500	...
GREENSBORO—																			
Asheboro Street	C	1899	J. B. Eller, 709 [illegible], Greensboro	all	44	32	5	50	5	9	...	...	1301	yes	1	...	[illegible]0	76000	...
Bessemer	C	1922	Ray W. Harrington, 507 Delancey, Gr.	all	25	4	15	24	1	...	...	...	555	yes	2	...	3000	23000	...
College Park	C	1906	[illegible]n [illegible]k, 508 Forrest Ave., Gr.	all	20	44	8	39	2	6	524	88	662	yes	...	...	[illegible]00	85000	...
Edgeville				...	...	...	...	...	...	...	...	...	...	...	...	...	...	...	...
Eller Memorial	C	1897	R. [illegible]n King, 1307 Summit Ave., Gr.	all	90	19	7	11	2	1	...	...	978	yes	3	722	9000	51000	...
First	C	1859	J. C. Turner, 2601 W. Market, G'boro	all	60	170	9	113	21	11	...	...	2532	yes	...	...	...	130000	...
Florida Street	C	1906	J. R. [illegible]n, 1110 Glenwood, G'boro	all	28	38	16	...	3	...	632	73	715	yes	2	...	6000	50000	...
Immanuel	C	1935	F. L. Fraser, [illegible]x 749, Greensboro	all	21	22	47	...	...	...	...	...	91	yes	2	...	...	3000	...
Latham Park	C	1916	None	...	5	...	...	...	...	...	60	...	60	...	2	151	...	3500	...
Magnolia Street	C	1912	W. T. [illegible]s, 103 E. Wendover, G'boro	all	17	7	2	7	2	...	208	17	225	yes	3	...	4000	11000	...
Pomona	T	1906	C. M. [illegible]s, 23 Boren, Pomona	all	28	6	10	2	...	...	...	...	286	yes	2	1318	...	3600	...
Revolution	C	1907	S. L. Riddle, 2218 Shober St., G'boro	all	4	...	1	4	...	2	...	...	378	yes	2	...	...	10000	...
Sixteenth Street	C	1907	W. Ad[illegible]n, 1504 16th St., G'boro	all	30	9	11	5	6	...	355	...	355	yes	2	...	...	3900	...
Stevens Memorial	C	1922	None	all	...	5	...	18	3	1	145	40	185	yes	...	6156	10000	25000	2000
Rankin	C	1935	B. L. Gupton, Rt. 5, [illegible]o	all	27	27	11	...	...	2	175	...	175	yes	2	...	11000	16000	2500
Guilford	V	1914	T. E. Kerley, 1704 Florida Ave., G'boro	½	12	13	3	9	...	...	...	...	107	yes	2	...	...	3800	...

[redacted]H POINT—																			
First	C	1832	W. W. [redacted]s, 225 [redacted]y, H. P.	all	29	77	2	70	14	....	1215	255	1560	yes	....	15748	7000	200000	......
[redacted] Street	C	1900	J. S. Hopkins, 324 [redacted]w Ave., H. P.	all	112	34	13	12	11	2	1500	344	1844	yes	1	4500	......	172000	......
Hilliard Memorial	C	1929	H. O. Miller, 2333 Edgewood Ave., H. P.	all	9	6	1	16	....	2	299	54	359	yes	1	721	......	35000	......
North Main	C	1908	N. J. [redacted]g, 111 Hillcrest Dr., H. P.	all	21	20	...	17	4	27	364	18	382	yes	2	943	7000	26500	......
[redacted]h Park	C	1929	J. W. [redacted]y, Jr., 915 [redacted]t Ave., H. P.	all	2	14	3	8	....	....	....	....	205	yes	3	......	......	4900	......
Southside	C	1916	W. H. [redacted]r, 415 South St., High Point	all	6	8	2	10	4	....	....	....	.....	yes	2	......	......	3500	......
West End	C	1913	W. C. [redacted]h, 918 [redacted]g St., [redacted]h Point	all	13	5	2	15	1	6	423	....	423	yes	2	......	3500	15000	......
Jessup [redacted]e	C	1933	J. E. Wiggs, P. O. Box 2769, [redacted]boro.	all	23	2	5	3	1	....	206	2	208	yes	2	1710	......	10000	......
Jewel	C	1941	A. H. Dunning, 806 [redacted]n, High Point	all	2	2	...	....	1	....	48	6	54	yes	1	241	......	2500	......
Lebanon	O	1911	C. C. [redacted]s, 208 Newlyn St., [redacted]ro	all	1	2	2	4	1	....	170	30	200	.....	....	......	......	......	......
Mt. Zion	O	1824	J. T. Swinson, Burlington	all	26	...	...	2	3	....	205	....	205	yes	2	......	......	5000	......
McConnell Road	O	1945	J. T. Ellis, 101 Dockery St., Greensboro	all	7	...	1	....	1	....	14	....	14	yes	2	1391	......	3000	......
McLeansville	V	1943	N. H. Blackburn, Greensboro	all	...	3	1	....	....	....	....	....	.....	yes	3	......	......	7000	......
Oak Grove	O	1916	R. L. Smith, 613 [redacted]y, High Point	all	16	4	...	3	1	....	....	....	134	yes	2	......	......	3500	......
Osceola	C	1915	W. S. Young	½	4	...	...	....	....	....	....	....	.....	.....	....	......	......	......	......
Ossipee	V	1933	L. M. King, Rt. 1, Graham	all	5	2	...	....	1	....	42	8	50	yes	2	238	......	3500	......
Pine Grove	O	1938	Robert Taylor, Rt. 3, High Point	all	1	2	...	1	....	....	....	....	86	yes	1	223	......	3500	......
Pilot View	V	1941	C. C. Roberts, Rt. 5, High Point	all	13	15	...	2	1	....	104	....	104	yes	2	1595	......	4500	300
Pisgah	C	1939	C. M. Floyd, 508 [redacted]r St., High Point	all	13	10	6	5	1	2	173	....	173	yes	4	......	3500	11500	......
Pleasant [redacted]n	V	1938	D. C. Austin, Pleasant [redacted]n	all	...	17	...	6	....	....	114	....	114	yes	2	175	5000	5000	3200
Pleasant Grove	O	1938	J. M. Allred, Pomona	all	2	3	...	6	1	....	100	25	125	yes	2	374	......	5000	......
Reedy Fork	O	1940	Elijah Lankford, Rt. 2, Brown [redacted]mit	all	14	8	2	1	....	1	....	....	156	yes	2	......	4264	10264	......
[redacted]—																			
Baptist Temple	C	1929	D. M. Clemmons, Reidsville	all	11	13	...	11	2	2	....	....	283	yes	2	......	4500	10500	......
First	C	1844	J. M. McGinnis, Reidsville	all	32	31	...	17	4	....	....	....	1007	yes	2	......	20000	......	......
Penn Memorial	T	1931	W. S. Holton, 103 Silver St., Reidsville	all	24	8	4	2	1	3	243	....	243	yes	1	663	3000	14000	......
Rocky Knoll	O	1934	G. A. [redacted]r, Rt. 1, Greensboro	all	3	5	...	4	....	....	....	....	284	yes	2	90	......	......	......
Ruffin Stacy	O	1931	J. T. London, Rt. 5, Reidsville	all	9	4	...	1	2	4	206	....	206	yes	2	500	......	3800	......
Smith Grove	O	1921	R. O. [redacted]s, [redacted]x	½	15	1	...	3	....	....	....	....	197	yes	2	......	......	2500	......
Summerfield	V		E. A. Long, Germantown	½	2	3	...	2	2	....	205	....	205	.....	1	......	......	9800	......
Temple	V	1939	John Burger, Rt. 4, High Point	all	6	4	4	6	1	....	....	....	99	yes	2	3700	......	3500	......
[redacted]d Memorial	V	1946	W. R. Smith, Rt. 1, Greensboro	all	...	19	6	....	....	....	25	....	25	yes		47	......	8000	......
Woodlawn	O	1945	A. B. Ashill, 2203 Green, High Point	all	33	55	5	....	....	4	....	....	93	yes	2	......	......	10000	1500
Totals				.....	944	823	219	578	110	127	8659	995	19148	.....	97	47988	130264	1283314	11103

TABLE TWO—SUNDAY SCHOOLS

CHURCHES	SUNDAY SCHOOL SUPERINTENDENTS AND ADDRESSES	Cradle Roll 3 Years and Under	Beginners 4-5 Years	Primaries 6-8 Years	Juniors 9-12 Years	Intermediates 13-16 Years	Young People 17-24 Years	Adults 25 Years and Up	Extension Department	General and Departmental Officers	Enrolment of Missions Sunday School	Total Enrolment—Main School, Missions, Officers & Teachers	Average Attendance	Does Church have 16mm Projector	Did You Have a Vac. Bible School?	What Was the Enrolment?	Average Attendance?
[illegible]n [illegible]y	[illegible]e Cumbie, [illegible] 1, [illegible]x 239, [illegible]h Point	12	15	20	43	38	36	125	.....	4	.....	289	217	*	**	62	48
[illegible]h	[illegible]y M[illegible], Reidsville	....	....	....	....	....	....	....	....	2	.....	66	35	*	**	66	35
[illegible]d	Lynn Strader, [illegible]r Br., [illegible]o	....	14	....	22	28	50	86	.....	3	.....	200	150	*	*	.....	.....
[illegible]	[illegible]h [illegible]d, Box 2760 [illegible]o	24	23	....	25	6	55	56	.....	....	.....	186	107	*	*	.....	.....
Calvary	J. W. [illegible]o, R. 2, [illegible]e	....	22	16	27	25	51	94	.....	....	.....	235	113	*	**	99	85
[illegible]y	[illegible]e [illegible]h, [illegible]n	....	26	....	26	.....	24	35	.....	3	.....	114	67	*	*	.....	.....
[illegible]d M[illegible]orial	R. F. [illegible]y, R. 1, High Point	....	14	29	39	22	25	86	.....	....	.....	221	141	*	**	48	42
[illegible]t [illegible]k	B. V. Broadway, Rt. 1, Thomasville	....	19	11	26	44	56	30	.....	1	.....	183	117	*	*	.....	.....
Fairview	A. D. [illegible]s, Rt. 1, Reidsville	....	15	....	....	.....	.....	.....	.....	....	.....	217	137	*	**	.....	.....
[illegible]le	[illegible]h [illegible]r, Gibsonville	....	....	87	128	122	113	426	43	8	.....	1066	448	*	**	250	177
[illegible]—																	
Asheboro Street	F. L. [illegible]l, 2420 [illegible]en Rd., G'boro	82	57	50	78	40	56	117	.....	17	.....	394	214	*	**	80	70
[illegible]r	C. E. [illegible]y, 611 [illegible]d St., [illegible]o	18	35	36	44	47	49	131	35	6	.....	146	237	*	**	65	52
College Park	N. B. Moury, 416 S. Mendenhall, [illegible]ro	67	31	76	111	90	84	177	12	4	.....	584	264	*	**	219	178
Edgeville	.....	....	....	....	....	.....	.....	.....	.....	....	.....	.....	.....	.....	.....	.....	.....
[illegible]r Memorial	[illegible]d Kincaid, 1103 Summit Ave., [illegible]	10	20	145	198	190	123	855	161	5	.....	1988	981	**	**	278	224
First	F. L. Stubbs, Greensboro	211	105	94	98	53	44	293	30	7	.....	683	307	**	**	255	165
[illegible]a Street	B. [illegible] [illegible]l, [illegible]x 1791, [illegible]o	29	35	15	20	13	26	22	.....	2	.....	134	70	*	**	69	60
[illegible]uel	W. C. Heilig, 2018 [illegible]o, [illegible]o	....	26	....	....	.....	.....	.....	.....			55	.....	.....	.....	.....	.....
[illegible]m Park	[illegible]y [illegible]s, Greensboro	....	....	14	19	12	25	54	.....	2	.....	150	75	*	**	60	45
[illegible]a Street	B. C. Scott, 1202 [illegible]a St., G'boro	2	24	26	56	43	43	88	.....	2	.....	299	179	*	**	73	58
Pomona	C. C. Patterson, Box 102, Pomona	....	41	35	49	20	25	72	18	7	.....	272	180	*	*	.....	.....
Revolution	J. C. Dennis, 2208 Poplar St., Greensboro	19	27	18	27	23	22	47	15	3	.....	158	123	*	**	55	48
Sixteenth Street	Rockford Hill, 4[illegible]5 [illegible]ss St., G'boro	5	15	56	99	45	40	90	7	6	.....	360	232	*	**	229	169
Stevens Memorial	[illegible]k [illegible], Rt. 2, Box 154, [illegible]o	14	8	20	24	20	30	60	.....	7	.....	183	116	*	*	.....	.....
[illegible]in	T. P. [illegible]n, 2404 [illegible]e St., G'boro	8	10	8	8	8	15	41	.....	1	.....	93	60	*	*	.....	.....
Guilford	Setzer [illegible]n, 635 S. [illegible], [illegible]o	3	10	8	8	8	15	41	.....	1	.....	93	60	*	*	.....	.....

HIGH POINT—																	
First	W. F. Clayton, 223 Lindsay St. H. P.	113	70	93	119	153	215	546	70	4	70	1379	661	**	**	312	249
Green Street	W. E. Crissman, 226 Woodrow Ave., H. P.	101	100	148	229	195	180	619		4		1576	730	**	**	368	259
Hilliard Memorial	A. L. Slate, Rt. 2, High Point	6	17	15	27	37	33	74		6		218	137	*	**	71	66
North Main	W. C. Edwards, 202 W. Lexington, H. P.	12	22	34	72	48	61	111		5		365	169	*	**	176	127
North Park	H. B. Chatham, 1434 N. Hamilton, H. P.	12	13	15	33	16	21	66		6		182	111	*	**	72	53
Southside	A. L. Bean, 504 Highland Ave., H. P.		31	30	36	30	89	65		4		281	175	*	*		
West End	R. G. Barlowe, 522 Barker, High Point	15	25	30	48	44	33	98	25	8		329	161	*	**	92	72
Jessup Grove	Paul Duggins, 1313 Lexington, G'boro		25		30		51	45		3		151	107	*	*		
Jewel	S. P. Stutts, Sr., Box 528, Rt. 5, H. P.		35		25		40	25		5		125	79	*	**	64	54
Lebanon	D. G. Davis, Rt. 2, Greensboro	17	13	18	17	17	57	71				203	117	*	*		
Mt. Zion	Winfred Shoffner, Rt. 2, Snow Camp		18		19	22	41	20		3		120	88	*	*		
McConnell Road	W. H. Bullock, Rt. 6, Greensboro		12		11		11	13				47	25	*	**	25	19
McLeansville			15		10		15	20				50	42	*	**	60	40
Oak Grove	A. L. Saunders, Box 928, High Point	13	9	10	10	17	16	39				144	70	*	*		
Osceola	E. J. Brown, Rt. 1, Brown Summit		13	8	14	12	11	27				85	38	*	*		
Ossipee	Leo Gerringer, Rt. 2, Elon College			13	18		14	23		3		71	50	*	*		
Pine Grove	J. W. Breedlove, Jamestown		18	8	11	9	27	33		2		108	57	*	**	57	
Pilot View	V. E. Webb, Rt. 5, High Point		23	17	15	26	27	44		1		152	96	*	*		
Pisgah	Z. V. Lanier, 2213 E. Green, High Point	22		16	34	33	53	77			45	280	170	*	**	85	65
Pleasant Garden	J. Rummage, Pleasant Garden		14	11	28	22	32	25		11		137	65	*	*		
Pleasant Grove	F. M. Atkins, Rt. 3, Greensboro		28	14	17	13	13	43				128	73	*	**	42	45
Reedy Fork	L. A. Beach, Rt. 2, Greensboro	15	13	21	14	22	23	52				160	119	*	*		
REIDSVILLE—																	
Baptist Temple	Milton Warf, Wentworth St., Reidsville	17	21	19	37	30	15	73	18	5		230	120	*	**	119	98
First	S. F. Wells, 233 Lindsay St., Reidsville	39	54	63	65	59	80	260		4		624	278	*	**	180	130
Penn Memorial	W. H. Ford, Box 988, Reidsville	5	13	12	32	15	29	64		3		173	110	*	*		
Rocky Knoll	E. H. Peele, Troy St., Greensboro	22	33	41	41	31	27	110				305	172	*	*		
Ruffin Stacy	R. W. Lane, Ruffin	24	27	25	30	22	15	96		3		242	100	*	*		
Smith Grove	Homer Westmoreland, Guilford College		34		22		68	65		2		189	79	*	*		
Summerfield	Marion Ayers, Summerfield		24	24	12	14	26	59				162		*	*		
Temple	R. S. Edmonds, Rt. 4, High Point	6	12	11	17		27	35				108	73	*	*		
Woodard Memorial	J. E. Peoples, Rt. 6, Greensboro											76	65	*	*		
Woodlawn	M. E. Turner, 111½ S. Hamilton, H. P.		11		20		64	46				141	125	*	*		
Totals		946	1310	1439	2388	1777	2421	5970	434	173	115	17210	9088			3683	2633

* No. ** Yes.

TABLE THREE—BAPTIST TRAININ GUNION

CHURCHES	TRAINING UNION DIRECTORS AND ADDRESSES	Adult Unions	Young People's Unions	Intermediate Unions	Junior Unions	Story Hours	Total Unions and Story Hours	Adults Enrolled	Young People Enrolled	Intermediates Enrolled	Juniors Enrolled	Story Hours Enrolled	Gen. & Dept. Officers Not Otherwise Enrolled	TOTAL ENROLLMENT	Average Attendance Per Sunday	Was Youth Week Observed?
Allen Jay	Roy Bennison, Archdale	1	1	1	1	1	5	12	7	8	23	7	1	57	30	*
Antioch																
[illegible]d																
[illegible]n																
[illegible]y	Mrs. Gladys Johnson, Rt. 2, Reidsville	1	1		1	1	4	15	8		5	5	1	33	14	*
Community																
Conrad Memorial	Mrs. Paul Jester, Rt. 6, High Point															
Fairmont Park		1	1	1	1	1	5	8	20	9	12	16	3	73	42	
Fairview																
[illegible]e	Ann Blythe, Whitsett		1				1		42					42	20	
GREENSBORO—																
[illegible]o [illegible]t	Mr. John R. Durham, 309 Burtner, G'boro	2	1	4	2	2	11						7	150	96	*
[illegible]r	[illegible]k [illegible], 911 Peterson, [illegible]o	1	1	1	1	1	5	12	17	10	20	5	4	64	28	*
[illegible]e [illegible]k	Fred L. Bell, 510 Forrest, [illegible]o		1	1			2		36	12			1	49	30	*
Edgeville																
Eller Memorial	H. E. May, 1504 Maple, Greensboro	1	1	2	1	1	6	20	8	24	17	18	2	89	56	*
First	Frank L. Stubbs, [illegible]o	3	4	4	2	1	14	77	60	43	25	7	5	212	164	*
Florida Street	E. M. Clark, 1410 Florida, Greensboro	3	2	2	3	1	11	48	12	36	23	9	3	131	90	**
Immanuel																
Latham Park																
[illegible]a Street	Baxter C. Scott, 1202 Magnolia, G'boro	1	1	1	1		4	9	18	10	10			47	21	*
Pomona	[illegible]v. D. E. Oates, 1921 Fargis, [illegible]o	1					1	19					1	20	15	*
Revolution	Hoyle C[illegible]ll, 1901 Poplar, [illegible]o	1		1	1	1	4	11		10	9	12	1	43	40	*
[illegible]th Street	[illegible]n A. Johnson, 2311 Hubbard, G'boro	1	1	1	1	1	5	10	13	17	21	14	5	83	83	*
[illegible]s Memorial																
Rankin	Mrs. Norman [illegible]n, Rt. 5, G'boro	1	1	1	1	1	5	10	12	7	8	7	6	50	28	*
Guilford	W. C. [illegible]h, Guilford	1	1			1	3	10	15			7		33	20	**

HIGH POINT—																	
F[illegible]t	Julia Liles, 09½ [illegible]h, [illegible]h Point	1	2	3	2	1	9	14	37	51	32	19	4	157	110		
[illegible]n [illegible]	R. L. [illegible]s, Box 1584, High [illegible]t	3	3	3	4	1	14	46	38	42	31	25	6	189	118	*	**
Hilliard Memorial	Everett Grubb, 1306 [illegible], High Point	1	1	1	1	1	5	10	14	17	7	3	3	52	32	**	*
North Main	Winfred Clinard	1		1	1	1	4	11		10	24	7	3	55	32	**	**
North Park	[illegible]s. L. [illegible] e[illegible]n, [illegible]x 702, [illegible]h Point	1	1	1	1	1	5	11	6	13	15	12	9	66	51	**	**
Southside	[illegible]y h[illegible]w, [illegible]8 Walker, High [illegible]t	1	1		1	1	4	8	4		10	11		33	24	*	*
West End	Leona Chappell, [illegible]5 Redding, [illegible] P.	1		1	1	1	4	10		5	13	8	4	40	25	*	*
Jessup Grove	Carrie [illegible]y, [illegible]t. 1, [illegible]d [illegible]e	2	2		1		5	22	24		10		4	65	63	*	*
Jewel	Billy t[illegible]s, [illegible]x 528, [illegible] 5, [illegible]h Point	1	1		1	1	4	10	20		20	10	4	60	40	*	*
Lebanon	J. L. [illegible]n, [illegible] 5, [illegible]x 224, G'boro	1	1	1			3	10	12	12				34	20	*	*
M[illegible] Zion																	
McConnell Road																	
McLeansville																	
Oak Grove																	
[illegible]a																	
Ossipee																	
Pine Grove																	
Pilot View	Joe Edwards, High Point	1		1	1		3							25		*	*
Pisgah	J. G. Ritch, 627 [illegible] [illegible]n, H. P.	1	1	1	1	1	5	19	15	25	10	7	5	86	50	*	*
P[illegible]t [illegible]n																	
P[illegible]t Grove	[illegible] H. Smith, Rt. 3, Box [illegible]8, [illegible]o	1		1	1	1	4	7		15	4	6	4	32	24	*	*
Reedy Fork	Parks Gregory, Rt. 2, Brown Summit	1	1	1	1	1	5	23	15	20	22	10		90	55	*	*
REIDSVILLE—																	
Baptist Temple	[illegible]n [illegible]k, 438 Lindsey, Reidsville	1	1	1	1	1	5	22	6	23	12	13	4	80	40	*	*
First	Paul Roach Reidsville	1	1	2	1	1	6	9	16	29	17	3		74		*	*
Penn Memorial	Mrs. [illegible]h [illegible]s, Reidsville	1	1	1	1	2	6	20	9	6	16	11	1	63		*	*
Rocky Knoll	W. T. Apple, Rt., Greensboro			1	1	1	3			8	15	12	1	36		*	*
Ruffin Stacy																	
[illegible]th Grove																	
Summerfield	Howard Pope, Summerfield	1		1	1		3	12		5	16			33	15	*	*
[illegible]e	Mrs. R. L. Rodden, Box 1545, High Pt.	1	1		1	1	4	13	17		15	5		50	20	*	*
[illegible]d Memorial																	
[illegible]n																	
Totals		41	35	41	39	30	187	538	501	467	462	270	92	2496	1496		

* No. ** Yes.

TABLE FOUR—W. M. U. ORGANIZATIONS AND GIFTS

CHURCHES	PRESIDENTS OF W. M. S. AND ADDRESS	Number of Woman's Missionary Societies	Number of Y.W.A.'s	Number of G.A.'s	Number of R.A.'s	Number of Sunbeams	Total W. M. U. Organizations	W. M. S. Members	Y. W. A.'s Members	G. A.'s Members	R. A.'s Members	Sunbeam Members	Total Members Enrolled	Total Enrolled in Mission Study Courses	Contributions (Local Work) Given by W. M. U.	Contributions (Missions) Given by W. M. U.
Allen Jay	Mrs. V. L. Maybry, Rt. 3, B. 316, H. P.	1					1	19					19	6		74.88
Antioch		1		1		1	3	11		9		12	32			56.57
Brightwood																
[illegible]n	Mrs. J. B. Clifton, 619 Waugh, G'boro	1	1	1	1	1	5	20	14	8	8	12	54	52		180.36
Calvary	Mrs. C. H. Lynn, Rt. 4, Reidsville	2	1	1	1	1	6	40	13	9	15	16	93		51.19	116.70
Community																
[illegible]d Memorial																
Fairmont Park	Mrs. O. C. Suggs, High Point	1	1	1	1	1	5	17		10	18	8	53		30.00	104.89
Fairview		1					1	16							4.50	77.64
Gibsonville	Mrs. C. C. Hammer, Gibsonville	1	1				2	16	13				29			78.85
GREENSBORO—																
Asheboro Street	Mrs. A. C. Lowe, [illegible]0 [illegible]h Ave., Gr.	1		2	1	1	5	187		41	16	46	290	192	6550.26	3372.84
Bessemer	Mrs. J. R. Medlin, 200 Sykes, Greensboro	1	1			1	3	51	12			33	96	22	127.81	417.96
College Park	Mrs. B. B. Stockard, 14 Springdale, G.	1	1	2	2	1	7	63	32	18	23	12	148	91	3673.48	1876.05
Edgeville																
Eller Memorial	Mrs. Lloyd Vornadore, 1209 Homeland, Gr.	1	1	1	1	1	5	35	12	7	6	10	70	39		1663.57
First	Mrs. H. D. Martin, 216 S. Men'hall, Gr.	1	2	4	4	2	13	434	17	29	42	59	[illegible]	95		13394.34
Florida Street	Mrs. C. D. [illegible]r, [illegible]0 McCor., G'boro	7	1	2	1	1	12	83	10	35	12	25	165	223	516.14	65.17
Immanuel	Mrs. S. W. [illegible]t, [illegible] 4, B. 446A, G.	1					1	17							6.25	18.00
Latham Park		1														33.20
Magnolia Street	Mrs. L. L. Jarvis, 2401 Lawndale, Gr.	1		1		1	3	27		10		25	62	19	1205.55	297.61
[illegible]a	Mrs. Ethel Wall, Pomona	1		1			2	25				20	45		17.17	108.89
Revolution	Mrs. Waldo Johnson, 2211 Shober, Gr.	1		1	1	1	4	17		10	8	11	46	21	318.71	393.92
Sixteenth Street	Mrs. Harry L. Moore, 1508 1[illegible]th St., G.	1	1	2	2	1	7	33	13	25	18	12	[illegible]	31	2122.36	1490.14
Stevens Memorial	Mrs. [illegible] Sutton, Spruce St., G'boro	1					1	15								171.96
Rankin	Mrs. C. L. Straughn, Rt. 5, G'boro	1		1		1	3	31		6		7	44	13	1964.98	138.86
Guilford	Mrs. I. E. Kerley, 1704 Fla. Ave., G'boro	1				1	2	15				8	23	6		33.00

HIGH POINT—																
First	Ms. W. F. Ellis, Jr., W. Lex., H. P.	1	1	4		1	7	216	18	75		40	349	612	524.08	6153.34
Gn Street	Mrs. Fred Culler, 518 Carter, High Point	1	2	2	2	1	8	134	19	19	26	15	213	56	6933.25	3498.91
Hilliard Memorial	Mrs. J. N. Ellis, 1006 Stauten, H. P.	1				1	2	18				20	38	26	798.67	205.75
N th Mn	Mrs. S. R. ld, Rt. 1, High Point	2					2	20					20	20	134.25	221.75
N th Park	Mrs. D. H. St, Box 1312, High Point	1		2	1	1	5	21		18	16	22	77	44	868.08	660.47
Sde	Mrs. J. S. n, 307 Greer St., H. P.	2					2	26						12	65.57	183.76
West End	Mrs F. M. Houser, Ennis St., h Point.	1		1	1	1	4	20		7	5	12	43	30		143.53
Jessup Grove																
Jewel																
Lebanon	Mrs. C. C. Cross, 8 Newlyn St., G'boro	1					1	34							200.00	243.00
Mt. Zion	Mrs. J. C. Lockamy, R. 2, y	1						15							123.00	314.00
ell Road																
sville																
k Grove																
Osceola																
Ossipee	Marie Tysinger, Rt. 2, Elon College	1					1	9								
he Grove																
Pilot View	Mrs. C. C. s, R. 5, h Point	1					1	22							96.50	23.00
h	Mrs. C. F. , 1505 l, H. P.	1		1			2	10		6			16	2	158.32	26.64
Pleasant Garden	Mrs. J. C. n, Pleasant n	1					1	20							24.00	7.20
Pleasant Grove		1					1	10								50.00
Reedy Fork	Mrs. R. P. Everage, Rt. 2, Brown Summit	1				1	2	9				16	25		864.58	153.00
REIDSVILLE—																
Baptist ple	s. J. I. s, Bx 224, Reidsville	1	1	2	1	1	6	55	11	35	16	33	150	69	2282.00	291.72
First	Mrs. S. F. Wells, 223 Lindsey, R'ville	1	1	2		1	5	178	16	21		34	249	231		4002.74
Penn Memorial	Mrs. G. V. Dalton, Box 414, Reidsville	1					1	27					27	17	231.54	98.88
Rocky Knoll	Mrs. W. T. Apple, Rt. 1, o	1	1	1			3	22	8	8			38		244.00	75.00
n Stacy																
Smith Grove																
Summerfield	Mrs. C. D. Robinson, ld	1				1	2	17				18	25			390.74
Temple																
d Memorial	s. Lee Roy r, R. 6, G'boro	1				1	20									
n																
Totals		52	17	36	20	26	167	2055	208	406	329	526	3231	2039	30136.24	41445.93

TABLE FIVE—MEN'S BROTHERHOODS

CHURCHES	DIRECTORS OF MEN'S BROTHERHOODS AND ADDRESSES	Does Church Have a Brotherhood Organization	Present Enrolment	Brotherhood Meetings Held Last Year	Pledged to Co-operative Program or United Budget Coming Year	Pledged to Associational Missions Coming Year	Number of Tithers in Church	Number Members Subscribing to Every Member Canvass	Building and Reserve Funds on Hand at End of Year	Is State Paper in Church Budget?	Does Church Have Library?
Allen Jay		*					40		12350	*	*
[illegible]ch		*			50				7		
Brightwood							80		1390		
Buchanon					365				500		
Calvary					250	15			937		**
Community							10		1185		
Conrad Memorial					400	120	18			**	
Fairmont Park						15					
Fairview											
Gibsonville							15		8855		
GREENSBORO—											
Asheboro Street	Earl Johnson, 2012 Asheboro, Greensboro	**	54	5		100		406	16377	*	**
Bessemer					480	30	35				
College Park							110		30994		**
Edgeville											
Eller Memorial					2400	55	75		8301	**	**
First							309		197952	**	**
Florida Street	Robert Barracks, 1009 Haywood, G'boro	**	20	12	3500		200	275		**	**
Immanuel							31		799		
Latham Park											
Magnolia Street					156	15	44	142	7523		**
Pomona							36				
Revolution											**
Sixteenth Street					2200	200	50		9778		
Stevens Memorial					6665		18				**
Rankin					400	20	22	66	820		**
Guilford		*					20		1576		**

HIGH POINT—												
First			*					150		7640		**
Green Street			*					240	1063	30040		**
Hilliard Memorial			*									**
North Main			*			1040	52	15		115		**
North Park			*					25		11000		**
Southside			*			100		32		7150	**	*
West End			*			660	184	33				
Jessup Grove			*				16	30		12	*	**
Jewel			*					12		361		
Lebanon			*					16				
Mt. Zion			*			50	5	17		1202		
McConnell Road			*					3		145		
McLeansville			*					6		87		
Oak Grove			*			15						
Osceola			*									
Ossipee			*			20	10	7		95	*	
Pine Grove			*									
Pilot View			*			92		20		579		
Pisgah			*			75		25		15168		
Pleasant Garden			*					20			**	**
Pleasant Grove			*			96	10	15		13		
Reedy Fork			*			156		24		1271		
REIDSVILLE—												
Baptist Temple			*									**
First			*							18100		
Penn Memorial			*					25		313		**
Rocky Knoll			*							2083		
Ruffin Stacy			*					12				
Smith Grove			*					7				
Summerfield			*							863		
Temple			*					8				**
Woodard Memorial			*									
Woodlawn			*									
Totals				74	17	19170	856	1862	1952	395589		

* No. ** Yes.

TABLE SIX—GIFTS FOR LOCAL CHURCH WORK

CHURCHES	TREASURERS AND ADDRESSES	Pastor's Salary Paid for Year	Incidentals—Janitor, Fuel, Water, Repairs, Insurance, Etc.	Assistant Pastor, Educational Director, Choir Leader, Etc.	Revival Expenses and Pastoral Supply	Paid on Church Debt Out of Current Funds	Literature—Quarterlies, Church Paper, Song Books, Etc.	Help for Local Poor	Minutes and Clerk of Association	Building Fund (Amount Given Last Year)	Other Objects	Total Given for Local Church Work
Allen Jay	W. R. Hobson, Rt. 1, Box 239, High Point	2610.00	4.[illegible]		535.22		345.50	558.81		4352.03	671.00	10607.23
Antioch	Mrs. T. H. Carter, Rt. 2, Reidsville	300.00	9.60		[illegible]		32.23		1.00			457.13
Brightwood	[illegible] Ham, 1216 Fairview St., Greensboro	2910.00	972.16		532.71	448.00	[illegible]	87.00	6.00	3700.00	339.07	9153.85
Buchanon	R. F. Carter, Rt. 6, [illegible]	2180.00	176.11	150.00	142.85		66.94	77.16	11.12	1040.54		4844.72
Calvary	J. F. Carroll, Rt. 3, Reidsville	1000.00	173.62		153.89		132.51	45.53	[illegible]	328.15	215.84	2052.54
[illegible]	Julia [illegible], Rt. 1, Greensboro	793.83	14.64		362.53		66.69		3.00		23.73	1264.42
Conrad [illegible]	[illegible] Mildred Jester, Rt. 6, High Point	747.00	12.00			500.00	66.47	18.00		906.00		2249.47
Fairmont Park	R. A. Teague, Rt. 2, High Point	2600.00	3580.45		462.97		310.08	150.21	19.50		252.60	7405.81
Fairview	D. E. Trantham, Rt. 2, [illegible]	600.00	285.32		201.12		98.42				86.00	1270.86
[illegible]	T. L. Robertson, [illegible]	1800.00	[illegible]	77.45	261.84	200.00	[illegible]	220.62	22.64	2713.11	300.00	6080.35
GREENSBORO—												
[illegible]ro Street	Mrs. A. C. Lowe, 150 0 Randolph Ave., G'boro	[illegible]	2982.58	3956.82	[illegible]		836.40	747.26		6686.25	2405.35	22072.61
Bessemer	C. L. Murray, 3909 E. Bessemer Ave., Greensboro	2600.00	1449.81	720.00	103.00		316.28		0.[illegible]	4047.00	264.00	9510.09
College Park	Mrs. C. O. [illegible]er, 2516 High Pt. Rd., Greensboro	2820.00	1592.28	1020.00	165.00		348.14	118.06	12.50	7890.68	831.51	14798.17
Edgeville												
Eller Memorial	Mrs. Robert Burgess, 512 E. Bessemer, Greensboro	3200.00	2037.32	2062.90	1 [illegible]		958.46	164.42	10.00	2382.78	1341.01	[illegible]
First	C. A. McKeel, 803 Longview, Greensboro	5850.00	[illegible]	11035.00	276.44		4935.34	1721.26		38020.05	4708.32	76312.16
Florida Street	D. M. Frazier, 1319 Florida St., Greensboro	3055.20	1527.68	298.50	400.00	337.07	1167.23			4440.00	1238.75	12404.43
Immanuel	W. C. Heilig, 2018 [illegible] St., Greensboro	[illegible]	264.32		370.00		63.54				577.96	3101.32
[illegible] Park	R. A. [illegible], 1312 W. [illegible], Greensboro	866.10	281.63		[illegible]		28.95					1353.18
Magnolia Street	H. S. Noah, 1700 Grove St., Greensboro	2990.00	902.92	[illegible] 00	244.50		120.38	105.02	5.00	280.47	218.70	[illegible]
Pomona	E. E. Henry, Pomona	2612.75	1582.62		433.62		268.11	438.32	5.00		316.38	5656.80
Revolution	[illegible] Johnson, 2211 [illegible]er St., Greensboro	2535.00	461.21		186.09		226.94	38.12	26.00		544.28	4017.64
Sixteenth [illegible]	L. F. Paris, 1507 15th St., Greensboro	3300.00	1509.22	130.00	250.00		322.35	154.98	25.00	4073.00	100.02	[illegible]
Stevens [illegible]	[illegible] C. B. Brisson, Rt. 2, Greensboro	1802.50	1621.03		135.16		127.78	18.50	4.00	3156.82		6865.79
Rankin	B. H. Scott, Rt. 5, [illegible]	2200.00	594.02	60.00	215.00		133.22	22.00		4632.93		7857.90
Guilford	Mrs. Dora Farrar, Guilford College	[illegible]	247.72		259.19		137.73	25.00	8.56		99.24	[illegible]

HIGH POINT—												
First	[illegible] [illegible] Patrick, 309½ [illegible] St., [illegible] Point	4425.00	5720.75	5656.71	145.00	15748.86	2210.73	112.82	122.88	[illegible]	6177.30	47960.28
Green Street	E. L. [illegible], 114 E. [illegible] St., High Point	3900.00	6582.42	1571.79	1446.93	....	1955.34	149.58	10.00	1 [illegible]	8094.06	35625.95
[illegible]	C. H. Farmer, 2108 English St., High Point	2290.00	1775.15	....	217.00	....	149.77	[illegible] 04	15.00	....	443.81	4939.54
North Main	J. E. Brawley, 916 N. [illegible] St., High Point	2600.00	1040.21	280.00	291.80	3157.62	573.80	135.32	8.00	198.55	....	8285.30
North Park	L. W. [illegible], 805 Dayton St., High Point	2585.00	310.68	....	313.83	....	362.00	....	......	3077.41	424.22	7197.34
Southside	W. R. Grant, 410 White St., High Point	2600.00	941.00	120.00	357.27	....	195.97	35.53	5.00	1510.60	230.57	5995.94
West End	C. M. Scott, [illegible]09 Ferndale Dr., High [illegible]	2442.06	669.90	....	199.12	....	366.11	25.00	33.76	2499.46	150.12	6660.93
Jessup Grove	Mrs. [illegible] Lewis, Rt. 1, Summerfield	2053.00	493.71	....	564.00	....	158.33	25.00	5.00	....	1954.00	5253.04
Jewel	Lela Weatherman, Rt. 5, High Point	892.13	241.59	....	62.00	....	87.84	86.50	3.00	199.72	310.17	1882.95
Lebanon	O. L. [illegible], Rt. 5, Box 223, [illegible]	2110.00	157.65	....	179.65	3080.70	154.31	185.57	......	1063.27	175.40	7106.55
Mt. Zion	Mrs. C. M. Johnson, Rt. 1, [illegible]	2600.00	214.94	....	359.90	....	79.12	179.27	5.00	1046.82	....	4485.55
[illegible] Road	C. G. [illegible], [illegible] [illegible] St., [illegible]	....	29.64	....	38.62	1351.10	24.48	....	1.00	1032.82	....	1446.85
McLeansville	E. V. Snow, McLeansville	250.00	84.57	....	....	390.00	54.37	....	2.40	....	209.54	990.88
Oak Grove	W. L. [illegible], Rt. 3, [illegible] [illegible]	2503.40	160.68	....	264.16	....	43.11	....	2.00	....	127.81	3101.16
Osceola	....	693.95	....	....	109.50	40.11	49.85	....	......	....	14.10	907.51
Ossipee	H. D. [illegible], Rt. 1, [illegible] College	543.00	355.23	....	[illegible]	....	45.00	....	2.00	231.57	20.00	1253.80
Pine Grove	Larson Tuttle, Rt. 3, High Point	186.64	350.00	....	69.93	....	58.54	....	2.50	....	119.98	787.59
Pilot View	[illegible]s. J. E. Rollins, Rt. 5, High Point	1680.00	275.87	....	132.50	....	155.29	....	5.00	1595.26	125.00	3968.92
Pisgah	L. C. Madden, [illegible] [illegible] St., High Point	2860.00	1194.71	....	600.00	[illegible]1.00	208.93	481.02	12.50	....	125.00	5583.16
Pleasant Garden	George Denny, Rt. 1, Greensboro	1500.00	213.16	....	241.91	1063.00	105.84	50.00	2.00	....	....	2075.91
Pleasant Grove	Virgil Ward, Rt. 3, Greensboro	1560.00	400.00	....	162.95	....	67.59	....	9.84	98.00	302.00	2600.38
Reedy Fork	Parks Gregory, Rt. 2, Brown Summit	2340.00	719.10	....	148.58	....	198.04	52.23	3.00	1271.18	24.10	4756.23
REIDSVILLE—												
Baptist Temple	Mrs. Odell Dellap, Box 283, Reidsville	3120.00	1338.30	245.00	474.73	....	413.22	....	21.92	6695.63	371.83	12680.63
First	J. P. Kemp, [illegible] Franklin St., Reidsville	3750.00	2875.97	2110.00	925.00	....	999.25	75.00	10.00	6000.00	[illegible]0.	19745.26
Penn Memorial	G. V. Dalton, Box 414, Reidsville	[illegible]0	636.73	160.00	390.37	....	160.01	114.07	5.00	313.70	1045.13	5015.01
Rocky Knoll	Mrs. R. A. Laughlin, Rt. 1, Greensboro	2105.00	584.63	....	178.01	....	287.63	278.00	5.00	1344.20	236.14	5018.61
Ruffin Stacy	Lillie Burton, Rt. 5, Reidsville	1500.00	208.50	....	280.00	....	[illegible]	11.00	4.00	....	678.09	2691.83
Smith Grove	Drew Smith, Rt. 1, Colfax	600.00	172.76	....	295.12	....	19.82	....	3.00	....	163.49	1254.19
Summerfield	Mrs. T. D. Carter, Summerfield	910.00	227.95	....	130.22	....	84.05	10.00	16.00	551.50	203.66	1581.86
Temple	R. L. Rodden, Box 1545, High Point	1291.30	378.94	....	266.40	....	60.34	30.00	2.00	....	....	2088.98
Woodard Memorial	Mrs. W. D. Neal, Rt. 6, Box 64, [illegible]	360.00	124.13	....	....	39.22	....	....	2.00	....	....	585.35
Woodlawn	E. D. Ridge, Rt. 1, High Point	....	....	....	....	....	....					
Totals	....	114647.52	61114.60	29788.17	16443.97	26556.68	20645.96	6847.22	494.12	136935.48	39159.28	452584.40

TABLE SEVEN—GIFTS FOR ALL MISSIONS, EDUCATION, ORPHANAGES, ETC.

CHURCHES	CLERKS OF CHURCHES AND ADDRESSES	Gifts to Co-operative Program or Unified Budget	Designated to Associational Missions	Designated to State Missions	Designated to Home Missions	Designated to Foreign Missions	Designated to Schools, Colleges, and Seminaries	Orphanage Cash and Conservative Estimate Value of Merchandise, Clothing, etc.	Designated to Hospitals	Designated to Red Cross and Foreign Relief	Relief and Annuity, Other Objects	Total for All Missions	Grand Total of All Contributions for All Purposes
Allen Jay	Hoy Yarborough, Rt. 4, Box 589, High Point	5.00	29.00					172.00	[illegible]	73.00	150.00	1024.00	181.23
Antioch	M. T. H. Carter, Rt. 3, Reidsville	50.00	5.28	11.28	3.50	59.50		85.00	22.50	15.02		185.12	642.25
Brightwood	Mrs. Dewey Fuller, 1501 18th St., Greensboro				1213.00			251.75	21.21			1485.96	10639.81
Buchanon	R. F. Carter, Rt. 6, Greensboro	545.46						52.00	20.00		41.60	659.06	5503.78
Calvary	J. E. McCargo, Rt. 2, Reidsville	250.00	12.00					199.00	65.05	87.30		613.35	2665.89
Community	Zelda March, Rt. 1, Randleman							62.00	46.17			108.17	1372.59
Conrad Memorial	D. B. Webb, Rt. 1, High Point												
Fairmont Park	Ray Moose, Rt. 2, High Point			100.00	100.00	100.00		165.06	100.00			669.95	8075.76
Fairview	William Cummings	216.32		15.00	[illegible]	20.00	20.00	228.42	46.19	134.52	36.00	737.23	2008.09
Gibsonville	Jim Laughlin, [illegible]le	100.00	.80	28.85		[illegible]		246.33	96.53	226.00	10.00	887.95	6968.30
GREENSBORO—													
Asheboro Street	J. B. Wills, 1026 Pearson St., Greensboro	5219.95	100.00	101.08		1027.00	30.00	1012.60	270.45	1538.59	210.00	9509.67	31552.28
Bessemer	R. F. Pace, 607 Sykes Ave., Greensboro	480				290.15		100.00	100.00	70.40	335.89	1376.44	10886.53
College Park	P. R. Venable, 1720 W. Lee St., [illegible]oro	550.00	..	72.58	87.70	1250.15	149.35	516.24	127.16	849.80	62.10	3673.48	18471.65
Edgeville													
Eller Memorial	E. P. Hinson, 1203 Homeland Ave., Greensboro	2325.00	55.00	32.62		618.87	119.72	533.80	223.66	1033.40	100.07	5042.14	18236.09
First	Vander Liles, 1326 Madison Ave., Greensboro	29028.93	600.00	986.03	1762.40	7110.15	720.00	5541.17	872.01	12243.20	740.57	59604.46	135916.62
Florida Street	Mrs. W. L. Jones, 1303 Oak St., Greensboro	1316.70	300.00		150.00	2083.30		736.66		816.06	127.40	5560.12	17964.55
I[illegible]nuel	Mrs. C. C. Stanley, Box 741, Greensboro	47.25	3.00	56.75	20.00	40.00		169.59	21.85			358.35	3459.67
Latham Park	Elizabeth Nelson, 1212 Northwood St., Greensboro												1353.18
Magnolia Street	Mary Scott, 1110 Walnut St., Greensboro	156.26	15.00	50.00	50.00	100.00		137.50	50.00	125.00	76.23	759.99	5633.48
Pomona	C. C. Patterson, Pomona	493.36		88.36		100.00		747.00	141.50	50.25	111.56	1732.03	7388.83
Revolution	Raymond Rogers, 2211 [illegible]er St., Greensboro	728.12		14.55	39.90	266.92		242.05	204.63	103.40	35.75	1626.37	5644.01
Sixteenth Street	Harry L. Moore, 1508 17th St., Greensboro	2883.97		28.21	29.02	104.82		412.43	100.00	209.42	280.06	4047.93	13912.51
Stevens [illegible]rial	Mrs. J. B. Brown, Rt. 2, Box 154, Greensboro	800.00			[illegible]	[illegible]		251.00	50.26	55.99		1281.40	8147.19
Pankin	G. E. [illegible]d, Rt. 5, Box 339, Greensboro	400.00		23.85	11.00	48.00		221.15	53.68	78.32	22.05	858.05	8715.95
Guilford	Mrs. Dora Farrar, Guilford College	173.82		5.00	6.00	15.00		50.00	[illegible]	40.00	24.92	369.74	2187.18

HIGH POINT—													
First	Mrs. W. K. [illegible]s, 310 E. Farriss Ave., High Point	6823.51	200.00	326.40	4 [illegible]	4298.04	100.00	2309.60	289.50	3618.25	[illegible]	18746 [illegible]	66706.47
Green Street	[illegible] Ayers, Rt. 3, [illegible]h Point	12203.00	120.00	95.02	150.00	4489.50		1473.13	650.00			[illegible]80 65	54806.66
Hilliard Memorial	Everett Grubb, 1306 [illegible] [illegible]h Point	227.53	15.00	25.00	31.00	25.00		287.16	77.84	157.56	91.60	[illegible]	5870.02
North Main	[illegible]s Ring, [illegible]09 Granby St., [illegible]h Point	[illegible]	52.00	131.15	101.81	138.69		234.00	79.56	130.00	232.00	2131.86	10417.16
North Park	Mrs. L. [illegible] [illegible], [illegible]5 [illegible]t Ave., High Point	637.30		24.00	20.50	63.15		346.50	55.00	61.00		1107.45	8304.79
Southside	Mrs. D. A. Parlier, 205 W. [illegible]le, High Point	10 [illegible]		183.76	65.57			145.00	42.82	6.00		543.15	6539.09
West End	Mrs. Vernon Coffey, 520 Barker St., High Point	712.41		184.00	218.35	103.31		537.42	1[illegible]	39.42		2505.55	9166.48
Jessup Grove	Mrs. D. H. Bryson, Rt. 5, [illegible]o		16.00		180.23		10.00	160.54	34.07		110.00	2130.61	7377.88
Jewel	Violet Craven, Rt. 5, High Point				25.18	25.18		68.00	35.18			153.54	2036.49
Lebanon	Mrs. Dolphus Stewart, Rt. 5, Greensboro	32 [illegible]	18.00	70.85	46.28	225.98		244.84	21.12	56.16		[illegible]	7821.78
Mt. Zion	C. D. [illegible]n, Rt. 3, Liberty	[illegible]		12.80	29.95	51.00		108.99	9.83		34.31	646.88	5132.43
[illegible] Road	J. T. Ellis, Jr., [illegible] [illegible] St., Greensboro								14.00			[illegible]	1535.76
[illegible]le	[illegible]a Harrell, [illegible]ville												
Oak Grove	Marion [illegible], Box 1622, High Point	[illegible]						105.95	15.00			138.95	3240.11
[illegible]la	T. J. Brooks, Rt. 1, Brown Summit			10.00			5.00	96.85	12.12	7.60		131.57	1039.08
Ossipee	Mrs. Leo Gerringer, Rt. 2, Elon College	20.00		10.00					10.00		20.00	60.00	1313.80
Pine Grove	Mrs. R. A. Pickard, Rt. 3, [illegible]h [illegible]t			5.00		20.00		101.34	20.00			146.34	933.93
Pilot View	Mrs. H. S. Fletcher, Rt. 5, High [illegible]t	92.16				10.00		69.60	77.58	30.00	13.00	292.34	4261.26
Pisgah	M. J. Bowen, 1902 Franklin St., [illegible]h Point	86.00		26.65		140.00		168.00		19.31	190.16	630.56	6213.72
Pleasant Garden	Mrs. Henry Foy, Rt. 1, Pleasant Garden	4.06			25.00	25.00		80.13	15.34			69.53	2145.44
Pleasant Grove	Virgil Ward, Rt. 3, Box 256, [illegible]ro	50.00						124.80	21.25		58.92	254.97	2855.35
Reedy Fork	Alvin Bullard, Denim Station, [illegible]oro	104.00		16.10	5.39	5.39		104.00	128.00	52.06	153.02	567.96	5324.19
REIDSVILLE—													
Baptist Temple	Mrs. Jessie Strader, 55 Wentworth St., Reidsville	651.15	17.00	47.82	24.78	72.61		210.00	89.85	44.05	105.60	1262.86	13943.49
First	E. S. Powell, 108 Franklin St., [illegible]sville	3517.70	375.00	100.25	126.25	[illegible]		1003.05		1796.15	96.50	7743.93	28829.77
Penn Memorial	Mrs. I. C. Gailey, 24 Turner Dr., Reidsville	[illegible]		29.20	18.00	118.37		36.35	50.00		83.20	403.50	5418.51
Rocky Knoll	Mrs. [illegible] T. [illegible]e			166.00	150.05	25.00		228.10	139.00	52.10	319.00	1079.25	6097.86
Ruffin Stacy	Ernest Lee, Box 1328, Reidsville							10.00	14.13			24.13	2691.33
Smith Grove	Mrs. Ray [illegible]k, Rt. 1, [illegible]k			11.00	3.20	6.80		139.00	75.00	14.00		239.00	1493.19
Summerfield	Myrtle [illegible]h, Summerfield	183.19		52.37	46.50	568.08		232.48	63.50	86.47	17.80	1250.39	2866.11
Temple	Mrs. R. L. [illegible]en, Box 1545, High Point			12.50	12.50				15.00			40.00	2128.98
Woodard [illegible]al	Mrs. [illegible] V. [illegible]l, Rt. 6, Box 87, Gr[illegible]boro			25.00		25.00		25.00	25.00			100.00	685.35
[illegible]	Mrs. M. E. Turner, 111½ S. [illegible]n, [illegible]igh Point												
Totals		72733.18	1933.08	3224.03	6817.82	24459.55	1164.07	[illegible]0703.49	6578.18	23919.80	4265.88	156860.04	617206.90

HISTORICAL TABLE—PIEDMONT BAPTIST ASSOCIATION

Year	Where Held	Moderator	Clerk	Preacher	Churches	Baptisms	Members	Gifts
1894	Greensboro	Dr. C. A. Rominger	W. L. Kivett	M. A. Adams	5	....	562	....
1895	Liberty	T. L. Chislom	W. L. Kivett	L. Johnson	12	16	1112	4695.50
1896	Moore's Chapel	R. W. Brooks	W. H. Eller	L. Johnson	14	66	1194	5128.94
1897	Summerfield	F. H. Jones	W. H. Eller	J. A. Munday	16	73	1540	7198.27
1898	Mount Zion	R. W. Brooks	W. H. Eller	L. Johnson	17	67	1557	6883.23
1899	Ramseur	R. W. Brooks	F. P. Tucker	John E. White	19	54	1570	7435.43
1900	Cherry Street	R. W. Brooks	W. H. Eller	Thomas Carrick	16	48	1538	7970.35
1901	Reidsville	F. H. Jones	W. H. Eller	L. Johnson	19	157	1657	8282.73
1902	Salem Street	F. H. Jones	W. H. Eller	W. C. Newton	19	135	1774	9950.97
1903	Gibsonville	F. H. Jones	W. H. Eller	C. L. Greaves	20	185	1868	12834.77
1904	Calvary	F. H. Jones	W. H. Eller	H. W. Battle	22	112	1832	12807.43
1905	Randleman	F. H. Jones	W. H. Eller	J. M. Hilliard	22	114	2096	17674.91
1906	High Point, First	F. H. Jones	W. H. Eller	W. R. Bradshaw	23	201	2333	29366.31
1907	Asheboro Street	F. H. Jones	W. H. Eller	Wm. Hedley	26	372	2798	39993.79
1908	Ramseur	F. H. Jones	W. H. Eller	C. E. Maddry	28	311	3086	26347.57
1909	Greensboro	F. H. Jones	W. H. Eller	Wm. Hedley	30	292	3429	49847.28
1910	Mount Zion	F. H. Jones	W. H. Eller	R. G. Hendrick	31	336	3731	28531.01
1911	Asheboro	W. F. Staley	W. H. Eller	W. F. Staley	29	182	3736	15887.56
1912	High Point, Green Street	F. P. Hobgood, Jr.	W. H. Eller	J. C. Turner	30	174	3647	29697.38
1913	Liberty	F. P. Hobgood, Jr.	W. H. Eller	R. P. Walker	31	409	3971	37700.97
1914	Asheboro Street	F. P. Hobgood, Jr.	W. H. Eller	A. W. Claxon	31	413	4202	42428.44
1915	Reidsville	J. M. Hilliard	W. H. Eller	J. M. Hilliard	42	313	4491	42577.68
1916	Forest Avenue	J. M. Hilliard	W. H. Eller	E. N. Johnson	36	369	4854	48418.92
1917	Green Street	J. M. Hilliard	W. H. Eller	W. R. White	39	308	4760	44609.05
1918	Moore's Chapel	J. M. Hilliard	W. H. Eller	J. W. Rose	39	374	5140	72538.46
1919	White Oak	J. M. Hilliard	W. H. Eller	W. H. Wilson	39	339	5359	76638.85
1920	Calvary	J. M. Hilliard	W. H. Eller	E. N. Johnson	39	543	5967	117682.35
1921	Summerfield	Clarence A. Smith	J. E. Lanier	B. K. Mason	39	480	6454	135561.79
1922	Glenola	Clarence A. Smith	J. E. Lanier	Jas. A. Clark	39	679	7226	149955.24
1923	Magnolia Street	Clarence A. Smith	H. O. Miller	E. E. White	38	365	7341	140553.25
1924	West End	Clarence A. Smith	H. O. Miller	W. E. Goode	40	672	7489	164658.19
1925	Fairview	Clarence A. Smith	H. O. Miller	A. T. Howell	41	610	8956	211792.21
1926	Ramseur	Clarence A. Smith	S. T. Hensley	Lloyd T. Wilson	42	620	9974	243500.68
1927	Trinity	Clarence A. Smith	S. T. Hensley	H. T. Stevens	40	656	10223	211846.40

1923	Bessemer	Clarence A. Smith	O. E. Lee	R. P. Ellington	41	531	10866	202002.30
1929	Liberty	Clarence A. Smith	O. E. Lee	C. F. Rogers	44	573	1	[illegible]87.61
1930	Asheboro	Clarence A. Smith	O. E. Lee	Geo. T. Tunstall	44	676	12012	198077.29
1931	Florida Street	Clarence A. Smith	O. E. Lee	A. B. Conrad	44	827	12789	[illegible]01.19
1932	Reidsville	Clarence A. Smith	O. E. Lee	J. C. Turner	46	778	13485	159000.60
1933	White Oak	Clarence A. Smith	O. E. Lee	T. L. Sasser	48	1561	15199	186041.40
1934	Franklinville	Clarence A. Smith	O. E. Lee	Wilson Woodcock	53	757	15365	172839.18
1935	South Side, High Point	Clarence A. Smith	O. E. Lee	J. S. Hopkins	41	623	12687	164135.92
1936	Calvary	Clarence A. Smith	O. E. Lee	J. Ben Eller	42	563	13958	166052.96
1937	Eller Memorial	Grover H. Jones	O. E. Lee	C. N. Royal	41	657	14086	195540.50
1938	Hilliard Memorial	Grover H. Jones	O. E. Lee	A. B. Conrad	42	814	14793	[illegible]46.20
1939	Reidsville	Grover H. Jones	O. E. Lee	J. C. Turner	46	975	15479	[illegible]24.34
1940	Florida Street	Grover H. Jones	O. E. Lee	Chas. E. Parker	51	804	16206	[illegible]25.45
1941	Green Street	Grover H. Jones	O. E. Lee	A. Lincoln Fulk	53	724	16929	284008.43
1942	Greensboro, First	Grover H. Jones	L. Grady Burgiss	A. A. Walker	55	794	16922	324184.15
1943	Greensboro, First	Grover H. Jones	L. Grady Burgiss	I. B. Jackson	55	772	17268	396139.14
1944	Greensboro, First	Grover H. Jones	Ray W. Harrington	G. H. Wallace	56	640	17958	[illegible]31.10
1945	Greensboro, First	Grover H. Jones	Ray W. Harrington	John McGinnis	56	921	18988	[illegible]03.36
1946	High Point	Grover H. Jones	Ray W. Harrington	W. W. Hutchins	60	944	19148	[illegible]06.90

MINUTES

of the

Piedmont Baptist Association
North Carolina

FIFTY-FOURTH ANNUAL SESSION

held with the

MOUNT ZION BAPTIST CHURCH
Liberty, N. C.

October 22-23

1947

★ ★ ★

Next meeting to be at the First Baptist Church, Reidsville, N. C.
October 19-20, 1948

R. C. Shearin .... Preacher
George Richman .... Alternate

MINUTES

of the

Piedmont Baptist Association
North Carolina

FIFTY-FOURTH ANNUAL SESSION

held with the

MOUNT ZION BAPTIST CHURCH
Liberty, N. C.

October 22-23

1947

★ ★ ★

Next meeting to be at the First Baptist Church, Reidsville, N. C.
October 19-20, 1948

R. C. Shearin .... Preacher
George Richman .... Alternate

Edited for the

Piedmont Baptist Association

by

Ray W. Harrington

INDEX

ASSOCIATIONAL DIRECTORY

Grover H. Jones, Moderator....................High Point
T. L. Gardner, Vice-Moderator..................Reidsville
Ray W. Harrington, Clerk-Treasurer............Greensboro

EXECUTIVE PROMOTION COMMITTEE

Grover H. Jones, Chairman...................High Point
T. L. Gardner..................................Reidsville
Carl Bell.....................................Greensboro
R. Von King...................................Greensboro
Mrs. W. C. Adkinson...........................Greensboro
Wilson Woodcock...............................Greensboro
Wilbur Hutchins...............................High Point
H. O. Miller..................................High Point
W. S. Holton...................................Reidsville
Mrs. C. H. Fryar.............................Summerfield
J. S. Hopkins.................................High Point
Dr. J. Clyde Turner...........................Greensboro
C. M. Scott...................................High Point
O. B. Teague..................................Greensboro
Mrs. C. W. Moseley............................Greensboro
W. E. Coates...................................Reidsville
George E. Williamson..........................Greensboro

CHURCH ADVISORY AND MISSIONS COMMITTEE

J. S. Hopkins.................................High Point
Grover H. Jones...............................High Point
Mrs. C. W. Moseley............................Greensboro
T. L. Garner...................................Reidsville
W. E. Coates...................................Reidsville
George E. Williamson..........................Greensboro
W. W. Hutchins................................Greensboro
Mrs. W. C. Adkinson...........................Greensboro
Ray W. Harrington.............................Greensboro

COMMITTEES SERVING DURING THE ASSOCIATIONAL YEAR

Executive Promotion Committee
Church Advisory and Missions Committee
Program Committee
Committee on Committees
Committee on Time, Place, and Preacher
Auditing Committee
Resolutions Committee
Program Committee for this year and next year
Committee to Nominate Officers
Committee to Nominate Executive Promotion Committee
Committee to Nominate Church Advisory and Missions Committee

CHURCHES BY DISTRICTS

District 1

Allen Jay, Conrad Memorial, Fairmont Park, Friendly, Green Street, High Point First, Hilliard Memorial, Jewell, North Main, North Park, Oak Grove, Pine Grove, Pilot View. Pisgah, Smith Grove, Southside, Temple, West End, Woodlawn.

District 2

Asheboro Street, Bessemer, Brightwood, Buchanan, College Park, Community, Edgeville, Eller Memorial, Florida Street, Gibsonville, Greensboro First, Guilford, Immanuel, Jessup Grove, Latham Park, Lebanon, Magnolia Street, McConnell Road, McLeansville, Mount Zion, Pleasant Garden, Pleasant Grove, Pomona, Rankin, Revolution, Reedy Fork, Rocky Knoll, Sixteenth Street, Stevens Memorial, South Elm, Southside, Summerfield, Ossipee, Woodard Memorial.

District 3

Antioch, Calvary, Fairview, Baptist Temple, Osceola, Penn Memorial, Reidsville First, Ruffin-Stacey.

OFFICERS OF BAPTIST TRAINING UNION

J. Carl Bell, Director........................Greensboro
Miss Thelma Patrick, Associate Director.......High Point
J. J. Norwood, Associate Director.............Greensboro
Mrs. Pearl Womack, Secretary-Treasurer.......Greensboro
E. C. White, Jr., Pianist.....................Greensboro
Anett Gounley, Chorister......................Greensboro
Miss Merdice Thomas, Story Hour Leader......Greensboro
Mrs. W. C. Adkinson, Junior Leader...........Greensboro
Allen Hancock, Intermediate Leader...........Greensboro
J. E. Hedrick, Young People's Leader...........High Point
R. C. Shearin, Adult Leader..................Greensboro
Everett Grubb, District No. 1.................High Point
George Williamson, District No. 2.............Greensboro
W. E. Coates, District No. 3....................Reidsville

PROGRAM COMMITTEE

W. W. Hutchins, Chairman.....................High Point
Mrs. C. A. Penn...............................Reidsville
Mrs. James R. Thompson.....................Greensboro
Shermon Young...............................Greensboro

OFFICERS OF PIEDMONT W. M. U.

Mrs. W. C. Adkinson.......................Superintendent
1504 16th, Greensboro

Mrs. A. C. Lowe.................Associate Superintendent
1500 Randolph, Greensboro

Mrs. Nettie Hoge................Superintendent Emeritus
1406 W. Market, Greensboro

Mrs. J. N. Turner...............................Secretary
705 Northridge, Greensboro

Miss Thelma Patrick..........................Treasurer
309½ Church, High Point

Mrs. James R. Thompson........................Y. P. L.
1110 Glenwood, Greensboro

Chairmen

Mrs. W. S. Fox............................Mission Study
807 Northridge, Greensboro

Mrs. W. C. Guth............................Stewardship
918 Redding St., High Point

Mrs. C. W. Moseley..................Community Missions
438 Mendenhall, Greensboro

Miss Cathrine Roddick.........................Literature
First Baptist Church, Reidsville

Group Leaders

Mrs. B. A. Teague..........204 Waverly Way, Greensboro
Mrs. C. D. Foster.................805 Dayton, High Point
Mrs. Guy Conrad...............Winston Road, High Point

Nominating Committee For Year

Mrs. Ben Spencer, Chairman..................Greensboro
Mrs. F. S. Wells............................Reidsville
Mrs. Fred Culler...........................High Point

ORDAINED MINISTERS NOT PASTORS

Barton, C. D., Retired.......................Greensboro
Barnes, E. S., Secular Work..................Greensboro
Bennett, Hubert..............................Greensboro
Blanchard, Chaplain Henry N., Retired........Greensboro
Billings, H. P...............................Jamestown
Boles, J. H..................................Greensboro
Coe, C. G., Secular Work.....................Greensboro
Conrad, Dr. A. B., Retired...................High Point
Cook, W. B., Secular Work....................Greensboro
Curl, L. D., Secular Work....................Greensboro
Davis, F. E..................................Greensboro
Dix, O. P....................................High Point
Farrington, B. H., Evangelist................Colfax
Fare, B. B...................................Leaksville
Hamilton, William............................Gibsonville
Harthnon, Vladwir............................Greensboro
Havner, Vance, Evangelist....................Greensboro
Hight, W. J., Retired........................Greensboro
Leonard, Dr. C. A., Missionary...............Hawaii
Loy, J. E., Jr...............................Salisbury
Matherly, W. F...............................Greensboro
McDowell, B. S...............................High Point
McDowell, Charles............................High Point
McGee, John S....................Missionary to Nigeria
Oates, D. E., Secular Work...................Greensboro
Overbey, D. W., Retired......................Reidsville
Plybon, C. T., Retired.......................Greensboro
Sasser, T. L., Associational Missionary......Reidsville

MINISTERS ORDAINED DURING THE YEAR

Charles L. Landreth..........................Greensboro
Richard Hanner...............................Greensboro
Luther M. King...............................Elon College
Troy Robbins.................................Louisville, Ky.

STUDENTS FOR THE MINISTRY

Rodger Snipes	Piedmont Bible Institute
Walter W. Stanley	Guilford College
Bob Johnson	Bob Jones College
John H. Lineberry	Moody Bible Institute
James B. Fleet, Jr.	Wake Forest
Ernest Holt	Bob Jones College
Connie Saliss	Bob Jones College
Henry Rutledge	Moody Bible Institute
Chas. C. Belch	Prairie Bible Institute
Dannie Lowe	Guilford College
Oscar Smith	Baylor University
Lonnie Shaw	Moody Bible Institute
Apol Deaton	Atlanta Bible Institute
Paul Duggins	Piedmont Bible Institute
Eugene Mason	Moody Bible Institute
Maurice McRea	Piedmont Bible Institute
Felton Carter	Southern Seminary
Arnold Ward	Piedmont Bible Institute
Charles Edward Bray	Campbell College
James Harrison	Tulane University
Nelson Harrison	Duke University
Carl Lackey	Piedmont Bible Institute
Kenneth G. Williams	Piedmont Bible Institute

MESSENGERS

ALLEN JAY—William Eberly, James Warren, Mrs. V. L. Mabry, Mrs. James Warren, Mary Warren.

ANTIOCH—Roy Moore, Mrs. Roy Moore, Mr. Curtiss Larrymore.

BRIGHTWOOD—Mr. and Mrs. Carl Ham, Mrs. Vernon Smith, Mrs. L. Welborn, Mrs. J. F. Jarrett, Mrs. Raymond Horner, Mrs. G. B. Cocklereece.

BUCHANON—Rev. James B. Clifton, Mrs. J. B. Clifton.

CALVARY—G. W. Gunn, Mrs. G. W. Gunn, J. E. McCargo, Mrs. J. E. McCargo, J. H. Johnson.

COMMUNITY—Herman Fentress, Robert Taylor, Mrs. Robert Taylor, Mrs. John May, T. M. Marsh.

CONRAD MEMORIAL — George Richman, Zeb Whitlow, Mrs. Glenn Mickey, Mrs. Paul Jester.

FAIRMONT PARK—J. E. Copple, Mrs. J. E. Copple, Mrs. J. H. Scalf, W. F. Thomas, B. V. Broadway.

FAIRVIEW—D. E. Trantham, Mrs. D. E. Trantham, Mrs. Henry Weber.

GIBSONVILLE—Mr. and Mrs. C. C. Hammer, Ed Riggins, Mrs. Daisy Thompson.

ASHEBORO STREET—F. L. Paschal, Austin Lovin, O. B. Teague, J. L. Fox, Mrs. Fred Murchison, Mrs. E. N. Bullock.

BESSEMER—Claude L. Murry, Mrs. Ray W. Harrington, Albert Sutton, E. C. Coble, M. P. Bullard.

COLLEGE PARK—Fred Bell, A. J. Hewitt, Mrs. B. B. Stockard, Mrs. Draper Leigh, Mrs. H. O. Weaver.

EDGEVILLE—Rev. Alton Riddle.

ELLER MEMORIAL — Mrs. Helen Shepherd, Mrs. Carl Beeker, Mrs. R. Von King, Mrs. G. A. Caviniss, W. P. Malone.

GREENSBORO FIRST—Frank L. Stubbs, Carl Bell, Mrs. H. D. Martin, R. W. Morton.

FLORIDA STREET—Mrs. J. R. Thompson, Mrs. Pugh, Mrs. C. D. Foster, Rev. and Mrs. T. C. Williams.

IMMANUEL—E. C. White, Jr., H. H. Altmon, C. C. Stanley, Mrs. C. C. Stanley, Rev. and Mrs. F. L. Fraser.

LATHAM PARK—

MAGNOLIA STREET—W. T. Adams, Mrs. J. A. Lewis, J. E. Poore, J. A. Lewis, Mrs. H. S. Noah.

POMONA—Mrs. Pearlie Brown, Mrs. E. E. Henry, Mrs. S. R. Young, S. R. Young, C. C. Patterson.

REVOLUTION—Mrs. Waldo Johnson, Miss Alice Miller, Mrs. Cletus Roddy, Mrs. C. A. Cagle.

SIXTEENTH STREET—Mrs. W. C. Adkinson, Mrs. Harry Moore, Mrs. Webster Owens, Fred Hester, W. C. Adkinson.

STEVENS MEMORIAL—Mrs. H. N. Sutton, R. V. Thornberry, Jr., Mrs. R. V. Thornberry, Mrs. A. C. Hilliard, Mrs. Roy Thornberry, Sr.

SOUTH ELM STREET—W. T. Lucas, Mrs. A. D Williams, Mrs. R. H. Wetmore.

SOUTHSIDE GREENSBORO—S. K. Brazil, Mrs. Alice Paschal, Mrs. Estelle Moon, H. W. Taylor.

RANKIN—A. Andrews, Mrs. A. Andrews, Mrs. Henry Bryson, Mrs. C. L. Straughn, Mrs. Mazie Nuckles.

GUILFORD—Mrs. Hattie Kennedy, Mrs. B. F. Butler, Mrs. F. R. Roberts.

HIGH POINT FIRST—W. Wilbur Hutchins, Miss M. Thelma Patrick, M. R. Shields, Mrs. M. R. Shields, John Reavis.

GREEN STREET—W. E. Crissman, J. L. Causby, Mrs. J. S. Hopkins, Mrs. E. M. Blakely, H. C. Hobbs.

HILLIARD MEMORIAL—Mrs. A. L. Langley, P. E. Grubb, Mrs. C. J. Hedrick, A. L. Slate, Boyce Moore, Mrs. J. B. Ellis, G. W. Underwood, C. H. Farmer.

NORTH MAIN—Mr. and Mrs. S. R. Clinard, Mr. and Mrs. R. L. Reeves, Rev. and Mrs. Neil Armstrong, Alice Davis, Mrs. S. J. O'Neal.

NORTH PARK—D. H. Short, Mrs. L. W. Glenn, Mrs. C. D. Jones.

SOUTHSIDE HIGH POINT—Mrs. Sara Aumnam, Mrs. J. Borland, Mrs. W. O. Elkins.

WEST END—C. M. Scott, Mrs. W. C. Guth, Mrs. C. M. Scott, Mrs. R. K. Hall.

JESSUP GROVE—James E. Wiggs, Mrs. James E. Wiggs, Mrs. Oscar Lewis, Elzie Smith.

JEWEL—Mrs. H. L. Hill, Mrs. Lela Weatherman.

LEBANON—Mr. J. B. Carter, Mrs. J. L. Goodwin.

MT. ZION—C. D. Branson, Geo. Spoon, Roy Coble.

McCONNELL ROAD—J. E. York, C. W. Yow.

McLEANSVILLE—W. R. Fuller, Mrs. W. R. Fuller, J. W. King, Mrs. Beatrice Howard, Earl Howard.

OAK GROVE—W. L. Shackelford, G. K. Saunders, Mrs. A. L. Saunders, Mrs. Alga Stevenson, Mrs. Charles Saunders.

OSSIPEE—R. C. Fitts, H. D. Smith, Leo Gerringer.

PINE GROVE—J. W. Breedlove, E. H. Eller, Mrs. E. H. Eller, Lanston Tuttle.

PILOT VIEW—Mrs. B. H. Webb, Mrs. A. J. Hussey, Mrs. Joe Edwards, Mrs. J. H. Miles, D. F. Kestler.

PISGAH—L. C. Madden, Mrs. L. C. Madden, Mrs. H. L. Maners, Mrs. J. T. Saunders.

PLEASANT GARDEN—J. H. Foy, I. F. Anderson, E. L. Routh.

PLEASANT GROVE—Mrs. J. T. Nunn, W. H. Smith, F. M. Atkins, Mrs. J. M. Allred.

REEDY FORK—Elijah O. Lankford, Mrs. Mail Kivett, William Presnell, Mrs. Romie Everage, Mrs. Eugene Brown.

BAPTIST TEMPLE—W. E. Coates, Mrs. W. E. Coates, Mrs. Gordon Roberts, Mrs. Bert Elliott, Otis Powell.

REIDSVILLE FIRST—Mrs. C. A. Penn, Miss Katherine Roddick, Mrs. R. H. Pleasants, Mrs. T. L. Sasser, Mrs. I. R. Humphreys, Miss Fannie Gardner, T. L. Gardner, T. L. Sasser.

PENN MEMORIAL—D. W. Overbey, Mrs. Maxel Thore, Mrs. W. S. Holton.

ROCKY KNOLL—Mrs. Ed Faccette, Mrs. Charlie Cooper, Mrs. J. A. Durham, Mrs. G. E. Williamson, Mrs. R. A. Laughlin.

RUFFIN STACEY—Mrs. John Burton, Mrs. Mary E. London, Mrs. J. T. Cardwell.

SMITH GROVE — Homer Westmoreland, Fairmae Pitts, Johan Pitts, Sanford Gray, Hettie Mae Westmoreland.

SUMMERFIELD—Mrs. F. F. Baynes, Mrs. Hettie Shields, G. T. Wilson.

TEMPLE—Mr. and Mrs. W. R. Swinson, Mrs. John Tuttle, Mrs. Eva Stevens, Mr. and Mrs. R. L. Rodden, A. J. Swinson.

WOODARD MEMORIAL—F. A. O'Briant, Mrs. J. E. Danes, Mrs. W. V. Bell.

WOODLAWN—A. B. Ashill, Mrs. C. S. Phillips, Mrs. M. E. Turner, Mrs. C. E. Abbott.

CONSTITUTION

ARTICLE 1.—The Association shall be called the Piedmont Baptist Association.

ARTICLE 2.—It shall be composed of the ordained ministers who are members of, and those who may have pastoral charges within the Associational District, and three delegates from each Church in the district aforesaid, and Churches having a membership exceeding 300 shall be entitled to one additional delegate for every 200 members or fraction thereof in excess of 300.

ARTICLE 3.—The said delegates shall, before taking their seats, produce letters from respective Church showing their appointment as delegates.

ARTICLE 4.—The Associational session shall be held at least once a year.

ARTICLE 5.—The officers shall be a Moderator, Vice-Moderator, Clerk and Treasurer. If deemed expedient by the Association, the offices of Clerk and Treasurer may be combined.

ARTICLE 6.—The officers of the Association shall be chosen annually by the Association.

ARTICLE 7—Association shall be clothed with authority only to advise the Churches touching all things pertaining to their interest but shall in no case presume to direct or control them in reference to their own government or internal policy.

ARTICLE 8.—A Committee of Arrangements, consisting of three members shall be appointed on the first day of each session to prepare and report the proceedings and suggest topics proper for the consideration and action of the next annual Association. It shall be the duty of this committee to outline and publish a program for the next annual Associational meeting or for any special or called meeting of the Association.

ARTICLE 9.—Baptist brethren, not members of the Association, who may be present at any session of the body, may on invitation by the body, take seats and participate in the debates of the Association.

ARTICLE 10.—

Section 1. The territory of the Association shall be divided into not less than three districts.

Section 2.—A committee composed of the Moderator, the Vice-Moderator, the Clerk of the Association, the Associational W. M. U. Superintendent, the Associational Sunday School Superintendent, the Associational B. T. U. Director, and twelve other members of churches in the Association, giving fair representation to the three districts, shall constitute the Executive Committee of the Association. This committee at its first meeting shall decide the number required for a quorum.

Section 3. Seven of the members of the Executive Committee

shall be named by the Association as members of the Church Advisory and Missions Committee.

Section 4. The duties of the Executive Committee are to act for the Association between the annual sessions of the Association. The Church Advisory and Missions Committee is charged with the task of seeking the cooperation of churches in the ordination of ministers, the location and organization of new churches, and the management of the Associational Mission Program in our Association.

ARTICLE 11.—All Committees shall be appointed by the Moderator, either directly or indirectly with the approval of the Association, unless otherwise authorized by the Association from time to time.

ARTICLE 12.—The Constitution may be altered only at an Annual Session of the Association and by a vote of two-thirds of the whole present.

ARTICLE 13.—The rules of this body shall follow Mell's Parliamentary Practice.

ARTICLE 14.—This Association shall cooperate with Baptist State Convention.

ARTICLE 15.—The time of the holding of the annual session shall begin on Wednesday before the fourth Sunday of October of each year, except where prevailing conditions make it advisable to change this date, in which event the Executive Committee shall be empowered to determine the date of meeting.

Adopted October 17, 1895.

Articles 2, 5, 6, 10, 15 Amended Sessions, July 23, 24, 1930.

Article 15 Amended Session, July 21, 1932.

Article 10 Amended Sessions, October 23, 24, 1935.

Articles 8, 10, 11 Amended Sessions, October 23, 24, 1940.

Article 10 Amended Session, October 19, 1944.

PROCEEDINGS

of the

FIFTY-FOURTH ANNUAL SESSION

of the

PIEDMONT BAPTIST ASSOCIATION

Held With the

MOUNT ZION BAPTIST CHURCH

Liberty, N. C.

October 22-23, 1947

WEDNESDAY MORNING SESSION—10:00 A. M.

1. The Piedmont Baptist Association was called to order at 10:00 a. m. by the Moderator, Grover H. Jones, and joined in singing, "What a Friend We Have in Jesus," led by Rev. J. E. Kirk, accompanied by Mrs. J. E. Kirk. After reading Matthew 25:31-46 and John 4:31-38 V. L. Mabry, pastor Allen Jay Baptist Church, led the invocation.

2. The Program Committee reported, and the printed program, with one change, was accepted.

3. Committee on Committees was appointed as follows: W. C. Adkinson, W. S. Holton, and H. O. Miller.

4. The new ministers of the Association were recognized by Rev. T. L. Sasser. They are: S. K. Brazil, Southside; A. S. Young, Pomona; Harvey Clark, Pilot View; W. W. Robbins, North Park; George Williamson, Rocky Knoll; T. C. Williams, Asst. Florida Street.

5. The following report, presented by W. C. Adkinson, Sixteenth Street Baptist Church, was accepted. Since Mr. Walter Crissman, who was to speak to the report, was not present, a motion was made and accepted to pass to the next business until Mr. Crissman arrives.

REPORT ON SUNDAY SCHOOL WORK

Studying the Scriptures is essential to the progress of the Kingdom. The Sunday School has set itself to this vital task. It has long since passed the experimental stage and has a record of achievement that inspires to ever widening action.

The Sunday School Board of the Southern Baptist Convention is one of our greatest Kingdom agencies. Their publications and periodicals are worthy of diligent study by the whole Baptist constituency. In a few of our Sunday School publications other than those of Southern Baptists are used instead of our own denominational literature. We have strong convictions that this is not a wise policy and should not be done. There is little likelihood that our own literature can be currently improved upon and there is great probability that the substitution will prove spiritually and otherwise unprofitable.

The Sunday School Board gives strong support to promotional work. We mention two phases of this activity. First, Sunday School Administration. Second, Improved Bible Teaching. The Sunday Schools of our Association have this year, as usual and with increasing force, been benefitted by this service.

In many of our churches now study courses in both administration and in teaching are regularly pursued. The benefits to the Sunday School work in general become more and more apparent.

Nearly all the Sunday Schools took part in the annual program planning promoted by the Sunday School Board and State Sunday School forces the last two years. This year more extensively than last and with larger beneficent results.

In our Association we were very fortunate this year in having the State Better Bible Teaching Clinic held in High Point. Many of our Sunday School officers, teachers and other workers took advantage of the clinic, attended constantly, greatly improved their teaching ability.

Vacation Bible Schools made fine progress in our Association this year. Many more schools than ever heretofore had schools. Six student missionaries who were paid small salaries by the Home Mission Board and by the Association, as well as a number of voluntary workers, made a large spiritual contribution in this organized effort for Bible study.

We recommend that our churches promote their Sunday School work along lines in keeping with our denominational life, and that all the churches give their full co-operation in the program planning project next year.

Respectfully submitted,
W. C. Adkinson.

6. The following report, presented by T. L. Sasser, Associational Missionary, was accepted. Mr. Sasser displayed pictures of the mission work in the association.

ASSOCIATIONAL MISSIONS

Despite the fact that more than half the people who live in the territory of our Association have no church affiliation of record they, in the main, are responsive to the Gospel appeal. This means that we are strategically located in a productive mission field.

No organization of Baptists have the opportunity and the responsibility so definitely as we to teach and to preach with a view to changing this mission field into a missionary force. No denomination of believers in Jesus have the opportunity and responsibility that Baptists of our time have.

We must therefore give ourselves to limitless effort to the work of Associational Missions. The whole Baptist program of world-wide missions in a very true sense is based upon local missions—the locality being the territory of the district association.

The Co-operative Program of Southern Baptists is a comparatively new device designed to support co-operatively and proportionately the whole work of Southern Baptists. The very success of the Co-operative Program demands its modification and its enlargement. Associational missions will become an integral part of it. So far as the growth and the readiness of our Association is concerned the time is ripe for such an adjustment now. This means that associational missions should be a worthy part of every church budget and that the Association have as large budget to support its work as the conscience, conviction and vision of the people will provide. The field is limited only by the will of the local Baptists.

I hereby offer a summary of my personal activities from October 1, 1946 to September 30, 1947:

Days on field	304
Days on other fields for State and Home Boards	46
Miles traveled on this and other fields	20025
Individual or personal conferences	376
Group conferences	56
Committee meetings	53
Associational meetings	6
Pastors conferences	51
State meetings	4
Census directed	2
Mission fields surveyed	9
Visits to churches	132
Visits to homes, hospitals, etc.	170
Visits to mission stations	19
Revival meetings conducted	1

Public professions of faith in revival	6
Sermons delivered	106
Addresses delivered	60
Classes taught	49
Number personally baptized	12
Church prayer meetings conducted	8
Articles published	24
Circular letters and mimeographed copies sent out	3000
Personal letters	160

Thanks to all for your unfailing kindness to me throughout the Association.

Respectfully submitted,
T. L. Sasser.

---

7. Mr. Walter E. Crissman, Attorney and Representative in North Carolina Legislature, addressed the association on the subject: "Baptists Must Teach the Word of God."

8. The Association joined in singing, "Rescue the Perishing."

9. After R. Von King read Mark 1:14-20, Rev. R. C. Shearin led in prayer; then the associational sermon was preached by the appointee—Rev. R. Von King, Eller Memorial. The subject: "The High Calling of Soul Winning."

10. The report of committee on Committees was accepted.

REPORT OF COMMITTEE ON COMMITTEES

EXECUTIVE PROMOTIONAL COMMITTEE:
J. Ben Eller, Chairman
Rev. Neil Armstrong
Rev. W. S. Holton

COMMITTEE ON TIME, PLACE AND PREACHER:
Rev. James B. Clifton, Chairman
H. P. Gauldin
W. C. Guth

AUDITING COMMITTEE:
Rev. S. L. Riddle, Chairman
George Richman
J. E. McCargo

COMMITTEE TO NOMINATE CHURCH ADVISORY AND MISSIONS COMMITTEE:
Rev. R. Von King, Chairman
C. M. Scott
W. D. Turner

NOMINATING COMMITTEE TO NOMINATE ASSOCIATIONAL OFFICERS:

Rev. Wilson Woodcock, Chairman
W. H. Barker
Jones E. Kirk

PROGRAM COMMITTEE:

Rev. Wilber Hutchins, Chairman
Mrs. C. A. Penn
Mrs. James R. Thompson
Rev. Sherman Young

COMMITTEE ON RESOLUTIONS:

Chairman, Rev. B. L. Gupton
V. L. Mabry, Mrs. R. H. Pleasants

Respectfully submitted,
T. L. Gardner,
H. O. Miller,
W. C. Adkinson.

---

11. Dr. A. B. Conrad, High Point, led the closing morning prayer.

12. Adjourned until the afternoon.

WEDNESDAY AFTERNOON SESSION—2:00 P. M.

13. The afternoon session opened with the singing of hymns.

14. The nominating committee reported and the following were elected:

Grover H. Jones, Moderator..................High Point
T. L. Gardner, Vice-Moderator..................Reidsville
Ray W. Harrington, Clerk-Treasurer...........Greensboro

Committee:
W. H. Barker,
J. E. Kirk,
Wilson Woodcock.

15. W. H. Barker conducted the devotional service, reading II Timothy 4:4-9.

16. The Association joined in singing, "Amazing Grace," led by J. E. Kirk, accompanied by E. C. White, Jr.

17. Address: "Christian Stewardship," by Dr. J. Clyde Turner, First Baptist Church, Greensboro.

18. The Association joined in singing, "When I Survey the Wondrous Cross."

19. The following report, presented by George Richman, Conrad Memorial, was accepted. Dr. W. K. McGhee, Director of Religious Activities, Baptist Hospital, Winston-Salem, spoke to the report.

REPORT BAPTIST HOSPITAL

Each year our hospital is able to admit approximately 8,000 patients as in-patients, or bed patients. In addition, the present out-patient facilities accommodate about 20,000 who are given complete examinations and are not admitted as bed patients. Also the medical school operates a private clinic for patients able to pay a physician and this clinic examines approximately 20,000 each year. This makes a grand total of 48,000 people who depend each year upon the Baptist Hospital for relief from pain.

Of the 8,000 patients admitted as bed patients, slightly over 4,000 of these are service patients who pay no doctors fee, and who pay reduced hospital expenses. During 1947 many of these service patients paid absolutely nothing toward their hospital bill.

Let me give you a concrete experience of a mother from one of our Baptist Churches. She was hurried to our Baptist Hospital. Local doctors had done their best and said she could not live unless she got other help right away. She had been sick for a year and had just spent six weeks in another hospital. She had been able to have her five-months-old baby with her only two weeks since he was born. Her stay in our Hospital was long and expensive costing over $1,200.00 though she was a service patient and there was no charge for all the work of the doctors. But there she was cared for by highly skilled physicians using the latest drugs and the best known methods of medical care.

Her family is almost without means and is able to meet only a portion of this large bill. The churches of the Association, through our Mother's Day offerings, helped to provide for her hospital care. Because we gave on Mother's Day she was given a chance and recently went back home, and to care for her baby.

What we did for this mother we are doing in larger or smaller measure for thousands of others throughout North Carolina who are sick and have little money. The past twelve months have been the most crowded year our Baptist Hospital has ever known. Its ministry has gone to more people than ever before.

Let us continue to pray that many more will be relieved of physical suffering by the work of our Hospital, but above all that it may be a means to an end to win precious souls to Christ.

Respectfully submitted,
George E. Richman.

20. The following report by J. Carl Bell, read by Fred Bell, Assistant Pastor of College Park Baptist Church, was accepted. W. W. Hill, Liberty Baptist Church, spoke to the report.

REPORT OF TRAINING UNION

The Baptist Training Union of the Piedmont Association closes its year's work with some accomplishments for which it can justly be proud and render thanks to Almighty God.

First among these are that we are again an A-1 Standard Organization. New Unions have been fully organized in ten churches. In most of these assistance was given by an Associational officer. According to our records there are now only fifteen churches in our Association without a Training Union organization. We had at least one study course in most of the churches where there are Training Unions. These resulted in approximately 1,500 awards.

Four mass meetings have been held in addition to the Twenty-Seventh Annual Convention, which was held in Reidsville in April. The afternoon session was utilized in the Associational eliminations in Training Union tournaments. Winners in these tournaments later competed in regional tournaments. At the evening session of the Convention approximately one thousand people attended the banquet, at which time we had the privilege of hearing Dr. I. G. Greer of Mills Home.

During the North Carolina week and the three Southwide weeks, a large number of our people attended Ridgecrest.

We herewith submit some goals which we hope to reach during the coming year:

1. An active Training Union in every church.
2. At least one study course in every church.
3. Every church represented in our mass meetings.

To attain these goals it is essential that we have the prayers and co-operation of ALL our pastors and other church leaders. We seek the attainment of these goals in order that our Training Program may reach not only into every church, but into the heart of every church member, to the end that we may indeed be, "....Workmen that needeth not to be ashamed, rightly dividing the Word of Truth."

Respectfully submitted,

J. Carl Bell.

---

21. The following report, presented by Floy Cox, Jr., was accepted. W. C. Reed, Kinston Orphanage, spoke to the report.

REPORT OF THE BAPTIST ORPHANAGE

North Carolina Baptists have found it necessary to support orphanages and other child caring agencies by reason of the poverty, poor health, illiteracy and instability in the home as well as an obedience to the teaching of Jesus.

The Baptist Orphanage was founded with the first superintendent, J. H. Mills, in 1885. There are now two branches: Mills Home, Thomasville, Miss Sara E. Elmore, Superintendent; Kennedy Home, Kinston, W. C. Reed, Superintendent. Dr. I. G. Greer serves as General Superintendent.

The purpose of this organization is the care for orphan children, though one of the chief concerns is the wrecked home. There are over one thousand children in the orphanages of North Carolina who have both parents living.

One of the greatest services that the orphanage renders is making it possible for parents and children to help themselves, and trying to preserve and improve homes that are in danger of breaking down. Through case work last year, this service helped to make adjustment for more than four hundred children where applications had been made to enter the orphanage.

A program of boarding home care has begun during these days of high building costs. This enables good homes to be provided for children with orphanage supervision. Sixty children were thus cared for last year.

There were seven hundred children cared for during the year in Mills Home and Kennedy Home, as well as through boarding homes.

One thousand, one hundred, and seven children were rendered serice through case work.

At the time of this report, there was reported 393 children at Mills Home, 145 at Kennedy. Fifty-two in foster homes, and 26 in Mother's Aid. The cost per day for care of the children runs over $675.00.

Charity and Children is published weekly to keep friends of the orphanage informed as to its activities. There is in Thomasville a commercial print shop operated by the boys of Mills Home under the management of the Orphanage.

One asset that means much to the children is the library. Here the children are guided to better reading under the direction of a skilled librarian.

Every Baptist would see the need of a larger Thanksgiving offering should he visit any branch of the orphanage and observe the skill of the staff that is dedicated to making, from the lives they touch, strong, clean, Christian men and women out of boys and girls who would not otherwise have the opportunity.

There would be spiritual enrichment in each church that put forth great effort to make monthly gifts as well as the Thanksgiving offering worthy of the name in which they are given.

Respectfully submitted,
Floy W. Cox, Jr.

22. The Church Advisory and Missions Committee recommended that Friendly and Southside Baptist Churches be accepted as members of the Piedmont Baptist Association. A motion was made and carried to accept both churches.

23. The following report, presented by J. S. Hopkins, chairman of the committee, was accepted.

SUGGESTED ANNUAL EXPENSE AND MISSIONS BUDGET FOR 1948

Associational Missionary's Salary	$ 2100.00
(To be supplemented by State and Home Mission Boards)	
Associational Missionary's Local Travel and Expense	900.00
Clerk's Compensation	200.00
Associational Minutes	400.00
Office Supplies and Expense	275.00
Tent. Fund for Insurance, Equipment, Repairs	300.00
Compensation Student Missionaries for Summer	300.00
Associational Pastor's School	200.00
Associational Sunday School, B.T.U. Expense	100.00
Aid Fund for Mission Churches	7500.00
Incidental and Unanticipated Expense Fund	400.00
TOTAL	$12675.00

Respectfully submitted,
J. S. Hopkins, Chairman
T. L. Gardner
Ray W. Harrington.

24. A motion was made and accepted to send greetings to J. C. Gillespie, James R. Thompson, and Clarence A. Smith.

25. Dr. A. B. Conrad asked the Association to be more careful in organizing Baptist Churches, and ordaining ministers.

26. Rev. Forrest L. Fraser led the closing prayer as the Association adjourned until tomorrow, Thursday morning.

THURSDAY MORNING SESSION—10:00 A. M.

27. The morning session opened with the hymn, "How Firm a Foundation," led by Forrest L. Fraser, accompanied by Mrs. W. S. Holton.

28. Rev. J. T. Ellis, McConnell Road Baptist Church, read Matthew 28:16-20, and led the invocation.

29. The following report, presented by F. L. Fraser, Immanuel Baptist Church, was accepted. Dr. E. L. Spivey spoke to the report.

STATE MISSIONS AND THE CO-OPERATIVE PROGRAM

"And Jesus came and spake unto them, saying, All power is given unto me in heaven and in earth. Go ye therefore, and teach all nations, baptizing them in the name of the Father, and of the Son, and of the Holy Ghost: Teaching them to observe all things whatsoever I have commanded you; and, lo, I am with you always, even unto the end of the world. Amen. (Matt. 28:18-20.)

"Last words" of our loved ones and true friends, are impressive and significant. How much more so, are the pronouncements and commands of our adorable Lord! Jesus nears the end of His earthly ministry. With His flawless mind He sees clearly, the full scope of His Plan of Salvation. Under such conditions our Master speaks forth "The Great Commission." This impressive command is still our mandate.

These words constitute the over-all program for "The Big Task of Making North Carolina Christian." (Biblical Recorder, October 8, 1947).

In this, necessarily brief report, it is utterly impossible to give a detailed picture of 1) Past, impressive victories won. 2) The insistent demands for greater accomplishments, and 3) The appalling need for increased service and investment of Time, Talent and Treasure; in an accelerated program, to save from sin and train for efficient and exalted Christian Service, the greatest number of people in the shortest possible time.

What is the actual challenge? The answer is: 2,000,000 unchurched people in North Carolina.

Of the 1,500,000 church members in our State; 600,000 are members of The Baptist State Convention of North Carolina. This constitutes a probable Baptist constituency of 1,200,000 people. What an impressive challenge!

What is being done by our State Mission Agencies to meet this challenge? In answer, we cannot do better than to quote Editor L. L. Carpenter's summation of the fact, published in Biblical Recorder of October 8, 1947.

Quote:—"Thousands of our Baptist people even among some of the best informed do not realize the bigness and importance of State Missions. Some think it means raising a little money to help weak and struggling churches. Secretary Huggins says, 'The aim of State Missions is through co-operative effort, to let Christ become regnant in North Carolina. The scope of State Missions is to provide a ministry of preaching, teaching and training to those inside and outside our churches, to those of other races, and to the sick and wayward in state institutions'."

"At least ten big and important causes are supported by State Missions. In order that you may see them as a whole, we list them together as follows: 1) The rich and well-rounded work of teaching, preaching and training carried on by our Field Secretaries, E. L. Bradley, E. L. Spivey, J. C. Pipes and Secretary of Evangelism, J. C. Canipe; 2) About forty Associational Missionaries; 3) Nearly 100 Missionary Pastors. (These get only a mere pittance, an average of about $25.00 per month to supplement their salaries on needy fields); 4) Aid in buying lots and re-locating church buildings; 5) Christian Education in the churches. (The work of training and enlistment carried on by our Sunday School, Training Union and Baptist Student Union force); 6) A ministry to other races, helping especially, work among Negroes and Indians; 7) A ministry to the sick at Oteen, sanatorium at Aberdeen, sanatorium at Black Mountain and some work at Samarcand; 8) Pastor's Schools and Conferences (Summer Schools and important Preacher's Schools at Fruitland; 9) Summer Assemblies, such as the one at Fruitland and the one that will be developed next summer near Carolina Beach; 10) Program of Visual Education and Publicity and also expenses in connection with the meeting of the State Convention and the work of the General Secretary and the General Board."

God works through consecrated human and dedicated material agencies. To do the work already outlined, (And greater things than these need to be done); it will take the imposing figure of $370,000.00. However, with 600,000 Redeemed, Praying, Bible-reading, Worshipping, Informed, Tithing and Sacrificing Baptists, within the bounds of our State Convention; $500,000, (Half a Million Dollars), would be easily at the disposal of our King Jesus and His Workers. Some will say: "You cannot expect 100% performance."....Well, 50%, under God, can do the greater work. Frankly, North Carolina Baptists should not be afraid to have $1,000,000 vision and treasury to match.

This report would be incomplete were we not to mention the untiring efforts of our efficient State Secretary, Mr. M. A. Huggins, a brother whose consecration, vision, faith and work are being so signally blessed by God. May his days be many; his powers unabated, and may he continually lead us to newer heights and greater victories is our earnest and sincere prayer.

Thus, the Baptist State Convention of North Carolina, with all the other State Conventions within the boundaries of the Southern Baptist Convention; humbly trusting God for strength and wisdom and "Doing with our might what our hands find to do," and through co-operative effort; will go far to obeying and implementing the Great Commission. God help us, so to do. Amen.

Respectfully submitted,
Forrest L. Fraser.

---

30. The following report, presented by W. T. Adams, Magnolia Street, was accepted. Rev. E. Norfleet Gardner, First Baptist, Henderson, spoke to the report.

MINISTERS RETIREMENT PLAN

For 29 years the Relief and Annuity Board has been serving the Southern Baptist Convention. During that time the Board has been invaluable in service rendered to the aged and disabled preachers of our Convention. And now, with the retirement plan of this board, a minister or full-time church worker need not live in fear of the day when he or she will be too old to carry on, for here is a fine plan for security in old age.

Nineteen hundred and forty-six was one of the most prosperous years the board has ever known and 1947 promises to be an even greater year. As of July 1, 1947 the number of certificates issued in all plans was 20,447, 10,859 of these being in the retirement plan. Since the last of 1946 eight other states have qualified for participation in the Widows Supplemental Annuity Plan, bringing the total to 14. Total assets of the Board as of June 30, 1947 were far above eleven millions of dollars. Benefits paid during the first six months of 1947 amounted to more than 574 thousand.

In North Carolina, the retirement plan is doing great service but many ministers have not yet availed themselves of this golden opportunity to be secure in old age. There are now between five and six hundred active members of the plan in the state. Forty-five members and ten widows are now receiving a check each month from the Relief and Annuity Board. There are at present about 250 members of the Widows' Supplement Plan. We note that there are only sixteen Pastors in the Piedmont Association who are members of the retirement plan. We commend this plan to you as the best insurance you can get against want in old age. A great blessing has been placed before us and we hope that more of the ministers and churches of our Association will accept this blessing by entering the Ministers Retirement Plan, and the Widows' Supplement Plan.

Respectfully submitted,
W. T. Adams.

31. Wilson Woodcock stated that the Association has a Missionary who will serve in Japan—Miss Frances Talley, a member of the College Park Baptist Church.

32. The following report, presented by B. L. Gupton, Rankin Baptist Church, was amended and accepted in part. The second part was referred to the Executive Promotion Committee.

REPORT OF THE RESOLUTION COMMITTEE

Whereas the Piedmont Baptist Association meeting in its fifty-fourth session with the Mt. Zion Baptist Church, we your Committee, offer the following Resolutions:

BE IT RESOLVED:

First: That a Resolution Committee be elected at this Associational Meeting to serve for the Associational year and that hereafter the Resolution Committee be elected to serve a year, making their report to the next Associational meeting after their election. Also that any person or persons wishing to submit a resolution, will submit said resolution to this committee prior to the Associational Meeting. We feel by doing this, each Resolution can be given a much more careful and prayerful consideration.

Second: That we express to Mt. Zion Church our sincere gratitude and appreciation for their courtesy, kindness, and entertainment.

Third: That we express our appreciation to the Program Committee for the splendid program.

Fourth: That we express our appreciation to the Daily News, for the publicity they gave the Association.

Respectfully submitted,
B. L. Gupton, Chairman
V. L. Mabry
Mrs. R. H. Pleasants.

33. The following report, presented by Mrs. W. C. Adkinson, President of W. M. U. in the Association, was accepted. Dr. L. Bun Olive, Missionary in China for twenty years, spoke to the report.

MISSIONS AT HOME AND ABROAD

In the beginning of my report, I shall make mention of some of the activities of the Piedmont Associational W. M. U. for the years 1946-1947. We have 60 churches in our Association and out of this 60 we have 45 W. M. S. and 88 Young Peoples organizations.

In January, Mrs. E. T. Howell, former superintendent, led the Association in a Leadership Conference at the First Baptist Church,

Greensboro, with eighteen churches represented and seventy-two women registering. The same conference was repeated at Reidsville First Church, with eight churches represented and seventy-three women registering.

In February the Associational Mission Study Chairman planned a very successful Mission Study Institute at Florida Street Church, Greensboro, with sixteen churches represented and seventy-seven women registering.

Mrs. E. T. Howell planned and conducted a very successful Annual Associational meeting at the First Church, Reidsville, with twenty-six churches represented and one hundred forty-four registering. The theme was, "Jesus Calls Us."

Our Community Mission Chairman, Mrs. C. W. Moseley, conducted a worthy project among the colored people of Greensboro, Reidsville, and High Point. There were two trained colored workers employed to give a month in each of the three points, mentioned above, during the summer. They conducted a Daily Vacation Bible School in ecah place. The result was gratifying.

Mrs. James R. Thompson, Associational Young People's Leader, planned and supervised two three-day camps in our Association; one for the R.A.'s and one for the G.A.'s. There were seventy girls and forty boys. There were eight who dedicated their lives for foreign mission service and one boy found Jesus as his Saviour.

The superintendent planned and conducted a two-day W.M.U. Clinic in Greensboro, High Point and Reidsville, using Mrs. John Wacaster, W.M.U. Field Representative for North Carolina, to direct the conferences. In the Greensboro Clinic there were eighteen churches out of the twenty-six represented and one hundred and twenty-five women registering. High Point had nine churches out of the eleven represented with seventy-two women registering. Reidsville had all eight churches represented, with 95 women registering. Thus we had 35 W.M.U. represented with a total of 292 women registering from the 45 W.M.S. Mrs. Wacaster spent two weeks in our association; one in September and one in October. We feel that all of our churches were strengthened by her visit with us.

We are grateful for what has been assomplished the past year, yet, we want to do even greater work for our Master the year ahead.

Now we shall turn our attention to our Home Mission Work. Dr. John R. Mott, an outstanding missionary leader speaking of the impact of Home Missions upon our foreign enterprise, says: "The ultimate triumph of a pure Christianity in non-Christian lands depends absolutely upon Christianizing the impact upon those lands. Only a Christianity strong enough to dominate our social, national, and international life and relationship will finally commend itself to the peoples to whom we go."

Again, Dr. Mott says that, "The United States of America is the largest, most difficult, and most important missionary problem in the world." Therefore in light of this information and from what we already know about the vast needs of the home base for Foreign Missions, Southern Baptists already have a substantial army of God-called men and women in the field, serving throughout the Home Mission Territory.

The task of the Home Mission Board of the Southern Baptist Convention is to evangelize the homeland and mobilize the evangelized for world conquest for Christ.

We need for this task an annual budget of two and one-half or three million dollars.

The field we have to cover stretches from the Atlantic seaboard to the Golden Gate of the Pacific in the homeland, the Canal Zone, Panama and Costa Rica, and the four western provinces of Cuba.

In this vast field there are approximately 66,000,000 people, of whom 36,000,000 are wholly un-churched. In the homeland alone there are 26,000,000 people un-churched—people who do not have a chance to hear the gospel of Christ.

The different groups with which our board is working are the Spanish-speaking people of Cuba, Mexico, and Central America; also groups in the Southwestern section of our country, near the Mexican border. We have missionaries among the French-speaking people of Louisiana, and among the Italian and Chinese in some of our larger cities. Besides the missionaries among the language groups, we have missionaries among the Indians and in the desolated rural sections of the Southland. We sponsor Rescue Missions and Good Will Centers in the larger cities. We have work with the deaf and sponsor Vacation Bible Schools in isolated sections, and in mission centers.

During the past year, Southern Baptists have maintained 920 active missionaries at the home base. Two hundred and three of these were College and Seminary students, who helped during the summer. The Home Mission Board reports during the past year, 27,474 conversions with 131 new churches organized, and 361 new Mission centers opened. Thus, we see the value of the efforts put forth by the Home Mission Board. The total contributions by Southern Baptists for the Home Mission Board amounted to $1,484,682.90 for the past year. If Southern Baptists would only respond by giving the tithe, no doubt we could soon double our income for Home Missions and thus hasten the task of evangelizing the Southland.

Let us now view the work of our Foreign Mission Board. All Southern Baptists have been anxious to learn how our work in the Foreign countries withstood the impact of the most devastating war in all history. Slowly, our missionaries are returning to their posts, vacated as a result of the war. According to all reports, our missionaries are encouraged to find great living examples of Christ, still carrying on in the Master's name. True, many of the church buildings and compounds have been destroyed, and most all bear the marks of war and destruction, but the thing that counts most is not houses made of brick and mortar, but, the Spirit of the Living Christ who dwells in the hearts of the native Christians in these mission fields.

During this year alone, approximately 100 new missionaries have been appointed or approved by the Foreign Mission Board to resume the work where it was interrupted by the war. Many of the older missionaries have reached the age of retirement and cannot return. Many others have been broken in health by the extreme hardships which many had to endure while in concentration camps during the war, thus preventing their return.

It is encouraging to note that many of our young people are volunteering for definite mission service. We realize that it will take time for these young people to prepare themselves for this all-important task of being a missionary. Yet, we want to have the means to send them when they are ready to go.

The W.M.U. is taking the lead in informing our people of the needs of both the home and foreign mission fields. They are also using every effort to help supply the needs with their prayers, means, and sons and daughters. The Lottie Moon Christmas Offering, for last December, amounted to $1,381,000 according to the last reports.

From all reports, Southern Baptists have already increased their gifts for Foreign Missions this year by 11% over last year. The needs of the Foreign Mission Board are very great. Last year, a special offering of almost four million dollars was given for World Relief and Rehabilitation, which gave relief to hungry people who would have starved had it not been given. Also a portion was used to help restore church property and mission stations, damaged by the war.

Our present need in missionary personnel is to add 150 new missionaries during th next year, to bring our number up to 800. Another great need is to enlist new tithers that we may increase our missionary giving. Our Foreign Mission Board now reaches out to eighteen different countries and areas of the world. Our task, for us whc remain at home, is to equip and supply these soldiers of the cross with every material and spiritual aid necessary for doing their task. Our total gifts for Foreign Missions last year, including the special offering for Relief and Rehabilitation, amounted to $7,065,133.29. Our goal as Southern Baptists is $10,000,000 for Foreign Missions. If our people would bring all of their tithes into the churches, the great task could be done.

Respectfully submitted,

Mrs. W. C. Adkinson, Supt.
Woman's Missionary Union,
Piedmont Association.

34. W. W. Woodcock led the closing prayer as the Association adjourned for lunch.

THURSDAY AFTERNOON SESSION

35. The afternoon session opened with the singing of selected hymns.

36. Rev. A. B. Ashill, Woodlawn Church, conducted the devotional service.

37. The following report, presented by J. Ben Eller, Asheboro Street Church, was accepted. Dr. Marc Lovelace, Professor in School of Religion at Wake Forest College, spoke to the report.

CHRISTIAN EDUCATION

We have New Testament authority for Christian Education. Jesus was the greatest of all teachers. He was called Teacher more often than preacher. The command to make disciples and baptize is no more binding than the command to teach.

There are three recognized ways of carrying out this part of the Great commission. The first is through the home. There is no adequate substitute for a Christian home. However, the home is measurably failing to do its part in Christian teaching. A second way we attempt to obey the command to teach is through the Sunday School, Training Unions, and W.M.U. organizations in our churches. But we must admit that many of our churches are playing at this task in this approach.

The third avenue through which we carry on Christian Education is through our Christian Colleges and Theological Seminaries. It is to this phase of the work that we address our thoughts at this time.

Our Southern Baptists today own and support three Theological Seminaries and one Training School. These are overcrowded with students. There is a growing need and demand for a fourth Seminary. A southwide committee is studying the advisability of such an institution and will report to the Southern Baptist Convention in May.

In North Carolina our Baptist State Convention owns and operates two senior colleges, Wake Forest and Meredith, and three junior colleges, Mars Hill, Campbell, and Gardner-Webb. Wingate Junior College is also a Baptist school. It is owned by Baptist Associations and partially supported by our State Convention. We also own Chowan College in eastern North Carolina which has been closed several years because of lack of students and money. All of our active schools are overflowing with students and many young people are being turned from their doors because there is no more room. Each school is endeavoring to raise money to meet these urgent needs. Just now the greatest Statewide emphasis is the campaign to raise enough money to move Wake Forest to Winston-Salem.

Two things should be said about our relationship to these schools. First we should keep them CHRISTIAN as well as standard schools. It is the privilege and responsibility of teachers and trustees to see to it that these schools are Christian. Otherwise they have no just claim to the support of our churches. In the second place it is our privilege and our responsibility, if these schools are Christian, to support them with our money, our prayers, and by sending to them our sons and daughters.

Respectfully submitted,
J. Ben Eller.

38. The following report, presented by J. H. Scalf, Fairmont Park, was accepted. Woodrow Bullard, Superintendent of Associational Missions of the State Convention, spoke to the report.

REPORT ON BAPTIST LITERATURE

Wherever the Bible is intelligently studied, there must be a definite and comprehensive plan—a guide for the work. This is true whether the study occurs in a Christian college, theological seminary, or in an individual church or Sunday school—whether the study is taken by individuals or by groups.

The Bible is a gigantic storehouse of all kinds of riches. Within its vastness there is the solvent for every problem, the balm for every wound, and the answer to every need the world has ever known. This great truth is the very reason why there must be a plan for its study. This is the value of Southern Baptist Literature. It carries a well-conceived, definite, comprehensive, and continuous plan for the study of the Bible.

We believe that the world today needs the Baptist message as much as it ever did. It is a message that is clearly and definitely based upon the New Testament. While the forces of darkness and error are doing all within their power to sow the field with tares we should double our efforts to see to it that every man, woman, boy and girl, within our reach shall receive the pure and unadulterated message of the Word of God.

No more doctrinely sound literature can be found anywhere than that written for our use by the spiritual leaders in our denomination. The needs of no one have been neglected, from the cradle roll to the oldest pupils in our Sunday schools. Study books on doctrine, missions, organization, and a host of other valuable subjects, have been prepared to add to the life of every group within our organization.

The Biblical Recorder, our state paper, is filled with information of every description that is invaluable to the pastor, teacher, and to all who read it. This great periodical is likened to a strong cord that ties the bundle together. It is through the information derived from this source that we learn we are a part of a great denomination.

Respectfully submitted,

John H. Scalf.

39. The Executive Promotion Committee names were presented by J. Ben Eller, Chairman, and they were elected. (See Index).

Committee:

J. Ben Eller, Chairman,
W. S. Holton,
Neil J. Armstrong.

40. The Committee on place, time and preacher reported and the following was accepted. Place: Reidsville, First Baptist Church. Time: Wednesday and Thursday after third Sunday in October, 1948. Preacher: R. C. Shearin. Alternate: George Richman.

Committee:

James B. Clifton, Chairman,
H. P. Gauldin,
W. C. Guth.

41. The Committee to nominate the Church Advisory and Missions Committee reported (See Index). The Committee was elected.

42. The following report, presented by the treasurer, was adopted:

THE FINANCIAL REPORT

Balance		$ 674.76

Received

Churches	$5,034.01	
Holden Road Mission	34.25	
Pastor's School	90.25	
Baptist State Convention	1,868.20	
Total	$7,028.06	$7,028.06
Grand Total		$7,701.47

Less Expenses

Supplement to Sasser (under other plan)	$ 75.00	
T. L. Sasser's Salary	3,510.00	
Living Supplement (by State Board)	135.00	
Convention Expenses (for T. L. Sasser)	82.50	
Checks (500) and Binder	3.50	
Clerk's Compensation	100.00	
Printing Minutes	355.00	
Office Supplies, Stamps, etc.	132.68	
Incidentals	830.18	
Insurance and Repairs on Tent	68.65	
Pastoral School	82.22	
York & Boyd for Legal Service	65.00	
R. W. Morton for Recording Fee	5.00	
Vacation Bible School Supplies	53.16	
Bulldozing Lot on Holden Road	260.00	
Associational Missions:		
Immanuel	100.00	
Pilot View	100.00	
South Elm Street	100.00	
Total	$6,057.89	$6,057.89
Balance in Treasury		$1,643.52

Respectfully submitted,

Ray W. Harrington.

43. The report of the Auditing Committee. The Auditing Committee has examined the treasurer's books and found them to be as represented in his report.

Respectfully submitted,

S. L. Riddle, Chairman,
G. E. Richman.

44. A request was made from the Antioch Baptist Church for a letter of dismission from the Piedmont Baptist Association to join a new association. A motion was made and carried to refer the matter to the Executive Promotion Committee with power to act.

45. The following Resolutions Committee was elected for the year: T. L. Sasser, Chairman; W. T. Adams, W. C. Guth.

46. The Association joined in singing, "When I survey the Wondrous Cross," led by Forrest L. Fraser, accompanied by Mrs. W. S. Holden.

47. The Address—"Putting Evangelism in the Forefront," by Charles B. Howard, Professor of Bible at Campbell College.

48. Dr. J. Clyde Turner led the closing prayer.

49. Adjourned from the 1946-1947 session.

IN MEMORIAM

ALLEN JAY
Mrs. Loraine Marion
ANTIOCH
BRIGHTWOOD
Mr. E. E. Hanner
BUCHANON
Mr. W. P. Brown
CALVARY
Mr. J. A. Johnson, Deacon
COMMUNITY
Miss Joan Morgan
FAIRMONT PARK
Mr. D. Floyd Frazier
Mrs. W. O. James
FAIRVIEW
Mrs. William Cummings
ASHEBORO STREET
Miss Betty Lee Baldwin
Mr. Thomas C. Crutchfield
Miss Sallie Cheek
Mr. B. S. Cheek
Mr. Hugh C. Apple, Sr.
Mrs. Hoyt E. Smith
Mrs. Marvin Patterson
BESSEMER
Mrs. Ida Creason
COLLEGE PARK
Mr. Kenneth Nelson
Mr. B. A. Scott
Mr. Hunter Bell
ELLER MEMORIAL
Mrs. Mae Harris
Mr. Elis Craven
Mr. C. N. Lowery
Mr. J. M. Lovings
Mrs. Theo Weaver
GREENSBORO FIRST
Mrs. Phoeba Parrish
Mr. C. E. Sloan
Mrs. J. M. Durham
Mr. P. O. Tatum
Mrs. A. F. Johnson
Mrs. S. H. Mitchell
Mr. Rankin Owen
Mr. George L. Crump
Miss Jessie Combs
Mr. L. J. Mills
Mrs. A. B. Creech
Mrs. J. N. Outen
Mr. Thos. E. Hunt
Mrs. E. A. Joyner
FLORIDA STREET
Mr. Guy Parker
Mr. C. H. Dodd
MAGNOLIA STREET
Mr. J. S. Oaks, Deacon
POMONA
Mrs. Johnsie Apple
REVOLUTION
Mr. D. C. Henson
Mr. J. L. Dowdy
SIXTEENTH STREET
Mrs. Jossie Hodges
Mrs. W. G. Somers
Mrs. C. V. Webster
Mr. M. R. Phillips
HIGH POINT FIRST
Mrs. Tyree Nabors
Miss Annie Grimes
Mrs. C. D. Goldsmith
Mr. James Ward
Mrs. E. D. Stephenson
Mrs. Thomas Carrick
Mrs. W. B. Thomas
Mrs. Ida McFarland
Mr. J. T. Lyda
Mr. C. H. Cecil
Mrs. Mary Michael
Mr. A. T. Moffitt
Mrs. J. T. Burrus
Mrs. W. A. Stutts
GREEN STREET
Mrs. Le Roy Barham
Mrs. A. L. McGhee
Mrs. G. H. Callicutt
Mr. N. G. Samuels
Miss Joyce Winfrey
Mrs. F. H. Hartgrove
Mr. C. L. Collins
Mrs. W. K. Collins
HILLIARD MEMORIAL
Mrs. Lizzie Webb
Mrs. E. M. Howerton
NORTH MAIN STREET
Mrs. C. F. Bowman
NORTH PARK
Mr. P. R. Archer
WEST END
Mrs. Nola Garner
JESSUP GROVE
Mrs. Mabel Roach, Teacher
LEBANON
Mrs. Annie Lamberth
Mrs. J. B. Carter
MT. ZION
Mr. Cisero Linens
Mr. John Suits, Deacon
Miss Beckie Linberry
Mrs. Lee Spoon
PILOT VIEW
Mr. Kelley Mosteller
REEDY FORK
Mrs. Viola Jones
BAPTIST TEMPLE
Mrs. H. H. Meadow
REIDSVILLE FIRST
Mrs. Belle Black
Mrs. J. R. Dunn
Mr. R. R. Saunders
Mrs. W. N. Duke
Mrs. Betty Lemons
Mr. W. L. Turner
Mr. George Somers
Mrs. J. C. Powell
Mrs. Agnes Johnson
PENN MEMORIAL
Mrs. D. S. Bray
RUFFIN-STACEY
Mr. George French
SMITH GROVE
Mr. O. J. Williams
SUMMERFIELD
Mrs. J. R. Thomas
Mrs. Alice Wilson
Mr. W. E. Strader, Deacon
TEMPLE
Mr. Roger Owens
WOODWARD MEMORIAL
Mrs. Mary Louise Brannock

TABLE ONE—CHURCH MEMBERSHIP

CHURCHES	Town, Vill., Country?	Year Organized	PASTORS AND ADDRESSES	Dates of Meeting	ADDITIONS: Baptisms	ADDITIONS: By Letter	ADDITIONS: Other Additions	LOSSES: By Letter	LOSSES: By Death	LOSSES: Other Losses	TOTAL: Present Resident Membership	TOTAL: Non-resident Membership	TOTAL: Grand Total Present Membership	SPECIAL INFORMATION: Are Weekly Prayer Meetings Held?	Number of Revival Meetings Held	Spent on Building or Remodeling Last Year	Value of Pastor's Home	Total Value of All Church Property	Total Debt on
Allen Jay	V	1934	V. L. [illegible]ry, Rt. 3, Box 316, H. P.	All	13	8	3	14	1	...	...	...	[illegible]	Yes	...	...	[illegible]	10000.00	...
Antioch	C	1935	J. C. Gillespie, Rt. 2, [illegible]	½	3	2	...	...	1	...	45	20	65	...	...	...	...	...	...
Brightwood	V	1940	H. P. Gauldin, Rt. 5, Greensboro	All	81	30	21	2	1		[illegible]	...	329	Yes	4	6662.27	6500.00	30163.00	2650.00
Buchanon	V	1936	J. B. Clifton, 619 Waugh Av. [illegible]ro	All	...	2	2	2	1	...	...	...	[illegible]	Yes	2	5351.30	...	12500.00	...
Calvary	O	1901	W. D. [illegible]er, Rt. 4, Reidsville	½	6	1	...	2	1	1	...	...	225	No	3	1287.00	2000.00	7000.00	...
Community	O	1934	[illegible]rt [illegible]r, Rt. 8, Greensboro	All	19	5	...	5	1	...	...	...	[illegible]	Yes	2	2051.95	...	7750.00	...
Conrad [illegible]orial	C	1946	George [illegible]an, Rt. 1, High Point	All	32	3	4	4	...	...	91	...	91	Yes	1	...	7500.00	10000.00	5000.00
Fairmont Park	V	1942	J. H. Scalf, Rt. 2, High Point	All	20	7	...	11	2	...	240	14	254	Yes	2	10320.16	17000.00	37000.00	7000.00
Fairview	O	1904	J. E. Kirk, Rt. 2, Reidsville	½	3	3	...	2	1	...	[illegible]	39	182	No	1	...	...	4000.00	...
[illegible]e	T	1884	J. L. Gamble, Box 85, Raleigh	All	5	9	1	8	...	...	200	85	285	Yes	1	...	700.00	...	5700.00
GREENSBORO—																			
[illegible]ro Street	C	1899	J. B. Eller, 709 [illegible]ro St., [illegible]ro	All	34	24	2	41	7	10	...	...	1303	Yes	2	...	6000.00	51000.00	...
Bessemer	C	1922	R. W. Harrington, 507 DeLancey St., Gr.	All	21	2	2	22	1	2	...	...	558	Yes	2	...	3000.00	23000.00	...
College Park	C	1906	[illegible]on [illegible]k, 508 Forest Ave., Gr.	All	17	40	9	26	3	60	543	75	[illegible]	Yes	...	150.00	17500.00	[illegible]	4600.00
Edgeville	C	1941	A. R. Riddle, 1530 [illegible]er St., Gr.	All	1	3	...	2	...	...	34	6	40	Yes	2	440.03	2500.00	7000.00	1600.00
Eller Memorial	C	1897	R. V. King, 1307 Summit Ave., Gr.	All	47	14	1	14	5	...	...	...	[illegible]	Yes	2	85.85	9000.00	51000.00	...
First	C	1859	J. C. [illegible]r, 2106 W. Mkt. St., Gr.	All	102	162	13	140	14	25	...	...	2630	Yes	1	...	...	130000.00	...
Florida Street	C	1906	J. R. [illegible]n, 1110 [illegible]od Ave. Gr.	All	34	54	...	50	2	...	651	100	751	Yes	2	...	7500.00	54500.00	...
Immanuel	C	1935	F. L. Fraser, 921 Spring [illegible]den St., Gr.	All	48	20	6	5	...	...	152	3	155	Yes	2	...	...	8900.00	...
Latham Park	C	1916	[illegible]rd [illegible]r, [illegible]le Ground Rd., Gr.	All	4	23	...	1	...	...	96	1	96	Yes	2	...	...	8000.00	...
Magnolia Street	C	1912	W. T. [illegible]s, 103 E. Wendover Ave. Gr.	All	4	18	5	4	1	...	213	...	213	Yes	1	...	4000.00	11600.00	...
Pomona	T	1906	S. R. [illegible]g, 23 Boren St., Pomona	All	...	4	...	11	1	6	...	...	[illegible]	Yes	2	1846.55	...	4600.00	...
Revolution	C	[illegible]	S. L. [illegible]e, 2218 Shober St., Gr.	All	10	2	2	6	2	2	...	...	382	Yes	2	...	...	10000.00	...
Sixteenth Street	C	1907	W. C. [illegible], 1504 16th St., Gr.	All	47	5	13	8	4	1	...	...	397	Yes	2	...	...	39000.00	...
Stevens Memorial	V	1922	R. C. Shearin, Rt. 5, Greensboro	All	38	13	1	12	...	...	[illegible]	55	235	Yes	2	5557.00	11000.00	26000.00	382.10
South Elm Street	V	1945	I. E. Kerley, 113 Robins St., Gr.	All	19	7	2	...	...	...	...	...	[illegible]	Yes	1	1009.66	6000.00	12000.00	5000.00
Rankin	C	1935	B. L. Gupton, Rt. 5, Box 446, Gr.	All	26	7	...	11	...	3	...	...	194	Yes	2	452.25	12500.00	17500.00	...
Guilford	V	1914	F. W. Cox, Jr, Guilford College	All	1	4	...	7	...	...	98	19	[illegible]	Yes	1	...	...	3800.00	...

HIGH POINT—																		
First	C	8[illegible]2	W. W. [illegible]s, 225 [illegible]y, H. P.	All	61	88	...	51	14	...	1482	216	[illegible]44	Yes	1	....	[illegible]000	200000.00	....
[illegible]en Street	C	1900	J. S. Hopkins, Box 1584, H. P.	All	101	40	...	40	8	...	1500	437	1937	Yes	1	....	1 [illegible]00	187000.00	....
Hilliard Memorial	C	1929	H. O. Miller, 2333 Edgewood Ave., H.P.	All	9	14	...	13	2	2	....	....	365	Yes	2	1226.49	....	40000.00	....
North Main	C	1908	N. J. Armstrong, 111 Hillcrest Dr., H.P.	All	44	10	1	6	1	1	435	70	505	Yes	2	....	....	40000.00	....
North Park	C	1929	W. W. [illegible]s, 914 Dayton St., [illegible]	All	15	6	2	12	1	...	....	....	209	Yes	1	....	....	....	....
Southside	C	1916	W. H. Barker, 415 S. St., High Point	All	16	16	2	9	...	3	....	....	368	Yes	3	....	....	3500.00	....
[illegible]st [illegible]	C	913	W. C. [illegible]h, 918 [illegible]g St., H. P.	All	20	5	...	11	1	...	....	....	426	Yes	2	....	5000.00	[illegible]	....
[illegible]p Grove	V	1933	J. E. Wiggs, Box 2769, Greensboro	All	4	13	3	4	1	...	237	3	240	Yes	1	8589.47	....	20000.00	5000.00
Jewel	O	1941	A. H. [illegible]g, 806 [illegible]n, H. P.	All	13	8	...	1	...	1	81	2	83	....	....	....	....	....	....
Lebanon	O	1911	E. D. Young, Rt. 5, Greensboro	All	....	4	1	4	2	...	147	35	182	Yes	1	338.00	7500.00	11000.00	2450.00
Mt. Zion	O	1824	J. T. Swinson, Rt. 1, Burlington	All	11	2	...	...	4	...	....	....	258	....	....	....	....	....	....
[illegible]ell Road	O	1945	J. T. [illegible]s, Jr., [illegible]01 [illegible]y, Greensboro	All	13	8	...	...	...	...	35	....	85	Yes	1	1351.10	....	4000.00	450.00
[illegible]le	C	[illegible]43	J. B. Clifton, 619 Waugh Ave., Gr.	All	4	6	...	...	...	...	....	....	39	Yes	2	-	....	8000.00	....
Oak Grove	O	1916	R. L. Smith, 613 [illegible]ry St., H. P.	All	4	...	2	7	...	...	133	....	133	Yes	2	....	....	3500.00	....
[illegible]la	O	1915	W. S. [illegible]g, 711 [illegible]le A[illegible]., [illegible]ton	All	....	...	...	...	...	...	....	....	....	No	2	-	....	....	....
[illegible]ee	V	1933	L. M. King, Rt. 1, Elon College	All	12	5	...	1	...	...	53	17	70	Yes	2	5000.00	5500.00	[illegible]	3889.80
Pine Grove	V	1938	....	All	5	4	3	4	...	...	....	....	94	Yes	3	....	....	4000.00	....
Pilot View	V	1941	J. H. Clark, 327 [illegible]w Ave., H. P.	All	1	5	2	6	1	...	....	....	105	Yes	2	[illegible]840	....	5000.00	....
[illegible]h	C	1939	C. M. [illegible], 508 Carter St., H. P.	All	22	8	4	4	...	1	....	....	199	Yes	3	769.00	4500.00	24525.00	1400.00
Pleasant Garden	T	1933	A. W. [illegible]s, Pleasant Garden	All	4	7	...	9	...	...	....	....	118	Yes	1	115.12	[illegible]	10000.00	3500.00
Pleasant Grove	O	1937	J. M. Allred, Pomona	All	7	...	...	3	...	2	115	10	125	Yes	2	....	....	4500.00	450.00
Reedy Fork	O	1940	E. O. Lankford, Rt. 2, Brown Summit	All	24	...	...	3	1	...	184	....	184	Yes	2	8476.81	4464.91	[illegible]00	10500.00
REIDSVILLE—																		
[illegible]st Temple	C	1929	W. E. [illegible]s, [illegible]h, Reidsville	All	26	21	6	14	1	6	....	....	313	Yes	2	....	4500.00	1050.00	....
First	C	1844	....	All	20	4	...	17	9	...	945	72	1017	Yes	2	....	20000.00	90000.00	....
Penn Memorial	C	1931	W. S. Holton, 103 [illegible]er St., Reidsville	All	13	5	6	9	1	...	....	....	260	Yes	1	....	3000.00	14000.00	....
[illegible]ky Knoll	O	1934	G. E. [illegible]n, Rt. 1, Greensboro	All	16	27	6	14	...	...	260	59	319	Yes	1	2221.86	4000.00	12500.00	....
Ruffin-Stacey	O	1931	J. T. London, Rt. 5, Reidsville	All	7	...	...	...	1	...	213	....	213	Yes	2	52.00	....	3900.00	....
Smith Grove	O	1921	R. O. [illegible]s, Rt. 1, Colfax	All	17	2	...	1	1	...	....	....	214	Yes	2	1698.15	....	4000.00	....
Summerfield	V		E. A. Long, Germantown	½	14	2	...	...	3	...	....	....	218	....	1	....	....	10675.70	....
Temple	V	1939	A. J. Swinson, Box. 507, H. P.	All	11	16	...	19	1	...	-	....	106	Yes	2	223.75	....	3500.00	....
[illegible]rd Memorial	V	1946	W. R. Smith, Greensboro	All	26	9	11	...	1	...	....	....	70	Yes	2	....	....	....	....
Woodlawn	O	1945	A. B. Ashill, 2203 E. [illegible]en, H. P.	All	32	10	3	7	...	...	129	1	130	Yes	3	850.00	....	10000.00	1250.00
Friendly	C	1943	W. L. Smith, 116 Springfield Ave. H.P.	All	35	4	4	5	...	...	....	....	....	Yes	2	200.00	....	20000.00	....
Southside	C	1947	S. K. Brazil, Rt. 8, Box 29, [illegible]ro	All	16	26	2	...	...	...	44	....	44	Yes	1	....	....	....	400.00
TOTALS				....	1258	856	143	684	103	142	8949	1339	21284	....	103	67256.17	203164.91	1542958.15	60721.90

TABLE TWO—SUNDAY SCHOOLS

CHURCHES	SUNDAY SCHOOL SUPERINTENDENTS AND ADDRESSES	Cradle Roll 3 Years and Under	Nursery—Attend (3 Years and Under)	Beginners 4-5 Years	Primaries 6-8 Years	Juniors 9-12 Years	Intermediates 13-16 Years	Young People 17-24 Years	Adults 25 Years and Up	Extension Department	General and Departmental Officers	Number of Mission Sunday Schools	Enrolment of Missions Sunday School	Total Enrolment—Main School, Missions,	Average Attendance	Did You Have a Vac. Bible School?	What Was the Average Attendance?
Allen Jay	Wade [illegible]e, Rt. 1, Box 239, High Point	....	24	16	28	35	38	48	152	....	....	....	....	341	225	107	85
Antioch	T. H. Carter, Rt. 2, Reidsville	....	....	....	....	....	....	....	....	....	5	....	....	....	35	....	....
Brightwood	Lynn Strader, Bessemer Branch, [illegible]nsboro.	....	....	14	....	40	48	80	125	....	3	....	....	307	212	105	85
Buchanon	R. M. Crane, Rt. 1, Box 144, McLeansville	22	....	24	....	35	4	41	55	....	....	....	....	181	95	68	60
Calvary	J. W. McCargo, Rt. 2, Reidsville	....	....	21	17	31	24	21	124	....	....	....	..	238	112	85	79
Community	G. B. [illegible]n, Rt. 8, [illegible]ro.	....	....	20	14	15	....	15	53	....	....	....	....	117	77	56	....
Conrad [illegible]orial	G. P. [illegible]ley, Rt. 6, High Point	....	....	....	21	35	....	34	42	....	....	....	....	132	82	....	....
Fairmont Park	A. L. Welborn, 2018 English, High Point	....	10	24	30	40	25	36	112	....	4	....	....	281	177	....	....
Fairview	A. D. Hopkins, Rt. 1, Reidsville	....	....	22	10	35	53	36	37	....	....	....	....	193	122	....	....
Gibsonville	[illegible]h Foster, Gibsonville	....	....	20	20	27	36	45	68	....	3	....	....	219	135	....	....
GREENSBORO—																	
Asheboro Street	Frank L. Paschal, 2420 Camden Road	23	40	67	85	127	130	111	453	43	6	....	....	1085	....	200	176
Bessemer	M. P. Bullard, 3911 Peterson, Greensboro	17	....	42	48	65	53	56	121	....	20	....	....	422	242	133	96
College Park	N. B. [illegible], Greensboro	28	34	41	41	41	55	45	152	40	7	....	....	477	263	112	75
Edgeville	David Pruitt, 1104 Maple St., Greensboro	....	....	16	10	17	6	25	15	....	....	....	....	89	60	50	40
Eller [illegible]al	Raymond Kincaid, 1101 Summit Ave., Greens.	52	8	35	79	132	102	111	171	12	3	....	....	705	308	185	156
First	Frank L. [illegible]s, 510 Edgeworth, Greens.	86	152	103	169	165	171	175	955	334	48	....	....	2358	904	196	161
Florida Street	B. H. Russell, 1520 Willomore, Greens.	....	32	30	58	76	55	29	223	41	7	....	....	551	322	247	168
Immanuel	Walter C. Heilig, Rt. 3, Box 440, Greens.	....	....	28	12	49	23	40	40	....	12	....	....	204	103	136	104
Latham Park	A. C. [illegible]in, 109 Wilson St., Greensboro	....	....	11	10	9	....	29	12	....	....	....	....	....	....	75	65
Magnolia Street	S. E. Louis, 1911 Palm St., [illegible]ro.	....	....	29	22	18	21	35	46	....	....	....	....	171	92	53	48
Pomona	C. C. Patterson, Box 102, Pomona	....	....	50	25	41	39	24	78	....	2	....	....	257	151	105	95
Revolution	J. C. Dennis, 2208 Poplar, Greensboro	12	20	32	42	66	36	28	78	....	4	....	....	320	181	140	116
Sixteenth Street	Rockford Hill, 604 Rollins St., [illegible]boro.	78	6	21	47	79	61	35	92	7	6	....	....	350	231	236	154
Stevens Memorial	Frank Pol, Rt. 5, Box 69, Greensboro	....	28	12	38	29	28	44	72	....	6	....	....	265	150	102	85
South Elm Street	Harvey H. Apple, Robbins St., Greensboro	5	....	7	26	18	28	....	55	....	....	....	....	139	85	60	55
Rankin	J. T. Pearman, 2404 Maple St., Greensboro	38	....	10	15	25	24	33	47	13	16	....	....	178	134	88	70
Guilford	Setzer [illegible]on, Guilford College	....	4	10	8	8	10	18	40	....	2	....	....	100	60	54	45

HIGH POINT—																	
First	Dr. W. F. [illegible]n, 223 Lindsay, High Point	65	92	64	98	117	150	252	572	56	6	....	....	1472	675	204	....
Green Street	W. E. Crissman, 226 Woodrow Ave., H. P.	....	49	115	138	212	212	218	630	....	....	....	....	1629	782	265	198
Hilliard Memorial	A. L. Slate, Rt 2, High Point	....	19	16	16	23	32	46	80	....	6	....	....	238	140	82	68
North Main	S. R. Clinard, Rt. 1, High Point	....	24	38	38	54	65	48	91	4	20	....	....	382	206	192	176
North Park	H. B. Chatham, 1434 N. Hamilton, H. P.	....	11	16	19	39	24	27	58	....	4	....	....	196	122	99	68
Southside	A. L. Bean, 502 Highland Ave., H. P.	....	4	28	41	37	24	90	67	....	4	....	....	291	175	....	....
West End	U. S. Coffey, 520 Barker St., H. P.	....	11	21	29	51	23	24	94	26	5	....	....	284	171	85	....
Jessup Grove	W. D. Price, Rt. 2, Box 414, [illegible]ensboro	23	....	23	64	....	....	53	57	....	....	....	....	167	127	....	....
Jewel	S. P. Stutts, Rt. 5, High Point	....	35	....	....	40	15	20	25	....	....	....	....	135	84	80	65
Lebanon	E. E. Lashley, Rt. 5, Box 493, [illegible]ro	14	....	17	19	12	24	45	67	....	5	....	....	203	99	....	....
Mt. Zion	Winfred Shoffner, Rt. 2, Snow Camp	3	3	13	11	12	20	40	40	....	....	....	....	142	105	....	....
McConnell Road	W. H. Bullock, Rt. 6, Greensboro	....	....	12	....	12	....	12	18	....	....	....	....	54	31	26	21
McLeansville	Robert Harrell, Rt. 6, Box 468, Greensboro	....	....	13	....	13	....	22	19	....	....	....	....	67	46	....	....
Oak Grove	A. L. Saunders, Box 928, High Point	....	....	13	10	12	7	11	49	....	....	....	....	102	74	....	....
Osceola	E. J. Brown, Rt. 1, Brown Summitt	....	....	13	9	14	8	13	16	....	2	....	....	....	46	....	....
Ossipee	R. C. Fitts, Rt. 2, Elon College	6	....	23	....	29	....	22	31	....	5	....	....	116	75	60	40
Pine [illegible]e	J. W. Breedlove, Jamestown	....	....	27	12	19	12	23	38	....	2	....	....	133	79	47	....
Pilot View	V. E. [illegible]bb, Rt. 5, High Point	....	....	25	8	19	24	17	38	....	2	....	....	132	85	....	....
Pisgah	Z. V. Lanier, Box 686, High Point	....	....	16	19	39	37	29	96	6	3	1	40	276	147	120	70
Pleasant Garden	Jay Rummage, Pleasant Garden	....	11	24	27	31	30	59	21	....	....	....	....	203	88	84	51
Pleasant Grove	F. M. Atkins, Rt. 3, Greensboro	....	....	36	13	17	14	20	45	....	....	....	....	145	77	60	50
Reedy Fork	A. L. Bullard, Denim Sta., Greensboro	22	....	23	16	23	32	31	67	....	....	....	....	214	127	....	....
REIDSVILLE—																	
Baptist Temple	Milton Warf, [illegible]th St., Reidsville	29	21	15	44	13	27	77	....	....	11	....	....	226	132	135	109
First	S. F. Wells, Reidsville	....	31	30	58	57	67	80	257	....	4	....	....	584	274	148	125
Penn [illegible]rial	W. H. Ford, 3 Uhles, Reidsville	....	13	13	11	36	22	28	80	....	4	....	....	207	122	105	89
Rocky Knoll	[illegible]d [illegible]n, Box 1292, Greensboro	....	26	35	34	55	26	37	137	....	4	....	....	354	184	116	96
Ruffin-Stacey	R. W. Lane, Rt. 1, Ruffin	....	26	30	28	35	25	22	98	....	3	....	....	267	98	....	....
Smith [illegible]e	W. H. Westmoreland, Guilford Col. Rt. 1	....	....	45	....	20	24	54	74	....	2	....	....	219	114	....	....
Summerfield	Marion Ayers, Summerfield	....	....	35	30	33	15	25	32	....	4	....	....	180	98	....	....
Temple	R S. Edmonds, Rt. 4, High Point	14	....	21	18	20	9	14	56	....	10	....	....	165	80	....	....
[illegible]rd Memorial	J. E. Peoples, 212 Cottage Grove Ave. Greens.	....	....	25	21	22	9	22	53	....	....	....	....	152	84	65	52
Woodlawn	M. E. Turner, 111½ Hamilton St., H. P.	....	....	....	21	25	17	29	52	....	....	1	77	221	125	95	65
Friendly	J. L. Lowe, Rt. 4, High Point	15	....	12	20	21	15	60	55	....	....	....	....	140	....	....	....
Southside	B. A. Green, Rt. 8, Box 29, [illegible]o	8	....	12	15	15	12	15	35	15	7	....	....	134	85	....	....
TOTALS		560	733	1553	1727	2435	2091	2749	6566	594	267	2	117	19138	9655	4660	3361

TABLE THREE—BAPTIST TRAINING UNION

CHURCHES	TRAINING UNION DIRECTORS AND ADDRESSES	Adult Unions	Young People's Unions	Intermediate Unions	Junior Unions	Story Hours	Total Unions and Story Hours	Adults Enrolled	Young People Enrolled	Intermediates Enrolled	Juniors Enrolled	Story Hours Enrolled	Gen. & Dept. Officers Not Otherwise Enrolled	TOTAL ENROLLMENT	Average Attendance Per Sunday	Was Youth Week Observed?	Was Christian Home Week Observed?
Allen Jay	Roy Be[illegible]n, Archdale	1	....	1	1	1	4	20	....	11	12	6	3	53	48	*	*
A[illegible]h	....	....	....	....	....	....	....	....	....	....	....	....	....	....	....	....	....
[illegible]od	....	....	....	....	....	....	....	....	....	....	....	....	....	....	....	....	....
Buchanon	....	....	....	....	....	....	....	....	....	....	....	....	....	....	....	....	....
Calvary	....	....	....	....	....	....	....	....	....	....	....	....	....	....	....	....	....
Community	....	....	....	....	....	....	....	....	....	....	....	....	....	....	....	*	*
[illegible]d [illegible]ial	Mrs. Paul Jester, Rt. 6, High Point	1	1	....	1	1	4	22	30	....	16	16	....	84	42	*	*
Fairmont Park	W. F. Thomas, 305 E. Russell, High Point	1	1	1	1	1	5	19	29	12	9	9	3	81	50	*	*
Fairview	....	....	....	....	....	....	....	....	....	....	....	....	....	....	....	....	....
[illegible]le	....	....	1	1	....	....	2	....	15	18	....	....	1	33	25	*	*
GREENSBORO—																	
Asheboro Street	Clayton Snead, 1101 Bellevue, Gbro.	2	1	3	2	3	11	41	22	46	38	18	8	173	84	**	*
Bessemer	Mrs. W. H. Layton, 714 Holt, Gbro.	1	....	1	1	0	4	8	....	30	25	....	6	63	44	*	*
College Park	W. B. Logan, Guilford College	1	1	1	1	1	5	32	54	14	19	12	....	181	59	*	*
Edgeville	....	....	....	....	....	....	....	....	....	....	....	....	....	....	....	....	....
Eller Memorial	Leah Andrews, 649 Chestnut, Gbro.	2	1	2	1	1	7	39	10	36	25	18	3	131	80	*	*
First	Frank R. Poole, Jr., 414 S. [illegible]h, Gbro.	3	4	4	2	2	15	72	50	49	35	22	16	244	159	*	*
Florida Street	V. A. Wilson, 1013 McCormick, Gbro.	2	2	1	2	1	8	34	34	11	20	12	....	111	85	**	**
Immanuel	Carson C. Stonley, 2401 [illegible]n, Gbro.	1	1	1	1	1	5	25	11	23	14	26	3	102	57	*	*
Latham Park	....	....	....	....	....	....	....	....	....	....	....	....	....	....	....	....	....
Magnolia Street	J. B. Wray, 1130 Magnolia, Gbro.	1	1	1	1	1	5	6	13	9	6	7	....	41	20	*	*
Pomona	James Albert, 907 Englewood, Gbro.	1	....	....	....	....	1	10	....	....	....	....	....	10	8	*	*
Revolution	Hoyle Campbell, 1901 Englewood, Gbro.	....	1	1	1	1	4	....	16	16	13	18	9	71	....	*	*
Sixteenth Street	S. G. Alers, Rt. 6, Gbro.	1	1	2	1	1	6	14	19	30	30	15	9	117	88	*	*
Stevens Memorial	S. G. Alers, Rt. 6, Gbro.	1	1	1	1	1	5	12	13	9	17	8	5	64	56	*	*
South Elm Street	J. A. [illegible]er, [illegible]he St., Gbro.	1	....	1	1	1	4	6	....	10	14	5	....	35	20	*	*
Rankin	Mrs. Henry Bryson, Rt. 5, Gbro.	1	1	1	1	1	5	14	10	10	12	4	2	62	35	*	**
Guilford	Mr. C. E. Gough, Guilford, N. C.	1	1	1	1	1	5	9	12	3	4	7	6	46	23	**	*

HIGH POINT—																	
First	...	1	2	3	2	1	9	22	54	60	59	25	6	226	113	*	*
Green Street	R. L. Phillips, Box 1584, High Point	3	2	3	4	1	13	37	35	52	74	29	6	233	128	**	*
Hilliard Memorial	...	1	1	1	1	...	4	14	9	17	13	...	3	56	41	*	*
North Main	Mrs. Eudora Moore, Rt. 2, High Point	1	1	1	1	1	5	17	16	16	13	8	3	70	55	**	*
North Park	Mrs. L. W. Glenn, Box 702, High Point	1	1	1	1	1	5	14	9	13	16	13	3	68	47	*	*
Southside	Daisy Shaw, 308 Walker St., High Point	1	1	...	1	1	4	6	5	...	6	7	2	26	23	**	*
West End	Miss Amy Darnell, 1206 Tryon St., H. P.	1	...	1	1	1	4	18	...	10	10	7	4	49	41	*	*
Jessup Grove	Elsie Smith, 29th St., Greensboro	2	2	...	1	1	6	20	20	...	14	6	3	69	67	*	*
Jewel	Billy Stutts, Rt. 5, High Point	1	1	1	...	1	4	10	20	15	...	10	...	55	36	*	*
Lebanon	...	...	...	...	...	...	...	...	...	...	...	...	...	...	...	...	...
Mt. Zion	Roy Wicker, Rt. 2, Liberty	1	...	1	1	1	4	24	...	17	12	13	...	66	48	*	*
McConnell Road	...	...	...	...	...	...	...	...	...	...	...	...	...	...	...	...	...
McLeansville	...	...	...	...	...	...	...	...	...	...	...	...	...	...	...	...	...
Oak Grove	...	...	...	...	...	...	...	...	...	...	...	...	...	...	...	...	...
Osceola	...	...	...	...	...	...	...	...	...	...	...	...	...	...	...	...	...
Ossipee	...	...	...	...	...	...	...	...	...	...	...	...	...	...	...	...	...
Pine Grove	...	...	...	...	...	...	...	...	...	...	...	...	...	...	...	...	...
Pilot View	...	...	...	...	...	...	...	...	...	...	...	...	...	...	...	...	...
Pisgah	J. G. Ritch, 627 W. Lexington, H. P.	1	1	1	1	1	5	13	15	10	9	5	3	55	40	*	*
Pleasant Garden	C. L. Yow, Pleasant Garden	1	...	1	1	...	3	15	...	10	17	...	...	59	...	*	*
Pleasant Grove	W H. Smith, Rt. 3, Box 420, Gbro.	1	...	1	1	1	4	6	...	13	7	8	...	30	27	*	*
Reedy Fork	L. A. Beach, Rt. 5, Box 144, Gbr.	1	1	1	1	1	5	27	7	24	22	13	6	99	62	*	*
REIDSVILLE—																	
Baptist Temple	Norman Cook, iLndsey St., Reidsville	1	1	1	1	1	5	16	5	19	16	11	4	71	47	*	*
First	C. H. Saunders, 110 Silver, Reidsville	...	1	2	1	...	4	...	13	39	29	...	...	81	39	**	*
Penn Memorial	Mrs. W. H. Ford, 3 Uhles St., Reidsville	1	1	1	1	1	5	19	10	7	10	2	5	63	20	*	*
Rocky Knoll	Mrs. J. A. Durham, Rt. 1, Gbro.	2	1	1	1	1	6	44	12	15	22	31	5	129	50	*	*
Ruffin-Stacey	...	...	...	...	...	...	...	...	...	...	...	...	...	...	...	...	...
Smith Grove	...	...	...	...	...	...	...	...	...	...	...	...	...	...	...	...	...
Summerfield	...	...	...	...	...	...	...	...	...	...	...	...	...	...	...	...	...
Temple	...	...	...	...	...	...	...	...	...	...	...	...	...	...	...	...	...
Woodard Memorial	Leroy Casey, RFD, Greensboro	...	...	1	1	1	3	...	...	10	26	10	12	61	43	*	*
Woodlawn	...	...	...	...	...	...	...	...	...	...	...	...	...	...	...	...	...
Friendly	Ermon Rudd, 1312 Franklin St., H. P.	1	1	1	1	...	4	9	20	15	25	...	...	69	35	*	*
Southside	Jesse Metz, Rt. 8, Box 29, Gbro.	1	1	1	1	1	5	18	5	5	15	5	...	48	...	...	...
TOTALS	...	44	37	48	44	36	212	732	593	704	724	406	139	3295	1945	...	...

* No. ** Yes.

TABLE FOUR—W. M. U. ORGANIZATIONS AND GIFTS

CHURCHES	PRESIDENTS OF W. M. S. AND ADDRESSES	Number of Woman's Missionary Societies	Number of Y.W.A.'s	Number of G.A.'s	Number of R.A.'s	Number of Sunbeams	Total W. M. U. Organizations	W. M. S. Members	Y. W. A. Members	G. A. Members	R. A. Members	Sunbeam Members	Total Members Enrolled	Total Enrolled in Mission Study Courses	Contributions (Local Work) Given by W. M. U.	Contributions (Missions) Given by W. M. U.
Allen Jay	M[illegible]. V. L. [illegible]ry, Rt. [illegible], [illegible]h Point	1	1	2	....	2	6	21	15	14	....	18	68	33	12.50	275.00
[illegible]h	....	1	....	....	....	1	2	14	....	....	....	12	26	....	....	34.00
[illegible]d	....	....	....	....	....	....	....	....	....	....	....	....	....	....	....	....
Buchanon	Mrs. I. B. Clifton, 619 [illegible]h St., Gbro.	1	1	1	1	1	5	16	11	11	5	17	60	48	....	152.85
[illegible]	M[illegible]. C. B [illegible]n, Rt. 4, Reidsville	1	1	2	2	1	7	35	11	15	14	12	87	23	122.42	213.51
Community	....	....	....	....	....	....	....	....	....	....	....	....	....	....	....	....
Conrad [illegible]al	....	....	....	....	....	....	....	....	....	....	....	....	....	....	....	....
Fairmont Park	Mrs. O. C. [illegible]gs, Box 464, H[illegible]h Point	1	1	1	1	....	4	23	20	18	8	....	[illegible]	40	3[illegible]0	230.73
Fairview	Mrs. J. E. Kirk, Rt. 2, Rei[illegible]le	1	....	....	....	....	1	25	....	....	....	....	26	12	17.70	75.12
Gibsonville	....	1	1	....	....	....	2	25	10	....	....	....	35	15	573.00	123.80
GREENSBORO—																
[illegible]o Street	Mrs. W. H. [illegible]ton, 453 [illegible]n St., Gbr	1	....	1	....	1	3	198	....	16	....	65	29	75	123.59	1127.47
Bessemer	Mrs. J. R. [illegible]n, 200 Sykes Ave., Gbro.	1	1	1	....	1	4	64	10	12	....	41	117	42	89.10	767.21
Coll ge Park	M[illegible]. B. B. Stockard, 111 Springdale Ct. Gbr	1	....	1	1	1	4	66	....	10	12	20	108	52	7131.47	128.75
Edgeville	Mrs. Gilmer Ashbey, 1308 [illegible]r St., Gbro.	1	....	....	....	....	1	15	....	....	....	....	15	....	80.00	9.30
Eller [illegible]orial	Leah [illegible]s, 549 Chestnut St., [illegible]o.	1	2	1	....	1	5	45	36	16	....	6	[illegible]3	9	....	2662.35
First	M[illegible]s. H. D. [illegible]n, 316 [illegible]ll St., Gbro.	1	2	4	4	1	12	407	27	24	32	45	[illegible]	352	....	14202.37
Florida Street	M[illegible]s. C. D. t[illegible]r, [illegible]o.	7	1	2	1	2	13	100	15	37	15	12	179	67	164.15	1169.40
[illegible]l	Mrs. E. C. White, [illegible]o.	1	....	....	....	....	1	19	....	....	....	....	18	....	30.00	73.00
[illegible]m Park	Mrs. [illegible]d [illegible], 1237 W. [illegible]dover Av.	1	....	....	....	....	1	16	....	....	....	....	16	....	140.00	....
[illegible]a Street	Mrs. L. L. r[illegible]is, 2401 [illegible]le Dr. Gbro.	3	....	1	....	1	5	36	....	13	....	25	74	30	3188.30	350.60
[illegible]	Mrs. W. H. Brown, Pomona	1	....	....	....	1	2	25	....	....	....	25	50	....	46.75	92.48
[illegible]on	Miss Sallie Burgess, 2103 Maple, Gbro.	1	....	1	1	1	4	14	....	8	4	10	30	....		1100.33
Sixteenth Street	(Mrs. Harry Moore, 1508 16th St., Gbro.	1	1	2	2	1	7	44	16	34	22	18	134	25	3338.40	2233.00
Stevens [illegible]al	Mrs. C. B. Brisson, Rt. 2, Box 155, Gbro.	1	1	....	....	....	2	19	10	....	....	....	[illegible]	12	....	175.84
South Elm Street	Mrs. H. H. Apple, [illegible]s St., Gbro.	1	....	....	....	....	1	20	....	....	....	....	[illegible]	....	31.15	64.10
Rankin	Mrs. C. L. Straughn, Rt. 5, Box 468, Gbro.	1	1	2	1	1	6	44	7	18	13	7	[illegible]	45	1976.60	378.65
Guilford	Mrs. [illegible]ie Kennedy, Rt. 7, Greensboro	1	....	....	....	1	2	19	....	....	....	20	39	..	....	....

HIGH POINT—																
First	Mrs. H. A. Knight, 1100 N. Main St., H. P.	1	2	3		1	7	212	33	41		59	845	282	685.48	[illegible]44.00
Green Street	Mrs. Fred Culler, Box 1584, High Point	1	1	2	2	1	7	143	6	22	30	23	224	149	6580.72	2922.16
Hilliard Memorial	Mrs. J. B. Ellis, 1006 Stanton St., H. P.	1		1	1	1	4	19		8	6	16	49	14	935.16	232.86
North Main	Mrs. Heil Armstrong, 111 Hillcrest, H. P.	2					2	34					34	25	150.00	299.33
North Park		1		2	2	1	6	22		23	27	19	91	63	1250.47	891.92
[illegible]e	Mrs. J. S. [illegible], 307 [illegible] St., H. P.	1					1	12					12	12	99.37	137.30
[illegible]st End	Mrs. Frank Causer, 306 Ennis St., H. P.	1				1	2	28				9	37			144.89
Jessup Grove																
Jewel																
Lebanon	Mrs. Ezra Lashley, Rt. 2, Liberty	1					1	23					23	11	329.42	274.55
Mt. Zion	Mrs. J. C. [illegible]kamy, Rt. 5, Liberty	1					1	20					20		87.50	141.00
McConnell Road																
[illegible]ville																
Oak Grove																
Osceola																
Ossipee	Mrs. [illegible]er Brown, Rt. 2, Elon College	1					1	6					6		12.00	5.25
Pine [illegible]e																
Pilot [illegible]w	M[illegible] J. E. Rollins, Rt. 5, High Point	1					1	15					15		61.91	13.00
Pisgah	Mrs. C. F. Beachamp, 1305 Thissell St., H. P.	1	1	1			3	10	9	7			26	10	43.00	18.00
Pleasant Garden	Mrs. I. F. [illegible]n, Rt. 1, Greensboro	1					1	20					20		25.00	20.80
Pleasant Grove	Mrs. Clyde Burris, Rt. 3, [illegible]o	1					1	13					13		10.00	20.00
Reedy Fork	Mrs. R. R. Everage, Rt. 2, Brown Summit	1				1	2	16				21	37		1353.72	143.33
REIDSVILLE—																
Baptist Temple	Mrs. Numa Baker, 16 Oak St., Reidsville	1	1	2	1	1	6	70	11	25	10	35	151	112	416.40	276.45
First	Mrs. T. L. Sasser, Reidsville	1	1	2		1	5	152	12	28		20	212	163	329.64	1043.09
Penn Memorial	M[illegible] Nash Wilkins, 241 Barnes St., Reids.	1					1	39					39	25	119.60	110.25
Rocky Knoll	M[illegible] W. T. [illegible]e, Rt. 1, Greensboro	1	1	2	1		6	22	9	19	9		59	12	198.79	131.19
Ruffin-Stacey																
[illegible]th Grove																
Summerfield	Mrs. C. D. Robinson, Summerfield	1					1	19					19			287.45
[illegible]ple		1					1	15					15			61.00
Woodard [illegible]al	M[illegible] Leo Chrismon, Rt. 6, Greensboro	1					1	23					23		25.00	148.86
Woodlawn													15			
Friendly																
Southside	Mrs. Estelle [illegible]n, Rt. 8, Box 63, Gbro.	1					1	12					12			7.00
TOTALS		56	21	37	21	26	162	2255	268	419	207	655	3712	1858	29760.81	40023.54

TABLE FIVE—MEN'S BRTHERHOODS

CHURCHES	DIRECTORS OF MEN'S BROTHERHOODS AND ADDRESSES	Does Church Have a Brotherhood Organization?	Present Enrolment	Brotherhood Meetings Held Last Year	Pledged to Co-operative Program or Unified Budget Coming Year	Pledged to Associational Missions Coming Year	Number of Tithers in Church	Number Members Subscribing to Every Member Canvass	Building and Reserve Funds on Hand at End of Year	Is State Paper in Church Budget?	Does Church Have Library?
Allen Jay		*				50.00	30		19253.54	*	*
Antioch		*			50.00	10.00	2			*	**
Brightwood		*				80.00	90		1000.99	*	*
Buchanon		*							240.78	*	*
Calvary		*								**	**
Community		*					9		280.47	*	*
Conrad Mal		*				180.00	18	91		**	*
Fairmont Park		*								*	*
Fairview		*					-			**	*
Gibsonville		*				25.00	20			*	*
GREENSBORO—											
Aero Street	R. Paul Greeson, 1200 Bellevue St., Greensboro	**	56	12		48.00	65	834	22085.11	*	**
Bessemer					435.00	130.00	53		15373.03	*	**
College Park		*					148		10219.19	*	*
Edgeville		*									
Eller Memorial						225.00	95		11921.91	**	**
First		*				1200.00	380		248793.50	**	**
Florida Street	Robert Barracks, 1009 Haywood St., Greensboro	**	10	12	2250.00	175.00	200	250	29543.98	**	**
Immanuel		*					67		449.94	*	*
Latham Park		*							237.74	*	*
Magnolia Street					324.00	63.00	52		6299.39	**	**
Pomona		*								*	*
Revolution		*				63.00			87 5.28	*	**
Sixteenth Street		*			2200.00	200.00	75		14582.91	*	*
Stevens Memorial		*			1000.00	60.00	75			**	**
Suth Elm Steet		*					10		211.81	*	*
Rankin		*			400.00	100.00	28	72	690.88	*	*
Guilford		*					20		1621.53	*	**

HIGH POINT—											
First		*				750.00	200	950	16395.90	*	**
Green Street		*					402		44048.90	*	**
Hilliard Memorial	L. E. Edwards, 1004 Stanton St., High Point	*			260.00	78.00	20	1400		*	**
North Main		*			900.00	132.00	81		680.00	*	*
North Park		*					25		10000.00	**	**
Southside		*			100.00		35		11652.27	**	*
West End		*			60.00	6.50	40				
Jessup Grove		*				15.00	32		1363.81	*	**
Jewel		*			235.00		10		569.51	*	*
Lebanon		*					19			*	*
Mt. Zion		*					32		420.27	*	*
McConnell Road		*					7		142.75	*	*
McLeansville		*							145.57		
Oak Grove		*			15.00						
Osceola		*								*	*
Ossipee		*			150.00	13.00	6		53.32	*	*
Pine Grove		*			92.16		11				*
Pilot View		*								*	*
Pisgah		*							1830.68	*	*
Pleasant Garden		*					24			*	**
Pleasant Grove		*					10		115.00	*	*
Reedy Fork		*			182.00		21		9258.28	*	*
REIDSVILLE—											
Baptist Temple		*							18514.95	*	*
First		*					62		3454.17	**	*
Penn Memorial		*							1565.52	*	**
Rocky Knoll		*			600.00	38.00	85		2221.67	*	**
Ruffin-Stacey		*				35.00	12			*	*
Smith Grove		*								*	*
Summerfield		*							1165.16	*	*
Temple		*					17			*	**
Woodard Memorial		*			25.00	100.00			9609.36	*	*
Woodlawn		*					30		170.00	*	*
Friendly		*					20			*	*
Southside		*							500.00	*	*
TOTALS			66	24	9278.16	4073.50	1201	3597	525178.10		

* No. ** Yes.

TABLE SIX—GIFTS FOR LOCAL CHURCH WORK

CHURCHES	TREASURERS AND ADDRESSES	Pastor's Salary Paid for Year	Incidentals—Janitor, Fuel, Water, Repairs, Insurance, Etc.	Assistant Pastor, Educational Director, Choir Leader, Etc.	Revival Expenses and Pastoral Supply	Paid on Church Debt Out of Current Funds	Literature— uarterlies, Church Paper, Song Books, Etc.	Help for Local Poor	Minutes and Clerk of Association	Building Fund (Amount Given Last Year)	Local Missions	Other Objects	Total Given for Local Church Work
Allen Jay	W. R. Hobson, Rt. 1, Box 239, High Point	3120.00	991.00		361.48		280.26	340.00	29.00			672.58	5804.32
Antioch	Mrs. T. H. Carter, Rt. 2, Reidsville	300.00	9.60		178.50		67.79		5.00			11.00	573.89
Brightwood	Carl Ham, 1216 Fairview St., Greensboro	3120.00	2184.43	125.00	660.68	622.63	321.14	355.57	6.00	6662.67		301.40	14359.52
Buchanon	R. F. Carter, Rt. 6, Greensboro	2340.00	162.50	64.50	107.62		78.65	116.09	68.12	1692.77			4630.25
Calvary	E. L. Terrell, Wentworth	1200.00	392.22		370.00	1078.40	138.76		5.00	209.60		177.49	3571.47
Community	Miss Julia Yow, Rt. 8, Greensboro	1120.00	102.00		149.09	2051.95	77.22		3.00			90.00	3592.26
Conrad Memorial	Mrs. Paul Jester, Rt. 6, High Point	2804.00	278.10		209.50	2091.78	366.84	25.00	10.00	2056.29		843.69	8683.20
Fairmont Park	L. G. Campbell, Rt. 2, High Point	3120.00	750.12		596.09	10320.16	298.44	177.00	20.00		46.05	779.80	16107.66
Fairview	B. B. Pearson, Rt. 2, Reidsville	900.00	412.93		104.82		160.60			438.00		252.50	2268.85
Gibsonville	F. L. Robertson, Gibsonville	2100.00	398.66	75.00	266.33	210.17	328.96	22.88	1650.00			743.00	5775.61
GREENSBORO—													
Asheboro Street	Mrs. A. C. Lwe, 1500 Randolph, Gbro	4147.78	5346.13	3234.19	748.92		1071.71	311.77		6947.23		4587.24	26394.97
Bessemer	E. C. le, 609 Willard St., o.	3003.00	3046.06	720.00	270.00		577.97			4261.66		115.00	11993.69
College Park	Mrs. C. O. Weaver, 2516 H.P. Rd., ensboro	2820.00	3414.32	3420.00	136.00		698.17		12.50	8824.03		2069.41	21394.43
Edgeville	Mrs. Ruth Greeson, 1506 Ball St., nsboro	1289.67	12.20		103.00	300.10	19.61	20.00	2.00	440.03	80.00		2266.51
Eller Memorial	Mrs. R. R. Burgess, 512 E. Bessemer Ave. Gr.	3608.80	1782.51	2519.30	931.35		468.86	55.86	10.00	2827.73		3136.32	15341.33
First	C. A. McKeel, 605 Northridge St., nsboro.	6000.00	9529.98	12920.00	1229.47		4560.50	1844.96		41005.45		4657.97	81748.23
Florida Street	R. E. Wash, 1219 Gregory St., Greensboro	3900.00	2951.53	1122.87	495.00		1017.46	250.00				500.00	10237.43
Immanuel	Mrs. W. C. Heilig, Rt. 3, Box 440, Gbro	2970.00	820.63	240.00	341.00		326.90	60.50		3543.08		1113.56	9415.67
Latham Park	R. A. Anderson, 1312 Wendover Ae., Gbro	909.66	767.04		390.64	41.35			2.00	40.00		23.85	2174.54
Magnolia Street	H. S. h, 1700 Grove St., Greensboro	3087.50	1083.16	108.10	128.46		357.26	205.00		905.03		330.77	6205.18
Pomona	E. E. Henry, Pomona	2389.70	2124.12		235.55		221.81	224.27	5.00		471.56	187.10	5859.11
Revolution	Waldo Johnson, 2211 Shober St., Greensboro	2957.50	767.19		376.26		414.46	10.00	5.00	1890.87		406.07	6827.35
Sixteenth Street	L. F. Paris, 1507 15th St., Greensboro	3700.00	1771.29		237.48		446.64	185.64	28.40	4593.00		610.07	11662.52
Stevens Memorial	Mrs. C. B. Brisson, Rt. 2, Box 155, oro	2227.50	865.73		291.75	5557.00	345.70		4.00			151.70	9443.38
Suth Elm Street	Miss Lillie Craven, 115 Robbins St., Greensboro.	725.00	332.25		73.80	2084.84	87.98	17.50		1009.66		90.84	4421.87
Rankin	B. H. Scott, Rt. 5, Greensboro	2340.00	1316.67	240.00	260.00	2737.84	341.07	92.25	5.00		160.00		492.83
Guilford	Mrs. Doro Farrar, Guilford College	1355.00	946.72		79.00		97.66		8.56				2486.94

HIGH POINT—													
First	Miss Thelma Patrick, 309½ Church St., H. P.	4766.61	10775.16	7837.90	436.52	......	2272.63	......	......	10046.46	1320.75	6430.12	43886.65
Green Street	E. L. Adams, Box 1584, High Point	4290.00	8338.24	957.00	2390.00	......	1737.41	188.05	......	15607.32	......	3550.82	37058.84
Hilliard Memorial	C. H. Farmer, 2108 English St., High Point	2600.00	1014.33	316.00	316.08	......	153.53	134.54	......	1226.49	......	804.52	6565.49
North Main	[illegible], 1916 N. Main St., High Point	3120.00	793.47	1640.00	190.00	696.86	579.70	230.86	8.00	1551.05	300.00	1843.91	10953.85
North Park	L. W. [illegible], Box 702, High Point	1310.00	491.24	150.00	1399.80	......	274.64	275.00	......	2133.45	......	597.50	6631.63
Southside	W. R. Grant, 410 White Oak St., High Point	2773.28	1076.86	80.10	625.40	......	252.51	121.85	5.00	3264.34	157.00	32.00	8348.33
West End	C. M. Scott, 1009 Ferndale Dr., High Point	2822.00	1094.18	813.50	691.85	......	379.25	......	......	1729.64	......	275.75	7806.17
Jessup Grove	Mrs. Ruth Lewis, Rt. 1, Summerfield	2406.86	368.86	121.00	280.00	4689.47	86.27	21.00	6.00	3946.15	259.41	......	13160.34
Jewel	Mrs. Maude Cannon, Rt. 5, High Point	989.75	282.61	......	108.50	117.82	112.27	97.73	4.00	1000.00	......	......	2712.68
Lebanon	C. L. Haynes, Rt. 5, Box 223, [illegible]	2550.00	514.64	25.00	67.72	400.00	86.48	......	......	5098.36	......	408.05	4051.89
Mt. Zion	Mrs. C. M. Johnson, Rt. 1, Burlington	2990.00	26.00	125.00	281.47	......	225.60	168.36	5.00	2657.90	......	......	6479.33
McConnell Road	J. E. York, Rt. 6, Greensboro	463.36	823.77	......	50.00	......	12.83	......	1.00	1351.10	......	......	2702.03
McLeansville	E. V. Snow, McLeansville	260.00	268.51	......	90.00	340.00	32.88	......	......	......	......	......	991.39
Oak Grove	W. L. Shackleford, Rt. 3, High Point	2696.38	182.84	......	302.02	......	53.18	50.00	2.00	......	......	157.46	3443.88
Osceola	Mrs. E. R. Brande, Brown Summitt	1713.46	185.18	......	210.54	......	41.56	......	5.87	......	10.00	33.93	2200.54
Ossipee	H. D. Smith, Rt. 1, Elon College	1076.50	154.45	......	224.46	396.05	111.12	......	2.00	309.74	17.25	35.80	2327.37
Pine Grove	Larston Tuttle, Rt. 4, High Point	583.72	103.55	......	271.94	......	66.50	......	3.00	......	......	32.00	1060.71
Pilot View	Mrs. J. E. Rollins, Rt. 5, High Point	2275.00	151.03	......	378.33	200.00	98.30	25.02	4.00	930.40	......	120.24	4182.32
Pisgah	L. C. Madden, 414 [illegible]ow St., High Point	2935.00	907.40	......	1009.10	400.00	205.13	67.02	12.50	......	689.82	1109.73	7335.70
Pleasant Garden	E. L. Routh, Pleasant [illegible]	1625.00	713.37	......	263.05	613.50	189.01	24.00	4.00	......	......	686.62	4118.55
Pleasant Grove	Virgil Ward, Rt. 3, Box 256, Greensboro	1589.65	313.31	......	138.35	168.00	103.80	28.00	......	109.84	......	......	2450.95
Reedy Fork	Parks Gregory, Rt. 2, Brown Summitt	2600.00	502.33	......	128.76	......	103.80	38.41	3.00	1342.93	......	192.39	5060.64
REIDSVILLE—													
Baptist Temple	Mrs. Odell Dellap, Box 283, Reidsville	2535.00	2321.53	420.00	476.29		590.37	......	22.64	8404.59	147.78	532.72	15450.92
First	Everette Pearson, Box 1139, Reidsville	3150.00	3896.78	2758.50	680.00	......	570.13	......	......	3495.67	......	1326.64	15877.72
Penn Memorial	G. V. Dalton, Box 414, Reidsville	2600.00	1288.89	881.26	565.93	......	249.13	278.51	5.00	1245.82	......	1871.57	8986.61
Rocky Knoll	Mrs. C. F. [illegible], Rt. 1, Greensboro	2109.00	2690.95	35.00	380.67	......	588.68	150.00	5.00	2221.67	956.58	609.51	9747.06
Ruffin-Stacey	E. J. Lee, Box 1328, Reidsville	1680.00	470.40	......	18.00	......	65.37	157.85	4.00	......	......	25.23	2420.85
Smith Grove	Drew Smith, Rt. 1, Colfax	1100.00	1769.15	......	672.55	......	55.00	......	3.00	......	83.33	59.89	3742.92
Summerfield	Mrs. T. D. Carter, Summerfield	970.00	211.25	......	131.00	......	195.40		13.00	......	......	79.00	1620.68
Temple	R. L. Rodden, Box 1545, High Point	1464.70	341.05	......	292.00	......	120.37	......	5.00	......	126.00	......	2329.12
Ward Memorial	Mrs. W. D. Neal, Rt. 6, Greensboro	1674.65	522.33	......	128.27	2380.20	194.95	61.75	6.11	62.94	16.00	40.25	5087.45
Woodlawn	Billy Kansy, Rt. 6, High Point	2880.00	110.32	......	800.00	......	108.39	300.00	......	850.00	......	200.00	5248.71
Friendly	[illegible]es Wardell, 406 Kennedy St., H. P.	3400.00	368.00	......	460.00	......	200.00	200.00	......	400.00	......	400.00	5428.00
Southside	H. W. Taylor, Rt. 8, Box 29, Greensboro	345.00	229.91	......	......	400.00	......	10.00	......	......	......	......	984.91
TOTALS		139899.99	85855.95	40949.52	23777.39	37898.12	23437.63	6942.24	2007.70	156332.96	4841.53	43307.51	560185.24

TABLE SEVEN—GIFTS FOR ALL MISSIONS, EDUCATION, ORPHANAGES, ETC.

CHURCHES	CLERKS OF CHURCHES AND ADDRESSES	Gifts to Co-operative Program or Unified Budget	Designated to Associational Missions	Designated to State Missions	Designated to Home Missions	Designated to Foreign Missions	Designated to Schools, Colleges, and Seminaries	Orphanages Cash and Conservative Estimate Value of Merchandise, Clothing, Etc.	Designated to Hospitals	Designated to Red Cross and Foreign Relief	Relief and Annuity, Other Objects	Total for All Missions	Grand Total of All Contributions for All Purposes
Allen Jay	Hoy Yarborough, Rt. 6, Box 589, High Point	481.15			23.50	28.35		275.18	75.00			903.18	670 .507
Antioch			10.00	4.00	3.50	57.00		27.07	25.00			119.57	692.66
Brightwood	Mrs. Dewey Fuller, [illegible]-15th St., Greensboro		80.00		1213.00			31.57	31.60			1626.17	15985.69
Buchanon	R. F. Carter, Rt. 6, Greensboro	227.00						103.00	19.03		91.00	440.03	5070.28
Calvary		303.50	17.20	23.00	24.00	46.50		239.00	77.21	105.00	21.71	857.12	4428.59
Community	Miss Zelda Marsh, Rt. 8, Greensboro		13.00					45.17	45.00			103.17	3695.43
Conrad Memorial	Mr. D. B. Webb, Rt. 1, High Point	352.00	90.00		352.00	520.70		51.62	14.25		25.00	1405.59	10088.79
Fairmont Park	Ray Moose, Rt. 2, High Point			100.00				100.00			147.18	347.18	16454.84
Fairview		315.81	12.00	32.20	10.00	20.00	20.00	151.50	54.40	100.00	73.11	789.02	3057.87
[illegible]	G. V. Laughlin, Box 172, [illegible]nville	12.00	11.00			399.63	100.00	293.25	78.31	[illegible]	10.00	1014.19	6789.80
GREENSBORO—													
Asheboro Street	J. B. Willis, Pearson St., Greensboro	5540.87	283.75			1311.10		1445.57	338.34	7.00	118.00	9044.63	36690.66
Bessemer		435.00	135.00	24.22		767.21	39.10	100.00	100.00	40.00	120.00	1760.53	13754.22
College Park		1306.39	357.50	42.55	12.43	1300.00	71.00	550.68	151.65	50.00	437.30	4279.50	25673.93
Edgeville	J. B. Barber, 1512 Ball St., Greensboro	5.30		1.00					10.60	8.81		25.71	2292.22
Eller Memorial		2850.00	280.00	50.00	72.00	1147.28	16.00	824.62	537.44	451.22	186.80	6415.36	21756.69
First	Vander Liles, 1326 Madison Ave., Greensboro	29417.57	900.00	1168.15	1234.73	9250.21	1140.00	6641.67	971.15	294.25	1773.18	52790.91	134539.14
Florida Street	Mrs. W. L. Jones, 1303 Oak St., Greensboro	2005.62			100.00	2000.00		950.00	63.75		308.86	5428.23	15565.66
Immanuel	Mrs. C. C. S[illegible]y, Box 741, Greensboro	103.75		130.00	80.96	77.00		384.43	29.00			805.14	10220.81
Latham Park							96.62	20.00	15.00			131.62	2306.16
Magnolia Street		269.74		32.31	30.00	4370	5.00	112.51			215.73	708.99	6914.17
Pomona	C. C. Patterson, Box 102, Pomona	442.33		36.13		27.32		584.21	125.00		34.74	1249.73	71[illegible]8.84
Revolution		1741.69	58.00	22.50	30.25	198.16		211.54	198.49	64.87	146.87	2672.37	9499.72
Sixteenth Street		3781.48	100.00	39.86	75.21	209.67		441.07	100.00	1170	179.16	4936.15	16598.67
Stevens Memorial	Mrs. J. B. Brown, Rt. 2, Box 69, Greensboro	950.00	47.25	19.75	51.39	65.41		243.60	47.62	4.44	74.00	1503.46	10946.84
South Elm Street	Mrs. O. W. Thomas, Box 2845, Greensboro	64.10	15.00			25.00		26.05	12.25			142.40	4776.08
Rankin	G. E. Norwood, Rt. 5, Greensboro	406.31	100.00	24.65		15.57		166.10	33.40	43.32		789.35	8282.19
Guilford	Mrs. Dora Farrar, Guilford College	229.35	27.50	21.70	1000	25.00	34.00	92.65	41.19		23.00	504.39	3381.33

HIGH POINT—													
First	Mrs. W. K. Dickens, 310 E. Farriss, High Po	9703.16	849.80	271.32	201.71	2117.02	1821.29	2392.03	447.15		1056.15	18805.63	62692.28
Green Street		12745.23	570.68	625.00	73.20	1223.22		2049.49	205.28	43.45	2511.95	20047.50	57106.34
Hrd eMial	P. E. Gaubb, 1306 W. Green, High Point	206.80	64.80	20.00	40.51	60.25		314.19	32.86		118.00	857.41	7422.90
North Main		1113.45	125.00	150.00	150.00	150.00	600.00	275.88	76.00	400.00	616.73	3357.06	14310.91
North Park	Mrs. L. R. McNeill, 915 Forrest, High Poin	874.50	64.00	29.00	58.29	80.00		439.25	85.00	5.00		1585.04	8216.67
Southside	Mrs. D. A. Parlier, 509 Flint, High Point	100.00		23.65				145.00	50.07	25.94		244.66	8692.99
Wst End	Miss Amy Darnell, 1206 Tn, High Point	797.65	80. 0	92.15	51.94	51.95		468.95	78.07	26.60	67.60	1715.11	9528.21
Jessup Grove			15.00	25.00	888.52	50.00		212.71	25.00			1415.23	14575.57
Jewel				20.00		20.00		120.00	65.00			211.06	2923.74
Lebanon		93. 0		100.00	62.27	25.00		221.40	25.00	52.50	48.00	727.17	9150.25
Mt. Zion		25.00				81.00		89.61	13. 7			209.32	6688.65
Mill Road			6.00		5.25	5.30			20.00			36.55	1387.84
McLeansville	Mattia Harrell, Rt. 6, Box 468, Greensboro		6.00						12.95	6.50		25.45	1016.84
Oak Grove	Miss Marion Boleman, Box 1622, High Point	18.00						105.35				223.35	3667.23
Osceola			13. 0	18.25	18.24	20.00			21.35			90.84	2291.38
Ossipee	Mrs. Walter Brown, Rt. 2, Elon College	125.60	13.00					25.00	9.25			172.25	2499.62
Pine Grove	Mrs. R. A. Pickard, Rt. 3, High Point				16.55			115.86	18.38			150.79	1211.50
Pilot View	Mrs. H. S. Fletcher, Rt. 5, High Point	92.16	25. 0		3.00	13.00		182.00	22.20		228.72	603.92	4444.66
Pisgah		86.00	69. 0	16.00				182.00	22.20		228.72	603.72	7939.62
Pleasant Garden		20.80	19.00			25.00		40.00	25.00			129.80	4248.35
Pleasant Grove			16. 0			100.00		140.10	26.39			282.49	2733.44
Reedy Fork		156.00	50.00	14.50	8.58	8.59		161. 0	137.83	6.00	143.33	685.83	5756.47
REIDSVILLE—													
Baptist Temple	Mrs. Jesse Strader, 55 Wentworth, Reidsville	282.45	119.50	15.65	57.20	25.40		161.48	46.43	20.43	26.40	754.94	16205.86
First		4165.67	500.00	158.43	507.40	1013.60	100.00	1071.14	91.85	1205.44		8913.53	25120.89
Penn Memorial	Mrs. W. S. Holton, 103 Silver, Reidsville	98.00		39.60	174.00			36.03	41.37		267.78	653.78	9640.39
Rocky Knoll					74.00			150. 0	125.00		25.00	374.00	10121.06
Ruffin-Stacey	E. J. Lee, Box 1328, Reidsville		3500					62.00	30.00			127.00	2547.85
Smith Gve	Mrs. Ray Clark, Rt. 1, Colfax						131.29	302.82	33.00			467.11	4210.03
Summerfield	Mrs. Myrtle Smith, Summerfield	161.93		96.51	79.76	295.68		192.58	33.98	25.58		915.97	2536.65
Temple	Mrs. R. L. Rodden, Box 1545, High Point			21.00	10.00	20.00		50.00				101.00	2430.12
Woodard Memorial	Mrs. W. V. Bell, Rt. 6, Box 14, Greensboro			25.00		25.00		25.00	25.00			100.00	5287.45
Woodlawn	Mrs. M. E. ier, 111½ S. Hamilton St., H.					15.00			25.00			40.00	5288.71
Friendly	Mrs. Selma Moe, Arch St., High Point							50.00	50. 0			110.00	5528.00
Southside	Mrs. Abie Paschal, Box 1366, o											45.42	1030.33
TOTALS		82102.76	5177.98	3480.08	5803.39	22952.82	3874.30	24095.95	5171.38	31 8.06	095.30	165325.24	731731.57

HISTORICAL TABLE—PIEDMONT BAPTIST ASSOCIATION

Year	Where Held	Moderator	Clerk	Preacher	Churches	Baptisms	Members	Gifts
1894	Greensboro	Dr. C. A. Rominger	W. L. Kivett	M. A. [illegible]	5	....	562	....
1895	Liberty	T. L. [illegible]	W. L. Kivett	L. Johnson	12	16	1112	4695.50
1896	Moore's Chapel	R. W. Brooks	W. H. Eller	L. Johnson	14	66	1194	5128.94
1897	Summerfield	F. H. Jones	W. H. Eller	J. A. [illegible]	16	73	1540	7198.27
1898	[illegible] Zion	R. W. Brooks	W. H. Eller	L. Johnson	17	67	1557	6883.23
1899	Ramseur	R. W. Brooks	F. P. Tucker	John E. White	19	54	1570	7435.43
1900	Cherry Street	R. W. Brooks	W. H. Eller	[illegible]	16	48	1538	7970.35
1901	Reidsville	F. H. Jones	W. H. Eller	L. Johnson	19	157	1657	8282.73
1902	Salem Street	F. H. Jones	W. H. Eller	W. C. [illegible]	19	135	1774	9950.97
1903	[illegible]	F. H. Jones	W. H. Eller	C. L. Greaves	20	185	1868	12834.77
1904	[illegible]	F. H. Jones	W. H. Eller	H. W. [illegible]	22	112	1832	12807.43
1905	Randleman	F. H. Jones	W. H. Eller	J. M. Hilliard	22	114	2096	17674.91
1906	High Point, First	F. H. Jones	W. H. Eller	W. R. [illegible]	23	201	2333	29366.31
1907	Asheboro Street	F. H. Jones	W. H. Eller	Wm. Hedley	26	372	2798	39993.79
1908	Ramseur	F. H. Jones	W. H. Eller	C. E. [illegible]	28	311	3086	26347.57
1909	Greensboro	F. H. Jones	W. H. Eller	[illegible] Hedley	30	292	3429	49847.28
1910	[illegible] Zion	F. H. Jones	W. H. Eller	R. G. Hendrick	31	336	3731	28531.01
1911	[illegible]	W. F. [illegible]	W. H. Eller	W. F. Staley	29	182	3736	15887.56
1912	High Point, [illegible] Street	F. P. Hobgood, Jr.	W. H. Eller	J. C. Turner	30	174	3647	29697.38
1913	[illegible]	F. P. Hobgood, Jr.	W. H. Eller	R. P. [illegible]	31	409	3971	37700.97
1914	Asheboro [illegible]	F. P. Hobgood, Jr.	W. H. Eller	A. W. [illegible]	31	413	4202	42428.44
1915	Reidsville	J. M. Hilliard	W. H. Eller	J. M. Hilliard	42	313	4491	42577.68
1916	Forest Avenue	J. M. Hilliard	W. H. Eller	E. N. Johnson	36	369	4854	48418.92
1917	Green Street	J. M. Hilliard	W. H. Eller	W. R. White	39	308	4760	44609.05
1918	Moore's [illegible]	J. M. Hilliard	W. H. Eller	J. W. Rose	39	374	5140	72538.46
1919	[illegible] Oak	J. M. Hilliard	W. H. Eller	W. H. Wil[illegible]	39	339	5359	76638.85
1920	[illegible]	J. M. Hilliard	W. H. Eller	E. N. Johnson	39	543	5967	117682.35
1921	Summerfield	Clarence A. Smith	J. E. Lanier	B. K. Mason	39	480	6454	135561.79
1922	Glenola	Clarence A. Smith	J. E. Lanier	Jas. A. Clark	39	679	7226	149955.24
1923	[illegible] Street	Clarence A. Smith	H. O. [illegible]	E. E. White	38	365	7341	140553.25
1924	[illegible] End	Clarence A. Smith	H. O. [illegible]	W. E. Goode	40	672	7489	164658.19
1925	Fairview	Clarence A. Smith	H. O. [illegible]	A. T. Howell	41	610	8956	211792.21
1926	Ramseur	Clarence A. Smith	S. T. Hensley	Lloyd T. Wilson	42	620	9974	243500.68
1927	Trinity	Clarence A. Smith	S. T. Hensley	H. T. Stevens	40	656	10223	211846.40

1928	Bessemer	Clarence A. Smith	O. E. Lee	R. P. Ellington	41	531	10866	2002.30
1929	Liberty	Clarence A. Smith	O. E. Lee	C. F. Rogers	44	573	11496	[illegible]87.61
1930	[illegible]ro	[illegible]ce A. Smith	O. E. Lee	Geo. T. Tunstall	44	676	12012	[illegible]77.29
1931	Florida Street	[illegible]ce A. Smith	O. E. Lee	A. B. Conrad	44	827	12789	[illegible]01.19
1932	Reidsville	Clarence A. Smith	O. E. Lee	J. C. Turner	46	778	13485	159000.60
1933	[illegible]te Oak	Clarence A. Smith	O. E. Lee	T. L. Sasser	48	1561	15199	[illegible]41.40
1934	Franklinville	Clarence A. Smith	O. E. Lee	Wilson Woodcock	53	757	15365	172839.18
1935	South Side, High Point	Clarence A. Smith	O. E. Lee	J. S. Hopkins	41	623	12687	[illegible]35.92
1936	Calvary	Clarence A. Smith	O. E. Lee	J. Ben Eller	42	563	13958	[illegible]52.96
1937	Eller [illegible]al	[illegible]er H. Jones	O. E. Lee	C. N. Royal	41	657	14086	[illegible]40.50
1938	Hilliard Memorial	Grover H. Jones	O. E. Lee	A. B. Conrad	42	814	14793	200246.20
1939	Reidsville	Grover H. Jones	O. E. Lee	J. C. Turner	46	975	15479	[illegible]24.34
1940	Florida Street	Grover H. Jones	O. E. Lee	Chas. E. Parker	51	804	16206	[illegible]25.45
1941	Green Street	Grover H. Jones	O. E. Lee	A. Lincoln Fulk	53	724	16929	284008.43
1942	Greensboro, First	Grover H. Jones	L. Grady Burgiss	A. A. [illegible]lker	55	794	16922	[illegible]84.15
1943	Greensboro, First	Grover H. Jones	L. Grady Burgiss	I. B. Jackson	55	772	17268	[illegible]39.14
1944	Greensboro, First	Grover H. Jones	Ray W. Harrington	G. H. Wallace	56	640	17958	[illegible]31.10
1945	Greensboro, First	Grover H. Jones	Ray W. Harrington	John McGinnis	56	921	18988	[illegible]03.36
1946	High Point	[illegible]er H. Jones	Ray W. Harrington	W. W. Hutchins	60	944	19148	617206.90
1947	Mt. Zion	Grover H. Jones	Ray W. Harrington	R. Von King	61	1258	21284	731731.57

Lightning Source UK Ltd.
Milton Keynes UK
UKHW020829271218
334508UK00011B/515/P

9 781528 13497